Fodor's Road Guide USA

Georgia
North Carolina
South Carolina

First Edition

Fodor's Travel Publications
New York Toronto London Sydney Auckland
www.fodors.com

WITHDRAWN

Fodor's Road Guide USA: Georgia, North Carolina, South Carolina

Fodor's Travel Publications
President: Bonnie Ammer
Publisher: Kris Kliemann
Executive Managing Editor: Denise DeGennaro
Editorial Director: Karen Cure
Director of Marketing Development: Jeanne Kramer
Associate Managing Editor: Linda Schmidt
Senior Editor: Constance Jones
Director of Production & Manufacturing: Chuck Bloodgood
Creative Director: Fabrizio La Rocca

Contributors
Editorial Production: Kristin Milavec
Editing: Jay Hyams (Georgia), Mayanthi Fernando (South Carolina), and Judith Wilson
(North Carolina), with Laurel Carroll, Dianne DiBlasi, Linda Downs, Robert Fleming,
Lorraine Martindale, Pat Hadley-Miller, Marty Munson, and Brian Rohan
Writing: James A. Crutchfield (Georgia), Jane Garvey (Georgia attractions and
restaurants), Mary Sue Lawrence (South Carolina), and Lisa Towle (North Carolina), with
Kelly Demaret, Hardy Griffin, Tenisha Light, Paula Margulies, Margarita Sorock, Karla
Tornabene, Lisa Towle, and Brendan Walsh
Research: Kim Bacon, Doug Hirlinger, Satu Hummasti, Keisha Hutchins, Hasan Khondker,
Carla Ranicki, Amanda Robinson, Frances Schamberg, Rupa Shah, and Alexei Taylor
Black-and-White Maps: Rebecca Baer, Robert Blake, David Lindroth, and Todd Pasini
Production/Manufacturing: Bob Shields
Cover: Rod Patterson/© Camera Arts Inc. (background photo), Bart Nagel (photo, illustration)
Interior Photos: Photodisc (Georgia and South Carolina), North Carolina Division of
Tourism, Film and Sports Development (North Carolina)

Copyright

First Edition
ISBN 0–679–00503–X
ISSN 1528–1477

Special Sales

Fodor's Travel Publications are available at special discounts for bulk purchases for sales promotions
or premiums. Special editions, including personalized covers, excerpts of existing guides, and
corporate imprints, can be created in large quantities for special needs. For more information,
contact your local bookseller or write to Special Markets, Fodor's Travel Publications, 280 Park
Avenue, New York, NY 10017. Inquiries from Canada should be directed to your local Canadian
bookseller or sent to Random House of Canada, Ltd., Marketing Department, 2775 Matheson
Boulevard East, Mississauga, Ontario L4W 4P7. Inquiries from the United Kingdom should be sent
to Fodor's Travel Publications, 20 Vauxhall Bridge Road, London SW1V 2SA, England.

PRINTED IN THE UNITED STATES OF AMERICA
10 9 8 7 6 5 4 3 2 1

CONTENTS

Great Road Trips

Of all the things that went wrong with Clark Griswold's vacation, one stands out: The theme park he had driven across the country to visit was closed when he got there. Clark, the suburban bumbler played by Chevy Chase in 1983's hilarious *National Lampoon's Vacation,* is fictional, of course. But his story is poignantly true. Although most Americans get only two precious weeks of vacation a year, many set off on their journeys with surprisingly little guidance. Many travelers find out about their destination from friends and family or wait to get travel information until they arrive in their hotel, where racks of brochures dispense the "facts," along with free city magazines. But it's hard to distinguish the truth from hype in these sources. And it makes no sense to spend priceless vacation time in a hotel room reading about a place when you could be out seeing it up close and personal.

Congratulate yourself on picking up this guide. Studying it—before you leave home—is the best possible first step toward making sure your vacation fulfills your every dream.

Inside you'll find all the tools you need to plan a perfect road trip. In the hundreds of towns we describe, you'll find thousands of places to explore. So you'll always know what's around the next bend. And with the practical information we provide, you can easily call to confirm the details that matter and study up on what you'll want to see and do, before you leave home.

By all means, when you plan your trip, allow yourself time to make a few detours. Because as wonderful as it is to visit sights you've read about, it's the serendipitous experiences that often prove the most memorable: the hole-in-the-wall diner that serves a transcendent tomato soup, the historical society gallery stuffed with dusty local curiosities of days gone by. As you whiz down the highway, use the book to find out more about the towns announced by roadside signs. Consider turning off at the next exit. And always remember: In this great country of ours, there's an adventure around every corner.

HOW TO USE THIS BOOK

Alphabetical organization should make it a snap to navigate through this book. Still, in putting it together, we've made certain decisions and used certain terms you need to know about.

LOCATIONS AND CATEGORIZATIONS

Color map coordinates are given for every town in the guide.

Attractions, restaurants, and lodging places are listed under the nearest town covered in the guide.

Parks and forests are sometimes listed under the main access point.

Exact street addresses are provided whenever possible; when they were not available or applicable, directions and/or cross-streets are indicated.

CITIES

For state capitals and larger cities, attractions are alphabetized by category. Shopping sections focus on good shopping areas where you'll find a concentration of interesting shops. We include malls only if they're unusual in some way and individual stores only when they're community institutions. Restaurants and hotels are grouped by price category then arranged alphabetically.

RESTAURANTS

All are air-conditioned unless otherwise noted, and all permit smoking unless they're identified as "no-smoking."

Dress: Assume that no jackets or ties are required for men unless otherwise noted.

Family-style service: Restaurants characterized this way serve food communally, out of serving dishes as you might at home.

Meals and hours: Assume that restaurants are open for lunch and dinner unless otherwise noted. We always specify days closed and meals not available.

Prices: The price ranges listed are for dinner entrées (or lunch entrées if no dinner is served).

Reservations: They are always a good idea. We don't mention them unless they're essential or are not accepted.

Fodor's Choice: Stars denote restaurants that are Fodor's Choices—our editors' picks of the state's very best in a given price category.

LODGINGS

All are air-conditioned unless otherwise noted, and all permit smoking unless they're identified as "no-smoking."

AP: This designation means that a hostelry operates on the American Plan (AP)—-that is, rates include all meals. AP may be an option or it may be the only meal plan available; be sure to find out.

Baths: You'll find private bathrooms with bathtubs unless noted otherwise.

Business services: If we tell you they're there, you can expect a variety on the premises.

Exercising: We note if there's "exercise equipment" even when there's no designated area; if you want a dedicated facility, look for "gym."

Facilities: We list what's available but don't note charges to use them. When pricing accommodations, always ask what's included.

Hot tub: This term denotes hot tubs, Jacuzzis, and whirlpools.

MAP: Rates at these properties include two meals.

No smoking: Properties with this designation prohibit smoking.

Opening and closing: Assume that hostelries are open year-round unless otherwise noted.

Pets: We note whether or not they're welcome and whether there's a charge.

Pools: Assume they're outdoors with fresh water; indoor pools are noted.

Prices: The price ranges listed are for a high-season double room for two, excluding tax and service charge.

Telephone and TV: Assume that you'll find them unless otherwise noted.

Fodor's Choice: Stars denote hostelries that are Fodor's Choices—our editors' picks of the state's very best in a given price category.

NATIONAL PARKS

National parks protect and preserve the treasures of America's heritage, and they're always worth visiting whenever you're in the area. Many are worth a long detour. If you will travel to many national parks, consider purchasing the National Parks Pass ($50), which gets you and your companions free admission to all parks for one year. (Camping and parking are extra.) A percentage of the proceeds from sales of the pass helps to fund important projects in the parks. Both the Golden Age Passport ($10), for those 62 and older, and the Golden Access Passport (free), for travelers with disabilities, entitle holders to free entry to all national parks, plus 50% off fees for the use of many park facilities and services. You must show proof of age and of U.S. citizenship or permanent residency (such as a U.S. passport, driver's license, or birth certificate) and, if requesting Golden Access, proof of your disability. You must get your Golden Access or Golden Age passport in person; the former is available at all federal recreation areas, the latter at federal recreation areas that charge fees. You may purchase the National Parks Pass by mail or through the Internet. For information, contact the National Park Service (Department of the Interior, 1849 C St. NW, Washington, DC 20240-0001, 202/208—4747, *www.nps.gov*). To buy the National Parks Pass, write to 27540 Ave. Mentry, Valencia, CA 91355, call 888/GO—PARKS, or visit www.national-parks.org.

IMPORTANT TIP

Although all prices, opening times, and other details in this book are based on information supplied to us at press time, changes occur all the time in the travel world, and Fodor's cannot accept responsibility for facts that become outdated or for inadvertent errors or omissions. So always confirm information when it matters, especially if you're making a detour to visit a specific place.

Let Us Hear from You

Keeping a travel guide fresh and up-to-date is a big job, and we welcome any and all comments. We'd love to have your thoughts on places we've listed, and we're interested in hearing about your own special finds, even the ones in your own back yard. Our guides are thoroughly updated for each new edition, and we're always adding new information, so your feedback is vital. Contact us via e-mail in care of roadnotes@fodors.com (specifying the name of the book on the subject line) or via snail mail in care of Road Guides at Fodor's, 280 Park Avenue, New York, NY 10017. We look forward to hearing from you. And in the meantime, have a wonderful road trip.

THE EDITORS

Important Numbers and On-Line Info

LODGINGS

Adam's Mark	800/444—2326	www.adamsmark.com
Baymont Inns	800/428—3438	www.baymontinns.com
Best Western	800/528—1234	www.bestwestern.com
	TDD 800/528—2222	
Budget Host	800/283—4678	www.budgethost.com
Clarion	800/252—7466	www.clarioninn.com
Comfort	800/228—5150	www.comfortinn.com
Courtyard by Marriott	800/321—2211	www.courtyard.com
Days Inn	800/325—2525	www.daysinn.com
Doubletree	800/222—8733	www.doubletreehotels.com
Drury Inns	800/325—8300	www.druryinn.com
Econo Lodge	800/555—2666	www.hotelchoice.com
Embassy Suites	800/362—2779	www.embassysuites.com
Exel Inns of America	800/356—8013	www.exelinns.com
Fairfield Inn by Marriott	800/228—2800	www.fairfieldinn.com
Fairmont Hotels	800/527—4727	www.fairmont.com
Forte	800/225—5843	www.forte-hotels.com
Four Seasons	800/332—3442	www.fourseasons.com
Friendship Inns	800/453—4511	www.hotelchoice.com
Hampton Inn	800/426—7866	www.hampton-inn.com
Hilton	800/445—8667	www.hilton.com
	TDD 800/368—1133	
Holiday Inn	800/465—4329	www.holiday-inn.com
	TDD 800/238—5544	
Howard Johnson	800/446—4656	www.hojo.com
	TDD 800/654—8442	
Hyatt & Resorts	800/233—1234	www.hyatt.com
Inns of America	800/826—0778	www.innsofamerica.com
Inter-Continental	800/327—0200	www.interconti.com
La Quinta	800/531—5900	www.laquinta.com
	TDD 800/426—3101	
Loews	800/235—6397	www.loewshotels.com
Marriott	800/228—9290	www.marriott.com
Master Hosts Inns	800/251—1962	www.reservahost.com
Le Meridien	800/225—5843	www.lemeridien.com
Motel 6	800/466—8356	www.motel6.com
Omni	800/843—6664	www.omnihotels.com
Quality Inn	800/228—5151	www.qualityinn.com
Radisson	800/333—3333	www.radisson.com
Ramada	800/228—2828	www.ramada.com
	TDD 800/533—6634	
Red Carpet/Scottish Inns	800/251—1962	www.reservahost.com
Red Lion	800/547—8010	www.redlion.com
Red Roof Inn	800/843—7663	www.redroof.com
Renaissance	800/468—3571	www.renaissancehotels.com
Residence Inn by Marriott	800/331—3131	www.residenceinn.com
Ritz-Carlton	800/241—3333	www.ritzcarlton.com
Rodeway	800/228—2000	www.rodeway.com

Sheraton	800/325—3535	www.sheraton.com
Shilo Inn	800/222—2244	www.shiloinns.com
Signature Inns	800/822—5252	www.signature-inns.com
Sleep Inn	800/221—2222	www.sleepinn.com
Super 8	800/848—8888	www.super8.com
Susse Chalet	800/258—1980	www.sussechalet.com
Travelodge/Viscount	800/255—3050	www.travelodge.com
Vagabond	800/522—1555	www.vagabondinns.com
Westin Hotels & Resorts	800/937—8461	www.westin.com
Wyndham Hotels & Resorts	800/996—3426	www.wyndham.com

AIRLINES

Air Canada	888/247—2262	www.aircanada.ca
Alaska	800/426—0333	www.alaska-air.com
American	800/433—7300	www.aa.com
America West	800/235—9292	www.americawest.com
British Airways	800/247—9297	www.british-airways.com
Canadian	800/426—7000	www.cdnair.ca
Continental Airlines	800/525—0280	www.continental.com
Delta	800/221—1212	www.delta.com
Midway Airlines	800/446—4392	www.midwayair.com
Northwest	800/225—2525	www.nwa.com
SkyWest	800/453—9417	www.delta.com
Southwest	800/435—9792	www.southwest.com
TWA	800/221—2000	www.twa.com
United	800/241—6522	www.ual.com
USAir	800/428—4322	www.usair.com

BUSES AND TRAINS

Amtrak	800/872—7245	www.amtrak.com
Greyhound	800/231—2222	www.greyhound.com
Trailways	800/343—9999	www.trailways.com

CAR RENTALS

Advantage	800/777—5500	www.arac.com
Alamo	800/327—9633	www.goalamo.com
Allstate	800/634—6186	www.bnm.com/as.htm
Avis	800/331—1212	www.avis.com
Budget	800/527—0700	www.budget.com
Dollar	800/800—4000	www.dollar.com
Enterprise	800/325—8007	www.pickenterprise.com
Hertz	800/654—3131	www.hertz.com
National	800/328—4567	www.nationalcar.com
Payless	800/237—2804	www.paylesscarrental.com
Rent-A-Wreck	800/535—1391	www.rent-a-wreck.com
Thrifty	800/367—2277	www.thrifty.com

Note: Area codes are changing all over the United States as this book goes to press. For the latest updates, check www.areacode-info.com.

Fodor's Road Guide USA

Georgia
North Carolina
South Carolina

Georgia

Georgia is the largest state east of the Mississippi River. Named for England's King George II, the colony was founded in 1733 by the English general and philanthropist James Oglethorpe as a private enterprise. Its first settlers were debtors and other unfortunates together with a small number of gentlemen. Georgia has come a long way since those early days of English exploration and colonization. The state's name is associated with peaches and cotton, and its history, especially scenes of lush antebellum plantation life, was made vividly memorable by Margaret Mitchell's best-selling novel, *Gone with the Wind,* and the movie, starring Clark Gable and Vivien Leigh, based on it. Georgia is today one of the nation's most productive and progressive states and serves as a shining example of what is meant by the term *New South.*

Georgia is a land of sharp geographical contrasts. From the lofty foothills of the Southern Appalachian Mountains in the north, with elevations approaching 5,000 feet, to the near–sea level, subtropical mysteries of the Okefenokee Swamp in the south; from the bleached, sandy beaches along the Atlantic Ocean in the east, to the flat peanut-rich croplands in the west, the Georgia landscape is among the most varied and inviting in the nation.

A leisurely four-hour drive separates one of the South's oldest, most charming, and historically significant towns—Savannah—and one of the entire nation's largest, most economically advanced, and ethnically diverse cities—Atlanta. And this dichotomy—the old and the new, the traditional and the high-tech, the native-born and the recently arrived newcomer, each existing next to the other in perfect harmony—seems to typify all that is good about Georgia.

CAPITAL: ATLANTA	POPULATION: 7,486,000	AREA: 58,910 SQUARE MI
BORDERS: TN, NC, SC, FL, AL	TIME ZONE: EASTERN	POSTAL ABBREVIATION: GA
WEB: HTTP://WWW.GEORGIA.ORG		

History

Thousands of years before European explorers first eyed its bountiful shores, Georgia was home to American Indians of several different culture groups. The first humans to reach the area were primitive hunters who had followed animal herds across the Bering Strait from Siberia into Alaska and then down ice-free corridors into the present-day United States. They arrived in the region during the last Ice Age, perhaps as early as 10,000 BC. Over the centuries, new groups of these Asiatic wanderers entered today's southeastern United States, mixing with the people already living there. The advent of agriculture was an important turning point, and soon after they had begun growing domestic crops, the natives were living in large settlements. By around 900 AD, the population of Georgia was living in large, agriculture-based villages covering many acres and supporting hundreds of residents.

This phase of prehistory, called the Mississippian Period, is most famous for the huge mounds the natives made from millions of buckets of earth. The mounds at Ocmulgee National Monument at Macon and those at Etowah Indian Mounds Historic Site and Archaeological Area at Cartersville are well-known examples of the creations of Mississippian builders and reflect the results of thousands of years of cultural evolution among the natives of the Southeast.

When the Spanish explorer Hernando de Soto entered Georgia in 1540, following landfall in Florida, he and his followers were amazed by the height of the native culture in the area. By then, the fires of Mississippian brilliance had waned somewhat, but they nevertheless remained bright enough to thoroughly impress the *civilized* Spaniards. De Soto and his men crossed Georgia in a generally southwest-to-northeast direction, passing near the present-day towns of Bainbridge, Albany, and Macon before entering South Carolina. Later in the year, he reentered Georgia from Tennessee and crossed the extreme northwestern corner of the state, near Rome.

A quarter of a century after De Soto's explorations, another Spaniard, Pedro Menéndez de Avilés, was ordered to the New World to drive out a French colony that had been organized in Florida. Menéndez successfully routed the French and built a fort on St. Catherines Island, south of present-day Savannah. In 1629 Charles I of England carved a large land grant out of much of the region, but it was nearly a century later before an English fort was built on the Altamaha River. Soon afterward, in 1732, King George II issued a large land grant to a corporation called the Trustees for Establishing the Colony of Georgia in America. One of the principles of the corporation was General James Oglethorpe, who volunteered to lead a party of 120 settlers to the mouth of the Savannah River. There, on February 12, 1733, Oglethorpe, by then designated governor of the new colony, and his small band of followers established the first permanent settlement in Georgia, aided greatly by the local Creek Indians and their chief, Tomochichi. Nine years after Oglethorpe's successful settlement at Savannah, England and Spain went to war, in part because of a dispute over the boundary between Georgia and Florida. When Oglethorpe defeated a Spanish invasion force at Bloody Marsh

GA Timeline

1540
Spaniard Hernando de Soto explores the southeastern United States, including Georgia.

1715
South Carolinian Thomas Nairne suggests to the English crown that it colonize the region that is now Georgia. For his reward, unhappy Indians burn him at the stake.

1733
James Oglethorpe and a small contingent of followers debark at the site of Savannah; by March of the following year, they have built 91 log houses overlooking the Savannah River.

1736
John Wesley, later to become famous as the father of Methodism, arrives in Savannah as a missionary for the Church of England; he establishes what has been called the world's first Protestant Sunday school.

on St. Simons Island in 1742, Spanish claims to Georgia were extinguished forever. The colony was never again seriously challenged.

When the Revolutionary War began, Georgia's population stood at around 50,000 residents, one-third of them slaves working on rice and indigo plantations along the seaboard. Georgia was left alone during the first few years of the war, but six months after the Articles of Confederation were approved in July 1778, British troops captured Savannah, and by the end of the next year they had taken control of every major town in Georgia. The fighting in Georgia, as in the nearby Carolinas, involved guerrilla bands as well as regular troops. The battles may have been small in scale, but they were bitterly contested. In 1779 American troops defeated a British force at Kettle Creek near the town of Washington in northeast Georgia; a short time later they were themselves bested at Brier Creek. The city of Augusta changed hands several times until Andrew Pickens and Light-Horse Harry Lee drove the British out in 1781. The British left Georgia forever when they lost Savannah to American forces in 1782. On January 2, 1788, five years after the Revolutionary War ended, Georgia joined the new United States. The last of the Thirteen Colonies to be founded, Georgia was the fourth state to ratify the Constitution and also the first Southern state to do so.

The state's economy received a dramatic boost in 1793, when Eli Whitney, who was visiting the plantation of the late General Nathanael Greene near Savannah, designed a cotton gin that could be inexpensively manufactured. Almost overnight, cotton became the number-one cash crop, not only in Georgia but in a large portion of the Southeast. Gins were installed all over the state, and, by the mid-1820s, Georgia's export figures for the crop led the world.

In 1828 the nation's first gold rush took place on Cherokee lands in the North Georgia mountains, setting the stage for the eventual removal of the native Cherokees from the homes of their ancestors. Even before the gold rush, thousands of acres of Indian lands in the state had been bargained away. When news of the gold discovery was made public, it was only a matter of time before the white settlers encroached on the tribal holdings and demanded that the Cherokees be expelled. President Andrew Jackson set the stage for the mass expulsion of all Indians east of the Mississippi River with his Indian Removal Act of 1830. A series of lengthy, high-level governmental discussions and lawsuits ended in the U.S. Supreme Court, and although the Cherokee eventually won their case, the state of Georgia ordered their removal, and they were forcibly escorted by the U.S. Army to lands beyond the Mississippi River.

By the time war clouds were again gathering over Georgia in the late 1850s, the state led all others in the number of plantations exceeding 1,000 acres in size. Contrary to popular belief, however, Georgia was still made up primarily of small, family-owned farms. Only 236 planters owned more than 100 slaves each, and the vast majority of the 50,000 farms in the state had no slaves at all. Even so, like the rest of the South, Georgia was caught up in the states' rights and slavery issues that had galvanized the nation's attention by 1860. Accordingly, soon after a specially called South Carolina conven-

INTRODUCTION
HISTORY
REGIONS
WHEN TO VISIT
STATE'S GREATS
RULES OF THE ROAD
DRIVING TOURS

1742 English forces under Oglethorpe defeat the Spanish in the battle of Bloody Marsh, assuring Georgia's survival and ending Spanish influence in the region.

1773 Georgia's slave population soars to over 15,000.

1776 Representing Georgia, Button Gwinnett, George Walton, and Lyman Hall travel to Philadelphia to sign the Declaration of Independence.

1777 Georgia's first constitution is adopted.

1778 During the Revolutionary War, Savannah falls to British naval forces; it is recaptured four years later by the Americans.

tion on December 20, 1860 dissolved the union between that state and the U.S., Georgia followed suit and announced its secession on January 20, 1861.

By mid-1863, most of Tennessee, Georgia's neighbor to the north, was occupied by elements of the Union army. On September 19–20 of that year, at Chickamauga in North Georgia, Confederate forces won their most important battle in the western theater. Their failure to follow up on the victory at Chickamauga, however, deprived them of nearby Chattanooga, which the fleeing Yankees occupied immediately. The Union high command set its sights on a prize it had been eyeing for months, Atlanta, situated at the southern end of the strategic corridor that split the state of Georgia in two from Chattanooga southward.

General William T. Sherman, commander of the Union armies in the West, advanced on Atlanta in May 1864. Following a lengthy siege of Atlanta, Sherman occupied the city in September and sent Confederate General John Bell Hood's Army of Tennessee fleeing. After burning the town, Sherman began his infamous March to the Sea in the fall. By the time he reached Savannah, just before Christmas, his army had cut a path of destruction 60 miles wide and caused an estimated $100 million worth of property damage. Railroads, factories, plantations, and farms were destroyed; livestock was commandeered; fields were burned; and in addition there was the terrible cost in human life.

With the fall of Savannah in December 1864, the Civil War was essentially over for Georgia. The official end came the following April at Appomattox Court House in Virginia, and Georgians began the long road to recovery. Following years of oppressive Reconstruction politics and policies, the state was finally permanently readmitted to the Union in 1870.

Good times returned fairly rapidly to Georgia, considering the amount of destruction that had been levied upon the state during Sherman's March to the Sea. By the mid-1870s sizable amounts of cotton were again being grown, and both Savannah and Brunswick had become important port towns for the export of the crop. Railroads were rebuilt, the state's timber was in demand, and the textile industry took a leap forward. By the turn of the 20th century, Georgia in general and Atlanta in particular were being universally hailed as prime examples of the South's remarkable recovery following the disastrous Civil War.

The early years of the 20th century brought a continuation of these healthy times. As new fibers for clothing were developed, cotton gradually lost its position as the number-one cash crop, succeeded by fruits, corn, livestock, and tobacco. In 1912 Juliette Gordon Low founded the Girl Scouts of America in Savannah. Rebecca L. Felton, the first woman to sit in the U.S. Senate, was sent to Washington in 1922 to replace the late Senator Thomas Watson, only to be unseated one day later by the newly elected replacement, Walter F. George. The Great Depression in 1929 brought days and years reminiscent of the poverty and anguish following the Civil War, but Georgians slowly pulled out of that dilemma much as an earlier generation had during Reconstruction.

Following World War II manufacturing overtook agriculture as Georgia's primary industry, and within a few years, more Georgians were living in urban settings than

1788	**1793**	**1820**	**1828**	**1838**
Georgia becomes the fourth state to ratify the new federal Constitution.	Eli Whitney invents the cotton gin while he is a guest at the Greene plantation near Savannah.	Georgia's population swells to nearly 341,000 people, including slaves.	The first gold rush in the United States begins at Dahlonega.	The Trail of Tears for the Cherokees begins. Before the long trek is over, thousands of men, women, and children will die from starvation and exposure.

INTRODUCTION
HISTORY
REGIONS
WHEN TO VISIT
STATE'S GREATS
RULES OF THE ROAD
DRIVING TOURS

in rural ones. Atlanta, the largest city in the state, witnessed a tremendous building boom, largely a result of the influx of Northern business interests that had suddenly discovered the economy and convenience of doing business in the New South.

During this same period, political and racial views were changing in Georgia. In 1964, for the first time since 1872, Georgians elected a Republican to the U.S. Congress. The same year, they also backed Barry Goldwater, the Republican candidate, for president. Continuing their bolt from the once-dominant Democratic party, voters supported Independent candidate George Wallace for president in 1968 and Republican Richard M. Nixon in 1972. Georgia's favorite son, former Governor Jimmy Carter, a native of Plains, recaptured the state for the Democrats in the presidential elections of 1976 and 1980.

In the meantime, Julian Bond, a black Democratic party member, civil rights advocate, and vocal anti–Vietnam War spokesman, was elected to the State House of Representatives in 1965. Following a lengthy battle by fellow representatives to deny him his seat, the U.S. Supreme Court ordered the House to allow Bond to claim his membership. In another black milestone, in 1973 Maynard Jackson was elected mayor of Atlanta, the first African-American mayor of a major Southern city.

The choice of Atlanta as the site for the 1996 Olympic Games was a spectacular indication of the growing importance of the city and its state. Today, Atlanta is a center of national and international transportation, business, and banking. Georgia is one of the most progressive states in the Union. Industry abounds, agriculture is still important, and tourism is at an all-time high.

Regions

1. NORTHEAST GEORGIA MOUNTAINS

The extreme northeastern section of Georgia lies in the Appalachian Mountains, and the area is one of majestic beauty and natural wonder. The first gold rush in American history occurred near Dahlonega, and the greed that surrounded it was directly responsible for the removal of the Cherokee Indians from this, their ancestral homeland. If you like the cool air of the high mountains, plenty of country-style and Old World–type resorts and B&Bs, or just plain relaxing along a rapidly flowing trout stream, this is the place for you.

Towns listed: Dahlonega, Helen, Gainesville, Hiawassee, Toccoa

2. CLASSIC SOUTH

The primary elements of Old South charm, from classical antebellum mansions to stately town squares and fragrant wisteria, are just a few among the many attractions to draw you to this region of Georgia, snuggled up alongside the South Carolina border. This

1842	1860	1861	1863	1864
A young physician living in Jefferson, Dr. Crawford Long, becomes the first person ever to use ether during a surgical procedure.	The Indian Removal Act sends practically all of Georgia's Indians—along with most of those living in the rest of the Southeast—to lands beyond the Mississippi River (today's Oklahoma).	On January 20, the state of Georgia secedes from the Union and joins the Confederacy.	Confederates win a major victory at Chickamauga, but fail to follow up, allowing the area to fall to Union troops.	After weeks of siege, Atlanta falls to the armies of Union General William Tecumseh Sherman. Shortly afterward, Sherman begins his famous March to the Sea, destroying literally everything

is also the home of the Masters' Golf Tournament, held annually at Augusta. You might prefer to watch one of the several fox hunts held in this part of the country or to go hunting in the midst of some of the finest bobwhite country in the United States.

Towns listed: Augusta, Washington

3. MAGNOLIA MIDLANDS

Southern cooking, fishing, and hunting are the favorite pastimes of natives of the Magnolia Midlands. Cotton is still king here, and fields of Vidalia onions contribute to the economic well-being of this agricultural heartland. Whether you celebrate St. Patrick's Day in Dublin or fête the famous onion in Vidalia, you'll always find something to do in this charming section that breathes images from the state's past.

Towns listed: Dublin, Statesboro, Vidalia

4. COLONIAL COAST

When James Oglethorpe first set foot on Georgia soil, in 1733, he couldn't have known that the spot where he was standing would one day grow into one of the most beautiful and charming cities in the United States. Today, Savannah anchors the northern end of the section of Georgia known as the Colonial Coast. Nearby Fort Pulaski, now a national monument, was one of Robert E. Lee's early construction projects as a young engineer in the U.S. Army.

Running the entire length of Georgia's Atlantic coast, the region includes the vacation wonderlands of Jekyll, Sea, and St. Simons islands, as well as Waycross, gateway to the wild and mysterious Okefenokee Swamp, one of the nation's largest freshwater marsh and swamplands.

Towns listed: Brunswick, Jekyll Island, Savannah, Sea Island, St. Simons Island, Waycross

5. PLANTATION TRACE

More plantations await you in the subtropical climate of the Plantation Trace region, which shares a common border with Florida in the southeastern part of the state. Pine and oak trees, plentiful wildlife, and a once-profitable timber industry are all part of the interesting story that this historic section of Georgia has to tell.

Today, peanuts, cotton, and soybeans are popular crops that help the economy of the region.

Towns listed: Albany, Bainbridge, Thomasville, Tifton, Valdosta

6. PRESIDENTIAL PATHWAYS

U.S. President Jimmy Carter, a native of Plains, Georgia, was a student at the U.S. Naval Academy in 1945 when the incumbent president, Franklin D. Roosevelt, died at his summer home at nearby Warm Springs. The location of both chief executive—related sites in this region of Georgia, which backs up to the Alabama border, gives it its name. Images

	1868	**1877**	**1886**	**1892**
between him and Savannah.	Georgia is readmitted to the Union.	Atlanta becomes the capital of Georgia.	Baseball great Ty Cobb is born in Banks County.	The Coca-Cola Company begins production in Atlanta.

of the Civil War are conjured up when you visit Andersonville, the huge Confederate prison, while more modern army equipment is on display at the Fort Benning National Infantry Museum near Columbus.

Towns listed: Americus, Andersonville, Columbus

7. HISTORIC HEARTLAND

Whether it's prehistoric Indian ruins, mouth-watering barbecue, or shops in the historic districts of antebellum towns, there is something waiting for you in the Historic Heartland. Situated smack in the middle of Georgia, the region boasts some of the state's most evocative villages, plantations, and churches, plus memories of Br'er Rabbit and Br'er Fox and the other Uncle Remus characters collected by native Joel Chandler Harris. This region lies on the path of General William T. Sherman's March to the Sea, but you'll see one town, Madison, that the fire-eating general refused to burn.

Towns listed: Eatonton, Macon, Madison, Milledgeville

8. ATLANTA METRO

The number of people living inside the city limits of Atlanta is about 400,000, but that figure swells to nearly 3 million when the greater metropolitan area is considered. Looked at that way, Atlanta is one of the largest cities in the United States. The capture of Atlanta was the primary goal of the Union army campaign led by General William T. Sherman in late 1864. The town's fall was the beginning of the end for the Confederacy. Today, the Atlanta Metro region is upbeat, progressive, and modern, truly a metropolis by any definition of the word. The arts abound in Atlanta, and you are never far away from a theater, museum, or other cultural site. There is plenty else to do as well, whether you are a shopper, music lover, outdoorsperson, or sports fanatic.

Towns listed: Atlanta, Marietta, Roswell, Stone Mountain

9. HISTORIC HIGH COUNTRY

Nestled in the extreme northwestern section of the state is Historic High Country, a region that shares its borders with Alabama and Tennessee. The area is dominated by the highlands created by the foothills of the Appalachian Mountains. It is richly steeped in prehistoric and Cherokee Indian lore and Civil War history. It is also the world *capital* for the carpet industry, with wayside outlets galore where you can shop till you drop and buy at deep discounts.

Towns listed: Calhoun, Cartersville, Dalton, Rome

When to Visit

Georgia's climate varies significantly, and the timing of your visit depends on two elements: where you plan to travel in the state, and whether you are fond of hot

INTRODUCTION
HISTORY
REGIONS
WHEN TO VISIT
STATE'S GREATS
RULES OF THE ROAD
DRIVING TOURS

1912	1929	1939	1945	1974
In Savannah, Juliette Gordon Low establishes the Girl Scouts of America movement.	Martin Luther King, Jr., is born in Atlanta.	The motion picture *Gone with the Wind*, based on Atlanta-native Margaret Mitchell's best-selling novel of the same name, premieres in Atlanta.	President Franklin D. Roosevelt dies at his summer home in Warm Springs.	The Atlanta Braves' Hank Aaron hits his 715th home run at home, breaking the old lifetime record held by Babe Ruth.

weather or prefer more moderate temperatures. Even in the summer, the temperatures in the northern mountains are tolerable, especially in the evenings, although it can get pretty warm in the daytime. In the southern half of the state, however, especially along the Atlantic coast and the Florida border, the heat and humidity in July and August can be stifling, day or night.

If you can stand the heat and humidity that prevail in southern Georgia during the summertime, then the timing of your trip there will not matter. On the other hand, if you can't tolerate temperatures approaching 100° F for days on end, with the humidity reading trailing closely behind, then by all means schedule your visit to coincide with the cooler and less humid days of spring, fall, or winter.

Some parts of southern Georgia are practically subtropical in climate, with many locales that get a daily shower that serves to increase the already elevated levels of humidity.

The average year-round temperature for Georgia is 65° F. Winters are relatively short and mild and average between 41° F and 57° F, while the summers tend to be very hot and humid with temperatures averaging between 81° F and 95° F. The coldest temperature ever recorded in Georgia was -17° F on January 26, 1936, in Floyd County. The hottest temperature was 113° F on May 26, 1974, at Greenville.

The state's annual rainfall averages 76 inches. Snow is infrequent in Georgia, the exception being in the northern mountains that lie near the Tennessee and North Carolina borders.

CLIMATE CHART
Average High/Low Temperatures (° F) and Monthly Precipitation (in inches)

	JAN.	FEB.	MAR.	APR.	MAY	JUNE
ATLANTA	52/36	54/38	63/43	72/52	79/61	86/67
	4.8	4.8	5.8	4.2	4.3	3.6
	JULY	AUG.	SEPT.	OCT.	NOV.	DEC.
	88/70	86/70	83/65	72/54	61/43	52/38
	5.0	3.7	3.4	3.1	3.9	4.4
	JAN.	FEB.	MAR.	APR.	MAY	JUNE
SAVANNAH	60/38	62/41	70/48	78/55	84/63	89/69
	3.6	3.2	3.8	3.0	4.1	5.7
	JULY	AUG.	SEPT.	OCT.	NOV.	DEC.
	91/72	90/72	85/68	78/57	70/48	62/41
	6.4	7.5	4.5	2.4	2.1	3.0

FESTIVALS AND SEASONAL EVENTS
WINTER

Dec. **Christmas in Roswell.** Features tours of the quaint town's historic district and antebellum homes. The town is gaily deco-

1976
Georgia-native James Earl Carter is elected president of the United States.

1996
The Summer Olympics are held in Atlanta.

INTRODUCTION
HISTORY
REGIONS
WHEN TO VISIT
STATE'S GREATS
RULES OF THE ROAD
DRIVING TOURS

rated with lights and greenery. Entertainment includes plays and storytelling. | 770/640–3253 or 800/776–7935.

Jan. **Georgia Heritage Festival.** This annual event in Savannah features a waterfront festival with concerts, craft shows, and a parade. There are walking tours and open house at many of the city's historic properties. | 912/233–7787.

SPRING

Mar. **Sacred Heart Garden Festival.** Augusta lives up to its nickname, Garden City, when it hosts this annual flower show. Seminars, panel discussions, and demonstrations of the *hows* and *whys* of gardening are presented by the region's leading gardeners and horticulturists. | 706/826–4700.

Apr. **A Taste of Toccoa.** Witness the wonderful world of northeastern Georgia at this festival, where music, food, children's events, and art come together for an evening not soon forgotten. | 877/686–2262.

May/Oct. **Cotton Pickin' Fair.** Held at Gay near Columbus, this is one of America's top arts and crafts festivals, featuring antiques, arts and crafts, and food against the backdrop of an old cotton plantation. The event is repeated on the first weekend in October. | 706/538–6814.

May/Oct. **National Indian Pow Wow.** Held annually in the Parks at Chehaw near Albany, in May and October. The festival features Indian crafts, storytelling, dances, food, and lectures. | 912/430–5275.

SUMMER

June **Country by the Sea Music Festival.** Some of the nation's biggest names in country music perform on Jekyll's Beach. | 877/635–4076.

Aug. **Georgia Mountain Fair.** This event in Hiawassee brings together a wide array of country and gospel music, arts and crafts, food, clogging contests, and lots of entertainment. | 706/896–4191.

AUTUMN

Oct. **Big Pig Jig.** The statewide Georgia Barbecue Championship is featured at this festival, held in Vienna near Cordele. A golf tournament, fireworks, carnival, and parade add to the fun. | 912/268–8275.

State's Greats

Whatever you're looking for in the way of a vacation destination, Georgia is sure to have it. For hikers, nature lovers, and white-water buffs, there are the cool mountains in the northern part of the state. For beachcombers, golfers, and sun worshipers, the **Golden Isles** that stretch along the Atlantic coast from Savannah to the Florida border can't be beat. If you want to visit historic sites, no town in America has more to offer than **Savannah,** and the state's **prehistoric Indian remains** and **Civil War sites** rank among the very best in America. And those who are happiest in a big-city environment will be very satisfied with Atlanta's rich mosaic of museums, restaurants, city parks, and shopping facilities.

Forests and Parks

Georgia has two national forests, the **Chattahoochee** and the **Oconee.** The Chattahoochee is a huge expanse of mountainous land—more than 1.5 million acres—that lies along the Tennessee and North Carolina borders on the north and the South Carolina border to the east. The state's highest elevations are in this region, and European-inspired villages dot the landscape. The many outdoor sports available include winter skiing; some of the larger resorts manufacture snow for off-season. Water sports on the area's many lakes are popular, as well as wilderness pastimes such as hiking, camping, and fishing. **Oconee National Forest** is farther south, along either side of I–20 between Atlanta and Augusta. Consisting of a quarter of a million acres, Oconee also features outdoor sports, but its location rules out skiing.

More than 50 state parks are scattered across Georgia, most of which offer swimming, hiking, and camping; those with lakes or rivers add fishing and boating.

Georgia's national parks and monuments include the **Andersonville National Historic Site,** the location of a Confederate prisoner-of-war camp during the Civil War; the **Chickamauga and Chattanooga National Military Park,** the nation's first military park, commemorating the decisive Civil War battle; **Ocmulgee National Monument,** which contains some of America's best preserved prehistoric mounds; and **Fort Frederica National Monument,** the remains of a fort built by James Oglethorpe to defend the new Georgia colony against Spanish attack.

No discussion of Georgia's natural assets can be made without mentioning **Okefenokee National Wildlife Refuge,** in the extreme southern part of the state near the Florida border. Nearly 400,000 acres of fresh-water swamp contain rare and endangered subtropical wildlife, including the American alligator, the Florida sandhill crane, and the red-cockaded woodpecker. Several other national wildlife refuges and wilderness areas are along the Atlantic coastline as well.

Culture, History, and the Arts

Mention of Georgia usually conjures up thoughts of antebellum plantations, cotton fields, and *Gone with the Wind.* The years before and during the Civil War were indeed important for the state, but history was being made in the region well before those perilous times. Scores of prehistoric Indian sites are scattered over the state, testifying to the high level of culture attained by these earliest settlers. **Ocmulgee National Monument** at Macon, the **Etowah Indian Mounds** at Cartersville, and the **Kolomoki Mounds State Park** at Blakely are just a few of the sites that are open to the public and that maintain exhibits interpreting the long and rich history of these ancient peoples.

The **city of Savannah** is a museum unto itself. Remnants of early architecture abound, and the town's design and well-laid-out streets are a prime example of early colonial city planning. Scores of houses and commercial buildings are on a regular tour, and a visit will give you a vivid sense of life along the Atlantic seaboard in the 18th and 19th centuries.

Of course, **the Civil War** is well documented in Georgia. Through a series of federally maintained parks, the history of the tragic conflict can be learned through museum exhibits, lectures, and battlefield tours. **Andersonville, Chickamauga, Fort Pulaski,** and **Kennesaw Mountain** are among the battle sites preserved in the national park chain.

The arts run rampant in Atlanta, home of the **Robert W. Woodruff Arts Center,** the Southeast's largest arts complex. One of its elements, the **High Museum,** features an outstanding collection of European art dating from the Renaissance to the present. The **Atlanta Symphony** performs regularly at Symphony Hall, also part of the Woodruff Center. The lavishly decorated **Fox Theatre** hosts artistic performances and trade conventions. The **Martin Luther King, Jr. National Historic Site** contains memorabilia of the civil rights leader, as well as a theater, library, and chapel.

INTRODUCTION
HISTORY
REGIONS
WHEN TO VISIT
STATE'S GREATS
RULES OF THE ROAD
DRIVING TOURS

Beaches

Georgia's waterfront is limited to a stretch of about 100 miles between the South Carolina and Florida borders—but Oh, what a stretch it is! Some of the most beautiful beaches in the East are on the famous **Golden Isles,** a series of subtropical barrier islands that lies just off the mainland coast. You can drive to three of them—**Sea, St. Simons, and Jekyll islands**—but to reach the others (Cumberland, Little St. Simons, Ossabaw, St. Catherines, and Sapelo) you have to go by boat, which adds to their romantic appeal. Once home to an enormous variety of exotic wildlife, the Golden Isles are today known for the number and variety of excellent resorts.

Sports

From winter **skiing** in the northern mountains, to **water-skiing** on the inland lakes, to world-class **golfing** at one of the state's many golf courses, to plantation **quail hunting** in the southwest, to salt-water **fishing** on the Golden Isles, Georgia is a sportsman's paradise. No matter where you are in the state, some kind of recreational facility or opportunity is nearby.

If spectator sports are your game, then there is plenty in Atlanta for you to watch. The city is the proud home of three major league sports teams. The **Atlanta Hawks** basketball team plays at the Georgia Dome, as does the **Atlanta Falcons** football team. The city's National League baseball team, the **Atlanta Braves,** plays at Turner Field. And, for those of you who like top-of-the-line golf competition, there is the **Masters Golf Tournament,** held annually at Augusta.

Rules of the Road

License Requirements: As a visitor driving an automobile in Georgia, you must have a valid driver's license from your home state.

Right Turn on Red: In Georgia, drivers can turn right on a red light *after* coming to a full stop, unless otherwise posted.

Seat Belts and Helmet Laws: A state law requires safety belts to be used by all persons riding in the front seat of a vehicle and all minors riding anywhere in the vehicle. Children ages 3 and 4 can use a regulation safety belt, but those ages 2 and under must be restrained in an approved safety seat.

Speed Limits: Individual speed limits are posted in all municipalities. Most interstates maintain a 50 mph speed limit in metropolitan areas and a 70 mph limit in rural areas.

For more information: Call the Georgia Department of Transportation at 404/656–5267.

Apple Orchards and Cotton Patches Driving Tour

FROM THE BLUE RIDGE MOUNTAINS OF APPALACHIA TO PLANTATION AND QUAIL COUNTRY

Distance: 360 mi   Time: 3–4 days
Breaks: You could spend the night in Rome or Columbus.

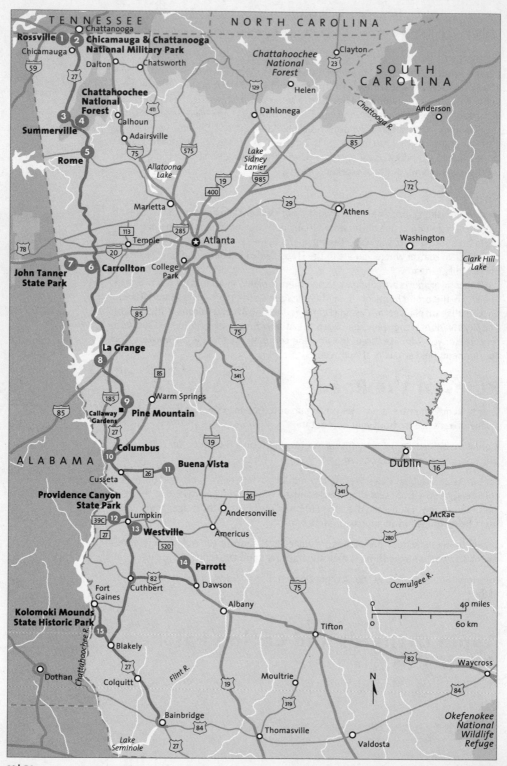

U.S. 27 south from the Appalachian Mountains in western Georgia links historic sites, busy cities, and quaint towns. The road courses through the state's rolling, hilly apple country to southwest Georgia where cotton fields spread to the horizon and where quail-hunting plantations have provided leisure for the rich and famous since the early 20th century.

❶ Begin the tour in the town of Rossville, near Chattanooga, Tennessee, with a visit to the John Ross House, named for the Cherokee leader who struggled valiantly against the removal of the Cherokee people to Oklahoma. When he failed, the Cherokee were rounded up and moved west under military escort in 1838. Thousands, including Ross's first wife, succumbed to the harsh rigors of the march. The house, which is the oldest structure in northwest Georgia, is open June through August.

❷ From the Ross House, continue south about 3 mi on U.S. 27 to Fort Oglethorpe and the **Chickamauga and Chattanooga National Military Park,** the nation's oldest military park. It was here, on September 19–20, 1863, that one of America's bloodiest battles was fought. More than 20,000 men died as General William T. Sherman marched from Chattanooga to Atlanta. U.S. 27 travels right through the park, but this visitors center merits a stop, and it would be a shame not to take some time to walk the grounds, which are well furnished with historical markers and monuments.

❸ Continue south on U.S. 27 to Summerville, where folk artist Howard Finster has his **Paradise Gardens.** The colorful, self-anointed minister paints religious themes, hewing to a strictly fundamentalist (from his perspective) interpretation of scripture. His paintings are very popular, especially among collectors of American folk art, for whom a stop at Paradise Gardens is almost a pilgrimage.

❹ Continuing south toward Rome, U.S. 27 passes through the exquisite **Chattahoochee National Forest,** an enormous (almost 750,000 acres) expanse of nationally preserved forest that takes in two substantial, but not contiguous, pieces of the North Georgia mountains. This segment runs north–south along Taylor Ridge.

❺ Approximately 10 mi south of the forest on U.S. 27, you'll come to **Rome,** named because, like its namesake in Italy, it was built on seven hills. The downtown section of Rome is charming, and there is an extensive rails-to-trails system for hiking and bicycling through the downtown area. In Rome, the **Chieftans Trail** begins, its first site being the **Chieftans Museum and the home of Major Ridge.** The Cherokee were known as excellent carpenters and builders, and the Ridge home typifies the plantation-plain style they preferred. Soon after the arrival of Europeans in their lands, the Cherokees abandoned their traditional costume along with other traditions, such as the longhouse style of abode, which they gave up in favor of the single-family house.

Also significant in Rome is **Berry College,** founded by Martha Berry to teach underprivileged mountain children. This beautiful 28,000-acre campus, the world's largest, is open to the public.

❻ From Rome, U.S. 27 continues south and crosses I–20, soon entering the town of **Carrollton,** named for John Carroll, a signer of the Declaration of Independence. It is also home to the State University of West Georgia. If you're a film buff, you might want to visit Susan Hayward's gravesite at Our Lady of Perpetual Help Catholic Church (770/832–8977). Hayward received five Oscar nominations and won the best actress Academy Award for her role in *I Want to Live*; she was married to Eton Chalkley, a businessman in Carrollton. They lived in Carrollton, which she considered her home, on a farm across the road from the church where they are both buried. To get there, turn east onto U.S. 78 where U.S. 27 crosses it to reach Temple, then turn south (right) 5 mi on Rte. 113 just before Abilene, which is barely a blip in the road now marked by a church. The church is just off Rte. 113, and a sign points the way. To reconnect to U.S. 27, go south on Rte. 113, which leads straight into U.S. 27.

7 Just 6 mi west of Carrollton, **John Tanner State Park** offers 2 lakes for swimming, boating, and fishing, plus camping and motor lodge rooms. There's a 1-mi nature trail for hiking around the upper lake. The park is about 5 mi south of U.S. 27. Turn right on Bowdoin Junction Rd., go 3 mi until it dead-ends at Rte. 16, turn left, and go 1.7 mi to Tanner Beach Rd. and turn right and go for .7 mi and through the gate.

8 From Carrollton, continue south on U.S. 27 to **La Grange,** named, so the story goes, by the marquis de Lafayette himself, who bestowed upon it the French term for farm and the name of his own country abode because the area so reminded him of that part of France. His likeness graces a fountain in the center of town, Lafayette Square. The statue was made in LePuy, France, from a mold of the original by Ernst Eugene Hyolle.
In La Grange, be sure to visit **Bellevue,** the exquisite antebellum Greek-revival home of Senator Benjamin Harvey Hill, and the **Chattahoochee Valley Art Museum.**

9 You should plan to spend a day or two in **Pine Mountain,** approximately 20 mi south of La Grange on U.S. 27. There is much to see in this area, beginning with a visit to **Callaway Gardens** on Rte. 18/354. The 14,000-acre gardens provide an amazing array of flower-filled vistas, especially in spring and summer. Here, you'll find hiking trails and bicycle paths. Also within the gardens, the **Cecil B. Day Butterfly Center** has more than 1,000 butterflies flying freely in a glassed-in space.

10 Continue south on U.S. 27 to **Columbus,** which is rich in military history. Here the **National Infantry Museum** as well as the **Port Columbus Civil War Center** will take up the better part of a day. To get a handle on the area and what made it important, start at the **Columbus Museum.** Don't miss a glimpse at the **Springer Opera House.**
During the day, weather permitting, Columbus begs to be explored on foot. The terrain is level, and it's an easy walk around the historic center. Columbus's Riverfront district, an ongoing restoration project, shows how old industrial buildings and neighborhoods can house excellent restaurants, new businesses, and living space. For guided tours and maps to the historic district, stop in at the Convention and Visitors Bureau.

11 Going from Columbus toward Cusseta on U.S. 27, turn east on Rte. 26 to Buena Vista. Follow the signs to **Pasaquan,** a painted environment by local iconoclastic artist Edward Owens Martin, who preferred to be known as St. EOM. This is a must-stop for anyone interested in self-taught art, as Martin crafted here, on his mother's farm, what can only be described as one of the country's most unusual works of art. Every surface, every stretch of concrete and every wall (and when he ran out of wall, he simply made more), is covered with his mythological anthropomorphic creatures painted in intense colors.

12 Returning to Cusseta, pick up U.S. 27 again south to Lumpkin, just west of which on Rte. 39C is **Providence Canyon State Park.** This Grand Canyon of Georgia is the result of erosion, but the site is a unique day-use park for hiking and picnicking.

13 Follow the signs southeast of Lumpkin to **Westville,** a reconstructed village where costumed docents explain the realities of rural life in west Georgia during the 19th century.

INTRODUCTION
HISTORY
REGIONS
WHEN TO VISIT
STATE'S GREATS
RULES OF THE ROAD
DRIVING TOURS

⑭ Back on U.S. 27 south through Cuthbert, take U.S. 82 east to Dawson, then Rte. 520 north to Parrott, whose restored storefronts capture the essence of 19th- and early 20th-century Georgia towns.

⑮ Retracing your steps to return to U.S. 27, you'll pass near the **Kolomoki Mounds State Historic Park** and then through Blakely, Colquitt, and finally Bainbridge, all historic towns, before exiting the state just north of Tallahassee, Florida. The most interesting of these sites is Colquitt, hometown of one of Georgia's official plays, *Swamp Gravy,* a folk opera presenting the lives and experiences of the local people performed by a cast of locals. The dish it's named for is a kind of stew made of bacon drippings, bits of fish, and whatever else comes to hand.

A Cultural Thread Driving Tour
VIEWING GEORGIA FROM U.S. 441

Distance: 380 mi   Time: 4 days
Breaks: After leaving the Okefenokee, the first natural break would be in McRae for lunch, then stay in Dublin. Then head to Milledgeville, Eatonton, or Madison, followed by Athens.

U.S. 441 traverses the state north to south from the Florida line near the Okefenokee National Wildlife Refuge to the North Georgia mountains. Along its path lie small towns and unique natural phenomena; art galleries, barbecue joints, and boiled peanut stands; state parks and national recreational facilities; pastures, dairy farms, and apple orchards; moss-draped trees and tall pine forests through which the moonlight gleams just as the song promises. No matter at which end of this varied landscape you choose to begin, you will find a wealth of cultural, visual, and culinary experiences.

❶ Entering Georgia from Florida on U.S. 441 brings you to Fargo, on the western edge of the **Okefenokee National Wildlife Refuge.** This amazing 700-square-mi environment harbors wildlife of the most exotic sort. Each season brings its own special time in the refuge, but perhaps spring is best: Unique blooms paint every bend in the water trails. It's mating season, and the bull frogs and bull alligators compete with one another for choral time. It's also bug season, and the size of these yellow flies will amaze you. Bring plenty of repellent and wear long sleeves and long pants.
   The closest entrance from this side of the refuge is **Stephen C. Foster State Park,** about 17 mi northeast of Fargo on Rte. 177. You can make your base camp here and enjoy a day trip into the refuge. The park has camp and RV sites, as well as cottages. In addition, there's a lake for fishing and boating, and you can canoe from the park into the refuge.

❷ Returning to Fargo, head north on U.S. 441 toward Homerville, then continue on to **Douglas. Lott's Country Store and Gristmill** is a bit out of the way (10 mi southwest of Douglas on Rte. 135 to the Atkinson County line, right 5 mi to a barnlike building, follow signs), but worth a trip to savor rural commercial reality and the grinding of corn.

❸ About 6 mi outside of Douglas on Rte. 32 is **General Coffee State Park,** with good campsites and a lodge, as well as RV and trailer facilities. An early 19th-century homestead, including a blacksmith shop, corn crib, and turpentine display, is in the park.

❹ U.S. 441 goes right through Little Ocmulgee State Park, which features a 30-room lodge and restaurant. The Little Ocmulgee River meanders northwest off the Ocmul-

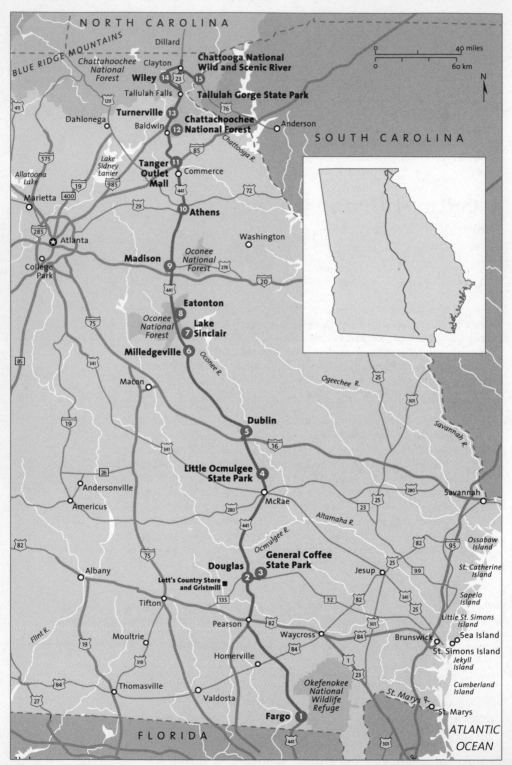

NORTH CAROLINA

BLUE RIDGE MOUNTAINS

Dillard

Chattahoochee
National
Forest

Clayton

Chattooga National
Wild and Scenic River

Wiley 14 23 15

Tallulah Falls

Tallulah Gorge State Park

76

Turnerville 13

Dahlonega

Baldwin

Chattachoochee
National Forest 12

Anderson

SOUTH CAROLINA

411

129

Tanger
Outlet
Mall 11

Chattooga R.

85

Commerce

441 72

Lake
Sidney
Lanier

575

Athens 10

Allatoona
Lake

19 985

400

29

Marietta

285

Atlanta

College
Park

Washington

Madison 9

441

Oconee
National
Forest

278

20

Eatonton 8

Oconee
National
Forest

Lake
Sinclair 7

Milledgeville 6

Oconee R.

Ogeechee R.

25

75

341

Macon

19

301

Savannah R.

85

Dublin 5

16

341

Little Ocmulgee
State Park 4

26

Andersonville

McRae

280

23

25

280

Savannah

Americus

441

Altamaha R.

82

95

Ossabaw
Island

75

Ocmulgee R.

St. Catherine
Island

Albany

General Coffee
State Park

Douglas 2 3

Jesup

25

99

Lott's Country Store
and Gristmill

82

135

32

82

341

25

Sapelo
Island

Tifton

Pearson

82

Waycross

301

84

Little St. Simons
Island

Sea Island

Flint R.

Moultrie

319

84

Homerville

Brunswick

St. Simons Island

1

Jekyll
Island

84

27

Thomasville

Valdosta

23

Okefenokee
National
Wildlife
Refuge

St. Marys R.

Cumberland
Island

St. Marys

Fargo 1

441

301

FLORIDA

ATLANTIC
OCEAN

40 miles
60 km

N

INTRODUCTION
HISTORY
REGIONS
WHEN TO VISIT
STATE'S GREATS
RULES OF THE ROAD
DRIVING TOURS

gee River, which, in turn, runs right up the middle of the state and once served as a major transportation conduit. This park has an 18-hole golf course, a lake with beach, nature trail, a restaurant, cottages, and tent, RV and trailer sites. Dating to 1935, the park is the work of the Civilian Conservation Corps.

5 Heading north from the park, U.S. 441 crosses I–16, the east–west interstate between Macon and Savannah. Crossing it, your next stop 25 mi later is **Dublin,** famous for its two-week-long celebration of St. Patrick's Day. If you choose to spend the night in Dublin, try the **Page House,** a fine Greek-revival residence and bed-and-breakfast inn.

6 From Dublin, U.S. 441 cuts northwest 50 mi toward **Milledgeville,** the capital of Confederate Georgia. There is much of historical interest here, so plan a day in this charming town rich with antebellum architecture, once home to novelist Flannery O'Connor.

7 **Lake Sinclair,** just north of Milledgeville on U.S. 441, lets you go fishing, boating, swimming, and camping.

8 From Lake Sinclair, head north on U.S. 441 to Putnam County, Georgia's dairy country, full of green rolling fields, grazing herds of Holstein cattle, and tree-lined country roads branching off U.S. 441 to beckon the curious traveler. **Eatonton** is the hometown of journalist and storyteller Joel Chandler Harris and modern novelist Alice Walker (*The Color Purple, Temple of My Familiar*). The *Br'er Rabbit* statue in the center of town acknowledges Harris's role as a gatherer of the African-origin tales that made up the Uncle Remus stories. You can also visit the **Uncle Remus Museum.**

For a good bed-and-breakfast, stay at **Crockett House,** a Victorian-era residence, and dine on Southern fare at **Magnolia House.**

9 From Eatonton north to **Madison** is only 25 mi, but on the way U.S. 441 curves along the southern section of the **Oconee National Forest.** Stop at **Rock Eagle,** the state 4-H camp, for a view of the eagle itself, a milky quartz bird sculpture about 5,000 years old. The forest is a two-part preserve featuring several wildlife management areas.

In Madison, you'll notice clusters of headstones on both sides of the railroad track. These are testimony to military activity in the region during the Civil War. Casualties were taken off passing trains and left alongside the tracks. The town's women interred the dead, but they were unable to carry the bodies any distance so buried them at random where they had been deposited. One headstone refers to an unidentified "colored" hospital corpsman, buried with his white compatriots.

In downtown Madison you'll want to get out of the car, pull on your walking shoes, and hit the pavement. Beginning at the imposing Victorian-era courthouse, you can explore the area, the main square of which is crowded with antique shops and restaurants. Loft living came to Madison some time ago, and several downtown commercial buildings have been remade as homes for some of the town's denizens. From there, walk into the residential area and explore the side streets. The **Madison-Morgan Cultural Center** is a good place to start this visit. In a former schoolhouse, the center houses art galleries and a history museum.

If you choose to spend the night in Madison, head 6 mi east of town on U.S. 278 to the **Farmhouse Inn** and dine in Rutledge, just 8 mi west on U.S. 278 at **Yesterday Café,** which serves a fabulous breakfast and lunch every day.

10 Continue along U.S. 441 to **Athens.** Home of the University of Georgia and site of numerous antebellum classical-revival residences, the town is known as the Classic City. Much modern music has spun out of Athens in recent years, as it's home to REM and the B–52s, among other groups. Music festivals abound, and there's always a performance somewhere.

Without question the largest employer and biggest single attraction is the University of Georgia itself, so you might want to begin your tour at the visitors center. **Founders' Memorial Garden,** on the campus, is an important site for anyone interested in gardening; Athens was site of the first Garden Club of America. After visiting the campus, pick up a walking-tour map at the **Athens Welcome Center** and visit the many architecturally worthy residences and commercial buildings, some of them open to the public. You can also arrange a driving tour in one of the center's tour buses, which travel around the historic district at 2 PM. It's a good idea to make reservations for the tour in the morning.

⑪ Continuing north from Athens, U.S. 441 slides just north of Commerce and then intersects Rte. 96 before crossing I–85 at Exit 53 (Banks Crossing). If your shopping demons are in fine tune, they'll be well exorcised at the outlet malls that surround Exit 53. Take a left at Rte. 96 off U.S. 441 and go about 3 mi toward I–85. On both sides of this exit (no. 52) are more shops. The Tanger Outlet Mall has three sections, on either side of I–85.

⑫ In another 15 mi U.S. 441 starts to curve along the western edge of the two-part **Chattahoochee National Forest.** This is the largest section of the forest and is the beginning of some of the most interesting traveling along U.S. 441. You're headed toward the **Blue Ridge Mountains,** part of the Appalachian Mountain chain. Each small town is a treasure trove where you can stop and enjoy local sights while shopping for antiques or local produce and preserves.

⑬ At Baldwin, take the modern, four-lane U.S. 441, which slides alongside Turnerville, where the **Glen-Ella Springs Inn and Conference Center** has a national reputation as one of the country's finest small resorts, noted for both its lodging and its dining. From here it's just 6 mi north to **Tallulah Falls,** where in 1970 the famous high-wire artist Karl Wallenda stepped delicately across a wire strung over Tallulah Gorge as the canyon's wind whipped around him and hundreds of spectators held their collective breath.

⑭ Head north on U.S. 441 toward Wiley, about 6 mi away. On the left is **Lofty Branch,** sitting high on a rise. Go up the winding driveway, and you'll find artists' studios producing textiles, hand-wrought iron, and works in other media. Across the road at **Bartow's Mountain Restaurant** it's barbecue time, with choices running from house-smoked pork and turkey to excellent barbecued chicken. Brunswick stew's good, too, and depending on the season, fruit-packed homemade ice cream (oh, the blackberry!) is simply divine.

Along this stretch of U.S. 441 are numerous fruit stands selling not only fruit in season (summer's blueberries and blackberries, fall's apples, and late summer's white peaches are not to be missed), but also local honey, and locally produced jams, preserves, and pickles. You can buy gourds, fresh cider, and pumpkins in the fall. Even if you don't buy a thing, the characters who run these places are worth a stop. Listen to their conversation with friends for an earful of the local language. As early as 1 PM, you might hear someone comment on what a beautiful evening it is. And if someone says, "You're a mess," take it as a compliment, for in fact it means "You're a lot of fun."

⑮ Spend your last day white-water rafting down the **Chattooga National Wild and Scenic River,** which forms the border between Georgia and South Carolina. From the Beechwood Inn, put-in is just 10 mi east on U.S. 76. Contact either **Southeastern Expeditions** or Wildwater Rafting for information, and don't even think about rafting this very dangerous river by yourself. Aptly named, its wildness ascends to level 5 rapids in some parts, while placid stretches allow you to catch your breath and gaze at the exquisite scenery. Day trips as well as overnight excursions are available. Nature lovers can trace the footsteps of the Philadelphia-born naturalist William Bartram, who first described much of Georgia's plants and wildlife. A trail map is available at the welcome center.

ALBANY

(Nearby towns also listed: Americus, Cordele)

This typical Southern town with a population of 78,000 was founded in 1836 by a Connecticut native, Colonel Nelson Tift. The Trail of Tears took most of the region's Indians westward in the late 1830s, and the vacuum created by their migration was quickly filled by American settlers. The pecan tree is king here, and the vicinity is famous for its production of the delicious nut, as well as for bobwhite quail hunting.

Information: Convention and Visitors Bureau | 225 W. Broad Ave., 31701 | 912/434–8700 | www.albanyga.com.

Attractions

Albany Civil Rights Movement Museum. Exhibitions housed in a turn-of-the-20th-century former African-American church focus on the music of the time, especially songs participants used to keep the spirit of the movement alive. Many African Americans from Albany were active in the movement. Mt. Zion Baptist Church, as the building was known then, heard Martin Luther King, Jr., preach in 1961. The congregation moved to a new, bigger church outside of town, and this church was made a museum. | 326 Whitney Ave. | 912/432–1698 | fax 912/432–2150 | $3 | Wed.–Sat. 10–4, Sun. 2–5.

Albany Museum of Art. This important regional museum is full of surprises. Among its outstanding holdings are a unique collection of African masks and pieces of 19th- and 20th-century European and American art. The museum hosts some six traveling exhibitions each year. The handsome postmodern building, by Albany architect Mack Wakeford, boasts a children's wing, AMAzing Space, featuring a youth art gallery and a hands-on participatory gallery where children can complete individual projects. | 311 Meadowlark Dr. | 912/439–8400 | fax 912/439–1332 | www.albanymuseum.com | Free | Tues., Wed., Fri., Sat. 10–5, Thurs. 10–7, Sun. 1–4.

The Parks at Chehaw. This 800-acre pine forest along the banks of Lake Chehaw and Muckalee Creek is the ideal setting for plants and wildlife typical of southwest Georgia. You must leave the park at dusk. | 105 Chehaw Park Rd. | 912/430–5275 | fax 912/430–3035 | www.parksatchehaw.org | $2 per car; $5 per van; $10 per bus | Memorial Day–Labor Day, daily 9–7; Labor Day–Memorial Day, daily 9–5.
Chehaw Wild Animal Park. More than 160 native and exotic animals representing 50 different species roam 150 fenced-in acres of Chehaw Park. The zoo, accredited by the Aquarium and Zoo Association, is a walk-through area, and there are picnic areas and a play park, as well as fishing, hiking, and bicycling areas. RV and tent camping. | 105 Chehaw Park Rd. | 912/430–5275 | fax 912/430–3035 | www.parksatchehaw.org | $2, in addition to the fee to enter the Parks at Chehaw; parking $2 per car; $5 per van; $10 per bus | Daily 9:30–5.
Lake Chehaw. Bordering the Parks at Chehaw, the lake has a dock for fishing and for launching boats. The Muckalee and Kinchafoonee creeks, both tributaries of the Flint River, join to form this lake. | Philema Rd. (Rte. 91) | Free | Daily.

Thronateeska Heritage Center. In a turn-of-the-20th-century railroad depot on a brick-paved street, this heritage center has a history museum, science discovery center, planetarium, and model railroad museum housed in a railroad car. | 100 W. Roosevelt Ave. | 912/432–6955 | fax 912/435–1572 | www.heritagecenter.org | $4 | mid-June–Aug., Wed.–Sat. noon–4; Sept.–mid-June, Thurs.–Sat. noon–4; Planetarium, Tues. 'til 7.

ON THE CALENDAR
MAY/OCT.: *National Indian Pow Wow.* Held in the Parks at Chehaw. Highlights are Indian crafts, storytelling, dances, food, and lectures. | 912/430–5275.

Dining
Aunt Fannie's Checkered Apron. Southern. Bright orange slabs of rutabaga, dusky turnip greens swimming in a dense potlikker, and crusty fried chicken are offered at this cream-colored cinderblock restaurant on a side street in a somewhat derelict neighborhood. At lunch, suits and laborers alike fill the 20-odd tables. Breakfast and lunch. | 826 Byron Rd. | 912/888–8416 | Closed Sat. | $6–$9 | No credit cards.

Austin's Steakhouse. Steak. Austin's has an incredible, five-page menu, but the locals head straight for the steak—cut fresh every day and never frozen, the meat will melt in your mouth. | 101 N. Slappey St. | 912/889–0699 | $10–$20 | AE, D, DC, MC, V.

Chef Gwen's Bistro. Caribbean. The interior, festooned with palm trees, is a riot of color. The Caribbean offerings—oxtails and various jerked meats and curried vegetables—are no less vibrant at this quaint and funky hideaway. Lunch only. | 303 W. Highland Ave. | 912/888–0401 | Closed Sat. and Sun. | $6–$9 | AE, D, DC, MC, V.

Fishbones. Seafood. The sea-foam-green decorations and fish prints on the walls make sure you get the point. You'll find chicken, pork, and steak entrées on the menu, but the specialties are fish and shellfish from the Gulf of Mexico. The all-time favorite is grouper prepared "Greek-style," broiled with tomatoes, mushrooms, and scallions. | 1504 Dawson Rd. | 912/439–2261 | No dinner Mon., no lunch Sat., closed Sun. | $9–$17 | AE, D, DC, MC, V.

Gus's BBQ. Barbecue. For the best barbecue in Albany, or even in southern Georgia, people will tell you to head to Gus's. Sit down at a table with a red-and-white checked tablecloth and enjoy your ribs or pork dripping with delicious sauce. But save some room—Gus gets orders for his chocolate pie from all over the United States. | 2347 Dawson Rd. | 912/883–2404 | $8–$12 | AE, D, MC, V.

Two Moon Coffee Saloon. Café. With an interior designed to resemble a 1950s soda-fountain, this place, 30 min from Albany, is perfect to stop off for a quick snack or light lunch. The chicken salad sandwiches are local favorites, and the array of sandwiches and salads leads to home-made ice creams and, of course, coffee. | 108 Main St., Parrott | 912/938–6547 | No dinner Mon.–Thurs. Closed Sun. | $5–$6 | No credit cards.

Lodging
Comfort Suites–Merry Acres. This two-story hotel is part of the Merry Acres complex, 10 landscaped acres of hotels, restaurants, and malls with specialty shops. There are touches of luxury and elegance, as in the flower displays, chandeliers, and Oriental carpets in the lobby, and the four-poster beds in some of the suites. | 62 suites. Restaurant, bar, complimentary Continental breakfast. In-room data ports, minibars, some microwaves, some refrigerators, some in-room hot tubs. Cable TV. Pool, wading pool. Beauty salon. Laundry service. Business services, airport shuttle. | 1400 Dawson Rd. | 912/888–3939 | fax 912/435–4431 | www.merryacres.com | $80–$150 suites | AE, D, DC, MC, V.

Days Inn. The Days Inn boasts the largest suites in the city. And you're in walking distance of Albany State University and nearby government offices. Microwaves, refrigerators. Cable TV. Pool. Laundry facility. Business services. | 422 W. Oglethorpe Blvd., off U.S. 82 | 912/888–2632 | fax 912/435–1875 | 150 rooms | $50 | AE, D, DC, MC, V.

Hampton Inn. The Hampton Inn is quite comfortable, with many amenities, but maybe you'll feel best knowing they stand behind their 100 percent satisfaction guarantee—they'll do everything in their power to make your stay enjoyable, or it's on them. In-room data ports. Cable TV. Pool. | 806 North Westover | 912/883–3300 | fax 912/435–4092 | www.hamptoninns.com | 82 rooms | $59 | AE, D, DC, MC, V.

Holiday Inn. This full-service hotel has nice, contemporary-styled rooms and a large pool to go along with the quiet setting. Staying here gives you complimentary access to the Gold's Gym in the mall across the street. Restaurant, bar, room service. In-room data ports. Pool. Hot tub. Business services, airport shuttle, free parking. | 2701 Dawson Rd. | 912/883–8100 | fax 912/883–5669 | 150 rooms | $89 | AE, D, DC, MC, V.

Holiday Inn Express. This typical chain hotel is convenient to Albany State University and the Convention and Visitors Bureau. It is one of the minimum-service branches of the Holiday Inn chain, but has many amenities. Complimentary Continental breakfast. In-room data ports, microwaves, refrigerators. Cable TV. Pool. Business services, airport shuttle. Pets allowed (fee). | 911 E. Oglethorpe Blvd. | 912/883–1650 | fax 912/883–1163 | www.holiday-inn.com | 151 rooms | $59–$69 | AE, D, DC, MC, V.

Quality Inn–Merry Acres. Though at its heart it's a motor hotel like the rest, this is Albany's nicest place to bed down. A 1934 frame house is the centerpiece of the hotel complex, with the rest of the cottage-style buildings, built in the 1950s, nestled around it, all within the landscaped grounds of Merry Acres. A mall and several restaurants are within walking distance. Restaurant, bar, complimentary Continental breakfast. In-room data ports, some kitchenettes. Cable TV. Pool, wading pool. Beauty salon. Exercise equipment. Playground. Laundry services. Business services, airport shuttle, free parking. No pets. | 1500 Dawson Rd. | 912/435–7721 | fax 912/439–9386 | www.merryacres.com | 110 rooms | $54–$80 | AE, D, DC, MC, V.

Ramada Inn. This colonial-style chain hotel with attractive landscaping is built around an atrium, over which some rooms have balconies. It is convenient to the medical center and business district, as well as to shops and sports facilities; the Hugh Mills Stadium is 5 min away, and a putting green is across the street. Restaurant, bar. In-room data ports, in-room safes. Cable TV. Pool, wading pool. Putting green. Basketball. Business services, airport shuttle. Some pets allowed. | 2505 N. Slappey Blvd. | 912/883–3211 | fax 912/439–2806 | www.ramada-albany.com | 158 rooms | $50 | AE, D, DC, MC, V.

Sleep Inn–Merry Acres. These quiet rooms, 1 mi from the mall, overlook landscaped grounds and a private courtyard swimming pool. This is the hotel to stay in for a good night's sleep and value for money. Complimentary Continental breakfast. In-room data ports, microwaves. Cable TV. Pool. Laundry service. Business services, airport shuttle, free parking. No pets. | 1525 Dawson Rd. | 912/888–5595 | fax 912/888–9833 | www.merryacres.com | 81 rooms | $55–$72 | AE, D, DC, MC, V.

AMERICUS

MAP 3, C9

(Nearby towns also listed: Albany, Andersonville, Cordele)

Once the center of agricultural production for the Creek Nation, Americus, with a population of 17,000, is noted today for its quality peanuts, corn, cotton, and small grains. The town is the second largest livestock sales center in Georgia. Former President Jimmy Carter's hometown of Plains is 9 mi west of town.

Information: Americus–Sumter County Tourism Council | 123 W. Lamar St., Americus, GA 31709 | 912/928–6059 | www.americustourism.com.

Attractions

Americus Historic Driving Tour. At the Americus–Sumter County Tourism Council, pick up a copy of this brochure, which lists 38 historic structures, including churches, residences, and commercial buildings. The linchpin in Americus's extraordinarily rich architectural heritage is the Windsor Hotel (1892), built in the style known as Richardson Romanesque after the American architect Henry Hobson Richardson. | 123 W. Lamar St. | 912/928–6059 | www.americustourism.com | Free | Mon.–Fri. 9–5, Sat. 10–2.

Georgia Southwestern State University. Founded in 1906 as the Third District Agricultural and Mechanical School, the university is known for its Asian studies, art (glassblowing), and computer science departments. The Rosalynn Carter Institute for Human Development, named for the university's most famous alumna, focuses on care giving. Individual and group tours can be arranged with a day or two advanced notice. The university hosts the state's largest and the nation's second largest Elderhostel (912/931–2171), an international educational program for those over 55. | 800 Wheatly St. | 912/928–1273 | fax 912/931–2983 | www.gsw.edu | Free | Daily.

James Earl Carter Library at Georgia Southwestern State University. Georgia Southwestern University's library is the James Earl Carter Library. Named for the president's father, the library displays items relating to the history of the Carter family. | 800 Wheatly St. | 912/931–2259 | fax 912/931–2265 | www.gsw.edu | Free | Daily.

Jimmy Carter National Historic Site. The old Plains High School, 9 mi west of Americus, now displays memorabilia and photographs of its most famous alum, James Earl Carter, Jr. | 300 N. Bond St., Plains | 912/824–3413 | fax 912/824–3441 | www.nps.gov/jica | Free | Daily 9–5.

Lake Walter F. George. With 640 mi of shoreline, this popular 45,180-acre lake sees around 5 million visitors annually. Several campgrounds ($16–$18 for those managed by the Army Corps of Engineers), marinas, boat ramps, state-managed cabins, a lodge, and picnic areas surround this lake, which was created in the early 1960s by damming part of the Chattahoochee River. Golden Age and Golden Access cards are accepted. Two campgrounds are open year-round. | Rte. 1, Hwy. 39C | 912/768–2516 | fax 912/768–2809 | www.usace.army.mil | Free; $2 boat-launch fee | Daily.

Providence Canyon State Conservation Park. This popular day-use park may remind you of the Grand Canyon, but on a much smaller scale. Sixteen canyons varying in length from ¼ to ¾ mi and reaching 150 ft deep covering 300 acres are the central feature of this 1,100-acre park, located 8 mi west of Lumpkin. Backpacking and pioneer camping for organized groups are draws. | Rte. 1, Hwy. 39C | 912/838–6202 | fax 912/838–6735 | www.gastateparks.org | $2 vehicle, $20 vans, $50 buses | mid-Apr.–mid-Sept. 7–9; mid-Sept.–mid-Apr. 7–6; Park Office 8–5.

ON THE CALENDAR
MID-OCT.–MID-NOV.: *Fair of 1850.* Head up U.S. Highway 19 to the historic town of Westville to catch a month of special demonstrations of harvest-time activities such as cane grinding and syrup making. The Westville folks also start up the last remaining antebellum animal-powered cotton gin from time to time. | Martin Luther King Blvd., Lumpkin | 912/838–6310 | fax 912/838–4000 | www.westville.org | $8 | Tues.–Sat. 10–5, Sun. 1–5.

Dining
Granny's Kitchen. Southern. The locals come for lace bread, a very thin cornbread, but you can also enjoy huge portions of tomato-laden meatloaf or excellent crisp fried chicken. The choice of dessert is a separate topic. There are traditional favorites such as coconut and lemon icebox, as well as more unusual specialties, such as buttermilk pie and sweet vinegar pie. The banana pudding is famous. Finish up with bracingly strong coffee. You'll find former President Jimmy Carter's signature in the guest book. No alcohol. | 188A U.S. Hwy 19S | 912/924–0028 | Reservations not accepted | Breakfast also available. Closed Sun. No dinner | $3–$8 | No credit cards.

Magnolia and Ivy Tea Room. Café. Homemade baked goods, both savory and sweet, are served for the "cream" tea of fruit and scones. The tray stacked with finger sandwiches and sweet things that is served for "light" afternoon tea makes a perfect lunch. The same stacked tray appears at the full afternoon tea with the addition of almond chicken croissants and vegetable quiche. | 100 W. Church St., Plains | 912/824–7252 | Closed Sun.–Tues. | $6–$15 | AE, MC, V.

VACATION COUNTDOWN Your checklist for a perfect journey

Way Ahead

- ❏ Devise a trip budget.
- ❏ Write down the five things you want most from this trip. Keep this list handy before and during your trip.
- ❏ Book lodging and transportation.
- ❏ Arrange for pet care.
- ❏ Photocopy any important documentation (passport, driver's license, vehicle registration, and so on) you'll carry with you on your trip. Store the copies in a safe place at home.
- ❏ Review health and home-owners insurance policies to find out what they cover when you're away from home.

A Month Before

- ❏ Make restaurant reservations and buy theater and concert tickets. Visit fodors.com for links to local events and news.
- ❏ Familiarize yourself with the local language or lingo.
- ❏ Schedule a tune-up for your car.

Two Weeks Before

- ❏ Create your itinerary.
- ❏ Enjoy a book or movie set in your destination to get you in the mood.
- ❏ Prepare a packing list.
- ❏ Shop for missing essentials.
- ❏ Repair, launder, or dry-clean the clothes you will take with you.
- ❏ Replenish your supply of prescription drugs and contact lenses if necessary.

A Week Before

- ❏ Stop newspaper and mail deliveries.
- ❏ Pay bills.
- ❏ Stock up on film and batteries.
- ❏ Label your luggage.
- ❏ Finalize your packing list—always take less than you think you need.
- ❏ Pack a toiletries kit filled with travel-size essentials.
- ❏ Check tire treads.
- ❏ Write down your insurance agent's number and any other emergency numbers and take them with you.
- ❏ Get lots of sleep. You want to be well-rested and healthy for your impending trip.

A Day Before

- ❏ Collect passport, driver's license, insurance card, vehicle registration, and other documents.
- ❏ Check travel documents.
- ❏ Give a copy of your itinerary to a family member or friend.
- ❏ Check your car's fluids, lights, tire inflation, and wiper blades.
- ❏ Get packing!

During Your Trip

- ❏ Keep a journal/scrapbook as a personal souvenir.
- ❏ Spend time with locals.
- ❏ Take time to explore. Don't plan too much. Let yourself get lost and use your Fodor's guide to get back on track.

Windsor Hotel. Southern. The hotel merits a visit because of its architecture, based on the Richardson Romanesque style. The dining room, colored deep eggplant trimmed in white, is also a classic and is worth visiting for such dishes as Cajun shrimp and stuffed and baked trout. Come for the lunch buffet during the week and the brunch on Sundays. | 125 W. Lamar St. | 912/924–1555 | No dinner Sun. | $13–$24 | AE, D, DC, MC, V.

Lodging

Americus Ramada Inn. Make sure you ask for a room that faces the curved and landscaped pool area. The rooms are all quite spacious, and the meeting room is the largest in town. Pool. Laundry facilities. | U.S. Highway 19 S. | 912/924–4431 | fax 912/924–9602 | 100 rooms | $60 | AE, D, DC, MC, V.

Pathway Inn. This Victorian-era home (1906) has the wide verandas, rockers, and colorful gardens associated with that period. All the rooms are furnished with antiques, and each is decorated individually—some have painted ceilings, some have rose wallpaper. | 5 rooms (2 with shower only). Complimentary breakfast. Some in-room hot tubs. Cable TV, VCRs. Some pets allowed. No smoking. | 501 S. Lee St. | 912/928–2078 or 800/889–1466 | fax 912/928–2078 | www.1906pathwayinn.com | $85–$115 | AE, D, MC, V.

Plains Bed-and-Breakfast. This pink-and-cream Victorian building is well situated in downtown Plains, just across from the old railroad depot. Though a bit worn at the edges, the inn is quite comfortable and reasonably priced. From Americus, 14 mi west via U.S. 280. Complimentary breakfast. | 100 W. Church St., Plains | 912/824–7252 | 4 rooms | $70 | MC, V.

Rees Park Garden Inn. Built in 1848, this B&B is situated on an acre of wandering walkways and gardens. In addition to the wraparound veranda and tall windows, you'll truly enjoy the engaging Miles family, not to mention the private garden tubs and stone fireplaces in a number of the suites. Laundry facilities. | 504 Rees Park St. | 229/931–0122 | 7 rooms | $75 | AE, MC, V.

Windsor Hotel. A splendid five-story redbrick hotel, built in 1892 in the style known as Richardson Romanesque and restored to its original glory. The building may remind you of a castle with towers, and two of the suites are set in those towers. Each room is decorated differently in deep rich colors and furnished with antiques. Restaurant, bar, complimentary Continental breakfast, room service. In-room data ports. Cable TV. Business services. No pets. | 125 W. Lamar St. | 912/924–1555 or 888/297–9567 | fax 912/924–1555, ext.113 | www.windsor-americus.com | 53 rooms | $90–$159 | AE, D, DC, MC, V.

ANDERSONVILLE

MAP 3, C4

(Nearby towns also listed: Americus, Cordele, Perry)

Andersonville is best known for the Andersonville National Historic Site, a Confederate military prison. During the last two years of the Civil War, roughly 33,000 Union prisoners were crowded into the 26-acre Camp Sumter prison grounds. Starvation, disease, and inadequate care took a tremendous toll on the prisoners, nearly 13,000 of whom died. The nearby Andersonville National Cemetery, dedicated four months after the war ended, holds the remains of these dead.

Information: Andersonville National Historic Site | 496 Cemetery Rd., Andersonville, GA 31711 | 912/924–0343.

Attractions

Andersonville National Historic Site. The Civil War prison at Andersonville was set up in 1864; by the time the war ended in 1865 nearly 13,000 of the prisoners had died. The stockade commander, Swiss-born Henry Wirz, was tried and convicted on the charge of conspiracy to destroy the lives of the prisoners. He sealed his fate by refusing to blame Confederate President Jefferson Davis for the prison's horrible conditions and was hanged, the only Confederate official executed by the Federal government for war crimes. Each state that had prisoners at Andersonville has erected monuments to the memory of its lost citizens. The site is off Highway 49. | 496 Cemetery Road, Andersonville | 912/924–0343 | fax 912/928–9640 | www.nps.gov/ande | Free | Daily, 8:30–5.

Andersonville National Cemetery. Both modern and Civil War–era graves are grouped around state monuments. | Andersonville National Historic Site | 912/924–0343, ext. 112 | fax 912/928–6330 | www.nps.gov/ande | Free | Daily 8:30–5.

National Prisoner of War Museum. Exhibitions detail the experiences of American prisoners of war from all U.S. wars. | Andersonville National Historic Site | 912/924–0343, ext. 205 | fax 912/924–1086 | www.nps.gov | Free | Daily 8:30–5.

Providence Spring. The spring appeared miraculously within the stockade when the prisoners, desperate for water, began digging. | Andersonville National Historic Site | 912/924–0343, ext. 205 | Free | Daily 8:30–5.

Andersonville Trail. Beginning at I–75 Exit 46 (Fort Valley/Byron), the Andersonville trail travels 75 mi through southwest Georgia to Plains, hometown of President Jimmy Carter. Along the way, you can catch many of the sights described in this chapter. The loop finishes at Cordele, where you can reconnect to I–75 at Exit 33. | Rte. 49/U.S. 280 | 912/924–2558 | fax 912/924–2558 | andersonville.tripod.com | Free | Daily.

Civil War Village of Andersonville. Founded in 1853, and with a current population of only 270, the town seems little changed since the Civil War. Nineteenth-century commercial buildings house antique shops; a monument honors Henry Wirz, the stockade commander of the Andersonville prison, executed for war crimes. The village hosts an arts and crafts show in May and October. A visitors center is housed in the old train depot. Tours available. | Church St. | 912/924–2558 | fax 912/924–2558 | Free | Daily 9–5 visitors center.

ON THE CALENDAR
MAY: *Memorial ceremonies.* On the Sunday preceding the legal observance of Memorial Day, memorial ceremonies are held in Andersonville, including a guest speaker and the placing of American flags on each of the 18,000 graves in the national cemetery. | 912/924–2558.

Dining
Andersonville Restaurant. Southern. Housed in the oldest building in Andersonville, a former schoolhouse. Hamburger steak and meatloaf are standouts of the lunch buffet; the vegetables are canned but well seasoned. Cakes, pies, and cobblers are homemade using canned fruit. Friday dinner is known for catfish, chicken livers, fried quail, and steaks. Buffet (lunch). No alcohol. | 213 W. Church St. | 912/928–8888 | No dinner Sun.–Thurs. | $5–$8 | No credit cards.

Lodging
A Place Away Cottage Bed-and-Breakfast. This plain but comfortable cottage was originally built for the principal of a nearby schoolhouse and his wife. The schoolhouse itself now serves as home to innkeeper and Andersonville booster Peggy Sheppard, a native of Yonkers, New York. One-half mile from Andersonville National Historic Site. Complimentary Continental breakfast. Kitchenettes, microwaves, refrigerators. Cable TV. | 109 Oglethorpe St. | 912/924–1044 | fax 912/924–2558 | 2 rooms | $45–$50 | No credit cards.

ATHENS

MAP 3, E5

(Nearby town also listed: Madison)

Athens dates its beginnings to 1801, when Franklin College, the forerunner of the University of Georgia, was built, after receiving its charter 16 years earlier. Today, the town of nearly 80,000 derives much of its income from the production of textiles and chemicals as well as from agriculture.

Information: Convention and Visitors Bureau | 300 N. Thomas St., Athens, GA 30601 | 706/357–4430, 800/653–0603.

Athens Welcome Center | 280 E. Dougherty St., Athens, GA 30601 | 706/353–1820 | www.visitathensgeorgia.com.

Attractions

Crawford W. Long Medical Museum. The museum occupies the office of Dr. Crawford W. Long, college roommate of Alexander Stephens, vice president of the Confederate States of America, and the first physician to use ether to sedate patients before surgery. | 28 College St., Jefferson | 706/367–5307 | fax 706/367–5307 | www.crawfordlong.org | $2 | Mon. noon–4, Tues.–Sat. 10–4.

Double-Barreled Cannon. This unique Civil War relic was designed by John Gilleland of Athens and built at the local foundry in 1863. The idea was to load each barrel with a ball, the two balls connected by a chain. When fired, balls and chain would whirl out and cut down approaching enemy soldiers. The concept was a failure, and the cannon was presented to the city of Athens for exhibition as a curiosity. | City Hall lawn, College Ave. and Hancock St. | Free | Daily.

Fort Yargo State Park. This nature center built on a 1,800-acre park is 10 mi outside of Athens. Camping, fishing, boat rental, beach, swimming, tennis courts, basketball courts, miniature golf, hiking trails, bicycling, and lots of picnic areas. | 210 S. Broad St., Winder | 770/867–3489 | fax 770/867–7517 | www.gastateparks.org | $2 vehicle, $20 vans, $50 bus; free Wed. | Daily 7–10.

Historic Houses. Athens is known for the richness of its residential architecture. Walk along the town's lush tree-lined streets and you'll see stunning examples of Southern mansions. Styles include Greek or classic revival, Victorian, and contemporary. For tour information, contact the Athens Convention and Visitors Bureau. | Visitors Bureau: 300 N. Thomas St. | 706/357–4430, 800/653–0603 | www.visitathensga.com | See individual houses for opening hours.
Church-Waddel-Brumby House. Housing the Athens Welcome Center, this Federal-period house, perhaps the oldest structure in the city, was built about 1820 for Alonzo Church, a professor of mathematics at the university. Its first resident was the university's president, Dr. Moses Waddel. Many of the period antiques are on loan from the Brumby family, source of the famous Brumby rocker. | 280 E. Dougherty St. | 706/353–1820 | fax 706/353–1770 | www.visitathensga.com | Free | Mon.–Sat. 10–6, Sun. noon–6.
Founders' Memorial Garden and House. With a trickling fountain, rare flora, winding walkways, and ornamental shrubbery, the garden serves as a refuge from the surrounding urban frenzy. On the grounds is an 1857 Federal-style house, former headquarters of the Garden Club of Georgia. The garden was designed in the 1940s by Hubert Owens, the first dean of the university's School of Environmental Design. The garden is open to the public daily, but to view the house call at least two days in advance to make an appointment. | 325 S. Lumpkin St. | 706/542–8972 | fax 706/542–4485 | www.visitathensga.com | Free | Daily.
Taylor-Grady House. A National Historic Landmark, this Greek-revival house was built in the 1840s by General Robert Taylor as a summer home. Major William S. Grady bought the home from the Taylors in 1863. The home is owned by Athens-Clarke County and is man-

THE STRANGE CASE OF THE DOUBLE-BARRELED CANNON

On a sunny spring day in 1862, several residents of Athens, Georgia, gathered in a large, partially wooded field at nearby Linton Springs. All those present kept their eyes on John Wesley Gilleland, Sr., a local physician who had doctored practically everybody in the crowd and a man who loved tinkering with machinery so much that he had invented prototypes for various bizarre mechanical tools, few of which had ever been put into production.

The invention Gilleland was demonstrating to his neighbors this day, however, had the potential to be far more important than anything he had yet dreamed up. The doctor had designed an awesome new weapon—a magnificent, double-barreled cannon that when mass-produced and adopted by the Confederate artillery would awaken such fear in the Yankees that they would go stay up north and leave the South alone. Some folks were even saying that Gilleland's innovative cannon would shorten the Civil War by months, maybe years!

For the demonstration, workmen cleared some of the trees along the pathway that stretched down the meadow for several hundred yards. Then the workers hauled out the artillery piece and pointed it down the lane between the remaining rows of trees. At the end of the cleared land they placed several upright poles to represent enemy soldiers.

In complete silence the crowd watched as powder was rammed down the twin barrels of the cannon. Then two assistants walked up to the muzzles. Each picked up a single cannonball, but the balls were connected to each other by a long chain! One ball was dropped down each barrel, with the chain left dangling from the muzzles of both barrels. Dr. Gilleland explained that when the two balls simultaneously left the side-by-side barrels they would be hurled away from each other until the chain was drawn taunt between them. Then, in the words of an early 20th-century historian, the balls and chain would *mow down the enemy somewhat as a scythe cuts wheat*.

When all was ready, the fuse was lit, and a second later came the violent roar. But it was a double roar: one barrel's powder charge exploded a tiny fraction of a second before the other one, causing its ball to leave its barrel first. The second ball flew out of its barrel immediately afterward, but the velocity and weight of the first ball, by now speeding through the air, broke the chain. The first ball, with the attached chain whipping about, landed among the uncut trees; the second missile struck *wide of the mark, and the poles which represented the hostile army stood uninjured*.

Dr. Gilleland was disappointed, as were all of the curious onlookers. After several more attempts over the next few months to fire his cannon successfully and to interest the Confederate government in his innovative weapon, Gilleland finally gave up his pursuit.

Admitting defeat, the dejected Dr. Gilleland donated his cannon to the city of Athens. The weapon was placed in front of the town hall to be used to fire warning shots in case of enemy attack. A quarter of a century after the Civil War, the cannon mysteriously disappeared from the town hall's lawn. For five years, the cannon's whereabouts were unknown, until, in 1898, a young Athens boy accidentally discovered it while playing. For four dollars, the boy peddled it to a junk dealer, who recognized the piece and passed it on to two men who remembered when it was manufactured and tested way back in 1862. The cannon eventually came back to rest on the lawn of city hall, where a Georgia Historical Commission monument was erected in 1957 to commemorate the weapon's interesting story.

aged by the Junior League of Athens. | 634 Prince Ave. | 706/549–8688 | fax 706/613–0860 | www.visitathensga.com | $3 | Weekdays 9–5 (closed 1–2:30), tours by appointment only. **University President's House.** Built in 1857–58, this Greek-revival mansion, with Corinthian columns that give the facade a singularly stately look, is one of the city's most distinguished historic homes. | 570 Prince Ave. | Free | Drive by only.

Lyndon House Arts Center. This arts center incorporates the Lyndon-Ware House, a restored Italiante mansion (1850) with a classic hip roof, deep eaves and brackets, and a fine wrought-iron balustrade. It is a rare example of the style in Athens. It has been restored and decorated in period antiques. The adjacent annex and art center are certified by the Smithsonian, making possible a high level of exhibition quality. | 293 Hoyt St. | 706/613–3623 | fax 706/613–3833 | www.itown.com/athens/lyndonhouse | Donations accepted | Tues., Thurs. noon–9; Wed., Fri.–Sat. 9–5.

Morton Building. Built in 1909–10 by Monroe Bowers "Pink" Morton, the theater provided entertainment for Athens's African-American community. The state's first black female dentist, Ida Mae Hiram Johnson, was among the professionals who had offices here. Performers who have appeared on its stage include the Preservation Hall Jazz Band, Cab Callaway, Ma Rainey, Bessie Smith, and Louis Armstrong. Local groups of national renown that have performed in the building include REM and Widespread Panic. | 195 W. Washington St. | 706/613–3770 | fax 706/613–3773 | www.mortontheatre.itgo.com | Free | Weekdays 9–6, tours by appointment only.

Sandy Creek Nature Center. The center's 225 acres of woodlands, fields, and marshland support a variety of wildlife, but the reptiles and amphibians are of particular interest. Ten miles of trails, as well as classroom and exhibit facilities, support special programs requiring preregistration, ranging from the Owl Prowl to lessons on buying a telescope. | 205 Old Commerce Rd. | 706/613–3615 | fax 706/613–3618 | sandycreeknc@hotmail.com | Free | Tues.–Sat. 8:30–5:30.

Sandy Creek Park. Trails, asphalt tennis courts, picnic shelters and areas, playgrounds, multipurpose fields, basketball courts, a community building, camp grounds, and access to boating are among the facilities in this 788-acre park. Unique are the fenced areas for dogs to frolic in, costing $1/hr per canine; one such area covers 5 acres. | 400 Bob Holman Rd. | 706/613–3631 | fax 706/613–3612 | $1 | Mar.–Oct., Tues.–Sun. 7–9; Oct.–Mar., Tues.–Sun. 7–6.

Tree That Owns Itself. Colonel William H. Jackson, a professor at the university, owned the land on which the white oak stands and loved the tree so much that he willed it the land within eight feet of it on all sides. The original tree was blown down in a windstorm in 1942, but a successor was nurtured from one of its acorns. The Junior Ladies Garden Club planted that acorn (Jackson Oak, Jr.), thus preserving the tree's progeny. | Intersection of Dearing and S. Finley Sts. | Free | Daily.

University of Georgia. Established in 1785, this is the oldest state-chartered land grant university in the nation, although the same claim is made by the University of North Carolina at Chapel Hill, which was chartered later but began classes earlier. The campus is a study in Greek-revival architecture and gardens. The university's alumni include Henry W. Grady, Texas Sen. Phil Gramm, TV anchor Julie Moran, Billy Payne (who brought the Olympic Games to Atlanta), TV newsperson Charlene Hunter-Galt, and Georgia Supreme Court Chief Justice Robert Benham. Tours are conducted daily, by van and on foot; reservations are essential. | University Visitors Center, 4 Towers Building, College Station Rd. | 706/542–0842 (tours) | fax 706/542–5151 | www.uga.edu | Free | Tours weekdays 9:15 AM, 1 PM and 3:30 PM; Sat. 10:30 AM and 2:30 PM; Sun. 2:30 PM; reservation required 3 weeks in advance; visitors center weekdays 9–5, Sat. 9–5, Sun. 1–5.
Butts-Mehre Heritage Museum. Built in 1987, the 78,000-square-ft building occupies 4 floors. Videos and displays chronicle the achievements of University of Georgia sports teams and individual athletes. Exhibits include the Heisman trophies won by Frank Sinkwich and Herschel Walker, as well as Olympic memorabilia. | Butts-Mehre Heritage Hall, 1 Selig Circle | 706/542–9036 | fax 706/542–2980 | www.visitathensga.com | Free | Weekdays 8–5.

Georgia Center for Continuing Education. Hotel and conference rooms, a good full-service restaurant (the Savannah Room), a lounge (the Tybee Lounge), and coffee shop (The Commons Cafe), television studios, and the NPR radio station for Athens are based in this 1957 building, built with Kellogg Foundation funding. | 1197 S. Lumpkin St. | 706/548–1311 | fax 706/542–5990 | www.gactr.uga.edu | Free | Daily.

Georgia Museum of Art. Alfred Heber Holbrook began his art collection in 1940 in honor of his late wife, Eva Underhill Holbrook. A retired New York City attorney, Holbrook donated 100 paintings to the university and served as the museum's first director. The two original galleries, on the ground floor of an old library, opened in 1948; in 1996, they were replaced by the 52,000-square-ft building. The collection has also grown and now contains more than 7,000 works. | 90 Carlton St. | 706/542–4662 | fax 706/542–1051 | www.uga.edu/gamuseum | Free | Tues., Thurs.–Sat. 10–5, Wed. 10–9, Sun. 1–5.

State Botanical Garden of Georgia. On the banks of the Oconee River, the garden features 313 acres and miles of winding trails. Its focal point is the conservatory, where tropical and semitropical plants grow along an indoor stream. The international garden focuses on the role of plants in the development of human civilization; its more than 17,000 plants cover 3.3 acres. | 2450 S. Milledge Ave. | 706/542–1244 | fax 706/542–3826 | www.uga.edu/botgarden | Donations accepted | May–Sept., daily 8–8; Oct.–Apr., daily 8–6; Conservatory Visitors' Center: Tues.–Sat. 9–4:30, Sun. 11:30–4:30.

U.S. Navy Supply Corps Museum. The school trains officers as managers to oversee the complex system that distributes supplies and materials throughout the world. Housed in the 1910 former Carnegie Library, the museum traces the growth and development of the corps, explain its functions in today's navy, and commemorates individuals associated with the corps. Displays include an 1841 purser's uniform; World War II galley gear and mess equipment; and naval-theme paintings. There is a garden with fountains and a gazebo. Archives contain manuals and cookbooks, photographs, newsletters, command histories, and other materials. | 1425 Prince Ave. | 706/354–7349 | fax 706/354–7239 | www.nscs.com | Free | Weekdays 9–5.

ON THE CALENDAR

SEPT.: AthFest. Given the success of Athens-area musicians, most notably the group REM, this festival is a great opportunity to hear truly high-quality rock and roll. In addition to plenty of free music, there's an arts fair in the park on Washington Street, and a number of local bars and pubs have bands for varying cover charges. | www.athfest.com | 706/548–1973.

Dining

East West Bistro. Eclectic. Downstairs, called Downtown, features a mixed menus of small plates, such as tapas, along with entrées from the world's cuisines, such as salmon bruschetta and Japanese tempura. The space is casual but elegant, with hardwood floors and a burgundy and beige color scheme. Upstairs, called Uptown, is more formal with linen tablecloths and a menu focused on classic Northern Italian food. One of the most popular dishes is the "Catch of the Day" with Kalamata olive sauce. Sunday brunch. | 351 E. Broad St. | 706/546–4240 | Reservations not accepted Downtown | Downtown: $9–$11; Uptown: $13–$19 | AE, D, MC, V.

Harry Bissett's. Cajun/Creole. This stylish restaurant, spacious and full of light, is in the two-story atrium of a converted bank building. The restaurant attracts a professional crowd; the bar is popular with students. Star dishes include soft-shell crab in season; duck confit, carpetbagger steak topped with fried oysters and Béarnaise sauce, and delicious bread pudding. | 279 E. Broad St. | 706/353–7065 | Reservations not accepted Fri., Sat. | No lunch Mon. | $14–$24 | AE, D, DC, MC, V.

The Grill. American. This diner is full of '50s nostalgia. Students appreciate the 24-hour service with many different hamburgers, excellent hand-made shakes, and lots of salads and egg dishes for noncarnivores. Beer only. | 171 College Ave. | 706/543–4770 | Reservations not accepted | Open 24 hours | $3–$6 | AE, D, DC, MC, V.

The Grit. Vegetarian. The high ceilings and starkly bare walls are enlivened by splashes of color from local artwork. Dishes are drawn from Italian, Indian, Middle Eastern, and Mexican cuisine and include a "Golden Bowl" of tofu, rice, and vegetables; quesadillas; and samosas. Beer and wine only. | 199 Prince Ave. | 706/543–6592 | Reservations not accepted | $4–$8 | MC, V.

The Last Resort. Eclectic. Before its incarnation as a restaurant, this was a college hangout featuring music groups, and its furnishings make novel use of materials—light fixtures made of paper and wood hang like hornets' nests, the ceiling is textured, and the chef's area is lined with copper. The artsiness extends to temporary exhibitions of local artists' work. Southwestern and California touches grace the most interesting dishes, which are also the best values, such as the black bean crêpes. The chocolate desserts are winners. | 174 W. Clayton St. | 706/549–0810 | Reservations not accepted | $8–$20 | AE, D, MC, V.

Weaver D's Delicious Fine Foods. Southern. Dexter Weaver's fried chicken is so good Athenians have twice voted it their city's best. But don't ignore the pork chops, fish, barbecue, macaroni and cheese, ox tails, squash casserole, or yummy lemon icebox pie, all served in homely and welcoming surroundings. No alcohol. | 1016 E. Broad St. | 706/353–7797 | Reservations essential for large parties | Closed Sun. No dinner | $4–$7 | No credit cards.

Lodging

Athens Days Inn. Close to campus and downtown, this Days Inn has a particularly friendly staff, along with the usual comforts. In-room data ports, cable TV. Pool. | 230 N. Finley St. | 706/543–6511 | fax 706/208–8467 | 75 rooms | $75 | AE, D, DC, MC, V.

Athens Hampton Inn. You really can't beat the price of this inn, and if everything is not to your satisfaction, this chain will gladly refund your money. Each room has cable and data ports, but you can also meet the staff and other guests for popcorn and snacks in the lobby every evening from 4 to 7. In-room data ports. Cable TV. Pool. | 2220 W. Broad St. | 706/548–9600 | fax 706/548–8268 | 112 rooms | $68 | AE, D, DC, MC, V.

Holiday Inn. Step out your door and you are on UGA's North Campus or in the midst of Athens's bustling downtown business district. The facilities mix motel-style lodging with newer rooms in an attached tower. You know what to expect from this type of chain hotel—floral bedspread, dismal curtains, peculiar artwork on the walls. However, there is a certain comfort in knowing in advance, and it makes this a reliable choice. | 308 rooms. Restaurant, bar. In-room data ports, some minibars, some microwaves, some refrigerators. Cable TV, some VCRs. Indoor pool. Exercise equipment. Business services. Pets allowed. | 197 E. Broad St. | 706/549–4433 | www.hdayn@hi-athens.com | $84–$104 | AE, D, DC, MC, V.

Magnolia Terrace. In the historic Cobbham neighborhood, this 1912 colonial-style inn is within walking distance of shops and restaurants along Prince Avenue. The cozy, plush Phinizy Parlor and the large front porch with comfortable wicker furniture provide welcoming common areas. Each bedroom is furnished in its own unique style with antiques and houseplants, making Magnolia Terrace a home away from home. The trimmings—fireplaces and fine linen—add luxury and comfort. Complimentary Continental breakfast (full on weekends). In-room data ports. Cable TV. Pets allowed. No smoking. | 277 Hill St. | 706/548–3860 | fax 706/369–3439 | www.bbonline.com/ga/magnoliaterrace | 8 rooms | $95–$115 | AE, MC, V.

Nicholson House Inn. The 1820 house is on 6 acres of an 18th-century land grant originally deeded to William Few, one of Georgia's two signers of the U.S. Constitution. At its core, it is a two-over-two log house. Later additions and changes hide this original structure beneath a 1947 colonial-revival exterior. The inn, which is only 3 mi from downtown Athens, has a wide front veranda with rocking chairs. Rooms are decorated in rich colors, and furnishings are a mix of antiques and reproductions. Deer routinely amble across the front lawn. Complimentary breakfast. Cable TV. No kids under 12. No pets. No smoking. | 6295

Jefferson Rd. | 706/353–2200 | fax 706/353–7799 | www.bbonline.com/ga/nicholson | 9 rooms (7 with shower only) | $95–$115 | AE, D, MC, V.

ATLANTA

(Nearby towns also listed: Cartersville, Roswell, Stone Mountain)

Atlanta was first named Terminus, for its location was the end of a railroad line. Founded in 1837, it was incorporated as Marthasville in 1843 and became Atlanta in 1845. Even before the Civil War it was a railroad and marketing hub. Then came the city's siege and destruction by the Union army in 1864, after which practically 90 percent of the city had to be rebuilt. Very little of the old town remains. After the Civil War, Atlanta recovered quickly, primarily because of the completion of several rail lines that put the struggling town in the center of a rapidly expanding transportation network. Because of its rapid rise, Atlanta was named the capital of Georgia in 1868. Today, with a metropolitan population of nearly 3 million, Atlanta and its environs constitute by far the largest city in the Southeast, home to many leading American corporations—among them Coca-Cola and CNN—as well as 29 colleges and universities.

Atlanta's character has evolved from a mix of peoples: Transplanted Northerners and people from elsewhere account for 50 percent of the population and have undeniably affected the mood and character of the city. Irish immigrants had a major role in the city's early history, along with Germans and Austrians; the Hungarian-born Rich brothers founded Atlanta's principal department store. In the past two decades, Atlanta has seen spirited growth in its Asian and Latin-American communities. Atlanta's Asian-American and Latino citizens can point with pride to their economic and civic accomplishments. Their restaurants, shops, and institutions have become part of the city's texture.

For more than four decades, Atlanta has been linked to the civil rights movement. Among the many accomplishments of Atlanta's African-American community is the Nobel Peace Prize that Martin Luther King, Jr., won in 1964. Dr. King's widow, Coretta Scott King, continues to operate the King Center, which she founded after her husband's assassination in 1968. In 1972 Andrew Young was elected the first black congressman from the South since Reconstruction.

The traditional and romantic image of the South, with lacy moss dangling from tree limbs, thick, sugary Southern drawls, a leisurely pace, and luxurious antebellum

CAR RENTAL TIPS

- ❏ Review auto insurance policy to find out what it covers when you're away from home.
- ❏ Know the local traffic laws.
- ❏ Jot down make, model, color, and license plate number of rental car and carry the information with you.
- ❏ Locate gas tank—make sure gas cap is on and can be opened.

- ❏ Check trunk for spare and jack.
- ❏ Test the ignition—make sure you know how to remove the key.
- ❏ Test the horn, headlights, blinkers, and windshield wipers.

*Excerpted from *Fodor's: How to Pack: Experts Share Their Secrets*
© 1997, by Fodor's Travel Publications

mansions, is rarely seen here. Even before the Civil War, the columned house was a rarity. The frenetic pace of building that characterized the period after the Civil War has continued unabated. Still viewed by die-hard Southerners as the heart of the Old Confederacy, Atlanta has become the best example of the New South, a fast-paced modern city proud of its heritage.

Information: **Convention and Visitors Bureau** | 233 Peachtree St. NE, Suite 100, Atlanta, GA 30303 | 404/521–6600 or 800/285–2682 | www.atlanta.com.

NEIGHBORHOODS

Downtown. Downtown Atlanta is centered on the hub known as Five Points. Here is the MARTA station that intersects north–south and east–west transit lines. On the surface, Five Points is formed by the intersection of Peachtree Street with Marietta, Broad, and Forsyth streets.

Midtown. This thriving area to the north of downtown was a hippie hangout in the late 1960s and '70s and is now home to a large segment of the city's gay population, along with young families, young professionals, artists, and musicians. Formerly in decline, Midtown has evolved into one of the city's most interesting neighborhoods. Its gleaming new office towers give it a skyline to rival Downtown's, and the renovated mansions and bungalows in its residential section have made it a city showcase.

Buckhead. Atlanta's sprawl doesn't lend itself to walking between major neighborhoods, so take a car or MARTA to reach Buckhead. Many of Atlanta's trendy restaurants, music clubs, chic shops, and hip art galleries are concentrated in this neighborhood. Finding a parking spot on the weekends and at night can be difficult, and waits of two hours or more are common in the most popular restaurants.

Virginia-Highland and the Emory Area. Restaurants and art galleries are the backbone of Virginia-Highland/Morningside, northeast of Midtown. Like Midtown, this residential area was down at the heels in the 1970s. Reclaimed by writers, artists, and a few visionary developers, Virginia-Highland today offers intriguing shopping and delightful walking. Nightlife hums here as well.

TRANSPORTATION INFORMATION

Airports: Atlanta and the surrounding areas are served by **Hartsfield Atlanta International Airport,** the busiest air terminal in the U.S. (10 mi south of downtown, off I–85 and I–285; 404/530–6600). All major domestic airlines, as well as a large number of foreign carriers, offer regularly scheduled flights.

Airport Transportation: Atlanta Airport Shuttle (Information: 404/766–5312; Reservations: 404/524–3400, ext. 6) operates vans every hour between 7 AM and 11 PM daily. The trip downtown ($12 one-way, $20 round-trip) takes about 30 minutes and stops at major hotels. If your luggage is light, take the **MARTA** (404/848–4711) high-speed trains between the airport and downtown and other locations. Trains operate 5 AM to 1 AM weekdays and 6 AM to 12:30 AM weekends. The trip downtown takes about 15 minutes to the Five Points station, and the fare is $1.50. From the airport to downtown, the **taxi** fare is $18 for one person, $20 for two, and $24 for three or more, including tax. From the airport to Buckhead, the fare is $28 for one person and $30 for two or more.

Amtrak serves the city from its station at 1688 Peachtree St. Call 404/881–3060 or 800/872–7245 for schedules and fare information.

Bus Lines: Greyhound Bus Lines serves Atlanta, with a depot at 232 Forsyth St. Call 404/584–1728 or 800/231–2222 for schedules and fare information.

Intra-city Transit: MARTA (Metropolitan Atlanta Rapid Transit Authority) operates a fleet of nearly 700 buses and a number of high-speed trains within the city and to the outlying communities. Call 404/848–4711 for information.

Other: Atlanta is easily accessible by **automobile,** being strategically located at the intersection of three interstate highways: I–20, I–75, and I–85.

Attractions

ART AND ARCHITECTURE

A.G. Rhodes Memorial Hall. Designed by Willis F. Denny, from Louisville, Georgia, this 1901 castle residence in the Romanesque revival style became the property of the state in 1929 and housed the Department of Archives. When restored, it will serve as headquarters for the Georgia Trust for Historic Preservation. It boasts a series of stained-glass windows depicting heroes of the Confederacy. | 1516 Peachtree St. NW | 404/885–7800 | fax 404/875–2205 | www.georgiatrust.org/rhodes.html | $5 | Weeekdays 11–4, Sun. noon–3.

City Hall Complex. Atlanta's city hall, a magnificent neo-Gothic structure, was built in 1930. It stands on the site of John Neal's house, which General William T. Sherman used as his headquarters after the battle of Atlanta. Attached is a modern annex, whose walls are covered with art. At the Justice Center, a sculpture given to Atlanta by Barcelona, also an Olympic City, celebrates the Catalan national dance, the Sardana. | 55 Trinity Ave. | 404/330–6100 | www.ci.atlanta.ga.us | Free | Weekdays 8:15–5.

Georgia Governor's Mansion. Built in 1968 and designed by Atlanta architect A. Thomas Bradbury, the columned mansion is open to tours of its public spaces. The superior collection of Federal-period furniture, 18th- and 19th-century paintings, and 18 acres of exquisite gardens are worth a visit. | 391 W. Paces Ferry Rd. | 404/261–1858 | www.ganet.org/governor/firstlady/tour | Free | Tours Tues.–Thurs. 10–11:30 AM; last admission 11:10.

Herndon Home. Alonzo Herndon emerged from slavery to found a chain of successful barber shops and the **Atlanta Life Insurance Company.** Herndon, who traveled extensively, widely influenced the cultural life around Atlanta's traditionally black colleges. Alonzo's son, Norris, willed the handsome Beaux Arts home his father built to a foundation to preserve it as a museum and heritage center. | 587 University Pl. | 404/581–9813 | fax 404/588–0239 | www.theherndonhome.org | $5 | Hourly tours Tues.–Sat. 10–4.

Margaret Mitchell House. Margaret Mitchell, author of *Gone with the Wind*, detested the turn-of-the-20th-century house where she lived when she wrote her masterpiece—she called it the Dump. Despite her opinion, determined volunteers braved fires and naysayers to restore the house as a tourist and cultural attraction. It looks a lot nicer today than when the famous writer and her husband, John Marsh, lived there. The visitor center exhibits photographs, archival material, and personal possessions, including her typewriter. There are also displays of memorabilia from the *Gone with the Wind* film, including costumes, fragments of the set, and photographs. Allow about 40 minutes for the tour. | 990 Peachtree St. | 404/249–7015 | fax 404/249–7118 | www.gwtw.org | $10 | Daily 9–4.

Atlanta Contemporary Arts Center. Founded in 1973, the center was first set up in a former schoolhouse. Now ensconced in a 40,000-square-ft restored warehouse, it includes a gallery and press, as well as performance and studio space for artists. | 535 Means St. | 404/688–1970 | fax 404/577–5856 | www.thecontemporary.org | $3 | Tues.–Sat. 11–5.

★ **State Capitol.** Chicago architects Edbrooke and Burnham designed this Renaissance-revival building, which was dedicated on July 4, 1889. Its dome was gilded with precious metal from Dahlonega, Georgia, where the nation's first gold rush fanned "get rich" fever. There is a small museum inside. | Capitol Sq. | 404/656–2844 | fax 404/463–7716 | www.sos.state.ga.us | Free | Weekdays 8–5:30.

Wren's Nest. This Victorian residence (1868–84) was home to Southern storyteller and humorist Joel Chandler Harris, best known for his Uncle Remus stories. The exterior has been restored to its 1884 appearance, while the rooms are restored to 1900. Educational tours focus on the African-American art of storytelling as well as architectural and decorative preservation/restoration. | 1050 Ralph D. Abernathy Blvd. SW. | 404/753–7735 | fax 404/753–8535 | www.accessatlanta.com/community/groups/wrensnest | $7 | Tues.–Sat. 10–2:30, Tues., Thurs., Sat. walk-ins, Wed., Fri. by appointment.

BEACHES, PARKS, AND NATURAL SITES

Centennial Olympic Park. Created for the 1996 Centennial Olympic Games entertainment area, the 21-acre urban landscape park is a spectacular study in urban reclamation. Dramatically lit at night, its presence has redefined this once-unfriendly part of Downtown, and today it is the site of concerts in its amphitheater and special events. Pathways formed by commemorative brick pavement meander through it, and there is a 6-acre great lawn. The Fountain of Rings holds the Olympic symbol at the center of a 24-flag court. | 265 Luckie St. NW | 404/223–441 | fax 404/223–4499 | www.gwcc.com/parkinfo.htm | Free | Daily 8:30–9.

Chastain Memorial Park. The amphitheater is used for popular concerts, ranging from classical to jazz and rock. Well before the music begins, Atlantans arrive with candles and picnic suppers, and as night settles on the town, the amphitheater begins to glow with soft light. Within the 158-acre park itself are sports facilities, including the North Atlanta Golf Course, an 18-hole, par 71 course; an equestrian center; tennis courts; and a swimming center. | 135 W. Wieucca Rd. | 404/252–9669 | fax 404/255–1993 | Free | Daily 6–11.

Chattahoochee River National Recreation Area. Fourteen individual units of land lying along the Chattahoochee River stretch north from U.S. 41 to Buford Dam on Lake Lanier. Because the river is unnavigable to large craft north of Columbus, Georgia, development along its shores did not occur until the 1970s. As pressure from both commercial and residential development grew, various groups eager to protect this unspoiled river area managed to get state and federal protection for designated parcels. By 1978 they had successfully begun to assemble the segments of shoreline they wanted. Today, the units serve a wide swath of residential areas, providing historic sites, jogging and hiking trails (some of the latter quite strenuous), and a chance to experience the wild in the heart of a metropolitan area. | 1978 Island Ford Pkwy. | 770/399–8070 | fax 770/399–8087 | www.nps.gov./chat | $2 per vehicle | Daily 7–30 minutes before sunset.

Grant Park. In 1882 Colonel Lemuel A. Grant, a native of Maine and a Confederate officer, donated 100 acres near his home to the city for a park. The park formed the centerpiece of a thriving Victorian neighborhood that flourished until World War II. Suburban development led to its decline until the early 1970s, when urban pioneers began to reclaim the neighborhoods and restore the homes. Today, the park is the setting for concerts. | Cherokee Ave. SE | 404/658–7538 | fax 404/624–0792 | Free | Daily 6 AM–11 PM.

Panola Mountain State Conservation Park. About 20 mi from the city, these 600 acres of rolling forest and farmland are crowned by Panola Mountain, a 100-acre granite outcrop geologically known as a monadnock. A registered national landmark, the mountain is a significant aspect of the Piedmont Plateau. Because of its role as a conservation environment, access to the park is controlled. Park naturalists conduct scheduled hikes on weekends at 2:30 PM. Self-guided walks begin at the visitors center, where you can view an orientation slide presentation that will help direct your visit. There are two moderately difficult trails, one of which winds up the face of the mountain, but no sports facilities. | Rte. 155 SW, Stockbridge | 770/389–7801 (information), 770/389–7275 (reservations) | fax 770/389–7925 | www.gastateparks.org | Free; parking $2 vehicle, $20 van, $50 bus | Daily 7–dark; Center: Tues.–Fri. 9–5, weekends noon–5.

Piedmont Park. The Gentlemen's Riding Club, now Piedmont Driving Club, acquired this undeveloped wooded area in 1887. It was the site of the Cotton States and International Exposition in 1895, for which John Philip Sousa wrote his "King Cotton" march. Earlier, in 1892, the first college football game in Georgia (University of Georgia vs. today's Auburn University: 10–0 Auburn) took place here. For years, it was the site of the now-suspended Atlanta Arts Festival. A public park since 1904, when nearby residential Ansley Park began to be developed, it is surrounded by commercial buildings and a restored residential neighborhood. Facilities include 12 excellent hard-surface tennis courts, plus trails for jogging and walking. | Piedmont Ave. between Monroe Dr. and 10th St. | 404/875–7275 | www.piedmontpark.org | Free | Daily 6 AM–11 PM.

Atlanta Botanical Garden. Lying on 30 acres within Piedmont Park, the facility features 15 acres of display gardens, including a serene Japanese garden, a 15-acre hardwood forest with walking trails, and the Fuqua Conservatory, featuring unusual and endangered flora from tropical and desert climates. There is also a children's garden, with Peter Rabbit's garden, Caterpillar Maze, and Butterfly Pavilion. | 1345 Piedmont Ave. | 404/876–5859 | fax 404/876–7472 | www.atlantabotanicalgarden.org | $7, free Thurs. after 3 | Oct.–mid-Mar., Tues.–Sun. 9–6; mid-Mar.–Sept., Tues.–Sun. 9–7.

Sweetwater Creek State Park. The ruins of a pre–Civil War textile plant built in 1847 and burned during the battle of Atlanta are the focus of this unusual park, which covers more than 2,000 acres. Fishing at George Sparks Reservoir, picnicking, and hiking are among its delights. A fairly strenuous trail descends through a forest and along an old wagon road that once connected the mill village to the outside world along Sweetwater Creek. | Mt. Vernon Rd., Lithia Springs (20 mi from Atlanta) | 770/732–5871 | fax 770/732–5874 | www.gastateparks.org | $2 vehicle; $20 vans; $50 bus | Daily 7 AM–dark.

CULTURE, EDUCATION, AND HISTORY

Alliance Theatre Company. This is the largest regional theater in the Southeast and is nearly four decades old. In addition to the mainstage theater, there is a studio theater and a children's theater. Strong community outreach programs, with an emphasis on diversity and education, are central to the company's contemporary success. Kenny Leon marked his 10th year as the theater's director with the 1999–2000 season. | 1280 Peachtree St. | 404/733–5000 | fax 404/733–4245 | www.alliancetheatre.org | Show tickets $16–$45 | Aug.–May.

College Park Historic District. Georgia's fourth largest urban historic district bases its claim on its early 20th-century architecture. The early 20th-century historic shopping district on Main Street is surrounded by a historic residential district; at its center is the Craftsman-style depot (1917). College Park, established in 1896, was designed by a group of professional landplanners as an affluent bedroom community. The MARTA stop is the first stop after the airport and exits right on to Main St. The visitors center is in Barrett Park, on Rugby Ave. | Main St. | 404/768–1342 | www.hcpna.org | Free | Daily.

Fort McPherson. "Fort Mac," as this 19th-century military installation is fondly known, was named for General James Birdseye McPherson, USA, the only Union general killed during the battle of Atlanta. On 500 acres, the facility is home to the Third United States Army and FORSCOM, once commanded by Colin Powell. Lining the post parade ground, Hedekin Field, is Staff Row, a street with 19 officers' residences on one side and two-story dormitory barracks (Troop Row) on the other. These structures are on the National Register of Historic Places. Tompkins Lane nearby was named for Captain Sally L. Tompkins, CSA, the only woman commissioned an officer in the Confederate army. | Lee St., U.S. 29 | 404/464–3556 | fax 404/464–3659 | www.mcpherson.army.mil | Free | Weekdays by appointment, at least three weeks ahead.

Fox Theatre. Built in 1929 in the then-popular Moorish-Egyptian style, the Fox was constructed as the headquarters for the Shriners. It is one of a few remaining classic movie palaces in the nation. Its twinkling faux sky ceiling—complete with clouds and stars above Alhambra-like minarets—elicits gasps of admiration. The Fox was saved from the wrecker's ball in the 1970s by concerted civic action and is still a prime venue for musicals, rock concerts, dance performances, and film festivals. One-hour tours are conducted by the Atlanta Preservation Center. | 660 Peachtree St. NE | 404/881–2100 | fax 404/872–2972 | www.thefoxtheatre.com | $5 | Mon., Wed., Thurs. 10 AM; Sat. 10 AM and 11 AM.

★ **Martin Luther King, Jr. National Historic Site.** The site encompasses the King Birth Home, Ebenezer Baptist Church, and the Visitors Center, all managed by the National Park Service, which also manages the exhibitions in the King Center at the Martin Luther King, Jr. Center for Nonviolent Social Change. | 450 Auburn Ave. | 404/331–5190, 404/331–6922 | www.nps.gov/malu | Free | Memorial Day–Labor Day, daily 9–6; Labor Day–Memorial Day, daily 9–5.

Ebenezer Baptist Church. Site of Dr. Martin Luther King, Jr.'s funeral service in 1968, this 1922 Gothic-revival church became the spiritual center for the civil rights movement after King won the Nobel Peace Prize in 1964. Members of the King family have preached in the church for three generations. In 1999 the congregation took possession of a new church, by the Atlanta architectural firm of Stanley Love-Stanley, directly across the street. The U.S. Park Service operates the tours in the historic church. | 407 Auburn Ave. NE | 404/688–7263 | www.nps.gov./malu | Donations accepted | Memorial Day–Labor Day, Mon.–Sat. 9–6, Sun. 1–6; Labor Day–Memorial Day, Mon.–Sat. 9–5, Sun. 1–5.

Martin Luther King, Jr. Birth Home. Part of the Martin Luther King, Jr. National Historic Site, this simple Queen Anne Victorian home was the childhood residence of Martin Luther King, Jr. Sign up for tours at Fire Station No. 6 at Auburn Avenue and Boulevard. | 501 Auburn Ave. | 404/331–3920 | www.nps.gov./malu | Free | Memorial Day–Labor Day, daily 9–6; Labor Day–Memorial Day, daily 9–5.

Oakland Cemetery. For a long time, this cemetery, a wonderland of Victorian funerary art, was Atlanta's only park. Among the famous buried here are Margaret Mitchell and her husband, John Marsh; thousands of Confederate and some Union soldiers; golf legend Bobby Jones; the city's first mayor, Moses Formwalt; and three Confederate generals. Magnificent sculptures include the *Lion of Atlanta,* modeled after the *Lion of Lucerne,* and a large monument to the Confederate dead. There is a large Jewish section, many of its monuments in Hebrew, and as proof that the cemetery is the resting place of Atlantans of all races and classes there is a haunting, markerless paupers' field. Tours are conducted by Historic Oakland Cemetery. A self-guided walking tour brochure costs $1. | 248 Oakland Ave. SE | 404/688–2107 | fax 404/658–6092 | www.oaklandcemetery.com | Free, guided tours $5 | Daily; tours Mar.–Oct. Sat. 10 AM, 2 PM, Sun. 2 PM.

Patrick Cleburne Confederate Memorial Cemetery. Cleburne, a native of Ireland, became a wealthy planter in Arkansas and rose to the rank of general in the Confederate army. The unknown soldiers who fell at the battle of Jonesboro (August 31–September 1, 1864), one of two decisive Civil War battles in Georgia (the other was Chickamauga), were first buried in mass graves in people's yards. In 1872 the Confederate soldiers were disinterred and reburied in individual coffins. The deceased Federals were reinterred at Marietta. The cemetery is named for Cleburne because he fought in the battle and because many of the unknown soldiers buried there served under him. | Johnson and N. McDonough Sts., Jonesboro | 770/477–8864 (tours) | Free | Daily dawn to dusk.

Robert W. Woodruff Arts Center. The center has its own production company and presents events in cooperation and conjunction with other entities around the city. Within the center lie the High Museum of Art, Symphony Hall, the Alliance Theatre Company, and the Atlanta College of Art. The center opened in 1968 as a memorial to Atlanta arts patrons killed in the crash of a chartered airplane returning them to the city from Orly Airport in Paris after an arts expedition. Funded at its launch by the Woodruff Foundation, the center is named for Coca-Cola magnate Robert Woodruff, a bronze statue of whom surveys the grounds. | 1280 Peachtree St. | 404/733–4200 or 404/733–5000 (box office) | fax 404/733–4245 | www.woodruff-arts.org | Free to Center | Daily.

Symphony Hall. The Atlanta Symphony Orchestra's current home is part of the Woodruff Arts Center. A new hall for the orchestra may someday be built on the site of First Baptist Church on Peachtree Rd. | 1280 Peachtree St. | 404/733–5000 (box office) | fax 404/733–4245 | www.atlantasymphony.org | Prices vary with event | Sept.–May and mid-June–mid-Aug.

MUSEUMS

APEX Museum. Begun in 1978 as the African-American Panoramic Experience, this museum is housed in the 1919 John Wesley Dobbs Building. In addition to traveling exhibitions from the United States and around the world, especially Africa, the museum has special materials on the history of "Sweet Auburn," as Dobbs called the 12-block stretch of Auburn Avenue that was once the economic, social, and spiritual heart of segregated black Atlanta. Each quarter there is a different exhibition on an aspect of the African-American contribution to culture or science. | 135 Auburn Ave. NE | 404/521–2739 | fax 404/523–3248 | www.apex-museum.org | $3 | Tues.–Sat. 10–5.

★ **Atlanta International Museum.** Rotating exhibits feature such diverse subjects as textiles, puzzles, arts and crafts, design, and culture from all over the world. | 285 Peachtree Center Ave. | 404/688–2467 | fax 404/521–9311 | $3 | Weekdays 11–5.

★ **Atlanta Cyclorama and Civil War Museum.** In Grant Park (named for a New England–born Confederate colonel, not the U.S. president), you'll find the Cyclorama, featuring a huge circular painting, completed by immigrant artists shortly after the Civil War, which depicts the 1864 battle of Atlanta. The museum has an excellent Civil War bookstore. | Grant Park, 800C Cherokee Ave. | 404/658–7625 or 404/624–1071 (recorded information) | fax 404/658–7045 | www.bcaatlanta.org | $5 | June–Labor Day, daily 9:20–5:30; Labor Day–May, daily 9:20–4:30.

★ **Carter Presidential Center.** This complex occupies the site where Union general William T. Sherman orchestrated the Battle of Atlanta (1864). The museum and archives detail the political career of former president Jimmy Carter. The center itself, which is not open to the public, focuses on conflict resolution and human rights issues. It sponsors foreign-affairs conferences and projects on such matters as world food supply. Outside, the Japanese-style garden is a serene spot to unwind. | 1 Copenhill Ave. | 404/331–3942 | $5 | Mon.–Sat. 9–4:45, Sun. noon–4:45.

★ **Center for Puppetry Arts.** In a former schoolhouse, the center houses a large museum exhibiting hand, body, rod, shadow, and string puppets from all of the world and from various historical periods, as well as a large collection of puppet-related posters. Puppet theater is presented for both children and adults; the shows for adults, which include puppet versions of theater classics and avant-garde pieces, have earned the center fame. The gift shop sells all manner of puppet-related items. | 1404 Spring St. | 404/873–3391 | fax 404/873–9907 | www.puppet.org | $8 | Mon.–Fri. 9–5.

Children's Arts Museum. One of the jewels of the Gwinnett Fine Arts Center complex, this museum is devoted to putting metro Atlanta children in touch with the arts, both visual and performance. The building, an expanse of glass and steel with a brick base, curves around sawtooth walls that provide exhibition space. Exhibitions include art for and by children. In addition, there are a black box theater, visual and performing arts classrooms, and a museum shop that sells educational and arts materials geared to young people. | 6400 Sugarloaf Pkwy., Duluth | 770/623–6002 | fax 770/623–3555 | www.hudgenscenter.org | $5 | Tues.–Thurs. 10–5, Fri. 1–5, Sat. 10–3.

City Gallery East. Atlanta's branch of city hall, City Hall East, is in a former Sears Roebuck building. Committed to fostering the city's arts community, Atlanta has developed a non-profit fine art gallery showcasing work by local, national, and international artists. | 1st Floor, 675 Ponce de Leon Ave. | 404/817–7956 | fax 404/817–6827 | Free | Weekdays 10–5.

Hammonds House Galleries and Resource Center. The handsome Eastlake Victorian house that once belonged to Dr. Otis Thrash Hammonds, along with his fine collection of Victorian furniture and paintings, was bequeathed to the city of Atlanta upon his death. The house now serves as an art gallery and resource center focused primarily on exhibiting work by African-American artists but also occasionally showcasing art from anywhere in the Africa-influenced world. | 503 Peeples St. | 404/752–8730 | fax 404/752–8733 | www.hammondshouse.org | $2 | Tues.–Fri. 10–6, weekends 1–5.

Hapeville Depot Museum. The centerpiece of Hapeville's downtown renewal, the museum displays materials relating to transportation (rail, air, and vehicle) and turn-of-the-20th-century life. The collection includes some early Delta airline archival photography. The depot anchors a fascinating urban area, including Chapman's Drugstore, complete with soda fountain; an antiques mall (Showcase Antique Mall); and a highly regarded restaurant (Cafe at the Corner). Hapeville is the home of the original Chic-Fil-A restaurant, the Dwarf House. | 620 S. Central Ave., Hapeville | 404/669–2175 | Free | Tues.–Fri. 11–3, Sun. 1–4.

High Museum of Art. Richard Meier's design is a high-tech showcase that has won rave reviews from architecture critics. The permanent collection includes the Uhry Print Collection, with works of French Impressionism, American decorative arts, and African art. In 1991 the American Institute of Architects listed the sleek museum, built in 1983, among the 10 best works of American architecture in the 1980s. There's an excellent gift shop and good food operation, serving sandwiches and salads. | 1280 Peachtree St., Woodruff Arts Center | 404/733–4444 (information line) | fax 404/733–4502 | www.high.org | $6 | Tues.–Thurs., Sat. 10–5, Fri. 10–9, Sun. noon–5.

★ **Michael C. Carlos Museum.** Drawn from all over the world, including Egypt, Greece, Rome, the Near East, the Americas, and Africa, this stunning permanent collection holds more than 16,000 objects. What you see here is the largest collection of ancient art in the South, from Mesopotamian cuneiform tablets to pre-Columbian pottery. European and American prints and drawings cover the Middle Ages through the 20th century. Designed by renowned American architect Michael Graves, the building is a visual delight, mixing Italian Renaissance and postmodern styles. The excellent gift shop sells hard-to-find art books, good copies of jewelry from the classical world, and art-focused items for children. In Caffè Antico, the museum's in-house dining establishment, the food approaches gourmet quality. | 571 S. Kilgo St., Emory University | 404/727–4282 | fax 404/727–4292 | www.emory.edu/CARLOS | $5 (suggested donation) | Mon.–Sat. 10–5, Sun. noon–5.

Museum of the Jimmy Carter Library. Part of the Carter Presidential Center, the museum exhibits memorabilia from the life and presidency of James Earl Carter, Jr. Special exhibits focus on life in the White House and the history of the U.S. presidency. There are frequent art exhibitions. A gift shop and a light lunch operation, the Copenhill Cafe, are part of the facility. This is a good spot for children. The view of the downtown skyline and the slightly westernized Japanese gardens enhance a visit. | 441 Freedom Pkwy. | 404/331–0296 | fax 404/730–2215 | www.cartercenter.org | $5 | Mon.–Sat. 9–4:45, Sun. noon–4:45.

Oglethorpe University Museum. Completed in 1992, the museum occupies 4,000 square ft on the third floor of the university library. The focus is realistic art from a wide range of cultures presented in rotating exhibitions. The gift shop keeps pace; you'll always find items related to the current exhibition. In addition to the permanent collection, the museum presents three or four special shows every year. | 4484 Peachtree Rd. NE | 404/364–8555 | fax 404/364–8556 | museum.oglethorpe.edu | Free | Sept.–May, Tues.–Sun. noon–5.

★ **SciTrek–The Science and Technology Museum of Atlanta.** With rotating exhibitions and daily science demonstrations, the Science and Technology Museum of Atlanta fills its 96,000 square ft with about 150 hands-on exhibits. The material is organized in four themed environments: Simple Machines; Light, Color, and Perception; Electricity and Magnetism; and Kidspace, for children ages 2 to 7. There's a Coca-Cola Science Show Theater and an Information Petting Zoo exhibiting "cybercritters." Other attractions include I Can Discover Nature in Kidspace and an eight-seat flight simulator. | 395 Piedmont Ave. | 404/522–5500 | fax 404/525–6906 | www.scitrek.org | $7.50 | Mon.–Sat. 10–5, Sun. noon–5.

The Teaching Museum South. Sponsored by the Fulton County School system, with funding from private donors, the museum is housed in a former elementary school. The neoclassical building was designed by one of Atlanta's foremost architects, Phillip Trammel Schutze. The displays include a replica of a one-room schoolhouse, a Native American exhibit, Holocaust-theme exhibits, and an African exhibit. | 689 North Ave., Hapeville | 404/669–8015 | fax 404/669–8016. | Free | Weekdays 8–4:30, weekends by appointment.

William Breman Jewish Heritage Museum. Exhibitions focus on the history of Jewish Atlanta from 1845 to the present in the Jewish Heritage Gallery. There is also a Holocaust gallery called Absence of Humanity: The Holocaust Years. Facilities include a special exhibitions gallery, a hands-on Discovery area, a library, an archives and genealogy section, a museum shop, and the Lillian and A. J. Weinberg Holocaust Education Center. The museum is administered by the Atlanta Jewish Federation. | 1440 Spring St. | 404/873–1661 | fax 404/874-7043 | www.jfga.org | $5 | Mon.–Thurs. 10–5, Fri. 10–3, Sun. 1–5.

SPORTS AND RECREATION

Atlanta Braves. The Atlanta Braves, professional sports' oldest continuously operating franchise, have been National League contenders since going from worst to first in 1991, finally winning the World Series in 1995. | Turner Field, Capitol Ave. | 404/522–7630 | fax 404/614–2480 | www.atlantabraves.com.

Atlanta Falcons. Dubbed "The Dirty Birds" by fond football fans, the Falcons won Atlantans' hearts with their spirited post-season play, resulting in the team's first NFC championship. Coach Dan Reeves in his first season won his fifth NFL Coach of the Year award in 1998. | Georgia Dome, 1 Georgia Dome Dr. | 770/945–1111 | fax 770/271–1221 | www.atlantafalcons.com | Call for schedule.

Atlanta Hawks. This basketball team was originally known as the Tri-City Blackhawks, with a home in the Midwest. Following stints in Milwaukee and St. Louis, the team found its home in Atlanta in 1968, and in 1977 media mogul Ted Turner bought it. The team has been in the NBA playoffs every year since 1993. | Philips Arena, 1 Philips Dr. | 404/827–3800 | fax 404/827–3880 | www.hawks.com.

Atlanta Thrashers. Professional hockey returned to Atlanta with the 1999 season, as the expansion Atlanta Thrashers, also owned by media guru Ted Turner, geared up for its first season. Curt Fraser, who played with the IHL Orlando Solar Bears, is the team's first coach. | Philips Arena, One CNN Center, 12 South Tower | 404/827–5300 | fax 404/827–5909 | www.atlantathrashers.com.

Six Flags Over Georgia. Built in 1967, the popular park is known for its excellent July 4 fireworks displays. Popular rides are the Mind Bender, the wooden-railed Georgia Cyclone, the Great American Scream Machine, and the Dahlonega Mine Train. The Georgia Scorcher is a stand-up rollercoaster; the Goldtown Racer is a Grand Prix racing cars ride (an upcharge starts at $5 per person). The Crystal Pistol is a music emporium that produces summer musical theater. | I–20 | 770/948–9290 | fax 770/819–8256 | www.sixflags.com | $39.99; parking $8 | June–Oct., daily; mid-Mar.–May, weekends.

SIGHTSEEING TOURS/TOUR COMPANIES

Cable News Network studio tour. You ride the tallest elevated escalator in North America to reach the starting point of this tour, an eighth-floor exhibit about Turner's global broadcasting empire. Then visit CNN's studios and newsrooms. Tours are not open to children under age 6. | At 1 CNN Center | 404/827–2300 (for reservations: Weekdays 9–5) | fax 404/827–4035 | www.cnn.com | $8 (45-minute tour); $25 (1 ¼-hour VIP tour) | Daily 9–6, every 20 minutes.

Gray Line bus tours. Tours focus on Downtown, Midtown, Buckhead, and the King Center. Stone Mountain is included on some tours. | 705 Lively Ave., Norcross | 770/449–1806 (charters); 404/767–0594 (tours); 800/965–6665 (tour office); 800/593–1818 (charter office) | fax 770/246–9397 | www.amebus.com | $35 | Tours run Mon.–Sat. 9–5, Sun. 1–5.

OTHER POINTS OF INTEREST

★ **Atlanta History Center.** This 33-acre site in the heart of elegant Buckhead was part of the grounds originally surrounding Phillip Trammel Schutze's elegant 1928 Swan House, which he designed for the Samuel Inman family in the early 20th century now functions as a hands-on historical complex. | 130 W. Paces Ferry Rd. | 404/814–4000 | www.atlantahistorycenter.com | $10 | Mon.–Sat. 10–5:30, Sun. noon–5:30.

Atlanta History Museum. With a floor of heart pine and polished Stone Mountain granite, materials native to Georgia, the museum displays provocative material and is not afraid to deal with the unattractive aspects of Georgia's history. *Gone with the Wind* romanticism contrasts with the grim reality of Ku Klux Klan racism. Exhibits include Civil War mem-

orabilia as well as the history of Atlanta's African-American community. | 130 W. Paces Ferry Rd. | 404/814–4000 | fax 404/814–2041 | www.atlantahistorycenter.com | $10 | Mon.–Sat. 10–5:30, Sun. noon–5:30.

McElreath Hall. This building, the original museum space, houses meeting rooms as well as the center's archives and extensive photographic collection. | 130 W. Paces Ferry Rd. | 404/ 814–4000 | fax 404/814–4186 | www.atlantahistorycenter.com | Free | Mon.–Sat. 10–5.

Swan House. The neo-Palladian, supremely formal residence was designed for Samuel Inman's family by Phillip Trammel Schutze, one of Atlanta's premier 20th-century architects. Look closely and you'll see how a swan motif is used throughout. The house and its surrounding grounds have become the nucleus of the Atlanta History Center. | 130 W. Paces Ferry Rd. | 404/814–4000 | www.atlantahistorycenter.com | $10 main admission plus $1 | Half-hour tours, Mon.–Sat. 11–4, Sun. 1–4.

Tullie Smith Farm. This 1840s plantation home, which originally stood in North DeKalb County, is displayed together with outbuildings and a garden to capture the feeling of a farmer's life in the mid-19th century. In season, you'll find a cotton crop growing. | 130 W. Paces Ferry Rd. | 404/814–4000 | www.atlantahistorycenter.com | $10 main admission plus $1 | Half-hour tours Mon.–Sat. 11–4, Sun. 1–4.

Fernbank Science Center. Geology, space exploration, and ecology are presented in ways entertaining to the youngest children. Special programs for children under 5, priced at 50¢, are offered four times a year on the weekends. | 156 Heaton Park Dr. | 404/378–4311 | fax 404/370–1336 | fsc.fernbank.edu | Free; planetarium shows $2 | Mon. 8:30–5, Tues.–Fri. 8:30–10 PM, Sat. 10–5, Sun. 1–5.

Georgia State Farmers' Market. Farmers bring their produce to this teeming market, where everyone from restauranteurs to institutional managers buys in large quantities. Stall tenants also sell such specialty items as pickles, honey, sorghum, and similar products in retail sizes. | 16 Forest Pkwy, Forest Park | 404/675–1782 | fax 404/362–4564 | www.agr.state.ga.us | Free | Daily.

Underground Atlanta. In the late 19th century a series of bridges was built across the center of Atlanta to ease traffic congestion. The bridges eventually became streets running along at the height of the second floor of the local buildings. The ground-floor storefronts of those buildings thus came to form an "underground." The merchants operated out of the second floor, abandoning the original street level. The area was rediscovered in the 1960s and developed as a wildly popular entertainment complex full of subterranean hideaways. But by the late 1970s the area's popularity had declined. It was rediscovered in the 1980s and is today home to 6 blocks of shops and restaurants. You'll find historical markers, including one that marks the zero mile spot where New Hampshire native Stephen Long drove the spike to mark the end of the Western and Atlantic Railroad. | 50 Upper Alabama St. | 404/523–2311 | fax 404/523–0507 | www.underatl.com | Free | Daily, Shops: Mon.–Sat. 10–9:30, Sun. noon–6.

The World of Coca-Cola. At this three-story, $15 million special-exhibit facility, you can sip samples of 38 Coca-Cola Company products from around the world and study memorabilia from more than a century's worth of corporate archives. The gift shop, called Everything Coca-Cola, sells Coke-emblazoned merchandise ranging from refrigerator magnets to evening bags. | 55 Martin Luther King, Jr. Dr. | 404/676–5151 | fax 404/676–5432 | $6 | Sept.–May, Mon.–Sat. 9–5, Sun. noon–6; June–Aug., Mon.–Sat. 9–7, Sun. 11–6.

Yellow River Game Ranch. This petting zoo claims to offer "people-friendly animals." Along with the highly pettable kid goats, fawns, and bunnies, there are also less strokable cougars, bears, and a large herd of buffalo. | 4525 U.S. 78, Lilburn | 770/972–6643 | fax 770/985–0150 | www.yellowrivergameranch.com | $6 | Daily 9:30–5.

Zoo Atlanta. Almost 1,000 animals abide in naturalistic habitats, such as the *Ford African Rain Forest, Flamingo Lagoon, Masai Mara* (re-created plains of Kenya), and *Sumatran Tiger* exhibits. Longtime resident gorilla Willie B. and his offspring, Kudzoo and Olympia, are always big hits. The zoo is lucky enough to have some rare giant pandas. | 800C Cherokee Ave. | 404/624–5600 | fax 404/627–7514 | www.zooatlanta.org | $13 | Mar.–Oct. weekdays 9:30–4:30, Sat. and Sun. 9–5:30; Oct.–Mar., daily 9:30–4:30.

ON THE CALENDAR

APR.: *Atlanta Dogwood Festival*. Early every April, as the dogwood trees around Atlanta are blooming, people make their way to Piedmont Park to enjoy various events and activities, including rock climbing on a portable wall, children's activities, an artist market during the day, hot air balloons, and local bluegrass and rock-and-roll bands. | 404/521–6600 or 800/285–2682.

Dining

INEXPENSIVE

ACE Barbecue Barn. Southern. Lively and open late most nights, this spot offers excellent barbecue, including hard-to-find rib tips, along with many of the special dishes of down-home Southern cooking, such as pig ears and such side dishes as pinto beans, greens, okra, and candied yams. For dessert, try the sweet potato pie. No alcohol. | 30 Bell St. | 404/659–6630 | Reservations not accepted | Closed Tues. | $6–$7 | No credit cards.

Agnes and Muriel's. Southern. Order collard greens here, and you'll find they come with a twist, lemon and sesame seeds. This is also the place to try salmon potpie. Such unexpected pleasures are standard in this funky but homey hangout, a restaurant in what was originally a family bungalow. The place is cluttered with original 1960s fixtures, furniture, and knickknacks. The outdoor dining area is on the patio. Salmon patties, buttermilk fried chicken, meatloaf and mashed potatoes, and Louisiana barbecued shrimp over grits are among the best main courses, with enough vegetable side dishes to compose a good meal. Don't overlook the chocolate chiffon pie. Beer and wine only. Brunch Sat. and Sun. | 1514 Monroe Dr. | 404/885–1000 | Reservations not accepted | $8–$14 | AE, D, DC, MC, V.

Anis Cafe. French. The small dining room is intimate and romantic. The cooking of the south of France comes through in such dishes as fish stews, grilled pork chop with figs, roast chicken with crêpes, mussels, Provençal grilled vegetables, tuna Niçoise, and the shrimp l'Anis. These guys even do some of the best iced tea in town, though they probably would never touch it themselves. You can eat outdoors on the patio. Wine only. | 2974 Grandview Ave. | 404/233–9889 | menus.atlanta.com/anis | Reservations essential | No lunch Sun. | $10–$20 | AE, D, DC, MC, V.

Annie's Thai Castle. Thai. The local business crowd is so fond of this place that lunchtime can be hurried, so if you prefer to eat leisurely come for dinner. The classics of Thai cooking, such as massaman curries, fish, basil duck, and pad Thai, are especially well done here. The candlelit dining area is decorated with Oriental wall-hangings. | 3195 Roswell Rd. | 404/264–9546 | Reservations not accepted for lunch | Closed Mon. No lunch weekends | $11–$17 | AE, MC, V.

Babette's Cafe. Mediterranean. This French country house was originally a turn-of-the-20th-century local residence. The food and the casual, friendly mood prove irresistible to young professionals. The menu mixes dishes of Italian and French inspiration, such as cassoulet, pasta, grilled fresh fish, vegetarian dishes, and espresso flan. For brunch there are Babette's eggs Benedict on tenderloin with superior home-fried potatoes and "assertive" coffee. Sun. brunch. | 573 N. Highland Ave. | 404/523–9121 | Closed Mon. No lunch | $11–$21 | AE, D, DC, MC, V.

Bajarito's. Eclectic. The humble tortilla wraps around gourmet ingredients that range from Thai curry peanut chicken to blackened salmon fillet. Salad wraps include a grilled chicken Caesar. More traditional items include fish burritos. Kids' menu. Beer and wine only. | 3877 Peachtree Rd. | 404/239–9727 | $5–$7 | AE, MC, V.

Basil's Mediterranean Cafe. Mediterranean. Come here when the weather is warm to sit on the large outdoor deck. The wood tables and wrought-iron and wicker chairs add a cosmopolitan style. Many dishes have a Middle Eastern touch, from pasta to grilled salmon on couscous, paella, tapas, or hummus to the traditional mezze dishes. Baklava is the dessert of choice. | 2985 Grandview Ave. | 404/233–9755 | Reservations essential | No lunch Sun., Mon. | $14–$24 | AE, D, DC, MC, V.

Bien Thuy. Vietnamese. Long-standing, popular, and authentic, this restaurant is known for soups, noodle dishes, and seafood heavily aromatic with cilantro and hot pepper: grilled, stuffed jumbo shrimp (lemongrass, onion, beef stuffing); hu tieu (glass-noodle soup with seafood); banh xeo (stuffed pancakes); cha gio (spring rolls). | 5095 Buford Hwy., Northwoods Plaza, Doraville | 770/454–9046 | $6–$20 | AE, MC, V.

Blue Ribbon Grill. American/Casual. This casual neighborhood grill is popular with the locals, both for its bar and its food. Try the burgers, especially the bleu cheese with house-made potato chips, or the meatloaf, served in portions big enough for three. The grilled salmon is popular, as are the fresh vegetables country style. Sun. brunch. | 4006 LaVista Rd., Tucker | 770/491–1570 | Closed Sun. | $6–$22 | AE, D, DC, MC, V.

★ **Brasserie Le Coze.** French. It's in the middle of a mall in downtown Atlanta, but it's also a true Parisian bistro. Its attitude marks the boundary between formal and casual dining. The food is classic French bistro fare: creamy onion soup, white bean soup with truffle oil, mussels, quiche, skate wing, coq au vin, and pâtés are the mainstays at this little sister to New York's Le Bernardin. | 3393 Peachtree Rd. | 404/266–1440 | Reservations essential | Closed Sun. | $11–$24 | AE, D, DC, MC, V.

The Bread Market. Café. Breads baked on the premises serve as the draw for excellent sandwiches. You'll find fresh salads and pastries, including quiches. Earlybird suppers. No alcohol. | 1937 Peachtree Rd., Brookwood Village | 404/352–5252 | Reservations not accepted | Breakfast also available. Closes at 5 | $5–$10 | AE, D, MC, V.

The Bridgetown Grill. Jamaican. These folks were serving jerk chicken to Atlantans before jerk was cool. Join the hipper-than-thou and slumming suburbanites for a supper of slightly Americanized Jamaican fare. Stick to the basics and you will be well rewarded. The brightly painted courtyard out back booms with the sound of reggae music. Lunch and dinner. | 1156 Euclid Ave. | 404/653–0110 | $6–$15 | AE, D, MC, V.

Broadway Cafe. Kosher. The fare in this casual place is supervised Kosher and also vegetarian, but it looks to the world's cuisines for inspiration. There are empanadas and pot stickers stuffed with tempeh and vegetables. Many of the dishes are made without eggs or dairy products. Beer and wine only. Sun. brunch. | 2166 Briarcliff Rd. | 404/329–0888 | Closed Sat. No dinner Fri. No lunch Sun. | $9–$15 | AE, D, MC, V.

Buckhead Bread Company and Corner Cafe. Café. It looks something like a French café, smells exactly like a bakery, and is the perfect place to grab a cup of coffee and a freshly baked pastry for an afternoon pick-me-up. If you come for breakfast or brunch you'll find yourself facing substantial dishes of pancakes or eggs. For lunch, there are good sandwiches, such as the fried green tomato BLT. All day there is that great coffee, those house-baked pastries, and the wonderful aromas of fresh baked goods. Kids' menu. Sat. and Sun. brunch. Beer and wine only. | 3070 Piedmont Rd. | 404/240–1978 | www.buckheadrestaurants.com | Reservations not accepted | Breakfast also available. No dinner | $8–$14 | AE, D, DC, MC, V.

Buckhead Diner. Eclectic. The self-proclaimed "ritziest diner in the country" doesn't take itself too seriously, and nor should you. The smoothly designed interior and the highly inventive food are aspects of the same laid-back, friendly mood. Even the menu has a sense of humor. Try the veal meatloaf with wild mushrooms and celery mashed potatoes. Or the calamari, pan-seared shrimp dumplings with ginger/soy sauce, or the salmon BLT. Rock shrimp popsicles with honey mustard glaze, house-made potato chips with Maytag blue cheese, and white chocolate banana creme pie are the high points. Kids' menu. Sun.

brunch. | 3073 Piedmont Rd. | 404/262–3336 | www.buckheadrestaurants.com | Reservations not accepted | $14–$19 | AE, D, DC, MC, V.

Cafe Sunflower. Vegetarian. The two branches of this colorful, artsy place make vegetarian life easy, and the quality of the food pleases those usually fond of meat. With dishes drawn from a range of cuisines–from Asian to Mexican–Cafe Sunflower is the city's vegetarian restaurant leader. Both branches do the outrageously delicious tofu peanut butter pie and offer good quality juices, teas, and other nonalcoholic drinks. Vegetarian dishes are available. Beer and wine only (Peachtree Rd.); no alcohol (Roswell Road). | 2140 Peachtree Rd. | 404/352–8859 | Closed Sun. | 5975 Roswell Rd., Suite 353 | 404/256–1675 | $9–$14 | AE, D, DC, MC, V.

Café Tu Tu Tango. Eclectic. This funky spot, with a working artist's garret upstairs, serves only appetizers. Grab a gang and assemble a table of tapas: small pizzas, cajun chicken egg rolls, hummus with pita bread, empanadas, pot stickers, skewers, croquetas. Homemade sangria. Kids' menu. | 220 Pharr Rd. | 404/841–6222 | www.cafetututango.com | Reservations not accepted | $4–$8 | AE, D, DC, MC.

Canton House. Chinese. Dim sum on Saturday brings out the Chinese community to nibble from carts deftly rolled among tables. There's a good full Cantonese menu, but the dim sum is the show. | 4825 Buford Hwy., Chamblee | 770/936–9030 | Reservations not accepted weekends | $6–$10 | AE, D, MC, V.

Chopstix. Chinese. A great place for a snack or even a major meal. Hong Kong–style fare delivers such treats as black pepper oysters, Peking duck, soft-shell crab in season, pot stickers, and dumplings. | 4279 Roswell Rd., Chastain Square | 404/255–4868 | No lunch weekends | $13–$40 | AE, D, DC, MC, V.

Coco Loco. Cuban. Caribbean touches give character to this classic Cuban establishment, famous for its croquetas, roast pork, Cuban sandwiches, and flan. Other dishes from the Hispanic world include huevos rancheros (eggs with smoked ham and tomato) and classic Spanish potato omelet (here called "tortilla gallega"), Dominican-style fried chicken (marinated in garlic and sour orange juice), and Argentine steak with chimichurri sauce (a kind of parsley, olive oil, and garlic pesto). | 2625 Piedmont Rd., Suite G-40 | 404/364–0212 | $9–$16 | AE, D, DC, MC, V.

★ **The Colonnade.** Southern. This stalwart has been here forever. Plump oysters dot the rich stew; perfect salmon patties, country ham steak and trout; chicken potpie; fresh-baked pies (coconut cream!). Plenty of hot and cold vegetables. | 1879 Cheshire Bridge Rd. | 404/874–5642 | Reservations not accepted | No lunch Mon. and Tues. | $8–$18 | No credit cards.

Don Taco. Mexican. All kinds of traditional Mexican dishes, from burritos, tacos and tortas, quesadillas, huarachas (like a corn patty) topped with meat, beans, and cheese, to flan, served in an authentically Mexican space. Try the homemade salsas. Beer only. | 4997 Buford Hwy., Chamblee | 770/458–8735 | Reservations not accepted | $2–$6 | AE, D, DC, MC, V.

Dusty's Barbecue. Barbecue. This family-style restaurant has checked tablecloths and touches of fun in the pigs painted on the walls. North Carolina–style 'cue comes with coleslaw on top of the meat, and that's how Dusty's does it. Excellent hot sauce. Vegetables, ribs, and peach cobbler are very good. Beer and wine only. | 1815 Briarcliff Rd. | 404/320–6264 | Reservations not accepted | $3–$13 | AE, D, DC, MC, V.

E. 48th Street Italian Market. Italian. With its freshly baked Italian breads and aromatic deli meats, the shop smells good enough to eat. Besides sandwiches, prepared foods include homemade lasagna, pasta, meatballs, vegetables, and superb house-made pastries. Espresso and house-made biscotti finish it off. Open-air dining is available. Beer and wine only. | 2462 Jett Ferry Rd., Suite 340, Williamsburg at Dunwoody Shopping Center, Dunwoody | 770/392–1499 | Reservations not accepted | $5–$8 | Closed Sun. | No credit cards.

Eclipse di Luna. Spanish. A popular and casual spot in an unglamorous wholesale decorating complex. Lunch is mostly sandwiches and salads, but if you come in the evening you'll find the specialty, which is Spanish-style tapas. Much of the inspiration comes from Spain: Spanish Serrrano ham sliced thinly off the leg; spicy potatoes; soups; flan. | 764 Miami Circle | 404/846–0449 | Closed Mon. No lunch Sun. | $3–$18 | AE, D, DC, MC, V.

Ethiopian Abbay Restaurant. Ethiopian. A favorite with the local Ethiopian community, this neighborhood restaurant does the classic dishes well, serving them with enjera, the traditional flat bread. Spicy (but not searingly hot) lamb, chicken, and vegetarian dishes are full-flavored. Entertainment weekends. | 3375 Buford Hwy. | 404/321–5808 | Reservations essential | No lunch weekdays | $8–$12 | AE, MC, V.

Fadó. Irish. The music and food, with Irish breakfast available all day, have the spirit and flavors of a traditional pub. Boxty (potato pancake), smoked salmon, cottage and shepherds' pies, rhubarb pudding with brown bread ice cream (made in-house), and homemade soda bread are just some of the Irish specialties. Irish music (traditional singers and instruments) Mon. and Wed. evenings. Sat. and Sun. brunch. | 3035 Peachtree Rd. | 404/841–0066 | www.fadoirishpub.com | $9–$15 | AE, D, DC, MC, V.

Floataway Cafe. Eclectic. A gleaming updated warehouse space holds one of the city's most inventive restaurants. Cooking is by Anne Quatrano, also of Bacchanalia. Dishes change daily, taking advantage of locally grown organic produce and seasonal specialties. Italian and French models inspire the treatments of such raw ingredients as skate wing and Georgia white shrimp. You can't go wrong with the hanger steak and frites. | 1123 Zonolite Rd. | 404/892–1414 | Reservations essential | Closed Sun., Mon. No lunch | $10–$22 | AE, DC, MC, V.

Frank's Famous Family Restaurant. American. Dining in a FINA gas station may not seem gastronomic, but Frank Promas adds Greek and Italian touches (minced red pepper and slices of black olive) to his excellent country-fried steak, smothered in onions and mushrooms. The side dishes are big enough to serve two. | 1188 Collinsworth Rd., Palmetto | 770/463–5678 | Closed Aug. Closed Sun. | $9–$20 | MC, V.

Fratelli di Napoli. Italian. This is the classic "ristorante," with red tablecoths covered with white paper, candles, and family-style service. Certain main courses are hefty enough to satisfy at least two people. Pastas, chicken, snapper, and veal dishes all reflect the Italian-American way with dinner. | 2101-B Tula St. | 404/351–1533 | No lunch | $10–$26 | AE, D, DC, MC, V.

French Quarter Too. Cajun. The chef comes from Lafayette parish, Louisiana, which is your guarantee that the Cajun cooking at this casual restaurant is authentic. The interior is decorated in warm yellows and reds; for outdoor seating you choose between the patio in front and the courtyard at the back. The menu offers such Cajun staples as jambalaya, gumbo, crawfish, and muffalettas. | 2144 Johnson Ferry Road | 404/770/458–2148 | Closed Sun. | $10–$12 | AE, D, DC, MC, V.

Fuzzy's Place. Cajun. This local pub/restaurant is popular with locals for the live music and the excellent mussels, salmon or vegetable quesadilla, carpetbagger steak (stuffed with shrimp or oysters), seafood "Patsy" in a rich béchamel sauce, and bread pudding. Music every night. | 2015 N. Druid Hills Rd. | 404/321–6166 | Reservations not accepted | $5–$17 | AE, D, DC, MC, V.

Georgia Grille. Southwestern. Named not for the state but for Southwestern artist Georgia O'Keeffe, this very popular spot fills up early with patrons eager for some of the lobster enchiladas, great fish and seafood, smoked chicken enchiladas, hand-cut Angus beef with chipotle barbecue sauce and fried onion rings, and stuffed jalapeños (Hot Shots). Vegetarian dishes by request. Yummy flan! | 2290 Peachtree Rd. NW | 404/352–3517 | No reservations | Closed Mon. No lunch | $12–$22 | AE, MC, V.

Gringo's. Mexican. Gourmet fare dished up in a converted garage focuses on such specials as picadillo-stuffed roasted poblano peppers, jalapeño ice cream in summer, sopa de lima, vegetable budins, and bread pudding. | 1238 DeKalb Ave. | 404/522–8666 | Reservations not accepted | Closed Mon. No lunch | $9–$15 | AE, MC, V.

Hae Won Dae. Korean. In a nondescript strip mall, you'll find one of the city's best Asian restaurants. Small private rooms for groups of about seven line one wall. Very authentic dishes. Korean barbecue done over wood charcoal, not gas, is the right way to do it. Open very late. | 5805 Buford Hwy., Doraville | 770/458–6999 | $7–$15 | AE, D, DC, MC, V.

Hanwoori. Korean/Japanese. Two restaurants in one: go to the right, and savor an all-Japanese menu in an elegant tatami room or sit at a sushi bar. To the left is the larger space, with a Korean menu, including Korean barbecue and other traditional dishes. Of course, you can get sushi there, too. | 4251 N. Peachtree Rd., Chamblee | 770/458–9191 | $14–$17 | AE, D, DC, MC, V.

Harvest. Eclectic. When they converted an old house to make room for this restaurant, they didn't go all the way and instead left behind a pleasantly quaint and homely quality. There are three fireplaces, with paintings and antiques among the decorations. The dishes come from the Mediterranean, Asia, and America. Pappardelle, rock shrimp (a Georgia specialty) on sweet corn risotto, maple-smoked grilled pork chop with cheddar-stuffed potato pancakes, and honey pecan chicken are finely honed dishes. Sun. brunch. | 853 N. Highland Ave. | 404/876–8244 | No lunch Sat. | $13–$18 | AE, DC, MC, V.

Holyfield's New South Grill. Eclectic. Atlanta boxing star Evander Holyfield's restaurant explores the globe with such dishes as shrimp and pork wontons with cilantro chile sauce and charred halibut with Cajun spices and an étouffée of crawfish ravioli. You can eat outdoors on a patio, but don't overlook the interior, which has its own blend of excitement, with blood-red ceilings and artwork that includes stone and metal sculptures. | 6075 Roswell Rd. | 404/531–0300 | www.holyfieldsrestaurant.com | Reservations essential | Closed Sun. No lunch Sat. | $10–$26 | AE, D, DC, MC, V.

Indigo Coastal Grill. Eclectic. You sample the world's coastal cuisines at this contemporary restaurant full of lively energy reflected in the vibrant orange and purple color scheme. Look around and you'll see an aquarium and a vintage 1950s jukebox. Start off with a key lime margarita, made with fresh key limes, then move on to sushi or seafood or pasta. Sit out on the covered patio to savor the great brunch dishes, such as jalapeño cheese grits. Fresh catch in parchment is superior, as is the key lime pie. | 1397 N. Highland Ave. | 404/876–0676 | Reservations essential | No lunch | $14–$22 | AE, D, MC, V.

Kurt's and Vreny's Biergarten. German. Two restaurants in one: Kurt's, the more formal of the two, does continental dishes with German touches: spaetzle with Black Forest ham and mushrooms; schnitzels; and house-made apple strudel. At the rear of Kurt's is the more casual Vreny's, which dishes out sausages, sauerkraut, rouladen, and other home-style German specialties. Back there you'll also find a beer garden in a landscaped courtyard for outdoor dining. Beer and wine only. | 4225 River Green Pkwy, Duluth | 770/623–9413 | Reservations not accepted at Vreny's | Kurt's: Closed Sun. No lunch. Vreny's Biergarten: Closed Sun., Mon. | Kurt's: $14–$27; Vreny's: $6–$14 | AE, D, DC, MC, V.

La Paz. Mexican. Owner Tom Nickoloff grows and roasts chiles for restaurants in North Georgia. Tortilla soup, roasted poblano chili strips, Santa Fe enchiladas, properly chunky freshly made guacamole, chili con queso with spinach, and amaretto flan for dessert. Kids' menu. | 6410 Roswell Rd. | 404/256–3555 | Reservations essential | No lunch weekends | 2950 New Paces Ferry Rd., Vinings | 770/801–0020 | $8–$13 | AE, D, DC, MC, V.

Little Szechuan. Chinese. Bring a gang and share dishes. Don't look for egg rolls or fortune cookies, which would be out of place amid the authentic and outstanding Szechuan cuisine. You'll find unfamiliar dishes worth trying, such as salt-and-pepper fish, and also reworked versions of old standards, including extraordinary egg foo yung. The string beans in garlic sauce are properly spicy. | 5091-C Buford Hwy. | 770/451–0192 | Closed Tues. | $8–$20 | MC, V.

Luna Sí. Eclectic. A funky loft-like space sectioned off with gauzy draping, this is a wildly popular bistro. The Latin music blares, and if you feel like it you can write on the walls. Seared salmon with a ginger crumb crust and roasted chicken with whipped potatoes are among the mainstays. The homemade desserts are worth trying. | 1931 Peachtree Rd. | 404/355–5993 | Reservations essential | Closed Sun. No lunch | $12–$19 | AE, D, DC, MC, V.

Mambo Restaurante Cubano. Cuban. This tiny neighborhood bistro is decorated with a 14-foot mural of Carmen Mulata. Go for the classics of Cuban cuisine: paella; black paella; ropa vieja; tapas; and especially Chinese Latino dishes, a specialty of Lucy Alvarez, chef and co-owner (with husband Hilton Joseph). | 1402 N. Highland Ave. | 404/876–2626 | Reservations essential | No lunch | $7–$16 | AE, DC, MC, V.

Manual's Tavern. American. The perfect neighborhood pub, rustic with a touch of the old style. The Manual's in Poncey-Highland marked a half century of life a few years back. Menus differ a bit (the original has a good vegetable burger, for instance), but both offer excellent steak sandwiches, beer-steamed hot dogs, and the city's best chicken wings with house-made bleu cheese dressing. | 602 N. Highland Ave. | 404/525–3447 | 4877 Memorial Dr., Stone Mountain | 404/296–6919 | $5–$9 | AE, D, DC, MC, V.

Marra's Seafood Grill. Seafood. Perfectly cooked fish and seafood, but also lamb and steak. You'll find some of the more exciting dishes taking you on a world tour, with Chilean seabass carpaccio, honey-ginger Caribbean grouper, New England giant natural sea scallops, or South African lobster tail. There are also good pasta dishes and house-made desserts ranging from cheesecake to pies. You can eat outdoors on a patio. | 1782 Cheshire Bridge Rd. | 404/874–7347 | menus.atlanta.com/marras | Reservations essential | No lunch | $13–$21 | AE, D, DC, MC, V.

Mary Mac's Tea Room. Southern. This local favorite has been around since 1945. When the legislature is in session, politicos hash out their differences over superior fried chicken, country-fried steak, fresh vegetables, and freshly baked cinnamon rolls. It's worth a visit just for the mashed potatoes and gravy. The service is fun, too—you fill out your own order, hand it to the waitress, and she brings your food. Don't be surprised if she calls you "honey" and pats your arm to assure you everything's all right. Sun. and Sat. brunch. | 224 Ponce de Leon Ave. NE | 404/876–1800 | No dinner Sun. | $7–$14 | No credit cards.

Max Lager's American Grill and Brewery. American/Casual. This downtown brew pub serves not only good suds but good food. Line up a tasting of the current brews and order some great gumbo, fish 'n' chips, or a vegetable pita. The beers include nonalcoholic house-made root and ginger beers. | 320 Peachtree St. | 404/525–4400 | www.maxlagers.com | $6–$22 | AE, D, DC, MC, V.

Mirage. Middle Eastern. The location is a typically characterless suburban shopping center, but as soon as you smell the aromas of this perfumed cuisine you'll know there's something different. This modern Iranian is not a vegetarian restaurant, but it offers more than a dozen intriguing vegetable dishes to sample. The lighter fare includes yogurt and shallots, herbs with feta cheese, and eggplant with garlic. There are such traditional desserts as rosewater ice cream with pistachios. Beer and wine only. | 6631C Roswell Rd. | 404/843–8300 | $6–$17 | AE, D, DC, MC, V.

Mi Spia. Italian. The space speaks fluent Tuscan, with marbelized walls and terra-cotta-like floors. The food ranges around Italy: good risotto, pasta, calamari, seafood, salads, and desserts. Grilled chicken on radiatore pasta with artichoke hearts and black olives is a signature dish. There is open-air dining on the small enclosed patio. | 4505 Ashford Dunwoody Rd., Dunwoody | 770/393–1333 | Reservations essential | No lunch weekends | $14–$23 | AE, D, DC, MC, V.

Murphy's. Contemporary. Regulars come back again and again to this neighborhood café for the inventive menu with its international array of dishes. Unusual soups such as sweet potato and vegetarian chili make good starters, and New Zealand green lip mussels in a Thai coconut curry broth and the BBQ vegetarian burrito suggest the range of the menu. This is a good place to drop in for late coffee and dessert, especially the nut tarts. Kids' menus. Sat. and Sun. Brunch. | 997 Virginia Ave. | 404/872–0904 | www.murphysvh.com | Reservations not accepted | $8–$16 | AE, D, DC, MC, V.

Nona's Italian Kitchen. Italian. With its bright, playful colors and fun chandeliers, this won't necessarily remind you of an Italian restaurant, but you'll know where you are when you taste the food, which is good, old-fashioned, traditional Italian. The selection of pastas is extensive, but this is a good place to try gnocchi instead, or the risotto di bosco or risotto with mushrooms and white truffle oil. A particular favorite is the chicken saltimbocca. Among the desserts is a flourless chocolate torte. | 3365 Piedmont Rd., Suite 1025 | 404/261–1312 | No lunch Sat. and Sun. | $12–$24 | AE, D, DC, MC, V.

Nuevo Laredo Cantina. Mexican. Inspired by the Cadillac bar in the border town of Nuevo Laredo, this lively spot features freshly made guacamole, refried beans, steak, and seafood, as well as good flan. Kids' menu. | 1495 Chattahoochee Ave. | 404/352–9009 | Closed Sun. | $6–$13 | AE, D, DC, MC, V.

OK Cafe. American. The turquoise-and-white-checked floor, wood walls, and displays of local artwork make this a pleasant place to eat. It's conveniently open very early and also very late on weekends. There is also take-out and kid-friendly fare. It's great for breakfast, especially for omelets and pancakes, but you'd do best to come later and focus on the American home-style classics: meatloaf, country-fried steak, mashed potatoes and gravy, fried chicken, pot roast. | 1284 W. Paces Ferry Rd. | 404/233–2888 | Reservations not accepted | Breakfast also available | $8–$11 | AE, D, DC, MC, V.

Panang. Malaysian. Classy and instantly popular, this addition to Atlanta's Asian line-up does Malaysian and Thai fare. Lots of spicy dishes, curries, and seafood, a wide range of soups, and traditional noodle dishes. | 4897 Buford Hwy. | 770/220–0308 | $7–$26 | MC, V.

Pasta da Pulcinella. Italian. Milanese-born Roberto Boratto's pasta trattoria is a simple affair: The only appetizer is salad (a Caesar so huge you might want to order a half). The pasta dishes are not the ordinary. Intriguing examples include round ravioli filled with browned Granny Smith apples, sausage, and Parmesan cheese and topped with browned butter and sage. At least one pasta is vegetarian. Check the frequently changing specials. | 1123 Peachtree Walk NE | 404/892–6195 | Reservations not accepted | Closed Mon. No lunch Fri.–Sun. | $12–$19 | AE, MC, V.

Poona. Indian. The true bargain here is the lunch buffet, a generous spread of dishes from the main menu. The lamb dishes and tandoori fare are excellent, and there are lots of vegetarian dishes. Don't hesitate if you're worried about spiciness—the heat levels can be adjusted to suit your taste. Buffet (lunch). Wine and beer only. | 1630 Pleasant Hill Rd., Duluth | 770/717–1053 | $8–$9 | AE, D, DC, MC, V.

Quality Kosher Emporium. Kosher. A few tables are available at the back of this kosher deli, and there are plans to expand the dining area. The food is strictly glatt kosher. Excellent potato salad, deli meats, sandwiches, good bagels. No alcohol. | 2153 Briarcliff Rd. | 404/636–1114 | Reservations not accepted | Closed Sat. No dinner Fri. | $6–$10 | AE, D, MC, V.

Rainbow Grocery. Vegetarian. At the rear of one of Atlanta's oldest health-food groceries, this casual spot dishes up meatless daily specials and sandwiches. Popular are the vegetable chili and lasagna, tofu dishes, walnut loaf, and luscious desserts. Smoothies are the drink of choice. No alcohol. | 2118 N. Decatur Rd. | 404/636–5553 | Reservations not accepted | Closed Sun. Closes at 8 | $4–$8 | No credit cards.

Rib Ranch. Barbecue. The Texas-style barbecue beef ribs are the best in town. The side dishes are excellent, too, but as you'll see if you look around, one of the big draws is the people watching. You'll see some real characters in here. The best bargain is a huge beef rib platter that feeds two or three people. Beer only. | 25 Irby Ave. | 404/233–7644 | www.theribranch.com | Reservations not accepted | $7–$11 | MC, V.

R. Thomas Deluxe Grill. American/Casual. You dine "outside" in all weather here, but that's because the dining room is a covered, climate-controlled patio. Adding to the sense of being in nature is a cage full of exotic birds. Stuffed baked potatoes are a complete meal, big salads, huge burgers and omelets, great malteds, some macrobiotic fare. Kids' menu. | 1812

Peachtree St. NE | 404/872–2942 | Reservations not accepted | Open 24 hours | $7–$15 | AE, D, DC, MC, V.

Seoul Garden. Korean. Start at the sushi bar, then repair to a table in this former chain-restaurant building to enjoy all manner of Korean barbecue, excellent Korean seafood pancakes, fish, and cold noodle dishes. The staff is very friendly. | 5938 Buford Hwy., Doraville | 770/452–0123 | No lunch weekends | $8–$25 | AE, DC, MC, V.

Silver Skillet. Southern. This establishment has been around so long and is so full of local color that it has been used in films and commercials. Locals know it for its eggs, grits, and country ham breakfasts, for its tender grilled pork chops, superb vegetables, and excellent pies. No alcohol. Sat. and Sun. brunch. | 200 14th St. | 404/874–1388 | Reservations not accepted | Breakfast also available. No dinner, no lunch weekends | $5–$6 | AE, D, DC, MC, V.

SoHo Restaurant. Eclectic. A lively, contemporary space decorated in neutral colors, mostly light tans, enlivened by local artwork hosts this upscale yet laid-back restaurant. Southwestern meets Asian to present a tasty, piquant chicken tortilla soup, seared elk loin with raspberry mustard, blue corn crusted fried calamari with Thai chili and honey vinaigrette. | 4200 Paces Ferry Rd., Suite 107, Vinings | 770/801–0069 | No lunch Sat. and Sun. | $9–$24 | AE, D, DC, MC, V.

Son's Place. Southern. Come here for breakfast and try a salmon croquette stuffed in a biscuit. Even better, come here for lunch and try authentic Southern food, most of all the legendary fried chicken, greens, pound cake, sweet potato pie, hoecakes, and similar substantial fare. The dining room is bright and cherry, and the service is cafeteria style. | 100 Hurt St. | 404/581–0530 | Reservations not accepted | Breakfast also available. Closed weekends. No dinner | $4–$6 | No credit cards.

Soto. Japanese. Sotohiro Kosugi, a third-generation master, has won nationwide acclaim for the quality of his sushi and sashimi. The Japanese dishes here are stunning both in taste and appearance; this is considered the best sushi restaurant in Atlanta, perhaps among the top five in the United States. The specials vary nightly and could include live flounder sushi. Orange cups stuffed with mango and minced scallop, gossamer salmon carpaccio, and for dessert ginger ice cream convey the idea. Wine and sake only. | 3330 Piedmont Rd. | 404/233–2005 | Closed Sun. No lunch | $10–$21 | AE, D, DC, MC, V.

Sotto Sotto. Italian. This hot spot close to downtown brings a fresh, authentic approach to Italian food. The space is tiny and noisy, full of activity, and the open kitchen provides diners with a great view. Owner and chef Riccardo Ullio, born in Italy but reared in Georgia, started at Pasta da Pulcinella. Grilled scallops with white beans and truffle oil, spaghetti with sun-dried mullet roe, and perfect panna cotta are just some of the tempting dishes. | 313 N. Highland Ave. | 404/523–6678 | Reservations essential | Closed Sun. No lunch | $13–$20 | AE, DC, MC, V.

★ **South City Kitchen.** Southern. A casual, contemporary grill offers a touch of sophistication to low-country fare from chef Fay Swift. Try rich she-crab soup, fried green tomatoes, catfish, poached eggs on crab hash, shrimp and scallops on stone-ground grits with garlic cream gravy, and chocolate pecan pie. Sun. brunch | 1144 Crescent Ave. | 404/873–7358 | Reservations essential | $13–$27 | AE, DC, MC, V.

Stringer's Fish Camp. Seafood. There's nothing closer to fish camp in the entire urban area. The seafood platters are huge and could easily feed two. The seafood stew, spicy and thick, is a lot like a gumbo. You can have the catfish deep-fried or broiled. Beer and wine only. | 3384 Shallowford Rd. | 770/458–7145 | $10–$16 | AE, MC, V.

Sundown Café. Southwestern. The warmth of the color scheme, yellow and red, echoes the warmth of the food at this casual cafe. Eddie's Pork, with jalapeño gravy, ancho-chili mashed potatoes, and turnip greens, corn chowder, and super chicken dishes are paired with the diner's choice of splendid house-made salsas. There's also the Budín al chipotle, a vegetable casserole. Kids' menu. | 2165 Cheshire Bridge Rd. | 404/321–1118 | Reservations not accepted | Closed Sun. No lunch Sat. | $10–$17 | AE, DC, MC, V.

The Tap Room. Eclectic. The dining here is casual, but you'll see right away that they're serious about drinking, with 43 beers on tap and 15 different martinis. The menu is standard, with a touch of Italian flair. Chicken satay, crab cakes, and grilled portobello mushrooms with port wine are among the appetizers; the main dishes include steaks, burgers, pastas, and chicken dishes along with a few more imaginative creations, such as Cajun crawfish linguine and tequila smoked salmon. | 231 Peachtree St. NE, Suite A5 | 404/577–7860 | www.taproom.net | Reservations essential | No lunch weekends | $11–$22 | AE, D, DC, MC, V.

Thai Chilli. Thai. Standard Thai dishes are well prepared. If you're looking for more heat try the specials, which are often substantially hotter. Soft-shell crab with spicy basil sauce, scallop curry, choochee curry salmon, spicy catfish, and catfish curry are super. Beer, wine, and BYOB wine (corkage fee). | 2169 Briarcliff Rd. | 404/315–6750 | No lunch weekends | $7–$14 | AE, D, MC, V.

Thelma's Kitchen. Soul. It's a special treat to drop in and find they've made their famous okra pancakes at this traditional Southern diner. If not, you'll have no trouble making do with the fried catfish, well-seasoned vegetables, macaroni and cheese, "cold" slaw, and pecan pie. No alcohol. | 768 Marietta St. | 404/688–5855 | Reservations not accepted | Closed Sun. No dinner. Breakfast also available | $6–$9 | No credit cards.

TomTom. Eclectic. In lively Lenox Square, TomTom offers a sushi bar and a menu combining Asian, Mediterranean, and Southern influences. Dishes range from barbecued salmon on white cheese grits with sesame slaw to individual pizzas and more substantial dishes, such as braised lamb or roast chicken with mashed potatoes. Crème brûlée and key lime pie are the best desserts. Sun. brunch. | 3393 Peachtree Rd. | 404/264–1163 | tomtom-atlanta.com | $14–$20 | AE, D, DC, MC, V.

Tortillas. Mexican. Great for people watching. Everything's made on the premises: wonderful fresh salsas, especially the tomatillo, excellent on the fine omelets and quesadillas. The bean and cheese burritos are delicious. Beer only. | 774 Ponce de Leon Ave. | 404/892–0193 | Reservations not accepted | $4–$8 | No credit cards.

Toulouse. Contemporary. The look is updated French rustic, the mood is casual, the cuisine is American-French. Hearty fare such as the country potato soup and buffalo meatloaf or sea bass with tarragon beurre blanc and roasted beet compote have made this hard-to-find Buckhead spot stand out. In good weather you can sit outside on the greenery-adorned deck. | 2293 Peachtree Rd. NE, Suite B | 404/351–9533 | www.toulouserestaurant.com | Reservations essential | No lunch | $10–$22 | AE, DC, MC, V.

★ **Veni Vidi Vici.** Italian. In the heart of the theater district, this is a great place to grab a bite to eat before or after a show. You can also enjoy an appetizer and drink on the patio while playing a game of boccie. The tastes of Northern Italy direct the kitchen, which produces tasty small plates (octopus and potato salad, for one) for light dining and fragrant rotisserie meats. Grilled suckling pig or rabbit braised with fennel on a fingerling potato and zucchini au gratin give an idea of these country-style flavors. For desserts, try the frozen white chocolate mousse with Georgia peach compote and caramelized pecans. | 41 14th St. | 404/875–8424 | www.buckheadrestaurants.com | Reservations essential | No lunch weekends | $13–$28 | AE, D, DC, MC, V.

Violette. French. This casual French bistro and bar is run by Guy Luc, from Alsace, so the food takes cues from that tradition. Try the quiche and veal meatloaf at lunch. Salmon rillettes, garlicky snails, house-made terrines and pâté, steak with Roquefort sauce or peppercorns, lamb, classic bistro desserts (chocolate mousse, crème brûlée, and pear tart, for instance) are all first rate. | 2948 Clairmont Rd., 30329 | 404/633–3363. | Closed Sun. No lunch Sat. | $9–$16 | AE, D, DC, MC, V.

Vortex. American/Casual. Open very late. The Moreland Avenue location is easy to find because the outside is decorated with a two-story skull, eyes spinning. The branch on Peachtree Street was clearly inspired by Peewee's Playhouse. Take your pick. Hamburgers in variety are the big draw, including vegetable burgers made of black beans or soy beans and turkey burgers. Chicken, fish, shrimp, and deli sandwiches are also available. The beer selection is outstanding. | 438 Moreland Ave. | 404/688–1828 | 878 Peachtree St. | 404/875–1667 | Reservations not accepted | $6–$8 | AE, D, DC, MC, V.

White House. Southern. Long famous for its Southern-style breakfasts, White House also does American fare for lunch. The owner has a convincing Southern accent, but he's a fourth-generation Greek-American, so don't be surprised by the dishes from the Aegean Sea tradition. At lunch, the steam table holds plenty of Southern fare, but if you look you'll recognize such Greek dishes as pastitsio and moussaka, not to mention gyros. No alcohol. No smoking. | 172 Peachtree St. | 404/237–7601 | Breakfast also available. No dinner | Reservations not accepted | $4–$11 | No credit cards.

Zócalo. Mexican. Lucero Martínez-Obregón runs one of the most popular restaurants in Atlanta, yet its only dining room is an enclosed patio. The food, rigorously authentic, explores the culinary variety of Mexico, from enchiladas to chiles en nogada to shrimp fajitas. Huge portions. Vegetarian items. The hibiscus tea is special. Beer and wine only. | 187 10th St. | 404/249–7576 | No lunch Sat. | $9–$17 | AE, D, DC, MC, V.

MODERATE

★ **The Abbey.** Contemporary. A deconsecrated church, complete with harpist in the choir loft, forms the spectacular backdrop for adventurous cuisine that features such luxury ingredients as ostrich, elk, quail, hen-of-the-woods mushrooms, lobster, and foie gras. The desserts are experiences—the crème brûlée is flavored differently each night. The menu changes seasonally. | 163 Ponce de Leon Ave. | 404/876–8532 | www.theabbeyrestaurant.com | Reservations essential | Jacket required | No lunch | $18–$28 | AE, D, DC, MC, V.

Abruzzi. Italian. This dining room exudes a golden glow. Pappardelle with game sauce, fresh game in season, excellent sweetbreads, and classic Italian desserts are the high points of the menu. Specials take advantage of the seasonal market. | 2355 Peachtree Rd. | 404/261–8186 | Reservations essential | Jacket required | $15–$25 | Closed Sun. No lunch Sat. | AE, D, DC, MC, V.

Anthony's. Continental. This is an old plantation house moved here from southeast Georgia. The continental standards include a huge surf & turf, salmon Wellington, and chateaubriand for two. You don't have to look hard to find Southern accents on the menu, such as crab cakes and she-crab soup, Carolina trout rolled in pecans, and pan-fried snapper. | 3109 Piedmont Rd. | 404/262–7379 | www.anthonysfinedining.com | Reservations essential | No lunch | $19–$25 | AE, D, DC, MC, V.

Aria. Contemporary. Chef Jerry Klafkala is a proponent of the "slow-food" movement, in which ingredients are slow-roasted to create fuller, more intense flavors. Fresh seafood is the speciality: soft-shell crabs, corn and crab risotto, and tuna steak are some of the stars. There are also meat dishes, and the flexible kitchen is happy to accommodate vegetarians. | 490 E. Paces Ferry Rd. | 404/233–7673 | Reservations essential | Closed Sun. No lunch | $17–$36 | AE, D, DC, MC, V.

Atlanta Fish Market. Seafood. The fish here is as fresh as fish gets inland. Southern, Asian, and Italian touches mark the menu: gumbo, blackened fish, fresh raw oysters, sea bass with Asian seasonings, and crab cakes are winners. Quieter seating is on the Geechee Porch. | 265 Pharr Rd. | 404/262–3165 | No lunch Sun. | $17–$33 | AE, D, DC, MC, V.

Blue Ridge Grill. American. The dark wood rafters, canoes on the walls, and fireplace make a welcoming, cosy environment. The soups change daily; keep an eye out for the hopping John and the vegetarian black bean, both of which are delicious. The main dishes include right-spiced gumbo, Southern-style vegetables (squash casserole), fish dishes (smoked trout crab cakes, horseradish crusted snapper), and filet mignon with potato-Stilton cheese cream and fried leeks. | 1261 W. Paces Ferry Rd. | 404/233–5030 | Reservations essential | No lunch Sat. | $18–$30 | AE, D, DC, MC, V.

Bone's. Steak. This popular local restaurant is reputed to make the city's best onion rings. The steaks are "wrestler-size," and the menu includes fish, lobster bisque, and crab cakes as well as vegetable side dishes such as sauteed spinach, potatoes, and vegetable hash au gratin. | 3130 Piedmont Rd. | Reservations essential | 404/237–2663 | No lunch weekends | $19–$35 | AE, D, DC, MC, V.

The Cabin. American. This recreation of a log cabin is no place for vegetarians, as is clear from the heads of elk, caribou, and moose displayed on the walls. Game and steaks are the focus, but there is also good fish and seafood, especially the crab cakes, as well as duck sausage. First-class key lime and pecan pies. | 2678 Buford Hwy. | 404/315–7676 | Reservations essential | Closed Sun. No lunch Sat. | $19–$28 | AE, D, DC, MC, V.

★ **Canoe.** Contemporary. The seasons and the region dictate the often-changing menu at this popular spot on the banks of the Chattahoochee River. Rock shrimp, a Georgia coastal specialty, are served as a cake with an Asian-inspired crispy noodle salad. There are tuna maki roll and pumpkin soup with Maine peekytoe crab meat, grilled Georgia quail and Carolina trout. You can sit on a patio overlooking lushly landscaped gardens dotted with walkways and benches. | 4199 Paces Ferry Rd. | 770/432–2663 | www.canoe-atl.com | Reservations essential | No lunch Sat. | $17–$24 | AE, D, DC, MC, V.

★ **City Grill.** Contemporary. The lobby of a landmark Federal Reserve Bank, built in 1912, has been transformed into an elegant restaurant. The architecture is stunning, with a sweeping marble staircase, marble columns, a rotunda, and chandeliers. It is old-fashioned formal though the food is regional with such Southern dishes as an appetizer of fried green tomatoes and house-made mozzarella, or quail with cream gravy and raspberry black pepper biscuits. Cornmeal-fried veal sweetbreads and onion-crusted sturgeon are more modern. The vegetable specials include a grilled vegetable roulade. | 50 Hurt Plaza | 404/524–2489 | Reservations essential | Jacket required | Closed Sun. No lunch Sat. | $15–$38 | AE, D, DC, MC, V.

Dish. Eclectic. This popular neighborhood spot, built from a converted gas station, draws crowds of locals. The menu swings east with a seafood trio in wonton cups, then heads south with eight-hour smoked baby-back ribs. You'll also notice a few Italian dishes. There's a covered patio if you want to eat outside. | 870 N. Highland Ave. | 404/897–3463 | No lunch | $15–$22 | AE, DC, MC, V.

★ **The Food Studio.** Contemporary. Like an artist's studio, this space is perched in a refurbished 1904 plow factory. The menu picks and chooses from a variety of cuisines: cassoulet, shrimp-and-feta stuffed cannelloni, grilled beef tenderloin. The frozen lemon basil bombe is heaven. | 887 W. Marietta St. | 404/815–6677 | Reservations essential | No lunch | $16–$28 | AE, DC, MC, V.

Hal's on Old Ivy. Cajun/Creole. Exposed brick walls and natural wood add a touch of the modern and stylish to the understated charm of this long-established restaurant. A touch of Cajun and Creole flavors do something similar to the food. Excellent soft-shell crabs, crawfish étouffée, and blackened filet rate alongside the veal and salmon. The homemade pastas include all-vegetable versions. There's live music Thurs.–Sat. | 30 Old Ivy Rd. | 404/261–0025 | Reservations essential | Closed Sun. No lunch | $16–$25 | AE, D, DC, MC, V.

★ **Horseradish Grill.** Southern. In a former horse barn, Chef David Berry, a native of South Carolina, presents his father's special barbecue recipe. The food is served on corn cake and is topped with coleslaw, Carolina style. Quail on sweet potato puree, catfish fingers, pork loin stuffed with dried peaches and Georgia peanuts, and the grill's famous fried chicken with macaroni and cheese are examples of the upscale Southern dishes. Try the pecan tart for dessert. Sun. brunch. | 4320 Powers Ferry Rd. | 404/255–7277 | www.horseradishgrill.com | Reservations essential | No lunch Sat. | $15–$27 | AE, D, DC, MC, V.

Japanese Restaurant Kamogawa. Japanese. Quiet and restrained, this is a good place to regain a sense of inner calm. The Tokyo-style fare offers such treasures as soft-shell crab in season, pristine sushi and sashimi presented with formal elegance, lobster tempura, traditional Japanese savory custard (chawan mushi). Excellent list of fine sakes, including Kurosawa, a limited-production Japanese special. | 3300 Peachtree Rd., Grand Hyatt Atlanta Hotel | 404/841–0314 | No lunch weekends | $28–$50 | AE, D, DC, MC, V.

La Grotta at Ravinia. Italian. A glass wall gives wonderful views of lush gardens. The menu differs in certain details from that of La Grotta in Buckhead, but the quality of the pastas, fish, and seafood is the same. Special dishes include cold roasted veal with sundried-tomato vinaigrette, veal chop with gorgonzola cream, and excellent panna cotta for dessert. | 4355 Ashford Dunwoody Rd. | 770/395–9925 | Closed Sun. No lunch Sat. | $15–$28 | AE, D, DC, MC, V.

La Grotta Ristorante Italiano. Italian. In Atlanta's oldest grand Italian restaurant, chef and owner Sergio Favalli does Northern Italian and regional dishes: bresaola (air-dried beef) with Parmesan cheese, snails and mushrooms on polenta; gnocchi with Swiss chard, tomatoes, walnuts, and cream; roast quail stuffed with Italian sausage. The setting in the basement of an apartment building is elegant and refined, with fresh flowers on the linen tablecloths. The kitchen responds happily to requests for vegetarian or other special dishes. | 2637 Peachtree Rd. | 404/231–1368 | www.la-grotta.com | Reservations essential | Jacket required | Closed Sun. No lunch | $15–$28 | AE, D, DC, MC, V.

Le Saint Amour. French. Provence is the guiding spirit behind the colors and flavors of this bustling bistro. Terrine of foie gras with red wine/onion compote, fish soup with garlic and grated cheese, sweetbreads, duck confit, game in season, and classic crème brûlée explain its growing popularity. | 1620 Piedmont Ave., 30324 | 404/881–0300. | No lunch Sat. | $15–$25 | AE, MC, V.

McKendrick's. Steak. Portions are generous in this very masculine, very classic steak house. The walls are paneled with dark wood, and the air is thick with noise. Red meat beyond beef includes buffalo and, in season, other game meats. The menu extends to grilled fish and good vegetable side dishes. | 4505 Ashford Dunwoody Rd., Park Place Shopping Center, Dunwoody | 770/512–8888 | No lunch weekends | $16–$49 | AE, D, DC, MC, V.

McKinnon's Louisiane. Cajun/Creole. There are two dining rooms at this restaurant; do you want to eat in a casual setting, or would you prefer something more upscale and formal? After that, the only questions are what to have from the popular menu, full of the special tastes of New Orleans. There are crab cakes, Creole and seafood gumbos, crab claws piquante, and snapper Patout. Choosing dessert is no easier: bread pudding with whiskey sauce or chocolate marquise? An adjacent lounge offers live piano music on weekends. | 3209 Maple Dr. | 404/237–1313 | Reservations essential | Closed Sun. No lunch | $15–$20 | AE, D, DC, MC, V.

★ **Mumbo Jumbo.** Contemporary. The long bar attracts the young single set and serves as the setting for familiar fare with regional touches. The famous Mumbo Gumbo points southward; other dishes show the sign of Asian or Italian inspiration. Emphasis is on the seasonal and regional, with lots of game in cool weather, fish and shellfish in the summer, and locally grown produce. | 89 Park Pl. | 404/523–0330 | Reservations essential | No lunch weekends | $16–$32 | AE, D, DC, MC, V.

★ **Nava.** Southwestern. A collection of Kachina dolls and other Southwestern art adorns the walls. Quesadillas with Vidalia onions and queso cabrales (a Spanish bleu cheese), tequila-cured salmon, blue corn muffins, bison strip loin with spicy passion fruit barbecue sauce capture the idea. Small plates, such as the quesadillas, are enough for a lunch entrée. | 3060 Peachtree Rd. | 404/240–1984 | www.buckheadrestaurants.com | Reservations essential | No lunch weekends | $15–$28 | AE, D, DC, MC, V.

Palisades. Contemporary. Exposed brick walls and hardwood floors, low lighting, and candles create an updated French bistro look. The menu changes often but stays focused on hearty fare. The grilled veal chop with basil whipped potatoes and Port wine sauce is heftier than the roasted sea scallops with whipped potatoes and onion salpicón. Crème brûlée for dessert is a must. On the weekends there is live jazz. | 1829 Peachtree Rd. | 404/350–6755 | Reservations essential | No lunch | $15–$26 | AE, D, DC, MC, V.

Pano's and Paul's. Continental. This opulently decorated restaurant is a hit with out-of-towners and locals bent on romance. It's also good for business dining. The dish of fame here is deep-fried lobster tail with Chinese honey mustard and drawn butter. Foie gras, veal steak, sweetbreads, and venison and ostrich in season also tempt. Vegetarians can also be accommodated. | 1232 W. Paces Ferry Rd. | 404/261–3662 | www.buckheadrestaurants.com | Reservations essential | Jacket required | Closed Sun. No lunch. | $17–$38 | AE, D, DC, MC, V.

Park 75. Contemporary. The flagship dining room of Atlanta's Four Seasons Hotel is marble lined and elegant. Classic dishes are given innovative treatment, as in the coddled salmon with sour cream and chive and caviar or the kobe carpaccio with juniper and cured foie gras. From squab to steak and lamb, dishes are individually garnished. If you're looking for something a little different, there's Montana bison with béarnaise sauce. There are also seasonally changing vegetarian menus. The peach, peach, and peach dessert pays homage to the Atlanta location. Wine only. Sun. brunch | 75 14th St. | 404/253–3840 | Reservations essential | Breakfast also available | $19–$38 | AE, D, DC, MC, V.

Pricci. Italian. A high-energy, contemporary space sporting lots of glass and wood, Pricci embraces all of Italy. Half orders of the freshly made pasta are perfect lunch entrées, and small pizzas, cooked in the wood-burning oven, make a good lunch or snack. Herbs from the restaurant's own herb garden enhance the classic Italian fare. A different risotto is offered every day. The whole roasted fish easily serves two people. | 500 Pharr Rd. | 404/237–2941 | www.buckheadrestaurants.com | Reservations essential | No lunch weekends | $15–$26 | AE, D, DC, MC, V.

Prime. Eclectic. Owner Tom Catherall, a native of Scotland, is a certified master chef, and the founder of TomTom. His unusual concept is to have a sushi bar incorporated into a steakhouse. The steaks (of corn-fed prime aged beef) and sushi are the focus, but the grilled salmon on stone-ground grits, grilled tuna, and veal chop are all first rate. | 3393 Peachtree Rd. | 404/812–0555 | www.prime-atlanta.com | Reservations essential | No lunch Sun. | $16–$33 | AE, D, DC, MC, V.

Villa Christina. Italian. An art-filled contemporary space with views onto a boccie court is a good scenario for Tuscan-style braised snails, buffalo ricotta gnocchi, and oven-roasted rabbit with any of several stellar desserts for a finish, such as roasted pear with praline crème brûlée. | 400 Summit Blvd. | 404/303–0133 | No lunch Sat. and Sun. | $21–$30 | AE, D, DC, MC, V.

EXPENSIVE

★ **Bacchanalia.** Contemporary. Set in a renovated Tudor-style home, the kitchen here is full of exciting ideas based on European country dishes with twists, sometimes Asian, sometimes Southern. Never have vegetables been handled more respectfully. A fixed-price menu has four courses and sorbet. The inventive wine list is restricted to American labels. Wine only. | 3125 Piedmont Rd. | 404/365–0410 | Reservations essential | Closed Mon. and Sun. | $50 (fixed price) | AE, D, DC, MC, V.

Imperial Fez. Moroccan. Slip off your shoes and get comfortable on plush cushions. Don't be surprised if a belly dancer spins through the room while you're eating. The fixed-price multicourse meal, which can be served vegetarian with advanced notice, includes traditional lentil soup, salads, b'stella (Cornish hen with cinnamon in savory pastry), and your choice of meat or fish main course. The dessert tray has an assortment of traditional sweets. | 2285 Peachtree Rd. | 404/351–0870 | www.imperialfez.com | Reservations essential | No lunch | $45 (fixed price) | AE, D, DC, MC, V.

Ruth's Chris Steak House. Steak. New Orleans–founded, this steak emporium offers a wide range of dishes other than steak. Everything is à la carte, but side dishes serve at least two or three people. Steak with gorgonzola sauce is outstanding—ask for it if it's not on the menu. Seafood items include sauteed shrimp, tuna, salmon, and fresh Maine lobster. | 950

E. Paces Ferry Rd., Atlanta Plaza | 404/365–0660 | webguide.com/steak.html | 5788 Roswell Rd. | 404/255–0035 | Reservations essential | No lunch | $40–$60 | AE, D, DC, MC, V.

VERY EXPENSIVE

The Dining Room, the Ritz-Carlton, Buckhead. Eclectic. As you might expect from the restaurant of the flagship hotel of the Ritz-Carlton chain, the dining room is classic Old World elegance, the service is impeccable, and there are fresh flowers and candles. Chef Joel Antunes takes dishes from his native France and blends them with his experiences cooking in southeast Asia and the American South. The menu changes daily, incorporating regional and seasonal specialties, such as king crab salad with daikon radish and pineapple dressing, diver's scallops with braised endive and a sesame emulsion, or roasted veal sweetbread with rhubarb, rutabaga, and seven spices. Thai minestrone with a tropical fruit sorbet is among the desserts. The fixed-price tasting menu with selected wines costs $45 extra, and the cheese course is an additional $12.50. | 3434 Peachtree Rd. | 404/240–7035 | Reservations essential | Jacket required | $68–$82 (fixed price) | AE, D, DC, MC, V.

Nikolai's Roof. Continental. Since the restaurant is on top of the Hilton you can enjoy the view of Atlanta's skyline while waiting for your dinner to be served. Rigorously classical dishes grace this fixed-price menu, which changes monthly: crêpe of duck confit and potatoes is topped with foie gras mousse for a first course, a seafood course of loup de mer with ginger olive oil, veal tongue and sweetbreads for an entrée, and pineapple tart tatin for dessert. | 255 Courtland St. NE | 404/221–6362 | Reservations essential | Jacket required | No lunch | $68 (fixed price) | AE, D, DC, MC, V.

★ **Seeger's.** Eclectic. World class, to put it simply. Guenter Seeger, a James Beard award–winner, has an extraordinary sense of food and wine. Both the restaurant, set in a converted home on the border of the Buckhead business district, and the food are stunning: foie gras shaped and formed to look pretty as well as taste good; pristine and sweet langostinos grilled and served with tiny cipollini onions, and good vegetarian dishes such as 25 different roasted vegetables with black truffle oil. The menu changes seasonally. | 111 W. Paces Ferry Rd. | 404/846–9779 | www.seegers.com | Reservations essential | Jacket and tie | $64–$80 (fixed price) | AE, DC, MC, V.

Lodging

INEXPENSIVE

Ansley Inn. Once the home of retailing magnate George Muse, this 1907 Tudor home is now one of the best B&Bs in town. Tucked away off Peachtree Street in the exclusive Ansley Park neighborhood, the inn has 22 rooms, some with fireplaces, and the common areas are rich with Oriental rugs. Complimentary breakfast. In-room data ports, in-room safes, some minibars, some refrigerators, in-room hot tubs. Cable TV, some in-room VCRs. No pets. No smoking. | 253 15th St. | 404/872–9000 or 800/446–5416 | fax 404/892–2318 | www.ansleyinn.com | 22 rooms | $99–$159 | AE, MC, V.

Atlanta International Hostel. Smack in midtown, almost on top of the Fox Theatre, this hostel is the envy of its kind—cheap, clean, and good. Laundry facilities. | 229 Ponce de Leon Ave. | 404/875–2882 | fax 404/870–0047 | 85 beds, 30 communal rooms | $15–$18 | MC, V.

Beverly Hills Inn. Each of the rooms in this pleasant inn has a balcony. The inn itself is tucked away on a residential side street just off Peachtree. Well equipped for business travelers, this European-style spot is a wonderful alternative to the nearby high-rise hotels. Complimentary Continental breakfast. In-room data ports. Cable TV. Business services. Pets allowed. | 65 Sheridan Dr. | 404/233–8520 | fax 404/233–8659 | www.beverlyhillsinn.com | 18 rooms | $120–$160 | AE, D, DC, MC, V.

Cheshire Motor Inn. Between Midtown and Buckhead, this friendly inn is attached to one of Atlanta's best soul-food restaurants, The Colonnade. Cable TV. | 1865 Cheshire Bridge Rd. NE | 404/872–9628 or 800/872–9628 | fax 404/872–3035 | 60 rooms | $75 | AE, MC, V.

Days Inn Peachtree. Once known as the York Hotel, this somber, brick-fronted hostelry is directly across the street from the Fox Theatre, making it the perfect choice for concert- and theatergoers. Decorated like a 19th-century men's club, the property displays a charm rarely, if ever, associated with a Days Inn. Complimentary Continental breakfast. In-room safes. Cable TV. Pets allowed. | 683 Peachtree St. | 404/874–9200 | fax 404/873–4245 | www.daysinn.com | 132 rooms | $99 | AE, D, DC, MC, V.

Emory Inn. Situated on more than 10 acres in the midst of the bustling Emory medical corridor, this hotel provides a tranquil and welcome respite from the harried activity just steps away. On wintry evenings, the lobby lounge with its fireplace is a favorite gathering spot. Restaurant, bar. Cable TV. 2 pools (1 indoor). Sauna. Gym. Business services, free parking. | 1615 Clifton Rd. | 404/712–6700 | 107 rooms | $89–$125 | AE, D, DC, MC, V.

Fallin Gate B&B. This Victorian cottage was built in 1895 and today holds a real treasure of a B&B. The flowers in the rooms are from the garden, the sheets are fringed with lace, and breakfast is served on china and crystal. The owners are very helpful in getting around Atlanta, and their special touches and personal attention make the Fallin Gate like a delightful home away from home. | 381 Cherokee Ave. SE | 404/522–7371 | 2 rooms | $99 | D, MC, V.

Gaslight Inn. A gaslight at the curb gives the name to this two-story bungalow situated near the heart of Virginia-Highland, and gaslight-style fixtures illuminate the inside. In addition to the main building there is a carriage house and a Victorian cottage. Each room is decorated in a different style, with names such as the Rose Room and the English Suite (both of which have four-poster beds). Complimentary Continental breakfast. Some kitchenettes, some minibars, some microwaves, some refrigerators. Cable TV, some in-room VCRs. No pets. No smoking. | 1001 St. Charles Ave. | 404/876–1001 | fax 404/876–1001 | www.gaslight-inn.com | 7 rooms | $95–$295 | AE, D, DC, MC, V.

Heartfield Manor. A refined, 1903 hunting lodge with wainscotting, stained-glass windows, and a grand balcony, this B&B overlooks quiet Springvale Park. You can get away from the city in the sunroom or on your own private deck, taking in all the period furniture and decorations, and once you are refreshed and again ready to enjoy Atlanta, there are two MARTA transit stations within a three-block stroll. | 182 Elizabeth St., NE | 404/523–8633 | 6 rooms | $80 | AE, MC, V.

Houston Mill House. In a graceful clapboard and fieldstone home near the Emory University campus, this B&B has two rooms upstairs, one with a queen bed and one with two twins. It's a peaceful retreat, and quite reasonable. Restaurant, complimentary breakfast. Minibars. TV. No pets. No smoking. | 849 Houston Mill Rd. | 404–727–7878 | fax 404/727–4032 | www.houstonmillhouse.net | 2 rooms | $95 | AE, D, MC, V.

Quality Hotel Downtown. This quiet, older downtown hotel, two blocks off Peachtree Street, has a marble lobby with sofas and a grand piano you can sit down and play. Modest-size rooms in teal and navy make the hotel inviting. It is popular for conventions due to its proximity to the World Congress Center and the show marts; prices go up when conventions are in town. Complimentary Continental breakfast. In-room data ports. Cable TV. Pool. Exercise equipment. Laundry service. Business services, parking (fee). No pets. | 89 Luckie St. | 404/524–7991 | fax 404/524–0672 | 75 rooms | $79–$119 | AE, D, DC, MC, V.

Sheraton Buckhead. This modern, eight-floor hotel has the advantage of being right across from the Lenox Square mall. Rooms have contemporary furnishings; some have a desk and chair, others have sofas. Restaurant, bar. In-room data ports, some minibars. Cable TV. Pool, gym. Laundry service. Business services, parking (fee). No pets. | 3405 Lenox Rd. | 404/261–9250 | fax 404/848–7391 | 369 rooms | $109–$210 | AE, D, DC, MC, V.

Sierra Suites Atlanta Brookhaven. This comfortable hotel, just north of Lenox Square, might remind you of the modern Southwest. Cream and green color schemes decorate the one- and two-bedroom suites. In-room data ports, kitchenettes. Cable TV. Pool. Gym. Laundry facilities. Business services, free parking. No pets. | 3967 Peachtree Rd. | 404/237–9100 | fax 404/237–0055 | www.sierrasuites.com | 92 suites | $89–$119 suites | AE, D, DC, MC, V.

Stonehurst B&B. This shingle-style house was built in 1896 and not only has period furnishings but still retains much of the original hardware, right down to the hinges on the doors. The Victorian poster beds are beautiful and comfortable, and the shops of Midtown are within walking distance. | 923 Piedmont Ave. NE | 404/881–0722 | fax 404/881–1378 | 4 rooms | $90 | MC, V.

Sugar Magnolia. The most opulent B&B south of Buckhead. Built in 1892, this Victorian has a rooftop deck that offers panoramic views of downtown Atlanta, and each of the three rooms has a working fireplace. Out back, there's a cottage suite. Complimentary Continental breakfast. Cable TV. Business services. No pets. No smoking. | 804 Edgewood Ave. | 404/222–0226 | fax 404/681–1067 | www.sugarmagnoliabb.com | 4 rooms | $90–$135 | MC, V.

Atlanta Super 8 Hotel. This is definitely not what you think of when you see the Super 8 sign—right in the heart of downtown, this ten-story hotel has a fitness center and both a Chinese and an American restaurant, all within walking distance of Peachtree Plaza and the CNN Center. 2 restaurants. In-room dataports. Cable TV. Gym. Laundry facilities. Business services, parking (fee). | 111 Cone St. | 404/524–7000 | fax 404/659–7521 | 238 rooms | $119 | AE, D, DC, MC, V.

Wyndham Hotel. At the epicenter of Midtown, just a short stroll from the park, the High Museum, and several good restaurants and bars, this property feels small despite its nearly 200 rooms. Rooms are well appointed, equipped with coffeemakers. Restaurant, bar. In-room data ports, some refrigerators. Cable TV. Pool. Hot tub. Exercise equipment. Laundry service. Business services, parking (fee). No pets. | 125 10th St. | 404/873–4800 | fax 404/870–1530 | www.wyndham.com | 191 rooms | $94–$139 | AE, D, DC, MC, V.

Wyndham Garden Hotel. The spacious rooms in this hotel are decorated with botanical prints. The rates are reasonable given the excellent location. The hotel offers complimentary transportation within 2 mi of the hotel and is next to the MARTA Buckhead station. Restaurant, bar. In-room data ports. Cable TV. Laundry service. Business services, parking (fee). No pets. | 3342 Peachtree Rd. | 404/231–1234 or 800/222–8733 | fax 404/231–5236 | www.wyndham.com | 230 rooms | $124–$134 | AE, D, DC, MC, V.

MODERATE

Atlanta Marriott Marquis. Immense and coolly contemporary, the Marquis seems to go on forever as you stand under the lobby's huge fabric sculpture that hangs from the sky-lighted roof 47 stories above. Guest rooms, which open onto this atrium, are decorated with dark greens and neutral shades. Major suites have live plants and fresh flowers; two suites have grand pianos and ornamental fireplaces. 2 restaurants, 2 bars. In-room data ports, in-room safes, some refrigerators. Cable TV. Indoor-outdoor pool. Health club. Laundry services. Business services, parking (fee). No pets. | 265 Peachtree Center Ave. | 404/521–0000 | fax 404/586–6299 | www.marriotthotels.com | 1,731 rooms | $179–$205 | AE, D, DC, MC, V.

Embassy Suites Hotel. This modern high-rise is just blocks from the Phipps Plaza and Lenox Square malls. The suites range from the deluxe presidential to more basic sleeping- and sitting-room combinations. Rates include afternoon cocktails. Restaurant, bar, complimentary breakfast. In-room data ports, in-room safes, microwaves, refrigerators. Cable TV. Indoor and outdoor pools. Hot tub, sauna. Gym. Laundry services. Business services, parking (fee). No pets. | 3285 Peachtree Rd. | 404/261–7733 or 800/362–2779 | fax 404/261–6857 | www.embassysuites.com | 317 suites | $169–$189 suites | AE, D, DC, MC, V.

Grand Hyatt Hotel. This 25-story postmodern skyscraper was built by a Japanese concern before being taken over by Hyatt. There's still a dash of the Orient about the place, as evidenced by the Japanese rock garden just beyond the lobby. Rooms are appointed with such luxuries as marble bathrooms. 3 restaurants. In-room data ports, minibars, some refrigerators. Cable TV. Pool. Sauna. Health club. Laundry services. Business services, parking (fee). Pets allowed (fee). | 3300 Peachtree Rd. | 404/365–8100 | fax 404/233–5686 | www.hyatt.com | 438 rooms | $220 | AE, D, DC, MC, V.

Hyatt Regency, Atlanta. This Hyatt was John Portman's first atrium-centered building. It became the model for other Portman-designed hotels, including the San Francisco Embarcadero and the Atlanta Marriott Marquis. You can spot it easily in the Atlanta skyline because of its blue bubble top. Expect the careful service and quality facilities typical of Hyatt hotels. 3 restaurants, bar. In-room data ports, in-room safes, minibars, some microwaves, some refrigerators. Cable TV. Pool. Gym. Laundry services. Business services, parking (fee). No pets. | 265 Peachtree St., (connected by skywalk to Peachtree Center) | 404/577–1234 or 800/223–1234 | fax 404/588–4137 | www.hyatt.com | 1,264 rooms, 58 suites | $184–$284; $550–$1,500 suites | AE, D, DC, MC, V.

King-Keith House. Each guest room in this Victorian "painted lady" has a private bath as well as a separate cottage with Jacuzzi and fireplace. Twelve-foot ceilings and ornate carved fireplaces give this inn a regal, if a slightly dowdy, air. Picnic area, complimentary breakfast. Some refrigerators. Cable TV. No pets. No smoking. Free parking (offstreet). | 889 Edgewood Ave. NE | 404/688–7330 | fax 404/584–0730 | www.kingkeith.com | 4 rooms with cottage | $175 | AE, D, MC, V.

Omni Hotel at CNN Center. The hotel is next to the home of Ted Turner's Cable News Network. The lobby combines Old World and modern accents, with marble floors, Oriental rugs, and exotic floral and plant arrangements. Rooms have large windows and contemporary-style furniture, including a sofa in each room. Staying here gives you access to the Downtown Athletic Club. 2 restaurants, bar. In-room data ports, some minibars. Cable TV. Indoor pool. Beauty salon. Gym. Laundry services. Business services, parking (fee). No pets. | 100 CNN Center | 404/659–0000 or 800/843–6664 | fax 404/818–4322 | www.omnihotels.com | 470 rooms | $175–$315 | AE, D, DC, MC, V.

Regency Suites Atlanta. Here you can get a lot of luxury for a reasonable price—each suite has a living room with a large, tasteful couch to relax on, and dinner is complimentary Monday through Thursday, along with a whole host of pampering touches such as HBO and a choice of a morning newspaper. In-room data ports. Cable TV. Laundry facilities. Parking (fee). | 975 W. Peachtree St. | 800/642–3629 or 404/876–5003 | 100 rooms | $144 | AE, D, DC, MC, V.

Shellmont. The Shellmont is named for the shell motif that adorns the house. Designed in 1891 by Massachusetts-born, Atlanta-reared architect Walter T. Downing for Dr. William Perrin Nicholson, the house has classical architectural elements, detailed stained-glass windows, and a reproduction of the original Victorian stenciling on the walls. Guest rooms have American Victorian antiques and CD players. Complimentary breakfast. In-room data ports, in-room safes, some kitchenettes. Cable TV, in-room VCRs. Laundry service. Business services, free parking. No pets. No smoking. | 821 Piedmont Ave. | 404/872–9290 | fax 404/872–5379 | www.shellmont.com | 5 rooms | $135–$170 | AE, D, DC, MC, V.

Sheraton at Colony Square Hotel. Theatricality and opulence are epitomized by the dimly lit lobby with overhanging balconies, piano music, and fresh flowers. Rooms are modern, with muted tones; those on higher floors have city views. The hotel is two blocks from MARTA's Art Center station and two blocks from the Woodruff Arts Center and the High Museum of Art; it anchors the Colony Square complex of office, residential, and retail buildings. Restaurant, bar. In-room data ports. Cable TV. Pool. Exercise equipment. Laundry service. Business services, parking (fee). Pets allowed. | 188 14th St. | 404/892–6000 or 800/325–3535 | fax 404/872–9192 | www.sheraton.com | 467 rooms | $129–$195 | AE, D, DC, MC, V.

The Suite Hotel at Underground Atlanta. All the rooms at this understated, elegant, 16-story hotel are suites. Restaurant, bar. Microwaves, refrigerators. Cable TV. Laundry service. Business services, parking (fee). No pets. | 54 Peachtree St. NE | 404/223–5555 or 877/477–5549 | fax 404/223–0467 | www.suitehotel.com | 157 suites | $159 | AE, D, DC, MC, V.

Swissôtel. Sleek and efficient, this stunner boasts a chic, modern exterior of glass and white tile, with curved walls and Biedermeier-style interiors. Convenient to Lenox Square Mall, a prime location for shopping and dining, the hotel is a favorite with business travelers.

The restaurant, the Palm, is noted for its steaks. The full-service fitness center has everything from facials to fitness trainers. Restaurant, bar. In-room data ports, in-room safes, minibars. Cable TV. Indoor pool. Beauty salon, massage. Gym. Laundry facilities. Business services, parking (fee). Pets allowed. | 3391 Peachtree Rd. | 404/365–0065 or 888/737–9477 | fax 404/365–8787 | www.swissotel.com | 365 rooms | $149–$289 | AE, D, DC, MC, V.

Virginia-Highland B&B. This 1920 Craftsman-style bungalow fits in well with its surroundings and is just a short walk from Piedmont Park or the intersection of Virginia and Highland avenues. Two rooms, each with private bath and separate entrance, are furnished with antiques. The flowers in the rooms are as fresh as they look, having been picked in the garden outside. Complimentary breakfast. Cable TV, VCRs. | 630 Orme Circle | 404/892–2735 or 877/870–4485 | fax 404/873–3128 | www.mindspring.com/~vahighlandbandb | 2 rooms | $125 | AE, MC, V.

EXPENSIVE

Four Seasons Hotel. A sweeping staircase leads up to a welcoming, refined bar and Park 75, the hotel's main restaurant. Rose-hue marble gives the public spaces a sense of warmth. Marble bathrooms, pale lemon or celadon color schemes, and polished brass chandeliers are among the guest-room appointments. Pets are allowed and even welcomed—a special pet menu is available. Restaurant, bar (with entertainment). In-room data ports, in-room safes. Cable TV, some VCRs. Indoor pool. Beauty salon, massage, sauna. Health club. Laundry services. Business services, parking (fee). Pets allowed. | 75 Fourteenth St. | 404/881–9898 | fax 404/873–4692 | www.fourseasons.com | 244 rooms | $175–$370. | AE, D, DC, MC, V.

Georgian Terrace. Spend a night where Enrico Caruso and the Metropolitan Opera stars once lodged. This fine old hotel (built in 1911), across the street from the Fox Theatre, is on the National Register of Historic Places and housed the rich and famous in its heyday. The hotel even hosted the party for the premier of *Gone with the Wind* in 1939. Now restored, and with an added matching tower, all units are suites. Restaurant, bar. In-room data ports, kitchenettes. Pool. Laundry facilities. Business services. | 659 Peachtree St. | 404/897–1991 or 800/651–2316 | fax 404/724–0642 | www.thegeorgianterrace.com | 326 suites | $149–$229 suites | AE, D, DC, MC, V.

★ **Ritz-Carlton, Atlanta.** The mood here is set by traditional afternoon tea served in the intimate, sunken lobby beneath an 18th-century chandelier. Notice the 17th-century Flemish tapestry when you enter from Peachtree Street. Some guest rooms are luxuriously decorated with marble writing tables, plump sofas, four-poster beds, and white-marble bathrooms. The Atlanta Grill is Downtown's only outdoor dining spot. The entrance to MARTA's Peachtree Center station is across the street. Restaurant, 2 bars. In-room data ports, in-room safes. Cable TV. Massage. Gym. Laundry facilities. Business services, parking (fee). No pets. | 181 Peachtree St. | 404/659–0400 or 800/241–3333 | fax 404/688–0400 | www.ritzcarlton.com | 447 rooms | $245–$280 | AE, D, DC, MC, V.

★ **Ritz-Carlton, Buckhead.** Decorated with the Ritz's signature 18th- and 19th-century antiques and art, this elegant gem bids a discreet welcome. Shoppers from nearby Lenox Mall and Phipps Plaza often revive here over afternoon tea or cocktails in the richly paneled Lobby Lounge. The Dining Room is one of the city's finest restaurants. The spacious rooms are furnished with traditional reproductions and have luxurious white-marble baths. From the hotel's club floors you get a view of Buckhead and an understanding of why Atlanta is known as a city of trees. Weekend musical performances are a delight. 2 restaurants, bar. In-room data ports, in-room safes, minibars. Cable TV, some VCRs. Pool. Hot tub, massage, sauna. Gym. Laundry services. Business services, parking (fee). Pets allowed (fee). | 3434 Peachtree Rd. | 404/237–2700 or 800/241–3333 | fax 404/239–0078 | www.ritzcarlton.com | 553 rooms | $230–$255 | AE, D, DC, MC, V.

Westin Peachtree Plaza. One of the tallest hotels in the world, this steel-and-glass tower has more than 1,000 rooms and a five-floor atrium lobby that bustles with activity. The Sun Dial bar and restaurant, 73 stories up, offers an amazing view of the Atlanta skyline. Restaurant, 2 bars (with entertainment). In-room data ports, in-room safes, minibars.

Cable TV. Indoor-outdoor pool. Massage, sauna. Exercise equipment. Business services. Some pets allowed. | 210 Peachtree St. NW | 404/659–1400 | fax 404/589–7424 | www.westin.com | 1,086 rooms | $235–$255 | AE, D, DC, MC, V.

AUGUSTA

MAP 3, G6

(Nearby town also listed: Thomson)

Georgia's "father," James Oglethorpe, founded Augusta in 1736, only three years after landing at the site of Savannah to organize the colony. Located on the headwaters of the Savannah River, the town soon attained a reputation for its cotton, and it was near here, on General Nathanael Greene's plantation, that Eli Whitney invented the cotton gin. Cotton is still an important product in Augusta, as is the production of fertilizer, textiles, and kaolin tiles, and bricks.

Information: **Augusta Metropolitan Convention and Visitors Bureau** | 14-50 Green St., Suite 110, Augusta, GA 30901 | 706/823–6600 or 800/726–0243 | fax 706/823–6609 | amcvb@augustaga.org | augustaga.org | Weekdays 8:30–5.

Attractions

Augusta Canal Authority. Built in 1845, the canal was enlarged in 1875. Now a National Heritage Area and a National Historic Landmark, the canal is popular for biking, jogging, and hiking. | 28th St. | 706/823–0440 | fax 706/823–1045 | www.augustacanal.com | Free | Daily.

Augusta Museum of History. Paintings, Native American artifacts from the region, and Civil War memorabilia fill the museum's permanent collection. The history of Augusta is presented from the prehistoric Indians to the late 1900s. | 560 Reynolds St. | 706/722–8454 | fax 706/724–5192 | www.rightguide.com/civilwar/poi/arcm.htm | $4 | Tues.–Sat. 10–5, Sun. 1–5.

Augusta State University. On the grounds of a former plantation, the old buildings, dating to the 1820s, were originally a U.S. arsenal, which started about 1819 near the site of the later Confederate Powder Works. Poet Stephen Vincent Benét grew up on the old arsenal grounds, for his father, Colonel J. Walker Benét, was its commandant from 1911 to 1919. The house in which they lived is one of the university's buildings today. Several original buildings were actually dismantled from the Powder Works site and reassembled on this spot. The college began as the Junior College of Augusta, founded in 1925 by the Richmond County Board of Education and housed at the Richmond Academy. In 1957, it moved to the arsenal grounds, and the following year it became a unit of the University System of Georgia. The institution was designated a university in 1996. You can pick up a history brochure to use in self-guided tours of the campus. | 2500 Walton Way | 706/737–1444 | fax 706/737–1774 | www.aug.edu | Free | Weekdays 8–5.

Confederate Powder Works Chimney. Standing in front of Sibley Mill, the chimney is the last remaining element in a 2-mi-long complex of buildings that made powder for the Confederate Army. The federal government ordered the destruction of the buildings after the Civil War, and much of the brick was recycled in the textile mill that was built beginning in 1880. The mill still makes cotton fabric and continues to use waterpower from the Augusta Canal. You can view the building from the exterior. | 1717 Goodrich St. | No phone | Free | Not open to the public.

Gertrude Herbert Institute of Art. This 1818 Greek-revival house, known as Nicholas Ware's Folly because of its outrageous construction cost ($40,000), offers rotating art exhibitions and an art school. | 506 Telfair St. | 706/722–5495 | fax 706/722–3670 | www.ghia.org | $2 (suggested) | Tues.–Fri. 8:30–5, Sat. 10–2.

Historic Augusta. This unusual late-18th-century gambrel-roofed frame house, with its unique space-saving exterior stairway, originally belonged to Ezekiel Harris. Harris was a tobacco entrepreneur, and his home was used as a lodging by traveling tobacco merchants. The exterior staircase allowed late arrivals to get into their rooms without disturbing the rest of the house. The furnishings date to the late 18th and early 19th centuries. Some come from the area; most are American, but a few are English. | 1822 Broad St. | 706/724–0436 | fax 706/724–3083 | $2 | Sat. 10–1.

Lucy Craft Laney Museum of Black History. Lucy Laney was born in 1854 in Macon to a family of freed slaves. She moved to Augusta, became an educator, and used money given to her by a wealthy white woman (Mrs. Haines) to establish educational institutions for African-Americans, including the Lamar Nursing School. Her house sits across from Lucy Laney High School, named in her honor. Permanent exhibits display art by Alice Davis, who taught at Paine College in Augusta, and the Ebony Legacy, which displays the contributions of area African-Americans, such as Jessye Norman and Butterfly McQueen. Delta Sigma Theta sorority's Augusta chapter owns and maintains the home, which its members also restored. Rotating exhibitions focus on art, in most cases by African-Americans. | 1116 Phillips St. | 706/724–3576 | fax 706/724–3576 | www.lucycraftlaneymuseum.com | $2 | tours weekdays 9–1 PM, weekends by appointment.

Meadow Garden. George Walton, the youngest signer of the Declaration of Independence, moved into this house in 1792 and named it Meadow Garden, for it then sat on 121 acres. The earliest part the house dates to around 1777, while the most recent addition dates to the early 1800s. | 1320 Independence Dr. | 706/724–4174 | $3 | Weekdays 10–4, weekends by appointment.

Morris Museum of Art. This unique collection of works by artists who are either Southern or who have lived and worked in the South is a treasure. Located on a floor of a commercial building, it also is a very comfortable, well-lit, and well-curated exhibition. Represented in the permanent collection is work by Jasper Johns, who was born in Augusta. Traveling special exhibitions add interest. | 1 10th St. | 706/724–7501 | fax 706/724–7612 | mormuse@themorris.org | www.themorris.org | $3; free Sun. | Tues.–Sat. 10–5:30, Sun. 12:30–5:30.

National Science Center's Fort Discovery. Hands-on exhibitions—about 270 of them— encourage children to experience science. They can sit at the controls of a flight simulator and practice taking off and landing an airplane. When the children aren't looking, you can have a go at it, too. Also promoting math, science, and technology, Fort Discovery is the smart place to have fun. | 1 7th St. | 706/821–0200 or 800/325–5445 | fax 706/ 821–0269 | www.nationalsciencecenter.org | $8; special rates for seniors and children | Mon.–Sat. 10–5, Sun. noon–5.

Springfield Baptist Church. Founded in 1787, this may be the country's oldest African-American congregation in continuous assembly. Members may have come from a plantation in South Carolina prior to the Revolution, settling in a village called Springfield that is now part of downtown Augusta. The original building dates from 1801, when it was a white Methodist Church; it was moved to this site in 1844. The main church building dates from 1897. Morehouse College in Atlanta was founded here as the Augusta Baptist Institute in 1866, then moved to its present location in Atlanta. The Georgia Equal Rights Association was founded here. | 114 12th St. | 706/724–1056 | fax 706/793–2929 | Free | Daily 11–3, and by appointment.

St. Paul's Church. This congregation, the city's oldest, dates from the mid-18th century. The present church building was completed in 1918, as the previous structures had either fallen apart, been destroyed in the Revolution, moved, or been consumed by the great Augusta fire of 1916. The adjacent cemetery dates to the mid-18th century, although its oldest marked graves go back to the 1780s. | 605 Reynolds St. | 706/724–2485 | fax 706/724–0904 | www.saintpauls.org | Free | Memorial Day–Labor Day, weekdays 9–4, Sat. 9 AM–noon; Labor Day–Memorial Day, weekdays 9–5, Sat. 9–noon.

MAR.: *Sacred Heart Garden Festival.* Augusta lives up to its name, Garden City, when it hosts this annual flower show, which is accompanied by seminars, panel discussions, and demonstrations by the region's leading gardeners and horticulturists. | 706/826–4700 | fax 706/722–2222 | $.60–$2 | Weekdays 9–5.

APR.: *Masters Golf Tournament.* The king of all golf competitions, held annually at Augusta, attracts pros from all over the U.S. and around the world to participate in the world-famous tournament. | Augusta National Golf Club | 706/667–6000 | fax 706/731–0611 | www.masters.org | Private club | Mon.–Sun. 8–9.

Dining

Bistro 491. Contemporary. Chef-owners Theo and Tod Schafer met in culinary school (Culinary Institute of America) in 1993. Dishes include French onion soup and foie gras, wild mushroom and potato lasagna, prawns with mushroom ragu, and braised short ribs. Homemade ice creams and sorbets, among other desserts. | 491 Highland Ave. | 706/738–6491 | Closed Sun. | $15–$25 | AE, D, MC, V.

French Market Grille. Cajun/Creole. The highly popular crab chop, shrimp po' boys, gumbo, and bread pudding with Chantilly cream rum sauce are the highlights. The relative spiciness of the dishes is indicated by the number of peppers next to the name; watch out for those with the maximum of three. | 425 Highland Ave. | 706/737–4865 | Reservations not accepted. | Closed Sun. | $13–$24 | AE, D, DC, MC, V.

Café Deatu. French. This high-energy spot is popular as a bar and restaurant and also for its live entertainment. The menu changes often, but target the snails, lamb, and venison specials, steaks, veal, grilled duck, pasta, and seafood. Good jazz accompanies dinner Thurs.–Sun. | 1855 Central Ave. | 706/733–3505 | Closed Mon. No lunch | $18–$30 | AE, D, DC, MC, V.

Calvert's. Continental. You'll find this candlelit delight nestled in a row of boutique shops. The salmon is light and soft, as is the filet mignon. | 475 Highland Ave. | 706/738–4514 | $23 | AE, D, DC, MC, V.

El Valle. Mexican. Although the decibel level here is decidedly high, the food's good, especially the enchiladas and tamales wrapped in corn husks. | 3830 Washington Rd. | 706/854–0051 | $7 | MC, V.

The King George Riverwalk Pub, Brewery and Cigar Bar. English. Come here for pub fare: good fish and chips, bangers-and-mash, Dublin pie (beef tips marinated in Guinness stout under pastry), cottage pie, and Scotch eggs. | 2 8th St. | 706/724–4755 | Closed Sun. | $6–$18 | AE, D, MC, V.

La Maison on Telfair. Continental. The best of the genre marks owner-chef Heinz Sowinski's elegant, refined restaurant in a former Victorian residence. German specialties and game are standouts. Nice appetizer menu. | 404 Telfair St. | 706/722–4805. | No lunch | $17–$38 | AE, D, MC, V.

Mikoto Japanese Restaurant. Japanese. The sushi and sashimi are delicious here, as is the slightly sweet tempura. You'll even find Kobe steak. The restaurant is comfortable if a bit bustling. | 3102 Washington Rd. | 706/855–0009 | $12 | AE, MC, V.

Sixth at Watkins. Eclectic. You'll find the finest luncheon experience in Augusta here, from chicken *ribier* (covered in a white wine cream sauce with crushed grapes) over fettuccine to a spice-filled, fried chicken salad. | 559 Watkins St. | 706/722–8877 | $24 | AE, D, DC, MC, V.

Sweet Basil Grille. Italian. Sweet Basil is a surprising mix—the restaurant is done almost entirely in mahogany, but is also light and open, with a veranda and a casual atmosphere. The pasta is quite good, as are the tuna steaks and the homemade desserts, such as the cappuccino crème brûlée and the cheesecake. | 399 Highlands Ave. | 706/736–6777 | $15–$18 | AE, DC, MC, V.

White Elephant Cafe. Brazilian. Chef Jean Louis Gamper is Swiss born, but was reared in Brazil. Brazilian, South Miami, South Pacific, and Caribbean sources show up in the dishes. Absolutely the best black beans and rice anywhere. Spicy all the way. Stellar coffee and desserts. Beer and wine only. | 1135 Broad St. | 706/722–8614 | Reservations not accepted | Closed Sun., Mon. No dinner Tues.–Thurs. | $10–$17 | D, MC, V.

Lodging

1810 West Inn. With its screened veranda and period furnishings, this early 19th-century inn is pleasantly romantic. Complimentary breakfast. Kitchenettes, microwaves, refrigerators. Pool. Hot tub. Business services, airport shuttle. Cable TV. No kids under 12. No smoking. | 254 N. Seymour Dr., Thomson | 706/595–3156 or 800/515–1810 | fax 706/595–3155 | www.gomm.com | 10 suites | $95–$245 | AE, D, MC, V.

Augusta Sheraton. The rooms in this typical chain hotel are furnished with writing desks. The rooms are spacious with various sizes of bed. Restaurant, bar, Continental breakfast. In-room data ports, some microwaves, refrigerators. Cable TV, in-room VCRs (in suites). 2 pools (1 indoor). Laundry facilities. Business services, airport shuttle. Some pets allowed. | 2651 Perimeter Pkwy. | 706/855–8100 or 800/325–3535 | fax 706/860–1720 | 179 rooms | $99–$159. | AE, D, DC, MC, V.

Augusta Wingate Inn. This modern hotel has everything from a pool, exercise room, and sauna to data ports and coffee in the rooms. If you bring the kids, be sure to visit the Funsville Park and Arcade just down the street. In-room data ports. Pool. Sauna. Gym. | 4087 Belair Rd. | 706/860–8223 | $85 | AE, D, DC, MC, V.

Amerisuites. This chain hotel offers living room area/bedroom combination suites. The kitchen area has dishes and silverware. Picnic area, complimentary Continental breakfast. In-room data ports, microwaves, refrigerators, cable TV. Pool. Exercise equipment. Laundry facilities. Business services. Pets allowed ($30 fee). | 1062 Claussen Rd. | 706/733–4656 or 800/833–1516 | fax 706/736–1133. | www.amerisuites.com | 111 suites | $59–$79 suites | AE, D, DC, MC, V.

Azalea Inn. Greene Street is lined with restored Victorian homes known as "painted ladies" because of their bright color schemes. At this eggplant-hued bed-and-breakfast—the reception center for a trio of renovated properties—all the guest rooms have private baths and the ceilings soar to dramatic heights. Complimentary Continental breakfast. Some kitchenettes, microwaves, refrigerators, in-room hot tubs, cable TV. Business services. | 312–316 Greene St. | 706/724–3454 | fax 706/724–1033 | azalea@theazaleainn.com | www.theazaleainn.com | 21 rooms | $79–$179 | AE, MC, V.

Best Western. Within a five-minute walk of two shopping centers, this hotel has a great sauna to relax in, and if that isn't hot enough for you, the sit-down breakfast will surely lift your spirits. Pool. Sauna. | 452 Park West Dr. | 706/651–9100 | 57 rooms | $55 | AE, D, DC, MC, V.

Columbus Hilton. Just a step away from the city's historic district and a couple of blocks from the riverfront, this modern hotel claims the best location in town. Set between the walls of an old gristmill, this property rises above the other chain accommodations in town. Restaurant. Pool. | 800 Front Ave. | 706/324–1800 | fax 706/327–8042 | 177 rooms | $65–$159 | AE, D, DC, MC, V.

Courtyard by Marriott. This renovated chain hotel is convenient to historic downtown. Restaurant, bar. In-room data ports, cable TV. Pool. Exercise equipment. Laundry facilities. Business services. Free parking. | 1045 Stevens Creek | 706/737–3737 or 800/321–2211 | fax 706/738–7851 | www.marriott.com | 130 rooms | $79–$89 | AE, D, DC, MC, V.

Days Inn. Though not a part of the well-known chain, this place offers similar accommodations and is a good value at its price. The two-story building has nice, large rooms and is convenient to restaurants. Restaurant, complimentary breakfast. In-room data ports, microwaves, refrigerators, some in-room hot tubs, cable TV. Pool. Laundry facilities. Business services. | 3026 Washington Rd. | 706/738–0131 or 800/329–7466 | fax 706/738–0131 | 124 rooms | $49–$66 | AE, D, DC, MC, V.

Fairfield Inn. The Fairfield staff are friendly and knowledgeable, and the price can't be beat. Unlike the hotels that line Washington Road, this inn is set back from all the noise in a quiet, residential setting. Cable TV. Pool. | 201 Boy Scout Rd. | 706/733–8200 | 117 rooms | $49 | AE, D, DC, MC, V.

Four Chimneys. A pre-1820s farmhouse in the plantation-plain style, probably built by Quakers who, around 1806, left the area, disgusted with slavery and the military situation. The rooms have colonial four-poster beds and a fireplace. Complimentary Continental breakfast. | 2316 Wire Rd., Thomson | 706/597–0220 | 4 rooms | $45–$70 | MC, V.

Gates House. This late Victorian cottage is the closest B&B to the Riverwalk. Furnished with period pieces, the rooms all have private baths. Wake up to the smell of fresh-baked bread and dark-roast coffee. There's a garden and a rocking chair on the porch. Complimentary breakfast. | 737 Broadway | 706/324–6464 or 800/891–3187 | fax 706/324–2070 | www.gatehouse.com | 3 rooms | $95–$135 | AE, MC, V.

Holiday Inn Express. Standard chain hotel, convenient to historic Augusta, Augusta State University, Paine College, and across the street from Medical College of Georgia. Complimentary Continental breakfast. In-room data ports, microwaves, refrigerators. Cable TV. | 1103 15th St. | 706/724–5560 | fax 706/774–6821 | holidayexp@aol.com | 38 rooms, 4 suites | $59, $63 suites | AE, D, DC, MC, V.

Holiday Inn Gordon Hwy. This renovated chain hotel is convenient to Fort Gordon, Bush Field Airport, and Augusta Mall. The rooms are spacious and nicely decorated. Restaurant, bar. In-room data ports, microwaves. Cable TV. Gym. Laundry facilities. Business services, airport shuttle, free parking. Some pets allowed ($35 fee). | 2155 Gordon Hwy. | 706/737–2300 or 800/465–4329 | fax 706/737–0418 | aghigm@shanerhotels.com | www.holiday-inn.com | 150 rooms | $72–$350 | AE, D, DC, MC, V.

Microtel Inn and Suites. The spacious, windowed suites—and pair of meeting rooms—make this one of the better hotels in Augusta. In-room data ports. Cable TV. Pool. Exercise equipment. | 2156 Gordon Hwy. | 706/736–6425 | fax 706/736–8219 | 61 rooms | $50 | AE, D, DC, MC, V.

The Partridge Inn. A National Trust Historic hotel, built in 1889 on "The Hill" in the Summerville Historic District, the restored inn sits at the gateway to Summerville, a hilltop neighborhood of summer homes dating to the 1800s. There's a splendid view of downtown Augusta from the rooftop concierge floor. The rooms are simple and sparsely decorated. The penthouse area on the rooftop floor is the Century Club, where you can enjoy views of the city and complimentary afternoon hors d'oeuvres. Restaurant, bar (with entertainment), complimentary Continental breakfast. In-room data ports, some kitchenettes, some microwaves, refrigerators. Pool. Tennis courts. Exercise equipment. Business services. | 2110 Walton Way | 706/737–2428 or 800/476–6888 | fax 706/731–0826 | www.partridgeinn.com | 156 rooms | $79–$149 | AE, D, DC, MC, V.

Perrin Guest House Inn. As you pass the 100-year-old magnolias in front of this inn, take a moment to enjoy the 3 acres of its walkways and gardens—right in the middle of Augusta. And once inside, revel in the period pieces this 1863 guest house has to offer, as well as the 11 stone fireplaces and six hot tubs. Cable TV. Hot tubs. | 208 Lafayette Dr. | 706/731–0920 | fax 706/731–9009 | www.bedandbreakfast.com/bbc/p20697.asp | 10 rooms | $85–$135 | AE, MC, V.

La Quinta. Of the Washington Road hotels, La Quinta boasts the largest rooms, along with all the ease of checking in and out that this chain is known for. In-room data ports. Cable TV. Pool. | 3020 Washington Rd. | 706/733–2660 | 129 rooms | $59 | AE, D, DC, MC, V.

Radisson Riverfront. Augusta's swankest hotel has more than 200 rooms, many of which have sweeping views of the Savannah River below. If you're planning to explore the downtown area, it just doesn't get any more convenient than this—the Morris Museum of Art is literally next door. The spacious rooms have beautiful furniture. Restaurant, bar. In-room data ports, some refrigerators. Cable TV. Pool. Driving range, putting green. Exercise equipment. Business services. Some pets allowed (fee). | 2 Tenth St. | 706/722–8900 or 800/333–3333 | fax 706/823–6513 | www.radisson.com/augustagariverfront | 234 rooms | $119–$149 | AE, D, DC, MC, V.

Radisson Suites Inn. A typical chain hotel; the room furnishings include writing desks. Restaurant, bar, complimentary breakfast, room service. In-room data ports, some microwaves, refrigerators, cable TV. Pool. Laundry facilities. Pets allowed (fee). | 3038 Washington Rd. | 706/868–1800 or 800/333–3333 | fax 706/868–9300 | www.radisson.com | 176 suites | $99–$129 | AE, D, DC, MC, V.

Rosemary and Lookaway Hall. Across the river in South Carolina. Each room has its own personality. Complimentary breakfast. Some hot tub tubs. Cable TV. Driving range. Business services. No smoking. | 804 Carolina Ave., North Augusta, SC | 803/278–6222 or 800/531–5578 | fax 803/278–4877 | 8 rooms in 15 buildings | $89–$195 | AE, D, DC, MC, V.

BAINBRIDGE

MAP 3, C11

(Nearby town also listed: Thomasville)

General Andrew Jackson was probably the first American to take note of the area around Bainbridge when he selected a nearby site for Fort Hughes during the First Seminole War. As settlement in the region increased during the mid- to late 19th century, Bainbridge found itself at the center of a large and lucrative timber industry. During the early 1900s, the town was recognized as the richest community in Georgia thanks to its lumber business.

Information: Bainbridge–Decatur County Chamber of Commerce | Box 736, Bainbridge, GA 31718 | 912/246–4774 or 800/243–4774 | bchamber@surfsouth.com | bainbridgega.com/chamber.

Attractions

Earl May Boat Basin and Park. In addition to the boat-launching area there is a children's park. Also available are 10 RV-friendly campsites with water and electrical hookups. The bathhouse has showers. There's a ball field, too. | 100 Basin Circle | 912/248–2010 | fax 912/248–2180 | blscity@surfsouth.com | Free | Daily.

The Firehouse Center and Gallery. The old public safety building (from the early 20th century) houses both the Decatur County Historical Society Museum and the Firehouse Gallery. The Decatur County Arts Council hosts art exhibitions, featuring work by local people as well as by artists from around the state. Artifacts, including some Native American material and some from the Civil War era, reflect the history of Decatur County. | 119 W. Water St. | 912/248–1719 (Museum) or 912/243–1010 (Gallery) | Free | Museum, weekends 1–5.

Seminole State Park. The 600-plus-acre park is located on Lake Seminole and has facilities for boat launching, canoes, pedal boats, and swimming. There are campsites and cabins. The flat topography makes it good for bicycling and hiking the 2.2-mi nature trail. | 7870 State Pkwy., Donalsonville | 912/861–3137 | fax 912/861–3711 | www.gastateparks.org | $2 vehicle, $20 vans; $50 bus | Daily 7–10.

ON THE CALENDAR

MID-SEPT.: *Bainbridge Bike Festival.* Come check out this wild, all-weekend event, with live bands Thursday through Saturday, a POW/MIA ceremony in George Willis Park (in downtown Bainbridge), and all kinds of motorcycle presentations. Be sure to catch the unicycle drag racing, in which competitors take off their front wheels and stand on skids behind their bikes to steer. | Just past Spring Creek Road on Highway 84 | 912/248–0505 or 800/243–4774 | $20 per day or $30 all weekend.

Dining

Charter House Inn. American. Smoked pork chops, blackened rib eye, seafood, and pastas come with a trip to the salad/soup bar. At lunch, sandwiches and salads rule. Salad bar. Kids' menu. | 1401 Tallahassee Hwy. | 912/246–8550 | chi@thecharterhouseinn.com | www.thecharterhouseinn.com | No dinner Sun. | $10–$18 | AE, D, DC, MC, V.

The Decatur House. Southern. Chef-owner Vorice Barr, with her husband, Stanley, does crab cakes, fried corn bread, bread pudding, occasional sweet-potato French fries, chicken and dumplings, and fried green tomatoes. Lots of seafood and hand-cut steaks. Kids' menu. Buffet Sun. brunch. Beer, wine, and BYOB wine. | 1697 Tallahassee Hwy. | 912/243–8811 | Closed Mon. No dinner Sun., no lunch Sat. | $8–$17 | AE, D, DC, MC, V.

Lodging

The Charter House Inn. Relax in one of the room recliners or by the large pool, or better yet take in the upscale restaurant and lounge, with karaoke on Thursdays, comedy on Fridays, and DJs all weekend. Restaurant, bar. In-room data ports. Cable TV. Pool. Business services, free parking. | 1401 Tallahasee Hwy. | 912/246–8550 | fax 912/246–0260 | 124 rooms | $52 | AE, D, DC, MC, V.

Tarrer Inn. From the veranda of this inn overlooking the courthouse square, all the world seems at peace. The rooms, which open off a grand, central hallway, are high-ceilinged and well appointed. Breakfast biscuits come with a crock of the famous local mayhaw jelly. Restaurant, complimentary breakfast. In-room data ports. Cable TV. | 155 S. Cuthbert St., Colquitt | 912/758–2888 or 888/282–7737 | fax 912/758–2825 | tarrer@surfsouth.com | www.tarrerinn.com | 12 rooms | $69–$105 | AE, D, DC, MC, V.

BLAKELY

MAP 3, B10

(Nearby town also listed: Albany)

Founded in 1821, this small town was named for U.S. Navy Captain Johnston Blakely, a hero of the War of 1812. Today it is an important peanut-producing area.

Information: Blakely-Early County Chamber of Commerce | 52 Court Square, Box 189, Blakely, GA 31723 | 912/723–3741 | fax 917/723–6876 | earlycoc@alltel.net | www.blakelyearlychamber.com | Mon.–Thu. 8:30–5:30, Fri. 8:30–4.

Attractions

Coheelee Creek Covered Bridge. The southernmost covered bridge in the United States was built in 1891. | Old River Rd. | Free | Daily.

Courthouse Square. The square has a monument honoring the peanut and also the South's last remaining Confederate flagpole, erected in 1861. | Downtown | Free | Daily.

Echodell House. While Blakely abounds with beautiful, turn-of-the-20th-century houses, be sure to look at the Echodell House right outside Blakely proper, as it was built in 1840 and predates the others by a good forty years. | 3 mi out of Blakely on U.S. Hwy. 84S | No longer open to the public.

Kolomoki Mounds State Park. Seven mounds built during the 12th and 13th centuries by the Swift Creek and Weeden Island Indians include the state's oldest temple mound. | Rte.

1, Blakely | 912/724–2150 | fax 912/724–2152 | kolomoki@alltel.net | www.gastateparks.org | $2 vehicle, $20 vans, $50 bus | Daily 7–10.

Indian Museum, Kolomoki Mounds State Park. The museum is built into the side of one of the excavated temple mounds, and an actual burial mound is enclosed in one end of the museum. Perhaps the most striking exhibit is a diorama of the funeral ceremony of a Kolomoki priest, a truly grim spectacle. Artifacts and art from native cultures in the area are among the other outstanding displays. | Rte 1, | 912/724–2152 | fax 912/724–2152 | kolomoki@alltel.net | www.gastateparks.org | $2 | Tues.–Sat. 9–5, Sun. 2–5:30.

ON THE CALENDAR
FOURTH WEEKEND IN OCT.: *Kolomoki Mounds Festival.* While no one may know exactly what these mounds were used for in the past, the people of Blakely now gather there at the end of every October for the annual arts and crafts fair at which you will find arrowheads and beaded leather, among other treasures. | 912/723–5296.

Dining
Brown's Busy Bee. American. Really good, straightforward fare makes this restaurant a local favorite—tender fried chicken, fresh biscuits, and renowned homemade pies. | Route 2 | 912/723–3588 | $7 | No credit cards.

Lodging
Days Inn. New to Blakely, the Days Inn has spacious rooms. In-room data ports. Cable TV. Pool. Laundry services. | 435 Allatoona St. | 229/723–5858 | fax 229/723–8213 | 30 rooms | $54 | AE, D, DC, MC, V.

BRUNSWICK

MAP 3, H11

(Nearby town also listed: St. Simons Island)

In addition to being the gateway to the resort communities of the Golden Isles of the Sea Islands, the coastal city of Brunswick is home to a sizable manufacturing and seafood-processing industry. It maintains an oceangoing harbor and is recognized as one of the largest shrimp-distribution centers in the world. Founded in 1771, the town was named in honor of George III of the house of Brunswick (Hanover). Brunswick's subtropical climate and its ocean-influenced economy give the town an exotic and romantic aura.

Information: **Brunswick–Golden Isles Visitors Bureau** | 4 Glynn Ave., Brunswick, GA 31520 | 912/265–0620 or 800/933–2627 | bgivbvisitorsb@technonet.com | www.bgivbvisitorsb.com | Mon.–Fri. 8:30–5.

Attractions
The Brunswick Farmers Market. This local market features great handpicked fruits, vegetables, and nuts plus homemade sauces, syrups, cakes, and pies. | At the Mary Ross Waterfront Park | Free | Tues., Thurs., and Sat. 7–7.

Hofwyl-Broadfield Plantation State Historic Site. Rice plantations were once the glory of the Altamaha River. This plantation, originally one of the rice-growing enterprises, was established in 1807 by Charlestonian William Brailsford. After rice declined as a crop around 1915, the plantation was turned into a dairy and operated as such until 1942, when it was willed to the state. The museum features fine silver and a model of a working rice plantation. You can wander the levees that controlled the water flow and watch a film about the life of both planters and slaves. | 5556 U.S. 17 N., Brunswick | 912/264–7333 | fax 912/264–7333 | hofwyl@darientel.net | $3.50 | Tues.–Sat. 9–5, Sun. 2–5:30.

James Oglethorpe Monument. General James E. Oglethorpe (1696–1785) laid out old Brunswick using a grid pattern, much as he did in Savannah. A cross commemorates his founding of the province, now state, of Georgia. Erected by Captain Charles Spalding Wylly and the Brunswick chapter of the Daughters of the American Revolution, the cross and monument note this soldier/philanthropist's devotion to men "of poor estate." | Queens Square | Free | Daily.

Marshes of Glynn. Immortalized in the poetry of the Macon-born poet Sidney Lanier (1842–81), the coastal marshes of Glynn County serve as feeding grounds for the famous Georgia white shrimp and dazzle the eye with their spectacular colors. As the sun sets, they change from gold to purple. You can visit the oak tree under which Lanier sat and "looked out over a world of marsh that borders a world of sea." The oak is immediately north of town in the median that bisects Hwy. 17. | 912/265–0620 | Free | Daily.

Mary Miller Doll Museum. Dollhouses, toys, and dolls from more than 90 countries spanning 150 years are represented in this extensive museum. | 1523 Glynn Ave. | 912/267–7569 | fax 912/267–7569 | $2 | Weekdays 11–4:30.

ON THE CALENDAR
MAY: *HarborFest and the Blessing of the Fleet.* This exuberant event on Mother's Day weekend features a parade through historic Downtown Brunswick, live music, arts and crafts booths, a farmers' market, and a U.S. Coast Guard helicopter search-and-rescue demonstration. In addition, Brunswick's Portuguese fishing community decorates its shrimp boats and pleasure craft, all of which are blessed with holy water for safety and good shrimp catches. | 912/265–0620 or 800/933–2627 | www.bgislesvisitorsb.com.

Dining
Borrell Creek. Steak and Seafood. Dark Entry Creek forms the backdrop for this casual restaurant, popular with the guys from the nearby Kings Bay submarine base. Lots of seafood dishes include crab-stuffed shrimp and very good fried shrimp. Kids' menu. | 1101 Rte. 40 E., St. Marys | 912/673–6300 | Closed Sun. No lunch Sat. | $11–$18 | AE, MC, V.

Seagles Waterfront Cafe. Steak/Seafood. This popular waterfront cafe is known for rock shrimp, a local delicacy, among other local seafood specialties (white Atlantic shrimp and deviled crab). You'll also find pasta and steak dishes. Kids' menu. | 105 W. Osborne St., St. Marys | 912/882–4187 | Closed Sun. | $11–$17 | AE, D, DC, MC, V.

Spanky's. American/Casual. Well-prepared seafood is served in a casual atmosphere. You'll find great wine and beer prices during happy hour, from after 4:30 to 7 on weekdays. Stay with the local specials, such as blue crab stew and fried oyster po' boys. Steaks, salads and pastas also available. Music Fri., Sat. nights. Kids' menu. | 704 Mall Blvd. | 912/267–6100 | Reservations not accepted | Mon.–Sun. 11–10 | $11–$17 | AE, D, MC, V.

Lodging
Brunswick Manor. This 1886 Victorian building is a good mix of historic touches and modern amenities. Wake up to a candelight breakfast in the grand dining room, where you can discuss your day's itinerary with the owners, then come home to tea or a cocktail in the parlor or on the wraparound veranda with the wicker swing. Take a quick soak in the hot tub before bed. Hot tub. | 825 Egmont St. | 912/265–6889 | fax 912/265–7879 | 7 rooms | $100 | MC, V.

Riverview Hotel. Most days the family pooch lounges on the couch in the black-and-white-tiled hallway. The rooms upstairs are calico-cute but nice, befitting what feels like an old railroad hotel. A balcony on the second level is outfitted with rockers and affords a grand view of the river. Restaurant, bar, complimentary Continental breakfast. | 105 Osborne St., St. Marys | 912/882–3242 | fax 912/729–6158 | gaila@eagnet.com | 18 rooms | $45–$60 | AE, D, DC, MC, V.

Spencer House Inn. This comfortable Victorian inn dates from 1872 and is named for the sea captain who built it as a hotel. Innkeepers Mike and Mary Neff reside here and will prepare picnic lunches if you ask. The inn makes a perfect base for a tour of historic St. Marys and the waterfront and is convenient to the *Cumberland Queen* ferry. This is a good selection for people who use wheelchairs, as there is an elevator. Complimentary breakfast. | 101 E. Bryant St., St. Marys | 912/882–1872 | fax 912/882–9427 | spencer@eagnet.com | 14 rooms | $80–$145 | Mon.–Sun. 9–8 | AE, D, MC, V.

CALHOUN

MAP 3, B4

(Nearby towns also listed: Dalton, Rome)

Formerly named Oothcaloga ("place of the beaver dams"), Calhoun sits in the middle of historic Cherokee Indian country. Nearby is New Echota, the last Cherokee capital before the removal took them west of the Mississippi River. The town is situated in the hilly countryside of North Georgia, along I–75 between Atlanta and Chattanooga. Calhoun's present-day economy is largely supported by the carpet industry.

Information: Gordon County Chamber of Commerce | 300 S. Wall St., Calhoun, GA 30701 | 706/625–3200 or 800/887–3811 | fax 706/625–5062 | info@gordonchamber.org | www.gordonchamber.org | Mon.–Fri. 8:30–5.

Attractions

Barnsley Gardens. When English-born Godfrey Barnsley set out to build his dream castle for himself and his Savannah-born wife, Julia, he little dreamed how short-lived their happiness would be. She died young, and he gave up construction. According to legend, she appeared to him in the garden and told him to resume the project, explaining how she wanted it done. In 1988, the mansion, then in ruins, was purchased by Prince Fugger of Germany, who opened the gardens to the public without restoring the mansion. It's now the site of a luxury resort. | 597 Barnsley Gardens Rd., Adairsville | 770/773–7480 | fax 770/773–3210 | barnsley@mindspring.com | www.barnsleyinn.com | $10 | Mon.–Sun. 9–6.

New Echota State Historic Site. A collection of one original and reconstructed buildings re-creates the last capital of the Cherokee Nation. The visitors center shows a film about life and culture in New Echota in the 1820s and 1830s, the period leading up to the Cherokee Removal. A nearby cemetery holds the graves, some of them marked, of town residents, including Chief Pathkiller and whites who lived among the Cherokee. | 1211 Chatsworth Hwy., Northeast Calhoun | 706/624–1321 | fax 706/624–1323 | www.gastateparks.org | $3 | Tues.–Sat. 9–5, Sun. 2–5:30.

Paradise Gardens. Famed folk artist Reverend Howard Finster began Paradise Gardens around 1961. The 3-acre collection of historic items and folk art is connected by a system of cement paths running from site to site. An L-shaped ramp, 6 ft above ground, leads to the bicycle museum and the tomb of the unknown body. The Finster Folk Art Gallery exhibits not only the reverend's work, but also that of his family and other regional artists. Weddings, christenings, and, on Sundays from 2–5 PM, sightings of the Reverend Finster himself take place. You can spend the night at the Paradise Cottage lodgings. | 84 Knox St., Summerville, Pennville | 706/857–2926 or 800/346–7837 | fax 706/857–2288 | www.finster.com | $5 | Daily noon–6.

Resaca Confederate Cemetery. Georgia's first Confederate cemetery created after the battle of Resaca (May 14–15, 1864), which took place on the plantation of Colonel John Green. When the family returned home, they found soldiers' bodies hastily buried in shallow graves, some of which had been uncovered by severe rains. Other bodies had simply been covered by dirt by advancing Federal soldiers. Colonel Green's two daughters, Mary and Pyatt, and some of the family's servants reburied the bodies in the plantation flower garden. Later, they gathered funds and, on the 2½ acres Colonel Green gave them, the women and their associates reinterred the soldiers again, grouping them by state. | U.S. 41 | Free | Daily.

ON THE CALENDAR
MID-AUG.: *Fifties Day in Downtown Calhoun.* Listen to local bands and marvel at the old cars, enjoy the outdoor food stands, the hula-hoop contest, and the people of Calhoun dressed in their favorite fifties outfits. Feel free to wear your own. | 706/602–5570.

Dining
Adairsville Inn. American. Basic steaks and seafood, chicken, pasta, and crêpes are the dinner dishes. Lunch tends more to sandwiches. Desserts range from chocolate mousse to fresh strawberries with crème anglaise. Kids' menu. | 100 S. Main St., Adairsville | 770/773–2774 | Reservations not accepted | Closed Mon. No dinner Tues.–Thurs., Sun. | $8–$17 | No credit cards.

Lodging
Barnsley Inn and Golf Resort. These guest cottages, which form a village, are inspired by American architect Andrew Jackson Downing's popular mid-19th-century book on country estates and gardens. No cars are allowed in the village. Each cottage is individually furnished. Room service. In-room data ports. Cable TV. Pool. Spa. Driving range, golf courses, putting green, 2 tennis courts. Hiking, fishing, bicycles. Free parking. | 597 Barnsley Gardens Rd., Adairsville | 770/773–7480 | fax 770/773–3210 | barnsley@mindspring.com | www.barnsleyinn.com | 30 cottages, 70 suites | $205–$800 suites | Mon.–Sun. 9–8 | AE, D, DC, MC, V.

Jameson Inn. The main balcony on this colonial-style inn is on the second floor, atop white columns; it's a good place to stand to breathe the fresh mountain air. The rooms have HBO, but it might be even more fun to grill some local produce in the hotel's picnic area. Cable TV. Pool. Gym. | 189 Jameson St. | 800/JAMESON | fax 706/629–7985 | 59 rooms | $59 | AE, D, DC, MC, V.

Paradise Cottage. This cottage and B&B is decorated with beautiful stained-glass windows and hardwood floors. The rooms are lined with folk art. Kitchenette and cable TV in the cottage. Phones in main house. | 84 Knox St., Pennville | 706/857–2926 | fax 706/857–2926 | www.finster.com | 3 rooms, 1 cottage | $100–$125, $60 cottage | AE, D, DC, MC, V.

CARROLLTON

MAP 3, B6

(Nearby towns also listed: Atlanta, Newnan)

Carrollton was named for one of the signers of the Declaration of Independence, Charles Carroll. Today this town near the Alabama border is home to one of the country's largest rod and cable manufacturing companies, Southwire. Sony also has a manufacturing plant here. The State University of West Georgia has an important presence in the town as well.

Information: Carroll County Chamber of Commerce | 200 Northside Dr., Carrollton, GA 30117 | 770/832–2446 | fax 770/832–1300 | www.carroll-ga.org | Weekdays 8:30–5.

Attractions
John Tanner State Park. Boasting the largest swimming beach of any Georgia state park, the two lakes also provide boating and fishing. Camping, a group lodge, motor lodge rooms (motel efficiency units without phone or TV), a nature trail, and picnicking are among the draws. | 354 Tanner's Beach Rd. | 770/830–2222 | fax 770/830–2223 | j_tanner@innerex.net | www.gastateparks.org | $2 vehicle, $20 vans, $50 bus | Daily 7–10.

McIntosh Reserve. As you approach this plantation house, it appears exactly as you might expect it to—a beautiful sweeping staircase meets the drive, and the hedges are perfectly trimmed. But once inside, there's a twist: this is the former plantation of Creek Indian Chief William McIntosh, and there are exhibits devoted to his life and ancestry throughout the mansion. | 11 mi south of Carrollton, off GA Hwy. 5 | 800/292–0871 | Free | Tues.–Sat. 9–5.

State University of West Georgia. Founded in 1906 as the Fourth District Agricultural and Mechanical School, the school was renamed West Georgia College in 1933 and designated a university in 1996. Today it has 8,600 students in undergraduate and graduate programs. Specialty degree programs include gerontology and an education doctorate in school performance improvement, and there's a focus in parapsychology in the psychology department. Michael Greene, president of the National Academy of Recording Arts and Sciences, is an alumnus, and so is Georgia author Terry Kay (*To Dance with the White Dog*). | 1600 Maple St. | 770/836–6500 | fax 770/836–6720 | www.westga.edu | Free | Daily.

Thomas Bonner House. Built in 1834 as a plantation home, this house is today located on the university campus. Bonner was an early sheriff of Carroll County. During the Civil War, passing Federal cavalry raided the farm. After the war, the B.A. Sharp family purchased the farm (1866), then the board of trustees of the Fourth District Agricultural and Mechanical School bought the farm in 1906. The house was moved to its present location in 1917 and now serves the office of tourism development. | 1600 Maple St. | 770/838–3221 | fax 770/838–3269 | www.westga.edu | Free | Tours by appointment only.

ON THE CALENDAR

SEPT.: McIntosh Reserve Festival. Arts and crafts, food and fun in an historic setting on the former plantation of Creek Indian Chief William McIntosh during the third weekend of the month. | 800/292–0871.

Dining

Lazy Donkey. Mexican. Not your basic beans-and-rice joint, this may well be Carrollton's most popular restaurant. Specials are the things to look at: garlic shrimp and lomitos tropicales (pork loin medallions with papaya/mango salsa) are good examples. Kids' menu. | 334 Bankhead Hwy. | 770/834–6002 | Reservations not accepted | Closed Sun., Mon. | $8–$15 | AE, D, DC, MC, V.

Lodging

Best Western. Here you'll find a lounge with live music on weekends, free HBO, good views of the surrounding hills, a business center with Internet access and fax service, and meeting rooms big enough for 350 people. Cable TV. Pool. Laundry services. | 1202 S. Park Street | 770/832–2611 or 800/352–6341 | fax 770/832–2612 | 103 rooms | $89 | AE, D, DC, MC, V.

CARTERSVILLE

MAP 3, B4

(Nearby towns also listed: Atlanta, Marietta, Rome)

Located north of Atlanta along I–75, Cartersville is home to the world-famous Etowah Indian Mounds. Between AD 1000 and 1500, the entire Etowah River valley was full of prehistoric Indian villages of the Mississippian culture. The Etowah mounds complex covers many acres and is the most impressive. Today, a healthy minerals industry, supported by textile manufacturing and the production of beer, contributes to the town's economy.

Information: Cartersville/Bartow County Convention and Visitors Bureau | Box 200397, Cartersville, GA 30120 | 770/387–1357 or 800/733–2280 | fax 770/386–1220 | cvb@notatlanta.org | www.notatlanta.org | Mon.–Fri. 9–5, Sat. 11–2.

Attractions

Allatoona Lake. More than 270 mi of shoreline surround this 12,000-acre lake, offering a full range of sporting activities. The visitors center is operated by the U.S. Army Corps of Engineers. | 1138 Rte. 20 Spur | 770/382–4700 | fax 770/386–6758 | www.sam.usace.army.mil/sam/op/rec/allatoon | Free; fees are charged for some activities. | Daily; visitors center: Apr.–Sept., daily 8–6:30; Oct.–Mar., daily 8–4:30.

Etowah Indian Mounds Historic Site and Archaeological Area. This major Mississippian Period cultural center flourished from about AD 950 until the mid-1500s. The largest mound stands more than 63 ft high and covers 3 acres. Artifacts are exhibited in the museum. | 813 Indian Mounds Rd. SE | 770/387–3747 | fax 770/387–3972 | www.gas-tateparks.org | $3 | Tues.–Sat. 9–5, Sun. 2–5:30.

Red Top Mountain State Park and Lodge. Once an important site for mining iron, the park sits on a 1,950-acre peninsula along Lake Allatoona. Abundant wildlife, a reconstructed 1860s homestead, and well-marked trails are among the draws. Now operated by a private concern, the 33-room lodge, restaurant, and meeting facility are added benefits. | 50 Lodge Rd. | 770/975–0055 | fax 770/975–3299 | www.gastateparks.org | $2 vehicle, $20 vans, $50 bus | Daily.

Roselawn Museum. This beautifully restored Victorian mansion began as a small, one-story structure in the 1860s. The attic was converted into bedrooms around 1872, a two-story wing was added in the 1880s, and in 1895 the existing two floors were *raised* and a third floor and basement were built underneath (an architectural feat at the time). | 224 West Cherokee Ave. | Adults $2, children 3–6 $1 | Tours Tues.–Fri. 10–noon and 1–5.

William Weinman Mineral Museum. The family of William Weinman, a pioneer in barite mining in Bartow County, donated funds to establish a museum in his honor. More than 2,000 specimens are featured in three exhibition halls. The Indian artifacts date to the Archaic Period (8,000 BC), although fossils date to the Cambrian Period of the Paleozoic Era. | 51 Mineral Museum Dr., White | 770/386–0576 | fax 770/386–0600 | wenman@mind-spring.com | www.chara.gsu.edu¢~weinman | $4 | Tues.–Sat. 10–4:30, Sun. 1–4:30.

ON THE CALENDAR

OCT.: *Halloween Hayrides and Storytelling.* On Halloween enjoy a hayride across the mountain, then gather around the bonfire for haunting tales from some of Georgia's best storytellers, but don't forget to make advance reservations and arrive before 6:30 PM. | Red Top Mountain Beach in Red Top Mountain State Park | 770/975–0055 | Adults $4, children 4–15 $2.50.

Dining

Doug's Place. *Southern.* This place looks like the usual steak house, but stands apart for its home cooking. The specialties to look for include fried okra, country fried steak with mashed potatoes, fried chicken, and roast beef. About 17 different vegetables are available daily along with four different desserts. Much of the fried foods are done in black cast iron, the traditional way. Breakfast is traditional, with real biscuits and gravy. No alcohol. | 696 Rte. 293 SE, Emerson | 770/382–9063 | Reservations not accepted | Breakfast also available. No dinner Sun.–Tues., Thurs., Sat. | $4–$6 | No credit cards.

Brindles. *American.* The atmosphere is both casual and romantic. The upscale dishes center on seafood, steaks, and pork. The desserts are homemade. | 119 W. Church St. | 770/382–6060 | brindlesofga@aol.com | Closed Tues. | $8–$38 | AE, D, MC, V.

Lodging

Red Top Mountain State Park Lodge. Right at dusk or in the early hours of the morning, the lodge gets a whole host of special visitors: the deer. These beautiful animals can be seen walking around the main building or the 18 cabins almost every day of the year, and they add to the experience of staying right in the park, with hiking, boat rental, and bird-watching just a few of the many nearby activities. Pool. | 653 Red Top Mountain Rd. | 770/975–0055 | fax 770/975–3299 | 103 rooms | $95 | AE, D, DC, MC, V.

CHICKAMAUGA AND CHATTANOOGA NATIONAL MILITARY PARK

MAP 3, A3

(Nearby town also listed: Dalton)

The oldest military park in the nation (authorized in 1890), this commemorates the bloody two-day battle at Chickamauga Creek in North Georgia in September 1863. The Confederacy's failure to capitalize on initial victory, coupled with the Union occupation of Chattanooga two months later, led to the loss of the vital rail link between Chattanooga and Atlanta, a loss that contributed immeasurably to the fall of Atlanta the following year.

Information: Chickamauga and Chattanooga National Military Park | Box 2128, Fort Oglethorpe, GA 30742 | 706/866–9241 | fax 423/752–5215 | chch_administration@nps.gov | www.nps.gov/chch/ | $2 | June–Aug. 8–5.

Attractions

Chickamauga and Chattanooga National Military Park. This military park is the site of one of the bloodiest battles in American history, the battle of Chickamauga, fought on September 19–20, 1863. In the end, more than 34,000 casualties were recorded. Monuments, battlements, and artillery dot the 8,000-acre park. | On Hwy. 27, Fort Oglethorpe | 706/866–9241 | fax 423/752–5215 | www.nps.gov/chch | Free | Mid-Aug.–mid-June, daily 8–4:45; mid-June–mid-Aug., daily 8–5:45.

Craven House. In 1863, as the Union and Confederate troops pressed nearer, the Craven family left their home for safety. Little did they know it would end up near the center of the Battle Above the Clouds (as the battle of Lookout Mountain, part of the Chattanooga campaign, came to be known). The original residence was destroyed during the battle as it rapidly changed hands back and forth, but in a testament to their strength, the Cravens later returned and rebuilt it, and today it stands as a museum honoring both the conflict and this remarkable family. | U.S. 27 | 706/866–9241 | www.nps.gov/chch | Free | Daily, summer 9–5; weekends in spring and fall 9–4.

ON THE CALENDAR
SEPT./NOV.: *Chickamauga and Lookout Mountain Battle Anniversaries.* In mid-September and mid-November, the military park hosts a variety of weekend events, including reenactments, walking tours, and evening lectures in the Craven House. | U.S. 27 | 706/866–9241.

Dining

Canyon Grill. American. The restaurant takes its name from nearby Cloudland Canyon. Certified black angus beef, grilled shrimp, and vegetables are the mainstays. You'll find plenty of vegetables, such as vegetable skewers and grilled cabbage, along with an extensive selection of fresh fish. The pasta dishes are good. No alcohol. | 28 Scenic Hwy., Rising Fawn | 706/398–9510 | cangrill@aol.com | Closed Mon.–Wed. No lunch | $8–$20 | No credit cards.

Lodging

Cloudland Canyon State Park. These spacious, functional cottages are perched on the canyon rim, high above the world at an ear-popping altitude. The best cabins are numbers 6 through 16, each with a screened porch and rocking chairs. There is also a lodge that sleeps up to 40, perfect for family reunions and the like. This is a great area for wildlife viewing. Kitchenettes. No room phones. Pool. Tennis court. Hiking. Laundry facilities. | 122 Cloudland Canyon Park Rd., Rising Fawn | 706/657–4050 or 800/864–7275 | www.gas-tatepark.org | 16 cabins, 1 lodge | $75–$95 cabins, $135 lodge | Mon.–Sun. 8–5 | AE, D, MC, V.

Gordon Lee Mansion. Four elegant rooms are available in the 1847 manor house. There are another two rooms in the former slave quarters. During the battle of Chickamauga this redbrick mansion served as headquarters for Union general Rosecrans, and there's a Civil War museum upstairs. Kitchenette (in cabin). Cable TV, no room phones. | 217 Cove Rd. | 706/375–4728 | fax 706/375–9499 | glmbb1@aol.com | www.fhc.org/gordon-lee | 4 rooms, 1 cabin | $75–$90, $125 cabin | AE, D, MC, V.

COLUMBUS

MAP 3, B8

(Nearby town also listed: Pine Mountain)

With much of its original town plan intact, Columbus is one of Georgia's most picturesque towns. Its 28-block historic district has been meticulously cared for and today offers a rare glimpse into what antebellum life in the state was like. At one time, Columbus was Georgia's number-two cotton producer, and although that crop is not as important to the economy as it once was, other forms of agriculture—bolstered by the proximity to the U.S. Army's Fort Benning—keep the economy thriving.

Information: **Columbus Convention and Visitors Bureau** | 1000 Bay Ave., P.O. Box 2768, Columbus, GA 31902 | 706/322–1613 or 800/999–1613 | fax 706/322–0701 | ccvb@msn.com | www.columbusga.com/ccvb | Weekdays 8–5, Sat. 11–5, Sun. 1–5.

Attractions

Coca-Cola Space Science Center. Founded in 1996 by Columbus State University, the Coca-Cola Space Science Center offers on-site learning experiences. Facilities include the Omni-sphere Planetarium, a Challenger Learning Center, exhibit areas, and observing sessions at the Mead Observatory. | 701 Front Ave. | 706/649–1470 | fax 706/649–1478 | www.ccssc.org | Free | Tues.–Fri. 10–4, Sat. 1:30–5, Sun. 1:30–4.

Columbus Georgia Convention and Trade Center. This historic building sits on the site of a Civil War cannon factory. Later a manufacturing plant, it was converted in 1979 to the convention center. A small area displays some of the items made at the manufacturing plan. | 801 Front Ave. | 706/327–4522 | fax 706/327–0162 | lcambell@columbusga.org | Free | Weekdays 8–5.

Columbus Museum. Georgia's second largest art museum exhibits regional history and a permanent collection focusing on American art. Visiting exhibitions draw from collections worldwide. | 1251 Wynnton Rd. | Free | 706/649–0713 | fax 706/649–1070 | www.colum-busmuseum.com | Tues.–Sat. 10–5, Sun. 1–5.

Port Columbus Civil War Naval Center. Displays tell the story of the Civil War navies, both Confederate and Union. The hulls of two of the only three surviving Confederate gunboats, rare naval cannon, swords, mines, ship models, artifacts, paintings of ships and battles, and period uniforms are among the displays. | 202 4th St. | 706/327–9798 | fax 706/653–4590 | www.portcolumbus.org | Donations accepted | Tues.–Fri. 10–5, weekends 1–5.

Fort Benning. Named for Henry Lewis Benning, soldier, attorney, politician, justice of the Georgia Supreme Court, and native Georgian, the fort began when the Infantry School of Arms, with all personnel, property, and equipment, moved to Columbus, Georgia, in

October 1918. The site, previously a plantation, grew to become one of the largest military installations in the state and in the nation. It takes up 182,000 acres and is an open post. Inside the stone gate on Benning Road is a welcome center where you can pick up brochures for self-guided tours. You may have the chance to catch some of the special events for visitors, such as parachute training jumps. Rangers sometimes put on demonstrations at the school's graduation. Be aware that the posted speed limits are fiercely enforced. | 4 Karker St. | 706/545–2238 | fax 706/545–1516 | www.benning.army.mil | Free | Daily.

National Infantry Museum. Exhibits trace the history of the U.S. Infantry from June 14, 1775, when the U.S. Infantry was established around Boston, MA, to the present. | Bldg. 396, Baltzell Ave., Fort Benning | 706/545–2958 | fax 706/545–5158 | www.benningmwr.com | Free | Weekdays 8–4:30, weekends 12:30–4:30.

Springer Opera House. Built in 1871, the stage here has hosted such notables as Edwin Booth and Oscar Wilde. Now lavishly restored, the 130-year-old Victorian theater houses the State Theatre of Georgia. A regional theater, it produces five mainstage shows per year, among other events. | 103 10th St. | 706/327–3688 | fax 706/324–4681 | www.springeroperahouse.org | $5 | Weekdays 10–5.

Pasaquan. Edward Owens Martin, who preferred to be known as St. EOM, was a visionary artist who painted every surface of his mother's home outside Buena Vista. When he ran out of surfaces, he made more, creating and then painting a series of undulating walls that crisscrosses the land. | Buena Vista | 912/649–2842 or 800/647–2832 | www.schockoestudios.com/steom.htm | $5 | Sat. 10–6, Sun. 1–6.

ON THE CALENDAR

MAY/OCT.: *Cotton Pickin' Fair.* Held annually in Gay, this is one of America's top arts and crafts festivals, featuring antiques and foods in addition to arts and crafts, all against the backdrop of an old cotton plantation. The event is repeated in October. | 38 mi from the Atlanta airport | 706/538–6814 | 1st weekend of May and Oct.

Dining

The Garlic Clove. Contemporary. Under new ownership since 1998, this establishment has raised its culinary sites a few notches. Shrimp brûlée in Parmesan phyllo dough rests on basil Chardonnay essence. Roast duck comes with potato puree, bacon-braised red cabbage, and port shallot sauce. Desserts go classic, such as bitter chocolate mousse. The dining room is comfortable, with white tablecloths and candles. Beer and wine only. | 6060 Veterans Pkwy. | 706/321–0882 | garlicclove@msn.com | Closed Sun., Mon. No lunch | $12–$25 | AE, D, DC, MC, V.

Goetchius House. Continental. This elegant Victorian mansion features old-fashioned flaming desserts, such as Cherries Jubilee and Bananas Foster. The veal and steak are good, but make sure the kitchen understands how well done you want them. | 405 Broadway | 706/324–4863 | Closed Sun. No lunch | $16–$46 | AE, D, DC, MC, V.

The Olive Branch Cafe. Mediterranean. This is a contemporary bistro with good food from around the world. Come here for such classic fare as escargots; for regional dishes such as Louisiana barbecued shrimp and gumbo; and for Italian favorites, such as traditional manicotti. | 1032 Broadway | 706/322–7410 | Closed Sun. No lunch Sat. | $12–$30 | D, DC, MC, V.

Lodging

The Rothschild Pound House. This B&B was built in 1870 and is on the National Historic Register. Complete with Victorian carved-wood furniture, a wraparound porch, and parlor, the Rothschild Pound house also has quite an understanding, history-savvy staff. | 201 7th St. | 706/322–4075 or 800/585–4075 | 7 rooms | $97 | MC, V.

CORDELE

(Nearby towns also listed: Albany, Perry)

If you like watermelons, Cordele is the place to go. Hailed as the "watermelon capital of the world," the town prides itself on being Georgia's number-one exporter of melons; it ranks high among soybean, sweet potato, cotton, and cantaloupe markets as well. Cordele, with a population exceeding 10,000, was founded in 1888 and is the seat of Crisp County.

Information: Cordele–Crisp Chamber of Commerce | 302 E. 16th Ave., Box 158, Cordele, GA 31015 | 912/273–1668 | fax 912/273–5132 | cccofc@sowega.net | www.cordele-crisp-chamber.com | Weekdays 8–5.

Attractions

Cotton Museum. A video explains the cultivation of cotton and the role of slaves in the production of cotton; old implements and old photographs are displayed in a small century-old schoolhouse that was moved into the town. | 1321 E. Union St., Vienna | 912/268–2045 | Donations accepted | Mon.–Sat. 9:15–4.

Georgia Veterans Memorial State Park. Formed in 1946, the park originally honored only World War II veterans but now depicts Georgia's role in all America's wars, from the Revolutionary through the Persian Gulf. There's a rare B-29 Super-Fortress on display, as well as artillery, planes, tanks, jets, and helicopters. The park is on Lake Blackshear and is Georgia's busiest park, hosting more than 1.5 million visitors. There's also a 18-hole golf course (912/276–2377). | 2459 A U.S. 280W | 912/276–2371 | fax 912/276–2372 | www.gastateparks.org | $2 vehicle, $20 vans, $50 bus | Daily 7–10.

Lake Blackshear. Covering nearly 7,000 acres, the lake is a natural habitat for many species of fish and wildlife. Boating, camping, and water-skiing attract outdoor enthusiasts year-round. Created in the 1930s by the Crisp County commissioners, who dammed the Flint River. A portion of the lake is in the Georgia Veterans Memorial State Park. | Off Hwy. 280W | 912/273–1668 | fax 912/273–5132 | cccofc@sowega.net | www.cordele-crisp-chamber.com | Free | Daily.

ON THE CALENDAR

JULY: Watermelon Festival. Celebrate the luscious fruit with watermelon-eating and seed-spitting contests. The festival also has arts and crafts and entertainment. | Box 308, Vienna | 912/273–3526 | fax 912/268–8200.

OCT.: Big Pig Jig. The statewide Georgia Barbecue Championship is featured at this festival, held in Vienna. A golf tournament, fireworks, carnival, and parade add to the fun. | Box 308, Vienna | 912/268–8275 | fax 912/268–8200 | bpjig@sowega.net | www.bigpigjig.com | $5 | Daily noon–midnight.

Dining

A.B.'s Barbeque. Barbecue. Traditional ribs, fried chicken, sliced and chopped barbecue, Brunswick stew, house-made coleslaw—everything but French fries is made from scratch. Kids' menu. No alcohol. | 328 Broad St., Hawkinsville | 912/892–3264 | Closed Sun. | $3–$7 | No credit cards.

Daphne Lodge. Southern. Susu and Sonny Burt greet regulars by first names. Traditional deep-fried fresh catfish, bacon-baked oysters, lightly battered sweet fried shrimp, and smothered quail (a traditional plantation dish) are specialties. Fried apple crescents for dessert. Beer and wine only. | U.S. 280W | 912/273–2596 | Closed Sun., Mon. No lunch | $9–$20 | AE, D, DC, MC, V.

Vienna Cafe. Southern. "I cook whatever comes to my mind," says owner Alene West. Homemade chicken potpie, stir-fried sausage with peppers and onions, cheeseburger pie are some of the specials. Broccoli casserole is popular. Kids' menu. No alcohol. | 14-12 East Union St., Vienna | 912/268–8809 | Closed weekends. No dinner Mon.–Fri. | $2–$8 | No credit cards.

Lodging
Marsh Pond B&B. Near Lake Blackshear, this B&B is right in the middle of 25 acres of certified backyard wildlife habitat—wake up and walk onto the porch to catch songbirds welcoming the day. All of the rooms are done in tasteful Southern stylings and include full baths. There's a meeting room large enough for 10 to 20. | 114 N. Valhalla Dr. | 912/273–9900 | $89 | MC, V.

CUMBERLAND ISLAND NATIONAL SEASHORE

MAP 3, H11

(Nearby towns also listed: Brunswick, Jekyll Island, St. Simons Island)

This 17- by 3-mi island off the coast of Georgia is the largest and most southerly of the barrier islands. It is a sanctuary of marshes, dunes, beaches, forests, lakes and ponds, estuaries, and inlets. Waterways shelter gators, sea turtles and otters as well as snowy egrets, great blue herons, ibis, wood storks, and more than 300 other species of birds. In the forests are armadillos, wild horses, deer, raccoons, and an assortment of reptiles.

The island is a unit of the National Park Service; the only way to reach it from the mainland is by passenger tour boat. (Mainland departures are from St. Marys; reservations are required.) There are no restaurants on the island, no shops, and no tourist attractions other than the wild beauty and the pristine wilderness of the island itself. Camping is allowed, but reservations are necessary (912/882–4335).

Cumberland Island was home to the Guale Indians and was visited by Spanish missionaries in the 16th century, English soldiers in the 18th century, and planters in the 19th. Thomas Carnegie (brother of industrialist Andrew) and his family built several lavish residences here in the 1880s. There are Indian, Spanish, and American historical sites worth visiting on the island.

Information: **Cumberland Island National Seashore** | Box 806, St. Marys, GA 31558 | 912/882–4335 | fax 912/673–7747 | www.nps.gov/cuis | Weekdays 10–4.

Attractions
Crooked River State Park. On the mainland near Cumberland Island, these 500 acres of coastal plain with moss-draped trees provide camping, cabins, rest rooms with hot showers, RV hookups, swimming, fishing, and boating. Crooked River is a tidal river. | Charlie Smith Sr. Hwy. (Spur 40), St. Marys | 912/882–5256 | fax 912/673–7747 | www.gastateparks.org | $2 vehicle, $20 vans, $50 bus | Daily 7–10; visitors center daily 8–5.

Cumberland Island National Seashore Museum. Native American relics and memorabilia from the Gilded Age, as well as exhibits about the natural history of Cumberland Island, are the focus of this museum. The museum is housed in an old bank building in St. Marys. | 129 Osborne St., St. Marys | 912/882–5496 | fax 912/882–5688 | www.nps.gov/cuis | Donations accepted | Daily 8–4:15.

Cumberland Queen. A reservations-only, 146-passenger ferry operating between St. Marys and Cumberland Island. | on the waterfront in downtown St. Marys | www.nps.gov/parklists/byname.htm | $10 round-trip; special rates for seniors and children | From St. Marys

Oct.–mid-May, Thurs.–Mon. 9 and 11:45; from Cumberland mid-May–Sept., daily 10:15 and 4:45; Oct.–mid-May, Thurs.–Mon. 10:15 and 4:45.

Orange Hall. Dating to circa 1829, this is an outstanding example of temple-form Greek-revival architecture. The building also serves as the Welcome Center and Museum. | 311 Osborne St., St. Marys | 912/882–4000 or 800/868–8687 | www.stmaryswelcome.com | $3 | Mon.–Sat. 9–5, Sun. 1–5.

Plum Orchard Mansion. This Carnegie mansion has fallen into a bit of disrepair, but the structure is as elegant as ever, with its marble stairs and Corinthian columns. | In the Cumberland Island State Park | 912/882–4335 | fax 912/673–7747 | www.nps.gov/cuis | $6 | Vans leave the main park campground at 10 on Wed., Sat., and Sun.

St. Marys Submarine Museum. Submarine exhibits from World War I, World War II, and on to the Trident era. There's a periscope that goes through the building's roof. | 102 W. St. Marys St. | 912/882–2782 | fax 912/882–2748 | www.eagnet.com/edipage/areaserv/submus/submus/htm | submus@eagnet.com | $2 | Tues.–Sat. 10–4, Sun. 1–5.

Lodging
Greyfield Inn. A Carnegie mansion built in 1900, the Greyfield now offers a magnificent setting to get away from the barrage of modern life—there are no televisions, phones, or newspapers (thankfully, they *do* have air-conditioning). Instead, you get to take a four-hour jeep tour of Cumberland Island with a naturalist guide, taking in the crocodiles, the herons, and everything in between. Afterward, enjoy the gourmet chef's selection, often focusing on local seafood combined with fresh herbs and French sauces. And don't forget the pristine beach (rated one of the ten best in the U.S.). Note, however, that they don't allow children under 6. Beach, boating, bicycles. | Box 900, Fernandina FL; you are taken to the inn by boat from Amelia Island, FL | 904/261–6408 | fax 904/321–0666 | 20 rooms | $350 | Closed Oct.–Apr. | AP | D, MC, V.

DAHLONEGA

INTRO
ATTRACTIONS
DINING
LODGING

DAHLONEGA

MAP 3, D4

(Nearby town also listed: Gainesville)

The gold that was discovered in 1828 in the region around the future town of Dahlonega spelled doom for the native Cherokee Indians who had called the area home for hundreds of years. White settlers immediately started pouring into the mountains, and the U.S. government passed legislation sending the Cherokees west of the Mississippi River. The area produced so much gold that the government had to open a mint nearby to dispose of the mineral. Today, agriculture and tourism have replaced gold as the major economic factor around Dahlonega, although the yellow stuff can still be found from time to time.

Information: Dahlonega–Lumpkin County Chamber of Commerce | 13 Park St. S., Dahlonega, GA 30533 | 706/864–3711 | www.dahlonega.org | Weekdays 9:30–5:30.

Attractions
Amicalola Falls State Park. Natural wonders at this state park center on a 729-ft waterfall, the highest in Georgia. Views of the Blue Ridge Mountains are exquisite. Nearby is the beginning point of the Appalachian National Scenic Trail at Springer Mountain (3,782 ft); you reach it by way of an 8½-mi approach trail that begins at the visitors center. The park adjoins the Chattahoochee National Forest on three sides. | 240 Amicalola Falls State Park Rd., Dawsonville | 706/265–4703 | fax 706/265–4705 | www.gastateparks.org | $2 vehicle, $20 vans, $50 bus | Daily 7–10.

Antique Rose Emporium. Alongside hundreds of more common rose varieties, there are quite a few historic strains to be found in these fragrant, outdoor gardens. | 5565 Cavender Creek Rd. | 706/864–5884 | $4 | Tues.–Fri. 9–5.

Chattahoochee National Forest. Two forests spread across the North Georgia mountains. Wissenhunt ORV Trails (an all-terrain vehicle area) is a close access point from Dahlonega, about 6 mi north off Campwahsega Rd. The Appalachian Trail starts 13 mi from Dahlonega. | Visitors Center, 400 Wal-Mart Way | 706/864–6173 | fax 706/864–6813 | www.fs.fed.us/conf | $2 | Mon.–Sat. 8–4:30, Sun. 10–4.

Appalachian National Scenic Trail. This 2,100-mi trail courses through 14 states and 7 national parks and takes about 6 months to traverse. It ends at Mount Katahdin, Maine; the approach trail begins right here at Amicalola Falls (the trailhead is at Springer Mountain, a day's hike to the north). | 240 Amicalola Falls State Park Rd. | 706/265–4703 | fax 706/265–4705 | Free | Daily.

Track Rock Gap. Hieroglyphs embedded within rock are found within the Chattahoochee National Forest. | U.S Forest Service, 1755 Cleveland Hwy., Gainesville | 770/297–3000 | fax 770/297–3011 | www.ss.fed.us/conf | Free | Daily.

Cohutta Wilderness. In the western Blue Ridge, this 60-square-mi wilderness embraces the Georgia–Tennessee border and lies within the 95,000-acre Cohutta Wildlife Management Area. Designated in 1975, it's the third largest mountain wilderness area in the East. Today it is strictly protected, and the damage done by logging and farming is slowly being repaired. Hiking trails—95 mi of them—attract the most stalwart. River crossings in bad weather can be difficult or impossible, so prepare accordingly. Camping is permitted, except at trailheads and in the trails themselves, but it's tough to find a flat spot. Horses are prohibited on some trails. | District Ranger's Office: 401 G.I. Maddox Pkwy. | 706/695–6737 | fax 706/695–1872 | www.fs.fed.us/conf | $2 vehicle | Daily.

Dahlonega Courthouse Gold Museum State Historic Site. Artifacts from the 1828 Gold Rush, America's first. The courthouse was built in 1828 of handmade brick. | Old Courthouse, center of town square | 706/864–2257 | fax 706/864–8730 | www.gastateparks.org | $2.50 | Mon.–Sat. 9–5, Sun. 10–5.

Consolidated Gold Mines. You can take a 40-minute tour of this underground mine, once the largest gold mine east of the Mississippi River. They'll also provide you with a pie tin so you can do your own panning. | 185 Consolidated Gold Mine Rd. | 706/864–8473 | fax 706/864–8367 | $10 | Daily 10–5.

Crisson Gold Mine. Go panning for your own gold and gems at this early strip mine. You can buy panning supplies, books, and gold jewelry at the gift shop. | 2736 Morrissonmore Pwky. | 706/864–6363 | fax 706/864–6363 | $2.50–9.50 gold; $4–$7 gemstones | Daily 10–6.

Gold Miners' Camp. A nature trail, gold panning, and gem grubbing are the attractions. | 15 S. Chestatee Rd. | 706/864–6373 | $2.50–$25 gold; $6 gems | May–Oct., Fri.–Sun. 9–6.

Lake Winfield Scott. This 18-acre U.S. Forest Service lake and campground has 35 campsites with hot showers (but no individual hookups), 15 day-use picnic sites, a swimming beach, and a handicapped-accessible fishing dock. There are two hiking trails, one encircling the lake and the other leading to the Appalachian Trail. Motorboats are not allowed on the lake, but canoes, kayaks, rafts, and bass-fishing boats are welcome. | Off Rte. 180 E | 706/745–6928 | fax 706/745–7494 | www.fs.fed.us/conf | $3 vehicle | Daily; facilities May–Oct.

North Georgia College and State University. Still the Military College of Georgia, this state institution offers a Corps of Cadets for all students, but it's mandatory for resident male students. They may graduate as commissioned officers. Strong fields are business, education, nursing, and criminal justice. Graduate programs are also offered in education, physical therapy, nursing, and public administration. Tours available at admissions office. | Rte. 60 | 706/864–1800 | fax 706/864–1478 | www.csu.edu | Free | Weekdays 8–5.

ON THE CALENDAR

APR.: *Gold Panning Competition.* This competition at the Consolidated Gold Mine always draws a great crowd of Dahlonegans and visitors alike. Watch or take part, as contestants try to glean eight nuggets of gold from a full pan of sand as fast as possible. Takes place the third weekend in April. | 706/864–8473 | $10.

Dining

The Fudge Factory. Café. Sit in the bay window or take your fudge right out to the town square—this fudge, with or without nuts, will keep you smiling for a long time (and you can always call and order more). | 8 N. Park St. | 706/864–2256 or 800/343–2256 | Weekdays 10–6, Sat. 10–8, Sun. 1–6 (closed Wed. Nov.–Apr.) | $8.95 | MC, V.

Renée's Café and Wine Bar. Eclectic. The setting is an old house with a lot of history dressed up to feel like a French country house. The cuisine begins with Southern-influenced dishes but takes off to Greek shrimp and Italian pasta. The restaurant is vegetarian friendly, with several excellent choices. Beer and wine only. | 135 N. Chestatee St. | 706/864–6829 | dero@alltel.net | www.dahlonega.com | Reservations not accepted | Closed Sun., Mon. No lunch | $15–$22 | MC, V.

Rick's. Contemporary. With flowers on the porch and original artwork by well-known Southern artists, this 1906 farmhouse holds a truly delightful restaurant, serving a variety of entrées from crawfish risotto cakes covered in black pepper sauce to smoked Cornish game hen with collard greens. | 47 S. Park St. | 706/864–9422 | $16 | AE, D, MC, V.

Lodging

The Black Mountain Lodge. Whether you stay in the main lodge or the deluxe log cabins, this B&B has beautiful views and lots of luxury. Each cabin or room comes with a private bath, hot tub, and private deck. | Black Mountain Lodge Dr. off Black Mountain Rd. | 800/923–5530 or 706/864–5542 | 18 rooms | $119 | AE, MC, V.

Blood Mountain Cabins. Hard by the roadside but somehow still remote in feel, this collection of cabins is perched on the side of the mountain. Simple and functional, the cabin interiors are accented by hand-hewn timbers. In-room VCRs, no room phones. | 9894 Gainesville Hwy, Blairsville | 706/745–9454 | bloodmtn@alltel.net | www.bloodmountain.com | 14 cabins | $74–$109 | AE, D, MC, V.

Blueberry Inn and Gardens. The inn crowns the crest of a low hill and takes its name from the wild blueberries that grow on its 55 acres. At the end of a busy day of touring, the rocking chairs on the porch can look truly welcoming. Gracious hosts Phyllis and Harry Charnley have made the inn reminiscent of a 1920s farmhouse. The rooms are decorated with antiques and family pieces. On the grounds are mountain laurel, oaks, and dogwoods, along with flowering plants of all kinds. No room phones, no TV in rooms, TV in common area. Pond. Hiking, fishing. | 400 Blueberry Hill | 706/219–4024 or 877/219–4024 | fax 706/219–4793 | 12 rooms | $85–$105 | MC, V.

Len Foote Hike Inn at Amicalola Falls State Park. Accessible only by a two- to four-hour hike, this inn has nothing but the Blue Ridge Mountains for miles around. Wake up and head to the Sunrise Room for a magnificent view, then enjoy the complimentary, family-style breakfast (dinner is also included). All linens are supplied, but the rooms are shared—two bunkbeds in each one. No smoking, pets, cell phones, beepers, or radios. | . Check-in at Amicalola Falls Park Visitors Center | 770/389–7275 or 800/864–7275 | 20 rooms | $89 | MC, V.

The Smith House. This is a country house with a shady front porch. The proprietors like to boast that it sits atop a rich vein of gold. The rooms upstairs are comfortable if not opulent. Conveniently located just off the town square. Restaurant, complimentary Continental breakfast. Cable TV. Pool. No smoking. | 84 South Chestatee St. | 706/867–7000 | fax 706/864–7564 | www.smithhouse.com | 16 rooms | $55–$149 | MC, V.

Worley Homestead Inn. This 1845 Victorian structure with a two-story front porch was renovated in 1984 by a descendant of the original owner, Captain William Worley of the CSA. Three of the rooms have fireplaces. | 168 Main St. W | 706/864–7002 | worleyhomestead@alltel.net | www.bbonline.com/gg/worley | 7 rooms | $95–$125 | MC, V.

DALTON

MAP 3, B3

(Nearby town also listed: Calhoun)

Dalton could well be called the carpet capital of the world, since a large portion of the world's output is produced right here. More than 100 carpet mills and outlets dot the countryside around Dalton, providing a shopper's paradise at discounted prices. Historically, the area around Dalton was home to the Cherokees, and later the young town (organized in 1837) found itself in the midst of the fierce fighting that took place in the Chattanooga–Atlanta corridor during the Civil War.

Information: Convention and Visitors Bureau | 2211 Dug Gap Battle Rd., Box 2046, Dalton, GA 30722-2046 | 706/272–7676 or 800/331–3258 | daltoncvb@alltel.net | www.daltoncvb.com | Weekdays 8:30–5.

Attractions

Fort Mountain State Park. An 855-ft-long rock wall on the mountain's highest point is the source of the park's name. Said to have been built by Native Americans as a fort against other hostile natives (or possibly as a ceremonial spot), the wall is near the Chattahoochee National Forest. The small park (3,500 acres) offers 14 mi of hiking trails (8 mi of it a strenuous backcountry trail), 15 cottages, a lake with a swimming beach, picnic tables, and shelters. | 181 Fort Mountain Park Rd., Chatsworth | 706/695–2621 | fax 706/517–3520 | www.gastateparks.org | $2 vehicle, $20 vans, $50 bus | Daily 7–10.

Hamilton House at Crown Garden and Archives. Dalton's oldest home (1840) was once used by the supervisor of the Crown Cotton Mill and is now open to the public. The Whitfield-Murray Historical Society purchased the house and uses its rooms for textile exhibitions. | 715 Chattanooga Ave. | 706/278–0217 | $3 | Tues.–Fri. by appointment.

John Ross House. This 1797 two-story log home sheltered John Ross, chief of the Cherokee Nation at the time of the Trail of Tears (1838). Restored to its original condition, it is furnished with period pieces, some of which belonged to Ross. | 826 Chickamauga Ave., Rossville | 706/861–3954 | Donations accepted | June–Aug., Thurs.–Tues. 1–4.

Prater's Mill. You can view (but not visit) an old gristmill (1855) and store, originally located on this site, as well as other historic structures moved to the property. There is much to enjoy in the surrounding grounds, with a 1-mi-long nature trail and sheltered picnic area. | 500 Praters Mill Rd. | 706/694–6455 (Prater's Mill Foundation) | fax 706/694–8413 | pratersmill@dalton.net | www.pratersmill.org | Free | Grounds: daily; buildings: only during festivals in May and Oct.

Spring Creek Preserve. A 200-acre water-quality and wildlife-habitat improvement project, sponsored and maintained by Dalton Utilities. The area was set aside to compensate for streams and wetlands that were altered or destroyed by construction of the Haig Mill reservoir. A marked 2-mi trail system runs through the property except for the wetlands themselves, although you can explore those as well. Get a brochure from the Dalton Convention and Visitors Bureau or from Dalton Utilities. | Voyles Mill Rd. | 706/278–1313 | fax 706/278–7230 | Free | Daily 9–6.

Tunnel Hill. Under restoration, the 1850 Western and Atlantic railroad tunnel is used as the site of Civil War battlefield reenactments. | Clisby Austin Rd., Tunnel Hill | 706/272–7676 or 800/331–3258 | fax 706/278–5811 | tunnlhll@catt.com | www.daltoncvb.com | Free | June–Sept., daily 8–8.

Vann House State Historic Site. Built in 1805 by Chief James Vann, of mixed Scottish and Cherokee parentage, the house exhibits an intricately carved interior. Owner of numerous slaves, Vann hired Moravian artisans to build it with slave labor. | 706/695–2598 | $2.50 | Tues.–Sat. 9–5, Sun. 2–5:30.

ON THE CALENDAR
MAY/OCT.: *Prater's Mill Country Fair.* Held twice each year on Mother's Day and Columbus Day weekends at the old water-powered mill, this country fair features mountain music, Southern food, living-history exhibits, and crafts demonstrations, including blacksmithing, weaving, quilting, rug hooking, and wood carving. | 10 mi northeast of Dalton on Hwy. 2 | 706/272–7676 or 800/331–3258.

Dining
The Cellar. Continental. An elegant, upscale place with traditional white tablecloths and candles, this is a top choice in Dalton. The menu centers on lamb, steaks, fresh fish, and veal. | 1331 W. Walnut Ave. | 706/226–6029 | Closed Sun. No lunch Sat. | $5–$45 | AE, D, DC, MC, V.

Flammini's Cafe Italia. Italian. The family is third-generation Italian from the Marches. Traditional home-style Italian-American dishes include seafood, pastas, and sometimes quail. The oversize grilled veal chop, penne with prosciutto and mushrooms in a pink sauce, and house-made sausage are specialties. Kids' menu. Beer and wine only. | 1205 W. Walnut Ave. | 706/226–0667 | Closed Sun. No lunch Tues., Wed., Sat. | $8–$16 | AE, D, DC, MC, V.

Los Reyes. Mexican. Built to resemble an authentic hacienda, this restaurant focuses on border fare: fajitas, carne asada, tacos alcarbón, steak Los Reyes, fajitas rancheras (shrimp, chicken, and beef). You can eat outdoors on a stone-floored patio. Mariachi and other live music on selected days. Kids' menu. | 817 S. Hamilton St. | 706/278–9112 | Reservations not accepted | $5–$11 | AE, D, MC, V.

Lodging
Country Hearth Inn Dalton. These well-appointed rooms have balconies from which you can see the beautiful surrounding mountains. In winter months, be sure to get hot chocolate in the Hearth Room. In-room data ports. Cable TV. | 2007 Chattanooga Rd. | 706/278–4300 | 51 rooms | $60 | AE, D, MC, V.

DARIEN

MAP 3, H10

(Nearby towns also listed: Brunswick, Jekyll Island, St. Simons Island, Sea Island)

The town of Darien dates its beginnings to 1736, when James Oglethorpe, in an attempt to protect the Altamaha River frontier, settled a group of Scots Highlanders in the area. The Scots founded their own community, named it Darien, and went on to become wealthy plantation owners. Darien became important as a major port from which rice and cotton were shipped. Lumber later replaced rice as the main export, but the shrimping industry and other forms of ocean harvesting are the major industries today.

Information: McIntosh Chamber of Commerce | Box 1497, Darien, GA 31305 | 912/437–4192 | fax 912/437–5251 | mcintosh@mcintoshcounty.com | Mon.–Sat. 9–5.

Attractions

Fort King George State Historic Site. Georgia's oldest fort was named for England's George I. The cypress blockhouse, earthen fort, and barracks were built in 1721 as the British Empire's southernmost outpost. | Fort King George Dr. | 912/437–4770 | fax 912/437–5479 | www.darientel.net/~ftkgeo | $3 | Tues.–Sat. 9–5, Sun. 2–5:30.

Sapelo Island. This barrier island has salt marshes that are home to abundant wildlife, a complex beach and dune system, and a unique African-American community, Hog Hammock, whose residents descend from slaves who first worked the island plantations. Settled first by Guale (pronounced Wale) Indians, Spanish missionaries, English pirates, and French royalists escaping the French Revolution, the island was purchased in part by Thomas Spalding in 1802. Later owned by Richard J. Reynolds, Jr., the tobacco magnate, it passed by his will to the University of Georgia for a marine research facility. Visited only by ferry and bus tours, reached at the visitors center in Meridian. | Rte. 1 | 912/437–3224 (visitors center) or 912/485–2251 (office) | fax 912/437–5526 | Free | Tues.–Fri. 7:30–5:30, Sat. 8–5:30, Sun. 1:30–5.

ON THE CALENDAR

MID-NOV.: *Drums Along the Altamaha.* Every year, for one weekend in the fall, Fort King George is the stage for battle reenactments and living-history demonstrations; you're a witness to exciting history as Britain's southernmost outpost comes under Revolutionary War American fire. | 912/437–4770 | $10.

Dining

Archie's. Southern. This no-frills establishment is famous for its perfect hush puppies and deep-fried seafood, such as catfish rolled in cornmeal. There are also grilled items, such as mahi-mahi, tuna, chicken breast along with oysters and homemade stuffed flounder. Kids' menu. Beer and wine only. | 1106 U.S. 17 Northway | 912/437–4363 | Reservations not accepted | No breakfast | $6–$19 | AE, D, DC, MC, V.

Highlander Barbeque. Barbecue. Superior Brunswick stew, homemade French fries, excellent coleslaw, plus some of the best ribs anywhere. The antique setting is pleasant. Kids' menu. BYOB. | Off Hwy. 57 at Exit 58, 3 mi on I–95, Eulonia | 912/832–4141 | Reservations not accepted | Closed Sun. | $4–$10 | AE, MC, V.

Hunter's Cafe. Seafood/Steak. The view of the water, Harris Neck, and Sapelo Island is part of the appeal, but you could come here just for the food: fresh seafood and steaks grilled over charcoal wood. Kids' menu. | At the waterfront near Eulonia, Shellman Bluff | 912/832–5771 | Closed Mon. No dinner Sun. | $5–$17 | MC, V.

Mudcat Charlie's. Southern. No frills; it's plastic forks and plates all the way. This casual popular eatery is known for local seafood, especially crab stew, fried oysters, and shrimp, plus, of course, fresh fish. Steaks, burgers, and pork chops are all good, too. Homemade peach and apple pies. | 250 Ricefield Way | 912/261–0055 | Reservations not accepted on weekends | $8–$21 | AE, D, DC, MC, V.

Lodging

Holiday Inn Express. This colonial-style Holiday Inn Express fits right into the historic buildings of Darien. Inside, you can enjoy the modern comforts of a nationwide hotel. Continental breakfast. In-room data ports, cable TV. | Exit 10 off I–95 | 912/437–5373 | $84 | AE, D, DC, MC, V.

Open Gates. Right in the center of Darien sits this comfortable white-frame Victorian house dating from 1876. Fine antiques fill the public spaces and guest rooms. Breakfast specialties include fresh fig preserves, plantation pancakes (puffed pancakes), and Hunter's casserole (a baked egg strata). Innkeeper Carolyn Hodges guides guests on tours of the Altamaha River. Complimentary breakfast. Cable TV. Pool. Some pets allowed. | 301 Franklin St. | 912/437–6985 | fax 912/437–8211 | 4 bedrooms (3 with shared bath) | $80–$90 | No credit cards.

DOUGLAS

(Nearby towns also listed: Tifton, Waycross)

Located in south-central Georgia, Douglas was organized in 1858, just three years before the Civil War began. Sometimes called the "city on the move," the town respects its past but is home to several Fortune 500 corporations.

Information: Chamber of Commerce | 211 S. Gaskin, Douglas, GA 31533 | 912/384–1873 | fax 912/383–6304 | ss@douglasga.org | www.douglasga.org | Weekdays 8–5.

Attractions

Jon's Sports Park. Batting cages, miniature golf, a driving range, go-carts, and an arcade compose this family-focused complex. There's also a snack bar. | 159 Thompson Dr. | 912/389–1250 | fax 912/389–1302 | Free; activities $3.98–$7.26 | Mon.–Thurs. 10–10, Fri.–Sat. 10–midnight, Sun. 2–10.

Lott's Country Store and Gristmill. A working gristmill, now more than 100 years old, grinds corn into grits and meal every day. Fresh products and crafts sold in the country store. There's a restaurant, too, serving country fare at lunch. | 5772 Mora Rd., Willacoochee | 912/384–6858 | Free | Mon.–Sat. 8–6.

General Coffee State Park. This popular park is named for General John Coffee, congressman, Indian fighter, and planter who fought in the War of 1812. Its 1,500 acres combine natural, recreational, and historic attributes. Part of the appeal is the wildlife, endangered plants, and agricultural history. There are four cottages, campsites, a lake, hiking, a group lodge that sleeps 32 people, picnic sites, and swimming. The perfect place to stay is the Burnham House, an elegant 19th-century cabin decorated with hand-stitched quilts and Persian rugs. | 46 John Coffee, Nicholls | 912/384–7082 | fax 912/389–1086 | www.gastateparks.org | $2 vehicle, $20 vans, $50 bus | Daily 7–10.

ON THE CALENDAR

MID-NOV.: *Pioneer Skills Day.* Nicholls Heritage Farm in General Coffee State Park exhibits cane grinding, syrup making, soap making, and home cooking. There are arts and crafts displays, a Civil War reenactment, and more music and food exhibits. | General Coffee State Park, 6 mi east of Douglas on Hwy. 32 | 912/384–7082.

Dining

Holt's Bakery and Cafe. American. The café fare focuses on fried chicken, turkey and dressing, roast beef, and fresh vegetables (sweet potato crunch is a special). Homemade donuts (chocolate and glazed), cakes, cookies, cheese crackers, and pecan divinity candy are the specialties in the bakery. You'll find potato and meringue pies, pecan pie, old-fashioned egg custard pie, and fruit pies—even the crust is homemade! Kids' menu. BYOB (call first). | 101 E. Fellers St. | 912/384–2202 | Closed Sun. No dinner | $2–$3 | AE, D, MC, V.

Pa Bill's. Barbecue. Good barbecue, potato salad, Brunswick stew, green beans, and baked beans. Home-baked pecan and coconut pie are among the desserts, as is red velvet cake. There is open-air dining at a porch table. No alcohol. | 1271 Bowen's Mill Rd. | 912/383–0642 | wendellg34@yahoo.com | Closed Sun. No dinner Wed. | $4–$11 | No credit cards.

Lodging

Jameson Inn. This Southern colonial–style inn is white with green trim, and the rooms are all spacious, two-room suites with well-stocked minirefrigerators. The fitness center is quite modern. Pool. Gym. Laundry services. | 1628 S. Peterson Ave. | 800/JAMESON | fax 706/629–7985 | 47 rooms | $59 | AE, D, DC, MC, V.

DUBLIN

(Nearby town also listed: Vidalia)

Dublin brings a bit of Ireland to Georgia with its elaborate, annual St. Patrick's Festival. On land once revered by Creek Indians, the progressive town today is best known for the production of textiles, missile-control and computer components, and agricultural produce. Dublin was the site of the nation's first aluminum extrusion plant.

Information: Dublin-Laurens County Chamber of Commerce | 1200 Bellevue, Dublin, GA 31021 | 912/272–5546 | fax 912/275–0811 | dublin1@accucomm.net | Weekdays 8:30–5.

Attractions

Dublin-Laurens Museum. Exhibits highlight Native American settlements in the area, 19th-century plantations and farmsteads, churches, and other sights in the region. The collection includes art by local artists. | 311 Academy Ave. | 912/272–9242 | history@nlamerica.com | Free | Tues.–Fri. 1–4:30, and by appointment.

Fish Trap Cut. On the Oconee River, the fish trap was formed when, over the course of time, an island in the river blended in with the riverbank. Its historical significance comes from the two Indian mounds—one of which is 7 ft tall and 300 ft at its base—that date back to the 13th century. On the National Register of Historic Places, Fish Trap Cut includes the remains of an Indian village that goes back about 2,200 years. Some scholars think it may be the oldest Woodland Period village in Georgia. | Oconee River, Rte. 19 | Free | Daily.

Historic buildings. Dublin was founded in 1807, and some of the commercial buildings in its downtown area are about 100 years old. Also of interest is the restored Theatre Dublin (1934). The local museum is in a former Carnegie library, built in the early 20th century. Ongoing renovation and upgrading of streetscapes and lighting began in 1999. | Downtown: Main St., Bellevue Ave., Veterans Blvd. | Free | Daily.

Revolutionary War Cemetery. Next to the United Methodist Church on the main square, this cemetery has weathered gravestones dating back to the early 17th century alongside those of many Revolutionary War soldiers. | Main St. | Free.

ON THE CALENDAR

MAR.: *St. Patrick's Festival.* A parade, golf tournaments, square dancing, a ball, and an arts and crafts show are among the features of this elaborate festival held in downtown Dublin. | 1200 Bellevue Ave. | 912/272–5546 | fax 912/275–0811 | Weekdays 8:30–5.
SEPT.: *Possum Hollow Arts and Crafts Fair.* The Dublin area arts and crafts fair has a great mix of mountain and Irish music, along with a grits cook-off during the last weekend of the month. | 12 mi outside Dublin on Hwy. 257 | 912/272–5546.

Dining

Ma Hawkins. Southern. Classic country fare with dishes that reflect rural tradition. Pork neckbones, an occasional specialty, illustrate the point. Everything, including very good cornbread, is homemade; strong, flavorful coffee. Breakfast also available. No alcohol. | 126 W. Jackson St. | 912/272–0941 | Reservations not accepted | Closed Sun. | $5–$7 | MC, V.

Lodging

Best Western Executive Suites Hotel. Within walking distance of the center of town and 10 minutes from antique and craft shopping and the two area hospitals. This is the only Dublin hotel with a fitness facility; it also has meeting rooms for up to 200. Pool. Gym. Business services. Laundry facilities. | 2121 Hwy. 441S | 478/275–2650 | 88 rooms | $69 | AE, D, DC, MC, V.

When it Comes to Getting Cash at an ATM,

Same Thing.

Whether you're in Yosemite or Yemen, using your Visa® card or ATM card with the PLUS symbol is the easiest and most convenient way to get cash. Even if your bank is in Minneapolis and you're in Miami, Visa/PLUS ATMs make getting cash so easy, you'll feel right at home. After all, Visa/PLUS ATMs are open 24 hours a day, 7 days a week, rain or shine. And if you need help finding one of Visa's 627,000 ATMs in 127 countries worldwide, visit **visa.com/pd/atm**. We'll make finding an ATM as easy as finding the Eiffel Tower, the Pyramids or even the Grand Canyon.

It's Everywhere You Want To Be.®

Holiday Inn. This typical chain hotel underwent major renovations in early 2000. The rooms are those familiar from chain hotels, with a writing desk in every one. Restaurant, bar (with entertainment), complimentary breakfast, room service. In-room data ports. Cable TV. Pool. Exercise equipment. Business services, free parking. Some pets allowed. | 2190 U.S. 441S | 912/272–7862 or 800/465–4329 | fax 912/272–1077 | dbnga@n1america.com | 124 rooms | $64–$79. | AE, D, DC, MC, V.

The Page House B&B. This fully restored Greek-revival residence (1900) has been filled with antiques, and there's a large ballroom for receptions and parties. A private library holds books, films, and a large-screen TV. Complimentary breakfast. Cable TV. Library. | 711 Bellevue Ave. | 912/275–4551 | fax 912/275–4551 | pagehous@accucomm.net | www.pagehousebb.com | 6 rooms | $90–$120 | AE, MC, V.

EATONTON

(Nearby towns also listed: Madison, Milledgeville)

Eatonton's most famous son was Joel Chandler Harris, creator of the Uncle Remus stories that were so popular a couple of generations ago. Alice Walker, author of *The Color Purple*, also calls the town home. Located at the center of a region known for its plantation culture, cotton growing, and typical Deep South life-style, Eatonton currently produces more dairy products than any other town in Georgia.

Information: Eatonton-Putnam Chamber of Commerce | 105 Sumter St., Eatonton, GA 31024 | 706/485–7701 | fax 706/485–3277 | epchamber@eatonton.com | www.eatonton.com | Weekdays 8:30–4:30.

Attractions

Alice Walker: A Driving Tour. This driving tour deals with the birthplace and private home of Eatonton native Alice Walker, author of *The Color Purple* and *The Temple of My Familiar*. Pick up a tour map at the Chamber of Commerce. | 105 Sumter St. | 706/485–7701 | fax 706/485–3277 | epchamber@eatonton.com | www.eatonton.com | Free | Weekdays 8:30–4:30.

Antebellum Trail Self-Guided Tour. All of downtown Eatonton is a National Register Historic District. You can pick up a tour map at the Chamber of Commerce with a list of the restored classical-revival homes in the area. | 105 Sumter St. | 706/485–7701 | fax 706/485–3277 | epchamber@eatonton.com | www.eatonton.com | Free | Weekdays 8:30–4:30.

Lake Oconee. Formed in 1979 and owned by Georgia Power Company, the lake offers three parks with campsites, beaches, and pavilions. Camping, boating, fishing, and swimming are the popular activities. Three golf resorts, two of them public, border the lake. | Rte. 44 | 706/467–2850 | www.georgiapower.com/gpclake | $2 vehicle | Sun.–Thurs. 7–9, Fri., Sat. 7–10; Camping and beaches May–Labor Day, daily.

Oconee National Forest. Covering more than 115,000 acres, this national forest is a hiker's paradise. There are also trails for horseback riding, and Lake Sinclair is popular for fishing, swimming, and boating. | Ranger District: 1199 Madison Rd. | 706/485–3180 | fax 706/485–7141 | www.fs.fed.us | Free | Daily.

Rock Eagle 4-H Center and Rock Eagle Effigy. Adjacent to the Oconee National Forest, the facility's eight conference buildings, auditorium, natural history museum, two open-air pavilions, and a chapel of natural stone are popular for meetings. There are 54 cottages for groups only. The Rock Eagle prehistoric effigy is shaped like a bird, with its head turned east and its wings outspread. It is made of milky quartz rocks, ranging from baseball size to boulders. | 350 Rock Eagle Rd. | 706/484–2831 | fax 706/484–2888 | Free | Daily dawn to dusk.

Uncle Remus Museum. Two log cabins hold shadow boxes, wood carvings of the Br'er Rabbit critters made famous by Joel Chandler Harris, and implements from the early 1800s. | U.S. 441 S. | 706/485–6856 | $.50 | June–Aug., Mon.–Sat. 10–5, Sun. 1–5; Sept.–May, Mon., Wed.–Sat. 10–5, Sun. 1–5.

ON THE CALENDAR
APR.: *Easter with Br'er Rabbit.* A number of Southern storytellers visit the Uncle Remus Museum every Easter Sunday for a retelling of the Br'er Rabbit stories by Joel Chandler Harris. | 706/485–6856.

Dining
Magnolia House. Southern. A restored 1850 farmhouse is the setting for updated regional fare, with such dishes as Vidalia onion–stuffed pork chops and, in season, fresh-peach fried pie for dessert. After dinner, enjoy the upstairs club/game room for a round of backgammon and perhaps a cigar or a postprandial drink in the downstairs tavern. Kids' menu, earlybird suppers Fri. and Sat. | 1130 Greensboro Rd. | 706/484–1833 | Reservations essential | Closed Sun. | $10–$25 | AE, D, DC, MC, V.

Paradise Country Barbecue. Barbecue. A family affair with the feel of a café, Paradise does delicious slow-smoked ribs and very good Brunswick stew. Watch for the pies, which are excellent. No alcohol. | 764 Milledgeville Rd. | 706/484–0037 | Reservations not accepted | Closed Sun.–Wed. | $5–$8 | No credit cards.

Lodging
The Crockett House B&B. This romantic, 1896 B&B has 100-year-old weeping willows and magnolias right beside the wraparound porch. In winter, it's a special treat to take a bath in your own claw-footed tub right by a fire in the fireplace. In the spring or fall, you can go on a nature outing with a picnic basket, quilt, and a book recommended by Christa or Peter Crockett. | 671 Madison Rd. | 706/485–2248 | 6 rooms | $89 | AE, MC, V.

ELLIJAY

MAP3, C3

(Nearby town also listed: Dalton)

Ellijay is situated in the beautiful North Georgia mountain country at the gateway to the Chattahoochee National Forest (see Gainesville). Originally Cherokee Indian land, the region around Ellijay produces some of the best apples anywhere, earning the town the nickname "Apple Capital of Georgia."

Information: Gilmer County Chamber of Commerce | 368 Craig St., East Ellijay, GA 30539 | 706/635–7400 | fax 706/635–7410 | chamber@ellijay.com | www.gilmerchamber.com | Weekdays 9–5, Sat. 10–3.

Attractions
Apple Alley. Visit apple-producing houses and watch the packing process, or maybe in season pick your own. Some orchards will let you ride the tractors, and one has a petting zoo. Some sell cider, apple bread, other apple products, and even fresh peach ice cream. Get a taped driving tour from the Chamber of Commerce. | 205 Craig St., East Ellijay | 706/635–7400 | fax 706/635–7410 | chamber@ellijay.com | gilmerchamber.com | Free | Daily; Chamber of Commerce weekdays 9–5.

Blue Ridge Scenic Railway. All aboard a century-old train for a 26-mi, 3-hour round trip along the Toccoa River to McCaysville, stopping about 45 minutes to visit this Tennessee/Georgia border town. Special packages include the Ocoee Rail Adventure, a com-

KODAK'S TIPS FOR TAKING GREAT PICTURES

Get Closer
- Fill the frame tightly for maximum impact
- Move closer physically or use a long lens
- Continually check the viewfinder for wasted space

Choosing a Format
- Add variety by mixing horizontal and vertical shots
- Choose the format that gives the subject greatest drama

The Rule of Thirds
- Mentally divide the frame into vertical and horizontal thirds
- Place important subjects at thirds' intersections
- Use thirds' divisions to place the horizon

Lines
- Take time to notice lines
- Let lines lead the eye to a main subject
- Use the shape of lines to establish mood

Taking Pictures Through Frames
- Use foreground frames to draw attention to a subject
- Look for frames that complement the subject
- Expose for the subject, and let the frame go dark

Patterns
- Find patterns in repeated shapes, colors, and lines
- Try close-ups or overviews
- Isolate patterns for maximum impact (use a telephoto lens)

Textures that Touch the Eyes
- Exploit the tangible qualities of subjects
- Use oblique lighting to heighten surface textures
- Compare a variety of textures within a shot

Dramatic Angles
- Try dramatic angles to make ordinary subjects exciting
- Use high angles to help organize chaos and uncover patterns, and low angles to exaggerate height

Silhouettes
- Silhouette bold shapes against bright backgrounds
- Meter and expose for the background illumination
- Don't let conflicting shapes converge

Abstract Composition
- Don't restrict yourself to realistic renderings
- Look for ideas in reflections, shapes, and colors
- Keep designs simple

Establishing Size
- Include objects of known size
- Use people for scale, where possible
- Experiment with false or misleading scale

Color
- Accentuate mood through color
- Highlight subjects or create designs through color contrasts
- Study the effects of weather and lighting

From *Kodak Guide to Shooting Great Travel Pictures* © 2000 by Fodor's Travel Publications

bination train ride and river-rafting trip. The trains depart from Blue Ridge. | 241 Depot St., Blue Ridge | 706/632–9833 or 800/934–1898 | fax 706/258–2756 | www.brscenic.com | $23 | Apr.–Nov., Fri., Sat. 10 AM and 2 PM, Sun. 2 PM.

Carters Lake. Begun in 1962 and completed in 1976, the lake was made by the tallest earthen dam east of the Mississippi River (450 feet). It comprises 3,200 surface acres and 62 mi of natural, undeveloped shoreline. The recreational facilities offer hiking trails, mountain-bike trails, fishing areas, and campgrounds that range from the primitive to the electric, with laundry and water hookups. There are also day-use facilities, game courts, boat-launching ramps, and hunting. | 1850 Carters Dam Rd., Chatsworth | 706/334–2248 | fax 706/334–2213 | www.sam.usace.army.mil/sam/op/rec/carters | Free | Apr.–Oct. daily.

ON THE CALENDAR
MID-SEPT.: *Apple Pickin' Jubilee at Hillcrest Orchards.* Pick your own apples, milk a cow, visit the petting farm, take a wagon ride, or just enjoy being in this beautiful countryside, eating delicious food and listening to great music. | 9 mi east of Ellijay on Hwy. 52 | 706/273–3838 | 9–dusk.

Dining
Holloway's Pink Pig. Barbecue. The memorabilia focus on photographs of Democratic Party luminaries from across the state and the nation. For more than 30 years, Bud Holloway has been making everything from scratch, including the fries. Good ribs and chops, an excellent barbecue sauce, and other menu items (the garlic Caesar salad, for instance) make this spot popular. No alcohol. | Old Hwy 5 off Rte. 515 N., Cherry Log | 706/276–3311 | Reservations not accepted | Closed Mon.–Wed. | $1–$15 | No credit cards.

Poole's. Barbecue. Poole is a retired preacher, but you may hear him called "Colonel" (the rank is honorary, from Kentucky). His popular mountain barbecue restaurant stands in front of a hillside covered in pig icons; inside it's decorated with signed photographs of local, state, and national Republican luminaries. Ribs and chopped pork with house-made barbecue sauce are the draws. Excellent coleslaw. Kids' menu. | 164 Craig St., E. Ellijay | 706/635–4100 | www.poolesbarbq.com | Reservations not accepted | Closed Mon.–Wed. | $5–$7 | AE, D, MC, V.

Toccoa Riverside Restaurant and General Store. Seafood. It really is by the side of a river; in fact, it's perched over the Toccoa. The trout, broiled or fried, is what most people come for. Also popular are the pasta, steak, prime rib, barbecued ribs, catfish, shrimp, and smoked trout. BYOB. | 8055 Aska Rd., Blue Ridge | 706/632–7891 | Closed Mon., Tues. | $9–$15 | AE, MC, V.

Lodging
Hearthstone Hall. Aptly named, this B&B has a stunning, massive stone fireplace upstairs, and yet the large windows keep the authentic mountain log house from feeling too dark. From the wood floors to the exposed beams of the Great Room, the Hearthstone has a peaceful, private feel while still only minutes away from the center of Ellijay. Cable TV. | 2755 Hwy. 282 | 706/695–6515 | 5 rooms | $85 | MC, V.

GAINESVILLE

MAP 3, D4

(Nearby town also listed: Dahlonega)

Located in the northeastern part of Georgia and situated on the beautiful 38,000-acre Lake Sidney Lanier, Gainesville is a poultry-producing center and headquarters for the Chattahoochee National Forest. Lanier, one of Georgia's most famous poets, was born in Macon and educated at Oglethorpe University.

Information: Gainesville/Hall County Convention and Visitors Bureau | 17 Jesse Jewell Pwky., Gainesville, GA 30501 | 770/536–5209 | fax 770/503–1349 | ghcvb@bellsouth.net | Weekdays 8:30–5.

Attractions

Brenau University. Founded in 1878 as the Georgia Baptist Female Seminary, the school was renamed Brenau in 1990. This coined word, joining the German word *brennan* (to burn) and the Latin word *aurum* (gold), gives the school its motto, "as gold refined by fire." Redesignated Brenau University in the fall of 1992, this unique private institution retains its four-year liberal arts women's college within the university. Also part of the campus is Brenau Academy, a residential secondary school for young women. Another unit is an evening and weekend college, catering to nontraditional students. Graduate programs are offered in education, business, nursing, and occupational therapy. Important international art exhibitions find good venues in several of the college's galleries. | 1 Centennial Circle | 770/534–6169 | fax 770/538–4300 | www.brenau.edu | Free | Weekdays 8:30–5.

Bete Todd Wages' Princess Luci Shirazi Collection. Brenau University holds this extensive collection of antique clothing, chiefly Victorian and Edwardian. Represented are some of the major New York designers of the 1940s to the 1960s. | 406 Academy St. | 770/534–6252 | $2 (suggested) | Weekends 1–5 and by appointment.

Green Street Fire Station. The old firehouse houses the Georgia Mountain History Museum of Brenau University. The collection of Ed Dodd, who did the "Mark Trail" comic strip, includes such material as woven catfish traps. The permanent collection includes work by self-taught and trained artists of the North Georgia mountains. Two real moonshine stills, donated by the Georgia Bureau of Investigation, are part of the exhibition. Chief Whitepath's cabin, originally in Ellijay, is on campus. Whitepath, who had taken the Cherokees' case against removal to the U.S. Supreme Court, died on the Trail of Tears. | 311 Green St., SE | 770/536–0889 | fax 770/534–9488 | $2 | Tues.–Fri. 10–5.

Chattahoochee National Forest. This two-part, 1-million-acre forest offers more than 500 mi of trails, for which guides are available at National Forests visitors centers. The facilities include campsites, boat ramps, and picnic shelters scattered about the forest. | 1755 Cleveland Hwy., Gainesville | 770/297–3000 | fax 770/297–3011 | www.fs.fed.us/conf | $2 vehicle.

Green Street Historical District. Gainesville's main thoroughfare is lined with vintage early 20th-century homes, ranging in style from neoclassical revival to Queen Anne Victorian and Tudor revival. | Green St. | Free | Daily.

Lake Lanier Islands. This resort on manmade Lake Lanier offers recreation and accommodations ranging from the organized and luxurious to the simple and basic. The Emerald Pointe Golf Course, Hilton, campgrounds, hiking, horseback riding, and fishing on the 38,000-acre lake are among the attractions. The resort is geared to both family and romantic getaway vacations. | 7000 Holiday Rd., Lake Lanier Islands Buford | 770/932–7200 | fax 770/614–5604 | www.lakelanierislands.com | $6 vehicle | Daily.

Lanier Point Softball Complex. Four adult softball fields, one high school regulated baseball field, picnic tables, and a boat ramp complete this unique facility on the edge of Lake Lanier. | 1530 Lee Waldrip | 770/287–0208 | fax 770/287–3139 | www.gainesville.org | Prices vary, some are free | Daily 8–11.

Main Street Museum. Memorabilia and photographs display the history of this important transportation and cotton-shipping town. | 37 E. Main St., Buford | 770/945–1660 | Free | Weekdays 11–5, Sat. 10:30–4:30.

Parks. Gainesville's urban park corridor includes Ivey Terrace, Wilshire Trails, and Longwood Park. **Ivey Terrace** is the oldest of these parks, some of it created by the Civilian Conservation Corps in the late 1930s. **Wilshire Trails** is a long, open park designed for walkers and joggers; it traverses a wooded area evocative of mountain terrain. A road separates it from **Longwood Park,** which sits on Lake Lanier. It has tennis courts, pavilions, and benches facing the lake. **Rock Creek** is a small creek that starts in Ivey Terrace and winds through the parks to Lake Lanier. | 770/536–1131 | fax 770/536–0144 | Free for all parks listed above | Daily dawn to dusk.

Railroad Museum. Three vintage 20th-century railroad cars—a caboose, an engine, and a baggage car—are set up in a downtown city park. You can't get into them, but they're fun to look at. | W. Academy St. | Free | Daily.

ON THE CALENDAR

MID-AUG.: *National Canoe and Kayak Championships.* Five miles outside Gainesville is magnificent Lake Lanier, where several watersport events were held for the 1996 Summer Olympics. The canoe and kayak courses are still maintained, and the national championship races have been held here every year since the Olympics. | 770/297–1141.

Dining

Breezes. Contemporary. The booths and tables are arranged around a curved space looking out onto Lake Lanier. Corn/crab meat chowder, smoked chicken quesadillas with fresh salsa, smoked salmon with leek and potato pancake are just a sampler. The vegetarian Natural Balance menu skimps on fat and calories, but not on flavor: try the four-onion risotto with red wine-black olive sauce. Live music nightly. | 9000 Holiday Rd., Lake Lanier Islands | 770/945–8921 | paulbrown195@yahoo.com | $16–$28 | AE, D, DC, MC, V.

Luna's. Caribbean. Owner Juan Luna, from the Dominican Republic, will dish up paella without advance notice. Macadamia-crusted snapper with mashed redskin potatoes, pasta Luna (spinach fettucine with shrimp in cream sauce), black bean soup, and lamb chops are terrific. In the dessert department there's Chocolate Divine. | Hunt Tower, 200 Main St. | 770/531–0848 | Closed Sun. No lunch Sat. | $12–$20 | AE, D, DC, MC, V.

Major McGill's Fish House. Seafood. Straightforward fare served in a rambling Victorian cottage known for walleye (or yellow) pike, one of several "when available" entrées, and North Georgia trout served any number of ways. Especially good is the smoked trout pâté. | 5603 Main St., Flowery Branch | 770/967–6001 | Closed Sun., Mon. | $16–$45 | AE, D, DC, MC, V.

Rudolph's. Contemporary. This popular standby, ensconced in a fine early 20th-century house, teams contemporary cuisine with regional specialties. A lunch sandwich puts fried green tomatoes and a smoked salmon BLT on crusty Portuguese bread. With the Jack Daniel's pork chop come mashed potatoes, thin beans, and a portobello tomato chowder. And how 'bout this? S'mores crème brûlée, complete with grahams, milk chocolate, and the requisite toasted marshmallows. | 700 Green St. | 770/534–2226 | Closed Sun. No lunch Mon., Sat. | $17–$19 | AE, D, DC, MC, V.

Lodging

Dunlap House. Built in 1910, this 10-room B&B has a large, welcoming front porch shaded by a tasteful green-and-white awning. Renovated in 1985, the inn has many modern conveniences and is furnished with traditional pieces. Complimentary breakfast. In-room data ports. Business services. No smoking. | 635 Green St. | 770/536–0200 | fax 770/503–7857 | dunlaphouse@mindspring.com | www.dunlaphouse.com | 10 rooms | $85–$155 | AE, DC, MC, V.

Hilton Lake Lanier Island Resort. Built on a 1,100-acre island in the middle of Lake Lanier, this Hilton has beautiful contemporary rooms with wood accents and offers a fine restaurant as well as a poolside bar and grill. The Emerald Points Golf Center and Lake Lanier Equestrian Center are also on the island. 2 restaurants, bar. In-room data ports. Cable TV. Pool. Spa. Gym. Laundry service. | 7000 Holiday Rd. | 770/945–8787 | 216 rooms | $199 | AE, D, DC, MC, V.

Tate House. Built in 1925 of locally quarried pink marble, this mansion has five suites within the main building and a clutch of log cabins out back, each equipped with a fireplace. Some in-room hot tubs (in cabins). | Rte. 53E, Tate | 770/735–3122 | fax 770/735–4730 | tatehouse@mindspring.com | www.tatehouse.com | 5 suites, 9 cabins | $131 suites, $110 cabins | MC, V.

HELEN

(Nearby town also listed: Toccoa)

The quaint town of Helen is located in the North Georgia mountains, and the place is so much like Germany you will swear that you are in Bavaria. Originally a logging town, Helen's economy today is centered around tourism. There is even an Oktoberfest to add to the charm of the Germanic surroundings. Museums, waterfalls, mountains, and cool climate all combine to make the area around one of the finest vacation destinations in the state.

Information: Alpine Helen/White County Convention and Visitors Bureau | P.O. Box 730, Helen, GA 30545 | 706/878–2747 or 800/858–8027. 706/878–2747 or 800/858–8027; | fax 706/878–4032 | maryann@helenga.org | www.helenga.org | Mon.–Sat. 9–5, Sun. 11–4.

Attractions

Anna Ruby Falls–CNF. A half mile trail leads to twin waterfalls measuring 115 ft. The 15-mi Lion's Eye Trail is designed for visually and physically challenged hikers. The falls are near Unicoi State Park | 3453 Anna Ruby Falls | 706/878–3595 | www.fs.fed.us/conf/ | Free; parking $2 vehicle, $20 van, $50 bus | Daily.

Babyland General Hospital/Cabbage Patch Kids. Witness the delivery of a Cabbage Patch kid. LPNs (Licensed Patch Nurses) assist Mother Cabbage in labor. Fathers may wait in a waiting room. There's an adoption process to be followed whenever someone adopts a Cabbage Patch Kid. | 19 Underwood St., Cleveland | 706/865–2171 | fax 706/865–5980 | www.cabbagepatchkids.com | Free | Mon.–Sat. 9–5, Sun. 10–5.

Dukes Creek Recreation Area–CNF. The spectacular 300-ft falls cascade into a scenic gorge and can be viewed from several observation points along a 1-mi trail. | Rte. 348 | 706/878–3087 | www.fs.fed.us/conf | Free; parking $2 | Daily.

Habersham Vineyards and Winery. There's a tasting room, gift shop, and a setup allowing visitors to view the winery operation. All of the wines are produced from Georgia-grown grapes. Pay special attention to a Seyval/Vidal blend called Signet, as well as the 1997 Chardonnay and Cabernet Sauvignon. There is also an excellent Chambourcin dessert wine. If you want to taste a Muscadine, make it this one. | 7025 S. Main St. | 706/878–9463 or 770/983–1973 | fax 706/878–8466 | www.habershamwinery.com | Free | Daily.

Mt. Yonah. This mountain's odd shape is due to its composition as a granite gneiss monolith. "Yonah" means bear in Cherokee, and from nearby Blood Mountain, Yonah does indeed look like a bear's head. It's a favorite spot for rock climbers, including U.S. Army Rangers, who repel its sheer cliffs. In recent years, access to the mountain has been restricted, as the existing road was closed by private landowners; however, the U.S. Forest Service has purchased land and is undertaking an environmental assessment to contruct access to the mountain. | Rte. 75 | 770/297–3000 or 706/754–6221 | fax 770/536–0544 | Free | Daily.

Museum of the Hills and Fantasy Kingdom. This wax museum depicts storybook characters set in rural Helen and the region at the turn of the century. More than 6,000 sq ft of exhibitions may be visited on a self-guided tour. | 8590-A Main St. | 706/878–3140 | fax 706/878–2470 | $5; special rates for seniors, students, and children | Jan.–Mar., daily 10–7:30; Apr.–Dec., daily 10–9.

Richard B. Russell Scenic Highway. Named for the late, long-serving U.S senator from Georgia, this 14-mi segment of Rte. 348 between Rte. 75A and Rte. 180 cuts across the main range of the Blue Ridge Mountains and through the Chattahoochee National Forest. At Hog Pen Gap, it crosses the Appalachian Trail. Parking areas, trails, and scenic over-

HELEN

INTRO
ATTRACTIONS
DINING
LODGING

looks invite dawdling. The road was built between 1962 and 1968 and follows early logging roads. | Free | Daily.

Sautee-Nacoochee Indian Mound. Said (apocryphally) to be the final resting place of two tragic lovers from different and warring Native-American tribes, the mound dates from 10,000 BC according to the artifacts found within it. | Intersection of Rtes. 17 and 75 | Free | Daily.

Smithgall Woods-Duke Creek Conservation Area. More than 5,000 acres of trout streams, along with hiking and biking trails, in exquisite woods, especially breathtaking in fall, make this a special place. You must check in at the visitor's center before entering the property. | 61 Tsalaki Trail | 706/878–3087 | fax 706/878–0301 | sgwoods@stc.net | $2; free Wed. | Mon.–Tues., Thurs.–Fri. 7–6, Wed., Sat., Sun. 6:30–8.

Stovall Mill Covered Bridge. Spanning Chickamauga Creek, Georgia's shortest (37 ft) clean-span covered bridge was built around 1895 according to a single-span King-post design. The bridge was seen in the film *I'd Climb the Highest Mountain.* Closed to traffic, and now restored, this is a good picnic spot. | Rte. 255 | 706/878–2181 | fax 706/878–4032 | www.helenga.org | Free | Daily.

Unicoi State Park. This popular state park, with more than 1,000 acres, offers a lodge, tent, trailer and RV sites, plus 30 cottages and a 53-acre lake and beach. Hike scenic trails, picnic on well-maintained grounds, enjoy swimming, fishing, or mountain biking. The craft shop specializes in handmade quilts. | Rte. 356, 4 mi from Helen | 706/878–2201 | fax 706/878–1897 | www.gastateparks.org | $2 vehicle, $20 van, $50 bus | Daily 7–10.

ON THE CALENDAR

OCT.: *Oktoberfest.* This annual event draws large crowds and offers live performances. | 706/878–2181.

Dining

Bernie's at Nacoochee Valley Guest House. Continental. This quaint mountain retreat serves the classics: Fench onion soup, chicken Florentine, duck with orange/raspberry sauce; Coquilles St. Jaques; and Beef Wellington. Your meal will be served with silver and crystal tableware on lace tablecloths. No alcohol. | 2220 Rte. 17, P.O. Box 249, Sautee Nacoochee | 706/878–3830 | fax 706/878–3843 | www.georgiamagazine.com/nvgh | Reservations advised | Closed Tues. No lunch | $14–$20 | No credit cards.

Stovall House. Contemporary. Stuffed breast of chicken, whole trout stuffed with crab meat, and apple praline pie for dessert are among the hallmarks of the quite good food at this Victorian mountain bed-and-breakfast inn. | 1526 Rte. 255 N, Sautee Nacoochee | Reservations essential | 706/878–3355 | www.georgiamagazine.com/stovall | No dinner Mon.–Wed. | $9–$15 | AE, MC, V.

Lodging

Chattahoochee Riverfront Motel. Just up the road from downtown, this low-slung motel is perched on the banks of the shallow Chattahoochee. Alpine Helen is but a short walk away, but this place is a far remove from the hubbub. Pool. | N. Main St. | 706/878–2184 | fax 706/878–1882 | chattmtl@alltel.net | 35 rooms | $65–$70 | Mon.–Sun. 7:30–11 | AE, D, DC, MC, V.

Dutch Cottage. An ivy-covered hillside and tranquil waterfall provide a beautiful setting for this B&B. Each room has a brass bed, Victorian antiques, lace curtains over the door to the central balcony, with views of the forest just beyond. There is a hot tub up the hill, as well as a honeymoon chalet by a stream, with a large fireplace. In-room cable TV, VCRs. | 114 Ridge Rd. | 706/878–3135 | 6 rooms | $99 | MC, V.

HIAWASSEE

(Nearby town also listed: Helen)

If the town of Helen is German-inspired, then its neighbor, Hiawassee, derives its flavor from Switzerland. Providing a gorgeous backdrop to the village are the beautiful Southern Appalachian mountains, capped by Brasstown Bald Mountain, the highest peak (4,784 ft) in Georgia. The Georgia Mountain Fair, held for 12 days every August, brings in folks from miles around to view the artifacts and to participate in the fun of a bygone age.

Information: Towns County Chamber of Commerce. | 1411 Fuller Circle, Young Harris, GA 30582 | 706/896–4966 | fax 706/896–5441 | towncoc@whitelion.net | www.towns-county-chamber.org | Weekdays 9–5, Sat. 10–2.

Attractions

Blood Mountain. This peak on Georgia's section of the Appalachian Trail tops out at about 4,460 ft. Legend says the name comes from bloody battle between the Creek and Cherokee Indians, but other theories reference the color of local flora. For information, contact the Walasi-Yi Interpretive Center, which sits at the base of the mountain. | U.S. 19/129, Blairsville | 706/745–6095 | fax 706/745–8651 | Free | Daily.

Brasstown Bald Mountain. This mountain goes 4,748 ft into the sky. Climb to the top or ride up and walk back down. The views are worth the trouble. | Rte. 180, Blairville | 706/896–2556 or 706/745–6928 (Chamber of Commerce) | Free; $2 round-trip shuttle to top | Daily; shuttle and information center: June–Oct., daily 10–6; late Apr.–May, weekends 10–5.

Fred Hamilton Rhododendron Garden. Planted along a mile-long, pine-bark trail running along Lake Chatuge, more than 3,000 plants bloom from early Apr. to late May. | U.S. 76 W | 706/896–4191 | fax 706/896–4209 | www.georgia-mountain-fair.com | Free | Daily 8–7.

Lake Chatuge. This 7,000-acre TVA reservoir spanning two states (Georgia and North Carolina) offers many recreational facilities, including numerous hiking trails in Chattahoochee and Nantahala National Forests, which flank the lake. Campsites, boating, picnic grounds, and fishing are among the facilities and attractions. | Rte. 288 | 706/745–6928 or 706/745–6928 | fax 706/896–2914 | www.fs.fed.us/conf | Free | Daily; camping May–Oct.

Vogel State Park. With 23 acres, this park sits at nearly 2,500 ft above sea level. Popular with urban folks seeking to escape summer's heat, its 35 cabins and 110 campsites, with power and water, fill quickly. The 12½-mi backcountry trail is pretty strenuous. | U.S. 19/129 | 706/745–2628 | fax 706/745–3139 | www.gastateparks.org | $2 vehicle, $20 van, $50 bus | Daily.

Walasi-Yi Interpretive Center. Built of native stone between 1934 and 1938, the center is listed on the National Register. The Appalachian Trail goes through its breezeway, the only spot where the trail intersects with a manmade structure. The store here is well-equipped with books, equipment, clothing, and all manner of camping gear. The trail up Blood Mountain starts across the road. | U.S. 19/129, Blairsville | 706/745–6095 | fax 706/745–8651 | www.synnergy.com/mtncross/index.htm | Free | Daily.

ON THE CALENDAR

AUG.: *Georgia Mountain Fair.* This festival brings together a wide array of country and gospel music, arts and crafts, fine food, clogging contests, and lots of entertainment. | 706/896–4191 | fax 706/896–4209 | www.georgia-mountain-fair.com.
EARLY OCT.: *Indian Summer Festival.* Among the many festivities in nearby Suches (or "Valley of the Clouds") is a play performed by the students of Woody Gap Elementary;

there is also an Irish clogging demonstration, mountain music, an auction, a 10-K race, and to top it all off square dancing in the evening. | 11 mi north of Hiawassee on Hwy.60 | 706/747–2401.

Dining

Dream Catchers. Contemporary. This tiny restaurant does a limited, but excellent, menu. Special dietary needs can be met with advance notice. Two entrees are featured each week, chicken, fish, or beef. Everything is made in-house, including the breads. No alcohol. | 568 Kanuga St. | 706/896–7023 | Reservations essential | Closed Mon.–Wed. No lunch | $16–$17 | AE, D, MC, V.

© Corbis

TOURING THE GOLDEN ISLES

One of Georgia's most popular travel destinations—and an absolute must-see for anyone touring the state for the first time—is the string of lovely offshore islands known as the Golden Isles. Situated between Savannah and the Florida border, these barrier islands have become a primary tourist attraction for the state, and several of them offer a variety of lodging, dining, and camping accommodations, ranging from simple, inexpensive motels to those on Sea Island, which rival the best hotels in the world.

A good place to start the tour is Savannah. After you've savored the flavor of this busy, historic seaport city and wined and dined in its fabulous restaurants, you should take in nearby Fort Pulaski and Tybee Island. Fort Pulaski protected Savannah Harbor during the Civil War, but when the Union army overwhelmed it with newly designed rifled artillery, it became a casualty. Coastal artillery emplacements can still be seen on Tybee Island, where a World War I post once thrived.

Heading south from Savannah along I–95 or U.S. 17 will bring you to the exits that will carry you to the first four of the Golden Isles: Ossabaw, St. Catherines, Sapelo, and Little St. Simons islands, which cannot be reached by automobile. The next three islands—Sea, St. Simons, and Jekyll—are all accessible by automobile and, consequently, they are where most of the accommodations are located. Sea Island is the home of the outstanding Cloister Hotel, where you feel like you are on a Mediterranean isle rather an island off Georgia. St. Simons Island is the site of Fort Frederica, built in the mid-1730s by James Oglethorpe's troops for protection against Spanish invasion from Florida. You can visit ruins of the fort and the adjoining town. Jekyll Island is probably the most commercialized of all of the isles; its amenities were once available only to the very wealthy, but today it offers a range of accommodations and recreational pursuits that can be enjoyed by anyone. Cumberland Island, the southernmost of the Golden Isles, is not accessible by automobile, but a ferry operates every 45 minutes. Industrialist Andrew Carnegie's brother, Thomas, owned much of this island in the late 1800s, upon which he built several luxurious mansions. Today, the Cumberland Island National Seashore takes up much of the isle, providing home to hundreds of species of rare wildlife species, including alligators, sea turtles, otters, great blue herons, wild horses, and armadillos.

If you want to combine abundant history with easy living, exceptional dining, and just plain good old sightseeing, Georgia's Golden Isles are definitely the place to go.

Brasstown Valley. Contemporary. Regional accents give the food a special lift in this dressy dining room, decorated in burgundy and green. From the windows, you can enjoy spectacular mountain views. Mountain trout with pecan crust, chicken pot pie, and bread pudding for dessert tap the strength of the menu. Inventive vegetarian items. Breakfast comes either off the buffet or from a lengthy menu including classic Benedict with grits. Buffet (breakfast). Kids' menu. | 6321 U.S. 76, Young Harris | 706/379–9900 or 800/201–3205 | www.brasstownvalley.com | Breakfast also available | $11–$22 | AE, D, DC, MC, V.

Fieldstone Inn. American. Local specialties include trout and ribs. Seafood buffet on Fri., and prime rib buffet on Sat. Sun. brunch features buffet and made-to-order omelettes. Buffet: Fri., Sat. supper; Sun. brunch. Kids' menu. Sun. brunch. Beer and wine only. | 3379 U.S. 76 | 706/896–2262 or 800/545–3408 | www.fieldstoneinn.com | sld1@alltell.net | No reservations | Sun.–Thurs. 11–10, Fri.–Sat. 11–11 | $9–$21 | AE, D, DC, MC, V.

Lodging

Brasstown Valley Resort. Set amid a 500-acre forest, this new resort features a beautiful lodge with a soaring central hall lit by antler chandeliers. Rooms and separate cottages are filled with "nouveau mountain" furnishings and folk art. Restaurants, bar, picnic area. In-room data ports, some microwaves, refrigerators, cable TV. Pool. Hot tub, sauna. Driving range, 18-hole golf course, putting green, tennis. Gym, hiking. Kids' programs, playground. Business services. | 6321 U.S. 76, Young Harris | 706/379–9900 | fax 706/379–9999 | www.brasstownvalley.com | 102 rooms; 8 cottages | $129–$250; $139–$159 cottages | AE, D, DC, MC, V.

Cabin Fever Cottages. The family room of each of these cottages looks onto Lake Chatuge. The bedrooms have vaulted ceilings with fans, and there is a Jacuzzi and separate shower in every cottage, along with a fully equipped kitchen, gas fireplace, and washer and dryer. The private dock affords great swimming and fishing. | 695 N. Main, Suite A | 706/896–7368 | 2 cottages | $125 per night, 2–night minimum | AE, MC, V.

Fieldstone Inn. On the shores of Chatuge Lake, this modern resort features more than 65 rooms, many of which overlook the lake. Picnic area. Microwaves, cable TV. Pool, lake. Tennis courts. Exercise equipment, marina, watersports. Business services. | 3379 U.S. 76 | 706/896–2262 | fax 706/896–4128 | www.fieldstoneinn.com | 66 rooms | $89–$115 | Dec.–Mar. | AE, D, DC, MC, V.

Henson Cove Place. This intimate B&B has a tasteful mix of mountain-wood stylings and Victorian antiques, along with a beautiful rose garden. The brass beds are covered with family quilts, and each room has its own shower bath. | 1137 Car Miles Rd. | 800/714–5542 or 706/896–6195 | 4 rooms | $75 | MC, V.

Town Creek Cabins. Perched on a hillside overlooking a stream, these new cabins feature porches with a view of the mountain scenery and flagstone fireplaces. Picnic area. Kitchenettes. Pond. Fishing. | 4863 Seabolt Rd., Blairsville | 706/745–8891 | www.towncreekcabins.com | 10 cabins | $99–$129 | AE, D, MC, V.

JEKYLL ISLAND

MAP 3, H11

(Nearby towns also listed: Brunswick, St. Simons Island, Sea Island)

This island resort community, one of the most visited places in Georgia, was the site of an early Spanish mission. Later, James Oglethorpe named it for Sir Joseph Jekyll, one of his financial backers. In 1886, the island became an exclusive private "paradise" for such wealthy New Yorkers as William Rockefeller, Joseph Pulitzer, and J. P. Morgan. The state of Georgia acquired all of the island in 1947 and maintains it as a year-round resort.

Today, the 7½-mi playground is no longer restricted to the rich and famous. Golf courses, tennis, some 20 mi of bike trails, fishing areas and public beaches are open to all.

Information: Jekyll Island Convention and Visitors' Bureau. | 381 Riverview Dr., 31527 | 912/635–3636 or 877/453–5955 | fax 912/635–4073 | www.jekyllisland.com | Mon.–Fri., 8–5.

Attractions

Horton House. The ruins of a tabby plantation house built by Mayor William Horton, of Oglethorpe's regiment, constitute an important landmark. The walls of the ruins were given some protective restoration by members of the Jekyll Island Club, who, in 1898, anted up $27 apiece for the project. | Riverview Dr. on north end of Jekyll Island | Free | Daily.

Jekyll Island Club Historic District. This 100-acre district features 19th- and early 20th-century Victorian-style cottages built by members of the Jekyll Island Club, including Rockefellers, Pulitzers, and Cranes. The Sans Souci apartments, which may be the country's first condominium, also is in the district, but not on tour as it's part of the Jekyll Island Club Hotel. | 381 Riverview Dr. | 912/635–2119 | fax 912/635–4420 | www.jekyllisland.com | Free | Daily; tours daily 10–3; tickets and information at the Visitors Center, the former Jekyll Island Club stables.

Sea Turtle Walks. During the summer, the island is home to nesting sea turtles and their hatchlings. A nightly two mile beach walk, led by the Georgia Department of Natural Resources, includes a brief video. | 196 Stable Rd. | 912/635–3636 | www.jekyllisland.com | $5 | June–Aug. Mon.–Sat. 9:30–11 PM.

Summer Waves. This 11-acre water park is geared to family activities, with an 18,000-sq-ft wave pool, water slides, a children's activity pool with two slides, and a circular river for tubing and rafting. Outside equipment is not permitted. | 210 S. Riverview Dr. | 912/635–2074 | fax 912/635–4068 | www.summerwavewaterpark.com | $14.95 | May–Sept., daily 10–6.

ON THE CALENDAR

JUNE: *Country by the Sea Music Festival.* The Southeast's largest country music beach party is held annually at Jekyll Island. Some of the nations's biggest names in country music attend, and the event also features exhibits, food and drink, and souvenirs. | 877/453–5955 | fax 912/635–4004 | csmith@jekyllisland.com | www.jekyllisland.com | $10.
NOV.: *Jekyll Island Fire Festival.* Fire engine rides, games, safety demonstrations and food. | 877/4JEKYLL.

Dining

SeaJay's. Seafood. Its famous dish is "low country boil," a mixture of fresh coastal shrimp, corn on the cob, smoked sausage, potatoes, slaw and seasonings. Live entertainment, riverfront seating and homemade key lime pie keep this place hopping. | 1 Harbor Rd. | 912/635–3200 | $5.95–$13.95 | AE, D, MC, V.

★ **Grand Dining Room, Jekyll Island Club Hotel.** American. Breakfast runs from eggs Benedict to pancakes. Lunch focuses on salads and sandwiches, freshly done and presented with style. Dinner specialties often reflect the upscale plantation tradition, with blue crab cakes, fried green tomatoes, soft-shell crab and plantation shrimp (Georgia white shrimp with andouille sausage, collards and rice). White tablecloths, candlelight, and a grand piano set the scene. Kids' menu. Early-bird suppers. | 371 Riverview Dr. | 912/635–2600 ot 800/535–9547 | fax 912/635–2818 | www.jekyllclub.com | Breakfast also available | $19–$25 | AE, D, DC, MC, V.

The Huddle House. American. Like meat? From its $3.49 burger to an $8.25 T-bone steak, Huddle House serves up some serious protein. If you have a craving at 4:30 AM, that's just fine– they're open 24 hours a day. | 901 Pkwy. Dr. | 912/635–3755 | Open 24 hours | $3.49–$8.25 | No credit cards.

Lodging

The Beachview Club. They literally raised the roof on an old motel to build this new luxury all-suites lodging in 1998. Stucco walls are painted light yellow, and big old oak trees shade the grounds. Kitchenettes. Pool. Hot tub. | 721 N. Beachview Dr. | 912/635–2256 or 800/299–2228 | fax 912/635–3770 | www.beachviewclub.com | bcach@darientel.net | 38 rooms | $43–$60 | AE, D, DC, MC, V.

Clarion Resort Buccaneer. There is rest for the weary at this beachfront hotel, with all the typical amenities of a Clarion. Cable TV. Outdoor pool. Hot tub. Tennis court. Games. | 85 S. Beachview Dr. | 800/253–5955 | fax 912/635–3230 | www.motelproperties.com | 230 rooms | $129 | AE, D, DC, MC, V.

Comfort Inn Island Suites. Most suites in this hotel have beautiful beach views; golf courses and bike trails are a few strides away. Complimentary Continental breakfast. Outdoor hot tub. Playground. | 711 N. Beachview Dr. | 800/204–0202 | www.motelproperties.com | 180 rooms | $149 | AE, D, DC, MC, V.

Jekyll Inn. This popular oceanfront complex has been freshly painted and upgraded with carpeting, furnishings, and modern conveniences. The 15 acres of grounds space the buildings generously apart. Popular with familes, the inn accommodates children under 17 for free when they stay with parents or grandparents. Packages include summer family-focused arrangements and romantic getaways. The restaurant has an Italian theme. Restaurant. Some in-room data ports. Pool. Volleyball. Playground, laundry facilities. | 975 N. Beachview Dr. | 912/635–2531 or 800/736–1046 | fax 912/635–2332 | 188 rooms; 76 villas | $99–$139, $139–$169 villas | AE, D, DC, MC, V.

★ **Jekyll Island Club Hotel.** Built in 1887, the four-story clubhouse with wraparound verandas and Queen Anne-style towers and turrets once served as the winter hunting retreat for wealthy financiers. In 1985, a group of Georgia businessmen spent $17 million restoring it. The guest rooms are custom-decorated with mahogany beds, armoires, and plush sofas and chairs. The nearby Sans Souci Apartments, built in 1896 by a group of club members, have been converted into spacious guest rooms. The hotel operates a free shuttle to area beaches. The b&b packages are a great deal. 2 restaurants, bar. In-room data ports, cable TV. Pool. Driving Range. 3 18-hole golf courses, putting green, 9 tennis courts. Beach, marina. Fishing. Bicycles. Shops. Kids programs'. Business services. Airport shuttle. Free parking. | 371 Riverview Dr. | 912/635–2600 or 800/535–9547 | fax 912/635–2818 | 134 rooms; 20 villas | $129–$189, $189–$259 suites | AE, D, DC, MC, V.

LA GRANGE

MAP 3, B7

(Nearby town also listed: Pine Mountain)

La Grange is located southwest of Atlanta, near the Alabama border. The story goes that, during the Civil War, after all of the available male population marched off to battle, the town was left defenseless. A home guard unit, made up entirely of females, was organized, and when the community was threatened with invasion by the Union army, the women met the Union troops head-on. So moved by the presence of the females was the invading army's commander, that he bypassed the town and left it untouched.

Information: La Grange-Troup County Chamber of Commerce | 111 Bull St., La Grange, GA 30241 | 706/884–8671 | fax 706/882–8012 | membership@lagrangechamber.com | www.lagrange-ga.org | Weekdays 9–5.

Attractions

Bellevue. Designed and built over a 2-yr period in the early 1850s, this Greek Revival Mansion, listed on the National Register, was home to Benjamin Harvey Hill, a U.S. congressman. Its facade is formed by Ionic columns, creating wide verandas. Massive carved-wood cornices over doors and windows, black Italian marble mantels, and plaster ceiling medallions are details to note. Original furnishings include the family rosewood piano, and upstairs are displayed family furnishings, mostly reflecting the style of the 1850s, and family momentos. | 204 Ben Hill St. | 706/884–1832 | $4 | Tues.–Sat. 10–12 and 2–5.

Chattahoochee Valley Art Museum. This refurbished 1892 commercial building– actually the county jail– exhibits 20th-century American art. Lamar Dodd, a native of La Grange, is a featured artist in the collection. 10 to 13 exhibits annually focus on work by contemporary regional artists. | 112 Lafayette Pkwy. | 706/882–3267 | fax 706/882–2878 | Free | Tues.–Fri. 9–5, Sat. 11–5.

Troup County Courthouse. The courthouse, recently added to the National Register of Historic Places, is an example of Art Moderne architecture. Details include stylized columns, globe lights on pedestals and wide front steps. | 118 Ridley Ave. | 706/883–1740 | Free | Weekdays 9–5.

West Point Lake. Managed by the Army Corps of Engineers, the lake was created by damming the Chattahoochee River in 1975. About 26,000 water surface acres and 30,500 acres of grounds, with 525 mi of shoreline, provide recreational facilities. There are six campgrounds, one of which is primitive and free. The others have water and electric hookups ($10–$16). Picnic areas, shelters (by reservation), boat-launching ramps, three beach areas, two marinas, and several day-use parks are among the facilities. | 500 Resource Management Dr., West Point | 706/645–2937 or 877/444–6777 (national reservation service) | fax 706/643–3200 | www.reserveusa.com (for campsite reservations) | $1 | Day-use parks: Apr.–Sept., daily sunrise to sunset; campgrounds: Apr.–Sept.; R. Shaefer Heard campground: year-round.

ON THE CALENDAR

DEC.: *Annual Christmas Parade.* A spirited local event. School bands, churches and businesses all participate. | 706/884–8671.

Dining

Taste of Lemon. American. Salad and vegetable plates, salmon croquettes, country-fried steak, crab au gratin, and chicken breasts over pasta. Banana pudding, brownies, buttermilk pie are typical desserts. Antique townhouse. No alcohol. | 100 S. Main St., Adairville | 706/882–5382 | Reservations not accepted | Closed weekends. No dinner | $6–$7 | MC, V.

MACON

MAP 3, D7

(Nearby town also listed: Milledgeville)

Today's modern city of Macon, with more than 100,00 people, belies its early beginnings as a trading post and fort. The community grew quickly after it was discovered that flat-bottomed boats could be used to connect the inland town with the seacoast. Cotton soon became king and after the railroad was completed through town, Macon became one of the most important rail facilities in the South, with three major lines connecting there. Poet Sidney Lanier, as well as rock and roller Little Richard and soul singer Otis Redding all hail from Macon.

Information: Macon-Bibb County Convention and Visitors Bureau | Terminal Station, 200 Cherry St., Macon, GA 31208 | 912/743–3401 or 800/768–3401 | fax 912/745–2022 | maconcbb@maconga.org | www.maconga.org | Mon.–Sat. 9–5.

PREHISTORIC GEORGIA

Two of America's most impressive prehistoric Indian sites lie within Georgia's boundaries. Ocmulgee National Monument, located 2 mi east of Macon on U.S. 80, was the first large prehistoric ruin in the South to be scientifically excavated. Almost as impressive are the Etowah Indian Mounds, located 35 mi north of Atlanta off I–75 near Cartersville. The Etowah remains, which consist of several mounds dominated by three unusually large ones, have been designated a National Historic Landmark.

Both the Ocmulgee and Etowah sites date from the period of American Indian prehistory known as the Mississippian. It was during this time that numerous large temple mounds and huge agricultural villages sprang up throughout the valley of the Mississippi River and its tributaries. Indian culture reached its zenith during Mississippian times, which lasted from about AD 700 to 1500.

The fires of Mississippian brilliance extinguished themselves shortly before the arrival of the Spaniard Hernando de Soto, and the lands of the South fell into a dark age that lasted until the advent of the so-called historic tribes of Indians—the Cherokees, Creeks, Chickasaws, and Choctaws.

Today, it is generally accepted that migrations of Asiatic hunters of Mongolian racial stock were responsible for the first peopling of North America. These Mongolians crossed the Bering land bridge during the last glaciation, when Siberia and Alaska were joined. As the hunters followed the herds upon which their survival depended, they crossed from one continent to another, becoming North America's first human inhabitants.

The massive migrations that brought with them America's first settlers took place perhaps 30,000 to 40,000 years ago. Hundreds and thousands of individual treks were made across the land bridge, the various groups spreading as they moved southward. Over many millennia, areas across the entire North American continent were settled by the migratory hunters.

Exactly when the vanguard of settlement reached Georgia is not known with absolute precision, but strong evidence suggests that the borders of today's state had been crossed by at least 10,000 BC. This first culture period is known as the Paleo and was purely hunting in nature. It lasted several thousand years.

The transition from Paleo to the next period, the Archaic, occurred about 10,000 years ago. During the Archaic people practiced a crude form of agriculture and lived in villages instead of constantly wandering like their predecessors.

The village life that began in Archaic times became more common during the Woodland Period, which began about 3,000 years ago. Because of their custom of burying the dead in mounds, the Woodland people are sometimes called Mound Builders. Pottery was introduced in this period, and the bow and arrow became the primary weapon.

By AD 700 Mississippian culture had begun to dominate. The large temple mounds, stockades, village plazas, and watchtowers—many remains of which can be seen today at Ocmulgee and Etowah—were being built, and the small villages of past years gave way to large towns covering many acres. Handicrafts reached a new level of beauty, and trade with neighboring parts of the continent became commonplace. Southeastern Indian culture reached its height during Mississippian times.

By the time Hernando de Soto and his men made their way through the pine woods and thickets of Georgia in the mid-1500s, all of this wonderful way of life had vanished forever. No white man's eyes ever witnessed the eerie beauty of a sacred ceremony atop one of the high temple mounds that had dominated Mississippian villages all over the South. All that is left today of this once-powerful culture—a culture that in its own way rivaled those of the Incas and the Aztecs—are the mysterious remains that can still be seen at Ocmulgee and Etowah.

© Artville

Attractions

City Hall. Built in 1836 as a bank, the Greek Revival building served as a fireproof cotton warehouse, then as Georgia's temporary capital. | 700 Poplar St. | 912/751–7170 | fax 912/751–7931 | www.maconga.us | Free | Weekdays 8:30–5:30.

Covered Bridge Trail of Georgia. At the state visitor Headquarters of the Covered Birdge Trail in Thomaston, there is a resource center and archives for the study of covered bridges. A free pamphlet details the 15 surviving Georgia covered bridges, which are scattered throughout the state. Two remain by master builder Horace King of La Grange. King was a slave who, in 1823 with his master John Godwin, studied bridge building under the engineering genius Ithiel Town. Town invented and patented the Town Lattice truss design, the basis of all modern bridge design. | 201 S. Center St., Thomaston | 706/647–9686 | Free | Daily; Chamber of Commerce: Mon.–Thurs. 9–5, Fri. 8:30–4:30.

The Douglas Theatre. The 1921 theater hosted musical greats, among them Ma Rainey, Bessie Smith, and Duke Ellington. Restored and reopened in 1997, it now offers tours. | 355 Martin Luther King, Jr. Blvd. | 912/742–2000 | fax 912/742–0270 | $2 (suggested) | Tues.–Fri. 9–5.

Georgia Music Hall of Fame. The 12,000-sq-ft exhibit hall re-creates a Georgia village enjoying a perpetual music festival. Period instruments, significant Georgia musicians, memorabilia, and Georgia music, heard at 20 CD listening stations, are the major draws. The gift shop features recordings of Georgia artists in all genres. | 200 Martin Luther King, Jr. Blvd. | 912/738–0017 | fax 912/750–0350 | www.gamusichall.com | $8; special rates for seniors, students, and children | Mon.–Sat. 9–4:30, Sun. 1–5.

Georgia Sports Hall of Fame. Opened in 1999, this latest of Georgia's state-sponsored museums honors sports at all levels, from prep to professional. The 43,000-sq-ft facility has a theater whose design is based on that of an early Atlanta ballpark. | 301 Cherry St. | 912/752–1585 | fax 912/752–1587 | www.gshf.org | $6; special rates for seniors, students, and children | Mon.–Sat. 9–5, Sun. 1–5.

Grand Opera House. Built in 1884, this performing arts center at Mercer University was the largest sound stage south of the Mason-Dixon line. W.R. Gunn, architect of the Hawkinsville opera house, also designed this one. | 651 Mulberry St. | 478/301–5470 | fax 912/751–7931 | Weekdays 10–5.

Hay House. This magnificent Italian Renaissance Revival mansion, completed just before the Civil War, was designed by T. Thomas & Son, a New York architectural firm. With its opulent finishes, including a magnificent stained-glass window, this was the most luxuriously appointed home of its day in Macon. Technological advances within the home included running water, central heating, and indoor plumbing. | 934 Georgia Ave. | 912/742–8155 | fax 912/745–4277 | $7 | Mon.–Sat. 10–4:30, Sun. 1–4:30.

High Falls State Park. A 100-ft natural gradual waterfall gives this park its name. There are three hiking trails, miniature golf and camping in this 1,000-acre park. | 76 High Falls Park Dr., High Falls | 912/933–3053 | fax 912/993–3054 | www.gastateparks.org | $2 vehicle, $20 van, $50 bus | Daily 8–10.

Indian Springs State Park. Healing springs valued by area Native Americans became a popular tourist resort, with luxury hotels and gambling, around the turn of the century. Today, the state park formed around the springs contains cottages, campsites, and areas for fishing, canoeing, and hiking. Thought to be the first state park in the country, it was the direct result of a treaty with the Creek Nation. Across the road, Chief William McIntosh of the Lower Creek Nation built the Indian Spring Hotel in 1823, with an addition, in 1825, as a tavern and an inn. Eight others followed, but only this one survives. Now undergoing restoration, it will be preserved as a historic site. | 678 Lake Clark Road (off I–75), Flovilla | 770/504–2277 | fax 770/404–2178 | www.gastateparks.org | $2 vehicle, $20 van, $50 bus | Daily 7–10.

Jarrell Plantation State Historic Site. This collection of more than twenty 19th- to mid-20th-century farm buildings and implements on wooded grounds accurately depicts the life and circumstances of an affluent family in middle Georgia. This was the home of John Fitz Jarrell, who built the first dwelling in the 1840s. Among the buildings open for tour are an 1847 plantation plain-style house, the mill complex, a carpenter shop, and other outbuildings. Seasonal programs demonstrate period crafts. Period implements and furnishings are displayed in the structures. | 711 Jarrell Plantation Rd., Juliette | 912/986–5172 | fax 912/986–5919 | jarrell@mylike.net | $3.50; special rate for children | Tues.–Sat. 9–5, Sun. 2–5:30.

Lake Tobesofkee. With about 750 acres and 35 mi of shoreline created by damming a creek as a state soil conservation project (1968), the lake provides facilities for camping, fishing, and boating, as well as playgounds. | 6600 Mosley Dixon Rd. | 912/474–8770 | fax 912/474–8996 | $3 | Daily 6AM–9:30PM.

Macon Historic District. Some 48 downtown buildings and homes cited for architectural excellence are individually listed on the National Register of Historic Places, with another 575 noted for their architectural significance. In acreage, this is the largest grouping of sites on the National Register in the country. | 912/743–3401 | www.gamusichall.com | Free | Daily.

Macon Museum of Arts and Sciences and Mark Smith Planetarium. Macon native Andrew Lyndon's diverse collection, including fine prints, a Picasso etching, and Asian artifacts, is one of the components of the museum's permanent collection. The three-story Discovery House and Artist's Garret are among the special child-focused exhibits. The planetarium uses special effects to bring astronomy to life. | 4182 Forsyth Rd. | 912/477–3232 | fax 912/477–3251 | www.masmacon.com | $5; special rates for seniors, students, and children | Mon.–Thurs., Sat. 9–5, Fri. 9–9, Sun. 1–5.

Mercer University. Affiliated with the Southern Baptist Convention, Mercer University was founded in 1833 in Penfield, Georgia. Prominent Georgia Baptist leader Jesses Mercer was its guiding light, and the institution is named for him. Moving to Macon in 1871, the university is the second-largest Baptist-affiliated institution in the world. With programs in liberal arts, business, engineering, education, medicine, pharmacy, law, and theology, it features a main campus located in Macon, as well as a satellite campus in Atlanta. | 1400 Coleman Ave. | 912/301–2715 | fax 912/301–4124 | www.mercer.edu | Free | Daily.

Ocmulgee National Monument. Ocmulgee is arguably the most explored, excavated, and researched prehistoric site in America. More than 12,000 years of continuous human presence have been unearthed here, the latest being the monumental Mississippian temple mounds that are still visible today. The Earthlodge is the oldest reconstructed building in the United States, dating back over a thousand years. You can see the original walls, floors, and seating arrangements. Part of the National Park Service, this site has been impressively arranged to give you a vivid sense of the prehistoric Indian cultures of the southeastern United States. There are a museum and visitors center, and you can take tours of the mounds, even an underground ceremonial center.

Old Cannonball House and Macon-Confederate Museum. The only house in Macon hit by Union forces, this Greek Revival home was built in 1853. A Confederate museum exhibits period clothing, uniforms, company flags, weapons, and there is a garden. The four-room house served as quarters for servants. | 856 Mulberry St. | 912/745–5982 | fax 912/745–5944 | $4 | Mon.–Sat. 10–4, Sun. by appointment.

Museum of Aviation. Nearly 100 vintage aircraft and missiles, inlcuding an MIG 17, a B-25, and B-29, depict the history of aviation from World War II through Desert Storm. Special exhibitions focus on the Tuskegee Airmen, the Hump Pilots of World War II, and the area Native American heritage. The Georgia Aviation Hall of Fame honors those who have made significant contributions to aviation in Georgia, such as Ben Epps Sr., the first Georgian to fly, and Eugene Jacques Bullard, the state's first black military aviator. Smithsonian aviation-theme films are shown every hour. There also are paintings of aircraft, a gift

MACON

INTRO
ATTRACTIONS
DINING
LODGING

shop, and a cafe serving decent food. | Rte. 247, Warner Robins | 912/926–6870 or 912/926–4242 | fax 912/923–8807 | www.museumofaviation.org | Free | Daily 9–5.

Sidney Lanier Cottage. Filled with period furnishings, this simple Victorian cottage was home to Sidney Lanier, poet, linguist, mathematician, lawyer, and one of the nation's finest flutists (first flute, Peabody Symphony, Baltimore, MD). | 935 High St. | 912/743–3851 | fax 912/745–3132 | $3 | Weekdays 9–1, 2–4, Sat. 9:30–12:30.

Tubman African American Museum. Quality exhibits focus on the history of Africans, on their contributions to American society, and on their art. A new facility is being planned. | 340 Walnut St. | 912/743–8544 | fax 912/743–9063 | www.tubmanmuseum.com | $3 | Weekdays 9–5, Sat. 10–5, Sun. 2–5.

Sightseeing Tours. Macon offers a wealth of architectural heritage, both commercial and residential, from antebellum to high Victorian periods. The most efficient way to see Macon's many sights is to take one of the tours available, many of them self-guided. For instance, "Lights on Macon Historic Intown" is a self-guided illuminated tour presented by the Intown Macon Neighborhood Association. It guides visitors through the historic district, beginng at the Hay House and serves as an excellent introduction to the various architectural styles represented in these homes. Maps available at the Visitors Bureau at Terminal Station.

Middle Georgia Historical Society, Sidney Tours. Custom-designed for the tourist's interest, the tours could focus on or combine historic sites, antiques, architecture, churches, or other history-centered themes. | 935 High St. | 912/743–3851 | fax 912/745–3132 | $3 | Weekdays 9–1, 2–4, Sat. 9:30–12:30PM.

Sidney's Tours of Historic Macon. Ride through historic Downtown as guides narrate the story of Macon. Stops include the Sidney Lanier Cottage, Hay House, and the Tubman African-American Museum. A self-guided tour brochure points out the area's many African-American landmarks. | 200 Cherry St. | 912/743–3401 or 800/768–3401 | fax 912/745–2022 | www.maconga.org | $15 | Mon.–Sat. 10 and 2.

Wesleyan College. The world's first degree-granting college for women, Wesleyan was founded in 1836 and continues its educational mission today. About 600 students study liberal arts, and the school is especially known for its music program. Neva Fickling, an alum, was Miss America. | 4760 Forsyth Rd. | 912/757–4030 | fax 912/477–1110 | www.wesleyancollege.edu | Free | Daily.

ON THE CALENDAR

ALL YEAR: *Macon, Georgia: An African American Experience.* More than twenty sites are included in this tour, which visits places such as the restored 1921 Douglass Theater and the Harriet Tubman museum, which is the largest of its type in Georgia. | 800/768–3401.

MAR.: *Cherry Blossom Festival.* Historic tours of Macon, concerts, fireworks, sporting events, and a parade are a part of this spring festival. | 912/751–7429 | fax 912/751–7408 | cbf@cherryblossom.com | www.cherryblossom.com | Free | Mar. 16th–25th.

SEPT.: *Indian Celebration at Ocmulgee National Monument.* The celebration, which costs $3, pays homage to Native American tribes through cultural exhibits, crafts, and food. | 912/752–8257.

Dining

Boulevard Serenade. Continental. Maconites really enjoy the fresh approach to classics, such as grilled duck à l'orange; grilled rack of lamb with mustard/rosemary crust; salmon with lemon-butter sauce; and rock lobster tails in basil, white wine, and cream. Piano entertainment nightly. | 401 Cherry St. | 912/742–2583 | Closed Sun.–Mon. No lunch | $20–$30 | AE, MC, V.

Buckner's Family Restaurant and Music Hall. Southern. Fried chicken, stewed tomatoes, and peach cobbler are presented family-style, with everybody seated at a lazy Susan table to dish up their own fare. Family-style service. Gospel singing Thurs., Fri., and Sat. No alcohol. | 1168 Bucksnort Rd., Jackson | 770/775–6150 | Closed Mon. and Tues. | $9–$10 | No credit cards.

The Cherry Corner. Italian. A corner café of surprising proportions, serving authentic, outstanding Italian pizzas, homemade bread, unusual soups and picture-perfect pastries. Espresso. Buffet (supper). Beer and wine only. | 502 Cherry St. | 912/741–9525 | fax 912/745–0751 | No dinner Sun.–Thurs. | $5–$8 | AE, MC, V.

City Kitchen. Southern/American/Café. Self-service salad bar and sandwiches to order on housemade bread are the draws. Salad bar. No alcohol. | 359 Third St. | 912/742–2255 | fax 912/742–6050 | Reservations not accepted | Closed weekends. No dinner | $5–$8 | AE, D, MC, V.

Downtown Grill. American. Pork tenderloin, lamb chops, steaks, and, for the vegetarian, lots of fresh vegetables. Scottish plaid red carpet, separate high booths, quiet setting. Take out. | 563 Mulberry St. | 912/742–5999 | fax 912/742–6050 | Closed Sun. No lunch | Reservations advised | $14–$25 | AE, D, MC, V.

Fincher's Barbeque. Barbeque. When astronaut Sonny Carter boarded a space shuttle flight in 1989, he took some of Fincher's barbeque into orbit with him—in the form of three dried-out shoulder steaks. Earthlings can savor the soupy sauce. | 891 Gray Hwy. | 912/743–5866 | $5.35–$7.99 | No credit cards.

Fresh Air. Barbecue. Chopped pork with a tangy vinegar/pepper sauce is the specialty of the house. Cole slaw and Brunswick stew are made on the premises. No alcohol. | 1164 U.S. 420, Jackson | 770/775–3182 | fax 770/775–0101 | Reservations not accepted | Mon.-Sun. 8–8 | $5–7 | No credit cards.

Gulf Coast Grill. American/Steak/Seafood. Generous seafood platters, fried seafood (crawfish, shellfish, and catfish both whole and filleted), grilled dinners, and good vegetables for the vegetarian are big hits. Kids' menu. | 3267 Vineville Ave. | 912/477–3534 | Reservations not accepted | Closed Sun. No lunch | $13–$19 | AE, DC, MC, V. .

The Isabella. American. Chicken breast artichoke, a sautéed breast with artichokes, cream, and mushrooms, is the town favorite. Buffet (Fri., Sat. supper). Kids' menu. Sun. brunch. Beer and wine only. | 111 Lyons St., Jackson | 770/775–6177 | Closed Mon. | $9–$15 | AE, D, DC, MC, V.

Jeneane's Cafe. Southern. Traditional southern breakfast with grits, eggs, country ham and all the trimmings. At lunch, savor roast pork and dressing, and excellent vegetables. Second location does dinner: Jeneane's at Pinebrook. Kids' menu. No alcohol. | 524 Mulberry St. | 912/743–5267 | 4436 Forsyth Rd., Pinebrook | 912/476–4642 | Mulberry: Breakfast also available. Closed weekends. No dinner; Pinebrook: Closed Mon. | $4–$10 | MC, V.

Len Berg's. American. If you like what you order at Berg's, you can press a special buzzer at your table that lets the cooks know. Popular requests are the salmon croquette, fresh veggies, and the macaroon pie. | 240 Post Office Alley | 912/742–9255 | $5.95–$11.95 | No credit cards.

Midtown Grill. American. A partner with Downtown Grill and Gulf Coast Grill (above), this was one of the first good restaurants to open in Macon in the past five years. From the menu: Steak, seafood, and chops. A casual restaurant with red walls and high booths. Open-air dining. Kids' menu. | 3065 Vineville Ave. | 912/745–8595 | Reservations not accepted | Closed Sun. No lunch | $9–$15 | AE, D, MC, V.

Nathalia's. Italian. Classic Italian cooking since 1984 is the hallmark of what may be Macon's most formal restaurant. Oyster appetizer, snails Roman style, traditional pasta with wild mushrooms, seafood, and grilled veal chop (frequent specials) define this menu. | 2720 Riverside Dr. | 912/741–1380 | Reservations essential | Closed Sun. No lunch | $17–$27 | AE, MC, V.

Peach Parkway Produce and B.B.Q. Barbecue. Sliced or chopped pork and ribs, good bar-becued chicken, and excellent side dishes make a stop here an imperative on I–75. The hot barbecue sauce is outstanding. Minimal seating, but take out is the way to go. This spot also sells fresh produce in season and "put-up" regional specialties, such as hot peppers, pickled peaches, and chow-chow. No alcohol. | Rte. 49, Byron | 912/956–4774 | Reservations not accepted | Mon.–Sun. 8–8 | $5–$11 | AE, D, DC, V.

Lodging

1842 Inn. The 1842 Inn offers the amenities of a grand hotel with the charm of a country inn and gracious Southern hospitality. Bar, complimentary Continental breakfast. Some in-room hot tubs, cable TV. No kids under 11. Business services. | 353 College St. | 912/741–1842 or 800/336–1842 | fax 912/741–1842 | the1842inn@worldnet.att.net | www.innbook.com/inns/1842 | 21 rooms | $125–$255 | AE, D, MC, V.

Best Western Riverside Inn. This chain hotel has a large lobby, a spiral staircase, oversized rooms, and a Southern atmosphere. Restaurant, bar. In-room data ports, refrigerators. Cable TV. Pool. Laundry facilities. Business services. | 2400 Riverside Dr. | 912/743–6311 or 888/454–4565 | fax 912/743–9420 | www.bestwestern.com | 125 rooms | $43–$59 | AE, D, DC, MC, V.

Comfort Inn. This typical chain hotel was renovated in early 2000. Contemporary furnishing, double and queen-sized beds. Bar, complimentary Continental breakfast. In-room data ports. Cable TV. Pool. Business services. | 2690 Riverside Dr. | 912/746–8885 or 800/847–6453 | fax 912/746–8881 | www.comfortinn.com | 120 rooms | $53–$74 | AE, D, DC, MC, V.

Courtyard by Marriott. This well-maintained, moderate hotel has all the amenities plus spacious rooms with contemporary furnishings. Bar. In-room data ports, some microwaves, refrigerators, cable TV. Pool. Hot tub. Exercise equipment. Business services. | 3990 Shera-ton Dr. | 912/477–8899 or 800/321–2211 | fax 912/477–4684 | www.courtyard.com | 108 rooms | $94–$119 | AE, D, DC, MC, V.

Crowne Plaza. This businessman's hotel is conveniently located close to downtown attrac-tions and the historic district. And since it's a large hotel that rarely fills up, you can often wrangle a deal. Rooms on the upper floors command a beautiful view of Coleman Hill, to the west. Restaurant, bar (with entertainment). In-room data ports, cable TV. Pool. Exer-cise equipment. Business services. | 108 First St. | 912/746–1461 or 800/227–6963 | fax 912/738–2460 | www.comfortinn.com | 298 rooms | $79–$289 | AE, D, DC, MC, V.

Holiday Inn Conference Center at Macon. Catering to business travelers, this Holiday Inn offers typical amenities, including in-room coffemakers. Although the hotel does not have a fitness center on the premises, you can use Gold's Gym down the road for free. Some microwaves and refrigerators. Cable TV. Pool. | 3590 Riverside Dr. | 912/474–2610 | 132 rooms | $72 | AE, D, DC, MC, V.

Holiday Inn Express. A renovated Holiday Inn offering complimentary newspaper and free local calls. Complimentary Continental breakfast. In-room data ports, some microwaves, refrigerators, cable TV. Pool. Business services. Free parking. Pets allowed (fee). | 2720 River-side Dr. | 912/743–1482 or 800/465–4329 | fax 912/745–3967 | www.holiday-inn.com | 94 rooms | $55–$63 | AE, D, DC, MC, V.

LaQuinta Inn. This newly renovated hotel is surrounded by restaurants and offers ameni-ties like in-room coffepots and hairdryers. Complimentary Continental breakfast. Pool. Hot tub. Gym. Laundry services. | 3944 River Place Dr. | 912/475–0206 or 800/531–5900 | 142 rooms | $75 | AE, D, DC, MC, V.

Rodeway Inn. A well-maintained hotel 1 mi off I–475 at Exit 3. Queen- and king-sized beds. Complimentary Continental breakfast. Microwaves, refrigerators, cable TV (and movies). Pool. Laundry facilities. Business services. Some pets allowed (fee). | 4999 Eisenhower Pkwy. | 912/781–4343 or 800/228–2000 | fax 912/784–8140 | www.rodeway.com | 56 rooms | $45 | AE, D, DC, MC, V.

THE GREAT LOCOMOTIVE CHASE

Thick, black smoke poured from the smokestack of the *General*, a state-of-the-art locomotive that was the pride and joy of the Western & Atlantic Railroad Company. Capable of running almost one mile per minute, the *General* was pulling a short train made up of a wood tender, three empty boxcars, and several passenger coaches. It was Saturday morning, April 12, 1862, and the train had left Atlanta at 6:00 AM, northbound for Chattanooga, Tennessee, some 130 mi away.

At Marietta, a station just a few miles north of Atlanta, 20 men, dressed in civilian clothes, boarded and took seats at various places on the train. Unbeknown to the rest of the passengers, the men were on an unusual mission—to hijack the very train they were riding and head toward Chattanooga, destroying as much Western & Atlantic property along the way as they could.

The next station was Big Shanty, today's village of Kennesaw, where the train was scheduled to make a 20-minute breakfast stop. After the *General* came to a halt at the depot and hotel at Big Shanty, most of the Atlanta passengers, as well as the entire crew, got off the train and headed for breakfast. Unnoticed to all were the activities of two of the 20 men who had boarded at Marietta. While one of them uncoupled the passenger cars from the rest of the train, the other—later identified as the group's leader, Captain James J. Andrews—quickly hustled 16 of his companions into the empty boxcars. Then Andrews, along with the man who had separated the cars and two remaining compatriots, mounted the engine, brought the *General* to a full head of steam, and sped northward toward the next town, leaving the surprised passengers and the train's crew wondering what had happened.

By the time the train's engineer and conductor reached the loading platform to see what was going on, the *General* was nearly out of sight around a bend. Big Shanty was not equipped with a telegraph, so a horseman was dispatched to Marietta to get the news of the train's theft on the wires as rapidly as possible. Unbeknown to the train's crew, however, Captain Andrews had already stopped the *General* just a few miles out of Big Shanty and cut the telegraph lines.

In the meantime, some of the *General*'s crew commandeered another locomotive several miles up the line at Etowah and took off after their hijacked train. Eventually, they encountered a southbound train, pulled by the locomotive *Texas* and, after uncoupling all of the boxcars, again headed north, in the backward-traveling engine.

For the next several miles, it was a touch-and-go situation for both Andrews, aboard the *General*, and his pursuers driving full speed on the *Texas*. At every opportunity, Andrews stopped his train and his men destroyed track, dumped cross ties across the rails, and cut telegraph wires. Their efforts to burn several railroad bridges failed, and Andrews realized that the wood used in the bridges' construction was soaking wet from recent heavy rains. At one point on the wild ride, the *Texas* pulled up to within just a few minutes of the *General*.

By the time he and his men were approaching the town of Ringgold, Georgia, located a few miles south of the Tennessee border, Andrews had lost all hope of accomplishing his mission. He was out of wood to feed the *General*'s hungry boilers, and the local militia had been alerted to be on the lookout for his command, with orders to shoot to kill. With no options left, he instructed his men to desert the train, flee into the woods, and *escape the best you can*. All of Andrews's followers were eventually caught and tried. Eight of them, Andrews included, were executed as spies in Atlanta.

The Andrews Raid, as this astonishing episode in Georgia history is known, was a failure as far as the grand design of the Union command was concerned. The exercise was futile, and the Western & Atlantic rail line was restored to full working order within a few days. But the men of the raid—all but one of whom were members of the 2nd, 21st, and 33rd Ohio Volunteer Infantry—and Andrews himself, who was a civilian, earned the first Medals of Honor ever presented by the U.S. Congress to American fighting men.

Scottish Inn I–475 Corner. Like those in many other Macon lodgings, the rooms at Scottish Inn have full kitchens with ovens, stovetops, and coffeemakers. Kitchenettes, microwaves, refrigerators. Pool. Pets allowed (fee). | I–475 and U.S. 80 | 912/474–2665 | 80 rooms | $35 | AE, D, MC, V.

Studioplus. Built in 1998, the rooms feature full-size kitchens and queen-size beds. No late arrivals (after 11pm) without reservations. Three types of rooms: queen, deluxe, and double. In-room data ports, cable TV. Pool. Exercise equipment. Laundry facilities. Business services. | 4000 Riverside Dr. | 912/475–8580 or 888/788–3467 | fax 912/474–2633 | www.extstay.com | 72 rooms | $49–$59 | AE, D, DC, MC, V.

Wingate Inn. An all-suite hotel built in 1997. The oversized rooms have either one king-size or two full-size double beds. Complimentary Continental breakfast. In-room data ports, refrigerators, some in-room hot tubs (in suites). Cable TV. Hot tub. Exercise equipment. Business services. | 100 Northcrest Blvd. | 912/476–8100 or 800/228–1000 | fax 912/477–8180 | www.wingateinn.com | 80 rooms | $79 | AE, D, DC, MC, V.

MADISON

MAP 3, D6

(Nearby towns also listed: Athens, Eatonton)

Madison was once the seat of government in a cotton-rich county—in fact, it was one of the economic linchpins of antebellum Georgia. The well-to-do local planters competed with one another in the building of luxurious homes, and unlike the case in many other Georgia towns, many of those exquisite mansions still exist. It seems that Madison was spared the torch during Sherman's March to the Sea. The popular explanation is that Madison was simply too beautiful to burn. There is also the story that Madison was home to a senator who resigned his seat rather than vote for the Articles of Secession; he is said to have met with Sherman and convinced him not to burn the town. Others say the simple fact is that the Yankees just didn't come that way. Whatever the truth, the historic district of Madison has more than 30 period homes and public buildings. It's no surprise that the town lures Hollywood filmmakers.

Information: Welcome Center | 115 E. Jefferson, Madison GA 30650 | 706/342–4454 or 800/709–7406.

Attractions

Lake Oconee. This manmade lake was created in 1978 by the construction of Wallace Dam, separating Lake Oconee and Lake Sinclair. Like its sister lake, Lake Sinclair, it is governed by its creator, Georgia Power Company. The reservoir covers 19,000 acres and has 374 mi of shoreline. There are public boat ramps and campgrounds ($2 parking fee and $12–$14 camping fee). | 125 Wallace Dam Rd. | 706/485–8704 or 888/GPCLAKE | fax 404/506–6449 | www.georgiapower.com/gpclake | $2 vehicle | Sun.–Thurs. 7–9; Fri.–Sat. 7–10.

Madison-Morgan Cultural Center. A restored 1895 Romanesque-revival school building, the first school in the state to have separate grades, the building today is used as museum and art gallery. It also has historical exhibits, including a recreation of home life in the late 19th century. Performances and festivals also take place here. | 434 S. Main St. | 706/342–4743 | fax 706/342–1154 | www.uncleremus.org/madmorg | $3 | Tues.–Sat. 10–5, Sun. 2–5.

Morgan County Historical Society/Heritage Hall. A Greek-revival home built in 1833, furnished with period antiques (one is original to the house), today it serves as headquarters for the Morgan County Historical Society. | 277 S. Main St. | 706/342–9627 | $5; Rogers House and Rose Cottage $2.50 | Mon.–Sat. 10–4:30, Sun. 1:30–4:30.

JULY: *Madison Theatre Festival.* Every third weekend of July, Madison kicks off its four day Theatre Festival. Previous performances have included plays by Gershwin and Miller. | 706/342–4454.

Dining
Yesterday Cafe. Southern. In a restored 1893 pharmacy and general store, Terri Bragg does traditional breakfast with biscuits and gravy, blueberry pancakes (made from locally grown berries), and country ham. At lunch enjoy country-fried steak with mashed red potatoes, fresh vegetables, and maybe buttermilk pie for dessert. Dinner's more upscale, with prime rib, fish, and fried shrimp among the selections. Beer and wine only. | 120 Fairplay St. | 706/557–9337 | Reservations essential for five or more | No breakfast Sat., Mon. No dinner Sun.–Wed. | $10–$15 | AE, MC, V.

Lodging
Brady Inn. The heart pine floors are polished to a sheen in this late-1800s Victorian cottage. The rooms have private baths, and there are plenty of rocking chairs out on the front porch. Complimentary breakfast. | 250 N. 2nd St. | 706/342–4400 | 7 rooms | $75–$150 | AE, D, MC, V.

Burnett Place. This early 19th-century inn has been restored by an interior designer who worked with the local historical preservation society to ensure that the home remained faithful to its original design. Rooms are well appointed and some feature canopy beds. Picnic area, complimentary breakfast. Cable TV. | 317 Old Post Rd. | 706/342–4034 | 3 rooms | $85 | MC, V.

Farmhouse Inn. Family-owned chickens supply the eggs at this inn, which has a mile long walking trail and a stocked pond for fishing. Melinda Hartney, the owner, designed the building herself. The result is a rambling red-roofed structure filled with quilts, wainscotting and Early-American style fabrics. Typical breakfasts include rosemary biscuits and carrot-cake muffins. Complimentary Continental breakfasts. Cable TV, some room phones. | 1051 Meadow La. | 706/342–7933 | members.aol.com/fhin | 3 rooms | $95 | MC, V.

MARIETTA

MAP 3, C5

(Nearby town also listed: Atlanta)

Marietta lies just north of Atlanta, and although a city unto itself with a population of nearly 55,000, it is still sometimes considered part of the metropolitan Atlanta area. The big battle at Kennesaw Mountain in the summer of 1864 was fought just north of town, and today military affairs are still foremost in the area with the presence of the nearby massive Warner Robins Air Force Base.

Information: Cobb County Convention and Visitors Bureau | 1 Galleria Pkwy., Atlanta, GA 30339 | 678/303–2622 or 800/451–3480 | www.cobbcvb.com.

Attractions
American Adventures. This is a family-focused entertainment complex, with 15 indoor and outdoor rides, an 18-hole miniature golf course, an arcade, and a race-car track. One of its attractions, Foam Factory, is a three-story fun house containing interactive games and 50,000 foam balls coming at you from every direction. | 250 N. Cobb Pkwy. | 770/424–9283 | fax 770/424–7565 | www.whitewaterpark.com | $13.99 | Weekdays noon–8, Sat. 10–8, Sun. 10–7; hours vary so call first.

The Big Chicken. Perhaps Marietta's most significant landmark, the 56-ft-tall Kentucky Fried Chicken Big Chicken marks one of the company's outlets. When a storm damaged the orig-

MARIETTA

INTRO
ATTRACTIONS
DINING
LODGING

inal chicken, the company planned to tear it down, but Marietta and the entire metro Atlanta area sent up howls of protest. The chicken was rebuilt on its original site in 1993–94 and now mechanically rolls its eyes and moves its beak. A KFC unit still operates here. | 100 N. Cobb Pkwy. | 770/492–4716 | Free | Daily.

Kennesaw Civil War Museum. Located near Kennesaw Mountain, the museum houses the *General*, the locomotive hijacked by the Union spies known as Andrews' Raiders. You can view a video giving details of the chase. Most of the exhibits are related to the Civil War, the raid, munitions, and armaments. You'll also find information about local history. The complex includes a gift shop and a caboose. | 2829 Cherokee St., Kennesaw | 770/427–2117 or 800/742–6897 | fax 770/429–4559 | www.thegeneral.org | $3; special rates for children and families | Apr.–Sept., weekdays 9:30–5:30, Sun. noon–5:30; Oct.–Mar., weekdays 10–5, Sun. noon–5.

Kennesaw Mountain National Battlefield Park. This national park preserves 2,884 acres near Marietta that commemorate one of the Civil War's decisive battles. The summer of 1864 witnessed Union General William T. Sherman making a concerted effort to get his massive army past the Confederate Army of Tennessee, settled in between Dalton and Kennesaw and commanded by Gerneral Joseph E. Johnston. Sherman's goal was Atlanta, and following several days of desultory fighting in the Kennesaw Mountain area, he forced Johnston to withdraw southward to the outskirts of Atlanta, wherupon he began his siege of the city. The park's visitors center, updated and expanded in the fall of 1999, exhibits memorabilia relating to the battle of Kennesaw Mountain. Stop here first for a map, which shows the hiking trails (16 mi) that loop around Little Kennesaw, Pigeon Hill, Cheatham Hill, and Kolb Farm; they're well groomed and marked. Dotting the grounds are monuments and re-created military positions. Two designated picnic areas (one with grills) and three designated recreation areas enhance the site. You can also view a 20-minute film in the visitors center. | 900 Kennesaw Mountain Dr., Kennesaw | 770/427–4686 | fax 770/528–8398 | www.nps.gov/kemo | Free | Daily 8:30–5.
Cheetam Hill. Most of the fighting at Kennesaw Mountain National Battlefield took place here; rangers say it is the soul of the park. | 900 Kennesaw Mountain Dr. | 770/427–4686 | fax 770/528–8399 | www.mps.gov/kemo | Free | Daily 7:30 AM–6:30PM.

Marietta/Cobb Museum of Art. The permanent collection focuses on 19th- and 20th-century American art. Special exhibitions focus on local artists or draw from important regional collections, both private and public. You may find special exhibitions that are free—it depends on the sponsorship. | 30 Atlanta St. | 770/528–1444 | fax 770/528–1440 | www.mariettasquare.com | $5 | Tues.–Sat. 11–5, Sun. 1–5.

Marietta Museum of History. Housed in the historic Kennesaw House, the museum details the history of the area, including Creek and Cherokee Indian material. Built in 1850 as a cotton warehouse, the Kennesaw House was also a hotel, in fact it was where James Andrews and his men lodged the night before they commandeered the *General* and began the Great Locomotive Chase. Later it was a Confederate army hospital and later still a headquarters for Union troops. | 1 Depot St., Suite 200 | 770/528–0431 | fax 770/528–0450 | www.mariettasquare.com/history | $3 | Mon.–Sat. 11–4, Sun. 1–4.

Marietta National Cemetery. Established in 1866 on 24 acres, the cemetery holds the graves of more than 10,000 Union soldiers. Henry Green Cole donated the land as a joint Confederate/Union cemetery, hoping it would help soothe ill feelings between North and South. When his plan didn't work, he gave the land to the Union. | 500 Washington Ave. | 770/428–5631 | fax 770/426–6092 | Free | Daily.

White Water, a Six Flags Park. The largest water park in the South features nearly 50 water attractions. Some 5,000 trees shape the grounds, and attractions are built in and around the trees. Especially popular are the 90-ft Cliffhanger Freefall, the Bahama Bobslide, and the Run-A-Way River, an enclosed family raft ride. | 250 N. Cobb Pkwy. | 770/424–WAVE | fax 770/424–7565 | www.whitewaterpark.com | $26.99 | Call for hours.

William Root House Museum. One of Marietta's oldest residences, built in 1844–45, this simple frame plantation-plain home, located just two blocks from its original site, showcases middle-class 19th-century life. Hannah and William Root were early settlers; he was one of the town's first merchants and its first pharmacist. The house is furnished with period pieces, and the re-created kitchen and flower and vegetable beds reflect the period. Operated by Cobb Landmarks & Historical Society. | 145 Denmead St. | 770/426–4982 | fax 770/499–9540 | www.mariettasquare.com/root.html | $3 | Tues.–Sat. 11–4.

ON THE CALENDAR
APR.: *Taste of Marietta.* This all-day festival on the last Sunday in April includes "Kids' Alley," a special section devoted to interactive games, safety demonstrations, tables devoted to artwork and entertainment. A free oldies concert usually winds down the day. | 770/429–1115.
JUNE: *Battle Anniversary Weekend.* The weekend of June 24th, Kennesaw Mountain National Battlefield offers artillery demonstrations and "living history" programs. | 770/427–4686.

Dining

Basil's Mediterranean Cafe. Mediterranean. Traditional dishes include good hummus, stuffed grape leaves, and tabbouleh. You can eat outdoors on a deck that is beautifully adorned with flowers. | 2985 Grandview Ave. | 770/578–0011 | Reservations essential for six or more | No lunch weekends | $13–$22 | AE, D, DC, MC, V.

Carey's Place. American/Casual. Scruffy, but who cares! These are some good burgers, big, hand-formed, and full of flavor. Good steaks, too. | 1021 Cobb Pkwy. | 770/422–8042 | Reservations not accepted | $7–$10 | No credit cards.

Don Taco. Mexican. All kinds of traditional Mexican dishes, from burritos, tacos, quesadillas, huarachas (like a corn patty) topped with meat, beans and cheese, to flan. Excellent house-made salsas. | 50 Cobb Pkwy. S | 770/792–8406 | $2–$7 | AE, D, DC, MC, V.

Grazie: A Bistro. Italian. This antiques-filled suburban bistro hits with good pastas, grilled salmon and Italian sausage, braised lamb shank with roasted vegetables and mashed potatoes. Pizzas, too. Piano nightly. | 1000 Whitlock Ave. | 770/499–8585 | grazie.home.mindspring.com | $12–$25 | AE, D, DC, MC, V.

Jimmy's. Mediterranean. This Mediterranean mainstay known for its succulent lamb counts several senators among its loyal patrons. Cozy tête-à-têtes, family dinners and corporate parties are all the norm at Jimmy's, which is filled with rich wood tones. | 164 Roswell St., Marietta | 770/792–4443 | $6.95–$16.95 | AE, MC, V.

Marietta Diner. American. In addition to steaks, burgers, and good meatloaf with vegetables and mashed potatoes, the menu features Greek specialties, such as pastitsio (baked meat and macaroni). Breakfast is great. Kids' menu. Beer and wine only. Open 24 hours. | 306 Cobb Pkwy. | 770/423–9390 | Reservations not accepted | $5–$19 | AE, MC, V.

1848 Plantation House. Southern. Traditional Low-country and contemporary Southern dishes, from she-crab soup to fried green tomatoes, maple-pecan crusted boneless Georgia trout and Sweet Georgia Brown with rhubarb *jus* and vanilla bean ice milk. The restaurant is constructed according to an old-fashioned Southern design and is decorated with furnishings from the Federal and Empire periods. Sun. brunch with Jazz. | 780 S. Cobb Dr. | 770/428–1848 | www.1848house.com | Closed Mon. No lunch | $18–$26 | AE, D, DC, MC, V.

Sukothai. Thai. Specials such as curry sauce or basil sauce on red snapper fillet and garlic basil lamb are well prepared, as are the classics of Thai cooking, such as pad Thai and other noodle dishes. | 1995 Windy Hill Road, Suite K, Smyrna | 770/434–9276 | Reservations essential for six or more | Closed Sun. No lunch Sat. | $7–$15 | AE, D, DC, MC, V.

Uncle Bud's Catfish, Chicken and Such. Southern. Catfish is the specialty, fried, of course, but you can also get it grilled. Excellent sides include white beans, hush puppies, and coleslaw. This outfit is based in Tennessee, and the white beans are a specialty there. Good fried chicken. The fish theme is made clear by the restaurant's decorations, with fishing poles and hats hung on the walls. Kids' menu. | 725 Concord Rd., Smyrna | 770/434–1881 | Reservations not accepted | $7–$15 | AE, D, DC, MC, V.

Vince et Christos. Italian. Linguine with clams, a variety of soups (lobster bisque or cream of asparagus), and tiramisu are fine work. Leg of lamb is the most popular dish. Highlighted in earth-tone colors, the restaurant has a hardwood bar and comfortable booths with leather seats. Mediterranean paintings line the walls. Live jazz Fri.–Sat. after 8. Kids' menu. | 1050 E. Piedmont Rd. | 770/971–9994 | Reservations essential for six or more | No dinner Sun., no lunch | $9–$27 | AE, MC, V.

Williamson Bros. Barbecue. Good chopped pork and ribs, house-made onion rings, coleslaw, Brunswick stew and beans, as well as homemade pies keep the place packed. The main decorations are antique wooden furniture. Kids' menu. Beer and wine only. | 1425 Roswell Rd. | 770/971–3201 or 770/971–7748 | www.williamsonbros.com | Reservations essential for eight or more | $3–$15 | AE, D, DC, MC, V.

Lodging

Comfort Inn. This Comfort Inn is 3 miles from the Kennesaw Battlefield and within walking distance of golf, cinemas and restaurants. Continental breakfast. In-room data ports. Cable TV. Pool. Hot tub. Business services. | 750 Cobb Pl. | 770/419–1530 | fax fax 770/421–8535 | www.comfortinn.com | 80 Rooms | $69 | AE, D, DC, MC, V.

The Whitlock Inn B&B. This painstakingly renovated Victorian mansion is just a block away from historic Marietta Square and within walking distance of theater, restaurants, and antique shops. Rich hardwood floors, leaded glass windows, period antiques, Chippendale reproductions, and plenty of floral fabrics decorate the inn, which is shaded by graceful trees. All rooms have private baths and AC. Complimentary Continental breakfast. Cable TV. Library. Business services. No kids under 12. No smoking. | 57 Whitlock Ave. | 770/428–1495 | fax 770/919–9620 | www.whitlockinn.com | 5 rooms | $100–$125 | AE, D, MC, V.

MILLEDGEVILLE

MAP 3, E7

(Nearby towns also listed: Eatonton, Macon)

This quaint town located 26 mi northeast of Macon was Georgia's capital from 1804 until 1868, when Atlanta took over the reins of government. The Old Governors' Mansion, which was home to the state's chief executives from 1839 to 1868, still stands and is just one of the outstanding examples of period architecture in the town.

Information: Convention and Visitors Bureau | 200 W. Hancock St., Milledgeville, GA 31061 | 912/452–4687 or 800/653–1804 | www.milledgevillega.com/cvb.htm.

Attractions

Georgia College and State University. The college was founded in 1889 as the Georgia Normal and Industrial College, and some of its buildings date to 1896. In 1922 it became a women's college, then went coeducational in 1967 and was renamed Georgia College. It was elevated to university status in 1996. With a student body numbering more than 5,000, this is one of the fastest growing units of the university system, offering 65 baccalaureate and 35 graduate degree programs. Besides the residential campus in Milledgeville, it has satellite campuses for commuters in Macon and Dublin and a commuter center in Warner Robins. | 231 W. Hancock St. | 478/445–5004 | fax 478/445–1914 | www.gcsu.edu | Free | Daily.

Old Governors' Mansion. This 1839 home was residence to nine Georgia governors, until 1868, when Federal authorities, to punish the state for its part in the Civil War, moved the capital to Atlanta. The governor's office is a replica, on a smaller scale, of the Oval Office in the White House. A part of Georgia College and State University since 1889, the building once served as dormitories. Now restored and open for guided tours, this National Historic Landmark Greek-revival house, its portico supported by classical Ionic columns, is furnished in period antiques. | 120 S. Clark St. | 912/445–4545 | fax 912–445–3045 | www.gcsu.edu/acad-affairs/ce-ps/mansion/default.html | $5 | Tues.–Sat. 10–4, Sun. 2–4.

Historic Guided Trolley Tour. This trolley tour offers an ideal way to view the historic district, including the Old Governors' Mansion, the Stetson-Sanford House, St. Stephen's Episcopal Church. | 200 W. Hancock St. | 912/452–4687 or 800/653–1804 | fax 912/445–4440 | www.milledgevillecvb.com | $10 | Weekdays 10 AM, Sat. 2 PM.

Lake Sinclair. Created in 1952, the lake covers 15,330 acres and has 417 mi of shoreline. Campgrounds and picnic areas, a day-use park (Rocky Creek Park), marinas, and a picnic area are popular attractions. You can find free parking at Georgia Power Company's Cosby's Boat Landing. | 125 Wallace Dam Rd. | 706/485–8704 or 888/GPCLAKE | fax 404/506–6449 | www.georgiapower.com | Free | Daily.

Old State Capitol Building. Seat of government for the state from 1807 to 1868, this may be the oldest public building in the U.S. built in the Gothic style. Since 1879 the building has been part of Georgia Military College. | 201 E. Greene St. | 912/445–2700 or 800/653–1804 | fax 478/445–2867 | www.gmc.cc.ga.us | $10 | Tours Tues.–Fri. 10 AM, Sat. 2 PM.

ON THE CALENDAR
NOV.: *Annual Arts and Crafts Festival.* The front campus of Georgia College is the site of this festival, which includes historical re-enactments and music. | 912/452–4687.

Dining
Cafe South. Southern. Housed in a former post office, this is really two restaurants in one. For lunch, it's a Southern buffet with traditionally prepared dishes such as salmon croquettes, fried chicken, or country-fried steak with fresh vegetables, including really good creamed corn. On weekday nights it's open only for catered banquets, but come here on a Fri. or Sat. night and you'll find an upscale restaurant, serving such dishes as Cornish hen with cranberry port wine sauce and cornbread dressing. Buffet (lunch). Kids' menu. Beer and wine only. | 132 Hardwick St., Hardwick | 912/452–3164 | cafesouth@alltel.net | No lunch Sat. | $6–$9 | AE, MC, V.

Choby's Landing. Seafood. On Lake Sinclair. Catfish, steaks, and seafood prepared Southern style (deep-fried, but grilled is available) are the focus at this very popular casual spot. You eat outside on a deck overlookng a beautiful lake. Kids' menu. | 3090 U.S. 441 N. | 912/453–9744 | Reservations not accepted | Closed Mon. No lunch | $8–$15 | MC, V.

Lodging
Antebellum Inn. Just a block from the Georgia College campus, this 1890 Greek-revival home has a wraparound porch and tall pillars; the rooms are decorated with a feminine flourish. Complimentary breakfast. Pool. | 200 N. Columbia St. | 912/454–5400 | antebellum@alltel.net | 2 rooms | $75–$99 | AE, D, MC, V.

Inns and Suites of Milledgeville. Lake Sinclair and Georgia College are only 4 miles away from the hotel, which has an indoor heated pool. Complimentary Continental breakfast. In-room data ports, microwaves, refrigerators. Cable TV. Indoor pool. Hot tub. Gym. | 2621 N. Columbia St. | 912/453–2212 | fax 912/453–0869 | 47 rooms | $60 | AE, D, DC, MC, V.

NEWNAN

(Nearby town also listed: Carrollton)

Newnan is the seat of government for historic Coweta County, and together they boast nearly 900 listings on the National Historic Register. Nearby is the birthplace of famed novelist Erskine Caldwell.

Information: Coweta County Welcome Center | 100 Walt Sanders Memorial Drive, Newnan, GA 30265 | 800/8CO–WETA | fax 770/254–2628 | welcometocoweta@mindspring.com | www.coweta.ga.us.

Attractions

Driving Tours. The Chamber of Commerce offers information on tours of the historic district and Newnan's Victorian homes. | 23 Bullsboro Dr. | 770/253–2270 | fax 770/253–2271 | www.ncchamber.org | Free | Weekdays 9–5.

Male Academy Museum. In 1883, with a total of 60 students, this building began life as a school for young men. The building was later moved and used as a residence. Later still, it was moved back to near its original site and restored, and now it serves as a museum for the Newnan Historical Society. You'll find both permanent and special exhibitions. | 30 Temple Ave. | 770/251–0207 | $2 | Tues.–Thurs. 10–noon and 1–3, weekends 2–5.

ON THE CALENDAR

SEPT.: *Powers' Crossroads Country Fair and Art Festival.* Every Labor Day weekend, Newnan welcomes over 300 artists and craftsmen from across the country, who exhibit and sell their work. In the past, the U.S. Marine Corps Band has performed, as have country, gospel, folk, and contemporary musicians. Local fare, provided by church and civic groups, includes a variety of choices for carnivores and vegetarians alike. | 770/253–2011.

Dining

Bulloch House. Southern. This is a popular spot: come at the right time, and you'll see tour buses pull up to unload their passengers for lunch. They come most of all for the buffet. If you bring your own alcohol, don't forget to bring your own glasses. Known for fried chicken, fried green tomatoes, homemade creamed potatoes, sweet potato souffle, macaroni and

PACKING IDEAS FOR HOT WEATHER

- ☐ Antifungal foot powder
- ☐ Bandanna
- ☐ Cooler
- ☐ Cotton clothing
- ☐ Day pack
- ☐ Film
- ☐ Hiking boots
- ☐ Insect repellent

- ☐ Rain jacket
- ☐ Sport sandals
- ☐ Sun hat
- ☐ Sunblock
- ☐ Synthetic ice
- ☐ Umbrella
- ☐ Water bottle

cheese. BYOB. | 47 Bulloch St., Warm Springs | 706/655–9068 | Reservations not accepted Sun. | No dinner Sun.–Thurs. | $6–$9 | AE, D, MC, V.

Jeff Spader's Original Hogan's Heroes. Italian. A surprising find in a tiny town. The specials may include ostrich and elk or even tournedos Rossini. Lunch features robust hero sandwiches on house-baked bread. The tables are small, with vinyl tablecloths, and the walls are lined with pictures. | 218 U.S. 29 N., Hogansville | 706/637–4953 | Closed Sun., Mon. | $8–$25 | AE, D, MC, V.

Ten East Washington St. American. Classical-based fare from Czech-born George Rasovksy makes this simple little spot fill quickly with repeat customers. Shrimp with apricot/orange sauce (a cold appetizer), excellent fish dishes, and superior crème caramel. | 10 E. Washington St. | 770/502–9100 | www.teneastwashington.com | Closed Sun., Mon. No lunch Sat. | $13–$20 | AE, MC, V.

Lodging

Hampton Inn. Historic downtown Newnan is just 2 miles away from the hotel, which frequently renovates its rooms. Complimentary Continental breakfast. Cable TV. Pool. | 50 Hampton Way. | 770/253–9922 | fax 770/253–3922 | Hampton.Newnan@Nobleinvestment.com | http://hampton-newnan.idmax.net | 91 rooms | $69 | AE, D, DC, MC, V.

OKEFENOKEE SWAMP

MAP 3, G11

(Nearby town also listed: Waycross)

The famed Okefenokee, straddling the Georgia-Florida border, is one of the largest and best preserved wetlands in the lower 48 states. Encompassing an area that measures roughly 25 mi by 35 mi, the swamp is home to hundreds of species of plants, insects, reptiles, amphibians, birds, and mammals. Most of the swamp's 4 million–plus acres are part of the Okefenokee National Wildlife Refuge, operated by the U.S. Fish and Wildlife Service.

Information: Refuge Manager | Okefenokee National Wildlife Refuge, Rte 2, Box 3330, Folkston, GA 31537 | 912/496–7836.

Attractions

Eye on Nature. Participants of all ages learn about the native animals of the Okefenokee Swamp. | U.S. 1 S. and Hwy. 77 | 912/283–0583 | $10 | Daily, 9–5:30.

★ **Okefenokee National Wildlife Refuge and Wilderness Area.** More than 730 square mi of southeastern Georgia and a bit of northeastern Florida constitute one of the most fascinating places on the planet. Alligators and bullfrogs vie for sound bites as they attract females in the spring; deer graze lazily, knowing they're protected; fish leap out of the brackish water into your boat. This is a wildlife refuge, so camping is very limited and primitive and must be reserved in advance. The best time to visit is between September and April to avoid the biting insects that emerge in May, especially in the dense interior. But compensation for swatting yellow flies is the exquisite flora that emerge in the spring. | Rte. 2, Box 3330, Folkston | 912/496–3331 (for canoe trips and reservations) or 912/496–7366 (for information) | fax 912/496–3332 | r4rwga.okr@fws.gov | $5 per vehicle | Daily.

ON THE CALENDAR

OCT.: *Okefenokee Festival.* Old-fashioned entertainment and craftsmanship characterize this festival in late October. Wood-burning stoves, basket weaving, soap making, and horseback riding keep kids and adults interested in local history. | 912/496–7836.

Dining

Okefenokee Restaurant. Southern. A good spot for breakfast before going over to the Okefenokee. Lots of good, deep-fried seafood, country-fried steak, fried chicken cooked to order and grilled ham steak. Kids' menu. No alcohol. | 103 S. 2nd St., Folkston | 912/496–3263 | Reservations not accepted | Breakfast also available. Closed Sun. | $4–$10 | MC, V.

Lodging

The Inn at Folkston. This Craftsman-style inn, located only 7 mi from the refuge, has a huge front veranda and four working gas-log fireplaces. The guest rooms are individually decorated. The Garden Room has a king-size bed. Some in-room hot tubs. | 509 W. Main St., Folkston | 912/496–6256 or 888/509–6246 | www.innatfolkston.com | 4 rooms | $85–$135 | AE, D, DC, MC, V.

Okefenokee Inn B&B. The unassuming, spunky owners of this ranch-style B&B are quick to tell you that they concentrate on making the house "comfy, but not frou-frou." Instead of strawberry crepes and china teacups, you can expect a lot of country grilling. The clean and neat house, which is 7 miles from Okefenokee Swamp, has some antique bone furniture. The owners have insider connections to swamp tours and entertainment. | 210 S. Magnolia St., Folkston | 912/496–3918 or 888/440–3918 | 5 rooms | $90 | No credit cards.

Western Motel. This motel with some extras, is within walking distance of shopping, dining, and entertainment. Complimentary Continental breakfast. Microwaves, refrigerators. Pool. Hot tub. | 1207 S. Second St., Folkston | 912/496–4711 | 31 rooms | $67 | AE, D, DC, MC, V.

PERRY

MAP 3, D8

(Nearby towns also listed: Andersonville, Cordele, Macon)

Perry is sometimes called the Crossroads of Georgia because of its location practically at the geographical center of the state. The town is known for its early blooming spring flowers and trees, a favorite of visitors to the region.

Information: Perry Area Convention and Visitors Bureau | 101 General Courtney Hodges Blvd., Perry, GA 31069 | 912/988–8000 | www.perryga.com.

Attractions

Massee Lane Gardens. Headquarters for the American Camellia Society, Massee Lane Gardens, outside Marshallville, totals about 100 acres and includes a Japanese garden, an environmental garden, a rose garden, and 10 acres of camellias in a formal garden. There are two museums of porcelain, including one that exhibits only birdhouse-theme pieces. | 100 Massee Lane, Fort Valley | 912/967–2722 or 912/967–2358 | fax 912/967–2083 | www.camellias-acs.com | $5 | Tues.–Sat. 10–4:30, Sun. 1–4:30.

Old Opera House. Built in 1907, the restored opera house originally served as city hall and auditorium. Designed by W. R. Gunn, who also built the Grand Opera House in Macon, it serves today as a performance space and houses the Hawkinsville-Pulaski County Arts Council. The Metropolitan Opera presented *Il Trovatore* in 1911, and comedian Oliver Hardy, born in Hiram, Georgia, performed on its stage. It is due soon for a major renovation. | 100 Lumpkin St., Hawkinsville | 912/783–1884 | fax 912/892–2333 | Donations accepted | Mon.–Thurs. 9–5, Fri. 9–midnight.

Sam Nunn Museum. Photographs and various memorabilia depict the boyhood and senate career of Perry native Sam Nunn. He attended school in the building. | Houston County Board of Education, 1100 Main St. | 912/988–6200 | fax 912/988–6259 | admin.houston.k12.ga.us | Free | Weekdays 8–4:30.

ON THE CALENDAR

FEB.: *Georgia National Rodeo.* The large PRCA-sanctioned rodeo in Perry brings cowboys and cowgirls together to compete in steer wrestling, barrel racing, bronc busting, calf roping, and more. | 401 Larry Walker Pkwy. | 912/987–3247 | fax 910/988–6526 | $17 | Thurs.–Sat. 7:30.

APR.: *Mossy Creek Barnyard Festival.* The craftsmen who exhibit their wares at this festival must be invited; their work is widely considered to be some of the best in the nation. Pottery, woodcarving, metal forging, and other crafts vie for your attention in the lovely countryside. | 912/988–8000.

Dining

The Langston House 1838 at Henderson Village. Contemporary. The restored Greek-revival house makes a fine setting for classical and regional traditions by Scottish chef Garry Kenley. A good example of the classical is squab with foie gras, but if you'd prefer something from the Southern tradition, try the country ham and peas. The extravagant brunch is less expensive, and lunch is even simpler, with sandwiches and salads. | 125 S. Langston Cir. | 912/988–8696 or 888/615–9722 | www.hendersonvillage.com | Closed Mon. No dinner Sun. | $18–$21 | AE, MC, V.

The New Perry Hotel. Southern. The hotel was built in 1925 and is somewhat worn around the edges, but that has not diminished its popularity. Tourists schedule stops for dinner in its expansive dining room hung with staghorn ferns. They come for fried chicken, pork chops, baked ham, chicken and dressing, and similar classics of Southern homestyle fare. Kid's menu. No alcohol. | 800 Main St. | 912/987–1000 | www.newperryhotel.com. | $11–$15 | AE, MC, V.

My Sister's Cafe. Southern. The country buffet focuses on chicken and dumplings, sausage and peppers, catfish fillets, butterbeans, and banana pudding. It's also a fine place for barbecue. Friday night's catfish and barbecue buffet is an "all-you-can-eat" affair. Buffet. Kids' menu. No alcohol. | 107 Perimeter Rd. | 912/987–3131 | Breakfast also available. No dinner Sun.–Wed. | $4–$7 | AE, MC, V.

Sharon's Kitchen. Southern. Country-style fare is freshly made: chicken and dressing, fried pork chops, homemade Vidalia-onion casserole, fresh vegetables in season, and barbecue. Kids' menu. No alcohol. | 1212 Peach Pkwy., Fort Valley | 912/825–4148 | Reservations not accepted | Closed Mon., Sat. No dinner. | $5–$6 | MC, V.

Yoder's. American. The men wear beards, and the women wear hair caps and long dresses. Long waits are frequent at lunch. Buffet steam tables hold classic Southern fare: stick-to-your-ribs portions of sauerkraut and sausage, sweet-and-sour pork chops, country-fried steak, excellent fried chicken, and great potatoes. Buffet. No alcohol. | Route 1, Montezuma | 912/472–2024 | Reservations not accepted | Closed Sun., Mon. No dinner Wed. | $7–$9 | No credit cards.

Lodging

Henderson Village. This village is actually a country resort made up of stunning 19th- and early 20th-century farm buildings, some original to the site. There are 13 buildings in all, clustered around a green. The guest rooms are rustic, the suites are more elegant, with fireplaces. Buttermilk-yellow walls give the fine 1838 Langston House restaurant a warm atmosphere, perfect for a meal of squab with foie gras on a potato haystack or wild game on buckwheat polenta. Restaurant. Some in-room hot tubs, in-room VCRs. Pool. | 125 S. Langston Circle | 912/988–8696 or 888/615–9722 | fax 912/988–9009 | www.hendersonvillage.com | 24 rooms, 5 suites | $145–$205, $205–$295 suites | AE, MC, V.

Holiday Inn of Perry. A standard Holiday Inn one exit away from the Georgia National Fair. The deluxe breakfast and clean rooms are the hotel's pride. Complimentary Continental breakfast. Cable TV. Pool. Gym. Business services. | 200 Bailey Dr. | 912/987–3313 or 800/808–8804 | fax 912/988–8269 | 117 rooms | $61 | AE, DC D, MC, V.

PERRY

INTRO
ATTRACTIONS
DINING
LODGING

New Perry Hotel. The main building is a mint-green concrete take on a colonial-style mansion, with simple, clean rooms. Out back, there's a motel court. Rooms are basic and affordable, with far more charm than you'd find at a similarly priced chain motel. Restaurant. Cable TV. Pool. Pets allowed (fee). | 800 Main St. | 912/987–1000 | 56 rooms in 2 buildings | $39–$49 | AE, MC, V.

The Plains B&B. This pink-and-cream Victorian building is well situated in downtown Plains, just across from the old railroad depot. Though a bit worn at the edges, the inn is quite comfortable and reasonably priced. From Americus, 14 mi west via U.S. 280. Complimentary Continental breakfast. | 100 S. Hudson St. | 912/824–7252 | 4 rooms | $70 | AE, V.

Swift Street Inn. This antebellum cottage has antique-filled rooms, each with private bath. The nicest is the Magnolia Room, with a four-poster bed and a fireplace. For breakfast, look for stuffed French toast or a cheese-grits casserole. Complimentary breakfast. | 1204 Swift St. | 912/988–9148 | 4 rooms | $65–$90 | MC, V.

PINE MOUNTAIN

MAP 3, B7

(Nearby towns also listed: Columbus, La Grange)

This resort town, located near President Franklin D. Roosevelt's summer White House at Warm Springs, is the home of the world-famous Callaway Gardens. Textile magnate Cason J. Callaway opened the 14,000-acre public garden and resort to the public in 1951, after using the property as a weekend getaway for several years. During all seasons of the year, the gardens are a delight. But it isn't all about flowers—there are 23 mi of hiking trails and back roads, hundreds of species of wildlife, 13 lakes, 4 golf courses, 17 tennis courts, even a private airport.

Information: Pine Mountain Tourism Association | 111 Broad St., Box 177, Pine Mountain, GA 31822 | 706/663–4000 or 800/441–3502.

Attractions

Callaway Gardens. The sweeping gardens developed in the 1930s to reinvigorate a languishing cotton economy bestow unparalleled spring splendor on this 14,000-acre family-style golf and tennis resort. Each season offers its unique natural display. Bicycle paths, most of them well protected from automobiles, wind throughout the gardens. Four nationally recognized golf courses, 10 tennis courts, and a lakefront beach are on the property, as well as such special facilities as a butterfly display (the Cecil B. Day Butterfly Center). | Rte. 18/354 | 706/663–2281 or 800/285–5292 | fax 706/663–6951 | www.callawaygardens.com | $10 | Mar.–Aug., daily 9–6; Sept.–Feb., daily 9–5.

Callaway Brothers Azalea Bowl. The world's largest azalea garden displays more than 5,000 native and hybrid azaleas. | Rte. 18/354 | 706/663–2281 or 800/285–5292 | fax 706/663–6951 | www.callawaygardens.com | Included with $10 general admission | Mar.–Aug., daily 9–6; Sept.–Feb., daily 9–5.

Cecil B. Day Butterfly Center. More than 1,000 butterflies from more than 75 species fly freely in this glass-enclosed space. | Rte. 18/354 | 706/663–2281 or 800/285–5292 | fax 706/663–6951 | www.callawaygardens.com | Included with $10 general admission | Mar.–Aug., daily 9–6; Sept.–Feb., daily 9–5.

Ida Cason Callaway Memorial Chapel. The ideal spot for meditation and reflection, the English Gothic-style chapel with exquisite stained-glass windows was designed by Cason Callaway in memory of his mother. | Rte. 18/354 | 706/663–2281 or 800/285–5292 | fax 706/663–6951 | www.callawaygardens.com | Included with $10 general admission | Mar.–Aug., daily 9–6; Sept.–Feb., daily 9–5.

John A. Sibley Horticultural Center. In an indoor/outdoor display garden, the plantings change seasonally. Don't overlook the gift shop, which focuses on unusual garden-theme items. | Rte. 18/354 | 706/663–2281 or 800/285–5292 | fax 706/663–6951 | www.callaway-gardens.com | Included with $10 general admission | Mar.–Aug., daily 9–6; Sept.–Feb., daily 9–5.

Mr. Cason's Vegetable Garden. This 7½-acre garden may be the nation's largest vegetable garden open to the public. The popular PBS program *The Victory Garden* films its Southern segment here. | Rte. 18/354 | 706/663–2281 or 800/285–5292 | fax 706/663–6951 | www.callawaygardens.com | Included with $10 general admission | Mar.–Aug., daily 9–6; Sept.–Feb., daily 9–5.

Virginia Hand Callaway Discovery Center. A new 35,000-square-ft facility is designed to give you an overall understanding of the garden. | Rte. 18/354 | 706/663–2281 or 800/285–5292 | fax 706/663–6951 | www.callawaygardens.com | Included with $10 general admission | Mar.–Aug., daily 9–6; Sept.–Feb., daily 9–5.

Franklin D. Roosevelt State Park. Features of this 10,000-acre park, originally a national park, include about 40 mi of hiking trails, 20 mi of horseback-riding trails, and a 500-gallon swimming pool shaped like the Liberty Bell. FDR became a state park in 1942. | Rte. 190 | 706/663–4858 | fax 706/663–8906 | www.gastateparks.org | $2 vehicle, $20 vans, $50 bus | Daily 7–10.

Little White House State Historic Site. Built in 1932 while Franklin D. Roosevelt was governor of New York, and just before his 1933 inauguration as president, the simple Greek-revival cottage became his favorite getaway. He had originally come to Warm Springs in 1924; after suffering polio in 1921, he found swimming in the warm spring waters improved his condition. It was here on April 12, 1945, that he had a stroke and died while posing for a portrait. The unfinished painting is displayed in the room where he was sitting. You can tour the grounds and wander through the rooms of the house. Among the more touching items are the president's wheelchair, various leg braces, and canes whittled by supporters unaware of how debilitated he was. Also on view are the guest house and Roosevelt's 1938 Ford roadster. | 401 Little White House Rd., Warm Springs | 706/655–5870 | fax 706/655–5872 | www.gastateparks.org | $5 | Daily 9–4:45.

ON THE CALENDAR

NOV.: *Fantasy in Lights at Callaway Gardens.* Glittering Christmas scenes are the focus of this event, which includes Santa's workshop, the nativity and "a pretty rainbow forest." | 800/441–3502.

Dining

Cricket's. Cajun/Creole. Cajun and Creole fare dominate the menu at this fun, elegant restaurant. Pictures of crickets and snakes adorn the walls of an Alpine house; its tables are set with paisley and white linen. Kids receive Mardi Gras beads. | Hwy. 18 | 706/663–8136 | Closed Mon. and Tues.; Sun brunch also available | $7.95–$16.95 | D, DC, MC, V.

The Georgia Room. Contemporary. Southern touches on this seasonally changing menu include very fine crab cakes, game (quail, rabbit, wild boar, wood grouse, duck), and heavenly muscadine ice cream. If you're feeling adventurous, there's ostrich, which is raised in Georgia. Kids' menu. | U.S. 27 | 706/663–2281 or 800/CALLAWAY | Jacket required | Closed Sun. No lunch | $19–$28 | AE, D, DC, MC, V.

Oak Tree Victorian Dinner Restaurant. Eclectic. An 1871 Victorian mansion is home to a casual restaurant serving dishes ranging from Italian to Southern country. Full bar. | U.S. 27, Hamilton | 706/628–4218 | Closed Sun. No lunch | $9–$25 | AE, D, DC, MC, V.

Lodging

Jameson Inn. This tidy hotel just down the road from Callaway Gardens offers free popcorn and fresh-baked cookies. Shopping, restaurants, and a cinema are right next door. Complimentary Continental breakfast. In-room data ports. Cable TV. Pool. Gym. | 110 Jame-

son Dr. | 706/882–8700 or 800/526–3766 | fax 706/845–1807 | www.jamesoninns.com/
lagrange-ga.html | 50 rooms | $58 | AE, D, DC, MC, V.

Pine Mountain Cabins. The creative and friendly owners of this unique 35-acre establishment
recently added a farmhouse, general store, barn, and schoolhouse to their property. Each
structure is filled with its appropriate set of antiques. Perks include Battenburg lace bed-
ding, a heart-shaped hot tub, cookouts, and Callaway Gardens, which is close by. | Hamil-
ton Rd. Exit off I–85 | 706/663–8790 | dreid@fiac.net | 3 rooms | $110 | AE, D, DC, MC, V.

ROME

MAP 3, B4

(Nearby towns also listed: Calhoun, Cartersville)

Rome stands on the site of a Cherokee village; it got its name because it was built on
seven hills. Once famous as "the stove center of the South," Rome is still an industrial
center and is the largest town in the Northwest Mountain region. Its main attractions
are its downtown district and the beauty of the Berry College campus, but there is
also the town's historical importance to the Cherokee Nation. You can visit the home
of Major Ridge (Chieftains Museum, *below*), one of the the tribe's leaders during the
saddest part of its history, when its members were marched under military guard from
their Georgia homes to lands beyond the Mississippi.

Information: Greater Rome Convention and Visitors Bureau | 402 Civic Center Hill, Rome,
GA 30162–5823 | 706/295–5576 or 800/444–1834 | lisa@romegeorgia.com | www.romege-
orgia.com.

Attractions

Berry College. The largest college campus in the world, with 28,000 acres, and certainly
also among the most beautiful, with towering oaks, rolling fields, stone buildings, and simple cabins. Founded in 1902 by Martha Berry, the school's original mission was the education of mountain children. The extensive grounds feature a gristmill, barns, an equine
center, hiking and bicycling trails, and a reservoir for fishing. A map is available at the gate
house. | 2277 Martha Berry Highway, Mount Berry | 706/232–5374 | fax 706/290–2658 |
www.berry.edu | Free | Daily 7–8.

Oak Hill and the Martha Berry Museum. This magnificent Georgian mansion, located on
the college campus, was the family home of Martha Berry, founder of Berry College. The
mansion is filled with family mementos and ringed by boxwood gardens. The museum
tells her story and the story of the college. | 2277 Martha Berry Highway, Mount Berry | 706/
291–1883 or 800/220–5504 | fax 706/802–0902 | www.berry.edu¢oakhill | $5; special rate
for children | Mon.–Sat. 10–5, Sun. 1–5.

Capitoline Wolf Statue. Like ancient Rome, Rome, Georgia, was set on seven hills. On the
Capitoline hill in the Italian city is a statue of Romulus and Remus, the mythical founders
of Rome suckled by a she-wolf. An identical statue stands in front of the Rome, Georgia,
city hall. If you look closely you'll see an interesting inscription: "From Ancient Rome to
New Rome during the consulship of Benito Mussolini in the year 1928." | In front of City
Hall, downtown | Free | Daily.

Chieftains Museum. The home of Cherokee chief Major Ridge, this plantation-plain house
was built in the 1790s and thus predates the founding of Rome. This is the first site on the
Chieftains Trail. | 501 Riverside Pkwy., Floyd | 706/291–9494 | fax 706/291–9494 | chmu-
seum@romannet.com | $3 | Tues.–Sat. 10–4.

Myrtle Hill Cemetery. Established in 1854 and named for the hundreds of crape myrtle bushes
that grace its grounds, the cemetery is the final resting place of Rome native Ellen Axson
Wilson, first wife of Woodrow Wilson. Located on one of the seven hills of Rome, it offers

THE TRAIL OF TEARS

In the spring of 1838, General Winfield Scott was sent to North Georgia with orders to forcibly remove the Cherokee tribe of Indians to lands beyond the Mississippi River. For eight years—ever since President Andrew Jackson signed the Indian Removal Act—federal authorities had attempted to expel the 15,000 members of the proud Cherokee Nation from their ancestral lands in Georgia, Tennessee, and North Carolina. Soon after the passage of the Removal Act, the tribe's chief, John Ross, had avoided the inevitable by taking the U.S. government to court. When the Cherokees' case was favorably ruled on by the U.S. Supreme Court in 1831, President Jackson's response had been *John Marshall* has made his decision. Now let him enforce it.

To complicate matters, Major John Ridge, who aspired to become chief of the Cherokee Nation, had signed a treaty in 1835 at New Echota, Georgia, that relinquished to the government all remaining Cherokee lands east of the Mississippi River. Questions were immediately raised as to the treaty's legality since only a small segment of the Cherokee leadership had approved it. Nevertheless, federal officials pointed to the controversial document as their authority to demand the Cherokees' immediate expulsion.

Time had nearly run out for John Ross and his stalwart followers who had no desire to relocate beyond the Mississippi River, when General Scott and 7,000 U.S. troops arrived in Cherokee country to ensure that the government's will was done. Stockades were built to house the Cherokees after they were forced to leave their homes and farmsteads. Supplies—one pound of flour and a half pound of bacon daily for each prisoner—were gathered to distribute among the disheartened Indians.

For the next several weeks, Scott oversaw the collection of thousands of Cherokees and their forced confinement in the log stockades that had been built to receive them. He admonished his troops to treat the natives with *every possible kindness,* warning them that *simple indiscretions, acts of harshness, and cruelty . . . may lead . . . to delays, to impatience, and exasperation, and in the end, to a general war and carnage.* The general suggested that *by early and persevering acts of kindness and humanity, it is impossible to doubt that the Indians may soon be induced to confide in the army, and, instead of fleeing to mountains and forest, flock to us for food and clothing.*

By summer, the Cherokees' long migration to the land of the setting sun had begun. About 4,000 of the 14,000 Indians who traveled the Trail of Tears died en route, including John Ross's wife. Ross himself went on to become a diligent worker for his people in their new homeland, present-day Oklahoma, eventually rising to become principal chief of the western branch of the tribe. In the meantime, a few hundred Cherokees in Georgia had escaped the watchful eye of the army and took refuge in the dense forests of the Southern Appalachians, where their descendants still live today.

a fine view of the city. Driving tours of the cemetery are available from the Greater Rome Convention and Visitors Bureau. | Myrtle Hill | 706/295–5576 | fax 706/236–5029 | www.romegeorgia.org | Free | Daily.

The Old Town Clock (1871) and Clocktower Museum. This four-faced clock tower once held the city's water supply. It is listed on the National Register of Historic Places. The museum displays artifacts from Rome's history. For a good view of the city, walk the 107 steps to the observation deck at the top. | Corner of East 2nd St. and 5th Ave. | 706/236–4430 | fax 706/236–4465 | www.romegeorgia.com/visitors/clocktowermuseum.html | Free | May–Oct., Sat. 10–4, Sun. 1–5; also by appointment.

Rome Area History Museum. Exhibits detail the history of the city of Rome and northwest Georgia, including Native Americans (Cherokees) and the Civil War. Some of it is home-spun, but it's charming and unusual. | 305 Broad St. | 706/235–8051 | fax 706/235–6631 | rahm@roman.net | $3 | Tues.–Sat. 10–5.

ON THE CALENDAR

OCT.: *Heritage Holidays.* This huge fall festival, lasting five full days, includes tours of downtown Rome and the museum, a craft show, music, and food. | 800/444–1834.

Dining

La Scala. Italian. Piero Barba, a native of Capri, Italy, focuses on authentic regional dishes. Salmon on a bed of spinach topped with a caper sauce or herb-scented fish broth over angel-hair pasta are examples. The dining room reflects the Italian theme and is pleasantly relaxing. Kids' menu. | 413 Broad St. | 706/238–9000 | Closed Sun. No lunch | $9–$22 | AE, D, DC, MC, V.

Lodging

Chandler Arms B&B. Listed on the National Register of Historic Places, this 1902 Victorian has rich woodwork, gaslight fixtures, and a wraparound porch. If you like, you can sit by the fireplace in your room with the wine and cheese that the owners provide. All rooms have private baths and fireplaces. No pets. No kids. | 2 Coral Ave. | 706/235–9883 | 4 rooms | $70–$100 | AE, MC.

The Woodbridge Inn. From its beginning in the middle years of the 19th century through the early years of the 20th century, the lodge was a railroad hotel. Now the original hotel is a restaurant, but there's a lodge out back with modern rooms, including the Eagle's Nest, a second-story loft that you reach by way of a spiral staircase. Restaurant. | 44 Chambers St. | 706/692–6072 | fax 706/692–9061 | www.woodbridgeinn.net | 12 rooms in lodge | $55–$80 | AE, D, MC, V.

ROSWELL

MAP 3, C5

(Nearby towns also listed: Atlanta, Marietta)

President Theodore Roosevelt's mother was from Roswell, and today you can stroll through her antebellum home, Bulloch Hall, which is still decorated much as it was in 1840, when it was built. Roswell's downtown historic district has been well preserved and offers an extensive walking and driving tour of the 1-square-mi area.

Information: Historic Roswell Convention and Visitors Bureau | 617 Atlanta St., Roswell, GA 30075 | 770/640–3253 or 800/776–7935 | www.cvb.roswell.ga.us.

Attractions

Archibald Smith Plantation Home. One of Roswell's founders, Archibald Smith, and his wife, Ann Margaret Magill, came to Roswell in 1838. Along with several preserved historic outbuildings, the house is furnished with more than 14,000 original artifacts and furnishings. | 935 Alpharetta St. | 770/992–1665 | fax 770/641–3978 | $5 | Tours weekdays 11 and 2, Sat. 11, 12, and 1.

Bulloch Hall. This temple-form Greek-revival mansion was built by Major James Stephens Bulloch in 1839–40. It was home to Martha (Mittie) Bulloch, who married Theodore Roosevelt; her sons were the president and Elliott, the father of Eleanor Roosevelt. Today the house serves as a cultural center and is open for hourly tours. The slave quarters were rebuilt following archeological research. | 180 Bulloch Ave. | 770/992–1731 | fax 770/587–1840 | $5 | Mon.–Sat. 10–3, Sun. 1–3.

Teaching Museum North. The museum is in an early 20th-century school building on the site of the original Roswell Academy. It presents the history of Roswell, Georgia, and the United States. | 791 Mimosa Blvd. | 770/552–6339 | fax 770/552–6340 | www.teachingmuseum.com | $3 | Weekdays 8–4.

ON THE CALENDAR
DEC.: *Christmas in Roswell.* Celebrate the season with tours of the historic district, which is gaily decorated with lights, greenery, and seasonal decor. | 770/640–3253 or 800/776–7935 | call for price | Nov. 17–Dec. 30, call for hours.

Dining
Dick and Harry's. Contemporary. Hefty crab cakes, roasted and grilled fish, and good meat (including game in season) mark the menu. One unusual dish is pan-seared farm-raised emu, similar to ostrich, which, in turn, is like lean beef. You'll find plenty of julienned vegetables. | 1570 Holcomb Bridge Rd. | 770/641–8757 | www.dickandharrys.com | Closed Sun. No lunch Sat. | $13–$30 | AE, D, DC, MC, V.

Greenwoods on Green St. Southern. A Southern instinct propels the menu, with excellent crab cakes (a special), fried chicken with mashed potatoes, duck, and luxuriously deep traditional pies. Beer and wine only. | 1087 Green St. | 770/992–5383 | Reservations not accepted | Closed Mon. and Tues. | $9–$17 | No credit cards.

Ferrera's Bistro. Eclectic. Chef/owner Michael Petrucci, an ex-New Yorker, ditched plastic surgery for the restaurant business. Dishes range from Italian specialties (pizzas and calzone, pastas, veal) to Thai ribs and Southern crab cakes. The decor is remarkably plain. | 635 Atlanta St. | 770/640–5345 | Reservations essential for six or more | Closed Sun., Mon. No lunch Sat. | $10–$24 | AE, D, MC, V.

Fratelli di Napoli. Italian. The family-style service means that many of the main courses are big enough to serve at least two people. Pastas, chicken, snapper, and veal dishes all reflect the Italian-American way with dinner. The setting is like that of most upscale dinner houses, but has a more casual feel than usual. | 928 Canton St. | 770/642–9917 | www.fratelli.net | No lunch | $10–$26 | AE, D, DC, MC, V.

Hi Life. Eclectic. This high-energy suburban restaurant does a wide-ranging menu, from excellent omelets to seasonal lobster. The menu changes often, with many international dishes. Grilled fish and meat, trout fillet wrapped like a spring roll with crisp stir-fried vegetables, sea scallops on spinach grits, and the popular stuffed omelet are examples. The restaurant is highlighted with natural accents of wood and sophisticated lighting. | 3380 Holcomb Bridge Rd., Norcross | 770/409–0101 | www.atlantahilife.com | No lunch weekends | $13–$34 | AE, DC, MC, V.

Pastis. French. Mediterranean cuisine rules at this suburban bistro, with such dishes as lamb osso buco, grilled salmon on lentil ragout, and linguine with seafood and Niçoise olives. The restaurant was modeled after a Provençal house and includes private dining rooms as well as outdoor dining on the balcony. Live jazz Wed.–Sun. | 936 Canton St. | 770/640–3870 | pastisone@aol.com | $10–$20 | AE, D, DC, MC. V.

Slope's BBQ. Barbecue. The Carolina-style barbecue, Brunswick stew, coleslaw, and baked beans are excellent. The ribs are good, too.This is meant to be a country-style restaurant, as you'll understand from the decorations based on stuffed pigs. Kids' menu. No alcohol. | 10360 Alpharetta Hwy. | 770/518–7000 | Reservations not accepted | Closed Sun. | $4–$9 | AE, D, DC, MC, V.

Stony River. Steaks. Come between 5 and 6 PM or 9 and 10 PM to avoid long waits. Terrific steaks (especially the filet mignon), good mashed potatoes, vegetables, chicken, and fish. The restaurant feels a lot like a lodge, with a fireplace with wooden mantle and those comfortable leather sofas. Kids' menu. | 10524 Alpharetta Hwy. | 678/461–7900 | 5800 State Bridge Rd., Duluth | 770/497–6676 | Reservations essential for nine or more | No lunch Mon.–Sat. | $15–$24 | AE, D, DC, MC, V.

Van Gogh's. Eclectic. Pacific Rim to Southwest touches are all over this menu. Wild rice egg rolls adorn the duck; chipotle peppers grace the pork tenderloin. The maximum expression of this must be the sashimi tuna crostini with poblano aïoli and habanero pepper jam. The setting is upscale. Kids' menu. | 70 West Crossville Rd. | 770/993–1156 | www.knowwheretogogh.com | No lunch Sun. | $15–$32 | AE, D, DC, MC, V.

Vinny's on Windward. Italian. This clean, contemporary space seems Italian in design, and the inventive dishes come from the Italian spirit and hearth: tomato ciabatta bread soup, reminiscent of Tuscan bread salad (panzanella); veal meatloaf with homemade potato gnocchi; really good crème brûlée. Kids' menu. | 5355 Windward Pkwy., Alpharetta | 770/772–4644 | www.knowwheretogogh.com | No lunch Sun. | $12–$26 | AE, D, DC, MC, V.

Lodging

Best Western Roswell Suites. Whether you're traveling for business, pleasure, or something in-between, this suite hotel is a comfortable stop. Pool. Hot tub. Gym. Baby-sitting. Business services. | 907 Holcomb Bridge | 770/552–5599 | fax 770/552–8437 | 167 rooms | $50–$80 | AE, DC, V.

ST. SIMONS ISLAND

MAP 3, I10

(Nearby towns also listed: Brunswick, Jekyll Island, Sea Island)

This secluded getaway is one of Georgia's famous Golden Isles. First settled in the mid-1730s by Governor James Oglethorpe when he built Fort Frederica on the north end of the island, St. Simons later became famous for its plantations supported by slave labor. After the Civil War destroyed the plantation system of farming, St. Simons Island was practically deserted except for a few stragglers, who made their meager livings from fishing. Today, St. Simons has been rediscovered and stands as one of Georgia's stellar tourist attractions.

Information: **St. Simons Visitors Center** | 530 B Beachview Dr., Neptune Park, St. Simons Island, GA 31522 | 912/638–9014 | bgivb@technonet.com | www.bgivb.com.

Attractions

Coastal Alliance for the Arts. The Glynn Art Association, with more than 650 members, promotes local and regional artists and stages five yearly festivals. The association publishes art books and has done both a members' cookbook and a book about Sapelo Island, as well as an annual arts calendar. | 319 Mallory St. | 912/638–8770 | fax 912/634–2787 | www.glynnart.org | Free | Weekdays 9–5, Sat. 10–5.

Fort Frederica National Monument. Built by James Oglethorpe in the late 1730s, Fort Frederica was once England's southern outpost in North America. Strategically located on St.

THE WESLEY BROTHERS' BRIEF STAY IN GEORGIA

The late days of autumn 1737 were trying ones for John Wesley. The 34-year-old preacher was looking for a way to get out of Savannah. When Wesley, who was entangled in immense legal difficulties, publicly announced that he would leave Georgia forever, he was threatened with immediate arrest if he dared depart the colony. Despite the warnings, on December 2, Wesley boarded a ship destined for Charleston, South Carolina. Several days later, he was bound for England.

Wesley's sojourn in Savannah had been a brief one. He and his younger brother, Charles, likewise a preacher, had arrived in the colony in February 1736, in the company of Georgia's founder, Governor James Oglethorpe. His desire to establish Protestant missions among the Indians prompted the governor to offer the Wesley brothers a berth on the ship *Simmonds* on his second trip to Georgia.

John's life had centered around religion, and he had been ordained a priest in the Church of England. He was more than anxious to travel to foreign shores and to try his powers of conversion. But John had another motive for making the trans-Atlantic journey. Before his departure from England, he wrote to a friend, *My chief motive is the hope of saving my own soul. I hope to learn the true sense of the Gospel of Christ by preaching it to the heathen.*

Brother Charles possessed deep religious convictions as well, although his faith was not as intense as John's, nor did he have a desire to spend several years in Georgia. Nevertheless, the Wesley brothers decided to accompany Governor Oglethorpe. John, to be paid an annual salary of 50 pounds, was to serve as *Minister to Savannah and Missionary to the Indians,* while Charles became Oglethorpe's private secretary.

A week after his arrival at Savannah, Charles was sent to a new town called Frederica, located several miles to the south on St. Simons Island. There, he quickly fell out of grace with the governor and eventually pleaded with John to come to his rescue. In the meantime, however, John stayed in Savannah and began his church duties in earnest. He soon became known as a zealot and, according to one churchgoer, he "drenched his parishioners with the physic of an intolerant discipline," and his sermons "tended to propagate a Spirit of Indolence and of Hypocrisy."

John finally made the trip to Frederica to check on his brother. He resolved the difficulties between Charles and the governor. Even so, Oglethorpe thought it best that Charles leave Georgia for good and return to England, which he did in August 1736. John, with his mission accomplished, returned to Savannah to take over the pulpit at Christ Church.

While preaching at Christ Church, John became infatuated with an 18-year-old girl named Sophia Hopkins. He considered asking for her hand in marriage, but all his closest friends advised against it. He distanced himself from Sophia for a while, hoping that the proper course of action would be divinely revealed to him. While the two were apart, however, Sophia married another, and John became hostile toward her, even to the point of refusing to serve her communion. Wesley was quickly served with a warrant for refusing Sophia the sacraments. Sophia's husband sued him for 1,000 pounds. John was hauled into court before a grand jury that had been rigged by Sophia's uncle and was indicted on all counts. As he awaited his trial, he made his decision to leave Savannah and Georgia once and for all.

Time soon healed Wesley's emotional and spiritual wounds. Less than two years after his return to England, he organized the Methodist Church, a denomination that had spread all the way to the backwoods of America before his death in 1791 at the age of 86. Charles remained active during that period as well. Before he died in 1788, he had written more than 6,500 church hymns, many of them still performed in Methodist churches around the world.

Simons Island, the fort was used by the English not only in frontier defense but also as a stepping-stone to the invasion of Spanish Florida. Spanish dreams of claiming Georgia were dashed in 1742, when Oglethorpe's army defeated a Spanish force at the battle of Bloody Marsh, the site of which is located nearby. Tabby, an indigenous building material made of oyster shell, was used in the construction of the fort; parts of tabby structures forming the bluff-based fort remain. | Rt. 9 | 912/638–3639 | fax 912/638–3639 | www.nps.gov¢park-lists¢index¢fofr.html | $4 vehicle | Daily 8–5; museum daily 9–5.

Gascoigne Bluff. This wooded area on Frederica River is a pretty picnic spot. Live-oak timber milled here in 1794 was used to build the frigate U.S.S. *Constitution*. Timber cut here later was used to build the Brooklyn Bridge. | West side of St. Simons Island, right on the Frederica River | www.gacoast.com/navigator/gascoigne.html | Free | Daily.

Museum of Coastal History. This museum, which is housed in a Victorian building by the lighthouse, depicts the history of St. Simons. | 101 12th St. | 912/638–4666 | http://www.glynncounty.com/stsimonslight/museum.shtml | $3 | Mon.–Sat. 10–4:45; Sun. 1:30-4:45.

St. Simons Island Lighthouse Museum. Exhibits detail the life of the lighthouse keepers. There are also replicas of the lights that once shone from the lighthouse and other period memorabilia from the area. | 101 12th St. | 912/638–4666 | fax 912/638–6609 | www.stsimonslighthouse.org | $3 | Mon.–Sat. 10–5, Sun. 1:30–5.

St. Simons Lighthouse. Built in 1872, this lighthouse is still used, it even has its original light. Climb the 129 steps to the top and a beautiful view. | 101 12th St. | 912/638–4666 | fax 912/638–6609 | www.coastalgeorgia.org | $3 | Mon.–Sat. 10–5, Sun. 1:30–5.

ON THE CALENDAR
OCT.: *Joe Burkhart's Antique Show at Neptune Park.* Each October, artisans and antique dealers show their wares on the pier. | 912/638–9014.

Dining
Blanche's Courtyard. Seafood. This "Bayou Victorian" house holds lots of antiques and nostalgic memorabilia. Seafood, such as blue crab soup and a huge seafood platter that could easily serve two, is the specialty. Try the mahi-mahi, which is outstanding. There are also basic steak and chicken. "Sweet puppies" are the ever-popular apple fritters. Kids' menu. | 440 King's Way Rd. | 912/638–3030 | Reservations not accepted | Closed Mon. No lunch | $14–$30 | AE, D, DC, MC, V.

Chelsea. Seafood. The lobster-tail fingers, bathed in a light egg wash, floured, then deep-fried or simply steamed, are memorable. Beef, veal, and lamb also available. Early bird specials, offered from 5:30 to 6:30 pm, come with salad. The casual dining room has an island setting. There is a bar, two no-smoking rooms, and one smoking room. Kids' menu, early-bird suppers. | 1226 Ocean Blvd. | 912/638–2047 | No lunch | $9–$33 | D, MC, V.

Frederica House. Seafood. Casual, comfortable, and friendly, this is a highly regarded area restaurant. The building has an unusually rustic feel because of the cypress logs used for both the exterior siding and the interior walls. Good fried and broiled seafood, excellent homemade coleslaw, and possibly the island's best blue crab stew are highwater marks. Steaks also available. Kids' menu, earlybird suppers. | 3611 Frederica Rd. | 912/638–6789 | No lunch | $10–$30 | AE, D, MC, V.

Georgia Sea Grill. Seafood. Classic dishes form the basis of the cooking in this tiny and very popular bistro. Specials go eclectic, with such dishes as lobster scallopini Oscar and spiced tuna loin. Look for the local specialties (blue crab melt and the key lime pot), but don't overlook the pasta. Kids' menu. Limited bar service. No smoking. | 310-B Mallory St. | 912/638–1197 | Oct.–Apr. closed Sun. and Mon.; June–Aug. closed Mon.; no lunch | $13–$22 | D, MC, V.

Mullet Bay. Seafood. This large restaurant is just off the pier in downtown. The deep-fried seafood sometimes tastes commercially prepared; other items, especially shellfish, come off better. Delicious smoked mullet spread is served with captain's crackers. | 512 Ocean Blvd. | 912/634–9977 | $6–$18 | AE, D, DC, MC, V.

The Redfern Café. Contemporary. Nightly specials focus on the seasonal and the regional, but there is also a regular menu. Fried oysters in a light cornmeal coating, shrimp/crab bisque with corn fritters, and the café's crab cakes are local specialties. This restaurant looks like everyone's idea of a bistro. Beer and wine only. | 200 Redfern Village | 912/634–1344 | Reservations essential | Closed Sun. No lunch | $18–$29 | MC, V.

Lodging

Epworth by the Sea. Located on the site of the old Hamilton Cotton Plantation, this complex of motel-style buildings is owned and operated by the Methodist church, which offers basic lodging at inexpensive rates. Meals are only served while conferences are held. Pool. Tennis court. Playground. No pets. | 100 Arthur Moore Dr. | 912/638–8688 | www.epworth-bythesea.org | 210 rooms | $55 | MC, V.

Hampton Inn. This Hampton Inn offers typical amenities and is family friendly. You can use the exercise facility nearby. Complimentary Continental breakfast. Cable TV. Pool. Hot tub. | 2204 Demere Rd. | 800/426–7860 | 79 rooms | $85 | AE, D, DC, MC, V.

Holiday Inn Express. With brightly decorated rooms at great prices, this new facility is an excellent choice if you're traveling on a budget. The executive suites have sofas and desks. Complimentary Continental breakfast. Pool. Bicycles. Laundry facilities. No smoking. | 299 Main St. | 912/634–2175 or 800/787–4666 | fax 912/634–2174 | 60 rooms, 6 suites | $50–$75, $70–$90 suites | AE, D, MC, V.

King and Prince Beach and Golf Resort. Guest rooms are spacious, and the villas offer two or three bedrooms. The villas are owned by private individuals, so the number available for rent varies. It's worth the trouble to get a beachfront room for easy access. 2 restaurants, bar. Some refrigerators. 5 pools (1 indoor). Hot tub. 4 tennis courts. Bicycles. Business services, airport shuttle. | 201 Arnold Rd. | 912/638–3631 or 800/342–0212 | fax 912/638–7699 | www.kingandprince.com | 140 rooms; 43 villas | $120–$160; $275–$380 villas | AE, D, DC, MC, V.

Lodge on Little St. Simons Island. The spacious, airy rooms are distributed among five buildings, including the 1917 Hunting Lodge, with two antiques-filled guest rooms; a two-bedroom cottage; and two houses with four guest rooms each. Each of the rooms in the houses has a private deck, and each house has a large living room with a fireplace. Houses also feature large screened porches, perfect for watching the sun set over the marshes. Rates include all meals, dinner wines, and cocktails. Meals are served family style in the main dining room and include platters heaped with fresh fish, homemade breads, and pies. Transportation from St. Simons Island, transportation on the island, and interpretive guides are included. Dining room, complimentary breakfast. Pool. Horseback riding, beach, boating, fishing, bicycles. Business services. | Little St. Simons Island, | 912/638–7472 or 888/733–5774 | fax 912/634–1811 | lssi@mindspring.com | www.littlestsimonsisland.com | 15 rooms in 5 buildings | $350–$525 | AP | AE, D, DC, MC, V.

Sea Palms Golf and Tennis Resort. Given the resort's emphasis on golf and tennis, this is an ideal location if you're interested in sports. Sea Palms is a contemporary resort complex with fully furnished villas nestled on an 800-acre site. As a guest you also enjoy beach club privileges. 2 restaurants, bar. Many kitchenettes. 2 pools. Golf courses, 12 tennis courts. Health club, volleyball, bicycles. Children's programs. | 5445 Frederica Rd. | 912/638–3351 or 800/841–6268 | fax 912/634–8029 | www.seapalms.com | 160 rooms, 79 suites, in 6 buildings | $114–$144, 145–260 suites | AE, DC, MC, V.

SAVANNAH

(Nearby town also listed: Tybee Island)

Savannah is Georgia's oldest city and also its third largest, following Atlanta and Columbus. Founded in 1733 when James Oglethorpe arrived with 120 settlers, the town began growing immediately. By the early days of the Revolutionary War Savannah was a thriving port city, a fact not overlooked by the British, who occupied it in December 1778. Despite a valiant American effort to regain the strategic port in 1779, Savannah remained in British hands until its liberation by General Anthony Wayne's troops in 1782. Savannah was Georgia's first state capital, a role it held from 1782 to 1785.

At the outbreak of the Civil War, Confederate troops seized Union-held Fort Pulaski. One year later, the superior firepower of Union artillery was more than Confederate defenders could resist, and the fort was retaken by the U.S. Army and was used as a Union hospital. In December 1864, General William T. Sherman marched on Savannah and, following intense fighting, took the city. A jubilant Sherman wired President Abraham Lincoln, advising the chief executive that Savannah was being given to him as a Christmas present.

Today, Savannah is one of the "crown jewel" cities of America's eastern seaboard. A vigorous and well-organized historic zoning effort has preserved the inner town much as it was in the days before and immediately following the Civil War. The city boasts 1,400 restored or reconstructed buildings dating from the time of its founding. Warehouses still line the banks of the Savannah River upon which oceangoing vessels haul cargo upstream for unloading.

Information: Savannah Area Convention and Visitors Bureau | 101 E. Bay St., Savannah, GA 31401 | 912/644–6401 or 877/728–2662 | cvb@savga.com | www.savannahvisit.com.

TRANSPORTATION INFORMATION

Airport: Savannah is served by the **Savannah International Airport,** 18 mi west of downtown. Delta, US Airways, and Continental Express offer domestic flights; despite the name, international flights to Savannah are virtually nonexistent. | 400 Airways Ave. | 912/964–0514.

Airport Transportation: Vans operated by **McCall's Limousine Service** leave the airport for downtown locations. The trip takes 15 minutes; fares vary, depending on the number of people traveling. | 912/966–5364 or 800/673–9365.

Amtrak serves the city from its station at 2611 Seaboard Coastline Drive | 912/234–2611 or 800/872–7245.

Bus Lines: Greyhound/Trailways provides bus service to and from Savannah. The depot is at 610 W. Oglethorpe Ave. | 912/232–2135 or 800/231–2222.

Other: Savannah sits astride two links of the Interstate highway system, I–16 and I–95, and is easily accessible by automobile.

Attractions

ART AND ARCHITECTURE

Andrew Low House. Andrew Low was a native of Scotland and one of Savannah's merchant princes. The 1848 home he built later belonged to his son William, husband of Girl Scouts founder Juliette Gordon. Besides its historical significance for scouting, the house has some of the finest ornamental ironwork in Savannah and is a treasure trove of fine 19th-century antiques and silver. | 329 Abercorn St. | 912/233–6854 | fax 912/233–1828 | andrewlow@aol.com | $7 | Guided tours on the hour and half hour, Mon.–Wed., Fri., Sat. 10:30–3:30, Sun. 12:30–3:30.

THE BEGINNINGS OF THE GIRL SCOUTS

On March 12, 1912, in the presence of 18 young girls sitting in the parlor of her towering three-story home located on the corner of Bull Street and Oglethorpe Avenue in downtown Savannah, Juliette Gordon Low, a petite, 51-year-old widow, organized what later became the Girl Scouts of America.

Born in Savannah on Halloween Day 1860, Juliette, called Daisy when she was growing up, was raised with her three sisters and two brothers. She loved to fish and learned to shoot, ride horses, and to appreciate fine art and literature. Daisy attended a well-to-do boarding school in Virginia and completed finishing school in New York. She traveled extensively on holidays between the cool mountains of North Georgia and such resorts as White Sulphur Springs in West Virginia.

When she was 25 years old Daisy was struck by a personal tragedy. For quite a while she had been suffering prolonged, excruciating pain from a series of ear infections. A dangerous and unsuccessful treatment of silver nitrate left her deaf on one side. Daisy's partial deafness only served to reinforce her love for life. She continued her busy schedule of attending every Savannah social event, and at one of these gala functions, she met her future husband.

William McKay Low, who maintained a residence and business office in Savannah, was the son of a wealthy British shipping family. On December 21, 1886, the couple was married at Savannah's historic Christ Episcopal Church. And then tragedy again visited Daisy. As the happy newlyweds exited the church into the barrage of rice being tossed by well-wishers, a single grain entered Daisy's *good* ear. Efforts to extract the rice failed, and within a few short months, Daisy's hearing in that ear was gone as well.

Her deafness aside, Daisy's next few years were among the happiest in her life. She and William Low loved each other deeply. They maintained three separate residences in England and traveled Europe extensively. However, the union between Daisy and William Low began to fall apart. In 1898, after returning to England from a trip to Florida where she assisted her mother with the establishment of a hospital for Spanish-American War veterans, Daisy was devastated to learn that William had taken a mistress. William sought a divorce. However, before it could be granted, he died, but not before guaranteeing that his entire estate was left to the mistress, not Daisy.

Embarrassed by her failed marriage, as well as the humiliation of helplessly watching her husband's legacy go to another woman, Daisy elected to maintain her residence in Great Britain. For the next several years, she lived alone, pursuing her social life and embarking on new artistic adventures, including sculpting and metalworking. Then, in May 1911, she made the acquaintance of General Sir Robert Baden-Powell, a man who would change her life forever.

Baden-Powell had seen a great deal of active service in India and Africa before making a name for himself in the South African War in 1900. He was a national icon and one of the most respected men in Great Britain. In 1908 he had established the Boy Scouts movement in England. Two years later, with the assistance of his sister, Agnes, he had founded the Girl Guides, a girls' organization similar to the Boy Scouts. Daisy was fascinated with the new program and visited Sir Robert and Agnes often, learning all she could about the newly formed girls' movement.

When Daisy returned to her Savannah home in 1912 she organized the Girl Guides in America. By the end of that year, the name of the Girl Guides was changed to Girl Scouts, and the organization's national headquarters was established in Washington, D.C. When Juliette Gordon Low died on January 17, 1927, the membership had soared to more than 100,000.

City Hall. In 1905 the Old City Exchange (1799–1904) was demolished to build City Hall, an imposing structure. Nearby is a bench commemorating Oglethorpe's landing on February 12, 1733. | 2 E. Bay St. | 912/236–7284 (automated information line) or 912/651–6410 (public information) | fax 912/651–6408 | www.ci.savannah.ga.us | Free | Weekdays 8–5.

Georgia Historical Society. Hodgson Hall, built in 1875 for the society, houses a library and archive. Display cases hold rotating exhibits drawn from the society's collections, and there's a lecture series as well. | 501 Whitaker St. | 912/651–2128 | fax 912/651–2831 | www.georgiahistory.com | Free | Tues.–Sat. 10–5.

★ **Green-Meldrim House.** Cotton merchant Charles Green commissioned New York architect John Norris to build this extravagant ($90,000 at the time) Gothic mansion, completed in 1850. General Sherman used the house as his headquarters after taking the city in 1864. Judge Peter Meldrim bought it in 1892, and his heirs sold it to St. John's Episcopal Church for use as a parish house. Gothic features include a crenellated roof, large bay windows called oriels, and an external gallery with filigreed ironwork. Within, its decorative finishes continue the Gothic motif. Fine antiques from several centuries are displayed, some original to the house. The house faces Madison Square. | 14 W. Macon St. | 912/233–3845 | fax 912/232–5559 | $5 | Tours on the half hour Tues., Thurs., Fri. 10–4, Sat. 10–1.

★ **Isiah Davenport House.** The threatened demolition of this fine Federal mansion jumpstarted Savannah's historic preservation movement. Master builder Isaiah Davenport began construction of his home in 1815 and completed it in 1820. The wrought-iron-trimmed semi-circular staircase leading to the front door, polished hardwood floors, fine woodwork and plasterwork, and a soaring elliptical staircase are among its significant features. Furnishings from the 1820s are Hepplewhite, Chippendale, and Sheraton. | 324 E. State St. | 912/236–8097 | fax 912/233–7938 | $6 | Mon.–Sat. 10–4:30, Sun. 1–4:30.

Juliette Gordon Low Birthplace. This majestic, Regency-style town house (built 1818–21) became Savannah's first National Historic Landmark in 1965. Juliette Gordon "Daisy" Low, founder in 1912 of the Girl Scouts, was born here in 1860, so the house is now owned and operated by the Girl Scouts of U.S.A. Mrs. Low's paintings and other artwork are on display in the house, restored to the style of 1886, the year of her marriage. There is a museum shop. Tours every 20 minutes. | 10 E. Oglethorpe Ave. | 912/233–4501 | fax 912/233–4659 | www.girlscouts.org | $8 | Mon., Tues., Thurs.–Sat. 10–4, Sun. 12:30–4:30.

King-Tisdell Cottage. An African-American cultural center, this Victorian cottage typifies the coastal urban middle-class residence of the late 19th century. There's a good gift shop with excellent books. | 514 E. Huntingdon St. | 912/234–8000 | fax 912/234–8001 | www.kingtisdell.org | $3 | By appointment.

U.S. Custom House. When it opened in 1852, the U.S. Custom House also housed both the U.S. Postal Service and the federal courts. The site itself is a historic one for Savannah, having held a house rented by James Edward Oglethorpe in 1733 as well as the building where John Wesley preached his first sermon in America. One of eight historic custom houses in the country, it was designed by New York architect John Norris and was his first Savannah commission. Norris worked in Savannah from 1846 to 1861 and also designed many of the warehouses along the river. Under his influence, Savannah moved from wooden buildings to sturdier, more fireproof brick-and-stone structures. | 1 E. Bay St. | 912/477–9400 | fax 912/447–9407 | www.customs.gov | Free | Weekdays 8–5.

BEACHES, PARKS, AND NATURAL SITES

Fort McAllister State Historic Park. The moss-draped, 250-mi-long Ogeechee River is the backdrop for this park, which preserves Confederate earthwork fortifications. Giant live oaks and salt marshes make a unique setting for camping, hiking, boating, and picnicking. The museum exhibits maps, a diorama, Civil War uniforms, artillery, naval artifacts, portraits of the generals involved in the Civil War battle that ended Sherman's March to the Sea, and period tools. | 3894 Fort McAllister Rd., Richmond Hill | 912/727–2339 | fax 912/

ELI WHITNEY AND THE COTTON GIN

As the 18th century drew to a close, cotton was in large demand in England and the rest of Europe for the manufacture of fine cloth and thus was a potential export for the United States. However, the variety of cotton that was grown in Georgia and neighboring states—and the type that could be easily processed by machine—grew only in the lowlands near the ocean, and production of marketable quantities was very limited. Another kind of cotton, the *short-staple* variety, was an easy grower anywhere in the warm, moist climes of the American South. The only problem with the short-staple variety was the extreme difficulty in separating the seeds from the fiber. The machine used with the other variety was of no avail on short-staple cotton, and consequently, to produce one pound of marketable, seed-free cotton required one person's labor for a full day. If only someone could come up with a device to remove the seeds from the fiber automatically, cotton could become an economic boon to farmers all over the region.

Sitting on the verandah of Mrs. Nathanael Greene's beautiful plantation house, Mulberry Grove, located just outside Savannah, 26-year-old Eli Whitney contemplated the chain of events that had brought him, a Massachusetts Yankee, to the Deep South. He had graduated from Yale College only a few months earlier and had been lured to Georgia in anticipation of filling a tutoring position that promised to pay well enough to get him out of the large debt he had incurred while putting himself through school. But, alas, when he arrived in Savannah, he learned that his future employer intended to pay him only half of the previously agreed salary. The kind-hearted Mrs. Greene, widow of the famed Revolutionary War general, insisted that he stay on her plantation until he could find more rewarding work.

With his friend Phineas Miller, who was Mrs. Greene's caretaker, Whitney discussed ideas that might make money for the two young men. Miller was also interested in a project that would help Mrs. Greene recover from the heavy debt that she had run up while trying to operate her large, but only marginally profitable, plantation. The subject soon turned to cotton and how the plant fibers could be economically processed. During the next few weeks, the notion that there must be some easy, inexpensive way to extract the cotton seeds from the fiber preyed on Whitney's mind. Finally, after hours of daydreaming and trial-and-error design work, he produced a prototype cotton gin that performed the desired functions without a hitch.

Whitney and Miller soon became partners and told nearby Georgia landowners that their goal was to build enough cotton gins to place them at convenient places throughout the region, thus allowing a grower to bring in his cotton, have it processed, and pay for it with a share of the "clean" fiber. Now, amid glowing success, a serious problem arose. The demand for the new machines outgrew the ability of the two men to build them. Whitney returned to New England where he hired skilled labor to manufacture the gins en masse, while Miller stayed in Georgia handling the administrative and logistical aspects of the new partnership.

It soon occurred to Whitney that his cotton gin, as revolutionary as it was, would be extremely easy to reproduce if some unscrupulous person had the notion. The partners had been careful not to divulge details of the design to anyone and even refused to allow cotton growers to watch the gin while it processed their cotton. Accordingly, in June 1793, Whitney applied for a patent on his machine. In the application he proudly wrote *That with the Ginn, if turned with horses or by water, two persons will clean enough cotton in one day, as a hundred persons could clean in the same time with ginns now in common use.*

Fewer than 200,000 pounds of cotton were exported in 1791, when the tedious work of separating the plant's seeds from the fiber was still largely performed by hand. A dozen years later, Southern growers were selling 41 million pounds of cotton a year, and the plant had become the basis for the plantation economy.

© Artville

727–3614 | www.gastateparks.org | $2.50; special rate for children; parking $2 vehicle, $20 vans, $50 bus | Daily 7–10; museum Mon.–Sat. 9–5, Sun. 2–5.

Melon Bluff Heritage and Nature Center. A private 3,000-acre nature and heritage preserve, the land has been in the same family since 1735. One of 17 sites on the Colonial Coast Birding Trail that runs from South Carolina to Florida, you'll find this perfect if you're seeking an eco-tourism experience. The big draws include bicycling, hiking, exploring adjacent Dickinson Creek in one of 15 kayaks, and studying the wildlife and history of the area. Excellent bed-and-breakfast accommodations are available on the property. | 2999 Islands Hwy. | 912/884–5779 or 888/246–8188 | fax 912/884–3046 | www.melonbluff.com | $5 | Tues.–Sun. 9–4.

Savannah National Wildlife Refuge. This refuge on the lower Savannah River covers over 38 mi of river and 25 mi of streams and creeks. The refuge is home to a variety of wildlife, especially migratory wading birds and waterfowl, including ducks and geese, along with bald eagles, great horned owls, and osprey. | South Carolina Rte. 170 | 912/652–4415 | fax 912/652–4385 | southeast.fws.gov/wildlife/nwrscr.html | Free | Daily dawn to dusk.

CULTURE, EDUCATION, AND HISTORY

★ **Colonial Park Cemetery.** The second burial ground for Savannah's founders (1750–1853) is the final resting place for many of the state's historic luminaries, including Button Gwinnett, who signed the Declaration of Independence, and Joseph Habersham, an early governor. | Corner of Oglethorpe Ave. and Abercorn St. | 912/651–6610 | Free | Daily dawn to dusk.

Congregation Mickve Israel. Founded in 1733, this Reform congregation (the country's third oldest) is housed in a splendid 19th-century Gothic synagogue on Monterey Square. Its founders, both Ashkenazic and Sephardic Jews, sailed from London to Savannah without the blessing of the colony's trustees and were welcomed by Oglethorpe despite orders from London to bar them. Among its members was Samuel Nunes, a Portuguese physician who saved the colonists from ravaging disease. | 20 E. Gordon St. | 912/233–1547 | fax 912/233–3086 | www.mickveisrael.org | Donations accepted; groups $2 per person | Weekdays 10–noon and 2–4.

Fort Jackson. On Salter's Island, just 3½ mi outside of Savannah, sits the oldest standing fort in Georgia, having been garrisoned in 1812. The brick fort, surrounded by a tidal moat, holds 13 exhibit areas. In the river under a red buoy, the scuttled ironclad CSS *Georgia* awaits raising, and a group of history enthusiasts is working feverishly to accomplish that goal. | 1 Ft. Jackson Rd. | 912/232–3945 | fax 912/236–5126 | www.chsgeorgia.org | $3.50 | Daily 9–5.

Laurel Grove Cemetery. There are two parts (north and south) to the cemetery. Laurel Grove North is the resting place for such well-regarded white Savannahians as Juliette Gordon Low, while Laurel Grove South, established in 1852, is for "free persons of color" and slaves. There, you'll find the final resting places of many of Savannah's leaders from the city's African-American community. Among these is Reverend Andrew Bryan, who succeeded George Leile as pastor of First African Baptist Church, the nation's oldest black church (1773). | 802 W. Anderson St. | 912/651–6772 or 912/651–6843 | fax 912/651–4254 | Free | Daily 8–5.

LeConte-Woodmanston Site, Rice Plantation and Botanical Gardens. The LeConte family left a major mark on American science: John LeConte compiled the basic work on Georgia ornithology, was a physician, and taught natural philosophy at the University of Georgia. In 1875 he became the first president of the University of California at Berkeley. Joseph LeConte, professor of biology at Berkeley, helped found the Sierra Club. The house is long gone, but this fascinating National Register site is being restored to resume the production of the rare Carolina Gold rice. A fascinating system of canals and drainage ditches attests to the presence of African rice-growing methods in Georgia. | Box 179, Midway | 912/884–6500 | fax 912/884–6700 | gwhalen@clds.net | www.hist.armstrong.edu/publichist/leconte/leconte-home.htm | $2 | Tues.–Sat. 9–5:30.

Wormsloe State Historic Site. A road lined with moss-draped live oaks leads to the ruins of Nobel Jones's fine mansion. Jones, a native of Surrey, England, was a physician and carpenter who came to Savannah with General James Oglethorpe in 1733. He survived hunger, plague, civil strife, and the difficulties of a new environment to establish himself and his family as colonists. A nature trail leads to the site, and when there you can watch a film and examine artifacts in the visitors center. Special programs often feature costumed docents. | 7601 Skidaway Rd. | 912/353–3023 | fax 912/353–3023 (call first) | www.gastateparks.org | $2.50 | Tues.–Sat. 9–5, Sun. 2–5:30.

New Ebenezer. In 1736 Lutheran religious refugees from Salzburg, Austria, arrived in Savannah, and Oglethorpe sent them upriver to found a new colony to grow food for Savannah. Devising a town plan similar to that of Savannah, the Salzburgers, as they came to be known, developed a thriving silkworm industry. The settlement did not survive long past the revolution. The historic cemetery is still used by their descendants. Today, surviving buildings include 1769 Jerusalem church, on its original site, and assorted buildings moved to the site for preservation. A retreat center accommodates up to 170 guests ($13–$40), mostly for groups. There's a museum and small gift shop with books about the Salzburgers. The Georgia Salzburger Society operates the enterprise and serves as caretaker of the site. | 2887 Ebenezer Rd., Rincon | 912/754–9242 | fax 912/754–7781 | www.newebenezer.org | Free | Museum Wed., Sat., Sun. 3–5 and by appointment.

MUSEUMS

Midway Museum and Church. This reproduction of an 18th-century raised cottage contains furniture, artifacts, and documents from early 18th- to 19th-century area families. At the museum, which has an excellent bookshop, get the key for the adjacent Puritan church, built in 1792. Two of its congregants were signers of the Declaration of Independence, Button Gwinnett and Lyman Hall. Don't miss the old cemetery, where significant colonial-era citizens, including two Revolutionary War generals—Daniel Stewart and James Screven—and a U.S. senator, are buried. Supreme Court Justice Oliver Wendell Holmes's grandfather is among the interred. | U.S. 17 in Midway | 912/884–5837 | $3 | Tues.–Sat. 10–4, Sun. 2–4.

★ **Owens-Thomas House and Museum.** English architect William Jay completed this Regency architectural marvel in 1819, soon after his arrival in Savannah. Curved walls, half-moon arches, and Greek-inspired ornamental details highlight its outstanding features. A National Historic Landmark, it is undergoing substantial, detailed conservation. | 124 Abercorn St. | 912/233–9743 | fax 912/233–0102 | $8 | Mon. noon–5, Tues.–Sat. 9–5.

Ralph Marks Gilbert Civil Rights Museum. Opened in 1996, the museum details in archival photographs the role of black and white Savannahians in ending the city's segregation era. Exhibits cover emancipation through the civil rights movement. In addition, the museum has touring exhibitions. | 460 Martin Luther King, Jr. Blvd. | 912/231–8900 | fax 912/234–2577 | $4 | Mon.–Sat. 9–5.

Savannah History Museum. The entire coastal region is the subject of the museum's numerous exhibits, which also deal with the founding of Savannah in 1733. The building sits on the site of the Revolutionary War Siege of Savannah; a diorama details the battle. On this site, it is thought, is a mass grave for the soldiers, who were interred where they fell. The gift shop offers souvenirs and books. | 303 Martin Luther King, Jr. Blvd. | 912/238–1779 | fax 912/651–6827 | www.chsgeorgia.org | $2; film $1.50; admission and film $2.90 | Weekdays 8:30–5, weekends 9–5.

Fashion Gallery. In a former theatrical space, the gallery exhibits garments from the long span of Savannah's history. | 303 Martin Luther King, Jr. Blvd. | 912/238–1779 | fax 912/651–6827 | www.chsgeorgia.org | Included with $2 admission ticket | Weekdays 8:30–5, weekends 9–5.

Exhibit Hall. Exhibits detail the city's military, maritime, and industrial activity. There's also a Johnny Mercer exhibit (including two of his Oscars), a collection of Savannah's monuments, and the Forest Gump bench. | 303 Martin Luther King, Jr. Blvd. | 912/238–1779 | fax 912/651–6827 | www.chsgeorgia.org | Included with $2 admission ticket | Weekdays 8:30–5, weekends 9–5.

Main Theater. Films on the history of Savannah are shown every half hour. | 303 Martin Luther King, Jr. Blvd. | 912/238–1779 | fax 912/651–6827 | www.chsgeorgia.org | Film $1.50; admission and film $2.90 | Weekdays 8:30–5, weekends 9–5.

Ships of the Sea Museum. Savannah merchant William Scarborough hired the brilliant designer William Jay to build his fine Greek-revival mansion. Today it houses a nautical museum, exhibiting scale models of famous ships. Included are models of *The Ann*, which bore James Oglethorpe and his settlers to the new colony; *The City of Savannah*; and many examples of the famous China clippers. | 41 Martin Luther King, Jr. Blvd. | 912/232–1511 | fax 912/234–7363 | www.shipsofthesea.org | $5 | Tues.–Sun. 10–4:15.

Telfair Mansion and Art Museum. William Jay, Savannah's principal architect in the early 19th century, designed the Telfair Mansion, now the oldest public art museum in the Southeast. Commissioned by Alexander Telfair, it features marbled rooms exhibiting American, French, and Dutch Impressionist paintings; German tonalist paintings; a large collection of works by Kahlil Gibran; plaster casts of the Elgin Marbles, the Venus de Milo, and the Laocoön, among other classical sculptures; and some of the Telfair family furnishings, including a Duncan Phyfe sideboard and Savannah-made silver. | 121 Barnard St. | 912/232–1177 | fax 912/232–6954 | www.telfair.org | $6 | Tues.–Sat. 10–5, Sun. 1–5, Mon. noon–5.

Mighty 8th Air Force Heritage Museum. Formed in Savannah during World War II, this famous squadron moved to the United Kingdom, and, flying borrowed aircraft, became the largest air force in the history of aviation. With about 200,000 combat crew personnel, many of whom lost their lives or were interned as prisoners of war, the unit saw extensive action in Europe. Opened in 1996, the museum exhibits memorabilia from the period, beginning with the buildup to World War II and the rise of Adolf Hitler. To make the experience more real, they show you a film in a Quonset hut. Vintage aircraft, an art gallery featuring aviation art, a library with archives, a tribute to the Tuskeegee Airmen, and displays about women in aviation and African-Americans in aviation are all within. Not limited to World War II, the museum's exhibits run through Desert Storm. The food service area, Heroes' Canteen, serves pretty decent fare, including local specialties. | 175 Bourne Ave., Pooler | 912/748–8888 | fax 912/748–0209 | www.mighty8thmuseums.com | $7.50 | Daily 9–6.

RELIGION AND SPIRITUALITY

Christ Church. This is the site of the home church to Georgia's first congregation; John Wesley, founder of Methodism, preached here and is believed to have established the colony's first Sunday school here. The building is the third on this site and dates to 1838, but the bell (Georgia's only Revere and Son) dates to 1816. Juliette Gordon Low, founder of the Girl Scouts, worshiped at this Episcopal church. | 28 Bull St. | 912/232–4131 | fax 912/232–4485 | Free | Tours: Wed., Fri. 10–3.

First African Baptist Church. Founded in 1773, this is the oldest black church in North America. George Leile was its first minister. The present structure was erected in 1859 by members of the congregation, who did the work themselves. Its contemporary importance is its role as the cradle of the civil rights movement in coastal Georgia. | 23 Montgomery St. | 912/233–6597 or 912/233–2244 | fax 912/234–7950 | www.oldestblackchurch.org | Free | Daily 10–4.

SIGHTSEEING TOURS/TOUR COMPANIES

Gray Line bus tours. Historic Savannah is the focus of the company's bus tours. | 215 W. Boundary St. | 912/234–8687 or 800/426–2318 | fax 912/233–3959 | www.grayline.com | $16–$21 | Daily 9–4:20.

Old Savannah Tours. City tours and weddings are their specialties. Tours run every 15 to 20 minutes. | 250 Martin Luther King, Jr. Blvd. | 912/234–8128 | fax 912/234–0493 | www.old-savtour.com | $15–$21 | Daily 9–4:30.

OTHER POINTS OF INTEREST

Factors Walk. The King Cotton–era center of commerce and trade housed merchants (factors) whose role was to set the world price of cotton. Elaborate iron bridgeways connect the buildings that once contained their offices. Today, it's filled with shops and galleries and is a good starting point for visiting the River Street area. | 100 E. Bay St. | Free | Daily.

Historic Savannah Waterfront Area. Stones carried in ships as ballast line the streets leading to River Street, where the waterfront has traded in its rough-and-tumble for fine shops and dining establishments. Lots of festivals and things to see keep the area busy and full of visitors. | John P. Rousakis Riverfront Plaza | Free | Daily.

ON THE CALENDAR

JAN.: *Georgia Heritage Festival.* Walking tours, open house at historic sites, concerts, a parade, and a waterfront festival are among the highlights. | Various locations throughout Savannah | 912/233–7787.
MARCH: *St. Patrick's Day Parade.* Purported to be the largest of its kind in the country, Savannah's St. Patrick's Day Parade is a waterfront celebration of life. Food vendors, music, and lots of green add to the fun. | 912/644–6401.
DEC.: *Christmas in Savannah.* House tours, parades, caroling, and musical performances are part of this month-long event. | Various locations throughout Savannah | 800/444–CHARM.

Dining

INEXPENSIVE

★ **Mrs. Wilkes' Dining Room.** Southern. Breakfast and lunch are totally traditional, with the dishes served family style at big tables. This restaurant is globally known, so you can find yourself chatting with folks from Britain or Japan. Wait times can be long, so arrive early. Fried or roast chicken, wonderful ham, sweet potatoes, collard greens, okra, mashed potatoes, corn bread are placed nonstop on the tables, which guests then help to clear. No alcohol. | 107 W. Jones St. | 912/232–5997 | Reservations not accepted | Closed Jan. and weekends. No dinner | $6–$12 | No credit cards.

★ **Nita's Place.** Southern. Owner Juanita Dixon cooks from pure tradition; try her salmon patties or sweet potato pie, the best in the state. Offerings are written on a board posted on the wall behind the steam table. Enjoy fresh-squeezed lemonade. Line-ups get thick around noon, so go early or late. No alcohol. No smoking. | 140 Abercorn St. | 912/238–8233 | Reservations not accepted | No dinner | $7–$19 | MC, V.

Red Hot and Blue Memphis Pit Barbecue. Barbecue. The place is a mite upscale for a 'cue joint, but the ribs are quite good. Do the Memphis thing and get the dry rub version. Kids' menu. | 11108 Abercorn St. | 912/961–7422 | $6–$12 | AE, D, MC, V.

MODERATE

★ **Bistro Savannah.** Southern. Textured brick walls, usually lined with paintings by local artists, provide a warm backdrop for chef Dan Kim's contemporary regional dishes, such as shrimp and tasso on grits, barbecued black grouper with peach and pear chutney, and fresh fruit cobblers. | 309 W. Congress St. | 912/233–6266 | No lunch | $15–$23 | AE, MC, V.

Garibaldi's. Italian. Brick walls warm to the touch of candlelight in this former firehouse. Despite the Italian base, Asian and Southern touches (shrimp Savannah and crab cakes with chutney) appear everywhere. Signature dish is whole flounder with apricot glaze, creation of a Thai chef. Focus on the specials, especially fish: grouper with fresh vegetables and pasta is outstanding. The wine list is good, with plenty of California varietals. Wish hard for the flourless chocolate torte for dessert. | 315 W. Congress St. | 912/232–7118 | No lunch | $15–$25 | AE, MC, V.

★ **Il Pasticcio.** Italian. Sicilian Pino Venetico turned this former department store, gleaming with steel, glass, and tile, into a high-energy spot buzzing with a young, hip crowd. The menu changes frequently, but fresh pastas with inventive sauces are a constant. Don't miss the second-floor art gallery. | 2 E. Broughton St. | 912/231–8888 | www.ilpasticcio.com | No lunch | $13–$25 | AE, D, DC, MC, V.

The Lady and Sons. Southern. Lines form early outside Paula Deen's City Market restaurant for lunch and supper buffets and for brunch. With her sons Bobby and Jamie, she serves specialties from the family repertoire. There's also a menu. Buffet (lunch and supper). | 311 W. Congress St. | 912/233–2600 | www.ladyandsons.com | No dinner Sun. | $10–$17 | AE, D, MC, V.

Old Pink House. Southern. Upstairs you're in the quiet, refined atmosphere you'd expect in a Georgian mansion dating to 1771. Downstairs in the tavern the environment is more lively, complete with entertainment. She-crab soup, a light version, is a Lowcountry specialty. Regional ingredients include black grouper stuffed with blue crab with Vidalia onion sauce. | 23 Abercorn St. | 912/232–4286 | No lunch | $15–$25 | AE, MC, V.

★ **Sapphire Grill.** Eclectic. Chef Chris Nason bases seasonal menus on local ingredients, such as Georgia white shrimp, crab, and fish. Elegant vegetable dishes include a seasonal vegetable tart. The chocolate flan defines ecstasy. | 110 W. Congress St. | 912/443–9962 | www.sapphiregrill.com | No lunch | $13–$26 | AE, DC, MC, V.

EXPENSIVE

★ **Elizabeth on 37th.** Southern. Founding chef Elizabeth Terry has won numerous awards, including the James Beard designation as Best Chef in the Southeast. This elegant restaurant, housed in a Beaux Arts mansion, focuses on regional and local specialties, including Bluffton oysters in season, shrimp on grits, and Savannah cream cake. | 105 E. 37th St. | 912/236–5547 | www.savannah-online.com/elizabeth | Reservations essential | No lunch | $21–$31 | AE, D, DC, MC, V.

★ **45 South.** Contemporary. Cuisine based on seasonal use of local and regional ingredients makes this quiet establishment hum with sophistication. Menu is à la carte, but the side dishes are sufficient for two. The service is impeccable. Rabbit, game, seafood, and stellar desserts are the draws, with specific preparations changing depending on the season. | 20 E. Broad St. | 912/233–1881 | www.thepirateshouse.com | Jacket required | Closed Sun. No lunch | $20–$32 | AE, D, DC, MC, V.

Lodging

INEXPENSIVE

B&B Inn. Said to be the first B&B to open in Savannah, the inn is a restored 1853 Federal-style row house on historic Gordon Row near Chatham Square. The rooms have four-poster queen-size beds. The building has four stories with no elevator. Some kitchenettes. | 117 W. Gordon St. | 912/238–0518 | fax 912/233–2537 | www.travelbase.com/destinations/savannah/bed-breakfast | 15 rooms, 6 suites | $80–$115, $115–$160 suites | AE, D, MC, V.

DeSoto Hilton. Built in 1968 on the site of the venerable DeSoto Hotel, this 15-story hotel is one of the largest in the historic district proper and is a short stroll from both Forsyth Park and the Riverfront. The rooms are luxurious, but lack the charm of those in the historic inns. Rooms on the upper floors command a sweeping view of the city. Restaurant, bar with entertainment. In-room data ports. Cable TV. Pool. Exercise equipment. | 15 East

Liberty St. | 912/232–9000 | fax 912/231–1633 | www.hilton.com | 246 rooms | $119–$179 | AE, D, DC, MC, V.

Holiday Inn. This Holiday Inn, 9 miles away from the airport, is within walking distance to the mall and dining. Restaurant. In-room data ports. Cable TV. Pool. Gym. Laundry service. Business services. Pets allowed. | I–95 and GA 204 | 912/925–2770 | fax 912/925–2770 | 176 rooms | $77 | AE, D, DC, MC, V.

The Olde Georgian Inn. Delores Ellis, Savannah's only African-American innkeeper, spent six years refurbishing this fine old Victorian house, built in 1890. Located on the edge of Forsyth Park. Amenities include gas-log fireplaces. Cable TV, in-room VCRs. Hot tub. | 212 W. Hall St. | 912/236–2911 or 800/835–6831 | fax 912/236–4010 | 5 rooms, 3 suites in 2 buildings | $110–$140 rooms, $150–$200 suites | MC, V.

MODERATE

East Bay Inn. Just a few steps away from River Street, this inn on the northern edge of the historical district is filled with reproductions rather than antiques. Some of the high-ceilinged rooms have exposed brick walls. Perks include wine and cheese, plus a deluxe nightly turn-down service. | 225 East Bay St. | 912/238–1225 | www.eastbayinn.com | 28 rooms | $179–$199 | AE, D, DC, MC, V.

Eliza Thompson House. Eliza Thompson was a socially prominent widow when she built her fine town house around 1847. In 1995 Carol and Steve Day purchased the house and repainted, refinished, and refurnished it in period style. Marble baths have been added to some rooms. Complimentary Continental breakfast. | 5 W. Jones St. | 912/236–3620 or 800/348–9378 | fax 912/238–1920 | www.elizathompsonhouse.com | 25 rooms in 2 buildings | $109–$260 | MC, V.

★ **Foley House Inn.** Two town houses, built 50 years apart, form this elegant inn. Most rooms have antiques and reproductions. A carriage house to the rear of the property has less expensive rooms. Complimentary Continental breakfast. In-room VCRs. Some in-room hot tubs. | 14 W. Hull St. | 912/232–6622 or 800/647–3708 | fax 912/231–1218 | www.foleyinn.com | 18 rooms in 2 buildings | $165–$325 | AE, MC, V.

Hamilton-Turner Inn. Experience *Midnight in the Garden of Good and Evil* with a stay in this 1873 mansion built by wealthy Savannah jeweler Samuel Hamilton. The house once belonged to Mandy Nichols, one of the principal characters in the book. It's furnished with fine Second Empire, Eastlake, and Renaissance antiques. Four rooms have large hot tubs, two have fireplaces, and two have both plus a balcony. In-room data ports. Some in-room hot tubs. | 330 Abercorn St. | 912/233–1833 or 888/448–8849 | fax 912/233–0291 | www.hamilton-turner.com | 14 rooms, 4 suites | $160–$275 | AE, D, DC, MC, V.

Jesse Mount. One of the six guest rooms at this 19th century brick rowhouse is a carriage house suite, complete with a full kitchen and a garden view. Most rooms have original oil paintings on the walls. All have polished hardwood floors and antiques. Complimentary Continental breakfast. Library. | 209 W. Jones St. | 912/236–1774 | 6 rooms | $195–$240 | AE, D, DC, MC, V.

Magnolia Place Inn. Overlooking verdant Forsyth Park, this grand Victorian mansion was built in 1878. Twelve guest rooms are available, many featuring a fireplace and hot tub. In the morning, breakfast is served on the veranda—if you're a late riser you can have it delivered to your room on a silver tray. Complimentary Continental breakfast. Some in-room hot tubs. Cable TV. | 503 Whitaker St. | 912/236–7674 or 800/238–7674 (outside GA) | fax 912/236–1145 | b.b.magnolia@mci2000.com | www.magnoliaplaceinn.com | 12 rooms | $145–$270 | A, D, MC, V.

Manor House. This 1830s style building hosted a group of federal officers during the Civil War. Today, the all-suites B&B has floor-to-ceiling windows that look out on old oak trees. Antiques and oriental rugs fill the rooms. Complimentary Continental breakfast. Some in-room hot tubs. Cable TV, in-room VCRs, room phones. | 201 S. Liberty St. | 912/233–9597 or 800/462–3696 | fax 912/236–9419 | www.bbonline.com/ga/savannah/manorhouse/index.html | 5 rooms | $185–$225 | AE, MC.

Marshall House. This restored hotel, with original pine floors, woodwork, and bricks, caters to business travelers while providing the intimacy of a bed-and-breakfast inn. Different spaces reflect different parts of Savannah's history, from its founding to the Civil War. Restaurant, bar. In-room data ports. Pets allowed (fee). | 123 E. Broughton St. | 912/644–7896 or 800/589–6304 | fax 912/234–3334 | www.marshallhouse.com | 68 rooms, 3 suites | $159–$209 | AE, D, MC, V.

★ **Mulberry Inn.** A unique Holiday Inn, with a beautiful courtyard and interesting history. Once the site of a livery stable, then a cotton warehouse and Coca-Cola bottling plant, the hotel has carved antiques and amenities for businessmen and tourists. Some suites with king-size beds and wet bars. Bar. In-room VCRs. Pool. Hot tub. | 601 East Bay St. | 912/238–1200 | 120 rooms | $145–$185 | AE, D, DC, MC, V.

★ **The President's Quarters.** Each room in the classic Savannah inn is named for an American president. The rooms are spacious, some with canopy four-poster beds. You'll be greeted with wine and fruit, and the complimentary afternoon tea tempts with sweet cakes. There are also rooms in an adjoining town house. Complimentary Continental breakfast. In-room data ports, refrigerators, some in-room hot tubs. Cable TV, in-room VCRs (and movies). Business services. | 225 E. President St. | 912/233–1600 or 800/233–1776 | fax 912/238–0849 | pqinn@aol.com | www.presidentsquarters.com | 11 rooms, 8 suites | $137–$177, $177–$225 suites | D, DC, MC, V.

River Street Inn. The interior is so lavish that it's hard to believe the building was once a vacant warehouse. Today, the structure, which dates to 1817, has guest rooms with antiques and reproductions from the era of King Cotton. One floor has charming shops and a New Orleans–style restaurant. 2 restaurants, 2 bars, complimentary breakfast. Shops. Business services. | 115 E. River St. | 912/234–6400 or 800/678–8946 | fax 912/234–1478 | www.riverstreetinn.com | 86 rooms in 2 buildings | $149–$275 | AE, DC, MC, V.

EXPENSIVE

★ **Ballastone Inn.** This sumptuous inn occupies an 1838 mansion that once served as a bordello. Rooms are handsomely furnished, with luxurious linens on canopy beds, antiques and fine reproductions, and a collection of original framed prints from *Harper's* scattered throughout. On the garden level, rooms are small and cozy, with exposed brick walls, beam ceilings, and, in some cases, windows at eye level with the lush courtyard. Most rooms have working gas fireplaces. Some in-room hot tubs. In-room VCRs. | 14 E. Oglethorpe Ave. | 912/236–1484 or 800/822–4553 | fax 912/236–4626 | www.ballastone.com | 16 rooms | $215–$275 | AE, MC, V.

★ **The Gastonian.** Actually two antebellum mansions joined by an above ground walkway, the Gastonian is among the most popular of Savannah's inns. Each of the rooms has a working fireplace, and Persian rugs cover the hardwood floors. The veranda is wide and welcoming. And there is even a sundeck. Complimentary breakfast. Some in-room hot tubs. Cable TV. Business services. No kids under 12. No smoking. | 220 E. Gaston St. | 912/232–2869 or 800/322–6603 | fax 912/232–0710 | www.gastonian.com | 17 rooms, 3 suites | $225–$375 | A, D, MC, V.

Hyatt Regency Savannah. When this riverfront hotel was built in 1981, preservationists opposed the construction of the seven-story modern structure in the historic district. The main architectural features are the towering atrium and glass elevators. Rooms have modern furnishings, marble baths, and balconies—you'll be overlooking either the atrium or the Savannah River. Restaurant, bar. Indoor pool. Gym. Business services. | 2 W. Bay St. | 912/238–1234 or 800/233–1234 | fax 912/944–3678 | www.hyatt.com | 347, 25 suites | $205–$230 | AE, D, DC, MC, V.

KODAK'S TIPS FOR PHOTOGRAPHING LANDSCAPES AND SCENERY

Landscape
- Tell a story
- Isolate the essence of a place
- Exploit mood, weather, and lighting

Panoramas
- Use panoramic cameras for sweeping vistas
- Don't restrict yourself to horizontal shots
- Keep the horizon level

Panorama Assemblage
- Use a wide-angle or normal lens
- Let edges of pictures overlap
- Keep exposure even
- Use a tripod

Placing the Horizon
- Use low horizon placement to accent sky or clouds
- Use high placement to emphasize distance and accent foreground elements
- Try eliminating the horizon

Mountain Scenery: Scale
- Include objects of known size
- Frame distant peaks with nearby objects
- Compress space with long lenses

Mountain Scenery: Lighting
- Shoot early or late; avoid midday
- Watch for dramatic color changes
- Use exposure compensation

Tropical Beaches
- Capture expansive views
- Don't let bright sand fool your meter
- Include people

Rocky Shorelines
- Vary shutter speeds to freeze or blur wave action
- Don't overlook sea life in tidal pools
- Protect your gear from sand and sea

In the Desert
- Look for shapes and textures
- Try visiting during peak bloom periods
- Don't forget safety

Canyons
- Research the natural and social history of a locale
- Focus on a theme or geologic feature
- Budget your shooting time

Rain Forests and the Tropics
- Go for mystique with close-ups and detail shots
- Battle low light with fast films and camera supports
- Protect cameras and film from moisture and humidity

Rivers and Waterfalls
- Use slow film and long shutter speeds to blur water
- When needed, use a neutral-density filter over the lens
- Shoot from water level to heighten drama

Autumn Colors
- Plan trips for peak foliage periods
- Mix wide and close views for visual variety
- Use lighting that accents colors or creates moods

Moonlit Landscapes
- Include the moon or use only its illumination
- Exaggerate the moon's relative size with long telephoto lenses
- Expose landscapes several seconds or longer

Close-Ups
- Look for interesting details
- Use macro lenses or close-up filters
- Minimize camera shake with fast films and high shutter speeds

Caves and Caverns
- Shoot with ISO 1000+ films
- Use existing light in tourist caves
- Paint with flash in wilderness caves

From Kodak Guide to Shooting Great Travel Pictures © 2000 by Fodor's Travel Publications

★ **Kehoe House.** A splendidly appointed bed-and-breakfast inn, the Victorian-style Kehoe House has brass-and-marble chandeliers, a courtyard garden, and a music room. Step into the double parlor, with two fireplaces, on the main floor, and your eyes will be swept upward to the 14-ft ceilings. The price of the room gives you access to the Downtown Athletic Club. Complimentary Continental breakfast. | 123 Habersham St. | 912/232–1020 or 800/820–1020 | fax 912/231–0208 | 15 rooms, 2 suites, in 2 buildings | $205–$275 | AE, D, DC, MC, V.

SEA ISLAND

MAP 3, H10

(Nearby towns also listed: Brunswick, Jekyll Island, St. Simons Island)

Separated from historic St. Simons Island by just a narrow strait, Sea Island, owned and operated by The Cloisters Hotel, is perhaps Georgia's—and indeed maybe the entire East Coast's—most luxurious resort. The hotel, in operation since 1928, is surrounded by scores of privately owned cottages that are available for rental. Practically every kind of outdoor sport is available here, including swimming, sailing, skeet, fishing—you name it, it's here. This standout facility is reminiscent of the old days when affluent people took vacations to do nothing more than sit and relax and maybe play a lawn game or two.

Information: The Cloister | Sea Island, GA 31561 | 912/638–5823.

Attractions
The Cloister. Sea Island is a long finger of land between St. Simons and Little St. Simons Islands. Its beaches are lined by the many structures that make up the resort. Originally designed by renowned Florida architect Addison Mizner more than 70 years ago, the Cloister hangs on to its landmark Spanish-Mediterranean architecture. Barrel-tile roofs and low-to-the-ground stucco walls shape both its earliest and its most recent buildings. The Dining Room and Club Room are open to the public. | Sea Island Dr. | 912/638–3611 or 800/SEA–ISLA | fax 912/638–5159 | www.seaisland.com | Free | Daily.

Dining
The Cloister, Main Dining Room. Eclectic. Spanish Mission architecture marks this popular, long-established resort. Meals are included for Cloister guests. Dishes range from pork loin stuffed with andouille sausage to classic navarin of lamb in a puff pastry crust. Sommelier John Capabianco maintains an excellent wine cellar. Breakfast is sumptuous, with classic eggs Benedict and fine jams and preserves. There are also spa dishes on the menu. Kids' menu. | Sea Island Dr. | 912/638–3611 | Jacket and tie | Reservations essential | Breakfast also available | $45 | AE, D, DC, MC, V.

Lodging
The Cloister. This famed resort has a Spanish-Mediterranean hotel, hundreds of privately owned cottages and villas available for rent, and abundant recreational facilities. The grand old resort prides itself on Southern hospitality. The spa is first-rate, and the building in which it is housed also has guest rooms. 4 restaurants, bar, room service. In-room data ports. Cable TV. 2 pools, wading pool. Hot tub, spa, steam room. Driving range, golf courses, putting greens, 18 tennis courts. Gym, horseback riding, beach, dock, boating, fishing, bicycles. Shooting school. Children's programs. Business services, airport shuttle. | Sea Island Dr. | 912/638–3611 or 800/SEA–ISLA | fax 912/638–5159 | www.seaisland.com | 286 rooms in 10 buildings; 250 cottages | $300–$370 | AP | AE, D, DC, MC, V.

STATESBORO

(Nearby town also listed: Savannah)

Statesboro is home to Georgia Southern University, in operation since 1906 and today accommodating 14,000 students. A vibrant, historic downtown district offers plenty of shopping, while close by is the unique Lamar Q. Ball, Jr. Raptor Center, which houses a variety of hawks, owls, and other birds of prey.

Information: Statesboro Convention and Visitors Center | 332 S. Main St., Statesboro GA 30458 | 912/489–1869 or 800/568–3301 | fax 912/489–2688 | visit-statesboro.com.

Attractions

Georgia Southern University. Founded in 1906 as a district agriculture school, the institution served as a teachers' college and a senior college before earning its university status in 1990. The 600-acre campus is a major part of Statesboro's urban landscape. Special centers focus on themed studies, including the Center for Irish Studies, in recognition of the region's Irish roots. The St. Catherines Sea Turtle Conservation Program studies the nesting ecology of Georgia's sea turtles. | U.S. 301 | 912/681–5611 | fax 912/681–5279 | www.gasou.edu | Free | Weekdays 8–5.

Lamar Q. Ball, Jr. Raptor Center. Founded in 1997, the center is home to 11 species of live birds of prey, including bald eagles, inhabiting six habitat displays. The birds in the displays have been injured in some way—perhaps they're blind or can no longer fly—making them unfit for life in the wild. These habitats—a wetlands area, an old-growth forest, and a mountain habitat—let you view native Georgia raptors in natural environments. Following a self-guided tour, you walk along an elevated pathway. | Forest Dr. | 912/681–0831 | fax 912/871–1779 | www.bio.gasou.edu¢wildlife | Free | Sept.–May, weekdays 9–5, weekends 1–5; June–Aug., weekdays 9–5, Sat. 1–5.

ON THE CALENDAR

DEC.: *The Christmas Parade.* Statesboro gets dressed up in its finest each December, as floats with Sugar Plum Fairies, Santas, and town officials parade past onlookers. | 912/764–7227.

Dining

Brinson's. Barbecue. A simple block building is the site of some of the state's best 'cue, best potato salad, and excellent "hash," which is to coastal folk as Brunswick stew is to the rest of the state. (Hash, which tastes like stew, is served over rice.) You can get ribs and chicken every day, but the standard is chopped pork on a bun. Great sauce! No alcohol. | 3924 W. Old Savannah Rd., Emmalane | 912/982–4570 | Closed Mon.–Tues. | $5–$7 | No credit cards.

Coleman House. American. In a classic Victorian mansion, locals enjoy lunches of light sandwiches and salads, with some grilled items, such as chicken Alfredo. For Sunday buffet, the line starts early to attack the hall tables laden with fried chicken, hearty casseroles, and salads. Dinner is simple grilled items, from steak to salmon. Lunch buffet every day. Beer and wine only. | 323 N. Main St., Swainsboro | 912/237–9100 | www.colemanhouseinn.com | No dinner Sun.–Fri. | $5–$8 | AE, D, MC, V.

Raines Room, Statesboro Inn. Contemporary. Michelle and Tony Garges have the city's best restaurant in their bed-and-breakfast. Specialties have a regional touch, with shrimp and grits and crab cakes. Pork medallions with currants and Scotch whiskey exemplify the fresh thinking in the kitchen. Michelle does most of the desserts, such as the coconut caramel pie. | 106 S. Main St. | 912/489–8628 or 800/846–9466 | www.statesboroinn.com | Closed Sun.–Tues. No lunch | $13–$20 | AE, D, MC, V.

Lodging

Coleman House. The Coleman House is an early 20th-century Victorian listed on the National Register. Fine tongue-and-groove wood ceilings and walls, broad verandas, and turrets. Complimentary breakfast. In-room data ports. Cable TV. | 323 N. Main St., Swainsboro | 912/237–9100 | fax 912/237–8656 | innkeeper@colemanhouseinn.com | www.colemanhouseinn.com | 9 rooms | $55–$85 | AE, D, MC, V.

Comfort Inn. Half of the rooms in this hotel include hot tubs and all include VCRs—making it almost a chore to leave the building. Restaurant. Microwaves, refrigerators. Business services. | 316 S. Main St. | 912/489–2626 or 800/228–5150 | www.comfortinn.com | 65 rooms | $80 | AE, D, DC, MC, V.

Days Inn. One block from Georgia Southern University. Complimentary Continental breakfast. Cable TV. | 461 Main St. | 912/764–5666 or 800/DAYS INN | www.daysinn.com | 42 rooms | $69–$79.

Fairfield Inn. This Fairfield Inn was built in 1996 and is very convenient to Georgia Southern University. Each of the spacious rooms has a desk with lamp. Complimentary Continental breakfast. In-room data ports, some microwaves, refrigerators. Cable TV. Indoor pool. Hot tub. Exercise equipment. | 225 Lanier Dr. | 912/871–2525 or 800/228–2800 | fax 912/871–3535 | www.statesboro.com | 63 rooms | $54–$64 | AE, D, DC, MC, V.

Georgia's B&B. You may want the Eggs Benedict for breakfast at this 1893 Victorian, where rooms are individually decorated and children are welcome. Bright colors and hospitality abound; the owner stresses that "this is a home." Cable TV. Pets allowed. | 123 S. Zetterower | 912/489–6330 | 4 rooms | $75 | No credit cards.

Hampton Inn. Across from Georgia Southern University, this well-maintained Hampton Inn underwent renovation in 1999. The standard rooms come with either two double beds, one queen-size, or one king-size. Complimentary Continental breakfast. In-room data ports, some microwaves, refrigerators. Cable TV. Pool. Free parking. | 616 Fair Rd. | 912/681–7700 or 800/HAMPTON | fax 912/681–9677 | www.hamptoninns.com | 81 rooms in 3 buildings | $49–$65 | AE, D, DC, MC, V.

Jameson Inn. This inn offers very well maintained rooms with many amenities. Each room is individually decorated with period antiques or reproductions, although they also include reclining chairs and king-size beds. Complimentary Continental breakfast. In-room data ports, some microwaves, refrigerators. Cable TV. Pool. Exercise equipment. Business services. | 1 Jameson Ave. | 912/681–7900 or 800/526–3766 | fax 912/681–7905 | www.jamesoninns.com | 39 rooms | $52–$67 | AE, D, DC, MC, V.

Statesboro Inn. This bed-and-breakfast is composed of an early 20th-century (1904) Victorian residence and its companion Craftsman-style cottage. To the rear of the main house and discreetly attached to it is a wing of especially quiet rooms. The rooms are individually decorated with antiques and period reproductions. Dining room, complimentary Continental breakfast, room service. In-room data ports, some in-room hot tubs. Cable TV. Business services. | 106 S. Main St. | 912/489–8628 or 800/846–9466 | fax 912/489–4785 | frontdesk@statesboroinn.com | www.statesboroinn.com | 18 rooms in 3 buildings | $85–$130 | AE, D, MC, V.

Trellis Garden Inn. The inn combines the ambiance of a bed-and-breakfast with the privacy of a large hotel. The rooms are decorated with unique wallpaper and draperies. Complimentary Continental breakfast. In-room data ports. Cable TV. Pool. Business services. | 107 S. Main St. | 912/489–8781 or 800/475–1380 | fax 912/764–4561 | trellis@frontiernet.net | www.trellisgardeninn.com | 40 rooms in 2 buildings | $55–$95 | AE, D, DC, MC, V.

STONE MOUNTAIN

(Nearby town also listed: Atlanta)

Stone Mountain is considered a suburb of Atlanta, although it is located 15 miles east of downtown. Today, the monolithic mountain contains what is considered to be the world's largest bas-relief carving. The sculpture shows the figures of Confederate Generals Robert E. Lee and "Stonewall" Jackson, as well as President Jefferson Davis. It was carved over a period of many years. The first of three primary sculptors to work on the project, Gutzon Borglum began carving in 1923 but was soon released amid controversy. Borglum went on to become famous for his work on Mount Rushmore. Augustus Lukeman was the next to try his hand, followed by Kirtland Hancock, who eventually finished the task in the 1970s.

Information: Stone Mountain Park | Box 778, Stone Mountain, GA 30086 | 770/498–5600. **The Atlanta Convention and Visitors Bureau** | 233 Peachtree St. NE, Suite 100, Atlanta, GA 30343 | 404/521–6600 or 800/285–2682.

Attractions

Historic Complex of DeKalb Historical Society. Three antebellum houses from the 1830s and 1840s include Swanton House, Decatur's oldest town house; Biffle Cabin, built by a Revolutionary War soldier; and the hand-hewn-log Thomas-Barber Cabin. | 750 W. Trinity St., Decatur | 404/373–1088 | fax 404/373–8287 | www.dekalbhistory.org | Donations accepted | Weekdays 9–4.

Old Courthouse on the Square. Built in 1898, this former courthouse now houses the DeKalb Historical Society. Museum spaces are devoted to the first 100 years of DeKalb County, established in 1822. Exhibitions include old farm tools, maps, and fashions. In the Civil War room you can see weapons and ammunition, musical instruments, and artifacts from the war at sea and on land. The 20th-century room deals with such matters as World War I–era Camp Gordon, where Sergeant Alvin York trained; East Lake Golf Course (Bobby Jones's home course); women's fashions; and an original Decatur street light. | 101 E. Court Square, Decatur | 404/373–1088 | fax 404/373–8287 | www.dekalbhistory.org | Donations accepted | Weekdays 9–4.

Stone Mountain Park. With its 3,200 acres, this popular state park now is managed by a private entity, Silver Dollar City. The mountain itself, with the Confederate Memorial on its northern face, is the largest exposed granite outcropping on the planet, at 825 ft high. Displaying images of Confederate leaders Robert E. Lee, Jefferson Davis, and Stonewall Jackson, the world's largest relief carving measures 90 ft by 190 ft. You can climb to the top of the mountain along a guided path (moderately strenuous) or get there with far less strain on the skylift. Special features include a steam locomotive that encircles the mountain's 5-mi-diameter base, an antebellum plantation, a swimming beach, a campground, a hotel, a resort, six restaurants, a paddle-wheel steamboat, wildlife preserve, and two Civil War museums. In summer, nights are capped with a laser light show played against the sculpture, beginning at 9:30 PM. | U.S. 78; 16 miles east of Atlanta | 770/498–5690 or 800/317–2006 | fax 770/413–5609 | www.stonemountainpark.org | Free; parking $6 per vehicle; all-attractions day pass $10 for Georgia residents, $17 for nonresidents | Daily 6–noon, Attraction shuttle 10–8, Family Fun Center, Museum, Plantation, Wildlife preserve, Scenic railroad, Skylift 10–8, Beach and water complex 10–6, Riverboat 11–8, Small craft rentals 11–7, Laser show 9:30 PM.

Village of Stone Mountain. About 60 stores and restaurants, very spiritedly decorated at holiday times, line the short main street of this 19th-century village. The town grew up around a railroad track, and the train still rumbles through on a regular schedule. There's a bed-and-breakfast, as well as several good restaurants. | Main St. | 770/879–4971 (visitors center) | fax 770/465–1116 (visitors center) | www.stonemountainvillage.com | Free | Daily.

ON THE CALENDAR

MAR.: *ARTStation's Annual "Raising of the Green."* Every March, the village hosts a silent auction. Locals and tourists alike bid on artwork, theater tickets, and dinner vouchers. Games, music, and food provided by local restaurants make this a fun way to spend an evening. | 404/521–6600.

Dining

Basket Bakery and Cafe at the Village Corner. Continental. Dishes from northern Germany (sausages, schnitzels, and frikadeller), pasta and chicken dishes, and homemade breads, cookies, and desserts are the draws. Entertainment second weekend of the month. | 6655 James Rivers Dr. | 770/498–0329 | www.germanrestaurant.com | Closed Mon. | $9–$14 | AE, D, DC, MC, V.

Café Alsace. French. Benedicte Cooper and Cecile Mignotte are two friends from France who joined up to cook in this tiny bistro. Alsatian dishes are the specialty, including, of course, quiche Lorraine, spaetzle, and coq au vin. Other French bistro classics as well. The walls, painted yellow and burgundy, are decorated with souvenirs and antiques from France. Beer and wine only. | 121 E. Ponce de Leon Ave., Decatur | 404/373–5622 | Reservations essential for six or more | Closed Mon. No lunch Sat., no dinner Sun. | $8–$14 | D, MC, V.

Crescent Moon. American/Casual. Wicked cheap and wicked good. Funky, super casual, tiny, this popular spot feeds students and yuppies alike who seek good vegetarian fare, omelets, superior breakfasts, stuffed baked potatoes, good barbecue, soups, and raging Mississippi Mud pie. Beer and wine only. | 274 W. Ponce de Leon Ave., Decatur | 404/377–5623 | bossmoon@mindspring.com | Reservations not accepted | Breakfast also available. No dinner Sun., Mon. | $5–$12 | AE, D, DC, MC, V.

The Food Business. Eclectic. This bustling uptown bistro is the place to go if you want a small meal—you'll find great sandwiches and salads and small plates of intriguing delights—but come here later too for more complex dinners, such as Georgia lake trout with pumpkin seed butter. The work of local artists decorates the dining rooms, which are also highlighted by tall ceilings and a skylight. Kids' menu. | 115 Sycamore St., Decatur | 404/371–9121 | Reservations essential for 10 or more | No lunch Sat. | $6–$14 | AE, MC, V.

Le Giverny. French. Bistro fare in a tiny, cozy environment focuses on good merlot-braised lamb shanks, baked fresh fish specials, mussels in pesto sauce, steak, country pâté, and homemade chocolate pâté. | 1355 Clairmont Rd., Decatur | 404/325–7252 | Closed Sun. No lunch Sat. | $10–$18 | AE, D, DC, MC, V.

The Supper Club. Eclectic. This romantic spot, with draped gauzy fabric separating the space into dining nooks, roams the culinary planet. Mango-tequila barbecued shrimp comes with cilantro sour cream. Tuscan-style white beans and penne are topped with tomato, crispy sage, and prosciutto and may be done vegetarian upon request. Beer and wine only. | 308 W. Ponce de Leon Ave., Decatur | 404/370–1207 | Closed Sun.–Tues. No lunch | $13–$21 | AE, MC, V.

Sycamore Grill. Contemporary. The building is an old hotel, built about 1836; a huge 150-year-old sycamore tree shades its veranda. Dishes are drawn from the plantation tradition. Updated Southern fare (fried green tomatoes and goat cheese) to salmon croquettes with lemon-dill cream sauce, this wide-ranging menu draws large crowds. | 5329 Mimosa Dr. | 770/465–6789 | Closed Sun., Mon. | $16–$26 | AE, MC, V.

Watershed. Contemporary. Ensconced in a former auto-repair garage, this enoteca (wine bar) does both retail and on-premises wine sales. The inventory is outstanding, with many unusual choices. One of the owners is Indigo Girl Emily Saliers. Continuous service, with dinner menu starting at 5 PM. Dishes draw from both Southern and Italian traditions, so range from organic pimento and sharp cheddar cheese sandwiches to truffled chicken salad sandwiches and magnificent soups. Beer and wine only. | 406 W. Ponce de Leon Ave., Decatur | 404/378–4900 | Reservations not accepted | Closed Sun. | $9–$15 | AE, MC, V.

Lodging
The Village Inn B&B. During the Civil War, the inn survived General Sherman's torch because it was in use as a Confederate hospital. Today, you can relax in one of the whirlpool baths instead of having bullets extracted. Period antiques fill the comfortable rooms, and the full breakfast includes Raspberry Stuffed French Toast with country sausage. Cable TV, some in-room VCR's, room phones. | 992 Ridge Ave. | 770/469–3459 or 800/214–8385 | reservations@villageinnbb.com | 6 rooms | $129–$169 | AE, D, MC, V.

THOMASVILLE

(Nearby town also listed: Bainbridge)

Located 54 mi south of Albany, near the Florida border, Thomasville is often called the City of Roses, and you'll find that several tours are offered of the town's beautiful rose gardens. The town was once frequented by affluent Northerners who traveled to this part of Georgia to participate in the excellent bird hunting.

Information: Thomasville Tourism Authority | 135 N. Broad St., Thomasville, GA 31799 | 912/227–7099 or 800/704–2350 | fax 912/227–2470 | www.thomasvillega.com.

Attractions
Big Oak. Thought to be 320 years old, the tree has been a tourist attraction for at least a century. The oak has its own trust fund for its ongoing maintenance. Its crown spreads more than 162 feet, and its circumference measures 24 feet. The tree was enrolled in the National Live Oak Society in 1936. | Monroe St. at the corner of Crawford St. | Free | Daily.

Cairo Antique Auto Museum. Antique vehicles from every decade of the 1900s are the focus of this museum, but there are also matchbox cars, antique bicycles, and motorcycles. Phone answers Mr. Chick's Restaurant, because the museum is behind it and owned by the same people. | 1125 U.S. 84E | 912/377–3911 | fax 912/378–8096 | $4 | First Sat. each month, 10–4, and by appointment.

Lapham-Patterson House State Historic Site. This house was built in 1885 for Chicago shoe merchant Charles W. Lapham, who moved south to seek warm weather for his health. His lungs had been scarred in the Great Chicago Fire of 1871, rendering him permanently, and ultimately terminally, ill. The last owners of the house were the Pattersons (1905–70), who had made their fortune in South Georgia's turpentine industry. This unusual Victorian house is strikingly geometric from the outside, with odd Japanese-style porch decorations; you won't be surprised to find that the rooms inside are anything but square, with no right angles in sight. No two rooms or floor patterns are exactly alike. The house has 19 rooms, 53 windows, and 45 doors, 24 of which exit to the exterior. Every room in the house has an outside door. | 626 N. Dawson St. | 912/225–4004 | fax 912/227–2419 | www.gastateparks.org | $4 | Tues.–Sat. 9–5, last tour at 4; Sun. 2–5:30, last tour at 4.

Pebble Hill Plantation. One of the classics of the Plantation South, the original house was built by English architect John Wind, who built many of the fine 19th-century homes in this area. Owned by Kate Hanna Harvey, one of the Cleveland Hannas who owned other plantations in the area, the existing house was designed by Abram Garfield, a Cleveland architect and son of President James Garfield. Its famous guests have included the Duke and Duchess of Windsor and President and Mrs. Jimmy Carter, who came for hunting expeditions. | 1251 U.S. 319 S. | 912/226–2344 | fax 912/226–0780 | www.pebblehill.com | $10 | Oct.–Aug., Tues.–Sat. 10–5, Sun. 1–5, last tour at 4, no kids under 6.

Thomas County Museum of History. Extensive photographic and archival displays deal with the history of Thomas County and the plantation country. There also is Civil War memorabilia, ladies' fashions from 1822 to 1947, and a growing exhibition on Thomasville native slave-born Lieutenant Henry O. Flipper, the first African-American to graduate from West Point Military Academy. The complex contains several structures: an 1860 log house, a 1877 Victorian cottage, an 1893 bowling alley, and the 1923 Flowers House, which houses the museum itself. | 725 N. Dawson St. | 912/226–7664 | fax 912/226–7466 | www.rose.net/~history/index.htm | history@rose.net | $5 | Mon.–Sat. 10–noon and 2–5.

Thomasville Cultural Center. This visual- and performing-arts center is housed in a restored 1915 school building, the city's first public school. An art gallery presents a variety of materials, from regional to important national artists. The theater shows classic films. Concerts, plays, and special events are presented in this National Register building. Exhibits display memorabilia on Thomas County. | 600 E. Washington St. | 912/226–0588 | fax 912/226–0599 | www.tccarts.org | Free | Weekdays 9–5, weekends 1–5.

ON THE CALENDAR
APR.: *Rose Festival* takes place every fourth week of April. | 912/227–7079.

Dining
J.B.'s Barbecue and Grill. Barbecue. James B. Jones is a retired Green Beret master sergeant. The superior barbecue, including barbecued chicken, attracted Jimmy Buffet when he owned one of the nearby plantations. Everything is made on the premises, coleslaw, potato salad, and sweet potato pie. You can sit at one of the long tables in the dining room or, if you prefer, in a small booth. The walls are hung with photos of celebrity fans. Kids' menu. No alcohol. | 2247 U.S. 319S | 912/377–9344 | Closed Mon. | $6–$9 | MC, V.

Melhana Plantation. Southern. Dine elegantly among magnolias on fried green tomatoes with a rosemary skewer of shrimp and Vidalia onion relish; chicken breast stuffed with goat cheese; "Plantation Trio" of lamb, duck breast, and roasted quail with Marsala wine reduction. After dinner join the other guests in the Hanna Room to listen to live music by a duo on electric guitar and the grand piano. Beer and wine only. | 301 Showboat Ln. | 912/226–2290 or 888/920–3030 | www.melhana.com | Reservations essential | Jacket and tie | No lunch | $48–$59 | AE, D, DC, MC, V.

Mr. Chick's. American. Once a month, an antique or modern car is displayed inside. Memorabilia lines the walls. Dishes focus on popular fried chicken, seafood, steaks on the weekends. Kids' menu. No alcohol. | 1125 Rte. 84E, Cairo | 912/377–3911 | Closed Sun. | $4–$8 | MC, V.

Lodging
Evans House B&B. Lee and John Puskar, the hospitable owners of this antiques-filled Victorian, believe in the little touches. After dinner liqueurs, pillow sweets, homemade cookies, and nightcaps are a few of the extras you can expect. Breakfasts vary, and have included fresh squeezed orange juice, peach crepes, bananas and strawberries in cream, and apple cinnamon muffins. Paradise Park is directly across the street; downtown Thomasville is just ¼ mile away. All rooms with private bath and/or shower. Library. Some pets allowed. No smoking. | 725 S. Hansell St. | 800/344–4717 | fax 912/226–0653 | 4 rooms | $75–$90 | No credit cards.

Melhana Plantation Resort. For a taste of the opulence that plantation life can offer, try this sprawling resort on the edge of town. You enter along a drive lined with majestic oaks and lustrous magnolias. In front looms the big house, but many of the outbuildings have been retained, too. Hunting, polo, and just plain lazing around the beautifully landscaped pool are favorite pastimes. Pool. Tennis courts. Gym, horseback riding. | 301 Showboat Ln.

| 912/226–2290 | fax 912/226–4585 | www.melhana.com | 26 rooms, 3 suites | $285–$450 | AE, D, DC, MC, V.

Paxton House Inn. This bright blue Victorian home features large rooms furnished with many amenities, including ironing boards, hair dryers, and bathrobes. Within easy walking distance of the shops of downtown Thomasville, the Paxton House boasts a wide and welcoming front porch. Indoor pool. Hot tub. | 445 Remington Ave. | 912/226–5197 | fax 912/226–9903 | www.1884paxtonhouseinn.com | 10 rooms, 4 suites, in 4 buildings | $110–$250 | AE, MC, V.

THOMSON

MAP 3, F6

(Nearby town also listed: Augusta)

The area around Thomson dates back to 1768, when Quakers settled nearby Wrights-borough. The old church dates from 1810, and it and the associated cemetery are historic sites to visit.

Information: Thomson-McDuffie Tourism Convention and Visitors Bureau | 111 Railroad St./Depot, Thomson GA 30824 | 706/595–5584 or 706/597–1000 | www.thomson-mcduffie.org.

Attractions
The Old Rock House. Built around 1785, the Rock House is now the oldest stone residence in Georgia. If the building reminds you of something up north, you're right: the Quakers who built it came from New Jersey. | Old Rock House Rd.

ON THE CALENDAR
NOV.: *"Blessing of the Hounds."* This annual event kicks off the traditional hunting season. Well-trained hounds and their scarlet-coated owners ride through the country-side. | 706/595–8000.

Dining
White Columns Restaurant. American. Steak, chicken, and seafood all make regular appearances on this menu, but the owners change their selctions from day to day. Directly across the road from Holiday Inn Express. | 1890 Washington Rd. NE | $6.95–$14.95 | MC, V.

Lodging
Holiday Inn Express. This new hotel is ultra-clean, with large rooms. Complimentary Continental breakfast. Microwaves. Pool. | 1893 Washington Rd. NE | 706/595–6500 or 800/465–4329 | 80 rooms | $100 | AE, D, DC, MC, V.

TIFTON

MAP 3, E10

(Nearby town also listed: Albany)

Tifton is the home of the Georgia Agrirama, a living-history museum that is often called the South's leading showcase of "agricultural products, history, and methods." Through year-around exhibits and demonstrations, special events on holidays, and tours of a reconstructed 19th-century farmstead, you learn the ins and outs of agriculture as it was practiced before the age of automation.

Information: Tifton-Tift County Chamber of Commerce | 100 S. Central Ave., Tifton GA 31793 | 912/382–6200 | fax 912/386–2232 | www.surfsouth.com/business/tiftchamber.

Attractions

Blue and Gray Museum. Rare Union and Confederate relics trace the town of Fitzgerald's beginning in 1895 as a colony of 2,700 former Union soldiers. A drought in the Midwest was the compelling reason for their migration to Fitzgerald. Confederate soldiers joined them later, but only three lived there its first year, a veritable metaphor of unification. Yankee and Rebel soldiers formed the first Blue and Gray parade in America. A new museum facility, much larger and grander, is being planned. | Old Depot, 116 N. Johnston St., Fitzgerald | 912/426–5069 | www.fitzgeraldga.org | $2 | Mon.–Sat. 10–4.

City Hall. The restored early 20th-century Mayan Hotel serves as city hall and houses private offices. The city government does a purchase award annually at a local arts festival and has assembled an extensive collection—the largest private collection in the city—to support the area's artists. | 130 E. 1st St. | 912/382–6231 | fax 912/386–9694 | www.tifton.com | Free | Weekdays 8–5.

Georgia Agrirama, 19th-Century Living History Museum. Experience life as it was in the rural South a century ago as you visit this living-history village with its authentic farm structures furnished with period antiques and staffed by costumed interpreters. Your understanding of history changes when you see a real sawmill, cotton gin, or gristmill; just walking the town's sandy roads evokes the past. Craft demonstrations, farm animals, a drugstore with a working marble-topped soda fountain, and a country store stocked with handmade goods, including crafts by local artists and stone-ground grits and meal, are among the features. | Whidden Mill Rd. | 912/386–3344 | fax 912/386–3386 | www.ganet.org-agriramamarket@ganet.org | $8; special rates for seniors, children, and families | Mon.–Sat. 9–5.

Jefferson Davis Memorial State Historic Site. This is the spot where Federal forces finally caught up with the former Confederate president and arrested him and his family. The 13-acre historic site includes a Civil War museum, picnic tables, and a group shelter. | 338 Jeff Davis Park Rd., Irwinville | 912/831–2335 | fax 912/831–2060 | www.gastateparks.org | $2.50 per adult, $2 vehicle, $20 vans, $50 bus | Tues.–Sat. 9–5; Sun. 2–5:30.

Tifton Museum of Arts and Heritage. This Methodist church, Tifton's oldest brick church, fell into disrepair but was restored following a large-scale community effort. Solid heart pine floors, walls, and ceilings, and 27 stained-glass windows now gleam with new brilliance. Plans call for professional exhibits on Southern crafts to be held here, together with readings and chamber music performances—the acoustics are excellent. | 255 Love Ave. | 912/386–4373 or 912/382–3600 | fax 912/382–1424 | Free | By appointment.

ON THE CALENDAR

MAY: *Love Affair*. Many people are involved in this Love Affair—artists, craftsmen, merchants, and vendors. Parents bring their children, who seem to have a great time. How did this family festival get its name? Why, it's held on Love Avenue, of course. | 912/386–3558.

Dining

Charlotte's. American. The seating is comfortable on leather chairs pulled up to tables with linen tablecloths. Steak, seafood, chicken, pork, and pasta come in generous portions and are cooked to order. The house soup is seafood bisque. Consider splitting orders for a $5 charge. Beer and wine only. | 260-B Sutton Rd. | 912/382–3300 | Tues.–Sat. dinner only | $9–$30 | AE, D, MC, V.

Lodging

Dorminy-Massee House. This charming B&B was built in 1915 in the classical-revival style. All rooms have king- and queen-size beds and private baths. Complimentary Continental breakfast. In-room data ports. Cable TV. | 516 W. Central Ave., Fitzgerald | 912/423–3123 |

mmassee@surfsouth.com | www.members.tripod.com/~dmhouse | 8 rooms | $75–$85 | AE, MC, V.

Econo Lodge Tifton. With restaurants, shopping, tennis, and cinemas nearby, Econo Lodge Tifton is a family-friendly place. Complimentary Continental breakfast. Microwaves. Cable TV. Playground. Pets allowed. | 1025 W. 2nd St. | 912/382–0280 | fax 912/386–0316 | $41–$56 | AE, D, DC, V.

TOCCOA

(Nearby town also listed: Gainesville)

Toccoa is located on the edge of the huge Chattahoochee National Forest in the mountains of northeast Georgia, about halfway between Atlanta and Greenville, South Carolina. Nearby is the 56,000-acre Hartwell Lake, which was filled when the U.S. Army Corps of Engineers built a dam across the Savannah River during their massive Savannah River project, begun in the late 1940s.

Information: Toccoa-Stephens County Chamber of Commerce | 901 E. Currahee St., Toccoa, GA 30577 | 706/886–2132 | toccoagachamber.com | toccoaga@alltel.net.

Attractions

Chattooga River. Made famous in the film *Deliverance,* this wild and scenic river on the border between Georgia and South Carolina is popular with rafters. You'll find many outfitters working the river and providing professionally guided trips. The Chattooga has a special rhythm, with wild rapids alternating with calm segments. There are some truly difficult spots, such as one eight-foot drop, so you should not consider rafting this dangerous river without professional guidance. | On U.S. 76 between Clayton, GA, and Long Creek, SC | Free | Daily.

Foxfire Museum and Center. The collection of artifacts you see displayed here were originally featured in the *Foxfire* books, I–XI. A gristmill, wooden toys, kitchen implements, old tools, animal traps, and hunting materials are among the items displayed. A gift shop sells folk art and handcraft items, as well as the books in the *Foxfire* series, begun by Eliot Wigginton, a teacher in the private Rabun Gap/Nacochee School. | 2837 Hwy. 441, Mountain City | 706/746–5828 | fax 706/746–5829 | www.foxfire.org | Donations accepted | Weekdays 9–4:30.

Hambidge Center. Founded in 1934 by mountain weaver Mary Crovatt Hambidge, this mountain institute for art is ensconced in a 600-acre site and includes cabins for resident artists and writers. Work by local artists and center residents is exhibited in the gallery, which is moving toward fine craft and contemporary art and away from folk art. The center, which also has a still-operating water-powered gristmill, is on the National Register. | Betty's Creek Rd., Rabungap | 706/746–5718 or 706/746–7187 (gallery) | fax 706/746–9933 | www.rabun.net/~hambidge | Free | Jan.–Apr., weekdays 10–4; June–Aug., Mon.–Sat. 10–4, Sun. 12:30–4:30; May, Sept.–Dec. Mon.–Sat. 10–4.

Mark of the Potter. This site was formerly an old water-powered cornmeal gristmill, which flooded in 1967, breaking the dam and destroying the millrace. It would have cost far too much to rebuild it, and in 1969 two potters, Glenn and John LaRowe, purchased it for a pottery shop. Jay Bucek, M.F.A. in ceramics, bought it in 1985, expanded it, and attracted better-quality potters. In addition to pottery by local artisans, the shop sells handcrafted jewelry. Another good reason to stop here is to feed the pet trout that live in the river below. You buy the fish food at a quarter a shot from a gumball machine on the back porch and toss it to the hungry finners below. | 9982 Rte. 197 N., Clarkesville | 706/947–3440 | fax 706/947–1418 | markpott@cyberhighway.net | www.markofthepotter.com | Free | Daily.

Raft Trips: Southeastern Expeditions. Come here for guided trips (sections III and IV on the Chattooga and Ocoee rivers), canoe and kayak lessons, overnight trips, and a ropes course (a team-building course), all on the Chattooga, using equipment that is provided to you. In business for nearly three decades, this is one of the more experienced river-guide companies. Special packages are available. | 50 Executive Park S, Suite 5016, Atlanta | 404/329–0433 or 800/868–7238 | fax 404/634–4946 | www.southeasternraft.com | $23–$79 Ocoee; $47–$235 Chattooga | Mar.–Oct.

Toccoa Falls College. The college was founded in 1907 to provide a nondenominational Christian education. | Chapel Dr. | 706/886–6831 | fax 706/282–6012 | www.toccoafalls.edu | Free | Weekdays 8:30–5:30.

Traveler's Rest State Historic Site. This rustic, naturally weathered plantation house was built by James Wyley 1815 and expanded by Devereaux Jarrett in 1833. It later served as a stagecoach inn, manor house, post office, and tavern. Most of what you see today is original, as are 80 percent of the furnishings. | 8162 Riverdale Rd. | 706/886–2256 | fax 706/886–6860 | $2.50 | Thurs.–Sat. 9–5, Sun. 2–5:30.

ON THE CALENDAR
APR.: *A Taste of Toccoa.* The world of northeastern Georgia is highlighted at this festival at which music, food, children's events, and art come together for an evening not soon forgotten. | 877/686–2262.

Dining
Bartow's Mountain Restaurant. Barbecue. Not just pork, but also turkey and chicken are smoked on the premises. Fork-tender ribs are melting delicious, and coleslaw, Brunswick stew, and baked beans are good side dishes. Steak, seafood, and poultry as well. Homemade blackberry ice cream is splendid. The country setting is not overly spectacular. No alcohol. No smoking. | U.S. 441, Wiley | 706/782–4038 | Reservations not accepted | Closed Mon., Tues. | $5–$12 | MC, V.

Copperhead's. Continental. The chef's specialty is snapper Vista del Mar (roasted peppers, onions, and tomatoes, baked in béarnaise sauce), crab cakes, prime rib, and steak, but don't overlook the daily specials. The restaurant features a full bar. | 415 N. Broad St. | 706/886–0373 | Closed Sun., Mon. No lunch | $12–$17 | AE, D, DC, MC, V.

Glen-Ella Springs Inn and Conference Center. Southern. The Lowcountry fare marks this North Georgia retreat's dining room. The rustic setting on the edge of a meadow is the perfect spot for enjoying trout pecan and pickled Gulf shrimp. BYOB wine (corkage fee). | 1789 Bear Gap Rd., Clarkesville | 706/754–7295 or 888/455–8891 | www.glenella.com | Reservations essential | No lunch | $17–$24 | AE, MC, V.

Soque River Steak House. Steak. Beef, yes, is the specialty, but you'll find good seafood, too, such as salmon in phyllo and grouper. Count on several pasta dishes as well. The restaurant is in the country, with a river running alongside the main building. The separate banquet room has vaulted hardwood ceilings and a fireplace. | 515 N. Grant St., Clarkesville | 706/754–1200 | No dinner Sun. | $10–$18 | AE, MC, V.

The Trolley. Eclectic. Fine dining in the mountains in a casual bistro. The dishes here give you a sense of outdoor dining—bison, veal sweetbreads with leeks and wild mushrooms, salsa verde with snapper, roasted duck, and filet mignon. Beer, wine, and BYOB wine (corkage fee). | 1460 N. Washington St., Clarkesville | 706/754–5566 | Closed Sun., Mon. No lunch | $14–$22 | DC, MC, V.

Lodging
Asbury House. Built in 1907 by W.R. Asbury, a local merchant, the neoclassical Greek-revival house has a veranda and a garden. The rooms have mahogany furniture; some have canopy beds, some have antique beds. Complimentary breakfast. Cable TV. No kids. No smok-

ing. | 1050 Washington St., Clarkesville | 706/754–9347 or 888/944–2466 | fax 706/839–7008 | asbury@hemc.net | www.asburyhouse.com | 4 rooms | $125–$145 | AE, MC, V.

The Burns-Sutton Inn. Built in 1901, this Victorian-style inn is furnished with antiques. The rooms feature oak four-poster beds as well as canopy beds. Some have a fireplace and double whirlpool tub. Picnic area, complimentary breakfast. Business services. No smoking. | 855 Washington St., Clarkesville | 706/754–5565 | fax 706/754–9698 | www.georgia-magazine/burnssutton.com | 7 rooms (2 with shared bath) | $75–$125 | AE, MC, V.

Days Inn. This Days Inn, 2 miles from Toccoa Falls, has a good selection of restaurants right around it. Complimentary Continental breakfast. Cable TV. Pool. | Hwy. 17 and Rte. 5 | 706/886–9461 | fax 706/282–0907 | 78 rooms | $56 | AE, DC, MC, V.

Glenn-Ella Springs Hotel. Just south of the new Tallulah Gorge State Park and bordered by Panther Creek, the hotel sits on 17 acres of meadows, flower and herb gardens, and original mineral springs. A swimming pool provides relaxing entertainment when the weather is warm. A great stone fireplace is the focal point of the parlor; two suites have one also. All rooms have local hand-crafted pieces and antiques. Complimentary Continental breakfast. Pool. Business services. | 1789 Bear Gap Rd. | 706/754–7295 | 16 rooms | $125–$195 | AE, MC, V.

LaPrade's Cabins. The fish camp of your dreams. Surrounding the lodge are rustic fisherman's cabins (all with bathroom) and cottages with full amenities. All the cottages have full kitchens, living rooms, and fireplaces. Cable TV (in cottages). | 68 Tradition Circle | 706/947–3312 | fax 706/947–3648 | www.laprades.com | 20 cabins; 3 cottages | $80, $125 cottages | Dec.–Mar. | AP (cabins only) | D, MC, V.

Mountain State Park Cottages. At the highest state park in Georgia, simple cottages are available to rent. Make your reservations early; these are among the most sought-after in the mountains. Each has a full kitchen. Cable TV. | U.S. 23/441, Mountain City | 706/746–2141 or 800/864–7275 | fax 706/746–7278 | brmpl@alltel.net | www.gastatepark.org | 10 cottages | $70–$105 | AE, D, DC, MC, V.

The York House. Begun as a two-room cabin, this is the oldest inn in the state in continuous operation—in fact, it has been in business since 1896. This attractive inn is full of antique furnishings and has rocking chairs on a veranda. There's another rocking chair in each of the rooms, along with a queen-size bed. A further unique touch is given each room by collectibles. Complimentary breakfast. Some cable TV. | York House Rd., Mountain City | 706/746–2068 | fax 706/746–0210 | www.gamountains.com/yorkhouse | 13 rooms, 4 suites | $69–$99, $89–$99 suites | MC, V.

TYBEE ISLAND

MAP 3, I9

(Nearby town also listed: Savannah)

This popular resort lies right on the Atlantic, some 18 mi east of downtown Savannah. There are a lighthouse, public pier, beaches, and the interesting remains of early coastal defenses that once protected the mainland with batteries of artillery.

Information: Tybee Island Beach Visitor Information | Box 491, Tybee Island, GA 31328 | 800/868–2322.

The Savannah Area Convention and Visitors Bureau, | 101 E. Bay St., Savannah, GA 31401–1628 | 912/644–6401 or 877/728–2662 | www.savannahvisit.com.

Attractions

★ **Fort Pulaski National Monument.** The fort was named for Casimir Pulaski, the son of a Polish noble who became a Revolutionary War hero and died during the siege of Savannah. Among the engineers to work on the fort was the young lieutenant and West Point graduate Robert E. Lee. Severely shelled by Federal troops during the Civil War, the fort is a well-preserved testament to 19th-century fortification engineering. The restored fort, operated by the National Park Service, is complete with moats, drawbridges, massive ramparts, and towering walls. An excellent gift shop sells not only memorabilia but numerous informative books on the Civil War. A nature trail (part of the area's Rails to Trails system) and picnic areas make this a must-visit. The fort is on Cockspur Island. You'll see the entrance on your left just before U.S. 80E reaches Tybee Island. | U.S. 80 | 912/786–5787 | fax 912/786–6023 | www.nps.gov | $12 | June–Aug., daily 8:30–6:45; Sept.–May, daily 8:30–5:15.

Tybee Island Marine Science Center. You can walk right off the beach into this museum, which educates young and old alike about Coastal Georgia's marine ecosystem. Eight aquariums, a touch tank, cross section of the beach and wave tank are just a few of the attractions. Libraries, classrooms, labs and tours add to the educational experience. | 1510 Strand | 912/786–5917 | www.tybeemsc.com | $1 | Summer, Mon.–Sat. 9–4, Sun. 1–4; winter, weekdays 9-4.

Tybee Museum and Lighthouse. The lower part of the lighthouse dates to 1773, with another 94 ft added in 1866. Today, at 154 ft, the lighthouse is Georgia's oldest and tallest. Its observation deck sits 135 ft above the sea. Leading to the Tybee Light are 178 steps. The head keeper's dwelling, built in 1881, has been under restoration. | 30 Meddin Dr. | 912/786–5801 | fax 912/786–6538 | www.tybeelighthouse.org | $4 | Apr.–Labor Day, Wed.–Mon. 9–6; Labor Day–Mar., Wed.–Mon. 9–4.

ON THE CALENDAR
SEPT.: *The Tybee Arts Association's Annual Festival of the Arts.* Over 30 artists from throughout the Southeast show and sell their paintings, prints, crafts and jewelry. | 912/786–5920.

Dining
The Breakfast Club. Southern. Start the day with the locals at this cherished hangout, opened in 1976. Friendly, simple service in a warren of interconnected rooms. Owner Jodee Sadowsky cooked breakfast for newlyweds John and Carolyn Bessette Kennedy at 4 AM when they needed to make a quick post-nuptial escape from paparazzi. Grits, eggs, sausage, pancakes, and similar substantial fare are the draws. Fish breakfast depends on what's in season but could include breaded red snapper with all the trimmings. If you're feeling courageous, ask for the Grill Cleaner's Special: sausage, cheese, eggs, and whatever else the cook decides to throw in. Kids' menu. No alcohol. | 1500 Butler Ave. (U.S. 80) | 912/786–5984 | eggmansky@aol.com | Reservations not accepted | Lunch also available. No dinner | $3–$11 | D, MC, V.

Georges' on Tybee. Contemporary. Owned by two partners named George, this upscale setting is unusual in this busy beach resort. So is the food: duck liver on frisée; marinated roasted beets; excellent venison; good crème brûlée. | 1105 E. U.S. 80 | 912/786–9730. | Closed Sun. No lunch | $18–$27 | AE, MC, V.

Hunter House. Seafood. With a bed-and-breakfast on the lower level and a fine dining establishment on the upper floor, this is a nice spot. You feel like you're at the beach and at the same time surrounded by Southern charm. Fresh seafood, such as grilled grouper with a red pepper coulis, is a typical special, and steaks and pasta dishes round out the menu. | 1701 Butler Blvd. | 912/786–7515 | www.tybeeisland.com | Closed Sun. in Sept.–May. No lunch | $15–$22 | AE, MC, V.

North Beach Grill. Caribbean. From this tiny kitchen on the ocean, partners George Jackson (host) and George Spriggs (chef) serve up tacos rolled around tilapia with cilantro pesto, topped with fresh salsa; jerk-seasoned chicken, pork, or salmon; and crab cake sandwiches with hand-cut coleslaw. Vegetarians will love the grilled okra. The pair also owns Georges' on Tybee. You eat outside, right on the beach at tables under umbrellas. | 41-A Meddin Dr.(on the beach at Fort Screven) | 912/786–9003 | www.northbeachgrill.com | Reservations not accepted | Closed weekdays in Dec.–Jan. | $11–$17 | D, MC, V.

Lodging

17th Street Inn. Steps away from the beach, the inn has two-story porches and rooms with generous kitchenettes, double iron beds, antique bureaus, and bright colors. Complimentary breakfast. Kitchenettes. Beach. | 12 17th St. | 912/786–0607 or 888/909–0607 | fax 912/786–0601 | 7 rooms | $110–$150 | D, MC, V.

Coach House B&B. In 1920, Coach House was built as the train station for Savannah Beach. Today, P.D. the Love Bird welcomes guests to the building, which has three regular guest rooms and one suite, which can sleep up to 4 adults. Canoeing, kayaking, fishing, hiking, tennis, sailing, swimming, and other water sports are nearby. Complimentary Continental breakfast. Cable TV, in-room VCRs. No kids. | 702 Butler Ave. | 912/786–5289 or 877/637–4416 | fax 912/786–5289 | CoachHouse@wans.net | 4 rooms | $100–$145 | AE, D, MC, V.

VALDOSTA

MAP 3, E11

VALDOSTA

INTRO
ATTRACTIONS
DINING
LODGING

(Nearby town also listed: Thomasville)

Valdosta had its beginnings in the mid-1800s, when it was known as Troupville. The citizens relocated the original community so that the railroad would pass through it, a wise decision since the town went on to become one of Georgia's most important rail centers. The town was later renamed Valdosta, after the Valle d'Aosta region of Italy, because Governor George Troup had a plantation to which he had given that name. Today Valdosta is a leading producer of timber, cattle, and tobacco.

Information: Valdosta-Lowndes County Convention and Visitors Bureau | 1 Meeting Pl., Valdosta, GA 31601–1964 | 912/245–0513 or 800/569–8687 | fax 912/245–5240 | hhampton@datasys.net | www.datasys.net/valdtourism.

Attractions

Brooks County Historical Museum and Cultural Center. Civil War artifacts, antique implements, and regional historical material, including genealogical and heritage archives, are in the museum. Art exhibits focusing on local artists occupy the cultural center. | 121 N. Culpepper St., Quitman | 912/263–4841 | fax 912/263–4822 | Free | Tues.–Sat. 1–5.

Converse-Dalton-Ferrell House. This 1902 neoclassical mansion, restored in 1983, serves as headquarters for the Valdosta Junior Service League. On the National Register, the three-story house once boasted a ballroom on its third floor. The intricate woodwork is fascinating; you'll see a laurel-wreath theme used in the decoration. The dining room features a recessed china cabinet and an oak-beamed and molded ceiling. The six-sided parlor has built-in louvered blinds and semidomed ceilings. | 305 N. Patterson St. | 912/244–8575 | Donations accepted | By appointment.

The Crescent (Valdosta Garden Center). Built in 1898 by U.S. and Georgia Senator William Stanley West, the house is best known for its crescent-shape front porch, which has 13 massive Doric columns that represent the 13 original colonies. Other features include a mirrored fireplace, a ballroom, and a gold-leaf tiled bath. In the garden are a chapel and an octagonal schoolhouse, built in 1913. | 904 N. Patterson St. | 912/244–6747 | Donations accepted | Weekdays 2–5, also by appointment.

Lowndes County Historical Society Museum. Photographs, artifacts, and documents relating to the history of Lowndes Country (1825) and its county seat, Valdosta, are displayed at this museum, which is housed in a 1913 Carnegie Library. | 305 W. Central Ave.

| 912/247–4780 | fax 912/247–2840 | www.surfsouth.com¢~lownhist | Free | Weekdays 10–5, Sat. 10–2.

Ola Barber Pittman House. Designed by a Valdosta architect and built in 1915, the house contains 52 pieces of original furnishings. It now serves as headquarters for the Valdosta Chamber of Commerce, but you can take a self-guided walking tour through the rooms. | 416 N. Ashley St. | 912/247–8100 | fax 912/245–0071 | www.chamber@mail.datasys.net | Free | Weekdays 8:30–5.

Valdosta State University. This institution began in 1906 as the South Georgia State Normal College, then became Georgia State Women's College in 1922. In 1950 the school, then coeducational, changed its name to Valdosta State College. On July 1, 1993, it became Valdosta State University. The 168-acre campus is academic home to 9,700 students, representing 48 states and 50 countries. | 1500 N. Patterson St. | 912/333–5800 or 800/618–1878 | fax 912/245–3891 | www.valdosta.edu | Free | Weekdays 8–8, Sat. 10–2, Sun. 3–5.

ON THE CALENDAR

APR.: *Spring Flower Show.* Lilies, Roses, orchids, and other beautiful flowers are exhibited by their proud growers. | 912/247–8100.

Dining

C. H. Mitchell's Barbeque. Barbeque. Try the fresh squeezed lemonade at this no-frills barbecue joint. Southern-style veggies, like collard greens and okra, are frequently ordered along with the usual ribs. | 515 S. Ashley St. | 912/244–2684 | $4.95–$11.95 | No credit cards.

The Fish Net. Seafood. Regulars at this country restaurant swear by the fried catfish, usually ordered with a side of grits. | 3949 Sportsman's Cove Rd., Lake Park | 912/559–5410 | $4.95–$8.85 | No credit cards.

Lulu's. Contemporary. Lunch in this restored late 19th-century building focuses on exceptionally nice sandwiches, such as grilled fillet of tuna, salads, and homemade soups. At dinner, breast of duck served medium rare with balsamic blackberry coulis is just an example. Salmon may come with Champagne Dijon mustard sauce. Kids' menu. Beer and wine only. | 132 N. Patterson St. | 912/242–4000 | Closed Sun., Mon. No lunch Sat., no dinner Tues.–Wed. | $12–$19 | AE, MC, V.

Ray's Mill Pond Cafe. Seafood. A real country restaurant, by a lake with huge oaks surrounding it. The fish is fresh; nets hang everywhere. | Hwy. 125, Ray City Exit | 912/455–4075 | $5.95–$8.95 | No credit cards.

Royal Cafe. Southern. Look around and you'll see a lot of Coca-Cola memorabilia on display in this country-style restaurant. Country-fare buffet at lunch features such old-time dishes as pork backbone and rice, chicken, dumplings, and fried hoecakes. The salad bar buffet at lunch has freshly made salads. Fri. and Sat. dinner is prime rib and seafood. All desserts are homemade; the specials to watch out for are Coca-Cola cake or Seven-Up cake. Kids' menu. No alcohol. | 304 Screven St., Quitman | 912/263–5443 | No dinner Mon.–Tues. | $6–$11 | No credit cards.

Lodging

Best Western King of the Road. This chain hotel is convenient to the Valdosta Mall. Restaurant, bar (with entertainment), complimentary Continental breakfast, room service. Some microwaves, refrigerators. Cable TV. Pool. Playground. Business services, airport shuttle. Some pets allowed. | 1403 N. St. Augustine Rd. | 912/244–7600 or 800/528–1234 | fax 912/245–1734 | www.bestwestern.com | 137 rooms, 5 suites, in 2 buildings | $48–$55. | AE, D, DC, MC, V.

Clubhouse Inn. This tidy inn is convenient to the Valdosta Mall. The rooms are also equipped with sofa beds. Complimentary Continental breakfast. In-room data ports, microwaves, refrigerator. Cable TV. Pool. Hot tubs. Business services. | 1800 ClubHouse Dr. | 912/247–7755 or 800/258–2466 | fax 912/245–1359 | www.chival@surfsouth.com | 104 rooms, 17 suites | $58–$68, $76–$86 suites | AE, D, DC, MC, V.

Comfort Inn. A typical chain hotel, convenient to the Valdosta Mall and outlet malls, the university, Moody Air Force Base, and Wild Adventure. The rooms have either two double beds or one king-size bed. The rooms also have ironing boards. Bar, complimentary Continental breakfast. Microwaves, refrigerators. Cable TV. Pool. Laundry facilities. Business services, airport shuttle, free parking. Some pets allowed. No smoking. | 2101 W. Hill Ave. | 912/242–1212 or 800/228–5150 | fax 912/242–2639 | www.hotelchoice.com | 138 rooms, 12 suites, in 3 buildings | $55–$65, $99–$129 suites | AE, D, DC, MC, V.

Fairfield Inn. With outdoor entrances for all its rooms, this Fairfield differs from its counterparts across the South. Cable TV. Pool. | 1309 St. Augustine Rd. | 912/253–9300 | 108 rooms | $63 | AE, D, DC, MC, V.

Hampton Inn Gornto Road. This typical chain hotel has been renovated, and the carpeting and furnishings have been replaced. Double rooms have a table, those with queen-size beds have a table and chair, and rooms with a king-size bed have a desk and ottoman. Complimentary Continental breakfast. In-room data ports. Cable TV. Pool. Business services. | 1705 Gornto Rd. | 912/244–8800 or 800/HAMPTON | fax 912/244–6602 | www.hampton-inn.com | 102 rooms | $60–$70 | AE, D, DC, MC, V.

Hampton Inn Timber Drive. This modern chain hotel has an atrium with a fountain. The rates are affordable, and the rooms, while basic, are spacious. They have queen-size beds, ironing boards, and hair dryers. Complimentary Continental breakfast. In-room data ports, some microwaves. Cable TV. Pool. Exercise equipment. Laundry facilities. Business services. | 2906 Timber Dr., Lake Park | 912/559–5565 or 800/426–7866 | fax 912/559–6548 | vldlp01@hi-hotel.com | 68 rooms, 2 suites | $59–$69, $99 suites | AE, D, DC, MC, V.

Holiday Inn. This Holiday Inn has a 24-hour shuttle service that takes you anywhere in the area. Cable TV. Pool. | 1309 Augustine Rd. | 912/242–3881 | fax 912/244–6272 | 167 rooms | $59 | AE, D, DC, MC, V.

Jameson Inn. The friendly staff, clean rooms, and in-town location are what brings people back. Access to workout facilities. Cable TV. Pool. | 1725 Gornto Rd. | 912/253–0009 | fax 912/247–4808 | 28 rooms | $63 | AE, D, DC, MC, V.

Ramada Inn. A standard chain hotel convenient to Wild Adventure and Valdosta State University. The standard rooms have two double beds and a desk. Complimentary Continental breakfast. Cable TV. Pool. Pets allowed (fee). | 2008 W. Hill Ave. | 912/242–1225 or 800/272–6232 | fax 912/247–2755 | 103 rooms | $42 | AE, D, DC, MC, V.

VIDALIA

MAP 3, F8

(Nearby town also listed: Dublin)

Vidalia has become famous the world over as the top producer of the Vidalia onion, the sweetest onion in the world. The town offers an onion festival in the spring, lots of onion factories to tour, and gobs of onion-inspired recipes and dishes to try.

Information: Vidalia Tourism Council | 2805 E. First St., Vidalia GA 30474 | 912/538–8687 | www.vidaliaga.com.

Attractions
Altama Museum of Art and History. Displayed in this 1911 house is a variety of works from the permanent collection, including more than 260 pieces of Staffordshire porcelain representing more than 210 patterns; 20th-century Southeastern art; antique prints, includ-

ing an Audubon series; a Victorian bedroom; and Southern wood carvings. | 611 Jackson St. | 912/537–1911 | Free | Mid-Jan.–mid-Dec., Mon., Tues., Thurs., Fri. 10–4.

Ladson Genealogical and Historical Library. One of the largest facilities of its kind in the Southeast, the library houses more than 30,000 books and pamphlets. | 119 Church St. | 912/537–8186 | Free | Weekdays 9–1 and 2–6, Sat. 9–1.

ON THE CALENDAR

APR.–MAY: *Vidalia Onion Festival.* This annual event celebrates Vidalia's world-famous onions with a variety of entertainment and, of course, onion dishes to sample. | Downtown | 912/538–8687 | www.vidaliaga.com.

Dining

Steeplechase. Steak/Seafood. Pastas, steaks, chicken Havanna (chicken breast on yellow rice with melted jack cheese), and fish dishes are the staple of this menu, served in a plain, casual setting. Kids' menu. | 306 E. 2nd St. | 912/537–7900 | Reservations not accepted | Closed Sun. No lunch Sat. | $5–$15 | AE, D, DC, MC, V.

Lodging

Vidalia–Days Inn. All the expected amenities from a Days Inn, restaurants and shopping nearby. Restaurant, bar, complimentary Continental breakfast. Microwaves, refrigerators. Cable TV. Pool. | 1503 Lyons Hwy. 280 E. | 912/537–9251 | fax 912/537–9251 | www.daysinn.com | 65 rooms | $36 | AE, D, DC, MC, V.

Little Ocmulgee State Park Lodge. A lodge and cluster of cabins set around the lake are available at this underappreciated jewel of a state park. Excellent facilities give this park the air of a small-town resort. The cabins, with fully fitted kitchens, are a home away from home, and the lodge rooms are comfortable. There are also tent and trailer sites. Restaurant, picnic area. Some kitchenettes (cabins). Cable TV. Pool, lake. 18-hole golf course, tennis courts. Hiking, beach, boating, fishing. No pets. | U.S. 441 in McRae, 3 mi north of the city | 912/868–2832 or 800/864–7275 | www.gastateparks.org | 30 rooms in lodge; 10 cabins | $60–$66 (lodge), $60–$90 (cabins) | AE, D, DC, MC, V.

WASHINGTON

MAP 3, F5

(Nearby town also listed: Athens)

This quaint antebellum town, chartered in 1780, was the first in the United States to be named in honor of George Washington. The first president visited nearby Augusta and environs in 1791, and his tour of the region no doubt inspired locals to bestow the name. During the Civil War, Confederate Secretary of State Robert Toombs made his home here, and the building is preserved today as a state historic site.

Information: **Washington-Wilkes Chamber of Commerce** | 104 E. Liberty St., Washington, GA 30673 | 706/678–2013 | www.washingtonga.org.

Attractions

Alexander H. Stephens State Park. Despite ill health and physical deformity, Stephens, a lawyer, served as a congressman, vice-president of the Confederacy, and later governor of Georgia. Stephens's Liberty Hall home and its 10 preserved outbuildings (kitchen, library wing, servants' quarters, privy, a gas plant that he purchased for his own lighting system) are the focal point of this park. The house has been restored to its 1875 appearance, when Stephens last renovated it. All but one of his 33 slaves, whom he always referred to as servants, remained with him after Emancipation. | 456 Alexander St. N. | 706/456–2602 | fax 706/456–2396 | www.gastateparks.org | $2.50 | Tues.–Sat. 9–5, Sun. 2–5.

Callaway Plantation. For a complete understanding of authentic 19th-century plantation life, Callaway Plantation may be unequaled. The land goes back to a 3,000-acre 1783 land grant for Job Callaway. In 1784 he built a cabin, but it burned; exhibited is a similar 1785 log cabin from the Heard plantation, also located in Wilkes County. Jacob Callaway's house, dating to 1790, in the Federal plain style, also is on the site. The main house, a redbrick Greek-revival structure, was built by Aristedes Callaway beginning in 1865 and finished in 1869. Period pieces, largely from Washington families, are on display together with simple items that reveal the character of daily life, such as kitchen implements. | 2160 Lexington Rd. | 706/678–7060 | www.washingtonga.org | $4 | Tues.–Sat. 10–5, Sun. 2–5.

Church of the Mediator. The windows in this Episcopal Church were designed by Wilbur Herbert Burnham, who designed and built the Lee and Jackson windows in Washington, D.C.'s National Cathedral. | 12 E. Robert Toombs Ave. | 706/678–7226 | Free | Daily.

Courthouse Square. At the base of this classic Southern town square is a Flemish-style courthouse, built in 1909. The spot is historic, for it was here that President Jefferson Davis, fleeing Federal arrest, held the last meeting of the Confederate government. And here on May 4, 1865, in the old Heard Building, the Confederacy was officially and finally dissolved, and its treasury, including gold, disposed of—but no one knows exactly where, which is why the woods here fill with treasure hunters each fall. In front of the courthouse stands the traditional Confederate memorial, a single soldier of common rank resting against his rifle. Shops fringing the square proclaim their construction dates: 1815, 1896, 1910. The 1898 Fitzpatrick Hotel, after languishing unoccupied, has been restored as apartments and will have a bed-and-breakfast. Local farmers often park their trucks full of produce to sell in front of the courthouse. | Free | Daily.

Elijah Clark State Park. This popular camping and recreational site is named for the Revolutionary War general, whose reproduced house is a museum. Besides 165 camping sites, facilities include cabins and miniature golf. | 2959 McCormick Hwy., | 706/359–3458 | fax 706/359–5856 | www.gastateparks.org | $2 vehicle, $20 vans, $50 bus | Mon.–Tues. 8–5, Wed.–Sun. 8–10.

J. Strom Thurmond Dam and Lake/Clarks Hill Lake. The Army Corps of Engineers dammed up this portion of the Savannah River in 1952 to create this multipurpose hydroelectric facility, still known as Clarks Hill Lake to many who live on the Georgia side. It forms the border between South Carolina and Georgia. The corps maintains an interpretive center at the lake, with displays about the lake and the Corps of Engineers. | Rte 1. Box 12, Clarks Hill, SC | 864/333–1100 or 800/533–3478; 877/444–6777 (campground reservations) | fax 864/333–1150 | www.sas.usace.army.mil/lakes/thurmond | Free; $1 (person) or $3 (carload) for beach access; $2 boat launch fee | Daily, some areas close Oct.–Mar. Visitors Center: 8:00–4:30.

Kettle Creek Battleground. A state historic marker and granite obelisk monument commemorate the site where the Revolutionary War ended in Georgia, on February 14, 1779. Managed by the Daughters of the American Revolution and the city of Washington. | War Hill Rd. | Free | Daily.

Mary Willis Library. Three confederate chests, Tiffany windows, a stuffed moose, and original Victorian furnishings make this library a noteworthy stop. | 204 E. Liberty St. | 706/678–7736 | Free | Mon., Wed., Fri. 8:30 AM–5:30 PM; Sat. 10–4.

Robert Toombs House State Historic Site. Born and reared in Wilkes County, Toombs, an impassioned orator, served as U.S. Senator (1853–61), resigning to become Confederate Secretary of State. He later held the rank of general in the Confederate army. As a lawyer, he earned as much as $50,000 in 1836, a fantastic sum for that day. Legend holds that he escaped out the back of his Greek-revival house just as Federal officers were coming to arrest him. Toombs fled to Cuba and then to England and France, an unreconstructed rebel, refusing ever to take the Oath of Allegiance. | 216 E. Robert Toombs Ave. | 706/678–2226 | fax 706/678–7515 | home.g-net.net/~toombs | $2.50 | Tues.–Sat. 9–5, Sun. 2–5.

Washington Historical Museum. This restored home was built on land once owned by the town's original surveyor, Micajah Williamson. The back part of the house was built in 1835 by Albert Semmes, and in 1847 Samuel and Elizabeth Barnett bought it and added the front three stories. Most furnishings come from the family of Francis Willis, who was Samuel's half brother. The museum showcases area Native American culture, Civil War artifacts, and other items related to local history. | 308 E. Robert Toombs Ave. | 706/678–2105 | $2 | Tues.–Sal. 10–5, Sun. 2–5.

ON THE CALENDAR

DEC.: *Washington Historic Homes Christmas Tour.* This tour makes its way through neighborhoods filled with antebellum homes, many of which are decorated for Christmas. | 706/678–2013.

Dining

Another Thyme Cafe. Contemporary. The dishes in this charming, high-ceilinged bistro have a Southern touch. Fine fried green tomatoes, first-rate breads, superior salads, ice creams (excellent!). Good coffee. Beer and wine only. | 5 East Public Sq. | 706/678–1672 | Reservations essential | Closed Sun. | $7–$15 | AE, D, MC, V.

Lodging

Holly Ridge Country Inn. This antique-filled 100-acre farm, 5 miles north of Washington, has two buildings: a Victorian inn and a plantation. You can wake up to the rooster crowing. All rooms have private baths; antiques abound. Complimentary breakfast. Golf. | 2221 Sandtown Rd., Tignall | 706/285–2594 | 10 rooms | $85 | No credit cards.

Maynard's Manor. This classical-revival structure, originally built in 1820, was transformed into a B&B in 1998. Fireplaces in the main house warm the public spaces. You can gather in the library and parlor for conversation with the other guests and light refreshments. Complimentary breakfast. Library. No pets. No kids under 12. No smoking. | 219 E. Robert Toombs Ave. | 706/678–4303 | www.bbonline.com/ga/maynard | 7 rooms | $85–$95 | MC, V.

WAYCROSS

MAP 3, G10

(Nearby town also listed: Brunswick)

Waycross is the gateway to the wild and wonderful Okefenokee Swamp and its associated Okefenokee National Wildlife Refuge. The town lies about halfway between Valdosta and Brunswick, and in its younger days it was the center of a vibrant timber and turpentine industry. Today a lot of the old mills are gone, and Waycross has reverted to the sleepy town it was before the boom days.

Information: Waycross-Ware County Convention and Visitors Bureau | 315 Plant Ave., Waycross, GA 31501 | 912/283–3744 | www.okefenokeetourism.com.

Attractions

Laura S. Walker State Park. Built in the 1930s as a WPA project, the park is named for a Waycross teacher who championed conservation. Facilities include boating, picnic areas, campsites, a playground, and a 120-acre lake that's good for boating and skiing. The 18-hole championship golf course offers all amenities. | 5653 Laura Walker Rd. | 912/287–4900 | www.gastateparks.org | $2 vehicle, $20 vans, $50 bus | Daily 7–10 PM.

Okefenokee Heritage Center. This local arts and history museum hosts artists from around the region, usually from south Georgia and north Florida. The history covers Waycross and the Ware County area, with exhibits focused on the Native American culture of the area and local African-American history. | 1460 N. Augusta Ave. | 912/285–4260 | fax 912/285–2858 | www.okeheritage.org | $3 | Mon.–Sat. 10–5, Sun. 1–5.

Okefenokee Swamp Park. This is the north entrance to the 700-acre Okefenokee Wildlife Refuge. You'll find a variety of available boat tours and canoe rentals. | 5700 Swamp Park Rd. | 912/283–0583 | fax 912/283–0023 | www.okeswamp.com | $10, boat tours $4–$12 extra | Daily 9–5:30.

Southern Forest World. This history museum tells the story of the forest industry through displays like dioramas, a loblolly pine you can walk inside to mount a spiral staircase, and a petrified dog stuck in a tree. | 1440 N. Augusta Ave. | 912/285–4056 | $2 | Mon.–Sat. 10–4:30, Sun. 1–4:30.

Obediah's Okefenok. The Henry Obediah Barber Historical Swampers Homesite, built in 1879, originally sat on 490 acres. A farmer and self-taught biologist, Barber mapped the swamp. You can view a blacksmith area, old railroad artifacts, turpentine and bee-keeping exhibits, and wildlife, including both domestic animals and native and exotic species. | 500 Obediah Trail | 912/287–0090 | www.okefenokeswamp.com | $4.50 | Mon.–Sun. 10–5.

ON THE CALENDAR
JUNE: *"Explore Georgia's Natural Wonders."* Search for gators along with your intrepid swamp ranger. | 912/283–0583.

Dining
Pond View. Contemporary. Lunch is country Southern style, while dinner goes more uptown, featuring freshly made crab cakes, duck breast with fig sauce, shrimp and pasta, and grilledpork tenderloin with blue cheese sauce. Buffet (Sun. lunch). Kids' menu. Beer and wine only. | 311 Pendelton St. | 912/283–9300 | No lunch Sat., Mon., no dinner Sun.–Tues., Thurs. | $17–$25 | AE, MC, V.

Lodging
The Comfort Inn at Waycross. This Comfort Inn provides you with a free newspaper; restaurants surround it. Complimentary Continental breakfast. Pool. Gym. | 1903 Memorial Dr. | 912/283–3300 | $56 | AE, D, DC, MC, V.

North Carolina

In 1629, King Charles I of England created a province and decreed that it would be called Carolina, from "Carolus," the Latin form of Charles. Into this region went all the land from Albemarle Sound in the north to the St. John's River in the south. When Carolina was divided in 1710, the southern portion became known as South Carolina, and the older northern settlement became North Carolina. From this came the sobriquet the "Old North State."

The Old North State is very old indeed, its ancient terrain shaped by a series of geological cataclysms that included the collision of continents hundreds of millions of years ago. A legacy of the pressure and molten heat created by those impacts and the repeated shuffling of rock is the amazing wealth of minerals and precious and semiprecious gemstones that make the western part of the state a heaven for rock hounds. Fossil hunters also have a lot to like about North Carolina. At one point the shoreline was west of where the Blue Ridge Mountains are now; sharks' teeth and whale bones are still unearthed by farmers who live nowhere near the ocean.

The breathtaking landscape of modern-day North Carolina—from the fragile, dune-dotted barrier islands that sit off the eastern coast in the Atlantic to the pristine forests, cascading waterfalls, and broad vistas in the west—is the most diverse in the Southeast, arguably the entire eastern United States. And it holds some surprises. At 560 mi wide, North Carolina is the widest state east of the Mississippi River. Horizontally, it ranges from flat, sandy, lush, semitropical, and swampy to rugged, rolling, tree-covered terrain crisscrossed by numerous mountain ranges. Sprinkled throughout this domain are wineries with vineyards that grow native muscadines; North Carolina was home to the nation's first cultivated grape. The earliest written account of the sweet, musky "big white grape" comes in the 1524 logbook of Florentine navigator Giovanni de Verrazano. In 1585, a report by Englishman Ralph Lane to Sir Walter

CAPITAL: RALEIGH	POPULATION: 7,428,194 (1997)	AREA: 52,669 SQUARE MILES
BORDERS: GA, SC, TN, VA, THE ATLANTIC OCEAN		TIME ZONE: EASTERN
POSTAL ABBREVIATION: NC	WEB SITE: WWW.VISITNC.COM	

Raleigh noted "grapes of such greatness, yet wild, as France, Spain, nor Italy hath no greater."

Greater still are the Appalachians in North Carolina, the oldest mountains in the United States. Their peaks are tallest east of the Mississippi (more than 200 mountains rise 5,000 ft or more), and their wilderness, a mosaic of woodlands, parks, and waterways, is immense. The New River, whose north and south forks run through three counties in the High Country, is the oldest river in America and the second oldest in the world, after the Nile. The Joyce Kilmer Memorial Forest, one of the nation's most impressive virgin forests, with trees measuring 20 ft in diameter, is here. So is Great Smoky Mountains National Park, the largest protected land area east of the Rockies and a very popular national park.

Connecting the Coastal Plain in the eastern third of the state to the mountains in the western third is the Piedmont Province in the center. The elevations here gradually rise from 300 to 600 ft above sea level to 1,500 ft. Gently rolling and well-rounded hills, long low ridges, meandering rivers, and large man-made lakes characterize the heartland, the most heavily developed region.

Once mostly farmland, the Piedmont, where growth has expanded along with the region's major arteries, is now a center of commerce, education, government, and manufacturing. For the sake of verbal convenience, North Carolinians group six of the urban centers into two threesomes: the Triad and the Triangle. The Triad is short for Greensboro, Winston-Salem, and High Point (a mouthful, to be sure), while the Triangle refers to the shape traced by Raleigh, Durham, and Chapel Hill, in whose center sits Research Triangle Park—a renowned complex of international companies and public and private research facilities. Yet shopping malls, world-class museums, sophisticated restaurants, and professional sporting venues aren't the only attractions here. The Piedmont is home to 15 large state parks best experienced on foot or by water. Indeed, one of the beauties of this region's cities—including Charlotte, which boasts the state's most dramatic skyline—is that they're characterized by canopies of hardwoods and pines.

Another plus is that you don't have to travel far—less than an hour—before reaching countryside where peaceful side roads lead to gristmills, gold mines, and general stores. History abounds in city center and countryside alike. Millions of people each year are drawn to meticulously preserved plantations and farmsteads, battlegrounds and burial grounds, Native American ceremonial sites and 18th-century villages settled by Europeans who came in search of, among other things, religious freedom.

Because North Carolina has four distinct yet temperate seasons, outdoor recreation is a big part of people's lives. For instance, the 36 parks and recreation areas run by the state preserve unique geological and biological resources; campers choose from hundreds of varied experiences—everything from primitive camping in the mountains' Nantahala National Forest to family camping along the shore; golfing is popular year-round on more than 400 courses; equestrians roam trails that wind through the heartland; and fishing and water activities are available at reservoirs near metropolitan centers.

Timeline

8000 BC	1524	1526	1540
The area that would become North Carolina is already inhabited.	Giovanni da Verrazano, an Italian navigator, explores the coast of North Carolina.	Lucas Vázquez de Ayllón of Spain tries to establish a colony near Cape Fear.	Hernando de Soto, a Spaniard, searches for gold in the mountains of North Carolina.

INTRODUCTION
HISTORY
REGIONS
WHEN TO VISIT
STATE'S GREATS
RULES OF THE ROAD
DRIVING TOURS

Population-wise, North Carolina is now more urban and suburban than rural. Due to a confluence of circumstance, custom, and capitalistic acuity, a number of centers of business, art, and education have grown up throughout the state. Each of them is vibrant and fiercely independent, but none of them is gritty, excessively noisy, or oversize. While traditional industries such as agricultural and textile production provided the money to build most of the cities, the engines driving the economy today are in the technology and service sectors. Also interesting is the fact that two of the state's most rapidly growing industries are filmmaking and tourism.

As much as geography or money, though, the state's landscape has been shaped by the people—Native Americans and African-Americans; settlers of English, German, and Scots-Irish descent; Moravians, Quakers, and Waldensians; and most recently Asians, Hispanics, and East Indians. The late Charles Kuralt, television journalist, author, and inveterate traveler, noted this truth in a moving 1991 tribute to his home state, both on videotape and book form. Kuralt pointed out that among those who have made a mark on his "state of grace" have been Whistler's mother, Billy Graham, Michael Jordan, three U.S. presidents, and Chief Manteo.

History

The first people arrived in North Carolina more than 10,000 years ago. At the time of European contact, 30 or so tribes inhabited different regions. Three major language families were represented: Iroquoian, Siouan, and Algonquian. The Iroquoian tribes (related to the Iroquois up north) included the Cherokee and Tuscarora. While the Cherokee, whose history dates to the pre-Columbian era, lived in the mountains on the state's western boundary, the Tuscarora occupied the Coastal Plain. Between those two were the Siouan, or Sioux, tribes living in the Piedmont: the Catawba Nation, numbering approximately 6,000, was the largest of these groups, while up in the tidewater area were 7,000 or so Algonquian-speaking people who had come south in a series of migrations from the Northeast.

They may have waged fierce battle against each other, but within their own communities the Indians lived peaceably, and for the most part the explorers found them to be hospitable people. The succession of Europeans making their way to and through North Carolina in search of glory and gold and new ground for the crown began during the summer of 1524. That's when Giovanni da Verrazano, an Italian in the service of France, navigated the area between the Cape Fear River and Kitty Hawk. Though he made no attempt to create a colony, he did note in his log that what he saw was "as pleasant and delectable to behold as is possible to imagine." Two years later Lucas Vásquez de Allyón of Spain formed a settlement near the Cape Fear River. It died a painful death; natives were furious at being enslaved. Next came Hernando de Soto, another Spaniard. So intent was he on finding gold that he completely overlooked the wealth of gemstones folded into the chain of ancient mountains that he crossed.

Ultimately, it was the English who won the settlement sweepstakes. In 1584 Sir Walter Raleigh, a soldier, explorer, and reported lover of Queen Elizabeth I, sent two

1584	1585	1587	1590	1629
English explorers led by Captains Arthur Barlowe and Philip Amadas are sent to North Carolina by Sir Walter Raleigh.	The first attempt to establishment an English colony is made on Roanoke Island. It fails but an earth fort built by the soldiers of fortune, and named Fort Raleigh, survives.	A second English colony is established, with John White as leader. His grandchild, Virginia Dare, is the first English child born in the New World.	John White returns to Roanoke from a supply trip to England, but all the colonists have disappeared without a trace.	King Charles I of England grants "Carolana" to Robert Heath.

ships to the New World. After anchoring in the Pamlico Sound, the captains, Arthur Barlowe and Philip Amadas, made their way ashore and promptly claimed everything in the name of their Virgin Queen (thus the area's first name, Virginia, and other place names such as Elizabeth City, Elizabethtown, and the Elizabethan Gardens). The men, who had noted that the natives were "most gentle . . . very handsome, goodly people," took two Indians, Wanchese and Manteo, back to London. Upon their return to North Carolina a year later, Manteo was an avowed ally of the English while Wanchese was their sworn enemy.

After hearing news of his captains' finds and after meeting the exotic men, Raleigh was convinced the time and place were right for a colony. Elizabeth granted him a charter, and in 1585 Ralph Lane, a military officer leading soldiers of fortune, landed on Roanoke Island. They built an earthworks, named it Fort Raleigh, and then for a year brutalized the locals before barely escaping to England with their lives. A second expedition of 110 settlers, including 17 women and 9 children, arrived near Hatteras in the summer of 1587. A month after the settlers arrived, Virginia Dare became the first child born to English-speaking parents in the New World. Shortly thereafter, her grandfather, the colony's leader, returned to England for supplies. It took John White three years to get back to the colony. Upon his return he found no signs of life, only the word *Croatan* carved into a tree or doorpost (depending on whose version is believed). The mystery of the "Lost Colony" remains. One popular theory, however, is that the frightened and destitute settlers eventually joined Manteo and the friendly Croatan people. Today, communities on the Outer Banks' Roanoke Island are named for Manteo and his onetime friend Wanchese.

Undeterred, the English pressed on. And for a while it was politics as usual. In the 17th century, Charles I gave Sir Robert Heath a chunk of land that included all of present-day North Carolina, South Carolina, and then some. The area was named Carolina in honor of the king. Settlers from coastal Virginia, seeking space of their own, began flowing into northeast North Carolina around 1650. In 1663 Charles II granted a charter to the Lords Proprietors, eight men who had helped regain the throne. For the next 66 years Carolina was under the control of these men and their descendants. During that time, John Locke wrote the "Fundamental Constitutions" as a model for the government of Carolina; Carolina was divided into North and South, the governors for which were appointed by the Lords Proprietors; and Bath, North Carolina's first town, was founded.

The setting was ripe for conflict, though. Already some colonists, displeased with their governor, had revolted and for more than a year governed themselves. Then the Tuscarora, unhappy at the loss of their land to settlers, were ready to rebel as well. The fiercely fought Tuscarora War, begun with attacks by Tuscaroras on farms and villages, lasted two years, ending in 1713. The white man's victory was a shallow one, and costly. About 800 Indians were killed or captured, and many of the remaining Tuscarora fled to New York—the land of their ancestors—and a good part of the colony of North Carolina was wiped out.

1650	1663	1706	1710	1711
The first permanent English settlers, immigrants from the tidewater area of southeastern Virginia, move into the Albemarle area of North Carolina.	King Charles II grants the Carolina colony to eight noblemen, known as Lords Proprietors, who helped him regain the throne of England.	Bath, the colony's first town, is founded.	North Carolina and South Carolina become separate colonies.	The brutal Tuscarora War between Native Americans and settlers begins.

In 1729 North Carolina became a royal colony when seven of the Lords Proprietors, in order to rid themselves of debt, not to mention the irritation of governing, sold their interests. The eighth proprietor, Lord Granville (as in modern-day Granville County), retained an economic interest and continued granting land in the northern half of the state. All political functions of the colony, which was fast filling not only with English but Irish, Scottish, and German settlers—120,000 in all—remained under the supervision of the Crown until 1775.

Missed opportunities, wars, and internal strife caused by deep fissures between the mainly English farmers, timbermen, and merchants in the east and by the disaffected German, Quaker, and Scots-Irish of the "backcountry" (Piedmont) temporarily faded in the face of a bigger issue, the Revolutionary War. North Carolina's role in the revolution was a key one from the beginning. On April 12, 1776, the state's delegates to the Continental Congress met in Halifax and authorized a vote for independence. The so-called Halifax Resolves, the first official action by a colony calling for independence, were directed to all the colonies. Virginia followed with its own set of recommendations.

More than 7,500 North Carolinians fought in George Washington's army, and the sites of their pivotal battles are marked with monuments and signs. The first action in North Carolina was at Moores Creek Bridge, near Wilmington. The Americans won, thus keeping the English from the goal of early on capturing much of the South. A much-needed boost to the war effort and the morale of the Patriots came in 1781 when at the Battle of Guilford Courthouse, near what is now Greensboro, Lord Cornwallis lost a fourth of his army. This staggering defeat led to Cornwallis's surrender and ultimately the Americans' victory in 1783.

Due to political wrangling and concern on the part of its representatives that the U.S. Constitution lacked the necessary amendments to ensure freedom of the people, North Carolina took a long time to ratify the document—so long, in fact, that for a brief while the state had the dubious status of a foreign country. Finally, in 1789, she joined the Republic and earned the flag's 12th star. By 1790, North Carolina, which had nearly 400,000 citizens, ranked as the third most populous state, behind Virginia and Pennsylvania. Yet it was called "a vale of humility between two mountains of conceit"— the mountains a reference to the wealthy plantation-based societies of Virginia and South Carolina.

While a few plantations used slave labor to produce large cash crops such as cotton, rice, and indigo, slavery was less common in North Carolina than in other Southern states. In fact, the majority of whites in North Carolina labored on small family farms producing their own food and cloth. But because it lagged behind its sisters when it came to things like schools and roads, North Carolina came to be known as the Rip Van Winkle State. The sleep lasted some 20 years, until the decades preceding the Civil War.

The 1795 founding of the University of North Carolina, the nation's first state-supported institution of higher learning, marked a turning point in the life of the state.

1713	1729	1767	1768	1774
The Tuscarora War ends as Native Americans are defeated.	Seven of the Lords Proprietors sell their interests in North Carolina, and it becomes a royal colony.	Andrew Jackson, seventh president of the United States, is born in the Waxhaw settlement, along the unsurveyed North Carolina–South Carolina border.	Charlotte, the city that will become the second-biggest banking center in the U.S., is founded.	North Carolina sends delegates to the First Continental Congress.

In the early 1800s, after a 17-pound "rock" lugged home by young Conrad Reed and used as a doorstop turned out to be gold, America's first documented gold rush was on. Dozens of mines were worked in the Charlotte area (now the second-largest banking center in the United States), and for the next three decades, all the native gold minted in the country came from the state. Pioneers in the mold of North Carolinian Daniel Boone set about exploring and settling the Appalachians to the west, and Cherokee land grew ever more valuable, so much so that eventually the federal government ordered the 15,000 members of the Cherokee Nation to leave their homeland and walk to a reservation in Oklahoma. While some escaped into the Smoky Mountains, many others participated in the sad and disquieting odyssey that became known as the "Trail of Tears."

In April 1861 came an even more sweeping upheaval: the Civil War. Though North Carolina was the last state to secede, it provided more troops and more materiel than any other member of the Confederacy. It was during this period that North Carolinians earned the nickname "Tar Heels" for their willingness to stand their ground. The price for that stand was steep. The Union Army's slash-and-burn policy decimated towns and cities across the state. North Carolina lost more than 40,000 men—more than any other Southern state. And while slaves, who had constituted one-third of the population, were finally free, they had no money, no property, no education, and nowhere to go. Many wound up staying where they had been, this time working as sharecroppers for former masters.

Economic renewal followed the bitter years of Reconstruction (the state wasn't readmitted to the Union until 1868). Factories and mills—something new for North Carolina—were built to process tobacco and cotton. Money from tobacco and textiles not only put food on the tables of farmers and factory workers, it funded universities, museums, symphonies, and medical centers. Then, realizing their abundant trees were the equivalent of "green gold," North Carolinians began turning wood into furniture and in the process created an industry in which the state still ranks number one.

As 20th century dawned, Governor Charles Aycock introduced a far-reaching program of education reform and recruited corporate leaders to actively support public education. In 1903 Orville and Wilbur Wright, acting on advice from the National Weather Bureau, prepared their flying machine for takeoff at the windswept site that is now known as Kill Devil Hills, near Kitty Hawk. A giant memorial now marks the spot of that first successful 12-second flight. In the 1920s a pioneer road-building program was instituted that not only caused the state to be known as the "Good Roads State" but also connected the mountains to the coast and cities to formerly isolate tiny hamlets. The construction of the Blue Ridge Parkway, begun during the Depression by the Works Progress Administration, laid the groundwork for the preservation of the scenic wilderness that flanks the road.

New military bases, new industries, new ideas, and new cultures marched into the state on the heels of the Second World War. In cities such as Durham, African-Ameri-

1776	1789	1792	1795	1799
North Carolina is the first colony to vote for independence.	North Carolina becomes the 12th state.	Raleigh, the state's capital, is founded.	The University of North Carolina, the nation's first state-supported university, opens in Chapel Hill; James Polk, 11th president of the United States, is born near Pineville (outside Charlotte).	Conrad Reed finds a yellowish rock in Cabarrus County. Three years later it is identified as gold.

INTRODUCTION
HISTORY
REGIONS
WHEN TO VISIT
STATE'S GREATS
RULES OF THE ROAD
DRIVING TOURS

can businesses thrived along "Black Wall Street." Booker T. Washington would enthusiastically tell people, "Wait 'til you get to Durham." Integration came slowly, but the process was, for the most part, peaceful, unmarred by the violent confrontations experienced at certain places in the North and other parts of the South. In 1898 a group of African-American businessmen founded the North Carolina Mutual Life Insurance Company. Today, with nearly a quarter of the state's population African-American, it remains one of the largest black-owned and -managed businesses in the world.

North Carolina's latest reinvention of itself came in the early 1960s, when, in an attempt to prevent brain drain, a public-private partnership established Research Triangle Park (RTP). Here, on 6,800 tree-filled acres, organizations engage in institutional, governmental, and high-tech research. Three major research universities—Duke in Durham, North Carolina State in Raleigh, and the University of North Carolina in Chapel Hill—are the base and the capstone of RTP, a magnet for people of different languages and cultures who seek to explore the world of ideas.

Regions

1. THE COASTAL PLAIN

The section of North Carolina broadly referred to as "the coast" is actually the sum of many parts (islands, shore, and inland Coastal Plain), all of which have economies built on farming, fishing, and tourism—here you can fish, surf, swim and see sights steeped in history dating from the pre-Colonial era. The state's eastern border has more than 300 mi of shoreline dotted with lighthouses, dunes, and vacation homes, while the Outer Banks,

a chain of barrier islands in the Atlantic, form a giant sandbar from the Virginia border to the Cape Fear area. The beautiful Albemarle region, in the north of the Coastal Plain, parallels a portion of the Outer Banks. Along with New Bern and Greenville, a bit farther inland in the central part of the Coastal Plain, it provides a close-up look at America during the Revolutionary and Civil wars. The historic port of Wilmington, on the Cape Fear River, is the coast's largest city. It has fine restaurants and museums. Surrounding it are golf courses, white-sand beaches, and resorts that have been voted some of the best in the nation by various sources. Though they're open for business year-round, thanks to an extremely mild climate, May through Labor Day is definitely the busy season.

Towns listed: Ahoskie, Atlantic Beach, Bath, Beaufort, Buxton, Cape Hatteras National Seashore, Cedar Island, Duck, Edenton, Elizabeth City, Greenville, Hatteras, Jacksonville, Kill Devil Hills, Kinston, Kitty Hawk, Kure Beach, Manteo, Morehead City, Murfreesboro, Nags Head, New Bern, Ocracoke, Outer Banks, South Brunswick Islands, Southport, Washington, Williamston, Wilmington, Wrightsville Beach.

1808	1861	1865	1868	1903
Andrew Johnson, 17th president of the United States, is born in Raleigh.	The Civil War begins in April; North Carolina secedes in May.	Confederate General Joseph Johnston surrenders his forces to Union General William T. Sherman, near Durham. The Civil War ends.	North Carolina is readmitted to the United States.	Orville and Wilbur Wright make the first successful airplane flight, near Kitty Hawk.

2. THE PIEDMONT

Directly connecting the Atlantic Ocean in the east to the Appalachians in the west, as well as Virginia to South Carolina, is the Piedmont, North Carolina's prosperous urban and commercial core. Universities and colleges, sprawling medical facilities and scientific think tanks, centers of banking, government, and military command call the heartland home. The region's major highways, Interstates 40, 85, and 95, are always crowded. But get on one of the many scenic byways outside any of the four largest metropolitan areas—Charlotte/Mecklenburg County, the Triad (Greensboro, Winston-Salem, High Point), the Triangle (Raleigh, Durham, Chapel Hill), and Fayetteville—and the soul of the Piedmont emerges. Leisurely journeys reveal small towns and farms, roadside produce stands, historic sites, inns and bed-and-breakfasts, parks and forests, and waterways, including the reservoirs of the Pee Dee River. NASCAR races and the potters of Seagrove, whose work is on display in museums around the world, have helped make this region famous.

Towns listed: Aberdeen, Albemarle, Asheboro, Burlington, Cary, Chapel Hill, Charlotte, Cherryville, Concord, Cornelius, Dunn, Durham, Fayetteville, Gastonia, Goldsboro, Greensboro, Henderson, Hickory, High Point, Kannapolis, Laurinburg, Lexington, Lumberton, Mount Airy, Pilot Mountain, Pinehurst, Pittsboro, Raleigh, Roanoke Rapids, Rocky Mount, Salisbury, Sanford, Shelby, Smithfield, Southern Pines, Statesville, Warsaw, Wilson, Winston-Salem.

3. THE MOUNTAINS

The Appalachians, the oldest mountains in the country and some of the oldest in the world, braid their way across the western part of North Carolina in a series of heavily forested ranges. The Blue Ridge, the easternmost range, runs parallel to the Atlantic Ocean. Behind them is a plateau filled with rolling pastures, fertile farmland, and streams. And beyond that, hugging the state's border with Tennessee, are the Great Smoky Mountains. A whole series of cross-ranges, including the Nantahala, begins not far from Asheville. Not only are these mountains rugged and largely protected by federal or state fiat, they provide particularly spectacular views given that they contain the highest peaks east of the Mississippi.

National and state parks and forests, hundreds of waterfalls, centers for folk art and handicrafts, and a major casino on the Cherokee reservation are the main draws, providing prime shopping, skiing, hiking, bicycling, backpacking, camping, fishing, canoeing, and gaming.

Towns listed: Asheville, Banner Elk, Blowing Rock, Blue Ridge Parkway, Boone, Brevard, Bryson City, Burnsville, Cashiers, Cherokee, Fontana Dam, Franklin, Great Smoky Mountains National Park, Hendersonville, Highlands, Hot Springs, Jefferson, Lake Toxaway, Lenoir, Linville, Little Switzerland, Maggie Valley, Marion, Morganton, Robbinsville, Tryon, Valle Crucis, Waynesville, Wilkesboro.

1930	1945	1959	1971	1992
North Carolina is the number one producer of cotton textiles, tobacco products, and wood furniture.	Fontana Dam, the largest dam east of the Rockies, is constructed.	North Carolina State University in Raleigh, the University of North Carolina at Chapel Hill, and Duke University in Durham become the anchors for what will be one of the largest planned research parks in the world.	The present state constitution goes into effect.	Eva M. Clayton becomes the first woman from North Carolina to be elected to serve in Congress.

INTRODUCTION
HISTORY
REGIONS
WHEN TO VISIT
STATE'S GREATS
RULES OF THE ROAD
DRIVING TOURS

When to Visit

Because of both the topographical variety that comes with its three distinct regions and the presence of the Gulf Stream, which makes its closest approach to land just off the coast, North Carolina has the broadest range of climatic conditions of any state east of the Mississippi. For example, the highest temperature of record, 110°F, was recorded in Fayetteville in August 1983. The state's low record of -34°F came in January of 1985 at Mt. Mitchell, the highest peak in the eastern United States (also the site of the greatest 24-hour snowfall: 36 inches). And the state has a long on-again, off-again history of destructive hurricanes; hurricane season runs from June to November, peaking in early September.

So the best time to visit depends on which region you're visiting. The state has four distinct seasons, marked by very warm summers and mild winters. Temperatures normally range from 22°F to 92°F. Snowfall averages 5 to 6 inches a year, and the mountains receive most of that. In summer, the Coastal Plain and Piedmont feel oppressive due to high temperatures and humidity levels; those seeking cooler and drier air find escape in air-conditioned buildings or cars, or in the mountains, on the Outer Banks, or on other breezy barrier islands. Winter in the mountains can be prolonged, and travel on narrow, winding roads dangerous. So many attractions close, save those catering to winter-sport enthusiasts. Temperatures along the coast rarely go below freezing because of the moderating effect of the ocean. The Piedmont and Coastal Plain can be rainy and cool—sometimes downright cold—with an occasional ice storm or snowstorm. The infrequency of such storms, though, means municipalities are loath to invest in lots of foul-weather equipment, so road clearing is not automatic.

It is, then, in spring and fall that all of North Carolina really shines. Late March to mid-May (and early June in the Appalachians) brings soft winds, a riot of blooming color to yards, roadways, and countryside, and smaller crowds. Autumn (mid-September to mid-November) brings gentle and dry Indian summer days.

CLIMATE CHART

Average High/Low Temperatures (°F) and Monthly Precipitation (in inches)

	JAN.	FEB.	MAR.	APR.	MAY	JUNE
ASHEVILLE	47/26	51/29	59/35	68/42	75/51	81/59
	3.9	3.9	4.6	3.5	4.5	4.4
	JULY	**AUG.**	**SEPT.**	**OCT.**	**NOV.**	**DEC.**
	85/63	83/62	77/56	68/44	59/36	51/29
	4.1	4.3	3.7	3.3	3.7	3.5
	JAN.	**FEB.**	**MAR.**	**APR.**	**MAY**	**JUNE**
BOONE	40/23	44/26	51/32	59/40	67/48	74/56
	4.1	4.5	4.8	4.5	4.7	4.4
	JULY	**AUG.**	**SEPT.**	**OCT.**	**NOV.**	**DEC.**
	78/60	83/62	71/52	62/42	52/34	44/26
	4.8	4.3	3.4	3.4	4.3	3.1
	JAN.	**FEB.**	**MAR.**	**APR.**	**MAY**	**JUNE**
CAPE HATTERAS	53/38	54/39	60/44	68/52	75/60	82/68
	5.8	4.1	5.0	3.2	3.8	3.8
	JULY	**AUG.**	**SEPT.**	**OCT.**	**NOV.**	**DEC.**
	85/73	81/68	76/58	73/59	65/50	57/42
	5.1	5.4	4.8	5.2	5.1	4.6

	JAN.	FEB.	MAR.	APR.	MAY	JUNE
CHARLOTTE	50/31	54/34	63/41	72/49	79/58	86/66
	3.9	3.7	4.5	2.8	3.7	3.3
	JULY	AUG.	SEPT.	OCT.	NOV.	DEC.
	89/70	85/72	87/69	81/63	72/51	62/41
	3.9	6.2	3.9	3.7	3.7	3.3
RALEIGH	JAN.	FEB.	MAR.	APR.	MAY	JUNE
	53/34	49/29	53/32	62/39	72/46	79/55
	3.4	3.8	3.6	4.1	2.6	3.9
	JULY	AUG.	SEPT.	OCT.	NOV.	DEC.
	85/64	89/68	87/67	81/61	72/48	62/39
	3.5	4.3	3.8	3.6	3.3	2.9
WILMINGTON	JAN.	FEB.	MAR.	APR.	MAY	JUNE
	53/33	56/35	59/37	66/44	74/51	81/60
	3.1	4.4	3.7	4.4	2.8	4.4
	JULY	AUG.	SEPT.	OCT.	NOV.	DEC.
	86/68	88/71	84/66	76/54	68/45	60/38
	5.5	7.4	5.9	3.2	3.2	3.9

FESTIVALS AND SEASONAL EVENTS

WINTER

Dec.　**Christmas at Biltmore Estate, Asheville.** The 250-room Biltmore, first opened on Christmas Eve 1895, is opulently decked out for the holidays, recreating the season as the original residents, George and Edith Vanderbilt, celebrated it. | 800/411–3807.

Dec.　**Christmas Town, U.S.A., McAdenville.** Right outside Gastonia, this town uses tens of thousands of lights to transform itself into one gigantic holiday display. There's also a parade and other activities. | 704/824–9696.

SPRING

Apr.　**Azalea Festival, Wilmington.** Home and garden tours, concerts, parades, and many other events take place among millions of the city's azalea blooms. | 910/763–0905.

Apr.　**MerleFest, Wilkesboro.** Flat-picking legend Doc Watson hosts this four-day acoustic and bluegrass music extravaganza in memory of his late son, Merle. | 800/343–7857 or 336/838–6267.

May　**Hang Gliding Spectacular.** The longest continuously running hang-gliding competition in the world, which takes place on the dunes of Nags Head. You'll also find air sports such as skydiving and paragliding (in nearby Currituck). | 800/334–4777.

SUMMER

June–July　**American Dance Festival, Durham.** This is the world's largest modern dance event, showcasing hundreds of dancers, choreographers, and original performances. | 919/684–6402.

INTRODUCTION
HISTORY
REGIONS
WHEN TO VISIT
STATE'S GREATS
RULES OF THE ROAD
DRIVING TOURS

| July | **Grandfather Mountain Highland Games, Linville.** The largest gathering of Scottish clans in the United States includes athletic competitions, folk music and dancing, a parade of tartans, and food. | 828/733–1333. |

FALL

| Sept.–Oct. | **Michaelmas, Asheville.** This harvest fair with roots in 6th-century England comes to life on the grounds of the Biltmore Estate. Music, dancing, crafts, food, and games are available on weekends. | 800/543–2961. |

| Oct. | **Barbecue Festival, Lexington.** More than 100,000 people gather annually for this event that extols one version of the state food with cook-offs, live entertainment, exhibits, a carnival, arts and crafts, dancing, and sporting events. | 800/555–2142 (dial the number; at the tone, enter 62952) or 336/956–1880. |

| Oct. | **North Carolina State Fair, Raleigh.** Amusement rides, music, games, food, animals, crafts, and exhibits converge on the state fairgrounds for 10 days. | 919/821–7400. |

State's Greats

North Carolina, identified by early visitors as "the goodliest land under the cope of heaven," is not just defined by breathtaking mountaintop vistas, secluded island beaches, and rolling hills, among which are some of the nation's fastest-growing and richest commercial cores. Making it even more of a standout is the fact that its landscape is an ecological crossroads, a mind-boggling mix of South and North. The firs on Roan Mountain and the hemlocks in Cary, a Piedmont town, are trees normally found in Canada, for example, while shells near Cape Lookout are more often seen on more southern shores.

Old South and New South intersect in North Carolina, now more urban and suburban than rural. Sophisticated shopping, dining, and cultural experiences are readily and widely available. Still, you come to know the state's heart and soul most intimately when you explore proud past and abundant natural beauty from top to bottom. Peaks soar higher and waterfalls cascade farther than most others in the country. Rivers, lakes, and marshes abound in both town and country—thousands of miles of them. The views from terra firma are lush, shifting from panoramic to intimate. But some history tours can only be in the form of scuba diving. A particularly treacherous section of North Carolina's coast has the dubious distinction of being known as the "Graveyard of the Atlantic." It's there that more than 2,000 ships rest on the ocean floor.

Beaches, Forests, and Parks

North Carolina's unique geological and biological resources give outdoors enthusiasts a spectrum of activities not available in many other places. The law forbids any man-made structures (such as seawalls) that restrict nature along the 300-mi coastline, so the beaches remain wide and unspoiled. The southernmost waterways, preserves, and conservatories, along the **South Brunswick Island chain,** are some of the most natural and environmentally diverse in the state, while the more northern parts of the coast— the **Outer Banks,** home to **Cape Hatteras,** the nation's first national seashore—boast the tallest natural sand dunes on the eastern seaboard.

In addition to 1,500 lakes of 10 acres or more and 37,000 mi of freshwater streams, there are 36 state parks and more than 1.2 million acres of national forest land in North

Carolina. Included in this count is **Fort Macon State Park.** Across from Morehead City east of Atlantic Beach, it provides everything from history lessons to swimming spots. Up in the southern mountains are the **Joyce Kilmer Memorial Forest,** where centuries-old virgin timber towers above the forest floor, and the **Great Smoky Mountains National Park,** the most popular national park in the country.

Cities have recreational lakes, greenways for walking, jogging, and bicycling, and parks with horse trails and facilities for year-round activities, including swimming, tennis, and even camping in some cases.

Culture, History, and the Arts

On the **Cherokee reservation,** in the shadow of the Smoky Mountains, elders pass on to children the secrets of finger weaving, wood carving, and mask and beaded jewelry making. The work is intricate and ageless, a connective thread to a time that predates the United States by thousands of years. North Carolina is rich with such examples of history, and seeks, through display and interpretation, to honor the complex inter-twining of cultures and art.

At Mt. Gilead, in the center of the state at the edge of the Uwharrie National Forest, is **Town Creek Indian Mound,** a rebuilt temple complex originally engineered, pyramidlike, by the Creek Indians who came to live in the area around AD 1250. In the 16th century, colonists settled on the coast, near what is now **Manteo,** and then suddenly and mysteriously disappeared. **Old Salem,** a meticulously restored 18th-century Moravian town within Winston-Salem, had one of the first public water systems in America, one of the first fire departments, and one of the first schools for girls. Scars North Carolina received during the only wars held on U.S. soil are still evident at **Guilford Battleground** in Greensboro (which historians say was the beginning of the end for the British in the American Revolution) and **Oakwood Cemetery** in Raleigh. The resting place of 1,400 Confederate soldiers and five Civil War generals, Oakwood contains many fine examples of Victorian mortuary art. The year 1895 brought the opening of George W. Vanderbilt's splendid **Biltmore Estate** in Asheville. Still the largest private home in America, the Biltmore is now open for public viewing with all its art, original furnishings, extensive gardens, and winery. Also in Asheville, and of special appeal to the literary-minded, is the childhood home-turned-museum of **Thomas Wolfe,** whose autobiographical novel *Look Homeward, Angel* recounts early 20th-century life in the mountain town. In the middle of the century, North Carolina became the first state to fund a museum devoted to art; the Old Master and Judaic collections at the **North Carolina Museum of Art** in Raleigh are must-sees. And in the 20th century's twilight years came another grand gesture, this one an homage to the long tradition of American, and especially North Carolina, crafts. The **Mint Museum of Craft and Design** in Charlotte is the largest museum of its kind in the nation.

Sports

The **Carolina Panthers** (NFL football) and the **Charlotte Hornets** (NBA basketball) are based in Charlotte, while the **Carolina Hurricanes** (NHL hockey) occupy a spacious state-of-the-art arena in Raleigh. But if you really want to see passions rise, particularly in the Triangle, mention college sports, especially basketball. The NCAA basketball championship has traded hands among the area's three schools: Duke, the University of North Carolina at Chapel Hill, and North Carolina State University. Competition is fierce, play top-rate.

Off the playing field, there's plenty to choose from. Dozens of scenic tours created just for bicycling include the 700-mi Mountains-to-Sea Trail and the 200-mi Piedmont Spur. There's lots of camping—everything from primitive camping in the mountain wilderness of **Nantahala National Forest** to family camping along friendly shores. Canoeists find scenic rides and still pools in the northern mountains, while the peace-

INTRODUCTION
HISTORY
REGIONS
WHEN TO VISIT
STATE'S GREATS
RULES OF THE ROAD
DRIVING TOURS

ful lakes and rivers of the Piedmont provide side creeks and lagoons. If you're search-ing for a bigger adrenaline rush, there is white-water adventure on the **French Broad, Nantahala, Nolichucky** and **New** rivers. Sailing and powerboating are enjoyed across the state. **Lake Norman,** the 34-mi-long "inland sea" of North Carolina, is the site of numerous sailing regattas, waterskiing exhibitions, and pontoon boat outings. **Wrightsville Beach** has nationally recognized courses that take sailors from novice skills all the way to bareboat certification.

Hang gliders from all over the country visit Nags Head to take off from the sandy dunes of **Jockey's Ridge State Park.** Skiers and snowboarders find an outlet for their passion at any of the state's eight ski resorts. **Beech Mountain,** with its 5,500-ft summit, is the East's highest ski area and nets 90 inches of annual snowfall. **Appalachian Ski Mountain** in Blowing Rock is the best choice if you're looking for a family-friendly, learn-to-ski experience.

To many travelers, North Carolina means golf. The state has more than 500 courses; 40 of them, championship courses, are in the **Sandhills** area alone. Pinehurst is home to eight legendary courses, including No. 2—site of the 1999 U.S. Open Championship, U.S. Senior Open Championships, and many historic U.S. Amateurs—No. 8, and Tom Fazio's No. 4.

State Parks

Throughout the state that has been endowed with much natural beauty, North Carolina has more than 35 state parks, recreation areas, and natural areas. These run the gamut from mountains and beaches to everything in between, including lakes, rivers, streams, forests, and historic forts. The North Carolina Division of Parks and Recre-ation does not charge entrance fees for it parks, but there is a per-car charge at Falls Lake State Recreation Area in Wake Forest and Jordan Lake State Recreation Area in Apex. Some parks also have fees for cabins, boat rentals, camping, and other ameni-ties. It's best to check with the individual park on such facilities.

Rules of the Road

License requirements: To drive without restrictions in North Carolina you must be at least 18 years old and have a valid driver's license. If you're under 18 (but at least 15), then graduated licensing applies. Under graduated licensing, you can obtain a lim-ited learner permit at age 15 if you have completed driver's education. You must keep this permit for at least 12 months. If you have not been convicted of motor vehicle mov-ing violations or seat belt infractions in the preceding six months, you may apply for a limited provisional license. You must keep the limited provisional license for at least six months. Then, if you have not been convicted of motor vehicle moving violations or seat belt infractions in the preceding six months, you may apply for a full provisional license. If you turn 18 before completing this process, you may apply for a regular license and are no longer under the graduated driver license law.

Speed limits: The top speed limit in cities and towns is 35 mph. Outside cities and towns, the maximum is 55 mph, and on interstates it's 70 mph. Speed limit signs change rather abruptly, though, so stay alert.

Right turn on red: Everywhere in the state you can make a right turn at a red light after a full stop. Exceptions to this rule are posted—usually at certain city intersections.

Seat belt and helmet laws: All drivers and front-seat passengers must wear a lap safety belt or lap and shoulder belt, whichever the seating position provides. All children between the ages of 5 and 12 must wear a belt. Children age 5 and under and less than 40 pounds must by properly secured in a weight-appropriate child restraint system. In a vehicle that has a passenger-side front air bag and a rear seat, a child less than 5 years old and less than 40 pounds must be properly secured in the rear seat unless the child restraint system is designed to be used with an air bag. Infants and small children must ride in safety seats that are designed for them and have been crash tested. When children outgrow their safety seats at about 40 pounds, they must ride in booster seats until they are big enough for seat belts. Children 12 and under must be secured in the rear seat. Infants in rear-facing child safety seats cannot ride in the front seat in vehicles that have passenger air bags. Small children must ride in rear seats that are approved for their age and size. Motorcyclists are required to wear helmets and to keep their headlights and tail lights on at all times.

For more information: Contact the state's Division of Motor Vehicles at 919/715–7000 or the Department of Transportation at 877/DOT–4YOU.

The Outer Banks Driving Tour

Distance: 96 mi   Time: 3 days
Breaks: Stay both nights on Roanoke Island, where you'll spend the second day, in between a day on the northern Outer Banks and another on the southern islands.

This tour covers most of the Outer Banks from Kitty Hawk at the north end to Ocracoke in the south, primarily along Route 12. After coming in from the mainland on U.S. 158, you continue to the south, with a detour to Roanoke Island. A summer trip finds beach life in full swing, but if you want to avoid crowds, try spring or fall.

❶ **Kitty Hawk** (off U.S. 158), with a few thousand permanent residents, is among the quieter of the beach communities. The **Aycock Brown Welcome Center,** operated by the Dare County Tourist Bureau, provides extensive resources, including area maps, tide charts, and ferry schedules.

❷ **Kill Devil Hills** is home to the **Wright Brothers National Memorial,** a granite monument that resembles the tail of an airplane and stands as a tribute to the two bicycle mechanics from Ohio who took to the air on December 17, 1903. You can see a replica of the *Flyer* and stand on the spot where it made four takeoffs and landings. **Nags Head Wood Preserve** is a quiet 1,400-acre maritime forest dedicated to preserving a barrier island ecosystem and is owned by the Nature Conservancy.

❸ **Nags Head** has 11 mi of beach with 33 public access areas, all with parking and some with rest rooms and showers. **Coquina Beach,** in the **Cape Hatteras National Seashore,** is considered by many to be the best swimming hole on the Outer Banks. The wide-beamed ribs of the shipwreck *Laura Barnes* rest in the dunes here. **Jockey's Ridge State Park** has the tallest sand dune in the East (about 88 ft). It is popular for hang gliding, kite flying, and sandboarding.

❹ **Roanoke Island** is a sleepy, well-kept place that hasn't succumbed to full-scale commercialism—much of the 12-mi-long island remains wild. The village of **Manteo** is the focal point. A history, education, and cultural arts complex opposite the waterfront in Manteo, **Roanoke Island Festival Park,** includes the *Elizabeth I* State Historic Site. Costumed interpreters conduct tours of the 69-ft ship, a re-creation of a 16th-century vessel. Clustered together on the outskirts of Manteo are the lush **Elizabethan Gardens,** a re-creation of a 16th-century English garden, established as a memorial to the first English colonists. **Fort Raleigh National Historic Site** is a restoration of the original 1585

INTRODUCTION
HISTORY
REGIONS
WHEN TO VISIT
STATE'S GREATS
RULES OF THE ROAD
DRIVING TOURS

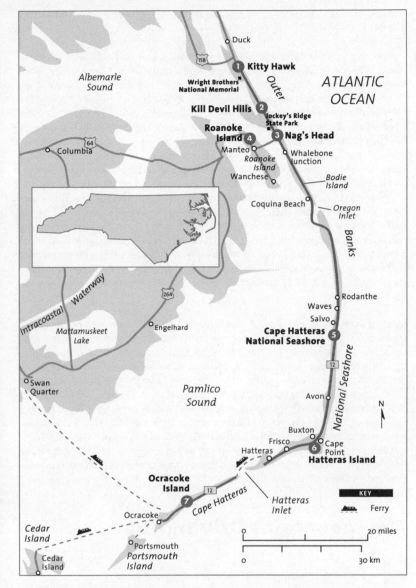

earthworks that mark the beginning of English Colonial history in America. The **North Carolina Aquarium at Roanoke Island,** next to the Dare County Regional Airport, is one of three aquariums in the state. The aquarium has a wetlands exhibit with turtles and amphibians, a shark exhibit, and a hands-on observation tank that is the aquatic equivalent of a petting zoo.

❺ **Cape Hatteras National Seashore** has more than 70 mi of unspoiled beaches stretching from south Nags Head to Ocracoke Inlet across three narrow islands: Bodie, Hatteras, and Ocracoke. The islands are linked by Route 12 and the Hatteras Inlet ferry. This coastal area is ideal for swimming, surfing, windsurfing, diving, boating, and many other water activities. It's easy to find a slice of beach all your own as you drive south down Route 12, but park only in designated areas. If you want to swim, beware of strong tides and currents—there are no lifeguard stations. Fishing piers are in Rodanthe, Avon, and Frisco.

❻ The Herbert C. Bonner Bridge arches for 3 mi over Oregon Inlet and carries traffic to **Hatteras Island,** known as the "blue marlin capital of the world." The island, a 33-mi-long ribbon of sand, juts out into the Atlantic Ocean; at its most distant point (Cape Hatteras), Hatteras is 25 mi from the mainland. About 85% of the island belongs to Cape Hatteras National Seashore, and the remainder is privately owned in seven small, quaint villages strung along Route 12, the island's fragile lifeline to points north. **Pea Island National Wildlife Refuge,** between Oregon Inlet and Rodanthe, is made up of more than 5,000 acres of marsh. This birder's paradise is on the Atlantic Flyway: more than 265 species are spotted regularly, including endangered peregrine falcons and piping plovers. Route 12 travels through marsh areas, and you can hike or drive, depending on the terrain. A visitor center, 5 mi south of Oregon Inlet, has an informational display. In Rodanthe, the restored 1911 **Chicamacomico Lifesaving Station** has a museum that tells the story of the 24 stations that once lined the Outer Banks. Living-history reenactments are performed June through August. **Cape Hatteras Lighthouse,** about 30 mi south of Rodanthe, is a beacon to ships offshore. At 208 ft, this is the tallest brick lighthouse in the world. Offshore lie the remains of the *Monitor,* the Confederate iron-clad ship that sank in 1862. The visitor center here provides information on the national seashore.

❼ Much of **Ocracoke Island** is part of Cape Hatteras National Seashore. A free ferry that leaves every hour during the day takes you from Hatteras to the island in 40 minutes. Ocracoke was cut off from the world for so long that locals still speak in quasi-Elizabethan accents; today, however, the island is a refuge for visitors. A village of shops, motels, and restaurants is around Silver Lake Harbor, where the pirate Blackbeard met his death in 1718. The **Ocracoke Lighthouse,** built in 1823, is the state's oldest and, at 75 ft, shortest operating lighthouse. You can walk up close to the light, but you cannot enter. There's an old graveyard behind the lighthouse. Ocracoke Island beaches are among the least populated and most beautiful in the Cape Hatteras National Seashore. Four public access areas have parking, as well as off-road vehicle access. At the **Ocracoke Pony Pen** you can observe from a platform the direct descendants of Spanish mustangs that once roamed wild on the island.

The Mountains Driving Tour

Distance: 225 mi   Time: 5–6 days
Breaks: Spend the first three nights in Asheville, the fourth along the Blue Ridge Parkway in Linville or Blowing Rock, and your final evening in Boone.

The majestic peaks, meadows, and valleys of the Appalachians' Blue Ridge and Smoky mountains characterize the western corner of the state. National parks, national forests, handmade crafts centers, and the Blue Ridge Parkway are the area's main draws, providing prime shopping, skiing, hiking, bicycling, camping, fishing, canoeing, or just taking in the breathtaking views. This tour samples the area's attractions, starting in the Asheville area and then continuing up the parkway.

❶ **Asheville** is the logical starting point for a tour of the North Carolina mountains. The largest and most cosmopolitan city in the mountains, Asheville has been rated America's favorite place to live among cities of its size. Particularly noteworthy is the renais-

INTRODUCTION
HISTORY
REGIONS
WHEN TO VISIT
STATE'S GREATS
RULES OF THE ROAD
DRIVING TOURS

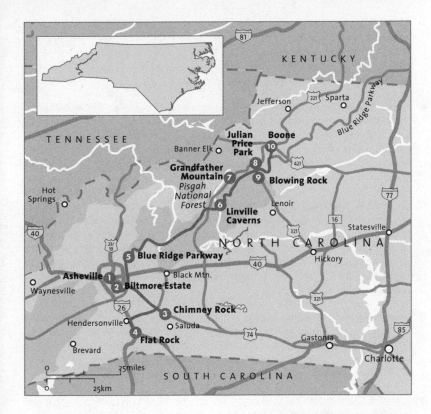

sance of the city's downtown, a pedestrian-friendly place with upscale shopping, art galleries, museums, restaurants, and nightlife. **Downtown Asheville** is also noted for its eclectic architecture. In fact, the city has the largest collection of Art Deco buildings in the Southeast, except for Miami. The 92,000-square-ft **Pack Place Education, Arts and Science Center,** in downtown Asheville, houses the **Asheville Art Museum, Colburn Gem and Mineral Museum, Health Adventure,** and **Diana Wortham Theatre.** The **YMI Cultural Center,** also maintained by Pack Place, is directly across the street. The **Thomas Wolfe Memorial,** built in 1880 in the Queen Anne style, is one of the oldest houses in downtown Asheville. Wolfe's mother ran a boardinghouse here for years, and he used it as the setting for his novel *Look Homeward, Angel.* Family pictures, clothing, and original furnishings filled the house before it was torched by an arsonist. The state historic site is being reconstructed and is expected to reopen in 2001. The visitor center and exhibit area behind the house remain open.

2 The astonishing **Biltmore Estate,** which faces Biltmore Village, was built in the 1890s as the private home of George Vanderbilt. This 250-room French Renaissance chateau is America's largest private house (some of Vanderbilt's descendants still live on the grounds but open the bulk of the home and grounds to visitors). It took 1,000 men five years to complete the gargantuan project. On view are the priceless antiques and art collected by the Vanderbilts and 75 acres of gardens and formally landscaped grounds. You can also see the state-of-the-art winery and take Christmas candlelight tours of the house. Allow a full day to tour the house and grounds. Ten years in the making, the **North Carolina Arboretum** is one of the state's jewels. On 426 acres that were part of the original Biltmore Estate, the arboretum completes the vision of Frederick Law Olmsted, who wanted a world-class garden in western North Carolina.

❸ Another day should be devoted to the attractions south of Asheville, including **Chimney Rock,** a town deep in the Blue Ridge Mountains. At **Chimney Rock Park** an elevator travels through a 26-story shaft of rock for a staggering view of Hickory Nut Gorge and the surrounding mountains. Trails, open year-round, lead to 400-ft Hickory Nut Falls, where *The Last of the Mohicans* was filmed.

❹ **Flat Rock** has been a summer resort since the mid-19th century. The **Carl Sandburg Home National Historic Site** is the spot to which the poet and Lincoln biographer Carl Sandburg moved with his wife, Lilian, in 1945. Guided tours of their house, Connemara, where Sandburg's papers still lie scattered on his desk, are given by the National Park Service. In summer, *The World of Carl Sandburg* and *Rootabaga Stories* are presented at the amphitheater.

❺ The beautiful **Blue Ridge Parkway** gently winds through mountains and meadows and crosses mountain streams for more than 469 mi on its way from Cherokee, North Carolina, to Waynesboro, Virginia. This is the most scenic route from Asheville to Boone and Blowing Rock. The parkway is generally open year-round but often closes during inclement weather. Maps and information are available at visitor centers along the highway. Mile markers (MM) identify points of interest and indicate the distance from the parkway's starting point in Virginia.

❻ **Linville Caverns** are the only caverns in the Carolinas. They go 2,000 ft underground and have a year-round temperature of 51°F. From the **Linville Falls Visitor Center,** a ¹/₂-mi hike leads to one of North Carolina's most photographed waterfalls. The easy trail winds through evergreens and rhododendrons to overlooks with views of the series of cascades tumbling into Linville Gorge. There's also a campground and a picnic area.

❼ Just off the parkway at Mile Marker 305, **Grandfather Mountain** soars to 6,000 ft and is famous for its **Mile-High Swinging Bridge,** a 228-ft-long bridge that sways over a 1,000-ft drop into the Linville Valley. There is also hiking and picnicking. The **Natural History Museum** has exhibits on native minerals, flora and fauna, and pioneer life. The United Nations has designated Grandfather Mountain a Biosphere Reserve. The annual **Singing on the Mountain** in June is an opportunity to hear old-time gospel music and preaching, and the **Highland Games** in July bring together Scottish clans from all over North America for athletic events and Highland dancing.

❽ Parks along the parkway include **Julian Price Park,** which has hiking, canoeing on a mountain lake, trout fishing, and camping. **Moses H. Cone Park** has a turn-of-the-century manor house (home of a textile magnate) that's now the **Parkway Craft Center.** The center sells fine work by area craftspeople.

❾ **Blowing Rock,** a mecca for mountain visitors since the 1880s, has retained the flavor of a quiet village. The rock looms 4,000 ft over the Johns River Gorge. If you throw your hat over the sheer precipice, it may come back to you, should the wind gods feel playful. The story goes that a Cherokee man and a Chickasaw maiden fell in love. Torn between his tribe and his love, he jumped from the cliff, but she prayed to the Great Spirit, and he was blown safely back to her. It's a gimmick, but the view from the observation tower is nice, and there's a garden landscaped with mountain laurel, rhododendron, and other native plants. The **Tweetsie Railroad** is a popular Wild West theme park centered on a narrow-gauge steam locomotive that's beset by "robbers."

❿ **Boone,** named for frontiersman Daniel Boone, is a city of several thousand residents. You'll find mountain crafts in stores and at crafts fairs here. **Mast General Store** at the Old Boone Mercantile is a classic general store. The **Appalachian Cultural Museum** examines the lives of Native Americans and African-Americans in the High Country, show-cases the successes of such mountain residents as stock-car racer Junior Johnson and country singers Lula Belle and Scotty Wiseman, and exhibits a vast collection of antique quilts, fiddles, and handcrafted furniture.

NOTE ABOUT NORTH CAROLINA RESTAURANTS

Be aware that in some areas of North Carolina restaurants do not serve alcoholic bever-ages. In addition, some dining spots do not serve alcohol but allow patrons to bring their own. In this book, listings for dining spots that serve beer and wine but no liquor say "beer and wine only." It's best to check with a restaurant before you go to find out about its alcohol policy and about what alcohol it serves, if any.

ABERDEEN

MAP 8, G5

(Nearby towns also listed: Pinehurst, Sanford, Southern Pines)

This small town of Scottish ancestry is just 5 mi south of Pinehurst. It was in the late 18th and early 19th centuries that the area's enormous virgin longleaf pine forests gave rise to a turpentine industry. Then came entrepreneurs such as the Page family who grew into "lumber kings" and branched out into railroading to ensure that their timber was efficiently transported. Eventually, the cut-over timberland was transformed into what Moore County, Including the 3,800-resident city of Aberdeen, is now known for: golf courses, lake-dotted resorts, and horse farms.

Information: Pinehurst Area Convention and Visitors Bureau | Box 2270, Southern Pines 28388 | 910/692–3926 or 800/346–5362 | cvb4golf@mindspring.com | www.home-ofgolf.com.

Attractions

Heart of Aberdeen. Downtown Aberdeen is only a few blocks long, yet it packs lots of archi-tectural punch. There's the beautifully restored train station, the Page Memorial Library, and the Page Memorial United Methodist Church, all from the turn of the 20th century. There are also plenty of shops with antiques and collectibles. The "old" Bethesda Presby-terian Church, just east of town on Bethesda Road, was founded in the late 1700s. Despite expansions, the wooden structure, which bears bullet holes from a Civil War battle, has remained true to its origins and wears its history well. It's still used occasionally for wor-ship services, as well as weddings, funerals, and reunions, and its cemetery, where many early settlers are buried, is always open. | Main and Poplar Sts., one block off U.S. 1 | 800/346–5362 | Free | Daily.

Malcolm Blue Farm. One of the few remaining examples of the 19th-century Scottish homes that dotted the area, this holds farm buildings and an old gristmill. A festival in late Sep-tember recalls life here in the 1800s, and there's a Christmas open house the second Sun-day in December. The farm and museum are part of the North Carolina Civil War Trails. | Bethesda Rd. at El Ives Dr. | 910/944–7558 or 910/944–9483 museum | Free | Thurs.–Sat. 1–4; tours by appointment.

The Old Silk Route. This Southeast Asian art gallery and shop is in a former bank build-ing and has six large showrooms containing a mind-boggling array of items from Afghanistan, Burma, India, Indonesia, Nepal, Pakistan, and Thailand. It was founded by Ann Magee, whose travels along the Old Silk Route began as a child. On display or for sale are everything from brass and copper artifacts to wall hangings. | 113 W. Main St. | 910/944–2900 | Free | Mon., Wed., Fri., Sat. 11–4.

ABERDEEN

INTRO
ATTRACTIONS
DINING
LODGING

ON THE CALENDAR
SEPT.: *Malcolm Blue Farm Festival.* The authentic 19th-century activities in this festival include crafts demonstrations, a puppet show, folk and country music, dancing, and a reenactment troop in a Civil War-type camp. You'll also find food and farm animals. The farm is on Rte. 5, 5 mi south of Pinehurst. | Bethesda Rd. | 910/944–7558.

Dining
Cafe Mediterraneo. Contemporary. When the more than 100-year-old Pinehurst (train) Station was moved lock, stock, and barrel a few miles down the road to Aberdeen, Pedro Zapater and his family decided its intimate size and richly-toned wood floors and walls would make the perfect backdrop for a restaurant whose menus combine the flavors of America and Spain. A lunch favorite is the Barcelona burger made of ground beef, spinach, onions, and spices. Seafood stew is a dinner specialty. Reservations are not accepted for lunch. | 300 Fields Ave. | 910/944–1717 | Reservations essential | $20–$30 | MC, V | Closed Sun., Mon., wk of July 4, and last wk in Dec.

Dave's Place. American/Casual. With its four TVs tuned to sports shows and its informal, rustic interior, Dave's feels like a bar. Families and individuals gather for the camaraderie as well as the pizzas, sandwiches, salads, and daily specials such as shrimp. Though there's no special kids' menu, the cook will halve portions and has been known to make baloney or peanut butter and jelly sandwiches upon request. Beer and wine only. | 1307 Sandhills Blvd. N | 910/944–9105 | Reservations not accepted | $6–$14 | MC, V.

Eva's Diner. American. Though it's in a former dance club, there's nothing disco about this family-owned restaurant. Portions of the country-style cooking, such as the pork chop and chicken plates, are ample. A house favorite is the Eagle burger, an oversized hamburger topped with just about anything you want. No alcohol. | 209 E. Rte. 211 | 910/944–4784 | Reservations not accepted | $2–$10 | No credit cards | Closed Sat., Sun.

Lodging
Motel 6. Near the intersection of U.S. 1 and US 15/501, this is a standard chain motel. In the rooms, everything is in neutral shades except the colorful bedspreads. All rooms are on the ground level and easily accessible. Some kitchenettes. Pool. Laundry facilities. | 1408 N. Sandhills Blvd. | 910/944–5633 or 800/466–8356 | fax 910/944–1101 | search.motel6.com | 80 rooms | $42 | AE, D, DC, MC, V.

Best Western Pinehurst Inn. There's a large front lawn, and some rooms overlook a courtyard that has a barbecue grill. The decorating scheme is fall colors, and there's a restaurant adjacent to the property. Complimentary Continental breakfast. Some refrigerators. Pool. Playground. Business services. Laundry facilities. | 1500 Sandhills Blvd. | 910/944–2367 or 800/944–2730 | fax 910/944–2730 | www.bestwestern.com | 50 rooms | $68–$80 | AE, D, DC, MC, V.

Inn at the Bryant House. This former home in the heart of Aberdeen's downtown historic district was expanded around 1913 and turned into a guest house. The liberal use of pastel colors, windows, and wicker furniture balances the heavier antiques. Complimentary Continental breakfast. Business services. | 214 N. Poplar St. | 910/944–3300 or 800/453–4010 | www.innatbryanthouse.com | 9 rooms | $70–$95 | AE, D, MC, V.

AHOSKIE

MAP 8, J3

(Nearby towns also listed: Edenton, Williamston)

Just 24 mi south of the Virginia line, Ahoskie has a population of approximately 5,000 and is the largest community in Hertford County. Numerous waterways and an abundance of wild game make it a haven for anglers and hunters.

Information: Ahoskie Chamber of Commerce | 310 S. Catherine Creek Rd., 27910 | 252/332–2042.

Attractions
Ahoskie Museum. Within the Garrett House is this museum that displays various artifacts relating to the history and development of the area. The building is a part of the Chamber of Commerce. Call ahead to make sure that someone will be there to let you in. | 310 S. Catherine Creek Rd. | 252/332–2042 | fax 252/332–8617 | Free | By appointment.

ON THE CALENDAR
APR.: *Chicken Fest.* In a nod to the economic impact of a major employer, a national chicken processor, a three-day party is held on West Main Street the last full weekend of the month, with amusement rides, music and dancing, games, an art show, and food. | 252/332–2042.

Dining
Bracy's Carolina Cookin'. American. Serving down-home, family food, this spot is known for its lunch buffet. It also serves breakfast. | 505 Academy St. (U.S. 13 N) | 252/332–5392 | Reservations not accepted | $6–$10 | No credit cards.

Catherine's 1770 Restaurant. American/Casual. Once a private home, this place which serves fried trout, crabcakes, stuffed flounder, and steak to local middle-aged business people both upstairs and down has a working fireplace in the dining room. | 706 Catherine Creek Rd. S | 252/332–5858 | $11–$28 | AE, D, MC, V.

O'Connor's. American. This no-frills, family-style place dresses up tables with linens on Sundays. It's known for chicken, pork chops, country ham, lots of vegetables, and sandwiches. | 1501 E. Memorial Dr. (U.S. 13 S) | 252/332–8242 | Reservations not accepted | $5–$9 | No credit cards | Closed 1 wk at Christmas.

Lodging
Ahoskie Inn. Thirty minutes from the Virginia border and one hour from Greenville, this inn has refurbished all rooms with carpeting, bedspreads, and amenities. Restaurant, bar with entertainment. Microwaves, no-smoking rooms, refrigerators. Cable TV. Indoor pool. Business services. | 343 Rte. 561 W | 252/332–4165 or 800/582–3220 | fax 252/332–1632 | 98 rooms | $52–$62 | AE, D, DC, MC, V.

Chief Motel. This basic drive-up motel has a king or two queen-size beds in each room. There's even a classic American "greasy spoon" diner on-site. Restaurant. Cable TV, room phones. Laundry facilities. | 700 Academy St. | 252/332–2138 | 28 | $35–$45 | AE, DC, D, MC, V.

Tomahawk Motel. A place in the heart of town, this single-story motel has simple accommodations and amenities. Cable TV. Business services. | 601 N. Academy St. | 252/332–3194 | fax 252/332–4665 | 58 rooms | $45 | AE, D, DC, MC, V.

ALBEMARLE

MAP 9, E5

(Nearby towns also listed: Charlotte, Concord)

In the Uwharrie Mountain range and bordered by Lake Tillery, the Albemarle area affords outdoor enthusiasts cabin lodging, camping, fishing, swimming, boating, canoeing, and walks along nature trails.

Through the 19th century, Albemarle was a quiet, rustic hamlet. The 20th century brought rail lines and industrialization in the form of textiles. The symbolic heart of Albemarle is the intersection of 2nd and Main streets. It's the highest point in downtown, and locals call it the Square.

Information: **Stanly County Chamber of Commerce** | Box 909, Albemarle, 28002 | 704/982–8116 | www.stanly-chamber.org.

Attractions

Badin Road Drive-In. You can load up on snacks at a convenience store, then head to this nostalgic throwback around dusk, where you can see two relatively new movies back-to-back in summer. | 2411 Badin Rd. | 704/983–4882 | $4.

Morrow Mountain State Park. A 4,693-acre natural resource area in the ancient Uwharrie Mountains, this park has overnight camping, family vacation cabins, hiking, pool swimming, boating, fishing, and picnicking. Attractions include the 1870s home site and infirmary of Francis Kron, the first doctor to settle and practice medicine in the southern Piedmont. | 49104 Morrow Mountain Rd. | 704/982–4402 | fax 704/982–5323 | www.ncsparks.net | Free, fee for camping and cabins | Jun.–Aug., daily 8 AM–9 PM; Sept., Apr., and May, daily 8–8; Nov.–Feb., daily 8–6.

Stanly Museum and Visitor Center. Here you'll see a permanent exhibit of the history of Stanly County and tour of two house museums: the Snuggs House (1873) and the Marks House (1847). | 245 E. Main St. | 704/986–3777 | fax 704/986–3778 | www.co.stanly.nc.us/departments/museum/info.htm | Free | Mon.–Fri. 8:30–5, 1st Sat. of month 10–2.

Town Creek Indian Mound State Historic Site. Six hundred years ago, Pee Dee people built a ceremonial site, including a major temple on an earthen mound. A minor temple, mortuary, game pole, and stockade surround the ceremonial area. Reconstruction of all this was based on 50 years of excavation. A visitor center has a slide presentation, exhibits, and a nature trail. | 509 Town Creek Mound Rd., Mt. Gilead | 910/439–6802 | fax 910/439–6441 | www.ah.dcr.state.nc.us/sections/hs/town/town.htm | Free | Apr.–Oct., Mon.–Sat. 9–5, Sun. 1–5; Nov.–Mar., Tues.–Sat. 10–4, Sun. 1–4.

ON THE CALENDAR

MAY: *Beach Blast.* Dance instruction, food, and rides provide the fun at this downtown street dance and beach music party. | 704/984–9415.

Dining

Blue Bay Seafood–Albemarle Inc. Seafood. Seascape murals and fishnets adorn the walls in this informal spot with family-style service. The menu includes some chicken and steak dishes, but it is dominated by all kinds of seafood that is mostly fried or broiled. | 2219 U.S. 52 N | 704/982–9277 | $5–$20 | AE, D, MC, V | Lunch Sun. only. Closed Mon.

Fifty Two North. American. Black-and-white decorations provide the backdrop at this casual family restaurant known for chicken, seafood, and steaks. There are also lunch and supper buffets. Kids' menu. | 1456 U.S. 52 N | 704/983–1813 | $9–$15 | AE, D, MC, V.

Firehouse Espresso Café. Delicatessen. Firehouse memorabilia create a fire-department theme at this casual, family-oriented restaurant. Potato soup, Firehouse reubens, Italian sandwiches, and subs are on the menu. Continental breakfast is also available. The open-air dining area has the same firehouse theme. Kids' menu. Beer and wine only. | 114 S. 2nd St. | 704/983–2320 | $5–$10 | MC, V | Closed Sun.

Harmancos. Cajun/Creole. Bright colors complement the Cajun dishes of jambalaya, shrimp creole, and crawfish. Steaks and ribs are also on the menu. Open-air dining, a full bar, and live music Wed.–Fri complete the picture. Kids' menu. | 1407 E. Main St. | 704/982–5414 | $15–$22 | AE, D, MC, V.

Lodging

Comfort Inn. Right off the highway in a small business district, this hotel is about 30 minutes from the outskirts of Charlotte and 45 minutes from downtown Charlotte. Some of the neutral-color rooms have kitchenettes and pull-out sofas. Complimentary Continental breakfast. Some refrigerators. Cable TV. Pool. Business services. | 735 Rte. 24/27 Bypass | 704/983–6990 | fax 704/983–5597 | 80 rooms | $60–$68 | AE, D, DC, MC, V.

The Pines Plantation Inn. A two-level porch welcomes you to this 1870s-era Southern mansion. It's about 15 mi southeast of Albemarle in the Uwharrie Lakes Region, on the western edge of Uwharrie National Forest. Each of the five guest rooms is different from the rest, each has a private bath, and some have a fireplace and access to the porch. Complimentary breakfast. Cable TV. | 1570 Lilly's Bridge Rd. | 910/439–1894 or 800/711–1134 | pinesinn@etinternet.com | 5 rooms | $55–$80 | MC, V.

ASHEBORO

MAP 9, F4

(Nearby towns also listed: Greensboro, High Point)

The weathered, tree-covered hills of the ancient Uwharrie Mountain range punctuate the gently rolling landscape of Asheboro. The Randolph County seat is part of the Uwharrie Lakes Region, which includes pieces of seven counties, a river, six man-made reservoirs, a national forest, and many scenic byways.

Information: Randolph County Tourism Development Authority | Box 4774, Asheboro, 27204 | 336/626–0364 or 800/626–2672 | tourism@visitrandolph.org | www.visitrandolph.org.

ASHEBORO

INTRO
ATTRACTIONS
DINING
LODGING

Attractions

American Classic Motorcycle Museum. A display of more than 30 Harley Davidson motorcycles, a complete 1948 dealership, and much more covers Harley Davidson motorcycle history from 1936 to 1972. You can enter the museum through the Heritage Diner. | 1170 U.S. 64 W | 336/629–9564 | fax 336/629–6819 | Free | Tues.–Fri. 8:30–5:30, Sat. 6–4:30 | Closed Mon.

North Carolina Pottery Center. The two-centuries-old history of North Carolina pottery comes to life with exhibits and activities at this museum and educational facility. The center provides information and displays to assist with more than 90 visiting potters in the immediate area and hundreds of potters across the state. | 250 East Ave., Seagrove | 336/873–8430 | fax 336/873–8530 | $4 | Tues.–Sat. 10–4.

★ **North Carolina Zoological Park.** The nation's largest walk-through, natural-habitat zoo is in the Uwharrie Mountains and houses more than 1,000 animals and 60,000 exotic and tropical plants. At 300 acres, the African Plains exhibit alone is larger than many zoos. In addition to an aviary, exhibits include animals and plants of North America and the Sonoran Desert. | 4401 Zoo Pkwy. (Rte. 159) | 336/879–7000 or 800/488–0444 | fax 336/879–2891 | $8; $4 when purchased at the gate Dec.–Feb. | Apr.–Oct., daily 9–5; Nov.–Mar., daily 9–4.

Peddycord F. A. C. Flying Museum. There are working war planes—from World War II, for example—and related memorabilia at this museum that's operated by the Foundation for Aircraft Conservation and dedicated to preserving aviation history. There's also a collection of model aircraft. | 2109 Pilots View Rd. | 336/625–0170 | $5 | Mon.–Sat. 10–4, Sun. noon–4.

Seagrove Area Potteries. More than 80 potteries are scattered along and off Route 705 and U.S. 220. Potters, some of whom are carrying on traditions that have been in their families for generations and others who are newer to the craft, make hand mugs, bowls, pitchers, platters, vases, and clay "face jugs." Specialties run the gamut from earthenware to porcelain. National museums, including the Smithsonian, exhibit the work of some of these local artisans. | 250 East Ave. | 336/873–7887 | fax 336/873–8530 | $3 | Most studios and shops Tues.–Sat. 10–4.

ON THE CALENDAR

MAR.: *North Carolina Potters Conference.* Potters travel from all over the world to listen to talks and see the works of potters at the height of their careers. The 2001 conference includes Welsh potters David and Margaret Frith, who are well known in the pottery community. The Randolph Potters Guild holds the conference, and the fee includes meals. | 336/629–0399 | $130.

MAR.: *Seagrove Lion's Fiddler's Convention.* A showcase for country and bluegrass musicians and devotees of all ages, this gathering tunes up at Seagrove Elementary School, 528 Old Plank Road. (Please do not call the school.) | 336/873–7621 | $6.

APR.: *Liberty Antique Show.* More than 150 antiques dealers from all over the United States descend on the small town of Liberty to participate in this show and sale. | 336/622–1901.

APR.: *Spring Kiln Opening.* Pottery studios throughout the Seagrove area display an array of their creations and open their kilns to the public. | 800/626–2672 or 336/873–7304.

JULY: *Summerfest.* Fourth of July fireworks, food, and entertainment light up this uptown holiday celebration. | 336/626–2626.

SEPT.: *Randolph Arts Guild Gem and Jewelry Show.* Gemstone and mineral dealers and jewelry artists from around the country display and sell their wares each Labor Day at the Days Inn Motel Albemarle. | 336/629–0399.

SEPT.: *Zoo-To-Do Gala.* A fund-raising social includes an auction, dinner, music, and dancing at the North Carolina Zoological Park. | 800/488–0444.

OCT.: *Asheboro Fall Festival.* More than 100,000 people fill the streets of uptown Asheboro for crafts, food, and entertainment. | 336/629–0399.

Dining

Blue Mist Barbecue. Barbecue. A no-frills, family-style place, this restaurant is known for pork barbecue, sandwiches, fried seafood, and lunch specials. Also serves breakfast. Kids' menu. | 3409 U.S. 64 E | 336/625–3980 | $7–$10 | MC, V.

Chin Song Restaurant. Chinese. Sesame chicken is the specialty at this spacious, older brick building downtown. The interior is done in shades of pink and jade green accents. | 615 S. Fayetteville St. | 336/626–3611 | $5–$10 | MC, V | No supper Sun.

Jugtown Café. American. With down-home cooking and 1950s decor, this restaurant is known for burgers and specials. | 7042 U.S. 220 S | 336/873–8292 | $3–$10 | No credit cards | Closed Mon. No supper Sun.

242 Café. American. Paraphernalia from all kinds of sports decorates the walls, as do license plates. This restaurant with family-style service is known for biscuits, bagels, omelettes, pancakes and waffles, salads, sandwiches, and blue-plate specials. Breakfast is also available. Kids' menu. | 242 S. Fayetteville St. | 336/625–5540 | $4–$12 | D, MC, V.

Lodging

Comfort Inn Asheboro. If you get tired of the outdoor swimming pool or the golf and fishing within 3 mi, you can burn off all that good, Southern food in the large fitness room. The rooms are standard hotel fare. Complimentary Continental breakfast. Cable TV, room phones. Pool. Exercise equipment. | 825 W. Dixie Dr. | 336/626–4414 | 90 rooms | $40–$90 | AE, D, DC, MC, V.

ASHEVILLE

MAP 9, B4

(Nearby towns also listed: Blue Ridge Parkway, Brevard, Hendersonville, Hot Springs, Marion, Waynesville)

The largest and most cosmopolitan city in the state's western mountains, Asheville has been rated America's favorite place to live among cities of its size. It has scenic beauty, a good airport and road system, a moderate four-season climate, and a thriving arts community.

Initially, development followed the French Broad River. Trade with the Cherokee was established as early as 1673, thanks to Indian paths that crossed the site of present-day Asheville. The area's natural riches and the promise of commerce drew settlers to the central mountains, and the paths became thoroughfares for traders, merchants, and others. Railroads brought the monied class in search of a healthful climate and a new way of socializing. With young George Vanderbilt and the construction of his Biltmore Estate came a legion of artists and craftsmen whose legacy remains.

Downtown Asheville brims with eclectic architecture; it has the largest collection of Art Deco buildings in the Southeast, except for Miami. Pack Square, the city's historic center, is now its cultural heart as well.

This urban center also benefits from the proximity of Pisgah National Forest and the Blue Ridge Parkway. These plus the French Broad provide numerous outdoor recreation options.

Information: Asheville Convention and Visitors Bureau | Box 1010, 28802 | 828/258–6101 or 800/257–1300. **Visitor Center** | 151 Haywood St., 28802 | cvb@ashevillechamber.org | www.ashevillechamber.org.

Attractions

Biltmore Estate. The focal point of this 8,000-acre property is America's largest private house, Biltmore House, a 250-room French Renaissance château that George Vanderbilt built in 1895. The estate also has gardens, a winery, and three restaurants. | 1 Lodge St. | 828/255–1700 or 800/624–1575 | www.biltmore.com | $32; prices vary for special events | Daily 8:30–5.

Biltmore Village Company. Next to the entrance to the Biltmore Estate, the village is a restored turn-of-the-20th-century community of shops, restaurants, and galleries. | 1 Kitchen Pl | 828/274–5570 | Free | Daily Mon.–Sat. 9:30–5, Sun. 1–5.

YOUR CAR'S FIRST-AID KIT

- ☐ Bungee cords or rope to tie down trunk if necessary
- ☐ Club soda to remove stains from upholstery
- ☐ Cooler with bottled water
- ☐ Extra coolant
- ☐ Extra windshield-washer fluid
- ☐ Flares and/or reflectors
- ☐ Flashlight and extra batteries
- ☐ Hand wipes to clean hands after roadside repair
- ☐ Hose tape

- ☐ Jack and fully inflated spare
- ☐ Jumper cables
- ☐ Lug wrench
- ☐ Owner's manual
- ☐ Plastic poncho—in case you need to do roadside repairs in the rain
- ☐ Quart of oil and quart of transmission fluid
- ☐ Spare fan belts
- ☐ Spare fuses
- ☐ Tire-pressure gauge

*Excerpted from *Fodor's: How to Pack: Experts Share Their Secrets*
© 1997, by Fodor's Travel Publications

Botanical Gardens. You can stroll along groomed paths through these 10 wooded acres with many plants native to the Appalachian region. | University of North Carolina–Asheville, 151 W. T. Weaver Blvd. | 828/252–5190 | Free | Reception daily 9–4; gardens, daily 9–sunset.

Chimney Rock Park. The biggest draw is a 26-story elevator ride through solid granite that leads to Chimney Rock level and a 75-mi view of the Blue Ridge. But there is also a 400-ft waterfall, as well as nature trails, wildlife, rare plant life, a picnic area, and sheer cliffs at this park 40 minutes from Asheville. | U.S. 74A and 64 | 828/625–9611 or 800/277–9611 | fax 828/625–9610 | www.chimneyrockpark.com | $10.95 | Daily 8:30–5:30, weather permitting.

Downtown Asheville. The downtown area showcases eclectic architecture. The Battery Park Hotel, built in 1924, is neo-Georgian; the Flatiron Building (1924) is neoclassical; the Basilica of St. Lawrence (1912) is Spanish Baroque; Pack Place, formerly known as Old Pack Library (1925), is Italian Renaissance; the S and W Cafeteria (1929) is Art Deco. In fact, the city has the Southeast's largest collection of Art Deco buildings outside Miami. | 828/258–6101 or 800/257–1300 | Free | Daily.

Folk Art Center. The nation's oldest crafts shop, Allanstand, makes its home in this 30,000-square-ft facility, which is headquarters for the Southern Highland Craft Guild. Included are the works of the guild's 700 members. Crafts demonstrations are given daily. The National Park Service also operates an information center here. | Blue Ridge Pkwy., MM 382 | 828/298–7928 | fax 828/298–7962 | www.southernhighlandguild.org | Free | Jan.–Mar., daily 9–5; Apr.–Dec., daily 9–6.

North Carolina Arboretum. These 426 acres, once part of the original Biltmore Estate, complete the dream of the master of landscape design, Frederick Law Olmsted, who wanted a world-class arboretum in western North Carolina. Showcased are southern Appalachian flora in a stunning number of spots, including the Quilt Garden, with bedding plants that are arranged in patterns reminiscent of Appalachian quilts. There is also the formal Stream Garden, which capitalizes on the Bent Creek trout stream that runs through the grounds. | I–26 Exit 2 | 828/665–2492 | Free; call about fees for group tours and special events | Visitor center Mon.–Sat. 9–5, Sun. 12–5; gardens and grounds dawn–dusk.

Pack Place Education, Arts and Science Center. This is a bustling complex in the historic district with four museums, a performing arts theater, a museum store, and lobby galleries. | 2 S. Pack Sq | 828/257–4500 | fax 828/251–5652 | main.nc.us/packplace | $4; $12 combination ticket to all museums | Tues.–Sat. 10–5, Sun. 1–5.
The **Asheville Art Museum** displays 20th-century American art, as well as contemporary crafts and art related to the Southeast region. | 2 S. Pack Sq | 828/253–3227 | fax 828/257–4503 | $4 | Tues.–Thurs. and Sat. 10–5, Fri. 10–8, Sun. 1–5.
The **Colburn Gem and Mineral Museum** displays gems and minerals from around the world; the *Washington Post* hailed it "a mini-Smithsonian of gems." The museum also showcases treasures from North Carolina, a gem-rich state. | 2 S. Pack Sq | 828/254–7162 | fax 828/251–5652 | main.nc.us/colburn | $4 | Tues.–Sat. 10–5, Sun. 1–5.
The **Diana Wortham Theatre** stages theatrical, dance, and musical performances at various times throughout the year. | 2 S. Pack Sq | 828/257–4530 | fax 828/251–5652 | Prices vary with shows | Call for schedule or see site www.dwtheatre.com.
Health Adventure contains 11 galleries of health- and science-related hands-on exhibits. | 2 S. Pack Sq | 828/254–6373 or 800/935–0204 | www.health-adventure.com | $4 | Tues.–Sat. 10–5, Sun. 1–5.
YMI Cultural Center is a celebration of African–American history, arts, and culture. | 39 S. Market St., next to Pack Sq | 828/252–4614 | fax 828/257–4539 | $4 | May–Oct., Tues.–Sat. 10–5, Sun. 1–5; Nov.–Apr., Tues.–Sat. 10–5.

Penland School of Crafts. This world-famous institution sits on a remote mountaintop and is the oldest and largest school for high-quality arts and crafts in North America. It offers classes in books and paper, glassblowing, ceramics, textile arts, and other mediums. A gallery displays work, some of which is for sale. Call to check hours and winter closing. Classes aren't open to the public, but you can arrange to tour the campus. | Penland Rd. | 828/765–

2359 (school) or 828/765–6211 (gallery and campus tours) | fax 828/765–7389 | www.pen-land.org | Free | Tours by reservation only.

River rafting. The French Broad River, which carves its way through the Biltmore Estate and some of the oldest mountains on earth, is ideal for quiet water trips led by outfitters such as Southern Waterways. The countryside surrounding Asheville has three rivers for white-water rafting. One of the white-water kings is Nantahala Outdoor Center (NOC). | NOC: 13077 U.S. 19 W, Bryson City | NOC: 828/488–2175 or 888/662–1662 | www.noc.com | Prices vary | Season varies, usually late Feb.–early Nov.

Riverside Cemetery. The burial place of authors Thomas Wolfe and O. Henry, this 87-acre parklike area, with more than 9,000 monuments, dates back to the early 1800s. Information about guided and self-guided tours is available during office hours, weekdays 8–4:30. | 53 Birch St. | 828/258–8480 | Free | Nov.–Mar., daily 8–6; Apr.–Oct., daily 8–8.

Thomas Wolfe Memorial. This is the famous novelist's boyhood home and setting for *Look Homeward, Angel.* | 52 Market St. | 828/253–8304 | $1 | Apr.–Oct., Mon.–Sat. 9–5, Sun. 1–5; Nov.–Mar., Tues.–Sat. 10–4, Sun. 1–4.

Western North Carolina Nature Center. At this "living" museum of animals and plants of the southern Appalachians, exhibits include both wild and domestic animals. | 75 Gashes Creek Rd. | 828/298–5600 | www.wildwnc.org | $4 | Daily 10–5.

Wolf Laurel Ski Resort. This resort has 54 acres of skiable terrain, 14 runs, and 100% snow-making capability. | Rte. 3, Mars Hill | 828/689–4111 | www.skiwolflaurel.com | Late Nov.–mid-Mar.

Zebulon B. Vance Birthplace State Historic Site. In spring and fall, artisans in period costume demonstrate early craftsmaking at this restored late-18th-century farmstead where the U.S. senator and Civil War governor was born. | 911 Reems Creek Rd., Weaverville | 828/645–6706 | www.ah.dcr.state.nc.us/sections/hs/vance/vance.htm | Free | Apr.–Oct., Mon.–Sat. 9–5, Sun. 1–5; Nov.–Mar., Tues.–Sat. 10–4, Sun. 1–4.

ON THE CALENDAR
JAN.: *Martin Luther King Jr. Annual Birthday Celebration.* Various events occur over several days at locations around town, honoring the birth of the civil rights leader. | 828/252–4614.
MAR.–APR.: *Festival of Flowers.* Elaborate Victorian floral arrangements in the Biltmore House, garden strolls, and live music highlight this popular festival. | 800/543–2961 | www.biltmore.com.
APR. AND SEPT.: *Pioneer Living Day.* At the birthplace of Zebulon B. Vance, a state historic site, there are demonstrations of domestic skills needed for life in the mountains in the 1800s, in addition to a re-created military encampment. It all happens at 911 Reems Creek Road in Weaverville. | 828/645–6706.
JULY: *Bele Chere.* One of the largest street festivals in the Southeast, this downtown event showcases multicultural crafts, food, and entertainment. There are many special events for kids. | 828/259–5800 | www.belechere.com.
JULY–SEPT.: *Shindig-on-the-Green.* Bluegrass and mountain dance liven up downtown every Saturday night until Labor Day. The "Green" is City/County Plaza. | 828/258–6101 | www.asheville.com.
JULY AND OCT.: *Craft Fair of the Southern Highlands.* Through exhibits and demonstrations of basket weaving, woodworking, pottery, and more, you peek into the lives and work of the craftspeople of the southern Appalachians. Held since 1948, this fair's current home is the Civic Center on Haywood Street. | 828/298–7928 | www.southernhighlandguild.org.
AUG.: *Asheville Antiques Fair.* This is believed to be one of the oldest continuously run antiques shows in the Southeast. Dealers from across the United States display antiques, including furniture, jewelry, china, and rugs at the Civic Center on Haywood Street. | 800/257–1300.

AUG.: _Goombay._ A West African word meaning rhythm translates to the name of this African–Caribbean festival on the fourth weekend of the month, which attracts 50,000 visitors a year and includes music, dancing, food, traditional African clothing, jewelry, and decorations. The first day's events are at the City/County Plaza, the second's at Eagle and South Market Streets. | 828/252–4614.

AUG.: _Mountain Dance and Folk Festival._ The nation's oldest continuing celebration of traditional music and dance includes hundreds of performers. The downtown festival gathers mountain musicians, cloggers, balladeers, and storytellers. | 828/258–6107 or 800/257–1300.

SEPT.–OCT.: _Michaelmas._ A traditional fair dating back to 6th-century England commemorates the harvest season with music, dance, food, and games at Biltmore Estate. | 800/543–2961.

OCT.: _Thomas Wolfe Centennial._ Exhibits, concerts, plays, and readings examine the life and writings of Asheville's famous native son at various downtown locations. | 828/253–8304.

NOV.–DEC.: _Christmas Candlelight Tours._ Available by reservation only, evening tours of the opulent Biltmore House show how the original owners, the Vanderbilts, would have celebrated the holiday. Thousands of lights illuminate elaborate ensembles, choirs, and family treasures at the Biltmore Estate. | 800/289–1895 | www.biltmore.com.

Dining

Asheville Pizza & Brewing Company. Pizza. Combining a restaurant, bar, and movie theater, this local hangout serves pizza and its own beers along with a second-run movie. The diverse crowd usually orders another Shiva pale ale and saunters back to the pool table room when the flick ends. | 675 Merrimon Ave. | 828/254–1281 | $5–$10 | AE, D, DC, MC, V | No lunch.

Barley's Taproom. Pizza. Downtown under an unmistakable red awning, Barley's serves creative pizzas and pints to a mixed college and townie crowd. You can try one of 40 beers on tap with your spinach and banana pepper pizza, the house specialty. | 42 Biltmore Ave. | 828/255–0504 | $5–$10 | AE, D, DC, MC, V.

Beanstreets Coffee. Café. The chalkboard menu at this hipster hangout near Pack Square changes daily but always includes a few vegetarian options. The tofu scrambler and Belgian waffles are popular in the morning; the hummus veggie wrap sells well at lunch. | 3 Broadway St. | 828/255–8180 | $4–$7 | No credit cards.

Café on the Square. Contemporary. This elegant and airy spot is known for fresh seafood and pastas cooked with salsas, chutneys, and simple marinades. | 1 Biltmore Ave. | 828/251–5565 | $15–$20 | AE, D, MC, V | No lunch Sun.

Fine Friends. Contemporary. A gazebo sits in the center of this restaurant, while Victorian surroundings and wood set the mood. Crab cakes and Waldorf salad are on the specialty list. Dress is casual. Kids' menu. Sun. brunch. | 946 Merrimon Ave. | 828/253–6649 | $17–$31 | AE, D, DC, MC, V.

Gabrielle's. Continental. A three-tiered chandelier and cherry-wood paneling contribute to the formality at this restaurant. A 7-course menu is available. Specialties include macadamia- and black sesame-crusted sea scallops. Pianist Thurs.–Mon. Kids' menu. | 87 Richmond Hill Dr. | 828/252–7313 or 800/545–9238 | Reservations essential | Jacket and tie | $22–$51 | AE, MC, V | No lunch.

The Greenery. Contemporary. Fresh flowers, candlelight, and antiques add a European flair. Maryland crab cakes, mountain trout, and confit de canard are some specialty items. Kids' menu. | 148 Tunnel Rd. | 828/253–2809 | $14–$25 | AE, MC, V.

Guadalajara Mexican Restaurant. Mexican. It's in a strip mall right next to K-Mart, but the spicy salsa, chicken tacos, basic beans and rice, and fresh-lime margaritas are anything but bland. | 4 S. Tunnel Rd. | 828/289–0702 | $4–$10 | AE, D, MC, V.

Horizons. Contemporary. Lanterns on the tables provide low lighting in this spot that's popular for birthday and anniversary celebrations. The menu evolves at this restaurant known for its lobster presentation and the chef's special with crawfish and crab cakes. Piano nightly. | 290 Macon Ave. | 828/252–2711 or 800/438–5800 | Jacket and tie | $24–$55 | AE, D, DC, MC, V | Closed Sun.

Il Paradiso. Steak. It's expensive—about $50 per person if you have wine—but the surroundings and service at this formal steak house are considered the best in town. Locals arrive a bit early to sip a martini at the La Taverna bar before being seated in one of three dining rooms. | 39 Elm St. | 828/281–4310 | Reservations essential | Jacket and tie | $25–$35 | MC, V | No lunch.

The Market Place. Contemporary. An evolving menu focuses on fresh, in-season foods, including local ingredients. Homemade bread, pasta, and pastries round out the selections. There is open-air dining on a canopied, wrought-iron-fenced patio. Kids' menu. | 20 Wall St. | 828/252–4162 | $16–$30 | AE, MC, V, DC | Closed Sun. No lunch.

McGuffey's. Eclectic. Murals and old books add to the schoolhouse theme of this restaurant. Known for pasta, steaks, prime rib, stir-fry, and many vegetarian entrées. Open-air dining in atrium. Kids' menu. Sun. brunch. | 13 Kenilworth Knoll | 828/252–0956 | $9–$17 | AE, D, DC, MC, V.

Max's Celebrity Grill. Deli. Despite the name, you probably won't bump into Michael Jordan here. The stars in this deli-style restaurant are the Mediterranean, Italian, and American salads, soups, and sandwiches—Max's famous grilled reuben is a specialty. | 130 College St. | 828/258–1162 | $5–$8 | DC, D, MC, V.

Mountain Smoke House. Southern. Mountain barbecue and pig-pickin' buffets join bluegrass by local musicians. Some items to try are bourbon yams and hopping John, a low-country, spicy dish with black-eyed peas and vegetables. Family-style service. Kids' menu. | Riverridge Business Ctr., 802 Fairview Rd. | 828/253–4871 | $9–$18 | AE, D, DC, MC, V | Closed Mon.

23 Page. Continental. This spot was voted "most romantic" by the *Asheville Mountain Times* in 1999. The menu changes seasonally, and specialties include wild game, grilled elk loin, prosciutto-wrapped Atlantic salmon with grilled scallops, grilled lamb chop with radicchio, and artichoke mousse. | 1 Battery Park Ave. | 828/252–3685 | Reservations essential | $19–$25 | AE, D, DC, MC, V | No lunch.

Vincenzo's Ristorante Bistro. Italian. There is a casual bistro section, as well as a more formal dining room. With pastel colors throughout, local art is exhibited. Menu items include filet medallions and veal dishes. Live music nightly. Kids' menu. | 10 N. Market St. | 828/254–4698 | $7–$30 | AE, D, MC, V.

West Side Grill. American. This 1950s-style diner has a little bit of everything. Known for blue-plate specials, from mile-high meat loaf to Southern-fried catfish, this restaurant also gives vegetarians a number of choices. Breakfasts are available weekends only. | 1190 Patton Ave. | 828/252–9605 | Reservations not accepted | $7–$15 | AE, D, MC, V.

Windmill European Grill. Eclectic. German, Italian, Middle Eastern, and Indian dishes are on the menu at this cool and dark cellar restaurant that also has a large vegetarian selection. | 85 Tunnel Rd. | 828/253–5285 | $13–$28 | AE, D, MC, V | No lunch.

Lodging

Acorn Cottage B&B. Queen Anne furnishings are prominent at this 1925 bungalow home. The guest rooms with private baths include the Red Room—just what it sounds like—and the Garden Room, complete with a hand-painted tree mural. The full breakfast may include Carolina coffee cake or blueberry cream cheese strata. Complimentary breakfast. In-room phones. | 25 St. Dunstans Cir | 828/253–0609 | www.acorncottagebnb.com/ | 4 rooms | $75 | AE, D, MC, V.

Albemarle Inn. High ceilings, antiques, and oak paneling dress up the rooms of this neo-classical Greek Revival mansion built in 1909 and on the National Register of Historic Places. No-smoking rooms are available. Complimentary breakfast. In-room data ports. No kids under 14. | 86 Edgemont Rd. | 828/255–0027 or 800/621–7435 | fax 828/236–3397 | www.albe-marleinn.com | 11 rooms, 1 suite | $125–$285 (2–night minimum stay weekends) | D, MC, V.

American Court. Just 1½ mi from the University of North Carolina–Asheville, 3 mi from the Biltmore Estate, and 2 mi from the Grove Park Inn, this family-run 1950s motel has white bedspreads and wall art in the rooms. Refrigerators. Cable TV. Pool. Laundry facilities. No smoking. | 85 Merrimon Ave. | 828/253–4427 or 800/233–3582 | fax 828/253–2507 | www.amer-icancourt.com | 22 rooms | $70–$80 | AE, D, DC, MC, V.

Applewood Manor Inn. High trees on 20 acres of rolling hills provide the backdrop for this antiques-filled inn. Many rooms have fireplaces, and the cottage has a kitchenette. Complimentary breakfast. No room phones. Business services. No kids under 12. No smoking. | 62 Cumberland Cir | 828/254–2244 or 800/442–2197 | fax 828/254–0899 | www.apple-wood.com | 4 rooms (2 with shower only); 1 cottage | $95–$115; $115 cottage | MC, V.

Beaufort House Victorian B&B. A wraparound porch signifies leisure, as does the guest care: down pillows and comforters in each room, filled-to-the-brim chocolate bowls, and on-site massage therapy are all close at hand. This 1894 Victorian sits on two acres of immac-ulately landscaped grounds in a residential neighborhood just north of downtown. The guest rooms in the main house or carriage house have private baths. Complimentary break-fast. Some in-room hot tubs. Cable TV, in-room VCRs, room phones. | 61 N. Liberty St. | 828/254–8334 or 800/261–2221 | www.beauforthouse.com | 12 rooms | $95–$235 | AE, MC, V.

Best Inns of America. This motel is 5 mi from downtown Asheville, 5 mi from the Biltmore Estate, and 25 mi from Chimney Rock Park. Rooms are mauve-colored with some wall art. Complimentary Continental breakfast. In-room data ports, some refrigerators. Cable TV. Pool. Business services. | 1435 Tunnel Rd. | 828/298–4000 | fax 828/298–4000 | www.bestinn.com | 84 rooms | $60–$75 | AE, D, DC, MC, V.

Best Western Asheville Biltmore. In the downtown area, this Best Western is 2⅓ mi from the Biltmore Estate, 25 mi from Chimney Rock Park, and 5 mi from the Blue Ridge Parkway. Housed in a 5-story, stucco building, the neutral-colored rooms are larger than standard. Restaurant, bar. Cable TV. Pool. Business services. | 22 Woodfin St. | 828/253–1851 | fax 828/252–9205 | www.bestwestern.com/ashevillebiltmore | 144 rooms, 3 suites | $49–$99, $119–189 suites | AE, D, DC, MC, V.

Blake House Inn. Confederate soldiers stayed at this neo-Gothic home when it served as a Civil War field hospital, and wounded Union soldiers were secreted into the tunnels under-neath the house and treated by sympathetic nurses. The house and guest rooms are filled with antique furnishings and Civil War memorabilia. Complimentary breakfast. In-room data ports. Cable TV, room phones. | 150 Royal Pines Dr. | 828/681–5227 or 888/353–5227 | fax 828/681–0420 | www.blakehouse.com | 5 rooms, 1 suite | $140–$225 | AE, D, MC, V.

Cedar Crest Victorian Inn. Victorian flower gardens and shrubs welcome you to this turn-of-the-20th-century B&B that is on the National Register of Historic Places. It's 3 blocks from the Biltmore Estate and 4 mi from the Blue Ridge Parkway. Period antiques, canopies of satin and lace, fireplaces, and claw-foot tubs furnish the rooms. Complimentary break-fast. Business services. No kids under 10. | 674 Biltmore Ave. | 828/252–1389 or 800/252–0310 | fax 828/253–7667 | www.cedarcrestvictorianinn.com | 9 rooms; 2 cottage suites | $135–$210; $135–$225 cottage suites | AE, D, DC, MC, V.

Comfort Inn River Ridge. Just 1 mi from the Blue Ridge Parkway and 3 mi from the Bilt-more Estate, this hotel is housed in three separate 3-story buildings. Each room has a cof-feemaker, iron, and ironing board. Hair dryers are also available. Rooms are neutral in color, and there is a two-room suite with a hot tub and kitchenette. Complimentary Continen-tal breakfast. Some microwaves, some refrigerators. Pool. Hot tub. Hiking. Playground. Laun-dry facilities, laundry service. Business services. Pets allowed. | 800 Fairview Rd. | 828/298–

9141 | fax 828/298–6629 | www.comfortinn.com | 178 rooms, 20 suites | $89–$139; $129–$159 suites | AE, D, DC, MC, V.

Comfort Suites. Although it's across from a shopping mall, the suites hotel is in a quite residential area. The property is 10 minutes from downtown and one exit away from the Biltmore Estate. Suites have double beds and separate living and sleeping areas. The colors are dark, and there's art on the walls. Complimentary Continental breakfast. In-room data ports, refrigerators. Cable TV. Pool. Hot tub. Exercise equipment. Laundry facilities. Business services. Airport shuttle. | 890 Brevard Rd. | 828/665–4000 or 800/622–4005 | fax 828/665–9082 | www.comfortinn.com | 125 suites | $69–$129 | AE, D, DC, MC, V.

Corner Oak Manor. Oak antiques, art, and handcrafted items adorn the rooms of this inn that's ringed with trees and shrubs. Just ½ mi from the Biltmore Estate and 1 mi from downtown, this 1920s Tudor-style house is in a small residential area. Rooms have private baths, and the cottage has a kitchenette. Picnic area, complimentary breakfast. No room phones. Outdoor hot tub. No kids under 12. No smoking. | 53 St. Dunstans Rd. | 828/253–3525 or 888/633–3525 | info@corneroakmanor.com | www.corneroakmanor.com | 3 rooms; 1 cottage | $110–$120; $160 cottage (2–night minimum stay weekends) | AE, D, MC, V.

Dogwood Cottage. The veranda at this 1910 home is a great place to relax after a busy day of sightseeing. Though it's just 2 mi from downtown, this inn feels like it's in the country and affords a great view of the Blue Ridge Mountains. Complimentary breakfast. TV in common area. Pets allowed. | 40 N. Canterbury Rd. | 828/258–9725 | 4 rooms | $110–$125 | AE, MC, V.

Econo Lodge Biltmore East. The main attraction at this motel is its proximity to the Biltmore Estate, but an outdoor pool, free Continental breakfast, and kitchenettes are also draws. Complimentary Continental breakfast. Some kitchenettes, some refrigerators. Cable TV, room phones. Outdoor pool. | 1430 Tunnel Rd. | 828/298–5519 | 139 rooms | $33–$96 | AE, DC, D, MC, V.

Flint Street Inns. Natural light streams into the second-story rooms at this Arts and Crafts–style structure in Montford Historic District, about 10 minutes from the Biltmore Estate, 5 minutes from the Thomas Wolfe Memorial, and 5 minutes from downtown. Rooms have antiques, and no two rooms are exactly alike in their furnishings. Complimentary breakfast. Cable TV, no room phones. | 116 Flint St. | 828/253–6723 | fax 828/254–6685 | 8 rooms in 2 buildings | $110–$125 | AE, D, MC, V.

Forest Manor Inn. Set on four wooded acres, this building has served as a roadhouse, gambling den, and restaurant. All rooms have wallpaper or knotty pine paneling. Complimentary Continental breakfast. Cable TV. Pool. | 866 Hendersonville Rd. | 828/274–3531 or 800/866–3531 | fax 828/274–3036 | 21 rooms | $69–$149 | AE, D, MC, V, DC | Closed mid-Dec.–Mar.

Grove Park Inn Resort. You can relax beside massive fireplaces or on a large outdoor terrace at this spot that is on the National Register of Historic Places. Built in 1913 and surrounded by the Blue Ridge Mountains, this resort prides itself on its mountain views. The surrounding area is residential, and the rooms have neutral color schemes. Restaurants, bar with entertainment. Cable TV. 2 pools (1 indoor). Hot tub, massage. 18-hole golf course, putting green, 9 tennis courts. Gym, racquetball, squash. Kids' programs (ages 3–16). Business services. | 290 Macon Ave. | 828/252–2711 or 800/438–5800 | fax 828/253–7053 | www.groveparkinn.com | 510 rooms, 10 suites; 1 cottage | $200–$380, $575 suites, $695 cottage | AE, D, DC, MC, V.

Hampton Inn. Across from Biltmore Square Mall and 6 mi from the Biltmore Estate, this hotel is right off the interstate in a commercial area. There are some trees on the grounds, and the rooms are simple. Suites have refrigerators. Complimentary Continental breakfast. In-room data ports, some refrigerators. Cable TV. Indoor pool. Hot tub. Exercise equipment. Business services. Airport shuttle. | 1 Rocky Ridge Rd. | 828/667–2022 | fax 828/665–9680 | www.hamptoninn.com | 121 rooms | $109–$129 | AE, D, DC, MC, V.

Hampton Inn. Trees and grass surround the building, and rooms are in neutral tones at this hotel in a commercial area a block from the Asheville Mall and 3½ mi from the Biltmore Estate. Complimentary Continental breakfast. Microwaves. Cable TV. Indoor pool. Hot tub. Exercise equipment. Business services. | 204 Tunnel Rd. | 828/255–9220 | fax 828/254–4303 | www.hamptoninn.com | 120 rooms | $109–$129, $145–$225 suites | AE, D, DC, MC, V.

Haywood Park. There is golden-oak woodwork and gleaming brass at this all-suites downtown hotel that was once a department store. All suites have custom-style furnishings, minibars, sitting areas, and soaking tubs, some with jets, separate from the showers. Restaurant, bar, complimentary Continental breakfast. In-room data ports, refrigerators. Cable TV, in-room VCRs. Exercise equipment. Business services. | 1 Battery Park Ave. | 828/252–2522 or 800/228–2522 | fax 828/253–0481 | www.haywoodpark.com | 33 suites | $165–$325 suites | AE, D, DC, MC, V.

Holiday Inn Sunspree Resort. With large windows, all rooms are designed to bring the outdoors in. This resort is less than a mile from the Biltmore Estate and 2 mi from the business district. Restaurant, bar, room service. Refrigerators. Cable TV. 2 pools. 18-hole golf course, putting green, tennis. Exercise equipment. Kids' programs. Business services. | 1 Holiday Inn Dr. | 828/254–3211 | fax 828/254–1603 | www.sunspree.com | 277 rooms | $79–$139 | AE, D, DC, MC, V.

Howard Johnson–Biltmore. Just a few blocks from the Biltmore Estate and built in the 1960s, this hotel is in an area that mixes residential and commercial. Outside, there is one acre of land with greenery and trees. The rooms are neutral in their color scheme. Restaurant. Cable TV. Pool. Business services. | 190 Hendersonville Rd. | 828/274–2300 | fax 828/274–2304 | www.hojo.com | 68 rooms | $89–$128 | AE, D, DC, MC, V.

Lake Lure Inn. Famous visitors to this Mediterranean-style hotel have included F. Scott Fitzgerald, Franklin D. Roosevelt, and Emily Post. Built on the lake in 1927, the place provides views of the Blue Ridge Mountains. The surrounding area is residential, and rooms have dark color schemes. Bar, dining room, complimentary Continental breakfast. Microwaves. Cable TV. Pool. Business services. | 2772 Memorial Hwy., Lake Lure | 828/625–2525 or 888/434–4770 | fax 828/625–9655 | www.lakelureinn.com | 50 rooms | $89–$99 | AE, D, DC, MC, V.

Lion and the Rose. Rooms have turn-of-the-20th-century furnishings and Oriental rugs at this inn that stands in the Montford Historic District, home to many fine examples of Victorian architecture. Complimentary breakfast. Data ports. No kids under 12. No smoking. | 276 Montford Ave. | 828/255–7673 or 800/546–6988 | fax 828/285–9810 | www.lionrose.com | 5 rooms | $135–$225 | AE, D, MC, V.

Mountain Springs. Spread out over 80 acres, this group of cabins and chalets trace a mountain stream. Cabins have antiques, fireplaces, porch swings, and rockers. You can also check out backpacks, fishing poles, games, and books. Picnic area. Kitchenettes, microwaves. Cable TV. | U.S. 151, Candler | 828/665–1004 | fax 828/667–1581 | mtnsprings@ioa.com | www.mtnsprings.com | 12 cottages | $80–$165 | MC, V.

Mountaineer Inn. This fixture for 40 years along Tunnel Road is in a commercial area 45 minutes from Chimney Rock Park and 3 mi from the Biltmore mansion. Rooms have dark color schemes, and no-smoking rooms are available. Complimentary Continental breakfast. In-room data ports, refrigerators. Cable TV. Pool. Business services. | 155 Tunnel Rd. | 828/254–5331 or 800/255–4080 | fax 828/254–5331 | 77 rooms | $48–$75 | AE, D, MC, V.

Old Reynolds Mansion. Once a private home, this B&B was built in 1885 and sits on four wooded acres. Rooms have private baths, and some have fireplaces. There is a separate cottage suite with a private deck. Some rooms and the cottage overlook the pool, and you can get afternoon tea and snacks. Complimentary Continental breakfast. No room phones. Pool. | 100 Reynolds Heights | 828/254–0496 or 800/709–0496 | innkeeper@oldreynoldsmansion.com | www.oldreynoldsmansion.com | 10 rooms, 1 cottage | $85–$120, $135 cottage | No credit cards.

Owl's Nest Inn at Engadine. Rooms have antiques and fireplaces, and three have original water closets at this Victorian inn built in 1885 and right outside of town, between the Blue Ridge and Great Smoky mountains. It's about a 15-minute drive from the Biltmore Estate and from music clubs, a theater, and museums. There are mountain views and 11.7 acres of rolling hills. The inn serves refreshments nightly. Complimentary breakfast. In-room hot tub in suite. Some room phones. No kids under 12. No smoking. | 2630 Smoky Park Hwy., Candler | 828/665–8325 or 800/665–8868 | fax 828/667–2539 | www.circle.net/owlsnest | 4 rooms, 1 suite | $110–$145, $175 suite (2–night minimum stay weekends) | AE, D, MC, V.

Pisgah View Ranch. This 2,000-acre ranch with trails to 6,000 ft was built in the 1960s. In a residential, country area with mountain views, this spot is 30 minutes from the Biltmore Estate. Many activities are available, including a game room and Ping-Pong, and you can pack a picnic lunch to enjoy while sightseeing. Each room is different—some are cottage-style, some motel-style, and some have fireplaces. Complimentary breakfast, lunch, dinner. Pool. Tennis. Hiking, horseback riding. Playground. Laundry facilities. Airport shuttle. | 70 Pisgah View Ranch Rd. | 828/667–9100 | 48 rooms | $65–$125 (2–night minimum stay) | No credit cards | Closed Nov. to mid-Apr.

Quality Inn–Biltmore. Set on several acres overlooking the Biltmore Estate, this modern brick-and-stone building with either two queen beds or one king bed in each room has a small business area. Restaurant, bar, room service. Some refrigerators. Cable TV. Pool. Business services. | 115 Hendersonville Rd. | 828/274–1800 | fax 828/274–5960 | biltsarms@ioa.com | www.qualityinn.com | 160 rooms, 20 suites | $99–$140 | AE, D, DC, MC, V.

Renaissance Hotel Asheville. From the restaurant on the top floor there is a view of the city's lights with the mountains in the background. In a valley surrounded by mountains in downtown Asheville, this 12-story hotel has undergone an $8 million renovation. The neutral-color rooms are done in Queen Anne style. Restaurant. In-room data ports, some refrigerators. Cable TV. Pool. Exercise equipment. Business services. | 1 Thomas Wolfe Plaza | 828/252–8211 | fax 828/236–9616 | www.renaissancehotels.com | 271 rooms, 10 suites | $169–$179, $199–$399 suites | AE, D, DC, MC, V.

Red Roof Inn. This motel sits in a residential area 6 mi from the Biltmore Estate and 5 minutes from the Blue Ridge Parkway. Business services. Some pets allowed. | 16 Crowell Rd. | 828/667–9803 | fax 828/667–9810 | www.redroof.com | 109 rooms | $30–$82 | AE, D, DC, MC, V.

Richmond Hill. Elegance is the keyword at this former congressman's home. Rooms in the mansion, with its grand entrance hall and library, are furnished with a Victorian theme, while the rooms in the Garden Pavilion are more contemporary and overlook the gardens and waterfall. The cottages are Shaker style. Restaurant, dining rooms, complimentary breakfast. Cable TV. Library. Business services. | 87 Richmond Hill Dr. | 828/252–7313 or 800/545–9238 | fax 828/252–8726 | www.richmondhillinn.com | 36 rooms, 2 suites; 9 cottages | $145–$395, $285–$450 suites; $195–$345 cottages | AE, MC, V.

Sleep Inn West. You can enjoy breakfast and a free newspaper each morning in the two-story atrium lobby at this basic, three-story hotel. It's 5 mi from town and 6 mi from the Biltmore Estate. Complimentary Continental breakfast. In-room data ports. Cable TV. No pets. | 1918 Old Haywood Rd. | 828/670–7600 | 74 | $54–$119 | AE, DC, D, MC, V.

Southern Safari. This camp with cushy touches—padded cots, crisp linens, and fluffy towels—is for the truly adventurous. The owners aim to make you feel like you're at an African safari base camp, so you can spend the day hiking, llama trekking, horseback riding, mountain biking, canoeing, or skydiving in the Blue Ridge Mountains. Then you join fellow safari-goers at the camp where you dine on gourmet cuisine, South African wine, and cognac. Complimentary breakfast. No TV. Hiking, horseback riding, water sports, fishing, bicycles. | 610 Barnardsville Hwy. | 828/626–3400 or 800/454–7374 | www.southern-safari.com | $162–$315 | AE, MC, V.

Wright Inn. This Queen Anne Victorian B&B has many family heirlooms and lovely gardens. Rooms are furnished with antiques, and all have private baths. The suite has in-room hot tub. Complimentary breakfast. Some in-room hot tubs. Cable TV. No kids under 12. No smoking. | 235 Pearson Dr. | 828/251–0789 or 800/552–5724 | fax 828/251–0929 | www.wright-inn.com | 9 rooms, 2-room suite that can be joined | $125–$235 | AE, D, MC, V.

ATLANTIC BEACH

MAP 8, J6

(Nearby towns also listed: Beaufort, Morehead City)

A small pavilion with a refreshment stand and dressing stalls built in 1887 on Bogue Banks gave rise to Atlantic Beach. Over the next six decades the area experienced a series of booms and busts. But today, thanks to a high-rise bridge connecting Atlantic Beach to Morehead City and a spruced-up appearance, the summer population swells to some 35,000, about 12 times the year-round count. The center of activity is a place called the Circle, at the site of the former pavilion.

Information: **Carteret County Tourism Development Bureau.** | Box 1406, Morehead City, 28557 | 252/726–8148 or 800/786–6962.

Visitor Center | 3409 Arendell St. (U.S. 70 E) | 252/726–8148 | vacation@sunnync.com | www.ncbeach.com or www.sunnync.com.

Attractions

The Circle. A good place for beach access, the Circle has a family environment during the daytime. In its center is a Ferris wheel and go-cart track. On its west side there's a bathhouse with outdoor showers, a gazebo, and picnic areas. | Atlantic Beach Causeway (Rte. 58) | 252/726–8148 | Free; prices for rides vary | Daily.

Fort Macon State Park. The centerpiece of this 365-acre park, 2 mi east of town, is pentagon-shaped Fort Macon, built in 1834 to protect the coast against foreign invasions. Today you can tour the soldiers' quarters and visit the museum. But don't forget to bring a bathing suit in summer: the park has swimming and picnic areas, and on the mile-long beachfront you can choose a spot for fishing. | 2300 East Fort Macon Rd. | 252/726–3775 | fax 252/726–2497 | www.ils.unc.edu/parkproject/ncparks.html | Free; $3 bathhouse | Daily 8 to sunset, fort 9–5:30.

North Carolina Aquarium at Pine Knoll Shores. Situated in a maritime forest on Bogue Banks, this facility offers a 2,000-gallon salt-marsh tank with live alligators and a loggerhead turtle nursery, both of which are crowd pleasers. A recent expansion includes exhibits on the state's five aquatic zones. | 1 Roosevelt Dr. (Mile 7) | 252/247–4004 | www.ncaquariums.com | $3 | Daily 9–7.

ON THE CALENDAR

JUNE: *North Carolina Kidfest.* Clowns, performances, amusement rides, games, and food mark the end of the school year and start of the beach season at the Circle. | 252/247–5433.

SEPT.: *Hardee's Atlantic Beach King Mackerel Tournament.* The claim is that this is the nation's largest all-cash king-mackerel fishing-competition event. You can check it out at Sea Water Marina, Atlantic Beach Causeway (Rte. 58). | 252/247–2334 or 800/545–3940.

Dining

Big Oak Drive-In. American/Casual. Known for pizza, burgers, and barbecue sandwiches, this restaurant also includes the shrimp burger on its specialty list. This is a walk-up place with no indoor seating. | Salter Path Rd. (Rte. 58), Salter Path | 252/247–2588 | $5–$14 | No credit cards | Closed Thanksgiving–Mar.

Bushwhackers. Seafood. Surfing-related paraphernalia surrounds you at this very casual place directly on the water, known for broiled fresh fish and shrimp. Also on the menu is flounder stuffed with crab or shrimp. Kids' menu. | Bogue Inlet Pier, 100 Bogue Inlet Dr., Emerald Isle | 252/354–6300 | Reservations not accepted | $12–$30 | MC, V | Closed Dec.–Feb. No lunch.

Channel Marker Restaurant. Seafood. Overlooking Bogue Sound and providing boat docks, this restaurant is known for grilled fish, steamed seafood, and aged beef. You can enjoy open-air dining on the waterfront deck, and there are nightly drink specials. Kids' menu, early-bird suppers. | 718 Atlantic Beach Causeway | 252/247–2344 | Reservations not accepted | $15–$20 | D, MC, V | No lunch.

New York Deli. Delicatessen. Breakfast is on the menu all day, and Wednesday night is pasta night. This restaurant is known for sandwiches, salads, and box lunches. Beer and wine only. Kids' menu. | 4709 Causeway Rd., Causeway Shopping Center | 252/726–0111 | Reservations not accepted | $5–$10 | MC, V.

Lodging

Days Inn and Suites. Each brightly colored room has a sunken sitting area and a view of Bogue Sound. This all-suites hotel is directly on the sound in a commercial area within walking distance of the beach. Some rooms have sleeper sofas and coffeemakers. Picnic area, complimentary Continental breakfast. In-room data ports, some microwaves, refrigerators. Cable TV. Pool. Beach, dock. Laundry facilities. Business services. | 602 W. Fort Macon Rd. | 252/247–6400 | fax 252/247–2264 | 90 rooms | $89–$129 | AE, D, MC, V.

Hollowell's. A family-oriented place built in 1948, this brick motel is three blocks from a swimming beach. It sits on a grassy area surrounded by pine trees, and the pool has a brick lattice fence. Rooms have pastel colors and Berber rugs. Boat parking available. Some kitchenettes. Cable TV. Pool. Beach. | 108 E. Fort Macon Rd. | 252/726–5227 | www.hollowellsmotel.com | 28 rooms, 1 suite | $50–$75, $120 suite | D, MC, V | Closed Nov.–Mar.

Ramada Inn. Rooms have ocean views and private balconies, and the hotel also has 300 feet of private beach. There are also an outdoor swimming pool and hot tub, as well as an on-site restaurant and lounge. Restaurant, bar, room service. Cable TV, room phones. Outdoor pool. Hot tub. Beach. | Rte. 58 and Salter Path Rd. | 252/247–4155 | 100 rooms | $49–$105 | AE, D, MC, V.

Sea Gull Motel. All rooms at this small, single-story motel are efficiencies and come with everything you'd need to make and eat a good meal, except the food. Pets are allowed in certain rooms for an additional fee. Kitchenettes, refrigerators. Cable TV, room phones. | 102 Henderson Blvd. | 252/726–3613 or 800/257–2196 | www.seagullmotel.net | 12 rooms | $56 | MC, V.

Seahawk Motor Lodge. All rooms have oceanfront views at this motel that has its own beachfront. It's 100 ft from a swimming beach, and rooms have white wicker furniture. Room service. Refrigerators. Cable TV. Pool. Fishing, bicycles. | 105 Salter Path Rd. | 252/726–4146 or 800/682–6898 | 38 rooms | $45–$135 | MC, V.

Sheraton Atlantic Beach Oceanfront Resort Hotel. Right on the beach and in an area of shops, this resort is steps from the ocean and has its own fishing pier, which is free for people staying here. All rooms provide either full or partial ocean views. They have wood furniture with brightly colored walls and wall art. Kids' programs are seasonal. Restaurant, bar with entertainment. Refrigerators. Cable TV. Indoor-outdoor pool. Hot tub. Exercise equipment. Kids' programs (ages 2–12). Business services. | 2717 W. Fort Macon Rd. | 252/240–1155 | fax 252/240–1452 | 200 rooms, 16 suites | $115–$205, $225–$275 suites | AE, D, DC, MC, V.

Windjammer Inn. There is a view of the beach from the glass-enclosed elevator. This hotel sits right on the beach, and all rooms have direct oceanfront views as well as private balconies with wood furniture. Some rooms have a seafoam green and pink color scheme with off-white wallpaper, while others are geared toward business customers, with stripes and darker, more conservative colors. Refrigerators. Cable TV. Pool. | 105 Salter Path Rd. | 252/ 247–7123 or 800/233–6466 | fax 252/247–0133 | www.windjammerinn.com | 46 rooms | $104–$125 (2–night minimum stay summer weekends, 3–night minimum holiday weekends) | AE, D, MC, V.

BANNER ELK

MAP 9, C3

(Nearby towns also listed: Blowing Rock, Blue Ridge Parkway, Boone, Linville, Valle Crucis)

In the rural northern Avery County are several exclusive enclaves, including Banner Elk. As in the last century, lowlanders flock to Christmas-tree country for cool summer getaways. In addition to being a popular skiing and golf resort community, 3,800-ft-high Banner Elk is the home of Lees-McRae College, which has a diverse cultural-arts calendar year-round.

Information: Avery/Banner Elk Chamber of Commerce | Box 335, Banner Elk, 28604 | 828/898–5605 or 800/972–2183 | chamber@averycounty.com | www.banner-elk.com.

THE HIGH COUNTRY

Alleghany, Ashe, Avery, Mitchell, and Watauga. Not only are these the northernmost of the state's counties, they contain the highest peaks on the Blue Ridge. Thus the "High Country" moniker. Up here where the Christmas trees grow, rambling, twisting roads soar and then dip. One minute you're on the crest of the Blue Ridge, facing stunningly beautiful vistas—wave upon wave of green-shouldered, mist-shrouded mountains. The next you're down in their folds among a rural patchwork quilt of old settlements, clapboard houses and cabins, tiny churches, general stores, farmland, state parks, and national forests bisected by unpaved trails and trout-filled streams and rivers—including the New River, one of the world's most ancient waterways.

Nature lovers and those in search of an adrenaline rush will find enough here to keep busy for weeks. Four of North Carolina's eight ski resorts are in the High Country. Boone, a busy university town, is the gateway to many of those resorts, typically open from mid-November to mid-March. There's guided white-water rafting on the Nolichucky ("Chucky") River. There's hiking into and then—the real challenge—out of Linville Gorge, which requires a special permit. There's mountain backpacking. And there's crossing Grandfather Mountain's Mile High Swinging Bridge, the country's highest suspension footbridge, which is in perpetual motion thanks to winds gusting through an 80-ft ravine.

Those in favor of quieter pursuits have rich choices as well: arts-and-crafts quests, concerts of mountain music, gemstone mining, garden walks, bird-watching, canoeing, or just lazing in a rocking chair on the front porch of an 18th-century inn.

Related towns: Banner Elk, Blowing Rock, Boone, Jefferson, Linville.

© Corbis

Attractions

Lees-McRae College. This private, four-year school is affiliated with the Presbyterian Church (U.S.A.), but its faculty and students are a diverse lot. Because it sits at 4,000 ft above sea level and is surrounded by mountains, Lees-McRae attracts lovers of winter sports. However, thanks to an impressive year-round cultural calendar, lovers of the arts are also attracted to the small but busy and attractive campus. | Rte. 194 | 828/898–8729 or 800/280–4562 | www.lmc.edu.

Ski Beech (Beech Mountain). The highest ski area in eastern North America, it has a peak elevation of 5,505 ft and a 4,675-ft base elevation. There's also a skating rink. | 1007 Beech Mountain Pkwy. | 828/387–2011 or 800/438–2093 | fax 828/387–4952 | www.skibeech.com | Late Nov.–mid-Mar.

Sugar Mountain Resort. Eight lifts, including two of the longest in North Carolina, carry patrons to 18 slopes. Particularly notable is the 1,200-ft vertical drop. | 1009 Sugar Mountain Dr. | 828/898–4521 | fax 828/898–6820 | www.skisugar.com | Late Nov.–mid-Mar.

Watauga River. This is a favorite with white-water rafters and canoeists. A popular outfitter is Edge of the World Outfitters in downtown Banner Elk. | Free | Daily.

ON THE CALENDAR
JULY AND AUG.: *Fine Art Festival.* Juried fine art is on exhibit and up for sale at this gathering held the second weekend in July and the last weekend in August at the Grandfather Home for Children, Hickory Nut Gap Road. | 800/972–2183.
OCT.: *Woolly Worm Festival.* Caterpillars are raced for prize money, public acclaim, and charity. A forecaster examines the victor's coloration and then announces the winter weather outlook. Music, crafts, and food are also included in this downtown festival. | 828/898–5605 or 800/972–2183.

Dining

Black Diamond Bistro and Grill. Contemporary. Black and white contrasts with wood accents and white tablecloths at this place that's known for crab cakes, grilled and sautéed seafoods, rack of lamb, and Peking duck. | 502 W. Main St. | 828/898–7556 | $12–$30 | AE, D, DC, MC, V | Closed Tues., Wed.

Jackalope's View. Continental. Floor-to-ceiling windows overlook the mountains and bring the outdoors in, and the walls display the works of local artists. The outdoor deck affords a long-range mountain view. This restaurant is known for beef tenderloin and Jamaican jerk shrimp. | 2489 Beech Mountain Pkwy. | 828/898–9004 | Reservations essential | $30–$36 | D, MC, V | Closed Tues.

Louisiana Purchase Food and Spirits. Cajun/Creole. Murals depict views of New Orleans at this place known for jambalaya. Live jazz Fri.–Sat. | Rte. 184 | 828/898–5656 or 828/963–5087 | $15–$35 | AE, D, DC, MC, V.

Stonewalls. Contemporary. Rustic, with a view of Beech Mountain, this restaurant is known for steak, prime rib, seafood, chicken, and a large salad bar. | Rte. 184 | 828/898–5550 | $12–$25 | AE, D, MC, V | No lunch.

Lodging

Archers Mountain Inn. A two-level, country-style inn built in 1885 at an elevation of 5,000 ft into the side of Beech Mountain, this spot overlooks Grandfather Mountain, Sugar Mountain, and the Elk River valley. Rooms are rustic and have stone fireplaces and wood furniture. Downhill skiing is 2 mi north, as well as 3 mi south of the inn. Restaurant, complimentary breakfast. Some refrigerators, some in-room hot tubs. Cable TV, some in-room VCRs. | 2489 Beech Mountain Pkwy. | 828/898–9004 | fax 828/898–9007 | www.archersinn.com | 15 rooms | $70–$200 | D, MC, V.

Holiday Inn at Banner Elk. This two-story hotel is ½ mi from Sugar Mountain Golf Course and 7 mi from Appalachian Ski Mountain in Blowing Rock. It sits on 30 acres of land, surrounded by trees and mountains. The neutral-color rooms afford pasture and mountain views. Cross-country and downhill skiing are 1 mi north of here. Restaurant, room service. Cable TV. Pool. Business services. | 1615 Tynecastle Hwy. | 828/898–4571 | fax 828/898–8437 | 101 rooms | $69–$79 | AE, D, DC, MC, V.

Inn at Elk River. You can take in panoramic views from this Colonial inn nestled between Beech and Sugar mountains. Its eight guest rooms have private baths, four have fireplaces, and all have access to a large, gracious, white-painted deck that runs the length of the house. Restaurant, complimentary breakfast. Cable TV. | 875 Main St. | 828/898–9669 | fax 828/898–9678 | www.elkriverinn.com | 8 rooms | $95 | D, MC, V.

Inns of Beech Mountain. Two Appalachian Mountain resorts—the Beech Alpen Inn and the Top of Beech Inn—are in eastern America's highest town. From here are views of the slopes of the Blue Ridge Mountains. Some rooms have stone fireplaces, exposed beams, or window seats, and all have private baths. Downhill skiing is 1 mi north of here. Dining room (at Beech Alpen), complimentary Continental breakfast. Cable TV. | 700 Beech Mountain Pkwy. | 828/387–2252 | fax 828/387–2229 | www.beechalpen.com | 50 rooms | $59–$159 | AE, D, MC, V.

Old Turnpike House. This restored 1902 farmhouse has a beautiful dark-wood interior, a large front porch with rocking chairs, and a common room with a wood-burning stove. Guest rooms have private baths, ceiling fans, and TVs. Complimentary breakfast. Cable TV. | 317 Old Turnpike Rd. | 828/898–5611 or 888/802–4487 | www.oldturnpikehouse.com | 5 rooms | $85–$119 | AE, D, MC, V.

Pinnacle Inn. All rooms have mountain and ski-slope views at this family-oriented inn with activities for all age groups. The property is across from Ski Beech on top of a mountain in a residential area. Ski suites and standard rooms are available; room styles vary from rustic to modern. Picnic area. Kitchenettes. Cable TV. Indoor pool. Hot tub, sauna. Tennis. Playground. Laundry facilities. Business services. | 301 Pinnacle Inn Rd. | 828/387–2231 or 800/405–7888 | fax 828/387–3745 | 242 rooms | $75–$190 | MC, V.

BATH

MAP 8, J5

(Nearby town also listed: Washington)

Founded in 1705 as Britain's first seat of power in Colonial North Carolina, the village, once home to Blackbeard the pirate, thrived as a trading center until the mid-1770s when a more geographically centered hamlet became the major town on the Pamlico River. Wars and developers passed by Bath, thus ensuring its tranquil and historic appearance. Today, much of the tiny town, with its green open spaces and tall Colonial houses, occupies its original boundaries.

Information: **Historic Bath Visitor Center** | Box 148, Bath, 27808 | 252/923–3971 | www.ah.dcr.state.nc.us/sections/hs/bath/bath.htm.

Attractions

Bath State Historic Site. Founded in 1705, Bath was North Carolina's first town. The historic district includes the state's oldest church, St. Thomas Episcopal, and three restored houses, now museums, from the 18th and 19th centuries. The original village limits are the boundaries of a National Register Historic District. Self-guided and guided tours are available. | 207 Carteret St. | 252/923–0174 | fax 252/923–3971 | House tours (2 homes) $2 | Visitor center Apr.–Oct., Mon.–Sat. 9–5, Sun. 1–5; Nov.–Mar., Tues.–Sat. 10–4, Sun. 1–4.

ON THE CALENDAR
JULY: *Independence Day Celebration*. A parade, fireworks, music, arts and crafts, and other activities light up the waterfront in downtown Belhaven on or near July 4. | 252/943-3770.

Dining
Old Town Country Kitchen. Southern. Small-town friendliness is easy to find at this casual spot known for cheese biscuits, barbecue, fried chicken, pork chops, and fried fish. It also serves breakfast. | Rte. 92 | 252/923-1840 | $5–$10 | No credit cards | No supper Sun.

Lodging
Pirate's Den B&B. After borrowing one of the inn's bicycles to explore town, you can relax in a rocking chair on the front porch. This modern home fits right in among the area's older, historic homes. The rooms have private baths, and outside there's a sun deck. Complimentary full breakfast. Cable TV in central room. No in-room phones. Bicycles. No smoking. No pets. | 116 S. Main St. | 252/923-9571 | www.bbonline.com/nc/piratesden | lcbrab@bathnc.com | 4 rooms | $65–$75 | AE, D, MC, V.

BEAUFORT

MAP 8, K6

(Nearby towns also listed: Atlantic Beach, Cedar Island, Morehead City, Ocracoke)

The third-oldest town in the state, Beaufort is a small seaport with an impressive historic district. The English influence is readily apparent in its architecture as well as in the names of its streets and structures. From the busy boardwalk you can glimpse seagoing crafts, dolphins, even wild horses grazing on a nearby island.

Information: Carteret County Tourism Development Bureau | Box 1406, Morehead City, 28557 | 252/726-8148 or 800/786-6962.

Beaufort Historic Site Visitor Center | 138 Turner St., Beaufort, 28516 | 252/728-5225 or 800/575-7483 | bha@bmd.clis.com | www.historicbeaufort.com.

© Corbis

SCENIC BYWAYS

The North Carolina Department of Transportation has instituted a scenic byway program. More than 1,500 carefully selected miles that meander throughout the state provide an alternative to the fast traffic and commercial areas along the major thoroughfares. In all, there are 44 such byways: 12 routes are in the Coastal Plain, and there are 16 each in the mountains and the Piedmont.

The routes, marked by blue and green NC SCENIC BYWAY signs, were selected because they have scenic, cultural, and/or historic value. They vary in length from 3 to 173 mi and in character from curvy mountain roads to ferry rides across coastal sounds.

These roads less traveled—with names such as Waterfall Byway, Devil's Stompin' Ground Road, and Alligator River Route—provide the public access to beautiful and sequestered locations. But they do even more than that, for in a hurry-up-and-get-there world they give travelers an opportunity to relax and reflect between ends.

To obtain more information about the North Carolina Scenic Byways Program or to order the North Carolina Scenic Byways guide, write to the North Carolina Department of Transportation, PO Box 25201, Raleigh, NC 27611.

Attractions

Beaufort Historic Site. Vintage double-decker English buses shuttle you between the historic spots of this 2-acre complex. Sights include the apothecary shop and doctor's office (circa 1859), the jail (circa 1829), and the county's oldest remaining public building (circa 1796). You can also opt to tour on foot. | 130 Turner St. | 252/728–5225 or 800/575–7483 | fax 252/728–4966 | Bus tour $6, house tour $6, bus-walking tour $10 | Bus tours Mon., Wed., and Fri. at 11 and 1:30; house tours Mon.–Sat. at 10, 11:30, 1, and 3; visitor center Mon.–Sat. 9:30–5.

Cape Lookout National Seashore. A barrier island in its natural state, this is the place to go for solitude. You can reach it only by toll ferry or private boat. Once you arrive, you find more than 50 mi of beach, no developed campsites, and no bathhouses. There's birding year-round. The Cape Lookout Lighthouse is closed to the public. | 131 Charles St., Harkers Island | 252/728–2250 | fax 252/728–2160 | www.nps.gov/calo | Free | Seashore daily, visitor center daily 8–4:30.

North Carolina Maritime Museum. Harpoons, duck decoys, outboard motors, and pirate-related artifacts fill this museum, and there's a vast collection of seashells. You can also see how wooden boats are built and restored in the watercraft center. Educational exhibits, programs, and field trips further enhance your visit. | 315 Front St. | 252/728–7317 | fax 252/728–2108 | Free | Weekdays 9–5, Sat. 10–5, Sun. 1–5.

Old Burying Ground. One of the state's oldest cemeteries, this one has legible dates on grave stones going back as far as 1756. The historical association has pamphlets to guide visitors to the more interesting graves, including that of a little girl buried in a rum keg and that of Otway Burns, the famous privateer. | Ann and Taylor Sts. | 252/728–5225 or 800/575–7483 | Free | Daily.

ON THE CALENDAR

APR.: *Beaufort-by-the-Sea Music Festival.* Free concerts of classical, country, traditional, jazz, rock, and reggae music are presented on various stages within a three-block area downtown. | 252/728–6894.

APR.: *Newport Pig Cookin' Contest.* More than 100 pigs are cooked every year at this barbecue competition, auction, and community fair held in the town park in nearby Newport. | 252/223–7447.

JUNE: *Old Homes Tour.* On the last weekend of the month some of the country's most historic homes and buildings are open for narrated tours, and there are crafts, music, demonstrations, and reenactments. Tours begin at the Beaufort Historic Site. | 252/728–5225 or 800/575–7483.

Dining

Beaufort Grocery Co. American/Casual. Colorful art hangs on the walls of this restaurant in a former grocery store known for fresh seafood, steaks, free-range chicken, veal, and lamb. Specialties include grouper encrusted with crab and asparagus, and there's a deli. Homemade breads and desserts are also on the menu. Open-air dining on sidewalk. Sun. brunch. | 117 Queen St. | 252/728–3899 | $15–$21 | AE, MC, V | Closed Jan. and Tues. from Labor Day to Memorial Day.

Captain's Choice. Seafood. Portholes serve as windows in this lively, family- and angler-oriented restaurant. It's known for the seafood buffet, shrimp, prime rib, fried chicken, and calves' liver. No alcohol. | 977 Island Rd., Harkers Island | 252/728–7122 | $5–$13 | MC, V | Closed Mon. and late Dec.–late Jan.

Clawson's 1905 Restaurant and Pub. Contemporary. Antiques decorate this restaurant that was a general store in the early 1900s. Ribs, burgers, steaks, pasta, and local seafood keep this restaurant crowded in summer. Other specialties are crab cakes, shrimp and grits, and grilled mahimahi. Kids' menu. | 425 Front St. | 252/728–2133 | $10–$20 | D, MC, V | No lunch Sun.

Loughry's Landing. Seafood. Tropical fish and beach memorabilia provide the theme at this waterfront restaurant that has open-air dining on a two-level deck. In summer, you can order pizza and ice cream on the upper level. Items to try include pecan-crusted grouper and champagne dijon orange roughy. Kids' menu. | 510 Front St. | 252/728–7541 | $15–$25 | AE, D, MC, V | Closed Jan.–mid-Mar.

Lodging

Captains' Quarters Bed & Biscuit. In a historic district and just a block from waterfront shops and restaurants is this inn with three guest rooms. They're furnished with antiques and have private baths and ceiling fans. This place is best known for the source of its name: the "Riz" biscuits that come with the gigantic breakfasts. Complimentary breakfast. | 315 Ann St. | 252/728–7711 or 800/659–7111 | captqtrs@costalnet.com | 3 rooms | $70–$110 | MC, V.

Cedars Inn by the Sea. Two side-by-side homes (circa 1768 and 1851) make up this B&B. In the historic district, this inn is close to shops and restaurants. Rooms have private baths, many have antiques, and no two are quite alike. Complimentary breakfast. Cable TV, no room phones. No smoking. | 305 Front St. | 252/728–7036 | fax 252/728–1685 | www.cedarsinn.com | 7 rooms, 4 suites; 1 cottage | $115–$125, $140–$150 suites; $165 cottage | AE, D, MC, V.

Cousins B&B. This house dates back to 1855, when it was known as the Ward-Adair home. Today, it's a B&B with central air-conditioning and four guest rooms. Cousins serves home-style Southern breakfasts in either the formal dining room or the light-filled sun room. Chef Elmo insists you will love grits by the time you leave. Complimentary breakfast. TV in common area. No pets. No smoking. | 303 Turner St. | 252/504–3478 or 877/464–7487 | fax 252/728–4696 | www.cousinsbedandbreakfast.com | 4 rooms | $95–$110 | MC, V.

Delamar Inn. An English courtyard garden borders this B&B in an 1866 house. There are porches upstairs and down and antiques in the guest rooms. This inn is one block from Beaufort historical spots and two blocks from the waterfront boardwalk. Complimentary Continental breakfast. No room phones. Business services. No kids under 10. No smoking. | 217 Turner St. | 252/728–4300 | fax 252/728–1491 | www.bbonline.com/nc/delamarinn | 4 rooms (3 with shower only) | $86–$112 | MC, V.

Langdon House. Dating from the mid-1700s, this is the oldest house in Beaufort that is run as a B&B. It's a block from the waterfront and across the street from the Old Burying Ground. Fishing and clamming equipment is available. Bicycles. No kids under 12. No smoking. | 135 Craven St. | 252/728–5499 | fax 252/728–1717 | innkeeper@coastalnet.com | www.langdonhouse.com | 4 rooms | $75–$135 | No credit cards.

Pecan Tree Inn. Turrets and gingerbread trim adorn this inn that has an English flower and herb garden with more than 1,000 identified plants. Rooms have canopy beds, antiques, and private baths. Complimentary Continental breakfast. No room phones. No kids under 12. No smoking. | 116 Queen St. | 252/728–6733 | www.pecantree.com | 7 rooms (2 with hot tubs) | $75–$135 | AE, D, MC, V.

BLOWING ROCK

MAP 8, C3

(Nearby towns also listed: Banner Elk, Blue Ridge Parkway, Boone, Lenoir, Linville, Valle Crucis)

Permanent residents of this beautiful mountain town on a ridge overlooking the John's River Gorge banded together to prohibit the development of large hotels and motels so they could keep the place semirural. The village environment is evident on Main Street, where specialty stores and small restaurants abound. Blowing Rock inspired one of its residents, contemporary novelist Jan Karon, to create the fictional town that is the setting for her Mitford series of books.

Information: Blowing Rock Chamber of Commerce | Box 406, 28605 | 828/295–7851 or 800/295–7851 | blowingrock@skybest.com | www.blowingrock.com.

Attractions

Appalachian Ski Mountain. Open since 1962, Appalachian provides a 4,000-ft elevation, nine slopes, two quad chairlifts, one double chairlift, and an outdoor ice-skating rink. | 940 Ski Mountain Rd. | 828/295–7828 or 800/322–2373 | fax 828/295–3277 | www.appskimtn.com | Late Nov.–mid-Mar.

Blowing Rock. Updrafts from the John's River Gorge below sweep a rocky, granite outcrop on a 3,000-ft-high cliff. The walk up is scenic; once you're there, the 180-degree view is majestic. | 432 Rock Rd. (at U.S. 321) | 828/295–7111 | $4 | May–Oct., weekdays 8:30–7, weekends 8:30–8; Nov.–Apr., weekdays 9–5, weekends 9–6.

Blowing Rock Stables. Expert riders and naturalists from Blowing Rock Stables guide one- or two-hour trail rides through Moses H. Cone Memorial Park. Reservations are recommended, and closed-toe shoes are required. | 2880 Laurel Rd. | 828/295–7847 | Horse rental $30–$50 | Daily 10–3:30 (last ride), Closed Dec.–Mar.

Julian Price Memorial Park. The 4,000-plus acres have a lake, campgrounds, hiking trails, and picnic areas. There's limited boating, fishing, and lakeside walking along an easy 2½-mi loop trail. | Blue Ridge Pkwy., MM 295 | 828/295–7591 or 828/963–5911 | Free | Grounds daily dawn–dusk, campground May–Oct., daily.

Moses H. Cone Memorial Park. A network of walking trails leads to a lake and trout ponds on the grounds of Moses Cone's former estate, which the textile magnate donated to the federal government in the 1950s. Today, Flat Top Manor serves as a Blue Ridge Parkway visitor center and houses a crafts shop. | Blue Ridge Pkwy., MM 294 | 828/295–7591 | Free | Call for hours.

Parkway Craft Center. Quilts, carvings, jewelry, pottery, and the like showcase the work of Southern Highland Handicraft Guild members inside historic Flat Top Manor. | Blue Ridge Pkwy., MM 294 | 828/295–7938 | Free | Mid-Mar.–Nov., daily 9–6.

Mystery Hill. Exploring the relationship between science, optical illusion, and natural phenomena, this museum invites you to defy gravity. You can see water running up-hill in the Mystery House and step into gigantic soap bubbles in the Hall of Mystery, where science is an interactive game. The site also has Native American exhibits in its Appalachian Heritage Museum. | U.S. 321 S | 828/264–2792 | $7 | June–Labor Day, daily 8–8; Labor Day–June, daily 9–5.

Tweetsie Railroad. Outlaws attack steam trains at this Wild West theme park. There are also shows, rides, shops, and a petting zoo. | U.S. 321/221, off Blue Ridge Pkwy. at MM 291 | 828/264–9061 or 800/526–5740 | fax 828/264–2234 | www.tweetsie.com | $20 | Mid-May–Oct., daily 9–6.

ON THE CALENDAR

JULY–AUG.: *Blowing Rock Charity Horse Show.* More than 600 horses and 300 accompanying riders come to Blowing Rock for three weeks of riding competition and classes in the oldest continuously running equestrian event of its kind in the country. The show at M. L. Tate Show Grounds and Broyhill Park raises money for charity and includes vendors selling crafts, clothing, food, and horse-related items. | 828/295–7851 or 828/295–4602.

OCT.: *Tweetsie Railroad Halloween Festival and Ghost Train.* Eerily lit grounds provide the backdrop for rides on a specially outfitted steam locomotive as a spook motif temporarily transforms the state's first theme park. Staff wear costumes, and there's a costume contest for kids, as well as a haunted house, trick or treating, entertainment, and games. Tweetsie Railroad is on U.S. 21 between Blowing Rock and Boone. | 828/264–9061 or 800/526–5740.

Dining

Artist's Palate. Contemporary. Sweeping views through plate-glass windows and white tablecloths set the scene at this restaurant. Menus change seasonally and include shrimp-bacon filet mignon, stuffed shrimp, Portobello boursin-cheese ravioli, and angel hair calamari. There's a sushi bar Thurs.–Sat. nights. | 711 Main St. | 800/467–6626 | $19–$32 | AE, D, DC, MC, V | No lunch.

Best Cellar. Continental. Fireplaces and pine floors decorate this former log cabin. On the menu are roast duckling, salmon, and banana cream pie. Beer and wine only. | 275 Little Spring Rd. | 828/295–3466 | $17–$25 | AE, MC, V | No lunch.

Mike's Inland Seafood. Seafood. With its fish trophies and large aquarium, this place feels like a fish camp. It's known as *the* seafood restaurant of the mountains. Specialties range from catfish, clams, and crab legs to perch and trout. There are also some chicken and beef items. Kids' menu. | Rte. 184 | 828/898–6005 | $10–$35 | AE, D, MC, V.

Parkway Cafe. American/Casual. A wide range of creative takes on American and Tex-Mex fare is on the menu at this casual spot in the Parkway Shoppes mall area. Mostly-pasta entrées, ranging from eggplant parmigiana to blackened tuna pasta, complement the diverse sandwich selections. | U.S. 321 | 828/295–0300 | $5–$13 | AM, D, MC, V.

Riverwood. Contemporary. A stone fireplace warms this former home built in the 1930s; white linen tablecloths and candlelight enhance the mood. Stuffed rainbow trout, marinated beef tenderloin, and a variety of vegetarian dishes are on the menu. | 7179 Valley Blvd. (U.S. 321) | 828/295–4162 | $15–$26 | D, MC, V | Closed Sun.–Tue.

Speckled Trout Cafe. American/Casual. Local landscape artists' work and mounted fish are on display at this restaurant with a neutral color scheme. At night, linen cloths dress the tables. This restaurant is known for fresh mountain trout and certified Angus beef. The dinner menu includes trout and seafood, pasta, pork, poultry, and steaks. There's also a raw bar, and outdoors you can dine by candlelight. Breakfast is also served. | 922 Main St. | 828/295–9819 | $19–$28 | AE, MC, V.

Woodlands Barbecue. American/Casual/Barbecue. This rustic place is popular with bus tours. It's known for barbecued beef, pork, chicken, and ribs. Some sandwiches and Mexican food are also on the menu. Live music nightly. | 8304 Valley Blvd. (off U.S. 321 Bypass) | 828/295–3651 | Reservations not accepted | $10–$25 | MC, V.

Lodging

Alpen Acres Motel. On a 2-acre hilltop between Boone and Blowing Rock, this basic hotel is 2 mi from the ski slopes. Besides standard rooms, a separate chalet is available, as well as rooms with kitchens that can accommodate families or groups. Picnic area. Some kitchenettes. Cable TV, room phones. Pool. Playground. | 318 Old U.S. Hwy. 321 | 828/295–7981 or 888/297–7981 | www.alpenacres.com | 19 rooms, 1 chalet | $40–$104, $75–$200 with kitchen | AE, D, MC, V.

Blowing Rock Inn. On Main Street two blocks from downtown shops and restaurants, this inn is surrounded by trees and a garden. In the back, you'll find a gazebo and rocking chairs. Rooms are white and light with wood furniture. Picnic area. Cable TV. | 788 N. Main St. | 828/295–7921 | 24 rooms | $89 | AE, D, MC, V | Closed Dec.–Mar.

Brookside Inn. A small lake, a garden, an orchard, and a winding brook add up to a relaxing pace at this inn. The rooms and cottages are Victorian in style, and Continental breakfast is in the central lobby lodge. Complimentary Continental breakfast. Cable TV, room phones. Lake. | 876 Valley Blvd. | 828/295–3380 or 800/441–5691 | www.thebrooksideinn.com | 19 rooms, 3 cottages | $89–$109 | AE, D, MC, V.

Chetola Resort. The name of this property was inspired by the Cherokee word meaning "haven of rest." There are a number of activities at the 7-acre lake and Moses Cone Memorial Park, less than 1 mi away. The lodge sits on 87 acres of the historic Chetola Estate. The rooms are all in dark, rustic yet sophisticated burgundy and green. All rooms sit hillside, with views of the lake and mountains. Cross-country and downhill skiing are 8 mi north of the resort. Dining room, picnic area. Refrigerators. Cable TV. Indoor pool. Hot tub. Tennis courts. Exercise equipment, hiking, racquetball. Water sports, fishing, bicycles. Kids' programs (4–12), playground. Laundry facilities. Business services. | N. Main St. | 828/295–5500 or 800/243–8652 | fax 828/295–5529 | www.chetola.com | 42 rooms | $116–$225 | AE, D, MC, V.

Cliff Dwellers Inn. A long, winding road takes you to the top of a hill, where this Bavarian-style inn overlooks a small lake. Rock walls dot the grounds, which also have a large perennial garden. The structure has high peaks and cutouts and was built of woods native to the area. Huge picture windows afford panoramic views of the mountains and lake. Rooms are done in soft whites and pinks, with dust ruffles and down comforters. Textured walls and upholstered rockers complete the decor. Rooms also have fireplaces, hot tubs, and coffeemakers, and outside there's a gazebo with a hot tub. Some kitchenettes, some microwaves, refrigerators, in-room hot tubs. Cable TV. Pool. | 116 Lakeview Terr | 828/295–3121 or 800/322–7380 | fax 828/295–3121 | info@cliffdwellers.com | www.cliffdwellers.com | 20 rooms, 3 suites | $110–$135, $165–$265 suites | DC, MC, V.

Crippen's Country Inn. Rural surroundings provide a perfect setting for relaxing at this casual inn. Each room is individually styled with quilts on the beds, wallpaper, bright colors, and wood floors with area rugs. There's cable TV in the common area. Kids under 12 are not permitted in rooms but are allowed in the cottage. Restaurant, complimentary Continental breakfast. Business services. No smoking. | 239 Sunset Dr. | 828/295–3487 | fax 828/295–0388 | www.crippens.com | 8 rooms (2 with shower only); 1 cottage | $59–$129, $199 cottage (2–night minimum stay) | AE, D, MC, V.

Days Inn. A chalet-style hotel in the mountains near skiing and other outdoor activities, this restful spot is also 9 mi from Appalachian State University and 2 mi from the Blue Ridge Parkway. Restaurant. Cable TV, room phones. Indoor pool. Hot tub. | 8412 Valley Blvd. | 828/295–4422 | fax 828/295–0313 | 118 rooms | $71–$164 | AE, DC, D, MC, V.

Gideon Ridge Inn. Inside this stone home is a library with fireplace and a breakfast room with original art. Outside there's a garden and stone patios with wicker furniture. All rooms have private baths, and some have fireplaces, floor-to-ceiling windows, and hot tubs. Afternoon tea is complimentary, and there's a TV in the common area on request. Complimentary breakfast. Some hot tubs. No pets. No smoking. | 202 Gideon Ridge Rd. | 828/295–3644 | www.gideonridge.com | 5 rooms | $115–$260 | AE, D, MC, V.

Green Park Inn. Sitting 4,300 ft up in the Blue Ridge Mountains, one of the South's finest resorts has been host to heads of state and business VIPs. Built in 1882, this Victorian inn has a grand veranda with white rockers. Some rooms have private balconies. All have Victorian wood furnishings and brightly painted, textured walls. Sunday brunch. Downhill skiing is 5 mi north of here. Dining rooms, bar, complimentary Continental breakfast. Cable TV. Pool. Business services. | 9239 Valley Blvd. | 828/295–3141 or 800/852–2462 | fax 828/295–3141 | www.greenparkinn.com | 86 rooms | $109–$175 | AE, D, MC, V.

Homestead Inn. All rooms are on the ground floor and have homemade quilts. Some have fireplaces. The inn is half a block off Main Street, 25 minutes from Grandfather Mountain and 5 minutes from Appalachian Ski Mountain. Gazebos and swings are on the property. Kids are welcome, and there's a playground down the street. Picnic area. Some microwaves, refrigerators, some in-room hot tubs. Cable TV. | 153 Morris St. | 828/295–9559 | fax 828/295–9551 | homestead-inn.com | 15 rooms | $49–$99 | AE, D, MC, V.

Hound Ears Lodge and Club. The resort is named for a 4,000-ft rock outcropping that looms above it in the Blue Ridge Mountains. The pool is secluded in a natural grotto, and there are massive stone fireplaces. Rooms have balconies with views. Golf and tennis packages are available. Dining room, complimentary Continental breakfast. Cable TV. Pool. 18-hole golf course, 6 tennis courts. Exercise equipment. Kids' programs. Business services. | 328 Shulls Mill Rd. | 828/963–4321 | fax 828/963–8030 | www.houndears.com | 28 rooms | $115–$150 | AE, MC, V | MAP available.

Inn at Ragged Gardens. Chestnut bark siding, which is on many older homes in the High Country, covers this inn that was built in 1900 and sits amid gardens in the village of Blowing Rock. The interior has wood walls and hardwood floors. Rooms vary in style from medieval to Japanese to Victorian to modern. Complimentary breakfast. Some in-room hot tubs. No kids under 12. No smoking. | 203 Sunset Dr. | 828/295–9703 | www.ragged-gardens.com | 12 rooms | $145–$275 (2–night minimum stay on weekends) | MC, V.

Maple Lodge. This is a two-story frame house built in the 1940s as a boardinghouse for tourists. The structure now sits in the heart of downtown Blowing Rock, and the landscaped yard is filled with perennial flowers. Rooms have hardwood floors, light-color wallpaper, and wood furniture. Cross-country and downhill skiing are 3 mi north of the lodge. Complimentary breakfast. No room phones. No kids under 12. No smoking. | 152 Sunset Dr. | 828/295–3331 | fax 828/295–9986 | innkeeper@maplelodge.net | www.maplelodge.net | 11 rooms | $95–$165 | AE, D, DC, MC, V.

Meadowbrook Inn. This inn is in the center of most of Blowing Rock's attractions. Rooms have traditional furnishings, and two suites have private pools. Downhill skiing is 3 mi north of here. Bar with entertainment, dining room, complimentary Continental breakfast. Cable TV. Indoor pool. Hot tub. Exercise equipment. Business services. | 711 N. Main St. | 828/295–4300 or 800/456–5456 | fax 828/295–4300 | www.meadowbrook-inn.com | 39 rooms, 22 suites | $129–$259, $149–$259 suites | AE, D, DC, MC, V.

BLUE RIDGE
PARKWAY

INTRO
ATTRACTIONS
DINING
LODGING

BLUE RIDGE PARKWAY

MAP 8, B5

(Nearby towns also listed: Asheville, Banner Elk, Blowing Rock, Boone, Brevard, Bryson City, Burnsville, Cherokee, Hendersonville, Jefferson, Lenoir, Linville, Little Switzerland, Maggie Valley, Marion, Mount Airy, Waynesville, Wilkesboro)

The parkway, an engineering marvel that took 50 years to complete, is a recreation-oriented scenic byway that connects the Great Smoky Mountains National Park in North Carolina with the Shenandoah National Park in Virginia. In North Carolina the parkway extends 252 mi and has five campgrounds, eight picnic areas, two lodges, and three restaurants.

Information: Superintendent, Blue Ridge Parkway | 400 BB&T Bldg., 1 Pack Sq., Asheville, 28801 | 828/298–0398 or 828/271–4779 | www.nps.gov/blri.

Attractions

Blue Ridge Parkway. This is a stunningly beautiful 469-mi road that winds through mountains and meadows and crosses mountain streams on its way from Waynesboro, Virginia, to Cherokee, North Carolina. The parkway closes during heavy snows and icy conditions. Maps and information are available at visitor centers along the highway. Mile markers (MM) identify points of interest and indicate the distance from the parkway's starting point in Virginia. | Free | Daily.

ON THE CALENDAR
OCT.: *Mountain Glory Festival.* Held in downtown Marion, the festival includes live bluegrass and gospel music, food vendors, craft booths and exhibits, children's events, and a quilt raffle. | 828/652–2215 or 828/652–3551.

Dining

Beam's Chinese-American Restaurant. Chinese. At this roadside diner dressed up as an Asian restaurant, classic dishes and American standbys are on menu. The Friday night dinner buffet is popular with locals at this spot that is 9 mi north of the Blue Ridge Parkway. | Rte. 19 E, Spruce Pine | 828/765–6191 | $6–$13 | No credit cards | Closed Sun.–Mon. No lunch.

Lodging

Pisgah Inn. Its location at 5,000 ft makes this a popular landmark; indeed, the place takes reservations a year in advance for prime foliage season (October). These four small, two-level buildings are a part of the National Parks Service Concession. All rooms have private decks and balconies with views of the forest. Restaurant. No room phones. Laundry facilities. | Blue Ridge Pkwy., MM 408.6 | 828/235–8228 | fax 828/648–9719 | pisgahinn@aol.com | www.pisgahinn.com | 50 rooms, 1 suite | $73–$85, $120 suite | MC, V | Closed Nov.–Mar.

BOONE

MAP 8, D3

(Nearby towns also listed: Banner Elk, Blue Ridge Parkway, Blowing Rock, Jefferson, Lenoir, Linville)

Boone is the seat of Watauga County's government, and Appalachian State University, a part of the University of North Carolina college system, is the educational and cultural heart of Boone. Students and tourists, who arrive in winter, summer, and fall, boost the permanent resident population in this sophisticated mountain town, which boasts a number of resorts for golfing, skiing, and other types of recreation.

Information: Boone Convention and Visitors Bureau | 208 Howard St., 28607 | 828/262–3516 or 800/852–9506 | chamber@boone.net | www.boonechamber.com.

Attractions

Appalachian State University. Atop a High Country peak sits "App State," a member of the University of North Carolina system. Its hilly campus is shaded by trees in the warm months; winter brings snow and ice. The school, which numbers some 12,000 students, is a cultural as well as educational anchor for the region. In addition to showcasing various performing arts, a formal lecture series includes nationally known speakers. | Stadium Dr. | 828/262–2000 or 828/262–2179 | www.appstate.edu.

A collection of artifacts from prehistoric times to the present illustrates the history and culture of southern Appalachia at the **Appalachian Cultural Museum.** An assortment of music, books, art, and documents tells the story of all who have helped shape the region: Native Americans, African-Americans, and European-Americans. Self-directed and guided tours are available. | University Hall, University Hall Dr. | 828/262–3117 | fax 828/262–2920 | www.museum-appstate.edu | $4 | Tues.–Sat. 10–5, Sun. 1–5.

Daniel Boone Native Gardens. Plants native to North Carolina thrive in an informal landscape. | 651 Horn in the West Dr. | 828/264–6390 | $2 | May–Sept., daily 9–6; call for Oct. hours.

Mast General Store. At the Old Boone Mercantile, this is a classic general store selling traditional clothing for all mountain seasons. | 630 W. King St. | 828/262–0000 | www.mast-generalstore.com | Free | Apr.–Dec., Mon.–Sat. 10–6, Sun. 1–6; Jan.–Mar., Mon.–Sat. 10–5, Sun. 1–5.

Wilcox Emporium Warehouse. More than 180 antiques, art, and collectible vendors sell their wares at this former warehouse in the historic district. | 161 Howard St. | 828/262–1221 | fax 828/264–1408 | Free | May–Dec., Mon.–Thurs. 10–6, Fri.–Sat. 10–8, Sun. 1–6; Jan.–Apr., Mon.–Sat. 10–6, Sun. 1–6.

ON THE CALENDAR

JUNE–AUG.: *Horn in the West.* Daniel Boone and his mountain men fight both the British militia and a feared Cherokee chief in this outdoor drama. The Daniel Boone Amphitheater stages this project of the Southern Appalachian Historical Association. | Shows Tues.–Sun. at 8 PM | 828/264–2120.

JULY: *Appalachian Summer Festival.* Performances by international headliners join the lineup at this monthlong series that also includes workshops, art competitions, concerts, exhibits. Theater, music, dance, and visual arts mingle at Appalachian State University, 229 Rivers Street. | 828/262–6084 or 800/841–2787 for box office.

JULY: *Firefly Festival.* Flat-pickin' musicians join this arts-and-crafts bonanza in the Horn in the West area. | 828/262–4532.

SEPT.: *Olde Boone Streetfest.* Traditional mountain foods, arts and crafts, and music combine in a country fair on the streets of downtown Boone. | 828/262–4532.

OCT.: *Apple Festival.* The northern mountains are apple country, and this festival is held during harvest season with crafts, entertainment, and food. You can check it out at Hickory Ridge Homestead, Horn in the West area. | 828/264–2120.

Dining

Caribbean Café. Caribbean. This is a casual party spot known for conch fritters, plantains, jerk chicken and pork, and warm smoked salmon with tomatillo sauce. Live music is also on the menu nightly. Kids' menu. Sun. brunch. | 489-B W. King St. | 828/265–2233 | Reservations not accepted | $12–$21 | AE, D, DC, MC, V.

Dan'l Boone Inn. American. In a building that once housed a hospital, this inn serves up old-fashioned dining in generous portions. With family-style service, the place is known for biscuits, ham, mashed potatoes, vegetables, and pies. Breakfast is served weekends only. Kids' menu. | 130 Hardin St. | 828/264–8657 | Reservations not accepted except for 15 or more | $12 | No credit cards | Lunch only on weekends Nov.–May.

Geno's Restaurant. American/Casual. Wood, ferns, and flags from many nations highlight the interior. This restaurant is known for chicken, beef, and pasta dishes. | 1785 Rte. 105 | 828/264–1000 | Reservations not accepted | $12–$18 | AE, D, MC, V | No lunch weekdays.

Makoto. Japanese. A Japanese steak house with casual family dining, this place dishes up sesame chicken, steak, and seafood. Lunch buffet. Kids' menu. | 2124 Blowing Rock Rd. | 828/264–7976 | $9–$23 | AE, D, DC, MC, V.

Lodging

Castle Hotel. Just off the Blue Ridge Parkway at Aho Gap (MM 288), the Castle Hotel is instantly recognizable as the only building around that looks like a medieval castle. The studio and one- or two-bedroom suites all have kitchens and fireplaces, and are available for daily or weekly rental. Kitchenettes, refrigerators. Cable TV, room phones. | 205 Sampson Rd., Boone | 828/264–4002 or 888/264–4003 | www.castlehotel.com | 29 | $55–$95 | MC, V.

Gragg House B&B. On a wooded ridge 1 mi from downtown Boone and Appalachian State University, the B&B is also close to downhill skiing at Beech and Sugar mountains. All three guest rooms are furnished with antiques; one has a private bath. Complimentary breakfast. No pets. No smoking. | 201 Ridge Point Dr. | 828/264–7289 | www.gragghousebandb.com/ | 3 rooms | $89–$99 | No credit cards.

Graystone Lodge. This place is just minutes away from skiing, golf, hiking, and Appalachian State University. The lodge's interior is fairly traditional, while the exterior has a contemporary look. Cross-country and downhill skiing are 20 mi north of the lodge. Complimentary Continental breakfast. Cable TV. Indoor pool. Business services. | 2419 Rte. 105 | 828/264–4133 or 800/560–5942 | fax 828/262–0101 | www.graystonelodge.com | 101 rooms | $50–$90 | AE, D, DC, MC, V.

Hampton Inn. Some rooms have hot tubs at this hotel that's within 30 minutes of three ski resorts and Grandfather Mountain and 10 minutes from Tweetsie Railroad. The five-level hotel is in a commercial area with limited grounds, and rooms have lightly colored paint and wood furniture. Complimentary Continental breakfast. In-room data ports. Cable TV. Indoor pool. Hot tubs. Business services. | 1075 Rte. 105 | 828/264–0077 | fax 828/264–4600 | 95 rooms | $89–$129 | AE, D, DC, MC, V.

High Country Inn. Native stone built this 3-story stucco inn that's on the side of a mountain. Blue, mauve, and green rooms provide views, and ponds surround the inn. It is in a commercial area, close to shops and attractions. Restaurant, bar. No-smoking rooms. Cable TV. Indoor-outdoor pool. Hot tub, sauna. Gym. Laundry facilities. | 1785 Hwy. 105 S | 828/264–1000 or 800/334–5605 | fax 828/262–0073 | info@highcountryinn.com | www.highcountryinn.com | 122 rooms, 2 suites; 2 cabins (off-site) | $34–$89, $75–$175 suites, $125–$250 cabins | AE, D, MC, V.

Holiday Inn Express of Boone. A mile from Appalachian State University, this two-story hotel has a courtyard in the back. Some of the rooms have fold-out sofas, and some have balconies overlooking the courtyard and pool. Complimentary Continental breakfast. In-room data ports. Cable TV. Pool. Exercise equipment. Downhill skiing. Laundry facilities. Business services. | 1855 Blowing Rock Rd. | 828/264–2451 | fax 828/265–3861 | holidayinn@boone.mail.net | www.holiday-inn.com | 138 rooms | $69–$119 | AE, D, DC, MC, V.

Lovill House. This restored country farmhouse was built in 1875 and sits on 11 wooded acres with gardens and a stream with a waterfall. There's a social hour with beer and wine each night. The rooms have antique iron bedsteads or sleigh beds, and you'll find the TV hidden away in a hardwood cabinet. Some rooms have fireplaces. Picnic area, complimentary breakfast. Cable TV. Cross-country skiing. No kids under 12. No smoking. | 404 Old Bristol Rd. | 828/264–4204 or 800/849–9466 | innkeeper@lovillhouseinn.com | www.lovillhouseinn.com | 6 rooms, 1 cottage | $145–$190 | MC, V | Closed Mar., 2 wks in Sept.

Quality Inn Appalachian Conference Center. Just ¼ mi from Appalachian State University and 20 mi from Grandfather Mountain, this seven-story white brick hotel is in the heart of the commercial district. Some rooms have mountain views. Cross-country and downhill skiing are 12 mi south of here. Restaurant. Refrigerators (in suites). Cable TV. Indoor-outdoor pool. Business services. | 949 Blowing Rock Rd. | 828/262–0020 | fax 828/262–9818 | www.qualityinnboone.com | 130 rooms, 4 suites | $95–$175, $125–$175 suites | AE, D, DC, MC, V.

River Farm Inn. Rocking chairs, a gazebo, and a two-person hammock are popular places to relax here at this rural retreat on the New River. Several types of accommodations are available: two suites are in a reconstructed 1800s barn, there's a carriage house on top of a garage, and there's a three-bedroom log house. Complimentary Continental breakfast. In-room hot tubs. Water sports. | 179 River Run Bridge Rd. | 336/877–1728 | 4 rooms | $165–$275 | MC, V.

Smoketree Lodge. From this three-story lodge you have great views of Grandfather Mountain. The large lobby has high wood-beam ceilings and a fireplace area. Rooms have neutral colors, and some provide mountain views. Downhill skiing is 3 mi north of here. Picnic area. Kitchenettes. Cable TV. Indoor pool. Hot tub. Exercise equipment, hiking. Video games. Laundry facilities. | 11914 Rte. 105 S | 828/963–6505 or 800/422–1880 | fax 828/963–7815 | www.smoketreelodge.com | 46 rooms | $75–$105 | AE, D, MC, V.

Windows View B&B. An advantage of a modern home like this one 3 mi outside of Boone is that the windows can be larger than usual. Here you get views of the Blue Ridge Mountains from an entire wall of windows in each guest room. There's no TV, but the views provide entertainment enough. Breakfast may include cinnamon coffee cake or apple pancakes. Complimentary full breakfast. Private bathrooms. No TV. | 204 Stoneleigh La. | 828/963–8081 or 800/963–4484 | www.windowviewsb-b.com | 2 rooms | $80–$100 | MC, V.

BREVARD

(Nearby towns also listed: Asheville, Blue Ridge Parkway, Cashiers, Cherokee, Hendersonville, Highlands, Lake Toxaway, Maggie Valley)

The town, in a tree-filled county known for its 200-plus waterfalls (many of which have appeared in movies), was named for Ephraim Brevard, a physician who authored the Mecklenburg Declaration of Independence, a document that preceded the national Declaration of Independence by a year. The town's progressiveness can also be measured by its big reputation as a year-round center for the performing and visual arts. Professionals, amateurs, and students alike flock to Brevard to hone their crafts.

Information: Brevard-Transylvania Tourism Development Authority | 35 W. Main St., Brevard, 28712 | 828/884–8900 or 800/648–4523 | waterfalls@citcom.net | www.visitwaterfalls.com.

Attractions
Land of the Waterfalls. Scenic waterfalls abound in Transylvania County, home to Brevard: Connestee Falls (U.S. 276 S), which are twin falls more than 110 ft high; 125-ft High Falls (2½ mi from Yellow Gap Road); 85-ft Looking Glass Falls (U.S. 276 N); 200-ft Rainbow Falls (on Horse Pasture River off Rte. 281 S); 123-ft Toxaway Falls (U.S. 64 W in Toxaway); and the highest waterfall in the eastern United States, Whitewater, which drops 411 ft (Rte. 281 S, near Sapphire). | 800/648–4523 | fax 828/883–8550 | www.vistwaterfalls.com | Free | Daily.

Pisgah National Forest. With more than 500,000 acres, Pisgah is a delight for hikers and nature lovers of all stripes. It's home to towering mountains, wildlife, trails, lakes, and streams. Campgrounds are available (some charge a fee). This forest also includes the Cradle of Forestry in America National Historic Site. | 160A Zillicoa St., Brevard | 828/257–4200 or 828/877–3130 for historic site | www.cs.unca.edu/nfsnc | Free | Daily.

Mount Pisgah. Standing at an elevation of 5,721 ft, this prominent peak, now part of Pisgah National Forest, is named after the biblical mountain from which Moses first viewed the Promised Land. | Blue Ridge Pkwy., MM 407.4 | 828/257–4200 | Free | Daily.

Pisgah Center for Wildlife Education. This center, designed to highlight the work of the N.C. Wildlife Resources Commission, is just off U.S. 276 near Pisgah Forest in Transylvania County. A stroll through the forest brings you to exhibits focusing on wildlife and fish management, law enforcement, and conservation education. There's a butterfly garden, wild flood plots, and viewing access to trout raceways at the adjacent Pisgah Fish Hatchery. Indoors, there are aquariums containing specimens found in the Coastal Plain, Piedmont, and mountains. | 475-C Fish Hatchery Rd., Pisgah Forest | 828/877–4423 | Free | Daily.

Sliding Rock. In summer, you can skid 150 ft on a natural water slide. Wear old jeans and tennis shoes and bring a towel. | Pisgah National Forest | 828/877–3265 | Free | Daily; lifeguards on duty Memorial Day–mid Aug., daily 10–6.

ON THE CALENDAR
JUNE–AUG.: *Music Festival.* Symphonies, soloists, operas, and jazz ensembles made up of students and internationally renowned professionals resound over a seven-week period at the Brevard Music Center Auditorium, 1000 Probart Street. | 828/884–2011 or 800/648–4523.

OCT.: *Forest Festival Day.* Crafters, exhibitors, and entertainers gather at the Cradle of Forestry to acknowledge the area's rich forest heritage. College forestry students vie in the Woodsmen's Meet, a lumberjack-type competition. This all happens at 1002 Pisgah Highway 276, Pisgah Forest. | 828/877–3130.

BREVARD

INTRO
ATTRACTIONS
DINING
LODGING

OCT.: *Transylvania County Halloweenfest.* A Dracula look-alike contest, costume and pumpkin contests, parades, a play, merchant sales, music, and dances stir up various downtown locations. | 800/648–4523.

DEC.: *Twilight Tour on Main.* Horsedrawn carriages carry people through streets illuminated by twinkling lights and luminaria at this downtown event. Merchants open house, carolers sing, musicians play, and actors are in character as Tiny Tim and his family. There are also food vendors. | 828/884–3278.

Dining

Chianti's Italian Café and Bar. Italian. Large brass gates, candles, low lighting, and floral arrangements set the mood. Some items to try are the seafood medley in basil sauce over pasta and veal medallions with mozzarella in cognac cream sauce. Open-air dining. | U.S. 64 and Rte. 280 | 828/862–5683 | $10–$16 | AE, D, MC, V | No lunch.

Corner Bistro. American/Casual. A relaxed mood prevails at this place known for sandwiches, tortilla wraps, vegetarian dishes, turkey chili, soups, salads, and pizza. There is open-air dining on the sidewalk. Kids' menu. Beer and wine only. | 1 E. Main St. | 828/862–4746 | $11–$18 | MC, V | Closed Sun. No supper Mon.

Falls Landing Restaurant. Contemporary. When owner Mike Young moved from the Virgin Islands to Transylvania County, he brought a love for the flavors of the Caribbean with him. That's evident in much of food served in this pleasantly appointed restaurant with handmade mahogany tables and Mexican tile floors. Fresh seafood is served with tropical fruit salsa. The conch fritters get raves. | 23 E. Main St., Brevard | 828/884–2835 | Reservations essential in summer | $14–$20 | AE, D, MC, V | Closed Sun., no dinner Mon.

Pisgah Fish Camp. Seafood. A local fixture. Items to try include calabash-style shrimp and homemade onion rings. There are also steaks and hot vegetable and salad bars. Kids' menu. | 663 Deavor Rd. | 828/877–3129 | $4–$12 | D, MC, V.

Raintree Restaurant. American/Casual. True to its name, this place has a pond with waterfall and greenery, as well as an atrium. The interior is rustic and casual. This restaurant is known for beef dishes, and dishes to try are Portobello mushrooms and stuffed filet mignon. Sun. brunch. BYOB. | 9001 Greenville Hwy. (U.S. 276) | 828/862–5832 | $11–$31 | D, MC, V | No supper Sun.

Lodging

Imperial Motor Lodge. Right on Brevard's main road in a commercial area, this place is ½ mi from downtown and about 30 minutes from the Blue Ridge Parkway. This multi-level brick lodge has some greenery. Rooms have wood furniture and a medium-to-dark color scheme. Kids are welcome. Complimentary Continental breakfast. Refrigerators. Cable TV. Pool. | U.S. 276 and 64 N | 828/884–2887 or 800/869–3335 | fax 828/883–9811 | 92 rooms | $80–$90 | AE, D, DC, MC, V.

Inn at Brevard. Entrance pillars greet you at this 1885 Southern mansion with blue awnings and carefully tended gardens. Stonewall Jackson's troops once held a reunion here. Five guest rooms in the main house have private baths, and the 10 guest rooms in the adjacent lodge have private showers. Complimentary breakfast. Cable TV. | 410 E. Main St. | 828/884–2105 | fax 828/885–7996 | www.innatbrevard.8m.com | 15 rooms | $110–$130 | AE, D, MC, V.

Sunset Motel. It's a short walk from here along a pretty street to Brevard's shops and restaurants. This is a classic 1950s-style urban motel. Rooms have outside entrances with screen doors and neutral-colored stucco walls. Windows in the rooms open, unlike many modern lodgings. There are some views of the Blue Ridge Mountains and Blue Ridge Parkway. Refrigerators. Cable TV, some room phones. | 415 S. Broad St. | 828/884–9106 | 20 rooms | $55–$85 | AE, D, MC, V.

BRYSON CITY

(Nearby towns also listed: Blue Ridge Parkway, Cherokee, Franklin, Maggie Valley, Robbinsville)

Outdoor activities are the bywords in Bryson City, a small but lively town on the banks of the Tuckasegee River. The elevation is about 1,800 ft, but only an hour's drive away the Smoky Mountains rise to more than 6,000 ft. Here you have access to some of the largest expanses of wilderness in the eastern United States.

Information: Swain County Chamber of Commerce | Box 509, Bryson City, 28713 | 828/ 488–3681 or 800/867–9246 | chamber@greatsmokies.com | www.greatsmokies.com.

Attractions

Great Smoky Mountains Railroad. Excursions of diesel-electric or steam trains take passengers through river gorges, across valleys, and through tunnels cut out of mountains. The open-sided cars are ideal for picture-taking. Dinner and holiday trips are available as well. | 119 Front St., Dillsboro | 828/586–8811 or 800/872–4681, ext. R | $20–$50 | Apr.–Dec.; call for schedule.

Nantahala River. A favorite with thousands of rafters and kayakers in search of white water, this scenic river, with its clear and very cold water, rushes through the Nantahala National Forest. | 828/488–3681 or 800/867–9246 | Free | Daily.

ON THE CALENDAR
JULY: *Folkmoot USA.* Groups from different countries travel throughout western North Carolina performing in native costumes. This festival at Swain County High School (1415 Fontana Road) showcases folk music, dance, and culture from around the world. | 828/ 488–3681 or 800/867–9246.
JULY: *Singing in the Smokies.* Nationally known gospel-music groups take the stage for this extravaganza at Inspiration Park, Exit 69 off U.S. 74 West. | 828/497–2060.
SEPT.: *Fireman's Day Festival.* A day and evening of music, entertainment, and crafts are on tap at this event sponsored by the local fire department, downtown on the square. | 828/488–9410.
OCT.: *Chili Cook-Off.* Teams of chili chefs compete for trophies, and as expected, there is lots of spicy food. This cooking happens at Bryson City Train Depot, Great Smoky Mountains Railroad, 119 Front Street. | 828/488–3681 or 800/867–9246.
DEC.: *Christmas Parade.* Floats, bands, horses, and clowns march in the holidays downtown. | 828/488–3681 or 800/867–9246.

Dining
Bar-B-Que Wagon. Barbecue. This casual, almost rustic spot serves Southern-style barbecue, specializing in pork sandwiches and rib tips. | U.S. 19 | 828/488–9521 | $5–$10 | No credit cards.

Hemlock Inn. Contemporary. On a small mountain overlooking three valleys, you get one-price, all-you-can-eat meals prepared with regional foods, including locally grown fruits and vegetables and mountain honey. Homemade yeast rolls and desserts round out the menu. | 911 Galbraith Creek Rd. | 828/488–2885 | Reservations essential | $15 | D, MC, V | Closed Nov.–Apr. No lunch Mon.–Sat., no supper Sun.

Nantahala Village Restaurant. American. This rock-and-cedar restaurant with front-porch rocking chairs has a menu that includes trout, chicken, and country ham, as well as some vegetarian dishes. An item to try is wild forest pasta. Sunday brunch serves up a few surprises like huevos rancheros and eggs Benedict. | 9400 U.S. 19 W | 828/488–2826 or 800/ 438–1507 | $10–$20 | D, MC, V | Closed Jan–Feb.

Lodging

Budget Host Inn Bryson City. Between Turkey and Bryson City (5 mi either way) and 20 minutes from whitewater rafting sits this 1950s style, single-story wood building with a wood interior. Rooms overlook the pool, and some face the river. Wallpaper and paint are light and bright; some walls have wood paneling. Picnic area. Cable TV. Pool. | 5280 Ela Rd. | 828/488–2284 | 21 rooms, 1 cottage | $36–$85, $120–$175 cottage | D, MC, V | Closed Nov.–May.

Chalet Inn. The German and Swiss influences are unmistakable; this is a Gasthaus down to the hand-carved woodwork. Rooms are European in style with authentic German pictures. One room is Dutch-style. Picnic area. Complimentary breakfast. No room phones. Driving range, putting green. No smoking. | 285 Lone Oak Dr., Whittier | 828/586–0251 or 800/789–8024 | fax 828/586–0257 | paradisefound@chaletinn.com | www.chaletinn.com | 4 rooms (2 with shower only), 2 suites | $82–$112, $130–$160 suites | MC, V.

Charleston Inn. The Victorian guest rooms in this 1920s home have hotel-quality bedding, air conditioning, and ceiling fans. The inn also includes a parlor with fireplace, a piano, an enclosed porch where you can watch movies, plus gardens and fountains. There's a TV in the common area. Complimentary breakfast. Some in-room hot tubs. Business services. No smoking. | 208 Arlington St. | 828/488–4644 or 888/285–1555 | fax 828/488–9459 | www.charlestoninn.com | 18 rooms | $89–$145 | AE, D, MC, V.

Folkestone Inn. Just ¼ mi from Great Smoky Mountains National Park, this inn was originally a 1920s mountain farmhouse. All rooms have private baths. Upstairs rooms have private balconies with views of the mountains, while the downstairs rooms have flagstone floors and pressed-tin ceilings. Picnic area. Complimentary breakfast. No room phones. Business services. | 101 Folkestone Rd. | 828/488–2730 or 888/812–3385 | fax 828/488–0722 | innkeeper@folkestone.com | www.folkestone.com | 10 rooms | $82–$108 | AE, D, MC, V.

Hemlock. The inn is built on a small mountain overlooking three valleys. This place emphasizes gracious hospitality. Breakfast and dinner are included in the room rates. Dining room. Some kitchenettes in cottages. | On Galbraith Creek Rd. off US 19S | 828/488–2885 | www.innbook.com/hemlock.html | 22 rooms, 3 cottages (1–3 bedrooms) | $137–$237, $142–$186 cottages | D, MC, V | Closed Nov.–mid-Apr. | MAP.

Randolph House Country Inn. This massive, turn-of-the-20th-century, 10-bedroom mansion (7 of which are rented) is owned by the third generation of the family that built it. Hearty breakfasts of bacon, country ham, grits, buttermilk biscuits from scratch, and more will get you ready for a day of antiquing in town. Restaurant. Breakfast and dinner included with lodging. Cable TV in common room. Some private baths. | 223 Fryemont Rd. | 828/488–3472 or 800/480–3472 | 7 rooms, 1 cottage | $75–$150, $160 cottage (3–day minimum stay) | MAP | AE, D, MC, V | Nov.–Mar.

BURLINGTON

MAP 8, G4

(Nearby towns also listed: Chapel Hill, Durham, Greensboro)

Because it's midway between the Blue Ridge Mountains in the west and the Atlantic to the east, Burlington, a part of the growing Piedmont Triad area (Greensboro, Winston-Salem, High Point), is a popular stopover. A multitude of outlet stores along I–40/85 attract bargain hunters. But there's a lot of history here as well, including Revolutionary War sites and the birthplace of the "Great Awakening," an evangelical movement that swept the South in the early 1800s.

Information: Burlington-Alamance County Convention and Visitors Bureau | Drawer 519, Burlington, 27216 | 336/570–1444 or 800/637–3804 | visitor@netpath.net.

Attractions

Alamance Battleground State Historic Site. This is a primary Revolutionary War site. It was here in 1771 that royal governor William Tryon led the North Carolina militia against the Regulators. There is a visitor center, an audiovisual program, exhibits, monuments, and a picnic area. | 5803 Rte. 62 S | 336/227–4785 | fax 336/227–4787 | Free | Apr.–Oct., Mon.–Sat. 9–5, Sun. 1–5; Nov.–Mar., Tues.–Sat. 10–4, Sun. 1–4.

Alamance County Historical Museum. This is a 19th-century house museum depicting the life of textile pioneer Edwin Michael Holt through period rooms, docent-hosted tours, and an audiovisual presentation. The upper floor includes rotating and permanent exhibits devoted to all aspects of local history. | Rte. 62 S | 336/226–8254 | Free | Tues.–Fri., 9–5, Sat. 10:30–5, Sun. 1–5.

Burlington Manufacturers Outlet Center. A shopper's dream, this is one of the state's largest outlet centers, with more than 75 factory outlet and designer stores. | I–85 Exit 145 | 336/227–2872 | Free | Mon.–Sat. 10–9, Sun. 1–6.

Dentzel Menagerie Carousel. The centerpiece of a 76-acre park, the carousel was restored in 1985. It has 46 hand-carved animals, and no two are alike. | S. Church St. (U.S. 70) | 336/222–5030 | fax 336/229–3106 | 50¢ | Call for hours.

ON THE CALENDAR

APR.: *Uncle Eli's Quilting Party.* Ladies of the rural Eli Whitney Community hold a quilting bee with hands-on demonstrations of various quilting and tatting techniques. There are displays of heritage quilts, as well as a potluck meal. The party is at Eli Whitney Community Center, Route 87 South, Exit 147. | 336/376–3149.

MAY: *Hospice League Horizons Balloon Fest and Airshow.* Dozens of hot-air balloons highlight the second-largest balloon festival in the Southeast and the largest in North Carolina. Daredevil air shows, arts and crafts, food, rides, games, and ground displays round out the agenda at the Burlington–Alamance Regional Airport, Route 62, ½ mi south of Interstate 40/85. | 336/538–8048.

JUNE–AUG.: *The Sword of Peace.* Quakers during the American Revolution are the subject of this outdoor drama at Historic Snow Camp Outdoor Theatre, 1 Drama Road, Route 49 Exit 145. | 336/376–6948 or 800/726–5115.

NOV.: *Molasses Festival.* Demonstrations on making molasses, apple butter, and apple cider whet the appetite at Historic Snow Camp Outdoor Theatre, 1 Drama Road, Route 49 Exit 145. | 336/376–6948.

Dining

Boston Sandwich Shop. American. All the standard sandwiches are available on several types of bread. Each sandwich is made to order, and vegetarian items are available. | 238 W. Front St. | 336/226–0266 | $4–$6 | No credit cards.

Hursey's Pig Pickin' Bar-B-Q. Barbecue. Drive-through and carry-out service are available, and items to try include homemade Brunswick stew, roasted chicken, and fruit cobblers. Kids' menu. | 1834 S. Church St. | 336/226–1695 | Reservations not accepted | $5–$9 | MC, V | Closed Sun.

Saffron. Continental. Country French with a Mediterranean influence, this restaurant completes the scene with candlelight, white linen, and recorded jazz. Specialties are prime beef, fowl, seafood, veal, and venison. The menu also includes pan-seared breast of Peking duck with asparagus, toasted almond saffron risotto, and Godiva-chocolate, dried-cherry bread pudding with Bailey's Irish Cream caramel sauce. Will prepare child-size meals. | 3328 S. Church St. | 336/585–1308 | $14–$32 | AE, MC, V | Closed Sun. No lunch.

Sidetrack Grill. American/Casual. This quiet side-street eatery is in an older building with dark wood and is popular with everyone from retirees to college students. The place is known for grilled fish, pastas, and fruit cobblers. Homemade soups, salads, and specialty sandwiches are favorites at lunchtime, while chicken, pork, and rib-eye steak are dinner-menu

standards. Kids' menu. Beer and wine only. | 110 W. Lebanon Ave., Elon College | 336/584–1769 | Reservations not accepted | $7–$17 | MC, V | Closed Sun. and late Dec.–Jan.

Lodging

Burke Manor Inn. A gigantic wraparound front porch is the focal point of this B&B 7 mi east of downtown Burlington. This place serves afternoon tea and an evening snack. Complimentary breakfast. In-room data ports. Cable TV, in-room VCRs. Outdoor pool. Outdoor hot tub, business services. | 303 Burke St., Gibsonville | 336/449–6266 or 888/287–5311 | fax 336/449–9440 | vbrady836@aol.com | 9 rooms | $90–$118 | AE, MC, V.

Burlington Comfort Inn. Burlington Manufacturers Outlet Center is within walking distance of this typical chain hotel on a main interstate highway. The two-story building is brick with outside entrances to the rooms. The rooms are in light and neutral colors. Complimentary Continental breakfast. Some refrigerators. Cable TV. Pool, wading pool. Laundry facilities. Business services. Some pets allowed. | 978 Plantation Dr. | 336/227–3681 | fax 336/570–0900 | 127 rooms | $66 | AE, D, DC, MC, V.

Hampton Inn. Rooms have safari themes at this hotel in a commercial area near Burlington Outlet Mall and about 50 other outlet stores. Complimentary Continental breakfast. Cable TV. Pool. Hot tub. Exercise equipment. Business services. | 2701 Kirkpatrick Rd. | 336/584–4447 | fax 336/721–1325 | 116 rooms | $72 | AE, D, DC, MC, V.

Kirk's Motor Court. Decor varies from room to room, from French provincial to modern, and colors are rich and bright at this two-story hotel near a miniature golf course and the bowling alley. Some kitchenettes. Cable TV. Pool. Business services. | 1155 N. Church St. | 336/228–1383 | fax 336/228–9786 | 102 rooms | $46–$56 | MC, V.

Ramada Inn Burlington. This hotel is near shops, outlets, and restaurants. There is a view of the highway. Rooms have pool views, and color schemes include burgundy, green, and blue. Restaurant, bar. Cable TV. Pool. Business services. | 2703 Ramada Rd. | 336/227–5541 | fax 336/570–2701 | 138 rooms | $65–$85 | AE, D, DC, MC, V.

Red Roof Inn. Antiques stores and outlet malls are within 5 mi of this motel that provides basic accommodations. Complimentary Continental breakfast. Cable TV. Pool. Business services. | 2133 W. Hanford Rd. | 336/227–1270 | fax 336/227–1702 | 121 rooms | $65 | AE, D, DC, MC, V.

Victorian Rose B&B. Just a couple of minutes away in Graham is the Victorian Rose, a three-story mansion dating from 1885. You can enjoy the gazebo with swing, porch with rocking chairs, a hammock in the yard, gardens, and one of eight guest rooms, all with private baths. Complimentary breakfast. Cable TV in common area. | 407 Graham Rd., Graham | 336/578–5112 or 888/767–3841 | fax 336/578–9918 | vicrose@netpath.net | 8 rooms | $85–$125 | AE, MC, V.

BURNSVILLE

MAP 8, B4

(Nearby towns also listed: Blue Ridge Parkway, Little Switzerland)

Yancey County, home to Burnsville, has the highest average elevation of any county in North Carolina. Within its boundaries are five of the highest peaks east of the Mississippi River, including Mt. Mitchell, the highest point in eastern America at 6,684 ft, and Grandfather Mountain, one of the most environmentally significant mountains in the world.

Information: Yancey County Chamber of Commerce | 106 W. Main St., Burnsville, 28714 | 828/682–7413 or 800/948–1632 | sharding@yanceychamber.com | www.yanceychamber.com.

Attractions

Mt. Mitchell State Park. Mt. Mitchell is the highest peak (6,684 ft) in the eastern United States. There's easy access to the park from the Blue Ridge Parkway. A restaurant, a museum, tent camping (fee), and picnic areas are available. Hiking trails connect the park with Pisgah National Forest. Look for the grave marker next to the observation tower. | Rte. 5, Box 700, Burnsville | 828/675–4611 | fax 828/675–9655 | ils.unc.edu/parkproject/momi.html | Free | Office daily 8–5; park daily 8 AM–9 PM.

ON THE CALENDAR

JULY: *Old-Fashioned July 4th on the Square.* Wagon trains parade through Town Square in this celebration that also includes crafts, food, and mountain music. | 828/682–7413 or 800/948–1632.
AUG.: *Mount Mitchell Crafts Fair.* Traditional mountain crafts, food, and music take up residence on the grass of Town Square. | 828/682–7413 or 800/948–1632.
SEPT.: *Folk Music Festival.* Mountain folk music and food are on the menu at Toe River Campground Park on Blur Rock Road. | 828/682–7215.

Dining

Li'l Smoky Drive In and Restaurant. American. Here is a chance to sample country-style dining at a small building with windows all around. This spot is known for hamburgers, hot dogs, and daily specials ranging from spaghetti to hamburger steak. Sun. brunch. Also open for breakfast. | 702 E. Main St. | 828/682–6802 | Reservations not accepted | $5–$7 | No credit cards.

Mount Mitchell View Restaurant. American. Photos of stock-car drivers adorn the walls of this restaurant done in autumn colors and with a NASCAR motif. The menu includes sandwiches, homemade hamburgers, fried seafood, grilled lemon-herb chicken, and daily specials such as country ham and barbecue. Kids' menu. Also open for breakfast. | 7989 Rte. 80 S | 828/675–9599 | Reservations not accepted | $6–$8 | No credit cards | Closed Sun.

Lodging

A Little Bit of Heaven B&B. Three miles east of Burnsville, this house sits at an elevation of 3,000 ft, on two acres next to the South Toe River valley and Pisgah National Forest. You can enjoy the mountain views or sit by the giant stone fireplace in the living room. Guest rooms are eclectic in style, and all have private baths. The large breakfast includes homemade bread, coffee cake, and fresh fruit. Complimentary breakfast. | 937 Bear Wallow Rd. | 828/675–5379 | fax 828/675–0364 | www.inngetaways.net/nc/features/alittle.html | 4 rooms | $70–$85 | MC, V.

Nu-Wray Inn. O. Henry, Thomas Wolfe, and Elvis Presley all slept in this 3-story country inn (circa 1833) that is filled with antiques and family memorabilia. It is registered as a National Historic Landmark. Most rooms have cable TV. Dining room, complimentary breakfast. No room phones. | Town Square | 828/682–2329 or 800/368–9729 | fax 828/682–2661 | 25 rooms | $75–$99 | AE, D, MC, V.

BUXTON

MAP 8, L5

(Nearby towns also listed: Cape Hatteras National Seashore, Hatteras, Ocracoke, Outer Banks)

While you're heading south along Hatteras Island, a winding drive leads you into the Outer Banks town of Buxton. It's full of quiet, family attractions, including brush-covered sand dunes and surf, fishing, the tallest brick lighthouse in the world, a Civil War ironclad shipwreck, and nature trails.

Information: **Dare County Tourist Bureau** | 704 S. U.S. 64, Manteo 27954 | 252/473–2138 or 800/446–6262 | visitinfo@outerbanks.org | www.outerbanks.org.

Attractions

Cape Hatteras Lighthouse. You can climb to the top of this 208-ft lighthouse, which sits 1,600 ft from the waterline. Offshore lie the remains of the *Monitor,* a Union vessel that fought the Confederate *Merrimack* in the first battle of ironclad vessels—and sank in 1862. The visitor center here has information on the national seashore. | Hatteras Island Visitor Center, off Rte. 12, Buxton | 252/995–4474 | $2 | Easter–Labor Day, daily 10–4.

ON THE CALENDAR

SEPT.: *Eastern Surfing Championships.* Only Eastern Surfing Championship Association members are allowed to compete in this event at the Buxton beach. But you can watch, and there are always large crowds. | 252/995–5785 or 800/937–4733.
NOV.: *Invitation Inter-Club Surf Fishing Tournament and Open Invitation Tournament.* Anglers of all skill levels gather and hope to catch the big one at the Buxton beach. | 252/995–4253.

Dining

Diamond Shoals Restaurant. Seafood. Serving a variety of local seafood as well as porterhouse and other steaks, this restaurant is known for formal food in a tourist-friendly, casual environment. | 46843 Rte. 12 | 252/995–5217 | $8–$15 | AE, D, MC, V.

Fish House. Seafood. This dockside spot is casual enough to have plastic tableware. Expect friendly service and large servings of fresh fried seafood, pastas, and steaks. Known for its crab cakes as well as its linguini with clams and mussels, steamed with olive oil, garlic, and basil. Kids' menu. | 27920 Rte. 12 S | 252/995–5151 | Reservations not accepted | $7–$19 | AE, D, DC, MC, V | Closed mid-Nov.–Easter.

Tides. Seafood. Locals gather in this family spot for crab cakes or the "tidal wave," which includes fresh local shrimp, scallops, fish of the day, and a homemade crab cake. Steaks, chicken, and other seafood are also on the menu. Breakfasts are good, too. The tables have paper placemats, and art by local artists adorns the walls. Beer and wine only. | 47048 Rte. 12 | 252/995–5988 | Reservations not accepted | $10–$20 | MC, V | Closed Dec.–Mar. No lunch.

Lodging

Cape Hatteras. Seven separate cedar-sided buildings make up this motel. It has oceanfront units, as well as some across the street from the beach, overlooking Pamlico Sound. There's a restaurant on premises, and kitchens are available in some units. Town houses can be rented by the week in summer. Some kitchenettes. Cable TV, no room phones. Pool. Hot tub. Laundry facilities. No pets. | Rte. 12 | 252/995–5611 or 800/995–0711 | 35 rooms in 7 buildings | $112–$195 rooms, $1463/wk town house | AE, D, MC, V.

Cape Hatteras B&B. Literally in the shadow of the Cape Hatteras Lighthouse, this small inn is just 500 ft from the beach. You can sit by the fireplace in the spacious lobby or on the large sundeck. Rooms are named after famous hurricanes. You can borrow beach chairs and bicycles. Complimentary breakfast. Beach, bicycles. No pets. No smoking. | 46223 Old Lighthouse Rd. | 252/995–6004 or 800/252–3316 | fax 252/995–3002 | 9 rooms, 1 suite | 9 rooms | $69–$109 | MC, V | Closed mid-Dec.–Mar.

Castaways Oceanfront Inn. People come to this secluded, family hotel to get away. All rooms have private balconies and a view of the water. Dining room, picnic area. Minibars, refrigerators. Cable TV. Pool. Hot tub. Beach. Game room with pool table. No pets. | Rte. 12, Avon | 252/995–4444 or 800/845–6070 | fax 252/995–5305 | www.lfwcorp.com/castaway.htm | 66 rooms | $29–$119 | AE, D, DC, MC, V | Closed mid-Dec.–mid-Jan.

Comfort Inn. This chain motel with bright rooms is about 200 yards from the beach and 1 mi from the Cape Hatteras Lighthouse. Complimentary Continental breakfast. In-room data ports, refrigerators. Cable TV. Pool. Laundry service. Business services. No pets. | Rte. 12 and Old Lighthouse Rd. | 252/995–6100 | fax 252/995–5444 | 60 rooms | $129–$149 | AE, D, DC, MC, V.

Falcon Motel. Designed for anglers and their families, this motel on Pamlico Sound has access to a boat ramp and fish-cleaning facilities. Rooms are large and bright, and each has a desk. There's a wide, covered porch, plus a shaded picnic area with barbecue grills. It's 1 mi from the beach and the lighthouse. Picnic area. Some kitchenettes, some refrigerators. Cable TV, no room phones. Pool. Bikes available. No pets. | 46854 Rte. 12 | 252/995–5968 or 800/635–6911 | fax 252/995–7803 | www.outer-banks.com/falconmotel | 35 rooms | $39–$75 | MC, V | Closed mid-Dec.–Mar.

Pamlico Inn. All four guest rooms at this seaside inn have queen beds, private baths, and large picture windows with views of the sea. Besides relaxing in the comfortable home or the hot tub, you can use the private beach. Complimentary breakfast. Cable TV. Hot tub. Beach. | 49684 Rte. 12 S | 919/995–6980 or 888/862–7547 | fax 919/995–6979 | 4 rooms | $75–$125 | MC, V | Closed Dec.–Mar.

CAPE HATTERAS NATIONAL SEASHORE

MAP 8, L5

CAPE HATTERAS
NATIONAL
SEASHORE

INTRO
ATTRACTIONS
DINING
LODGING

(Nearby towns also listed: Buxton, Duck, Hatteras, Kill Devil Hills, Manteo, Nags Head, Ocracoke, Outer Banks)

★ This first seashore to be added to the national park system has more than 70 mi of unspoiled beaches—from wild to more developed—stretching from south Nags Head to Ocracoke Inlet across three narrow islands: Bodie, Hatteras, and Ocracoke. Route 12 and the Hatteras Inlet ferry link the islands.

You can swim, surf, windsurf, dive, and boat, but beware of the strong and unpredictable currents—there are no lifeguard stations. There are fishing piers in Rodanthe, Avon, and Frisco.

Information: Cape Hatteras National Park | Rte. 1, Box 675, Manteo 27954 | 252/473–2111 | www.nps.gov/caha.

ON THE CALENDAR

JUNE–AUG.: *Fish With A Ranger.* Join a ranger from the National Park Service at 8 AM on Tuesday or Thursday morning throughout the summer to learn the art of surf fishing on Hatteras Island. Only 15 people are allowed per session, so advance reservations are a good idea. | 252/473–5772.

Dining

Down Under. Seafood. On the pier at Hatteras Island Resort, this spot is known for some of the best fried shrimp on Hatteras, and you'll also find ocean views and a very casual atmosphere. À la Australia, try spicy fish burgers and the "Great Australian Bite"—a beef burger with fried egg, grilled onions, cheese, and bacon. | Rodanthe Pier, Rte. 12, Rodanthe | 252/987–2277 | $11–$16 | AE, MC, V | Closed Dec.–Mar.

Quarterdeck. Seafood. You'll find all varieties of local fish and shellfish at this unpretentious local favorite. Try the crab cakes with jumbo crab, flounder, or the fish of the day. | Rte. 12, Frisco | 252/986–2425 | Reservations not accepted | $10–$19 | D, MC, V | Closed late Nov.–mid-Mar.

Lodging

Seaside Inn. This first hotel on Hatteras Island has been refurbished into a B&B, where some rooms are light and airy while others have classic tongue-and-groove pine paneling. Rooms have private baths, and some have hot tubs. The pace is casual, and from here you can enjoy the scenery as well as the area's swimming, fishing, surfing, bicycling, and canoeing. Complimentary breakfast. Some in-room hot tubs. Cable TV. Beach. | 57303 Rte. 12, Hatteras | 252/986–2700 | www.seasidebb.com | 10 rooms | $85–$150, $65–$95 off–season | MC, V.

CARY

MAP 8, G4

(Nearby towns also listed: Chapel Hill, Durham, Pittsboro, Raleigh)

At the beginning of the 1900s, Cary was a little village that served as a railway center and had one of the best co-ed boarding schools on the East coast. That school would become the state's first public school. Today, given Cary's proximity to Research Triangle Park, area universities, and the Raleigh-Durham International Airport, it's one of the fastest-growing cities in North Carolina. Downtown is still a small square of service shops, but the town has an extensive system of parks and greenways, and its shopping centers attract people from miles around.

Information: Cary Chamber of Commerce | Box 4351, 27519 | 919/467–1016. **Visitor Center** | 307 N. Academy St. | 919/467–1016 | cnorman@carychamber.com | www.carychamber.com.

Attractions

Fred G. Bond Metro Park. The largest municipal park in Wake County has 310 acres with picnic shelters, athletic fields, a fishing and recreational lake, boat rentals, fitness and hiking trails, an outdoor amphitheater, and a playground. | 801 High House Rd. | 919/469–4100 | Free | Daily 9–6.

Hemlock Bluffs Nature Preserve. Cool, north-facing bluffs sit on the roughly 150 acres along Swift Creek. Growing on the bluffs are Canadian hemlocks and other vegetation that's typically 200 mi away in the Appalachian Mountains. A 2-mi system of walking trails includes observation decks overlooking scenic areas. Nature programs take place in the park at the Stevens Nature Center. | 2616 Kildaire Farm Rd. | 919/387–5980 | Free | Grounds daily 9–sunset; nature center Mon.–Sat. 10–7, Sun. 1–7.

Page–Walker Arts and History Center. Built in 1868 by Cary's founding family, the Pages, the building was sold to the Walkers and used as a hotel for train travelers. Later, this Second Empire–style building was a boardinghouse and then a private residence. Today it has classes and performances of all kinds. Art exhibits in the main gallery on the first floor change monthly. On the third floor is the Cary Museum, which gives, via multimedia exhibits and artifacts, the story of the area from Colonial times to the present. | 119 Ambassador Loop | 919/460–4963 | Free | Mon.–Wed. 10–9:30, Thurs. 10–5, Fri. 10–1.

ON THE CALENDAR

APR.: *Spring Daze.* Local artisans display and sell their work at Page–Walker Arts and History Center; the festival includes food and entertainment. | 919/469–4061.

MAY: *Peak Week Festival.* A weeklong series of activities in downtown Apex, including a gospel sing and a golf tournament, that culminates in a street festival with arts and crafts, food, and entertainment for all ages. | 919/362–6456.

JUN.–MID-JULY: *Summerfest.* The North Carolina Symphony plays concerts with a variety of guest artists. Performances run through mid–July at a lakeside amphitheater in Regency Park, at the intersection of U.S. 1 south and U.S. 64 west. | 919/733–2750.

AUG.: *Jimmy V Celebrity Golf Classic.* Greats and near-greats from the world of sports and entertainment draw crowds during their visit to Cary for a weekend of golf, tennis, parties, and concerts at the Prestonwood Country Club. Money goes to cancer research. | 300 Prestonwood Pkwy. | 919/319–0441.

AUG.: *Lazy Daze Arts and Crafts Festival.* Artists and craftspeople from around the country exhibit their work in this juried show, held on Academy and Chatham Streets. With food vendors and live entertainment, the festival draws tens of thousands of people to downtown Cary on the fourth Saturday of the month. | 919/469–4061.

SEPT.: *Today and Yesteryear Festival.* The day starts with a pancake breakfast, then builds with arts and crafts, antiques, Civil War reenactments, music, entertainment, and food in downtown Apex. A charity bingo game is held the night before the festival. | 919/387–9550.

NOV.: *Cary Band Day.* A lengthy parade through downtown Cary kicks off the longest-running high-school marching band competition in the Southeast. Following this are various competitions at Cary High School, including field shows, music, marching, and drum lines. | 919/460–3572.

Dining

Chef John Café. Contemporary. The landscapes and accessories that fill this tiny storefront are vaguely reminiscent of the Mediterranean. This place is known for crab cakes, blackened salmon, pastas, and enormous fruit cobblers, and you can also try shrimp brochettes with apples and Thai dipping sauce. There's open-air dining on the sidewalk. | 969 N. Harrison Ave. | 919/462–0500 | $10–$30 | AE, MC, V | Closed Sun. No lunch Sat.

Coyote Café. Southwestern. Bandanas on tabletops add the final touch to the Western theme set up by the desert sunset hues of the walls and upholstery. Fresh, authentic ingredients are a priority. You can try gulf shrimp grilled in garlic and lime, and chicken breast stuffed with jack cheese and covered with tomatillo sauce. There's an umbrella-topped picnic table on the patio and live music on weekends in summer. Kids' menu. | 1014 Ryan Rd. | 919/469–5253 | $9–$20 | AE, DC, MC, V | No lunch Sat.–Mon.

Fox and Hound Restaurant and Pub. English. The dark wood and framed literary prints turn this into something of a British pub. Food ranges from British, Irish, and Scottish pub grub to more daring dishes. You can try shepherd's pie, spiced venison, or trout stuffed with bacon, onion, and smoked Gouda. There's an excellent bar with a large selection of draft beers and single-malt Scotches, and in nice weather you can eat on the tiny, covered patio. Live music on Thursday nights. Kids' menu. | 107 Edinburgh Dr., Suite 119 | 919/380–0080 | $8–$23 | AE, D, DC, MC, V | No lunch Sun.

Gypsy's Shiny Diner. American. This chrome-plated diner à la 1950s has Formica tables, plastic seats, and tabletop jukeboxes, and comes complete with a friendly staff. It's known for the classics like blue-plate specials, burgers, sandwiches, and milk shakes. It is also open for breakfast. Kids' menu. | 1550 Buck Jones Rd. | 919/469–3663 | Reservations not accepted | $3–$7 | No credit cards.

Il Sogno. Italian. The storefront, filled with white tablecloths and blue, black, and silver accents, is sleek and contemporary, but the friendly hosts make you feel at home. Known for veal Portobello, gnocchi, and calamari. Kids' menu. | 1301–03 N.W. Maynard Rd. | 919/469–6600 | $9–$20 | AE, DC, MC, V | Closed Sun. No lunch Sat.

Jasper's. American. Large and inventive burgers are king in this comfortable, casual place. A specialty is the kahuna burger, which is blackened and topped with guacamole, sour cream, and finely diced jalapeño peppers. Many pasta dishes are also on the menu. Kids' menu. Sun. brunch. | 4300 N.W. Cary Pkwy. | 919/319–3400 | Reservations not accepted weekends | $7–$15 | AE, MC, V.

Kabuki. Japanese. Oversize photographs of Kabuki theater scenes loom over a dramatic black-and-white color scheme and a large sushi bar. Known for chicken, seafood, steak, vegetables, rice, and noodles in many combinations—and cooked on a grill right in front of you. Kids' menu. | 220 Nottingham Dr. | 919/380–8081 | $7–$13 | AE, D, DC, MC, V | No lunch Sat.

The King and I. Thai. Find an extensive menu of authentic dishes in a simple space with linen tablecloths, a painted-glass ceiling light and a fountain. Try the spicy fish—deep-fried whole red snapper topped with a spicy pepper basil sauce. | 926 N.E. Maynard Rd. | 919/460–9265 | $13–$26 | AE, MC, V | Closed Sun. No lunch Sat.

Ruth's Chris Steak House. Steak. Dark wood and cut glass make you think you're walking into a VIP club. This place is known for large, expertly cooked steaks that they serve very hot, as well as potatoes and other sides prepared in a number of innovative ways. | 1130 Buck Jones Rd. | 919/468–1133 | $18–$31 | AE, D, MC, V | No lunch.

Semolina. Eclectic. If you get tired of looking at the columned dining area or the reproductions of famous art with pasta inserted in key places, you can check out what's happening in the open kitchen. Known for pasta of all ethnic persuasions, as well as pan-seared veal and chicken dishes. Try the chicken enchilada pasta. | 1144 Kildaire Farm Rd. | 919/462–0444 | $8–$14 | AE, D, DC, MC, V.

Spartacus Grill. Greek. Columns, grape vines, and Greek music evoke the Mediterranean. So does the food. Try lamb kleftico, slow-cooked on the shank. Kids' menu. Sun. brunch. | 104-A New Waverly Rd. | 919/852–5050 | $10–$15 | AE, D, DC, MC, V | Closed Mon.

35 Chinese Restaurant. Chinese. Pink and black accents, silk trees, fish tanks, and a small waterfall and stream run through this traditional restaurant. An extensive and popular buffet, open every day for lunch and dinner, has items from many of China's 35 provinces, including citrus chicken and smoky lo mein noodles. Kids' menu. | 1135 Kildaire Farm Rd. | 919/467–4262 | $8–$20 | AE, D, MC, V.

Tony's Bourbon Street Oyster Bar. Cajun/Creole. You can find festive New Orleans in North Carolina with the red walls and Mardi Gras masks here. Known for Louisiana crab cakes, jambalaya, and crawfish étouffée. Raw bar. Live music (usually blues) Fri.–Sat. evenings. | 107 Edinburgh Dr., Suite 129 | 919/462–6226 | $12–$24 | AE, D, DC, MC, V | No Lunch.

Torero's. Mexican. Among the happy chaos of Mexican hangings and wall paintings, you'll find a good selection of dishes and generous portions. Adding real noise to visual noise, TVs in the bar area are tuned to Spanish-language stations. Known for flautas, taquitos, and spinach enchiladas. Kids' menu. | 1207-C Kildaire Farm Rd. | 919/468–8711 | $7–$13 | AE, D, DC, MC, V.

Lodging

Best Western Inn and Suites. This hotel, 15 minutes from Research Triangle Park and North Carolina State University, has an outdoor pool and workout facilities. Standard rooms come with a hair dryer and coffeemaker; two-room suites include microwaves, refrigerators and 25-inch TVs. Some microwaves, some refrigerators. Cable TV. Outdoor pool. Outdoor hot tub, exercise equipment. | 1722 Walnut St. | 919/481–1200 or 800/227–9466 | fax 919/467–7535 | 140 rooms, 42 suites | $59–$99 | AE, DC, D, MC, V.

Comfort Suites. The suites at this hotel come with a kitchenette, two phones, T1 access to the Internet, and a Sony Play Station video game unit. The indoor pool overlooks majestic pine trees. Complimentary Continental breakfast. In-room data ports, kitchenettes. Cable TV. Indoor pool. Exercise equipment. Business services. | 350 Asheville Ave. | 919/852–4318 | 122 rooms | $69–$109 | AE, DC, D, MC, V.

Courtyard by Marriott. Just off U.S. 1 and 6 mi from I–40, this motor inn is adjacent to the MacGregor Village Shopping Center. It's across the street from a golf course and the Silver Lake Water Park. Some rooms overlook the courtyard and pool; most have balconies. Bar. In-room data ports, some refrigerators. Cable TV. Pool. Hot tub. Gym. Laundry facilities, laundry service. Business services. No pets. No-smoking floors. | 102 Edinburgh Dr. S | 919/481–9666 or 800/321–2211 | fax 919/460–0380 | courtyard.com | 149 rooms | $55–$104 | AE, D, DC, MC, V.

Courtyard by Marriott–Airport. A fireplace in the lobby welcomes you to this mostly business hotel. It's 3 mi from the Research Triangle Park and ¼ mi from Triangle Factory Outlet Mall, a major upscale outlet mall. Some rooms have balconies. Restaurant, dining room, complimentary Continental breakfast. In-room data ports, refrigerators (in suites). Cable TV. Pool. Hot tub. Exercise equipment. Laundry facilities. Business services. Airport shuttle. No pets. No-smoking rooms. | 2001 Hospitality Ct., Morrisville | 919/467–9444 or 800/321–2211 | fax 919/467–9332 | courtyard.com | 152 rooms, 12 suites | $122 rooms, $139 suite | AE, D, DC, MC, V.

Embassy Suites–Airport. Four miles from the Raleigh-Durham International Airport, and 15 mi from the Research Triangle Park, you'll find this classic, businessperson's hotel. All rooms face the atrium, filled with a waterfall, plants, and a small stream with fish. Rooms have video-game play stations. No-smoking rooms are available. Restaurant, bar, complimentary breakfast. Some microwaves, some refrigerators. Cable TV. Indoor pool. Hot tub. 2 tennis courts. Gym. Laundry service. Business services. Airport shuttle. No pets. | 201 Harrison Oaks Blvd. | 919/677–1840 or 800/362–2779 | fax 919/677–1841 | 273 rooms | $159–$250 | AE, D, DC, MC, V.

Hampton Inn–Airport. Business travelers like this hotel because the Raleigh-Durham International Airport is only 1 mi away. Complimentary Continental breakfast. Satellite TV. Pool. Laundry service. Airport shuttle. No-smoking rooms. | 1010 Airport Blvd., Morrisville | 919/462–1620 | fax 919/462–3217 | 102 rooms | $69–$105 | AE, D, DC, MC, V.

Hampton Inn and Suites. This light and modern family hotel is 6 mi from the Raleigh Entertainment and Sports Arena and 3 mi from the state fairgrounds. No-smoking floors are available. Complimentary Continental breakfast. Cable TV. Pool. Gym. Baby-sitting. Laundry service. Business services. No pets. | 111 Hampton Woods La. | 919/233–1798 or 800/426–7866 | fax 919/854–1166 | www.hamptoninn-suites.com | 123 rooms | $89–$139 | AE, D, DC, MC, V.

Holiday Inn & Suites Cary. This basic business hotel has some romantic touches: you can sign up for the hot-tub suite or enjoy the romance of the fireplace in the lounge. Restaurant, bar, room service. In-room data ports, some in-room hot tubs. Cable TV. Laundry service. Business services. | 5630 Dillard Dr. | 128 rooms | $65–$119 | AE, DC, D, MC, V.

Homewood Suites. Although this is behind MacGregor Village Shopping Center, it's in a semi-secluded wooded area. Earth tones in the rooms accent the nature outside. There are videos for rent and no-smoking floors. Complimentary Continental breakfast. Kitchenettes. Cable TV, in-room VCRs. Pool. Hot tub. Gym. Shop. Laundry service. Business services. | 100 MacAlyson Ct | 919/467–4444 or 800/225–5466 | fax 919/467–3074 | 150 rooms | $99–$199 | AE, D, DC, MC, V.

La Quinta Inn and Suites. This might be the South, but inside this hotel it's the Southwest, with Mexican-influenced colors. The hotel is 1 mi from MacGregor Corporate Park and 16 mi from Research Triangle Park. There are no-smoking rooms. Complimentary Continental breakfast. In-room data ports, some microwaves, some refrigerators. Cable TV. Pool. Hot tub. Gym. Laundry service. Business services. Pets allowed. | 191 Crescent Commons | 919/851–2850 or 800/642–4258 | fax 919/851–0728 | 123 rooms, 5 suites | $65–$89 rooms, $105 suites | AE, D, DC, MC, V.

CASHIERS

MAP 8, A5

(Nearby towns also listed: Brevard, Franklin, Highlands, Lake Toxaway)

If you're looking to escape the heat and humidity of the flatlands, follow the locals to Cashiers (pronounced "*cash*-urs"). For 100 years, North Carolina residents have been heading to this mountain valley for an escape. Stunning vistas, lakes for fishing, boating, and canoeing, and amenity-laden resorts are part of the scene.

Information: **Cashiers Travel and Tourism Authority** | Box 238, 28717 | 828/743–5941 | cashcham@dnet.net | www.cashiers-nc.com.

Attractions

Lake Glenville. Although the 1,400-acre lake was officially renamed Thorpe Reservoir in the early 1950s, everyone still refers to it by its original name, Lake Glenville. It has 26 mi of shoreline, and at an elevation of nearly 3,500 ft it is the highest major lake in eastern America. It teems with fish and it's also a good place to canoe, swim, and waterski. | Rte. 107 | 828/743–5941 | Free | Daily.

Sapphire Valley Ski Area. Twenty acres of skiable area include a 425-ft vertical drop, night skiing, and snowboarding. | 4000 U.S. 64 W | 828/743–1171 or 800/522–8268 | fax 828/743–2641 | Late Nov.–mid-Mar.

ON THE CALENDAR

APR.: *Tour de Cashiers Bicycle Road Ride.* A total of 500 cyclists are allowed on a 50-mi road ride (with 5,000 ft of climbing), a 25-mi ride, or an 11-mi family fun ride on a plateau of the Blue Ridge Mountains. Rides vary in length from year to year. | 828/743–5191.
JUNE: *Dillsboro Heritage Festival.* Arts and crafts, food, and regional musicians are this downtown Dillsboro street festival's biggest draws. | 828/586–4060.
SEPT.: *Cashiers Chili Cook-Off.* Demonstrations, music, and sales accompany this popular chili cooking contest, held at the Village Green in downtown Cashiers. | 828/743–5191.
SEPT.: *Mountain Heritage Day.* Many consider this to be the granddaddy of all heritage festivals. This event, now in its third decade, attracts tens of thousands to the campus of Western Carolina University for chain-saw demonstrations, ax-throwing contests, mountain arts and crafts, clogging, square dancing, line dancing, food, and more. | Rte. 107, Cullowhee | 828/227–7237.

Dining

Carolina Smokehouse. Barbecue. The smoker is on premises at this roadside establishment. Takeout is popular, but you can also dine inside on pork spare ribs, chicken, and several kinds of southern barbecue sandwiches. | U.S. 64 W | 828/743–3200 | $8–$12 | No credit cards.

Cornucopia Restaurant. Contemporary. You can have a gourmet sandwich for lunch while overlooking Cashiers Lake, either inside the restaurant or on the deck. Or you can try the coconut shrimp and Coca-Cola ribs. Kids' menu. Sun. brunch. | Rte. 107 S | 828/743–3750 | $18–$22 | MC, V | Closed mid-Oct.–Mar. No dinner Sun.

Martine's. French. Considered the finest restaurant in town by most locals, the emphasis at this spot is on Old World, traditional steak and seafood dishes. | Rte. 107 S | 828/743–3838 | $20–$30 | MC, V | No lunch.

Lodging

The Cottage Inn. Up here at 3,500 feet you can choose from one- or two-bedroom cottages scattered throughout the grounds, or B&B rooms in the Knoll Top Lodge that include a complimentary breakfast in the price. The grounds have a tennis court, picnic areas, and an indoor swimming pool. There are 19 waterfalls within 20 miles. Picnic area. Cable TV, no room phones. Indoor pool. Tennis court, hiking trails. | 71 Brocade Dr. | 828/743–3033 or 877/595–3600 | fax 828/743–0199 | www.cottageinncashiers.com | 4 rooms, 13 cottages | $95 rooms, $85–$145 cottages | MC, V.

High Hampton Inn and Country Club. On a 1,400-acre mountain estate stands this tranquil, rustic resort, established in 1924. It is the former hunting lodge of a Civil War general (Hampton), and some of the rooms have views of either a lake or the mountains. All meals are included in the rate. Kids' programs are available June through August and Thanksgiving weekend. Dining room, complimentary breakfast. No room phones, cable TV in common area. Two lakes. Driving range, 18-hole golf course, putting greens. Tennis courts. Exercise equipment. Hiking. Water sports. Bicycles. Library. Kids' programs (2–11). Laundry facilities. Business services. Airport shuttle. Some pets allowed. | 1525 Rte. 107 S | 828/743–2411 or 800/334–2551 | fax 828/743–5991 | www.highhamptoninn.com | 30 rooms; 90 rooms in 15 cottages | $172–$218 | AE, D, DC, MC, V | Closed Dec.–mid-Apr.

Innisfree Victorian Inn. One block from Lake Glenville, these accommodations have a romantic touch: some rooms have views of the lake and hot tubs. Others have private verandas. The lobby holds a large Count Rumford fireplace. Complimentary breakfast. Minibars, refrigerators. Satellite TV in some rooms, some room phones. Business services. No kids under 17. No smoking. | 7 Lakeside Knoll, Glenville | 828/743–2946 | www.innisfreeinn.com | 10 rooms | $119–$290 | AE, D, MC, V.

Laurelwood Mountain Inn. Stores and restaurants are within walking distance of this downtown inn. Rooms are all different, but all use natural wood and have earth-tone accents. Picnic area. No air-conditioning in some rooms, microwaves, refrigerators, some in-room hot tubs. Cable TV. Playground. Business services. No pets. | Rte. 107 and U.S. 64 | 828/743–9939 or 800/346–6846 | www.laurelwoodmountaininn.com | 22 rooms (10 with shower only) | $57–$145 | AE, D, DC, MC, V.

Millstone Inn. At a 3,500-ft elevation, the inn provides a grand view of the Nantahala Forest and the surrounding countryside. Exposed beams and a stone fireplace add a rustic feeling to the inn, whose owners can point you to a trout pond, waterfalls, and scenic hiking trails that are less than 3/4 mi from the lobby. Complimentary breakfast. Cable TV. Library. No pets. No smoking. | U.S. 64 W | 828/742–2737 or 888/645–5786 | fax 828/743–0208 | www.millstoneinn.com | 11 rooms | $103–$154 | D, MC, V | Closed Jan.–Feb.

Oakmont Lodge. This family resort is almost parklike: there's a pond right on the secluded property. Rooms are rustic and oversize. You'll find shops within walking distance, and waterfalls, horseback riding, and hiking are 3 mi away. Restaurant, picnic area, barbecue grills available. No air conditioning, some refrigerators. Cable TV. Pets allowed ($10 fee). | U.S. 63 | 828/743–2298 | fax 828/743–1575 | 20 rooms, 3 cabins | $55–$150 | AE, MC, V.

Woodlands Inn of Sapphire. Seven mi east of Cashiers, and 9½ mi from the border of the Nantahala and Pisgah forests, this modern home has 250 waterfalls in its vicinity, easy access to hiking trails, and modern comforts. All guest rooms have private baths, phones, and cable TV; some have hot tubs. Complimentary Continental breakfast. Some in-room hot tubs. Cable TV. Hiking. | 1305 U.S. 64 W, Sapphire | 828/966–4709 | fax 828/884–6233 | www.woodlandsinn.net | 15 rooms | $70–$125 | AE, D, MC, V.

CEDAR ISLAND

MAP 8, K5

(Nearby towns also listed: Atlantic Beach, Beaufort, Buxton, Hatteras, Morehead City, Ocracoke, Outer Banks)

This is part of what locals call "down east"—an area stretching from the east side of Beaufort to Cedar Island—and the land is untamed, filled with canals and wetland marshes. The island itself has homes dating from the 1880s. Tourists come for its rich bird-watching, fishing, and hunting, and its beach horseback riding.

Information: Carteret County Tourism Development Bureau | 3409 Arendell St., Morehead City 28557 | 252/726–8148 or 800/786–6962. **Visitor Center** | 3409 Arendell St. (U.S. 70 E) | 252/726–8148 | vacation@sunnync.com | www.ncbeach.com or www.sunnync.com.

Attractions

Cedar Island National Wildlife Refuge. Formed in 1964 to build waterfowl impoundments (primarily to help the black duck), this refuge has grown to 14,700 acres, most of it marsh. It's managed by the U.S. Fish and Wildlife Service. This is where bird-watchers gather, especially in the spring and fall. There's also hiking, hunting, and boat launch and picnic areas. | 879 Lola Rd. | 252/225–2511 | Free | Daily dawn–dusk.

Cedar Island to Ocracoke Ferry Service. Reservations are essential. Crossing time is 2¼ hours. | Ferry entrance: 3619 Cedar Island Rd. (Rte. 12) | 252/225–3551 or 800/856–0343 | One way pedestrians $1, bicycles $2, motorcycles $10, cars $10, more for larger vehicles | Office daily 6–9; call for schedule.

ON THE CALENDAR

MAY: *Nelson Bay Challenge Sprint Triathlon*. This benefit event includes a 750-meter swim, a 20K bike ride, and a 5K run. For a small fee, spectators can join the post-race clambake. | Rte. 12, in Sea Level | 252/247–6902.

Dining

Pirate's Chest Restaurant. Seafood. The restaurant in the Driftwood Motel on the shore of Core Sound has a nautical theme. Dine on fried, broiled, and steamed seafood, or try the shrimp alfredo. Kids' menu. Beer and wine only. | Rte. 12 | 252/225–4861 | Reservations not accepted | www.clis.com/deg | $11–$18 | AE, D, MC, V | Closed late Jan.–mid-Mar. Lunch Sun. only.

Oriental Marina. Seafood. You can dine on the outdoor patio overlooking the harbor, or enjoy your locally harvested shrimp, flounder, or crab in the indoor dining room. The most popular dish is the seafood nirvana—shrimp, scallops, and crabmeat in a puff pastry with lobster sauce. | Hodges St., Oriental | 252/249–2204 | $10–$20 | D, MC, V.

Lodging

Driftwood. This motel sits right on the beach, though not all rooms face the ocean. There is also a 65-site campground, 55 with hookups. Restaurant. Complimentary Continental breakfast. Cable TV, no room phones. Beach. Pets allowed. | Cedar Island Beach, Rte. 12 N | 252/225–4861 | fax 252/225–1113 | 37 rooms | $60–$70 | AE, D, MC, V | Closed mid-Jan.–mid-Mar.

Oriental Marina Motel. You can arrive at this working marina and motel by car or boat. Most rooms have private balconies overlooking the sea, and a lounge and restaurant are on premises. Restaurant. Cable TV, room phones. Outdoor pool, dock, boating, fishing. | Hodges St., Oriental | 252/249–1818 | 18 rooms | $55–$89 | D, MC, V.

CHAPEL HILL

MAP 8, G4

(Nearby towns also listed: Burlington, Cary, Durham, Pittsboro, Raleigh)

Chapel Hill is the smallest city in the Research Triangle area—an area defined when you connect the cities of Raleigh, Durham, and Chapel Hill on a map. Yet its reputation looms large as a seat of learning and liberalism.

Home to the University of North Carolina, the nation's first public university, Chapel Hill sits on a tree-shaded rise. While the downtown area is filled with shops and restaurants and bustles with students, businesspeople, and retirees, it still feels like a quiet, tree-lined village.

Information: Chapel Hill/Orange County Visitors Bureau | 501 W. Franklin St., Suite 104, Chapel Hill 27516 | 919/968–2060 or 888/968–2060. **Visitor Center** | 104 Estes Dr., Chapel Hill | 919/967–7075 | chvisbur@bellsouth.net | www.chocvb.org.

Attractions

Arts Center. With exhibits and classes of all kinds for all ages, this is home to a nationally recognized jazz program as well as numerous dance, theater, and music events. | 300-G

E. Main St., Carrboro | artscenter@aol.com | 919/929–2787 | fax 919/969–8574 | Prices vary for shows | Weekdays 10–6, Sat. 10–2.

North Carolina Botanical Garden. A part of the University of North Carolina at Chapel Hill, the garden is made up of minigardens and trails. There's a special emphasis on plants native to the southeastern United States; these are arranged by sandhill, coastal plain, and mountain habitats. Very popular are the extensive herb garden and the collection of carnivorous and aquatic plants. | Old Mason Farm Rd., off U.S. 15/501 and Rte. 54 Bypass | 919/962–0522 | fax 919/962–3531 | www.unc.edu/depts/ncbg | Mid-Mar.–mid-Nov., weekdays 8–5, Sat. 10–5, Sun. 1–5; mid-Nov.–mid-Mar., weekdays 8–5.

University of North Carolina at Chapel Hill. The nation's first state university was chartered in 1789, and was the only public university in the nation to give students degrees in the 18th century. Trees, flowering shrubs, and buildings dating back to the 1850s fill the 700-acre campus, which is the flagship for the 16 schools within the the UNC system. | W. Franklin St. | 919/962–1630 | www.unc.edu | Free | Daily.

Ackland Art Museum. The permanent collection includes more than 14,000 works of art from around the world. Holdings are particularly rich in Old Master paintings and sculptures. Galleries also show Asian art, North Carolina folk art, prints, drawings, and photographs. | S. Columbia St. at E. Franklin St. | 919/966–5736 | fax 919/966–1400 | www.ackland.org | Free | Wed.–Sat. 10–5, Sun. 1–5.

Coker Arboretum. Established in 1903, this 5-acre area houses one of the oldest arboretums in the Southeast and contains more than 1,000 varieties of ornamental plants, shrubs, and trees. Brick and sand paths wind through groves of oak, sugar maple, Japanese maple, cyprus and evergreen, many of which are over 80 years old. Most of the paths are wheelchair-accessible. | Cameron Ave. and Raleigh St., on UNC-Chapel Hill campus | 919/962–0522 | Free | Daily dawn–dusk.

Graham Memorial Building. Built in 1931, the structure was designed as a student union. Now Public Radio shows such as Garrison Keillor's *Prairie Home Companion* are broadcast from its Memorial Hall. The North Carolina Symphony also performs here when on tour. | Cameron Ave. and E. Franklin St. | 919/962–1630 | Free | Call for hours.

Kenan Stadium. One national sports magazine rated Kenan one of the five best places in America to watch a college football game. UNC's Tar Heels have called the stadium home since 1927; a recent expansion brought seating capacity to 60,000. | Stadium Drive, behind bell tower | 919/962–2123 | www.tarheelblue.com | Call for schedule.

Louis Round Wilson Library. Containing more than 5 million volumes, the handsome building (circa 1929) serves mostly as a research library in the humanities and social sciences. Standouts among the more than a dozen special collections are the Southern Historical Collection and the North Carolina Collection. Adjoining the latter are the Sir Walter Raleigh rooms, furnished as rooms were in 1600 and paneled in English oak of the period. | South Rd., off Raleigh St., across from bell tower | 919/962–0114 | Free | Weekdays 9–5, Sat. 9–1, Sun. 1–5.

Morehead-Patterson Memorial Bell Tower. With bells that ring on the hour and on special occasions such as commencement, the tower is named for the cousins who built it. | South Rd., off Raleigh St. | 919/962–1630 | Free | Daily.

Morehead Planetarium. Many astronauts, including those on the *Mercury, Gemini,* and *Apollo* missions, have trained at this planetarium. Star shows run regularly, and, in addition to the observatory's art collection you can often find exhibits on astronomy. | 250 E. Franklin St. | 919/962–1247 or 919/549–6863 for show information | www.morehead.unc.edu | $4.50 | Building Wed.–Fri.12:30–5 and 7–9:30, Sat. 10–5 and 7–9:30, Sun.–Tues. 12:30–5. Shows Wed., Thurs. at 7:30 and 8:30, Fri. at 3:30, 7:30, and 8:30, Sat. at 10:30, 11:30, 1:30, 2:30, 3:30, 7:30, and 8:30, Sun. at 1:30, 2:30, and 3:30.

Old East. For 200 years, both the residential and instructional life of the university centered in this building. In 1996, the dorm, the oldest state university building in the nation (1793), was designated a National Historic Landmark. You have to see it from the outside; no access is permitted. | Cameron Ave. | 919/962–1630 | Free | Daily.

The Old Well. A favorite meeting place for students and alumni, the Old Well is the campus landmark most associated with the University of North Carolina at Chapel Hill. Modeled after the Temple of Love in the garden at Versailles, it once served as the sole water supply for Old East and Old West dormitories. | Cameron Ave., at McCorkle Place Quadrangle | 919/962–1630 | Free | Daily.

Paul Green Theater. This 500-seat theater is headquarters for the PlayMakers Repertory Company, the state's only member of the League of Resident Theatres. The League is the national organization for full-season, not-for-profit professional theaters. | Country Club Rd., at Paul Green Theater Dr. | 919/962–7529 | Prices vary with shows | Call for schedule.

Old PlayMakers Theatre. To some, this 1851 Greek Revival building is the most beautiful on campus. In recent years it's been used for student productions. | 919/962–7529 | Prices vary with shows | Call for schedule.

South Building. Built between 1798 and 1814, this was a combined classroom and dormitory whose most eminent resident was a future president, James Polk. Today the porticoed structure houses central administration and an information desk. | Cameron Ave., across from the Old Well | 919/962–1630 | Free | Daily.

ON THE CALENDAR

APR.: *Apple Chill.* Chapel Hill's Parks and Recreation Department hosts this downtown street fair, which includes music, food, and arts and crafts. | E. Franklin St. | 919/968–2784.

JUNE: *Hog Day Festival.* A barbecue cook-off, crafts, live music, and children's activities are on tap at this downtown Hillsborough event. | 919/732–8156.

JUNE: *Native American Spring Cultural Festival and Pow-Wow.* Members of the Occaneechi Band of the Saponi Nation present storytelling, music and dance, arts and crafts, food, and traditional tribal ceremonies on the banks of the Eno River in Hillsborough. The festival is near the site of an 18th-century Occaneechi village. | www.occaneechi-saponi.org | 919/304–3723.

SEPT.: *La Fiesta del Pueblo.* Dance troupes in costume and continuous music in the Latin-American tradition accompany the food and crafts at this festival. There's also a soccer tournament with Hispanic league teams from around the state. | Chapel Hill High School, 1709 High School Rd. | 919/932–6880.

NOV.: *Artists Open Studio Tour.* For two weekends, artists all over Orange County open their studios, letting you glimpse their lives and how they work. The tour is self-guided and much of the art is for sale. | 919/542–6511.

DEC.: *Christmas Candlelight Tour.* On the first Sunday in December, you can visit some of the finest homes in Hillsborough, which have been dressed for the holidays. | 919/732–8156.

Dining

Allen and Son Barbecue. Barbecue. Inside a large cinder-block building by the side of a country road is a large room filled with long, oilcloth-covered tables. It is here, in this laidback place, that a die-hard and diverse clientele—farmers, truckers, surgeons, students—pig out on hickory-smoked pork barbecue, baked beans, hush puppies, slaw, and catfish. Those without an appetite for barbecue can order burgers. Fruit pies and cobblers are popular desserts. | 6203 Millhouse Rd. | 919/942–7576 | Closed Sun. | $7–$10 | No credit cards.

Aurora. Italian. Find fresh is the specialty in this spacious, airy, pastel-color place. The chef uses local poultry, dairy products, and produce for the ever-changing menu. The place is known for grilled meats, seafood, and wood-fired pizzas and breads. A tiny, partially-covered patio is filled with plants and a fountain, so you think you're dining in the woods. | 1350 Raleigh Rd. (Rte. 54 Bypass) | 919/942–2400 | $4–$8 | AE, MC, V | No lunch weekends.

Carrburritos Taqueria. Mexican. After you order at the counter, you take your generous portions to one of the few tables in this colorful, funky café. Known for salsas, guacamole, oven-roasted meats, and grilled fresh vegetables and fish. Open-air dining. | 711 W. Rosemary St., Carrboro | 919/933–8226 | $12–$19 | AE, MC, V | Closed Sun.

Crook's Corner. Southern. You could call this small, sometimes noisy café "Southern chic," for the classic menu and the genteel dining on the bamboo-walled patio. Try shrimp and grits–sautéed shrimp with bacon, scallions, mushrooms, and Tabasco lemon juice served over grits. Sun. brunch. Kids' menu. | 610 W. Franklin St. | 919/929–7643 | $7–$25 | AE, D, DC, MC, V | No lunch.

Elmo's Diner. American. Vegetarians come here for the hummus and salads. Families come for the simple and hearty, made-from-scratch meals, including breakfast all day. Try the chicken and dumplings. Kids' menu. Sun. brunch. | 200 N. Greensboro St., Carrboro | 919/929–2909 | $5–$9 | MC, V.

411 West. Mediterranean. Old World stucco and brick walls adorn the inside, and there's a glass-enclosed patio adjacent to the main dining area. The menu includes many pasta dishes and wood-fired pizzas. Kids' menu. | 411 W. Franklin St. | 919/967–2782 | Reservations not accepted | $7–$19 | AE, D, DC, MC, V | No lunch Sun.

Il Palio Ristorante. Italian. You can dine to the sound of a harp and surrounded by columns at this restaurant that has Tuscan cuisine with a twist. Specialties include osso buco, almond pesto, and gnocchi with a fresh tomato and basil sauce. This place serves everything with top-notch service at breakfast, lunch, and dinner. Entertainment nightly and at Sun. brunch. | 1505 E. Franklin St. | 919/929–4000 or 919/918–2545 | $19–$25 | AE, DC, MC, V.

La Residence. French. The menu at this restaurant changes according to what's succulent and in season, which means food is always fresh and from scratch. Dine indoors on white tablecloths or on the open-air garden patio, surrounded by flowers and trees. | 202 W. Rosemary St. | 919/967–2506 | $19–$26 | AE, D, DC, MC, V | Closed Sun. No lunch.

Mama Dip's Kitchen. Southern. Meals here are as authentically Southern as it gets: pork chops, ribs, stews, fried chicken, chicken and dumplings, salmon cakes, vegetables such as okra and string beans, melt-in-your-mouth biscuits, banana pudding, and a half-dozen other desserts. Try the fried chicken and famous pecan pie at this family-friendly restaurant. Family-style servings are available if you're with 8 or more people. Notching up the hospitality, there's a wraparound porch, and you can dine there, too. Locals also go for breakfast and lunch. Kids' menu. | 408 W. Rosemary St. | 919/942–5837 | Reservations not accepted | $6–$15 | MC, V.

Pyewacket. Eclectic. A plant-filled sunroom plus a celery-green and white color scheme make for a light-filled dining experience within the Courtyard, a shopping/dining area. The menu changes regularly, but the place remains known for seafood, pasta, and vegetarian dishes. The plaki is always available–baked fish in white wine, lemon juice, garlic, and onions. On fair evenings, you can dine on the veranda. | 431 W. Franklin St. | 919/929–0297 | $9–$20 | AE, D, DC, MC, V | No lunch weekends.

Lodging

Best Western University Inn. An expansive lawn welcomes you to this red-brick building 2 mi east of the University of North Carolina Chapel Hill campus. Most rooms have views of UNC's Finley golf course. Complimentary Continental breakfast. Satellite TV. Pool. Business services. Laundry services. No pets. | Rte. 54 E | 919/932–3000 or 800/WESTERN | fax 919/968–6513 | www.bestwestern.com/universityinnchapelhill | 84 rooms | $80–$115 | AE, D, DC, MC, V.

Carolina Inn. Owned by the University of North Carolina and operated by Doubletree Hotels Corp., this landmark was built in 1924. The edge-of-campus inn was placed on the National Register of Historic Places in 1999 and is just a block from the town's main drag. Restaurant, bar. In-room data ports. Cable TV. Exercise equipment. Laundry facilities, laundry service. Business services. | 211 Pittsboro St. | 919/933–2001 or 800/962–8519 | fax 919/962–3400 | 184 rooms | $154–$164 | AE, D, DC, MC, V.

Days Inn. Built in 1999, this hotel has refrigerators and microwaves in all rooms, and suites with hot tubs are available. It's two miles from UNC and 10 miles from Duke University. In-room data ports. Microwaves, refrigerators, some in-room hot tubs. Cable TV. Business services. | 1312 N. Fordham Blvd. | 919/929–3090 or 800/544–8313 | fax 919/929–8170 | 51 rooms | $69–$129 | AE, D, MC, V.

Governors Club. Here you have access to the 27-hole, Jack Nicklaus championship golf course, as well as the fitness center, tennis courts, and indoor and outdoor pool. You can stay in a four- to seven-bedroom villa, or in a standard hotel room. In-room data ports, some kitchenettes, some minibars, some refrigerators. Cable TV, room phones. Indoor pool, outdoor pool. Hot tub. Golf privileges. Exercise equipment. | 11000 Governors Dr. | 919/918–7260 | 110 rooms | $139–$194 | AE, DC, MC, V.

Hampton Inn. This branch of the chain is 2 mi from the University of North Carolina and within walking distance of shops and restaurants. Complimentary Continental breakfast. Cable TV. Pool. Laundry service. Business services. No pets. | 1740 U.S. 15/501 | 919/968–3000 or 800–HAMPTON | fax 919/929–0322 | www.hamptoninnchapelhill.com | 122 rooms | $69–$82 | AE, D, DC, MC, V.

Holiday Inn. Chapel Hill memorabilia fills the lobby and rooms here. The hotel is in the middle of Chapel Hill, within walking distance of several restaurants and 2 mi from movies, shops, and clubs. Restaurant, bar, room service. In-room data ports. Cable TV. Pool. Laundry service. Business services. No pets. | 1301 N. Fordham Blvd. | 919/929–2171 or 888/452–5765 | fax 919/929–5736 | 135 rooms | $89 | AE, D, DC, MC, V.

Inn at Bingham School. This inn was first built as a two-story log cabin in 1790, and a Federal-style extension was added in 1801. Finally, a main building was created in Greek Revival style in 1835. It was a boy's prep school from 1845 to 1865. Now, it's secluded and in the country, giving you forest views and hiking trails. Spanish and French are spoken. Complimentary breakfast. In-room data ports, some in-room hot tubs. Some in-room VCRs. Business services. No pets. | Rte. 54 and Mebane Oaks Rd. | 919/563–5583 or 800/566–5583 | fax 919/563–9826 | fdeprez@aol.com | www.chapel-hill-inn.com | 4 rooms (1 with bath only, 2 with shower only) | $80–$130 | AE, D, MC, V.

Joan's Place. Three miles south of downtown is this ranch house on a wooded property, where you can enjoy a wooden deck out back. Joan has lived in the area for 30 years and can advise you on activities and attractions. Complimentary Continental breakfast. Room phones, TV in common area. | 1443 Poinsett Dr. | 919/942–5621 | 2 rooms | $65–$75 | No credit cards.

Sheraton Chapel Hill. This sunny, modern hotel is surrounded by six acres of pines. Restaurant, bar, room service. In-room data ports. Cable TV. Pool. Business services. Airport shuttle. | 1 Europa Dr. | 919/968–4900 | fax 919/968–3520 | www.sheratonchapelhill.com | 168 rooms | $79–$154 | AE, D, DC, MC, V.

Siena. The imported furniture and artwork remind you of the Italian Renaissance when you're in this first-class hotel. Out the window, you have a view of Chapel Hill. 15 minutes from airport; close to UNC. Restaurant, bar with entertainment, picnic area, complimentary breakfast. In-room data ports, some refrigerators. Cable TV. Laundry service. Business services. Airport shuttle. Some pets allowed ($50 fee). | 1505 E. Franklin St. | 919/929–4000 or 800/223–7379 | fax 919/968–8527 | 80 rooms, 12 suites | $169–$300 | AE, DC, MC, V.

CHARLOTTE

MAP 8, E5

(Nearby towns also listed: Albemarle, Concord, Cornelius, Gastonia, Kannapolis)

Though Charlotte dates from Revolutionary War times (it is named for King George III's wife), its Uptown, with gleaming skyscrapers, is distinctively New South. Uptown encompasses all of Charlotte's business and cultural heart and soul. It's also home to the government center and some residential neighborhoods.

Within the Uptown area, at the intersection of Trade and Tryon streets, is Independence Square, with sculptures symbolizing Charlotte's beginnings: a gold miner (Commerce), a mill worker (Textile Heritage), a railroad builder (Transportation), and a mother holding her baby aloft (the Future). Residents of the Queen City like the fact that their sprawling city is the largest in the Carolinas; they're proud of the major-league sports franchises based in Charlotte; and they are happy with the prosperity that comes with being the nation's second-largest banking center (Bank of America and First Union are headquartered here).

Heavy development has created some typical urban problems, like heavy rush hour traffic. But the locals' courtesy is contagious, lots of green spaces remain, and people still love the traditional pleasure of picnicking in Freedom Park.

You can explore Uptown and the Fourth Ward neighborhood on foot, and buses are adequate for getting around within the city limits. You'll need a car for touring beyond these places.

Information: Charlotte Convention and Visitors Bureau | 122 E. Stonewall St., 28202 | 704/334–2282 or 800/722–1994. **Visitor Center** | INFO! Charlotte, 330 S. Tryon St. | 704/331–2753 or 800/231–4636 | info@charlottecvb.org | www.charlottecvb.org.

TRANSPORTATION

Charlotte is off I–77 and I–85. I–40, which runs east–west across the country, is about one hour north.

Airports: Charlotte is about two hours by air from cities in more than half of the country. **Charlotte/Douglas International Airport,** a hub for US Airways, is 7 mi west of downtown. | 704/359–4013.

Airport Transport: Cabs run between the airport and downtown. Cost is about $14 with **Crown Cab Co.** (704/334–6666) and about $18 via **Yellow Cab Co. of Charlotte/Carolina Airport Express** (704/332–6161).

Bus: Charlotte is served by **Greyhound Bus Lines.** | 704/372–0456.

Intra-city Transport: Free shuttle service within the few blocks of the center of the city is provided by **Center City Circuit** (704/332–2227). Municipal bus service is also available via **Charlotte Transit** (704/336–3366) and **Charlotte Transportation Center** (704/336–3159). Fares are $1 ($1.40 for express buses). Many routes start as early as 5:30AM and run until 1:30AM.

KODAK'S TIPS FOR NIGHT PHOTOGRAPHY

Lights at Night
· Move in close on neon signs
· Capture lights from unusual vantage points

Fireworks
· Shoot individual bursts using a handheld camera
· Capture several explosions with a time exposure
· Include an interesting foreground

Fill-In Flash
· Set the fill-in light a stop darker than the ambient light

Around the Campfire
· Keep flames out of the frame when reading the meter
· For portraits, take spot readings of faces
· Use a tripod, or rest your camera on something solid

Using Flash
· Stay within the recommended distance range
· Buy a flash with the red-eye reduction mode

From *Kodak Guide to Shooting Great Travel Pictures* © 2000 by Fodor's Travel Publications

WALKING TOURS

Park your car in an open lot a few blocks east of Independence Square. This is the center of Uptown Charlotte. Start at the Bank of America Corporate Center. Walk two blocks west on Trade Street to the First Presbyterian Church and begin exploring the Fourth Ward, the "new" old city. (You can pick up walking maps for Center City and Fourth Ward tours at INFO! Charlotte, 330 S. Tryon Street). There are more than 18 historic sites in this area. After exploring the Fourth Ward walk south to North Tyron Street, just above 6th Street, where you will find Discovery Place, a science and technology museum. Finish your walk at the Mint Museum of Craft and Design, which showcases the craft tradition of North Carolina.

Attractions

CULTURE, EDUCATION, AND HISTORY

Afro-American Cultural Center. This arts center in the former Little Rock A.M.E. Zion Church has galleries and a theater. | 401 N. Meyers St. | 704/374–1565 | www.aacc-charlotte.org | Free | Tues.–Sat. 10–6, Sun. 1–5.

Bank of America Corporate Center. Built in 1992, this 60-story structure with a crownlike top, designed by Cesar Pelli, is one of the city's most striking buildings. Its main attraction is its three massive philosophical frescoes by Ben Long that symbolize the city's past, present, and future. Also in the tower are the North Carolina Blumenthal Performing Arts Center and the restaurants and shops of Founders Hall. | 100 N. Tryon St. | 704/386–0120 | www.foundershallcharlotte.com | Free | Daily.

© Corbis

A STOCK-CAR STAR

In the post–World War II days, moonshine runners relied on their wiles and speed to get their product to, ah, market. It didn't take long for people to start betting against each other to see who had the fastest car and for cow pastures to become racetracks. Thus was stock-car racing born, and it has been part of the fabric of life for thousands upon thousands of North Carolinians ever since.

Now, though, millions of others have found religion, and the evolution from dirt roads and jalopies to the glass and chrome of corporate America and automobiles of stunning speeds and excessive horsepower is complete.

NASCAR is the organization that owns and runs most of stock-car racing, and by any measure it's been one of the phenomenal success stories of American sports. TV ratings are up; corporate America can't splash logos on cars, drivers, and articles of clothing fast enough; and the Winston Cup series, the top level of racing, draws crowds that approach and sometimes exceed hundreds of thousands each week.

North Carolina is the driving force behind this multimillion-dollar enterprise, thanks to several key factors: numerous short tracks around the state that nurtured the sport have become veritable shrines; it hosts more Winston Cup races than any other state; numerous high-tech racing shops have clustered around the state-of-the-art speedway near Charlotte; and, perhaps most important, it keeps producing drivers whose personalities capture imaginations. Of the state's racing families, three can boast three generations of champions—the Pettys, the Jarretts, and the Earnhardts.

Charlotte Coliseum. Professional as well as Atlantic Coast Conference (ACC) basketball, the circus, and a variety of shows ranging from the Ice Capades to rodeos are crowd pleasers in this 24,000-seat facility. | 100 Paul Buck Blvd. | 704/357–4700 | Prices vary with events | Call for hours.

Fourth Ward. Charlotte's newly popular old neighborhood began in the mid-1800s as a political subsection created for electoral purposes. The architecture of this quiet, home-spun neighborhood takes you back to life in a less hectic time. A brochure available at INFO! Charlotte includes 18 historic places of interest, such as the First Presbyterian Church and the Old Settlers Cemetery. Fourth Ward Park is an oasis in the middle of the city on the NE side of downtown, bordered by Graham St., South Tryon St., 6th St., and 11th St. | 704/331–2700 | Free | Daily.

First Presbyterian Church. This Gothic Revival church, which takes up a city block and faces West Trade Street, reflects the prosperity of the early settlers and their descendants. Behind it is the city's Old Settlers Cemetery. | 200 W. Trade St. | 704/332–5123 | Free | Week-days 8:30–5.

Spirit Square Center for the Arts and Education. An interdisciplinary arts center that includes seven galleries, three theaters, and classrooms is in what used to be the sanctu-ary for the First Baptist Church. | 345 N. College St. | 704/372–9664 (box office) | Prices vary with events | Weekdays 8–5.

Historic Latta Plantation. The last remaining Catawba River plantation (circa 1800) open to the public, this 62-acre property consists of the original home and smokehouse, plus 11 other outbuildings. Fields, farm animals, gardens, and interpreters in period clothing complete the experience. | 5225 Sample Rd., Huntersville | 704/875–2312 | www.lattaplan-tation.org | $4 | Tues.–Fri. 8–4, Sat. 12:30–4, Sun. 1:30–5.

James K. Polk Memorial State Historic Site. Exhibits, artifacts, and film are used to illus-trate the life and times of the 11th U.S. president at his birthplace. You can also take a guided tour through reconstructed log buildings furnished in the style of the 1700s to early 1800s. | 308 S. Polk St., Pineville | 704/889–7145 | Free | Apr.–Oct., Mon.–Sat. 9–5, Sun. 1–5; Nov.–Mar., Tues.–Sat. 10–4, Sun. 1–4.

N.C. Blumenthal Performing Arts Center. Operatic, symphonic, choral, dance, and theatri-cal performances are mounted in the five-level center with a dramatic marble and mosaic-tile interior. | 130 N. Tryon St. | 704/333–4686 | Prices vary with shows | Call for schedule.

MUSEUMS

★ **Discovery Place.** One of the city's premier attractions, Discovery Place contains a science museum, an aquarium, a planetarium, and an Omnimax theater, as well as a three-story rain forest and ever-evolving hands-on exhibits. | 301 N. Tryon St. | 704/372–6261 or 800/935–0553 | $6.50–$10.50 | Weekdays 9–5, Sat. 9–6, Sun. 1–6.

Hezekiah Alexander Homesite and Charlotte History Museum. The home, built in 1774, is the oldest dwelling in the county. Here, Hezekiah and his wife, Mary, reared 10 children and farmed the land. Costumed docents give guided tours every day except Monday. | 3500 Shamrock Dr. | 704/568–1774 | Free | Tues.–Sun. 10–5; tours Tues.–Sun. at 1:15 and 3:15.

Mint Museum of Art. The first branch of the U.S. Mint became North Carolina's first art museum. Today, the Mint has holdings that include paintings, furniture, porcelain, pot-tery, costumes, and decorative arts. Collections include African, pre-Columbian, and Span-ish colonial works. | 2730 Randolph Rd. | 704/337–2000 | fax 704/337–2101 | www.mintmuseum.org | $6 | Tues. 10–10, Wed.–Sat. 10–5, Sun. noon–5.

★ **Mint Museum of Craft and Design.** A crosstown sister to the Mint Museum of Art, the Craft and Design branch is the largest museum in the nation focused on crafts. Housed in what used to be an upscale women's clothing store, the museum displays objects in ceramics, glass, fiber, metal, and wood. There's a special emphasis on the long tradition of

North Carolina crafts. | 220 N. Tryon St. | 704/337–2000 | fax 704/337–2101 | www.mint-musuem.org | $6 | Tues. 10–10, Wed.–Sat. 10–5, Sun. noon–5.

Museum of the New South. A regional (Charlotte and 13 surrounding counties) history repository focusing on the New South period from 1877 to the present. | 324 N. College St. | 704/333–1887 | fax 704/333–1896 | $2 | Tues.–Sat. 11–5.

Nature Museum. This affiliate of Discovery Place is an educational resource that provides programs on wildlife, and has hands-on exhibits, live creatures, a scenic trail, and a puppet theater. | 1658 Sterling Ave. | 704/372–0471, ext. 605, or 800/935–0553 | fax 704/337–2670 | $3 | Weekdays 9–5, Sat. 10–5, Sun. 1–5.

Ovens Auditorium. Everything from Broadway productions to children's shows is put on here. The seating capacity is 2,500. | 2700 E. Independence Blvd. | 704/372–3600 | Prices vary with events | Call for schedule.

PARKS, NATURAL AREAS, AND OUTDOOR RECREATION

Latta Plantation Park. This 1,290-acre nature preserve on Mountain Island Lake centers around the plantation house of James and Jane Latta. The park is a diverse place: attractions include the Carolina Raptor Center (where injured birds are cared for), a full-service equestrian center, hiking trails, canoeing, kayaking, fishing, and picnicking. | 5225 Sample Rd., Huntersville | 704/875–1391 | Free | Daily.

Wing Haven Gardens and Bird Sanctuary. In Myers Park, one of Charlotte's loveliest neighborhoods, a four-acre garden developed by the Clarkson family is home to more than 135 species of birds. The park also has many pools and fountains. | 248 Ridgewood Ave. | 704/332–5770 | Free | Tues. 3–5, Wed. 10–noon, Sun. 2–5, or by appointment.

RELIGION AND SPIRITUALITY

Belmont Abbey College. Ten miles west of Charlotte you will find what is most likely the oldest Catholic parish in the south. The original abbey has a lovely landscape as its setting. | 100 Belmont-Mt.Holly Rd., Belmont | 704/825–6890.

Calvary Church. This non-denominational church is famous for its largesse and is worth a visit even if you just drive around the lot. | Corner of Hwy 51 and Ray Rd. | 704/543–1200.

St. Mary's. This non-denominational chapel is on the site of a former orphanage, the Thompson's Children's Home. Behind the chapel is the local Vietnam veterans' memorial. | 1129 E. Third St. | 704/333–1235.

St. Peter's Catholic Church, the first Catholic Church in Charlotte, is home to the frescos of Ben Long. Long's work can be seen throughout Charlotte but is best exemplified in this beautiful setting. | Triumph St. | 704/332–2901.

St. Peter's Episcopal Church. Jefferson Davis and the cabinet of the Confederacy met here before Lee's surrender. Built in 1834, the church is one of the area's oldest. This St. Peter's is also home to Charlotte's best-known soup kitchen. | 115 W. 7th St. | 704/332–7756.

SHOPPING

Charlotte Regional Farmers Market. You'll find the produce, handmade crafts, baked goods, and plants of vendors from 13 counties surrounding Charlotte at this indoor market. | 1801 Yorkmont Rd. | 704/357–1269. | Mar.–Nov. Tues.–Sat. 8–5.

Concord Mills. Located about 10 mi north of downtown Charlotte at the intersection of, this mall has nearly 200 stores including manufacturer outlets, off–price retailers, and specialty stores. You will also find a food court, restaurants, and a 24–screen theater. | I–85 and Concord Mills Blvd. | 704/979–3000 or 877/NC–MILLS | Mon.–Sat. 10–9:30, Sun. 11–7.

Eastland Mall. This mall has about 120 stores and many special events throughout the year. | 5471 Central Ave. at Sharon Amity Rd. | 704/537–2626 | Mon.–Sat 10–9, Sun. 12:30–6.

Phillips Place/Lincoln Harris. Centrally located, this upscale strip mall in the SouthPark neighborhood features specialty markets like Dean & Deluca as well as other stores, restaurants, and a movie theater. | Cameron Valley Pkwy. at Fairview Rd. | 704/556–1717 | Weekdays 8 –5.

SouthPark Mall. Charlotte's largest mall has more than 100 stores, three restaurants, and a food court and is at the corner of Sharon and Fairview Roads. | 4400 Sharon Rd. | 704/364–4411 or 888/346–4411. | Mon.–Sat. 10–9, Sun. 12:30–6.

SIGHTSEEING TOURS

Gray Line Charlotte. Hour-long trolley tours are available. | Box 7348 | 800/922–3492 or 704/332–8687 | fax 803/329–8657 | $18.

SPECTATOR SPORTS

Carolina Panthers. The professional football team for both North Carolina and South Carolina, the Panthers are one of the newest entries on the NFL roster. Their home is the 73,000-seat open-air Ericsson Stadium. | 800 S. Mint St. | 704/358–7800; schedule and tickets 704/372–1000 | www.nfl.com/panthers | Prices vary with events | Sept.–Jan., stadium tours year-round.

Charlotte Hornets. Home court for the NBA Hornets, who typically play some 40 home games, is the Charlotte Coliseum. | 100 Hive Dr. | 704/357–0252 | www.charlottehornets.com | Prices vary with events | Oct.–Apr.

Lowe's Motor Speedway. In the heart of stock-car racing country, the Speedway attracts crowds of 150,000. In addition to hosting two NASCAR Winston Cup and two NASCAR Busch Series races each year, this mecca for motor sports hosts NASCAR's all-star event, the Winston. Guided tours are available except during race weeks, primarily in May and October. | 5555 Concord Pkwy. S., Harrisburg | 704/455–3200 | fax 704/455–2547 | www.lowesmotorspeedway.com | $6 | Mon.–Sat. 9–5, Sun. 1–5.

OTHER POINTS OF INTEREST

Paramount's Carowinds. There's a campground and amphitheater, but the biggest draw at this 100-acre complex is WaterWorks, a rides and water entertainment area. | 14523 Carowinds Blvd. | 704/588–2600 or 800/888–4386 | www.carowinds.com | $32 | Call for hours.

ON THE CALENDAR

APR.: *Festival of India.* Folk dances, people modeling fashions from India, displays of art and artifacts, and food from the country's many states mark this annual celebration in the First Union Atrium. | 301 S. Tryon St. | 800/231–4636.

APR.: *Center City Fest.* Locals get together to share live music, food, and arts and crafts in the city's Uptown section. | 704/332–2227 or 800/231–4636.

MAY–OCT.: *Auto racing.* Lowe's Motor Speedway hosts NASCAR (stock car) events, including two of the biggest and longest-running: the Coca-Cola 600 (May) and the the UAW-GM 500 (October). | 5555 Concord Pkwy. S | 704/455–3200.

JULY: *Bon Odori Festival.* A celebration of Japanese culture sponsored by the Japan-American Society, with folk dancing, drumming, origami, flower arranging, a tea ceremony, food, art, and performances. | 2 First Union Plaza | 704/333–2775.

SEPT.: *Festival in the Park.* One of Freedom Park's most popular events has entertainment, food, and arts and crafts from regional artisans. | 1900 East Blvd. | 704/336–2663.

OCT.: *Latin American Festival.* The popularity of this festival mirrors the growth of Mecklenburg County's Latin-American community. Two dozen countries are represented. You'll find dancing, from Colombian folk to flamenco, plus music, ethnic dress, food, and children's activities. | Mint Museum of Art, 2730 Randolph Rd. | 704/337–2000.

OCT.: *Latta Plantation Folklife Festival.* This early-19th-century harvest celebration includes demonstrations and a crafts sale at Historic Latta Plantation, a living-history farm. | 5225 Sample Rd., Huntersville | 704/875–2312.

Dining

INEXPENSIVE

College Place Restaurant. Southern. You can load up on Southern food at this cafeteria, where there are five entrées and a dozen vegetables, as well as homemade rolls, cornbread, and cobblers. Breakfast is made to order. | 300 S. College St. | 704/343–9268 | Reservations not accepted | $3–$4 | No credit cards | Closed weekends. No dinner.

Landmark Restaurant–Diner. American. The restaurant is spacious, the menu vast, but it's the desserts—more than 30 choices—that get rave reviews. | 4429 Central Ave. | 704/532–1153 | $6–$20 | AE, MC, V.

MODERATE

Atlantic Beer and Ice Co. Contemporary. This three-floor spot includes a cigar and Scotch bar with billiards on the top floor, a restaurant and bar on the main floor, and a jazz club in the cellar. The menu's signature is a fusion of American and Southern foods, and one item to try is the apple-wood-smoked prime rib. There's open-air dining on the sidewalk and live entertainment Thurs.–Sat. evenings. Kids' menu. | 330 N. Tryon St. | 704/339–0566 | $8–$18 | AE, MC, V.

Mert's Heart and Soul. Southern. Art and photographs related to famous African-Americans adorn the walls, while bright colors, a neon EAT sign, and R-and-B background music complete the scene. The menu holds updated classics and new creations. Specialties include shrimp and grits, salmon cakes, and cornbread. | 214 N. College St. | 704/342–4222 | $6–$10 | AE, D, MC, V | No dinner Mon.–Wed.

Palomino Euro Bistro. Mediterranean. Bright colors, leather booths, background jazz music and a fountain make for a welcoming place. The kitchen is on display to the diners, and you can watch the cooks make thin pizzas, spit-roasted meats, and the fish they're known for. The menu changes according to what's in season. Dine inside or on the patio, which has a fountain, and which faces an old church. Kids' menu. | 525 N. Tryon St. | 704/373–9499 | $11–$25 | AE, D, DC, MC, V | No lunch Sun.

Providence Café. Contemporary. Many of the dishes at this chic, upscale spot center on the focaccia that's baked daily. Try the prime rib or the rainbow trout. People-watch from the canopied patio on the street. Live music Wed. and weekend evenings. Kids' menu. | 110 Perrin Pl | 704/376–2008 | Reservations essential for 8 or more | $10–$20 | AE, D, DC, MC, V.

Ranch House. Contemporary. The chefs put contemporary twists on the classics here. The shrimp cocktail has a special sauce, and salads have unique dressings. Everything is made fresh daily and served in a setting of dark paneling, red curtains, and candles. Kids' menu. | 5614 Wilkinson Blvd. | 704/399–5411 | Reservations essential for 6 or more | $10–$25 | AE, D, MC, V | Closed Sun. No lunch.

Smoky's Grill. Southern. Mustard-yellow walls and upholstery, portraits of birds, and a china collection make this restaurant in the Park Hotel warm and airy. Known for Carolina barbecue tuna with sweet-potato pancake and Carolina mountain trout with sesame seeds and julienned vegetables. Or, try the tea-seared salmon with red wine butter. Breakfast is also served. Sun. brunch. | 2200 Rexford Rd. | 704/364–8220 | $12–$25 | AE, D, DC, MC, V.

Thai House. Thai. Carved wood sculptures stand in the three locations of this traditional restaurant. If you're looking for a romantic evening, you can nestle into the booths at this dimly lit spot. There's an extensive seafood list and a separate vegetarian menu, and the place is known for Thai curry and pad Thai noodles. | 3210 N. Sharon Amity Rd. | 704/532–6868 | 8652 Pineville–Matthews Rd., No. 1000 | 704/542–6300 | 4918 Central Ave. | 704/717–8006 | $8–$16 | AE, D, DC, MC, V.

300 East. Eclectic. This house has been lovingly restored to its early-1900s roots. Indoors there are deep-red walls with photographs and artwork. Known for enormous filet burgers, made of ground filet mignon, jack cheese, jalapeños, and bacon. Other favorites are the turkey salad club and black bean tortillas. Locals love the place's famous drink, the Matilda Wong—a giant, fruity drink with four different types of alcohol and three different fruity mixers. The patio, filled with plants, is like a garden. | 300 East Blvd. | 704/332–6507 | Reservations essential for 6 or more | $10–$17 | AE, D, MC, V.

Townhouse. Contemporary. The oldest freestanding restaurant in Charlotte used to be a diner, but in 1988 was converted into an upscale restaurant. Specialties include almond-crusted grouper and Pauleys Island crab cakes. | 1011 Providence Rd. | 704/335–1546 | $18–$28 | AE, D, DC, MC, V | Closed Sun. No lunch.

EXPENSIVE

Bravo! Ristorante. Eclectic. The mostly northern Italian cuisine here is accented by a wait-staff that sings arias and Broadway tunes. Cuisine breaks out into international flavors: one of the best dishes is Australian lamb chops. Live jazz for Sunday brunch. Kids' menu. | 555 S. McDowell St. | 704/372–5440 | $17–$35 | AE, D, DC, MC, V.

Campania. Italian. Warmth emanates from the rich wood, candlelight, and the golden, textured walls. The food is authentic Italian and not just pasta-focused. Veal chops are a main category on the menu. Try the gamberone Mergellina, shrimp sauteed in garlic butter and herbs. | 6414 Rea Rd. | 704/541–8505 | $18–$35 | AE, D, DC, MC, V | Closed Sun. No lunch.

Hereford Barn Steak House. Steak. The name of the place says it all: enjoy your prime cuts in a place that looks like a country barn gone upscale, with farm implements and a fireplace. Try the T-bone steaks and lobster while dining by lantern light. Kids' menu. | 4320 N. I–85 Service Rd. | 704/596–0854 | $15–$40 | AE, D, DC, MC, V | Closed Sun.– Mon. No lunch.

La Bibliothèque. French. You'll be surrounded by white-linen-covered tables and bookshelves at this formal restaurant. Specialties include the rack of lamb or the chateaubriand. Open-air dining on terrace. Pianist Tues.–Sun. | 1901 Roxborough Rd. | 704/365–5000 | Jacket required | $17–$32 | AE, D, DC, MC, V | Closed Sun.

★ **Lamplighter.** Continental. This one-time Spanish mansion is now the place for very intimate, sophisticated dining. Known for fresh seafood and wild game; crab cakes are the house specialty. Private rooms are available for groups of 8 to 50-plus. | 1065 E. Morehead St. | 704/372–5343 | Reservations essential | Jacket required | $18–$29 | AE, D, DC, MC, V | No lunch.

McNinch House. Continental. This one-time home, owned by the McNinch family, hosted U.S. president Taft when he visited Charlotte in 1909. When the final McNinch died in 1978, it was sold to the woman who's currently the chef. They serve a 6-course Continental dinner, featuring specialties like rack of lamb and crab cake appetizers, to six tables a night. It's a "highly choreographed evening," as the proprietors put it. "We're qualified to be snobs about it, but I guess you could say we epitomize Southern hospitality because we really just enjoy a nice dinner and having people in here," they say. | 511 N. Church St. | 704/332–6159 | Reservations essential | $89 fixed price per person | AE, MC, V.

Monticello. Continental. You can experience a little bit of history at this restaurant in the Dunhill Hotel, built around 1929. The food is largely French, and locals come for the specialty veal dishes. Other specialties are tournedos duxelle and chicken roulade, stuffed with roasted red and yellow peppers, mushrooms, and cheese, then served over champagne sauce with couscous and vegetables. There's open-air dining on the sidewalk, and no tennis shoes or jeans are allowed. | 235 N. Tryon St. | 704/342–1193 or 800/354–4141 | $15–$34 | AE, D, DC, MC, V.

Morton's of Chicago. Steak. Between the Sinatra in the background, the dark, wood-paneled walls, and its cigar friendliness, this place is clublike. Known for enormous steaks—including a 24-oz portion. Try the double-cut filet mignon. | 227 W. Trade St. | 704/333–2602 | Reservations essential | $25–$33 | AE, DC, MC, V | No lunch.

Scalini. Italian. Nestled among the greenery in the lobby of the Hyatt Southpark Hotel, this restaurant is a favorite of couples. Known for lobster ravioli and shrimp with angel-hair pasta. It also serves breakfast. | 5501 Carnegie Blvd. | 704/554–1234 | $13–$23 | AE, D, DC, MC, V.

Lodging

INEXPENSIVE

Bradley Motel. The NASCAR theme in the lobby, complete with old posters and other memorabilia, is appreciated by the truckers and construction workers who tend to land here. The motel is 1½ mi from the airport and 2 mi from the Coliseum, but about 25 minutes from Lowe's Motor Speedway. Family-owned and -operated since 1959. Cable TV. Some pets allowed. No-smoking rooms. | 4200 S. I–85 Service Rd. | 704/392–3206 | fax 704/392–5040 | 21 rooms | $31–$34 | AE, D, MC, V.

Fairfield Inn by Marriott. Just off I–85, this standard chain hotel is 3 mi from the University of North Carolina at Charlotte and 6 mi from downtown Charlotte, the Charlotte Coliseum, and Lowe's Motor Speedway. Complimentary Continental breakfast. In-room data ports. Cable TV. Outdoor pool. Business services. | 5415 N. I–85 Service Rd. | 704/596–2999 or 800/228–2800 | fax 704/596–3229 | www.fairfieldinn.com | 133 rooms | $44–$49 | AE, D, DC, MC, V.

La Quinta–South. Just south of Charlotte, this hotel has bright, clean rooms and an inviting lobby area with fireplace. The hotel is 6 mi from the airport, 4 mi from the Coliseum, and 3 mi from shops and restaurants. Complimentary Continental breakfast. In-room data ports, some microwaves. Cable TV. Pool. Laundry service. Business services. Some pets allowed. | 7900 Nations Ford Rd. | 704/522–7110 | fax 704/521–9778 | www.laquinta.com | 118 rooms | $45–$76 | AE, D, DC, MC, V.

Red Roof Inn–Coliseum. This family-friendly hotel is 3 mi from Charlotte Coliseum. Rooms are cozy, with landscape paintings on the walls. Cable TV. Business services. Some pets allowed. | 131 Red Roof Dr. | 704/529–1020 | fax 704/529–1054 | 124@redroofinn.com | 115 rooms | $45–$55 | AE, D, DC, MC, V.

Rodeway Inn. The oversized rooms are spiced up with paintings in this otherwise standard chain. It's 7 mi from downtown and 6 mi from the Concord Mills outlet shopping center. Complimentary Continental breakfast. In-room data ports. Cable TV. Pool. | 1416 W. Sugar Creek Rd. | 704/597–5074 | fax 704/597–5074 | 56 rooms | $48–$59 | AE, D, DC, MC, V.

MODERATE

AmeriSuites Charlotte. Large suites with desks and data ports, plus a pool for relaxing, are included at this hotel five miles from the Douglas International Airport. In-room data ports. Cable TV. Outdoor pool. Business services. | 7900 Forest Point Blvd. | 704/522–8400 | 128 rooms | $69–$129 | AE, D, MC, V.

Best Inn. All rooms have desks at this hotel 10 mi from the Coliseum; some include loveseat sofas. Complimentary Continental breakfast. Some microwaves. Cable TV. Pool. Business services. No pets. | 305 Archdale Dr. | 704/525–3033 | fax 704/525–3033 | 69 rooms | $50–$60 | AE, D, DC, MC, V.

Comfort Inn–Airport. This modest hotel is 1 mi south of the airport and 3 mi from the Coliseum. Bar, complimentary Continental breakfast. Some microwaves, refrigerators. Cable TV. Pool. Exercise equipment. Business services. Airport shuttle. | 4040 I–85 S | 704/394–4111 | 120 rooms | $63–$115 | AE, D, DC, MC, V.

Comfort Inn–Sugar Creek. An easy-to-get-to branch of the chain, 11 mi north of the airport, just off I–85. Complimentary Continental breakfast. Some microwaves. Cable TV. Pool. Hot tub. Exercise equipment. Business services. | 5111 N. Sugar Creek Rd. | 704/598–0007 | fax 704/319–2683 | 87 rooms | $69 | AE, D, DC, MC, V.

Courtyard by Marriott. From the guest rooms, you'll see an actual courtyard. Step outside and it's easy to get just about anywhere: it's 1½ mi from Westingwood Industrial Park, 15 minutes from downtown, and 15 minutes from the airport. Bar. In-room data ports, some refrigerators. Cable TV. Pool. Hot tub. Exercise equipment. Laundry facilities. Business services. | 800 W. Arrowood Rd. | 704/527–5055 or 800/321–2211 | fax 704/525–5848 | www.marriott.com | 146 rooms, 12 suites | $69–$94 | AE, D, DC, MC, V.

Days Inn Uptown. Hotels in the Uptown area can be expensive, but the Days Inn provides an alternative. Though your room will be pretty basic, you're still close to shopping, restaurants, and nightlife. Complimentary Continental breakfast. Cable TV. Outdoor pool. | 601 N. Tryon St. | 704/333–4733 or 800/329–7466 | 100 rooms | $59 | AE, D, MC, V.

Doubletree Club. From here you can walk to the convention center or Carolina Panthers stadium. Restaurant, bar. In-room data ports. Cable TV. Pool. Hot tub. Exercise equipment. Business services. No pets. | 895 W. Trade St. | 704/347–0070 or 800/222–8733 | fax 704/347–0267 | 187 rooms | $68–$165 | AE, D, DC, MC, V.

Drury Inn & Suites. Close to the University of North Carolina at Charlotte campus, the modern Drury Inn has regular guest rooms and multi-room suites. An on-site spa and pool provide relaxation. In-room data ports. Cable TV. Outdoor pool, spa. | 415 W. W. T. Harris Blvd. | 704/593–0700 | 143 rooms, 15 suites | $78–$100 | AE, D, MC, V.

Four Points Sheraton. There are a restaurant and two lounges on the premises of this hotel, which is within walking distance of the Charlotte Convention Center and Marshall Park. With your room, you get a discount at the Mecklenburg Acquatic Center across the street. Restaurant, 2 bars, room service. In-room data ports. Cable TV. Indoor pool. Business services. | 201 S. McDowell St. | 704/372–7550 | 198 rooms, 2 suites | $53–$211 | AE, D, MC, V.

Hampton Inn. Reasonably priced rooms in a classic chain hotel about 5 mi from downtown Charlotte and 2 mi from the Coliseum. Complimentary Continental breakfast. In-room data ports, some microwaves. Cable TV. Pool. Exercise equipment. Business services. Airport shuttle. | 440 Griffith Rd. | 704/525–0747 or 800/HAMPTON | fax 704/522–0968 | 161 rooms | $70–$80 | AE, D, DC, MC, V.

Hampton Inn. Not your typical Hampton Inn, this one has a large fountain in the circle drive-in front, plus a spacious outdoor pool and hot tub. There are two-room suites with fireplaces and whirlpool baths. In-room data ports, some in-room hot tubs. Cable TV. Pool. Hot tub, spa. Business services. | 6700 Phillips Place Ct | 704/319–5700 | 124 rooms, 24 suites | $117–$160 | AE, D, MC, V.

Holiday Inn–Woodlawn. The garden atrium adds a refreshing touch here, at one of the largest hotels in the city catering to business travelers. Restaurant, bar with entertainment, room service. In-room data ports. Cable TV. Pool. Exercise equipment. Business services. Airport shuttle. | 212 Woodlawn Rd. | 704/525–8350 | fax 704/522–0671 | www.travelbase.com/destinations/charlotte/holiday-woodlawn | 425 rooms | $89–$95 | AE, D, DC, MC, V.

Omni. Rooms are spacious and tastefully decked in earth tones at this upscale hotel in the heart of the city, within walking distance of the business and entertainment districts. A rooftop pool and deck, fine dining, and a world class gym facility are some of the extra perks here. Restaurant, bar, room service. In-room data ports, some minibars, refrigerators. Cable TV. Pool. Barbershop, beauty salon. Exercise equipment. Laundry service. Business services. No pets. | 132 E. Trade St. | 704/377–0400 or 800/theomni | www.omnihotels.com | fax 704/347–0649 | 347 rooms, 8 suites | $99–$169, $219–$395 suites | AE, D, DC, MC, V.

Residence Inn by Marriott–South. Suites have full-sized kitchens, and some rooms have fireplaces in this hotel catering to long-stay business travelers. Complimentary Continental breakfast. In-room data ports, kitchenettes, microwaves, refrigerators. Cable TV. Pool. Hot tub. Laundry facilities. Business services. Some pets allowed (fee). | 5816 Westpark Dr. | 704/527–8110 | fax 704/521–8282 | 116 suites | $99–$169 | AE, D, DC, MC, V.

Sheraton Airport Plaza. Rooms are bright in this chain hotel 2 mi from airport and 5 mi from convention center. A large atrium lobby with a waterfall and tropical plants invites relaxation. Restaurant, bar with entertainment, room service. In-room data ports, some microwaves. Cable TV. Indoor-outdoor pool. Hot tub. Exercise equipment. Business services.

Airport shuttle. No Pets. | 3315 S. I-85 | 704/392-1200 or 800/325-3535 | fax 704/393-2207 | www.sheraton.com | 222 rooms | $89-$154 | AE, D, DC, MC, V.

Still Waters B&B. Fifteen minutes from downtown Charlotte, this B&B is on two acres of heavily wooded property on Lake Wylie. Outside there's a boat launch, fishing, and swimming off the dock. Inside, there's a glass-enclosed porch and a common room with TV and VCR. Rooms have private baths; the largest one has a TV and phone. Picnic area, complimentary breakfast. Lake. Basketball, dock, fishing. No pets. No smoking. | 6221 Amos Smith Rd. | 704/399-6299 | members.aol.com/bbdyer399/homepage/index.html | 4 rooms | $55-$95 | DC, MC, V.

Summerfield Suites. This standard, well-maintained chain hotel is 5 mi from Charlotte-Douglas International Airport and downtown Charlotte. Picnic area, complimentary breakfast. In-room data ports, kitchenettes. Cable TV, in-room VCRs. Pool. Hot tub. Exercise equipment. No-smoking floors. Business services, Airport shuttle. Some pets allowed (fee). | 4920 S. Tryon St. | 704/525-2600 | fax 704/521-9932 | 135 suites | $89-$109 | AE, D, DC, MC, V.

Wyndham Garden Hotel. Popular with businesspeople for being right in Lake Pointe Business Park, this hotel is also only 2 minutes from the Coliseum. The lobby has a library and a fireplace; some guest rooms face the pool. Restaurant, bar, room service. In-room data ports, refrigerators. Cable TV. Pool. Hot tub. Exercise equipment. Business services. Airport shuttle. | 2600 Yorkmont Rd. | 704/357-9100 | fax 704/357-9159 | www.wyndham.com | 167 rooms, 6 suites | $79-$119, $99-$159 suites | AE, D, DC, MC, V.

EXPENSIVE

Adam's Mark. The dark wood in the lobby of this convention hotel makes it cool and clubby. It's only a short commute from the Uptown financial district. Restaurant, bars with entertainment. In-room dataports, some minibars, some refrigerators. Cable TV. 2 Pools (1 indoor). Hot tub. Exercise equipment, racquetball. Business services. | 555 S. McDowell St. | 704/372-4100 | fax 704/348-4645 | 613 rooms, 21 suites | $99-$165, $200-$800 suites | AE, D, DC, MC, V.

Carmel B&B. A modern home with a country floral style, the Carmel has four guest rooms, all with private baths and queen size beds. Upscale shopping at Southpark Mall is 3 mi north of the inn. | 4633 Carmel Rd. | 704/542-9450 or 800/229-5860 | fax 704/544-8278 | lmoag@carolina.rr.com | 4 rooms | $95-$109 | AE, MC, V.

Courtyard by Marriott-University. Visiting scholars tend to appreciate the desks in the rooms of this hotel about 4 mi from the University of North Carolina-Charlotte. Bar. In-room data ports, some refrigerators. Cable TV. Pool. Hot tub. Exercise equipment. Laundry facilities. Business services. | 333 W. T. Harris Blvd. | 704/549-4888 or 888/270-8582 | fax 704/549-4946 | www.marriott.com | 152 rooms, 12 suites | $124 | AE, D, DC, MC, V.

★ **Dunhill.** Built in 1929, this is Charlotte's oldest hotel. Furnishings in the rooms and lobby are all antiques or reproductions. It's in the heart of Charlotte's arts and business district, which puts it within walking distance of theaters, museums, and restaurants. Restaurant, bar. In-room data ports, refrigerators. Cable TV. Business services. Airport shuttle. | 237 N. Tryon St. | 704/332-4141 or 800/354-4141 | fax 704/376-4117 | cltdun@bellsouth.net | www.dunhillhotel.com | 60 rooms | $199 | AE, D, DC, MC, V.

Embassy Suites. A high ceiling and lots of indoor plants give the lobby here a tropical garden look. It's 1 mi from Charlotte Coliseum. Restaurant, bar, complimentary breakfast. In-room data ports, some minibars, microwaves, refrigerators. Cable TV. Indoor pool. Hot tub. Exercise equipment. Laundry facilities. Airport shuttle. | 4800 S. Tryon St. | 704/527-8400 or 800/EMBASSY | fax 704/527-7035 | www.embassy-charlotte.com | 274 suites | $119-$169 | AE, D, DC, MC, V.

Hilton at University Place. This is in the northeast section of the city, and is close to the university, businesses, shops, and restaurants. From some rooms, you get a view of the city. Restaurant, complimentary Continental breakfast, bar with entertainment. In-room data ports, some refrigerators. Cable TV. Pool. Exercise equipment. Business services. No pets. | 8629 J. M. Keynes Dr. | 704/547–7444 | fax 704/549–9708 | www.travelbase.com/destinations/charlotte/hilton-univ | 393 rooms | $129–$169 | AE, D, DC, MC, V.

Hilton Charlotte and Towers. The bar of this hotel, called Union Station, is a popular after-hours gathering spot. It's right downtown, within walking distance of many attractions. All rooms have city views. Restaurant, bar. In-room data ports, minibars, some refrigerators. Cable TV. Business services. Airport shuttle. | 222 E. 3rd St. | 704/377–1500 | fax 704/377–4143 | 407 rooms | $145–$299 | AE, D, DC, MC, V.

Hilton Executive Park. Fifteen minutes from the airport, this Hilton is on the outskirts of town, just south of I-77, in a business district. It's 5 mi from the Coliseum, 10 minutes from a shopping mall, and walking distance of some restaurants. Restaurant, bar. In-room data ports, some refrigerators. Cable TV. Pool. Hot tub. Exercise equipment. Business services. Airport shuttle. No pets. | 5624 Westpark Dr. | 704/527–8000 or 800/445–8667 | fax 704/527–4278 | 178 rooms, 34 suites | $79–$165, $100–$190 suites | AE, D, DC, MC, V.

★ **Homeplace.** This turn-of-the-20th-century Victorian gem sits on 2½ acres in southeast Charlotte. The house, including guest rooms, is filled with antiques. Complimentary breakfast. Some cable TV. No kids under 10. No smoking. | 5901 Sardis Rd. | 704/365–1936 | fax 704/366–2729 | www.bbonline.com/nc/homeplace | 2 rooms, 1 suite | $120, $150 suite | AE, MC, V.

Hyatt Charlotte at South Park. The four-story atrium houses a Mexican fountain surrounded by 25-ft olive trees and Scalini, one of the city's best restaurants. Rooms are light and designed for the business traveler. Restaurant, bar, room service. In-room data ports, some microwaves, refrigerators. Cable TV. Indoor pool. Hot tub. Exercise equipment. Business services. Laundry service. Airport shuttle. No pets. | 5501 Carnegie Blvd. | 704/554–1234 | fax 704/554–8319 | 262 rooms | $119–$200 | AE, D, DC, MC, V.

Inn Uptown. See the city from the windows of this 1891 brick château on the edge of the Fourth Ward neighborhood. All rooms are different but carefully designed. One, for instance, is crisp and elegant with navy-blue wallpaper and a blue-and-white stripe bedspread. The lobby of this family-run business is cozy and has a fireplace. It's close to Uptown businesses and attractions. Complimentary breakfast. In-room data ports, some in-room hot tubs. Business services. No kids under 9. No smoking. | 129 N. Poplar St. | 704/342–2800 or 800/959–1990 | fax 704/342–2222 | 6 rooms | $129–$169 | AE, D, DC, MC, V.

Marriott–City Center. Just steps from the convention center, Discovery Place, and Blumenthal Performing Arts Center, this is a classic chain hotel. Some rooms have city views; others look over a park. Restaurant, bar. In-room data ports, some microwaves, refrigerators. Cable TV. Indoor pool. Hot tub. Exercise equipment. Laundry facilities, laundry service. Business services. Airport shuttle. | 100 W. Trade St. | 704/333–9000 | fax 704/342–3419 | www.marriotthotels.com | 423 rooms, 11 suites | $169–$179, suites $209 | AE, D, DC, MC, V.

Morehead Inn. This B&B in the Dilworth area caters to corporate clients but is cozy and homey. Some rooms have private balconies, fireplaces, or private gardens. Complimentary Continental breakfast. In-room data ports. Cable TV. | 1122 E. Morehead St. | 704/376–3357 or 888/667–4323 | fax 704/335–1110 | morehead@travelbase.com | www.moreheadinn.com | 12 suites | $120–$190 | AE, D, DC, MC, V.

★ **Park Hotel.** Some of the bright rooms in this downtown hotel have city views, and all are appointed with antique-style furniture, artwork, and marble vanities. Fresh flowers in the lobby, nightly turn-down service, and attentive staff members are added luxuries. Restaurant, bars with entertainment, room service. In-room data ports, some microwaves, some refrigerators. Cable TV. Pool. Hot tub. Exercise equipment. Business services. Airport shuttle. | 2200 Rexford Rd. | 704/364–8220 or 800/334–0331 | fax 704/365–4712 | www.theparkhotel.com | 184 rooms, 7 suites | $109–$185, $395–$750 suites | AE, D, DC, MC, V.

Southpark Suite. These spacious suites are south of town, and each overlooks a courtyard and has a dining area. The Southpark shopping mall is right next door. Restaurant, bar. Kitchenettes. Cable TV. Pool. Hot tub. Exercise equipment. Laundry facilities, laundry ser-

vice. Business services. No pets. No-smoking rooms. | 6300 Morrison Blvd. | 704/364–2400 or 800/647–8483 | fax 704/362–0203 | spsh-res@destinationtravel.com | www.south-parksuite.com | 208 suites | $99–$149 | AE, D, DC, MC, V.

CHEROKEE

MAP 8, A5

(Nearby towns also listed: Blue Ridge Parkway, Bryson City, Maggie Valley, Waynesville)

The 56,000-acre Cherokee Indian Reservation is known as the Qualla Boundary, and the town of Cherokee is its capital. It sits at the southern end of the Blue Ridge Parkway and at the entrance to the Great Smoky Mountains National Park.

Cherokee has two distinct personalities. There's the side that caters to pop culture, designed to appeal to mass numbers of tourists—this includes fun parks and gaming. The other Cherokee explores the rich heritage of the tribe's Eastern Band. Though relatively small in number, these people have been responsible for keeping Cherokee culture alive. They are descendants of those who hid in the Great Smoky Mountains to avoid the forced removal of the Cherokee Nation to Oklahoma in the 1800s on the "Trail of Tears." They are survivors, extremely attached to the hiking, swimming, trout fishing, and natural beauty of their homeland.

Information: Cherokee Tribal Travel and Promotion | Box 460, Cherokee, 28719 | 828/497–9195 or 800/438–1601. **Visitor Center** | U.S. 441 Business | 828/497–9195 or 800/438–1601 | cherokeeinfo@cherokee-nc.com | www.cherokee-nc.com.

Attractions

Cherokee Reservation. More than 30 mi of stocked trout streams and abundant hiking and mountain biking trails are just some of the attractions on this 56,000-acre reservation bordering the Great Smoky Mountains. Mingo Falls, 6 mi north of downtown Cherokee on Big Cove Road, is one of the largest waterfalls in the western Carolinas, with a 210-ft drop. Rafting and tubing trips can be arranged on the Ocanaluftee and Raven Fork Rivers, and camping is available at numerous private campgrounds in the area. | Visitor Center, U.S. 441 Business | 828/497–9195 or 800/438–1601 | fax 828/497–3220 | Free; $7 per day for fishing permit | Daily.

Harrah's Cherokee Casino. The more than 60,000 square ft of gaming area is filled with thousands of video gaming machines. There's also a 1,500-seat theater that draws a variety of headliners, three restaurants, and a child-care facility. | 777 Casino Dr. | 828/497–7777 | fax 828/497–5076 | Free | Daily 24 hrs.

Museum of the Cherokee Indian. After a $3.5 million renovation, the museum is able to combine technology (computer-generated images, specialty lighting, and audio, holographic imaging) with an artifact collection dating back 10,000 years to give you a multisensory trip through Cherokee history. | U.S. 441 at Drama Rd. | 828/497–3481 | fax 828/497–4985 | $6 | Mon.–Sat. 9–8, Sun 9–5.

Oconaluftee Indian Village. Guides in native costume take you through this authentically re-created 18th-century Indian community while artisans demonstrate the traditional skills of their ancestors, such as weaving, pottery, canoe making, and hunting techniques. | U.S. 441 | 828/497–2315 | fax 828/497–6987 | www.oconalufteevillage.com | $12 | Mid-May–late Oct., daily 9–5:30.

Qualla Arts and Crafts Mutual. Across the street from the Museum of the Cherokee Indian, this cooperative displays and sells baskets, masks, pottery, and wood carvings handcrafted by 300 Cherokee artisans. | U.S. 441 | 828/497–3103 | Free | June–Aug., daily 8–8; Sept.–Oct., daily 8–6; Nov.–May, daily 8–4:30.

Santa's Land. This "fun park" has rides, a zoo, a Christmas theme, and yes, Santa and his elves. There are specialty shops as well as demonstrations of broom making and black-smithing. | U.S. 19 N | 828/497–9191 or 800/648–7268 | fax 828/497–9188 | $14 | May–Oct., weekdays 9–5, weekends 9–6; Nov., weekends 9–6.

ON THE CALENDAR
JUNE–AUG.: *Unto These Hills Outdoor Drama.* Mountainside Theater holds this color-ful and well-staged history of the Cherokee from the time of Spanish explorer Her-nando de Soto's visit in 1540 to the infamous Trail of Tears, the forced removal of the North Carolina natives to Oklahoma. | U.S. 441 N | Mon.–Sat. at 8:30 PM | 828/497–2111.
JULY: *Fourth of July Pow-Wow.* Native American dance and crafts demonstrations as well as athletic competitions take place on the tribal ceremonial grounds behind the Museum of the Cherokee Indian. | U.S. 441 at Drama Rd. | 828/497–3481 or 800/438–1601.

Dining
Grandma's Country Cooking Buffet. American. Come-as-you-are family-style dining is on tap with breakfast, lunch, and dinner buffets. You'll find lots of chicken entrées, some seafood, and at least 10 vegetables. On nice days, you can sit outside at picnic tables. Kids' menu. No alcohol. | U.S. 441 and 19 | 828/497–4504 | Reservations not accepted | $5–$9 | D, MC, V.

Grandma's Pancake and Steak. Steak. Locals feast on buttermilk pancakes and drain bot-tomless pots of coffee at this popular breakfast spot. By afternoon, budget steaks are the meal of choice. | U.S. 19 | 828/497–9801 | $5–$10 | No credit cards.

Little Princess Restaurant. American. Hamburgers, sandwiches, homemade soups, and sal-ads draw diners to this café-style eatery with placemats and flatware rolled in paper nap-kins. | Aquoni Rd. | 828/497–6624 | $5–$8 | MC, V.

Tee Pee Restaurant. American. Overlooking the Oconaluftee River, this casual, family-ori-ented restaurant has daily all-you-can-eat lunch and dinner buffets. Dinner has at least three different types of meats, as well as a range of vegetable choices, and there's also a full à la carte menu. Friday is seafood night, but locals come for the broiled or fried rain-bow trout any night of the week. There's open-air dining on the deck. Buffet breakfast, lunch, and dinner. Kids' menu. No alcohol. | U.S. 441 N | 828/497–5141 | Reservations not accepted | $9–$14 | MC, V | Closed Nov.–Jan.

Lodging
Best Western–Great Smokies Inn. Across the street from the Great Smokies Convention Center is this hotel serving both business and leisure travelers. For business travelers, there are the usual amenities. For leisure travelers, there's a free shuttle to the casino. The log-cabin-style lobby has antique furniture and a fishing theme. Restaurant, room service. Cable TV. Pool, wading pool. Laundry facilities. Business services. Pets allowed ($10 fee). | U.S. 441 | 828/497–2020 or 800/528–1234 | fax 828/497–3903 | 152 rooms | $90 | AE, D, DC, MC, V.

Comfort Inn. All rooms have balconies and a view of the Oconoluftee River. Some include French doors and love seats. The inn is within walking distance of restaurants, 1 mi from downtown Cherokee, and 5 mi from the U.S. 441 entrance to the Great Smoky Mountains National Park. Complimentary Continental breakfast. In-room data ports, some refriger-ators. Cable TV. Pool. Hot tub. Business services. | U.S. 19 S | 828/497–2411 or 800/228–5150 | fax 828/497–6555 | 87 rooms | $59–$89 | AE, D, DC, MC, V | Closed Jan.–Feb.

Cool Waters. This long, low motel is ½ mi from the casino. It offers a playground, swim-ming pool, and picnic area. The standard motel rooms are done either in blue or maroon. Restaurant, picnic area. Cable TV. Pool, wading pool. Tennis courts. | U.S. 19 E | 828/497–3855 | 50 rooms | $65–$75 | D, MC, V.

Days Inn. Kick back in the king executive rooms with a 25-inch TV and reclining chair. Other rooms have desks, and some face a small creek. The hotel is ½ mi from the casino and 3 mi from the entrance to Great Smoky Mountains National Park. Free shuttle to the casino and theater. Cable TV. 2 pools, wading pool. Playground. | U.S. 19 | 828/497–9171 or 800/daysinn | fax 828/497–3424 | 57 rooms | $49–$95 | AE, D, DC, MC, V.

Econo Lodge Cherokee. The fact that this standard hotel is 1 mi from the Blue Ridge Parkway, 2 mi from Harrah's, and has shopping within walking distance makes it a handy overnight spot. Complimentary Continental breakfast. Cable TV. Outdoor pool. | 1593 Acquoni Rd. | 828/497–2226 | 66 rooms | $49–$75 | AF, DC, D, MC, V.

Holiday Inn. Rooms are standard chain fare, but the staff at this well-equipped motel is very friendly. The lobby is decorated with Native American art, and some rooms have

© Corbis

ARTS AND CRAFTS

When it comes to arts and crafts in western North Carolina, there's so much more going on than first meets the eye. And that's the fun of it—the hunt. Handmade treasures are also out in the open, however. More than 85 crafts fairs are held annually throughout the rural 21-county region.

More than 4,000 people in the mountains earn part or all of their living from crafts, and many of them are "around the bend" and in homes tucked back in forested hollows. They patiently coax form from clay and wood and metal, and because art is close to the heart, they are usually happy to talk about what they do. Interesting roads that are off the map can lead to workshops. If hours are posted, however, it's best to respect them; time is precious.

In the beginning, it was practical function, not notions of folk art, behind all the quilting, weaving, woodworking, and pottery making. By the latter part of the 19th century, though, missionaries, social workers, and women of means—Frances Goodrich and Edith Vanderbilt among them—began to recognize that the things of day-to-day life contained artistry and thus economic salvation.

Today, utility and aesthetics have melded. From furnaces in the northwest counties of Mitchell and Yancey come gobs of hot liquid that are shaped by hand into art glass prized by collectors and dealers worldwide. Many glassblowers have perfected their métier at the prestigious Penland School of Crafts, whose courses include printmaking, wood, surface design, metals, drawing, clay, and fibers. The work of students and graduates, much of it contemporary, is on display in area galleries including Penland's own extensive gallery shop.

In the tiny village of Crossnore in southern Avery County, a rock cottage houses the Crossnore School's Weaving Room. Favored here are patterns used by the early settlers of the Appalachians; however, in a nod to modernity the ladies spin with easy-care rayon and synthetics as well as with cotton, wool, and linen.

And on the Cherokee Reservation, in the shadow of the Smoky Mountains, elders pass on to children the secrets of finger weaving, wood carving, and mask and beaded-jewelry making. Their work, intricate and colorful and in shops such as Medicine Man Crafts in downtown Cherokee, is ageless, a connective thread to a time that predates the United States by thousands of years.

mountain views. Restaurant, room service. In-room data ports. Cable TV. 2 pools (1 indoor), whirlpool. Hot tub, sauna. Game room with pinball and pool table. Fitness center. Playground. Laundry facilities. Shop. | U.S. 19 S | 828/497–9181 | fax 828/497–5973 | 154 rooms | $59–$130 | AE, D, DC, MC, V.

Pioneer. This standard small motel is in the heart of downtown Cherokee, and you can fish right on the premises (if you have a license), since it's right on the Oconoluftee River. Kitchenettes (in cottages). Cable TV. Pool. Fishing. | U.S. 19 S | 828/497–2435 | 21 rooms, 6 cottages | $48–78, $75–$150 cottages | AE, D, MC, V.

Quality Inn Cherokee. This two-story hotel has chairs outside each room, where you can relax and look over the small outdoor swimming pool and concrete sundeck, or just chat with neighbors. A free newspaper is available every morning. Complimentary Continental breakfast. Some in-room hot tubs. Cable TV. Outdoor pool. | U.S. 441 N Bypass | 828/497–4702 | 121 rooms | $45–$149 | AE, DC, D, MC, V.

CHERRYVILLE

MAP 8, D5

(Nearby towns also listed: Gastonia, Shelby)

CHERRYVILLE

INTRO
ATTRACTIONS
DINING
LODGING

Settled in the last half of the 18th century by Scots-Irish and German families, Cherryville, first known as White Pine, has changed from farming settlement to textile community to trucking center. This Gaston County town has a vital, central commercial district and continues to place a heavy emphasis on families, area ministries, civic clubs, and baseball teams.

Information: Gaston County Travel and Tourism | Box 2339, Gastonia 28053 | 704/867–2170 or 800/849–9994 | kminter@gastongov.org | www.gaston.org.

Attractions

C. Grier Beam Truck Museum. This museum, only one of three in the country devoted to trucks, is built in an old-style service station. The oldest trucks displayed date from 1927. | 111 N. Mountain St. | 704/435–3072 | www.beamtruckmuseum.com | $1 | Fri. 10–5, Sat. 10–3.

Cherryville Historical Museum. Old City Hall, a local landmark, is where you can follow the history of Cherryville from the early 1800s to the present through a number of exhibits. | 109 E. Main St. | 704/435–8011 | Free | Fri. and Sun. 2–5, Sat. 10–5.

Crowders Mountain State Park. The park's 2,758 acres include 1,625-ft Crowders Mountain and 1,705-ft Kings Pinnacle, peaks that attract even experienced climbers. You'll also find a 9-acre lake and fishing pier, more than 15 mi of hiking and nature trails, plus backpack camping and picnic facilities. | 522 Park Office La., Kings Mountain | 704/853–5375 | fax 704/853–5391 | www.crowders@vnet.net | Free | Daily.

ON THE CALENDAR

JAN.: *Annual Shoot-In.* Continuing a tradition begun in Germany centuries ago, some 100 dues-paying members of the New Year's Shooters bring in the New Year with a chant for good luck and the firing of black-powder muskets. The chants and shoot take place between midnight on New Year's Eve and the evening of New Year's Day at several locations in and around Cherryville. A finale is held at the high-school football stadium. | 704/435–1714.

APR.: *Cherry Blossom Festival.* Locals welcome spring with a festival that has arts and crafts, food and entertainment, and a children's area with rides and a petting zoo. | Main St. | 704/435–1714.

Dining

Black's Grill. American/Casual. In this simple, large room, you can settle into a booth and order one burgers, sandwiches, pork barbecues, or milk shakes. No alcohol. | 1915 Lincolnton Hwy. | 704/435–5666 | $3–$6 | No credit cards | Closed Sun.–Mon.

Fish Box. Seafood. This take-out-only shop opens at 3:30 PM and supplies locals with fried seafood (shrimp, catfish, perch, flounder) with coleslaw, hush puppies, and fries. | 108 W. 1st St. | 704/435–9717 | $5–$8 | No credit cards | Closed Sun.–Tues.

Home Folks Café. American. You'll know what season it is by what's on the walls in this family-owned restaurant, as it changes to reflect the seasons and holidays. Locals like the hearty, country-style food, including fried chicken (Friday special), baked ham, livermush (a fried, sausagelike mixture of liver, cereal, and spices), flounder, and liver and onions. Pies and puddings are all homemade. No alcohol. | 209 E. Main St. | 704/435–9336 | $6–$11 | No credit cards | Closed Sun., Mon., and wk before Labor Day.

Lodging

Ramada Limited. Rooms in this standard chain have a maroon and beige color scheme. The hotel is 10 mi from restaurants and a movie theater. Complimentary Continental breakfast. Some microwaves, refrigerators. Cable TV. Pool. Hot tub. Business services. Conference room. Banquet center. | 728 York Rd., Kings Mountain | 704/739–2544 | fax 704/739–6586 | 104 rooms | $40–$80 | AE, D, DC, MC, V.

Robin's Nest B&B. This 1914 Classical Revival home has four guest rooms with private baths and televisions, a fireplace for relaxing, and a stone pond in the backyard. Mount Holly is about 20 mi southeast of Cherryville. Complimentary breakfast. Cable TV. Pond. | 156 N. Main St., Mount Holly | 704/827–2420 or 888/711–6378 | www.robinsnestbb.com | 4 rooms | $70–$100 | MC, V.

CONCORD

MAP 8, E5

(Nearby towns also listed: Albemarle, Charlotte, Cornelius, Kannapolis, Salisbury)

In the 18th century, gold was discovered 5 mi from downtown Concord, and the country's first documented gold rush began in this Cabarrus County town. In the latter half of the 19th century, after Reconstruction, James Cannon started a cotton mill in Concord that would grow to become a textile manufacturing giant. The money generated by that business and Cannon's civic-mindedness combined to produce grand homes, a library, a hospital, and some of the most beautiful churches in the area. Important to Concord's present economy is a major motor speedway, just west of town.

Information: Cabarrus County Convention and Visitors Bureau | 2319 Dale Earnhardt., Kannapolis, 28083 | 704/938–4550 or 800/848–3740 | info@cabarruscvb.com | www.cabarruscvb.com.

Attractions

Concord Mills. Proving that not all shopping malls are the same, Concord Mills seeks to provide "shoppertainment," that is, they try to make spending money fun. Eight themed entrances take you to seven themed shopping areas laid out on a circle as well as a food court. Look out for the in-house TV channel spouting out messages encouraging you to shop. | 8111 Concord Mills Blvd. | 704/979–3000 | www.concordmills.com | Free | Daily.

Reed Gold Mine State Historic Site. The nation's first gold rush began here, just 12 mi south of Concord, after young Conrad Reed found a 17-pound gold nugget in 1799. This history is preserved with a museum, an orientation film, a guided underground tour, a stamp mill, and walking trails. Gold panning is available for a fee on a seasonal basis. | 9621 Reed Mine

Rd., Stanfield | 704/721–4653 | fax 704/721–4657 | Free; gold panning $2 per pan | Apr.–Oct.,
Mon.–Sat. 9–5, Sun. 1–5; Nov.–Mar., Tues.–Sat. 10–4, Sun. 1–4.

ON THE CALENDAR
OCT.: *Share Cabarrus Festival.* Downtown Concord celebrates with crafts, food, enter-
tainment, and a car show. | 704/782–4111.
OCT.: *FallFest.* This autumn event is designed around hayrides, music, and children's
games. | 704/784–4208.
NOV.–DEC.: *Santa Scramble.* A 5K road race leads the annual Concord Christmas
Parade. | 704/788–9840.

Dining
Austin's. Jamaican. Get traditional specialties at this take-out only spot, including jerk chicken,
Jamaican stew beef, curry goat, and ox tail. Special sides include rice and peas, yams,
greens, and Jamaican sodas. | 345 S. Kings Dr. | 704/331–8778 | $6–$12 | MC, D, V | Closed Sun.

Concord Family Restaurant. Eclectic. One of the three dining rooms has a 1950s theme,
complete with diner-style booths. The food is an eclectic blend of down-home American
fare such as seafood and steak as well as Greek, Italian, and some vegetarian entrées. Break-
fast is served all day. | 921 Concord Pkwy. N | 704/786–5614 | Reservations not accepted |
$6–$11 | AE, D, DC, MC, V.

Lodging
Colonial Inn. This inn is within walking distance of restaurants and the theater, yet is secluded.
Rooms are done in a Colonial style. Cable TV. Pool. | 1325 Concord Pkwy. N | 704/782–2146 |
fax 704/786–9856 | 65 rooms | $45–$80 | AE, D, MC, V.

Essex House B&B. Lowe's Motor Speedway, Concord Mills mall, Carowinds Amusement Park,
and other area attractions are not far from this Colonial home. You can borrow movies to
watch in your room, golf clubs to use at courses 2–5 mi away, and bicycles to pedal around
town. Complimentary breakfast. In-room data ports. Cable TV, in-room VCRs. Business
services. | 2577 Essex Dr. | 704/262–7059 or 888/760–8666 | fax 704/795–5910 | essex-
housebandb@aol.com | 3 rooms | $80–$125 | AE, D, MC, V.

CORNELIUS

MAP 8, D5

(Nearby towns also listed: Charlotte, Concord, Kannapolis, Statesville)

Cornelius is a community in North Mecklenburg County, a part of the Charlotte region,
yet it has its own identity as a strong manufacturing center—Cornelius has retained
its original cotton mill. Lately, growth has been fueled by its proximity to both Lake
Norman, a man-made inland sea where you can enjoy all types of water sports, and
academically acclaimed Davidson College, 2 mi from town.

Information: Lake Norman Chamber of Commerce | Box 760, Cornelius, 28031 | 704/
892–1922. **Visitor Center** | 20216 Knox Rd., in Shops on the Green | 704/892–1922 |
www.lakenorman.org or www.lakenormanchamber.org.

Attractions
Lake Norman. Lake Norman was created by the Duke Power Company when it built the
Cowan Ford Dam to generate hydroelectric power. Completed in 1963, the lake totals 525
square mi and is claimed by towns in four counties: Mecklenburg, Iredell, Lincoln, and
Catawba. Homes, restaurants, and shopping areas are clustered around central areas of
the lake. Campgrounds and community parks abound, with everything from canoe rentals
and nature trails to picnic areas and tennis courts. | 704/382–8587 | Free | Daily.

North Carolina Auto Racing Hall of Fame. Just 10 mi north in Mooresville stands this museum, which displays more than 35 race cars, has a movie theater with films about racing, and holds other exhibits on the history of racing in North Carolina. | 119 Knob Hill Rd., Mooresville | 704/663–5331 | www.ncarhof.com | $5 | Mon.–Sat. 9–5.

ON THE CALENDAR

SEPT.: *LakeFest*. Life on Lake Norman, a man-made "inland sea" with 520 mi of shoreline, is celebrated with two days of live music, games and contests, children's activities, a dog show, boat rides, and food and drink. | 19000 Jetton Rd. | 704/896–9808.

SEPT.: *Davidson College Homecoming*. You can participate in the all-American tradition of a college football homecoming as you cheer on the Davidson Wildcats against the team's Division I-AA opponents. | 704/894–2000.

Dining

Captain's Galley. Seafood. Curbing your seafood craving is easy at this casual dining spot with a nautical look. You can try the crab legs or the fried seafood platter, which includes flounder, crab, clams, oysters, and shrimp. Reservations aren't accepted for dinner on Friday and Saturday, but you can reserve on other nights. Kids' menu. | 105 J Statesville Rd., Huntersville | 704/875–6038 | $5–$15 | MC | Closed Sun.

Kobe Japanese House of Steak and Seafood. Japanese. You get a show with your meal here; the chef comes and cooks at your table. This casual, family restaurant also has a sushi bar and a regular menu. From the latter, you can try the Kobe filet mignon or the sesame chicken. Kids' menu. Early-bird dinners on weekdays. | 20465 Chartwell Center Dr. | 704/896–7778 | $12–$30 | AE, D, DC, MC, V | No lunch weekends.

South Shore Grill. Contemporary. The dark wood and palm trees in the dining room have a Cuba-in-the-1950s look, but the food here is Louisiana style. This place is known for Cajun specialties including gumbo and jambalaya, though the large menu includes surf and turf, pastas, and seafood. You can dine on the deck overlooking the water and have a drink at the outdoor tiki bar. Or you can pull up your boat to the slips on the dock outside. On Tuesday the dining room is decked out for Mardi Gras night; Thursdays are Caribbean Cruise nights. Kids' menu. | 20210 Henderson Rd. | 704/895–6011 | $9–$25 | AE, D, DC, MC, V.

Lodging

Best Western Lake Norman. Guest rooms in this typical chain hotel have 25-inch TVs and coffeemakers. Restaurants and a movie theater are within walking distance. Complimentary Continental breakfast. In-room data ports, some microwaves, refrigerators. Cable TV on request. Pool. Exercise equipment. Business services. Laundry services. No pets. | 19608 Liverpool Pkwy. | 704/896–0660 | fax 704/896–8633 | 80 rooms, 10 suites | $74–179 | AE, D, DC, MC, V.

Comfort Inn–Lake Norman. The rooms are oversized and the lobby rustic in this chain hostelry. It's 1 mi from Ramsey Creek Park, Jetton Creek Park, and Lake Norman. Complimentary Continental breakfast. In-room data ports, some microwaves, refrigerators. Cable TV. Pool. Laundry facilities. Business services. No pets. | 20740 Torrence Chapel Rd. | 704/892–3500 or 800/848–9751 | fax 704/892–6473 | 82 rooms, 8 suites | $72–$120; $90–$125 suites | AE, D, DC, MC, V.

Davidson Village Inn. All rooms in this small, friendly inn all have four-poster beds and overlook the town of Davidson, 2 mi from Cornelius. Because of its location across the street from Davidson College, the place books up months and even years in advance for homecoming and other school-event weekends. There's no restaurant, but the inn serves breakfast and afternoon tea, or you can get room service from neighboring restaurants. Complimentary Continental breakfast, room service. Minibars, some microwaves, refrigerators. Cable TV. Business services. | 117 Depot St., Davidson | 704/892–8044 or 800/892–

0796 | fax 704/896–2184 | www.davidsoninn.com | 14 rooms, 4 suites | $100–$110, $115–125 suites | AE, D, DC, MC, V.

Dove House Inn. This three-story home was built by the Dove family in 1907, and many of the home's furnishings are in the early 1900s style. An outdoor hot tub sits in a small garden and patio area. Complimentary breakfast. Cable TV in common room. Outdoor hot tub. No smoking. | 19309 Old Statesville Rd. | 704/896–8511 | fax 704/896–8113 | www.the-dovehouse.com | 3 rooms | $80–$110 | MC, V.

Hampton Inn. These bright, basic accommodations are just 1 mi from Lake Norman and Jetton Creek Park, and 2 mi from shops, restaurants, and bars. Complimentary Continental breakfast. In-room data ports, some refrigerators, some microwaves. Cable TV. Pool. Exercise equipment. Business services. Laundry services. | 19501 Statesville Rd. | 704/892–9900 | fax 704/896–7488 | www.hampton-inn.com | 117 rooms | $79–$84 | AE, D, DC, MC, V.

Holiday Inn. The only full-service hotel in the area is only 500 ft from Lake Norman. Restaurant, bar, room service. Some microwaves, some refrigerators. Cable TV. Pool. Exercise equipment. Laundry facilities. Some pets allowed ($25 fee). | 19901 Holiday La. | 704/892–9120 | fax 704/892–3854 | 119 rooms | $80 | AE, D, DC, MC, V.

Holiday Inn Express. This simple, clean, modern hotel is five minutes from Lake Norman. Complimentary Continental breakfast. In-room data ports, some microwaves, some refrigerators. Cable TV. Pool. Business services. No pets. No smoking. | 14135 Statesville Rd., Huntersville | 704/875–1165 or 800/HOLIDAY | fax 704/875–1894 | www.basshotels.com | 60 rooms | $84 | AE, D, DC, MC, V.

Microtel Inn Lake Norman. Off I–77 at Exit 28, this basic multistory hotel is 2 mi from Davidson College, a mile from Lake Norman, and just a few blocks from Mom's Restaurant and the Stock Car Cafe. Cable TV. | 20820 Torrence Chapel Rd. | 704/895–1828 or 800/642–7622 | fax 704/895–1258 | 90 rooms | $55 | AE, D, MC, V.

Quality Inn & Suites. Davidson College is less than 5 mi from this hotel that is also within walking distance of a movie theater and restaurants. You can read a free newspaper every morning. Complimentary Continental breakfast. Cable TV. Pool. Hot tub. Business services. | 19521 Liverpool Pkwy. | 704/896–7622 | 105 rooms | $75–$120 | AE, DC, D, MC, V.

DUCK

MAP 8, L3

(Nearby towns also listed: Kill Devil Hills, Kitty Hawk, Manteo, Nags Head, Outer Banks)

It's said that in the lucrative hunting years, those before World War I, the waterfowl were so abundant during migratory season that they darkened the daytime sky. "Market hunters" could sell as many ducks as they could kill and still not appease northern city folks' insatiable appetite for the meat. Back then, most of the land between Duck and Corolla, 15 mi to the north, was held by hunting clubs. Today Duck teems with humans during the high season, yet the beaches at this northern end of the Outer Banks remain pristine. The leafy neighborhoods of this upscale resort village, which has views of both ocean and sound, are most easily navigated on foot or bike. You won't find chain restaurants or motels here, but you will find a shopper's paradise.

Information: Dare County Tourist Bureau | Box 399, Manteo, 27954 | 252/473–2138 or 800/446–6262 | visitorinfo@outerbanks.org | www.outerbanks.org.

Attractions

Currituck Lighthouse. The Keeper's House at the base of the light has been recognized for its architectural significance and placed on the National Register of Historic Places. It's 212 steps to the top of this northernmost lighthouse on the Outer Banks. First beamed in 1875, its beacon continues to flash warnings to ships approaching North Carolina's barrier islands. The lighthouse is open for tours; the entry fee is donated to the Corolla Wild Horse Fund. | Rte. 12, Corolla Village | 252/453–4939 | www.currituckbeachlight.com | $5 | Daily.

Corolla Wild Horses. Descended from Spanish mustangs brought to the Outer Banks hundreds of years ago by explorers, these hardy wild horses have been protected from encroaching development by being in a refuge area north of Duck. Accessible only by 4-wheel-drive vehicles, their sanctuary is protected by state and federal authorities. They roam at will. Though some are very friendly, stay at least 50 yards away from them. | Rte. 12, between Sanderling and Corolla | www.corollawildhorses.com | Daily.

ON THE CALENDAR

JULY: *Independence Day Festival.* The Currituck Chamber of Commerce hosts this party, which typically begins in early afternoon. A day of live music, arts and crafts, and food culminates with a fireworks show. The festival is on the grounds of the Whalehead Club, now owned by the county. Proceeds benefit the restoration of the club, once the grandest private home and hunting retreat on the Outer Banks. | Off Rte. 12, Corolla | 877/287–7488.

Dining

Blue Point Bar and Grill. Contemporary. A diner theme sets the busy pace at this restaurant on the sound. Though the place is known for crab cakes, the rest of the menu is creative and varied. On nights when the weather is nice, you can dine on the porch overlooking the water. Sun. brunch. | 1240 Rte. 12 | 252/261–8090 | fax 252/261–7284 | www.goodfood-goodwine.com | Reservations essential | $20–$40 | AE, MC, V | Closed Mon. and Nov.–Mar.

Elizabeth's Café and Winery. Eclectic. At this small bistro under oaks, you can dine either in the French country dining room or the stone grotto. The menu changes constantly to reflect the day's purchases, whether it's Norwegian salmon, rack of lamb, Angus beef tenderloin, or seasonal vegetable. *Wine Spectator* has said that this restaurant has "one of the most outstanding wine lists in the world." | Rte. 12 | 252/261–6145 | elizcafe@pinn.net | Reservations essential | Fixed price $80 or $125 | AE, D, DC, MC, V | No lunch.

Nicoletta's Italian Cafe. Italian. White linen tablecloths, flowers, and a view of the Currituck Beach Lighthouse enhance the mood at this small café in the Corolla Light Village Shops. You can also sit outside on the porch and enjoy such specialties as fresh seafood, Angus beef, and a variety of southern Italian and other pasta dishes. Kids' menu. | Rte. 12, Corolla | 252/453–4004 | Reservations essential | $24–$28 | AE, D, MC, V.

Sanderling Inn Restaurant and Bar. Eclectic. In a former lifesaving station listed on the National Register of Historic Places, this place has a menu that ranges from crab cakes to roast Carolina duckling with black cherry sauce and fricassee of shrimp. Kids' menu. Sun. brunch. | 1461 Duck Rd., Sanderling | 252/261–4111 or 800/701–4111 | fax 252/261–1638 | www.sanderlinginn.com | Dinner reservations essential | $23–$35 | AE, D, MC, V.

Lodging

Advice 5¢. The name may be quirky, but this contemporary B&B in the North Beach area is very serious about guest care. It's within walking distance of the beach, less than ¼ mi from downtown shops and restaurants, and it has an arrangement that allows you to use the tennis courts and swimming pool at Sea Pines, a property across the street. Crisp, colorful linens dress the beds in each room. All rooms have ceiling fans, shuttered windows, and baths stocked with thick cotton towels. Complimentary Continental breakfast. Pool. Tennis court. | 111 Scarborough La. | 252/255–1050 or 800/238–4235 | www.theouter-banks.com/advice5/ | 4 rooms, 1 suite | $155–$185 | MC, V | Closed Dec.–Jan.

Inn at Corolla Light. The inn is a part of the Corolla Light Resort and sits on Currituck Sound, about 10 mi from Duck. You can access the ocean, ¼ mi away, by bike or open-air trolley service. Even the smaller rooms feel big thanks to richly toned fabrics, large beds, and windows with views of the garden, pool, or sound. Restaurant, complimentary Continental breakfast. Some kitchenettes, refrigerators. In-room VCRs. Pool, wading pool. Hot tub, sauna. Golf privileges, 9 tennis courts. Health club, hiking, racquetball, volleyball. Beach, water sports, boating, fishing, bicycles. Shops, video games. | 1066 Ocean Terr, Corolla | 252/453–3340 or 800/ 215–0772 | fax 252/453–6947 | www.corolla-inn.com | 43 rooms | $159–$279 | D, MC, V.

Sanderling Inn Resort & Conference Center. The Sanderling, on a remote beach 5 mi north of Duck, is a fine place to be pampered. Recreation choices include boating and nature walks through the Pine Island Sanctuary. Although it was built in 1985 and has contemporary conveniences, the inn has the look of old Nags Head. Rooms are casual with ceiling fans, wicker, and neutral tones. Restaurant, bar. Some kitchenettes, minibars, some microwaves, some refrigerators. Indoor pool. Hot tub. 4 tennis courts. Health club, water sports, boating. Library. Business services. | 1461 Duck Rd., Sanderling | 252/261–4111 or 800/701–4111 | fax 252/ 261–1638 | www.sanderlinginn.com | 88 rooms, 29 efficiencies | $204–$261 | AE, D, MC, V.

DUNN

MAP 8, H5

(Nearby towns also listed: Fayetteville, Smithfield)

A century ago, Dunn was settled as a logging town and turpentine distilling center. Today it is the largest of five towns in Harnett County. Two religious colleges call Dunn home, and Campbell University, which regularly presents concerts, plays, and musicals, is 10 mi away in Buies Creek. North–south links through the town include I-95 and U.S. 301, while I-40 and U.S. 421 provide east–west routes.

Information: Dunn Area Tourism Authority | Box 310, Dunn, 28335 | 910/892–3282 | tourism@dunnchamber.com | www.dunntourism.org.

Attractions

Averasboro Civil War Battlefield. The battle of Averasboro was the first deliberate, tactical resistance to the march of Union forces through Georgia and the Carolinas. Historic markers outline the events of this action, which took place in 1865. Highlighted are Lebanon, a plantation home used as a Confederate hospital, and Chicora Cemetery, a burial ground for the battle's heroes. The battlefield museum outlines the Averasboro battle with displays of uniforms, weapons, and plans used by the Confederate Army. | 910/892– 3282; museum 910/891–5019 | fax 910/892–4071 | Free | Daily.

Bentonville Battleground State Historic Site. Bentonville was the largest battle fought on North Carolina soil and the last full-scale Confederate offensive. The Harper House on the site served as a Union field hospital during the battle. Both a driving tour and walking tour are available. | 5466 Harper House Rd., Four Oaks | 910/594–0789 | fax 910/594–0222 | www.ah.dcr.state.nc.us/sections/hs/bentonvi/bentonvi.htm | Free | Apr.–Oct., Mon.–Sat. 9–5, Sun. 1–5; Nov.–Mar., Tues.–Sat. 10–4, Sun. 1–4.

ON THE CALENDAR

JUNE: *National Hollerin' Contest.* There's singing, dance, games, arts and crafts, and food at this festival, but the whole point is the entertainment that includes all manner of whistles, hoots, and hollers: conch shell and fox horn blowin', hollerin' for juniors, and callin' for ladies. Often, the winner of the internationally known competition at Midway High School's athletic field appears on national television. | Spivey's Corner | 910/892–3282.

OCT.: *Denim Days.* The town of Erwin celebrates its moniker "Denim Capital of the World" with arts and crafts, a car show, a street dance, military displays, and a parachute jump. | 910/892–4113.

Dining

Brass Lantern Steak House. Steak. The dimly lit interior makes this popular with couples; since you can see it from I–95, the restaurant also attracts travelers. In addition to beef dishes, the menu lists a number of seafood entrées. Beer and wine only. | I–95 and Springbranch Rd. | 910/892–6309 | $12–$20 | AE, D, MC, V | Closed Sun.

Howard's Barbecue. Barbecue. Two sides are all glass, giving you a beautiful view of the Cape Fear river from any seat in the house. This place is known for chopped-pork barbecue, all-you-can-eat hush puppies, a fried seafood platter, and desserts. | 100 S. Main St., Lillington | 910/893–4571 | $5–$12 | MC, V | Closed Sun.–Mon.

Lodging

Best Western Midway. Guest rooms all have desks; some have pool views. The affordable price is a big draw of this chain hotel. Restaurant. Cable TV. Pool, wading pool. Business services. Pets allowed ($5 fee). | 603 Springbranch Rd. | 910/892–2162 or 800/528–1234 | fax 910/892–3010 | 146 rooms | $40–$50 | AE, D, DC, MC, V.

Ramada Inn. This standard chain hotel is about eight blocks from the battlefield museum and golf courses. Restaurant, complimentary Continental breakfast. In-room data ports, some microwaves, some refrigerators. Cable TV. Pool. Laundry service. Business services. Pets allowed. | 1011 E. Cumberland St. | 910/892–8101 or 800/2RAMADA | 100 rooms | $48–$69 | AE, D, DC, MC, V.

Simply Divine B&B. A 1,000-volume library graces this Southern Colonial inn that was built in the early 1900s and later became the first B&B in town. A 100-year-old hardwood tree still stands in the back. Guest rooms have 10-foot ceilings, queen-size beds, and period furnishings in styles ranging from English countryside to Art Deco. Two rooms have gas-log fireplaces. Complimentary breakfast. Cable TV. No pets. No smoking. | 309 W. Divine St. | 910/891–1103 or 800/357–9336 | fax 910/891–1427 | simplydivine@dockpoint.net | 3 rooms | $69 | MC, V.

DURHAM

MAP 8, G4

(Nearby towns also listed: Burlington, Cary, Chapel Hill, Henderson, Raleigh)

Ethnically and racially diverse Durham long ago shed its tobacco-town image and is now known as the "City of Medicine" for the medical and research center at Duke University, one of the top schools in the nation. With tens of thousands of employees, Duke is not only the largest employer in Durham but also one of the largest in the state. Additionally, the majority of the 6,800-acre Research Triangle Park, one of the largest research parks in the United States, lies in Durham County.

Mills and tobacco warehouses around the city have been converted to chic shops, offices, and condos. This city of 212,000 is home to three art centers and hosts 18 cultural festivals a year, and the Durham Bulls, a AAA baseball team immortalized in the hit movie *Bull Durham,* set national attendance records at their 9,000-seat stadium downtown.

Information: Durham Convention and Visitors Bureau | 101 E. Morgan St., 27701 | 919/687–0288 or 800/446–8604 | tc@durham-cvb.com | www.durham-nc.com.

Attractions

Bennett Place State Historic Site. Union general William Sherman and Confederate general Joseph Johnston met at the Bennett farmstead 17 days after Robert E. Lee's Appomattox surrender to arrange the largest troop surrender of the Civil War. Reconstructed farmhouse, outbuildings, interpretive center, and museum. | 4409 Bennett Memorial Rd. | 919/383–4345 | fax 919/383–4349 | www.ah.dcr.state.nc.us/sections/hs/bennett/bennett.htm | Free | Apr.–Oct., Mon.–Sat. 9–5, Sun. 1–5; Nov.–Mar., Tues.–Sat. 10–4, Sun. 1–4.

Duke Homestead State Historic Site. Here are the ancestral farm home (circa 1852) and other outbuildings of the Washington Duke family, who built a worldwide financial empire based on the production of tobacco and the development of electricity in the two Carolinas. The Tobacco Museum, with interactive displays that tell the history of the "golden leaf," is also on the grounds. | 2828 Duke Homestead Rd. | 919/477–5498 | fax 919/479–7092 | www.ah.dcr.state.nc.us/sections/hs/duke/duke.htm | Free | Apr.–Oct., Mon.–Sat. 9–5, Sun. 1–5; Nov.–Mar., Tues.–Sat. 10–4, Sun. 1–4.

Duke University. Consistently rated as one of the nation's top schools, Duke was founded as Trinity College and renamed in 1924 after an endowment by James Buchanan Duke as a memorial to his father, Washington. The neo-Gothic West Campus stretches in an arc around downtown Durham to the neo-Georgian East Campus. A bus system and bike paths connect the campuses. | Undergraduate admissions and information office: West Campus, 2138 Campus Dr.; East Campus: between Main and Broad Sts. | 919/684–3214 | www.duke.edu | Free | Daily, tours Mon.–Fri. at 9, 11, and 3, Sat. at 11.

★ **Duke Chapel.** The centerpiece of West Campus and spiritual home for an interdenominational congregation, the chapel features a 5,200-pipe organ, a 210-ft tower housing a 50-bell carillon, and 77 intricate stained-glass windows. It was modeled after Canterbury Cathedral. Guided tours are available for groups of 12 or more, by appointment. | Chapel Dr. | 919/681–1704 | www.chapel.duke.edu | Free | May–Aug., daily 8–8; Sept.–Apr., daily 8 AM–10 PM.

Duke Libraries. The libraries of Duke University consist of the William R. Perkins Library, its seven branches, and the independently administered libraries of the schools of divinity, law, medicine, and business. They contain more than 4.6 million volumes (excluding the law library), 11 million manuscripts, and 2 million public documents. | 919/684–3009 | www.lib.duke.edu | Free | Call for hours.

Duke Medical Center. The year of his death, James Buchanan Duke made an additional bequest to Duke University for the establishment of a medical school, hospital, and nurses' home. Less than four years after the new school and hospital opened in 1930, the American Medical Association placed it among the top 20 schools in the country. Today, the teaching hospital, which occupies a 210-acre campus, is hailed as one of the crown jewels of American medicine. | Erwin Rd. | 919/684–8111 | www.mc.duke.edu | Free | Daily.

Duke Museum of Art. Among the Georgian buildings on East Campus is DUMA. The museum's collection includes decorative arts from the classical and medieval periods, complemented by ancient Peruvian weavings and Oriental and Navajo rugs. There's also pre-Columbian art, African sculpture, and Chinese jade and porcelain. European and American artists are represented as well. | East Campus, Buchanan Blvd. and Trinity Ave. | 919/684–5135 | www.duke.edu/web/duma | Donations accepted | Sept.–Apr., Tues., Thurs., and Fri. 10–5; Wed. 10–9; Sat. 11–2; Sun. 2–5; May–Aug. same, except Wed. 10–5.

★ **Sarah P. Duke Memorial Gardens.** Bordered by 35 acres of pine forest, the gardens lie in a valley on Duke's West Campus. A wisteria-covered pergola nestles in formal terraced garden beds surrounded by a large lily pond. Plants native to the Southeast grow along the wooded trails. | Anderson St. | 919/684–3698 | fax 919/864–8861 | www.hr.duke.edu/dukegardens/dukegardens.html | Free | Daily 8–dusk.

Wallace Wade Stadium. Home of the Blue Devils since 1929, the horseshoe-shape stadium, named for a former head coach, seats 33,941. It occupies a special niche in college football history in that it is the only facility outside Pasadena, California, to have hosted the Rose Bowl. | Whitford Dr. | 919/684–2120, ext. 0 | www.goduke.com | Aug.–Nov; call for schedule and admission prices.

Eno River State Park. The park's 2,733 acres include hiking trails, a picnic area, primitive camping, and Class II rapids (after a heavy rain). | 6101 Cole Mill Rd. | 919/383–1686 | www.ils.unc.edu/parkproject/enri.html | Free | Daily 8–sunset.

Hayti Heritage Center. St. Joseph's A. M. E. Church, one of Durham's oldest religious structures, houses this center for African-American art. In addition to exhibitions of traditional and contemporary art by local, regional, and national artists, the center hosts such special events as the Black Diaspora Film Festival. | 804 Old Fayetteville St. | 919/683–1709 or 800/845–9835 | www.hayti.org | Free | Weekdays 9–5, Sat. 10–2:30.

Historic Stagville. Built in 1860, this former plantation's well-preserved barn and slave quarters now serve as examples of historic preservation. Programs and lectures on black history and 19th-century culture, with a particular emphasis on architectural preservation, are frequently given. | 5825 Old Oxford Hwy., Bahama | 919/620–0120 | www.ah.dcr.state.nc.us/sections/do/stagvill/ | Free | Weekdays 9–4.

North Carolina Central University Art Museum. African-American art is showcased at the nation's first liberal arts college for African-Americans. Besides the permanent collection, you can see work by students and local artists. | 1801 Fayetteville St. | 919/560–6211 | Free | Mon.–Fri. 8–5, Sun. 2–5.

North Carolina Museum of Life and Science. A 78-acre, 55,000-square-ft regional, interactive science technology center. The museum includes hands-on exhibits dedicated to aerospace, Carolina wildlife, scientifica, and the farmyard. A railway that runs through the wildlife park is popular, as is the three-story Magic Wings Butterfly House and Garden, home to more than 1,000 exotic butterflies in open flight. | 433 Murray Ave. | 919/220–5429 | www.ncmls.citysearch.com | $8, train rides $1.50 | Mon.–Sat. 10–5, Sun. noon–5.

West Point on the Eno Park. This is a natural and historic city park located on 371 acres along the Eno River. In addition to picnicking, hiking, and fishing, the park contains a working water-powered gristmill, a photography museum, and a restored 1850s farmhouse. | 5101 N. Roxboro Rd. (U.S. 501 N) | 919/471–1623 | Free | Daily 8–sunset; historic buildings weekends 1–5.

ON THE CALENDAR

APR.: *Bennett Place Living History Civil War Surrender.* A reenactment of the negotiations between Generals Sherman and Johnston that once and for all ended the Civil War. | 4409 Bennett Memorial Rd. | 919/383–4345 | Free | Apr.–Oct., Mon.–Sat. 9–5, Sun. 1–5; Nov.–March, Tues.–Sat. 10–4, Sun. 1–4.

APR.: *DoubleTake Film Festival.* This was the first international festival to recognize the artistry of documentary cinema. Screenings and discussions. | 1926 Beaux Arts Carolina Theatre | 919/660–3699 | $100, $50 students.

MAY: *Bimbe Cultural Festival.* Music, art, and dance, from African and Caribbean to reggae and rap. | Historic Durham Athletic Park, 428 Morris St. | 919/560–4355.

JUNE–JULY: *American Dance Festival.* World's largest modern dance festival features more than two dozen dance companies and hundreds of choreographers, writers, and students participating in classes, seminars, and performances that are open to the public. | Page Auditorium and Reynolds Industries Theater, Duke University West Campus, Campus Drive | 919/684–6402 | www.americandancefestival.org | www.adfinternational.org | Call for information on programs and fees.

JULY: *Festival for the Eno.* A three-day folklife festival centering on the Fourth of July. Musicians, artists, and craftspeople come from around the region to Eno City Park. Lots of food. | 5101 N. Roxboro Rd. (U.S. 501 N) | 919/471–1623.

JULY: *Tobacco Harvest Festival.* A glimpse into the harvest, curing, and sale of Bright Leaf tobacco as it was done from the late 1930s to the mid-1940s. Hands-on demonstrations, home-style food, antique cars, and the Durham blues style of music help re-create the color of the times. | Duke Homestead and Tobacco Museum, 2828 Duke Homestead Rd. | 919/477–5498 | Free.

SEPT.: *Bull Durham Blues Festival.* National, regional, and local bands play a range of the blues, from Mississippi Delta to Piedmont. | Historic Durham Athletic Park, 428 Morris St. | 919/683–1709 | $20 | 5 PM–midnight.

Dining

Anotherthyme. Contemporary. This is a quiet, dimly lit space with walls decorated with trompe-l'oeil objects and artwork. Heart-healthy items are featured, such as artichokes with low-fat aioli and tomato-caper vinaigrette. There are also entrée salads, pasta combinations, seafood, and a few beef dishes. Specialties include lemon-baked salmon with roasted red pepper sauce, scalloped potatoes and asparagus, or vegetarian dishes like smoked mozzarella ravioli and asparagus and porcini mushrooms served with snow peas and shiitake mushrooms in mornay and marinara sauces, topped off with fried leeks. | 109 N. Gregson St. | 919/682–5225 | Reservations essential | $10–$24 | AE, MC, V | No lunch.

Bullock's Bar-B-Cue. Barbecue. Autographed portrait gallery of celebrities, many of whom declare their appreciation for Bullock's. Known for side dishes, including onion hush puppies, coleslaw, and fried okra. Kids' menu. No alcohol. | 3330 Wortham St. | 919/383–3211 | $6–$15 | No credit cards | Closed Sun.–Mon.

Café Parizäde. Contemporary. Dramatic lighting, brown and yellow leather chairs, and surrealist murals create an artistic space. The menu circles the globe and tends to lean toward seafood, but there are plenty of meat and poultry dishes as well. Vegetarians, however, shouldn't bother. Typical dishes include lobster cocktail with mango and fresh oranges, Moroccan chicken skewers, udon noodles with shrimp and scallops or roast duck confit. Open-air dining is available on a fountain-side patio in the garden at the back of the restaurant. | 2200 W. Main St. | 919/286–9712 | Reservations essential | www.fuzz.com/giorgios/parizade | $16–$38 | AE, D, DC, MC, V | No lunch weekends.

Fairview. Continental. The dining room of the Washington Duke Inn is becoming one of Durhams's top restaurants. A star dish is breast of Muscovy duck with mashed white beans, roasted garlic, and sweet-and-sour cranberry sauce. There are outside tables overlooking the trees and clipped lawns of the golf course. Pianist Tues.–Sat. and Sun. brunch. Kids' menu. | 3001 Cameron Blvd. | 919/493–6699 or 800/443–3853 | www.washingtondukeinn.com | No collarless shirts | $17–$38 | AE, D, DC, MC, V | No lunch Sun.

★ **Magnolia Grill.** Contemporary. This bistro in a former private residence is decorated with the work of local artists. The open kitchen lets you watch your meal being prepared. The menu changes daily, but some examples are cucumber soup with vermouth shrimp, grilled yellowfin tuna on warm green lentils with Mediterranean salsa and red pepper vinaigrette, pan-seared sea scallops on fennel polenta with lobster bordelaise, and grilled Black Angus strip steak with mushroom ragout. | 1002 9th St. | 919/286–3609 | www.magnoliagrillcookbook.com/maggrill.htm | Reservations essential | $16–$25 | AE, MC, V | Closed Sun.–Mon. No lunch.

Nana's. Contemporary. Abstract art is the backdrop in this restaurant where the menu changes frequently. Entrées have featured red snapper over a white beans and mussels stew and beef short ribs braised in hazelnut stout over horseradish mashed potatoes, kale, and balsamic roasted onions. | 2514 University Dr. | 919/493–8545 | www.durham-nc.com | Reservations essential | $16–$22 | AE, D, DC, MC, V | Closed Sun. No lunch.

Papas Grill. Greek. The Papanikas family owns and runs this restaurant, where Greek and Mediterranean specialities are served in a semiformal setting. Their lamb and grilled octopus are renowned, but steaks, pastas, salads, and other kinds of seafood are also served. Kids' menu. | 1821 Hillandale Rd. | 919/383–8502 | www.durham-nc.com | $16–$35 | AE, D, DC, MC, V | Closed Sun. No lunch Sat.

Pop's. Contemporary. This is a former tobacco warehouse transformed by industrial sculptures and an open kitchen into a popular and hip trattoria. Dishes like slow-roasted lamb shank with a port wine and mint reduction sauce with wild mushrooms and sweet red peppers, or seared sashimi tuna with tempura potatoes, a ginger frisée salad, and garlic tamari vinaigrette, show that plenty of thought has gone into the gastronomics as well as the visuals. | 810 W. Peabody St. | 919/956–7677 | www.durham-nc.com | Reservations essential | $9–$19 | AE, MC, V | No lunch weekends.

Shanghai. Chinese. Chinese lanterns, silk-embroidered pictures, and contemporary sculpture fill the interior what was one of the first Chinese restaurants in Durham when it was started in 1980. This eatery's reputation is based on the many tofu dishes, freshly made egg rolls, and vegetable dumplings as well as crispy duck, whole flounder, and breaded chicken in brown sauce. | 3433 Hillsborough Rd. | 919/383–7581 | www.durham-nc.com | $12–$33 | AE, D, MC, V.

Lodging

Arrowhead. A plantation home built in 1775 and converted into a charming B&B. The rooms (some with fireplaces) are furnished with 18th-century antiques, and the three buildings—the manor house, a carriage house, and a replica log cabin—are set on 6 acres of landscaped gardens and magnolia trees, some of which are over 200 years old. Dining room, picnic area, complimentary breakfast. In-room data ports, in-room hot tubs (in suites and cabin), cable TV in most rooms, in-room VCRs and movies (in suites and cabin). Business services. No pets. No smoking. | 106 Mason Rd. | 919/477–8430, 919/471–9538, or 800/528–2207 | www.arrowheadinn.com | 6 rooms, 2 suites; 1 cabin | $98–$185, $150–$185 suites, $225 cabin | AE, D, DC, MC, V.

Best Western Skyland Inn. Situated atop a hill, this chain motel is 5 mi from Duke University and 12 mi from the University of North Carolina at Chapel Hill. There is an adjacent restaurant, and golf and tennis facilities are also nearby. All rooms are on the ground floor and have their own entrances. Picnic area, complimentary Continental breakfast. In-room data ports, refrigerators. Cable TV. Pool. Playground. Business services, free parking. Pets allowed (fee). | 5400 U.S. 70, I–85 Exit 170 | 919/383–2508 | fax 919/383–7316 | www.best-western.com | 31 Northgate rooms | $58–$68 | AE, D, DC, MC, V.

The Blooming Garden Inn. In the historic part of downtown Durham, this charming 1890 gated Victorian home features a huge wraparound columned porch with swing and handcrafted woodwork. Shops, restaurants, Research Triangle Park and Duke University are all within a mile. All rooms have private baths, and are furnished with antiques. Two rooms are spacious oversize Jacuzzi suites. Complimentary breakfast. | 513 Holloway St. | 919/687–0801 or 888/687–0801 | fax 919/688–1401 | www.call.to/BGI.com | 4 rooms, 2 suites | $100–$225 | AE, D, DC, MC, V.

Campus Arms Motel and Apartments. In a commercial area less than 8 mi from Northgate Mall and Duke University. Several restaurants are within walking distance. All rooms have spacious closets and queen-sized beds. Microwaves, refrigerators. Cable TV. Laundry service. Free parking. | 2222 Elba St. | 919/286–9133 | fax 919/416–9267 | www.campusarms.citysearch.com | 29 rooms | $250/wk, $900/mo | AE, D, DC, MC, V.

Comfort Inn–University. This stucco-exterior chain hotel is 5 mi from the University of North Carolina and the historic Duke Gardens, and is landscaped with perennial beds, trees, and shrubs. Some restaurants are adjacent and there is shopping nearby, and there's easy access to I–40 and I–85. Complimentary Continental breakfast. In-room data ports, some microwaves, some minibars, some in-room hot tubs. Cable TV, some VCRs. Pool. Exercise equipment. Laundry facilities. Business services. No pets. | 3508 New Mount Moriah Rd. | 919/490–4949 | fax 919/419–0535 | www.comfortinn.com | 138 rooms, 18 suites (with whirlpool) | $79 | AE, D, DC, MC, V.

Doubletree Guest Suites. Next to the Research Triangle Park, this seven-story hotel overlooks a landscaped area with a large man-made lake. Although geared toward business travelers, it offers many facilities for non-business travelers as well. Restaurant, bar. Microwaves, minibars, refrigerators, some in-room hot-tubs. Cable TV. Two heated pools (one indoor), lake. Hot tub. Tennis courts. Exercise equipment. Laundry facilities. Business services, airport shuttle. No pets. | 2515 Meridian Pkwy. | 919/361–4660 | fax 919/361–2256 | www.doubletree.com | 203 suites | $149–$175 | AE, D, DC, MC, V.

Fairfield Inn by Marriott. This stucco-faced chain motel is landscaped with perennial beds, trees, and shrubs and is near restaurants and shops. Complimentary Continental breakfast. In-room data ports. Cable TV. Pool. Laundry service. Business services. Free parking. No pets. | 3710 Hillsborough Rd. | 919/382–3388 | fax 919/382–3388 | www.fairfieldinn.com | 135 rooms | $69 | AE, D, DC, MC, V.

Hawthorn Suites. A three-building complex 10 minutes from North Carolina Central University. The airport is 6 mi away. There are one- and two-bedroom suites available. Complimentary breakfast (full during week, Continental on weekends). In-room data ports, kitchenettes, microwaves. Cable TV. Pool. Laundry service. Business services, airport shuttle. Free parking. Pets allowed (fee). | 300 Meredith Dr. | 919/361–1234 | fax 919/361–1213 | www.citysearch.com/rdu/hawthornsuites or www.hawthorn.com | 100 suites in 3 buildings | $135–$169 | AE, D, DC, MC, V.

Hillsborough House Inn. In the Hillsborough historic district, this B&B with an 80-ft wraparound veranda was originally an Italianate mansion built in 1790. It is surrounded by seven acres of partly landscaped and partly wooded grounds. Each room is distinguished by its own style, with an eclectic mix of antiques and contemporary furnishings. Some rooms have four-poster beds, and the Kitchen House features a bed bowered with white poplar branches. Complimentary breakfast. Refrigerator in suite, no room phones except in suite. Cable TV in sitting room and suite. Pool. Business services. No pets. No kids under 10. | 209 E. Tryon St., Hillsborough | 919/644–1600 or 800/6616–1660 | fax 919/644–1308 | www.hillsboroughinn.citysearch.com | 5 rooms, 1 suite | $95–$125, $200 suite | AE, MC, V.

Hilton. This hotel is within 5 mi of the University of North Carolina and 2 mi of Duke Medical Hospital and Duke University. A low building surrounded by trees, it is in a quiet area, close to I–85. Restaurant, bar. In-room data ports. Cable TV. Pool. Hot tub. Exercise equipment. Business services. No pets. | 3800 Hillsborough Rd. | 919/383–8033 | fax 919/383–4287 | 152 rooms | $119–$139 | AE, D, DC, MC, V.

Marriott Civic Center. This chain hotel is in the heart of Durham and part of an entertainment complex. The fountains in the lobby are an elegant touch. Restaurant, bar, room service. In-room data ports, in-room safes, some microwaves, minibars. Cable TV. Exercise equipment. Laundry service. Business services. Free parking. No pets. | 201 Foster St. | 919/768–6000 | fax 919/768–6037 | www.marriott.com/marriott/rducv | 187 rooms, 2 suites | $129 | AE, D, DC, MC, V.

Morehead Manor B&B. This 8000-square-ft Colonial Revival home is within walking distance of the downtown area, the Durham Bulls Athletic Park, and historic Brightleaf Square. Choose from four individually decorated rooms—the Magnolia Suite, the Tiger Room, the Eagle's Inn, and the Jasmine room. All rooms have private baths and have a king, queen, or full-size bed. Complimentary breakfast. No pets. | 914 Vickers Ave. | 919/687–4366 or 888/437–6333 | fax 919/687–4245 | moheadmanr@aol.com | 4 rooms | $100–$165 | AE, D, MC, V.

Old North Durham Inn. This restored, early 1900 Colonial Revival home is in one of Durham's oldest residential neighborhoods. It's only a mile from Duke University, the Durham Bulls Ballpark, and the historic Carolina Theatre, and just 20 minutes from Raleigh/Durham Airport. Guest rooms feature 10-ft ceilings, ceiling fans, queen-size beds, and period furnishings. Complimentary breakfast. In-room VCRs. | 922 North Mangum St. | 919/683–1885 | fax 919/682–2645 | dvick1885@aol.com | 4 rooms | $100–$165 | No credit cards.

Red Roof Inn. This red brick chain motel is landscaped with trees and shrubs and is near a shopping mall. In-room data ports. Business services. Pets allowed (under 25 pounds). | 1915 N. Pointe Dr. | 919/471–9882 | fax 919/477–0512 | www.redroof.com | 117 rooms | $54–$58 | AE, D, DC, MC, V.

Sheraton Imperial Hotel and Convention Center. Just minutes from the airport, this 10-story glass-and-stone hotel lies inside the Research Triangle Park. It caters mainly to business travelers. Restaurant, bar. Minibars (in suites). Cable TV. Pool. Hot tub, massage. Tennis courts. Gym. Business services, airport shuttle. Free parking. No pets. | 4700 Emperor Blvd.,

Research Triangle Park | 919/941–5050 | fax 919/941–5156 | www.sheratonrtp.com | 331 rooms | $167–$177 | AE, D, DC, MC, V.

Super 8. This 2-story motel is in a commercial area only 2 mi from Duke University. Restaurants are only 3 blocks away. Complimentary Continental breakfast. Cable TV. Laundry facilities. | 2337 Guess Rd.; I–85 Exit 175 | 919/286–7746 or 800/800–8000 | fax 919/286–1855 | www.super8.com | 48 rooms | $49–$53 | AE, D, DC, MC, V.

★ **Washington Duke Inn and Golf Club.** This inn's richly colored rooms, furnished with lots of antiques, are designed around an English country inn theme. The inn is named for Washington Duke, founder of the American Tobacco Company. Golf championships are held here, and the inn is hosting the 2001 NCAA Men's Gold Championship. Restaurant, bar. In-room data ports, safes, minibars. Cable TV. Pool. Driving range, 18-hole golf course, putting green. Hiking trails. Laundry service. Business services. Free parking. No pets. | 3001 Cameron Blvd. | 919/490–0999 or 800/443–3853 | fax 919/688–0105 | wdi@netmar.com | www.washingtondukeinn.com | 164 rooms, 7 suites | $135–$275 | AE, D, DC, MC, V.

Wyndham Garden Hotel. Seven-story chain hotel 6 mi from the airport. If you like to luxuriate at bath time, this is the place to go: there are scented bath oils in every room. The flower-filled lobby is scented with aromatherapy oils, and also the place where, on Wednesdays, the house chef presents a free sampling of his creations. Restaurant, bar. In-room data ports. Cable TV. Pool. Hot tub. Exercise equipment. Business services, airport shuttle. Free parking. Pets allowed (fee). | 4620 S. Miami Blvd. | 919/941–6066 | fax 919/941–6363 | www.wyndham.com | 172 rooms | $125 | AE, D, DC, MC, V.

EDENTON

MAP 8, K4

(Nearby towns also listed: Ahoskie, Elizabeth City, Williamston)

The first permanent settlement in North Carolina, Edenton, on Albemarle Sound, is sometimes called the "mother town" of the state. At one time this port town was the capital of the colony and the home of the Royal Governors. Its 18th- and 19th-century buildings have been wonderfully preserved.

Information: Edenton-Chowan Tourism Development Authority | 116 E. King St., Edenton 27932 | 252/482–3400 or 800/775–0111 | nicholls@interpath.com | www.edenton.com.

Attractions

Historic Edenton. Settled in about 1600 along the shores of Edenton Bay and Albemarle Sound, Edenton was a prosperous port in 1774 when 51 women gathered at a home, held their own "tea party," and vowed to support the American cause. Blackbeard the pirate sailed into Edenton Bay on many occasions. Today the year-round population numbers around 5,000. You can enter structures in the historic district only during daily guided tours, which vary from 45 minutes to 2 hours. | Visitor center, 108 N. Broad St. | 252/482–2637 | fax 252/482–3499 | www.ah.dcr.state.nc.us/sections/hs/iredell/iredell.htm | Free, tours $3–$7 | Apr.–Oct., Mon.–Sat. 9–5, Sun. 1–5; Nov.–Mar., Tues.–Sat. 10–4, Sun. 1–4.

Chowan County Courthouse. This structure has been under restoration for 2 years, but interpretive tours are still given. Architecturally it is described as the finest public building in the South. Erected in 1767, it is North Carolina's oldest courthouse, and has served a variety of purposes—it was a Whig center during the Revolutionary War, a speaking venue for governors from the time of Josiah Martin, and President Monroe held a reception upstairs in the assembly room in 1819. Tours are given from the Historical Edenton State Historical Site visitor's center, from where several other sites can be visited as well. | 108 N. Broad St. | 252/482–2637 | fax 252/482–3499. | www.ah.dcr.state.nc.us/sections/hs/iredell/iredell.htm | $3–$7 | Apr.–Oct., Mon.–Sat. 9–5, Sun. 1–5; Nov.–Mar., Tues.–Sat. 10–4, Sun. 1–4.

Cupola House. Furnished with period pieces and accented by a garden that has been re-created using a 1769 map, the Cupola House (built in 1758) operates as a house-museum. Check out the message carved in a window pane by a long-ago resident of the Colonial home. | W. Water and S. Broad Sts. | 252/482–2637 | Free | For hrs, see Historic Edenton; tours available.

Historic Edenton Visitor Center. The center offers a 14-minute audiovisual program as well as exhibits, visitor information, and guided walking tours of the area's architecturally diverse buildings. | 108 N. Broad St. | 252/482–2637 | Free | Call for hrs.

James Iredell House. James Iredell was appointed a justice to the Supreme Court by George Washington. Iredell's Federal house was constructed in two stages, the first in 1800 and the second 1827. | E. Church St. | 252/482–2637 | Free | For hrs, see Historic Edenton; tour available.

St. Paul's Episcopal Church. St. Paul's has the oldest charter and is the second oldest standing church in the state. It was built between 1736 and 1760 on grounds dotted with ancient oaks, and is the site of a historic graveyard. | W. Church and S. Broad Sts. | 252/482–2637 | Free | For hrs, see Historic Edenton; tours available.

. . . .

Merchants Millpond State Park. A coastal pond and a swamp forest mingle to create one of the state's rarest ecological communities. The 760-acre mill pond is stocked with a variety of fish, which makes flyfishing a popular pastime here. For a fee, campers and canoeists are welcome to enjoy the eerie beauty of the park, where towering bald cypress and tupelo gum trees are draped in Spanish moss. | 71 U.S. 158 E, Gatesville | 252/357–1191 | fax 252/357–0149 | www.ils.unc.edu/parkproject/memi.html | Free | Daily 8–sunset.

USEFUL EXTRAS YOU MAY WANT TO PACK

- ❏ Adapters, converter
- ❏ Alarm clock
- ❏ Batteries
- ❏ Binoculars
- ❏ Blankets, pillows, sleeping bags
- ❏ Books and magazines
- ❏ Bottled water, soda
- ❏ Calculator
- ❏ Camera, lenses, film
- ❏ Can/bottle opener
- ❏ Cassette tapes, CDs, and players
- ❏ Cell phone
- ❏ Change purse with $10 in quarters, dimes, and nickels for tollbooths and parking meters
- ❏ Citronella candle
- ❏ Compass
- ❏ Earplugs
- ❏ Flashlight
- ❏ Folding chairs

- ❏ Guidebooks
- ❏ Luggage tags and locks
- ❏ Maps
- ❏ Matches
- ❏ Money belt
- ❏ Pens, pencils
- ❏ Plastic trash bags
- ❏ Portable TV
- ❏ Radio
- ❏ Self-seal plastic bags
- ❏ Snack foods
- ❏ Spare set of keys, not carried by driver
- ❏ Travel iron
- ❏ Travel journal
- ❏ Video recorder, blank tapes
- ❏ Water bottle
- ❏ Water-purification tablets

Newbold–White House. The oldest authentically restored brick house (circa 1730) in North Carolina. Built by a Quaker planter, it features enormous fireplaces, pine woodwork, a winding corner staircase, and period furniture. Flemish bond brick walls are plastered on the first-floor interior. | Harvey Point Rd. | 252/426–5123 | fax 252/426–3538 | www.albemarle-nc.com/newbold-white | $3 | Mar.–Thanksgiving Day, Tues.–Sat. 10–4:30, Sun. 2–5.

Somerset Place State Historic Site. An example of the slave-supported economy of the antebellum South. Home to two generations of the Collinses, a wealthy planter family, and more than 300 slaves. Guided tours of the mansion, dependencies, slave cabins, and grounds with transportation canal are offered. Descendants of Somerset's enslaved community hold family homecomings here. | 2572 Lake Shore Rd., Creswell | 252/797–4560 | fax 252/797–4171 | www.ah.dcr.state.nc.us/sections/hs/somerset/somerset.htm | Free | Apr.–Oct., Mon.–Sat. 9–5, Sun. 1–5; Nov.–Mar., Tues.–Sat. 10–4, Sun. 1–4.

ON THE CALENDAR

MAR.: *Historic Edenton Annual Antique Show and Sale.* Exhibitors feature a broad range of furniture, porcelain, silver, china, glassware, linens, toys, and other household effects from the late 18th, 19th, and early 20th centuries. Experts in antiques and restoration are also on hand. | New National Guard Armory, 739 Soundside Rd. | 252/482–7800 | Free.

APR.: *Biennial Pilgrimage Tour of Homes and Countryside.* Private homes and public buildings of historic and architectural significance are open to the public. A series of meals sponsored by local churches and organizations complements the weekend's activities. | 252/482–3400 or 800/775–0111.

OCT.: *Sound Country Celebration.* Canoe and kayak races, demonstrations by paddle-powered watercraft, guided canoe outings, contests related to water activities, arts and crafts, music, raffles, and food. | 252/482–3400 or 800/775–0111.

Dining

Dram Tree. Contemporary. Murals span the formal front dining room in this building that once housed a bottling company and antiques shop. Great view of Edenton Bay. Seafood, steak, and some Italian dishes. The salmon and crab cakes are particularly popular. Live music Fri.–Sat. evenings. Kids' menu. Sun. brunch. | 112 W. Water St. | 252/482–2711 | $20–$40 | AE, D, MC, V | No supper Sun., Wed.–Thurs.

Lane's Family Barbecue. Barbecue. Casual family dining is the mode in this simple aluminium-sided house with a porch. Pork barbecue, seafood, hamburgers, steaks, and a large choice of vegetables are offered. Kids' menu. | 421 E. Church St. | 252/482–4008 | $6–$11 | No credit cards.

Waterman's Grill. Seafood. Choose from a variety of dishes on the menu or the list of fresh-caught daily specials. Crab cakes, oysters, and smothered chicken with rice pilaf are available, as well as the popular waterman's trio, steamed crabmeat, shrimp, and scallops seasoned with oil bay and hushpuppies. | 427 S. Broad St. | 252/482–7733 | $11–$17 | AE, D, MC, V.

Lodging

Albemarle House. Guided tours of several historic homes depart daily from the visitor center next to this two-story country Victorian house, which is in the heart of the Edenton historic district. Each room is individually decorated and has a queen-size bed, cable TV, and private bath. The home also features a two-room suite with a connecting bath. Complimentary breakfast. No pets. No smoking. | 204 W. Queen St.; 1 block west of Broad St. | 252/482–8204 | albemarlehouse@inteliport.com | 3 rooms, 1 suite | $80, $125 suite | AE, MC, V.

Captain's Quarters Inn. A turn-of-the-20th-century (1907) inn with anchors and model ships throughout. Each room has its own nautical theme. Popular packages are offered: Mystery Weekend from October to March, Sail and Snooze from April to October. Complimentary breakfast. One in-room hot tub. Cable TV. Kids over 8 only. No pets. No smoking. | 202 W. Queen St. | 252/482–8945 or 800/482–8945 | www.captainsquartersinn.com | 8 rooms | $85–$95 | MC, V.

Governor Eden Inn. A striking home with a wraparound porch, built at the turn of the century, has been converted to this B&B offering a peaceful retreat from the stresses of modern life. Complimentary breakfast. Cable TV, no room phones. Airport shuttle. Free parking. No pets. No kids under 12. No smoking. | 304 N. Broad St. | 252/482–2072 | fax 252/482–3613 | 4 rooms | $85 | AE, MC, V.

Lords Proprietors'. The beds, many of them four-posters, were crafted by a local cabinet-maker. Attention to detail is evident in the rest of this B&B as well, from the dining room's gourmet fare to the fresh flowers and blend of antique and reproduction period furniture in each room. Dining room, complimentary breakfast. Some minibars. Cable TV, VCRs. Library. Business services. No pets. No smoking. | 300 N. Broad St. | 252/482–3641 or 800/348–8933 | fax 252/482–2432 | www.lordspropedenton.com | 16 rooms and 2 suites in 3 buildings | $170 | AE, D, MC, V.

Trestle House. This B&B was built in 1972 as a wildlife retreat. The interior features massive redwood beams that were originally Southern Railway Company trestles. This place is particularly attractive to bird-watchers and nature lovers: it borders Albemarle Sound, the largest freshwater sound in the world, and links up with over 1,200 mi of canoe trails. The front borders the North Carolina biking highway. On staff are an ornithologist, a fishing guide, and a hunting guide. The rooms are named after birds, and all have antiques and hand-made quilts. Picnic area, complimentary breakfast. Cable TV, VCRs, and movies in common area. Lake, pond. Canoeing, fishing. No pets. No smoking. | 632 Soundside Rd. | 252/482–2282 or 800/645–8466 | fax 252/482–7003 | www.edenton.com/trestlehouse | 5 rooms | $60–$100 | AE, MC, V.

ELIZABETH CITY

MAP 8, K3

(Nearby town also listed: Duck, Edenton)

Elizabeth City (population 18,475) is the commercial, industrial, medical, and educational center of the Albemarle region, and the role of water in its development is unmistakable. Pasquotank, an Indian word meaning "where the currents divide," is the name of the county and its major river. Trade with the West Indies and the construction of the Dismal Swamp Canal—the nation's oldest canal still in operation—made fortunes rise. Elizabeth City remains a waterfront community and is home to the largest U.S. Coast Guard command complex in the nation.

Information: Elizabeth City Area Chamber of Commerce | 502 E. Ehringhaus St., 27907 | 252/335–4365 | ecacc@interpath.com | www.elizcity.com.

Attractions

Historic Main Street Commercial District. You can take a self-guided tour of one of Elizabeth City's five National Register historic districts, which includes the largest number of antebellum brick commercial buildings in the state. The early 19th- and 20th-century storefronts house specialty shops, restaurants, art galleries, and antiques shops. Also included in the tour are historic homes, churches, municipal buildings, and a waterfront park. Free tour brochures are available from the Museum of the Albemarle and the Chamber of Commerce's outside brochure rack. | 502 E. Ehringhaus St. | 252/335–4365 | fax 252/335–5732 | Free | Daily.

Museum of the Albemarle. The permanent and temporary galleries of this museum, a branch of the North Carolina Museum of History, tell the story of the people who have lived in the Albemarle region—from Native Americans to the English-speaking colonists to adventurers, farmers, and fishermen. | 1116 U.S. 17 S | 252/335–1453 | fax 252/335–0637 | www.albemarle-nc.com/MOA | Free | Tues.–Sat. 9–5, Sun. 2–5.

Pasquotank County Farmers Market. This place gets lots of local traffic because of its wide variety of locally grown fresh fruits and in-season produce. | Pritchard St. | 252/338–3954 | fax 252/338–6442 | Free | May 15–Dec. 25, Tues., Fri., and Sat. 8–5.

ON THE CALENDAR
SEPT.: *A Day on the River.* A regatta, pontoon-boat river tours, a juried art show, live music, children's activities, and food are all part of the fun at this event. | Elizabeth City waterfront | 252/335–1453.
OCT.: *Ghost Walk.* At this event you'll find tours of homes, public buildings, and a cemetery in Elizabeth City's historic district, along with ghost tales, a reenactment of a famous murder trial, and an otherworldly magic show. | 252/338–2242 | $10 | Fri. and Sat. 5–9.
NOV.: *Mistletoe Show.* Seventy crafts booths, many with holiday-oriented items. Music and food. | Knobbs Creek Recreation Center, 200 E. Ward St. | 252/335–1424 or 252/336–4411 | Fri. noon–9, Sat. 10–6, Sun. 12:30–4.

Dining
Marina. Seafood. The owner, Clarence Munden, is a fisherman, and whatever he catches on any given day is what's on the menu that evening. The waterfront restaurant provides a view over the sound and a deck for outdoor dining. The Marina special, a combination of shrimp, scallops, and crab meat sautéed in butter, is one of the most popular dishes. Steak and chicken are also on the menu. Sun. brunch. Kids' menu. | 35 Camden Causeway | 252/335–7307 | $13–$25 | MC, V | Closed Mon. No lunch Tues.–Sat.

Mulligan's Waterfront Grille. Contemporary. Lots of dark wood, greenery, and boat models decorate this waterfront restaurant that provides dockage for boats. Among the restaurant's most popular offerings are fish, steaks, pastas, and hefty sandwiches. The shipyard pasta, with shrimp and scallops, is a perennial favorite. There's open-air dining on a deck overlooking the Pasquotank River. Live music Wed.–Sat. evenings. Kids' menu. | 400 S. Water St. | 252/331–2431 | $9–$27 | AE, D, DC, MC, V | Closed Sun.

Topside. Contemporary. A former navy man established this family-friendly place in what was the auditorium of a historic high school. Wooden tables and chairs, nautical memorabilia, and old movie posters constitute the decor. The hearty, country-style dinner buffet is popular, as are the seafood, beef (steaks, burgers, and prime rib), and chicken. Kids' menu. Beer and wine only. | 910 S. Rte. 343, Shiloh | 252/336–2611 | $8–$15 | MC, V | Closed Mon. No lunch Tues.–Sat.

Lodging
Comfort Inn. This chain hotel near the waterfront, restaurants, and shops has a pale yellow stucco exterior and landscaped islands of trees and shrubs around the parking lot. Complimentary Continental breakfast. In-room data ports, refrigerators (in suites). Cable TV. Pool. Laundry service. Business services. No pets. | 306 S. Hughes Blvd. | 252/338–8900 | fax 252/338–6420 | www.comfortinn.com | 80 rooms, 28 suites | $95 | AE, D, DC, MC, V.

Hampton Inn. Just 1½ mi from downtown, this 5-story building is a farmers' market, and the Museum of the Albemarle. King deluxe and king study rooms are available in addition to the single and double accommodations. Complimentary Continental breakfast. In-room data ports. Cable TV. Pool. Hot tub. Exercise equipment. Laundry facilities. Airport shuttle. | 402 Halstead Blvd.; near U.S. 17 Bypass | 252/333–1800 or 800/426–7866 | fax 252/333–1801 | www.ramada-inn.com | 101 rooms | $56–$100 | AE, D, DC, MC, V.

Holiday Inn. This stucco-and-brick chain hotel is 2 mi from the waterfront, with landscaped grounds. Restaurant, bar, room service. In-room data ports. Cable TV. Pool. Laundry facilities. Business services. Pets allowed (fee). | 522 S. Hughes Blvd. | 252/338–3951 | fax 252/338–6225 | www.basshotels.com | 157 rooms | $64 | AE, D, DC, MC, V.

FAYETTEVILLE

(Nearby towns also listed: Aberdeen, Dunn, Lumberton, Sanford, Southern Pines)

In addition to being the Cumberland County seat, Fayetteville—the first place in America named for the Marquis de Lafayette—is Cumberland's largest city (population 115,000) and a hub for shopping, dining, services, lodging, health care, entertainment, and, with three colleges, education. Residential areas are quiet and leafy, and the historic Haymount District is filled with stately homes and antiques stores. Undeniably, this is a military town. The army's Fort Bragg and Pope Air Force Base sit side by side, forming one of the largest military complexes in the world.

Information: Fayetteville Area Convention and Visitors Bureau | 245 Person St., Fayetteville 28301 | 910/483–5311, 800/255–8217, or 888/622–4276 | facvb@facvb.com | www.facvb.com.

Attractions

Cape Fear Botanical Garden. The garden includes a gazebo, an old farmhouse, perennial gardens, wildflowers, towering oaks, nature trails, and numerous species of native plants. | 536 N. Eastern Blvd. | 910/486–0221 | fax 910/486–4209 | $3, free first Sat. of month | Mon.–Sat. 10–5, Sun. noon–5.

Cumberland County Coliseum Complex. A multipurpose facility that hosts a variety of national and regional shows and events—everything from circuses to symphonies to truck pulls. There are four venues, including the state-of-the-art, 13,500-seat Crown Coliseum. | 1960 Coliseum Dr. | 910/323–5088 | fax 910/323–0489 | www.crowncoliseum.com | Prices vary with events | Call for schedule.

Fayetteville Museum of Art. Each year the museum sponsors 8 to 10 regional, national, and international traveling exhibitions. There is a permanent collection of art that includes many African artifacts. Educational programs and an entertainment series for all ages are also offered. | 839 Stamper Rd. | 910/485–5121 | fax 910/485–5233 | Free | Weekdays 10–5, weekends 1–5.

Museum of the Cape Fear Historical Complex. The museum, a branch of the North Carolina Museum of History, has exhibits and programs that interpret the history and cultures of southeastern North Carolina. Next to the museum, the 1897 Poe House examines the social, economic, and political struggles of the region's upper-middle-class families from 1897 to 1917. And Arsenal Park reveals the history of an 1840s federal arsenal. | 801 Arsenal Ave. | 910/486–1330 | fax 910/486–1585 | Free | Tues.–Sat. 10–5, Sun. 1–5.

ON THE CALENDAR

FEB.: *Black History Month.* Concerts, lectures, exhibits, and plays take place on the campus of Fayetteville State University. | 910/486–1474 | www.uncfsu.edu | Call for schedule and fees.

APR.: *Dogwood Festival.* Entertainment (including live music), social, cultural, sporting, and historical events, as well as an 18-mi scenic Dogwood Trail. | 910/323–1934 | www.fayettevillenc.com/dogwood.

MAY: *Pope AFB/Fort Bragg Joint Open House and Air Show.* Aerial demonstrations, aircraft and equipment displays, working-dog demonstrations, and military drill-team performances highlight this two-day event. | 910/394–4183 | Free | Call for dates.

AUG.: *Greek Fest.* Greek foods, music, and arts. | Cumberland County Coliseum Complex, 121 E. Mountain Dr. | 910/323–5088 or 910/484–2010 | Call for times and fees.

SEPT.: *International Folk Festival.* International cuisines, costumes, crafts, entertainment, dancing, and a Parade of Nations with colorful, sometimes elaborate, native dress. | 910/323–1776.

OCT.: *Cape Fear Folk Festival.* Demonstrations of traditional 18th- and 19th-century crafts, skills, and customs. Folk music, food vendors, and children's activities. | Museum of the Cape Fear Historical Complex, 801 Arsenal Ave. | 910/486–1330 | Free.

NOV.: *Holly Day Fair.* Southeastern North Carolina's largest holiday craft and gift show. | Cumberland County Coliseum Complex, 121 E. Mountain Dr. | 910/323–5509.

Dining

The Barn. Contemporary. The original barn has been updated with glass solariums, white linen, candles, and a baby grand piano, and has a pleasant and relaxing atmosphere. The extensive menu includes steaks, chicken, seafood, pasta, and veal. Specialties are prime rib and more elaborate dishes, like pan-seared salmon stuffed with Gouda cheese, topped with shrimp, scallops, artichokes, and lemon-dill sauce. Live music Fri.–Sat. | 1021 Bragg Blvd. | 910/678–0686 | Reservations essential | $11–$59 | AE, D, MC, V | Closed Sun. No lunch.

Bella Villa. Italian. This spot has a cafélike atmosphere and friendly service, as well as authentic recipes cooked to order, particularly chicken, seafood, and veal. The seafood special—shrimp, clams, and mussels in a marinara sauce over pasta, and chicken fricassee with mushrooms and marinara and white wine sauce, are typical dishes. Buffet lunch weekdays. Kids' menu. Beer and wine only. | 201 S. McPherson Church Rd. | 910/867–1199 | Reservations not accepted | $5–$14 | AE, D, MC, V.

Canton Station. Chinese. In addition to the buffet lunch and supper, there's a Japanese grill, with meats and vegetables cooked to order in full view and an à la carte menu selection of Cantonese and Szechuan dishes. Kids' menu. | 301 N. McPherson Church Rd. | 910/864–5555 | Reservations essential | $7–$9 | AE, D, MC, V.

Chris's Open Hearth Steak House. Steak. Forest-green and burgundy hues color the interior for a slightly rustic look. Although charcoal-grilled steaks are the featured menu item here, there's also chicken, prime rib, and veal chops; the seafood selection includes swordfish and lobster tails. | 2620 Raeford Rd. | 910/485–2948 | $12–$22 | AE, D, DC, MC, V | No lunch.

Cross Creek Brewing Company. Contemporary. This is a California-style brew pub with a wood-fired brick oven and a cigar room. There's also Sterling Silver beer, steak, gourmet pizzas, and Texas-style chili made with steak and without beans. | 4150 Sycamore Dairy Rd. | 910/867–9223 | $11–$15 | AE, MC, V.

De Lafayette. Continental. A restored gristmill with some lake-view tables, this restaurant contracts with organic farmers for custom-grown vegetables, herbs, and edible flowers. Featured are duck, steaks, rack of lamb, fresh fish, pasta, and vegetarian dishes. Of particular note are the lobster ravioli and a vegetarian dish of grilled Creole-spiced Portabello mushrooms filled with roasted vegetables and sun-dried tomatoes, served with angel-hair pasta and roasted tomato-basil sauce. | 6112 Cliffdale Rd. | 910/868–4600 | $15–$32 | AE, D, DC, MC, V | Closed Sun. and Mon. No lunch.

Haymount Grill. American. Fresh seafood, Italian, Greek, and daily specials like hamburger steak and mashed potatoes, as well as breakfast made to order from a whopping 57-item menu explain this place's popularity. Kids' menu. | 1304 Morganton Rd. | 910/484–0261 | $6–$12 | MC, V.

Hilltop House Restaurant. Contemporary. This restaurant is in a gracious early 20th-century home in the historic Haymount section, with large rooms, high ceilings, and antiques. It offers seafood, steak, pasta, and Greek specialties, like kadaife shrimp and moussaka. There are some outdoor tables in a garden patio at the back of the house. Sun. brunch buffet. | 1240 Fort Bragg Rd. | 910/484–6699 | $12–$22 | AE, D, MC, V | No lunch Sat.

Mary Do's Deli. American. Images of Betty Boop cover the walls, and the large mural of cartoon characters (painted by one of the waitresses) reminds you that it's time to relax and enjoy the wind-up toys, free jukebox, and, oh, yes, the food. You'll find salads, sandwiches, seafood, and nightly dinner specials like cube steak in mushroom gravy. Kids' menu. Beer and wine only. | 1940-A Skibo Rd. | 910/826–9900 | Reservations not accepted | $6–$11 | AE, DC, MC, V | Closed Sun. No dinner Mon. and Sat.

Lodging

Comfort Inn. Perennials, shrubs, and trees provide the backdrop for this red brick chain hotel with Shaker-shingled roof that stands on a strip with many other hotels and restaurants. It's 8 mi southeast of the airport and near the interstate, just off Exit 49. Complimentary breakfast. Some in-room data ports, refrigerators, microwaves. Cable TV. Outdoor pool. Exercise equipment. Shop. Business services, free parking. Pets allowed. | 1957 Cedar Creek Rd. | 910/323–8333 or 800/621–6596 | fax 910/323–3946 | www.comfortinn.com | 120 rooms | $65 | AE, D, DC, MC, V.

Days Inn. This stucco chain hotel is next to a Denny's restaurant, near I–95, and about 10 mi from shopping malls. The sofa-and-chair-filled lounge area allows you to sit and enjoy your morning coffee. Complimentary Continental breakfast. Some refrigerators. Cable TV. Outdoor pool. Pets allowed (fee). | 2065 Cedar Creek Rd. | 910/483–6191 | fax 910/483–4113 | www.daysinn.com | 122 rooms | $69 | AE, D, DC, MC, V.

Days Inn Fayetteville. King-size beds are available at this 2-story hotel, which is 7 mi from Fayetteville Municipal Airport. The downtown area is 3 blocks away. Restaurant, picnic area. Outdoor pool. Basketball. Free parking. | 333 Person St. | 910/483–0431 | fax 910/483–0432 | 54 rooms | $39–$58 | AE, D, DC, MC, V.

Econo Lodge. This standard chain hotel is 2 blocks from Cracker Barrel and Beaverdam Steak and Seafood, 3 blocks from Shoney's, and directly off the exit from I–95. Complimentary Continental breakfast, Cable TV. Outdoor pool. Business services. No pets. | 1952 Cedar Creek Rd. | 910/433–2100 | fax 910/433–2009 | www.econolodge.com | 150 rooms | $50 | AE, D, DC, MC, V.

Four Points by Sheraton. This four-story hotel is about 6 mi from downtown and conveniently close to I–95. It's the last hotel before the highway, at Exit 49. Restaurant, bar, room service. In-room data ports, some refrigerators. Cable TV. Indoor and outdoor pools. Hot tub. Exercise equipment. Laundry service. Business services, airport shuttle. Free parking. No pets. | 1965 Cedar Creek Rd. | 910/323–8282 | fax 910/323–5052 | www.sheraton.com | 137 rooms | $89 | AE, D, DC, MC, V.

Hampton Inn. Across from Cross Creek Mall, this landscaped, stucco-exterior hotel is only 5 minutes from Fort Bragg and 10 minutes from the university. The wood-paneled interior is filled with plants, and a book-lined lobby invites you to relax and read. Complimentary Continental breakfast. In-room data ports. Cable TV. Outdoor pool. Laundry service. No pets. | 1700 Skibo Rd. | 910/864–1007 | fax 910/487–5773 | www.hamptoninn.com | 131 rooms | $67–$75 | AE, D, DC, MC, V.

Holiday Inn Bordeaux. Across from a regional medical center, this chain hotel is in one of the largest convention hotels in North Carolina. Restaurant, bar with entertainment. Some in-room data ports. Cable TV. Outdoor pool. Exercise equipment. Laundry service. Business services, airport shuttle. | 1707 Owen Dr. | 910/323–0111 | fax 910/484–9444 | www.basshotels.com | 289 rooms, 7 suites | $88 | AE, D, DC, MC, V.

Linden Inn B&B. This quiet, 3-story 1890s mansion features fine English furniture and modern amenities in the center of Linden. Each room is individually decorated and has ceiling fans and English country-style furniture. Complimentary full breakfast. Data ports (available). | 4922 Main St., Linden; 18 mi outside Fayetteville | 910/980–5504 | fax 910/980–5504 | wdmimi@aol.com | thelindeninn.com | 5 rooms | $69–$89 | AE, MC, V.

Quality Inn Ambassador. This one-story chain hotel is 6 mi from shops and restaurants. Restaurant, picnic area. Some microwaves, some refrigerators. Cable TV. Outdoor pool. Play-

ground. Business services. Pets allowed. | 2035 Eastern Blvd. | 910/485–8135 | fax 910/485–8682 | 62 rooms | $52–$62 | AE, D, DC, MC, V.

Ramada Inn. Just a mile from historic downtown Fayetteville, this 2-story hotel is also 4 mi from the Fayetteville Airport. The Cumberland County Civic Center is just 2 mi away. Restaurant. No-smoking rooms. Cable TV. Outdoor pool. | 511 Eastern Blvd. | 910/484–8101 | fax 910/484–2516 | 138 rooms | $60 | AE, D, DC, MC, V.

FONTANA DAM

MAP 8, B2

(Nearby town also listed: Robbinsville)

Fontana Village, a large resort area with a moderately high elevation (1,727 ft), was once home to the workers who built Fontana Dam in the early 1940s as a project of the Tennessee Valley Authority. It offers a deep-water lake, horseback riding, and many other recreational opportunities.

Information: Graham County Travel and Tourism Authority | 427 Rodney Orr Bypass, Robbinsville, 28771 | 828/479–3790 or 800/470–3790 | grahamchamber@graham.main.nc.us | www.wncguide.com/graham.

Fontana Village Resort | Rte. 28 N, Fontana Dam, 28733 | 828/498–2211 or 800/849–2258 | fontana@fontanavillage.com | www.fontanavillage.com.

Attractions

Fontana Dam. This dam, the largest east of the Mississippi, was constructed during the early 1940s to generate the electricity needed to fuel the war efforts of World War II. Today it impounds the water that forms 29-mi Fontana Lake, around which a resort community, Fontana Village, was formed. The powerhouse, reached by Fontana's Incline Tram, is open for tours, and both the observation deck and the overlook provide views of the dam, its discharge tunnels, and surrounding mountain scenery. The Appalachian Trail crosses the top of the dam (featured in a few movies, including *The Fugitive*), and the Smoky Mountains National Park borders its reservoir. Boat docks and launching ramps are located at various sites on the lake. | Rte. 28, Fontana Village | 828/498–2234 or 800/467–1388 | Free, tram $2 | Daily, visitor's center May–Oct. 9–7.

ON THE CALENDAR
OCT.: *Harvest Festival.* Fireworks, dancing, games, entertainment, food, arts and crafts, and more are on tap in Stecoah. | 828/479–3364.

Dining
Peppercorn Restaurant. Contemporary. The Smoky Mountains and Fontana Village through picture windows create the setting for the casual dining at this restaurant. The menu includes beef, chicken, and seafood, but it's the catfish and blackened chicken that make it popular. Kids' menu. BYOB. Breakfast and dinner buffet, and lunch occasionally. | Rte. 28 | 828/498–2211 | $15–$20 | AE, D, DC, MC, V.

Village Café. Casual. Sandwiches, burgers, and pizzas are what to order if you're in the center of Fontana Village and need a quick and light bite to eat. There's open-air dining on the deck. | Rte. 28 | 828/498–2211 | Reservations not accepted | $3–$16 | No credit cards | Closed Mon.–Wed. and Nov.–Apr.

Lodging
The Hike Inn. Built in the 1950s, this small, single-story motel in Graham County is 6.5 miles from Fontana Dam and is surrounded in beautiful outdoor settings that are great for hiking, fishing, and mountain biking. Some rooms have kitchens and stoves. On the premises

there is a museum with 12,000-year-old pieces from North, South, and Central America. Some refrigerators. | Rte. 28 | 828/479–3677 | 5 rooms | $45–$55 | No credit cards.

Fontana Village Resort. On Fontana Lake, at the southern border of Great Smoky Mountains National Park, this secluded resort has three types of accommodations: rooms, cabins, and a hostel. Cabins have kitchenettes, and there's cable TV (except in some cabins). 3 restaurants. Some refrigerators. Some room phones. 3 pools (1 indoor). Hot tub. Miniature golf, lighted tennis court. Gym, hiking, horseback riding. Water sports, fishing, bicycles. Children's programs, 2 playgrounds. Laundry facilities. Pets allowed (fee). | Rte. 28 N | 800/849–2258 | fax 828/498–2209 | fontana@fontanavillage.com | www.fontanavillage.com | 84 rooms, 100 cabins; 16-bunk hostel | $49–$79 | AE, D, MC, V.

FRANKLIN

(Nearby towns also listed: Bryson City, Cashiers, Highlands)

In 1540, Hernando de Soto came to what is now Franklin (population 3,000) in search of gold. So intent was he on the precious metal that he completely overlooked the wealth of gemstones for which this area is now so famous. Franklin sits in Macon County at an elevation of 2,800 ft and at the convergence of three highways: U.S. 441, U.S. 64, and Route 28.

Information: Franklin Area Chamber of Commerce | 425 Porter St., Franklin 28734 | 828/524–3161 or 800/336–7829 | facc@franklin-chamber.com | www.franklin-chamber.com.

Attractions

Franklin Gem and Mineral Museum. Examples of rocks, minerals, and gems from around the world, as well as Indian artifacts, are on display here in what once was the old jail on the square. | 25 Phillips St. | 828/369–7831 | Free | May–Oct., Mon.–Sat. 10–4.

Gem mines. Today Franklin is home to nearly two dozen gem mines and shops; some carry native stones only, others a combination of native and "enriched" stones (i.e., those not native to this locale). The Franklin Area Chamber of Commerce provides a complete listing. | 425 Porter St. | 828/524–3161 or 800/336–7829 | fax 828/369–7516 | www.franklin-chamber.com | Prices vary | Call for hrs.

Macon County Historical Museum. There are displays on education, the Civil War, early medicine, textiles, and photographs, as well as a reference for genealogical research. | 36 W. Main St. | 828/524–9758 | Free | May–Oct., Tues.–Fri. 10–5, Sat. 1–8; Nov.–Apr., Tues.–Fri. 10–5.

Nantahala National Forest. The national forest, protecting an area first explored in 1540 by Hernando de Soto, was established in 1920 and is the largest of four national forests in North Carolina. The Wayah—Cherokee for "wolf"—is in Franklin. There are 87 mi of trails and mountaintop vistas, including those from 5,342-ft-high Wayah Bald, where wild flame azaleas bloom in June. | Visitor's center, 90 Sloan Rd. | 828/524–6441 | www.cs.unca.edu/nfsnc/ | Free | Daily; visitor's center weekdays 8–4:30.

Scottish Tartans Museum and Heritage Center. The museum contains an official registry of all publicly known tartans and is the American extension of the Scottish Tartans Society in Edinburgh, Scotland. | 86 E. Main St. | 828/524–7472 | fax 828/524–1092 | www.scottishtartans.org | $1 | Mon.–Sat. 10–5, Sun. 1–5.

Sheffield Mine. You can expect to find this ruby mine open rain or shine—there's a partially covered flume in case of rain, but expect to get a little wet while you prospect using their equipment and guidance. Once owned by Tiffany's, this is one of the oldest ruby mines still in operation in the Cowee Valley. You can purchase Native Ruby Dirt, Rainbow Dirt, or

Emerald Dirt to take home. Try to get here before 3:30 PM to avoid crowds. | 385 Sheffield Farms Rd. | 828/369–8383 | ruby@sheffieldmine.com | $12 | April–Oct., daily 9–5.

ON THE CALENDAR

JULY: *Leaf Lookers Gemboree.* Rough and cut gems, minerals, fine jewelry, jewelers' supplies, and gem-related books and lectures. | Macon County Community Bldg., 1288 Georgia Rd. (U.S. 441) | 828/524–3161 or 800/336–7829.

SEPT.: *Gem Capital Auto Club Car Show.* American and European cars, sports cars, antiques, custom-builts, and classics, and all manner of trucks are lined up for inspection and sometimes for driving. There's also food, music, and a flea market. | Macon County Fairground | 828/369–9570.

Dining

Fortune House Restaurant. Chinese. This small family restaurant is very popular with local residents. Every day there is a rotating three-dish lunch special, with pork, beef, shrimp, and chicken dishes. Try the crispy duck for dinner. | 305 Highlands Rd. | 828/524–2804 | $6–$15 | AE, D, MC, V | Closed Sun., Mon. and 2–5 Tues.–Sat.

Frog and Owl Kitchen. Eclectic. This small, casual bistro is owned by Jerri Fifer, a former bar-jumper, whose nickname at school was Froggy. Deli items are popular for take-out. Try onion-encrusted salmon, grilled tuna, or one of the many salads, including raspberry citrus. | 46 E. Main St. | 828/349–4112 | $6–$10 | MC, V | Closed Sun. No dinner.

Gazebo Café. Casual. The restaurant is entirely outdoors, where patio levels overlook a mountain creek. Soups, specialty salads, and sandwiches are served. One popular choice is the chicken framboise, made with ham, Swiss cheese, lettuce, and tomato and raspberry preserves. Wine only, BYOB (beer). Kids' menu. | 103 Heritage Hollow Dr. | 828/524–8783 | $5–$13 | MC, V | No supper weekends.

Lodging

Colonial Inn. Several restaurants, as well as the Scottish Tartans Museum, are within 3 mi of this motel. Scenic waterfalls are 7 mi away. Complimentary Continental breakfast. Refrigerators. Cable TV. Outdoor pool. Laundry facilities. Free parking. Pets allowed. | 3157 Georgia Rd. | 828/524–6600 | fax 828/349–1752 | 42 rooms | $35–$65 | AE, D, MC, V.

Country Inn Town. All rooms are on the ground floor of this hotel set on a riverbank on 4½ acres of landscaped grounds. It's in the center of town and just a short walk from restaurants and shops. Cable TV. Outdoor pool. Pets up to 20 pounds allowed (fee). | 668 E. Main St. | 828/524–4451 or 800/233–7555 | fax 828/524–0703 | www.switchboard.com | 46 rooms in 2 buildings | $45–$98 | AE, D, MC, V.

Days Inn. All the rooms at this small motel are at ground level and have their own entrances. Some rooms have porches and rocking chairs, and there are restaurants within walking distance. Picnic area, complimentary Continental breakfast. Some microwaves, some refrigerators. Cable TV. Outdoor pool. Playground. Business services. Pets allowed (fee). | 1320 E. Main St. | 828/524–6491 | fax 828/369–9636 | www.daysinn.com | 41 rooms | $84–$95 | AE, D, DC, MC, V.

Hampton Inn. This three-story hotel is just 1 mi from the Gem and Mineral museum. There's a shopping plaza down the street. In-room data ports. Outdoor pool. Fitness center. | 244 Cunningham Rd. | 828/369–0600 or 800/426–7866 | fax 828/369–0700 | www.hampton-inn.com | 81 rooms | $89 | AE, D, DC, MC, V.

Heritage Inn. Perched atop a stone wall above a quiet street, this tin-roofed country inn offers a peaceful stay in the private village of Heritage Hollow, a part of Franklin. The interior is country style: plain, homey, and welcoming. Complimentary breakfast. Some kitchenettes, no room phones. Cable TV in common area. Laundry facilities. Art gallery and gift shop. No pets. No kids under 14. No smoking. | 43 Heritage Hollow Dr. | 828/524–4150 or

888/524–4150 | www.heritageinnbb.com | 5 rooms, 1 suite | $75 (3–night minimum stay Oct. and holidays) | AE, DC, MC, V.

GASTONIA

MAP 8, D5

(Nearby towns also listed: Charlotte, Cherryville, Shelby)

The Catawba Indians were the first inhabitants of Gaston County; next came Scots, Irish, German, Dutch, and English settlers from the Northeast. They were followed by miners who'd heard about deposits of gold, iron, and sulfur. Now home to more than 75,000 people, the area relies on textile operations and metalworking. Low mountains grace the gently rolling landscape, and the Catawba River affords boating and fishing.

Information: Gaston County Travel and Tourism | 110 W. Main Ave., Gastonia 28052 | 704/867–2170 or 800/849–9994 | ascott@gastongov.org | www.gaston.org.

Attractions

American Military Museum. Next to the police department and operated by volunteers from American Legion Post 23, this museum houses collections of uniforms, weapons, scale models, flags, pictures, and other war and service memorabilia. | Memorial Hall, 115 W. 2nd Ave. | 704/866–6068 | Free | Sun. 2–5, or by appointment.

Daniel Stowe Botanical Garden. The garden is undergoing a 20-year-long renovation. Check the Web site or call for information about what exactly is on show. | 6500 S. New Hope Rd., Belmont | 704/825–4490 | fax 704/829–1240 | www.dsbg.org | $6 weekdays, $8 weekends | Mar.–Oct., daily 9–6; Oct.–Mar. daily 9–5.

Gaston County Museum of Art and History. In the historic Hoffman Hotel (1852), the museum features period furnishings in parlor settings, artifacts of early home textile manufacturers, and exhibits exploring art, architecture, and regional history. An adjoining carriage house holds a collection of carriages and sleighs. | 131 W. Main St., Dallas | 704/852–6025 | fax 704/922–7683 | Free | Tues.–Fri. 10–5, Sat. 1–5, 4th Sun. of each month 2–5.

Schiele Museum of Natural History and Planetarium. Inside, changing exhibits explore art, wildlife, and regional history. Costumed docents bring to life the re-created backcountry farm and Catawba Indian village outside. The gristmill and wooded paths along a stream enhance the natural beauty of the setting. | 1500 E. Garrison Blvd. | 704/866–6900 | www.schielemuseum.org | $2, free to residents and 2–8 on the 2nd Tues. of each month; planetarium shows $2.50 | Mon.–Sat. 9–5, Sun. 1–5; planetarium shows Mon.–Fri. at 2, Sat. at 1, 2, and 3, Sun. at 2 and 3; Indian village Mon.–Sat. 10–noon and 12:30–2, Sun. 1–4:30.

ON THE CALENDAR

AUG.: *Balloon Glow.* On the last Saturday of the month, from 5 PM into the evening hours, a dozen or so hot-air balloons that have been grounded and strategically placed throughout the Daniel Stowe Botanical Garden are lit up from the inside for dramatic effect. There's also food and entertainment. | 6500 S. New Hope Rd., Belmont | 704/825–4490.

OCT.: *Fish Camp Jam.* Fried fish and trimmings, catfish races, children's games, artist displays, and entertainment on the third Saturday only. | 704/853–3474.

DEC.: *Christmas Town, USA.* For the entire month, lights on private homes, public buildings, churches, and trees (including evergreens encircling a lake)—a million lights in all—turn a small textile town into one gigantic holiday display. This coordinated effort extends to the Yule Log Parade and accompanying festivities. Free hay rides are available weekends only with a reservation. | Town of McAdenville | 704/824–9696.

Dining

Billie Jean's Grasshopper Farm. American. Memorabilia from the 1940s, 1950s, and 1960s includes a jukebox in the bar area. An extensive lunchtime sandwich menu and burgers, fajitas, chicken, and prime rib on weekends. Kids' menu. | 911 Union Rd. | 704/853–8661 | Reservations not accepted | $11–$24 | AE, D, MC, V.

Purple Rose. Eclectic. With casual dining in a burgundy and heather-green space and soft lighting at dinner, this place is popular for steaks, seafood, pasta, and stir-fry. Also on the menu are early bird suppers, such as pork loin, mountain trout, and grilled rib eye. Buffet and Sun. brunch. Kids' menu. | 1007 Union Rd. | 704/864–6113 | $6–$21 | AE, D, MC, V | No lunch Sat.

Rodi. Continental. This restaurant is decorated in shades of blue and with hand-painted tables, and birds and trees create an aviary-like environment. The menu includes lots of grilled items, especially seafood, and there's always a pasta and pizza of the day. Specials change weekly, and the Greek sandwiches are popular. The grilled garlic shrimp over polenta, pan-seared almond-crusted trout, tuna niçoise, grilled lamb kebabs over tabbouleh, and spiced duck breast are particularly delicious. A wisteria-covered patio provides open-air dining. Live music some Fri.–Sat. evenings. Kids' menu. | 245 W. Garrison Blvd. | 704/864–7634 | $15–$20 | AE, D, MC, V | Closed Sun.– Mon.

Lodging

Hampton Inn. This chain hotel is within walking distance of a movie theater and shopping and is also near museums. The building is five stories high, and there's a landscaped pool. Complimentary Continental breakfast. In-room data ports. Cable TV. Outdoor pool. Laundry service. Business services. No pets. | 1859 Remount Rd. | 704/866–9090 | fax 704/866–7070 | www.hamptoninn.com | 108 rooms | $76–$84 | AE, D, DC, MC, V.

Super 8. Just 2 mi from the Schiele Museum and shopping malls, this 2-story motel is also within a mile of several restaurants. Charlotte Airport is 13 mi away. In-room data ports. Cable TV. | 502 Cox Rd. | 704/867–3846 | fax 704/868–3764 | www.super8.com | 45 rooms | $42–$50 | AE, D, DC, MC, V.

GOLDSBORO

MAP 8, H5

(Nearby towns also listed: Kinston, Smithfield, Warsaw, Wilson)

Goldsboro and Wayne County, with a collective population of nearly 50,000, and home to three state supreme court justices and two governors, have played key roles in several of this country's major wars. Today they're home to the Seymour Johnson Air Force Base, a training center for the F-15E fighter jet.

Information: Wayne County Chamber of Commerce | 308 N. Williams St., Goldsboro 27533 | 919/734–2241 | info@waynecountychamber.com | www.waynecountychamber.com.

Attractions

Cliffs of the Neuse State Park. On the Neuse River, this 750-acre park contains a 90-ft-high sand cliff, three hiking trails (½ mi each), a picnic area, family and group camping, and fishing. At the northern end of the cliffs is a small natural history museum. There's a fee for camping and swimming. | 345-A Park Entrance Rd., Seven Springs | 919/778–6234 | fax 919/778–7447 | ils.unc.edu/parkproject/clne | Free | Apr.–Nov. daily; Dec.–Mar., weekends only 8–sunset; museum daily 10–5.

Governor Charles B. Aycock Birthplace State Historic Site. This was the simple boyhood home of the man who would come to be known as North Carolina's education governor.

The rural site still retains the restored mid-19th-century home and outbuildings, an heirloom garden, and one-room schoolhouse, and has a visitor center. Special living-history programs are scheduled throughout the year. | 264 Governor Aycock Rd., Fremont | 919/242–5581 | fax 919/242–6668 | www.ah.dcr.state.nc.us/sections/hs/aycock/aycock.htm | Free | Apr.–Oct., Mon.–Sat. 9–5, Sun. 1–5; Nov.–Mar., Tues.–Sat. 10–4, Sun. 1–4.

Willowdale Cemetery and Confederate Monument. A cast-iron fence surrounds this circa-1853 cemetery that is the burial place of many early citizens. The Confederate Monument, a life-sized statue of a cloaked infantryman, was erected in 1883 to honor the 800 unknown Confederate and Union soldiers killed at the Battle of Bentonville. | 306 E. Elm St. | 919/734–2241 | Free | Daily dawn–dusk.

ON THE CALENDAR
APR.: *North Carolina Pickle Festival.* Mt. Olive, home to the largest independent pickle company in the United States, hosts a two-day ode to the pickle, with bike and car races, airplane rides, arts and crafts, entertainment, children's activities, commercial vendors who sell everything from flags to futons, and foods, including—what else?— pickles! | 800/334–6713.

Dining
Captain Bob's Seafood. Seafood. A casual, family kind of place with a deep-sea decor, this spot has walls covered with fishing nets and a boat parked outside. Seafood selections like lobster and clams are standard items, as are steaks and other non-seafood options. Kids' menu. | 430 N. Berkeley Blvd. | 919/778–8332 | $11–$16 | MC, V | Closed Mon. No lunch Sat.

Madison's Prime Rib and Steak. Steak. A Louisiana-style, riverboat-theme restaurant that offers lunch and dinner buffets and prides itself on a loyal clientele, this place serves two types of dinner buffets: country (fried chicken, roast beef, vegetables), and seafood. À la carte items include prime rib, rib-eye steaks, and lobster tails. | 413 New Hope Rd. | 919/751–2009 | $7–$22 | AE, MC, V | Closed Mon. No lunch Sat. No dinner Sun.

Wilber's Barbecue and Restaurant. Barbecue. This family-style restaurant with a red brick, roomy, family atmosphere, offers an authentic eastern North Carolina chopped pork barbecue, cooked over hardwood coals with a vinegar and pepper–based sauce, as well as a variety of side dishes including collards, baked beans, coleslaw, and potato salad. Kids' menu. | 4172 U.S. 70 E | 919/778–5218 | Reservations not accepted | $5–$10 | MC, V.

Lodging
Best Western Goldsboro Inn. This two-story hotel is 13 mi from Cliffs of the Neuse State Park. Restaurant, bar. Refrigerators, microwaves. Cable TV. Outdoor pool. Fitness center. Laundry facilities. Free parking. Pets allowed. | 801 U.S. 70 Bypass E | 919/735–7911 or 800/528–1234 | fax 919/735–5030 | www.bestwestern.com | 116 rooms | $51–$59 | AE, D, DC, MC, V.

Days Inn. This chain motel is within walking distance of restaurants, a 5-minute drive from the Berkeley Mall, and 5 mi from the center of town. Some in-room data ports, some refrigerators. Cable TV. Outdoor pool. Laundry facilities. Business services. Pets allowed (fee). | 2000 Wayne Memorial Dr. | 919/734–9471 | fax 919/736–2623 | www.daysinn.com | 121 rooms | $52–$57 | AE, D, DC, MC, V.

Hampton Inn. This standard chain hotel is within walking distance of restaurants, 1 mi from the Air Force base, a 5-minute drive to Berkeley Mall, and 15 mi from the state park. Complimentary Continental breakfast. In-room data ports, some refrigerators. Cable TV. Outdoor pool. Exercise equipment. Laundry facilities. Business services. No pets. | 905 N. Spence Ave. | 919/778–1800 | fax 919/778–5891 | www.hamptoninn.com | 111 rooms | $59–$72 | AE, D, DC, MC, V.

Holiday Inn Express. Just 3 blocks from restaurants, this chain hotel is 1 mi from the Seymour Johnson Air Force Base and a 5-minute drive to several other restaurants. Complimentary Continental breakfast. In-room data ports, some refrigerators, some in-room hot tubs. Cable TV. Outdoor pool. Exercise equipment. Business services. No pets. | 909 Spence Ave. | 919/751–1999 | fax 919/751–8299 | www.basshotels.com | 122 rooms | $69 | AE, D, DC, MC, V.

Ramada Inn. The Air Force base is 5 mi from here, and I–95 is 20 minutes away. Its wing-chair-stuffed lobby is a bit homier than most, a good place to sit and relax, watch TV, chat, and get acquainted with the 20-yr-old potted house plant. Restaurant, bar with entertainment. Some in-room data ports, some microwaves, some refrigerators. Cable TV. Outdoor pool. Laundry facilities. Business services. Some pets allowed (fee). | 808 W. Grantham St. | 919/736–4590 | fax 919/735–3218 | 128 rooms, 4 suites | $52 | AE, D, DC, MC, V.

GREAT SMOKY MOUNTAINS NATIONAL PARK

MAP 8, A4

(Nearby towns also listed: Asheville, Charlotte, Hot Springs)

With 276,000 acres in North Carolina and 244,000 acres in Tennessee, this national park is the largest nationally protected area east of the Rockies. Its mountains are some of the oldest in the world and represent the southernmost limit of many northern species of trees and other plants. Because of this, many federally funded biological studies are conducted here. The Appalachian Trail runs along the crest of the moun-

© Corbis

BARBECUE

A guaranteed one-word conversation-starter in any gathering of Tar Heels? Barbecue. Sociologist John Shelton Reed, director of the University of North Carolina's Institute for Research in Social Science, has called it "the most southern meat of all, long associated with political rallies and fire department fund-raisers, and ideally served from a cinder-block building with a sign that says BBQ."

The barbecue tradition is a long one, linked to Native Americans from the region. And in North Carolina—where barbecue means pork—the word is used as a noun (a dish or an event) as well as a verb.

The line that divides east and west is method. In eastern North Carolina (that's east of I–95), either a whole hog or its shoulder is smoked, and the meat is chopped or "pulled" and dressed with a vinegar and pepper-based sauce. Side dishes include coleslaw, hush puppies, boiled potatoes, and Brunswick stew (a kind of gumbo). At Wilber's in Goldsboro, mecca for many when it comes to eastern-style 'cue, the pigs are cooked up to 12 hours over oak coals in a smokehouse behind the restaurant.

West of I–85, the meat can be sliced or chopped and the spicy sauce is tomato-based. That sauce also gets mixed into the coleslaw. The favorite side with all this is deep-fried hush puppies. In Lexington, where barbecue has become an economic force, the majority of pig-out spots would rather be caught dead than using anything but pork shoulders and hickory coals. What both sides agree on is that the line of good taste has got to be drawn somewhere. In this case, it's at that distinctive sweet mustard–based sauce used south of the border.

tains, and U.S. 441 is the only paved road that passes all the way through the park. Within the park's boundaries are more than 800 mi of trails, 600 mi of trout streams, 10 developed campgrounds (five of them in North Carolina), and historical structures of early white settlements.

Information: **Park Headquarters** | 107 Park Headquarters Rd., Gatlinburg, 37738 | 865/436–1200 or 800/365–2267 (campground reservations) | www.nps.gov/grsm.

ON THE CALENDAR
APR.: *Spring Wildflower Pilgrimage.* A three-day program of conducted nature walks, motorcades, and photographic tours that includes both the North Carolina and Tennessee sides of the park and a designated wildlife sanctuary. In addition to field trips for those with a botanical bent, there are also bird, insect, spider, amphibian, and geological jaunts offered. | 865/436–1200.

Lodging
LeConte Lodge. No electricity and the absence of showers may keep away some, but camping is the only other alternative inside Great Smoky Mountains National Park. It's a 5–8 mi hike to this wilderness lodge, but the food could be worth it. Breakfast and supper is served family-style in the dining room. Complimentary breakfast and dinner. | 865/429–5704 | 5 rooms | $78 | No credit cards.

GREENSBORO

MAP 8, F4

(Nearby towns also listed: Asheboro, Burlington, High Point, Winston-Salem)

With over 200,000 citizens, Greensboro is the largest population center in the Triad (a verbal convenience for Greensboro, Winston-Salem, and High Point). Thanks to its spacious convention facilities, it is a destination for business travelers. The city, named in honor of Revolutionary War hero General Nathanael Greene, is proud of the role it has played in American history, and has taken great pains to preserve and showcase the sights of other eras.

With the exception of Old Greensborough and the downtown historic district, however, walking is not a comfortable sightseeing option. To tour grand historic homes, glimpse monuments to famous native sons and daughters (e.g., Dolley Madison, Edward R. Murrow, O. Henry), or visit one of the many recreation areas, you need a car.

Information: **Greensboro Area Convention and Visitors Bureau** | 317 S. Greene St., 27401 | 336/274–2282 or 800/344–2282 | gso@greensboronc.org | www.greensboronc.org.

Attractions
Blandwood Mansion. The former home of two-term North Carolina governor John Motley Morehead is open as a house-museum depicting life in the mid-19th century. Built in 1844, it is the oldest example of Italianate architecture in the United States. A National Historic Landmark, Blandwood contains many of its original furnishings and is on four landscaped acres. To see the interior, you must take a guided tour. | 447 W. Washington St. | 336/272–5003 | fax 336/271–8049 | www.blandwood.org | $5 | Tues.–Sat. 11–2, Sun. 2–5.

Charlotte Hawkins Brown Memorial State Historic Site. In 1902, Dr. Charlotte Hawkins Brown, an African–American, founded Palmer Memorial Institute (PMI), an accredited prep school for African–Americans. Over time, its size and national reputation expanded. The memorial links Brown and PMI to the larger themes of Black women, education, and social history. | 6136 Burlington Rd., Sedalia | 336/449–4846 | fax 336/449–0176 |

www.ah.dcr.state.nc.us/sections/hs/chb/chb.htm | Free | Apr.–Oct., Mon.–Sat. 9–5, Sun. 1–5; Nov.–Mar., Tues.–Sat. 10–4, Sun. 1–4.

★ **Chinqua-Penn Plantation.** An English country-style mansion built in 1927 by tobacco and utility magnates Jeff and Betsy Penn. The world-traveling Penns filled their 27-room home with an eclectic collection of furniture and decorative arts. On the grounds are gardens, pools, fountains, greenhouses (with plants for sale), a clock tower, and a pagoda. Entrance to the house is by guided tour only. Call ahead if you want a guided tour of the garden, but you can also tour the gardens on your own. | 2138 Wentworth St., Reidsville | 336/349–4576 | fax 336/342–4863 | www.chinquapenn.com | $13 house and garden, $6 garden only, greenhouses free | Mar.–Dec., Tues.–Sat. 9–5, Sun. noon–5.

Greensboro Children's Museum. Exhibits and activities are designed with 1- to 12-yr-old children in mind. They can dig for buried treasure, wrap themselves in a gigantic bubble, or stroll through "Our Town," a miniature town that comes complete with a grocery store and bank. Transportation, theater, and environmental awareness are other exhibit themes. | 220 N. Church St. | 336/574–2898 | fax 336/574–3810 | www.gcmuseum.com | $5.50, special rates for seniors and children | Tues.–Thurs. and Sat. 9–5, Fri. 9–9, Sun. 1–5.

Greensboro Cultural Center at Festival Park. An architectural showplace that houses 25 visual- and performing-arts organizations, five art galleries, rehearsal halls, a sculpture garden, a restaurant with outdoor café-style seating, and an outdoor amphitheater. | 200 N. Davie St. | 336/373–2712 | Free | Daily; call for gallery hours.

Greensboro Historical Museum. Ten galleries and two restored houses present American history with a local perspective. Of special note are exhibits featuring the Greensboro civil rights sit-ins, area natives like first lady Dolley Madison, author O. Henry, and journalist Edward R. Murrow. Piedmont furniture and military history are also highlighted. | 130 Summit Ave. | 336/373–2043 | fax 336/373–2204 | www.greensborohistory.com | Free | Tues.–Sat. 10–5, Sun. 2–5.

Guilford Courthouse National Military Park. This was the first Revolutionary War battlefield set aside as a national park. It preserves the site of the epic battle that crippled the British Army and set the stage for the American victory at Yorktown. It includes a visitor center with a film and exhibits of arms and equipment, a tour road, walking trails, and 28 monuments. | 2332 New Garden Rd. | 336/288–1776 | fax 336/282–2296 | www.nps.gov/guco | Free | Daily 8:30–5.

Natural Science Center of Greensboro. A hands-on museum, zoo, and planetarium featuring a 36-ft model of Tyrannosaurus rex, virtual reality, a walk-through maze, an aquarium, a reptile lab, and "exploratorium" for young children. | 4301 Lawndale Dr. | 336/288–3769 | fax 336/288–2531 | www.greensboro.com/sciencecenter | $6, $1 more for planetarium | Science Center Mon.–Sat. 9–5, Sun. 12:30–5; zoo Mon.–Sat. 10–4:30, Sun. 12:30–4:30.

Old Greensborough. Elm Street, with its turn-of-the-20th-century architecture, is the heart of this area, which is listed on the National Register of Historic Places. | Elm Street and surrounding area | 336/274–2282 | Free | Daily.

Replacements Ltd. The world's largest inventory of discontinued and "active" china, crystal, flatware, and collectibles. More than 5 million pieces and 100,000 patterns are in stock. Tours of the facility, which is the size of four football fields, are offered every 30 minutes all day. | 1089 Knox Rd. | 336/697–3000 or 800/737–5223 | fax 336/697–3100 | www.replacements.com | Free | Daily 8 AM–9 PM, tours every ½ hr.

Tannenbaum Park. This hands-on history experience near Guilford Courthouse National Military Park draws you into the lives of early settlers. With advance notice, costumed reenactors escort you through exhibits at the Colonial Heritage Center in the visitor center. The restored 1778 Hoskins House (tours by appointment), with a blacksmith shop and barn, are on the property. | Visitor center, 2200 New Garden Rd. | 336/545–5315 | fax 336/545–5314 | Free | Apr.–Nov., Tues.–Sat. 9–5, Sun. 1–5; Dec.–Mar., Tues.–Sat. 10–4:30, Sun. 1–4:30.

Weatherspoon Art Gallery. On the campus of the University of North Carolina at Greensboro, the Weatherspoon emphasizes contemporary art in its six galleries and sculpture courtyard. It is recognized for its permanent collections and changing exhibits of 20th-century American art. | Anne and Benjamin Cone Building, Spring Garden and Tate St. | 336/334–5770 | fax 336/334–5907 | www.weatherspoon.uncg.edu | Free | Tues. and Thurs.–Fri. 10–5, Wed. 10–8, Sun. 1–5.

ON THE CALENDAR

JAN.–MAR.: *African-American Arts Festival.* A series of cultural and artistic events, including performances. | 336/373–7523, ext. 245.

MAR.: *Battle of Guilford Courthouse Historic Re-enactment.* A retelling of a key Revolutionary War battle, historic exhibits, and demonstrations. | Guilford Courthouse National Military Park, 2332 New Garden Rd. | 336/288–1776.

APR.: *Greater Greensboro Chrysler Classic Golf Tournament.* One of the oldest and richest stops on the PGA Tour. | Forest Oaks Country Club, 4600 Forest Oaks Dr. (U.S. 421 S) | 336/379–1570.

MAY: *Blues Festival.* The Piedmont Blues Preservation Society hosts blues performers from all over the state at this one-day jam session held at Emerald Pointe Water Park. | 336/275–4944.

JUNE–JULY: *Eastern Music Festival.* Six weeks of music competitions and concerts by students, professors, and internationally recognized performers. The alumni list includes Wynton Marsalis. The majority of events takes place at Guilford College. | 5800 W. Friendly Ave. | 336/333–7450 | www.easternmusicfestival.com.

SEPT.: *Native American Festival.* A party to celebrate the cultures of a number of Native American tribes. Food, dance, crafts, music, and competitions. | Country Park | 336/273–8686.

Dining

Bear Rock Café. American. Rustic wooden rails, antler chandeliers, and stone fireplaces fill the dining room at this casual restaurant. Have anything from an Adirondack (smoked turkey) sandwich to a Sasquash (grilled eggplant and squash) sandwich. Create your own sandwich for $4.75. | 705 Friendly Center Rd. | 336/292–1977 | fax 336/292–7786 | $4–$6 | AE, MC, V.

Casaldi's Café. Italian. This sleek tile-and-marble trattoria offers such recommended dishes as spinach and walnut ravioli, chicken cacciatore, spaghetti bolognese, or the house speciality, lasagne bolognese with béchamel sauce and fresh pasta. | 1310 Westover Terr | 336/379–8191 | Reservations not accepted | $9–$18 | D, MC, V | Closed Sun. No lunch Sat.

Fuzzy's Barbecue. Barbecue. A down-home, family-style place specializing in spicy chopped pork barbecue, creatively shaped hush puppies, red slaw, and banana pudding. | 407 Highway St., Madison | 336/427–4130 | Reservations not accepted | $8–$20 | MC, V.

Lo Spiedo Di Noble. Italian. A wood-burning tile oven and spit are the highlights at this primarily Tuscan restaurant adorned with murals. A fried oyster salad is very popular; lamb, filet mignon, and fresh fish are some of the other stars on the menu. Piano bar; jazz Fri. and Sat. evenings. | 172 Battleground Ave. | 336/333–9833 | $22–$44 | AE, D, MC, V | Closed Sun. No lunch.

Paisley Pineapple. Continental. This formal dining spot with an extensive menu is in a restored 1920s building. The inventive soups change daily. Rack of lamb, grilled veal tenderloin, and sautéed beef tenderloin share the menu. | 345 S. Elm St. | 336/279–8488 | Reservations essential | $30–$51 | AE, MC, V | Restaurant closed Sun.–Mon.; sofa bar open daily.

Sapporo. Japanese. Traditional Japanese decorations are the backdrop for steak, shrimp, and chicken combinations prepared in full view in the classic Teppanyaki style. All-vegetable selections are available. Sushi bar. Kids' menu. | 2939-C Battleground Ave. | 336/282–5345 | Reservations essential | $10–$30 | AE, D, MC, V | No lunch Sat.

Stamey's Barbecue. Barbecue. A bit more upscale than is usual for a pig palace with a bustling dining room. Try western North Carolina–style chopped pork with tomato-based sauce, spicy coleslaw, and hot peach cobbler. | 2206 High Point Rd. (Rte. 6) | 336/299–9888 | Reservations not accepted | $4–$14 | No credit cards | Closed Sun.

Stephen's Steakhouse and Oyster. Seafood. Only 5 mi outside of downtown Greensboro, this is one of the only places in town where you can find karaoke, on Friday and Saturday nights from 10 PM–2 AM. Steamed and raw oysters, and Stephen's favorite, fillet stuffed with Cajun oysters, are great dishes to try. There are also pasta and chicken specialties. | 2702 High Point Rd. | 336/292–8907 | $11–$25 | AE, D, MC, V.

Sunset Café. Contemporary. Art Deco in style and slightly bohemian, this spot emphasizes fresh ingredients and careful preparation. There's a definite Middle Eastern flavor to meat, seafood, and appetizers. | 4608 W. Market St. | 336/855–0350 | $15–$25 | AE, MC, V | Closed Mon.

Lodging

Amerisuites. Within a 15-min drive of Haganstone Park, Greensboro Jaycee park, Bryan Park, and Carolyn Allen park, this chain hotel is also within walking distance of restaurants and shops and 1 mi from the Four Seasons Mall and the Greensboro Coliseum. Complimentary Continental breakfast. In-room data ports, microwaves, minibars, refrigerators. Cable TV, in-room VCRs. Outdoor pool. Exercise equipment. Laundry facilities. Business services, airport shuttle, free parking. Pets allowed. | 1619 Stanley Rd. | 336/852–1443 or 800/833–1516 | fax 336/854–9339 | www.amerisuites.com | 126 suites | $79–$114 | AE, D, DC, MC, V.

★ **Biltmore Greensboro Hotel.** Original architectural features like beveled-glass front doors, a walnut-paneled lobby, floor-to-ceiling windows, and a cage elevator, are just a few of the details that give period charm and character to this 1895 hotel in the heart of Greensboro's business district. Complimentary Continental breakfast. Minibars, refrigerators. Cable TV. Business services, airport shuttle. Some pets allowed. | 111 W. Washington St. | 336/272–3474 or 800/332–0303 | fax 336/275–2523 | http://members.aol.com/biltmorenc/index.html | 25 rooms, 4 suites | $85–$95 | AE, D, DC, MC, V.

Coliseum Motel. There's a Mexican restaurant on the premises of this 3-story motel, and the Greensboro Coliseum is only 4 blocks away. Cable TV. Free parking. | 2428 High Point Rd. | 336/292–1831 | fax 336/292–6001 | 126 rooms | $35–$49 | AE, D, DC, MC, V.

Comfort Inn. Near restaurants, movie theaters, a park, and I–40 Exit 217, this hotel is just 10 mi from the airport. With contemporary-style rooms, this motel is also less than 1 mi from horseback riding, 5 mi from water theme park, and 10 mi from golf. Complimentary Continental breakfast. Some in-room data ports, some microwaves, some refrigerators. Cable TV. Outdoor pool. Business services, free parking. No pets. | 2001 Veasley St. | 336/294–6220, ext. 199 | fax 336/294–6220 | www.comfortinn.com | 122 rooms | $64–$135 | AE, D, DC, MC, V.

Days Inn. This chain hotel is 4 mi from the Emerald Point water park, just south of the city center. The tree-shaded pool is right next to a children's play area. Complimentary Continental breakfast. In-room data ports. Cable TV. Pool. Playground. Free parking. No pets. | 120 Seneca Rd. | 336/275–9571 | fax 336/275–9571 | www.daysinn.com | 122 rooms | $49–$75 | AE, D, DC, MC, V.

Embassy Suites. In an office park 2 mi from the airport, at the intersection of I–40 and Route 68, this hotel is well situated for business travelers. It is centered around an elegant, seven-story atrium lit by skylights and filled with plants. Three shopping malls are 5 mi away. Restaurant, bar, complimentary breakfast. In-room data ports, microwaves, refrigerators. Cable TV. Indoor pool. Hot tub. Gym. Gift shop. Laundry facilities. Business services, airport shuttle, free parking. No pets. | 204 Centreport Dr. | 336/668–4535 | fax 336/668–3901 | www.embassysuites.com | 221 suites | $109–$159 | AE, D, DC, MC, V.

Fairfield Inn by Marriott. Across the street from a shopping mall, this chain hotel is also less than 1 block from many restaurants. Complimentary Continental breakfast. In-room data ports. Cable TV. Outdoor pool. Business services, free parking. No pets. | 2003 Athena Ct | 336/294–9922 | fax 336/294–9922 | www.fairfieldinn.com | 135 rooms | $49–$62 | AE, D, DC, MC, V.

Greenwood B&B. Eclectic antiques and art fill this 1905 Craftsman home in historic Fisher Park and just seven blocks north of downtown and a 20-minute drive from High Point furniture shops. Owned by a former New Orleans chef (who does all the cooking) and his decorator wife. Each room is treated in a different way; for instance, the taupe, lavender, and green Morning Glory Room has a canopy-backed bed. Complimentary breakfast. No TVs in rooms, cable TV in common area. Outdoor pool. Free parking. No smoking. No kids under 12. | 205 N. Park Dr. | 336/274–6350 or 800/535–9363 | fax 336/274–9943 | www.greenwoodbb.com | 5 rooms | $130–$140 | AE, D, DC, MC, V.

Hampton Inn. A chain hotel within 4 mi of the water park and 3 mi from downtown, with restaurants nearby. Complimentary Continental breakfast. In-room data ports. Cable TV. Outdoor pool. Business services, free parking. No pets. | 2004 Veasley St. | 336/854–8600 | fax 336/854–8741 | www.hamptoninn.com | 121 rooms | $79–$125 | AE, D, DC, MC, V.

Marriott. On 17 landscaped acres that include a small lake and 2 lighted tennis courts, this standard chain hotel is within walking distance of the airport. Restaurant, bar. In-room data ports. Cable TV. Indoor-outdoor pool. Hot tub. Tennis courts. Exercise equipment. Gift shop. Laundry service and facilities. Business services, airport shuttle, free parking. No pets. | 1 Marriott Dr. | 336/852–6450 | fax 336/665–6522 | www.marriott.com | 299 rooms | $149 | AE, D, DC, MC, V.

Motel 6. This two-story building is in a commercial area 9 mi from the Greensboro Coliseum Complex. There's a restaurant within a mile of the motel. Cable TV. Outdoor pool. Laundry facilities. Pets allowed. | 605 S. Regional Rd.; I–40 Exit 210 | 336/668–2085 or 800/466–8356 | fax 336/454–6120 | www.motel6.com | 125 rooms | $37–$40 | AE, D, MC, V.

Park Lane Hotel at Four Seasons. This hotel is a sister facility to the Sheraton Four Seasons; there's a shuttle that regularly runs between the two. The building itself is 1960s style concrete, but the common areas are filled with plants and wall-hangings. Restaurant, bar, complimentary Continental breakfast, room service. In-room data ports, some microwaves, minibars (in suites), some refrigerators, some in-room hot tubs. Cable TV. Outdoor pool. Exercise equipment. Laundry facilities. Business services, airport shuttle, free parking. No pets. | 3005 High Point Rd. | 336/294–4565 | fax 336/294–0572 | 161 rooms, 4 suites | $79–$89 | AE, D, DC, MC, V.

Radisson Inn. Greensboro Coliseum is 7 mi from this four-story chain, which is located about 10 minutes from downtown Greensboro. Spacious rooms and a business-class floor make up the inside. Restaurant, complimentary breakfast. In-room data ports. Cable TV. Outdoor pool. Hot tub. Fitness center. Business services, airport shuttle. | 415 Swing Rd. | 336/299–7650 | fax 336/854–9146 | www.radisson.com | 195 rooms | $89–$129 | AE, D, DC, MC, V.

Ramada Inn–Airport. A chain hotel, this spot is 5 mi from the airport and 10 mi from downtown. Restaurant, bar, room service. Indoor-outdoor pool. Sauna. Business services, airport shuttle, free parking. Pets under 15 pounds allowed. | 7067 Albert Pick Rd. | 336/668–3900 | fax 336/668–7012 | www.ramada.com | 168 rooms | $67–$79 | AE, D, DC, MC, V.

Sheraton Four Seasons/Joseph S. Koury Convention Center. A 28-story mini-city, this is the largest hotel in the state. Across the street is a mall with 250 stores. The rooms are basically upgraded versions of the typical chain hotel style. 4 restaurants, 4 bars with entertainment, room service. In-room data ports, some refrigerators. Cable TV. Indoor and outdoor pool, wading pool. Hot tub, sauna. Gym, racquetball. Laundry service. Business services, airport shuttle, free parking. No pets. | 3121 High Point Rd. | 336/292–9161 or 800/242–6556 | fax 336/294–3516 | www.kourycenter.com | 1,014 rooms | $119–$139 | AE, D, DC, MC, V.

Super 8 Motel. Four Seasons Mall is 2 blocks away and Greensboro Coliseum is ½ mi from this three-story building built in 1987. Suites are also available. Bar, complimentary breakfast. Cable TV. Free parking. | 2108 W. Meadowview Rd. | 336/855–8888 or 800/800–8000 | fax 336/855–8888, ext. 323 | www.super8motel | 62 rooms | $45–$65 | AE, D, DC, MC, V.

Travelodge-Coliseum. The exposed-brick lobby of this hotel is filled with potted plants. It is 9 mi from the airport, a 10-minute drive from downtown, and within walking distance of restaurants and shops. It is off I-40 Exit 217. In-room data ports, some microwaves, some refrigerators. Cable TV. Pool. Business services. No pets. | 2112 W. Meadowview Rd. | 336/292–2020 | fax 336/852–3476 | www.travelodge.com | 108 rooms | $64–$84 | AE, D, DC, MC, V.

Troy Burnpass Inn B&B. Built in 1847, this B&B opened its doors in 1992 as one of the oldest remaining homes in the Greensboro College Hill historic district. Within walking distance of Greensboro College, downtown Greensboro, and the campus of the University of North Carolina at Greensboro. All rooms are individually decorated with period antiques and reproductions, and all have an shared bath. Complimentary breakfast. Cable TV. Free parking. | 114 S. Mendenhall St. | 336/370–1660 | fax 336/274–3939 or 800/370–9070 | www.troy-bumpasinn.com | 4 rooms | $95–$110 | AE, D, DC, MC, V.

GREENVILLE

MAP 8, J4

(Nearby towns also listed: Kinston, Washington, Williamston, Wilson)

Home to East Carolina University, a major medical center, and a diverse number of businesses and industries, Greenville is a hub for the eastern part of the state. While the city of nearly 60,000, situated on the Tar River, is urban, what fans out from it quickly turns from suburban to rural. Point of fact: Pitt County, of which Greenville is the seat, grows more bright-leaf tobacco than any other comparable region in the world.

Information: **Greenville–Pitt County Convention and Visitors Bureau** | 525 S. Evans St., Greenville 27835 | 252/329–4200 or 800/537–5564 | info@visitgreenvillenc.com | www.visitgreenvillenc.com.

Attractions

East Carolina University. With an enrollment of 18,000, East Carolina University, commonly known as ECU, is the third-largest school in the University of North Carolina system. The school serves as the focal point for cultural events, theater and the arts, research, and public service in the eastern part of the state. Its School of Medicine is across town in west Greenville on a campus next to a regional medical center. | Main campus between E. 5th and E. 10th Sts. | 252/328–6131 | www.ecu.edu | Free | Daily.

East Carolina Village of Yesteryear. A cluster of 19 once-endangered historic buildings that date from 1840 to 1940 include a country store filled with its wares and a log church. Designed to preserve and interpret rural farm life, the village holds more than 1,000 artifacts of early North Carolina history. | 117 W. 5th St. | 252/329–4200 | $2 | Apr.–Nov., Fri.–Sat. 10–5, Sun. 1–5; tours by appointment.

Greenville Museum of Art. Founded in 1939 as a Works Progress Administration gallery, the museum has four galleries and now houses a collection of 20th-century American art and the largest permanent display of Jugtown pottery in eastern North Carolina. Contemporary work by North Carolina artists and exhibits of national, regional, and local importance round out the offerings. | 802 Evans St. | 252/758–1946 | Free | Tues.–Fri. 10–4:30, weekends 1–4.

May Museum and Park. A celebration of the history, heritage, and culture of the Pitt County area and the family instrumental in colonizing it, the Mays. Family items on display in the house-museum represent a 200-year time span. Especially notable is the quilt collection, one of the oldest in the state. | 213 S. Main St., Farmville | 252/753–5814 | fax 252/753–3190 | Free | Tues.–Sat. 12–5, or by appointment.

ON THE CALENDAR
MAR.: *A Taste of Greenville.* Noshers sample cuisine from more than 30 Greenville area restaurants. Proceeds benefit charity. | 252/752–5093.
APR.: *Farmville Dogwood Festival.* Music, arts, crafts, rides, races, and exhibits centered on the Farmville Town Common in celebration of North Carolina's state flower. | 200 N. Main St. | 252/753–5814.
JUNE: *Michael Jordan Celebrity Golf Classic.* Sports and entertainment celebrities accompany basketball superstar Michael Jordan to his home state for a weekend of golf competition and social events for charity. | Brook Valley Country Club, 311 Oxford Rd. | 252/355–3222.
JUNE–JULY: *Guitar Festival.* A week of public concerts by members of the artist-faculty at East Carolina University's School of Music. Recitals by award-winning guitarists, solo guitar competitions, and classical guitar workshops. | E. 10th St. | 252/328–6245.
AUG.: *Watermelon Festival.* All manner of watermelon concerns, from contests surrounding the watermelon—the largest watermelon, watermelon eating, seed spitting—to exhibits and entertainment. | Rte. 11, Winterville | 252/756–1068.
SEPT.: *Collard Festival.* Collard cooking and eating contests, sports events, beauty contests, arts and crafts, live entertainment, and rides. | Rte. 11, Ayden | 252/746–2270.

Dining
Beef Barn. Steak. This casual, country-style restaurant has a barnlike look and is filled with antiques. Not surprisingly (given the name), beef and steak figure largely on the menu, though there are also daily seafood specials. The steaks go up in size to 30 oz., and there's a salad bar. Kids' menu. | 400 St. Andrews Dr. | 252/756–1161 | $15–$30 | AE, D, DC, MC, V | No lunch Sat.

Chico's Mexican Restaurant. Mexican. Students and faculty from East Carolina University give this place a thumbs-up. Five TVs are often tuned to sporting events. Full list of Mexican food, plus items like cheeseburgers, calamari, and chicken soup. Kids' menu. | 521 Contanche St. | 252/757–1666 | $6–$13 | AE, D, MC, V.

Marathon Restaurant. Greek. This casual family restaurant is full of woodwork and plants. The menu offers a very unique selection of pizzas specialties, as well as a souvlaki (grilled, marinated pork tenderloin) sandwich, chicken kebab sandwich, eggplant pita, or grilled tuna. | 706 S. Evans St. | 252/752–0326 | $6–$10 | No credit cards | Closed Sun.

Parker's Bar-B-Que. Barbecue. The emphasis at this family-owned eatery is on hearty, traditional Southern fare, like pork barbecue and fried chicken, but you can also order fish, oysters, and shrimp. Kids' menu. | 3109 S. Memorial Dr. | 252/756–2388 | $6–$8 | No credit cards | Closed 1 week mid-June.

Lodging
Days Inn. Eastern Carolina University and shopping malls are within 2 mi of this two-story hotel. There are various restaurants within a mile as well. Restaurant. Complimentary breakfast. Refrigerators. Cable TV. Outdoor pool. Free parking. | 810 S. Memorial Dr. | 252/752–0214 or 800/544–8313 | fax 242/752–4565 | www.daysinn.com | 47 rooms | $56–$75 | AE, D, DC, MC, V.

Fairfield Inn by Marriott. This two-story chain hotel is just 10 minutes from Arlington Village, Explora Town, and the Greenville Museum of Art, with some chain restaurants also nearby. There's a free shuttle to the hospital, which is only ½ mi away. Complimentary Continental breakfast. In-room data ports. Cable TV. Pool. Laundry service. Business services, airport shuttle, free parking. No pets. | 821 S. Memorial Dr. | 252/758–5544 | fax 252/758–1416 | www.fairfieldinn.com | 112 rooms | $74 | AE, D, DC, MC, V.

Hampton Inn. This chain hotel has a landscaped area outside and a plant-filled lobby where you can relax, watch TV, and drink some of the coffee that's available 24 hours a day. On Route 11 S, right across from Carolina East Mall and Winn Dixie Plaza, and about 5 mi from downtown. There are restaurants and a movie theater within walking distance. Complimentary Continental breakfast. In-room data ports, some microwaves, some refrigerators. Cable TV. Pool. Laundry service. Business services, airport shuttle, free parking. No pets. | 3439 S. Memorial Dr. | 252/355–2521 | fax 252/355–0262 | www.hamptoninn.com | 121 rooms | $55–$65 | AE, D, DC, MC, V.

Hilton Inn. This chain hotel is on Greenville's main thoroughfare, Greenville Boulevard/U.S. 264 Alternate—just minutes from corporate businesses and 3½ miles southeast from downtown. There are two malls and a movie theater within a mile. The in-house restaurant offers Greek and Italian specialities, as well as seafood and steak; Kosher food is available through room service. Restaurant, bar, room service. In-room data ports, refrigerators, microwaves (in suites). Cable TV. Pool. Hot tub, spa. Exercise equipment. Laundry service. Business services, airport shuttle, free parking. No pets. | 207 S.W. Greenville Blvd. | 252/355–5000 | fax 252/355–5099 | www.greenvillenc.hilton.com | 141 rooms | $99–$104 | AE, D, DC, MC, V.

Holiday Inn Express Greenville. This four-story hotel is 2½ mi from downtown Greenville. It has rooms with two double beds or a king size bed with sleeper sofa. Complimentary breakfast. In-room data ports, refrigerators. Cable TV. Hot tub. | 909 Moye Blvd. | 252/754–8300 | fax 252/754–8301 | www.holiday-inn.com | 118 rooms | $69 | AE, D, DC, MC, V.

Ramada Plaza. This four-story chain hotel with a plant-and-tree-filled lobby is on the main thoroughfare, just minutes from the airport and the medical center. Restaurant, bar with entertainment, complimentary breakfast (weekdays), room service. In-room data ports, microwaves, refrigerators. Cable TV. Pool. Exercise equipment. Laundry service. Business services, free parking. No pets. | 203 W. Greenville Blvd. | 252/355–8300 | fax 252/756–3553 | www.ramada.com | 192 rooms | $64 | AE, D, DC, MC, V.

Super 8. This two-story, stucco-faced chain hotel is 3 mi from the airport and close to restaurants and malls. Upholstered chairs and potted trees grace the lobby. Complimentary Continental breakfast. In-room data ports. Cable TV. Laundry facilities. Business services, free parking. No pets. | 1004 S. Memorial Dr. | 252/758–8888 | fax 252/752–0523 | www.super8.com | 52 rooms | $35–$55 | AE, D, DC, MC, V.

HATTERAS

MAP 8, L5

(Nearby towns also listed: Buxton, Cape Hatteras National Seashore, Ocracoke, Outer Banks)

The forces of nature are moving Hatteras (population 5,000) to the south and west, just as it is doing to all of the Outer Banks. Exploring it on foot means the opportunity to take paths less traveled. The island is rich in wildlife, and the fishing situation is unrivaled, as both northern and southern species of fish are found in its waters.

Information: **Outer Banks Visitor's Center** | 704 S. U.S. 64/264, Manteo 27954 | 252/473–2138 or 800/446–6262 | info@outer-banks.com | www.outer-banks.com.

Attractions

Chicamacomico Lifesaving Station. In Rodanthe, this restored 1911 structure has a museum that tells the story of the 24 stations that once lined the Outer Banks. Living-history reenactments of lifesaving drills are performed on Thursdays June through August. | Rte. 12, Rodanthe | 252/987–1552 | www.outer-banks.com/history.cfm | Donations accepted | May–Oct., Wed.–Sat. 11–5.

Hatteras Island. The Herbert C. Bonner Bridge arches for 3 mi over Oregon Inlet and carries traffic to Hatteras Island, known as the "Blue Marlin Capital of the World." The island, a 33-mi-long ribbon of sand, juts out into the Atlantic Ocean; at its most distant point (Cape Hatteras), Hatteras is 25 mi from the mainland. About 85% of the island belongs to Cape Hatteras National Seashore, and the remainder is privately owned in seven small, quaint villages strung along Route 12, the island's fragile lifeline to points north. | 252/473–2138 or 800/446–6262 | www.hatteras-nc.com | Free | Daily.

Pea Island National Wildlife Refuge. Between Oregon Inlet and Rodanthe, the refuge is made up of more than 5,000 acres of marsh. This birder's paradise is on the Atlantic Flyway: more than 265 species are spotted regularly, including endangered peregrine falcons and piping plovers. Route 12 travels through marsh areas, and you can hike or drive, depending on the terrain. There are also guided canoe tours, special wildlife and children's tours, and bird and turtle walks. A visitor center, 5 mi south of Oregon Inlet, has an informational display. | Pea Island Refuge Headquarters, Rte. 12 | 252/473–1131 | www.hatteras-nc.com/peaisland | Free, tours extra | May–Sept., daily 9–4; Oct.–Apr., weekdays 9–4.

ON THE CALENDAR
MAY: *Hatteras Village Offshore Open Billfish Tournament.* For one week, anglers contend for prizes in this Governor's Cup–sanctioned event. The goal is to catch and release the biggest billfish. | The tournament is held at a different marina each year. Call for details | 252/986–2555.
JUNE–AUG.: *Living-History Re-enactments.* In Rodanthe, at the restored 1911 Chicamacomico Lifesaving Station, one of 24 such stations that once lined the Outer Banks, rescue and lifesaving techniques employed in the early part of the 20th century are commemorated at 2:00 each Thursday. | Rte. 12 | 252/987–1552.
DEC.: *Christmas Parade.* Floats, a best-decorated home and business contest, refreshments, and caroling at the Community Center. | Hatteras Village, Rte. 12 | 252/986–2381.

Dining
Breakwater Restaurant. Seafood. Fat daddy-crab cakes rolled in potato chips, then fried and served on pineapple-jalapeño salsa, as well as Carolina shrimp served either fried or broiled in white wine and butter are the menu toppers at this restaurant, which overlooks Oden's dock. Seafood pastas, fried oysters and roast duck are also on the menu. | Hwy. 12, Odens dock | 252/986–2733 | $11–$25 | AE, MC, V | No lunch.

Channel Bass. Seafood. A casual, family-style seafood joint, with mounted fish on the walls and a nautical theme. Basically known for a variety of fresh fish, though a nod is given to steaks, chicken, and ribs. The seafood platters are very popular, as is the homemade crab imperial, used for crab cakes and stuffings. The seafood delight—scallops, shrimp, and crabmeat with mushrooms and onions topped with cheese—is also a favorite. Kids' menu. | Rte. 12 | 252/986–2250 | $20–$30 | D, MC, V | Closed Tues. and Dec.–Mar. No lunch.

Lodging
Hatteras Marlin Motel. This hotel is spread out over three buildings and is located in the village of Hatteras, within walking distance of restaurants and shops and 1 mi from the beach. Suites have sundecks and all rooms have porches. Picnic area. Some kitchenettes. Cable TV. Pool. Business services. No pets. | Rte. 12 | 252/986–2141 | fax 252/986–2436 | 37 rooms, 2 suites | $54 | MC, V | Closed late Dec.

Holiday Inn Express Hatteras Island This two-story modern hotel is within ½ mi of several shops and restaurants. Historic Cape Hatteras Lighthouse is 13 mi away. Complimentary breakfast. In-room data ports, refrigerators, microwaves. Laundry facilities. | Rte. 12 | 252/986–1110 | fax 252/986–1131 | www.holiday-inn.com | 72 rooms | $109–$149 | AE, D, DC, MC, V.

Sea Gull. Since the 1950s, one family has owned this three-building motel, which stands on the waterfront near Hatteras Village, within 1 mi of marinas. In addition to rooms and housekeeping apartments, there are cottages that rent by the week. Picnic area. Some kitchenettes, some microwaves, some refrigerators. Cable TV. Pool, wading pool. Beach. No pets. | Rte. 12 | 252/986–2550 | fax 252/986–2525 | www.seagullhatteras.com | 45 rooms, 10 apartments, 2 cottages | $75–$100 | D, MC, V | Closed Dec.–Feb.

HENDERSON

MAP 8, H3

(Nearby towns also listed: Durham, Raleigh)

About 20 mi from the Virginia border, Henderson (population 18,000) is the seat of small Vance County. Life here moves at a quiet pace. The downtown shopping and business area has been designated a National Register historic district and a North Carolina Main Street City, and townspeople are proud of one of their most famous sons, journalist Charlie Rose, host of the eponymous PBS interview show. Recreational life in Henderson revolves around Kerr Lake, one of the largest lakes in the Southeast.

Information: **Vance County Tourism** | 934K W. Andrews Ave., Henderson 27536 | 252/438–2222 | vctourism@gloryroad.net | www.vancecounty.com; www.kerrlake-nc.com.

Attractions

Kerr Lake State Recreation Area. A 50,000-acre lake stretching from North Carolina to Virginia, Kerr has 800 mi of shoreline and 1,000 tent-trailer campsites in seven recreation areas. You can picnic, hike, go boating, skiing, and fishing (which includes tournaments). | 6254 Satterwhite Point Rd., Henderson | 252/438–7791 | fax 252/438–7582 | www.kerrlake-nc.com or ils.unc.edu/parkproject/kelaindex.html | Free | Daily 8–sunset.

Vance County Historical Museum. Seven permanent exhibits explore the history of Vance County from 18,000 BC to the present. There's one exhibit that changes every 6 months. The museum has no phone; the number listed here is for the local chamber of commerce. | 213 S. Garnett St. | 252/438–2222 | Free | Wed. 2–5, and by appointment.

ON THE CALENDAR

JUNE: *Governor's Cup Regatta.* Skippers from around the region sail racing-class boats for two days in this Carolina Sailing Club–sponsored event. | Henderson Point at Kerr Lake | 252/438–2222.
JULY: *Independence Day Celebration.* Fireworks, food, and entertainment make this a great place to celebrate the Fourth. | Satterwhite Park, Satterwhite Point Rd.; I–85 Exit 217 | 252/438–2222.
SEPT.: *Labor Day Weekend Parade of Lights on Water.* Decorated boat parade, fireworks, entertainment, and food. | Satterwhite Point at Kerr Lake | 252/438–2222.

Dining

Nunnery-Freeman Barbecue. Barbecue. The staff is friendly and the portions generous at this casual spot directly off U.S. 1. Known for seafood, shrimp, oysters, trout, and their famous barbecue chicken, this place also has the menu favorite chopped pork with vinegar-pepper-tomato sauce and hush puppies. | Norlina Rd. (U.S. 158) | 252/438–4751 | $6–$8 | No credit cards | Closed Mon.

Lodging

Comfort Inn. Kerr Lake, North Carolina's largest lake, is 6 mi east of this chain hotel. Restaurants are less than a block away in this mixed commercial-residential neighborhood.

Complimentary Continental breakfast. Cable TV. Outdoor pool. | 112 Parham Rd. | 252/438–8511. | fax 252/492–2215 | www.comfortinn.com | 51 rooms | $46–$66 | AE, D, DC, MC, V.

Howard Johnson. This two-story redbrick and stucco chain hotel is 8 mi from Kerr Lake and next to I–85. Several fast-food restaurants are within 2 blocks. Complimentary Continental breakfast. In-room data ports, some microwaves, some refrigerators. Cable TV. Pool. Laundry services. Business services. No pets. | I–85 (Exit 215) and Parham Rd. | 252/492–7001 | fax 252/438–2389 | www.hojo.com | 98 rooms | $56–$63 | AE, D, DC, MC, V.

Quality Inn. This chain hotel is convenient to the lake, camping sites, and hiking. You can relax in the plant- and flower-filled lobby and watch a little TV. Restaurant, bar, complimentary breakfast. In-room data ports, some microwaves, some refrigerators. Cable TV. Pool, wading pool. Laundry service. Business services. Pets allowed (in carrier). | I–85 Tarham Road | 252/492–1126 | fax 252/492–2575 | 156 rooms | $60–$65 | AE, D, DC, MC, V.

HENDERSONVILLE

MAP 8, B5

(Nearby towns also listed: Asheville, Blue Ridge Parkway, Brevard, Tryon)

With a prosperous economy, a pretty and busy downtown, a nearly 360-degree view of the mountains, rich cultural environment, and upscale suburbs, Hendersonville (population 10,000), which was a resort town in the 19th century, has become a magnet for retirees as well as scores of artisans. This is still apple country, though, and during the spring bloom period, the nearly million apple trees are a sight to behold.

Information: Henderson County Travel and Tourism | 201 Main St., Hendersonville 28792 | 828/693–9708 or 800/828–4244 | www.historichendersonville.org.

Attractions

Carl Sandburg Home National Historic Site. Pulitzer Prize–winning poet, historian, author, and lecturer Carl Sandburg spent the final 22 years of his life at his estate, Connemara. At that time Connemara was a 240-acre working farm, and today it is pretty much as Sandburg and his wife, Lilian (known for her goat herd), left it. There's a visitor center on the ground floor of the 22-room house. | 1928 Little River Rd., Flat Rock | 828/693–4178 | www.nps.gov/carl | Free | Daily 9–5; tour available.

Historic Johnson Farm. A late 19th-century farm turned early 20th-century tourist retreat, and now listed on the National Register of Historic Places. Owned by the local public school system and operated as a heritage education center and museum, the farm is a mini-complex complete with nature trails and special events. | 3346 Haywood Rd. | 828/891–6585 | fax 828/890–7001 | www.johnsonfarm.org | $3 | May–Oct., Tues.–Sat. 9–3; Nov.–Apr., Wed.–Sat. 9–3.

Holmes Educational State Forest. A managed forest with picnic and tent areas designed to promote better understanding of the value of forests through exhibits, audio stations ("talking" trees), signage, and ranger-conducted classes. | Rte. 4; 9 mi west of Hendersonville on Kanuga Rd./Crab Creek Rd. | 828/692–0100 | fax 828/698–0086 | www.dfr.state.nc.us/esf/holmes_esf.htm | Free | Mid-Mar.–mid-Nov., Tues.–Fri. 9–5, weekends 11–8 (daylight savings time) or 11–5 (standard time).

Western North Carolina Air Museum. Antique and vintage aircraft from the 1930s and 1940s are on display at this hometown airport. Pilots often take these aircraft up for a spin, departing and landing from the grass field outside the museum. | Hendersonville Airport, 1340 Gilbert St. | 828/698–2482 | Free | Wed. and weekends noon–5.

ON THE CALENDAR

MAY: *Garden Jubilee.* Plant sale, garden talks, garden and lawn accessories exhibited and sold, arts and crafts, and entertainment. | Memorial Day weekend | 828/693–9708 or 800/828–4244.

MAY: *Folk Music Festival.* Folk music and poetry readings at a national historic site, Connemara, the home of Carl Sandburg. | 1928 Little River Rd., Flat Rock | Memorial Day | 828/693–4178.

MAY–OCT.: *Flat Rock Playhouse.* High reputation for summer stock theater: comedy and American classics, musicals, farces, and whodunits. In midsummer, in the outdoor theater, the Apprentice Company gives lively and dramatic renditions of Carl Sandburg's writings, including his *Rootabaga Stories.* | 2661 Greenville Hwy., Flat Rock | 828/693–0731.

SEPT.: *North Carolina Apple Festival.* Cooking contest for apple-based recipes, food, music, arts, crafts, sporting events, and activities for kids. | Labor Day weekend | 828/697–4557.

OCT.: *Farm City Day.* Entertainment, food, games, demonstrations, antique engines, and cars. | Jackson Park | 828/697–4884.

Dining

Expressions. Contemporary. China and candlelight give this downtown, 1800 storefront with exposed-brick walls a romantic and elegant setting. The menu changes daily, making the most of locally grown produce, fresh fish, lamb, beef, and veal. There are usually about 12 entrées to choose from. Kids' menu. | 114 N. Main St. | 828/693–8516 | Reservations essential | $16–$29 | DC, MC, V | Closed Sun. and mid-Jan.–mid-Feb. No lunch.

Highland Lake Inn. Contemporary. Menus change seasonally to make abundant use of produce from inn's own organic herb and vegetable garden. Trout, shrimp, crab, lamb, prime rib, and pasta, as well as heart-healthy dishes, are available. Many specialty sandwiches for lunch. Themed Sun. brunches (pioneer, southern bayou, summer garden), and Sun. dinner and holiday buffets. Breakfast also available. | Highland Lake Rd., Flat Rock | 828/693–6812 or 800/762–1376 | Reservations essential | $16–$26 | AE, D, MC, V | Closed Sun.–Wed. from Nov.–Apr.

Sinbad. Mediterranean. In this century-old former residence, hand-hammered brass trays serving as tabletops and seascape murals on the walls help to create a Mediterranean-themed setting. The entrées reflect a culinary mix of Italy, Greece, Lebanon, India, and France. The lunch menu ranges from a simple BLT sandwich and eggplant Parmesan to Greek salad, falafel, and grilled vegetable focaccia. Try stuffed grape leaves, marinated lamb, or shrimp kebabs. Open-air dining on deck. | 202 S. Washington St. | 828/696–2039 | $12–$23 | AE, D, MC, V | Closed Sun.–Mon.

Squire's Restaurant. American. The antique coverlet wall hangings and fireplace make this a cozy place to stop for dinner. The menu is prix-fixe, and particularly noted for the fresh seafood and locally grown vegetables. The surrounding 28 mostly wooded acres have trails. | 2905 Greenville Hwy. (U.S. 25 S). | 828/693–6016 or 800/533–6016 | Reservations essential. | $35 | AE, D, MC, V | Closed Mon., Tues.

Lodging

Budget Host Inn. This two-story chain hotel is only 6 mi from Kerr Lake, and restaurants are within 2 mi. Cable TV. Free parking. | 1727 N. Garnett St.; I–85 Exit 215 | 252/492–2013 or 800/283–4678 | fax 252/482–7908 | www.budgethost.com | 25 rooms | $32–$55. | AE, D, DC, MC, V.

Comfort Inn. This chain hotel is a block from Blue Ridge Mall and 5 mi from the Carl Sandburg Home and Flat Rock Playhouse. The rooms are floral-themed, more elaborately than is typical for this level of chain hotel, and the building is constructed around the pool. Complimentary Continental breakfast. In-room data ports, some microwaves, some refrigerators, in-room hot tubs (in suites). Cable TV. Pool. Laundry services. Business services. Pets allowed (fee). | 206 Mitchell Dr. | 828/693–8800 | www.comfortinn.com | 85 rooms | $94–$135 | AE, D, DC, MC, V.

Echo Mountain Inn. You can relax in this restful, 1896 inn, out of the reach of the sounds of the city. Its turn-of-the-century-themed interior is furnished with antiques and reproductions. Many have fireplaces and some have views of the mountains. The in-house restaurant offers gourmet specialties like escargots with artichokes, button mushrooms, and a garlic saffron cream sauce, or pecan-crusted mountain trout with orange herb sauce. Restaurant, bar, complimentary Continental breakfast. Some kitchenettes. Cable TV. Pool. Business services. No smoking. No pets. | 2849 Laurel Park Hwy. | 828/693–9626 | fax 828/697–2047 | www.echoinn.com | 37 rooms | $75–$150 | AE, MC, V.

Hampton Inn. This chain hotel is only 2 mi from the historic downtown area and within walking distance of a mall and restaurants. Complimentary Continental breakfast. In-room data ports, some microwaves, some refrigerators. Cable TV. Pool. Laundry service. Business services. No pets. | 155 Sugarloaf Rd. | 828/697–2333 | fax 828/693–5280 | www.hampton-inn.com | 119 rooms | $66–$97 | AE, D, DC, MC, V.

Hendersonville-Days Inn. The Ashville Regional Airport is 9 mi east of this chain hotel, and restaurants are within a block or two. The Flat Rock Playhouse is 5 mi to the east and the downtown Henderson area just 1½ mi away. Complimentary breakfast. Cable TV. Free parking. | 102 Mitchell Dr. | 828/697–5999 or 800/544–8313 | fax 828/697–5999 | www.daysinn.com. | 46 rooms | $36–$100 | AE, D, DC, MC, V.

Quality Inn and Suites. This hotel is 8 mi from Asheville Municipal Airport, near Biltmore Estate, businesses, and shops, and only 2 mi from a movie theater. The interior's major feature is its enclosed-atrium lobby. Some of the rooms overlook the atrium. Restaurant, bar, room service. In-room data ports, refrigerators, microwaves (in suites). Cable TV. Indoor pool. Hot tub, sauna. Exercise equipment. Putting green. Game room. Laundry services. Business services, airport shuttle, free parking. No pets. | 201 Sugarloaf Rd. | 828/692–7231 | fax 828/693–9905 | www.comfortinn.com | 149 rooms | $59–$69 | AE, D, DC, MC, V.

Ramada Inn. Downtown Henderson is 3½ mi west of this chain hotel; there are some restaurants on the same block in this mixed residential-commercial neighborhood. The Flat Rock Playhouse is 5 mi to the east, and Chimney Rock Park is about 18 mi away (also to the east). Complimentary breakfast. Cable TV. | 150 Sugarloaf Rd. | 828/697–0006 or 888/298–2054 | fax 828/697–0006 | www.ramada.com | 53 rooms | $54–$78 | AE, D, DC, MC, V.

Waverly Inn. This inn is on the National Register of Historic Places, and is the oldest inn in Hendersonville. A mix of Victorian antiques and reproductions helps reinforce its turn-of-the-20th-century theme. Each room is distinctive; some are colored lavender and white, others are done in pinks and blues. There are several rooms with four-poster beds and claw-footed tubs, and one room has a sunporch. If you're not staying in that one, then the verandah that runs along the front of the building has plenty of rocking chairs for you to enjoy as you watch the twilight at day's end. Complimentary breakfast. In-room data ports. Cable TV. Business services, free parking. No smoking. No pets. | 783 N. Main St. | 828/693–9193 or 800/537–8195 | fax 828/692–1010 | www.waverlyinn.com | 14 rooms | $119–$159 | AE, D, DC, MC, V.

Woodfield Inn. You are invited to find the secret room in this circa 1852 house, where Confederate soldiers hid valuables from Union troops and renegades. Some of the Victorian-themed rooms have homespun touches like handmade quilts. Other yesteryear reminders include four-poster beds, claw-foot baths, and French windows that open onto a private verandah, with views of the 28 acres of estate gardens. Dining rooms, complimentary Continental breakfast. Some in-room hot tubs. Cable TV, some VCRs. Hiking. Tennis courts. Laundry service. No pets. No smoking. | 2905 Greenville Hwy. (U.S. 25 S), Flat Rock | 828/693–6016 or 800/533–6016 | fax 828/693–0437 | www.woodfieldinn.com | 19 rooms | $109–$189 | AE, D, MC, V.

HENDERSONVILLE

INTRO
ATTRACTIONS
DINING
LODGING

HICKORY

MAP 8, D4

(Nearby towns also listed: Lenoir, Morganton, Statesville)

The largest municipality in Catawba County, Hickory has twice received the All-America City award. Its 31,000 residents have fused the traditional and the new. Long a center noted for textiles and furniture making, this Blue Ridge Mountains town has also begun to distinguish itself with the high-tech manufacturing of fiber-optic and telecommunication cable. Another distinction: the Hickory Motor Speedway is the longest continuously operating NASCAR-sanctioned track in the United States.

Information: Hickory Metro Convention and Visitors Bureau | 1055 S. Gate Corp. Park SW, Hickory 28602 | 828/322–1335 or 800/509–2444 | hickory_cvb@w3link.com | www.hickorymetro.com.

Attractions

Arts and Science Center of Catawba Valley. At the heart of Catawba County's and Hickory's cultural activities is the Arts and Science Center, which houses the Catawba County Council for the Arts, the Hickory Museum of Art, and the Catawba Science Center. The center also provides offices and rehearsal space for the Western Piedmont Symphony and the Hickory Choral Society. | 243 3rd Ave. NE, on the "SALT" block (Sciences, Arts, and Literature Together) | 828/322–8169 | Free | Tues.–Fri. 10–5, Sat. 10–4, Sun. 1–4.

Catawba Science Center. A hands-on museum that offers three levels of exhibits: permanent, temporary, and traveling. Permanent exhibits include a Hall of Life Science, RaceWays, EarthWatch Center, and the Footprints Preschool Gallery. | 243 3rd Ave. NE | 828/322–8169 | www.catawbascience.org | $2 | Tues.–Fri. 10–5, Sat. 10–4, Sun. 1–4.

Hickory Museum of Art. The second-oldest art museum in North Carolina—and the first museum in the Southeast to collect American art—offers classes, tours, lectures, and films for all ages. | 243 3rd Ave. NE | 828/327–8576 | fax 828/327–7281 | www.hickorymuseumofart.org | $2 | Tues., Wed., and Fri. 10–5, Thurs. 10–7:30, Sat. 11–4, Sun. 1–4.

Bunker Hill Covered Bridge. Listed on the National Register of Historic Places, the 85-ft-long bridge spans Lyle's Creek and is one of only two remaining covered bridges in the state. | U.S. 70 A | 828/465–0383 | fax 828/465–9813 | Free | Wed. and Fri. 9–4, Sun. 1–5, or by appointment.

Catawba County Museum of History. Housed in the former Catawba County Courthouse, and a National Register structure built in 1924, the museum is regional in scope. Exhibits include Catawba Valley pottery, car racing, and early industries, as well as a large military collection. | 30 N. College Ave., Newton | 828/465–0383 | fax 828/465–0928 | www.catawbahistory.org | Free | Tues.–Fri. 9–4, Sat. 10–4, Sun. 2–5, or by appointment for groups of more than 15.

Hickory Furniture Mart. This marketplace is the largest of its kind on the East Coast, and has 80 showrooms with more than 1,000 lines of furniture, accessories, bedding, lighting, wall coverings, and the like. There are items from all over the world within more than 20 acres of showrooms, galleries, and outlets. From downtown Charlotte, take I–77 north to Statesville, then I–40 west to Hickory, Exit 126. Turn left at the off-ramp and right onto Highway 70 W. You will see the mall on your left. | 2220 U.S. 70 SE | 828/322–3510 or 800/462–6278 | fax 828/322–1132 | www.hickoryfurniture.com | Free | Mon.–Sat. 9–6.

Hickory Motor Speedway. Opened in 1951, this short-track speedway has a storied history in the world of NASCAR. Fans flock to weekly Saturday evening races (gates open at 5:30; races begin at 8:00), which are part of the Winston Series and feature late-model stock cars and trucks. | 3130 U.S. 70 SE | 828/464–3655 | fax 828/465–5017 | www.hickoryspeedway.com | $10 | Mar.–early Nov.

Historic Murray's Mill. A turn-of-the-20th-century gristmill featuring one of the largest water wheels in the state. A general store, a folk art museum, and the restored residence of the owner-miller add interest. | 1489 Murray's Mill Rd., Catawba | 828/465–0383 | fax 828/465–9813 | $3 | Wed.–Sat. 10–5, Sun. 1–5.

ON THE CALENDAR

MAY, JUNE, SEPT.: *Hickory Alive.* Two and a half hours of live music and dancing every Friday night in downtown Hickory. | Union Square | 828/322–3125.

JULY: *Furniture Festival.* The Hickory Furniture Mart is in the heart of furniture-making country and carries a thousand lines of furniture and accessories. Seventeen acres are filled with showrooms, galleries, and factory outlets. Every year at the end of July, art, pottery, and woodwork are sold at deep discounts during a Mart-wide clearance, and it's every bargain hunter for him- and herself. | 828/322–3510 or 800/462–6278.

OCT.: *Oktoberfest.* Hickory's largest festival. Three days of arts, crafts, dozens of food vendors, musical entertainment (everything from oompah bands to barbershop quartets), dancers, and rides for children. Peripheral activities include a fun run and a car show. | Union Square | 828/322–3125.

Dining

1859 Café. Contemporary. Three formal dining rooms in a restored home from the antebellum period, serving elegant gourmet food such as veal with sun-dried tomato and artichoke sauce, lamb with a wild mushroom demi-glaze, and salmon with tomato and basil sauce over angel-hair pasta. There are no vegetarian menu items, but the chef will happily accommodate you if would prefer just veggies. There is open-air dining on a deck. Live music Sat. | 433 2nd Ave. SW | 828/322–1859 | Reservations essential | $15–$24 | AE, D, DC, MC, V | Closed Sun. No lunch.

Giovanni's of Hickory. Italian. Tablecloths and candlelight add a touch of elegance to this casual restaurant located in a commercial district. The cordon bleu heads the list of most asked for entrées, but you can also get sandwiches, pizza, and pastas. Kids' menu. | 2601 N. Center St. | 828/322–8277 | $5–$11 | AE, MC, V | Closed Sun. No lunch.

Hickory Station Restaurant. American. This restaurant is in a restored railway station, where diners can watch trains go past on their way downtown while enjoying all-American fare like sandwiches, seafood, ribs, and—the most popular menu item—steak. There's a deck with outdoor tables; a buffet lunch is available. | 232 Government Ave. | 828/322–1904 | $9–$19 | AE, DC, MC, V | Closed Sun.

McGuire's Pub. Casual. A downtown pub with a large wood bar and two entrances: one at street level, the other down a metal spiral staircase. Hot and cold deli-type sandwiches, soups, and salads. Kids' menu. | 46 3rd St. NW | 828/322–7263 | Reservations not accepted | $10–$15 | D, MC, V | Closed Sun.

Lodging

Comfort Suites. A chain property just five minutes from Hickory Furniture Mart. Bowling, boating, and miniature golf are available very nearby, as are a barber shop and beauty salon. All rooms are suites, and if you aren't happy with them you can take advantage of the chain's 100% satisfaction guarantee. Complimentary breakfast. In-room data ports, some kitchenettes, microwaves, refrigerators. Cable TV. Pool, hot tub. Exercise equipment. Laundry facilities. Business services. No pets. | 1125 13th Ave. Dr. SE | 828/323–1211 | fax 828/322–4395 | www.comfortsuites.com | 116 suites | $69–$82 | AE, D, DC, MC, V.

Fairfield Inn by Marriott. The Hickory Motor Speedway is about 3 mi from this chain hotel, downtown Hickory about 5 mi, and the Valley Hills Mall is 1 mi away. Complimentary breakfast. In-room data ports. Cable TV. Indoor pool. Exercise equipment. Laundry facilities. Free parking. | 1950 13th Ave. Dr. SE | 828/431–3000 | fax 828/431–4714 | www.marriott.com | 108 rooms, 6 suites | $62–$69 | AE, D, DC, MC, V.

Hampton Inn. This chain accommodation is two minutes from a shopping mall and five minutes from Hickory Furniture Mart. It is just off the interstate and only 3 mi northeast of downtown. Complimentary Continental breakfast. In-room data ports. Cable TV. Pool. Laundry service. Business services. No pets. | 1520 13th Ave. Dr. SE | 828/323–1150 | fax 828/324–8979 | www.hamptoninn.com | 119 rooms | $65–$72 | AE, D, DC, MC, V.

Hickory B&B. This beautiful 1908 Georgian house is set on 1½ acres of parklike grounds and has a Victorian-themed interior with lots of antiques. Some of the rooms have fireplaces. Common areas include a parlor, a library, and various porches with flowers and bird feeders. Complimentary breakfast. No TV in rooms, cable TV in common area. Pool. Library. Business services. No kids under 14. No smoking. No pets. | 464 7th St. SW | 828/324–0548 or 800/654–2961 | fax 828/324–7434 | www.hickorybedandbreakfast.com | 4 rooms | $90–$110 | AE, D, MC, V.

Holiday Inn. Lenoir Rhyne College and the Valley Hills shopping mall are both within 2 mi of this chain hotel, and there are restaurants less than a block away in this commercial district. For a small fee you can use the facilities at the next-door YMCA. Complimentary breakfast. In-room data ports. Cable TV. | 2250 U.S. 70 SE | 828/328–2081 | fax 828/328–2085 | www.holiday-inn.com. | 60 rooms | $60–$72 | AE, D, DC, MC, V.

Holiday Inn Select. This Holiday Inn has won many awards (from Holiday Inn's parent company, Bass Hotels). It's within walking distance of the Valley Hills Mall and 1 mi from the Hickory Furniture Mart. Restaurant, bar, complimentary breakfast, room service. In-room data ports, some microwaves, some refrigerators. Cable TV. Indoor pool. Hot tub, sauna. Exercise equipment. Laundry facilities. Business services, free parking. No pets. | 1385 Lenoir Rhyne Blvd. SE | 828/323–1000 | fax 828/322–4275 | www.basshotels.com/hickorync | 201 rooms | $89–$129 | AE, D, DC, MC, V.

Quality Inn and Suites. Several Hickory furniture marts (a major city attraction) are just about 3 mi away from this chain hotel; the Hickory Crawdads Baseball Stadium is right next door; and the Hickory Art Museum is 5½ mi to the east. Complimentary breakfast. In-room data ports. Cable TV. Outdoor pool. Exercise equipment. Laundry facilities. | 1725 13th Ave. Dr. NW | 828/431–2100 | fax 828/431–2109 | 100 rooms | $79–$145 | AE, D, DC, MC, V.

Red Roof Inn. This chain hotel is just a short drive from the main road, 1 mi from a shopping mall and movie cineplex, and 1½ mi from the Hickory Furniture Mart. There are plenty of restaurants nearby, and the rooms are enlivened by brightly colored bedspreads. In-room data ports, some microwaves, some refrigerators. Cable TV. Business services. Pets allowed. | 1184 Lenoir Rhyne Blvd. SE | 828/323–1500 | fax 828/323–1509 | www.redroof.com | 108 rooms | $45–$60 | AE, D, DC, MC, V.

Sleep Inn. This chain hotel is about 10 minutes from the Hickory Furniture Mart. It won the Sleep Inn of the Year award in 1995, so you know you'll be getting the best of what the Sleep Inn chain has to offer. Complimentary Continental breakfast. In-room data ports, some microwaves, some refrigerators. Cable TV. Some in-room hot tubs. Laundry facilities. Business services. No pets. | 1179 13th Ave. Dr. SE | 828/323–1140 | fax 828/324–6203 | www.sleepinn.com | 100 rooms (94 with shower only) | $67 | AE, D, DC, MC, V.

HIGH POINT

MAP 8, E4

(Nearby towns also listed: Asheboro, Greensboro, Lexington, Winston-Salem)

Originally settled by Quakers in the 1700s, High Point was incorporated in 1859. Its name comes from its former position as the highest point on the railroad between Goldsboro and Charlotte.

Today, when people think of High Point they think of furniture. High Point is home to the International Home Furnishing Market, the largest wholesale furniture market in the world (not open to the public). Tens of thousands of buyers and others associated with the trade "go to market" in April and October. In the process, they bring sophistication to this small city (and take virtually every available hotel room and rental car for miles around). Retail outlets here offer furniture and home accessories at bargain prices to consumers from around the country.

Information: High Point Convention and Visitors Bureau | 300 S. Main St., 27260 | 336/884–5255 | fax 336/884–5256 | www.highpoint.org | Weekdays 9–5.

Attractions

Angela Peterson Doll and Miniature Museum. The museum is thought to be the largest doll museum in the South, housing one woman's own collection. It contains over 1,700 dolls, costumes, miniatures, and dollhouses. | 101 W. Green Dr. | 336/885–3655 or 336/887–3876. | fax 336/887–2159 | $4; combination ticket with Furniture Discovery Center $8.50 | Apr.–Oct., weekdays 10–4:30, Sat. 9–4:30, Sun. 1–4:30; Nov.–Mar., Tues.–Sat. 10–4:30, Sun. 1–4:30.

Furniture Discovery Center. An interactive center that shows how furniture is designed, manufactured, and marketed. You can also design your own furniture, if you wish. | 101 W. Green Dr. | 336/887–3876 | fax 336/887–2159 | www2.hpe.com/discovery | $5; combination ticket with Angela Peterson Doll and Miniature Museum $8.50 | Apr.–Oct., Mon.–Sat. 10–5, Sun. 1–5; Nov.–Mar., Tues.–Sat. 10–5, Sun. 1–5.

High Point Museum/Historical Park. The museum focuses on Piedmont history and includes the 1786 Haley House and a mid-1700s blacksmith shop and weaving house. The exhibits highlight furniture, pottery, communication, transportation, and military artifacts. Costumed tours of the buildings are available on weekends. | 1859 E. Lexington Ave. | 336/885–6859 | fax 336/883–3284 | www.ci.high-point.nc.us/dept/museum | Free | Museum Tues.–Sat. 10–4, Sun. 1–4; Historical Park daily dawn–dusk; tours Sat. 10–4, Sun. 1–4.

Mendenhall Plantation. A few miles northeast of High Point you can admire a well-preserved example of 19th-century Quaker domestic architecture. The Mendenhalls opposed slavery, and here you will find one of the few surviving false-bottomed wagons used to help slaves escape to freedom on the Underground Railroad. | 603 W. Main St., Jamestown | 336/454–3819 | $2 | Weekdays 11–2, Sat. 1–4, Sun. 2–4.

World's Largest Chest of Drawers. The facade of a building shaped like a chest of drawers was erected in 1926 to call attention to High Point as the "Home Furnishings Capital of the World." Restored as a four-story 18th-century chest of drawers, it is now the home of the High Point Jaycees. | 508 N. Hamilton St. | 336/883–2016 or 800/720–5255 | fax 336/884–4352 | www.highpoint.org | Free | Daily for drive-bys.

ON THE CALENDAR

FEB.: *Mary Washington's Famous African-American Heritage.* African-American dolls are on display at the Angela Peterson Doll and Miniature Museum. (The dolls are not for sale.) The event takes place the whole month of February. | 101 West Green Dr. | www.highpoint.org | $4 | 336/884–5255 or 336/885–3655.

JULY: *Drag Boat Championships.* Dozens of drag-boat drivers compete for cash in this two-day event sanctioned by the International Hot Boat Association. Food vendors are on-site. | Oak Hollow Lake | 336/883–20.

AUG.–OCT.: *North Carolina Shakespeare Festival.* A critically acclaimed professional troupe mounts several productions in late summer and early autumn at the High Point Theatre. | 220 E. Commerce Ave. | 336/841–2273 | fax 336/883–3533 | www.people-places.com/ncsf.highpointticketctr@excite.com | $15–$22.

SEPT.: *Day in the Park Festival.* A day-long festival including arts, crafts, rides, and entertainment at City Lake Park. | 336/889–2787 or 336/883–3498 | fax 336/889–2789 | $40.

SEPT.: *Heritage Day.* A collection of living-history Quaker crafts, food, and demonstrations at Mendenhall Plantation, built in the 19th century by a prominent member of the area's large Quaker community. | 603 W. Main St., Jamestown | 336/454–3819.

Dining

Atrium Café. American. Nestled on the third floor of the Atrium Furniture Mall and adorned with fine art, frescos, and pastel murals, the Atrium Café can be a welcome spot for weary shoppers trying to make a decision on a new living-room set. Try the homemade soup, veal, duck, and fish. | 430 S. Main St. | 336/889–9934 | fax 336/889–2804 | $15–$22 | AE, D, DC, MC, V | Closed Sun. No dinner.

B Flat Café. Contemporary. This down-home café-style bistro has a definite Southern flair. A reconstructed tobacco barn sits in the center of the dining area, surrounded by murals with southern food-and-drink themes. You could say it's Low Country with some Cajun-Creole thrown in. Try the seafood pasta, pistachio-encrusted pork tenderloin, grilled pork chop with apple rum chutney, New York strip with brandied peppercorn sauce, black bean cakes, and shrimp and grits. | 3805 Tinsley Dr. | 336/887–0094 | fax 336/887–0098 | $10–$23 | AE, D, DC, MC, V | Closed Sun. No lunch.

J. Basul Noble. French. This cosmopolitan yet laid-back, contemporary French restaurant is a favorite of locals. Try the grilled veal tenderloin or the fresh fish rotisserie, though the eclectic menu changes daily. A spirited jazz combo appears on Thursday, Friday, and Saturday evenings. | 101 S. Main St. | 336/889–3354 | fax 336/889–6499 | reservations@hp.noblesrest.com | www.noblerest.com | $20–$35 | AE, DC, MC, V | Closed Sun.

Rosa Mae's Café. American. A historic storefront graces the exterior of Rosa Mae's café, in heart of downtown. Comfortable booths and tables make up the interior. Known for country-style steak, grilled chicken breast, pork chops, roast beef, pasta dishes, sandwiches, and salads, Rosa Mae's also serves up delicious homemade soups and desserts. Kids' menu. No alcohol. | 106 N. Main St. | 336/887–0556 | fax 336/887–0682 | Reservations not accepted | $7–$12 | AE, D, MC, V | Closed Sun.

Lodging

Bouldin House. This bed-and-breakfast sits on three acres of a former tobacco farm and gives guests a charming version of country living. It's only 4 mi from downtown, America's largest concentration of furniture showrooms. It took two years to restore this country home to its original beauty, demonstrated in the expertly crafted oak paneling of the dining room and in the patterns of the hardwood floors. Each room has its own particular character, with a king-size bed and a fireplace. Complimentary breakfast. No room phones. No TV in some rooms, cable TV in common room. Kids over 10 only. Business services. No smoking. | 4332 Archdale Rd. | 336/431–4909 or 800/739–1816 | fax 336/431–4914 | relax@bouldinhouse.com | www.bouldinhouse.com | 4 rooms | $90–$120 | AE, D, MC, V.

Radisson. The Radisson is 1 mi from the downtown discount furniture stores and is only one block from the High Point Theatre. Selected suites are tastefully furnished by furniture companies of High Point. Restaurant, bar. In-room data ports, minibars (in suites), refrigerators (in suites). Cable TV. Indoor pool, hot tub, exercise equipment. Business services. | 135 S. Main St. | 336/889–8888 | fax 336/885–2737 | www.radisson.com/highpoint.tnc | 252 rooms, 10 suites | $79–$139, $199–$248 suites | AE, D, DC, MC, V.

Super 8 Motel. This chain motel is in the heart of downtown; there's one restaurant across the street and others about 2 mi away. Complimentary breakfast. Some microwaves, refrigerators. Cable TV. | 400 S. Main St. | 336/882–4103 or 800/800–8000 | fax 336/882–7125 | www.super8.com | 43 rooms | $45–$155 | AE, D, DC, MC, V.

HIGHLANDS

(Nearby towns also listed: Cashiers, Franklin, Lake Toxaway)

Some of the most expensive real estate in the mountains can be found in the Macon County town of Highlands, a community of 3,000 that was founded in 1875 and is now known for fine shops, restaurants, and cultural events. Unique plant life also thrives in the town, thanks to rainfall that averages 70 inches a year. Scientists from around the world come to study the area's forests and flowers.

Information: Highlands Area Chamber of Commerce | Box 404, Highlands 28741 | 828/526–2112 | fax 828/526–0268 | hilands@dnet.net | www.highlands-chamber.com | Mon.–Sat., 9–5.

Attractions

Highlands Area Waterfalls. Bridal Veil Falls (U.S. 64/28 W) cascades 120 ft. You can pull off of the highway, go onto an underpass and drive underneath the waterfall. Dry Falls, also at U.S. 64/28 W, is a 75-ft waterfall that visitors can walk behind. Glen Falls (Route 106 S) is actually a series of three large falls, dropping approximately 60 ft each. And the Lower Cullasaja (meaning "sweet water") Falls on U.S. 64/28 (7 mi from town) is considered one of the most magnificent falls in North Carolina. It has a 250-ft cascade. | U.S. 64/28 W | 828/526–3765 | Free | Daily.

Highlands Civic Center. The Woodruff Building is the hub of year-round activities and special events. There's a Nautilus room, gymnasium, meeting rooms, and a kitchen; pool and tennis courts are located on the grounds. | U.S. 64 E | 828/526–3556 | Free | Daily.

Highlands Nature Center and Biological Station. Botanical gardens and a lake are just two of the many ecosystems found here. A variety of programs, scheduled weekly, discuss the animals, reptiles, and plants of the plateau. The Biological Station is one of the oldest in the United States. | E. Main St. (Horse Cove Rd.) | 828/526–2623 | fax 828/526–2797 | hibio@wcu.edu | www.wcu.edu/hibio | Free | Weekdays 10–5.

Scaly Mountain Ski Area. This small, family-oriented ski resort has beginner and intermediate skiing on four slopes, as well as snowboarding and snowtubing. The vertical drop is 225 ft. | Dillard Rd. | 828/526–3737. | 828/526–3737 | Late Dec.–mid-Mar., weekends 9 AM–10 PM.

ON THE CALENDAR
JULY–AUG.: *Highlands–Cashiers Chamber Music Festival.* Chamber music concerts are held throughout July and the first part of August. Children's performances as well as "festival feasts" make up the season. The performances and festivities alternate between Highlands Performing Art Center and the Albert Carlton Community Library in Cashiers. | 828/526–9060 | fax 828/526–1865 | hcmf@juno.com | www.h-cmusicfest.org or www.main.nc.us/hcmf | $20.

Dining

Fireside Inn. Contemporary. You can truly dine by the fireside at this informal inn, as one of its features is a large open fireplace. Dishes include steaks, chicken, pasta, and salads—try the grilled fresh mountain trout. After your meal, peruse the gift shop, where food items and work from local artists, among other treasures, are for sale. Breakfast is also served. Kid's menu. Wine only. | Wright Square/ Main St. | 828/526–3636 | Reservations not accepted | $5–$10 | MC, V | No supper.

Nick's. Continental. This restored home turned restaurant is enclosed in an idyllic garden, and work by local artists hangs in the four dining rooms. Try the veal, prime rib, and

INTRO
ATTRACTIONS
DINING
LODGING

NC | 289

seafood. Kids' menu. Sun. brunch. | Route 28 | 828/526–2706 | fax 828/526–2150 | $13–$32 | MC, V | Closed Wed. and Jan.–Feb.

On the Verandah. Contemporary. This rustic place with an international theme over-looks Lake Sequoyah. You can dine outdoors and enjoy the view or stay inside and lis-ten to a live pianist in the evening, who performs seasonally. The dishes, with a Caribbean, Latin American, and Asian flair include some use of chile peppers, and you will have your choice of a varied collection of hot sauces. Sun. champagne brunch. | 1536 Franklin Rd. (U.S. 64 W) | 828/526–2338 | fax 828/526–4132 | otv1@ontheverandah.com | www.ontheverandah.com | Reservations requested | $19–$30 | D, MC, V | Closed Jan.–mid Mar. No lunch.

Ristorante Paoletti. Italian. Dine by candlelight at Ristorante Paoletti, where the favored dishes of the classic traditional cuisine include the prime veal, coastal fish, lamb, and nightly specials. Extensive wine list. | 440 E. Main St. | 828/526–4906 | fax 828/526–4149 | www.ris-torantepaoletti.com | $15–$29 | AE, MC, V | Closed Sun. and Jan.–Feb. No lunch.

Wolfgang's on Main. Eclectic. This old house with cozy fireplaces is known for its New Orleans specialties, steaks, veal, pastas, and Bavarian food. You can dine in the garden pavilion or on outdoor decks, and listen to live music on Mon. and Thurs. evenings in season. Sun. brunch. | 474 E. Main St. | 828/526–3807 | fax 828/526–5754 | www.wolfgangs.net | Reservations Accepted | $29–$34 | AE, D, MC, V | Closed Wed. No lunch Mon., Tues, Thurs.

Lodging

Chandler Inn. This inn actually comprises several barn board–sided, turn-of-the-century buildings, each with brass or wrought-iron beds, eyelet sheets and comforters, natural wood paneling, and private baths and entrances. Complimentary breakfast. Cable TV. | U.S. 64 E and Martha's La. | 828/526–5992 | www.thechandlerinn.com | 15 rooms | $76–$172. | MC, V.

Hampton Inn Highlands. Shopping and restaurants are within 1 mi of this chain hotel in a mountain resort area. Some suites are available with jacuzzis and fireplaces. Compli-mentary Continental breakfast. In-room data ports. Cable TV. Exercise equipment. Laun-dry facilities. Airport shuttle. | Rte. 106 and Spring St. | 828/526–5899 or 800/426–7866 | fax 828/526–5979 | www.hampton-inn.com | 59 rooms | $64–$84 | AE, D, DC, MC, V.

Highlands Inn. Each room of the Highlands Inn is provided with period furnishings and has its own character. A sitting room adjoins the lobby. Complimentary Continental breakfast. Cable TV. | 4th and Main Sts. | 828/526–9380 or 800/964–6955 | fax 828/526–8810 | www.highlandsinn_nc.com | 32 rooms, 5 suites | $89–$110 | MC, V | Closed mid-Dec.–Apr.

Highlands Suites Hotel. A fireplace and balcony are included in the suites, and a fold-out couch converts the separate sitting room into a second bedroom. The hotel is one block from antique and gift shops, and four to five blocks from restaurants in the area. Com-plimentary Continental breakfast. Whirlpool bath, refrigerators, coffeemakers, minibars, microwaves. 2 cable TVs, VCRs, two phones. Business services. | 205 Main St. | 828/526–4502 or 800/221–5078 | fax 828/526–4840 | www.highlandssuitehotel.com | 27 suites | $147–$200 | AE, MC, V.

Mountain High. Mountain High is on a hilltop, with a front porch overlooking Main Street. The spacious double rooms contain antique furniture and ornate four-poster beds; the bath is oversized with marble floors and a Jacuzzi in the mountain brook superior rooms, where a fireplace and a balcony look out onto a small creek. Picnic area, complimentary Continental breakfast. Refrigerators, some in-room hot tubs. Cable TV. Business services. Pets allowed. | W. Main St. and 2nd Ave. | 828/526–2790 or 800/445–7293 (outside NC) | www.mountainhighinn.com | 55 rooms | $95–$165 | AE, D, MC, V.

HOT SPRINGS

MAP 8, B4

(Nearby town also listed: Asheville)

Hot Springs is an idyllic—and tiny—resort village 30 mi northwest of Asheville on the French Broad River. Among other things, it functions as a way station for hikers on the Appalachian Trail, which runs through the center of town.

Information: Madison County Tourism Development Authority | Box 1527, Mars Hill 28754 | 828/680–9031 or 877/262–3476 | fax 828/689–2217 | madisontourism@main.nc.us | www.madisoncounty-nc.com | Mon.–Sat., 9–5, Sun. 1–5.

HOT SPRINGS

INTRO
ATTRACTIONS
DINING
LODGING

Attractions

Hot Springs Mineral Baths. Hot tub–type pools are outside by the French Broad River in a wooded area, and natural hot mineral water is piped to them from the bubbling springs nearby. Temperatures are a constant 98°F–100°F. Testimonials to the curative power of the water date from the 18th century. Long before that, the Cherokee used the fizzy pools to relax in. Therapeutic massage is available by appointment, and campsites for recreational vehicles as well as tents are within walking distance. | 315 Bridge St. | 828/622–7676 or 800/ 462–0933 | fax 828/622–7615 | Spa rates start at $12/hr but vary depending on number of people and time spent in tubs; massages cost $35–$75; campground rates start at $10 per night, depending on type of site | Mid-Feb.–Nov., weekdays 8:30 AM–11 PM, weekends 8:30 AM–1 AM; Dec.–mid-Feb., weekends 8:30 AM–11 PM.

ON THE CALENDAR

MAY: *Festival on the French Broad.* You can raft, kayak, and experience canoe races on the French Broad River; listen to live music; play in a volleyball tournament; and partici- pate in a raffle for prizes. | Hot Springs Spa, 315 Bridge St. | 828/649–9205 | fax 828/649– 2784 or 828/622–7676 | www.madisoncounty-nc.com.
JUNE: *Bluff Mountain Music Festival.* Started by the Bluff Mountain Defense Fund to save the mountain from logging, the daylong festival is now sponsored by the Madison County Arts Council. There's live old-time and bluegrass music, a silent auction, door prizes, and refreshments. | Hot Springs Spa, 315 Bridge St. | 828/656–8208.
OCT.: *Heritage Festival/Bascum Lamar Lunsford Festival.* During the day, the her- itage portion of this event features local musicians, dancing, food, crafts booths, baked goods, and an animal petting area for kids, as well as craftspeople and artists showing how things were done in yesteryear (blacksmithing, yarn spinning). In the evening, bal- lads and traditional music are offered in Moore Auditorium on the Mars Hill College campus in remembrance of Mr. Lunsford, "the Minstrel of the Mountains." | Downtown Mars Hill and Mars Hill College | 828/689–5974 or 828/689–1424.

Dining

Bridge Street Café and Inn. Italian. A renovated storefront, circa 1922, is a feature of this earthy café that rests along the Appalachian Trail. French doors open onto an outdoor din- ing area that overlooks Spring Creek. The cuisine has a distinctive Mediterranean flair; rec- ommended are the pizzas cooked in a wood-fired brick oven, the seafood and chicken specials, and the dishes made with local organic vegetables. Fine wines from Italy and California are served here, as well as imported beers and microbrews. You can listen to live music many weekend evenings. Sun. brunch. | 145 Bridge St. | 828/622–0002 | fax 828/622–7282 | bridgecafe@main.nc.us | www.bridgestreetcafe.com | $8–$22 | AE, D, MC, V | Mon.–Wed. No lunch. Closed Dec.–March.

Lodging

Mountain Magnolia Inn and Retreat. Huge, mature trees give a parklike quality to the extensively gardened grounds of this 1868 Victorian home with mountain views. You can sit in one of the quiet sanctuaries found throughout that are provided with hammocks and chairs; there's also a meditation room, and massage is available. The inn's kitchen prepares breakfast and dinner (extra), using its own organically grown vegetables. | 204 Lawson St. | 828/622-3543 | mountainmagnolia@juno.com | www.mountainmagnoliainn.com | 5 rooms, 1 cottage | $110-150 | MC, V.

JACKSONVILLE

MAP 8, J6

(Nearby towns also listed: Morehead City, New Bern)

Two bases house the nation's largest U.S. Marine expeditionary force, so the military has become a major contributor to the economic success of Jacksonville and Onslow County. Strong community support for the military presence is shown by the Beirut Memorial, which sits in a small forest of dogwood and oak trees and pays tribute to the 268 marines and sailors from Camp Lejeune who were killed by terrorists in Lebanon in 1983.

Information: Onslow County Tourism | Box 1226, Jacksonville 28541 | 910/455-1113 or 800/932-2144 | fax 910/455-8014 | octour@co.onslow.nc.us | www.onslowcounty-tourism.com.

Attractions

Camp Lejeune Marine Corps Base. Lejeune, the largest Marine base on the east coast, is home to more than 47,000 marines and sailors. It is here at the 246-square-mi training facility that NATO often sponsors exercises. You can take your own driving tour of the base, which has 14 mi of beaches capable of supporting amphibious operations, 54 live-fire ranges, and 89 maneuver areas. To get a visitor's pass and base map, stop by the visitor center at the main gate and present a valid driver's license, vehicle registration, and proof of insurance. | Main gate, Rte. 24 E | 910/451-5655 | fax 910/451-5882 | www.lejeune.usmc.mil | Free | Daily 8-5.

Lynnwood Park Zoo. A landscaped 10-acre park that is home to 50 animals, including mammals, birds, and reptiles. | 1071 Wells Rd. (Rte. 24) | 910/938-5848 | $5, special rates for children | Weekdays 10-6.

Onslow County Museum. Two exhibit galleries and a research room hold the artifacts that tell of the heritage of Onslow County, a coastal and farming area with a large military presence. The county was named for Arthur Onslow, speaker of the British House of Commons for 33 years. | 301 S. Wilmington St., Richlands | 910/324-5008 | fax 910/324-2897 | ocmuseum@co.onslow.nc.us | Free | Tues.–Fri. 10-4:30, weekends 1-4.

ON THE CALENDAR

APR.: *Air Show.* Aerial displays of military and civilian aircraft draw observers by the tens of thousands. On-ground exhibits allow a close look at the military's high-tech airplanes. The show alternates between the Marine Corps Air Station New River in Jacksonville, just down the road from Camp Lejeune, and the Marine Corps Air Station Cherry Point in Havelock, right outside New Bern. | U.S. 17 (Jacksonville show) and U.S. 70 (Cherry Point show) | 252/466-4241 | fax 252/466-5201 | www.cherrypoint.usmc.mil.
APR.: *Topsail Island Spring Fling.* Surf and Turf Triathlon—½-mi ocean swim, 12-mi bike race, and 5K run—vendor booths, boat show, and live entertainment. | Surf City on Topsail Island | 910/329-4446 or 800/626-2780 | fax 910/329-4432 | topsail@topsail.net | www.topsail.coc.com | Free.
AUG.: *Kuumba Festival.* African-American culture is explored through food, dancing, singing, clothing, jewelry, and literature. | American Legion Building, Georgetown Rd. | 910/455-5538.

AUG.: *Sneads Ferry Shrimp Festival.* This celebration of shrimp includes "Shrimp-a-Roo," pageants, a parade, a fishing tournament, arts and crafts, live entertainment, and a carnival. | Sneads Ferry | 910/327–4911 or 800/626–2780.

Dining

Golden Corral Family Steak House. Steak. You have a choice between the buffet (140 hot and cold items) and the non-buffet foods. Pizza, pastas, fresh veggies, and carved meats are some of the buffet foods, and the non-buffet menu offers steaks, seafood, and chicken. The bakery makes fresh muffins, cookies, brownies, and rolls every 15 minutes. Kids' menu. | 2055 N. Marine Blvd. | 910/455–3773 | $7–$14 | AE, D, MC, V.

Ragazzi's Restaurant. Italian. All meals are homemade in this family-style restaurant with booths and lots of windows. The fettuccine Alfredo, chicken Parmesan, and white clam sauce are particularly good. | 1439 Lejeune Blvd. | 910/577–2782 | $7–$13 | AE, MC, V.

Yanna's Ye Olde Drugstore Restaurant. American. Memorabilia and neo-hippie decor make up Yanna's, a casual drugstore restaurant featuring 1950s diner cuisine. Try the "Bradburger," a hamburger with egg, bacon, and cheese. Breakfast and lunch are served all day. | 109 Front St., Swansboro | 910/326–5501 | $5–$10 | No credit cards | No supper.

Lodging

Days Inn Hotel. This two-story hotel is in a commercial area only 2 mi from downtown Jacksonville. Complimentary breakfast. In-room data ports. Cable TV. Outdoor pool. | 603 N. Marine Blvd. | 910/455–4100 | fax 910/455–4100 | 124 rooms | $34–$56 | AE, D, DC, MC, V.

Hampton Inn. This chain hotel is 1 mi from shops and restaurants. Complimentary Continental breakfast. In-room data ports. Cable TV. Pool, laundry facilities. Business services. | 474 Western Blvd., Jacksonville | 910/347–6500 | fax 910/347–6858 | www.hamptoninn.com | 120 rooms | $69–$89 | AE, D, DC, MC, V.

Holiday Inn Express. These accommodations are 4 mi from downtown. Complimentary Continental breakfast. In-room data ports, some refrigerators. Cable TV. Pool. | 2115 U.S. 17 N | 910/347–1900 | fax 910/347–7593 | www.basshotelsandresort.com | 118 rooms | $64–74 | AE, D, DC, MC, V.

Onslow Inn. Each standard-size room has its own unique furnishings in this hostelry. A fishing pier is not far from the inn. Restaurant, picnic area. In-room data ports. Cable TV. Pool, wading pool. Business services. | 201 Marine Blvd. | 910/347–3151 or 800/763–3151 | fax 910/346–4000 | lodging@onslowonline.net | 92 rooms, 5 buildings | $50–$55 | AE, D, DC, MC, V.

Super 8 Motel. A 30-mi stretch of beach is about a 15-minute drive away (depending on traffic) from this chain motel. The Mill Avenue Historic District, the Jackson Mall, and several restaurants are about 1 mi away. Complimentary breakfast. In-room data ports, in-room safes. Cable TV. Outdoor pool. | 2149 N. Marine Blvd. | 910/455–6888 or 800/800–8000 | fax 910/455–3214 | www.super8motel.com | 60 rooms | $61 | AE, D, DC, MC, V.

JEFFERSON

MAP 8, D3

(Nearby towns also listed: Blue Ridge Parkway, Boone)

Jefferson and West Jefferson are the biggest towns in remote and rural Ashe County, which has been shaped literally and figuratively by the New River, one of the country's few north-flowing streams. Canoeing, camping, hiking, golfing, and, in season, Christmas tree picking are popular activities here.

Information: **Ashe County Chamber of Commerce** | 6 N. Jefferson Ave., Jefferson 28694 | 336/246–9550 | fax 336/246–8671 | ashechamber@skybest.com | www.ashechamber.com | Weekdays, 9–5, Sat. 10–4.

Attractions

Ashe County Cheese Company. The only cheese manufacturer in the Carolinas is in the northwesternmost corner of North Carolina, and the company has been in operation since 1930. You can watch the varieties of cheese being made and then select a favorite from the in-house shop. | 106 E. Main St. (Rte. 194), West Jefferson | 336/246–2501 or 800/445–1378 | fax 336/246–6135 | Free | Mon.–Sat. 8:30–5.

Blue Ridge Mountain Frescoes. In the 1970s and 1980s, artist Ben Long painted four luminous, internationally acclaimed frescoes in two Ashe County Episcopal churches. Three of the wall-size frescoes are at St. Mary's: *Mary Great with Child* (1974), *John the Baptist* (1975), and *The Mystery of Faith* (1977). A wall of Holy Trinity bears *The Last Supper* (1980). | St. Mary's: Rte. 194, West Jefferson; Holy Trinity: 195 J. W. Luke Rd., Glendale Springs | 336/982–3076 | Free | Daily.

Mt. Jefferson State Natural Area. From Luther's Rock you can get a spectacular view of the New River. You can also take a self-guided nature tour of Mt. Jefferson and learn about the natural history of the area. On request, park naturalists will lead a guided walk explaining the area's natural history and legends. | Off Rte. 163 | 336/246–9653 | fax 336/246–3386 | www.ils.unc.edu/parkproject/moje.html | Free | Call for information.

New River. This American Heritage River, renowned at the age of 300 million years as the second-oldest river in the world (after the Nile), was first surveyed by Thomas Jefferson's father. Three state parks flank the river, each a day's canoe ride apart for primitive riverside camping and picnicking. Within Ashe County the river is formed by two branches: the North Fork and the South Fork. The South Fork is the most developed for recreational use. Six outfitters rent canoes, tubes, and the like. Among them: New River Outfitters (800/982–9190); Wahoo's Adventures (800/444–7238); and Zaloo's Canoes (800/535–4027). | 336/246–9550 or 336/946–4871 | Free | Daily.

ON THE CALENDAR

JULY: *Christmas in July Festival.* Christmas tree farms are a mainstay in the northern mountains, and this party offers a sneak peek at the season. Decorated trees and Christmas crafts are on display in downtown West Jefferson along with traditional mountain crafts. Music, food, and children's activities round out the event. | June 30–July 2 | 336/264–9550.

OCT.: *New River Festival.* The ancient New River flows through the hamlet of Todd, which hosts an old-fashioned community social with gospel music, art displays, storytelling sessions, a fishing tournament, and more. | 336/877–1067 | sjmorgan@skydust.com.

Dining

Glendale Springs Inn and Restaurant. New American. Choose from three different dining rooms in this authentic country inn built in 1892. The Arbor room overlooks an herb and flower garden, and is ideal for groups. In summer you can dine on the porch and experience the mountain breeze. Try the classic fish, beef, chicken, or pork dishes. Sun. brunch. Wine and beer. | 7414 Rte. 16, Glendale Springs | 336/982–2103 | fax 336/246–3999 | www.glendalespringsinn.com | $9–$31 | AE, D, MC, V | Closed Wed.

Shatley Springs. Southern. This rustic place with old wooden furnishings provides family-style dining and live music. Try the home-cooked country ham, fried chicken, and vegetables. Kids' menu. No alcohol. | 407 Shatley Springs Rd. (Rte. 16) | 336/982–2236 | fax 336/246–3999 | $5–$13 | No credit cards | Closed Nov.–Apr.

Smokey Mountain Barbecue. Barbecue. You can dine outdoors at this very casual cafeteria-style restaurant known for its whole-hog barbecue, fried chicken, fried fish, and Danish baby-back ribs. Kids' menu. No alcohol. | 1008 S. Jefferson Ave. (U.S. 221 Business), West Jefferson | 336/246–6818 | fax 336/246–6085 | $4–$16 | MC, V | Closed Sun.

Lodging

Best Western Eldreth Inn at Mount Jefferson. This chain hotel stands in a rural, scenic mountain setting. Restaurant, complimentary breakfast. In-room data ports, microwaves, refrigerators. Cable TV, room phones. Sauna. Exercise equipment. Free parking. No pets. | 829 E. Main St. | 336/246–8845 or 800/221–8802 | fax 336/ 246–9109 | 75 rooms | $52–$78 | AE, D, DC, MC, V.

KANNAPOLIS

MAP 8, E5

(Nearby towns also listed: Charlotte, Concord, Cornelius, Salisbury)

Almost since its inception, Kannapolis has been a company town, and though the names of the companies may have changed, the business remains the same: household textiles—sheets, towels, bedspreads, and the like. Its refurbished downtown area, known as Cannon Village, has been recognized nationally for its Williamsburg-inspired style and tree-lined streets.

Information: Cabarrus County Convention and Visitors Bureau | 2391 Dalearnhart Blvd., Kannapolis 28083 | 704/938–4550 or 800/848–3740 | fax 704/782–4333 | info@cabarruscvb.com | www.cabarruscvb.com.

KANNAPOLIS

INTRO
ATTRACTIONS
DINING
LODGING

Attractions

Cannon Village Home Furnishings Market. Restored in the style of the Colonial era, this community of shops has off-price, outlet, and specialty stores selling everything from antiques and accessories to linens and rugs. The market's centerpiece is the Fieldcrest Cannon Textile Museum and Multi-Image Theatre, located in the visitor center. Here are samples of 1,000-year-old textiles, interactive displays, and a 20-minute show about the history and making of textiles. | 200 West Ave. | 704/938–3200 or 800/438–6111 | fax 704/938–2990 | www.cannonvillage.com | Free | Mon.–Sat. 9–6.

ON THE CALENDAR

MAY: *Cottonstock Arts and Crafts Festival.* A festival of crafts, food vendors, children's games, and entertainment. | 704/932–4164 | fax 704/782–4050.
NOV.–DEC.: *Christmas in the Village.* This party presents a festive holiday light display, carolers à la Dickens, and a Santa Claus in a Colonial-style atmosphere. | Cannon Village | 704/938–3200.

Dining

Gary's Bar-B-Que. Barbecue. Old enamel drink signs and Lone Ranger memorabilia line the walls of this pleasant, comfortable place. Try the authentic chopped pork barbecue, slaw, and hush puppies. Kids' menu. No alcohol. | 620 U.S. 29 N, China Grove | 704/857–8314 | $5–$6 | No credit cards | Closed Sun.

Towel City Junction Restaurant. American. You can sit on unique booths made from seats of 1950s cars, listen to tunes on the jukebox, and wax nostalgic for that bygone decade at this restaurant known for its biscuits, grits, eggs, country-style steak with gravy, meat loaf, roast beef, and vegetables all prepared from scratch. Breakfast is also served. | 119 S. Main St. | 704/938–2913 | Reservations not accepted | $4–$7 | AE, D, DC, MC, V | No supper.

Lodging

Best Western Kannapolis. Charlotte-Douglas International Airport is 23 mi from this chain on I–85. The hotel is 3 mi from Concord, 2½ mi from restaurants, and 14 mi from Charlotte Motor Speedway. Complimentary Continental breakfast. Some microwaves, some refrigerators. Cable TV. Outdoor pool. Free parking. Laundry facilities. No pets. | 815 Lane St. | 704/933–5080 | fax 704/933–5057 | 41 rooms | $49–$139 | AE, D, MC, V.

Comfort Inn. The Comfort Inn is about 7 mi from Winston NASCAR racetrack. Complimentary Continental breakfast. Some kitchenettes, some microwaves, no-smoking rooms. Cable TV. Pool. Exercise equipment. Laundry service. Business services. | 3100 Cloverleaf Pkwy. | 704/786–3100 | fax 704/784–3114 | 71 rooms | $60–$85 | AE, D, DC, MC, V.

Fairfield Inn by Marriott. The NASCAR racetrack is 11 mi from the Fairfield Inn. Complimentary Continental breakfast. In-room data ports, no-smoking rooms. Cable TV. Pool. Gym. Laundry service. Business services. | 3033 Cloverleaf Pkwy. | 704/795–4888 | fax 704/784–4888 | www.fairfieldinn.com | 84 rooms | $59–$64 | AE, D, DC, MC, V.

KILL DEVIL HILLS

MAP 8, L4

(Nearby towns also listed: Cape Hatteras National Seashore, Duck, Kitty Hawk, Manteo, Nags Head, Outer Banks)

Kill Devil Hills, on U.S. 158 Bypass, has been the site of rapid development over the last decade. Its population explodes in the summer, and though many businesses are seasonal, most anything one needs can be found here year-round. It's most popularly known as the site of man's first motorized flight.

Information: **Dare County Tourist Bureau** | 704 S. U.S. 64, Manteo, 27954 | 252/473–2138 or 800/446–6262 | fax 252/473–5106 | visitorinfo@outerbanks.org | www.outerbanks.org.

Attractions

Nags Head Wood Preserve. This quiet, 1,400-acre maritime forest dedicated to preserving a barrier-island ecosystem is owned by the Nature Conservancy. More than 5 mi of hiking trails wind through forest, dune, swamp, and pond habitats. No camping, bicycling, picnicking, or pets are allowed. Educational programs are offered; the preserve has a small visitor center. | 701 Ocean Acres Dr. | 252/441–2525 | fax 252/441–1271 | rparis@tmc.org | Free | Weekdays 10–3, or by appointment.

★ **Wright Brothers National Memorial.** This dramatic granite monument at the site of the world's first powered flight resembles the tail of an airplane. Orville and Wilbur Wright camped on this windswept spot as they prepared to take flight in 1903. At the visitor's center you will find a full-scale reproduction of their plane and glider, and on the grounds are the brothers' camp buildings. | Off U.S. 158, between Mile Markers 7 and 8 | 252/441–7430 | fax 252/441–7730 | $2 per adult, $4 per car | Call for hrs.

ON THE CALENDAR

JULY: *Wright Kite Festival.* This festival offers kite flying for all ages, kite stunt demonstrations, and contests. Kids can make their own kites and then fly them atop a dune. | Wright Brothers National Memorial | 252/441–4124 or 800/334–4777 | www.kittyhawk.com.

DEC.: *Wright Brothers Anniversary of First Flight.* Wilbur and Orville Wright first took to the air from the Outer Banks on December 17, 1903. The First Flight is commemorated annually at the Wright Brothers National Memorial with fly-overs and speeches by military personnel, dignitaries, and those who have devoted their lives to flight. | 252/441–7430 | fax 252/441–7730.

Dining

Colington Café. Eclectic. This old house nestled amid oak trees is known for seafood, steaks, and French dishes. Try the crab bisque and crab dip. | 1029 Colington Rd. | 252/480–1123 | Reservations essential | $17–$26 | DC, MC, V | Call for hrs.

J.K.'s. Contemporary. You can dine privately in large booths and enjoy simply prepared food at J.K.'s—known for its mesquite-grilled dishes: beef, veal, chicken, and fresh seafood. The tables are covered with linen, and the lustrous dark walnut floors add to the restaurant's character. | U.S. 158 Bypass, Mile Marker 9 | 252/441–9555 | fax 252/441–8079 | www.jksfoods.com | Reservations not accepted | $13–$23 | AE, D, MC, V | Closed 2 wks mid-Dec. No lunch.

Jolly Roger. American. Old World charm, nautical motifs, and pirate-era artifacts make up the Jolly Roger. Live music livens up the place on weeknights. If you wish, enjoy an early-bird supper, or breakfast. | 1336 N. Virginia Dare Trail | 252/441–6530 | fax 252/408–3241 | Reservations not accepted | Call for hrs | $15–$27 | AE, D, DC, MC, V.

Mako Mikes. American. Murals, local artwork, and big-game fish hang on the walls of this place, which is unusual in its being open year-round. The menu's favorites include chicken Marsala, Cajun pasta, shrimp scampi, and Mediterranean fresh spinach. The place is patronized by a mix of locals and tourists. Kids' menu. | 1630 N. Croatan Hwy. | 252/480–1919 | $9–$20 | AE, D, DC, MC, V.

Port O' Call. Continental. Near the beach, you can listen to live music nightly in season and enjoy dishes of beef, tuna, and lamb in this casual setting. Kids' menu. Sun. brunch. | 504 Virginia Dare Trail | 252/441–7484 | fax 252/441–5725 | portocall@eagnet.com | $9–$15 | AE, D, MC, V | Closed Jan.–mid-Mar.

Lodging

Best Western Ocean Reef Suites. This Best Western is made up of all suites, in contemporary beach decor, and each room has a balcony that overlooks the Atlantic Ocean. Restaurant. Kitchenettes. Cable TV. Pool. Hot tub. Exercise equipment. Laundry facilities. Business services. | 107 Virginia Dare Trail | 252/441–1611 or 800/528–1234 | fax 252/441–1482 | www.bestwestern/oceanreefsuites.com | 70 suites | $164–$204 | AE, D, DC, MC, V.

Budget Host Inn. Walk a block or two to ocean fishing, swimming, and restaurants. Complimentary breakfast, room service. Microwaves, refrigerators. Cable TV, phones. Free parking. Pets allowed (fee). | 1003 S. Croatan Hwy.; 1 mi south of Wright Brothers Memorial on U.S 158 Bypass | 252/441–2503 or 252/441–4671 | fax 252/441–4671 | www.budgethost.com | 40 rooms | $50–$150 | AE, D, MC, V.

Cypress House Inn. Built in the 1940s as a hunting and fishing lodge, the inn is adorned with cypress tongue-and-groove paneled walls and ceilings. Cheerful white ruffled curtains line the windows; rooms also have a private bath and a queen-sized bed. The common room has a fireplace and can be a nice place to read, play cards, or converse with other guests. Complimentary breakfast. Cable TV, no room phones. No kids under 14. No smoking. | 500 N. Virginia Dare Trail | 252/441–6127 or 800/554–2764 | fax 252/441–2009 | cypresshse@aol.com | www.cypresshouseinn.com | 6 rooms | $115–$130 (2–night minimum stay weekends) | AE, D, MC, V.

Comfort Inn North. Exterior corridors lead to rooms with mauve and teal finishes. This hotel is near the beach, and is 2 mi from the Avalon fishing pier. Complimentary Continental breakfast. In-room data ports, some refrigerators. Cable TV. Pool. Laundry facilities. Business services. | 401 Virginia Dare Trail | 252/480–2600 or 800/854–5286 | fax 252/480–2873 | 121 rooms | $112–$165 | AE, D, DC, MC, V.

Days Inn–Ocean Front. The lobby, with its hardwood floors, Oriental rugs, and fireplace, gives a flavor of the old Nags Head. The rooms are refurnished, and many have views of

the ocean. Complimentary Continental breakfast. In-room data ports, some kitchenettes. Cable TV. Pool. Business services. | 101 N. Virginia Dare Trail | 252/441–7211 or 800/329–7466 | fax 252/441–8080 | 54 rooms | $90–$160 | AE, D, DC, MC, V.

Holiday Inn. There's a seasonal beach bar as well as entertainment in the lounge at this beachfront chain hotel, which is about 5 mi from the Wright Brothers Museum. All rooms have balconies, some with ocean views. Restaurant, complimentary breakfast. Some in-room data ports, microwaves, refrigerators. Cable TV, room phones. Outdoor pool. Exercise equipment. Laundry facilities. Free parking. No pets. | 1601 S. Virginia Dare Trail | 252/441–6333 or 800/843–1249 | fax 252/441–7779 | www.holiday-inn.com | 105 rooms | $154–$209 | AE, D, DC, MC, V.

Nags Head Beach Hotel. This beachside property is 1 mi from shops and restaurants, and is right across the street from the Wright Brother's Memorial. Complimentary Continental breakfast. Microwaves, refrigerators. Cable TV. Pool. Some pets allowed (fee). | 804 N. Virginia Dare Trail | 252/441–0411 | fax 252/441–7811 | 96 rooms | $99–$115 | AE, D, DC, MC, V.

Quality Inn. This chain hotel is in a commercial area and right on the beach. Most rooms have beachfront views. The Wright Brothers Monument is about 1½ mi away. Picnic area. Microwaves, refrigerators. Cable TV. Outdoor pool. Playground. | 2009 S. Virginia Dare Trail | 252/441–7141 | fax 252/441–4277 | www.qualityinn.com | 107 rooms | $109–$209 | AE, D, DC, MC, V.

Ramada Inn. The rooms in this oceanfront hotel include a private balcony. Restaurant, bar with entertainment. In-room data ports, microwaves, refrigerators, room service. Cable TV. Indoor pool, hot tub. Business services. Some pets allowed (fee). | 1701 S. Virginia Dare Trail | 252/441–2151 or 800/635–1824 | fax 252/441–1830 | www.ramadainnnagshead.com | 172 rooms | $158–$209 | AE, D, DC, MC, V.

KINSTON

MAP 8, I5

(Nearby towns also listed: Goldsboro, Greenville, New Bern)

Urban and rural mix easily in Kinston (site of some Fortune 500 manufacturing companies), where produce stands pop up like wildflowers in the spring and summer. Farmers from Lenoir County wish to capture the business of people on U.S. 70 headed to or from the beach.

Information: Kinston Convention and Visitors Bureau | Box 157, 28502 | 252/523–2500. Visitor Center | 301 N. Queen St. | fax 252/527–1914 | chamber@ns1.eastlink.net | www.chamberofcommerce.kinstonlc.com | Weekdays 8:30–5.

Attractions

CSS *Neuse* State Historic Site and Governor Richard Caswell Memorial. You can learn why this ironclad, one of 22 commissioned by the Confederate Navy, was ill-fated. You can also learn the story of Richard Caswell, the man who founded Kinston and North Carolina's first elected governor. | 2612 W. Vernon Ave. (U.S. 70 Business) | 252/522–2091 | fax 252/522–7036 | cssneuse@ncsl.dcr.state.nc.us | www.ah.dcr.state.nc.us/sections/neuse/neuse.htm | Free | Apr.–Oct., Mon.–Sat. 9–5, Sun. 1–5; Nov.–Mar., Tues.–Sat. 10–4, Sun. 1–4.

Neuseway Nature Center. Nature trails and exhibits emphasizing live reptiles, fish, and mammals are found in the area, as well as three aquariums, two fish ponds, and a salt-water touch tank. Hikers can climb various rocks on the paths. Sites for RV and primitive camping are available. | Rte. 11 | 252/939–3367 | fax 252/939–3129 | Free | Tues.–Sat. 9:30–5, Sun. 1–5.

MAY: *Festival on the Neuse.* Eastern North Carolina–style pig pickin' with entertainment, including live music, arts and crafts, children's events, and a rubber-ducky race down the Neuse River for big prizes. | 252/523–2500.
OCT.: *Fireman's Day Festival.* Food, crafts, contests, fire-truck rides, and entertainment. | 252/939–3220.

Dining
King's Restaurant. Barbecue. Casual, family-friendly dining and down-home service are the hallmarks of King's Restaurant. Known for the chicken and collards—try the eastern North Carolina chopped pork vinegar-pepper barbecue and fried pork skins. Kid's menu. Beer and wine only. | 405 A E. New Bern Rd. (U.S. 70 E) | 252/527–2101 | fax 252/527–6465 | www.kingbbq.com | $4–$10 | AE, D, MC, V.

Lodging
Comfort Inn. The inn is less than ½ mi from specialty shops and restaurants. Complimentary Continental breakfast. Microwaves, refrigerators. Cable TV. Pool, sauna, exercise equipment. Business services. | 200 W. New Bern Rd. | 252/527–3200 | fax 252/527–3200, ext. 420 | 60 rooms | $55–$60 | AE, D, DC, MC, V.

Super 8 Motel. There's a shopping center right across the street from this two-story chain motel, and restaurants are also nearby. Complimentary breakfast. Cable TV. Free parking. No pets. | 212 East New Bern Rd. (U.S. 70 Bypass | 252/523–8146 or 800/800–8000 | fax 252/523–8146 | 48 rooms | $45–$50 | AE, D, DC, MC, V.

KITTY HAWK

MAP 8, L3

(Nearby towns also listed: Duck, Kill Devil Hills, Manteo, Nags Head, Outer Banks)

Kitty Hawk was one of the first popular beach settlements on the Outer Banks; this is clear when older, weather-beaten cottages are compared to modern beach houses.

KODAK'S TIPS FOR PHOTOGRAPHING WEATHER

Rainbows
- Find rainbows by facing away from the sun after a storm
- Use your auto-exposure mode
- With an SLR, use a polarizing filter to deepen colors

Fog and Mist
- Use bold shapes as focal points
- Add extra exposure manually or use exposure compensation
- Choose long lenses to heighten fog and mist effects

In the Rain
- Look for abstract designs in puddles and wet pavement
- Control rain-streaking with shutter speed
- Protect cameras with plastic bags or waterproof housings

Lightning
- Photograph from a safe location
- In daylight, expose for existing light
- At night, leave the shutter open during several flashes

From Kodak Guide to Shooting Great Travel Pictures © 2000 by Fodor's Travel Publications

Though recent storms have hit the beaches hard, the maritime forest on the west side of the island has survived and remains beautiful. U.S. 158 is the commercial corridor, but quiet spots can still be found along Route 12 ("Beach Road") and dolphins still swim in Kitty Hawk Bay.

Information: **Outer Banks Visitors Bureau** | 74 S. U.S. 64/264, Manteo, 27954 | 252/473–2138 or 800/446–6262 | dctb-info@outer-banks.com | www.outerbanks.org | Weekdays 8 AM–6 PM.

Attractions

Aycock Brown Welcome Center. Operated by the Dare County Tourist Bureau, this haven for travelers has extensive resources, including area maps, tide charts, and ferry schedules. | U.S. 158 | 252/261–4644 | fax 252/261–1053 | www.outerbank.org | Free | Memorial Day–Labor Day, daily 8:30–6:30; Labor Day–Memorial Day, daily 9–5.

Kitty Hawk Public Beach and Bathhouse. Across the road from the ocean rests a small parking area and bathhouse with rest rooms and showers. People who arrive too early for check-in to their room or condo will often change into bathing suits here and spend time in the water before heading to their beach retreat. | Rte. 12 | 252/261–3552 | Free | Memorial Day–Labor Day, daily 10–6.

ON THE CALENDAR

OCT.: *Kelly's Kup Regatta.* 25 to 30 boats compete in a 6- to 8-mi race. | Colington Harbor | 252/441–4116.

Dining

Rundown Café. Caribbean. A popular and fun place with a Caribbean flair, this restaurant is very Jimmy Buffett-like and tropical. Items to try are the Jamaican stew and conch fritters, and there's live music. Kids' menu. | 5300 Beach Rd. | 252/255–0026 | fax 252/255–0028 | Reservations not accepted | $18–$26 | AE, D, DC, MC, V | Closed Dec.–Jan.

Lodging

Beach Haven. Independently owned and well-maintained, this unique little inn has its own quiet beach overlooking the Atlantic Ocean. Each room has a deck with outdoor furniture. Picnic area. Refrigerators. Cable TV. Putting green. Beach. Laundry facilities. No smoking. | 4104 Virginia Dare Trail | 252/261–4785 | www.beachhavenmotel.com | 6 rooms | $75–$121 | AE, MC, V | Closed mid-Nov.–mid-Mar.

Holiday Inn Express. Located on the U.S. 158. Complimentary Continental breakfast. Refrigerators. Cable TV. Pool. Beach. Business services. No smoking. | U.S. 158 | 252/261–4888 or 800/836–2753 | fax 252/261–3387 | www.hiexpress.com/kittyhawk.nc | 98 rooms | $129 | AE, D, DC, MC, V.

Holiday Inn Express–Kitty Hawk Beach. A lifeguard beach is about a block away from this chain hotel, and there are several restaurants on the same block. Complimentary Continental breakfast. Refrigerators. Cable TV, phones. Outdoor pool. No pets. | 3919 N. Croatan Hwy. | 252/261–4888 or 800/836–2753 | 98 rooms | $129 | AE, D, MC, V.

KURE BEACH

MAP 8, I7

(Nearby towns also listed: South Brunswick Islands, Southport, Wilmington, Wrightsville Beach)

The year-round population of Kure (pronounced "cure-ee") Beach is less than 1,000, so the community is tightly knit. It's always been quiet in this small, mostly residential town, which lies just south of rowdier Carolina Beach. A Dane, Andersen Kure, began buying large tracts of land in the 1870s, but things moved slowly and Kure Beach wasn't even incorporated until 1947. Instead of amusement parks and high-rise development there are modest cottages and old-style beach hotels in this town, which claims the oldest fishing pier on the Atlantic coast.

Information: Cape Fear Coast Convention and Visitors Bureau | 24 N. 3rd St., Wilmington, 28401 | 910/341–4030 or 800/222–4757 | info@cape-fear.nc.us | www.cape-fear.nc.us.

Attractions

Carolina Beach State Park. You can camp, fish, boat, and picnic in this park, but a favorite activity is to hike the trails where you can see the rare Venus flytrap and other species of insect-eating plants. The cypress, lily, and grass ponds are also of special interest. | Carolina Beach | 910/458–8206 or 910/458–7770 marina | fax 910/458–6350 | ils.unc.edu/parkproject/cabe.html | Free | Call for hrs.

Fort Fisher State Historic Site. This is the largest and one of the most important Confederate earthworks fortifications of the Civil War. You'll find here a reconstructed battery, Civil War relics, and artifacts from sunken blockade-runners. The fort is part of Fort Fisher Recreation Area, with 4 mi of undeveloped beach. | 1910 Fort Fisher Blvd. | 910/458–5538 | fax 910/458–0477 | www.ah.dcr.state.nc.us/sections/hs/fisher/fisher.htm | Free | Call for hrs.

North Carolina Aquarium at Fort Fisher. One of three state aquariums, this one has a 20,000-gallon shark tank, a touch pool, and whale and alligator exhibits. It's undergoing renovations in 2000 and 2001, and is closed in those years. The park is also a natural area where wildflowers, birds, and small animals thrive. A World War II bunker on the grounds stood guard against sea attack. | 2201 Fort Fisher Blvd. | 910/458–8257 | fax 910/458–6812 | $3 | Closed until the end of 2001.

ON THE CALENDAR

DEC.: *Civil War Reenactment.* Visit the past with authentic camp conditions, battles with participants in period dress, and evening campfires at Carolina and Kure beaches. | 910/458–7116.

Dining

Big Daddy's Seafood Restaurant. Seafood. A Kure Beach institution known for its family-oriented, casual setting, maritime memorabilia, and gift shop. Steaks, prime rib, and chicken are offered but it's the all-you-can-eat salad and seafood specials that are especially popular. | 202 K Ave. | 910/458–8622 | $13–$18 | AE, D, MC, V.

The Cottage. Contemporary. This renovated 1916 beach cottage has several modern and airy dining areas as well as an outdoor dining deck that catches the ocean breezes. The menu offers beef, chicken, and vegetarian dishes, but the mix-and-match pasta and sauce dishes and the seafood are real standouts. Try the buttery Masonboro fish in foil. | 1 N. Lake Park Blvd., Carolina Beach | 910/458–4383 | $14–$19 | AE, MC, V | Closed Sun.

Freddie's Restaurante. Italian. Small, made of cinder block, and standing near the Kure Beach pier, Freddie's seems as unassuming as they come. Look past the knickknacks and tablecloths checkered in the colors of the Italian flag, though, and you'll find food that's anything but unassuming. The bread is fresh, the salads large, and the entrées, such as Portobello mushroom lasagna, inventive. Reservations are accepted only for parties of 5 or more. | 111 K Ave. | 910/458–5979 | $13–$18 | AE, MC, V | Closed Mon.–Tues.

Lodging

Docksider Oceanfront Inn. The Docksider, which dates from the 1980s, is close to the Kure Beach pier. All gray shingles and balconies outside, it is furnished inside with beachy furniture set off by marine art and artifacts, including a set of 1930s British Admiralty signal

KURE BEACH

INTRO
ATTRACTIONS
DINING
LODGING

flags. A Docksider tradition from mid-April to mid-October is a complimentary Continental breakfast served poolside on Sunday morning. In-room data ports, kitchenettes, microwaves, refrigerators. Cable TV. Pool. Beach. | 202 Fort Fisher Blvd. (U.S. 421) | 910/458–4200 or 800/383–8111 | fax 910/458–6468 | beachnow@bellsouth.com | www.docksiderinn.com | 34 rooms | $120–$219 | AE, D, MC, V.

Seven Seas Inn. People who visited the family-owned Seven Seas as children in the 1950s and 60s are now returning with their children. Since then it has expanded to include three buildings on the ocean side of Fort Fisher Boulevard. The little extras—a picnic area with grill, breakfast served poolside on Sunday between Memorial Day and Labor Day, and a fish-cleaning area—add to the appeal. Picnic area. Some kitchenettes, microwaves, refrigerators. Some in-room VCRs. Pool. Beach, fishing. Video games. Laundry facilities. No pets. | 130 Fort Fisher Blvd. (U.S. 421) | 910/458–8122 | 32 rooms | $85–$155 | AE, D, MC, V.

Kure Keys Motel. You can't miss Kure Keys—it's the one about 100 ft from the ocean with the seascape murals on the outside. The rooms are done in shades of blue, all beds are extra-long and amenities include on-site therapeutic massage (if scheduled in advance), a picnic area with grill and fryer, fish-cleaning area, beach carts and boogie boards, even an inflater for water toys. Picnic area. Some kitchenettes, refrigerators. Cable TV. Pool. Hot tub, massage. Beach, water sports, fishing, bicycles. Laundry facilities. No pets. | 310 Fort Fisher Blvd. (U.S. 421) | 910/458–5277 | kurekeys@mindspring.com | www.kurekeysmotel.com | 10 rooms | $71–$136 | D, MC, V.

LAKE TOXAWAY

MAP 8, A5

(Nearby towns also listed: Brevard, Cashiers, Franklin, Highlands)

A century ago, a group calling itself the Toxaway Company created a 640-acre lake in the Blue Ridge Mountains between Brevard and Cashiers. Nearby, a grand 500-room hotel made of the finest materials, using the most modern conveniences and serving European cuisine, attracted many of the country's elite—the Fords, Edisons, Rockefellers, Wannamakers, and Dukes. That hotel is long gone, but the scenic area that some still call "America's Switzerland" holds a number of resorts, the state's largest private lake, some of the priciest real estate in the North Carolina mountains, and the highest average rainfall east of the Pacific Northwest.

Information: Brevard-Transylvania Tourism Development Authority | 28 E. Main St., Brevard, 28712 | 828/884–8900 or 800/648–4523 | waterfalls@citcom.net | www.visitwaterfalls.com.

Attractions

Toxaway Falls. These falls, more than 300 ft wide and just over the Jackson County line between Brevard and Cashiers, are visible from the road. Water slides 125 ft over a massive dome-shaped granite shelf and then plunges 350 ft. About halfway down, a curve in the rock causes the current to dramatically spout upward. | U.S. 64 | 828/884–8900 or 800/648–4523 | www.visitwaterfalls.com | Free | Daily.

Toxaway Tower. Just 6 mi east of Cashiers off U.S. 64 is an observation tower. Sitting atop Hogback Mountain (elevation 4,777 ft), it offers stunning 360–degree views. | Tower Rd. | Free | Daily.

Dining

October's End. American/Casual. This restaurant is open from April until the end of October—thus its name. The view of Toxaway Falls from the enclosed deck is worth a visit alone. The food, a mix of American and Italian flavors, only adds to the experience. Lunch fare ranges from sandwiches and pizzas to eggplant parmigiana. The dinner menu is more expansive and includes a variety of seafood. Try the house specialty, Veal October stuffed with cheese, spinach, and prosciutto and topped with fresh tomatoes, basil and olives. | 115 U.S. 64 W | 828/966–9226 | $13–$18 | D, MC, V.

Lodging

Earthshine Mountain Lodge. You can have as much solitude or adventure as you want at this spacious cedar-log cabin with stone fireplaces. The lodge sits on 70 acres midway between Brevard and Cashiers on a ridge that adjoins the Pisgah National Forest, and offers horseback riding, hiking, fishing, climbing, even an opportunity to gather berries, feed the goats, or master some Cherokee skills. In the evening, guests may gather around an open fire to sing songs, square dance, or exchange stories. A minimum stay of two nights is required and prices include all meals. Hiking, horseback riding, fishing. Baby-sitting, children's programs (ages 6 and up). Business services. | Golden Rd.; U.S. 64 to Silversteen Rd. | 828/862–4207 | www.earthshinemtnlodge.com | 10 rooms | $220 | D, MC, V | AP.

Fairfield Sapphire Valley. Each cottage and condo is individually designed on this 6,000-acre resort. Its 3,500 ft altitude, between Lake Toxaway and Cashiers, makes for stunning views. You can take advantage of the on-site ski slopes, the private beach on Fairfield Lake, and the private gem mine 4 mi away. Golf, fishing, and tennis are available. 2 restaurants, dining room. Some microwaves, some refrigerators, some in-room hot tubs. Cable TV. Indoor-outdoor pool. Hot tub. Driving range, 18-hole golf course, miniature golf, tennis courts. Exercise equipment, beach, boating. Downhill skiing. Kids' programs (3–12), playground. | 70 Sapphire Valley Rd. W, Sapphire | 828/743–3441 or 800/533–8268 | fax 828/743–2641 | 100 cottages, 8 houses | $90–$260 cottages; $1,600–$2,750/wk houses (1 wk minimum stay) | AE, D, MC, V.

Greystone Inn. The main mansion, built in 1915, is listed on the National Register of Historic Places. Rooms in the mansion and in the Hillmont Building next door have antiques or period reproductions, while the two suites that border the lake of this mountain resort are modern. Picnic area, complimentary breakfast. Minibars, refrigerators. Cable TV, in-room VCRs. Pool, lake. Massage. Driving range, 18-hole golf course, putting green, tennis courts. Business services. | Greystone La. | 828/966–4700 or 800/824–5766 (outside NC) | fax 828/862–5689 | greystone@citcom.net | www.greystoneinn.com | 33 rooms, 2 suites | $340–$540 | MC, V | Closed Sun.–Thurs. in Jan.–Mar.

LAURINBURG

MAP 8, G6

(Nearby towns also listed: Aberdeen, Lumberton, Southern Pines)

The earliest settlers in what is now Scotland County were Highland Scots, and the fruit of their labor is visible everywhere one turns in Laurinburg, the county seat. Laurinburg and Scotland County retain a rural, small-town flavor. However, four decades ago they launched a passionate and savvy campaign to be chosen the site for St. Andrews Presbyterian College. Since then, the school, with its many international students, has touched every aspect of life here and has developed a reputation as a great innovator.

Information: Laurinburg/Scotland County Area Chamber of Commerce | Box 1025, Laurinburg, 28353 | 910/276–7420 | fax 910/277–8785 | scotcoc@carolina.net | www.laurinburgchamber.org | Weekdays 8:30–5.

Attractions

St. Andrews Presbyterian College. St. Andrews is a private four-year liberal arts and sciences college in the Sandhills region near the South Carolina border. Situated on 600 acres around a lake, St. Andrews was designed to have an accessible, barrier-free campus decades before the notion was popular. The school has made a public commitment to promoting independence for students with special needs; today, about 6% of the student body is physically challenged. | 1700 Dogwood Mile | 910/277–5000 or 800/763–0198 | fax 910/277–5020 | www.sapc.edu | Free | Daily.

Lake Ansley C. Moore. Academic and administrative buildings occupy the south shore of this lovely 70-acre lake, while the residence halls, student center, and gym are on the north shore. A walkway ties the two together. Wildlife has made a home here and there is a cypress grove. | St. Andrews campus | 910/277–5000 or 800/763–0198 | fax 910/277–5020 | www.sapc.edu | Free | Daily.

Scottish Heritage Center. Dedicated to preserving and highlighting the Scottish history, culture, music, and traditions of the Carolinas and beyond, the center maintains links with Scottish organizations in North America and Scotland. In addition to an extensive collection of old and rare books, a genealogy research area, visual exhibits, and programs, there is what the center believes to be largest listening library of Celtic music in the United States. | DeTamble Library | 910/277–5047 | fax 910/277–5663 | www.sapc.edu | Free | Weekdays 8:30–5.

ON THE CALENDAR

OCT.: *John Blue Cotton Festival.* Entertainment, food, arts, crafts, antiques, displays, and demonstrations, such as a team of mules powering a pre–Civil War cotton gin, make up this festival. Costumed docents give tours of the 19th-century John Blue house in western Laurinburg. Adding to the historic flavor are old-time games and an old-style Sunday church service on the grounds. | X-Way Rd. | 910/277–3582 or 910/277–2585.

Dining

Captain Larry's Seafood Restaurant. Seafood. This casual, family-style restaurant is just about 1 mi outside of downtown Laurinburg. The seafood platter and lobster tail are the most popular choices here. | 1695 S. Main St. | 910/276–1880 | $5–$20 | AE, D, MC, V.

Champs Fine Foods and Spirits. Contemporary. This casual sports bar-like restaurant has prime rib, buffalo wings, and steaks on its menu. If you want something lighter, they have a salad bar. The live music on Tue.–Sat. is loud and festive. Kid's menu. | U.S. 15/401 Bypass | 910/276–4386 | fax 910/277–0828 | $11–$23 | AE, D, DC, MC, V | Closed Sun.–Mon.

Lodging

Comfort Inn. This spot is 2 mi from St. Andrews College and 3 mi from the John Blue House. Complimentary Continental breakfast. Refrigerators, some in-room hot tubs. Cable TV. Pool, exercise equipment. Business services. | 1705 U.S. 401 S | 910/277–7788 | fax 910/277–7229 | 80 rooms | $59–$125 | AE, D, DC, MC, V.

Hampton Inn. Right off U.S. 74 you'll find the Hampton Inn. Complimentary breakfast. In-room data ports. Cable TV. Pool. Business services. | 115 Hampton Circle | 910/277–1516 | fax 910/277–1514 | 50 rooms | $58–$74 | AE, D, DC, MC, V.

Ramada Inn. What makes this chain hotel stand out in the minds of golf lovers is the nearby 18-hole golf course. Restaurant, complimentary Continental breakfast. In-room data ports. Outdoor pool. Putting green. Free parking. | 1609 U.S. 15/401 Bypass, South Laurinburg | 910/276–6555 or 888/298–2054 | fax 910/277–0138 | 118 rooms | $65 | AM, D, DC, MC, V.

LENOIR

MAP 8, C4

(Nearby towns also listed: Blowing Rock, Blue Ridge Parkway, Boone, Hickory, Morganton)

Lenoir, in the foothills of the Blue Ridge Mountains, is a major furniture center. The lifestyle here is quiet and focuses on the arts as well as outdoor pursuits, thanks to the presence of national and state forests, streams, and gardens.

Information: Caldwell County Chamber of Commerce | 1909 Hickory Blvd. SE, Lenoir 28645 | 828/726–0616 or 800/737–0782 | fax 828/726–0385 | visitors@caldwell-cochamber.org | www.caldwellcochamber.org | Weekdays 8–5.

Attractions

Fort Defiance. The home of General William Lenoir, a Revolutionary War hero, was built in 1792. On display are more than 300 pieces of original clothing and furnishings. Special events include the annual Colonial Christmas celebration held the second weekend of December. | Rte. 268 | 828/758–1671 | fax 828/874–6548 | $4, special rates for children | Thur. and Sat. 10–5, Sun. 1–5.

Tuttle Educational State Forest. Outdoor education is a feature of the Tuttle Educational State Forest, especially for children. You can enjoy the trails with "talking" trees and exhibits, picnic facilities, and ranger-conducted programs. | Rte. 6 | 828/757–5608 | www.dfr.state.nc.us | Free | Tues.–Fri. 9–5, weekends 11–8.

ON THE CALENDAR

AUG.: *Blue Grass Festival.* The Blue Grass Festival features entertainment, kids' activities, and food. | 828/757–2177. | www.ci.lenoir.nc.us.

SEPT.: *Cycling Challenge Bridge to Bridge.* An endurance ride for bicyclists referred to as "100 miles of pure hill." It begins at the Lenoir Mall (elevation 1,081 ft) and ends at Grandfather Mountain's swinging bridge (elevation 5,280 ft). | 828/726–0616 | www.caldwellcochamber.org.

SEPT.: *Sculpture Celebration.* A nationally recognized event with dozens of sculptors competing for purchases and merit awards. Exhibits of indoor and outdoor sculptures, food vendors, and musical performances make up this celebration of sculpture. | J. E. Broyhill Park | 828/754–2486.

Dining

Acapulco. Mexican. This festive Mexican restaurant is known for its carmeacavas, enchiladas, burritos, and fajitas. There are two stories—one for smokers and one for non-smokers. Live mariachi music livens up the place once a month on Thurs. night. Kid's menu. | 110 Valencia Pl. NE | 828/754–1879 | Reservations not accepted except for large parties | $11–$30 | AE, MC, V.

Supreme Restaurant. American. This downtown storefront with a very casual flavor is known for its comfort food—eggs, grits, hash browns and homemade gravy, club sandwiches, Reubens, and grinders. Or, for lighter fare, sample the salad bar. It is also open for breakfast. | 813 West Ave. NW | 828/758–1268 | Reservations not accepted | $3–$6 | No credit cards | No supper.

Lodging

Comfort Inn. This chain is centrally located between Boone and Hickory. The Hickory Airport is 18 mi away and Appalachian State University 25 mi away. Complimentary breakfast. In-room data ports. Cable TV. Outdoor pool. Exercise equipment. Laundry facilities. | 970 Blowing Rock Blvd. | 828/754–2090 | fax 828/757–4595 | 78 rooms | $76–$92 | AE, D, DC, MC, V.

Ramada Limited. The Ramada is 2 mi from the furniture mall. Complimentary Continental breakfast. Cable TV. Pool, laundry facilities. | 142 Wilkesboro Blvd. SE | 828/758–4403 | fax 704/758–1349 | 100 rooms | $59–$68 | AE, D, DC, MC, V.

LEXINGTON

MAP 8, E4

(Nearby towns also listed: Asheboro, High Point, Salisbury, Winston-Salem)

Lexington is known for its famous barbecue. But Bob Timberlake, who was mentored by Andrew Wyeth, is nearly as well known. He left the family business to paint full-

time, and was soon presenting sold-out shows in major cities. Now he is a grandfather and a corporate force, and his hometown is a mecca for the millions who desire his original artwork, reproductions, home furnishings, collectibles, and other branded merchandise.

Information: Lexington Area Chamber of Commerce | 16 E. Center St., Lexington 27292 | 336/248–5929 | fax 336/248–2161 | chamber@lexingtonncchamber.org | www.lexingtonncchamber.org | Weekdays 8–5.

Attractions

Boone's Cave State Park. A 110-acre day-use park with a hiking trail, river fishing, and picnicking. The most intriguing characteristics are a cave that, according to legend, Daniel Boone slept in and several large rock outcrops that serve as rest stops along the Yadkin River Canoe Trail. | Boone's Cave Rd. | 336/982–4402 | fax 336/982–5323 | Free | Call for hrs.

Davidson County Historical Museum. Listed on the National Register of Historic Places, the museum features permanent and changing exhibits that spotlight the history of the area, which was settled in 1775 and named in honor of the Revolutionary War battle in Massachusetts. | Old Courthouse, 2 S. Main St. | 336/242–2035 | choffmann@co.davidson.nc.us | www.co.davidson.nc.us | Free | Tues.–Sat. 10–4, Sun. 2–4.

Art United for Davidson County Actually, two museums are found in the 1911 U.S. Post Office: an art museum featuring a public art gallery and monthly exhibits, and the Chairs Museum, a hands-on museum for children. | 220 S. Main St. | 336/249–2742 | fax 336/249–6302 | artsdavidsonco@hotmail.com | Free | Tues.–Fri. 10–4:30, Sat. 10–2.

ON THE CALENDAR

OCT.: *Barbecue Festival.* This town of 17,000, home to more than 20 barbecue restaurants, swells when 130,000 people attend this whopper of a festival held the last two Saturdays of October. In addition to piles and piles of Lexington-style barbecue, there are six stages with live entertainment, exhibits, a carnival, a juried arts-and-crafts show, dancing (including a "clog-off"), sporting events, and lots of stuff for kids. A month's worth of activity, including the cycling and walking event, Tour de Pig, leads up to these weekends. | 336/956–1880 or 800/248–2118.

Dining

Lexington Barbecue. Barbecue. A famous destination with friendly and quick service and a very family-like spirit. Try the chopped pork barbecue with western North Carolina–style tomato-based sauce, slaw, and hush puppies. Kid's menu. | 10 U.S. 29/70 S/I–85 Business | 336/249–9814 | $3–$7 | No credit cards | Closed Sun.

Lodging

Comfort Inn. What's especially noteworthy about this chain hotel are the rooms with whirlpool baths. The place is just about 10 minutes from downtown Lexington, the Davidson Museum is about 4 mi west. Complimentary breakfast. In-room data ports, microwaves. Cable TV. Outdoor pool. Exercise equipment. Laundry facilities. | 1620 Cotton Grove Rd.; I–85 Exit 91 | 336/357–2333 | fax 336/357–2359 | 120 rooms | $72–$150 | AE, D, DC, MC, V.

Holiday Inn Express. About halfway between Raleigh and Charlotte, this hotel is also 15 minutes from the North Carolina Transportation Museum and 45 mi from the zoo. Complimentary Continental breakfast. Some microwaves and refrigerators, no-smoking floors. Cable TV. Pool. Business services. | 101 Plaza Pkwy. | 336/243–2929 | fax 336/249–7003 | 57 rooms | $62–$69 | AE, D, DC, MC, V.

LINVILLE

(Nearby towns also listed: Banner Elk, Blowing Rock, Blue Ridge Parkway, Boone, Valle Crucis)

Close to Boone, bordering Route 105, is Linville, a resort area that has attracted seasonal visitors and the wealthy for a century. There's a rugged serenity and sophistication to all of surrounding Avery County. Christmas tree farms abound on the hillsides. Skiers flock to the peaks in winter, and cool temperatures in summer attract Lowlanders.

Information: Avery County–Banner Elk Chamber of Commerce | Shoppes of Tunecastle, 28604 | 828/898–5605 or 800/972–2183 | fax 828/898–8287 | chamber@averycounty. com | www.banner-elk.com | Weekdays 9–5.

Attractions

Grandfather Mountain. Famous for its scenery and singled out by the United Nations as a natural heritage site of global importance, Grandfather is the highest peak in the Blue Ridge chain. It's known for its Mile High Swinging Bridge and a plethora of wildlife—black bears, otters, panthers, deer, and eagles. Picnic sites, hiking trails, woodland walks, and a nature museum add to the diversity of the experience. | 2050 Blowing Rock Hwy., Mile Marker 305 | 828/733–2013 or 800/468–7325 | fax 828/733–2608 | www.grandfather.com | $10, special rates for children | Apr.–mid-Nov., daily 8 AM–dusk; mid-Nov.–Mar., daily 8–5, weather permitting.

Linville Caverns. The only caverns in the Carolinas go 2,000 ft underground and have a year-round temperature of 51°F. You can also explore a stream with blind trout. | U.S. 221 between Linville and Marion | 828/756–4171 or 800/419–0540 | www.linvillecaverns.com | $5 | Mar.–Nov., daily 9–6; Dec.–Feb. weekends only 9–6.

Linville Falls Visitor Center. From here it's an easy ½-mi hike to one of North Carolina's most photographed waterfalls. The easy trail winds through evergreens and rhododendrons to overlooks with views of the series of cascades tumbling into Linville Gorge. There's also a campground and a picnic area. | Rte. 1 | 828/765–1045 or 828/298–0398 | Free | Apr.–Oct., daily 8–4:30.

ON THE CALENDAR

JUNE: *Nature Photography Weekend.* Shutterbugs of all skill levels gather at Grandfather Mountain's Nature Museum to share notes, listen to nature photographers talk about various aspects of their work, and view exemplary pictures. A highlight is an informal photography contest, the subjects of which can be found right outside the museum's doors. | Blue Ridge Pkwy. and U.S. 221 | 828/733–4337 or 800/468–7325.
JUNE: *Singing on the Mountain.* An opportunity to hear old-time gospel music and preaching on the slopes of Grandfather Mountain. | MacRae Meadows | 828/733–4337 or 800/468–7325.
JULY: *Grandfather Mountain Highland Games.* Scottish clans from all over North America converge on MacRae Meadows for the Parade of the Tartans, athletic competitions, sheep herding, Celtic and Scottish folk music, dancing, picnicking, and more. | Blue Ridge Pkwy. and U.S. 221 | 828/733–4337 or 800/468–7325.
JULY: *On the Square Arts and Crafts Festival.* Eighty artists and craftspeople from all over the Southeast come to Newland, the Avery County seat, for a signature-event show. The auction is especially popular, which features select items from vendors in addition to products donated by local businesses. Also featured are a children's area, live entertainment, and food. | Town Square, Newland | 828/733–0065.

Dining

Eseeola Lodge and Restaurant. Contemporary. Executive chef John Hofland describes the food at this rustic lakeside lodge as "an eclectic blend of international cuisine with a Southern accent." Entrées may include sautéed local trout with candied pecans, white grapes and chervil butter, or grilled fillet of Black Angus beef with Sonoma valley foie gras with truffled Armagnac sauce. There is a seafood buffet on Thurs. evenings, and a pianist plays every night but Thursday. | 175 Lenville Ave. | 828/733–4311 or 800/742–6717 | fax 828/733–3772 | www.eseeola.com | Reservations essential | Jacket and tie at supper | Prix–fixe $36, Thurs. $43 | MC, V | Closed late Oct.–late May.

Spear's Barbecue and Grill. Barbecue. Casual and family-friendly with a broad menu including steaks, chicken, pork, fish, seafood, barbecue, and vegetarian dishes, Spear's is known for fresh local rainbow trout. You can dine outdoors on their deck, and feast upon a seafood buffet Fri. evenings or a barbecue buffet Sat. evenings. Kid's menu. Beer and wine only. | U.S. 221 N and Rte. 183 | 828/765–0026 | fax 828/765–6788 | $9–$19 | D, DC, MC, V | Closed weekdays Nov.–Apr.

Lodging

Linville Lodge and Cottage B&B. This turn-of-the-20th-century Victorian farmhouse is just about 2 mi from Grandfather Mountain, a major tourist attraction. There are over 4,000 acres of hiking trails here, and a museum as well. The property is accessible to the Appalachian Trail and 20 mi away from golf, skiing, horseback riding, and Tweetsie Railroad. The rooms have featherbeds and country-style antiques. Mom's Cabin is pet- and children-friendly. Complimentary breakfast. | 154 Ruffin St.; Rtes. 221 and 183 | 828/733–6551 or 877/797–1885 | www.highsouth.com/linville | 4 rooms, 1 suite | $65–$150 | AE, D, MC, V.

LITTLE SWITZERLAND

MAP 8, C4

(Nearby towns also listed: Blue Ridge Parkway, Burnsville, Marion)

Settled in the early 1900s, Little Switzerland, as its names implies, has a decidedly Swiss quality. Gingerbread-trimmed chalets and cabins abound in a lush mountain setting.

Information: McDowell County Tourism Development Authority | Box 1028, Marion, 28752 | 828/652–1103 or 888/233–6111 | fax 828/652–3862 | www.mcdowellnc.org.

Attractions

Emerald Village. You can mine for gemstones and watch artisans cut and mount jewelry, then see authentic mining equipment in an underground mine. | Blue Ridge Pkwy., MM 334 | 828/765–6463 | fax 828/765–4367 | gemmine@m-y.net | www.emeraldvillage.com | Museum $4, plus cost of gem bucket chosen ($3–$500). A $50 bucket guarantees you a stone, which will be cut free of charge; $100 guarantees 2 | Apr.–Oct., daily 9–6.

Museum of North Carolina Minerals. The visitor center at the Mitchell County Chamber of Commerce gives a unique sampling of the more than 300 varieties of North Carolina rocks and minerals. Numerous gemstones such as ruby, aquamarine, and emerald are shown in both rough and polished states. | 214 Pkwy. Maintenance Rd. | 828/765–2761 | Free | Daily 9–5.

Springmaid Mountain. Guided horseback riding and river sports are offered here in Altapass near Little Switzerland. Accommodations include cabins, lodge, and camping facilities. Other activities are fishing, rafting trips, tubing, and hiking. There is also a children's recreation center that has a playground and a pool. | Huntback Mountain Rd.; Hwy. 19 to Altapass Rd. | 828/765–2353 | $12 or $17 per person | Daily 9–4.

AUG.: *Spruce Pine Mineral and Gem Festival.* A retail show with dozens of dealers from around the world displaying minerals, precious gems, fossils, and crafted jewelry, which includes demonstrations of faceting, jewelry making, and other mineral- and gem-related arts and crafts. | Pinebridge Center, Spruce Pine | 828/765–9483 or 800/ 227–3912.

Dining

Big Lynn Lodge. American. An atrium dining room at 3,100 ft and knotty pine walls and ceiling enhance this lodge known for its hearty breakfasts, mountain trout, baked ham, roast turkey, and roast sirloin of beef. Beer and wine only. | Rte. 226A | 828/765–4257 | fax 828/765–0301 | biglynn@m-y.net | www.biglynnlodge.com | Prix–fixe $12 | MC, V | Closed Nov.–Apr. 15. No lunch.

Chalet Restaurant at Switzerland Inn. Contemporary. Three dining areas make up the Chalet Restaurant, including one with a breathtaking mountain view. White-linen service and candlelight can add to your experience. They are known for filet mignon, prime rib, pot roast, and rainbow trout. You can eat outdoors on the deck at lunch. Supper buffet is on Fri. Kid's menu. | Blue Ridge Pkwy. MM 334 | 828/765–2153 | fax 828/765–0049 | www.switzerlandinn.com | Reservations not accepted | $15–$29 | AE, MC, V | Closed Nov.–Apr.

Mountain View Restaurant. American. Mountain View overlooks the valley of Marion, with spectacular views of Mt. Mitchell. Known for its salads, burgers, sandwiches, steak, shrimp, ribs, and chicken and rice. You can dine outside on the deck, and occasionally listen to live music. Kid's menu. Sun. brunch. Beer and wine only. | Marion Hwy. | 828/765–4233 | $11–$15 | D, MC, V | Closed Wed.

Skyline Restaurant. American. A roadside restaurant with views of the mountains. Try the mountain trout, grilled steaks, and local dishes. Beer and wine only. Breakfast is also served. | Off Rte. 221 | 828/765–9394 | $7–$11 | MC, V | No supper Sun.–Thurs.

Lodging

Alpine Inn. For those seeking a mountain getaway, these rustic rooms with a private bath have a view of the valley. Picnic area, complimentary Continental breakfast. No room phones, no TV in rooms, TV in common area. | Hwy. 226A | 828/765–5380 | www.inside-enc.com | 14 rooms (11 with shower only) | $40–$65 | MC, V | Closed Nov.–Apr.

Big Lynn Lodge. A contemporary facility that overlooks the breathtaking Catawba River Valley, the lodge is 1½ mi from the town and less than an hour away from many Little Switzerland sites, including Mt. Mitchell, Grandfather Mountain, and Roan Mountain. Room rates include home-cooked meals. Restaurant, complimentary breakfast. No TV in some rooms, TV in common area. Hiking. Library. Laundry facilities. | Rte. 226A | 828/765–4257 or 800/ 654–5232 | fax 828/765–0301 | www.biglynnlodge.com | 26 rooms, 4 suites; 12 cottages | $85– 129 | MC, V | Closed Nov.–mid-Apr.

Mountain View Motel. The views of the Blue Ridge Mountains from this 1930s motel are spectacular. The in-house restaurant serves breakfast, lunch, and dinner, and you can relax and take in the panoramic views of the mountains from the wraparound porch. Restaurant. Cable TV. | Rte. 226 | 828/765–4233 or 800/304–1715 | 12 rooms | $49–$55 | D, MC, V.

Pinebridge Inn and Executive Center. In a former high school, the rooms and suites of this inn have high ceilings, and tall windows have nice views of the grounds. The Principal's Cottage presents a completely furnished three-bedroom, one-and-one-half bath bungalow, featuring a full kitchen, fireplace, and large deck. Picnic area. Cable TV. Cross-country and downhill skiing. Business services. | 207 Pinebridge Ave., Spruce Pine | 828/765–5543 or 800/356–5059 | fax 828/765–5544 | www.pinebridgeinn.com | 44 rooms and suites | $53– $125 | AE, D, MC, V.

LITTLE SWITZERLAND

Switzerland Inn. Built in 1910, this inn is near Tweetsie Railroad Theme Park. Restaurant, bar, complimentary Continental breakfast. Outdoor pool. Golf, tennis. | Rte. 226A and Blue Ridge Pkwy. | 800/654–4026 | 50 rooms | $95–$180 | AE, D, DC, MC, V | Closed Nov.–late Apr.

LUMBERTON

MAP 8, G6

(Nearby towns also listed: Fayetteville, Laurinburg)

Lumberton, in Robeson County, through which the dark Lumber River flows, is arguably the most racially balanced community in North Carolina. About one-third of its residents are white, one-third black, and one-third Native American. The Lumbee, the largest Indian tribe east of the Mississippi, have lived here for centuries. Some believe the tribe includes the English-speaking descendants of Sir Walter Raleigh's Lost Colony and runaway slaves.

Information: **Lumberton Area Visitors Bureau** | 3431 Lackey St., Lumberton 28360 | 910/739–9999 or 800/359–6971 | fax 910/739–9777 | info@i95travel.org | www.i95travel.org | Weekdays 9–5.

Attractions

Native American Resource Center. Exhibits on crafts and arts depicting tribal Indian life are found at the University of North Carolina at Pembroke, established more than a century ago as a school for Native Americans. Major displays include an authentic log canoe and a log cabin. A tour includes a 30-minute film. | Old Main, University of North Carolina at Pembroke, Pembroke | 910/521–6282 | knick@nat.uncp.edu | www.uncp.edu/native-museum/ | Free | Weekdays 8–5.

Robeson County Museum. Here you'll find a collection of artifacts pertaining to Lumberton and Robeson County. | 101 S. Elm St. | 910/738–7979 | Free | Call for hrs.

Robeson Planetarium–Science and Technology Center. Planetarium presentations teach astronomy using multimedia, exhibits, photographs, and displays. The science center has ongoing live TV when NASA is telecasting from space. | 420 Canton Dr. (Rte. 72/711) | 910/671–6015 | fax 910/671–6017 | $2 | Weekdays 8–5.

ON THE CALENDAR

MAY: *White Lake Water Festival.* White Lake, with its smooth, sandy bottom and clean, quiet water, is the centerpiece of this weekend-long event. There's a foot race and a parade in addition to live bands and dancing, roaming magicians, an arcade, and amusement rides, arts-and-crafts booths, and a waterskiing show. | White Lake | 910/862–4368.

JUNE OR JULY: *Lumbee Indian Homecoming.* A weeklong festival recognizing the heritage of Robeson County's Lumbee Indians, this event features Lumbees parading in native dress, making baskets, and selling their arts and crafts, as well as scholarship pageants and an antique-car show. | Pembroke | 910/521–8602.

OCT.: *Fairmont Farmers' Festival.* Cloggers and square dancers, gospel and country-and-western singing groups, horseshoe pitching and puppet shows, arts-and-crafts booths, and homemade food make up this festival. | Fairmont | 910/628–9766.

OCT.: *Flora MacDonald Highland Games.* Scottish music, dance, Scottish heritage booths, vendors, and athletics are all a part of the Flora MacDonald Highland Games. | Flora MacDonald Academy campus, Rte. 211, Red Springs | 910/843–5000.

Dining

Fuller's. Seafood. This traditional seafood place includes extensive lunch and dinner buffets with Southern food selections, including steak. Kid's menu. Sun. brunch. No alcohol.

| 87 W. Broad St., Elizabethtown | 910/872–0122 | $12–$20 | MC, V | Closed Mon. No lunch Sat., no supper Sun.

John's. Continental. A local favorite with a casual mood. Try the baby veal with wine mushroom garlic sauce or the prime rib. | 4880 Kahn Dr. | 910/738–4709 | $12–$25 | AE, D, DC, MC, V | Closed Sun.–Mon. and first wk in July. No lunch.

New China. Chinese. Szechuan-style dining, serving lunch and supper buffets as well as a full menu. If you are waiting for a take-out order, you can take a look at one of the many books on China's history that the owners have put out for customers. Try the pepper steak with onion, the chicken broccoli, or the General Tso's chicken. | 3534 Capuano Rd. | 910/671–1628 | $7–$18 | MC, V.

Lodging

Best Western Inn. Jerry Giles Park, Biggs Park Mall, and Cross Creek Mall are just about 1 mi from this chain hotel, and a restaurant is adjacent. Complimentary Continental breakfast. Microwaves, refrigerators. Cable TV. Outdoor pool. | 201 Jackson Ct; I–95 Exit 22 | 910/618–9799 | fax 910/618–9057 | www.bestwestern.com | 62 rooms | $55–$65 | AE, D, DC, MC, V.

Comfort Suites. Near movie theaters and restaurants, this place has a separate sitting room in each suite. Complimentary Continental breakfast. In-room data ports, refrigerators. Cable TV. Pool, exercise equipment, laundry facilities. Business services. | 215 Wintergreen Dr. | 910/739–8800 | fax 910/739–0027 | comfort@nc.online.com | 93 suites | $65–$100 | AE, D, DC, MC, V.

Fairfield Inn by Marriott. The Fairfield Inn is 6 mi from golf courses. Complimentary Continental breakfast. Refrigerators (in suites). Cable TV. Pool. Business services. | 3361 Lackey St. | 910/739–8444 | fax 910/739–8466 | 105 rooms, 4 suites | $55, $70 suites | AE, D, DC, MC, V.

Hampton Inn. A good rest stop along I–95, the inn is also near several restaurants. Complimentary Continental breakfast. Microwaves, refrigerators. Cable TV. Pool. Exercise equipment. Laundry facilities. Business services. | 201 Wintergreen Dr. | 910/738–3332 | fax 910/739–8671 | 68 rooms | $69–$119 | AE, D, DC, MC, V.

Holiday Inn. About 7 mi from the University of North Carolina at Pembroke, and less than 1 hour from the NASCAR racetrack at Darlington, this hotel is also near shops and restaurants. Restaurant, room service. In-room data ports. Cable TV. Pool. Business services, airport shuttle, free parking. | 101 Wintergreen Dr. | 910/671–1166 | fax 910/671–1166 | www.holiday-inn.com | 107 rooms | $53–$69 | AE, D, DC, MC, V.

Quality Inn. Close to a shopping area and restaurants, the Quality Inn also houses its own popular Italian restaurant and has coffeemakers in all rooms. Bar, complimentary Continental breakfast. In-room data ports, refrigerators (in suites). Cable TV. Pool. Business services. | 3608 Kahn Dr. | 910/738–8261 | fax 910/671–9075 | 120 rooms, 28 suites | $60–$92 | AE, DC, MC, V.

Ramada Inn Limited Lumberton. Several restaurants are within 2 mi of the property. Complimentary Continental breakfast. Cable TV. Outdoor pool. Free parking. | 3510 Capuano Rd.; I–95 Exit 20 | 910/738–4261 or 888/298–2054 | fax 910/738–4261 | www.ramada.com | 133 rooms | $45–$50 | AE, D, DC, MC, V.

MAGGIE VALLEY

MAP 8, A4

(Nearby towns also listed: Blue Ridge Parkway, Bryson City, Cherokee, Waynesville)

Named for the daughter of the town's first postmaster, Maggie Valley is a very small but very busy vacation spot. North Carolina's oldest ski resort is here.

Information: Maggie Valley Area Convention and Visitors Bureau | 2487 Soco Rd., Maggie Valley 28751 | 828/926–1686 or 800/785–8259 | cmaggie@primeline.com | www.maggievalley.org | Weekdays 9–5, Sat. 10–3.

Attractions

Cataloochee Ski Area. This ski area is a mile high with ten slopes and trails and a 740-ft vertical drop. | 1080 Ski Lodge Rd. | 828/926–0285 or 800/768–0285 | fax 828/926–0354 | www.cataloochee.com | Weekdays $22, weekends $36 | Late Nov.–mid-Mar.

Ghost Town in the Sky. Gunfights, jail breaks, a saloon, and country music shows all play on the Wild West theme of Ghost Town in the Sky. There are also more than 30 rides. Getting to the top of this family amusement park means taking the inclined railroad or, for the more adventurous, the chairlift. Restaurants are available throughout the park. | Soco Rd. (U.S. 19) | 828/926–1140 | fax 828/926–8811 | www.ghosttownsky.com | $20, special rates for children | Early May–late Oct., daily 9–6.

Santa's Land Fun Park and Zoo. This is the largest zoo in the Smokies. There are bears and monkeys, a magic show, Santa (naturally), rides, and lakes with paddle boats. | Rte. 1 Cherokee; About 20 mi from Maggie Valley | 828/497–9191 | $15 | Apr.–Nov.

Soco Gardens Zoo. Soco Gardens Zoo is just what the title says: a zoo with garden areas. Guided tours with nonvenomous and venomous snake shows are given, though visitors may opt to tour by themselves. There's also a petting area, reptile exhibits, large and small cats, bears, monkeys, and exotic species including lemurs. | 3578 Soco Rd. | 828/926–1746 | fax 828/926–0940, ext. 51 | $6 | May–Labor Day, daily 9–8; Labor Day–Oct., daily 10–6:30.

ON THE CALENDAR

JUNE: *Balloon Festival.* Hot-air balloon displays and rides, music, and vendors are all a part of the Balloon Festival. | 828/456–3021.

Dining

Eddie's Bar-B-Que. Barbecue. This place offers a large selection of barbecue fare. Beef, pork, chicken, ribs, and smoked turkey are accompanied by fried apples, sweet-potato pie, hush puppies, and baked beans. | 3028 Jonathan Creek, Rte. 276 | 828/926–5353 | $7–$11 | MC, V.

© Corbis

WILDFLOWER WATCH

The nonprofit Wildflower Program began in 1985 as a highway beautification project. Today, it is one of the largest and most successful in the country, with 22 varieties of flowers giving dazzling bursts of color to 3,500 acres of roadsides. Most of the flowers are in full bloom by the first of May, and they continue to bloom until the first frost in late October or early November.

Roadside Environmental personnel in 14 divisions across the state maintain the beds, many of which are marked by small, brightly colored NCDOT WILDFLOWER PROGRAM signs. The plantings involve upward of 30,000 pounds of seed. So great is the interest in this seasonal rite that beginning in May, NCDOT engineers submit weekly wildflower-watch reports. These reports, posted on the department's Web site (www.dot.state.nc.us), showcase the beds in full bloom.

Revenue from the sale of personalized license plates provides the principle source of funding for the gardening effort.

Guaybito's. Mexican. The authentically prepared food here makes this a great lunch spot. The Speedy Gonzalez is very good; it comes with one taco, an enchilada, and choice of beans or rice. Kids' menu. | 3422 Soco Rd. | 828/926–7777 | $4–$7 | AE, D, MC, V | Closed weekends.

J. Arthur's. American. This steak place has a rustic, log-cabin quality. Try the steak or the Gorgonzola salad. Kid's menu. | 2843 Soco Rd. | 828/926–1817 | Reservations not accepted except for groups of 10 or more | $10–$27 | AE, DC, MC, V | Closed Wed.–Sat. in winter, call for hrs.

Maggie Valley Resort and Country Club. Contemporary. You can enjoy a relaxing dinner in the Valley Room of the country club, which overlooks the Great Smokey Mountains and the first nine holes of the golf course. Try the filet mignon, New York strip steak, baby-back ribs, mountain trout almondine, or veal piccata. You can enjoy the fresh air and dine on the terrace; live music entertains Thursday–Saturday from May to October. Sample the lunch deli buffet May–October. Breakfast is served in season. | 1819 Country Club Dr. | 828/926–1616 | fax 828/926–2906 | golf@maggievalleyresort.com | www.maggievalleyresort.com | Reservations essential | Collared shirts only | $15–$31 | AE, MC, V, D.

Lodging

Abbey Inn. Mountain and valley views from every room have brought guests back to this inn perched about 1,000 ft above Maggie Valley. The rooms are individually treated in a country theme. Picnic area. Some kitchenettes, some refrigerators. Cable TV. Pets allowed. | 6375 Soco Rd. | 828/926–1188 or 800/545–5853 | fax 828/926–2389 | tours@abbeyinn.com | www.abbeyinn.com | 20 rooms | $49–$89 | AE, DC, MC, V | Closed Nov.–Mar.

Best Western Mountainbrook Inn. You can relax on rocking chairs on the porch and appreciate the grand view of the Great Smokey Mountains at this hotel. The rustic rooms have two queen-sized beds. The Ghost Town amusement park is one block from the inn, and a miniature golf course is two mi away. Picnic area, complimentary Continental breakfast. Microwaves, refrigerators. Cable TV. Pool. Hot tub. Driving range, 18-hole golf course, putting green. Business services. | 3811 Soco Rd. (U.S. 19) | 828/926–3962 | fax 828/926–2947 | 49 rooms | $75–$85 | AE, D, DC, MC, V.

Cataloochee Ranch. The rooms and cabins on this ranch have names such as Bluebird, Willow, or Cedar. Some rooms have fireplaces and cathedral ceilings; most have a breathtaking view of the Great Smoky and Blue Ridge mountains. Cookouts and mountain music entertainment make up the activities on this comfortable ranch. Hot tub. Tennis courts. Horseback riding. Downhill skiing. Business services. | 119 Ranch Dr. | 828/926–1401 or 800/868–1401 | fax 828/926–9249 | info@cataloochee-ranch.com | www.cataloochee-ranch.com | 15 rooms in 2 buildings, 2 suites, 11 cabins | $165, $210 suites, $195–$275 cabins | AE, MC, V.

Comfort Inn. The zoo, amusement park, and many other attractions are close to the Comfort Inn. Restaurant, complimentary Continental breakfast. Some in-room hot tubs (in suites). Cable TV. Pool. | 3282 Soco Rd. | 828/926–9106 | fax 828/926–9106 | 68 rooms | $79–99 | AE, D, DC, MC, V.

Four Seasons Inn. Creekside patio rooms have French doors that open up to the back patio, where oak rockers provide comfortable seating. Some kitchenettes, microwaves, refrigerators. Cable TV, in-room VCRs, room phones. | 4040 Soco Rd. (Rte. 19) | 828/926–8505 or 888/909–8505 | fax 828/926–8964 | www.fourseasons.com | 20 rooms | $59–$150 | AE, DC, MC, V.

Jonathan Creek Inn. Hand stenciling on the walls and decorative country wreaths give the rooms of Jonathan Creek Inn a homey, country-like touch. Private decks, included with some rooms, overlook a rushing creek. Restaurant, picnic area. Microwaves, refrigerators. Cable TV. Indoor pool. Fishing. Playground. | 4324 Soco Rd. | 828/926–1232 or 800/577–7812 | fax 828/926–9751 | www.jonathancreekinn.com | 42 rooms, 3 cottages | $80–$105, $1,000/wk cottages | AE, D, MC, V.

Ramada Inn. The Ghost Town In the Sky amusement park is just ½ mi from this chain hotel. Some rooms have balconies with creekside mountain views. Complimentary Continental breakfast. Microwaves, refrigerators. Cable TV. Indoor pool. Hot tub. Free parking. | Rte. 19 and Soco Rd. | 828/926–7800 or 888/289–2054 | fax 828/926–2176 | 46 rooms | $79–$129 | AE, D, DC, MC, V.

Rocky Waters. A quiet, idyllic place with well-maintained rooms. Picnic area. Some kitchenettes, some refrigerators. Cable TV. Pool, wading pool. Playground. | 4898 Soco Rd. | 828/926–1585 | 32 rooms | $65–$78 | AE, D, MC, V | Closed Nov.–Apr.

Stony Creek. As the owner says, you can "sleep on a creek" here, as a rambling stream runs through the back of the property. Stony Creek is near the Ghost Town amusement park. Picnic area. Some refrigerators. Cable TV. | 4494 Soco Rd. | 828/926–1996 | mandyh@brinet.com | 20 rooms | $40–$90 | MC, V.

MANTEO

MAP 8, L4

(Nearby towns also listed: Cape Hatteras National Seashore, Duck, Kill Devil Hills, Kitty Hawk, Nags Head, Outer Banks)

In addition to housing a lot of the commercial business area for Roanoke Island, Manteo has many sights related to the island's history. The waterfront is a pleasant place and is easily navigated.

Information: **Dare County Tourist Bureau** | 704 S. U.S. 64/264, Manteo 27954 | 252/473–2138 or 800/446–6262 | fax 252/473–5106 | visitorinfo@outerbanks.org | www.outerbanks.org/visitor-info | Weekdays 8–6, weekends 12–4.

Attractions

Elizabethan Gardens. These gardens are a lush re-creation of a 16th-century English garden, established as a memorial to the first English colonists who arrived between 1584 and 1587. | 1411 U.S. 64/264 | 252/473–3234 | fax 252/473–3244 | $5 | Mar.–Nov., daily 9–5; Dec.–Feb., weekdays 9–4.

Fort Raleigh National Historic Site. A restoration of the original 1585 earthworks that mark the beginning of English Colonial history in America. You can view the orientation film and then take a guided tour of the fort. A nature trail leads to an outlook over Roanoke Sound. | 252/473–5772 | fax 252/473–2595 | www.nps.gov/fora | Free | Daily 9–5; hrs may be extended June–Aug.

North Carolina Aquarium at Roanoke Island. One of three aquariums in the state, this one has a wetlands exhibit with turtles and amphibians, a shark exhibit, and a hands-on observation tank that is the aquatic equivalent of a petting zoo. | 374 Airport Rd.; off U.S. 64 | 252/473–3493 | fax 252/473–1980 | www.ncaquariums.com | $4 | Daily 9–7.

Roanoke Island Festival Park. *Elizabeth II* State Historic Site is across the street from the waterfront in Manteo. Costumed interpreters conduct tours of the 69-ft ship, a re-creation of a 16th-century vessel, except when it is on educational voyages in the off-season (call ahead). The park also has plays, concerts, arts-and-crafts exhibitions, and special programs. | 1 Festival Park | 252/475–1506 or 252/475–1500 information | fax 252/475–1507 | rift.information@ncmail.net | www.roanokeisland.com | $8 | Apr.–Oct., daily 9–6; Mar. and Nov.–Dec., daily 10–5.

Tuna Fever Charters. Full-day fishing for tuna, dolphin fish, wahoo, sailfish, and blue marlin. Boats go out when at least six people have made reservations; make reservations one week in advance. You must call ahead to be sure the boat has been filled. Offered through the Oregon Inlet Fishing Center. | 111 Gilbert St. | 800/272–5199 | $172 | Mar.–Nov. | D, MC, V.

ON THE CALENDAR
JUNE: *Wanchese Food Festival.* After the Blessing of the Fleet come educational displays, crab races, seafood, children's games, arts and crafts, and more seafood. | Harbor Rd., Wanchese | 252/441–8144.

JUNE–AUG.: *Lost Colony.* The country's first and longest-running outdoor drama reenacts the story of the first colonists who settled here in 1587 and then vanished without a trace. | Roanoke Island's Waterside Amphitheater, 1409 U.S. 64/264 | Sun.–Fri. 8:30 PM, no shows Sat. | 252/473–3414 or 800/488–5012.

SEPT.: *Oktoberfest.* For nearly 20 years the Weeping Radish Bavarian-style restaurant has hosted a two-day party with German oompah bands, traditional dancing, ethnic costumes, food, beer, and children's activities. | U.S. 64 | 252/473–1157 or 800/896–5403.

Dining
Clara's Seafood Grill. Seafood/Steak. Three dining rooms with an art deco look have spectacular views of the bay. You can feel the ocean breeze if you dine outdoors on the porch. Favored dishes are the she-crab soup, the tuna, and the baked Atlantic salmon. Kids' menu. Beer and wine only. | Sir Walter Raleigh St. | 252/473–1727 | fax 252/473–1723 | Reservations not accepted | $12–$20 | AE, D, MC, V | Closed Jan.–Feb.

1587. Contemporary. Nestled in the Tranquil House Inn, this dining spot is surrounded by beautiful boardwalks, sailboats, and the lulling sounds of the Shallowbag Bay lapping the shore. Inventive, artistically prepared entrées include tasty vegetarian dishes, sesame-crusted tuna with wasabi vinaigrette and shiitake mushrooms. Kids' menu. | 405 Queen Elizabeth Ave. | 252/473–1587 or 800/458–7069 | fax 252/473–1526 | www.1587.com | $18–$25 | AE, D, MC, V | Closed Dec.–Feb. No lunch.

Queen Anne's Revenge. Seafood. Queen Anne's Revenge is a stately old home with a plethora of art on its walls. Kids' menu. They serve beer and wine only. | 1064 Old Wharf Rd., Wanchese | 252/473–5466 | $24–$34 | AE, D, DC, MC, V | Closed Tues. No lunch.

Weeping Radish Brewery and Restaurant. German. A bavarian-style restaurant and microbrewery known for its schnitzel and sausages, this place has an annual post-Labor Day Oktoberfest weekend showcasing German and blues bands. Brewery tours are offered. | 525 S. Virginia Dare Trail | 252/473–1157 | $15–$26 | D, MC, V.

Lodging
Island House of Wachese B&B. Built in 1902, this two-story B&B is on the northern, inner portion of Roanoke Island, surrounded by Roanoke Sound. You can enjoy an acre of wooded scenery on the wraparound front porch. The house is in the center of this small fishing town, and you can walk to shops, restaurants, and beaches. Fishing, boating, and water sports are also available in town. Complimentary breakfast. Cable TV. Laundry facilities. No pets. No smoking. | 104 Old Wharf Rd. | 252/473–5619 | 4 rooms, 1 suite | $89–$135 | V.

Tranquil House Inn. This lodging stands on the Manteo waterfront, with views of Roanoke Sound and Shallowbag Bay. You can choose from rooms with canopy, four-poster, queen, or king-size beds, and even mini-suites with cozy sitting areas. Designer wallpapers, hardwood floors, Oriental rugs, Berber carpets, and flower arrangements enhance each room. | 25 rooms. Restaurant, complimentary Continental breakfast. No-smoking rooms. Cable TV. Business services. | 405 Queen Elizabeth St. | 252/473–1404 or 800/458–7069 | fax 252/473–1526 | www.1587.com | AE, D, MC, V.

MARION

(Nearby towns also listed: Asheville, Blue Ridge Parkway, Little Switzerland, Morganton)

About 40,000 people live in McDowell County; 5,000 of them make their home in Marion, the county seat. During the Civil War, deserters from both armies made their way to Marion to hide out in the area's caverns. Today visitors come looking not for refuge but for gold and gems in the area's mines.

Information: McDowell County Tourism Development Authority | 629 Tate St., Marion 28752 | 828/652–1103 or 888/233–6111 | www.mcdowellnc.org | Weekdays 9–5.

Attractions

Gem Mountain. Just north of Marion, Gem Mountain offers you the chance to pan along the flume line of the mountain for 20 types of gems, including amethysts, topazes, and emeralds. The guided mine tour runs June–August; reservations are required. Tours take you into the mountain where you are given mining tools to dig for your own gems. | 13780 Rte. 226 | 888/817–5829 | Free; $10 for gem collection bucket | March–Labor Day 9–7, Labor Day–Dec. 9–5, Mining Tours, June–Aug., Sat. 10–2.

ON THE CALENDAR

APR.: *Pioneer Day.* Revolutionary War reenactors, crafts, demonstrations, exhibits, food, and music make up Pioneer Day. | Mountain Gateway Museum, Old Fort | 828/668–9259.

MAY: *Gold Prospector's Meet.* Recreational mining equipment is displayed and sold, and there are nugget races, gold panning contests, treasure hunts, food, entertainment, and music—all at Vein Mountain's Lucky Strike Mine. | Polly Sprout Rd. | 828/738–4893.

OCT.: *Mountain Glory Festival.* Original arts and crafts, food vendors, entertainment with an emphasis on music, a quilt show, a 100K bike ride, and pet contests are all part of the festivities. | 828/652–2215.

DEC.: *Appalachian Potters Market.* Pottery is the main focus here, and the work of some 100 potters is represented. People line up very early to ensure they're first through the door at the start of the day. | McDowell High School, U.S. 70 W | 888/233–6111.

Dining

Harvest Drive-In. American. You will go back in time when you visit this curb-service and carry-out 1950s drive-in diner. The burgers, steaks, seafood, chicken, barbecue, ham, and a variety of sandwiches and side dishes are all favorites. | 423 N. Main St. (U.S. 70 W) | 828/652–4155 | $4–$14 | No credit cards | Closed Sun.

Little Siena Restaurant. Italian. A latticed ceiling intertwined with greenery adorns the main dining area of Little Siena. The Italian dishes are applauded (try the manicotti, spaghetti, or lasagna), as well as the rainbow trout, prime rib, and country ham. Kids' menu. Sun. brunch. | U.S. 70 and Rte. 80, Pleasant Gardens | 828/724–9451 | $6–$16 | D, MC, V | No lunch Sat.

Lodging

Comfort Inn. Situated 60 mi from Grandfather Mountain and 40 minutes from Linville Caverns, this hotel is also minutes from the home-turned-museum of Civil War general Rutherfordton, who also founded McDowell County. Complimentary Continental breakfast. Some microwaves, no-smoking rooms, refrigerators (in suites). Cable TV. Indoor pool. Hot tub. Exercise equipment. Laundry facilities. Business services. | U.S. 70/221 Bypass | 828/652–4888 | fax 828/652–3787 | 56 rooms, 6 suites | $89–$110 | AE, D, DC, MC, V.

Super8. This motel is at I–40 Exit 85. Complimentary Continental breakfast. Cable TV. No pets. | 4281 U.S. 221 S | 828/659–7940 | fax 828/659–3713 | www.super8.com | 60 rooms | $46–$65 | AE, D, MC, V.

MOREHEAD CITY

MAP 8, J6

(Nearby towns also listed: Atlantic Beach, Beaufort)

Morehead's history begins in the early 1700s with a land prospector. During the Civil War it was a stronghold for Union forces. Today it's a busy fishing and port city whose waterfront, thanks to a major face-lift, is attractive and spacious. On summer weekends, though, parking is still at a premium as people make their way to restaurants and specialty shops near the docks. Away from the waterfront, on side streets, are many refurbished historic residences serving as inns, galleries, and shops.

Information: Carteret County Tourism Development Bureau | 3409 Arendett St., Morehead City 28557 | 252/726–8148 or 800/786–6962. **Visitor Center** | 3409 Arendell St., Morehead City (U.S. 70 E) | 252/726–8148 | vacation@sunnync.com | www.ncbeach.com or www.sunnync.com | Weekdays 9–5, weekends 10–5.

Attractions

Carteret County Museum of History and Art. You can't miss the museum, which is housed in a yellow church building (circa 1907) with a big anchor out front. Inside are rotating exhibits that show how life used to be in this coastal community. There's an emphasis on the Native American heritage, schools, businesses, and homes. A research library attracts genealogists. | 100 Wallace Rd. | 252/247–7533 | fax 252/247–7533 | cchs@clif.com | www.roosweb.com/~hcchs | Free | Tues.–Sat. 1–4.

Fort Macon State Park. The park centers on the five-sided brick-and-stone fort built in 1834 to guard Beaufort Inlet. Activities include hiking, sunbathing, picnicking, swimming, and fishing. | E. Fort Macon Rd., Atlantic Beach | 252/726–3775 | fax 252/726–2497 | www.clis.com/friends | Free | Daily 9:30–5.

ON THE CALENDAR

JUNE: *Big Rock Blue Marlin Tournament.* With a purse near the $1 million mark, this tourney is one of the largest and oldest sportfishing contests. Also involved are fish-fries, parties, and daily weigh-ins of the catch. | Waterfront on Evans St. | 252/247–3575.
OCT.: *North Carolina Seafood Festival.* Lots of seafood, Blessing of the Fleet, ship tours, coastal educational exhibits, arts, crafts, entertainment—including storytelling and musicians—and rides make up this festival. | Waterfront on Evans St. | 252/726–6273.

Dining

Anchor Inn Restaurant. Seafood. You can savor seafood or steak in this quiet, romantic place. Favored dishes include prime rib, filet mignon, rib eyes, shrimp, flounder, oysters, or crab cake. Kids' menu. | 109 N. 28th St. | 252/726–2156 | $13–$21 | AE, D, MC, V | No lunch.

Bistro by the Sea. Continental. An upscale bistro known for fresh local seafood, where you can listen to live music on weekends. | 4031 Arendell St. | 252/247–2777 | Reservations not accepted except for 6 or more | $20–$35. | AE, D, DC, MC, V | Closed Sun.–Mon. and Jan.–early Feb.

Lodging

Comfort Inn. Next to the Morehead Shopping Center, ¼ mi from the Civic Center, and 2 mi from the beach. Complimentary Continental breakfast. In-room data ports. Cable TV, room phones. Outdoor pool. No pets. | 3100 Arendell St. | 252/247–3434 | fax 252/247–4411 | comfort@moreheadhotels.com | 101 rooms | $36–$150 | D, DC, MC, V.

Dill House. Built in 1918, this residence of former Mayor George Dill is a few blocks from the waterfront, shops, and restaurants. The house has some of its original French doors, Oriental carpets, and antiques. One of the rooms has a working fireplace. Dining room, complimentary breakfast. No air-conditioning in some rooms. Cable TV. Laundry facilities. Some pets allowed. No children under 10. | 1104 Arendell St. | 252/726–4449 | 2 rooms | $50–$125.

MORGANTON

MAP 8, C4

(Nearby towns also listed: Banner Elk, Blowing Rock, Boone, Hickory, Lenoir, Marion)

Backed by the foothills of the Blue Ridge Mountains in western North Carolina, Morganton was established by German and Scots–Irish immigrants in 1777 and incorporated in 1784 as Morganborough. The town was named for Revolutionary War General Daniel Morgan and is the seat of Burke County.

Today, many of Morganton's 16,500 residents work in the area's manufacturing and health-care industries. The town is home to the North Carolina School for the Deaf, as well as a number of correctional and mental-health facilities. Downtown Morganton is the city's historic district, with dozens of buildings dating back to the early 1900s and nearly 100 unique shops and boutiques. The downtown area has been undergoing extensive refurbishing and landscaping since the mid-90s and has lots of greenery, trees, and shady benches upon which to sit and people-watch. The Catawba River cuts through the center of town, and Lake James is just outside the city limits for boating, swimming, and soaking in the sun.

Information: Burke County Travel and Tourism Commission | 102 E. Union St. in Courthouse Square 28655 | 828/433–6793 or 888/46–2921.

Attractions

Brown Mountain Lights. On clear nights, strange lights of unexplained origin illuminate the sky outside of town. Witnesses first documented the phenomenon at the turn of the century, but local legend maintains that the lights have been appearing for hundreds of years. The best vantage points are along Hwy. 181 N. and from Wiseman's View in the Linville Gorge Wilderness Area west of town. | Hwy. 181 N | 828/433–6793 | Free.

Jailhouse Gallery. Since the mid-70s, this overhauled jailhouse has served as a public forum for local artists and traveling exhibits. In historic downtown Morganton. | Meeting St, on Courthouse Square | 828/433–7282 | Free | Mon.–Fri. 10–4.

Old Rock Schoolhouse. This structure was hand-built by Waldensian immigrants from Italy in the mid-1800s. The schoolhouse now houses an art gallery and performance space for local and touring theater and musical performers. | On Main St. in downtown Valdese, 4 mi. SE of Morganton | 828/879–2129 | Varies by event | Mon.–Fri. 9–5.

Old Burke County Courthouse. Built in 1837, this building once served as the summer quarters for the North Carolina Supreme Court. Now, it's home to the Burke Historical Foundation, a museum, and the Visitor Information Center. | On Courthouse Square, downtown Morganton | 828/437–4104 | Free | Mon.–Fri. 9–5, Sat. 10–1.

ON THE CALENDAR
MAY.: *Riverfest.* Held every year at Greenway Park, this spring fling features canoe trips on the Catawba river, plentiful food booths, games for kids, and live music. | 828/438–5266.

SEPT.: *Historic Morganton Festival.* This downtown event celebrates Morganton's rich history with tours, music, and a varying roster of themed activities and attractions. | 828/438–5280.

Dining

The Emporium. Contemporary. Panoramic mountain views spread in every direction from this casual establishment. The dining room has plenty of windows to capitalize on the vistas, and the blazing sunset makes for a majestic accompaniment to dishes like chicken Maui—a boneless, skinless chicken breast marinated and grilled with Hawaiian barbeque sauce, then covered with bacon and sautéed mushrooms and doused with melted monterey cheese. Seafood and pasta dishes are also on the menu. | Hwy. 321 between Morganton and Blowing Rock | 828/295–7661 | $5–$13 | AE,D,MC,V.

Lodging

Fairway Oaks B&B. Built specifically as a B&B in 1997, this modern farmhouse is just off the 5th tee of the meticulously maintained 18-hole Fairway Oaks golf course. Guest rooms have mountain views, and you can either head out onto the green for some putting, or relax on the vast front porch and watch the action from there. Golf packages available. Complimentary Continental breakfast. Cable TV, in-room VCRs. Golf. | 4640 Plantation Dr. | 828/584–7677 or 87/584–7611 | fax 828/584–8878 | 4 rooms | $65 | AE, D, MC, V.

Red Carpet Inn. This motel is near many restaurants and businesses in downtown Morgantown. Pets are allowed for a $5 fee, and you can rent videos at the front desk. Complimentary Continental breakfast. Some in-room microwaves, some in-room refrigerators. Cable TV, in-room VCRs. Outdoor pool. Pets allowed (fee). | 2217 S. Sterling St. | 828/437–6980 | 70 rooms | $48–$58 | AE, D,MC, V.

MOUNT AIRY

MAP 8, A3

(Nearby town also listed: Winston-Salem)

At the foot of the Blue Ridge Mountain range, only 3 mi from the Virginia border, Mount Airy was settled in the late 1700s by English, Scots–Irish, and German immigrants.

The economy of Mount Airy was for many years—and still is, though to a lesser extent—based on the area's granite quarries, which produce raw material for buildings and monuments far beyond the town borders.

Today, Mount Airy is perhaps best known as the birthplace and childhood home of television personality Andy Griffith. Griffith used his hometown as the inspiration for the fictional community of Mayberry, which was the setting for his popular TV program *The Andy Griffith Show.* Mayberry memorabilia can be found all over Mount Airy, as can Griffith's boyhood house and the shops and diners upon which he patterned the iconic TV town.

Information: Mount Airy Visitors Center | 615 N. Main St., Mount Airy, 27030 | 336/789–4636 or 800/576–0231.

Attractions

Andy Griffith Playhouse. In 1920, this building was constructed as a public school, but the area arts council purchased it in the mid-80s and overhauled it into a theater and arts center. Concerts, theater productions, and art exhibits pepper the schedule of events here. | 218 Rockford St. | 336/786–7998 or 800/286–6193 | Varies per event.

Mayberry Jail. This used to be a real, functioning jail and municipal building post WWII, but now the space has turned into a reproduction of the jail from *The Andy Griffith Show,* complete with Andy's desk and "Justice of the Peace" sign. Outside, a genuine 1962 Ford

Galaxie police cruiser is permanently parked at the curb. | 215 City Hall, downtown | 336/789–4636 or 800/576–0231 | Free | Mon.–Fri. 8–4:30. Closed Sat.–Sun.

Mt. Airy Visitors Center. The small house that holds the main community visitor center also has the largest collection of Andy Griffith memorabilia in the nation, including TV props, personal effects, and promotional materials. Other exhibits at the Center include local mining history displays, and information on the famous Chang and Eng Bunker—the "original" Siamese Twins, who made their home in nearby White Plains in the mid-1800s. | 615 N. Main St. | 336/789–4636 or 800/576–0231 | Free | Mon.–Sat. 9–5, Sun. 11–4:30.

Pilot Mountain State Park. Encompassing 3,800 acres in two counties, this wilderness area has two sections joined by a 5 mi-long, 300-ft-wide hiking corridor. You can go canoeing, horseback riding, birdwatching, or camping here. | Rte. 3, in Pinnacle | 336/325–2355 | $5 per car, camping fees vary.

Pilot Mountain. Area Native Americans used this huge, cylindrical rock formation as a navigational guide, and early settlers christened it "Mt. Ararat," after the rock upon which Noah's ark came to rest. The 1,400-foot peak is the geological centerpiece of Pilot Mountain State Park. The main peak itself is not open to the public, but a park visitor center at the base offers informational literature and wagon-trail tours of the area. | Hwy. 52 to the west of Mount Airy | 336/325–2355 | Free.

ON THE CALENDAR

SEPT.: *Mayberry Days.* Celebrate Andy Griffith's contributions to Hollywood and the town that inspired him to create Mayberry and its cast of memorable characters. The yearly event includes a celebrity golf tournament, a talent show, Mayberry trivia competitions, and a pie-eating contest. | 366/786–7998 or 800/286–6193.

OCT.: *Autumn Leaves Festival and Craft Show.* Juried craftspeople, food vendors, bluegrass musicians, and a carnival atmosphere converge on downtown Mount Airy to celebrate the changing seasons. | 336/786–6116 or 800/948–0949.

YEAR-ROUND: *Bluegrass Jam Sessions.* These free concerts not only give you the chance to hear some genuine, down-home bluegrass music, but if you happen to bring along your fiddle or harmonica, you can join in the fun. Held most weekends in various spots throughout town. | 336/786–7998.

Dining

Bluebird Diner. American. Right downtown, this old-school diner is a piece of classic Americana. Summer brings lots of tourists, but locals still gather here for coffee and chat. Hearty sandwiches, casseroles, and handmade soups and desserts are on the menu. | 206 N. Main St. | 336/783–0006 | $3–$7 | No credit cards.

Snappy Lunch. American. Bologna sandwiches used to be a nickel at this classic American diner. The owner's been plying his trade since 1950, and not much has changed in the place that invented the "pork chop sandwich" made famous by Barney Fife on *The Andy Griffith Show*. You can grab a booth or sit at the counter to dig into an old-fashioned burger and fries. | 125 N. Main St. | 336/786–4931 | $2–$5 | No credit cards | No dinner. Closed Sun.

Lodging

Carriage House B&B. Right in the middle of Mount Airy's historic district, this Georgian brick home offers something that few of its ilk can claim; horse-drawn carriage tours of the area and downtown Mount Airy conducted by the innkeeper. Guest rooms are outfitted with a cozy blend of antique and reproduction furniture, and a patio out back provides space and quiet after a day of sightseeing. Complimentary Continental breakfast. No room phones, TV in common area. | 218 Cherry St. | 336/789–7864 or 800/707–8789 | fax 336/786–6258 | 4 | $60–$125 | AE, MC, V.

Comfort Inn. This motel is a few blocks from the shops and restaurants in Mount Airy. Complimentary Continental breakfast. Cable TV, room phones. Outdoor pool. Pets allowed. | 2136 Rockford St. | 336/789–2000 | 98 rooms | $60–$90 | AE, D, DC, MC, V.

MURFREESBORO

(Nearby towns also listed: Ahoskie, Roanoke Rapids)

Located in the Albemarle region, between the Roanoke and Chowan Rivers, the Murfreesboro area was first visited by John White of Roanoke Island in the 16th century, then by an expedition from Jamestown, Virginia in the 17th century. During this time the principal inhabitants were several Indian tribes, including the Meherrins. In Colonial times it became a port of call for sailing vessels that brought goods from New England, the West Indies, and Europe in exchange for local naval stores (products including turpentine and pitch) and agricultural products. In fact, it was the abundance of raw materials that led many New England shipping families to relocate to northeastern North Carolina. Evidence of their presence is still strongly felt in this quiet college town, which was incorporated in 1787 and named for a Revolutionary War hero.

Information: Roberts-Vaughan Visitor Center | 116 E. Main St., Murfreesboro 27855 | 252/398–5922 | fax 252/398–5871 | histassn@albemarlenet.com | www.murfreesboronc.com.

Attractions

Brady C. Jefcoat Museum of Americana. The old Murfreesboro high school (circa 1922) was restored by the historical association and filled with over 10,000 artifacts collected by one man. It's the nation's largest collection of washing-machine equipment, irons, and butter churns. | 201 W. High St. | 252/398–5922 | $3 | Sat. 11–4, Sun. 2–5.

Chowan College. Founded in 1848, this four-year liberal arts school stands between the Roanoke and Chowan rivers. Thanks to its 300 acres of woodlands and lakes, it has one of the most scenic campuses in the state. While its landmark building is an antebellum mansion known as McDowell Columns, a state-of-the-art fiber optic system connects all buildings to a campus network and the Internet. The study of ethics is an integral part of the curriculum. Students hail from at least 27 states and several countries. | 200 Jones Dr. | 252/398–6500 or 800/488–4101 | fax 252/398–1190 | admissions@chowan.edu | www.chowan.edu | Daily.

Historic Murfreesboro. There are 62 historic buildings and sites in Murfreesboro, an architectural treasure trove. Guided tours of the 12-block National Register historic district in the center of town begin at the circa 1814 Roberts-Vaughan House, home to the historical association, chamber of commerce, and public library. Beautifully preserved examples of 18th- and 19th-century buildings, including a country store and the childhood home of famed military doctor Walter Reed are on the tour. | 116 E. Main St. | 252/398–5922 | $5 | Mon.–Fri. 8–5.

ON THE CALENDAR

AUG.: *Watermelon Festival.* Parades, contests (including seed spitting), rides, crafts, food, live entertainment, and fireworks over a three day period in early August celebrate summer and this most summery food. | Historic district | 252/398–5922.

DEC.: *Candlelight Christmas in Historic Murfreesboro.* Held evenings the first Tuesday and Wednesday in December, this event features caroling and instrumental music, horse and buggy rides, costumed street vendors, and food served in historic buildings dressed for the holiday. | Historic district | 252/398–5922 | $20 adults, $7 children.

Dining

China Garden. Chinese. For nearly 20 years, locals have flocked to this small, family-owned restaurant not far from the town's center. They come not only for the atmosphere—soft music, black-lacquer furniture, and colorful silk screens—but for the inexpensive lunch specials and a dinner menu that always features the favorites: orange chicken, sesame chicken, pepper steak, and an assortment of teas. | 611 E. Main St. | 252/398–3725 | fax 252/398–4986 | $10–$20 | MC, V | Closed Mon.

Napoli Pizza & Italian Restaurant. Italian. The interior of this independently-owned restaurant is familiar territory, just what you'd find in pizzerias across the country—a red, white, and green color scheme, lots of booths, and a salad bar. But the large specialty salads and pizzas served for both lunch and dinner are standouts. Beer and wine are sold as well. | 331 E. Main St. | 252/398–3687 | $10–$15 | No credit cards.

Whitley's Barbecue. Barbecue. All self-respecting towns in the eastern part of the state have a joint like this: a plain, roomy building, often wood-paneled, filled with long wood tables at which copious quantities of barbecued chicken or pork, fried chicken, hush puppies, cole slaw, various greens (collards, turnips), and iced tea (but no alcohol) are served. An array of homemade cakes and pies is always displayed. | 315 Beechwood Blvd. | 252/398–4884 | $5–$10 | AE, D, MC, V | Closed Mon.

Lodging
Piper House B&B. Sitting on nearly an acre of landscaped grounds near Chowan College, this spacious, tree-shaded 1935 country French house has a dramatic vestibule with a hung stairway. Breakfast is served in the dining room under a crystal chandelier, and one guest bathroom has the epitome of Art Deco luxury: a big, square, black bathtub. Complimentary breakfast. Some room phones. No pets. No children under 12. No smoking. | 809 E. High St. | 252/398–3531 | cmpiper@coastalnet.com | 3 rooms | $60–$70 | MC, V.

Winborne House B&B. The original woodwork and painted flooring in this Greek Revival home, built in 1818 and renovated in 1850, remain intact. Antique furniture and wavy window glass add interest to this lodging 1 from town, as do the marbleized baseboards. A large front porch welcomes guests, many of whom are visiting Chowan College. The owners, active in the local historical society, offer tours of significant sites. Complimentary breakfast. No pets. No children under 10. No smoking. | 333 Jay Trail | 252/398–5224 | 2 rooms share bath | $35–$40 | No credit cards.

Woodson Manor B&B. The exterior of this Cape Cod-style home, with its goldfish pond, jasmine-covered gazebo, natural-plant fence, and profusion of flowers, is a garden-lover's delight. The interior, featuring original art and a large collection of blue-and-white porcelain, is well-coordinated. The ceiling of the red dining room is trellised with ivy, and the cheery sunroom, with its French doors, is a favorite quiet spot. Complimentary breakfast. TV in common area. No pets. No children under 12. No smoking. | 301 Holly Hill Rd. | 252/398–4142 | fax 252/398–5142 | 2 | $80 | MC, V.

NAGS HEAD

MAP 8, L4

(Nearby towns also listed: Cape Hatteras National Seashore, Duck, Kill Devil Hills, Kitty Hawk, Manteo, Outer Banks)

Nags Head has been a vacation destination since the 1830s, when mainland planters came to the shore to take the cool sea breezes and get away from the stifling heat of inland areas. Before its settlement as a vacation community, the portion of the Outer Banks that Nags Head now occupies was a haven for both land and sea pirates, who legend has it used lanterns mounted on horseback to lure ususpecting ships in to shore where they ran aground in shallow waters and were sittng ducks for the plundering pirates.

Today, Nags Head's towering sand dunes and woodland areas attract kite-flying enthusiasts, hang-gliders, swimmers, anglers, and nature-lovers. The shipwrecks left behind by the pirates of the last century still lie beneath the waves, tempting treasure-hunters and scuba-divers with the promise of wealth—or at least an afternoon's adventure.

Information: Outer Banks Visitors Bureau | 704 S. Hwy. 64/264, Manteo, 27954 | 252/473–2138.

Attractions

Jockey's Ridge State Park. Home to the largest "living" sand dune on the East Coast, this 400-acre park (and its 140-ft dune) is a favorite among kite-flyers and hang-gliders. A visitor information center is on-site. | 5 mi north of Nags Head on BR 158 | 252/473–2138 | Free.

Bodie Island Lighthouse. The third-oldest working lighthouse in the area, this black-and-white banded tower stands 156 ft above the ground. Though the lighthouse itself is not open to the public, the keeper's house below serves as an information center, and the surrounding marshland is open for self-guided nature and bird-watching tours. | Hwy. 12 between Nags Head and the Oregon Inlet | 252/473–2138 | Free.

ON THE CALENDAR

MAY: *Hang-Gliding Spectacular and Air Games.* The oldest hang-gliding competition in the nation, this event draws gliders and flyers from all over the world who come to execute aerial stunts over the Jockey's Ridge Park at Nags Head and Currituck County Airport. | 252/441–4124 or 800/334–4777.
NOV.: *Wings Over Water.* This three-day event, held the first weekend in November, celebrates the wildlife and wildlands of North Carolina, with field trips, workshops, and seminars held throughout Nags Head and its surrounds. | 252/441–4966.

Dining

Nags Head Fishing Pier. Seafood. Perched on one end of the oldest and longest pier on the Outer Banks, the dining room here commands some serious water views. The room is very casual, with lots of light pine planking and plastic deck furniture for seating. The menu features crab, shellfish, and fish filets, but the real bonus is that after a successful day on the end of the pier, you can bring in your own pre-cleaned catch and have it cooked to your specifications. | On the fishing pier, downtown Nags Head | 252/441–5141 | $7–$18 | AE, D, MC, V.

Tortuga's Lie. Seafood. Hunkered down against the dunes in a bright, aqua-blue building, this smallish spot has a distinct Carribbean flavor. Colored pennants and wooden beams shade the spacious patio, and the varied menu has items like porkloin chops rubbed with jerk sauce, grilled, and topped with habanero pepper jelly. You can get fresh-from-the-water local seafood, too, and there's a sushi bar on Wednesday nights. Sand volleyball courts out back provide friendly pre-meal competition, and the adjacent souvenir shop has caps and T-shirts. | At milepost 11.5 on Beach Rd. | 252/441–7299 | $11–$14 | AE, D, MC, V.

Lodging

Nags Head Beach Inn. A 70-year-old cedar shake cottage, this inn is 100 yards from the dune line. Complimentary breakfast. Some in-room safes. No pets. No smoking. | 303 Admiral St. | 252/441–8466 | 8 rooms, 2 suites | $45–$155 | AE, D, MC, V.

Nags Head Tar Heel Motel. A basic motel in the center of Nags Head. Some microwaves, some refrigerators. Cable TV. Outdoor pool. No pets. | 7010 S. Virginia Dare Tr. | 252/441–6150 | 29 rooms, 4 efficiencies | $58–$80 | AE, MC, V.

Ocean Veranda Oceanfront Motel. This beach motel has a playground, grill area, and outdoor showers. It is adjacent to a resort, golf course, and restaurants and is 5 mi from miniature golf, an amusement park, go-carts, and Jockey's Ridge State Park. Two rooms have an ocean view. Two restaurants, picnic area. Some kitchenettes, some microwaves, some refrigerators. Cable TV. Outdoor pool. No pets. No smoking. | 2603 S. Virginia Dare Trail | 800/582–3224 or 252/441–5858 | 30 suites | $45–$170 | AE, D, MC, V.

NEW BERN

MAP 8, J5

(Nearby towns also listed: Atlantic Beach, Jacksonville, Kinston, Morehead City)

Occupying some prime real estate at the junction of the Trent and Neuse Rivers and the northern edge of the Croatan National Forest, New Bern is a nature-lover's paradise. The town was originally settled in 1710 by Swiss and German exploerers led by Christopher de Graffenreid, who named the town after his hometown in Switzerland. In the 19th century, New Bern's strategic location made it a major trading port—and a target for Union soldiers during the Civil War. Raized by fire and war, New Bern has had to rebuild itself more than once.

The modern incarnation of New Bern has three major historic districts around the downtown area and scores of Registered Historic Landmarks. Over 150 buildings in town have been recognized for their historical or architectural significance.

Information: Convention and Visitors Bureau | 314 S. Front St.,New Bern, 28560 | 252/637–9400.

Attractions

Cherry Point MACS. Home of the largest Marine Corps Air Station in the nation, this spot has year-round tours that may include military working dogs, search-and-rescue helicopters, a crash fire and rescue demonstration, or flying squadrons, depending on the season. | Highway 101 and Roosevelt Blvd. | 252/466–4906 | www.visitnewbern.com | Free | June–Aug., Thurs. 9–11 AM; Sept.–May, first and third Thurs. 9–11 AM.

Croatan National Forest. 157,000 acres of unspoiled wilderness along the Neuse River is home to countless species of wildlife and plants, including the rare and unusual, bug-eating Venus Flytrap. | Hwy. 70 6 mi E. of downtown New Bern | 252/636–4060 | Free.

Firemen's Museum. An extensive assembly of antique firefighting equipment, including steam-engine fire trucks, hooks, ladders, and hoses, is showcased here, along with photos and Civil War-era relics. | 410 Hancock St. | 252/636–4087 | Free | Mon.–Fri. 10–4.

New Bern Academy. In New Bern's oldest residential district, this small museum traces the community's history from the early 1700s to the Civil War. Exhibits change periodically. | Corner of Hancock and New Sts. | 252/672–1690 | Free | Mon.–Fri. 10–4.

Tryon Palace. This gradiose structure anchors New Bern's largest historic district. It was originally the home of Governor William Tryon, who ruled the colony of North Carolina for the British Crown before the Revolutionary War. Today, the mansion is full of antiques and an extensive art collection and is surrounded by beautifully landscaped gardens. Two other homes make up the Tryon Palace complex, and costumed re-enactors lead tours and demonstrations throughout the day. | 600 block of Pollock St. | 800/767–1560 | Free | Mon.–Fri. 9–4.

ON THE CALENDAR

MAY: *Strawberry Festival.* Anything and everything good that can be made with strawberries makes an appearance at this yearly celebration, along with music, food, and amusements. | 252/244–0017.

OCT.: *Ghost Walk.* You can tour some of New Bern's possibly haunted (but definitely beautiful) old mansions during this Halloween-time event. Keep your eyes open for spectral activity. | 252/638–8558.

DEC.: *Tryon Palace Holiday Candlelight Tours.* Period decorations adorn the interior of the fabulous Tryon Palace for the holidays. The gardens are open to the public, and costumed tour guides lead you through room after room of opulent antiques and one-of-a-kind works of art. | 252/514–4900.

Dining

Billy's Ham 'n Eggs. American. If you're feeling the need for some down-home comfort food, Billy's is the place to go in New Bern. Fried hash browns, waffles, flapjacks, and (of course) ham and eggs are all on the menu here, but if you're not in the mood for breakfast, you can get a juicy burger, or some broiled trout, or even deep-fried clam strips. All the soups and desserts are homemade. Open 24 hours. | 1300 S. Glenburnie Rd. | 252/633–5498 | $3–$6 | AE, MC, V.

The Chelsea. Contemporary. The historic building that now houses the Chelsea used to contain the pharmacy of Caleb Bradham, the inventor of Pepsi-Cola. The menu has hearty-yet-creative sandwiches—like the smoked turkey with raspberry mayonnaise—as well as burgers and grilled chicken. Live music. | 325 Middle St. | 252/637–5409 | $12–$20 | AE, D, MC, V | Closed Sun.

Friday's 1890 Seafood. Seafood. The dimly lit, dark-wood interior of this street-level eatery brings to mind the innards of a pirate ship, or an 18th-century schooner. Seating is intimate, and the food is mostly aquatic—you can consider the crab legs, or perhaps ultra-fresh river trout. The menu has steak and chicken dishes as well, but the seafood is the real standout here. | 2307 Neuse Blvd. | 252/637–2276 | $10–$14 | AE, MC, V.

Henderson House. Continental. A restored historic home provides the backdrop for a romantic evening, with private dining rooms, white-linen tablecloths, and lots of soft, gold light. Menu choices are classic Continental cuisine—medallions of veal, pheasant with port-wine sauce, and duck a l'orange. Jacket required. Reservations essential. | 216 Pollock St. | 252/637–4784 | $30–$40 | AE, D, MC, V | No lunch. Closed Sun.–Mon.

Lodging

Days Inn. This spot is four blocks from Tryon Palace and downtown. Complimentary Continental breakfast. Some in-room data ports, some microwaves, some refrigerators. Cable TV, room phones. Outdoor pool. Health club. No pets. | 925 Broad St. | 800/325–2525 | 101 rooms, 8 suites | $50–$60 | D, DC, MC, V.

Holiday Inn Express. Four miles from Tryon Palace historic sites and gardens, this hotel is the same distance from restaurants and shops. Complimentary Continental breakfast. In-room data ports, some in-room minibars, some microwaves, some refrigerators, some in-room hot tubs. Cable TV. Outdoor pool. Health club. Baby-sitting. Laundry service. No pets. | 3455 Dr. Martin Luther King Blvd. | 252/638–8266 | 57 rooms, 3 suites | $70–$110 | AE, D, MC, V.

OCRACOKE

MAP 8, L5

(Nearby towns also listed: Buxton, Cape Hatteras National Seashore, Cedar Island, Hatteras, Outer Banks)

Ocracoke Island, only about 16 mi long, is the end of the road for those traveling south on the Outer Banks. The pace is slower on this sliver of sand, which has changed shape through time thanks to the operation of the elements.

Much of the island is part of Cape Hatteras National Seashore and is only accessible by water or air. Ocracoke Village, the only town on the island, was cut off from the world for so long that locals still speak in quasi-Elizabethan accents. Today, shops, motels, and restaurants here are clustered around Silver Lake Harbor, the site of Blackbeard's death in 1718.

Information: Greater Hyde County Chamber of Commerce | Box 178, Swan Quarter 27885 | 888/493–3826 | hydecocc@beachlink.com.

Attractions

Ocracoke to Hatteras Ferry. This ride takes 40 minutes and leaves on the half hour or hour depending on the time of day. Reservations for autos are recommended. | Rte. 12 | 252/928–3841 or 800/345–1665 | www.ncferry.org | Free | Daily.

Ocracoke Island Visitor Center. Operated by the National Park Service as part of the Cape Hatteras National Seashore, the center has an information desk, a small bookshop, and exhibits. | Ocracoke Village | 252/928–4531 | Free | Memorial Day–Labor Day, daily 8:30–6.

Ocracoke Lighthouse. Built in 1823, this is the state's oldest and, at 75 ft, shortest operating lighthouse. You can walk up close to the light, but you cannot enter. There's an old graveyard behind the lighthouse. | Point Rd. | 252/473–2111 | Free | Daily.

Ocracoke Pony Pen. From a platform you can observe the direct descendants of Spanish mustangs that once roamed the island. The unruly herd is now cared for by the National Park Service. During rough weather these rugged horses take shelter near the southwest end of the island, where they have a retreat. | Rte. 12 | 252/928–4531 | Free | Daily.

ON THE CALENDAR

MAY: *British Cemetery Ceremony.* Held to honor the sailors of the HMS *Bedfordshire*, buried in Ocracoke after their ship was torpedoed offshore in 1942. A British official attends the U.S. Coast Guard's memorial service each year. | 252/928–6711.

Dining

Back Porch. Seafood. Crab beignets, smoked local fish, and crab cakes are the stars in the juniper-paneled dining room. Or eat outside on the screened porch. Beer and wine only. | 110 Back Rd. | 252/928–6401 | Reservations not accepted | No lunch | $20–$30 | D, MC, V.

Café Atlantic. Seafood. Known for grilled and sautéed local seafood, this restaurant serves meals in simple surroundings on two levels. Beer, wine, and spirits are available. Sunday brunch. Kids' menu. Reservations accepted for parties of five or more. | Rte. 12 | 252/928–4861 | Closed late Oct.–early Mar. | $25–$35 | AE, D, MC, V.

Creekside. American/Casual. There's a great view of the harbor from this second-floor location that's decked out in nautical attire. Crab cakes, fresh fish, and local catches of the day are all on the menu. Oyster burgers and shrimp salad pitas make for something a little different. You can also try the homemade "blackened" seasoning. | 368 Rte. 12 | 252/928–3606 | Closed Nov.–March; call for hrs in spring and fall | $4–$14 | D, MC, V.

Howard's Pub and Raw Bar. American/Casual. Large oak and walnut tables accommodate larger groups for a hearty lunch or dinner. Live music attracts a younger set at night. Burgers, sandwiches, and seafood are served along with home-smoked ribs and local catches. Come for a full meal or just for the raw bar and a beer. | Rte. 12 | 252/928–4441 | Reservations not accepted | $9–$24 | D, DC, MC, V.

Island Inn and Dining Room. Seafood. Central to the village, this eatery specializes in crab cakes, hush puppies, and oyster omelets. Piano and fiddle music is performed on Tuesdays. Breakfast is also served. | 100 Lighthouse Rd. (Rte. 12) | 252/928–7821 | Closed Dec.–Feb. No lunch | $10–$16 | D, MC, V.

Pony Island Motel Restaurant. Seafood. You can bring your own fish in to be cooked. Otherwise, the menu is mostly fried seafood. Try the "pony potatoes"—hash browns with salsa and cheese. Breakfast is also served. | Rte. 12 and Oceanview Rd. | 252/928–5701 | Closed Nov.–Mar. No lunch | $15–$25 | D, MC, V.

Lodging

Anchorage Inn. The four stories of this hotel overlook the Ocracoke Harbor. The beach is 2 mi away. Complimentary Continental breakfast. Cable TV. Pool. Some pets allowed. | Rte. 12 | 252/928–1101 | fax 252/928–6322 | www.theanchorageinn.com | 35 rooms | $114–$125 | D, MC, V.

Berkley Manor. The main building of this Ocracoke Village inn was built in the 1860s. The four-story tower affords a good view of the island. Rooms have a Caribbean getaway theme. Complimentary breakfast. Some in-room hot tubs. Cable TV in common area. Library. No kids under 15. No smoking. | Rte. 12 | 252/928–5911 or 800/832–1223 | fax 252/928–7945 | berkleymanor@beachlink.com | www.berkleymanor.com | 12 rooms in 2 buildings | $125–$195 | AE, D, MC, V.

Bluff Shoal. Every room opens onto a porch at this inn adjacent to the harbor. Rooms have twin or queen beds. You can fish or relax on the private dock and deck. Refrigerators. Cable TV. | Rte. 12 | 252/928–4301 or 800/292–2304 | 7 rooms | $75–$85 | D, MC, V.

Boyette House. The two buildings of this inn are connected by a large deck. Take a nap on one of the hammocks or rocking chairs on the wide porch. Some microwaves. Cable TV. Outdoor hot tub. | Rte. 12 | 252/928–4261 or 800/928–4261 | www.boyettehouse.com | 22 rooms, 2 suites | $60–$90, $145–$160 suites | D, MC, V.

Crews Inn B&B. This B&B is in the center of town but set back from the road. Bedrooms are furnished with turn-of-the-20th-century iron beds. You can stroll in the English garden, sit in the main dining area, or sit on the screened-in wraparound porch. Dining room, complimentary Continental breakfast. No pets. No smoking. | 460 Back Rd. | 252/928–7011 | www.ocracoke.com | 5 rooms share 3 baths | $45–$65 | D, MC, V.

Pirates Quay Hotel. Across the road from Silver Lake, which is visible from all units. Each two-bedroom unit has a living area and a private courtyard where you can grill, picnic, and sunbathe. In the center of town. Kitchenettes, microwaves, refrigerators, hot tubs. Cable TV, some in-room VCRs. Lake. No pets. | 95 Silver Lake Rd. | 252/928–3002 | fax 252/928–4102 | corrinnes@beachlink.com | 5 2-bedroom units | $1,200–$1,500 | MC, V.

Pony Island. Within walking distance of Ocracoke Lighthouse, this three-story wood building is served by the restaurant next door. Picnic area. Some kitchenettes. Cable TV. Pool. Bicycles. | 252/928–4411 | fax 252/928–2522 | 50 rooms | $87–$142 | Call for winter schedule | D, MC, V.

OUTER BANKS

INTRO
ATTRACTIONS
DINING
LODGING

OUTER BANKS

MAP 8, L6

(Nearby towns also listed: Beaufort, Buxton, Cape Hatteras National Seashore, Cedar Island, Duck, Hatteras, Kill Devil Hills, Kitty Hawk, Manteo, Morehead City, Nags Head, Ocracoke)

North Carolina's Outer Banks, a series of barrier islands on the Atlantic Ocean, stretch from the Virginia state line south to Cape Lookout. Throughout history these waters have been the nemesis of shipping, earning the nickname "the Graveyard of the Atlantic". The network of lighthouses and lifesaving stations draws people today; many of the submerged wrecks attract scuba divers. English settlers landed here in the 16th century and attempted to colonize the region, but they disappeared without a trace. The islands' coves and inlets provided a safe haven for pirates. For many years, the Outer Banks remained isolated, home to only a few families who made their living by fishing. Today, linked by bridges and ferries, the islands have become popular destinations. Much of the area is included in the Cape Hatteras and Cape Lookout national seashores.

The 120-ml stretch of Route 12 from Corolla, at the northern tip, to Ocracoke, the southernmost point, can be driven in a day, but plenty of time must be allowed during the summer months for ferry connections and heavy traffic.

The islands are most beautiful when experienced in their natural state: dune-rimmed white-sand beaches and dense maritime forests. Mile markers (MM) or mile posts (MP) are used to indicate addresses for sites where there aren't many buildings. During major storms and hurricanes the roads and bridges become clogged with traffic. In that case, follow the blue-and-white evacuation signs.

Information: Dare County Tourist Bureau | Box 399, Manteo 27954 | 252/473–2138 or 800/446–6262 | dctb-info@outer-banks.com | www.outer-banks.com/visitor-info.

(For listings, see the individual towns: Buxton, Cape Hatteras National Seashore, Hatteras, Kill Devil Hills, Kitty Hawk, Nags Head, Ocracoke)

PILOT MOUNTAIN

MAP 8, E3

(Nearby towns also listed: Mount Airy, Winston-Salem)

The Indians called Surry County's most prominent geographical feature "Jomeokee," which roughly translates to "great guide" or "piiot." (Andy Griffith referred to it as "Mt. Pilot" on numerous episodes of his early television show.) This formation is a quartzite monadnock, a highly resistant rock. Scientists estimate that it has survived millions of years while the elements eroded the surrounding foothills.

Information: Greater Mount Airy Chamber of Commerce | Box 913, Mount Airy 27030 | 336/786–6116 or 800/948–0949 | www.visitmayberry.com.

Attractions

The Hacker House Haunted Adventure. The expansive Hacker House grounds includes the Enigma Theater, the Garden, the Dark Forest, the Hacker Mortuary, and Macabre Midway. There are two tours available. Not recommended for kids under eight. | 712 Old Westfield Rd. | 336/351–3275 | www.hackerhouse.com | $9–$13 | October.

Pilot Mountain State Park. Rising out of nowhere, 1,400 ft above the surrounding countryside, this mountain is capped by two vegetation-covered knobs: Big Pinnacle and Little Pinnacle. Rock climbing and rappelling are favorite activities here. Hiking, horseback riding, picnicking, canoeing, camping, fishing, and educational programs are also popular. | U.S. 52, Pinnacle | 336/325–2355 | fax 336/325–2751 | ils.unc.edu/parkproject/pimo.html | Free, fee for camping | Nov.–Feb., daily 8–6; Mar.–Oct., daily 8–7; Apr., May, Sept., daily 8–8; June–Aug., daily 8 AM–9 PM.

ON THE CALENDAR

OCT.: *Cornshucking Frolic*. Harvesting, shucking, shelling, and grinding of corn highlight the happenings at the Horne Creek Living Historical Farm. Cider making, quilting, woodworking, cooking, and other crafts demonstrations as done a century ago. | 336/325–2298.

Dining

Cousin Gary's. American. Down-home Southern cooking is complemented by all-American staples at this restaurant. Daily specials include chicken casserole, lasagna, ribs and sauerkraut, and chicken and dumplings. Breakfasts. Lunch and dinner buffets. Kids' menu. | 606 S. Key St. | 336/368–1488 | $4–$6 | MC, V.

Mountain View. American. Known for beef, fish, and ham dinners, as well as vegetables and breads, the restaurant also has a selection of Italian entrées. A buffet breakfast is served every Saturday, a buffet lunch is prepared on weekdays. | Rte. 268 | 336/368–9180 | Reservations not accepted | $5–$7 | MC, V.

Lodging

Scenic Overlook B&B. This three-story brick building is set on 100 acres of land about 4 mi from the center of town. Pilot Mountain can be seen from every room. Hardwood floors and antique furniture are accented by handmade quilts and fresh flowers in all the rooms. Each of the six cabins, formerly Civil War-era tobacco barns, has a bedroom, living room with stone fireplace, bathroom with dry-sauna, kitchen, and front porch. Dining room, picnic area, complimentary breakfast. Some in-room data ports, some in-room safes, some kitchenettes, some microwaves, some refrigerators, some in-room hot tubs. Cable TV, in-room VCRs, room phones. Outdoor pool, lake. Exercise equipment. Boating, fishing. Library. No pets. No kids under 18. No smoking. | 144 Scenic Overlook La. | 336/368–9591 | info@scenicoverlook.com | 2 rooms, 3 suites, 6 cabins | $125–$155 | AE, D, DC, MC, V.

PINEHURST

(Nearby towns also listed: Aberdeen, Sanford, Southern Pines)

Even if you are not a golfer, it's hard not to appreciate the emerald oasis of golf greens in the leafy village of Pinehurst. The town is home to 40-plus courses and boasts the world's largest golf resort.

Golf isn't the only game in town. There are bicycling races and tennis competitions that often include the U.S. Clay Court Championships. At the venerable Pinehurst Racetrack, standardbreds are put through paces year-round. Harness races, polo games, fox hunts, and Olympic trials are also staged there.

Information: **Pinehurst Area Convention and Visitors Bureau** | Box 2270, Southern Pines 28388 | 910/692–3330 or 800/346–5362 | cvb4golf@mindspring.com | www.home-ofgolf.com.

Attractions

Tufts Archives. These archives document the founding of Pinehurst through the 1895 letters, pictures, and news clippings of James Walker Tufts. Tufts served as president of the United States Golf Association. Golf memorabilia is on display. | Given Memorial Library, 150 Cherokee Rd. | 910/295–6022 or 910/295–3642 | Free | Weekdays 9:30–5, Sat. 9:30 AM–12:30 PM.

ON THE CALENDAR

AUG.: *Farmer's Day and Wagon Train Festival.* Music and dancing, arts and crafts, special demonstrations, a gospel sing, and a parade of horses are held for this community gathering. | Downtown Robbins | 910/948–3746.

Dining

Carolina Dining Room. Contemporary. Five-course meals are served in the formal restaurant of the Carolina Hotel. Linen table cloths, fresh flowers, and a Venetian glass chandelier grace the large dining area. The menu changes daily and has included entrées such as sautéed veal medallions with applejack cream sauce, grilled apples, and caramelized Vidalia onions. Live music is performed nightly. Sunday brunch. Kids' menu. | 1 Carolina Vista Dr. | 910/295–6811 or 800/487–4653 | fax 910/295–8503 | Jacket required at dinner | Prix–fixe $41 | Reservations essential | AE, D, DC, MC, V.

Chef Warren's. Contemporary. This restaurant with an open kitchen has the look of a turn-of-the-20th-century French bistro. The menu changes monthly, but it usually includes a skirt steak or double-cut center-cut pork chop as well as a choice of fresh fish. | 215 N.E. Broad St. | 910/692–5240 | Closed Sun. No lunch | $13–$22 | AE, D, MC, V.

Dugan's Pub. Irish. Golf is the theme at Dugan's, which serves pints, steak, and chicken. Live music Fri.–Sat. | 2 Market Sq | 910/295–3400 | $8–$20 | D, MC, V.

★ **Pinehurst Playhouse Restaurant.** American. Primarily a luncheonette, this small but busy spot in the Theater Building shopping complex serves soup and sandwiches. | W. Village

Green | 910/295–8873 | Reservations not accepted | Closed Sun. No dinner | $4–$5 | No credit cards.

Lodging

Comfort Inn. Opened in 1996, this hotel is near horseback riding and tennis. The shops and restaurants of Pinehurst Village and downtown Southern Pines are a mile away. Complimentary Continental breakfast. Some microwaves, some refrigerators. Cable TV. Pool. Exercise equipment. Laundry facilities, laundry services. | 9801 U.S. 15/501 | 910/215–5500 or 800/831–0541 | fax 910/215–5535 | www.comfortinns.com | 80 rooms | $69–$99 | AE, D, DC, MC, V.

The Inn at Rainbow Bend Farm B&B. On a 17-acre horse farm, with a private lake where you can fish. All rooms overlook the lake and the gardens. The inn is 5 mi from Pinehurst, and close to golf courses, horseback riding, antiques stores, and restaurants. Horses are welcome; there is a stall charge. Complimentary breakfast. Room phones. Lake. Horseback riding. Fishing. No pets. No smoking. | P.O. Box 824, Pinebluff | 800/447–5071 | gstanton@pinehurst.net | 2 rooms | $65–$80 | AE, D, MC, V.

Pine Crest Inn. Owned by famous golf architect Donald Ross until his death in 1948, this inn was opened in 1913. The main attraction is the golf course, steeped in history; it is considered to be one of the finest in the world. Antiques and specialty stores are one block away. No two rooms are the same, as each has its own theme. Dining room, complimentary breakfast and dinner, bar. Cable TV. | Dogwood Rd. | 910/295–6121 or 800/371–2545 | fax 910/295–4880 | www.pinecrestinnpinehurst.com | 40 rooms | $104–$212 | AE, D, DC, MC, V | MAP.

★ **Pinehurst Resort and Country Club.** Designated a National Historic Landmark, this resort was built in 1895. This 2,000-acre facility has a 200-acre lake with sailing, swimming, and beach activities. There are four buildings of accommodations. The largest is the Carolina with 210 rooms and 12 suites. The Holly Inn pays homage to the natural world with floral-motif carvings, decorative tile, and glass fixtures. 9 restaurants, bar, complimentary dinner, room service. In-room data ports, minibars, no-smoking rooms, refrigerators. Cable TV. 3 outdoor pools. Massage. 8 golf courses (18 hole), 24 tennis courts. Health club. Water sports. Bicycles. Kids' programs (up to 12 years old). Laundry service. Business services. Free parking. | 1 Carolina Vista | 910/295–6811 or 800/487–4653 | fax 910/295–8503 | www.pinehurst.com | 338 rooms, 130 apartments | $194; call for packages | AE, D, DC, MC, V | MAP.

PITTSBORO

MAP 8, G4

(Nearby towns also listed: Asheboro, Cary, Chapel Hill, Sanford)

Turn-of-the-20th-century buildings and bridges, 200-year-old mills, and ancient natural springs are an integral part of the rolling pastoral landscape of Chatham County, whose seat was named in 1787 in honor of William Pitt, the Earl of Chatham. In downtown Pittsboro, with its walkable main shopping district, all main roads circle a historic courthouse.

People choose to live and play in Pittsboro precisely because of its small-town nature and rural surroundings; they find it an antidote to the pressures associated with urban areas such as the nearby Research Triangle region. The Haw River, which runs between Chatham and Alamance counties, and the Deep River, which forms Chatham's southern border, are magnets for paddlers. Antiques lovers will find bliss here as well, for two dozen antiques stores dot the area. Pittsboro and Chatham County boast a wonderfully eclectic citizenry. Many artists call the area home, as do academics, professionals, farmers, and an ever-growing number of Hispanic immigrants.

Information: Chatham County United Chamber of Commerce | 1609 E. 11th St., Siler City 27344 | 919/742–3333 or 800/468–6242 | fax 919/742–1333 | ccucc@enji.net.

Attractions

Calhoun's Apple Nursery. Lee Calhoun has spent years searching for and researching old apple varieties all over the South. The author of the heralded *Old Southern Apples* propagates tasty vintage apples, the kind you can no longer get in groceries. Some custom grafts or trees can be purchased at the nursery, which is open to the public. Tours are available. | 295 Blacktwig Rd. | 919/542–4480 | Free | Call for hrs.

Historic Chatham County. The Chatham County Historical Association, which maintains an office and museum (open Fridays 10–2) in the 1881 Chatham County Courthouse in downtown Pittsboro, has identified nearly 20 historic sites throughout the county. They include public buildings such as a U.S. post office as well as churches, a mill, a cemetery, and private homes. Contact the association for information about self-guided driving or walking tours of Pittsboro and Siler City, the county's largest towns. Maps are also available in the courthouse and Pittsboro library. | 12 East St. | 919/542–3603 | Free | Daily.

Jordan Lake State Recreation Area. Special hiking trails near the lake's edge, abundant wildlife, including flying squirrels, birds of prey, and deer, plus picnic facilities are all a part of this spot. There's even a ½-mi "talking trees" trail, along which you can push buttons and let trees tell you about themselves. | 2832 Big Woods Rd., off U.S. 64 | 919/542–1154 | fax 919/542–1707 | www.dfr.state.nc.us | ncdfrjordanlake@mindspring.com | Free | Mon.–Fri. 9–5, weekends call for hrs.

ON THE CALENDAR

DEC.: *Artists Open Door Studio Tour.* On the first weekend of the month, dozens of artists in all mediums throughout Chatham County open their studios so the public can glimpse how they live and work. The driving tour, sponsored by the Chatham County Arts Council, is self-guided, and much of the art is for sale. | 919/542–0394 | www2.emji.net/chatham_arts.

Dining

Pittsboro General Store. Eclectic. The small café within this store, which sells everything from fresh bread and goat cheese to locally made crafts, coffee, and homeopathic remedies, is headed by a chef with vegetarian sensibilities. East Indian and Mediterranean flavors (stuffed grape leaves, couscous salad) frequently find their way onto the menu. There are also sandwiches and homemade soups, but the house specialty and overwhelming favorite is the too-big-for-the-plate green chili burrito. | 39 West St. | 919/542–2432 | www2.emji.net/jnitsch/pgs/store.html | Reservations not accepted | Closed Sat., Sun. No dinner | $5–$7 | D, MC, V.

★ **Fearrington House.** Contemporary. Appropriate to the restaurant's pastoral surroundings, the dining rooms are done in pastels, floral arrangements, and candles. The menu is filled with regional food prepared in a classic manner, such as the collard-pecan pesto stuffed chicken breast with Hoop cheddar grits over a chicory morel gravy. The desserts are showstoppers. | 2000 Fearrington Village Center, U.S. 15/501 | 919/542–2121 | fax 919/542–4202 | www.fearringtonhouse.com | Reservations essential | Jacket and tie | Closed Mon. | Prix-fixe $65 | AE, MC, V.

Lodging

★ **Fearrington House.** A member of the Relais & Châteaux group, this country inn is on a 200-year-old farm that has been remade into a residential community resembling a country village. The village square has upscale shops and offices for professional services. The village mascots, the "Oreo cows" (black on the ends, snow white in the middle), roam the pasture at the entrance. The inn's modern guest rooms are individually furnished with antiques, original art, English pine, and a variety of lush fabrics. A courtyard and fountain welcome you at the entrance. Dining room, complimentary breakfast, room service. Cable TV. Pool. Hot tub. Tennis. Exercise equipment. Business services. No pets. No smoking. | 2000 Fearrington Village Center, U.S. 15/501 | 919/542–2121 | fax 919/542–4202 | fci@mail.inter-path.net | www.fearrington.com | 32 rooms | $180–$300 | AE, MC, V.

The Inn at Celebrity Dairy. The owners of this 200-acre, oak-shaded farm (circa 1820) orig-inally bought goats to clear the overgrown ground. A few grew to many, and a license to run a dairy on the property was secured. The goat cheese is now produced for gourmet restaurants, grocers, and farmer's markets in addition to meals served at the inn. The goats are named for celebrities, and the rooms within the inn's two buildings, which are con-nected by a carefully designed, sunlight-filled atrium, are named for goats past and present. The heart of the inn, the Old House Suite, is the original settler's cabin. It has rough-hewn walls, heart-of-pine floors and a stone fireplace. The newer part of the inn is a three-story, Greek Revival farmhouse. The decorations in its rooms are simple but comfortable and artful. One has walls of periwinkle blue stenciled with a lace-pattern border. Another has teal tones and an ornate Victorian headboard. Complimentary breakfast. TV in com-mon area. Massage. No pets. No smoking. | 2106 Mt. Vernon Hickory Mtn. Rd., Siler City | 919/742–5176 or 877/742–5176 | fax 919/742–1432 | TheInn@celebritydairy.com | www.celebri-tydairy.com | 8 rooms | $60–$130 | MC, V.

RALEIGH

MAP 8, H4

(Nearby towns also listed: Cary, Chapel Hill, Durham, Pittsboro, Smithfield)

Legislators founded Raleigh, North Carolina's capital city, in 1792. It is the only state capital to have been planned and established by a state as the seat of government. Nicknamed "City of Oaks" because of its many trees and parks, Raleigh is the largest of the cities that compose the Research Triangle (Raleigh, Durham, Chapel Hill)—an area that's been characterized as full of "trees, tees, and Ph.D's."

Raleigh is Old South and New South, down-home and upscale, all in one. Named for Sir Walter Raleigh (who attempted to establish the first English colony on the Carolina shores), the city now thrives on high-tech industries, government, education, service industries, research, and medicine. In addition to North Carolina State, there are six other universities and colleges in town.

In 1947, the General Assembly made headlines when it voted to appropriate $1 million for art. No state had ever used public funds to buy art, so the move was controversial. Joining the North Carolina Museum of Art are two other state-funded museums. All are large, all are free, and all are in or near downtown, a section of the city containing 18th-century homes built within Raleigh's original boundaries. Maps of the historic areas can be obtained at Capitol Area Visitor Center across from the governor's mansion.

Over the past decade Raleigh has capitalized on its "land of opportunity" reputa-tion. Thanks to the Triangle area's appearance on a slew of "best of" lists, its growth has been rapid. A lot of the development has occurred in the sprawling, suburban area known as North Raleigh. In recent years, downtown revitalization has taken off, and the result has been the rapid development of housing, museums, shops, restaurants, and night spots infusing energy into downtown and surrounding areas. Wake County includes Raleigh and 11 other municipalities; the red clay farmland that used to stretch between them has all but disappeared as residential and commercial development (even more shopping centers and entertainment venues) continues. The fact that there are so many newcomers who hail from colder climates helped convince the National Hockey League that greater Raleigh would support a new professional franchise, the Carolina Hurricanes.

Still, the area's agrarian roots aren't ignored. The sizable State Farmers Market, on the city's southeastern edge, draws more than a million people annually.

Growth has its price. During rush hour, certain corridors (I–40 through Research Triangle Park, for example) should be avoided at all costs. On Friday and Saturday nights, the wait to be seated in some restaurants can stretch to an hour or more. Nonetheless, sunshine, lush green areas, and courtly manners soothe the soul. As Sadie Delaney, a native North Carolinian, commented in *Having Our Say,* an autobiography written with her sister, Bessie: "Bessie and I have lived in New York for the last seventy-five years, but Raleigh will always be home."

Information: Greater Raleigh Convention and Visitors Bureau | Box 1879, 27602 | 919/ 834–5900 or 800/849–8499. **Visitor Center** | Bank of America Building, 421 Fayetteville St. Mall, Suite 1505 | 919/834–5900 or 800/849–8499 | visit@raleighcvb.org | www.raleighcvb.org.

TRANSPORTATION

Airports: Raleigh-Durham International Airport (919/840–2123), off I–40 between Raleigh and Durham, is served by 19 airlines, including American, Continental, Delta, Midway, Northwest, Southwest, TWA, United, and US Airways. Passengers take off and arrive at 1600 Terminal Boulevard.

Rail: Amtrak (919/833–7594 or 800/872–7245) provides local and regional rail service. The *Carolinian* route has one daily train northbound and one southbound, it stops in Raleigh, Durham, and 10 other Piedmont cities. The in-state *Piedmont* line connects nine cities between Raleigh and Charlotte each day. Leave from the station in Raleigh at 320 W. Cabarrus Street.

Intra-City Transit: Capitol Area Transit (919/828–7228) is Raleigh's public transport system. Fares are 75¢. The **Triangle Transit Authority** (919/549–9999) links downtown Raleigh with Cary, Research Triangle Park, Durham, and Chapel Hill. It runs weekdays except on major holidays. Rates start at $1.

Bus: Greyhound/Carolina Trailways (800/231–2222 or 919/834–8410) serves Raleigh.

Attractions

CULTURE, EDUCATION, AND HISTORY
★ **Executive Mansion.** Home to 25 of North Carolina's governors, this is a brick turn-of-the-20th-century Queen Anne cottage with gingerbread trim and manicured lawns. Tours are available through the Raleigh Visitor Center with advance notice. | 200 N. Blount St. | 919/ 733–3456 | fax 919/733–1991 | Free.

Joel Lane House. The oldest dwelling in Raleigh, dating from 1760, was the home of the "Father of Raleigh." Joel Lane sold the state the property on which the capital city grew. Costumed docents tell the story and show the authentically restored house and period gardens. | 728 W. Hargett St. | 919/833–3431 | $3 | Mar.–mid Dec., Tues.–Fri., 10–2; 1st and 3rd Sat. 1–4, and by appointment.

Memorial Auditorium. Traveling Broadway troupes and local groups perform here often. This building, constructed in the Greek Revival style, is also the home stage for the North Carolina Symphony and the professional Carolina Ballet Company. | 1 E. South St. | 919/831–6060 | Box office daily 10–5.

Mordecai Historic Park. Here you can see the Mordecai family's plantation home and other structures. President Andrew Johnson was born in one of the park's homes in 1808. | 1 Mimosa

St. | 919/834–4844 | fax 919/834–7314 | $4 | Mon. and Wed.–Sat. 10–3, Sun. 1–3; tours on the ½ hr.

North Carolina State University. This school, the largest university (more than 28,000 students) in the state, was founded in 1887. It is known for its humanities and professional programs, agriculture, engineering, and veterinary medicine curriculums. | Hillsborough St. | 919/515–2011 or 919/515–2434 | www.ncsu.edu | Free | Daily.

College of Veterinary Medicine. Ranked as one of the top five schools of veterinary medicine in the nation, this college has more than 20 buildings at its main site. It sits atop a slight rise on 182 green and rolling acres where cows and horses graze. | 4700 Hillsborough St. | 919/513–6200 | Free | Daily.

Harrelson Hall. This hall is known to have the first round classroom facility on a college campus in the United States. | Stinson Dr. | 919/515–2434 | Free | Daily.

KODAK'S TIPS FOR PHOTOGRAPHING THE CITY

Streets
- Take a bus or walking tour to get acclimated
- Explore markets, streets, and parks
- Travel light so you can shoot quickly

City Vistas
- Find high vantage points to reveal city views
- Shoot early or late in the day, for best light
- At twilight, use fast films and bracket exposures

Formal Gardens
- Exploit high angles to show garden design
- Use wide-angle lenses to exaggerate depth and distance
- Arrive early to beat crowds

Landmarks and Monuments
- Review postcard racks for traditional views
- Seek out distant or unusual views
- Look for interesting vignettes or details

Museums
- Call in advance regarding photo restrictions
- Match film to light source when color is critical
- Bring several lenses or a zoom

Houses of Worship
- Shoot exteriors from nearby with a wide-angle lens
- Move away and include surroundings
- Switch to a very fast film indoors

Stained-Glass Windows
- Bright indirect sunlight yields saturated colors
- Expose for the glass not the surroundings
- Switch off flash to avoid glare

Architectural Details
- Move close to isolate details
- For distant vignettes, use a telephoto lens
- Use side light to accent form and texture

In the Marketplace
- Get up early to catch peak activity
- Search out colorful displays and colorful characters
- Don't scrimp on film

Stage Shows and Events
- Never use flash
- Shoot with fast (ISO 400 to 1000) film
- Use telephoto lenses
- Focus manually if necessary

From *Kodak Guide to Shooting Great Travel Pictures* © 2000 by Fodor's Travel Publications

J. C. Raulston Arboretum. This 8-acre garden is home to a 300-ft perennial border, the White Garden, a Japanese Garden, a French parterre, and a special plant house. | 4301 Beryl Rd. | 919/515–3132 | Free | Mon.–Sat. 8–sunset, Sun. 8–2; guided tours mid-Apr.–mid-Oct.

Libraries. There are five libraries at North Carolina State, including the main D. H. Hill Library and the Burlington Textiles Library. The collections include nearly 3 million volumes, the papers and drawings of architect George Matsumoto, and the Winston Music Collection. | 919/515–2935 | Free | Daily; hrs vary.

Memorial Tower. A symbol of the school, the bell tower was completed in 1937 and built in memory of those students who died in defense of the country. It rings not only to mark time but to announce or celebrate events of importance to the university community. Guided tours of the campus begin here. | Hillsborough St. | 919/515–2434 | Free | Daily.

Oakwood Historic District. Trees shade this neighborhood containing many examples of Victorian architecture. Self-guided walking tours of the area, which encompasses 20 blocks bordered by Person, Oakwood, East, and Lane streets, are available at the Capitol Area Visitor Center. | 301 N. Blount St. | 919/733–3456 | Free | Visitor center weekdays 8–5, Sat. 9–5, Sun. 1–5.

Historic Oakwood Cemetery. Established in 1869, this is the resting place of 2,800 Confederate soldiers, Civil War generals, governors, and numerous U.S. senators. The 100 acres are filled with impressive monuments, lawn crypts, and tombstones. Free maps are available at the cemetery office. | 701 Oakwood Ave. | 919/832–6077 | fax 919/832–2982 | Free | Daily 8–5.

State Capitol. A beautifully preserved example of Greek Revival architecture from 1840, the capitol once housed all the functions of state government. Today it's part museum, part executive offices. Tours are available with advance notice. | Capitol Sq., 1 E. Edenton St. | 919/733–4994 | fax 919/715–4030 | Free | Mon.–Sat. 9–5, Sun. 1–4.

State Legislative Building. One block north of the State Capitol, this complex hums with the comings and goings of lawmakers and lobbyists when in session. You are welcome to watch from the gallery. A free guided tour is also available through the Capitol Area Visitor Center. | 16 W. Jones St. | 919/733–7928 | fax 919/733–2599 | Free | Weekdays 8–5, Sat. 9–5, Sun. 1–5.

MUSEUMS

Artspace. Next to the Moore Square art district, this visual-arts center is in a refurbished warehouse. There are 25 studios open to the public, exhibition galleries, and a variety of arts education programs. Most of the art can be purchased. | 201 E. Davie St. | 919/821–2787 | fax 919/821–0383 | www.artspace.citysearch.com | Free | Tues.–Sat. 10–6, 1st Fri. 10–10; call for studio hrs.

Exploris. Most children's museums and science centers focus heavily on health and natural sciences. This architectural showplace, an 80,000-square-ft, multi-level learning center, is specifically geared to convey a global perspective through hands-on exhibits. Exhibits include language, culture, geography, global trade, and communications. | 201 E. Hargett St. | 919/834–4040 | fax 919/834–3516 | www.exploris.org | $6.95 | Mon.–Sat. 9–5, Sun. noon–5.

★ **North Carolina Museum of Art.** Sitting on a large, grassy tract near Raleigh's western edge, this museum exhibits art ranging from the ancient Egyptian to the contemporary. The Museum Café, which looks out on a performance space, is a popular spot for lunch or Friday night entertainment. Outdoor concerts, movies on the lawn, and other special events take place on the grounds in summer. | 2110 Blue Ridge Rd. | 919/839–6262 or 919/833–3548 restaurant | fax 919/733–8034 | www.ncartmuseum.org | Free | Tues.–Thurs. and Sat. 9–5, Fri. 9–9, Sun. 11–6; guided tours at 1:30.

★ **North Carolina Museum of History.** Founded in 1902, this museum is now housed in an airy state-of-the-art facility on Bicentennial Plaza near the capitol. Artifacts, audiovisual programs, and interactive exhibits bring the state's history to life. The Folklife and Sports Hall of Fame galleries are two of the more popular exhibits. | 5 E. Edenton St. | 919/715–0200 | fax 919/733–8655 | nchistory.dcr.state.nc.us/museums | Free | Tues.–Sat. 9–5, Sun. noon–5.

North Carolina Museum of Natural Sciences. The museum houses ten major exhibits and a two-story waterfall. The skeleton of Acrocanthosaurus, a giant carnivore that lived in the South 110 million years ago, is displayed in a multistory glass-enclosed tower. | 11 W. Jones St. | 919/733–7450 or 877/462–8724 | fax 919/733–1573 | www.naturalsciences.org | Free | Mon.–Sat. 9–5, Sun. noon–5.

PARKS, NATURAL AREAS, AND OUTDOOR RECREATION

Falls Lake State Recreation Area. One of the state's largest recreation areas (12,000-acre lake, 26,000-acres of woodlands) offers swimming, boating, fishing, camping, hiking, and picnicking. There are seven recreation sites within the park. The park office is 10 mi north of Raleigh off Rte. 50. | 13304 Creedmoor Rd., Wake Forest | 919/676–1027 | fax 919/733–3499 | ils.unc.edu/parkproject/falaindex.html | $4 per car in season.

Pullen Park. Large crowds come to picnic and ride the 1911 Dentzel carousel, the train, and the pedal boats. You can swim in a large public aquatic complex, explore an arts-and-crafts center, or, if the timing is right, see a play at the Theater in the Park. | 520 Ashe Ave. | 919/831–6468 or 919/831–6640 | Free; fees for rides and programs | Memorial Day–Labor Day, Mon.–Thurs. 10:30–6:30, Fri.–Sat. 10:30–8, Sun. 1–8; call for off-season hrs.

William B. Umstead State Park. The 5,300-acre urban green space of this park has three small lakes, horse trails, a campground, a cabin, and a mess hall. Facilities for hiking and biking are also on hand. | 8801 Glenwood Ave. (U.S. 70) | 919/571–4170 | ils.unc.edu/parkproject/wium.html | Free, fee for camping | Daily 8–dusk.

RELIGION AND SPIRITUALITY

Christ Church. On Capitol Square, this Episcopal church is a Raleigh landmark. Founded in 1821, the building contains large stained glass windows with biblical scenes. | 120 E. Edenton St. | 919/834–6259 | www.christ-church-raleigh.org | Free.

First Baptist Church I. The lower level of this church was used as a Confederate hospital during the Civil War; today the church is home to more than 1,350 members. | 99 N. Salisbury St. | 919/832–4485 | www.fbcraleigh.org | Free | Weekdays 8:30–5.

First Baptist Church II. When the Baptist population of Raleigh was organized in 1812 on the second floor of the Capitol building, there were 23 charter members. Nine were white and 14 were African–American. Following the Civil War in 1868, there was a peaceful separation of the two races; this church was founded by the African–American members. | 101 S. Wilmington St. | Free.

St. Paul African Methodist Episcopal Church This 148-year-old church was orginally the slave membership of Edenton Street United Methodist Church. When the group grew large enough, the church became the "first independent African–American congregation. Today, the red brick and wood American Gothic Revival-style church continues to grow. | 402 W. Edenton St. | www.stpaulmechurch.org | Free.

SHOPPING

City Market. This 1914 Spanish Mission–style marketplace has been converted into an outdoor shopping center filled with specialty shops, art galleries, restaurants, and a comedy club. It is part of the growing Moore Square Art District, a nucleus for the art community. | Martin St. and Moore Sq | 919/828–4555 | fax 919/856–8873 | Free.

Fayetteville Street Mall. Extending from the State Capitol to the Raleigh Civic and Convention Center, this pedestrians-only walkway, with a statue of Sir Walter Raleigh, provides an entrance to a number of high-rise office buildings. The shops and restaurants in the area cater to the weekday business crowd. | Free | Daily.

SPECTATOR SPORTS

Carter-Finley Stadium. Home of Wolfpack football and other special events, the stadium holds 50,000 spectators in its two levels. An expansion has been promised by university officials and supporters of the athletic program. | Wade Ave. and Trinity Rd. | 919/515–2106 or 800/310–7225 | Varies.

OTHER POINTS OF INTEREST

Playspace. "Creative Play" is the mission of this museum geared to children ages 6 months to 7 years and their caregivers. There's a pretend grocery store, a hospital, café, water area, and puppet theater. | 400 Glenwood Ave. | 919/832–1212 | fax 919/821–5649 | $2 per 50-min session | Mon. 9–1, Tues.–Sat. 9–5.

ON THE CALENDAR

JAN.: *Antiques Extravaganza.* Nearly 200 exhibitors gather to display and sell antiques and collectibles over a three-day period every January at the Raleigh Convention and Conference Center. | 336/924–8337 or 919/831–6011 | www.raleighconvention.com.

JAN.: *Dr. Martin Luther King Jr. Celebration.* A memorial march, speeches, prayer services, and dramatic and musical performances acknowledge the accomplishments and sacrifices of the slain civil rights leader, Dr. King. Events are held up and down MLK Boulevard. | 919/834–6264 | www.king-raleigh.org.

FEB.: *Home and Garden Show.* This botanical gathering showcases over 100,000 square ft of flowers, plants, home plans, and designer rooms at the Raleigh Convention and Conference Center. There are also a garden competition, seminars, and home product displays. | 919/831–6011.

MAR.: *N.C. Renaissance Faire.* Crafts, entertainment (including jousting), food, games, and reenactments from 16th-century England mark this fair held at the State Fairgrounds in Raleigh. | 919/755–8004 | www.ncrenfaire.com.

APR.: *Civil War Living History.* In this reenactment in the Capitol building, actors portray citizens who lived during the final days of the Civil War during the 1865 Union occupation. | 919/733–4994.

MAY: *Artsplosure Spring Jazz and Art Festival.* International jazz and regional blues performers, hundreds of juried visual-artist exhibits, children's activities, and food vendors gather at Moore Square in Raleigh every May. Over 75,000 people generally attend. | 919/832–8699 | www.artsplosure.org.

MAY: *Meet in the Street.* Downtown Wake Forest plays host to this arts and crafts festival with more than 100 vendors, food, and music. | 919/556–1519.

JUNE: *Tar Heel Regatta.* The American Power Boat Association sanctions this event, which attracts drivers from all over North America. Food vendors are on-site at the Lake Wheeler Park venue. | 919/834–6441 or 919/662–5704.

JUNE–JULY: *Nike Carolina Classic.* This $350,000 tournament, held at Raleigh Country Club, is part of the PGA Tour and attracts many up-and-coming golfers. | 919/380–0011.

JULY: *July 4th Celebration.* Exhibits, games, rides, and a huge fireworks show on the North Carolina State Fairgrounds celebrate the nation's birth. | 919/831–6640 or 919/890–3291.

SEPT.: *Gourd Festival.* A 60-year tradition at the North Carolina state fairgrounds, this festival has displays of gourds of every shape and size, gourd art, crafts demonstrations, slide lectures, contests, and sales. | Blue Ridge Rd., Raleigh | 919/362–4357.

SEPT.: *Grecian Festival.* Members of the Holy Trinity Greek Orthodox Church organize this event held at the State Fairgrounds. Traditional Greek foods, music, dance, and gift items highlight the activities. | 919/781–4548.

SEPT.: *Oktoberfest.* German cuisine and beverages, music and dancing, and activities for kids are conducted during this "stein hoist" at the North Hills Mall. | 919/828–0890.

SEPT.: *Pops in the Park.* The expansive lawn of Meredith College is where the North Carolina Symphony performs a program of pop music to conclude the Labor Day holiday. A fireworks show tops off the evening. | 919/821–8655.

OCT.: *International Festival.* International foods, cultural exhibits, demonstrations, a bazaar, ethnic dress, dancing, and music celebrate diversity at the Raleigh Convention and Conference Center. | 919/832–4331 | www.internationalfestival.org.

OCT.: *North Carolina State Fair.* Games, rides, sideshows, concerts by headliners, food, craft demonstrations, livestock exhibits, and competitions invade the State Fairgrounds for 10 days in mid-October. | 1025 Blue Ridge Rd. | 919/733–2145 or 919/821–7400.

NOV.: *Carolina Christmas Show.* More than 400 exhibits with craftspeople, holiday displays, food, and entertainment welcome in the holiday season at the Raleigh Convention and Conference Center. | 800/232–4936.

NOV.: *The Old Reliable Run 10K.* Some 2,000 entrants, including wheelchair racers and race walkers, participate in this event and compete for trophies. It's sanctioned by USA Track and Field and listed by *Runner's World* magazine as one of the top races in the nation. The starting line is in downtown Raleigh. | 919/829–4843.

DEC.: *Executive Mansion Holiday Open House.* Built in 1891 in the Queen Anne style, the governor's official residence is decked out for the holidays and open to the public for a limited time. | 919/733–3456.

DEC.: *First Night.* This alcohol-free New Year's Eve celebration, held at venues throughout downtown Raleigh, is loaded with numerous food vendors, live music, dance, theater, a parade, children's activities, and fireworks at the countdown to midnight. | 919/832–8699.

DEC.: *Messiah "Sing-In."* Music by the North Carolina Symphony and the National Opera Company celebrates the Christmas season. The public is invited. | Edenton Street United Methodist Church, 228 W. Edenton St. | 919/890–6063.

Dining

INEXPENSIVE

Big Ed's City Market Restaurant. Southern. Antique farm implements and the owner's political memorabilia set the scene for down-home cooking. The changing menu always includes barbecued chicken. Sit at big wooden tables and listen to the Dixieland band on Saturday mornings. | 220 Wolfe St. | 919/836–9909 | Closed Sun. No dinner | $6.50–$9 | No credit cards.

Char-Grill. Fast food. This drive-in, with glass-enclosed cooking area, has outdoor seating and a take-out counter. Char-grilled burgers, hot dogs, french fries, shakes, and apple turnovers round out the menu. | 618 Hillsborough St. | 919/821–7636 | $4–$7 | No credit cards.

Courtney's. American. Drink coffee with eggs Benedict, frittatas, pancakes, waffles, and biscuits. At lunch, sandwiches such as grilled chicken, salads, and burgers are served. There is a kids' menu. | 407 Six Forks Rd. | 919/834–3613 | No dinner | $6–$9 | MC, V.

Greenshields Brewery and Pub. English. Beer is brewed on site at this multilevel pub with oak paneling and fireplaces. British staples such as fish-and-chips and shepherd's pie comprise the menu. You can stop by after shopping at nearby stores to listen to live music on the weekend. | 214 E. Martin St. | 919/829–0214 | $6–$15 | AE, D, MC, V.

Lilly's Pizza. Pizza. One of the creative pizzas you can try at this lively restaurant is the "Buddha," which is doused with olive oil, feta, fresh garlic, spinach, tomatoes, and zucchini. Another popular choice is the white pizza, which includes riccotta cheese. | 1813 Glenwood Ave. | 919/833–0226 | $5.75–$16 | AE, D, MC, V.

Neo-China. Chinese. Original art and modern sculptures set the tone for contemporary preparations of Chinese favorites with fresh local ingredients, particularly vegetables. Sunday buffet. | 6602 Glenwood Ave. | 919/783–8383 | No lunch Sat. | $7–$15 | AE, D, DC, MC, V.

Third Place. Coffeehouse. The work of local artists covers the reddish-orange marbleized walls in this funky coffeehouse; specialty drinks and sandwiches are on the menu. The "Plethora," a popular choice, is stuffed with hummus, tabbouli, pico de gallo, sprouts, havarti, sunflower seeds and a mustard-vinaigrette dressing. For the less adventurous, there's a hearty baked cheese and tomato sandwich. | 1811 Glenwood Ave. | 919/834–6566 | $1–$5.50 | Cash only.

MODERATE

Bistro 607. Contemporary. Creative and dramatically presented dishes are served in this 1912 bungalow with large windows, white linens, and fresh flowers. The mainly French menu changes monthly. | 607 Glenwood Ave. | 919/828–0840 | Closed Sun. No lunch Sat. | $8–$20 | MC, V.

Casa Carbone. Italian. Traditional Italian dishes such as chicken marsala and veal scaloppine are the staples of this small Oak Park Shopping Center eatery. Pizza, vegetarian dishes, and salads are available for a quick lunch. Beer, liquor, and wine are served. Kids' menu. | 6019A Glenwood Ave. | 919/781–8750 | Closed Mon. | $10–$16 | AE, DC, MC, V.

Charter Room. Contemporary. China and Chippendale accent the dining room. Sea bass, New York steak, Maryland crab cakes, and linguine are served with an emphasis on presentation. Breakfast is also an option. | 1505 Hillsborough St. | 919/828–0333 | $17–$31 | AE, MC, V.

Caffé Luna. Italian. Seasonal Italian dishes are served in this palm-lined dining room. Terrace dining is available. | 136 E. Hargett St. | 919/832–6090 | Closed Sun. | $12–$22 | AE, MC, V.

Dos Taquitas. Mexican. Tequila flows at this Mexican eatery, which is popular for its poblanos with beef, pork and three cheeses. Brightly colored hats festoon the bamboo walls of this cantina. | 5629 Creedmor Rd. | 919/787–3373 | $8–$16.

Enotica Vin. Contemporary. Exposed brick walls, modern art, track lighting, and a climate-controlled storage area set the tone at this restaurant, which serves wine in "flights," or groups of tastes. In addition to the extensive wine selection, there are many rare European cheeses, along with entrees like pan roasted grouper with leek and endive fondue. Popular choices for dessert include the hot chocolate cake with caramel ice cream and the poached pear with red wine and white chocolate marscapone. | 410 Glenwood Ave., Ste. 350 | 919/834–3070 | fax 919/834–3163 | Closed Mon. | $5–$23.

Fins. Contemporary. Simple white linen and abstract paintings are the backdrop for Asian-influenced flavors and seafood. The menu changes daily. | 7713–39 Lead Mine Rd. | 919/847–4119 | Reservations essential | Closed Sun. No lunch | $15–$37 | AE, DC, MC, V.

518 West Italian Café. Italian. Unique pasta combinations, wood-fired pizzettes, and breads are served under the vaulted painted ceilings simulating a sky at this Mediterranean-theme bistro. | 518 W. Jones St. | 919/829–2518 | Reservations not accepted | No lunch Sun. | $8–$19 | AE, D, DC, MC, V.

Irregardless Café. Contemporary. Vegetarian, seafood, chicken, beef, and lamb choices are joined by specialties like grilled quail and rich desserts. Live jazz, folk, or classical music is performed nightly. | 901 W. Morgan St. | 919/833–8898 or 919/833–9920 (menu) | No lunch Sat. No dinner Sun. | $13–$21 | AE, D, DC, MC, V.

Jean Claude's French Café. French. Linen tablecloths and live French music provide the backdrop for soups, salads, crepes, salmon in puff pastry, grilled sirloin, and rack of lamb. Beer and wine are available. Reservations are required for five or more. | 6112 Falls of the Neuse Rd. | 919/872–6224 | Closed Sun.–Mon. | $10–$26 | AE, D, MC, V.

Peppercorn Restaurant. American. Lunch and dinner dishes such as veal, chicken, shrimp, pasta, soups and salads are on the menu at this casual restaurant, which has indoor and outdoor seating. | 208 Wolf St. | 919/863–0048 | $10–$15 | AE, MC, V.

Rathskellar. Contemporary. Vegetarians and carnivores alike frequent this restaurant and lounge, which offers a wide variety of dishes. The cashew, black bean, and sweet potato casserole is one of the popular vegetarian options, and it may appear on the same table as the filet mignon provencale with bearnaise sauce. The "Rat" also offers salads, burgers, sandwiches, seafood, specialty coffee drinks, foreign and domestic beers and wine. | 2412 Hillsborough St. | 919/821–5342 | $8–$17 | AE, MC, V.

The Rockford. Sandwiches. Original art hangs on the seafoam green and mustard yellow walls of this sandwich shop. Light streams in the windows, as patrons chow down on sandwiches like the ABC, with apple, bacon, and cheddar, or the Cubana, which has turkey, ham, and spicy pepper jelly. The veggie burgers are also popular. | 320-1/2 Glenwood Ave. | 919/821–9020 | $6.50–$8 | MC, V.

Southend Brewery and Smokehouse. Contemporary. Shiny beer vats double as decoration in this brewery and restaurant, which has high ceilings with exposed beams and ductwork. Giant salads, garlic fettucini pasta, and applewood smoked bacon pizza are popular choices here, as are the many different kinds of beer. Lively and loud, the restaurant draws a large crowd of 20-somethings, who come for the drinks and live entertainment. | 505 W. Jones St. | 919/832–4604 | $7–$20 | AE,D,DC,MC,V.

Sushi Blues. Sushi. Miso soup, salad, and spicy noodles with cucumbers, tomatoes, and sauce precede each dish at this sushi place, which serves its food against a backdrop of blues music. The chef's choice sushi platter includes an assortment of California rolls, a surf clam, eel, salmon, tuna and snapper. The spicy chicken tempura is also popular. | 301 Glenwood Ave., Ste. 110 | 919/664–8061 | fax 919/664–8062 | Not accepted | No lunch Sun. | $7–$19 | AE, D, DC, MC, V.

Tír Na Nóg. Irish. The name means "land of eternal youth." Stone and farm implements pay homage to the Irish agricultural tradition. Authentic fare from pub grub to nouveau Irish cuisine is served. Irish entertainers play live Tue.–Sat. | 218 S. Blount St. | 919/833–7795 | No dinner Mon. | $8–$17 | AE, DC, MC, V.

EXPENSIVE

Angus Barn. Steak. A gun collection welcomes patrons to the lobby of this Raleigh institution. Downstairs is more family oriented and can get loud. Upstairs dining has live jazz, big leather chairs, and a wine collection. Certified Black Angus steaks are the focus, but lobster, crab cakes, oysters, pork, and lamb are also served. Kids' menu. | 9401 Glenwood Ave. | 919/787–3505 | No lunch | $25–$40 | AE, D, DC, MC, V.

Bloomsbury Bistro. Contemporary. White linens, lace curtains, and murals accent this eatery. The French-inspired menu changes seasonally. | 509–101 W. Whitaker Mill Rd. | 919/834–9011 | Closed Sun. No lunch | $17–$26 | AE, D, DC, MC, V.

Butterflies Restaurant. Contemporary. The ever-changing menu emphasizes seafood with light sauces such as pan seared grouper in warm citrus sauce. Australian rack of lamb and Montana-raised filet mignon are keystone entrées. The dining room is adorned with fresh flowers, a butterfly mural, and original ceramic tiles. | 6325 Falls of the Neuse Rd. | 919/878–2020 | Closed Sun. No lunch | $16–$25 | AE, D, MC, V.

42nd Street Oyster Bar. Seafood. Always bustling but particularly crowded on weekends, this Raleigh institution has been in business since 1931. Steamed oysters, clams, and shrimp, steak, pastas, and Cajun-style seafood selections are served. You can come for a full meal or just for the oyster bar. There's live blues Thurs.–Sat. | 508 W. Jones St. | 919/831–2811 | No lunch weekends | $12–$40 | AE, DC, MC, V.

Glenwood Grill. Contemporary. A seasonal menu of modern Southern cuisine is served in a setting of art-deco, metallic shades accented by cobalt blue. Seafood with an Asian influence is the house specialty. | 2929 Essex Circle | 919/782–3102 | No lunch weekends | $17–$33 | AE, MC, V.

Kanki Japanese House of Steaks. Japanese. Chefs prepare food right at the teppanyaki tables at both of the restaurant's locations. Entrées utilize shrimp, scallops, chicken, filet mignon, lobster, and vegetables. Most meals start with sushi. | 4500 Old Wake Forest Rd., North Market Sq.; 4325 Glenwood Ave., Crabtree Valley Mall | 919/876–4157; 919/782–9708 | Reservations not accepted Sat. | No lunch weekends at North Market Sq. location | $15–$40 | AE, DC, MC, V.

Margaux's. Contemporary. A massive stone fireplace adds warmth to this spot. The choices, which change daily, are diverse, consisting of beef, poultry, and seafood combinations. Try bacon-wrapped lobster and the raw bar. Reservations accepted only for five or more. | 8111 Creedmoor Rd. | 919/846–9846 | No lunch | $15–$35 | AE, DC, MC, V.

Second Empire. Contemporary. A historic Victorian building is the home for this restaurant and tavern that changes its menu monthly to serve the freshest seasonal dishes, such as the autumn pan roasted Manchester quail. Its tavern menu, available Monday to Friday, includes crispy chips and steak. In summer you can sit outside on the covered patio for cocktails, dinner, and entertainment. | 330 Hillsborough St. | 919/829–3663 | Closed Sun. No lunch | $22–$40 | AE, MC, V.

Simpson's Beef and Seafood. Steak/Seafood. Dine on steak and seafood such as oysters Rockefeller, lobster, or grilled salmon by candlelight. Chicken, pasta, and filet mignon round out the entrées. Jazz is played on the weekends; weeknights a pianist takes requests. | 5625 Creedmoor Rd. | 919/783–8818 | Closed Sun. and July–Aug. No lunch | $20–$30 | AE, D, DC, MC, V.

Sullivan's. Steakhouse. Dark mahogany wood, Art Deco-style furniture, and low lighting fill this steakhouse, which also includes a jazz bar. The 20 oz. Kansas City strip is the most frequently ordered dish, but there are also selections for those who shy away from red meat. The tequila–lime shrimp with black bean pico de gallo is a popular choice. | 414 Glenwood Ave. | 919/833–2888 | Closed Sun. | $15–$56 | AE, D, DC, MC, V.

Vinnie's Steakhouse and Tavern. Steak. Cigars, wine, and prime beef form this steak house's menu. All items are ordered à la carte. Reservations are accepted only for five or more. | 7440 Six Forks Rd. | 919/847–7319 | No lunch | $20–$40 | AE, D, DC, MC, V.

Winston's Grille. Contemporary. Popular with the business crowd at lunchtime, this place has a side patio with umbrellas. Steak, mahimahi, salmon, and some vegetarian dishes are typical items. Sunday brunch. Kids' menu. | 6401 Falls of Neuse Rd. | 919/790–0700 | No lunch Sat. | $23–$37 | AE, D, DC, MC, V.

Lodging

INEXPENSIVE

Days Inn–Crabtree. This motel is 2 mi from the Crabtree Mall and 5 mi from the Raleigh Airport. A fitness club is across the street. Restaurant. Some microwaves, some refrigerators. Cable TV, room phones. Outdoor pool. Laundry facilities. Pets allowed. | 6329 Glenwood Ave. | 919/781–7904 | fax 919/571–8385 | www.daysinn.com | 122 rooms | $49–$79 | AE, D, DC, MC, V.

Extended Stay America. A motel 10 mi from downtown Raleigh in a business area with its own shops and restaurants. Look for the big sign in front of this tan-colored, 3-story building next to the Studio Plus. In-room data ports, some kitchenettes, some microwaves, some refrigerators. Cable TV, room phones. Outdoor pool. Exercise equipment. Laundry facilities. No pets. | 911 Wake Towne Dr. | 919/829–7271 | fax 919/571–8385 | www.daysinn.com | 101 rooms, 3 suites | $49–$54 | AE, D, DC, MC, V.

Innkeeper North. Ten miles outside of downtown Raleigh sits this two-story white brick motel. Complimentary Continental breakfast. Some in-room data ports, some microwaves, some refrigerators. Cable TV, room phones. No pets. | 3401 North Blvd. | 919/872–9114 | fax 919/872–9114 | 61 rooms | $45–$69 | AE, D, DC, MC, V.

MODERATE

Comfort Inn–North. These are simple accommodations close to shops and restaurants. Complimentary breakfast weekdays. In-room data ports, some refrigerators. Cable TV. Indoor-outdoor pool. Hot tub. Exercise equipment. Laundry services. Business services. | 2910 Capitol Blvd. | 919/878–9550 | fax 919/876–5457 | www.comfortinns.com | 149 rooms | $69 | AE, D, DC, MC, V.

Fairfield Inn by Marriott–Northeast. Next to a major medical center, this three-story hotel provides frills-free lodging. Complimentary Continental breakfast. In-room data ports. Cable TV. Pool. Business services. Free parking. | 2641 Appliance Ct | 919/856–9800 | fax 919/856–9898 | www.fairfieldinn.com | 132 rooms | $58–$65 | AE, D, DC, MC, V.

Hampton Inn–Crabtree. Select from single, double, or king rooms at this hotel just 2 mi from the largest shopping mall in the state, the Crabtree Valley Mall. Complimentary Continental breakfast. In-room data ports, microwaves (in suites), refrigerators, some in-room hot tubs. Cable TV. Pool. Exercise equipment. Business services, airport shuttle, free parking. | 6209 Glenwood Ave. | 919/782–1112 or 800/426–7866 | fax 919/782–9119 | 141 rooms, 17 suites | $69–$99 | AE, D, DC, MC, V.

Holiday Inn Crabtree. Across the street from Crabtree Valley Mall, this 12-story hotel was refurbished in 1998. Complimentary breakfast, room service. In-room data ports, cable TV. Outdoor pool. Exercise center. Laundry facilities. Free parking. Pets allowed. | 4100 Glenwood Ave. | 919/782–8600 | 176 rooms | $69–$109 | AE, D, DC, MC, V.

Plantation Inn Resort. Spacious grounds, banquet facilities, and attractive landscaping make this a popular spot for weddings. Choose from king, queen, or twin beds in the guest rooms, they are appointed with a floral motif and oak furniture. 2 restaurants, bar, room service. In-room data ports, some refrigerators. Cable TV. Pool, lake, wading pool. Putting green. Fishing. Playground. Business services, airport shuttle. Some pets allowed (fee). | 6401 Capital Blvd. | 919/876–1411 or 800/521–1932 | fax 919/790–7093 | plan_inn@mindspring.com | www.plantationinnraleigh.com | 94 rooms | $58–$75 | AE, DC, MC, V.

Red Roof Inn–North. Within walking distance of restaurants and two shopping malls, this two-story structure underwent a renovation in 1997. Complimentary Continental breakfast. Cable TV. Pool. | 3201 Old Wake Forest Rd. | 919/878–9310 | fax 919/790–1451 | 148 rooms | $46–$80 | AE, D, DC, MC, V.

EXPENSIVE

Best Western. Across the street from the Crabtree Mall, this motel is outside downtown Raleigh. Complimentary Continental breakfast. In-room data ports, microwaves, refrigerators. Cable TV, room phones. Pets allowed (fee). | 6619 Glenwood Ave. | 919/782–8650 | fax 919/782–8650 | www.bestwestern.com | 88 rooms, 2 suites | $78–$84 | AE, D, DC, MC, V.

Brownestone. Popular among visiting parents, this hotel is adjacent to North Carolina State University. The mid-rise hotel is 1 mi from downtown Raleigh. Restaurant, bar. In-room data ports, some microwaves. Cable TV. Pool. Business services. Airport shuttle. Free parking. | 1707 Hillsborough St. | 919/828–0811 or 800/331–7919 | fax 919/834–0904 | www.brownstonehotel.com | 190 rooms | $59–129 | AE, D, DC, MC, V.

Courtyard by Marriott–North. This three-story hotel is convenient to shops, restaurants, and a movie theater. Restaurant (breakfast only), bar. In-room data ports, some microwaves, some refrigerators (in suites). Cable TV. Pool. Hot tub. Exercise equipment. Laundry facilities and services. Business services. Free parking. | 1041 Wake Towne Dr. | 919/821–3400 | fax 919/821–1209 | www.courtyard.com | 153 rooms, 13 suites | $59–$114 | AE, D, DC, MC, V.

6 "I'm thirsty"s, 9 "Are we there yet"s, 3 "I don't feel good"s,
1 car class upgrade.
At least something's going your way.

Hertz rents Fords and other fine cars. ® REG. U.S. PAT. OFF. © HERTZ SYSTEM INC., 2000/005-00

Make your next road trip more comfortable with a free one-class upgrade from Hertz.

Let's face it, a long road trip isn't always sunshine and roses. But with Hertz, you get a free one car class upgrade to make things a little more bearable. You'll also choose from a variety of vehicles with child seats, Optional Protection Plans, 24-Hour Emergency Roadside Assistance, and the convenience of NeverLost, the in-car navigation system that provides visual and audio prompts to give you turn-by-turn guidance to your destination. In a word: it's everything you need for your next road trip. Call your travel agent or Hertz at **1-800-654-2210** and mention PC# **906404** or check us out at **hertz.com** or AOL Keyword: **hertz**. Peace of mind. Another reason nobody does it exactly like Hertz.

Hertz
exactly.®

Crabtree Summit Hotel. Adjacent to Crabtree Valley Mall, in downtown Raleigh, and the State Fairgrounds, this gray four-story structure is noted for its spacious rooms and marble-floored lobby. Complimentary breakfast. In-room data ports, some microwaves, refrigerators. Cable TV. Pool. Exercise equipment. Business services, airport shuttle. | 3908 Arrow Dr. | 919/782–6868 or 800/521–7521 | fax 919/881–9340 | www.crabtreesummithotel.com | 84 rooms, 7 suites | $99–$124, $125–$175 suites | AE, D, DC, MC, V.

Embassy Suites Crabtree. One of the larger high-end hotels in central Raleigh, the nine-story, tropical-theme atrium welcomes you. Shopping, dining, and other attractions are nearby. Restaurant, bar, complimentary breakfast. In-room data ports, kitchenettes, microwaves. Cable TV. Indoor pool. Hot tub. Exercise equipment. Laundry service. Business services, airport shuttle. | 4700 Creedmoor Rd. | 919/881–0000 or 800/362–2779 | fax 919/782–7225 | www.embassy-suites.com | 225 suites | $124–$174 | AE, D, DC, MC, V.

Four Points by Sheraton. Across the street from Crabtree Valley Mall, this three-story hotel is a mile from downtown Raleigh at I–440 Exit 301. Restaurant, bar. In-room data ports. Cable TV. Indoor pool. Exercise equipment. Business services. Airport shuttle. | 4501 Creedmoor Rd. | 919/787–7111 | fax 919/783–0024 | fourptshotel@mindspring.com | www.four-pointsraleigh.com | 317 rooms | $69–$109 | AE, D, DC, MC, V.

Holiday Inn–Crabtree. This hotel is 8 mi from the airport and 2 mi from North Carolina State University. Some rooms have a Nintendo video game system. Restaurant, bar. In-room data ports. Cable TV. Pool. Exercise equipment. Laundry services. Business services, airport shuttle, free parking. Pets allowed. | 4100 Glenwood Ave. | 919/782–8600 | fax 919/782–7213 | www.basshotels.com | 176 rooms | $80–$120 | AE, D, DC, MC, V.

Holiday Inn–Downtown. Near the Crabtree Mall and many shops, restaurants and businesses in downtown Raleigh. Complimentary breakfast. In-room data ports. Cable TV, room phones. Health club. Laundry services. Pets allowed. | 320 Hillsborough St. | 919/782–8600 | fax 919/571–8385 | www.holiday-inn.com | 176 rooms | $109–$119 | AE, D, DC, MC, V.

Oakwood Inn. Close to downtown Raleigh, this Victorian home is in the 20-block Oakwood historic district. Each room has 19th-century antiques and a private bath. Complimentary breakfast. Cable TV. | 411 N. Bloodworth St. | 919/832–9712 or 800/267–9712 | fax 919/836–9263 | 6 rooms | $85–$150 | AE, D, DC, MC, V.

Quality Suites. Five miles north of downtown Raleigh, in the area known as "mini-city," the suites of this hotel all have separate living and sleeping rooms. Bar, complimentary breakfast. In-room data ports, microwaves, refrigerators. Cable TV. Pool. Exercise equipment. Laundry services. Business services, free parking. | 4400 Capital Blvd. | 919/876–2211 | fax 919/790–1352 | www.qualityinn.com | 114 suites | $86–$104 | AE, D, DC, MC, V.

Sheraton Capital Center Hotel. Four blocks from the Capitol building and next to the Civic Center. Restaurant, bar, complimentary breakfast, room service. In-room data ports, some refrigerators. Cable TV, some in-room VCRs. Indoor pool. Health club. Laundry services. Airport shuttle. No pets. | 421 South Salisbury St. | 919/834–9900 | fax 919/833–6342 | www.sheratoncapital.com | 355 rooms, 4 suites | $89–$200 | AE, D, DC, MC, V.

Velvet Cloak Inn. This property is two blocks from North Carolina State University, and four museums are within a 2 mi radius. It has a brick exterior with a balcony upstairs and white columns in front. The spacious rooms have Southern-style, dark-wood furnishings. Restaurant, bar, room service. In-room data ports, microwaves, refrigerators. Cable TV. Indoor pool. Laundry services. Business services, airport shuttle, free parking. | 1505 Hillsborough St. | 919/828–0333 or 800/334–4372 reservations | fax 919/828–2656 | www.velvetcloakinn.com | 172 rooms, 8 suites | $117 | AE, D, DC, MC, V.

William Thomas House. Now a bed-and-breakfast on the edge of downtown Raleigh, this Victorian home was built in 1881. Step off the front porch and you are only a block away from the governor's mansion. 19th-century antiques and high ceilings grace each room. Complimentary breakfast. In-room data ports, refrigerators. Cable TV. Free parking. No kids except by prior arrangement. No smoking. | 530 N. Blount St. | 919/755–9400 or 800/653–3466 | fax 919/755–3966 | www.williamthomashouse.com | 4 rooms | $108–$165 | AE, D, DC, MC, V.

ROANOKE RAPIDS

MAP 8, I3

(Nearby towns also listed: Murfreesboro, Rocky Mount)

Roanoke Rapids is a familiar name to those who traverse I–95. The small city, which sits in the northeastern part of the state, is just a few miles from the Virginia border.

What weary travelers may not know is that this Halifax County town, founded in 1893 as a cotton-mill site, has voluntarily extended hospitality to strangers in times of need. City employees have turned the civic center into a shelter for hundreds when inclement weather or other unforeseen circumstances have halted traffic, and local businesses have readily donated food to the stranded.

Information: Halifax County Tourism Development Authority | Box 144, Roanoke Rapids 27870 | 252/535–1687 or 800/522–4282 | halifaxcountytourism@coastalnet.com | www.visithalifax.com.

Attractions

Historic Halifax State Historic Site. The home of the Halifax Resolves, the first official action for independence by any colony, these seven restored buildings and two exhibit areas tell the story of this early river port. | St. David and Dobbs Sts., Halifax | 252/583–7191 | fax 252/583–9421 | Free | Call for hrs.

Roanoke Canal Trail. Some of the best-preserved early 19th-century canal constructions in the nation are on the 7 mi of this trail. Listed on the National Register of Historic Places, rustic bridges, earthen steps, wildflowers, stands of pines, and wildlife can be discovered on this self-guided hike. | 252/533–2847 or 800/522–4282 | Free | Daily 8–dusk.

ON THE CALENDAR

JUN.–JULY: *First for Freedom.* Performed outdoors, this drama tells the story of the events leading up to the signing of the Halifax Resolves, the first formal declaration of independence from Great Britain by an American colony. | Joseph Montford Amphitheater, King St., Halifax | 252/583–7191.

SEPT.: *Festival in the Park.* Food, live bands, children's games, and a 5K road race are held at Doyle Field. | 252/533–2847.

SEPT.: *Peanut Festival.* Enfield, 25½ mi south of Roanoke Rapids, calls itself the "Peanut Capital of the World". The town celebrates the peanut every third Saturday in September with peanut confections, Southern food, children's games, crafts, and entertainment. | 252/445–3146.

Dining

Ryan's Steakhouse. American. Lots of I–95 travelers stop here for fresh-cut steaks. The 200-item buffet has everything from macaroni and cheese to chicken potpie. No reservations on weekends. Kids' menu. | 1500 Julian Allsbrook Hwy. | 252/535–4266 | $9–$15 | AE, D, DC, MC, V.

Lodging

Comfort Inn. East of Lake Gaston, this hotel is 7 mi north of Halifax. Restaurant, Complimentary Continental breakfast. Cable TV. Pool. Business services. | Rte. 46, north of Virginia line; I–95 Exit 176 | 252/537–1011 | fax 252/537–9258 | www.comfortinns.com | 100 rooms | $54–$60 | AE, D, DC, MC, V.

New Yorker Motel. Open since 1950, this motel was built by a New Jersey native and is directly off the highway, 3 mi from downtown Roanoke Rapids. It's a one-story white brick building. Picnic area. Some kitchenettes, some refrigerators. Cable TV, some room phones. No pets. | U.S 301 S., Weldon | 252/536–3148 | 34 rooms | $35–$40 | D, MC, V.

ROBBINSVILLE

MAP 8, B2

(Nearby towns also listed: Bryson City, Fontana Dam)

Robbinsville is the largest town in Graham County, the wild and rugged southwestern boundary of the Great Smoky Mountains. There are only three traffic lights in the entire county; two-thirds of it lies in Nantahala National Forest.

Moviemakers, attracted by the isolated, pristine small-town charm of Robbinsville, filmed *Nell,* starring Jodie Foster, here, as well as parts of *The Fugitive,* with Harrison Ford.

ROBBINSVILLE

INTRO
ATTRACTIONS
DINING
LODGING

Information: Graham County Travel and Tourism Authority | Box 1206, Robbinsville 28771 | 828/479–3790 or 800/470–3790 | grahamchamber@graham.main.nc.us | www.wncguide.com/graham.

Attractions
Cherohala Skyway. One of the nation's 20 national scenic byways, this 50 mi stretch, 12 miles west of Robbinsville, crosses scenic ridges at altitudes higher than 5,000 ft. On clear days you can see into Great Smoky Mountains National Park. | 828/479–3790 or 800/470–3790 | Free | Daily.

Chief Junaluska's Grave Site. A prominent Cherokee leader credited with saving the life of Andrew Jackson at the Battle of Horseshoe Bend, Chief Junaluska was driven from North Carolina to Oklahoma on the Trail of Tears. He later returned on foot and was granted citizenship for his heroic deeds. His grave is on a hill marked with a memorial stone. | Rte. 143 Business | 828/479–3790 or 800/470–3790 | fax 828/479–9130 | Free | Daily.

Joyce Kilmer–Slickrock Wilderness. Named for the author of the poem "Trees", the refuge is 12 mi west of Robbinsville. Today this wilderness remains in a primitive state. The 2-mi Joyce Kilmer National Recreation Trail adjoins the 60-mi trail system of the Slickrock Wilderness Area. | Cheoah Ranger District, Rte. 1, Massey Branch Rd. | 828/479–6431 | Free, no-fee camping | Daily.

ON THE CALENDAR
OCT.: *Harvest Fest and Country Fair.* Mountain music, mountain dancing, handmade local arts and crafts, food, and antiques celebrate the county's rural tradition at the Stecoah Valley Center, 12 mi northeast of Robbinsville. | 828/479–3364 or 800/470–3790.

Dining
Aura's. American. Serving scampi, steak, and catfish, this Thunderbird Mountain Resort eatery overlooks Lake Santeetlah. Bread is baked fresh daily. | U.S. 129, Santeetlah | 828/479–6442 or 800/479–6442 | Closed Nov.–Mar. No lunch | $12–$23 | AE, D, DC, MC, V.

Tootie's Café. American. Country-fried steak, ham, and beef stew typify the country menu at this restaurant 11 mi northeast of Robbinsville. Live music (mountain, bluegrass, gospel) is performed Fri. nights May–Oct. | Rte. 28, Stecoah | 828/479–8430 | Closed Sun. and 2 wks Dec.–Jan. | $5–$13 | No credit cards.

Lodging

Snowbird Mountain Lodge. This roomy stone lodge is surrounded by 100-acres of the Joyce Kilmer Memorial Forest. The main structure was built in 1939 of native stone. Rooms have locally crafted hardwood tables and hand-stitched quilts. Dining room, complimentary breakfast, lunch, dinner. No TVs in rooms, no room phones. Hiking. No kids under 12. | 275 Santeetlah Rd. | 828/479–3433 or 800/941–9290 | fax 828/479–3473 | innkeeper@snowbirdlodge.com | www.snowbirdlodge.com | 20 rooms | $160–$275 | Closed Dec.–Mar. | MC, V | AP.

Tuskeegee Motel & Restaurant. In a rural farming area 7 mi from the 10,000-acre Fontana Dam site. Restaurant. Some kitchenettes, some microwaves, some refrigerators. Cable TV, no room phones. No pets. | Rte. 28 | 828/479–8464 | 11 rooms | $40–$68 | D, MC, V.

ROCKY MOUNT

MAP 8, I4

(Nearby towns also listed: Roanoke Rapids, Wilson)

Grand old homes reflect the money made in Rocky Mount from cotton, the railroad, and tobacco industries. The Tar River, a navigable waterway, spurred the town's settlement and development. Today, aeronautics, food-service distribution, manufacturing, pharmaceuticals, and agriculture dominate the business environment.

Information: Nash County Travel and Tourism | Box 392, Rocky Mount 27802 | 252/451–4705 or 800/849–6825 | mlamm@rockymountchamber.org.

Attractions

City of Rocky Mount Children's Museum. Open since 1954, this museum provides educational and fun exhibits for kids and adults. Many hands-on experiences for children. | Sunset Park | 252/972–1167 | museum@cirocky-mount.nc.us | $2; free Wed. 2–4 | Weekdays 10–5, Sat. 12–5, Sun. 2–5.

Down East Festival. Held the second Saturday in October in the uptown streets of Rocky Mount, this festival showcases music, food, dancing, and arts and crafts. | 252/972–1151 | events@ci.rockymount.nc.us.

ON THE CALENDAR

FEB.–MAY: *Artists on the Mall Series.* Bagpipe players, square dancers, and other entertainers perform here at Tarrytown Mall. | 2320 Sunset Ave. | 252/451–4705 or 800/849–6825.

MAY: *Happening on the Common.* Art, crafts, children's games, live music, food, and historic reenactments take place all month in the historic district. | 252/823–4159.

MAY: *Harambee Festival.* You can celebrate African–American culture through dance, music, and costumes. | Harambee Sq | 252/451–4705 or 800/849–6825.

SEPT.: *Heritage Festival.* This annual celebration has arts and crafts, games and contests, entertainment, food, and rides for the kids. | Indian Lake Park, U.S. 64 | 252/823–7241.

OCT.: *Pumpkin Festival.* Tiny Spring Hope ushers in fall with parades, entertainment, games, and food. | 252/451–4705 or 800/849–6825.

Dining

Bob Melton's Barbecue. Barbecue. You can choose from eastern North Carolina-style barbecue, seafood platters, or chicken here at the oldest sit-down barbecue restaurant in the state. There's a view of Tar River. | 631 E. Ridge St. | 252/446–8513 | $6–$15 | MC, V.

Carleton House Restaurant. American/Casual. In business since 1961, this restaurant's slogan is "Southern home-cooked food like mom used to make." It serves roast beef, greens, potatoes, and other simple classics, sometimes from a buffet. You can call in advance if you prefer to order a la carte. This restaurant has an inn of the same name in its backyard. | 213 N. Church St. | 252/977–6576 | No lunch Sat. | $10–$25 | AE, MC, V.

Kay's Restaurant. American. For more than 80 years, this restaurant with counter seating has served home-cooked fried chicken, country steak, shrimp, vegetables, rolls, and desserts. | 111 Tarboro St. | 252/442–5328 | Reservations not accepted | Closed weekends. No dinner | $2–$10 | D, MC, V.

Lodging

Best Western. Next to a bowling alley and a gas station, this two-story red and white motel is near shops and restaurants. A business conference room and services are available. Restaurant, complimentary Continental breakfast. Some microwaves, some refrigerators. Cable TV, room phones. Outdoor pool. Health club. Laundry services. No pets. | 1921 N. Wesleyan Blvd. | 252/442–8101 | fax 252/442–1048 | www.bestwestern.com | 72 rooms | $59–$74 | AE, MC, V.

Bright Leaf Motel. In a quiet, rural area 10 mi outside downtown Rocky Mount, this one-story white brick motel has typical services and facilities. Cable TV, room phones. Pets allowed. | U.S. 301 S., Sharpsburg | 252/977–1988 | fax 252/977–3269 | 28 rooms | $40–$70 | AE, D, MC, V.

Carleton House. Established more than 40 years ago, this hotel two blocks from the train station was remodeled in 1994. There are two floors with outside entrances. Restaurant, complimentary breakfast. Cable TV. Pool. Business services. | 215 N. Church St. | 252/977–0410 | fax 252/985–2115 | 42 rooms | $50–$56 | AE, DC, MC, V.

Comfort Inn. You can walk to restaurants next door to this five-story hotel that's 5 mi from the Children's Museum. You can also order room service from Coach's Sports Bar and Grill in the neighboring Holiday Inn. Complimentary Continental breakfast. Some in-room data ports. Cable TV. Pool. Exercise equipment. Laundry service. Business services, airport shuttle. Pets allowed. | 200 Gateway Blvd. | 252/937–7765 | fax 252/937–3067 | www.comfortinns.com | 125 rooms | $73–$90 | AE, D, DC, MC, V.

Hampton Inn. Near the lake and the park, this 1995 four-story hotel is 3 mi west of the Children's Museum, 1 mi from I–95 Exit 138. Complimentary Continental breakfast. Some refrigerators. Cable TV. Pool. Business services. | 530 Winstead Ave. | 252/937–6333 or 800/426–7866 | fax 252/937–4333 | www.hamptoninn.com | 124 rooms | $68 | AE, D, DC, MC, V.

Holiday Inn–Dortches. In a quiet, secluded area and about 7 mi north of downtown, this two-story hotel has outside entrances. You can order room service from the hotel's restaurant. Restaurant, room service. In-room data ports, some microwaves, some refrigerators. Cable TV. Pool. Exercise equipment. Laundry facilities, laundry services. Business services. Pets allowed (fee). | 5350 Dortches Blvd. | 252/937–6300 or 800/HOLIDAY | fax 252/937–6312 | holiday-inn.com | 154 rooms | $62–68 | AE, D, DC, MC, V.

SALISBURY

MAP 8, E4

(Nearby towns also listed: Concord, Kannapolis, Lexington, Statesville)

Salisbury's history is old money made from textiles and chemicals, and Cheerwine, a cherry-flavored soft drink with no alcohol, despite its name. The town is now headquarters for Food Lion, a supermarket chain, and 23 downtown blocks are on the National Register.

Information: **Rowan County Convention and Visitors Bureau** | Box 4044, Salisbury 28145 | 704/638–3100 or 800/332–2343 | www.visitsalisburync.com.

Attractions

North Carolina Transportation Museum. At the Southern Railway Company's largest steam locomotive facility, you can see antique autos, a "Bumper to Bumper" exhibit, and airplanes and railroad rolling stock. For a fee, you can also take a steam or diesel engine ride. | 411 S. Salisbury Ave., Spencer | 704/636–2889 or 877/628–6386 | fax 704/639–1881 | Free | Apr.–Oct., Mon.–Sat. 9–5, Sun. 1–5; Nov.–Mar., Tues.–Sat. 10–4, Sun. 1–4.

Old Stone House. A German immigrant built this two-story Georgian house with carefully shaped and matched stones in 1766. | Old Stone House Rd., Granite Quarry | 704/633–5946 | fax 704/633–9858 | $3 | Apr.–Nov., weekends 1–4, or by appointment.

Rowan Museum. This 1854 courthouse, with artifacts and historical displays, survived Stoneman's raid. | 202 N. Main St. | 704/633–5946 | fax 704/633–9858 | $3 | Thurs.–Sun. 1–4.

Salisbury Historic District. You can see the 1820 Dr. Josephus Hall House, built first as the Salisbury Female Academy, then home to Dr. Hall, chief surgeon at the Salisbury Confederate Prison. The district is downtown and in residential West Square. | 132 E. Innes St. | 704/638–3100 or 704/636–0103 | fax 704/642–2011 | Free | Visitor center weekdays 9–5, Sat. 10–4, Sun. 1–4.

Salisbury National Cemetery. There are 11,700 Union soldiers buried here in 18 trench graves. The soldiers died at the Salisbury Confederate Prison during the Civil War. | 202 Government Rd. | 704/636–2661 | Free | Daily.

Waterworks Visual Arts Center. The city's first waterworks building, built in 1913, hosts regional and national gallery exhibits, studio classes, workshops, and lectures. You can experience art through touch, sound, smell, and sight at a sensory garden. | 1 Water St. | 704/636–1882 | fax 704/636–1985 | www.waterworks.org | Free | Weekdays 9–5, Sat. 10–4, Sun. 1–4.

ON THE CALENDAR

JUNE: *Rail Days.* You can take a ride on 1920s and 1930s steam engines and diesel locomotives here at the North Carolina Transportation Museum. You can also enjoy model train layouts, kids' games, music, and a "railroadiana" show and sale. | 411 S. Salisbury Ave., Spencer | 704/636–2889.

SEPT.: *O. O. Rufty's General Store Basement Tour.* On Labor Day, browse antiques in the basement of this 1905 store with everything from dry goods, cider presses, and liquid blueing to stick candy and salves. Hear live music and enjoy soda-fountain drinks. | 126 E. Innes St. | 704/633–4381 or 800/611–6055.

Dining

DJ's Restaurant. American. This is a family-oriented spot, with a menu of souvlaki, gyros, pasta, pizza, burgers, and sautéed dishes. Kids' menu. | 1502 W. Innes St. | 704/638–9647 | $7–$15 | AE, D, DC, MC, V.

Farm House Restaurant. Southern. There's a wraparound porch with rocking chairs at this family-style restaurant and a fireplace inside. Kids' menu. | 1602 Jake Alexander Blvd. | 704/633–3276 | Closed Sun. | $8–$11 | AE, MC, V.

La Cava. Italian. Built in 1897, this former church has hardwood floors, exposed brick, and leaded stained glass. Try seafood, veal, crêpes suzette, or a soufflé. | 329 S. Church St. | 704/637–7174 | Reservations essential | Closed Sun. No lunch Sat. | $16–$42 | AE, MC, V.

Wrenn House. American. Once an all girls academy, this restaurant has a pub, sunroom, and separate dining room for nonsmokers. Choose from sandwiches, salads, soup, pasta, and salmon. Kids' menu. | 115 S. Jackson St. | 704/633–9978 | Closed Sun. | $6–$18 | AE, D, MC, V.

Lodging

Chanticleer Motel. In a wooded area 2 mi from the Salisbury Historic District, Salisbury National Cemetery, and the Waterworks Visual Arts Center. Room service. Cable TV. No pets. | 1285 Old Union Rd. | 704/636–6520 | fax 704/637–9271 | 20 rooms | $35–$45 | AE, D, MC, V.

Holiday Inn. The two- and three-story hotel with four buildings is in a secluded area at I–85 Exit 75. Restaurant, bar with entertainment, room service. In-room data ports, some in-room refrigerators. Cable TV. Indoor-outdoor pool. Hot tub. Basketball, exercise equipment. Laundry service. Business services. | 530 S. Jake Alexander Blvd. | 704/637–3100 or 800/465–4329 | fax 704/637–9152 | holiday-inn.com | 181 rooms | $60–$80 | AE, D, DC, MC, V.

SANFORD

MAP 8, G5

(Nearby towns also listed: Aberdeen, Fayetteville, Pinehurst, Southern Pines)

Sanford, a railroad village named after a railroad engineer, was incorporated into Moore County in 1874. Portions of Moore County were merged into Lee County in 1907, and Sanford is now the county seat. The town's historic downtown renovation started with the makeover of the Temple Theatre, an elegant 1920s movie and opera house.

Information: Sanford Area Chamber of Commerce | Box 519, Sanford 27331 | 919/775–7341 | ccsanford@wave-net.net.

SANFORD

INTRO
ATTRACTIONS
DINING
LODGING

Attractions

House in the Horseshoe State Historic Site. Bullet holes are still visible in this 1772 house where Whigs and Tories fought. Named for the horseshoe-shaped bend in Deep River, the house belonged to a North Carolina governor. | 324 Alston House Rd. | 910/947–2051 | fax 910/947–2051 | Free | Mar.–Oct., Mon.–Sat. 9–5, Sun. 1–5; Nov.–Apr., Tues.–Sat. 10–4, Sun. 1–4.

Temple Theater. This 1925 theater is the centerpiece for the historic district renovations. The nonprofit theater attracts large audiences from all over the state for chamber music, jazz recitals, film, and drama. | 120 Carthage St. | 919/774–4155 | Tours by appointment.

Raven Rock State Park. You can see the 152-ft-high rock jutting out at 45 degrees over the Cape Fear River in this 3,549-acre park 20 mi east of Sanford. There are 11 mi of hiking trails, 7 mi of bridle trails, and picnic areas, canoeing, and fishing for bass, crappie, warmouth, bluegill, catfish, and sunfish. You can backpack camp for a permit fee. | 3009 Raven Rock Rd., Lillington | 910/893–4888 | fax 910/814–2200 | ils.unc.edu/parkproject/raro.html | Free | Daily.

ON THE CALENDAR

JULY: *Brick City Fat Tire Festival.* You can see an 8K race, biathlon, classic car show, fat-tire bike races, street races, and kids' games. | 919/775–7341.
AUG.: *House in the Horseshoe Battle Reenactment.* Watch a reenactment of the Revolutionary War's Whig-Tory militia skirmish. | 324 Alston House Rd. | 910/947–2051.

Dining

Brick City Chop House. Continental. Lots of rich wood, white table cloths, and a cigar lounge characterize this downtown restaurant with a menu of steaks, chops, and fresh seafood. | 101 S. Steele St. | 919/774–8898 | Closed Sun. | $18–$39 | AE, D, MC, V.

W B Joyce & Co. American. This restaurant has large banquet rooms, balconies, and a patio. Try the beef tips or quail. Kids' menu. | 808 Spring La. | 919/774–5559 | Reservations not accepted | Closed Sun. | $8–$20 | AE, D, MC, V.

Lodging

Comfort Inn. The rooms here are quiet, simple, and affordable. Bar, complimentary Continental breakfast. In-room data ports, some refrigerators. Cable TV. Pool. Sauna. Exercise equipment. Laundry facilities. | 1403 N. Horner Blvd. | 919/774–6411 | fax 919/774–7018 | 122 rooms | $54 | AE, D, DC, MC, V.

SHELBY

MAP 8, D5

(Nearby towns also listed: Cherryville, Gastonia)

Shelby is in the upper Piedmont, on the way to the mountains. Arching trees shade Colonial Revival buildings, and the farmer's market sells handpicked fruits and vegetables and homebaked breads and cakes. You can see a 1919 Herschell-Spillman Carousel that operated in City Park for three decades.

Information: Cleveland County Travel and Tourism | Box 1210, Shelby 28151 | 704/484–4999 or 800/480–8687 | www.co.cleveland.nc.us.

Attractions

Central Shelby Historic District. A walking tour showcases 1850s buildings, the house of former Governor O. Max Gardner, the Cleveland County Historical Museum, and a 1907 Classic Revival courthouse. Get a map at the Shelby Chamber of Commerce, 200 S. Lafayette Street. | 704/481–1842 or 704/487–8521 | Free | Daily.

Cleveland County Historical Museum. The geodetic center has 1-inch-square marble tiles embedded in the central hallway. Fixed and rotating exhibits, with many artifacts donated by locals, relate county history. A 1950s courtroom can be seen by appointment. | Court Sq | 704/482–8186 | Free | Tues.–Fri. 9–4.

ON THE CALENDAR

JUNE: *Cleveland County Bluegrass Festival.* Hear live bluegrass bands, taste home-cooked food, and take a mule train ride at this lively event. | 704/484–5483.
SEPT.–OCT.: *Cleveland County Fair.* Exhibits include horticulture, home and gardens, school, cattle, barns, and horses. See demolition derbies, tractor pulls, a circus, talent shows, cheerleaders, a grandparents contest, a beauty pageant, and live entertainment. | 704/487–0651 or 704/487–0652.

Dining

Bridges Barbecue Lodge. Barbecue. Built in 1953, this cookhouse has wood-paneled walls and ceiling, and a teal-colored counter. The family-style menu has chopped pork barbecue and hush puppies. No liquor. | 2000 E. Dixon Blvd. (U.S. 74 Bypass) | 704/482–8567 | Closed Mon.–Tues. | $5–$10 | No credit cards.

Chen's. Chinese. You can try the daily buffet lunch or one of the house dinner specials of spicy ginger shrimp and Peking pork at this casual place that's full of Chinese ornaments. | 209 W. Dixon Blvd. | 704/484–9669 | Reservations not accepted | No lunch Sat. | $6–$15 | AE, MC, V.

Lodging

Days Inn. This two-story hotel with exterior entrances is within 2 mi of stores and restaurants. Restaurant, room service. Cable TV. Pool. Laundry facilities. | 1431 W. Dixon St. (U.S. 74) | 704/482–6721 | fax 704/480–1423 | 97 rooms | $54 | AE, D, DC, MC, V.

Econo Lodge. This one-story motel is ½ mi from shopping and dining in downtown Shelby. Complimentary Continental breakfast. Some refrigerators. Cable TV, room phones. Outdoor pool. No pets. | 825 W. Dixon Blvd. | 704/482–3821 | fax 704/482–3821 | www.econolodge.com | 62 rooms | $34–$80 | AE, D, DC, MC, V.

SMITHFIELD

(Nearby towns also listed: Dunn, Goldsboro, Raleigh)

Ava Gardner was born and is buried here. The town, founded in 1746, still nurtures its agricultural, Civil War, and railroad heritage with museums and historic sites. There are also lots of factory outlet stores here, near Interstates 95 and 40.

Information: Johnston County Visitors Bureau | 1115 Industrial Park Dr., Smithfield 27577 | 919/989–8687 or 800/441–7829 | www.johnstonco-cvb.org.

Attractions

Ava Gardner Museum. Film clips and scripts, costumes, U.S. and foreign posters, and scrapbooks of Gardner's life fill the 3,000-square-ft memorial. | 325 E. Market St. | 919/934–5830 or 800/441–7829 | fax 919/934–5830 | www.avagardner.org | $3 | Daily 1–5.

ON THE CALENDAR

APR.: *Ham and Yam Festival.* Watch cooking contests, taste ham biscuits, barbecued pork, and sweet potatoes, and see arts and crafts, exhibits, a 5K run, a carnival, and live entertainment. | 919/934–0887.

MAY: *Brookhill Steeplechase.* More than 60 horses take part in this race sanctioned by the National Steeplechase Association. Elaborate tailgating parties and fancy hats are part of the one-day event. | Brookhill Farm, Clayton | 919/838–1492.

SEPT.: *Benson Mule Days.* Mule contests, rodeos, a parade, an arts-and-crafts show, live music, street dancing and clogging, and lots of food draw 70,000 people here. | Grove Park and other areas, Benson | 919/894–8204 or 919/894–3825.

OCT.: *Railroad Days Festival.* Hot-air balloon rides, crafts shows, a 10K run, and a street dance highlight this Selma event on the first October weekend. | 919/965–9841.

Dining

Golden Choice Buffet and Brass Bell Bakery. Southern. You can watch the bakers make pies, cookies, breads, and brownies at this restaurant-bakery. It serves a wide range of Southern food, such as fried chicken, cornbread, and sweet tea. Selections include inch-thick steaks, homemade meat loaf, and locally grown sweet potatoes. | 1319 Brightleaf Blvd. | 919/934–0508 | $6–$9 | D, MC, V.

Smithfield's Chicken and Bar-B-Q. Barbecue. The eatery offers family-style dinners and drive-thru service for eastern North Carolina–style pork barbecue, fried chicken, and Brunswick stew. Kids' menu. | 924 Brightleaf Blvd. | 919/934–8721 | $5–$10 | No credit cards.

Lodging

Comfort Inn. This two-story hotel is next door to a restaurant and is 1 mi from outlet and antiques shopping and restaurants. Complimentary Continental breakfast. Some refrigerators. Cable TV. Pool. Hot tub. Exercise equipment. Business services. | 1705 Industrial Park Dr., Selma | 919/965–5200 or 800/228–5150 | www.comfortinns.com | 80 rooms | $60–$84 | AE, D, DC, MC, V.

Four Oaks Lodging. This motel is near the Tobacco Museum, Bentfield Battlegrounds, the outlet shopping mall, Atkinson Mill, the Benson Museum, and Benson State Park. You can swim in the pool at the Holiday Travel Park Camping Resort ½ mi from the motel. Cable TV. Pets allowed. | 4606 U.S. 301 S | 919/963–3596 | 15 rooms | $19–$52 | AE, D, DC, MC, V.

Howard Johnson Express. This orange and tan stucco hotel is ¼ mi from the outlet mall and has plenty of parking. Complimentary Continental breakfast. Cable TV. Pool. Playground. Business services. | 2200 E. Market St.; I–95 Exit 95 | 919/934–7176 or 800/406–1411 | fax 919/934–6995 | www.hojo.com | 60 rooms | $40–$90 | AE, D, DC, MC, V.

Log Cabin Motel. Poplar-wood furniture gives this motel its rustic charm. It is across from the outlet shopping mall and 5 mi from town. You can use the motel's private trout- and bass-stocked fishing pond. Restaurant, bar. Some microwaves, some refrigerators. Cable TV. Pond. Laundry facilities. Pets allowed (fee). | 2491 U.S. 70 | 919/934–1534 | fax 919/934–7399 | 61 rooms | $40–$42 | AE, D, MC, V.

Masters Economy Inn. Just off Highway 70 at Exit 97, this two-story, red brick motel is near the outlet mall, train station, and restaurants. Restaurant. Cable TV. Pool. Laundry facilities. Business services. | U.S. 70A and I–95, Selma | 919/965–3771 | fax 919/965–5565 | 119 rooms | $36–$40 | AE, D, DC, MC, V.

SOUTH BRUNSWICK ISLANDS

MAP 8, H7

(Nearby towns also listed: Kure Beach, Southport, Wilmington)

These secluded barrier islands stretch east to west across the southern coast. There are seven community beaches, some arcades and amusement rides, and more than 30 golf courses.

Information: **NC Brunswick Islands** | Box 1186, Shallotte 28459 | 800/795–7263 | www.ncbrunswick.com.

Attractions

Oak Island Lighthouse. Built in 1958 on Oak Island's Caswell Beach, this 17-story beacon can be seen from 24 mi out. Its light, the brightest in the western hemisphere, flashes four times every 10 seconds. | 300A Caswell Beach Rd. | 910/278–5592 | Free | Daily.

ON THE CALENDAR

OCT.: *North Carolina Oyster Festival.* See oyster-shucking contests, 5K and 10K runs, more than 100 arts-and-crafts booths, and live entertainment. | West Brunswick High School, 550 Whiteville Rd. NW, Shallotte | 800/426–6644.
DEC.: *Christmas by the Sea Festival.* In mid-month there's a parade, home tours, best-decorated home and business contests, and *The Nutcracker* ballet. | 800/457–6964.

Dining

Crabby Oddwaters. Seafood. Above a seafood market, the restaurant has dinners and an in-season raw bar. Kids' menu. | 310 Sunset Blvd. (Rte. 179), Sunset Beach | 910/579–6372 | $20–$30 | MC, V.

Ella's of Calabash. Seafood. The big tables here can accommodate families in smoking and nonsmoking areas. There are huge portions of food, and very fresh seafood. Kids' menu and early-bird suppers. | 148 River Rd., Calabash | 910/579–6728 | $13–$22 | MC, V.

Lodging

Sea Trail Plantation Golf Resort. This expansive facility has one-, two-, and four-bedroom villas with dishwasher, washer-dryer, living room, dining room, and porch. There are two pro shops, and a village activity center. The indoor-outdoor pool and kiddie pool are flanked by a snack bar. It is near activities such as canoeing, pier fishing, and kayaking. You can also buy ferry tickets to Myrtle Beach. 2 restaurants, 2 bars. Some kitchenettes, some microwaves. Cable TV, in-room VCRs. Indoor-outdoor pool, wading pool. Hot tub. Massage.

Three 18-hole golf courses, one tennis court. Health club. Bicycles. Shops. Baby-sitting. Children's programs. Laundry facilities. Business services, airport shuttle. No pets. | 211 Clubhouse Rd. SW | 910/287–1100 | fax 910/287–1104 | www.seatrail.com | 434 villas | $70–$270 per person | AE, D, MC, V.

Winds Inn and Suites. This hotel has standard rooms, suites, and a six-bedroom house. Golf packages are offered. Picnic area, complimentary breakfast. Some kitchenettes, some minibars, refrigerators. Cable TV. 3 pools. Hot tub. Putting green. Exercise equipment. Beach. Laundry facilities. Business services. | 310 E. 1st St., Ocean Isle Beach | 910/579–6275 or 800/334–3581 | fax 910/579–2884 | 72 rooms, 48 suites; 6 cottages | $120–$156 | AE, D, DC, MC, V.

SOUTHERN PINES

MAP 8, G5

(Nearby towns also listed: Aberdeen, Fayetteville, Laurinburg, Pinehurst, Sanford)

Filled with longleaf pine trees, dogwoods, and azaleas, Southern Pines attracts writers and artists with a year-round program in arts and humanities. The small downtown has many restaurants, specialty stores, and offices. Route 2 connects Southern Pines to Pinehurst.

Information: Pinehurst Area Convention and Visitors Bureau | Box 2270, Southern Pines 28388 | 910/692–3330 or 800/346–5362 | www.homeofgolf.com.

THE SANDHILLS

Because of its sandy soil—it once was Atlantic beach, though it is now more than 100 mi from the sea—the area now known as the Sandhills wasn't of much use to early settlers, mostly Scots. So they switched from farming to lumbering and making turpentine for a livelihood. Since the early 1900s, however, Moore County, with its gently undulating hills, spring-fed lakes, and mild climate, has proved ideal for tennis, cycling, all manner of equine activities, and golf. Most especially golf. The county has the highest concentration of golf courses per person in the country and enough year-round golf packages to suit just about any budget.

No major highways feed directly into this part of the Sandhills, which is in the south-central portion of the Piedmont. This is an additional plus for the millionaires and presidents, movie stars, and athletes, even sharpshooters (namely Annie Oakley), who've found refuge here. It also means that forests (including one of the Southeast's few remaining virgin long-leaf pine forests), meandering country roads, historic sites and inns, and villages filled with antiques shops such as Cameron, founded in the 19th century, remain virtually untouched.

Another draw, especially in the spring, summer, and fall, are the gardens. Dozens of gardens at Sandhills Community College, for example, serve as living and learning laboratories not just for the public but for the school's horticulture and landscaping program, whose graduates work worldwide.
Related towns: Pinehurst, Southern Pines.

© Corbis

Attractions

Cameron. Browse for goodies in 60 antiques stores here in this 19th-century historic town. | 12 mi north of U.S. 1 | 910/245–7001 | Free | Most shops Tues.–Sat. 10–5, Sun. 1–5.

Sandhills Horticultural Gardens. See the wetlands from elevated boardwalks in 15 acres of roses, fruits and vegetables, herbs, conifers, hollies, a formal English garden, pools, and a waterfall. | Sandhills Community College, 2200 Airport Rd. | 910/695–3882 or 800/338–3944 | Free | Daily.

Shaw House. Built around 1840, this house is now home to the Moore County Historical Association. The 1770 Garner House and Britt-Sanders cabin have also been moved to this site. | S.W. Broad St. and Morganton Rd. | 910/692–2051 | fax 910/692–8051 | Free | Apr.–Dec., Wed.–Sun. 1–4.

Weymouth Center for the Arts and Humanities. This former home of author and publisher James Boyd has concerts, lectures, and literary events sponsored by the North Carolina Literary Hall of Fame, which is housed here. See the vast gardens. | 555 E. Connecticut Ave. | 910/692–6261 | fax 910/692–1815 | Free | Weekdays 10–12 and 2–4, tours by appointment.

Weymouth Woods Nature Preserve. A 571-acre wildlife preserve on the eastern outskirts of town, the preserve has 4 mi of hiking trails, a beaver pond, and a museum, and there's a naturalist on staff. | 1024 N. Fort Bragg Rd. | 910/692–2167 | Free | Mon.–Sat. 9–6, Sun. 12–5.

ON THE CALENDAR

OCT.: *Cameron Antiques Fair.* More than 300 dealers show antiques and collectibles in historic-district shops and on Main Street. | 910/245–7001.

NOV.: *Festival of Trees and Lights.* Each tree has its own theme, and Santa makes a visit at the century-old Pine Needle Lodge in Southern Pines, 4 mi east of Pinehurst. A brilliant array of flashing bulbs, music, and entertainment ring in the holiday season. | 910/692–3323 or 910/295–8415.

Dining

La Terrace. French. Tables have white cloths, silverware, and fresh flowers, and there's a terrace surrounded by large trees. You can try the duck albarine, which is roasted duck breast with goose-liver stuffing and port wine–shittake mushroom sauce. There's imported wine. Kids' menu. Early-bird suppers. | 270 S.W. Broad St. | 910/692–5622 | Closed Sun. No lunch Sat. | $13–$26 | D, MC, V.

Lob Steer Inn. American. There's a fireplace, and autographed photos of race-car drivers and golfers are on the walls. The salad and dessert bars complement house specials of mahi mahi, pork loin, salmon, and steaks. Kids' menu. Early-bird suppers. | U.S. 1 N | 910/692–3503 | Reservations essential | No lunch | $13–$30 | AE, DC, MC, V.

195. Eclectic. Wooden tables, tablecloths, and candles at night describe this restaurant next to Nature's Own Market. Choose from fresh fish, beef, pork, or grilled Portobello mushrooms. Listen to classical guitar music once a month. | 195 Bell Ave. | 910/692–3811 | Closed Sun.–Mon. No dinner Tues. | $15–$20 | D, MC, V.

Squire's Pub. English. See British artifacts, maps, and photographs on the walls here. There's a large selection of beers, and a menu with steak and and seafood dishes. Kids' menu. | 1720 U.S. 1 S | 910/695–1161 | Reservations not accepted | Closed Sun. | $7–$17 | AE, D, MC, V.

Lodging

Days Inn. This one-story, peach-colored brick motel has golf packages for the Little River Golf Course, which is 5 mi away. Complimentary Continental breakfast. Some microwaves, some refrigerators. Cable TV, room phones. Outdoor pool. Pets allowed. | 1420 U.S. 1 S | 910/692–7581 | fax 910/692–7581 | www.daysinn.com | 120 rooms | $35–$70 | AE, D, DC, MC, V.

Hampton Inn. There are 21 golf courses within 5 mi of the property. Two floors have outside entrances, and some rooms have been upgraded with sofabeds, microwaves, and refrigerators. Complimentary Continental breakfast. Cable TV. Pool. Laundry facilities. Business services. | 1675 U.S. 1 S | 910/692–9266 or 800/333–9266 | fax 910/692–9298 | www.hampton-inn.com | 126 rooms | $79–$89 | AE, D, DC, MC, V.

Holiday Inn. There's cherry-wood furniture in this lodging with exterior entrances 4 mi from Pinehurst Resort and Country Club. Restaurant, bar, room service. In-room data ports. Cable TV. Pool. Tennis courts. Exercise equipment. Video games. Business services, airport shuttle. | U.S. 1 at Morganton Rd. | 910/692–8585 or 800/262–5737 | fax 910/692–5213 | www.holiday-inn.com | 160 rooms | $64–$90 | AE, D, DC, MC, V.

Hyland Hills Resort. This resort is near 87 golf courses, and is to be the site of the LPGA US Open in 2001. The Olympic Equestrian Team trains in town, and there are a number of horse shows held throughout the year. The resort is 5 mi south of Cameron, home of the popular Piners Antique Village. Picnic area. Some microwaves, some refrigerators. Cable TV, room phones. Golf packages. Outdoor pool. No pets. | 4110 U.S. 1 N | 910/692–7615 | fax 910/692–6983 | 60 rooms | $42–$136 | D, MC, V.

Mid Pines Inn and Golf Club. In Georgian 1920s style, the inn has rooms with deep-blue or forest-green carpeting and French wallpaper. No two rooms are alike, and there are five villas on the 10th fairway. All meals are included in the room price. Dining room, bar, room service. Some minibars, some refrigerators. Cable TV. Pool. 18-hole golf course, putting green, 4 tennis courts. Business services, airport shuttle. | 1010 Midland Rd. | 910/692–9362 or 800/323–2114 | fax 910/692–4615 | www.golfnc.com | 112 rooms; 7 apartments; 5 cottages | $140 | AE, D, DC, MC, V | AP.

Pine Needles Lodge and Golf Club. Run by the legendary golfer Peggy Kirk Bell, the 1920s hotel has rooms with two double beds and a sitting area. Dining room, bar, room service. Some refrigerators. Cable TV. Pool. Driving range, 18-hole golf course, putting green, tennis courts. Bicycles. Business services. | 1005 Midland Rd. | 910/692–7111 or 800/747–7272 | fax 910/692–5349 | www.golfnc.com | 71 rooms in 10 lodges | $210–$460 (2–night minimum stay) | AE, MC, V.

SOUTHPORT

MAP 8, I7

(Nearby towns also listed: Kure Beach, South Brunswick Islands, Wilmington)

★ For 200 years, life in Southport, a small fishing village at the Cape Fear River, has revolved around boats and water. In town you can stroll through small parks, take bike rides on streets lined with stately homes and ancient oaks, browse in antiques shops, and watch pelicans. From 1792 to 1887 Southport was called Smithville. The town was portrayed in Robert Ruark's novel *The Old Man and the Boy*, and *Crimes of the Heart* was filmed here. The town is listed on the National Register of Historic Places.

Information: | Southport–Oak Island Chamber of Commerce: 4841 Long Beach Rd. | 910/457–6964 | www.southport-oakisland.com | Free | Daily; Chamber of Commerce weekdays 8:30–5, Sat. 9–4.

Attractions

Bald Head Island. A reservation-only passenger ferry (910/457–5003; $15 round-trip, operates 8 AM–11 PM) links Southport and Bald Head Island. On the island, take a tour (reservations) to the 1817 109-ft Old Baldy Lighthouse, watch loggerhead turtles, tour the maritime forest with a naturalist, picnic or lunch at the restaurants, and play golf, swim, or fish. | Bald Head Island | 910/457–5000, 910/457–5003, or 800/234–1666 | fax 910/457–9232 | www.baldheadisland.com | Free | Daily.

Brunswick Nuclear Plant Visitors Center. See 30 energy-related exhibits on the production of electricity, electrical safety, alternative energy sources, and energy conservation. | 8520 River Rd. SE | 910/457–6041 | fax 910/457–6266 | Free | Tues.–Thurs. 9–4.

Brunswick Town–Fort Anderson State Historic Site. Explore the excavations of a Colonial port town, see the remains of Fort Anderson, a Civil War earthworks fort, and picnic. The visitor center has exhibits and artifacts. | 8884 St. Phillips Rd. SE, Winnabow | 910/371–6613 | fax 910/383–3806 | Free | Apr.–Oct., Mon.–Sat. 9–5, Sun. 1–5; Nov.–Mar., Tues.–Sat. 10–4, Sun. 1–4.

Southport–Fort Fisher Ferry. From Fort Fisher and Route 421, the car ferry connects Old Federal Point at the tip of the spit to the mainland. Arrive 30 minutes before the ferry departs to ensure your spot. | Price's Creek Rd. | 910/458–3329, 800/293–3779, or 910/457–6942 | Pedestrians 50¢, bicycles $1, motorcycles $3, cars $3, all one-way; larger vehicles additional | Mid-Mar.–mid-Nov., daily every 45 mins 9:15–5:30; mid-Nov.–mid-Mar., daily every 1½ hrs.

Southport Maritime Museum. See area history through exhibits, artifacts, programs, and a research library. | 116 N. Howe St. | 910/457–0003 | fax 910/457–0003 | $2 | Tues.–Sat. 9–5.

ON THE CALENDAR

APR.: *Robert Ruark Foundation Chili Cook-Off.* Chili cooking and eating, entertainment, and arts and crafts sales at this event benefit charity. | Franklin Square Park | 910/457–5494 or 800/457–6964.

NOV.: *US Open King Mackerel Tournament.* Anglers of all ages and skill levels compete for a cash purse the first weekend of the month. Or, if you don't fish, you can watch fish weigh-ins, eat at a fish fry, and see entertainment. | Southport Marina | 800/457–6964.

Dining

Eb and Flo's. Seafood. Eat inside or outside on an uncovered deck overlooking the harbor. The house specials are steamed oysters and clams. Hear live local music Wed., Fri., and Sun. Kids' menu. | Ferry Landing and Marina, Bald Head Island | 910/457–7217 | Closed Nov.–Mar. | $10–$35 | AE, D, MC, V.

Mister P's Waterway Seafood Restaurant and Oyster Bar. Seafood. On the mouth of Cape Fear River, the restaurant has two screened decks. Try the shrimp and grits or the raw bar. Kids' menu. | 317 W. Bay St. | 910/457–0832 | Closed Sun. No lunch | $10–$22 | D, MC, V.

River Pilot Café and Lounge. American/Casual. Eat soups, sandwiches, pizza, or seafood inside or outside at a few tables. Live music some nights. Kids' menu. Early-bird suppers. Sun. brunch buffet. | Ferry Landing and Marina, Bald Head Island | 910/457–7390 | Reservations not accepted | No supper Sun. Nov.–Feb. | $19–$32 | AE, D, MC, V.

Sandfiddler Restaurant. Seafood. The menu includes barbecue and pasta, along with tuna, catfish, and other seafood. Stuffed flounder and Seafood Wando, a seafood casserole, are some of the specialties. Colorful fish cover the walls at this family place. Kids' menu. | 1643 Howe St. (Rte. 211) | 910/457–6588 | Reservations not accepted | $20–$30 | MC, V.

Thai Peppers. Thai. This small, wood-paneled restaurant is known for its authentic curries and satay. | 115 E. Moore St. | 910/457–0095 | Closed Sun. No lunch Sat. | $8–$35 | AE, D, MC, V.

Lodging

Island Inn. One block from the ocean, this inn on Oak Island is just a few blocks from a few shops and restaurants and 2 mi from Southport. The one apartment in the facility has two bedrooms and cooking facilities. Refrigerators. Cable TV, room phones. Outdoor pool. Pets allowed. | 5611 E. Oak Island, Oak Island | 910/278–3366 | 18 rooms, 1 apartment | $40–$125 | AE, D, MC, V.

Lois Jane's Riverview Inn. This 19th-century home, a block from antiques shops and with views of Cape Fear River, has rooms with antiques, queen beds, and upstairs-downstairs porches. Complimentary breakfast. Cable TV, no room phones. | 106 W. Bay St. | 910/457–6701 or 800/457–1152 | www.southport.net/riverview.html | 4 rooms (2 with shared bath) | $85–$100 | MC, V.

Port Motel. Three miles from a swimming beach, this one-story motel is also a movie theater. Picnic area. Some kitchenettes, refrigerators. Cable TV. Pool. | 4821 Long Beach Rd. | 910/457–4800 | fax 910/457–0620 | 36 rooms | $55 | D, DC, MC, V.

STATESVILLE

(Nearby towns also listed: Cornelius, Hickory, Salisbury)

The town was called Fourth Creek, meaning the fourth creek west of Salisbury, in the mid-1700s. In 1789 it was incorporated as Statesville. It was named the state capital in the last months of the Civil War while Union troops occupied Raleigh. Today old textile plants have been replaced by modern industries such as hot-air balloon manufacturing.

Information: Greater Statesville Chamber of Commerce | Box 1064, Statesville 28687 | 704/873–2892 | chamber@i-america.net.

Attractions

Duke Power State Park. See Lake Norman, the largest man-made lake in the state, where fish are plentiful. The 1,458-acre park has nature trails, swimming, boating, and camping. | 159 Inland Sea La., Troutman | 704/528–6350 | fax 704/528–5623 | ils.unc.edu/parkproject/dupo.html | Free | Call for hrs.

Fort Dobbs State Historic Site. This is the site of a French and Indian War fort with artifacts, nature trails, and recreation. | 438 Fort Dobbs Rd. | 704/873–5866 | fax 704/873–5866 | Free | Apr.–Oct., Mon.–Sat. 9–5, Sun. 1–4; Nov.–Mar., Tues.–Sat. 10–4, Sun. 1–4.

Iredell Museum of Arts and Heritage. The museum has rotating exhibits and, on permanent view, an Egyptian mummy. | 1335 Museum Rd. | 704/873–4734 | $1 | Tues.–Fri. 10–5, Sun. 2–5.

ON THE CALENDAR

APR.: *Carolina Dogwood Festival.* Food vendors, a beauty pageant, horseshoe-pitching contests, a golf tournament, and live concerts go on all week at Lakewood Park. | 704/873–2892.

APR.: *Militia Encampment.* See the reenactment of an 18th-century militia camp, along with artillery and small-arms demonstrations. | Fort Dobbs State Historic Site, 438 Fort Dobbs Rd. | 704/873–5866.

MAY: *Ole Time Fiddler's and Bluegrass Festival.* Hear master fiddlers and banjo players, listen to storytellers, and see cloggers and contra dancers at this Memorial Day weekend event. There's also shape-note and gospel singing, many workshops, and a musical instrument competition. | Fiddler's Grove Campground, Union Grove | 704/539–4417.

SEPT.: *National Balloon Rally.* You can enjoy hot-air balloon demonstrations, "Moon Glow" flights at night, tethered balloon rides, entertainment, food, and crafts. | Troutman | 704/873–2892.

Dining

Glutton's Restaurant & Bar. American. This pub-style restaurant has casual dining and hearty food. The burgers are large, and the menu lists many standard appetizers and entrées. | 1539 E. Broad St. | 704/872–6951 | fax 704/871–0926 | $10–$20 | AE, D, MC, V.

Lodging

Best Western. This two-story motel is outside the business district, in a quiet area but less than a mile from I-77. It is 5 mi from JR Tobacco. Complimentary Continental breakfast. In-room data ports, some kitchenettes, some microwaves, some refrigerators, some in-room hot tubs. Cable TV, room phones. Outdoor pool. Health club. Laundry facilities, laundry service. Pets allowed (fee). | 1121 Moreland Dr. | 704/881–0111 | 69 rooms | $50–$109 | AE, D, DC, MC, V.

Fairfield Inn by Marriott. This two-story hotel is 1 mi from the downtown historic area, as well as restaurants and shops. It's also close to I–77 and I–40. Complimentary Continental breakfast. In-room data ports. Cable TV. Pool. Laundry services. Business services. | 1505 E. Broad St. | 704/878–2091 | fax 704/873–1368 | 117 rooms | $59–$64, $129 suite | AE, D, DC, MC, V | www.fairfieldinn.com.

Hampton Inn. One mile from the mall, many fast food restaurants, and stores, this hotel is the same distance from the Iredell Museum. Rooms have single beds, two doubles, or a king-size bed. Complimentary Continental breakfast. In-room data ports. Cable TV. Pool. Business services. | 715 Sullivan Rd. | 704/878–2721 or 800/426–7866 | fax 704/873–6694 | www.hamptoninn.com | 122 rooms | $63 | AE, D, DC, MC, V.

The Kerr House. This small, 109-year-old guest house is a half block from town and a mile from the city park and three antiques malls. There are fresh flowers in all the rooms, and each room has genuine and replica antique furnishings. The common parlor houses the cable TV. All fifth nights are free, consecutive or not. Complimentary breakfast. Room phones. No pets. No kids under 12 years. No smoking. | 519 Davie Ave. | 877/308–0353 | 4 rooms | $80–$95 | AE, D, DC, MC, V.

Red Roof Inn. There are three floors with exterior entrances at this motel just off I–77. Shops and restaurants are across the street. Cable TV. Pets allowed. | 1508 E. Broad St. | 704/878–2051 or 800/733–7663 | fax 704/872–3885 | www.redroof.com | 115 rooms | $46–$57 | AE, D, MC, V.

TRYON

MAP 8, C5

(Nearby town also listed: Hendersonville)

This area is known as the "thermal belt," where inversions of warm air create a temperature higher than other areas of the Blue Ridge foothills. The weather is perfect for growing apples, grapes, and peaches.

Information: Polk County Tourism Development Authority | 425 N. Trade St., Tryon 28782 | 828/859–8300 or 800/440–7848 | www.nc-mountains.org.

Attractions

Foothills Equestrian Nature Center (FENCE). This nonprofit center at the South Carolina border has more than 300 acres of trails for hiking and riding, meadows, a pond, a restored log cabin, and an equestrian facility. Enjoy the nature and birding programs. | 500 Hunting Country Rd. | 828/859–9021 | fax 828/859–9315 | www.fence.org | Free | Daily.

Pacolet River Scenic Byway. Drive 10 mi from Tryon to Saluda in the central Blue Ridge Mountains and see waterfalls, the Pacolet River, wildflowers, and vistas. | U.S. 176 | 828/859–8300 or 800/440–7848 | Free | Daily.

ON THE CALENDAR

APR.: *Block House Steeplechase Races.* The Tryon Riding and Hunt Club sponsors this event at the Foothills Equestrian Nature Center. Also, there's tailgate picnicking, hat contests, and a parade of hounds. | 800/438–3681.

APR.: *Tryon Home Tour.* You can tour many homes and gardens at this event. | 910/296–2180 or 828/859–0200.

MAY: *Saluda Spring Garden Festival.* There are private garden tours, an art show, music, crafts, and nature-related classes to attend. | Downtown Saluda | 828/749–1165.

JUNE: *Blue Ridge Barbecue Festival.* Watch a barbecue cook-off, entertainment, and browse crafts. | Harmon Field | 828/859–6236.

JULY: *Coon Dog Day.* See dog contests and judging, crafts, hear live music, and watch a parade and a street dance at this festival. | Downtown Saluda | 828/749–2581.

DEC.: *Tryon Christmas Stroll.* You can enjoy holiday caroling, refreshments, carriage rides, and entertainment. | Downtown | 828/859–8300.

Dining

Orchard Inn. Contemporary. View the mountains while eating from tables with white linen and fresh flowers. Try swordfish over beet latke with fresh carrot coulis, or pan-seared duck with fresh bing cherry cabernet sauce. Bring your own wine to the seating at 7 PM. | U.S. 176, Saluda | 828/749–5471 or 800/581–3800 | Reservations essential | Jackets required | Closed Sun.–Mon. | Prix–fixe $39 | D, MC, V.

Pine Crest Inn. Contemporary. Antique pine tables fill the dining room here. House specials are Alaskan halibut with chardonnay orange sauce and pork tenderloin with apple-cider shallot reduction. Breakfast is also served. | 200 Pine Crest La. | 828/859–9135 | Closed Sun. | $33–$39 | AE, D, MC, V.

Lodging

Mimosa Inn. This stunning inn was built in 1903 and is on the original site of the Mills Plantation. Set back off the road, it provides privacy and a great view of the Blue Ridge Mountains and Tryon Peak. An expansive veranda, a living room with a fireplace, a formal dining room, and a pine-paneled sitting room are some of the amenities. Dining room, picnic area. Cable TV, room phones. No pets. No smoking. | One Mimosa Inn La. | 877/859–7688 | fax 828/859–6766 | www.carolina-foothills.com | 10 rooms | $95–$115 | AE, D, MC, V.

Orchard Inn. Built on 12 acres in 1910 by the Southern Railroad company as a summer retreat, the cottages have fireplaces, hot tubs, private decks, or balconies. Some rooms have four-poster beds. Eat breakfast on an enclosed porch overlooking the mountains. Restaurant, complimentary breakfast. Some in-room hot tubs. TV in common area, no room phones. Hiking. Business services. No kids under 12. No smoking. | U.S. 176, Saluda | 828/749–5471 or 800/581–3800 | fax 828/749–9805 | www.orchardinn.com | 9 rooms; 4 cottages | $119–$189, $169–$245 cottages | D, MC, V.

Pine Crest. The main house, where folks came to "take the cure," is 100 years old. The buildings and a 200-year-old log cabin are on 6 acres in the foothills. Restaurant, complimentary Continental breakfast, room service. Cable TV. Library. Business services. | 200 Pine Crest La. | 828/859–9135 or 800/633–3001 | www.pinecrestinn.com | 32 rooms in 10 buildings, 10 suites | $160–$180 | AE, D, MC, V.

VALLE CRUCIS

MAP 8, C3

(Nearby towns also listed: Banner Elk, Blue Ridge Parkway, Blowing Rock, Boone, Jefferson, Linville)

This speck of a town is nestled in a valley between Boone and Banner Elk at an altitude of 2,726 ft. Actually a non-incorporated community with no recorded geographic boundaries, it has a year-round population of somewhere around 100 residents and the distinction of being the state's first and only rural historic district. Four families—the Bairds, Masts, Schulls and Taylors—were most instrumental in helping to settle the fertile area over 200 years ago, but it was an Episcopal bishop who named the town. The story goes that he saw in the confluence of three streams on the valley's floor the shape of a St. Andrew's Cross. Valle Crucis comes from the Latin, meaning "vale of the cross."

Information: Boone Convention and Visitors Bureau | 208 Howard St., Boone, 28607 | 828/262–3516 or 800/852–9506 | chamber@boone.net | www.boonechamber.com.

Attractions

Mast General Store. Everything from handmade baskets, overalls, and old-time toys to brogans, candy, and yard art is sold in this classic in the center of Valle Crucis—one of the oldest, continuously operated general stores in the United States. Built in 1882, the two-story emporium has squeaky plank floors worn to a soft sheen and a potbellied stove as well as a working post office. Advertising posters remain where they were hung decades ago, and a back porch with rocking chairs invites you to sit a spell. | Rte. 194 | 828/963–6511 | fax 828/963–1883 | www.mastgeneralstore.com | Free | Late Apr.–Dec., Mon.–Sat. 7–6:30, Sun. 1–6; Jan.–late Apr., hours vary slightly.

Church of the Holy Cross. Built in 1925, Holy Cross continues the work of the Episcopal mission established in the Wautauga River valley in 1842. With its stained-glass windows, red doors, and ivy-covered stone walls crowned with a Celtic cross, the church looks as though it would be equally at home on England's moors. | Rte. 194 | 828/963–4609 | fax 828/963–4619 | Free | Daily.

ON THE CALENDAR

OCT.: *Valle Country Fair.* This celebration of the harvest season is held on the third Saturday in October. Truth be told, it's really a church bazaar run wild. Along with 130 juried craft booths, there's mountain music, food, freshly pressed apple cider, games, storytellers and a children's stage. Proceeds underwrite a variety of nonprofit community organizations. | Off Rte. 194 | 828/963–6511.

Dining

Columbine Restaurant. Continental. Lunch and dinner are served on a covered porch or in the French country–style dining room with views of a pasture and raised-bed organic kitchen garden. Walls are a cheery light yellow. By day, tables are dressed with vinyl cloths, at night the linen comes out. Lunch fare is on the lighter side—salads, frittatas and pastas, while the dinner menu runs the gastronomic gamut—escargots to lamb to mountain trout. Specialties include risotto and osso buco. It's BYOB here. | Rte. 194 S | 828/963–6037 | Closed Nov.–Apr. No lunch Mon.–Tue. No dinner Sun.–Thurs. | Reservations essential | $16–$30 | AE, MC, V.

Mast Farm Inn. Southern. During warm months, diners have the option of eating on the terrace at this pastoral inn. In colder weather, you enjoy meals in the dining room that has wood paneling and a fireplace. Both locations serve traditional Southern dishes with a twist. Try the sweet-potato cornbread fritters and seared sea scallops with grilled Portabello mushroom and smoky pineapple salsa. The apple-orange spice cake is a popular dessert. Beer and wine are available. Sun. brunch. BYOB. | 2543 Broadstone Rd. | 828/963–5857 | fax 828/963–6404 or 888/963–5857 | www.mastfarminn.com | Closed Wed. May–Oct. Open mostly weekends only Oct.-May; call for hrs | $21–$38 | MC, V.

Lodging

Inn at the Taylor House. Set back among trees, the rambling, white, multistory farmhouse with its big wraparound porches is an attention-grabber. Outbuildings have been transformed into a massage cottage and gift shop. The owner, who used to run a cooking school in Atlanta, has adorned the interior of the inn with antiques and original art. Extras include terrycloth robes and afternoon tea. Complimentary breakfast. No air-conditioning in some rooms. TV in common room. Massage. No pets. Children by prior arrangement. No smoking. | Rte. 194 | 828/963–5581 | fax 828/963–5818 | taylorhouse@high-south.com | www.highsouth.com/taylorhouse | 10 rooms | $150–$265 | Closed mid-Dec.–early Apr. | MC, V.

Mast Farm Inn. One of the area's founding families built this farmhouse in the 1800s; it's now on the National Register of Historic Places. Distinct rooms, some with fireplaces, others with dormer windows, exposed wooden beams, or claw-foot tubs, are in the main house or in log outbuildings. The second floor has a sunroom, while the third has a sitting room with game tables. The sisters who own the place do organic gardening demonstrations in the inn's expansive flower and vegetable gardens. Restaurant, complimentary breakfast. No air-conditioning in some rooms. TV in common room. Hot tubs. | 2543 Broadstone Rd. | 828/963–5857 | fax 828/963–6404 or 888/963–5857 | www.mastfarminn.com | 9 rooms, 6 cottages | $125–$175 | MC, V.

WARSAW

MAP 8, I5

(Nearby town also listed: Goldsboro)

The people of Duplin County know theirs is a rural environment. They like it that way. There's pride in the fact that the original Welsh, Scots-Irish, English, German, and Swiss settlers would likely still recognize considerable chunks of the area's landscape and its well-preserved historic structures. There have been changes, though. Manufacturing and big-time agribusiness have come to Warsaw and its nine sister towns.

Information: Duplin County Tourism Development Commission | Box 929, Kenansville 28349 | 910/296–2180 or 800/755–1755 | www.duplincounty.com.

Attractions

Duplin Winery. Wines are made here from native muscadine grapes, which are said to contain high levels of resveratrol, an antioxidant that helps prevent heart disease and cancer. You can attend tastings and tours all year—and the annual grape stomp in September. | U.S. 117 N, Rose Hill | 910/289–3888 or 800/774–9634 | fax 910/289–3094 | www.duplinwinery.com | Free | Mon.–Sat. 9–5.

ON THE CALENDAR
MAY: *Springfest.* The downtown area's Veterans Park becomes a lively scene of cooking competitions, street vendors, contests, and entertainment. | 910/293–7804.
SEPT.: *Grape Stomp.* If you've ever wanted to take part in an old-fashioned grape-crushing, you can take off your shoes and join in at Duplin Winery's annual celebration of the grape-gathering season, with tastings and entertainment. | U.S. 117 N | 910/289–3888 or 800/774–9634 | Free.
NOV.: *Veterans Day Celebration.* It's believed to be the oldest continuous Veterans Day celebration in the nation, with a parade through downtown as well as military displays and food. | 910/293–7804.

Dining
Country Squire. Eclectic. English Tudor is the style for this building in the Squire's Vintage Inn complex. Inside are five dining rooms, candlelit for dinner, that carry out various historic themes in a medieval spot with open beams. Specialties include prime rib and Korean barbecued beef. Pianist Saturday evenings. Kids' menu. | 748 Rte. 24/50 | 910/296–1831 | No lunch Sat. | $12–$40 | AE, DC, MC, V.

Lodging
Squire's Vintage Inn. Just 2 mi west of Kenansville, the Tudor-style inn makes its sunken gardens a focal point, and all the rooms along the back have a view of the floral displays.

Restaurant (*see* Country Squire), complimentary Continental breakfast. Cable TV in many rooms. Business services. | 748 Rte. 24/50 | 910/296–1831 | fax 910/296–1431 | 18 rooms | $72 | AE, DC, MC, V.

WASHINGTON

MAP 8, J4

(Nearby towns also listed: Bath, Greenville, Williamston)

Little-known fact: Washington was the hometown of legendary producer and director Cecil B. DeMille. Another fact: the town, which played a strategic role during the War of Independence, calls itself "the original Washington," as it was the first community in the nation named for General George Washington. Its historic district along the Pamlico River, which is listed in the National Register of Historic Places, includes some 30 noteworthy structures dating from the late 1700s.

Information: Washington–Beaufort County Tourism Development Authority | Box 665, Washington 27889 | 252/946–9168 or 800/999–3857 | www.washnctourism.com.

Attractions

Goose Creek State Park. Swampland, a marsh, and live oaks draped with Spanish moss lend a sense of mystery to this 1,596-acre area. You can rough it overnight at one of the 12 primitive campsites (tent camping, no showers) or just go for a day of picnicking, hiking

CAROLINA BAYS

They are mysterious natural wonders—the great, thumb-shaped freshwater lakes that dot the flat Coastal Plain like so many shallow bowls rimmed with white sand. Theories abound as to their prehistoric origins. One hypothesis holds that peat fires hollowed out depressions that filled with rainwater. Another supposes that gigantic meteors were responsible for the basins, some of which are in forested areas, while others are in boggier spots.

Locals call them Carolina bays, "Carolina" because both North Carolina and South Carolina have them and "bay" because of the shape of their foliage. Uniting them further is a tranquil, untamed beauty.

The largest of North Carolina's bays is Lake Mattamuskeet. Despite attempts to drain it for farmland and mine it for peat, it is the centerpiece of a wildlife refuge that echoes with the calls of trumpeter swans in the winter and shorebirds in the summer. At 16,600 acres, Lake Phelps has long been considered a treasure by boaters and swimmers. But in the mid-1980s researchers began to prize it for other reasons: discovered underneath the water were ancient American Indian artifacts, including 30 dugout canoes.

Unlike its sisters, White Lake does not have dark, tannin-stained water. Instead, its white, sandy bottom is clearly visible. A clean appearance, plus the tree-shaded summer cottages that rim its shore, and the public boat ramp and dock have helped fuel this bay's reputation as the "nation's safest beach."

on the 7 mi of nature trails, swimming off a sandy beach, or boating on the Pamlico River. | 2190 Camp Leach Rd. | 252/923–2191 | fax 252/923–0052 | ils.unc.edu/parkproject/gocr.html | Free; camping $8.

Historic Washington. The Arts Council suggests that you begin your walking tour of this nationally noted district at the old Atlantic Coast Line railroad station. As you wend your way through the riverside area, you'll see nearly 30 buildings constructed when George Washington himself was alive and probably the best-known person in the young United States. | Main, 2nd, and Gladden Sts. | 252/946–9168 or 800/999–3857 | fax 252/946–9169 | Free | Daily.

North Carolina Estuarium. In the United States, the Pamlico River estuary is second in size only to Chesapeake Bay, and this aquarium, on the Pamlico waterfront in downtown Washington, was the first in the state to focus exclusively on North Carolina's ecologically important ocean inlets and coastal rivers. | 223 E. Water St. | 252/948–0000 | fax 252/948–4747 | $3 | Tues.–Sat. 10–4.

ON THE CALENDAR

JUNE: Riverfest. More serious business gives way to food and fireworks, arts and crafts, street dancing, and children's events during this festival on Washington's downtown waterfront. | 252/793–4804.

NOV.: Mattamuskeet Fun Ride. Routes of 35, 45, 55, and 70 mi take you cycling around and across North Carolina's largest natural lake and, along the way, spread out views of many of nature's creatures in the Lake Mattamuskeet National Wildlife Refuge. | 2 Mattamuskeet Rd. | 252/926–9311.

DEC.: Swan Days Festival. You may see thousands of tundra swans, as well as the other waterfowl that have returned to the state's largest natural lake, on guided tours through Lake Mattamuskeet National Wildlife Refuge. The program also includes lectures, workshops, demonstrations, and arts and crafts exhibits. One of the largest flyways on the east coast. Nature writing workshops and other exhibits take place in the Mattamuskeet Lodge, which was previously the old pumping building. | Mattamuskeet National Wildlife Refuge, 38 Mattamuskeet Rd., Swan Quarter | 252/925–5201 or 888/HYDE–VAN | separate fees for some specific tours but otherwise free, $7.

Dining

Blackbeard's Restaurant and Lounge. Seafood/Steak. Named after the infamous pirate who roamed the seas out of Carolina in the 1700s (and was often mentioned in old swashbuckling films), this restaurant carries out its theme with nautical decorations. Locals prize the prime rib special on Friday night—by no coincidence, the busiest night of the week. If you get tired of the seafood or beef, try the pastas. Kids' menu. | 1000 Washington St. (U.S. 17) | 252/975–1172 | Closed Sun. No lunch | $10–$30 | MC, V.

The Curiosity Shop. Continental. This restaurant is in a 100-year-old building with hardwood floors and brick walls. You can try one of their ever-changing "genteel" Southern dishes. The menu includes hand-cut steaks, fresh local seafood, and their most popular dish, crab cakes. There is a full bar. Dinner only. | 201 W. Main St. | 252/975–1397 | Reservations recommended | Closed Mon. | $13–$20 | AE, D, MC, V.

Lodging

Acadian House. Built in 1902, this inn is two blocks from the downtown area and one block from the Pamlico River and the Estuarium. It is 6 mi from Goosecreek State Park. You can sit on the large, herringbone-brick front porch or walk around the yard. Dining room, complimentary breakfast. Cable TV, room phones. No pets. No kids under 6 years. No smoking. | 129 Van Norden St. | 888/975–3393 | www.theacadianhouse.com | 4 rooms | $60–$70 | AE, MC, V.

Comfort Inn. Right on Rte. 17, this two-story chain hotel sits in a cluster of hotels 2 mi south of downtown Washington. Complimentary Continental breakfast. In-room data ports, some microwaves, some refrigerators. Cable TV. Pool. Exercise equipment. Business service. | 1636 Carolina Ave. | 252/946–4444 | fax 252/946–2563 | 56 rooms | $69 | AE, D, DC, MC, V.

Covered Wagon Motel. This small motel has been in business for 40 years. It is 10 mi from downtown Washington, and is surrounded by woodlands and farms. TV. No pets. | 9553 U.S. 17 N | 252/946–8347 | 8 rooms | $25–$35 | No credit cards.

Days Inn. This chain option is 2 mi south of downtown Washington on U.S. 17, where the Pamlico River meets the Tar River. Bar with entertainment. In-room data ports. Cable TV. Pool. Business services. | 916 Carolina Ave. | 252/946–6141 | fax 252/946–6167 | 72 rooms | $49 | AE, D, DC, MC, V.

Pamlico House. This B&B in Washington's historic district is in a Colonial Revival building that's listed on the National Register of Historic Places. But its wraparound porch and parlor are classically Victorian in style, with many antiques. You can choose from a king-size white wicker bed, a canopied queen-size four-poster, brass twin beds, or a hand-painted antique Eastlake queen bed. All rooms have a cozy sitting area. Complimentary breakfast. In-room data ports. Cable TV, VCRs. No kids under 6. No smoking. | 400 E. Main St. | 252/946–7184 or 800/948–8507 | fax 252/946–9944 | www.pamlicohouse.com | 4 rooms | $85–$95 | AE, D, MC, V.

River Forest Manor and Marina. River views abound at this site halfway between Albemarle Sound and the Neuse River, a onetime lodge converted in 1941 into a restaurant, country inn, and marina. It still has a full-service shipyard and marina, and the inn maintains its ties to the past with many antiques. Restaurant. Complimentary Continental breakfast. Cable TV. Pool. Hot tub. Tennis. Business services. | 738 E. Main St., Belhaven | 252/943–2151 or 800/346–2151 | fax 252/943–6628 | www.riverforestmanor.com | 11 rooms | $50–$125 | AE, MC, V.

WAYNESVILLE

MAP 8, B5

(Nearby towns also listed: Asheville, Blue Ridge Parkway, Cherokee, Maggie Valley)

This is where the Blue Ridge Parkway meets the Great Smokies. Pretty and arty, Waynesville is the seat of Haywood County, about 40% of which is within Great Smoky Mountains National Park, the Pisgah National Forest, or the Harmon Den Wildlife Refuge.

Information: **Haywood County Tourism Development Authority** | 1233 N. Main St., Suite 1–40, Waynesville 28786 | 828/452–0152 or 800/334–9036 | hctda@smokeymountains.net.

Attractions

Cold Mountain. About 15 mi from Waynesville in the Shining Rock Wilderness Area of Pisgah National Forest, this 6,030-ft rise has stood in splendid and relative isolation. Now people want to see the region called home by Inman and Ada, the Civil War–era protagonists of the best-selling book *Cold Mountain*. Hikes up the mountain are for the more experienced. You can camp out, although there are no designated campsites, no campfires are allowed, and groups may be no larger than 10 campers. It is visible from several overlooks on the Blue Ridge Parkway (near MM 411.9, 412.2, and 451.2) at the Waterrock Knob interpretive station. | 828/877–3350 ranger station | Free | Daily.

Museum of North Carolina Handicrafts. This collection in the Shelton House, circa 1875, presents a comprehensive exhibit of 19th-century crafts and furniture, as well as Native American artifacts. | 307 Shelton St. | 828/452–1551 | $5 | May–Oct., Tues.–Fri. 10–4.

APR.: *Razzle Dazzle Street Fest.* Held at the Performing Arts Center on the second Saturday of April, this festival for the kids has live performances, hands-on art, face-painting, and food. | U.S. 276, off Main St. | 828/452–0152 or 800/334–9036.

MAY: *Great Smoky Mountain Trout Festival.* You can watch—or enter—the Trout Race or other competitions or just view the exhibits, crafts displays, and entertainment at this annual Memorial Day event at Maggie Valley, 6 mi northwest of Waynesville. | 828/452–0152 or 800/334–9036.

MAY: *Ramp Festival.* This typical southern Appalachian hoedown honoring the ramp, a cousin to the onion, focuses on the many ways people try to make the pungent wild vegetable palatable. At the American Legion Post downtown, it also showcases bluegrass music, square dancing, and clogging. | 828/452–0152 or 800/334–9036.

JUNE: *Smoky Mountain Auto Show.* Classic cars of all vintages cruise down Waynesville's main streets in this annual event, while various entertainments raise money for worthy causes. | 828/452–0152 or 800/334–9036.

JUNE–OCT.: *Farmer's Tailgate Market.* Each Tuesday and Thursday from 8 to noon, farmers from throughout the region sell their homegrown fruit, vegetables, honey, and flowers in a parking lot off North Main Street. | 828/456–3021 or 800/334–9036.

JULY: *Folkmoot USA.* Costumed performers from 10 to 12 other countries demonstrate their traditional dances, music, and art against the backdrop of the Great Smoky Mountains in a 12-day series of individual and group exhibitions, plus a parade. | 828/452–2997 | www.folkmoot.com.

JULY–AUG.: *Arts in the Mountains.* Jackson County residents present their own arts and crafts in this two-month-long exhibition at the Balsam Mountain Inn in Balsam. | Seven Springs Dr. | 800/224–9498.

SEPT.: *Smoky Mountain Folk Festival.* The music traditions of the region sound through the Labor Day weekend as folk musicians, many of them family groups, stage shows of bluegrass and gospel tunes, along with some spirited clogging, at this event 26 mi from Asheville. | Lake Junaluska | 828/452–0152 or 800/334–9036.

OCT.: *Church Street Art and Craft Show.* A showcase for original arts and crafts by regional artists, this event in downtown Waynesville also includes music and dance presentations, and food, of course. | 828/452–0152 or 800/334–9036.

Dining

Lomo Grill. Eclectic. The menu changes weekly at this restaurant where the food includes traditional Argentine dishes as well as Italian and other Mediterranean specialties. Beef ranks as the local favorite. Beer and wine only. | 44 Church St. | 828/452–5222 | Closed Sun. and Jan.–spring. No dinner Tues. | $27–$38 | AE, D, DC, MC, V.

Old Stone Inn. Contemporary. Exposed stone walls set the decorative theme here, along with wood floors and a beamed ceiling. Try the filet mignon topped with shiitake mushrooms, wrapped in applewood bacon, and baked in puff pastry—like an individual beef Wellington—topped with Marsala cream sauce. | 109 Dolan Rd. | 828/456–3333 or 800/432–8499 | Reservations essential | Closed Jan.–Mar. No lunch | $23–$33 | AE, D, MC, V.

The Swag. Contemporary. Enjoy lunch, dinner, and Sunday brunch 5,000 ft up in the Smoky Mountains. Limited reservations for Sunday brunch, lunch Mon.–Fri., and dinner Sun.–Sat. Four-course meals include soup, salad, main entree, and dessert. Rainbow trout and beef tenderloin are among the daily specials. | 2300 Swag Rd. | 828/926–0430 | Reservations required | Jacket required | Closed 3rd weekend Nov.–end of Apr. | $15–$30 | AE, D, MC, V.

Lodging

Balsam Mountain Inn. Standing like a sentinel on a high ridge above Balsam Gap, this three-story inn welcomed its first guests in 1908. Brightly patterned fabrics and colors like teal now give guest rooms a more modern look, although there is frequent use of such details as beaded-board walls and rustic twig furniture in sitting areas. Dining room.

Some no-smoking rooms. No room phones. Library. Business services. | Seven Springs Dr., Balsam | 828/456–9498 or 800/224–9498 | fax 828/456–9298 | balsaminn@earthlink.net | www.balsaminn.com | 50 rooms, 21 with shower only, 8 suites | $102–$118, $133–$153 suites | D, MC, V.

Boyd Mountain Log Cabins. This facility covers 130 acres of mountains, pine forests, and walking-biking-horse trails. You can fish in one of three stocked ponds, cut your own Christmas tree, or play basketball, badminton, or volleyball. Each cabin has one, two, or three bedrooms, with a full kitchen, washer/dryer, fireplace, and porch. Cable TV, in-room VCRs, room phones. Basketball, hiking, horseback riding, volleyball. Fishing. Cross-country skiing, tobogganing. No pets. | 445 Boyd Farm Rd. | 828/926–1575 | www.boydmountain.com | 6 cabins | $130–$210 | AE, MC, V.

Grandview Lodge. Just outside Waynesville and 5 mi from the Blue Ridge Parkway, the lodge sits on 2½ rolling acres of apple orchards, grape arbors, and rhubarb patches that add their homier vistas to the grandeur of the Great Smoky Mountains around them. All rooms, including the six off the rocker-lined porch, have private baths and two beds; the three rooms within the inn have gas-burning fireplaces. Dining room. Picnic area. Kitchenettes in apartments, some refrigerators. Cable TV, no room phones. VCR in common room. No smoking. | 466 Lickstone Rd. | 828/456–5212 or 800/255–7826 | fax 828/452–5432 | innkeeper@grandviewlodgenc.com | www.bbonline.com/nc/grandview | 9 rooms, 6 with shower only; 2 apartments available May–Oct. | $105–$125 | MC, V | MAP.

Ketner Inn and Farm. This unusual lodging is in a 102-year-old farmhouse on a 27-acre working farm. It is 30 mi from the Great Smoky Mountain Railway, the Biltmore House, and the Cherokee Indian Reservation, and Harrod's Casino. Picnic area, complimentary breakfast. Cable TV. Exercise equipment. No pets. No kids under 6 years. No smoking. | 1154 Jonathan Creek Rd. | 828/926–1511 | ketinn@primeline.com | www.bbonline.com/nc/ketner | 5 rooms | $60–$75 | MC, V.

Old Stone Inn. If you like to walk, this rustic onetime hunting lodge is only a ½-mi stroll from the center of town, even though it's 3,200 ft high in the Great Smokies. Homemade quilts and many antiques keep furnishings are true to the inn's heritage. Dining room (see Dining, *above*). Some refrigerators. Cable TV, no room phones. No kids under 12. No smoking. | 109 Dolan Rd. | 828/456–3333 or 800/432–8499 | www.bbonline.com/nc/oldstone | 17 rooms; 4 cottages | $94–$139, $144–154 cottages | Closed Jan.–Mar. | AE, D, MC, V.

Parkway Inn. The rooms are simple, but the inn is 13 mi from the many attractions, including an amusement park, a casino, and an Indian reservation. Picnic area. Some microwaves, some refrigerators. Cable TV. | 2093 Dellwood Rd. W | 828/926–1841 or 800/537–6394 | fax 828/926–6093 | 30 rooms | $32–$99 | D, MC, V.

The Swag. Guest rooms and cabins have handmade quilts, woven rugs, rustic Early American antiques, and original artwork. Many rooms have private balconies, fireplaces, and steam showers. Each cottage has a sitting room and private porch. Dining room. In-room safes, refrigerators. Pond. Hot tub, massage, sauna. Hiking, racquetball. Library. Laundry service. Business services. No kids under 7 in cabins. | 2300 Swag Rd. | 828/926–0430 or 800/789–7672 | fax 828/926–2036 | letters@theswag.com | www.theswag.com | 12 rooms; 3 cottages | $240–$560, $360–$525 cottages | Closed Dec.–Apr. | AE, D, MC, V.

Waynesville Country Club Inn. At the main lodge of this golfers' oasis only 6 mi from the national park, you'll have a view of both the mountains and the first tee from the 270-ft-long Main Terrace. Several groups of cottages and the country villas will put you even closer to the fairways, some right on the course, some with their own private porches or balconies. 3 restaurants, bar with entertainment. Cable TV. Pool. Golf courses, tennis courts. Business services, airport shuttle. | 176 Country Club Dr. | 828/456–3551 or 800/627–6250 | fax 828/456–3555 | www.wccinn.com | 92 rooms; 8 cottages, 1 house | $80–$118; golf packages available | AE, MC, V.

Windsong. When the weather's chilly, this inn in a secluded Smoky Mountain cove provides the wood for your fireplace, and year-round you'll have panoramic mountain views from your room. Room decorations follow particular themes—safari or Santa Fe, for example—and each room has a deck or patio. If you're in the suites up the hill, you'll see the owners' llamas on the walk to your room. Complimentary Continental breakfast. In-room TVs, VCRs. Fireplace and tub for two in all rooms but one. Pool. Tennis. Business services. No kids under 12 in main house. No smoking. | 459 Rockcliffe La., Clyde | 828/627–6111 | fax 828/627–8080 | russ@windsongbb.com | www.windsongbb.com | 5 rooms, 2 suites | $125–$160, $175–$195 suites | D, MC, V.

Yellow House. The bedrooms in this house borrow their colors from the Impressionists, who often liked to apply bold strokes of yellow to their canvases. At a 3,000-ft elevation in the countryside just outside of Waynesville and only 25 mi from Asheville, the main house dates from 1885. Complimentary breakfast. Some minibars, refrigerators, some in-room hot tubs. No TVs in rooms. Driving range, putting green. Business services. No kids under 12 in main house. No smoking. | 89 Oakview Dr. | 828/452–0991 or 800/563–1236 | fax 828/452–1140 | yellow.house@asap-com.com | www.theyellowhouse.com | 6 rooms, 1 with shower only, 4 suites; 1 cottage | $115–$175, $205–$230 suites, $220 cottage | MC, V.

WILKESBORO

MAP 8, D3

WILKESBORO

INTRO
ATTRACTIONS
DINING
LODGING

(Nearby towns also listed: Blue Ridge Parkway)

Wilkes County has a rich and varied history through both the Revolutionary War and the Civil War, and if you take a walking tour of the Wilkesboro area itself, you'll find 13 stops on the National Register of Historic Places. Much of the community is outdoor-oriented and popular activities are fishing, boating, and hiking.

Information: Wilkes County Chamber of Commerce | Box 727, North Wilkesboro 28659 | 336/838–8662 | wilkescoc@wilkes.net.

Attractions
Old Wilkes Jail Museum. An excellent example of mid-19th-century jails and one of the few intact old-time "jugs" in the state, Old Wilkes was completed in 1860 and was used as a lock-up until 1915. Civil War figure Tom Dooley, made famous in the Kingston Trio song, was an inmate here. | 203 N. Bridge St. | 336/667–3712 | Free | Weekdays 9–4; closed last 2 wks in Dec.

Stone Mountain State Park. The mountain, a dome-shaped mass of granite, is reminiscent of a moonscape. Climbing is permitted only in designated areas, although you'll have a choice of streams, trails, camping sites, and places for picnics below the big rock. | 3042 Frank Pkwy., Roaring Gap | 336/957–8185 | fax 336/957–3985 | ils.unc.edu/parkproject/stmo.html | Free | Call for hrs.

ON THE CALENDAR
APR.: *MerleFest.* Staged the last weekend in April in memory of Eddy Merle Watson, late son of the flat-picking legend Doc Watson, MerleFest is a celebration of American music that draws 60,000 people. Food and entertainment abound. | Wilkes Community College | 800/343–7857 or 336/838–6267 international | www.merlefest.org.
OCT.: *Brushy Mountain Apple Festival.* You'll find crafts, food, entertainment, and lots of apples at this harvest observance in downtown North Wilkesboro. | 336/948–3022.

Dining
Fine Friends Café. American. Hand-painted murals and touches of Victorian style set the mood in this dining spot known for chicken and prime rib. When the weather's nice, you

can dine outdoors on the veranda. | 101 6th St., Melody Square, North Wilkesboro | 336/838–3331 | Closed weekends. No supper | $5–$12 | MC, V.

Ole Wilkes Plantation House. Contemporary. It may be in town instead of out in the countryside, but this "plantation house" actually is in an old house, with wainscoting and wallpaper in classic motifs. Try the pecan salmon and the crab cakes. Kids' menu. | 210 6th St., North Wilkesboro | 336/838–8207 | Closed Sun.–Mon. No lunch | $20–$40 | AE, MC, V.

Roselli's Italian Restaurant. Italian. Movie posters on the walls help build a casual mood in this bit of Italy known for its pasta dishes. Live music three times a month. Kids' menu. | 910 Main St., North Wilkesboro | 336/838–7070 | Closed Sun.–Mon. No lunch | $15–$30 | AE, D, DC, MC, V.

Lodging

Best Western Wilkesboro. Formerly called the College Park Inn, this two-story structure built in 1970 is across from Wilkesboro Community College. After a $1 million renovation, all rooms now are now outfitted with a table and two chairs, and great work desks. Restaurant, complimentary Continental breakfast. Cable TV. Pool. | 1206 River St. | 336/667–2176 or 888/667–4001 | fax 336/838–9103 | 100 rooms | $50–$60 | AE, D, DC, MC, V.

Williams Motel. This motel is 30–45 minutes from Blowing Rock and Smoot Park. Cable TV, room phones. Outdoor pool. No pets. | 107 Boone Trail, Old Hwy. 421, North Wilkesboro | 336/838–4138 | 34 rooms | $32–$51 | AE, MC, V.

WILLIAMSTON

MAP 8, J4

(Nearby towns also listed: Ahoskie, Edenton, Greenville, Washington)

Williamston is the largest town in Martin County. On the Coastal Plain and bounded on the north by the Roanoke River, this area is, indeed, a very watery place, with more than 20 creeks, streams, and swamps in the vicinity.

Information: **Martin County Travel and Tourism Authority** | Box 382, Williamston 27892 | 252/792–6605 or 800/776–8566 | tourism@visitmartincounty.com | www.visit-martincounty.com.

Attractions

Fort Branch. This restored Confederate fort on the Roanoke River, 21 mi north of Williamston and close to Hamilton, includes a museum with maps, artifacts, original cannons, and living-history programs. | Fort Branch Rd., Fort Branch | 252/792–6605 or 800/776–8566 | fax 252/792–8710 | Free | Apr.–Nov., weekends 1:30–5:30.

Hope Plantation. Built in 1803 by Gov. David Stone, the clapboard mansion has Federal and Georgian architecture, the governor's library, and period furnishings. The King-Bazemore House, a gambrel-roofed structure that dates from 1763, is also here. | 132 Hope House Rd., Windsor | 252/794–3140 | fax 252/794–5583 | $6.50 | Mon.–Sat. 10–5, Sun. 2–5.

Morningstar Nature Refuge. You can take guided or self-guided tours of this small, privately owned wildlife sanctuary. Along the eight short trails, you can see feeding stations and visit an observation area overlooking a swamp. The complex also includes a museum and visitor center, a research lab, a library, and a picnic area. | 1967 Meadow Branch Rd. | 252/792–7788 | Free | Afternoons by appointment only.

ON THE CALENDAR

SEPT.: *North Carolina Country Stampede.* Run in conjunction with a regional country-music talent search, the annual event in downtown Williamston has food vendors and exhibits of handmade arts and crafts as well as the musical performances. | 800/776–8566.

NOV.: *Battle Reenactment.* The first weekend of November, Blue meets Gray once again as actors relive the events of a Civil War battle at an old fort that once guarded the Roanoke River for the Confederacy (*see* Fort Branch). | Fort Branch Rd., Fort Branch; 21 mi north of Williamston, close to Hamilton | 252/792–6605 or 800/776–8566.

Dining

Cobb's Corner. American. Family-style service gives the feeling of being in someone's Southern home, though this family-run restaurant is actually in a Holiday Inn. Specialties include pork chops, chicken, steak, seafood, loads of vegetables, and a dozen daily specials. You can also try the banana fritters. Kids' menu. Beer and wine only. | 101 East Blvd. | 252/792–6493 | $5–$10 | AE, D, DC, MC, V.

Deadwood. Steak. Part of a Wild West theme park with saloon and jailhouse, the restaurant is known for char-broiled steaks, big hamburgers, and grilled chicken. Kids' menu. Sun. brunch. Beer only. | 2302 Ed's Grocery Rd., Bear Grass | 252/792–8938 | Closed Mon.–Thurs. No lunch | $10–$18 | MC, V.

Lodging

Big Mill Bed and Breakfast. Surrounded by farmland, streams, and lakes, this 50-acre working farm is 4 mi from the Senator Bob Martin Equestrian Center and the Hope Plantation, and 13 mi from Fort Branch. Each room has vaulted ceilings with Portuguese and Spanish painted tiles in the bathrooms, and bars and fireplaces. You can fish in the bass-stocked private lake. Complimentary Continental breakfast. Some minibars, some refrigerators. TV, room phones. No pets. No kids under 12. No smoking. | 1607 Big Mill Rd. | 252/792–8787 | 2 rooms | $55–$70 | AE, D, DC, MC, V.

Comfort Inn. Rooms in this chain hotel only a mile from downtown have tables and chairs to use for breakfast, snacks, or work on the road. Complimentary Continental breakfast. Cable TV. Exercise equipment. Business services. | 100 East Blvd. | 252/792–8400 or 800/827–8400 | fax 252/809–4800 | 59 rooms | $56–$66 | AE, D, DC, MC, V.

Holiday Inn. This chain hotel is 5 mi from the rodeos held at the Bob Martin Equestrian Center. Rooms are off-white with wood furniture. Restaurant, bar, room service. In-room data ports. Cable TV. Pool. Business services. Some pets allowed. | 101 East Blvd. | 252/792–3184 | fax 252/792–9003 | 100 rooms | $65 | AE, D, DC, MC, V.

WILMINGTON

MAP 8, I7

(Nearby towns also listed: Kure Beach, South Brunswick Islands, Southport, Wrightsville Beach)

Its white-sand beaches are considered Wilmington's biggest draw, and New Hanover County maintains almost 100 public access sites along the shoreline (look for the orange-and-blue signs). Fishing piers dot the coast, and in the spring and the fall, when the blues and the king mackerels run, anglers are everywhere.

Its location also gave the small but busy city a noteworthy place in history: it played a major role in the American Revolution, and it was the main port of the Confederacy during the Civil War. The 200-block historic district, the largest in the state, is not far from the tannin-colored Cape Fear River.

The hometown of basketball superstar Michael Jordan is also a college town full of clubs, shops, and restaurants, the University of North Carolina at Wilmington adding much to the cultural scene. Pretty all year, Wilmington really shines in the spring, when banks of azaleas bloom underneath trees draped in Spanish moss.

Information: **Cape Fear Coast Convention and Visitors Bureau** | 24 N. 3rd St., Wilmington 28401 | 910/341–4030 or 800/222–4757 | info@cape-fear.nc.us | www.cape-fear.nc.us.

Attractions

Bellamy Mansion Museum of History and Design Arts. Built as the city residence of a prominent planter, the mansion is a spectacular example of antebellum architecture. You can go on tours and also view exhibits (changed from time to time) about North Carolina arts, architecture, and preservation. | 503 Market St. | 910/251–3700 | $6 | Wed.–Sat. 10–5, Sun. 1–5.

Burgwin-Wright Museum House. In April 1781, the British leader General Cornwallis used this three-story 1770 house as his headquarters. It has been restored to the style of a Colonial gentleman's town house and includes a period garden. | 224 Market St. | 910/762–0570 | fax 910/762–8650 | $6 | Feb.–late Dec., Tues.–Sat. 10–4; last tour at 3:30.

Cape Fear Museum. The oldest history museum in the state traces the natural, cultural, and social history of the lower Cape Fear region from its beginnings to the present. One exhibit covers the youth of famous native son Michael Jordan. | 814 Market St. | 910/341–4350 | fax 910/341–4037 | $4 | Tues.–Sat. 9–5, Sun. 2–5.

***Captain J. N. Maffitt* Riverboat.** You can board the riverboat for cruises on the Cape Fear from the Cape Fear Riverboats site at the end of Market St. | 910/343–1611 or 800/676–0162 | fax 910/343–8636 | $8.

Carolina Beach State Park. On some of the trails that wind through this park, you can see the rare Venus flytrap and other species of insect-eating plants, as well as cypress, lily, and grass ponds. If you want a more active outing, you'll also find fishing, boating, hiking picnicking, and camping areas. | 1678 Sate Park Rd. | 910/458–8206 or 910/458–7770 marina | fax 910/458–6350 | ils.unc.edu/parkproject/cabe.html | Free.

Cotton Exchange. This shopping-dining complex is housed in eight restored buildings on the Cape Fear River that have flourished as a trading center since pre-Civil War days. | 321 N. Front St. | 910/343–9896 | fax 910/251–1040 | Free | Call for hrs.

Greenfield Lake and Gardens. You can picnic or rent canoes or paddleboats at this 180-acre lake bordered by cypress trees laden with Spanish moss. In April, the area is ablaze with azaleas. | 302 Willard St.; behind Parks and Recreation building | 910/341–7855 | fax 910/763–9371 | Free | Daily dawn–dusk.

***Henrietta II* Riverboat.** You can choose narrated sightseeing cruises or dinner–dance cruises aboard this old-fashioned two-deck paddle wheeler. Each sightseeing tour lasts 1½ hours. | Downtown riverfront | 910/343–1611 or 800/676–0162 | $10 | Apr.–Oct., Tues.–Sun., noon and 2:30; dinner–dance cruises Fri. 7:30–10, Sat. 7–10.

Moores Creek National Battlefield. American patriots defeated the Loyalists here in 1776. You can view an audiovisual program and exhibits in the small museum, go off on your own self-guided history tours, or stroll along the nature trails. | 200 Moores Creek Rd., Currie | 910/283–5591 | Free | Daily 9–5.

New Hanover County Arboretum. You'll find 100 varieties of shade-loving camellias among the 33 exhibits here, which also include magnolia and patio gardens, a salt-spray garden, and a children's garden with a maze. | 6206 Oleander Dr. | 910/452–6393 | Free | Daily dawn–dusk.

★ **Orton Plantation Gardens.** The house is not open to the public, but you can stroll through its 20 acres of gardens. The former rice plantation has magnolias, ancient oaks, and all kinds of ornamental plants, and the grounds have become a a refuge for waterfowl. | 9149 Orton Rd. SE, Winnabow | 910/371–6851 | $8 | Call for hrs.

Poplar Grove Historic Plantation. You have several options at this plantation site where you can tour the 1850 Greek Revival-style house, visit the outbuildings, eat at the restaurant, see crafts demonstrations, and even pet the farm animals. | 10200 U.S. 17 N | 910/686–9518 or 910/686–2476 restaurant | fax 910/686–4309 | www.poplargrove.com | $7 | Feb.–Dec., Mon.–Sat. 9–5, Sun. noon–5; restaurant Tues.–Fri. 11–10, Sat. 4–10.

St. John's Museum of Art. Three buildings house temporary exhibits and the permanent collections of 18th-, 19th-, and 20th-century North Carolina art, plus an acclaimed group of prints by Mary Cassatt. One structure was built in 1804 as a Masonic Lodge building, the oldest such lodge in the state. There is also a sculpture garden. | 114 Orange St. | 910/763–0281 | fax 910/341–7981 | $3 | Tues.–Sat. 10–5, Sun. noon–4.

USS *North Carolina* Battleship Memorial. When you move about the *North Carolina,* you are trodding the passages of a ship that participated in every major naval offensive in the Pacific during World War II. You can rent a casette narration to guide your exploration, and a 10-minute film on the ship is shown throughout the day. Parking is available next to the site, or, from Memorial Day to Labor Day, you also can get here by river taxi from downtown's Riverfront Park. | Eagle Island, U.S. 74/76, 17, and 421 | 910/251–5797 or 910/350–1817 (24–hr information line) | www.battleshipnc.com | $8, taxi $2 | Mid-May–mid-Sept., daily 8–8; mid-Sept.–mid-May, daily 8–5.

Wilmington Railroad Museum. For more than a century, railroading was Wilmington's chief industry. Specifically, the museum preserves the history of the Atlantic Coast Line Railroad, but also covers the general story of trains and tracks in the Southeast. You'll see extensive model railroad displays and real cars and cabooses. Children's Corner. | 501 Nutt St. | 910/763–2634 | fax 910/763–2634 | $3 | Jun.–Sept., Mon.–Sat. 10–5, Sun. 1–5; Oct.–May, Mon.–Sat. 10–4.

Zebulon Latimer House. Throughout this house-museum you are greeted by reminders of opulent antebellum living. Built in 1852 in the Italianate style, the house is headquarters for the Lower Cape Fear Historical Society, which conducts the guided tours. | 126 S. 3rd St. | 910/762–0492 | fax 910/763–5869 | $6 | Weekdays 10–3:30, weekends noon–5.

ON THE CALENDAR
MAR.: *Cucalorus Film Festival.* You can screen all sorts of independently made films and videos during this series, since sponsors have no restrictions on subject matter or length. There also are speakers and live music at the various sites. | Main venue: Thalian Hall, 310 Chestnut St. | 910/343–5995.
MAR.: *Herb Fair.* In March, Poplar Grove Plantation conducts this event that includes classes on herbs as well as sales of live plants, garden items, and related products. | 10200 U.S. 17 N | 910/686–9518.
APR.: *North Carolina Azalea Festival.* If nature cooperates, the azaleas are at their peak for these four days of garden and home tours, music concerts, a street fair, a parade and fireworks, a circus, a juried art and master crafts show, and other events around the city. | 910/763–0905.
MAY: *Annual Memorial Day Observance.* The holiday observance aboard a famous warship has a decidedly military tone. A tradition since 1968, the USS *North Carolina* ceremonies honor the dead of our past conflicts with a marine band, an all-service color guard, a gun salute, a high-ranking military speaker, taps, and a memorial wreath cast onto the water. | Eagle Island, U.S. 74/76, 17, and 421 | 910/251–5797.
MAY: *Port of Wilmington Maritime Day Celebration.* The North Carolina state port facility has an important role in the economy of this coastal city. At its annual open house you can share a behind-the-scenes look at harbor operations through tours of port and cargo ships, demonstrations, and exhibits. There's also a forklift rodeo and maritime flotilla. | 2202 Burnett Blvd. | 910/763–1621.
MAY: *WE Festival.* At least three dozen bands from around the world play "mostly headbanger music" at the Wilmington Exchange event downtown. You also can see independent/underground films and samples of 'zines and small-press output and try lots of microbrewed beer during the week-long event. | 800/222–4757 | www.wefest.indiegroup.com.

JULY: *Cape Fear Blues Festival.* The soft, sweet sounds so many Southerners love echo all around the town in this four-day blues extravaganza. You can hear them at club performances, a concert, a talent contest, workshops, or on "blues cruises" down the Cape Fear River. | 910/350–8822.

JULY: *Coastal Carolina Antique Arms and Military Collectors Show.* Dealers and collectors buy, sell, and trade here, but you can go to just have a look at the displays of old arms and military memorabilia. | Elks Lodge, 5102 Oleander Dr. | 704/282–1339.

OCT.: *Riverfest.* Besides music, arts and crafts exhibitors, and food booths, this street fair along the river in the historic downtown district has ship tours, a gun show, a stamp-coin-card show, and a carnival for the kids. | 910/452–6862.

NOV.: *Classic Creations of North Carolina.* Every November, the Zebulon Latimer House presents this holiday sale of works by about 150 craftspeople from 30 states. | 126 S. 3rd St. | 910/762–0492.

DEC.: *Old Wilmington by Candlelight Tour.* The holly, the ivy, and all the other signs of the season await on tours of holiday-bedecked homes and churches, with horse-drawn carriage rides through the historic downtown area, which is lit by luminaria. | 910/762–0492.

Dining

Annabelle's Restaurant & Pub. American/Casual. Known for prime ribs, sandwiches, and Sunday brunch, this place has a rustic interior with exposed brick and wood paneling. You can dine in the old Wrightsville Beach Trolley and top off your meal by indulging in Annabelle's Hot Fudge Cake. Kids menu. | 4116 Oleander Dr. | 910/791–4955 | fax 910/799–4261 | $15–$25 | AE, D, DC, MC, V.

Caffe Phoenix. Mediterranean. Displays of art bedeck a bright, busy, and posh bistro known for seafood, soups, and salads. Outdoors there's a small awning-shaded dining patio. Sun. brunch. Kids' menu. | 9 S. Front St. | 910/343–1395 | $14–$28 | AE, D, DC, MC, V.

Doxey's Market and Cafe. Delicatessen. A combination gourmet grocery and organic deli with daily specials, this place has eggplant parmesan on its specialty list. Carrot juice, smoothies, and the like are also on the menu. | 1319 Military Cutoff Rd. | 910/256–9952 | Closed Sun. | $7–$10 | AE, D, MC, V.

Dragon Garden. Chinese. It's an Oriental restaurant with only one dining choice—a supper buffet—but you'll find many options among its dishes, plus a variety of "exotic" drinks. | 341–52 S. College Rd. | 910/452–0708 | Reservations not accepted | $10–$20 | AE, D, MC, V.

Eddie Romanelli's. Italian. Hanging plants and skylights add a light and contemporary note to the open-rafter ceilings of this restaurant that's won praise from *Encore* magazine. You'll find fresh fish here, as well as pastas. Kids' menu. | 5400 Oleander Dr. | 910/799–7000 | $10–$20 | AE, DC, MC, V.

Elijah's. Seafood. Nautical paintings and historic photos set the mood in the large space; the Cape Fear River lends its own natural appeal to a meal on the deck outside. The American seafood and grill specialties include an oyster bar and other raw seafood. Kids' menu. Sun. brunch. | 2 Ann St. | 910/343–1448 | $12–$20 | AE, D, DC, MC, V.

Harvest Moon. Contemporary. A Neil Young song inspired the name, although the menu from the wood-fired oven changes with every season. Local artwork hangs on the walls, and dining at the bare wooden tables is always by candlelight. Try the shrimp with grits or the oyster bar. Kids' menu. | 5704 Oleander Dr. | 910/792–0172 | Closed Sun. No lunch | $13–$21 | AE, D, DC, MC, V.

Hieronymus Seafood. Seafood. The nearby sea sets the theme for both the menu and the decorative boat, fish, and lighthouse motifs of this large family restaurant. If you're not in the mood for any of the fresh local seafood, you can opt for prime rib. The fireplace blazes on chilly evenings, and an open-air dining area beckons on warmer days. There's an oyster bar in the lounge, with a pianist on weekends. Kids' menu. | 5035 Market St. | 910/392–6313 | $14–$25 | AE, DC, MC, V.

Market Street Casual Dining. Contemporary. This eatery builds a turn-of-the-century look with subdued lighting and lots of ornamental knicknacks. It's known for having a variety of daily specials. | 6309 Market St. | 910/395–2488 | Reservations not accepted | Closed Mon. No lunch | $10–$25 | AE, D, MC, V.

Pilot House. Seafood. Awnings and fans help keep the riverside dining deck pleasant no matter what the actual temperature might be. Many of the specialties take on a decidedly Southern touch, in dishes like shrimp with grits, Carolina bisque, and crunchy catfish, but the restaurant is also known for its pastas and fresh vegetables. Kids' menu. Sun. brunch. | 2 Ann St. | 910/343–0200 | $11–$25 | AE, D, DC, MC, V.

Rucker Johns. Contemporary. Artifacts and collectibles come together to create an eclectic spot that bemuses the eye. The "Black Jack Specials," like the rib eye marinated in Jack Daniels whiskey, have become local menu favorites. Kids' menu. | 5511 Carolina Beach Rd. | 910/452–1212 | Reservations not accepted | $9–$17 | AE, MC, V.

Vinnie's Steak House. Steak. Beef is the big thing here, but nightly specials add such choices as Brazilian dishes or wild boar. In good weather you can have your all-American or more exotic fare out on the patio. Live music. Sun. brunch. | 1900 Eastwood Rd., Suite 2 | 910/256–0995 | Reservations not accepted | No lunch | $15–$60 | AE, D, DC, MC, V.

Water Street Restaurant and Sidewalk Café. Eclectic. In this restored two-story brick waterfront warehouse dating from 1835 you can choose from Greek, Mexican, Middle Eastern, and other ethnic cooking, as well as seafood chowder. Live entertainment Wednesday through Sunday ranges from dinner theater to jazz or blues music. Open-air dining area. Kids' menu. | 5 S. Water St. | 910/343–0042 | Reservations essential for some entertainment | $13–$25 | AE, MC, V.

Lodging

Anderson Guest House. This is actually a 20-year-old detached carriage house behind a main house, which was built in 1851. There is a private patio looking over the garden, and a fireplace in each room. It is in downtown Wilmington, and just 10 mi from the beaches. Complimentary breakfast. Pets allowed. No kids under 18 years. No smoking. | 520 Orange St. | 910/343–8128 | 2 rooms | $90 | No credit cards.

Best Western. All rooms at this motel on the outskirts of downtown Wilmington face the Cape Fear riverfront. Stores are about a mile away, and the property has landscaping, trees, and flowers surrounding it. Complimentary Continental breakfast. In-room data ports, some microwaves, some refrigerators. Cable TV, room phones. Health club. Laundry services. No pets. No smoking. | 2916 Market St. | 910/763–4653 | fax 910/763–0486 | 47 rooms, 6 suites | $79–$149 | AE, D, DC, MC, V.

Camellia Cottage B&B. This B&B is four blocks from Cape Fear River and 10 mi from the ocean. Complimentary breakfast. Some microwaves, some refrigerators. Cable TV, room phones. Laundry facilities. Pets allowed. No kids under 18 years. No smoking. | 118 South 4th St. | 910/763–9171 | www.capefearconventionsbureau.com | 3 rooms, 1 suite | $125–$150 | AE, MC, V.

Catherine's Inn. Just beyond the back lawn and its sunken garden you can see the Cape Fear River. Inside the 1883 house, guest rooms are done in varying styles, but all have some antique pieces. Complimentary breakfast. No TV in rooms; cable TV and VCRs in common area. No kids under 12. No smoking. | 410 S. Front St. | 910/251–0863 or 800/476–0723 | fax 910/772–9550 | www.catherinesinn.com | 5 rooms | $99–$120 | AE, MC, V.

Comfort Inn–Executive Center. Four blocks from the University of North Carolina at Wilmington, this motel caters to the business crowd. Monday through Thursday evenings, the manager hosts a reception in the lobby with hors d'oeuvres from nearby restaurants. Complimentary Continental breakfast. Some refrigerators. Cable TV. Pool. Business services. | 151 S. College Rd. | 910/791–4841 | fax 910/790–9100 | 146 rooms | $69–$100 | AE, D, DC, MC, V.

NORTH CAROLINA | WILMINGTON

Courtyard by Marriott. This hostelry has serene off-white guest rooms with sparkles of color in the accessories. Amenities include complimentary morning newspapers, hair dryers, and two-line phones. Restaurant, bar. In-room data ports, safes, microwaves, minibars, refrigerators, irons and ironing boards, some in-room hot tubs, whirlpools. Cable TV. Pool. Hot tub. Exercise equipment. Laundry facilities. Business services. Free parking. | 151 Van Campen Blvd. | 910/395–8224 | fax 910/452–5569 | 128 rooms | $99–$129 | AE, D, DC, MC, V.

Curran House. Three blocks from the Cape Fear River and 8 mi from the ocean, this B&B was built in 1883 in the Victorian Italianate and Queen Anne style. The antique furnishings are mostly English, with an iron scroll bed in one guest room and an Oriental rug in another. Complimentary breakfast. Cable TV. Laundry service. Airport shuttle. No kids under 12. No smoking. | 312 S. 3rd St. | 910/763–6603 or 800/763–6603 | fax 910/763–5116 | www.bbonline.com/nc/curran | 3 rooms | $89–$119 | AE, MC, V.

Days Inn. Half a mile from the University of Wilmington campus and right at the end of I-40, this motel gives you a choice of a queen bed or two doubles. It's within walking distance of restaurants and stores. Restaurant. Cable TV. Pool. Business services. | 5040 Market St. | 910/799–6300 | fax 910/791–7414 | 122 rooms | $66–$75 | AE, D, DC, MC, V.

Fairfield Inn by Marriott. This chain option, half a mile from the University campus and 4 mi from historic downtown Wilmington, helps you start the day with complimentary newspapers awaiting you in the lobby each weekday morning. Complimentary Continental breakfast. Cable TV. Pool. Business services. | 306 S. College Rd. | 910/392–6767 | fax 910/392–6767 | 134 rooms | $75–$92 | AE, D, DC, MC, V.

French House. Built in 1850, much of this inn's original floors, mantels, doors, and fixtures remain. There is a common parlor, dining room, and fireplace, and each suite has its own porch and fireplace. It is four blocks from Cape Fear. Dining room, complimentary breakfast. Some kitchenettes. Cable TV, in-room VCRs, room phones. Laundry facilities. No pets. No smoking. | 103 South 4th St. | 910/763–3337 | www.thefrenchhouse.com | 2 suites | $85–$125 | No credit cards.

Front Street Inn. Earth tones, natural fibers, and many plants lend a modern twist to a 1923 building that was home to the first Salvation Army in North Carolina. There's an art collection to view and a pool table and dart board for more active relaxation, or you can just watch the river and sunset views from the balcony. Complimentary Continental breakfast. In-room data ports, microwaves, refrigerators. Cable TV. Massage. Exercise equipment. Business services. | 215 S. Front St. | 910/762–6442 | fax 910/762–8991 | www.seewilmington.com/streetin.htm | 9 suites | $95–$165 suites | AE, D, DC, MC, V.

Graystone Inn. When this 1906 building was young its turn-of-the-century antiques would have been the latest rage. The period pieces especially lend grace to the music room, just off the sunlit parlor, and to the large suites with fireplaces. Complimentary breakfast. In-room dataports. Cable TV. Exercise equipment. No kids under 12. No smoking. | 100 S. 3rd St. | 910/763–2000 | fax 910/763–5555 | 5 rooms, 2 suites | $139–$189, $249–$299 suites | AE, D, DC, MC, V.

Green Tree Inn. Built in the 1970s, this good-sized inn ranks as one of the relatively newer additions to the Wilmington scene, and at a mile from downtown, not quite 5 mi from the beach, and less than 4 mi from the Cape Fear River, its location is a strong point. Complimentary Continental breakfast. Cable TV. Pool. Business services. | 5025 Market St. | 910/799–6001 or 800/225–7666 | fax 910/799–6001 | grntreenc@aol.com | 123 rooms | $50–$80 | AE, D, DC, MC, V.

Hampton Inn. The portico entrance to this low-rise motel in gray is just 6 mi from Wrightsville Beach. Complimentary appetizers are served Monday through Thursday evenings, and there's freshly popped popcorn every night. Complimentary Continental breakfast. In-room data ports. Cable TV. Pool. Business services. | 5107 Market St. | 910/395–5045 | fax 910/799–1974 | 118 rooms | $99–$115 | AE, D, DC, MC, V.

Hampton Inn and Suites–Landfall Park. In this inn in the prestigious Landfall area of Wilmington, 1½ mi from the Wrightsville Beach drawbridge, you can relax in the rocking chairs on the veranda overlooking the courtyard or start your day with runs on the adjacent jogging trail. Golf packages. Bar, picnic area, complimentary Continental breakfast. In-room data ports, minibars and kitchenettes in suites, some microwaves, some refrigerators, some in-room whirlpools. Cable TV. Pool. Driving range, putting green. Exercise equipment. Laundry facilities. Business services. Some pets allowed. | 1989 Eastwood Rd. | 910/256–9600 | fax 910/256–1996 | www.landfallparkhotel.com | 120 rooms, 30 suites | $99–$129, $119–$399 suites | AE, D, DC, MC, V.

Hilton-Riverside. When the alarm radio sounds, you can start the day with coffee brewed in your own coffeemaker and a complimentary newspaper that waits at your door on weekday mornings. Rising from the east bank of the Cape Fear River and directly across from the USS *North Carolina* battleship memorial, the mid-rise hotel provides views in several directions. Restaurant, bar, room service. In-room data ports. Cable TV. Pool. Hot tub. Exercise equipment. Dock. Business services, airport shuttle. | 301 N. Water St. | 910/763–5900 | fax 910/763–0038 | info@wilmingtonhilton.com | www.wilmingtonriverside.hilton.com | 178 rooms, 8 suites | $99–$159 | AE, D, DC, MC, V.

Holiday Inn. Print fabrics and easy chairs give a quaint feeling to many rooms in this two-story hotel 4 mi from downtown, but you'll also find work desks and phones with 25-ft cords for laptop computers. About three-quarters of the rooms are no-smoking, and some have whirlpools that seat up to three people. Restaurant, bar, room service, complementary breakfast buffet. In-room data ports. Cable TV. Pool. Laundry facilities. Business services, airport shuttle. | 4903 Market St. | 910/799–1440 | fax 910/799–2683 | howdenr@bellsouth.net | 227 rooms | $89–$129 | AE, D, DC, MC, V.

Holiday Inn Express. On I–40 about a mile from the Corning plant and about 7 mi from downtown, this motel presents a tall neo-modern entrance above a red-roofed portico. Rooms have hair dryers, iron, and ironing board. Complimentary Continental breakfast. Some microwaves, refrigerators in suites. Cable TV. Pool. Exercise equipment. Laundry facilities. Business services. | 160 Van Campen Blvd. | 910/392–3227 | fax 910/395–9907 | hixwilm@earthlink.net | 131 rooms, 45 suites | $84–$109, suites $105–$159 | AE, D, DC, MC, V.

Howard Johnson Express. Just ½ mi from the University of North Carolina at Wilmington and 3 mi from downtown, this motel has kitchenettes in some rooms and a table and chairs in all. Complimentary Continental breakfast. Some microwaves, some refrigerators. Cable TV. Business services. | 3901 Market St. | 910/343–1727 | fax 910/343–1727 | 80 rooms | $50–$70 | AE, D, DC, MC, V.

Inn at St. Thomas Court. When you go through the entrance court to this suites complex, you can see that the inn actually includes five buildings—turn-of-the-century commercial structures, a former convent, and an antebellum mansion. Guest spaces have many antiques. Complimentary Continental breakfast. In-room data ports, microwaves, some minibars. Cable TV. Some washers and dryers. Business services. No kids under 12. | 101 S. 2nd St. | 910/343–1800 or 800/525–0909 | fax 910/251–1149 | 40 suites | $129–$149 | AE, D, DC, MC, V.

Ramada Inn Conference Center. Though it is right in the center of town, this motel has free parking, including some spaces just for trucks and RVs. It caters to business people and is within a mile of restaurants and shops. The mall is about 5 miles away. Restaurant, bar with entertainment, room service. Some refrigerators. Cable TV. Pool. Business services, airport shuttle. | 5001 Market St. | 910/799–1730 | fax 910/799–1730 | 100 rooms | $79–$109 | AE, D, MC, V.

Sheraton–Four Points. Just 4½ mi from downtown and only 5 mi from the beach, this pale-toned low-rise hotel emphasizes calming light colors in guest rooms, too. If you want a quick swim without having to drive to the beach, there is an indoor heated pool. Restaurant, bar, room service. Some microwaves, refrigerators in suites. Cable TV. Hot tub. Exercise equipment. Business services. | 5032 Market St. | 910/392–1101 | fax 910/397–0698 | 124 rooms, 7 suites | $89 | AE, D, DC, MC, V.

Super 8. As you go up the drive to this buff-colored motel 1 mi from downtown you can see the extensive plantings that have brought the site a special award from the chain's management. Cable TV. Business services. | 3604 Market St. | 910/343–9778 | fax 910/343–9778, ext. 125 | 62 rooms | $49–$69 | AE, D, DC, MC, V.

Taylor House. When you step from the cobblestone streets and into this Classic Revival house you'll find that many architectural elements are as they always were: a large open staircase, stained-glass windows, parquet floors, along with fireplaces and the original clawfoot tubs in the guest rooms. Complimentary breakfast. Airport shuttle. No smoking. | 14 N. 7th St. | 910/763–7581 or 800/382–9982 | www.bbonline.com/nc/taylor/index.html | 5 rooms | $110–$225 | AE, MC, V.

Worth House. A short stroll from the riverwalk, this gracious Queen Anne–style inn is surrounded by gardens. Guest rooms have decorative fireplaces and ceiling fans to ward off the summer heat. Complimentary breakfast. In-room data ports. No TV in rooms, cable TV in common area. Laundry service. No kids under 10. No smoking. | 412 S. 3rd St. | 910/762–8562 or 800/340–8559 | fax 910/763–2173 | worthhouse@aol.com | www.worthhouse.com | 7 rooms | $100–$150 | AE, D, MC, V.

WILSON

MAP 8, I4

(Nearby towns also listed: Goldsboro, Greenville, Rocky Mount)

Wilson is the town that tobacco built. Tobacco barons made the place one of the wealthiest communities in North Carolina, as well as one of the most attractive. Today, though, the action takes place in another arena: antiques. Wilson boasts more than two dozen antiques shops and more than 100,000 items from the 17th, 18th, 19th, and early 20th centuries.

Information: Wilson County Tourism Authority | Box 2882, Wilson 27894. **Visitor Center** | 124 E. Nash St. | 252/243–8440 or 800/497–7398 | info@wilson-nc.com | www.wilson-nc.com.

Attractions

Imagination Station. You'll discover live animals and plants in the rain forest of this interactive science museum with 200 exhibits. Demonstrations are given daily. | 202 W. Nash St. | 252/291–5113 | fax 252/291–2968 | $3 | Mon.–Sat. 9–5.

Vollis Simpson's Wind Art. Giant, colorful sculptures in the form of windmills are scattered about the countryside around Vollis Simpson's home. Many of them have reflective pieces, and when the wind kicks up, the sculptures appear to come alive. The artist, who was commissioned to do a work for the 1996 Olympics, is also in museum collections. | Willing Worker Rd. | 252/243–8440 or 800/497–7398 | Free | Daily.

ON THE CALENDAR

AUG.: *WilsonFest.* Organized by the city's Human Relations Commission, with the help of arts groups, the festival presents food, art, music, dance, clothing, and games, from many nations. | Nash St. | 252/399–2308.

SEPT. or OCT.: *Golden Leaf Gala.* A celebration of the town's tobacco and agricultural heritage, this program includes music and dance, arts and crafts, speakers, and food. | 252/243–8440.

Dining

Parker's Barbecue. Barbecue. A slew of photos bears testimony that this eatery has been serving its eastern North Carolina chopped pork barbecue and corn sticks for almost 60 years. You can have your samples inside, where service is family-style, or on the picnic tables outside. Kids' menu. | U.S. 301 S | 252/237–0972 | Closed 1 wk following Father's Day | $3–$10 | No credit cards.

Lodging

Comfort Inn. All rooms have both a table and a work desk, although you can have a choice of bed size. Complimentary Continental breakfast. Some refrigerators. Cable TV. Pool. Business services. | 4941 U.S. 264 W | 252/291–6400 | fax 252/291–7744 | 76 rooms | $60–$90 | AE, D, DC, MC, V.

Days Inn. This motel provides basic accommodations in the middle of the antiques shopping area. Complimentary Continental breakfast, bar. Cable TV. Pool. Business services. | 1815 U.S. 301 S | 252/243–5111 | fax 252/291–9697 | 100 rooms | $50–$62 | AE, D, DC, MC, V.

Hampton Inn. Rooms are categorized by bed size, but you can expect an alarm radio and coffeemaker in all of them—along with a free newspaper weekdays. Complimentary Continental breakfast. In-room data ports. Cable TV. Pool. Business services. | 1801 S. Tarboro St. | 252/291–2323 | fax 252/291–7696 | 100 rooms | $60–$73 | AE, D, DC, MC, V.

Miss Betty's. Is your choice old or really old? This B&B in the downtown historic section is composed of four restored houses built between 1858 and 1910, all furnished as in those days gone by. Complimentary breakfast. Cable TV. Business services. No kids under 15. No smoking. | 600 W. Nash St. | 252/243–4447 or 800/258–2058 | fax 252/243–4447 | 10 rooms, 3 with shower only; 4 suites with 10-day minimum stay | $60–$80, $51 suites | AE, D, DC, MC, V.

WINSTON-SALEM

MAP 8, E3

(Nearby towns also listed: Greensboro, High Point, Lexington, Pilot Mountain)

The Moravians, a Protestant sect that settled here in the mid-1700s, fostered an industrious ethic on this area that was then the edge of America's western frontier. They created a solid economic base for the region, later expanded by the makers of cigarettes, textiles, and furniture.

Originally, the two towns were separate—Salem, founded as a Moravian settlement in 1766, and Winston, dating from 1849. Many residents objected when the U.S. Post Office began to consider them as one hyphenated address in 1899, but the towns officially merged in 1913.

Today, Winston-Salem bills itself as the City of the Arts. Residents' donations to the arts are among the highest per capita in the nation, and Broadway directors bring shows here for try-outs. In addition to several museums, the city is home to the North Carolina School of the Arts, as well as the Wake Forest Bowman Gray School of Medicine, Salem College, the oldest women's college in the country, and Wake Forest University, where author Maya Angelou teaches.

Information: Greater Winston-Salem Convention and Visitors Bureau | Box 1409, Winston-Salem 27102 | 336/728–4200 or 800/331–7018 | fax 336/728–4220 | info@wscvb.com | www.wscvb.com.

Visitor Center. The convention bureau maintains this place with many materials to help you explore the region and with a sampling of traditional Moravian sugar cookies. | 601 N. Cherry St. | 336/728–4200 or 800/331–7018 | fax 336/728–4220. | info@wscvb.com | www.wscvb.com.

Attractions

Hanging Rock State Park. If you're a climber, you can bring your equipment here. The 6,192-acre park in the Sauratown Mountains has designated several areas for rock climbing and rappelling. Within its boundaries, you'll also find five waterfalls, a small cave, three ridgetops with panoramic views, more than 18 mi of hiking trails, and camping, picnicking, and swimming sites. | 1005 Visitors Center Dr., Danbury | 336/593–8480 | fax 336/593–9166 | www.ncsparks.net | Free.

Historic Bethabara Park. On a wooded 195 acres, this site, now on the National Register of Historic Places, became home to the first Moravian settlement in North Carolina in 1753. You can tour Colonial gardens and such restored buildings as the 1788 Gemeinhaus, or church, and explore the foundations of the town. | 2147 Bethabara Rd. | 336/924–8191 | fax 336/924–0535 | $1 | Mon.–Fri. 9:30–4:30, weekends 1:30–4:00.

Museum of Anthropology. This collection on the Reynolda campus of Wake Forest University presents the stories of the peoples of the Americas, Asia, Africa, and Oceania through exhibits of their household and ceremonial items, textiles, hunting and fishing gear, and objects of personal adornment. | Wingate Rd. | 336/758–5282 | fax 336/758–5282 | Free | Tues.–Sat. 10–4:30.

★ **Old Salem.** Costumed interpreters re-create the everyday life of the Moravians in the Salem of the late 18th and early 19th centuries. The village includes more than 80 restored and original buildings. | 600 S. Main St. | 336/721–7300 or 888/653–7253 | www.oldsalem.org | $15; combination ticket with Museum of Early Southern Decorative Arts $20 | Mon.–Sat. 9:30–4:30, Sun. 1:30–4:30.

★ **Museum of Early Southern Decorative Arts (MESDA).** You can gain a real picture of the Old South from 24 painstakingly designed period rooms and six galleries showcasing the furniture, painting, ceramics, and metalware made and used regionally through 1820. | 924 S. Main St. | 336/721–7360 or 888/653–7253 | fax 336/721–7335 | $10; combination ticket with Old Salem $20 | Mon.–Sat. 9:30–3:30, Sun. 1:30–3:30.

Reynolda House, Museum of American Art. The former home of tobacco magnate Richard Joshua Reynolds and his wife, Katherine, is filled with American paintings, prints, and sculptures by such artists as Thomas Eakins, Frederick Church, and Georgia O'Keeffe. There's also a costume collection, as well as clothing and toys used by the Reynolds children. The museum is next to Reynolda Village, a collection of shops and restaurants that fill the estate's original outer buildings. | 2250 Reynolda Rd. | 336/725–5325 | fax 336/721–0991 | reynolda@reynoldahouse.org | $6 | Tues.–Sat. 9:30–4:30, Sun. 1:30–4:30.

R. J. Reynolds Whitaker Park. At this facility, where the tobacco company conducts a lot of research, you can take a guided tour through exhibits on tobacco growing and view historic memorabilia related to the industry. | 1100 Reynolds Blvd. | 336/741–5718 | Free | Weekdays 8–6.

SciWorks. Besides scanning the skies at the 120-seat planetarium, you can visit a 15-acre Environmental Park and 45,000 square ft of interactive or hands-on exhibits, including the Coastal Encounters wet lab. | 400 W. Hanes Mill Rd. | 336/767–6730 | fax 336/661–1777 | www.sciworks.org | Museum $7; planetarium, park, and museum $8 | Science center Mon.–Sat. 10–5; Environmental Park Mon.–Sat. 10–4:30.

Southeastern Center for Contemporary Art (SECCA). Across the street from Reynolda House, this series of galleries sits on 32 wooded acres and showcases both regional arts and crafts and nationally known artists. | 750 Marguerite Dr. | 336/725–1904 | fax 336/722–6059 | www.secca.org | $3 | Tues.–Sat. 10–5, Sun. 2–5.

Tanglewood Park. Part of territory claimed by Sir Walter Raleigh for Queen Elizabeth I in 1584 and the site of a fort during the French and Indian Wars, this land later became the estate of the late William and Kate Reynolds. You now can boat, hike, fish, ride horses, and swim here, as well as view the formal gardens Mrs. Reynolds installed. | U.S. 158, Clemmons

| 336/778–6300 | fax 336/778–6322 | www.tanglewoodpark.org | $2 per car, plus activity fees | Daily dawn–dusk.

ON THE CALENDAR

MAR. or APR.: *Moravian Easter Sunrise Service.* Thousands of people make their way to the restored town of Old Salem for the hour-long predawn service that, as tradition dictates, begins in front of the Home Moravian Church and proceeds to God's Acre cemetery as the sun rises. The ritual, which takes place rain or shine, uses hymns, brass instruments, and the spoken word. | 529 S. Church St. | 336/722–6171.

MAY: *Crosby National Celebrity Golf Tournament.* Named for Bing Crosby and over-seen by his widow, the tournament draws politicians, entertainers, and sports stars to help raise money to combat drug abuse. | Bermuda Run Country Club | 336/519–7500.

MAY: *Greek Festival.* This program at and around St. Nicholas Greek Orthodox Church presents an abundance of traditional Greek food and entertainment, including, of course, the pulse-pounding music and dance. | 435 Keating Dr. | 336/765–7145.

JULY: *Flow Motors Tennis Invitational.* Wake Forest University is the home of this com-petition, which pits some of the top professional tennis players, including stars from the male and female circuits, against each other. | 336/722–6111.

AUG.: *National Black Theater Festival.* Since 1989, nationally and internationally known actors, playwrights, musicians, dancers, and singers have come to Winston-Salem every other year for performances, workshops, and seminars during this week-long program. | 336/723–2266 or 336/723–7907.

SEPT.: *Vantage Championship Golf Tournament.* Many are the oohs and aahs when legends of the game make great shots at the Vantage, which has one of the largest purses on the Senior PGA Tour. | Tanglewood Park Golf Club, U.S. 158 off I–40, Clemmons | 336/766–2400.

NOV.: *Piedmont Crafts Fair.* Crafts artisans from around the region showcase their work for three days of exhibits and sales, workshops, and demonstrations at the Benton Convention Center. | 301 W. 5th St. | 336/725–1516.

NOV.–JAN.: *Tanglewood Festival of Lights.* A million lights form giant decorations and more than 60 animated exhibits in this event. With more than 3 mi of displays, the drive-through holiday light show in Tanglewood Park is one of the largest in the South-east. | U.S. 158 off I–40, Clemmons | 336/778–6300.

DEC.: *The Nutcracker Ballet.* Dancers from the North Carolina School of the Arts and musicians from the Winston-Salem Piedmont Triad Symphony collaborate on perfor-mances of the fairy-tale ballet, always a favorite of kids. | Stevens Center for the Per-forming Arts, 405 W. 4th St. | 336/721–1945.

Dining

Leon's Café. Contemporary. You can have your dinner in the building near Old Salem, where there's live music Tuesday nights and some Saturdays, or out on the quiet patio, set among the trees. Known for fresh seafood, chicken, and lamb. | 924 S. Marshall St. | 336/725–9593 | No lunch | $19–$25 | AE, D, MC, V.

Noble's Grille. Contemporary. The musical entertainment comes from live jazz Monday nights, but if you're a food buff, you may be just as interested in watching as the specials—often with French and Mediterranean flavors—are grilled or roasted over an oak-and-hickory fire. The umbrella-bedecked patio provides open-air dining beside a small garden. Kids' menu. | 380 Knollwood St. | 336/777–8477 | Closed Sun. No lunch Sat. | $20–$35 | AE, DC, MC, V.

Old Salem Tavern Dining Room. Eclectic. You'll find everything from meat loaf to seafood at this site that's part of the Old Salem complex and has several dishes inspired by the Moravian tradition. In summer, you can dine out on the porch. | 736 S. Main St. | 336/748–8585 | $20–$30 | AE, MC, V.

Paul's Fine Italian Dining. Italian. This simple restaurant is known for its veal dishes but lists a range of other traditional choices. Vegetarian dishes and lighter fare include lin-guini primavera and manicotti stuffed with cheese. Desserts include chocolate dream, rum cake, and ice cream. | 3443B Robin Hood Rd. | 336/768–2645 | Reservations essential | No lunch weekends | $11–$25 | AE, DC, MC, V.

The Vineyards. Contemporary. Out on the patio, next to a garden, the iron tables are topped with umbrellas for shaded open-air dining. The menu, which has many seasonal changes, puts an American touch to such specialties as grilled swordfish and stuffed eggplant. Entertainment Thursday–Saturday. Kids' menu. | 120 Reynolda Village Rd. | 336/748–0269 | Closed Sun. | $13–$21 | AE, MC, V.

Zevely House. Contemporary. Costumed servers in Moravian-style dress are visible reminders of the heritage of this 1816 building where the six rooms have been left as separate dining spaces. Outside, there's a tree-shaded patio. Kids' menu. Sun. brunch. | 901 W. 4th St. | 336/725–6666 | Closed Mon. | $20–$30 | AE, MC, V.

Lodging

Adam's Mark at Winston Plaza. You have stunning views of the city from the two skywalk-connected towers of what is now the second-largest hotel in North Carolina. Especially known as a convention destination, the hotel underwent a $10 million expansion and renovation in recent years. Rooms often have deep, serene tones against paler walls, and all are furnished with work desks. Restaurants, bar with entertainment, room service. In-room data ports, refrigerators in suites. Cable TV, Indoor pool. Hot tub, sauna. Gym. Laundry service. Business services. | 425 N. Cherry St. | 336/725–3500 | fax 336/721–2240 | www.adams-mark.com | 605 rooms, 26 suites | $139–$185, $450–$800 suites | AE, D, DC, MC, V.

Augustus T. Zevely Inn. Electrified beeswax candles in the windows welcome you to this bed-and-breakfast in the heart of Old Salem. Many rooms in the 1844 house have been closely returned to their original appearance, often using reproductions especially made from the Moravian originals in the Old Salem restored village. Complimentary Continental breakfast, complete breakfast on weekends. Some in-room hot tubs. Cable TV. No kids under 16. Business services. | 803 S. Main St. | 336/748–9299 or 800/928–9299 | fax 336/721–2211 | ctheall@dddcompany.com | 11 rooms, 1 suite | $80–$135, $205 suite | AE, MC, V.

Brookstown Inn. If you've had a busy day, you may especially appreciate the wine and cheese served every evening. Early American furnishings keep the interiors true to the inn's origins in the 1800s. Complimentary Continental breakfast. In-room data ports. Cable TV. Business services. | 200 Brookstown Ave. | 336/725–1120 or 800/845–4262 | fax 336/773–0147 | 40 rooms, 31 suites | $125, $135–$150 suites | AE, DC, MC, V.

Coliseum Courtyard by Marriott. Work desks and an iron and ironing board are standard in this motel next to Wake Forest University and one block from Lawrence Joel Veterans Coliseum. To help you start the day, a morning newspaper is delivered weekdays, and there is complimentary in-room coffee. Cable TV. Pool. Hot tub. Exercise equipment. Laundry facilities. Business services. | 3111 University Pkwy. | 336/727–1277 or 800/321–2211 | fax 336/722–8219 | 123 rooms, 1 suite | $78, $135 suite | AE, D, DC, MC, V.

Colonel Ludlow Inn. This inn in a National Historic District consists of two large adjacent Victorian homes, more than 100 years old, and is itself listed on the National Register of Historic Places. Rooms are furnished with Victorian antiques, art and books, but have such modern touches as a stereo system, two-person whirlpool tub with candles, and towel warmer. Restaurants, complimentary breakfast. In-room data ports, microwaves, refrigerators. Cable TV. In-room hot tubs. Exercise equipment. Business services. Free parking. No kids under 12. | 434 Summit | 336/777–1887 or 800/301–1887 | fax 336/777–0518 | innkeeper@bbinn.com | www.bbinn.com | 9 rooms, 2 suites | $109–$209 | AE, D, MC, V.

Comfort Inn–Cloverdale. Rooms at this five-story motel 5 mi from downtown are in light colors and include table and chairs. A drug store and grocery store are within walking distance. Complimentary Continental breakfast. In-room data ports, some microwaves, some refrigerators, some no-smoking rooms. Cable TV. Pool. Hot tub, sauna. Exercise equipment. | 110 Miller St. | 336/721–0220 | fax 336/723–2117 | 122 rooms | $69–$85 | AE, D, DC, MC, V.

Days Inn. Furnishings are quietly modern in this hotel 4 mi from Wake Forest University and Hanes Mall, the second-largest mall on the East Coast. Morning newspapers are complimentary. Complimentary Continental breakfast. Cable TV. Pool. Hot tub. Business services. | 3330 Silas Creek Pkwy. S | 336/760–4770 | fax 336/760–1085 | 135 rooms | $50–$54 | AE, D, DC, MC, V.

Hampton Inn. Behind the giant Hanes Mall, this motel uses a lot of floral themes in furnishings, often with companion borders, and some rooms have wing chairs. Complimentary Continental breakfast. Minibars, some refrigerators. Cable TV. Pool. Exercise equipment. Business services. Free internet access. | 1990 Hampton Inn Ct | 336/760–1660 | fax 336/768–9168 | 131 rooms | $89–$129 | AE, D, DC, MC, V.

Hampton Inn–University. This buff-colored multistory motel is 3 mi from Wake Forest University. Inside, you'll find free coffee or tea served in the lobby 24-hours a day. Complimentary Continental breakfast. Some in-room data ports. Cable TV. Pool. Business services. | 5719 University Pkwy. | 336/767–9009 | fax 336/661–0448 | 117 rooms | $69 | AE, D, DC, MC, V.

Henry F. Shaffner House. Wraparound porches remind of more leisurely times. Outside, the inn has Tudor-style detailing, and the interior has a bounty of tiger-oak paneling beneath beamed ceilings. Wine and cheese are served with the sunset. Restaurant, complimentary Continental breakfast. In-room data ports. Cable TV. Business services. No smoking. | 150 S. Marshall St. | 336/777–0052 or 800/952–2256 | fax 336/777–1188 | 9 rooms | $99–$239 | AE, MC, V.

Holiday Inn Select. Furnishings have a modern air, and you'll find such oft-requested conveniences as hair dryers and irons. You can go jogging or walking along the path that connects to the back of the hotel grounds. This hotel is within walking distance of chain restaurants and stores. Restaurant, bar, room service. In-room data ports, minibars, some refrigerators. Cable TV. Pool. Exercise equipment. Business services. | 5790 University Pkwy. | 336/767–9595 | fax 336/744–1888 | jmerriott@wsholidayinn.com | 150 rooms, 8 suites | $79–$99, $110 suites | AE, D, DC, MC, V.

Residence Inn by Marriott. If you—or your family—want to have munchies available at any hour, you can stock the kitchenettes for late-night snacking, or even a full-blown picnic outdoors. This spot is within walking distance of some restaurants, and movie theaters are less than a block away. Picnic area, complimentary Continental breakfast. Kitchenettes, microwaves, refrigerators. Pool. Hot tub. Laundry facilities. Free parking. Some pets allowed. | 7835 N. Point Blvd. | 336/759–0777 | fax 336/759–9671 | 88 suites | $94–$160 | AE, D, DC, MC, V.

Tanglewood Manor House B&B. In 1921, magnate William Neal Reynolds bought this land that traces its deeds back to Sir Walter Raleigh. Now the estate has become Tanglewood Park, and the manor house and adjoining lodge apartment are part of a lodging complex that also includes four rustic cottages in the woods overlooking Mallard Lake and a guest house where wood is supplied for the fireplaces. Park entrance is free if you stay at the manor house. Picnic area. Cable TV. Pool, wading pool. Driving range, two 18-hole golf courses, tennis courts. Playground. | 4061 Clemmons Rd., Clemmons | 336/778–6300 | fax 336/778–6379 | www.tanglewoodpark.org | 28 rooms; 4 cottages, 1 house | $45–$107; $425/wk cottages, $575/wk guest house | AE, MC, V.

WRIGHTSVILLE BEACH

MAP 8, I7

(Nearby towns also listed: Kure Beach, Southport, Wilmington)

For more than a century, Wrightsville Beach has been a family resort dotted with upscale hotels, summer cottages, and one of the oldest yacht clubs on the East Coast. The beach, on an island just the other side of the Intracoastal Waterway drawbridge from Wilmington, also draws many day-trippers, but there's nothing honky-tonk here: no boardwalks, no carnivals, no arcades. Just clean, wide beach.

WRIGHTSVILLE
BEACH

INTRO
ATTRACTIONS
DINING
LODGING

Information: Cape Fear Coast Convention and Visitors Bureau | 24 N. 3rd St., Wilmington 28401 | 910/341–4030 or 800/222–4757 | info@cape-fear.nc.us | www.cape-fear.nc.us.

Attractions

Wrightsville Beach Island. In summer, this small island grows from 3,050 year-round citizens to 12,000 overnighters and 30,000 day-trippers. The beach is wide and clean and easily accessible, but be warned that free parking spaces are limited—if you're not there by 9:30 AM, you may need to come stocked with quarters to feed a meter. | 910/341–4030 or 800/222–4757 | Free | Daily.

Wrightsville Beach Museum of History. The island's fourth-oldest cottage has been restored to display both rotating and permanent exhibits on the island's history, including a scale model, circa 1910, complete with working trolley and studies of hurricanes and barrier islands. | 303 W. Salisbury St. | 910/256–2569 | $2 | Daily noon–6.

ON THE CALENDAR

MAY: *Cape Fear Marlin Tournament.* You can try your hand at catching a big one in this sportfishing contest at the Bridge Tender Marina. Cash awards are given for various categories. | 1418 Airlie Rd. | 910/256–6550.

JULY: *Lumina Daze Festival.* You'll find a range of options at this event sponsored by the Wrightsville Beach Preservation Society, from dancing to big-band music to viewing displays or vintage movies to taking a midnight swim in the Atlantic—or

© Corbis

OPERATION BUMBLEBEE

Topsail (pronounced *top*-sil) was the first barrier island south of Bogue Inlet subject to commercial development. But before there was commerce, and definitely before there were tourists, there was a secret.

The island, 26 mi long and only about ½ mi wide, is home to eight evenly spaced, squat reinforced-concrete towers. These lookouts, along with a concrete patio and a museum, are all that's left of Operation Bumblebee, a U.S. Navy rocket program that was the precursor to NASA. In the 1940s, Topsail, an isolated place that had experienced some military buildup during World War II, was selected as the top-secret site for the development and testing of defense missiles—the granddaddies of supersonic missiles.

These first rockets were put together in the large Assembly Building, now a museum. They were then transferred via underground tunnels to a seaside launching pad that presently serves as a patio at the Jolly Roger Motel. Observers stationed in either the concrete watchtowers or safer underground bunkers would track the flight of the guided missiles and measure their speed. Between 1947 and 1948, some 200 two-stage rockets blasted out over the ocean. The experiments made Topsail as significant to jet flight as Kitty Hawk was to propeller flight.

Ultimately, salt air, humidity, and increased traffic within the 20-mi firing range did in the project. Many of the buildings and much of the equipment associated with the operation were donated or sold, and two years after the military moved out, Topsail Island had its first incorporated town, Surf City.

just enjoying the food and tiki bar. | Blockade Runner Beach Resort, 275 Waynick Blvd. | 910/256–2251 or 800/541–1161 | $8 in advance, $10 at the door.

SEPT.: *Wrightsville Beach King Mackerel Tournament.* You can join anglers from many states who enter this competition year after year. After the fishing, there is a dance ceremony. | Bridge Tender Marina | 910/256–6550.

NOV.: *Holiday Flotilla.* The holiday fair includes arts-and-crafts shows, children's art activities, rides, food, and fireworks, but the big pull is the water parade of brightly lit, sometimes wildly decorated boats. The flotilla begins at 7 PM. | Banks Channel | 910/791–4122.

Dining

Blue Water Grill. Caribbean. Light-blue walls hung with paintings and photos of the beach help make this place feel like a beach resort, although you may notice a few items connected to the *Titanic*. You can try the island-style fish, cocoanut shrimp, or marinated hanger steak, and for entertainment there's occasional live music and DJs. Kids' menu. | 4 Marina St. | 910/256–8500 | Reservations not accepted in pub | No lunch upstairs | $11–$30 | AE, MC, V.

Bridge Tender. Seafood. This white-tablecloth dining room is on the waterfront in an otherwise residential beach neighborhood and has a view of the Intracoastal Waterway from the deck. Locals recommend the herb-crusted grouper and the prime rib. | 1414 Airlie Rd. | 910/256–4519 | No lunch weekends | $21–$41 | AE, D, DC, MC, V.

Dockside. Seafood. Beachy fish motifs and hurricane photos are eye candy while you wait for this casual spot's grilled catch of the day or the popular hamburger. Or you can place your order out on the deck and view the beach of today. Live entertainment Wednesday and Sunday. Kids' menu. | 1308 Airlie Rd. | 910/256–2752 | Reservations not accepted | $7–$14 | D, MC, V.

Middle of the Island. American. This no-frills eatery serves breakfast, lunch, and supper all day, as well as Sunday brunch. Try one of the seafood breakfasts. Kid's menu. | 216 Causeway Dr. | 910/256–4277 | Reservations not accepted | No supper Sun. | $5–$10 | No credit cards.

Ocean Terrace Restaurant. Contemporary. Part of the Blockade Runner Resort, this restaurant attracts the crowds to its Friday lobster night, when there is a pianist, and the Saturday seafood buffet and Sunday brunch. Try grilled New York strip steak with Bourbon-shallot butter; sautéed almond-breaded flounder with shrimp; and sautéed chicken breast with toasted pecans, pears, and apples. Walls of big windows open up to the breezes and views of the ocean. Kids' menu. | 275 Waynick Blvd. | 910/256–2251 or 800/541–1161 | Reservations essential | $20–$35 | AE, D, DC, MC, V.

Oceanic Restaurant and Grill. Seafood. The theme is definitely nautical, in the decorative touches and the real-life views of beach and boats from this open-air restaurant on a huge pier. You can try the "Super Duper Grouper" or the "Very Fresh Fish Special." Kids' menu. Sun. brunch. | 703 S. Lumina Ave. | 910/256–5551 | $15–$25 | AE, MC, V.

Lodging

Blockade Runner Beach Resort. Right on the beach and the Intracoastal Waterway, this is the largest facility on the island. Rooms have a quietly modern feeling, but no vinyl wallpaper or typical hotel carpeting, since mold can grow under them in the sea air. Restaurant, bar with entertainment, room service. Cable TV. Pool. Hot tub. Gym. Beach. Boating. Kid's programs. Business services, airport shuttle. | 275 Waynick Blvd. | 910/256–2251 or 800/541–1161 | fax 910/256–5502 | www.blockade-runner.com | 150 rooms | $120–$320; 2–night minimum stay weekends | AE, D, DC, MC, V.

The Cottage. Originally built as a boarding house, this two-story structure is a splendid example of the classic beach cottages that are landmarks of Wrightsville Beach. Now

WRIGHTSVILLE
BEACH

INTRO
ATTRACTIONS
DINING
LODGING

owned by the Blockade Runner, it usually rents by the group, as it sleeps 26 and has a 1,000-sq ft living area/meeting space. Large covered porches provide panoramic harbor views; oceanside, there is an open sundeck on the second floor. Complimentary breakfast. Pool. Hot tub, sauna. No smoking. | 225 S. Lumina Ave. | 910/256–2251 or 800/805–2252 | fax 910/256–5502 | www.blockade-runner.com | 3 rooms, 5 suites | $1,000–$2,500 | AE, D, DC, MC, V.

One South Lumina. This 21-condo community requires a two-night minimum stay on weekends. Each one-bedroom unit has a full kitchen and washer and dryer, and only owners and those staying at the community can use the oceanside pool. Microwaves. Cable TV. Pool. Beach. | 1 S. Lumina Ave. | 910/256–9100 or 800/421–3255 | fax 910/509–1639 | 21 suites | $145–$190 | AE, D, MC, V.

Silver Gull. You'll have an ocean view from any room at this modernized motel on the ocean where U.S. 74 begins, since each room has its own private balcony. Kitchenettes. Cable TV. Laundry facilities. | 20 E. Salisbury St. | 910/256–3728 or 800/842–8894 | fax 910/256–2909 | 32 rooms | $135–$210 | AE, D, DC, MC, V.

Surf Suites. Each of these oceanfront suites has a fully equipped kitchen and a queen-sized sleeper sofa in the living room—and a private balcony facing the sea. Kitchenettes. Cable TV. Pool. Beach. Laundry facilities. | 711 S. Lumina Ave. | 910/256–2275 | fax 910/256–1206 | 45 suites | $165–$215 | AE, D, DC, MC, V.

Waterway Lodge. The Waterway Lodge complex at the Intracoastal Waterway drawbridge has one-bedroom condominiums, large hotel rooms, and an apartment. Each hotel room has a microwave oven, a refrigerator, and a coffeemaker. Larger units have full kitchens, plus sleeper sofas in condo living rooms. Cable TV. Pool. Business services. Some pets allowed ($15 fee). | 7246 Wrightsville Ave. | 910/256–3771 or 800/677–3771 | fax 910/256–6916 | www.waterwaylodge.com | 42 rooms | $90–$170 | AE, D, MC, V.

TOP TIPS FOR TRAVELERS

Smart Sightseeings

Don't plan your visit in your hotel room. Don't wait until you pull into town to decide how to spend your days. It's inevitable that there will be much more to see and do than you'll have time for: choose sights in advance.

Organize your touring. Note the places that most interest you on a map, and visit places that are near each other during the same morning or afternoon.

Start the day well equipped. Leave your hotel in the morning with everything you need for the day—maps, medicines, extra film, your guidebook, rain gear, and another layer of clothing in case the weather turns cooler.

Tour museums early. If you're there when the doors open you'll have an intimate experience of the collection.

Easy does it. See museums in the mornings, when you're fresh, and visit sit-down attractions later on. Take breaks before you need them.

Strike up a conversation. Only curmudgeons don't respond to a smile and a polite request for information. Most people appreciate your interest in their home town. And your conversations may end up being your most vivid memories.

Get lost. When you do, you never know what you'll find—but you can count on it being memorable. Use your guidebook to help you get back on track. Build wandering-around time into every day.

Quit before you're tired. There's no point in seeing that one extra sight if you're too exhausted to enjoy it.

Take your mother's advice. Go to the bathroom when you have the chance. You never know what lies ahead.

Hotel How-Tos

How to get a deal. After you've chosen a likely candidate or two, phone them directly and price a room for your travel dates. Then call the hotel's toll-free number and ask the same questions. Also try consolidators and hotel-room discounters. You won't hear the same rates twice. On the spot, make a reservation as soon as you are quoted a price you want to pay.

Promises, promises. If you have special requests, make them when you reserve. Get written confirmation of any promises.

Settle in. Upon arriving, make sure everything works—lights and lamps, TV and radio, sink, tub, shower, and anything else that matters. Report any problems immediately. And don't wait until you need extra pillows or blankets or an ironing board to call housekeeping. Also check out the fire emergency instructions. Know where to find the fire exits, and make sure your companions do, too.

If you need to complain. Be polite but firm. Explain the problem to the person in charge. Suggest a course of action. If you aren't satisfied, repeat your requests to the manager. Document everything: Take pictures and keep a written record of who you've spoken with, when, and what was said. Contact your travel agent, if he made the reservations.

Know the score. When you go out, take your hotel's business cards (one for everyone in your party). If you have extras, you can give them out to new acquaintances who want to call you.

Tip up front. For special services, a tip or partial tip in advance can work wonders.

Use all the hotel resources A concierge can make difficult things easy. But a desk clerk, bellhop, or other hotel employee who's friendly, smart, and ambitious can often steer you straight as well. A gratuity is in order if the advice is helpful.

© Artville

South Carolina

From its Lowcountry shoreline with wide sand beaches, large bays, and forests of palmet- tos and moss-draped live oaks, South Carolina extends inland into an undulating region rich with fertile farmlands, then reaches toward the Blue Ridge Mountains, whose foothills are studded with lakes, forests, and wilderness hideaways.

Textiles remain the state's biggest industry, thanks in great part to an innovative technical training system that has brought scores of new industries to the state. New factories line the Upcountry stretch of I–85 between Anderson, Greenville, Spartan- burg, and Gaffney, and much of this industrial corridor is owned by European corpo- rations. In fact, the state has the third highest per-capita foreign investment in the nation—85,000 people in South Carolina are employed by nearly 500 foreign-based companies.

Tourism is also booming and is now South Carolina's second largest source of income, bringing more than 29 million people each year to the state. The Grand Strand resorts around Myrtle Beach, historic Charleston, and the Sea Island resorts such as Hilton Head bring in the most revenue (in that order). As is often the case with popu- lar travel destinations, visitors return to retire, and the growth rate of retirees settling in South Carolina is now higher than that of Florida.

These pockets of development around the state coexist, however, with traditional and soothingly slow-paced rural life. About 75% of South Carolina's workers commute to their jobs from nearby small towns. Most South Carolinians are, like many South- erners, very church- and community-oriented. Church is the main event on Sunday, and restaurants and clubs must have a special liquor permit to serve alcoholic bever- ages after midnight on Saturday and on Sunday.

Agriculture remains an important factor in the economy, though tobacco, peaches, and soybeans, as well as pulpwood pine farms, bring in far more money now than cotton.

CAPITAL: COLUMBIA	POPULATION: 3,684,000	AREA: 32,007 SQUARE MI
BORDERS: GA, NC	TIME ZONE: EASTERN	POSTAL ABBREVIATION: SC
WEB SITE: TRAVELSC.COM		

A number of small farm market towns across South Carolina have also lured new industrial plants, usually apparel manufacturers, and many are confidently finding a new niche for their wares in the burgeoning tourism industry.

One of the great things about the state's small size and geographic diversity is that it's possible to have a varied visit: the sun-soaked beaches of the Lowcountry coast are only a few hours from the excellent hiking and nature trails of the hilly Upcountry. South Carolina, a state whose history changed the course of the nation, also has a rich cultural heritage. Most South Carolinians were born, live, and die right here—so history and heritage are not only their past but their present and their future as well.

History

The first European adventurers to reach South Carolina were the Spanish, who entered St. Helena Sound near Beaufort in 1520. A few years later, in 1526, the Spanish don Lucas Vázquez de Ayllón of Toledo established San Miguel at Winyah Bay, making it the first European settlement in the state and predating the English settlement at Jamestown, Virginia, by 81 years. After a year and a bitter winter, however, the Spanish abandoned San Miguel.

A group of French Huguenots fleeing religious persecution came next, then—again—the Spanish. The English finally made a go of it during the 1670s, after King Charles II granted Carolina—which encompassed everything from Virginia down to Cape Canaveral in Spanish Florida—to eight of his lord proprietors. Recruited by the lords, planters from the English colony of Barbados in the West Indies began settling the area, the first arriving in 1670 at Albemarle Point on the Ashley River. During the next decade, they and other settlers would move across the river to found Charles Town, today's Charleston, which would soon become England's wealthiest American colony.

By 1700, there were plantations throughout the Lowcountry and Sea Islands; by the 1730s, development of the area had spread north. Settlements near North Augusta, Camden, Lexington, York, Chester, and Lancaster included Welsh Baptists from Pennsylvania and Swiss, Irish, Scottish, and German immigrants from northern colonies. In the 1740s, there were 22,000 slaves in the colony, most of whom had been taken from what are today the African nations of Senegal and Sierra Leone. They outnumbered the colony's white population three to one. Most worked Lowcountry plantations, clearing swamps and building dikes and canals along rivers to plant rice, a crop they had cultivated in Africa. The colony's rice crop produced an extraordinary concentration of wealth in the hands of a few hundred plantation owners, Charleston merchants, and seaport shippers.

From one month after the Revolutionary War battle at Bunker Hill in 1775 until the British surrender at Yorktown, Virginia, in 1781, virtually the entire state of South Carolina became a battleground. More battles and skirmishes were fought here than in any other state. In many South Carolina towns it is referred to as the real civil war, because it pit father against son, neighbor against neighbor. In general, Lowcountry

SC Timeline

1400s	1521	1562	1600
15,000 to 20,000 indigenous people reside in the Carolinas.	Spaniards from Santo Domingo (present-day Dominican Republic) visit South Carolina.	French Huguenots build Charlesfort on what is today Parris Island, predating St. Augustine in Florida by three years.	15,000 Native Americans live in South Carolina. Forty-six separate tribes are represented, the largest being the Cherokee and the Catawba.

INTRODUCTION
HISTORY
REGIONS
WHEN TO VISIT
STATE'S GREATS
RULES OF THE ROAD
DRIVING TOURS

planters took up the rebel cause; the small farmers of the Upcountry, unaffected by British import and export taxes, remained Loyalists. During a major battle—the Tory attack on the Patriot fort at Ninety-Six—there was not one British officer on the field. Upcountry colonists finally joined forces with Lowcountry rebels against Cornwallis's forces at the Battle of Kings Mountain, in what many historians consider the turning point of the Revolution.

Cotton meant almost nothing to the Low County until 1793, when Eli Whitney's cotton gin went into production. By the outbreak of the Civil War in 1861, cotton accounted for 57% of the entire nation's exports. As early as 1832, the state threatened to secede from the Union over federal export taxes on cotton. It did so in 1860; on April 15, 1861, state troops bombarded the Union's Fort Sumter. By May, 10 states had joined South Carolina to form the Confederate States of America in 1861. The Union's General Sherman began his infamous march across the state in 1865. Congress officially removed federal troops from the Confederate states in 1877, ending the occupation of the South and Reconstruction. The collapse of slavery ended the plantation system, sending much of the state's economy into depression. Thousands of freed slaves moved to industrial jobs in northern cities during World War I, a migration that continued until 1970 and is one of the greatest emigrations in American history. Since the 1980s, however, there has been a reverse migration, as African-Americans have begun to return to their home states in the South.

By the 1880s, the upper part of the state had become a textile mill center, a tradition that continues today. From the 1920s to the 1940s, many Lowcountry plantations were bought by wealthy Northerners to use as hunting preserves and winter retreats. Today, some of them are protected by conservation easements, some are commercial hunting clubs, and some are owned by timber companies that harvest the pine forests. Charleston's historic district's fate was also sealed in the early 20th century. A meeting to protest the widening of its streets for cars—which would have meant the destruction of historic structures—resulted in the preservation laws that have made the city a model for historic districts across the country. During the civil rights movement, South Carolina succumbed to desegregation with nonviolent but prolonged resistance. Tourism started booming in the late 1960s and is now the second largest source of income in the state, after textiles.

Regions

1. CHARLESTON AND THE LOWCOUNTRY

Over a hundred years older than the nation itself, Charleston is the jewel of South Carolina. The historic port city, though lovingly preserved, is not a museum city. While many of its treasured antebellum and Colonial homes are authentically furnished house museums, even more are home to Charlestonians and newcomers. Residents air their quilts over piazzas, walk their dogs down cobblestone streets, and tend their famous gardens in much the same way their ancestors did 300 years ago. Locals bravely rebounded

1665	1670	1670s	1680	1680s
King Charles II of England grants the "Carolinas," stretching from Virginia to Cape Canaveral in Spanish Florida, to several of his financial backers, the Lords Proprietors.	First permanent European (English) settlement is established on the west bank of the Ashley River at Albemarle Point.	British planters from Barbados arrive in Carolinas with African slaves and begin cultivating the land.	First English settlement moves to the location of present-day Charleston.	Scots and French Huguenots settle in the Carolinas.

from Hurricane Hugo, which hit in 1989, painstakingly rebuilding and renovating the city, making it perhaps as gleaming and fresh as it was in the 18th century. Renovation continues to expand to the far reaches of the downtown historic district, and development extends across the Cooper River Bridge and out of the town of Mount Pleasant into Awendaw and McClellanville. Culturally vibrant, Charleston nurtures theater, dance, music, and visual arts, showcased each spring during the internationally acclaimed Spoleto Festival USA.

There are several suburban beach communities near Charleston, where locals and visitors alike can swim, surf, golf, and play tennis. Folly Beach is just south of the mouth of Charleston Harbor, while Sullivans Island and Isle of Palms are to the north of the harbor entrance. All three islands have vacation homes for rent.

Towns listed: Charleston, Folly Beach, Isle of Palms, Kiawah Island, McClellanville, Sullivans Island, Walterboro

2. MYRTLE BEACH AND THE GRAND STRAND

Myrtle Beach is the glitzy bauble of the Grand Strand, a 60-mi stretch of wide white-sand beaches—nearly all of which are covered with beach towels in summer. The area abounds with recreational activities, especially golf, a major attraction throughout the state. It's almost one continual community south from Myrtle Beach to historic Georgetown, which enjoys a healthy tourism trade and offers a small-town respite smack-dab between the big-city sophistication of Charleston and the amusement park excitement of Myrtle Beach. Brookgreen Gardens, with its extensive collection of American sculpture, lies in quiet splendor at the south end of the Strand in Murrell's Inlet, famous for its row of seafood restaurants.

Towns listed: Conway, Georgetown, Litchfield Beach, Murrells Inlet, Myrtle Beach, Pawleys Island

3. HILTON HEAD AND THE SEA ISLANDS

The sea islands, separated from the mainland by expanses of estuaries and salt marshes, make up more than half of South Carolina's coastline. To the south, tasteful, low-key Hilton Head—divided into several sophisticated, self-contained resorts—has beautiful beaches and wonderful opportunities for golf and tennis. A new toll expressway was completed in 1997 to help handle traffic to the resort areas. Sun City, a large, newly developed retirement community, attracts scores of fifty-somethings to the area.

The port city of Beaufort, its lovely streets dotted with preserved 18th-century homes, is a popular stopover with New York to Florida commuters. It's also the favorite of early retirees in search of small-town life and great deals on real estate; many have

1708	1720	1730s	1731	1738
Colony's population includes 3,960 free white men, women, and children, and 4,100 African slaves.	European population reaches 19,000.	New immigrants move into the area, including Germans (to the Midlands) and Welsh (along the Big Pee Dee River).	Present-day Georgia is separated out of the southern part of the original Carolinas land grand.	Smallpox epidemic kills half the Catawbas and Cherokees.

converted their historic houses into bed-and-breakfasts. Nearby, at the Penn Center on St. Helena, freed slaves first found schooling. Edisto Island remains undiscovered, sleepy, and bucolic.

Towns listed: Beaufort, Edisto Island, Hilton Head

INTRODUCTION
HISTORY
REGIONS
WHEN TO VISIT
STATE'S GREATS
RULES OF THE ROAD
DRIVING TOURS

4. COLUMBIA AND THE MIDLANDS

Columbia, the state capital, is a busy and historic city blessed by three rushing rivers. Besides museums and a good minor-league baseball team, the city has one of the country's top zoos and a riverside botanical garden. The University of South Carolina, with a student body of 40,000, means that nightlife and cheap and cheerful restaurants are plentiful. Nearby lakes and state parks provide abundant outdoor recreation and first-rate fishing, and the Congaree Swamp National Monument has the oldest and largest trees east of the Mississippi.

Towns listed: Bennettsville, Camden, Cheraw, Chester, Columbia, Darlington, Florence, Hartsville, Latta, Newberry, Orangeburg, Santee, Sumter

5. THOROUGHBRED COUNTRY

Thoroughbred Country, centered around the town of Aiken, is a peaceful area of rolling pastures where top racehorses are trained. In this part of the state, charming, old-fashioned towns such as Abbeville draw more and more visitors with their history, abundant outdoor activities, sleepy main streets, and friendly residents.

Towns listed: Abbeville, Aiken, Allendale, Edgefield, Greenwood

6. THE UPCOUNTRY

Upcountry South Carolina, at the northwestern tip, is the land of the outdoors, with dramatic mountain scenery, excellent hiking, and challenging white-water rafting. The Greenville–Spartanburg area, often considered one place, has had a dramatic growth spurt in the last few years. A longtime textile center, the area has recently become headquarters to companies including BMW. Downtown Greenville is changing and growing rapidly; new cafés, shops, and boutiques, plus a newfound cultural diversity, are breathing fresh life into the old city.

Towns listed: Anderson, Clemson, Greenville, Pendleton, Rock Hill, Spartanburg, York

When to Visit

South Carolina is loveliest in spring when azaleas, dogwood, and other flowering bushes and trees are in bloom, but flowers brighten every season—even winter, when pansies and camellias thrive. Between mid-March and mid-April, you can tour private mansions in Charleston, and the city is alive with Spoleto events in May and June. In the Upcountry, rafting and trails are at their best in spring and fall.

1750s	1770	1776	1780	1783
Scotch-Irish move into the Piedmont area through the 1760s.	College of Charleston is founded; charter in 1785.	South Carolina sends four delegates to the Continental Congress in Philadelphia. They sign the Declaration of Independence. During the Revolutionary War, 127 battles are fought in South Carolina up until 1783.	British troops occupy Charles Town.	The city of Charles Town is incorporated, and officially becomes Charleston.

South Carolina's climate is mild and humid. Throughout the lower part of the state and the coast, spring and fall are very busy, especially in the Charleston and Hilton Head area, where the climate is subtropical. Summer here is simply too hot and humid for extended outdoor activities, except directly on the water, where the ocean breezes help cool you down. With day temperatures in the high 80s and low 90s and lows mostly in the 70s, the hot days of summer are prime beach time: the ocean warms to the high 70s from early June through late August.

Savvy beach travelers know the off-season means big bargains: 30%–70% discounts on accommodations and rentals. If you go to the beach for shelling and quiet walks, spring and fall are wonderful times to visit. Winter, when freezing weather is possible but not common, can be pleasant, with spectacular sunsets and even better shelling.

CLIMATE CHART
Average High/Low Temperatures (°F) and Monthly Precipitation (in inches)

	JAN.	FEB.	MAR.	APR.	MAY	JUNE
CHARLESTON	59/41	60/43	66/49	73/56	81/64	86/71
	3.3	3.0	4.3	2.4	3.5	5.8

	JULY	AUG.	SEPT.	OCT.	NOV.	DEC.
	88/74	88/73	84/69	76/59	67/49	59/42
	6.0	7.3	4.7	2.8	2.3	2.9

	JAN.	FEB.	MAR.	APR.	MAY	JUNE
COLUMBIA	55/32	60/34	68/42	77/50	84/59	89/66
	4.4	4.1	4.8	3.3	3.7	4.8

	JULY	AUG.	SEPT.	OCT.	NOV.	DEC.
	92/70	90/70	85/63	76/50	68/42	59/35
	5.5	6.0	3.7	3.0	2.9	3.6

FESTIVALS AND SEASONAL EVENTS
WINTER

Dec. **First Night Charleston.** A downtown celebration of the visual arts, dance, music, and theater, with street performances, food, and crafts vendors. | 843/853–8000.

First Night Greenville. A performing and visual arts festival in downtown Greenville. | 864/467–6627.

Feb. **Southeastern Wildlife Exposition.** In Charleston with wildlife paintings, sculptures, auctions, live animal demonstrations, and a barbecue at 15 venues downtown. | 843/723–1748.

1786	1788	1800s	1801	1860
Capital moves from Charleston to Columbia.	South Carolina ratifies the U.S. Constitution and becomes the eighth state in the Union.	Nearly one-third of the slaves who arrive in the U.S. come through Sullivans Island.	University of South Carolina is chartered; opens in 1805.	South Carolina secedes from the Union. Ten states follow to form the Confederate States of America in February 1861.

SPRING

Mar.   **Aiken Triple Crown.** Showcases for fine horse racing and thoroughbreds for three weekends. | 803/641–1111.

Mar.   **Festival of Houses and Gardens.** Charleston opens its treasured homes and gardens, most of them private, to visitors. | 843/722–3405.

Apr.   **Cooper River Bridge Run.** In Charleston a 10K run or $4^4/_{10}$-mi walk. | 843/792–1586.

Apr.   **MCI Heritage Classic.** Brings 120 top golfers to Hilton Head. | 843/234–1107 or 800/234–1107.

May   **Mayfest.** In Columbia, one of the state's largest arts and entertainment festivals, with hundreds of vendors and big-name acts. | 803/343–8750.

May   **Freedom Weekend Aloft.** In Greenville, a colorful hot-air balloon event. | 864/232–3700.

May–June   **Spoleto USA.** Founded by Pulitzer prize–winning composer Gian Carlo Menotti in 1977, this internationally acclaimed celebration of music, dance, theater, and visual art takes place in Charleston for two weeks. | 843/722–2764.

SUMMER

June   **Sun Fun Festival.** This Myrtle Beach festival features, among other activities, beauty queen contests and sand sculpting. | 843/626–7444 or 800/356–3016.

FALL

Sept.   **Pepsi 7500.** Darlington rounds up the best road racing drivers. | 843/395–8892.

Sept.–Oct.   **Fall Candlelight Tour of Homes and Gardens.** Visitors get a glimpse into Charleston's private historic homes and gardens. | 843/722–4630.

State's Greats

One of South Carolina's most outstanding features is surely its history, for this small state changed the course of the nation. South Carolina played a pivotal role in the American Revolution, experiencing the war "with a constancy and severity unparalleled in the North," according to historian David Duncan Wallace. Later, in 1860, South Carolina became the first state to secede from the Union, sparking the Civil

1861	1865	1867	1880s	1918
First engagement of the American Civil War begins on April 12, when Confederate troops attack Union-held Fort Sumter in Charleston Harbor.	The Union's General Sherman invades South Carolina. Confederate General Robert E. Lee surrenders at Appomattox.	Reconstruction begins. During the next 10 years, under the Union's military and political supervision, the state reestablishes its government.	Textile mills are built in the Upcountry.	During World War I, more than 70,000 men from South Carolina join the armed services.

War. Yet South Carolina's rich past is not simply locked away in museums but is everywhere apparent—in the antebellum houses, throughout the historic port city of Charleston, and in the remaining Gullah communities of the Sea Islands, to name only a few examples.

South Carolina also garners praise for its varied and lush landscape: The wide sand beaches along the coast are home to famous resorts such as Hilton Head and Myrtle Beach. To the west are the rolling fields of Thoroughbred Country and the Blue Ridge Mountains. Upcountry, at the northwestern tip of South Carolina, there is spectacular mountain scenery, excellent hiking, and white-water rafting.

Beaches

South Carolina's mild climate makes the surf enjoyable from April through October. The beaches are expanses of white sand—some serene and secluded, others bustling and lined with high-rises. The Grand Strand of South Carolina begins at the North Carolina state line and runs exuberantly down the coast for about 60 mi, through North Myrtle Beach, a favorite of college kids and shag dancers, to booming Myrtle Beach, with its Miami-style high-rises and country music theaters, down to the quieter, tonier part of the Strand, at Pawleys Island, Hunting Beach, and Georgetown. Charleston also has three beaches nearby. South of Charleston are a series of less well-known but appealing beach communities the upscale and private: Kiawah and Seabrook Islands; comfortable-as-an-old-shoe Edisto Beach; and Beaufort, Hunting Island, and Fripp Island, each very different but with a lot to offer. Then you're on Hilton Head. Although the resort beaches here are reserved for guests and residents, there are four public entrances to Hilton Head's 12 mi of ocean beach. Two main parking and changing areas are at Coligny Circle, near the Holiday Inn, and on Folly Field Road, off U.S. 278. Signs along U.S. 278 point the way to Bradley and Singleton beaches, where parking space is limited.

Gardens

Gardening devotees can and do build vacations around South Carolina gardens, where camellias, azaleas, other flowering shrubs, and blooming trees abound. Along the coast are some of the nation's most famous, including Middleton Place, with the oldest landscaped garden in America; Cypress Gardens, where cypress trees tower in dark waters with azaleas on the banks; and Brookgreen Gardens, with a superb outdoor sculpture collection set amid giant oaks and colorful flowers. Inland, remarkable gardens planted with roses, irises, or mountain laurel make some small towns a worthwhile side trip. Along the way, you can see peach orchards in bloom in spring.

Rivers and Lakes

You can swim, fish, waterski, and boat year-round on the rivers and lakes throughout the state. They are so plentiful in the Upcountry that it's called South Carolina's Freshwater Coast. Both the Upcountry and the heart of the state have white-water rapids

1923	1928	1941	1960	1961
Revenue from manufactured goods exceeds that of agricultural products for the first time.	Julia Peterkin (born in Calhoun County) is awarded a Pulitzer Prize for her novel *Scarlet Sister Mary.*	Military training centers are established at Fort Jackson, Camp Croft, and Shaw Field; 173,642 South Carolinians serve in World War II.	Civil rights demonstrations begin.	Desegregation is extended to city buses, railway, and bus station facilities.

for rafting or kayaking. Canoeing and kayaking are popular on waters near Columbia, as well as on the rivers in the Lowcountry. Anglers frequently break records with hauls of largemouth bass, stripers, crappie, and catfish caught in Lakes Marion and Moultrie.

INTRODUCTION
HISTORY
REGIONS
WHEN TO VISIT
STATE'S GREATS
RULES OF THE ROAD
DRIVING TOURS

Culture, History, and the Arts

Charleston is well known for its cultural and architectural heritage, set in motion by the city's planter aristocracy in the early 1700s. By 1734, Charleston's first playhouse, the original Dock Street Theatre, was entertaining these early supporters. The Charleston Museum, founded in 1773, is the oldest museum in the United States. The city's famed religious tolerance and the African heritage of most of its residents guaranteed an enduring tradition of various forms of music and architectural styles. Some of the city's churches, including St. Michael's, are the oldest in the country.

Charleston spawned the famed dance, the opera "Porgy and Bess" (written by native Dubose Heyward), the architecture of Robert Mills, the character Rhett Butler, and, more recently, the author Josephine Humphreys, artist Alice Ravenel Huger Smith, and Mary Jackson, whose sweetgrass baskets are on display in the Vatican and the Smithsonian.

Throughout South Carolina, Revolutionary War sites and battlefields dot the landscape. Many, such as the Historic Camden Revolutionary War Site, give visitors a progressive view of the period and the events leading to the war. The graveyard at Old St. David's Church in Cheraw has soldiers from every war buried there; it also has the oldest Confederate monument in the country. Civil War buffs will also want to visit Abbeville and the Burt–Stark Mansion, dubbed the birthplace and deathbed of Confederacy.

Several South Carolina towns, including Charleston, Beaufort, Georgetown, McClellanville, and Edisto Island, offer annual tours of their historic buildings and gardens. Cultural traditions live on in Edgefield, where potters continue to create the famed clayware of the region, in Rock Hill at the Catawba Cultural Center, and in Blackville at the Healing Springs, where Native Americans brought wounded Revolutionary soldiers to the waters.

Plantations

Plantation life flourished in South Carolina, and many of the state's Colonial and antebellum cotton, rice, and indigo plantations are now open to the public. Drayton Hall, Magnolia Plantation and Gardens, and Middleton Place come one after another in a 10-mi stretch of SC Scenic Highway 61, which parallels the Ashley River from Charleston to the headwaters. Drayton Hall is considered the finest early Georgian house in the nation. It is the only Ashley River plantation to have survived the Civil War, spared by Union troops because it was being used as a smallpox hospital for just-freed slaves. Magnolia Plantation is best known for its 50 acres of lawn and gardens, begun in the 1840s, with 250 varieties of azaleas and 900 kinds of camellias. Middleton Place has

1975	**1977**	**1990s**	**1994**
James Edwards becomes the first Republican governor in 100 years.	Spoleto Festival USA begins in Charleston.	Myrtle Beach becomes known as the country music capital of the East Coast.	The Citadel military college opens its doors to women.

the nation's oldest landscaped gardens, complete with butterfly lakes, colorful blooms year-round, and stable yards. Boone Hall in Mt. Pleasant has a stunning avenue of oaks and original slave cabins and a gin house.

There are dozens of old plantations along the five rice rivers of Georgetown, a region that by 1840 produced almost half the rice in the nation. Hampton Plantation, brought to greatest prosperity by a widow in the 1780s, is now a state park. Brookgreen Gardens is on the site of an old rice plantation; visitors can take boat tours to learn more about the former plantation's rice culture. Mansfield Plantation, now a bed-and-breakfast, has old slave cabins and offers rice culture tours. The best way to see less-public Georgetown plantations is by boat or van tours from Georgetown. Redcliffe Plantation, near North Augusta, is one of the few preserved inland plantations. Near Union, Rose Hill, another state park, offers a glimpse into cotton plantation life with the original mansion, slave house, and carriage house. Clemson University is on the site of a plantation; at its heart is the plantation mansion Fort Hill, furnished with original mementos and furnishings.

Shopping

Charleston has many unique boutiques and trendy shops, as well as a colorful produce market in the three-block Old City Market and, adjacent to it, an open-air flea market with crafts, antiques, and memorabilia. You'll find locally produced sweetgrass and other baskets here. Shopping complexes in the historic district include the **Shops at Charleston Place** with Gucci, Gap, and Brookstone; and **Rainbow Market** in two interconnected 150-year-old buildings. **King Street** has many first-class antiques shops with 18th- and 19th-century pieces; it also has some of Charleston's oldest and finest shops, as well as **Saks Fifth Avenue.** From May until September, the festive **farmers' market** takes place each Saturday morning in Marion Square.

The Grand Strand has plenty of sprawling malls and outlet parks, including **Barefoot Landing,** built over marshland and water, with scores of shops and restaurants; and Broadway at the Beach, with over 75 shops, restaurants, and nightlife venues.

Many of Columbia's antiques outlets are in the Congaree Vista around Huger and Gervais streets, between the State House and the river. A number of intriguing shops and cafés are in Five Points, around the intersection of Blossom and Harden streets. The **State Farmers' Market** is one of the 10 largest in the country. Fresh vegetables are sold each weekday, along with flowers, plants, seafood, and more, from 6 AM to 9 PM.

Sports

BIKING

The historic district in Charleston, as well as local beaches, are ideal for bicycling, and many city parks have biking trails. Palmetto Islands County Park in Mount Pleasant also has trails. There are pathways in several areas of Hilton Head (many in the resorts), and pedaling is popular along the firmly packed beach. Bicycles can be rented at most hotels and resorts.

The Palmetto Trail (803/771–0870; www.sctrails.net), a hiking, biking, and equestrian trail that will eventually encompass 400 mi over the entire state, is being opened in passages. Three are open: High Hills of Santee Passage, which joins Mill Creek Park to Poinsett State Park; Lake Moultrie Passage, which stretches 26 mi along the Santee Cooper dike system on the northeast side of Lake Moultrie; and Swamp Fox Passage, a 27-mi trail starting at Hwy. 17 near Awendaw and traveling inland.

BOATING

Outside Hilton Head is an ecologically sensitive company that rents canoes, kayaks, bikes, and rollerblades; it also has nature tours. In the Columbia and Midlands area, self-guided canoe trails traverse an alluvial floodplain bordered by high bluffs at the 22,200-acre Congaree Swamp National Monument. Rafting, kayaking, and canoeing on the Saluda River near Columbia offer challenging Class III and Class IV rapids. Guided river and swamp excursions can be arranged as well.

INTRODUCTION
HISTORY
REGIONS
WHEN TO VISIT
STATE'S GREATS
RULES OF THE ROAD
DRIVING TOURS

FISHING

The Gulf Stream usually makes for good fishing from early spring through December. Anglers can fish from 10 piers and jetties for amberjack, sea trout, and king mackerel. Surfcasters can snare bluefish, whiting, flounder, pompano, and channel bass. In the South Strand, salt marshes, inlets, and tidal creeks yield flounder, blues, croakers, spots, shrimp, clams, oysters, and blue crabs.

On Hilton Head, you can pick oysters, dig for clams, or cast for shrimp. Local marinas offer in-shore and deep-sea fishing charters. Each year a bill-fishing tournament and two king mackerel tournaments attract anglers.

Anglers go to lakes Marion and Moultrie in search of bream, crappie, catfish, and several kinds of bass. Supplies, camps, guides, rentals, and accommodations abound.

GOLF

One of the most appealing aspects of golfing in the Charleston area is the relaxing pace. With fewer golfers playing the courses than in destinations that are primarily golf oriented, you can find choice starting times and an unhurried atmosphere. For a listing of area golf packages, contact the Charleston Area Convention and Visitors Bureau. Many of the Grand Strand's 91 courses are championship layouts; most are public. Many of Hilton Head's 29 championship courses are open to the public.

TENNIS

Charleston has public tennis courts in every community, including the historic district. There are more than 200 courts on the Grand Strand. Facilities include hotel and resort courts, as well as free municipal courts in Myrtle Beach, North Myrtle Beach, and Surfside Beach. There are more than 300 courts on Hilton Head.

SPECTATOR SPORTS

The minor-league **RiverDogs** baseball team plays at the Joe Ballpark in Charleston from April through August. The Charleston **Stingrays** play hockey at the North Charleston Coliseum to record-breaking crowds from October through March.

In Columbia, the **Capital City Bombers,** a Class-A affiliate of the New York Mets, play from mid-April through August at Capital City Stadium downtown.

The **Greenville GRRRowl** hockey team plays October through March, and the **Greenville Braves** are a AA minor-league baseball team of the Atlanta Braves. The **Carolina Panthers** Football Training Camp is in Spartanburg, where the team trains during mid-July at practice sessions open to the public.

In Aiken, polo matches are played at Whitney Field on Sunday afternoon September through November and March through July. Three weekends in late March and early April are set aside for the famed **Triple Crown.**

Rules of the Road

License Requirements: South Carolina's minimum driving age is 16 with a valid driver's license.

Speed Limits: The maximum speed allowed on South Carolina highways is 55 mph unless otherwise noted.

Right Turn on Red: Everywhere in the state, you can make a right turn at a red light *after* a full stop, unless a sign is posted forbidding it.

Seat Belt and Helmet Laws: All persons in the front seat of a moving vehicle must wear safety belts. Children six years of age and younger must be secured in a child safety seat that meets National Safety Commission standards. All persons under age 21 must wear a helmet while riding a motorcycle in South Carolina.

Other: South Carolina has a headlight law: If windshield wipers are on because of weather conditions, headlights must also be on.

It is against the law to have any type of open alcoholic beverage in moving vehicles, including buses.

For More Information: Contact the State Department of Motor Vehicles at 803/737–4000, or 800/442–1368 (automated information only).

Sea Islands Driving Tour
THE LOWCOUNTRY

Distance: 90 mi   Time: 2 days

Breaks: Try stopping overnight in Beaufort, where you can enjoy a walking tour of the historic district and stay in one of the many old homes now converted into bed-and-breakfasts.

This tour takes you through the romantic, saltwater marsh–studded coastal lands of the South Carolina Lowcountry, once the domain of rice and cotton planters. You'll pass pristine wetlands framed by palmettos and oaks dripping with Spanish moss. Half of the state's 190-mi ocean shoreline is on these islands, which reach south from Charleston to the Savannah River. If you're looking for prime beach weather but would like to avoid the crowds, go in May or September. Fall and spring are generally lovely and mild—not too chilly or too hot to stroll historic districts or take a canoe ride down gentle rivers. The seafood is fresh and plentiful in these parts, and golf courses have spectacular coastal views.

❶ Start the tour on Hilton Head Island (108 mi southwest of Charleston, 164 mi southeast of Columbia, access from I–95, Exit 8 over bridge on U.S. 278). The **Welcome Center and Museum of Hilton Head** offers background information on the island, as well as information about tours. Harbour Town on **Sea Pines,** the oldest and best known of Hilton Head's resort developments, occupies 4,500 thickly wooded acres and has three golf courses, a wide beach, tennis clubs, stables, and shopping plazas. There's quite a bit of outlet shopping on Hilton Head, too.

❷ From Hilton Head, you can take a ferry to nearby **Daufuskie Island** (south of Hilton Head) for a day tour. Though there is now a resort on the island and development continues to encroach, many inhabitants—the descendants of former slaves—live on small farms among remnants of churches, homes, and schools.

❸ The 40-mi route between Hilton Head and Beaufort is one of the most beautiful. In **Beaufort,** which was settled by rich planters, graceful antebellum homes and churches are generally all within walking distance. Tour it by foot or by bike with a map from the chamber of commerce, or take a carriage tour. A few miles away is the **Parris Island U.S. Marine Corps Base,** which welcomes visitors and even offers guided tours. The **Parris Island Museum** exhibits uniforms, photographs, and weapons chronicling military history since 1562, when the French Huguenots built a fort here.

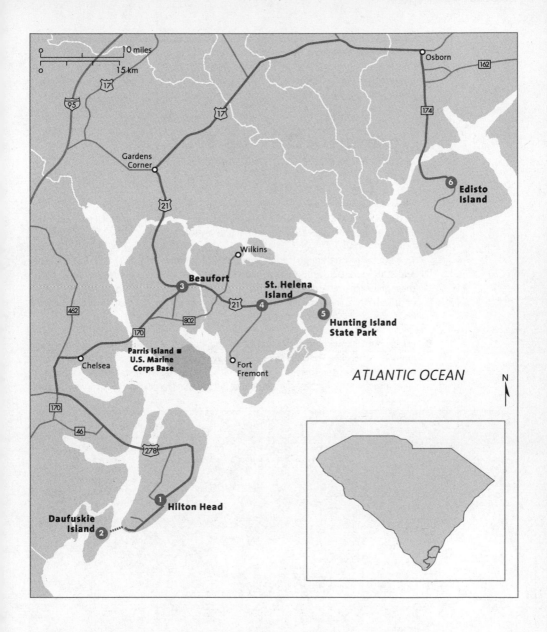

④ **St. Helena Island** is the site of the historic **Penn Center,** where freed slaves first found schooling. Now unofficial headquarters of the Gullah culture, the center is devoted to the preservation of the language, culture, and history of the Sea Island's Gullah community.

⑤ From St. Helena Island, head south on U.S. 21 to Hunting Island. **Hunting Island State Park** has a secluded domain of beach, nature trails, camping, and fishing along its 3 mi of public beach—some of it dramatically eroding. The 1,120-ft fishing pier is among the longest on the East Coast. You can climb the 181 steps of the 140-ft Hunting Island Lighthouse (built in 1859 and abandoned in 1933) for sweeping views.

⑥ **Edisto Island.** Ancient tomato fields and Colonial-era plantations and churches flank country roads that wind through bucolic scenes of simple wood frame homes sitting on the edge of tidal creeks and salt marshes. Mostly undeveloped, Edisto Beach has modest, one-family rental beach houses and a couple of no-frills restaurants. **Edisto Beach State Park** has cabins by the marsh and campsites by the ocean.

Upcountry Driving Tour
ALONG THE CHEROKEE FOOTHILLS SCENIC HIGHWAY

Distance: about 75 mi   Time: 2 days

Break: You may wish to stop and spend the night at Table Rock State Park (12 mi north of Pickens on SCII), which has rustic cabins in the midst of its natural wonders, or in Pendleton, where historic B&Bs and an old-time town square will take you back in time.

This tour takes you through the Carolina Upcountry, renowned for its magnificent scenery and state parks. Traveling along the Cherokee Foothills Scenic Highway, you'll go through peach orchards, tiny mountain towns, and wooded and rocky foothills spiked with waterfalls. The more adventurous can add an extra day to head farther west from Pendleton and raft the Chattooga River.

❶ Begin your tour at the junction of U.S. 85 and Route 11 outside of **Gaffney.** Head west along the **Cherokee Foothills Scenic Highway.** Cherokees, and then English and French fur traders, once used this route, which winds through lush forests and along sparkling lakes and has striking views and brilliant fall foliage. The section that travels through

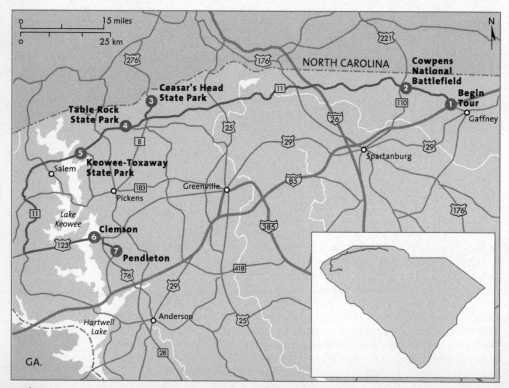

Cherokee County is studded with peach orchards; you can see the colorful blossoms each spring and eat the fruit at busy roadside stands in summer.

❷ **Cowpens National Battlefield** is a rustic Colonial site where the American militia defeated the British. A walking trail takes visitors through the battlefield; there are also a marked road tour and a visitor center with exhibits.

❸ **Caesar's Head State Park.** On a clear day, you can see the sweep of the Blue Ridge Mountains from the elevation of 3,208 ft. The view of **Raven Cliff Falls,** a 420-ft-high cascade, is easily worth the 2-mi hike.

❹ **Table Rock State Park,** with its landmark rounded dome, has rustic cabins, campsites, lake swimming, canoe and boat rentals, hiking trails, and a Sunday-morning breakfast buffet served in the stone lodge that's worth planning around.

❺ **Keowee-Toxaway State Park** has camping, hiking and picnic areas along Lake Keowee on this land that once belonged to the Cherokees. The Cherokee Indian Interpretive Center traces the history and culture of the Cherokee Indian Nation.

❻ Continue along Route 11, then take Route 123E for 12 mi into **Clemson.** The **South Carolina Botanical Garden** covers 270 acres with blooming plants and trees, heirloom gardens, nature trails, plus a log cabin and Colonial home (circa 1716). On-site is the Discovery Center for Region One of the Heritage Corridor, a tourism trail—a suggested driving route dotted with Discovery Centers with exhibits on regional agriculture, history, and industry—that stretches 240 mi across the state. Also on the Clemson University campus are several must-sees: **Fort Hill** and **John C. Calhoun's plantation home,** now a house museum and National Historic Landmark, with items that once belonged to Calhoun and his son-in-law, Thomas Clemson. **Uniquely Clemson Agricultural Sales Center** sells the town's famous Clemson blue cheese, plus superb ice cream and milk shakes.

❼ In **Pendleton,** the historic district, anchored by a charming town square, has more than 40 points of interest, antiques shops, and cafés. The **Pendleton Visitor Center,** in the 1850 mercantile **Hunter's Store,** has an impressive archive library upstairs. The 1828 **Farmer's Society Hall,** on the town square with a restaurant on the ground floor, is the oldest farmers' hall still in continuous use in the United States.

ABBEVILLE

MAP 9, C4

(Nearby town also listed: Greenwood)

Abbeville (pop. 6,200) has a distinguished town square, surrounded by a restored Victorian hotel and opera house, shops, restaurants, and small businesses—but not frantic traffic—and feels like a step back in time. The square is still the hub of the business district, as it was in 1785, when it was first built. At its center is a Confederate monument: the "Southern Cause" was born and died at Abbeville's Burt–Stark Mansion, where the first secession meeting was held and where, on May 2, 1965, Confederate President Jefferson Davis disbanded his defeated armies of the South during the last meeting of his war council. Gothic-style churches and Victorian mansions dot the historic district; the area also has a long, rich Cherokee history. A local Mennonite community adds flavor with its popular restaurants.

Information: **Abbeville Chamber of Commerce and Welcome Center** | 107 Court Sq. Abbeville, SC 29620 | 864/459–4600 | www.emraldis.com/abbeville.

Attractions

Abbeville County Museum. Occupying an 1850s jail, this museum contains area memorabilia. | Poplar and Cherry Sts. | 864/459–4600 | Free | Wed., Sun. 3–5, or by appointment.

Abbeville Opera House. Built in 1908, the opera house was renovated to reflect the grandeur of the days when Jimmy Durante and Sarah Bernhardt performed here. Current productions, from light, contemporary comedies to Broadway-style musicals, take place most weekends. | Town Square | 864/459–2157 | Weekdays 8–5.

Burt–Stark Mansion. Jefferson Davis held his last War Cabinet meeting of the Confederacy in this Greek Revival 1830 home; the period furnishings remain. | 400 N. Main St. | 864/459–4297 or 864/459–2181 | $4 | June–Sept., Tue.–Sat, 1–5; Sept.–June, Fri. and Sat., 1–5.

John de la Howe School and The Barn. Land donated by a French Huguenot immigrant has become the beautiful campus of a state-operated children's school. You can buy handmade crafts (some made by the children), food items, and more in the school's rustic barn each Saturday. | Rte. 1 (Hwy. 81) | 864/391–2131 | Free | Campus, daily; barn, Sat. 9–4.

Town Square. Attractive gift and specialty shops in restored historic buildings dating from the late 1800s line the town square. | Free.

ON THE CALENDAR

DEC.: *Holiday House Tour.* You can visit eight authentic Victorian homes in Abbeville's extensive historic district during the first weekend of the month. The tour, sponsored by the Abbeville Women's Club, raises funds for charity and is held between 1 and 5 on Saturday and Sunday. You can buy tickets ($10) at the Welcome Center on Court Square. | 107 Court Square | 864/459–4600.

Dining

Village Grille. American. Pomegranate-colored walls, booths, and antique mirrors highlight the high-ceilinged dining room, where the atmosphere is trendy and friendly. The restaurant serves herb rotisserie chicken, ribs, homemade pastas, and cordial-laced desserts. | 110 Trinity St. | 864/459–2500 | Casual | Closed Sun., Mon. | $13–$24 | AE, D, DC, MC, V.

Yoder's Dutch Kitchen. Pennsylvania Dutch. An unassuming red-brick building with a mansard roof is home to authentic Pennsylvania Dutch cooking, including shoofly pie, fried chicken, stuffed cabbage, and Dutch meat loaf. | 809 E. Greenwood St. | 864/459–5556 | Closed Sun.–Tues. No supper Wed., Thurs. | $5–$9 | No credit cards.

Lodging

Abbewood B&B. Built in the 1860s, the Abbewood has Victorian decor, a wraparound porch, and some antique furnishings. Theater packages are available. Complimentary breakfast. Cable TV. No kids under 12. | 605 N. Main St. | 864/459–5822 | fax 864/459–5822 | www.innsgetaways.net | 3 rooms (2 with shared bath) | $65–$75 | AE, MC, V.

Belmont Inn. Popular with Opera House visitors, this 1903 Victorian house has a marble veranda that overlooks the square. Antique furnishings decorate the rooms, and the Belmont offers play packages in conjunction with the Opera House. Bar, dining room, complimentary Continental breakfast. Cable TV. Business services. | 104 E. Pickens St. | 864/459–9625 | fax 864/459–9625 | www.belmontinn.net | 25 rooms | $54–$79 | AE, D, MC, V.

The Vintage Inn. A verandah wraps around this two-story fully restored Queen Anne home, which is a 15-min walk from the center of town. Ceiling fans and antique furnishings decorate the rooms. Complimentary breakfast. No kids under 8. No pets. | 1205 North Main St. | 800/890–7312 or 864/459–4784 | www.thevintageinn.com | 3 rooms with baths, 1 suite with hot tub, 1 suite with kitchenette | $65–$125 $65–$75, suites $100–$125 | AE.

AIKEN

(Nearby towns also listed: Augusta, GA, Edgefield)

The center of South Carolina's Thoroughbred Country first earned its fame in the 1890s, when wealthy Northerners (including the Vanderbilts and the Whitneys) built winter "cottages" and entertained one another with lavish parties, horse shows, and hunts. Many of the cottages—most of them are actually stately mansions with up to 90 rooms—remain as a testament to that era. The town is the starting point for some of the nation's finest thoroughbreds. In March, horse trainers, owners, and equestrian industry folks descend for the Triple Crown. Unpaved roads, equestrian stoplights, fox hunting, polo, steeplechasing, track racing, and the equestrian heaven Hitchcock Woods clearly define Aiken's character. Tennis and golf are also popular; the area is fast becoming a retirement haven as well.

Information: Aiken Chamber of Commerce | 121 Richland Ave. E, Aiken, SC 29801 | 803/641–1111 or 800/542–4536 | fax 803/641–4174.

Attractions

Aiken County Historical Museum. Housed in what was a 32-room, 15-bath mansion, the collection includes Native American artifacts, firearms, locally mined kaolin, and Civil War artifacts. On site are an authentically furnished 1808 log cabin and an 1890 one-room schoolhouse. | 433 Newberry St. SW | 803/642–2015 | fax 803/642–2016 | Donations accepted | Tues.–Fri. 9:30–4:30, weekends 2–5.

Aiken Equestrian District. Dirt roads meander past polo fields, training farms, and three racetracks. Horses and trainers abound from November through March. | 2 blocks east of Whiskey Rd., 3 blocks south of Boundry Ave. | 803/641–1111 | Free | Daily 6–11.

Aiken State Park. Along with four lakes created by natural springs, this 1,067-acre park on the South Edisto River also has camping, swimming, fishing boat rentals, canoeing, and 3 mi of nature trails. | 1145 State Park Rd. | 803/649–2857 | Free | Daily 9–6.

Hitchcock Woods. Aiken literally surrounds this 2,000-acre forest of hiking trails and bridal paths—the nation's largest urban nature preserve. During three weeks in March, the Aiken Trials, which is Aiken's Triple Crown, are held here. | Enter at the western dead-end of South Boundary Ave. | 803/643–8202 | Free | Daily dawn to dusk.

Hopeland Gardens. Fourteen acres of winding paths, quiet terraces, reflecting pools, and a Touch and Scent Trail with braille plaques. From mid-July to August, there are open-air free concerts and plays on Monday evenings. | Whiskey Rd. and Dupree Pl. | 803/642–7630 | fax 803/642–7639 | www.aiken.net | Free | Daily 10–dusk.
The **Thoroughbred Racing Hall of Fame** at the Hopeland Gardens used to be a carriage house; it now contains horse-related decorations, paintings, sculptures, racing silks, and trophies, including those of national champions trained in Aiken from 1942 on. | Dupree Pl | 803/642–7630 | fax 803/642–7639 | www.aiken.net | Free | Sept.–May, Tues.–Sun. 2–5.

Montmorenci Vineyards. You can visit this winery and taste its award-winning wines. | 2989 Charleston Hwy. | 803/649–4870 | Free | Tastings Wed.–Sat. 10–6.

Polo Games. Sunday afternoons mean polo matches at Whitney Field. | Mead Ave. | 803/648–7874 or 803/643–3611 | $2 | Games played Feb.–July and Sept.–Nov. Call for times.

Redcliffe Plantation State State Historic Site. Governor James H. Hammond and his family lived here until they donated the 1859 plantation home to the state in 1973. The 350 acres on the banks of the Savannah River include nature trails, picnic areas, and Magnolia Lane. | 181 Redcliffe Rd. | 803/827–1473 | Grounds free, house $2 | Grounds, Thurs.–Mon. 9–6; house, Thurs.–Mon. noon–4.

ON THE CALENDAR

MAR.: *Triple Crown.* During three weekends in March, young thoroughbreds trained in Aiken debut on the racing circuit. Call the Aiken Chamber of Commerce for more information. | 803/641–1111.

MAY: *Lobster Race and Oyster Parade.* Festivities include lobster races, beach music, and lobster and oyster cooked every which way. | Downtown Aiken | 803/648–4981.

DEC.: *Christmas in Hopelands Gardens.* Over 50,000 lights illuminate the 14 acres of these public gardens as choral groups perform and the Rye Patch Estate within the gardens hosts a crafts exhibit. | 803/642–7650.

Dining

Malia's. Contemporary. This casual, romantic dining room serves inventive soups, sandwiches, and seafood entrées, including grouper with crabmeat and salmon. | 120 Laurens St. | 803/643–3086 | Reservations essential | No dinner weekdays | $16–$23 | D, MC, V.

No. 10 Downing Street. Continental. Working fireplaces warm this one-story clapboard house with a garden in the back. Built in 1835, it's the oldest home in Aiken and was previously a boarding house. Separate rooms make for intimate dining; you can try the almond baked sea bass with lemon butter sauce, or the rack of lamb. | 241 Laurens St. SW | 803/642–9062 | Closed Sun.–Mon. No lunch | $14–$20 | AE, D, DC, MC, V.

Olive Oils Italian Restaurant. Italian. Chicken with pesto, and seafood in garlic and white wine sauce over pasta, as well as pizza and calzones are served at this renovated home with grape vines and faux bricks painted on the dining room walls, a glassed-in patio, and outdoor dining areas. | 232 Chesterfield St. | 803/649–3726 | No lunch | $9–$18 | AE, D, DC, MC, V.

Track Kitchen. American. This unpretentious mint-green cinder-block building near the racetrack and stables comes complete with simple Formica counters. The who's who of Aiken's horsey set can be found here most mornings, feasting on the heavy and hearty breakfasts. | 420 Mead Ave. | 803/641–9628 | Breakfast only | $5–$7 | No credit cards.

Up Your Alley. American. Steak, seafood and healthful alternatives are the basic fare at this renovated early 1900s brick warehouse. | 222 The Alley | 803/649–2603 | Closed Sun. No lunch | $12–$18 | AE, D, DC, MC, V.

West Side Bowery. American. Locals and tourists mix at this casual but classy eatery, housed in what was previously a stable. You can eat out on the terrace as well, and the bar stays open until 1 AM. Popular dishes include steak, seafood, and Phillie cheesesteaks. | 151 Bee La. | 803/648–2900 | fax 803/643–8106 | Reservations recommended | Closed Sun. | $13–$17 | AE, D, DC, MC, V.

Lodging

Annie's Inn. Cotton fields surround this 1830s plantation farmhouse with large white columns, fireplaces, pine plank floors and a wraparound front porch 5 mi east of town. Long-term stays are available. Complimentary breakfast. Refrigerators. Pool. | 3083 Charleston Hwy. Montmorenci, | 803/649–6836 | fax 803/642–6709 | annizin@aol.com | 5 rooms; 6 cottages | $70–$125 | AE, D, DC, MC, V.

Briar Patch. The owners created this B&B out of two former tack rooms in Aiken's stable district. French provincial furnishings decorate one rooms; the other rooms has pine antiques and a weather vane. The house itself is on the National Historic Register. Complimentary Continental breakfast. Golf privileges, 1 tennis court. | 544 Magnolia La. SE | 803/649–2010 | briarfox@prodigy.net | 2 rooms | $60 | No credit cards.

Holley House and Holley Inn. Built in 1910, this plantation house downtown remains a favorite of the horse set. Complimentary breakfast. Some refrigerators. Pool. | 235 Richland Ave. | 803/648–4265 | fax 803/649–6910 | 60 rooms | $60–$70 | AE, D, MC, V.

Rosemary Hall Inn. Period antiques, including antique linens, decorate the rooms of this 1902 home complete with luxurious parlors and verandas. It's 1 mi from the riverwalk in Augusta, Georgia, and 17 mi west of Aiken. Complimentary breakfast. Cable TV. Pool. | 804 Carolina Ave., North Augusta | 803/278–6222 or 800/531–5578 | fax 803/278–4877 | www.bbhost.com | 23 rooms | $89–$195 | AE, D, DC, MC, V.

Willcox Inn. Winston Churchill, Franklin D. Roosevelt, and the Astors all slept at this elegant Second Empire inn built in 1928 by Frederick Sugden Wilcox. Majestic white columns adorn the front of the huge tree-ringed white mansion. Many rooms have four-poster beds. Restaurant, bar (with entertainment), complimentary Continental breakfast, room service. Refrigerators. Cable TV. Business services. | 100 Colleton Ave. | 803/649–1377 or 800/368–1047 | fax 803/643–0971 | www.willcoxinn.com | 24 rooms, 6 suites | $95, $125–$150 suites | AE, D, DC, MC, V.

ALLENDALE

MAP 9, F7

(Nearby town also listed: Walterboro)

Allendale maintains its strong agricultural tradition; small prosperous farms with fields of cotton, grain, watermelon, peaches, peanuts, and corn surround the area. Roadside stands, pastures, bucolic churches, and private hunting clubs dot the coastal plain landscape, though there's quite a bit of industry here, too, much of it tied to the nearby Savannah River Site, a federal facility for atomic products. Highway 301, which passes through Allendale, was the main north–south road before I–95, and shows signs of its glory days.

Information: Allendale County Chamber of Commerce | 186 Main St., Allendale, SC 29810 | 803/584–0082 | fax 803/584–0082 | www.allendalecountychamber.org.

Attractions

Barnwell State Park. There are two lakes on this 307-acre park 20 mi northeast of Allendale, where you can rent boats, swim, camp, or stay in cabins. | 223 State Park Rd., Blackville | 803/284–2212 | Free | Daily 9–6.

Healing Springs. Native Americans brought wounded Civil War soldiers to these artesian wells outside Blackville 40 mi northeast of Allendale; today pilgrims from across the state come for the legendary mineral waters to heal all kinds of ailments. | Hwy. 3 | 803/259–7446 | Free | Daily dawn to dusk.

Jim Harrison Gallery. Nationally known artist Jim Harrison specializes in rural Americana scenes and is one of only 150 authorized licensees worldwide in partnership with Coca-Cola. His gallery showcases his paintings and prints of old barns, soft-drink signs, and country stores, as well as his collection of old signs, gas pumps, and ice chests. The gallery is 38 mi north of Allendale. | 1 Main St., Denmark | 803/793–5796; 800/793–5796 | www.jimharrison.com | Free | Tues., Thurs.– Fri. 11–5; Wed., Sat. 11–3.

Rivers Bridge State Historic Site. These old Confederate fortifications, now in ruins, were built to hold back Sherman's Union army. You can camp, swim, fish, and walk the nature trails at this state park, the only one in South Carolina to commemorate the Confederacy. The park is 25 mi east of Allendale. | 803/267–3675 | fax 803/267–3675 | www.southcarolinaparks.com | Free | Apr.–Aug. 9–9, Sept.–Oct. Thurs.–Mon. 9–9, Nov.–Mar. Thurs.–Mon. 9–6.

ON THE CALENDAR
NOV.: *Holiday Arts and Craft Fair.* You can find displays of local and regional crafts the National Guard Armory and Brandt Agricultural Building in Barnwell 15 mi north of Allendale. | Hwy. 278, Exit 39B | 803/584–4207.

Dining

Miller's Bread Basket. American. This old brick store on Blackville's main thoroughfare serves old-fashioned Pennsylvania Dutch fare with a Southern touch: homemade bread, shoofly pie, fried chicken, and meat loaf. | 322 Main St., Blackville | 803/284–3117 | Closed Sun. No supper Mon., Wed., Sat. | $10–$20 | AE, MC, V.

Lodging

Executive Inn. This L-shape motel serves tourists, business people, and—as the parking facilities for large trucks indicates—truckers. Cable TV, room phones. Pets allowed (fee). | 671 N. Main St. | 803/584–2184 | fax 803/584–2184 | 65 rooms | $35–$50 | AE, D, DC, MC, V.

ANDERSON

MAP 9, C3

(Nearby towns also listed: Clemson, Greenville, Pendleton)

Anderson has a 16-block historic district with the Blue Ridge Mountains in the background. The town is part of the upstate industrial corridor along I–85 that extends to the Spartanburg area. The downtown area, with its new courthouse, original 1897 courthouse-turned-museum, and scattering of shops and restaurants in renovated historic buildings, seems in transition. Empty cotton mills at the end of town remain as a testament to the area's cotton legacy. Nearby Lake Hartwell and Sadlers Creek Park are the top attractions.

Information: Anderson Area Chamber of Commerce | 706 E. Greenville St., Anderson, SC 29621 | 864/226–3454.

Attractions

Anderson County Arts Center. Year-round special programs here give art instruction to adults and children. You can also view changing displays and art exhibits. | 405 W. Main St. | 864/224–8811 | Free | Weekdays 9:30–5:30. Closed Sun.

Hartwell Dam and Lake. The Hartwell Dam on the Savannah River created this man-made lake—one of the Southeast's largest—as part of a flood-control and hydropower project. The lake covers nearly 56,000 acres and has a 962-mi sandy shoreline; several state parks surround it. The 3-mi-long dam rises 204 ft. You can take guided tours of the dam and power plant. | Hartwell Lake Visitor Information Center, 5625 Anderson Hwy., Hartwell | 706/376–4788 or 888/893–0678 | www.sas.u706/856–0358sace.army.mil/hartwell.htm | Free | Weekdays 8–4:30; tours Wed. 2:30, Sat. 10.
The 680-acre **Lake Hartwell State Park** has camping, picnic facilities, and a boat launch. | 19138 South Hwy., Fairplay | 864/972–3352 | fax 864/972–3352 | www.southcarolinaparks.com | Free; camping fee $17 | Daily 10–6.

You can find nature trails, camp sites, and picnic facilities at **Sadlers Creek State Park.** | 940 Sadlers Creek Rd., Anderson | 864/226–8950 | fax 864/226–8950 | www.southcarolinaparks.com | Free | Daily 7 AM–dusk.

"The Old Reformer." This small brass cannon, originally from England, saw military action during the Revolutionary War and the War of 1812. | Main and Whitner Sts. | Free | Daily.

ON THE CALENDAR

MAY: *Pontiac GMC Freedom Weekend Aloft.* This four-day hot air balloon festival held on Memorial Day weekend features over 100 hot air balloon competitions daily. Four music stages provide entertainment for spectators on the ground, as do children's rides, a crafts show, and sponsor displays. | 864/232–3700.
SEPT.: *Anderson County Fall Fair.* You can see the only railroad carnival left in the country at this nine-day fair. There is special entertainment every night in the grand-

stand, plus juried art and photography shows, along with all the other usual fair events. | 431 Williamston Rd. | 864/226–6114.

Dining

1109 South Main Restaurant, Sushi Bar and Evergreen Spa. Continental. The sushi bar upstairs adds an eclectic touch to this restored 1903 Greek Revival–style mansion with three formal dining rooms. There, you can dine on seafood, veal, and wild mushroom dishes; try the potato horseradish-crusted salmon fillet. | 1109 S. Main St. | 864/225–1109 or 800/241–0034 | Closed Sun.–Wed. No lunch | $15–$20 | AE, D, DC, MC, V.

Outback Steak House. Steakhouse. Kangaroos, koala bears, boomerangs, and Australian flags provide the background for this Aussie eating experience. | 110 Interstate Blvd. | 864/261–6283 | fax 864/261–0491 | No lunch | $9–$20 | AE, D, DC, MC, V.

Sullivan's Metropolitan Grill. American. Basil, garlic, and oregano give a Mediterranean flair to the meat, fish, poultry, and pasta dishes served under high ceilings and balconies in this renovated hardware store. A pastry chef makes all desserts on the premises. | 208 S. Main St. | 864/226–8945 | Closed Sun.–Mon. | $15–$24 | AE, D, DC, MC, V.

Lodging

Anderson Hotel. This former Holiday Inn 4 mi from downtown was built in 1962 but it's still a good bet for simple, reasonably priced rooms. Restaurant, bar (with entertainment), room service. In-room data ports. Cable TV. Pool. Laundry facilities. Business services. Some pets allowed. | 3025 N. Main St. | 864/226–6051 | fax 864/964–9145 | 130 rooms | $59–$99 | AE, D, DC, MC, V.

Comfort Suites. This relatively new business-district hotel tends to cater to corporate clients, and rooms come with iron, ironing board, and hair dryers. Complimentary Continental breakfast. Microwaves, refrigerators. Cable TV, room phones. No pets. | 118 Interstate Blvd. | 864/622–1200 | fax 864/622–1202 | www.choicehotels.com | 60 rooms | $78–$125 | AE, D, DC, MC, V.

Hampton Inn. Less than ½ a mile from I–85, this three-story hotel is next to two restaurants. Complimentary Continental breakfast. In-room data ports. Cable TV. Outdoor pool. Exercise equipment. Business services. No pets. | 120 Interstate Blvd. | 864/375–1999 | fax 864/375–1099 | 70 rooms | $69–$86 | AE, D, DC, MC, V.

La Quinta Inn. Two stories with outside entrances to the rooms mark this chain hotel 3 mi north of downtown. Complimentary Continental breakfast. In-room data ports. Pool. Business services. | 3430 N. Main St. | 864/225–3721 | fax 864/225–7789 | 100 rooms | $60 | AE, D, DC, MC, V.

Super 8. Though cheap and simple, this three-floor concrete motel is peaceful and quiet and rooms are tastefully decorated. Cable TV. | 3302 Cinema Ave. | 864/225–8384 | fax 864/225–8384 | 62 rooms | $41–$57 | AE, D, DC, V.

BEAUFORT

MAP 9, G8

(Nearby towns also listed: Edisto Island, Hilton Head Island)

The historic town of Beaufort (pronounced Bew-fort) is some 40 mi north of Hilton Head, on Port Royal Island. Its compact historic district's lavish 18th- and 19th-century homes and churches evoke Beaufort's prosperous antebellum days as a cotton center. Although many private houses in Old Point, the historic district, are not usually open to visitors, some may be on the annual Fall House Tour in mid-October and the Spring Tour of Homes and Gardens in April or May. The Greater Beaufort Chamber of Commerce can provide more information about house-tour schedules.

Information: **Greater Beaufort Chamber of Commerce** | Box 910, 106 Carteret St., Beaufort, SC 29901 | 843/524–3163 or 800/638–3525.

Attractions

Beaufort Arsenal/Museum. You can see prehistoric relics, native pottery, and Revolutionary and Civil War exhibits on display in this brick and tabby arsenal, built in 1798. | 713 Craven St. | 843/525–7077 | fax 843/525–7013 | www.beufortcity.sc.com | $2 | Mon.–Tues., Thurs.–Sat. 10–5.

Hunting Island State Park. A dramatically eroding beach sets the scene at this park 17 mi east of town, where you can walk nature trails, rent cabins, camp, or fish from one of the east coast's longest fishing piers (1,120 ft). You can also climb the 140-ft Hunting Island Lighthouse (built in 1859). | 2555 Sea Island Parkway, Hunting Island | 843/838–2011 | Free | Daily 8 AM–dusk.

John Mark Verdier House Museum. This Federal-style 1790 home served as the headquarters for Union forces during the Civil War. The Marquis de Lafayette visited it in 1825. | 801 Bay St. | 843/524–6335 | fax 843/524–6240 | www.historic beaufort.org | $4 | Mon.–Sat. 11–4.

Marine Corps Air Station. With two weeks' notice, support units at the Marine Corps Atlantic Base can give you tours of some of the seven operational F/A-18 Hornet fighter squadrons on the base. | U.S. 21 | 843/228–7201 | www.beaufort.us.sc.mil | Free | Call to arrange tours.

National Cemetery. This cemetery, created by Abraham Lincoln in 1863 for those who died in battles in the South, holds the remains of 9,000 Union soldiers and 122 Confederates. | 1601 Boundary St. (U.S. 21) | 843/524–3925 | www.beaufortus.sc.com | Free | Daily dawn to dusk.

Parris Island. You can take a self-guided driving tour through this boot camp, which trains about 17,000 U.S. Marines a year. The tour includes a visit to a small historic district, the drill instructor school, a rifle range, the parade field, and the Iwo Jima monument. | Hwy. 21 (then follow signs), Beaufort | 843/525–3650 | www.parrisisland.com | Free | Daily 7:30–5.

The **Parris Island Museum** exhibits uniforms, photos, and weapons depicting military history since 1562, when the French Huguenots built a fort on nearby St. Helena. | Marine Corps Recruit Depot, Parris Island Bldg. #111 | 843/525–2951 | Free | Fri.–Wed. 8–4:30, Thurs. 10–4:30. Spaniards built **Fort San Felipe** and the village of **Santa Elena** just a year after the founding of St. Augustine. **Fort San Marcos** was added after Indians destroyed the town in 1576. Each summer there are archaeological digs; maps are available at the Parris Island Visitors Center. | Parris Island | 843/228–3650 | Free | Weekdays 7:30–5, weekends noon–4.

WHAT TO PACK IN THE TOY TOTE FOR KIDS

- ❑ Audiotapes
- ❑ Books
- ❑ Clipboard
- ❑ Coloring/activity books
- ❑ Doll with outfits
- ❑ Hand-held games
- ❑ Magnet games

- ❑ Notepad
- ❑ One-piece toys
- ❑ Pencils, colored pencils
- ❑ Portable stereo with earphones
- ❑ Sliding puzzles
- ❑ Travel toys

*Excerpted from *Fodor's: How to Pack: Experts Share Their Secrets*
© 1997, by Fodor's Travel Publications

Penn Center. In 1862, Quaker missionaries from the North founded this center for freed slaves; it is now one of the most important African-American historical sites in the United States. In the early 1960s, Dr. Martin Luther King, Jr. used the center as a training and meeting facility for civil rights workers. Today, it preserves the language, culture, and history of the Sea Island's Gullah community. The campus 6 mi east of town has 19 buildings, which may be visited on a self-guided tour. | 16 Penn Circle W, St. Helena Island | 843/838–2432 | Free; museum $4 | Grounds open daily; museum Mon.–Sat. 11–4.

Red Piano Too Art Gallery. Quirky folk and Southern art, colorful beads, and pottery fill this huge old wooden building on the way to St. Helena Island. | 870 Sea Island Pkwy. | 843/838–2241 | Free | Daily 10–5.

St. Helena's Episcopal Church. The gravestones at this historic church were used as operating tables during the Civil War, when the church served as a hospital. | 501 Church St. | 843/522–1712 | Free | Mon.–Thurs. 9–4, Fri., Sat. 9–1.

Sheldon Church Ruins. Massive brick pillars and an imposing outer shell tell the history of this church, built in 1753 and burned by the British in 1779, then rebuilt but burned again by Sherman in 1865. Once a year (on the second Sunday after Easter), services are held at the ruins. | Old Sheldon Church Rd. | Free | Daily.

Sightseeing Tours. You can see Beaufort on foot, by mule-drawn carriage, or by car. **Carolina Buggy Tours** focus on Beaufort's historic district. | Corner of Charles and Craven Sts. | 843/525–1300 | $14.50 | Mon.–Sat. 9:30–5; call for tour schedule.
You can take mule-drawn carriage rides of the historic district with **Carriage Tours of Beaufort.** | 1002 Bay St. | 843/521–1651 | fax 843/524–5371 | $15 | Mon.–Sat. 10–4, Sun. noon–4.
The **Greater Beaufort Chamber of Commerce** offers self-guided walking or driving tours of Beaufort. | 106 Carteret St. | 843/524–3163 | Free | Daily 9–5:30.
Gullah 'n' Geechie Mahn Tours have tours of Beaufort and sea islands such as St. Helena that focus on the traditions of African-American culture. | 847 Sea Island Pkwy. | 843/838–7516 | $17 | Office daily 9:45–4:30; tours 9:45 and 1:45.
Costumed guides sing and act out history during the **Spirit of Old Beaufort** walking tours. | 103 West St. | 843/525–0459 | $10 | Call ahead for tour schedule.

U.S. Naval Hospital. This military hospital was formerly a Civil War army base where the Emancipation Proclamation had its first reading south of the Mason Dixon Line. You need to get an entry pass at the front gate. | 1 Pickney Blvd. | 843/525–5600 | Free.

ON THE CALENDAR
MAR.–APR.: *St. Helena's Episcopal Church Spring Tours.* You can tour Beaufort's Colonial homes and lovely plantations in the Lowcountry. | Church St. and North St., Box 1043 | 843/524–0363.
JULY: *Beaufort County Water Festival.* Boats galore turn up for this event in the Waterfront Park on Bay Street, which includes water sports and entertainment. | 843/524–0600.
OCT.–NOV.: *Beaufort Fall Festival of Homes and Gardens.* Private homes and gardens open up to the public; you can also tour historic sites, and attend lectures and special events. | 208 Scott St. | 843/524–6334.
NOV.: *Heritage Days Festival.* This three-day festival at the Penn Center celebrates Gullah culture with storytelling, crafts, tours, and food. | 16 Penn Center Circle, St. Helena | 843/838–8563.

Dining
Beaufort Inn. Continental. The mahogany-paneled dining room in this Victorian inn exudes a formal atmosphere, while the wine bar is clubby, with booths and black leather. You can try the crispy flounder with yucca chips, or have an appetizer at the bar. You can also dine outside on the porches. Sunday brunch. | 809 Port Republic St. | 843/521–9000 | Breakfast also available. No lunch | $17–$24 | AE, D, MC, V.

Bistro De Jong. Contemporary. The chef here blends European style with local ingredients in a garden-like space, with a long bar counter and and café tables. The peanut-and-cilantro fried shrimp is good; you can also try apple bellies and pasta with sun-dried tomatoes, artichokes, and Portobello mushrooms. | 205 West St. | 843/524–4994 | Resevations essential | Closed Sun. | $17–$26 | AE, D, MC, V.

11th Street Dockside. Seafood. Nearly every table looks out over the water at this classic wharfside restaurant with a screened porch. As would be expected, it's known for fried oysters, shrimp, fresh fish, a steamed seafood pot, and seafood pasta. | 1699 11th St. W, Port Royal, | 843/524–7433 | No lunch | $13–$20 | AE, D, DC, MC, V.

Emily's. Continental. This wood-panelled restaurant, one block off the main thoroughfare, begins serving tapas at 4:30 and continues with a full course dinner—choices range from steak au poivre and wienerschnitzel to soft-shelled crabs—at 6. | 906 Port Republic St. | 843/522–1866 | Closed Sun. No lunch | $21–$23 | AE, D, MC, V.

Plum's. American. Bright yellow predominates in this casual, arty restaurant with a full bar and extensive wine list. Lunch includes light sandwiches, salads, homemade soup, ice cream, and desserts. Dinner features sashimi, pasta, prawns, and dishes with a Mediterranean flair. | 904 ½ Bay St. | 843/525–1946 | fax 843/986–9052 | $15–$24 | D, DC, MC, V.

Shrimp Shack. Seafood. Shrimp burgers—deep-fried ground shrimp meat patties—are the specialty at this tiny, ramshackle shack on the way to Hunting Island and across from the marina where boats unload fresh catches. | 129 Sea Island Pkwy., St. Helena Island | 843/838–2962 | No lunch | $6.50–$13 | No credit cards.

Lodging

Beaufort Inn. Built in 1897 as a second-home by a prominent Hampton (SC) attorney, this peach-color Victorian inn was later sold to become one of Beaufort's first boarding houses. It became the Beaufort Inn in the early 1930s, catering to vacationers seeking the sea-breezes and seafood of the Lowcountry, before falling on hard times in the 1960s. In 1993, Debbie and Russell Fielden purchased the boarded-up structure. Their extensive renovations and expansion ended in July 1994, when the Beaufort Inn re-opened and was named "One of the Top Ten Inns in the Country" by American Historic Inns. Gables decorate the exterior, and antique reproductions and comfortable chairs furnish the rooms, some of which also have fireplaces; the inn is also home to the Beaufort Inn restaurant. Restaurant, complimentary breakfast. In-room data ports, refrigerators. Cable TV. Business services. No kids under 8. No smoking. | 809 Port Republic St. | 843/521–9000 | fax 843/521–9500 | beaufortinn@hargray.com | www.beaufortinn.com | 12 rooms, 4 suites | $125–$300 | AE, D, MC, V.

Best Western Sea Island Inn. The entrance of this well-maintained chain hotel faces the Beaufort Historic Waterfront on the Intracoastal Waterway. Rooms are basic but clean, and the hotel is in the historic district, walking distance from 18th century homes, gourmet dining, shops and art galleries. Complimentary Continental breakfast. In-room data ports. Cable TV. Pool. Exercise equipment. Bicycles. Business services. | 1015 Bay St. | 843/522–2090 | fax 843/521–4858 | www.bestwestern.com | 43 rooms | $85–$109 | AE, D, DC, MC, V.

Craven Street Inn. Built as a private residence in 1870, this lovely Victorian home was used in *Forest Gump, The Prince of Tides,* and *The Big Chill.* You can sit outside on rockers on the sweeping double porches or stroll in the 2-acre garden. Most rooms have private entrances. Complimentary Continental breakfast. Some kitchenettes, refrigerators. Cable TV. Business services. No smoking. | 1103 Craven St. | 843/522–1668 or 888/522–0250 | fax 843/522–9975 | cravensinn@hargray.com | www.cravenstreetinn.com | 10 rooms | $139–$219 | AE, MC, V.

Cuthbert House Inn. Original Federal fireplaces, crown and rope molding, 18th- and 19th-century antiques, mahogany furniture, and pine floors distinguish this pillared 1790 home overlooking the bay. Complimentary breakfast. In-room data ports, refrigerators. Cable TV. Bicycles. Business services. | 1203 Bay St. | 843/521–1315 or 800/327–9275 | fax 843/521–1314

| cuthbert@hargray.com | www.cuthberthouseinn.com | 7 rooms, 1 suite | $115–$195, $195–$225 suite | AE, D, MC, V.

Fripp Island Resort. The Atlantic coast stretches for 3½ mi of beach along this resort made up of modern villas and condos, most of which overlook the ocean. Some of the rentals have walk-on porches, and some come complete with garages. 5 restaurants. Microwaves, refrigerators. Cable TV. 4 pools. Driving range, two 18-hole golf courses, putting green, 10 tennis courts. Beach, boating, fishing, bicycles. Children's programs ages 3–12, playground. Business services. | 1 Tarpon Blvd., Fripp Island | 843/838–3535 or 800/845–4100 | fax 843/838–9079 | sales@frippislandresort.com | www.frippislandresort.com | 240 2- and 3-bedroom cottages | 2 bedrooms $250; 3 bedrooms $300 | AE, D, DC, MC, V.

Hampton Inn. This three-story hotel is near movie theaters, shops, and exercise facilities. Rooms come equipped with iron, ironing board, clock radio, and hair dryer. Complimentary Continental breakfast. In-room data ports, refrigerators. Cable TV. Outdoor pool. No pets. | 2342 Boundary St. | 843/986–0600 | fax 843/986–0494 | www.hampton-inn.com | 74 rooms, 2 suites | $73–$125 | AE, D, DC, MC, V.

Holiday Inn Beaufort. Although not remarkable for its decor, this chain hotel is centrally located: 1 mi from Beaufort, 1 mi from Savannah, GA, 2 mi from downtown, and 3 mi from Parris Island. Restaurant, bar, room service. In-room data ports. Cable TV. Pool. Laundry service. Business services. | 2001 Boundary St. (Hwy. 21) | 843/524–2144 | fax 843/524–1704 | 150 rooms | $65–$95 | AE, D, DC, MC, V.

Howard Johnson Express Inn. Large trees shade the white stucco building surrounded by greenery and on the edge of the marsh. Rooms overlook the river, and sunlight streams in through the large windows. The hotel is 5 mi from beaches and 5 mi from Parris Island. Complimentary Continental breakfast. Microwaves, refrigerators. Cable TV. Pool. Fishing. Business services. Pets allowed. | 3651 Trask Pkwy. (Hwy. 21) | 843/524–6020 or 800/406–1411 | fax 843/524–2070 | 63 rooms | $75 | AE, D, DC, MC, V.

Port Republic Inn Guest Room and Luxury Suites. Four-poster beds and antiques furnish this home, a stylish example of Federal architecture in Beaufort's historic district. Complimentary Continental breakfast. In-room data ports, some kitchenettes. Cable TV, room phones. No pets. | 915 Port Republic St. | 888/305–7499 or 843/770–0600 | fax 843/521–4858 | www.port-republic-inn.com | 1 room, 4 suites | $115–$195 | AE, D, DC, MC, V.

★ **Rhett House Inn.** This former plantation house bordering the historic district and the Intracoastal Waterway dates back to 1820, its sprawling verandahs and white columns harking back to the Old South. Many rooms have gas fireplaces, private balconies, and whirlpool baths; all bathrooms come equipped with hair dryers and robes. The newly renovated historic cottages have private entrances and porches. Fresh cut flowers throughout the inn add a nice touch. Complimentary breakfast. Some in-room hot tubs. Cable TV. Bicycles. Business services. No kids under 5. | 1009 Craven St. | 843/524–9030 or 888/480–9530 | fax 843/524–1310 | rhetthse@hargray.com | www.rhetthouseinn.com | 17 rooms | $125–$225 | AE, MC, V.

Royal Frogmore Inn. This family vacation beach spot is in St. Helena, 7 mi from Beaufort and 8 mi from the ocean. Local crafts, including wicker baskets and woven fabrics, decorate the rooms, and guests receive complimentary coffee and a newspaper. In-room data ports. Cable TV, room phones. No pets. | 863 Sea Island Pkwy., St. Helena | 843/838–5400 | fax 843/838–7137 | 50 rooms | $60 | AE, D, MC, V.

Sleep Inn of Beaufort. This very modern inn is 3 mi from the historic downtown. Complimentary Continental breakfast. In-room data ports, microwaves, refrigerators. Outdoor pool. Exercise equipment. | 2523 Boundary St. (Hwy. 21) | 843/522–3361 | fax 843/522–9929 | 86 rooms | $60–$95 | AE, D, DC, MC, V.

Two Suns Inn. Built as a private residence in the historic district in 1917, the Keyserling home later became the Beaufort County School's "Teacherage" from 1943–66, accommodating up to twenty single female teachers at a time. Its new owners, Carrol and Ron Kay, substantially restored it between 1990 and 1994, and in 1996, the inn received a U.S. Department of the Interior "Certified Historic Structure" designation. In the historic district, it overlooks the bay. Complimentary breakfast. Cable TV in most rooms. Business services. No kids under 12. No smoking. | 1705 Bay St. | 843/522–1122 or 800/532–4244 | fax 843/522–1122 | twosuns@islc.net | www.twosunsinn.com | 5 rooms | $95–$155 | AE, D, DC, MC, V.

BENNETTSVILLE

MAP 9, I3

(Nearby towns also listed: Cheraw, Darlington, Hartsville, Latta)

Bennettsville is in Marlboro County, once one of the state's wealthiest counties as a result of rich farmland and bumper crops of cotton. Victorian and Greek Revival homes and buildings—many studded with colorful stained glass—are among the 118 in the town's National Historic District. The 1881 courthouse anchors the downtown business district, which is struggling toward renewal. Nearby, Lake Wallace offers water sports and nature breaks.

Information: **Marlboro County Chamber of Commerce and SC Cotton Trail Visitor Center** | 300 W. Main St., Bennettsville, SC 29512 | 843/479–3941.

Attractions

Jennings–Brown House. This 1826 house served as headquarters for Sherman's army during the Union occupation of Bennettsville. It has a rare hand-painted and stenciled ceiling in one of the upstairs bedrooms and furnishings from the 1850s. | 123 S. Marlboro St. | 843/479–5624 | $2 | Weekdays 10–2, or by appointment.

Lake Paul Wallace. The world's largest man-made controlled-fishing lake, 500-acre Lake Wallace has a fishing and sailing area stocked by the Department of Natural Resources. The swimming and boating area has a 1-mi skiing channel, as well as sandy beaches, and wild geese, swans, ducks, and coots inhabit the waterfowl refuge. There's also a walking trail. Park in the lot on Jefferson St. to swim or launch your boat, or in the lot on Country Club Dr. to fish. | Jefferson St. and Country Club Dr. | 843/479–3312 | Free | June–Labor Day, dawn to dusk.

Marlboro Civic Center. This old movie house, once a major stop for vaudeville and music shows on the New York–Miami circuit, has been turned into a modern auditorium for community programs and events. | 106 Clyde St. | 843/454–9496 | Prices vary | Call for schedule.

Marlboro County Historical Museums. You can find a rare copy of the South Carolina Ordinance of Secession at this 1902 home, along with a Victorian parlor, medical museum, textiles room, corn liquor still, and old plantation tools. Also on site is the 1834 two-room Bennettsville Female Academy. | 123 S. Marlboro St. | 843/479–5624 | $2 | Weekdays 10–5.

ON THE CALENDAR
MAY: *Jubilee Arts Festival.* This festival in Lindsay Park on Hwy. 9 features large exhibits of arts and crafts, food, and entertainment. | 843/479–6982.

Dining
Southern Oaks Restaurant. Southern. Homemade barbecue chicken and a family atmosphere accompanies buffet style service and salad and dessert bars at this 110-yr-old two-story house. | 509 Beauty Spot Rd. W | 843/479–3964 | Reservations not accepted | Closed Sat., Mon. No dinner | $6.50–$7.50 | No credit cards.

Lodging
Breeden Inn and Carriage House. In 1886, on land gifted from his bride-to-be's parents, Thomas Bouchier, an attorney, farmer and politician, built this Beaux Arts mansion as a

wedding gift to his bride. Today, stained glass, wood floors and paneling, and antique furnishings decorate the historic district house, its carriage house, and garden cottages. Lake Wallace is 1 mi away. Complimentary breakfast. Pool. | 404 E. Main St. | 843/479–3665 or 888/335–2996 | fax 843/479–7998 | www.bbonline.com/sc/breeden | 6 rooms | $85–$135 | AE, D, DC, MC, V.

Ellerbe House. Gardens and trees surround this suburban, country-style inn downtown 20 mi west of I–95. Columned porches front the 1885 structure, and antique reproductions decorate the suites. No alcohol permitted. Complimentary Continental breakfast. Cable TV. | 106 Jennings St. (Box 826), Bennettsville | 843/479–2066 or 800/248–0128 | fax 843/479–0730 | guestservice@marlboroelectric.net | www.bbhost.com/ellerbe | 5 rooms | $75–$125 | AE, D, MC, V.

Holiday Inn Express. A burgundy color scheme distinguishes this modern chain hotel across the street from shopping. Complimentary Continental breakfast. In-room data ports, some kitchenettes, microwave in lobby, refrigerators, some in-room hot tubs. Cable TV, room phones. Outdoor pool. No pets. | 213 U.S. 15 (401 Bypass E) | 843/479–1700 | fax 843/479–4190 | www.basshotels.com | 52 rooms | $69–$89 | AE, D, DC, MC, V.

CAMDEN

MAP 9, G3

CAMDEN

INTRO
ATTRACTIONS
DINING
LODGING

(Nearby towns also listed: Bishopville, Columbia, Sumter)

Dating from 1732, Camden is South Carolina's oldest inland town. British general Lord Cornwallis established a garrison here during the Revolutionary War and burned most of Camden before evacuating it. Many of the town's antebellum homes still stand, spared by General Sherman during the Civil War. From the late 19th century through the 1940s, Camden was a center of textile trade and attracted Northerners escaping the cold winters. The DuPont family is still one of Camden's major employers. Horse training and breeding are now major industries, and some of the roads in the fanciest and oldest neighborhoods are unpaved. The Carolina Cup and Colonial Cup are run here; in addition to the races, you'll get to see champagne tailgate parties with elegant crystal and china.

Information: **Kershaw County Chamber of Commerce** | Box 605, 724 S. Broad St., Camden, SC 29020 | 803/432–2525 or 800/968–4037.

Attractions
Bethesda Presbyterian Church. Designed by Robert Mills, this 1822 church is a graceful example of his use of Greek Revival style. Note that he placed the steeple at the rear, rather than at the front, of the building. | 502 DeKalb St. | 803/432–4593 | Free | Weekdays 9–5; services Sun. 9:30 and 11.

DeKalb Monument. Robert Mills designed this monument featuring the names of the 24 states in existence at the time, in honor of Revolutionary hero Baron Johann de Kalb, who is buried here. | 502 DeKalb St. | 803/432–2525 or 800/968–4037 | Free.

Camden Antique District. You can find nearly 20 antiques stores within several blocks, offering an array of furniture, china, glassware, sterling, porcelain dolls, and Confederate and equestrian collectibles. | Broad St.

Camden Archives and Museum. The exhibits of local and regional history include Camden's circa 1825 town clock and a rare early American medical chest. You can search for your ancestry in the extensive materials on genealogical research. | 1314 Broad St. | 803/425–2525 | Free | Weekdays 8–5, 1st Sun. of month 1–5.

Hampton Park. Named for General Wade Hampton, Confederate cavalryman and later governor of the state, this park has a drinking fountain funded by coins contributed by Camden schoolchildren. Both people and horses can drink here. | Lyttleton St. | 803/432–2525 | Free.

Historic Boykin. A handful of historic buildings 10 mi north of Camden make up this small but scenic farm community, including the working Boykin Grist Mill, Swift Creek Baptist Church (circa 1827), Boykin Company Store, and Broom Place (in a restored 1760 slave cabin), where you can see brooms being made on 100-yr-old equipment. | Rte. 261, Boykin | 803/425–6724 or 803/425–0933 | Free | Broom Place: weekdays 10–5, Sat. 10:30–2; other sites by appointment.

Historic Camden Revolutionary War Park. General Cornwallis established a post here, and 14 battles of the Revolutionary War were fought in the area. The park represents 18th- and early 19th-century Camden (with emphasis on the British occupation) through fort sites, log cabins, and period homes, including the Joseph Kershaw house, which Cornwallis made his headquarters. | 222 S. Broad St. | 803/432–9841 | fax 803/432–3815 | www.historic-camden.net | $5 | Tues.–Sat. 10–5, Sun. 1–5; Mon. grounds open 10–5, shop closed.

Lake Wateree State Park. Pine woods surround a 14,000-acre lake with a 190-mi shoreline. You can also camp or walk the nature trails, and there's a boat ramp and a tackle shop. | 122 State Park Rd. | 803/482–6401 | Free | Daily 6 AM–9 PM.

Mills Court House and Kershaw County Visitors Center. At press time, there were plans to move the Kershaw County Chamber of Commerce to this 1826 building designed by Robert Mills and recently renovated, where you'll be able to pick up maps and rent cassette tapes ($5) for self-guided walking tours. | 603 Broad St. | 803/432–2525 or 800/968–4037 | fax 803/432–4181 | www.camden-sc.org | camden@camden.net | Free | Daily 9–5.

N. R. Goodale State Park. Cypress trees cover this 735-acre park, where you can swim, fish, and boat on the spring-fed lake or play the nine-hole golf course. | Old Wire Rd. | 803/432–2772 | Free | Apr.–Sept., daily 9–9; Oct.–Mar., Thurs.–Mon. 9–6.

Quaker, Beth El, and Cedar Cemeteries. Early settlers, including many early Irish Quakers from the late 1700s, are buried in these three adjoining cemeteries. This was also the spot of the original Quaker Meeting House. | Broad and Meeting Sts. | Free | Daily.

Rectory Square. A six-columned pantheon dedicated to six Civil War generals from Kershaw County dominates this square. There's also a recreational activity station for children as well as tennis courts. | Chestnut and Lyttleton Sts. | Free | Daily.

Old South Carriage Co. You can take 1-hr narrated tours of Camden's historic district by horse-drawn carriage. | 14 Anson St. | 843/577–0042 | fax 843/722–3880 | www.oldsouth-carriagetours.com | $17 for 1-hr tour | Oct.–Apr., daily 9–5; Nov.–Mar, daily 10–4.

Springdale Race Course. Two national races take place at this racecourse: the Carolina Cup in late March or early April and the Colonial Cup in November. The Carolina Cup draws more than 50,000 fans and includes tailgate picnics, some with china and sterling silver. The Colonial Cup includes kids' activities, a market, and terrier races. You're most likely to get a look at trainers working with their horses in the morning or midday. The on-site museum chronicles steeplechasing with winners' silks and other memorabilia. | 200 Knights Hill Rd. | 803/432–6513 | www.carolina-cup.org | $15 general admission | Museum: Sept.–Apr. Mon.–Fri. 9–5, May–Aug. by appt. Races: Sundays, open at 9, races begin at 1. The **Carolina Cup Racing Museum** includes exhibits of the area's steeplechasing legacy. Exhibit halls and a library display decades of competition and pageantry, including jockey silks, photographs, and trophies. | 200 Knights Hill Rd. | 803/432–6513 | Free | Nov.–Mar., weekdays 9–5.

Westfall Arena and Entertainment Complex. This busy arena hosts more than 22 horse shows a year. There are events most weekends, including rodeos, barrel racing, team penning, musical events, horse shows, and sales. | 443 Cleveland School Rd. | 803/432–9100 | Prices vary | Call for events schedule.

ON THE CALENDAR

OCT.: *Carolina Down Home Blues Festival.* The Fine Arts Auditorium and 10 other downtown venues showcase top Blues talent during this three-day event during the first or second week of the month. Auditorium events cost $10; a three-day subscription pass is available from the Fine Arts Center of Kershaw County. | 810 Lyttleton St. | 803/425–7676.

NOV.: *Revolutionary War Field Days.* You can see battle skirmishes, living history demonstrations, military courts and competitions, a period fashion show, frontier weddings, and traditional craftsmen. | 803/432–9841.

Dining

Avanti's Restaurant. Italian. Cane-back chairs, fox-hunting prints, and elaborately tiled fireplaces set the tone for an elegant meal in the Victorian Greenleaf Inn (*see below*). You can try the pastas, family-style side dishes, and cannoli. | 1308 Broad St. | 803/713–0089 | Closed Sun. | $15–$30 | AE, D, MC, V.

Lucy's. Continental. Low lighting, hardwood floors, and mason brick walls define this classic Old South dining room in a historic building. Locals and tourists congregate at the bar, from the Willard Hotel in Washington, D.C. | 1043 Broad St. | 803/432–9096 | Closed Sun.–Mon. | $10–$25 | AE, D, DC, MC, V.

Mulberry Market Bakery. Café. This downtown bakery makes fantastic Southern cheese straws and a variety of Danish pastries, including the popular almond Danish. Takeout only. | 536 E. DeKalb St. | 803/424–8401 | Breakfast served. Closed Sun. No lunch or supper | $1–$6 | No credit cards.

The Paddock. American. A horsey atmosphere pervades this restaurant, with dark paneling, booths, and a bar. On some evenings, the lounge has entertainment. You can try the Paddock's Reubens, chicken, and steak. | 514 Rutledge St. | 803/432–3222 | Closed Sun. | $14–$18 | AE, DC, MC, V.

Lodging

Camden B&B. Working fireplaces and Belgian stained-glass windows decorate this original Federal-style home, surrounded by acres of pine forest. Complimentary breakfast. In-room data ports, microwaves, refrigerators. Cable TV, in-room VCRs, room phones. Pets allowed. No smoking. | 127 Union St. | 803/432–2366 | fax 803/432–9767 | jerixon@tech-tech.com | www.camdenscbandb.com | 1–3 bedroom suite; 2 cottages | $85–$109 | AE, D, DC, MC, V.

Candlelight Inn. A brick driveway circles this 1928 Cape Cod–style home in the historic district. Quilts, needlework, and antiques furnish the rooms, and candles burn in all the windows. Complimentary breakfast. TV in common area. | 1904 Broad St. | 803/424–1057 | www.bbhost.com | 3 rooms | $90–$105 | AE, D, DC, MC, V.

Colony Inn. Rooms in the two two-story brick buildings of this mom-and-pop hotel a 1½ mi from downtown have either interior or exterior entrances. The building with interior entrances is entirely non-smoking and without pets. Restaurant. Cable TV. Pool. Some pets allowed. | 2020 W. DeKalb St. | 803/432–5508 or 800/356–9801 | fax 803/432–0920 | 53 rooms | $55 | AE, D, DC, MC, V.

The Greenleaf Inn of Camden. Three buildings comprise this inn: the main inn, with four rooms on the second floor; a nearby carriage house with seven rooms; and a guest cottage, which is well suited to families. Classic Victorian furniture and wallpaper decorate the spacious rooms. Restaurant (*see* Avanti's), complimentary breakfast. Cable TV. | 1310 Broad St. | 803/425–1806 or 800/437–5874 | fax 803/425–5853 | 11 rooms | $75–$95 | AE, MC, V.

Holiday Inn Camden. Although in a commercial area, this particular concrete, two-story branch of the classic chain hotel has a courtyard. Rooms are simply furnished. Restaurant, bar, complimentary breakfast, room service. In-room data ports, some in-room hot tubs. Cable TV. Pool, wading pool. Business services. | 850 Hwy. 1S, Lugoff | 803/438–9441 | fax 803/438–5784 | 117 rooms | $69 | AE, D, DC, MC, V.

CAMDEN

INTRO
ATTRACTIONS
DINING
LODGING

Inn at Camden. This two-story brick hotel, 2 mi from downtown, was built in the 1980s. The lobby is in a separate building, and rooms are simple, cozy, and reasonably priced. Cable TV. Pool. | 928 U.S. 1S | 803/438–4961 or 800/578–7878 | fax 803/438–4961 | 82 rooms | $40–$60 | AE, D, DC, MC, V.

Travel Lodge. This motel is in Lugoff, 5 mi south from Camden on I–20 and next to a number of restaurants. Complimentary Continental breakfast. In-room data ports, microwaves, refrigerators. Cable TV, room phones. Outdoor pool. Pets allowed (fee). | 928 Hwy. 1S, Lugoff | 803/438–4961 | fax 803/438–4961 | www.travelodge.com | 83 rooms | $49–$59 | AE, D, DC, MC, V.

CHARLESTON

MAP 9, H7

(Nearby towns also listed: Folly Beach, Isle of Palms, Kiawah Island, Sullivans Island)

Routinely named one of the top visitor destinations in America, Charleston is both sophisticated and charmingly historic. This peninsular city between the Ashley and Coopers rivers was founded in 1670 and became a leading colonial port by the early 1700s. Its prosperity continued until the Civil War and is still apparent in the city's splendid, double-galleried antebellum homes. Reconstruction was a difficult time for the city, but because of the poor economy, residents made do with what they had and, consequently, the city's historic buildings were left untouched.

Today, Charlestonians have lovingly restored old downtown homes and commercial buildings, as well as many historic churches—more than 180 churches in all, so many that natives sometimes refer to Charleston as "the holy city." Each spring the city celebrates its rich heritage with candlelight tours of historic homes, symphony galas, and the famous Spoleto Festival USA.

Information: Charleston Area Convention and Visitors Bureau | Box 975, 81 Mary St., Charleston, SC 29402 | 843/853–8000 or 800/868–8118 | fax 843/853–0444.

Attractions

ART AND ARCHITECTURE
Aiken–Rhett House. The 1819 mansion, kitchen, slave quarters, and work yard (one of the most complete examples of African-American life in the United States) exist much as they were when last occupied. The original wallpaper, paint, and some furnishings still remain in the un-air-conditioned house. | 48 Elizabeth St. | 843/723–1159 | $7, combination with Nathaniel Russell House (see below) $12 | Mon.–Sat. 10–5, Sun. 2–5.

Boone Hall Plantation. An impressive ½ mi of moss-draped oaks leads up to this former cotton plantation 13 mi east of Charleston. Its slave street, made up of nine brick cabins (circa 1743), is one of the few remaining in the United States. The original smokehouse, cotton gin house, and 1935 mansion (only the main floor is open for tours) also remain. | 1235 Long Point Rd., Mt. Pleasant | 843/884–4371 | $12.50 | Apr.–Labor Day, Mon.–Sat. 8:30–6:30, Sun. 1–5; Labor Day–Mar., Mon.–Sat. 9–5, Sun. 1–4.

Drayton Hall. This circa 1738 plantation mansion survived the Civil War—the only one on the Ashley River to do so. Many consider it one of the nation's finest examples of Colonial architecture; neither restored nor furnished, it remains little changed, with original plaster moldings and paint, opulent hand-carved woodwork, and other details. | 3380 Ashley River Rd. | 843/766–0188 | www.draytonhall.org | $8; $10 Mar.–Apr. and Sept.–Oct. | Mar.–Oct., daily 10–4; Nov.–Feb., daily 10–3.

SPOLETO USA

Outdoor jazz against the backdrop of the early 19th-century campus of the College of Charleston, under giant oaks draped with moss . . . Classic theater at the historic Dock Street Theater . . . Stunningly futuristic opera at the Gaillard Auditorium . . . Choral and chamber music in some of the nation's best preserved churches . . . Site-specific art exhibitions rooted in Charleston's history, in venues such as an 1850s jail, former slave quarters, a pump house, and a Confederate widow's home . . . A festival finale, with fireworks and a lakeside concert, at 18th-century Middleton Plantation . . .

For 17 days in late May and early June during Spoleto USA, Charleston reverberates with the works of artists from Verdi to Philip Glass, from Balanchine to Twyla Tharp, from the Westminster Choir to Laurie Anderson. Charlestonians often say they are "Spoletoing" during the two-plus weeks of the festival. From morning to midnight, more than 100 performances (with as many as 10 performances a day) of 30 programs take place all over the city. Renowned artists and emerging performers alike present works of opera, theater, musical theater, dance, and chamber, symphonic, and choral music. There are world premieres, national debuts, and regional favorites; the experimental and the established; performances indoors and out, contemporary and traditional, funky and familiar.

Another 200 events make up Piccolo Spoleto, the city's companion fringe festival, many of them free and family-oriented, including street dances, puppet shows, fireworks, circuses, arts and crafts, and children's theater. Piccolo highlights local and regional artists with an emphasis on the affordable: Prices range from free to $15. It all takes place in the heart of the historic district, within walking distance of the city's most famous sites, best inns, and restaurants.

Pulitzer prize–winning composer Gian Carlo Menotti founded Spoleto USA in 1977 as the American counterpart to his Festival of Two Worlds in Spoleto, Italy. It grew under his leadership until he resigned a few years ago after a bitter dispute with the festival's board of directors, and Spoleto USA faltered—but only fleetingly. In recent years the festival continues to break all previous sales records and enjoys rave critical and audience reviews.

Artists from all over the world submit proposals to perform in the festival, yet few are invited based on these proposals alone. "Our mission is not just to entertain; it is to present challenging as well as popular works," says festival producer Nunnelly Kersh, "even works that make you uncomfortable." Because it lacks the budget of many European festivals, Spoleto relies on its prestige and freedom of expression to draw performers. Often it's a career-making move for these "young stars of tomorrow," as *Newsweek* magazine called Spoleto performers. Nationally, the festival occupies a unique niche, mostly because it continues to uphold Menotti's founding focus on opera. "It has become very important to produce our own operas," explains Kersh. "It's our unique signature."

Edmondston–Alston House. Antiques, silver, porcelain, portraits, and an impressive library furnish this 1825 stately home with beautiful harbor views. | 21 E. Battery St. | 843/722–7171 | www.middletonplace.org | $8, combination ticket with Middleton Place Gardens and Middleton Plantation House (see below) $27 | Tues.–Sat. 10–4:30, Sun.–Mon. 1:30–4:30.

Heyward–Washington House. Thomas Heyward, signer of the Declaration of Independence used to live in the 1772 house, now a National Historic Landmark. Its original kitchen building provides a rare glimpse into the past. The three-story brick house is on Cabbage Row, a neighborhood central to Charleston's African-American history. | 87 Church St. | 843/722–0354 | www.charlestonmuseum.com | $8, for combination ticket, see Charleston Museum (below) | Mon.–Sat. 10–5, Sun. 1–5.

Joseph Manigault House. Considered by many to be the finest example of Adam-style architecture in the country, this 1803 home has a fantastic "flying" staircase, outstanding plasterwork and mantels, and notable Charleston-made furniture. | 350 Meeting St. | 843/723–2926 | $8, for combination ticket, see Charleston Museum (below) | Mon.–Sat. 10–5, Sun. 1–5.

Middleton Place Gardens, House, and Stableyards. The stable yards of a self-sustaining, working plantation—including roaming peacocks and other animals—have been recreated at this 18th-century rice plantation, and you can dip candles, grind corn, and milk cows. The restored wing of the original mansion, destroyed during the Civil War, showcases silver, furniture, paintings, and historic documents. A lovely stretch of lawn ends in the Butterfly Lakes. The Middleton Place restaurant serves Lowcountry specialties for lunch and dinner. | 4300 Ashley River Rd. | 843/556–6020 | www.middletonplace.org | $15, house tours $8 | Daily 9–5; house tours Tues.–Sun. 10–4:30, Mon. 1:30–4:30.

★ **Nathaniel Russell House.** You can marvel at the famous "flying" staircase (it circles upward with no visible support) at this house museum completed in 1808. It is richly furnished with period pieces and has extensive gardens. | 51 Meeting St. | 843/724–8483 | www.middletonplace.org | $7, combination ticket with Old Powder Magazine (see below) and Aiken–Rhett House (see above) $12 | Mon.–Sat. 10–5, Sun. 2–5.

BEACHES, PARKS, AND NATURAL SIGHTS

Battery and White Point Gardens. Stede Bonnet was one of the pirates who was hanged at these former gallows, now a harborfront park at the southern-most point of the peninsula. The artillery that remains protected the area from maritime invasions. | Battery St. | 843/853–8000 | Free | Daily.

Charles Towne Landing Historic Site. The English built their first permanent settlement here, a 1670 fortification of which you can take a tram tour. There are English garden trails, a replica of a 17th-century trading ketch, an animal forest, and a re-creation of the settlers' village. | 1500 Old Town Rd. (Hwy. 171) | 843/852–4200 | fax 843/852–4205 | charlestownelandingsp@prt.state.sc.us | www.southcarolinaparks.com | $5 | Daily 8:30–6.

★ **Cypress Gardens.** Water trails and nature paths crisscross this swamp garden 28 mi north of Charleston, where there are also a small rice field, a butterfly house, and a freshwater aquarium. Boats are available for rent. | 3030 Cypress Gardens Rd., Moncks Corner | 843/553–0515 | $7 | Feb.–late Dec., daily 9–5.

Folly Beach County Park. This park, with 4,000 ft of ocean frontage and 200 ft of river frontage, is ideal for beach lovers. You can rent chairs, rafts, and umbrellas, and there are dressing areas as well as parking. The 1,045-ft Folly Beach fishing pier also extends from this island. | 1010 W. Ashley Ave. | 843/588–2426 | fax 843/462–2713 | www.ccprc.com | Free, parking $5 per car | May.–Aug. 9–7, Nov.–Mar. 10–5, Sept., Oct., Apr. 10–6.

Francis Beidler Forest. You can find the world's largest remaining virgin stand of bald cypress and tupelo trees in Four Holes Swamp, which has a 6,500-ft boardwalk. | 336 Sanctuary Rd. | 843/462–2150 | $5 | Tues.–Sun. 9–5.

★ **Magnolia Plantation and Gardens.** This 300-yr-old plantation has the oldest Colonial estate garden in South Carolina. There are 50 acres of blooming azaleas and camellias (one of the largest collections in the country), plus nature trails, a petting zoo, tram rides, rental bikes and canoes, and a wildlife refuge. | 355 Ashley River Rd. | 843/571–1266 | www.magnoliaplantation.com | $10 | Apr.–Oct., daily 8–5:30, Nov.–Mar., daily 9–5.

The **Audubon Swamp Garden** is a 60-acre black-water cypress and tupelo swamp, on the grounds of Magnolia Plantation and bordered with flowers and ferns. | 550 Ashley River Rd. | 843/571–1266 | $5.

Old Dorchester State Historic Site. You can see the ongoing archaeological excavation of the ruins of this fort and 18th-century town, which overlook the Ashley River. The nearby picnic tables make for a nice lunch spot. | 300 State Park Rd. | 843/873–1740 | Free | Thurs.–Mon. 9–6.

Palmetto Islands County Park. Biking and rollerblading paths meander through the scenic marshland at this park 12 mi east of Charleston near Boone Hall Plantation. You can take the kids to the seasonal Splash Island family water park. You can also fish, go crabbing, climb the 50-ft observation tower, rent pedal boats, play volleyball on the courts, try your hand at the horseshoe pits, or just picnic. | 444 Needlerush Pkwy., Mt. Pleasant | 843/884–0832 | $1 | Daily 10–5.

CULTURE, EDUCATION, AND HISTORY

Citadel, Military College of South Carolina. One of the last military state colleges in the United States lies behind the historic Waggner–Terrace suburb along the Ashley River. Established in 1842, the Citadel only recently admitted women. There's a dress parade almost every Friday afternoon at 3:45 during the academic year. | 171 Moultrie St. | 843/953–5000 | www.citadel.edu | Free | Daily 8–6.

Photographs, uniforms, and military artifacts and equipment at the **Citadel Archives Museum** tell the history of the college since its founding in 1842. | 171 Moultrie St. | 843/953–6846 | fax 853/953–6956 | Free | Sun.–Fri. 2–5, Sat. 1–5.

College of Charleston. The 1828 Randolph House, the graceful main building designed by Philadelphia architect William Strickland, complements the lovely tree-shaded campus, founded in 1770. It also forms a romantic backdrop for the Cistern, which functions as a grassy stage for concerts and other activities. | 66 George St. | 843/953–5507 | www.cofc.edu | Free | Daily dawn to dusk, Tours Sept.–Dec., Feb.–May Mon.–Fri. 10, 2.

The college's **Avery Research Center for African-American History and Culture,** at the corner of George and St. Phillips streets, traces the heritage of Lowcountry African-Americans. | 125 Bull St. | 843/953–7609 | www.cofc.edu/~averyrsc/front.html | Free | Mon.–Sat. noon–5, or mornings by appointment.

Dock Street Theatre. Built on the site of one of the nation's first playhouses, the building combines the reconstructed early Georgian playhouse and the preserved Old Planter's Hotel (circa 1809). The theater, which offers fascinating backstage views, welcomes tours except when technical work for a show is underway. | 135 Church St. | 843/965–4032 or 888/577–5967 | Weekdays 9–5; call for show times.

★ **Fort Sumter National Monument.** In 1861, the first shots of the Civil War were fired at this Union-occupied fort, which lies on a man-made island in Charleston Harbor. By the war's end, Fort Sumter lay in ruins after bombardment by both sides as it continually changed hands. National Park Service rangers conduct free guided tours; tour boats (*see* Sightseeing Tours/Tour Companies, *below*) provide transportation. | 1214 Middle St., Sullivans Island | 843/883–3123 (fort) or 843/722–1691 (boat tours) | www.nps.gov.fosu | Boat fare $11 | Tours usually leave from City Marina daily at 9:30, noon, and 2:30, but they vary by season. Tours also leave from Patriots Point daily at 10:45 and 1:30; Apr.–Labor Day, additional tour at 4.

Lowcountry Legends Music Hall. Charleston's Preservation Hall serves up regional music and folktales. | 30 Cumberland St. | 843/722–1829 or 800/348–7270 | Call for performance times.

Medical University of South Carolina. Founded in 1847, this was the first medical school in the South. With a busy campus in downtown Charleston serving 2,200 students, MUSC functions as the state's major teaching hospital, with nationally recognized research programs. | 171 Ashley Ave. | 843/792–3621 | Free | Daily dawn to dusk.

You can see tooth keys and molds, early x-ray units, and various instruments at MUSC's **Macaulay Museum of Dental History,** a re-creation of a 100-yr-old dental office. | 175 Ashley Ave. | 843/792–2288 | www.waring.library.edu/ | Free | Weekdays 8:30–5.

This 1893 arsenal-style building houses MUSC's **Waring Historical Medical Library,** which holds rare books, including the Medical Society of South Carolina's collection dating to 1791, plus archives and a museum in which medical chests, anesthesia and bleeding instruments, and surgery kits are on display. | 175 Ashley Ave. | 843/792–2288 | waring.library.musc.edu | Free | Weekdays 8:30–5.

Old Exchange and Provost Dungeon. Originally used as a customs house, the British confined prisoners in this 1771 structure during the Revolutionary War. On a more uplifting claim to fame, George Washington danced in its ballroom. | 122 E. Bay St. | 843/727–2165 | $4 | Thurs.–Mon. 9–6.

Old Powder Magazine. The oldest public building in the Carolinas was completed in 1712 and used to store gunpowder. It has since been restored as a National Historic Landmark and now offers an audiovisual tour of costumes, armor, and other artifacts from 18th-century Charleston. | 79 Cumberland St. | 843/723–1623 | Free, combination ticket with Aiken–Rhett House (see above) and Nathaniel Russell House (see above) $14 | Mon.–Sat. 10–5, Sun. 2–5.

MUSEUMS

★ **Charleston Museum.** Charleston silver, fashions, toys, and snuffboxes make up a small part of the 500,000 items in this collection, housed in a contemporary complex. Children can enjoy the "Discover Me" room, with interactive exhibits. The Joseph Manigault Mansion and Heyward–Washington House are also part of the museum. | 360 Meeting St. | 843/722–2996 | www.charlestonmuseum.com | $8, combination ticket for museum and houses $18, for 2 sites $12 | Mon.–Sat. 9–5, Sun. 1–5.

City Hall Art Gallery. John Trumbull's famous 1791 painting of George Washington is among the many portraits of leaders that hang in the Council Chamber. City Hall is part of what is known as the Four Corners of Law, the intersection of Meeting and Broad streets where the laws of nation, state, city, and church are represented. | 80 Broad St. | 843/724–3799 | Free | Weekdays 9–5.

Gibbes Museum of Art. The museum displays a collection of miniature portraits that ranks among the world's best. It also exhibits American art, including 18th- and 19th-century portraits of Carolinians. In the Miniature Rooms, detailed replicas show various period architecture and furnishings. | 135 Meeting St. | 843/722–2706 | $7 | Tues.–Sat. 10–5, Sun.–Mon. 1–5.

Museum on the Common. The Hurricane Hugo exhibit at this small museum 8 mi east of Charleston shows the 1989 storm damage through videos and photographs. It also has an outdoor maritime exhibit. | 217 Lucas St., Shem Creek Village | 843/849–9000 | Free | Mon.–Sat. 11–4.

RELIGION AND SPIRITUALITY

Emanuel African Methodist Episcopal Church. Home of the South's oldest African Methodist Episcopal congregation, the church was founded in 1818. Authorities closed it in 1822 when they learned that Denmark Vesey had used the sanctuary to plan his slave insurrection. The church reopened in 1865. | 110 Calhoun St. | 843/722–2561 | Free | Daily 9–4.

French Protestant (Huguenot) Church. The only church in the country still using the original Huguenot liturgy (during a special spring service) was built in 1844 in Gothic style. | 110 Church St. | 843/722–4385 | Donations accepted | Weekdays 9–2, Sun. 10:30 (service).

Kahal Kadosh Beth Elohim. This was the 1824 birthplace of American Reform Judaism. Though the original temple burned down, this 1840 structure is one of the nation's finest examples of Greek Revival architecture. | 90 Hasell St. | 843/723–1090 | Free | Weekdays 10–noon, services Fri. 8:15 PM, Sat. 11 AM.

St. John's Lutheran Church. Imposing wrought-iron gates and a fence surround this Greek Revival church, built in 1817 for a congregation founded in the 1750s. | 5 Clifford St. | 843/723–2426 | Free | Weekdays 9:30–3:30, services Sun. 8:30 and 11.

St. Mary's Church. The mother church of Catholicism in the Carolinas and Georgia was established in 1789. Spectacular stained glass decorates this 1839 Classical Revival building. | 93 Hasell St. | 843/722–7696 | Free | Weekdays 10–2, services Sun. 9:30.

St. Michael's Church. The 186-ft steeple, Charleston's most famous, punctuates the cityscape. The church, modeled after London's St. Martin-in-the-Fields, dates to 1761, the clock tower to 1764. Inside, the original pulpit remains in front of old-fashioned pews. | Corner of Meeting and Broad Sts. | 843/723–0603 | Free | Weekdays 9–4:45, services Sun. 8, 9, 10:30, and 6.

St. Philip's Church. The graceful late Georgian church, built in 1838 and restored in 1994, is the second on its site. Charlestonians are buried in the graveyard on the church's side of the street; foreigners (including John C. Calhoun, who was from Abbeville, South Carolina) lie in the graveyard on the other side. | 146 Church St. | 843/722–7734 | Free | Call for hours; services Sun. 8:15 and 10:30, Wed. 10 and 5:30.

Unitarian Church. First completed in 1787, this church was remodeled in the mid-19th century using plans inspired by the Chapel of Henry VII in Westminster Abbey. The Gothic fan-tracery ceiling was added during that renovation. You can enter the church grounds on 161½–163 King Street, amid the antiques shops there. The secluded and romantically overgrown graveyard invites contemplation. | 4 Archdale St. | 843/723–4617 | Free | Open only for services, Sun. 11.

SHOPPING

Old City Market. A series of low sheds that once housed produce and fish markets, this area is often called the Slave Market, though Charlestonians dispute that slaves were ever sold here. Restaurants, shops, and gimcracks and geegaws for children now occupy the area, along with vegetable and fruit vendors and local "basket ladies" who weave and sell distinctive sweetgrass, pine-straw, and palmetto-leaf baskets—a craft passed down through generations from their West African ancestors. | Market St. (from Meeting St. to E. Bay St.) | 843/724–3796 | Free | Daily 8:30–5, open evenings Thurs.–Sat. 8:30–11.

SIGHTSEEING TOURS/TOUR COMPANIES

Charleston Tea Party Walking Tour. This informative tour takes participants into private gardens and ends with tea in the guide's garden. Tours start at 198 King Street. | 198 King St. | 843/577–5896 or 843/722–1779 for 2 PM tour | $15.00 | Mon.–Sat. tours at 9:30 and 2.

Fort Sumter Tours and Spirit Line Cruises. You can take boat tours to Fort Sumter, tours of Charleston Harbor, and deep-sea fishing charters, as well as a dinner cruise aboard a 102-ft yacht. | City Marina on Lockwood Blvd. and Patriots Point, Mt. Pleasant | 843/722–2628 or 843/722–1691 | www.spiritcruises.com | Fort Sumter $11, Harbor Tour $10 | Fort Sumter 9:30, noon, and 2:30; Harbor Tour 12:30.

Gray Line Bus Tours. This company offers tours of the historic district, as well as seasonal trips to gardens and plantations. Tours either pick you up from your hotel, or meet you at the Visitors Center. | Box 219, Visitors Center, 374 Meeting St. | 843/722–4444 | $17–$22 | Daily 9:30–4; tours leave every 30 min.

Gray Line Water Tours. Daytime narrated harbor tours include all the sites surrounding Charleston Harbor. You can also take a weekend dinner cruise (call for details). | 196 Concord St. | 843/723–5858 | $10 | Tours depart 11:30, 1:30 and 3:30.

Gullah Tours. This bus tour, which leaves from Gallery Chuma, focuses on African-American influences on Charleston architecture, history, and culture, and includes Gullah stories. Both English and Gullah are spoken on the tour. | 43 John St. | 843/763–7551 | fax 843/763–7551 | www.gullahtours.com | $15 | Weekdays 11 and 1, Sat., 11, 1, and 3.

Lowcountry Carriage Co. You can take a 1-hr narrated tour of Charleston's historic district by horse-drawn carriage. | 14 Anson St. | 843/577–0042 | fax 843/722–3880 | www.old-southcarriagetours.com | $17 | Daily 9–dusk.

On the Market, Get Set, Tour! This company offers walking tours that describe Charleston's history as well as ghost tours. Tours depart from corner of Meeting and Market Sts. | 843/853–8687 | $14 | History tours daily 11, 1, and 3. Ghost tours daily 6, 8.

Palmetto Carriage Tours. These horse-drawn 1-hr narrated carriage tours are handicap accessible. There's also free parking and a children's petting zoo. | 40 N. Market St. (Rainbow Market) | 843/723–8145 | fax 843/722–6363 | www.carriagetour.com | $17 | Daily 9–5.

Tour Charleston. These specialty tours include Ghosts of Charleston and the history-laden Daytime Story tour of Charleston. Tours depart from Waterfront Park at the end of Vendue Range. | 184 E. Bay St. | 843/723–1670 or 800/854–1670 | fax 843/223–0180 | www.tour-charleston.com | $14 | Ghost Tour daily 5, 7:30, 9:30; Daytime Story Mon.–Sat. 10 and 5; Pirates Tour Mon.–Sat. 10 and 4.

Watercolors about Charleston. This tour combines two hours of walking with a basic watercolor and drawing class and lunch. | 24 Vendue Range | 843/937–9357 | fax 843/937–0957 | www.aboutcharleston.com | $65.

OTHER POINTS OF INTEREST

Charleston Visitor Center. This center in an old train depot provides an introduction to the city, tickets for shuttle services to downtown, and Forever Charleston, an entertaining 20-min film. Parking is 65¢ per hour, with the first hour free if you purchase a shuttle pass ($2). | 375 Meeting St. | 843/853–8000 or 800/868–8118 | fax 843/853–0444 | www.charleston-cvb.com | Film $2.50 | Mar.–Oct., daily 8:30–5:30; Nov.–Feb., daily 8:30–5; film screening daily 9–5 on the ½ hr.

South Carolina Aquarium. North America's tallest aquarium window flanks the 322,000-gallon Great Ocean Tank. The aquarium lets you travel through the five major regions of the Southeast Appalachian Watershed found in South Carolina: the Blue Ridge Mountains, the Piedmont, the Coastal Plain, the Coast, and the Ocean. More than 60 exhibits display more than 10,000 living organisms, representing more than 500 species. The saltwater marsh aviary has a tide that rises and falls, with free-flying birds including egrets and herons. There are interactive displays and special toddler exhibits. | 100 Aquarium Wharf | 843/720–1990 or 800/722–6455 | www.scaquarium.org | $14 | July–Aug., daily 9–7; Sept.–Oct. and Mar.–June, daily 9–5; Nov.–Feb. daily 10–5.

ON THE CALENDAR

FEB.: *Southeastern Wildlife Exposition.* Wildlife paintings, sculptures, and collectibles accompany auctions, live animal demonstrations—trained elephants performing tricks, and a barbecue contest at 11 sites throughout downtown. | 843/723–1748.

MAR.–APR.: *Festival of Houses and Gardens.* You can take walking tours of some of Charleston's finest private homes and gardens, and enjoy an oyster roast. | 843/722–3405 | www.historiccharleston.com.

MAY–JUNE: *Spoleto Festival USA.* This huge, internationally acclaimed 14-day festival features theatre, dance, musical performances, and art in downtown venues, many of them historic. Call for details. | 14 George St. | 843/722–2764 | www.spoletousa.org.

SEPT.–OCT.: *Fall Candlelight Tour of Homes and Gardens.* This self-guided walking tour takes you along candlelit sidewalks and into private homes and gardens. You can pick up a map at the Preservation Society Book Shop. No high-heeled shoes allowed. | 147 King St. | 843/722–4630.

SEPT.–OCT.: *MOJA Arts Festival.* Dance, theatre, visual arts, and a parade celebrate the area's African and Caribbean influences. Check with the Charleston Office of Cultural Affairs for more information. | 133 Church St. | 843/724–7305.

DEC.: *First Night Charleston.* The main part of the city is closed off for this alcohol free New Year's Eve festival, with a variety of street performances including theater, music, puppetry, and fireworks. | 843/853–8000, 843/224–8604, or 843/937–6423 | www.first-nightcharleston.com.

Dining

INEXPENSIVE

★ **Alice's Fine Foods.** Southern. This is the place for no-fuss Lowcountry food. Entrées such as fried chicken, baked chicken, barbecue, and fried fish all come with three home-cooked vegetables, including collard greens and green beans. There's live music during Sunday brunch. | 468 King St. | 843/853–9366 | $7–$14 | DC, MC, V.

Blossom Cafe. Mediterranean. Classy booths and funky lighting decorate the courtyard dining area, where you can find hummus, couscous, gnocchi, and bruschetta. There's also a bar. Kids' menu. Sunday brunch. | 171 E. Bay St. | 843/722–9200 | $15–$25 | AE, DC, MC, V.

★ **Gaulart and Maliclet Cafe.** French. This casual, chic eatery is known for its changing specialties, such as fondue, seafood Normandy, bouillabaisse, and Indian curry. It also serves fresh soups, inventive salads, croque monsieur sandwiches—French grilled cheese and ham, chicken sesame, and, of course, escargots. | 98 Broad St. | 843/577–9797 | Closed Sun. No supper Mon. | $7–$15 | AE, D, DC, MC, V.

MODERATE

Barbadoes Room. Continental. Palm trees fill this elegant and formal dining room in the Mills House Hotel, where a pianist often accompanies your meal. Buffet breakfast. Sunday brunch. | 115 Meeting St. | 843/577–2400 | Reservations essential | $13–$19 | AE, D, DC, MC, V.

Fulton Five. Italian. Olive-oil colored walls and muted gold touches decorate this 45-seat, candle-lit spot where osso bucco and antipasta spiletto—mozzarella and proscuitto rolled around romaine and grilled—highlight the menu. | 5 Fulton St. | 843/853–5555 | Closed late Aug.–first week Sept. and Sun. No lunch | $17–$29 | AE, DC, MC, V.

Garibaldi's. Seafood. Hard pine floors, exposed beams, and fireplaces create an intimate, romantic dining space, where the crispy flounder has been a house specialty for 23 years. | 49 S. Market St. | 843/723–7153 | Reservations recommended | No lunch | $15–$20 | AE, MC, V.

Hominy Grill. Southern. This restaurant, a few blocks off the beaten path from the historic district, serves fish, crab cakes, fried green tomato salad, shrimp and grits, and skillet fried chicken. You can eat inside in what used to be a barbershop or outside in the garden. | 207 Rutledge Ave. | 843/937–0930 | Breakfast also available. No supper Sun. | $9–$17 | MC, V.

J. Bistro. Southern. Steel cutouts decorate the walls and lighting stays low on both dining levels. You can sit in the booths and dine on dishes such as sautéed black grouper and garlic whipped potatoes with crabmeat in a champagne cream sauce. The restaurant is known for its soufflés served Fridays and Saturdays. Sunday brunch. | 819 Coleman Blvd. | 843/971–7778 | Closed Mon. No lunch | $10–$20 | AE, MC, V.

Pinckney Café and Expresso. American. You can enjoy superfresh soups, pastas, and seafood dishes prepared in Lowcountry style inside this casual, artsy Charleston house or outside on the porch. All entrées come with quality salads; a half order of pasta is a great deal, as

ROYAL RICE

The Lowcountry is rice country and, although the crop has not been commercially produced here since the 1920s, the taste for the small grain is deeply ingrained in South Carolinians. In his cookbook, *Hoppin' John's Lowcountry Cooking,* local culinary historian John Martin Taylor quotes another cookbook author, Verta Grosvenor: "I was 16 years old before I knew that everyone didn't eat rice everyday. Us being geechees, we had rice everyday. When you said what you were eating for dinner, you always assumed that rice was there."

The Carolina Rice Kitchen contains more than 300 historical receipts for rice: red rice, Hoppin' John, rice soups, rice casseroles, rice sausages, rice pâtés, rice pilaus (usually pronounced "puhr-LO" and consisting of rice cooked in a broth until the liquid is absorbed and the rice dry), and rice breads and cakes. There is even such a thing as rice pie, its shell made from twice-cooked rice. And, of course, all good hosts serve their rice with a rice spoon, after which they sleep in a rice bed.

A local citizen, Dr. Henry Woodward, is said to have obtained the first rice seeds around 1685 when a ship sailing from Madagascar was temporarily stranded in Charleston's port. Thanks to the knowledge of West African slaves, whose own native rice lands resembled those of the Lowcountry, by 1700 rice was established as a major crop in the state. The West Africans brought vast information not only to the fields but also to kitchens and tables: "Africans brought the secret of cooking rice with them," says historian Karen Hess in *The Carolina Rice Kitchen.*

As early as 1690, growers were producing rice in large quantities and petitioning the British government to allow them to pay their taxes with the grains. At its height in the mid-19th century, rice was the number one crop in the region, with more than 75,000 acres of Lowcountry land producing the grain. Carolina Gold (so named because of the golden hue of the ripe grain in the field) made up 3½% of the nation's total crop of 5 million bushels and was exported to Europe and Asia. Growing Carolina Gold became so profitable that even physicians and attorneys left their professions to become rice planters.

The last crop of commercial rice in South Carolina was harvested in the 1920s. The end of slavery had shrunk the labor pool, but it was only a matter of time before new farming tools, developed in the late 1800s, would make growing rice easier in the drier western United States than in the boggy swamps of South Carolina. In 1988, however, Richard and Patricia Shulze harvested the first successful crop of Carolina Gold in half a century at their plantation near Savannah, after convincing the U.S. Department of Agriculture to dig into its seed bank and find a few of the grains that had been stored there for 60 years. You can usually find bags of Carolina Gold at Hoppin' John's Cookbook store in Charleston.

is the black bean burrito. Sunday and Monday brunch. | 18 Pinckney St. | 843/577–0961 | No supper Sun. | $10–$18 | D, MC, V.

Poogan's Porch. Southern. This old house has two separate dining rooms in which to enjoy Southern classics like chips and grits. You can also eat outside on the porch. Sunday brunch. | 72 Queen St. | 843/577–2337 | $13–20 | AE, MC, V.

Saracen. Mediterranean. The 35-ft ceilings with sky lights make this restaurant unusually airy, complementing the Moroccan architecture. You can try honey-and-sesame–encrusted Chilean sea bass served over roasted beet couscous. There's jazz on Fridays and Saturdays. Kids' menu. | 141 E. Bay St. | 843/723–6242 | fax 843/723–0530 | Closed Sun.– Mon. No lunch | $17–$22 | AE, DC, MC, V.

Sermet's. Mediterranean. The chef is also an artist whose colorful and bold work decorates the walls of this lively eatery. It's known for great appetizers; entrées include seafood, flavorful pastas, and lavender-and-honey–scented pork. | 276 King St. | 843/853–7775 | $10–$17 | AE, MC, V.

Slightly North of Broad. Contemporary. Several seats look directly into the exposed kitchen at this high-ceiling haunt with brick and stucco walls. You can get many of the entrées as appetizers. Kids' menu. | 192 E. Bay St. | 843/723–3424 | No lunch weekends | $12–$25 | AE, D, DC, MC, V.

Slightly Up the Creek. Eclectic. The dining room overlooking Shem Creek serves sautéed quail-filled sausages, Thai noodles with shrimp or pork, and Southern grilled vegetables. There's also an 8-ft deck on the water and an outdoor gazebo bar. Kids' menu. | 130 Mill St., Mt. Pleasant | 843/884–5005 | fax 843/856–9828 | No lunch | $17–$22 | AE, D, DC, MC, V.

EXPENSIVE

Anson. Southern. Wrought iron, plantation home doors, pale yellow shades, subtle lighting, and cozy booths create an elegant, romantic dining room. Dishes include Lowcountry barbecue grouper. | 12 Anson St. | 843/577–0551 | $17–$28 | AE, D, DC, MC, V.

Beaumont's Cafe. French. Frame paintings decorate this salon-like dining room, where you can dine on grilled lamb chop baked in chartreuse with a herb jus reduction and seasonal vegetables. | 12 Cumberland St. | 843/577–5500 | $16–$30 | AE, D, DC, MC, V.

Carolina's. Southern. Terra-cotta tiles, 1920s French posters, and a black-and-white motif create a bistro-like atmosphere at this lively restaurant. Dishes include fried calamari, almond-crusted grouper stuffed with crabmeat in lemon-butter sauce, and pasta with crawfish and tasso (spiced ham) in cream sauce. | 10 Exchange St. | 843/724–3800 | Reservations recommended | No lunch | $15–$30 | AE, D, DC, MC, V.

Charleston Grill. Contemporary. Rich mahogany accentuates this intimate dining room serving Lowcountry cuisine with a slight French inflection, where nightly jazz accompanies your meal. | 224 King St. | 843/577–4522 | Reservations essential | No lunch | $23–$29 | AE, D, DC, MC, V.

Louis's. Southern. Louis Osteen's fans have followed him from his former restaurant at Charleston Place to this new spot just across the street, which has a light, contemporary, almost Japanese vibe. It still serves the New South cuisine for which the chef is famous, including she-crab soup, crab and lobster cakes, roasted Chilean sea bass, roast duck, and lamb medallions. You can also sit at the sleek bar and order items such as tuna burgers from the inventive menu. | 200 Meeting St. | 843/853–2550 | No lunch | $14–$32 | AE, D, DC, MC, V.

★ **Magnolias.** Southern. Artwork by Rod Gobel and white tablecloths decorate what has become a local favorite and therefore a tourist attraction as well. Dishes include the Down South egg rolls (chicken, tasso, and collard greens) served with a trio of sauces, and shellfish over grits. | 185 E. Bay St. | 843/577–7771 | $15–$25 | AE, DC, MC, V.

McCrady's. Contemporary. Exposed brick walls and antique mirrors in the elegant dining room complement this lovely old Colonial building, a favorite of local businesspeople and tourists. The restaurant gets its Chilean sea bass fresh, not frozen, the only one to do so in Charleston. | 2 Unity Alley | 843/577-0025 | Reservations recommended | No lunch | $17-$29 | AE, MC, V.

★ **Peninsula Grill.** Contemporary. Portraits hang on the velvet walls of this restaurant styled after the jazz clubs of the 1930s and '40s. You may choose to sit outside among the palmettos and gas lanterns, where candles and white linen decorate the tables. The intricate dishes include roasted and sliced Muscovy duck breast and savoy cabbage, and wild mushroom grits with Lowcountry oyster stew. Kids' menu. | 112 N. Market St. | 843/723-0700 | No lunch | $19-30 | AE, D, MC, V.

82 Queen. Southern. You can eat Lowcountry cuisine such as barbecue shrimp and grits in the elegant dining room or the romantic courtyard. | 82 Queen St. | 843/723-7591 | $18-$23 | AE, DC, MC, V.

VERY EXPENSIVE

★ **Dining Room at Woodlands.** Contemporary. Chef Ken Vedrinski has created a four-course menu that includes Angus beef in a Barolo wine reduction with celery-root home fries, soft-shell crab with mushrooms, lemongrass, and ginger, and Asian spiced whole Maine lobster. There's also a more expensive chef's tasting menu, an excellent wine list, and a pianist to accompany your meal. | 125 Parsons Rd. | 843/875-2600 | Jacket required | Breakfast also available | Entrés $45-$60. Prix fixe menu $89, $120 | AE, D, DC, MC, V.

Robert's of Charleston. Southern. Four rich, generously portioned courses come with fine wines, impeccable service, and the best of Broadway tunes in a warm, intimate dining room. You can try scallop mousse with lobster sauce, duckling with grilled vegetables, or the roast tenderloin with bordelaise sauce. | 182 E. Bay St. | 843/577-7565 or 800/977-4565 | www.robertsofcharleston.com | Reservations essential | $75 prix fixe | Tue.-Sat. 7:30 only | MC, V.

Lodging

INEXPENSIVE

Ashley Inn. Alexander Black, an inventor of rice and cotton processing equipment, built this house in 1832 on the edge of the historic district. The property changed hands several times after that, and one of the more recent owners converted the complex into three apartments: two in the main house and one in the former slave quarters. Bud and Sally Allen bought the property in 1992 and restored the original plaster medallions, crown moldings, and beautiful heart pine floors to their original state. They also paved the drive and planted a new garden with brick walks, a fish pond and a fountain. Four poster, pencil post, or canopied rice beds now furnish the rooms, which are also filled with antiques. Complimentary breakfast. Cable TV. Bicycles. Business services. Free parking. No kids under 10. No smoking. | 201 Ashley Ave. | 843/723-1848 | fax 843/579-9080 | www.charleston-sc-inns.com | 6 rooms, 1 suite | $110-$155, $180 suite | AE, D, MC, V.

Barksdale House. George Barksdale, a wealthy Charleston planter and former member of the South Carolina House of Representatives, built this house in 1778 to serve as the family residence when they weren't at Youghall Plantation in the country. In 1817, George's nephew and then owner Thomas sold the town house, which passed through numerous hands until 1985, when Robert and Suzanne Chestnut bought it, meticulously restored it, and turned it into one of Charleston's most elegant accommodations. Complimentary Continental breakfast. Cable TV. Business services. Free Parking. No kids under 10. | 27 George St. | 843/577-4800 | fax 843/853-0482 | 14 rooms | $90-$95 | MC, V.

Best Western Charleston International Airport Inn. A long driveway wraps around this elegant four-story chain hotel 12 mi from downtown. The simple, modern rooms are well maintained. Restaurant, bar, complimentary breakfast buffet. Microwaves, room service. Cable

TV. 2 pools (1 indoor). Hot tub. Exercise equipment. Video games. Business services, airport shuttle, free parking. | 7401 Northwoods Blvd. | 843/572–2200 | fax 843/863–8316 | www.best-western.com | 197 rooms | $99 | AE, D, DC, MC, V.

Best Western King Charles Inn. The modern architecture and cement building stand out a little in the historic district, but this chain hotel is warm and cozy nonetheless. Restaurant. Cable TV. Pool. Laundry service. Business services, free parking. | 237 Meeting St. | 843/723–7451 | fax 843/723–2041 | www.bestwestern.com | 93 rooms | $129–$189 | AE, D, DC, MC, V.

Days Inn–Airport. This two-story chain hotel is ½ mi the from Charleston Coliseum and about 10 mi from beaches. Restaurant. Some refrigerators. Cable TV. Pool. Playground. Laundry facilities. Business services. Free Parking. Some pets allowed (fee). | 2998 W. Montague Ave., North Charleston | 843/747–4101 or 800/544–8313 | fax 843/566–0378 | 147 rooms | $37–$89 | AE, D, DC, MC, V.

1837 B&B and Tearoom. Romantic canopy beds furnish the rooms at this 1837 home and carriage house near the College of Charleston. While not as fancy as some B&Bs in town, this inn is long on hospitality. Complimentary breakfast. Free parking. | 126 Wentworth St. | 843/723–7166 | fax 843/722–7179 | www.1837bb.com | 9 rooms | $69–$149 | AE, MC, V.

Elliott House Inn. Since its construction in 1861, this inn has always been used for lodging. Canopy beds and other antebellum decor furnishes the rooms, and guests can snack on afternoon wine and cheese while reading their complimentary newspapers. Complimentary Continental breakfast. TV, room phones. Outdoor hot tub. Bicycles. Free parking. No pets. No smoking. | 78 Queen St. | 843/723–1855 | fax 843/722–1567 | www.elliotthouse-inn.com | 24 rooms | $94–$160 | AE, D, MC, V.

Guilds Inn. White picket fences surround this inn built in the mid-1800s in Colonial revival style in the historic district of Mt. Pleasant. Beige and green shutters complement the white exterior, and trees shade the building. Complimentary Continental breakfast. Cable TV, in-room VCRs. Free parking. No kids under 10. | 101 Pitt St., Mount Pleasant | 843/881–0510 or 800/331–0510 | fax 843/884–5020 | www.guildinn.com | 6 rooms | $110–$175 | AE, DC, MC, V.

★ **Hampton Inn–Historic District.** A courtyard garden, hardwood floors and a fireplace in the lobby make this inn a cut above the usual chain hotel (which is reflected in the price). Complimentary Continental breakfast, room service. In-room data ports, some refrigerators. Cable TV. Pool. Business services, parking (fee). | 345 Meeting St. | 843/723–4000 | fax 843/722–3725 | www.hamptoninn.com | 171 rooms | $109–$189 | AE, D, DC, MC, V.

Hampton Inn–Riverview. Some rooms in this five-floor cement high-rise overlook the pool and small gardens. The hotel is next to the Ripley Light Marina, about 2 mi from the Charleston Museum, the Citadel, and downtown Charleston. 12 mi northwest of Charleston International Airport. Complimentary Continental breakfast. In-room data ports. Cable TV. Pool. Laundry facilities. Business services, parking (fee). Some pets allowed. | 11 Ashley Pointe Dr. | 843/556–5200 | fax 843/571–5499 | 175 rooms | $89–$109 | AE, D, DC, MC, V.

Holiday Inn–Riverview. This 14-story circular high-rise on the banks of the Ashley River overlooks historic downtown. It's accessible from I–95 and I–26 via Hwy. 17N. Restaurant, bar, room service. In-room data ports. Cable TV. Pool. Exercise equipment. Laundry facilities. Business services, free parking. | 301 Savannah Hwy. (U.S. 17) | 843/556–7100 | fax 843/556–6176 | www.holiday-inn.com | 181 rooms | $101–$139 | AE, D, DC, MC, V.

King George IV B&B. This "Charleston Historic House," named the Peter Freneau House after the prominent Charleston journalist and newspaper owner, is in the heart of the historic district. Three levels of lovely porches adorn the four stories, and 10-ft ceilings and 7-ft windows distinguish the rooms, all of which have decorative fireplaces, 8-ft oak doors and wide-planked hardwood floors. Complimentary Continental breakfast. Refrigerators. Free Parking. No smoking. | 32 George St. | 843/723–9339 or 888/723–1667 | fax 843/723–

7749 | www.kinggeorgeiv.com | 6 rooms, 4 suites (4 with shower only, 4 with full bath, 2 with shared bath) | $89–$175 | MC, V.

Knights Inn Motel. Two miles from the Coliseum Convention Center, this chain hotel in North Charleston is also 2 mi from the airport. You enter rooms off an interior corridor. Complimentary Continental breakfast. Some kitchenettes, some refrigerators. Cable TV. 2 pools. Laundry facilities. Business services, airport shuttle, free parking. | 2355 Aviation Ave., North Charleston | 843/744–4900 | fax 843/745–0668 | www.knightsinn.com | 293 rooms | $35–$55 | AE, D, DC, MC, V.

La Quinta Inn Charleston. Red tile roofing and teal trim on a white stucco building are the trademark style of this budget hotel. Some rooms have walk-on porches. Picnic area, complimentary Continental breakfast, room service. In-room data ports, refrigerators. Cable TV. Pool. Business services, free parking. Some pets allowed. | 2499 La Quinta La., North Charleston | 843/797–8181 | fax 843/569–1608 | www.laquinta.com | 122 rooms, 2 suites | $59–$69, $89 suites | AE, D, DC, MC, V.

Maison Du Pré. Frenchman Benjamin Du Pré built this property in 1804. Three restored Charleston "single houses" and two carriage houses comprise the inn, which is in Charleston's historic Ansonborough district, next to the Gaillard Auditorium. Period pieces and antiques furnish the 15 deluxe guest rooms, including the executive suite and honeymoon suite. Complimentary Continental breakfast. Kitchenettes. Cable TV. Free parking. | 317 E. Bay St. | 843/723–8691 or 800/844–INNS (4667) | fax 843/723–3722 | www.maisondupre.com | 13 rooms, 2 suites | $98–$175, suites $185–$215 | D, MC, V.

Middleton Inn. Next to America's oldest landscaped gardens, this inn is secluded among tall pines and oaks on a bluff overlooking the Ashley River. Hand-crafted furniture, cypress wall paneling, and a wood-burning fireplace decorate each of the 55 rooms, and floor-to-ceiling windows afford magnificent views of the surrounding woodlands. Restaurant. Refrigerators. Cable TV. Pool. Hiking, horseback riding. Boating, bicycles. Business services, free parking. No pets. | Ashley River Rd. (Rte. 61) | 843/556–0500 or 800/543–4774 | fax 843/556–0500 | www.middletoninn.com | 55 rooms | $119–$189 | AE, D, MC, V.

Quality Suites. This stucco and concrete chain hotel is on a frontage road along with a strip of hotels by I–26, 3 mi from the airport. Complimentary breakfast. In-room data ports, mini-bars, microwaves, refrigerators. Cable TV, in-room VCRs. Pool. Exercise equipment. Laundry facilities. Business services, airport shuttle, free parking. | 5225 N. Arco La. | 843/747–7300 | fax 843/747–6324 | www.hotelchoice.com | 168 suites | $99–$199 | AE, D, DC, MC, V.

Radisson Inn Airport. A covered awning greets you at this eight-floor brick high-rise 10 mi from downtown. Restaurant, bar (with entertainment), room service. In-room data ports. Cable TV. Pool. Hot tub, sauna. Business services, airport shuttle, free parking. | 5991 Rivers Ave. | 843/744–2501 | fax 843/744–2501 | www.radisson.com | 159 rooms | $119–$129 | AE, D, DC, MC, V.

Ramada Inn. Tall trees and greenery surround this limestone, Southern deco-style building off I–26 and I–526 in North Charleston. Restaurant, bar (with entertainment). In-room data ports, some refrigerators. Cable TV. Pool. Laundry service. Business services, airport shuttle, free parking. | 2934 W. Montague Ave. | 843/744–8281 | fax 843/744–6230 | www.charlestownmanagement.com | 155 rooms | $59–$89 | AE, D, DC, MC, V.

Red Roof Inn. This white stucco and stone building with triangular slanted roofs is convenient to restaurants and shopping, 12 mi from the Citadel, and 21 mi from Fort Sumter. You enter rooms on both floors from exterior corridors. Cable TV. Microwaves, refrigerators. Laundry facilities. Free parking. Some pets allowed. | 7480 Northwoods Blvd., North Charleston | 843/572–9100 or 800/RED–ROOF (733–7663) | fax 843/572–0061 | 109 rooms | $57 | AE, D, DC, MC, V.

Red Roof Inn. This particular branch of the budget chain sits at the foot of Cooper River Bridge, 5 mi from the historic district and 9 mi from the Isle of Palms. Rooms on two floors have exterior entrances. Cable TV. Pool. Free parking. Some pets allowed. | 301 Johnnie Dodds Blvd., Mt. Pleasant | 843/884–1411 or 800/RED–ROOF (733–7663) | fax 843/971–0726 | 124 rooms | $65–$90 | AE, D, DC, MC, V.

Shem Creek Inn. You can eat breakfast on the pool deck at this hotel on Shem Creek, 4 mi from the historic district downtown and near restaurants. Complimentary Continental breakfast. Microwaves, refrigerators. Cable TV. Pool. Exercise facilities. Business services, free parking. | 1401 Shrimp Boat La., Mt. Pleasant | 843/881–1000 or 800/523–4951 | fax 843/849–6969 | www.charlestownmanagement.com | 50 rooms | $89–$165 | AE, D, DC, MC, V.

Sheraton North Charleston. An elegant, warm lobby is the first thing that greets you at this typical eight-floor chain hotel off I–26, 5 mi from the airport, and 8 mi from downtown. Restaurant, bar (with entertainment). In-room data ports. Cable TV. Indoor-outdoor pool. Hot tub. Exercise equipment. Business services, airport shuttle, free parking. | 4770 Goer Dr., North Charleston | 843/747–1900 or 888/747–1700 | fax 843/744–6108 | hilton@charleston.net | www.charleston.net/com/hilton | 295 rooms 296 rooms | $99–$149 | AE, D, DC, MC, V.

MODERATE

Anchorage Inn. Ensconced within the walls of a 19th-century harbor-side warehouse, this inn sits to the east of where the harbor's active shipping industry developed. It follows the decor of the 17th-century English buildings with which Charleston's early inhabitants were familiar. Complimentary Continental breakfast. Cable TV. Library. Business services, parking (fee). | 26 Vendue Range | 843/723–8300 or 800/421–2952 | fax 843/723–9543 | www.anchoragencharleston.com | 17 rooms, 2 suites | $145–$185, $185–$249 suites | AE, MC, V.

Ansonborough Inn. Period reproductions and a rooftop terrace distinguish this spacious, all-suite inn, formerly a warehouse. Complimentary Continental breakfast. Business services. | 21 Hasell St. | 843/723–1655 or 800/522–2073 | fax 843/577–6888 | 37 suites | $139–$199 | AE, MC, V.

Battery Carriage House. Facing Charleston harbor, this structure, filled with period-style pieces, is set in the gardens of the Stevens–Lathers 1843 antebellum mansion, in a residential neighborhood. Shops and restaurants are less than a mile away. Complimentary Continental breakfast. Some in-room hot tubs. Cable TV, room phones. No pets. No kids under 12. No smoking. | 20 South Battery | 800/775–5575 or 843/727–3100 | fax 843/727–3130 | www.charleston-inns.com | 11 rooms | $159–$269 | AE, D, MC, V.

Cannonboro Inn. Antique four-poster and canopied beds decorate this 1853 historic house. You can have your breakfast and afternoon tea on the piazza overlooking a low country garden and fountain. Complimentary breakfast. Cable TV. Bicycles. Business services, free parking. No kids under 10. No smoking. | 184 Ashley Ave. | 843/723–8572 or 800/235–8039 | fax 843/723–8007 | www.charleston-sc-inns.com | 6 rooms (4 with shower only) | $79–$210 | AE, D, MC, V.

Church Street Inn. Antique reproductions furnish this inn in a historic market area. Some suites overlook the courtyard. Bar. Kitchenettes. Cable TV. Business services, free parking. | 177 Church St. | 843/722–3420 or 800/552–3777 | fax 843/853–7306 | www.church-streetinn.com | 31 suites | $149–$199 | AE, MC, V.

Doubletree Guest Suites Historic Charleston. Three lush gardens surround this deluxe hotel across from the City Market. Canopied beds and 18th-century reproductions decorate the spacious suites. Bar. In-room data ports, some kitchenettes, some minibars, microwaves. Cable TV, in-room VCRs. Exercise equipment. Laundry facilities. Business services, free parking. | 181 Church St. | 843/577–2644 | fax 843/577–2697 | doubletree@awod.com | www.doubletree.com | 182 rooms | $159–$259 | AE, D, DC, MC, V.

Hayne House. In the historic area south of Broad Street near the Battery, this 18th-century inn consists of the original home plus the old kitchen and slave quarters. Antiques, books, a piano, and Charleston art furnish the house. Complimentary breakfast. Free parking. | 30 King St. | 843/577-2633 | fax 843/577-5906 | www.haynehouse.com | 6 rooms | $165–$270 | MC, V.

Jasmine House Inn. This inn comprises a carriage house with four rooms and an 1840s Greek Revival mansion with 6 rooms, 14-ft ceilings, Italian marble baths, and hardwood floors. Two rooms also have working fireplaces. Complimentary Continental breakfast. In-room data ports, some in-room hot tubs. Cable TV, room phones. Outdoor hot tub. No pets. No kids under 12. Free parking. No smoking. | 64 Hasell St. | 800/845-7639 or 843/577-5900 | fax 843/577-0378 | www.jasminehouseinn.com | 10 rooms | $125–$285 | AE, D, DC, MC, V.

Lodge Alley. This inn takes its name from the adjoining 10-ft wide alley, Lodge Alley. Paved in Belgian blocks, the alley was created in 1773 by adjacent land owners to allow access from their homes on State Street to their ships and docks one block away on East Bay Street. The French Huguenots once had warehouses and homes in this area, close to Charleston's wharves. The Lodge Alley Inn opened in 1983, incorporating more than 15 separate warehouse buildings, thereby allowing many of the Inn's rooms to retain their original 18th-century pine floors and brick walls. Bar (with entertainment), dining room, complimentary Continental breakfast, room service. Many kitchenettes, minibars, refrigerators. Cable TV. Business services, parking (fee). | 195 E. Bay St. | 843/722-1611, 800/845-1004 (except South Carolina), or 800/821-2791 (in South Carolina) | fax 843/722-1611 | www.lodgealleyinn.com | 95 rooms | $139–$375 | AE, MC, V.

Meeting Street Inn. High ceilings, wood floors, and four-poster rice beds mark the spacious rooms at this salmon-color former tavern built in 1874 across from the City Market in the historic district. Bar, complimentary Continental breakfast. Some in-room hot tubs. Cable TV. Business services, parking (fee). | 173 Meeting St. | 843/723-1882 or 800/842-8022 | fax 843/577-0851 | www.aesir.com/meetingstreet/ | 56 rooms | $125–$199 | AE, D, DC, MC, V.

Phoebe Pember House B&B. Spectacular architectural details and porches adorn this 200-yr-old Federal-style B&B. Antiques furnish the individually decorated rooms. Long-term stays are available. Complimentary Continental breakfast. Cable TV. Beauty salon, massage. Business services. | 26 Society St. | 843/722-4186 | fax 843/720-0557 | info@phoebepemberhouse.com | www.phoebepemberhouse.com | 4 rooms, 1 carriage house | $125–$185 | AE, MC, V.

Rutledge Victorian Guesthouse. Rare decorative Italianate details and beautiful ceiling moldings decorate this house, originally the Brodie–Pinkussohn House and built in 1880. All rooms have mahogany and oak fireplaces, 12-ft ceilings with beautiful plaster moldings, hardwood floors, 10-ft doors and windows, and antiques. You can sit in rocking chairs out on the 120-ft round porch. Complimentary Continental breakfast. Some refrigerators. Bicycles. Free parking. No smoking. | 114 Rutledge Ave. | 843/722-7551 or 888/722-7553 | fax 843/727-0065 | www.bbonline.com/sc/rutledge | 10 rooms (2 with shared bath), 1 cottage | $89–$199, $399 cottage | MC, V.

Seabrook Island Resort. Set on a private barrier island 22 mi south of historic Charleston are a scattering of 175 fully equipped one- to three-bedroom cottages, some of which have fireplaces. Trees and marshes surround the resort, which has a private beach and sunset cruises. *Golf Digest* has recognized both golf courses here as some of the finest in America. Dining room, bar. Kitchenettes, microwaves, refrigerators. Cable TV. 7 pools, wading pool. Driving range, two 18-hole golf courses, putting green, 13 tennis courts. Gym, horseback riding. Boating, fishing, bicycles. Kids' programs (4–10). Business services, free parking. | 1002 Landfall Way, Seabrook Island | 843/768-1000 or 800/845-2475 | fax 843/768-4922 | www.seabrookresort.com | 170 cottages and houses | $165–$235 one–bedroom, $200–$310 two–bedrooms, $225–$475 3–bedrooms | AE, D, MC, V.

27 State Street B&B. An interior courtyard, central verandah, and marble stairway reflect this early 19th-century home's European influence. Two blocks from the waterfront, it is also within the old walled city, in close proximity to shops, dining, and tourist attractions. Rooms come with complimentary coffee, tea, soft drinks, a fresh basket of fruit, and fresh flowers, as well as a complimentary newspaper. In-room data ports, kitchenettes. Bicycles. Parking (fee). No pets. No smoking. | 27 State St. | 843/722–4243 | fax 843/722–6030 | www.charleston-bb.com | 5 rooms | $145–$185 | No credit cards.

Two Meeting Street Inn. Oriental rugs, family antiques, and carved oak paneling decorate the rooms in this Victorian home built in the 1890s and situated on the battery. Its two Tiffany windows look out onto the water. Complimentary Continental breakfast. Cable TV. No kids under 12. No pets. Free parking. No smoking. | 2 Meeting St. | 843/723–7322 | www.twomeetingstreet.com | 9 rooms | $165–$295 | Closed Christmas week | No credit cards.

Vendue Inn B&B. Several warehouses in the French Quarter were renovated over the years to become this elegant, friendly inn near the Waterfront Park and harbor. Four-poster beds, antiques, Oriental rugs, and art furnish the rooms, and fireplaces and sleigh beds decorate the suites. Restaurant, bar, complimentary breakfast. In-room data ports. Cable TV. Hot tub. Exercise equipment. Library. Business services, free parking. | 19 Vendue Range | 843/577–7970, 800/845–7900 (except SC), or 800/922–7900 (in SC) | fax 843/577–2913 | www.bedandbreakfast.com | 22 rooms, 23 suites | $120–$295 | AE, D, DC, MC, V.

EXPENSIVE

Embassy Suites Historic Charleston. The courtyard of the Old Citadel military school (1822) has been transformed into a skylit atrium with stone floors, palm trees, and a fountain. Some of the guest rooms contain the original gun ports, a reminder that this hotel was originally a fortification. Bar, complimentary breakfast. In-room data ports, minibars, microwaves, refrigerators, some in-room hot tubs. Cable TV. Pool. Exercise equipment. Laundry facilities. Business services, parking (fee). | 337 Meeting St. | 843/723–6900 or 800/362–2779 | fax 843/723–6938 | www.embassy-suites.com | 153 suites | $169–$269 | AE, D, DC, MC, V.

Fulton Lane Inn. The Confederate blockade runner John Rugheimer built this 1890s inn, where the charm and spirit of the Old South live on. Large whirlpool baths and luxurious canopied beds draped with handstrung netting come with many rooms; cathedral ceilings and fireplaces distinguish others. The soaring windows, complemented by shutters, look out onto Charleston's historic skyline, while the natural textures and soft pastels that decorate the inn invite you to indulge in the simple pleasures of a more gracious time. In-room data ports, refrigerators, some in-room hot tubs. Cable TV. Business services, parking (fee). | 202 King St. | 843/720–2600 or 800/720–2688 | fax 843/720–2940 | www.charminginns.com | 21 rooms, 6 suites | $195, $260–$285 suites | MC, V.

Governor's House Inn. Piazzas run the length of this 1760 Georgian home with Victorian touches, now a historic landmark. The home belonged to Edward Rutledge, the youngest signer of the Declaration of Independence and Governor of South Carolina. You can stay in the main part of the house or in one of the suites in the original kitchen. Every afternoon, tea and sherry are served, along with homebaked foods. Complimentary Continental breakfast. In-room data ports, minibars, refrigerators. Cable TV, room phones. No pets. No kids under 13. No smoking. Free parking. | 117 Broad St. | 843/720–2070 | fax 843/805–6549 | www.governorshouse.com | 7 rooms and 2 suites | $165–$330 | Closed Christmas week | No credit cards.

Indigo. The 1850s Greek Revival Jasmine House Inn and carriage house comprise this hotel nestled in the heart of Charleston's historic district. Period correct fabrics, antique reproductions, and queen-size beds furnish the rooms, and plants fill the lush courtyard. Complimentary Continental breakfast. In-room data ports. Cable TV. Business services, free parking. Some pets allowed (fee). | 1 Maiden La. | 843/577–5900 or 800/845–7639 | fax 843/577–0378 | indigoinn@awod.com | www.aesir.com/indigoinn | 40 rooms | $189–$225 | AE, D, DC, MC, V.

★ **John Rutledge House.** The Revolutionary-era main house—built by one of the framers of the U.S. Constitution—and two carriage houses (each with four rooms) comprise this luxurious 1763 inn. High ceilings make the guest rooms airy, while wood floors, antique furnishings, fireplaces, and four-poster beds make them appealing. Complimentary Continental breakfast. In-room data ports, refrigerators. Cable TV. Business services, free parking. | 116 Broad St. | 843/723–7999 or 800/476–9741 | fax 843/720–2615 | www.charminginns.com | 19 rooms, 3 suites | $135–$325 | AE, D, DC, MC, V.

Kings Courtyard Inn. Built in 1853, Kings Courtyard Inn is one of the largest and most historic on King Street, which used to be the main "trail" leading into old Charles Towne. Architect Francis D. Lee designed this three-story antebellum structure in Greek revival style, with unusual Egyptian detail. Oversize beds furnish all rooms, many of which overlook the courtyard or rear garden. Two period suites have four poster canopied beds and living rooms with original architectural features. Complimentary Continental breakfast. In-room data ports, refrigerators. Cable TV. Hot tub. Business services, parking (fee). | 198 King St. | 843/723–7000 or 800/845–6119 | fax 843/720–2608 | www.charminginns.com | 37 rooms, 4 suites | $185–$205, $260 | AE, D, DC, MC, V.

Mills House Hotel. Dark green canopied porches on the second floor distinguish this seven-story hotel which originally opened in the 18th-century. Rooms are somewhat small, but the hotel has a fine restaurant, the Barbadoes Room Restaurant, bar. In-room data ports. Cable TV. Pool. Business services, parking (fee). | 115 Meeting St. | 843/577–2400 or 800/874–9600 | fax 843/722–2112 | www.millshouse.com | 214 rooms | $199–$600 | AE, D, DC, MC, V.

Planters Inn. Tasteful antiques and four-poster beds decorate the high-ceilinged rooms. The new wing overlooks a garden courtyard, and the Peninsula Grill makes for a classy resident restaurant. Restaurant, bar, complimentary Continental breakfast. In-room data ports. Cable TV. Business services, parking (fee). | 112 N. Market St. | 843/722–2345 or 800/845–7082 | fax 843/577–2125 | plantersinn@charleston.net | www.plantersinn.com | 62 rooms, 21 suites | $200–$225, suites $225—$600 | AE, D, DC, MC, V.

Victoria House. This hotel is one of Charleston's rare Victorian-era structures, built in the Romanesque style popular in the 1880s. Armoires, wicker chairs, large windows, and Victorian furniture decorate rooms, some of which have working fireplaces. Complimentary Continental breakfast. In-room data ports, refrigerators, in-room hot tubs. Cable TV. Business services, parking (fee). | 208 King St. | 843/720–2944 or 800/933–5464 | fax 843/720–2930 | www.charminginns.com | 18 rooms, 4 suites | $215, suites $225 | D, DC, MC, V.

VERY EXPENSIVE

★ **Charleston Place.** Narrow cobblestone streets, antiques stores, art galleries, and spectacular antebellum homes surround one of the city's most luxurious hotels. You can marvel at the grand double staircase and soaring windows and eat at the fine Charleston Grill inside the hotel. Soft linen covers the beds, and soaring windows, antique reproductions, and chandeliers decorate the rooms. Restaurants, bar (with entertainment), room service. In-room data ports. Cable TV. Indoor-outdoor pool. Hot tub, massage. Gym. Summer children's programs (2–12). Business services, parking (fee). | 305 Meeting St. | 843/722–4900 or 800/611–5545 | fax 843/722–0728 | charleston-place.com | 440 rooms | $360 | AE, D, DC, MC, V.

Wentworth Mansion Inn. This spectacular brick mansion built in 1886 is a pristine example of America's Gilded Age. Tiffany glass, Second Empire antiques, grand chandeliers, and fine woodwork decorate the interior. Heavy velvet curtains dress the soaring windows, and many rooms have fireplaces. You can sit outside on the sun porches. Complimentary Continental breakfast. In-room data ports, some in-room hot tubs. Cable TV. Business services, free parking. | 149 Wentworth St. | 843/853–1886 or 888/466–1886 | fax 843/720–5290 | www.wentworthmansion.com | 21 rooms | $295–$695 | AE, D, DC, MC, V.

The Westin Francis Marion Hotel. Named for Revolutionary War hero Francis Marion, the "Swamp Fox," and built by local investors at a cost of $1.5 million from plans by noted New York architect W. L. Stoddard, this hotel opened in 1924 as the largest and grandest in the Carolinas. It now combines 1920s style and grace—high ceilings and decorative moldings—with 21st century comfort and convenience in the heart of historic Charleston on Marion Square, with scenic views of the harbor. Restaurant, bar. In-room data ports. Cable TV. Massage, spa. Exercise equipment. Business services, parking (fee). | 387 King St. | 843/722–0600 or 888/625–5144 | fax 843/723–4633 | www.westin.com | 312 rooms | $299, $159–$329 suites | AE, D, DC, MC, V.

Woodlands Resort and Inn. The warmth of the Old South and decor in the English tradition combine at this distinctive country-house hotel, surrounded by 42 acres of private woodland 30 mi northwest of Charleston. Six white columns and a porch greet you at the entrance, and you can amuse yourself playing tennis and croquet. This hotel is also the site of the fabulous Dining Room at Woodlands. Restaurant, bar, room service. In-room hot tubs. Cable TV, in-room VCRs (and movies). Pool. Massage, spa. Two tennis courts. Bicycles. Business services, free parking. No smoking. | 125 Parsons Rd., Summerville | 843/875–2600 or 800/774–9999 | fax 843/875–2603 | www.woodlandsinn.com | 20 rooms | $295–$350 | AE, D, DC, MC, V.

CHERAW

MAP 9, I2

(Nearby towns also listed: Bennettsville, Darlington, Hartsville)

The historic town of Cheraw was founded as a trading post in 1740, and later became a commercial and shipping center due to its location at the head of navigable water on the Great Pee Dee River. Its historic district has 50 antebellum mansions, gardens, and colonial buildings.

Information: **Cheraw Visitors Bureau** | 221 Market St., Cheraw, SC 29520 | 843/537–8425 | fax 843/537–5886.

Attractions

Carolina Sandhills National Wildlife Refuge. You can find one of the largest remaining populations of the threatened red-cockaded woodpecker at this 45,586-acre forest and preserve. There are two observation towers, a photography blind, hiking and biking trails,

KODAK'S TIPS FOR USING LIGHTING

Daylight
· Use the changing color of daylight to establish mood
· Use light direction to enhance subjects' properties
· Match light quality to specific subjects

Dramatic Lighting
· Anticipate dramatic lighting events
· Explore before and after storms

Sunrise, Sunset, and Afterglow
· Include a simple foreground
· Exclude the sun when setting your exposure
· After sunset, wait for the afterglow to color the sky

From *Kodak Guide to Shooting Great Travel Pictures* © 2000 by Fodor's Travel Publications

an auto tour route, and interpretive displays. | R.R. 2 | 843/335–8401 | Free | Weekdays dawn to dusk.

Cheraw Historic District. Cheraw's well-preserved 213-acre historic district holds the Town Green, part of the original 1768 plan. The district encompasses more than 50 antebellum public buildings and houses, as well as later structures, including the Market Hall, Town Hall, Lyceum Museum, and Inglis–McIver law office. You can stop by the Chamber of Commerce and Visitors Bureau for a key. | 221 Market St. | 843/537–7681 | Free | Daily 9–5.

Cheraw State Fish Hatchery. From this 7,300-acre warm-water fish hatchery come three million bass, bream, catfish, and other fish that supply lakes and farm ponds. The aquarium can give you close-up views. | Hwy. 1 | 843/537–7628 | Free | Daily 7:30–3.

Cheraw State Park. The state's oldest park (7,800 acres) features the rare red-cockaded woodpecker and lovely Lake Juniper, shaded by cypresses. You can camp or stay in cabins, play the championship 18-hole golf course, fish, rent boats, or swim in the lake. | 100 State Park Rd. | 843/537–2215 or 800/868–9630 | Free | Apr.–Oct., daily 6 AM–9 PM; Nov.–Mar., daily 7–7.

Old St. David's Episcopal Church. The last church built in South Carolina under King George III, this is one of Cheraw's oldest buildings. During the Revolutionary War the British used it as a hospital, and both Union and Confederate troops found the same use for it during the Civil War. The cemetery contains graves of all faiths. The Cheraw Visitors Bureau on Market Street has a key to the church. | 100 Church St. | 843/537–8425 or 843/537–7681 | Free | Weekdays 9–5, Weekends by appt.

ON THE CALENDAR
APR.: *Spring Festival.* Locals celebrate spring with entertainment, canoe races, trolley rides, and arts and crafts throughout downtown and in Riverside Park. | 803/537–8425.
JULY: *Independence Day Celebration.* Fireworks, music, and food at the Cheraw High School playing field celebrate American independence. | 843/537–8420.

Dining
Cole's Diner. Southern. You can indulge in home cooked specialties such as cornbread, biscuits, barbecue ribs, and chicken at this plain, informal restaurant. | 821 Kershaw St. | 843/537–6311 | Breakfast also served. Closed Sun. | $5.50 | No credit cards.

Quincy's Family Steak House. American. This cafeteria-style restaurant counts steak and shrimp among its specialties, served in a casual, comfortable, family-friendly setting. | 315 Second St. | 843/921–4306 | $5–$11 | AE, D, MC, V.

Lodging
Cheraw State Park. For instant access to hiking, canoeing, biking, and kayaking, you can stay in the fully furnished cabins in South Carolina's oldest and largest state park. There are also equestrian trails and golf. Kitchens, microwaves, refrigerators. Golf privileges. Hiking, horseback riding. Boating. Pets allowed. | 100 State Park Rd. | 800/868–9630 or 843/537–2215 | fax 843/537–1009 | 8 cabins | $65 for up to 4 people | D, DC, MC, V.

Days Inn. Although not particularly distinctive, this chain hotel is just 2 mi from golf courses and tennis courts and 1 mi from restaurants and shopping. Complimentary Continental breakfast. In-room data ports, some microwaves, refrigerators, some in-room hot tubs. Cable TV, room phones. Outdoor pool. Pets allowed (fee). | 820 Market St. | 800/329–7466 or 843/537–5554 | fax 843/537–4110 | www.daysinn.com | 55 rooms | $45–$55 | AE, D, DC, MC, V.

Spears Guest House. Antiques and reproductions furnish this wooden guest house built in 1940 in the historic district, across from the Public Library and near the South Carolina Cheraw State Park. One furnished corporate apartment is also available. Complimentary Continental breakfast. Cable TV. | 501 Kershaw St. | 843/537–7733 or 888/4–CHERAW (888/424–3729) | fax 843/537–0302 | 4 rooms | $60–$75 | AE, MC, V.

Inn Cheraw. A little balcony greets you at the entrance of this simple, affordable accommodation about two blocks from the downtown historic area and near restaurants and shops. Restaurant, complimentary Continental breakfast. Refrigerators. Cable TV, in-room VCRs. Free parking. Some pets allowed. | 321 Second St. | 843/537–2011 or 800/535–8709 | fax 843/537–0227 | 50 rooms | $40–$70 | AE, D, DC, MC, V.

314 Market Street B&B. This charming old Greek Revival home, built in 1906, has five porches and is convenient to the NASCAR races held in Darlington and Rockingham, 25 mi away. Complimentary Continental breakfast. Cable TV. | 314 Market St. | 843/537–5797 | 3 rooms | $65 | MC, V.

CHESTER

MAP 9, F2

(Nearby towns also listed: Rock Hill, York)

Named by settlers who came from Pennsylvania in 1755, the town of Chester has a historic downtown with an antebellum courthouse, Confederate monument, 19th-century cistern, and many original Victorian buildings, churches, and homes. You can do some great antiquing here.

Information: Chester County Chamber of Commerce | Box 489, 109 Gadsden St., Chester, SC 29706 | 803/581–4142 | fax 803/581–2431.

Attractions

Chester State Park. You can camp, picnic, fish, try out the archery range, and rent boats at this hilly woodland park 4 mi south of town on Highway 72. Nature trails and bridle paths cross the path. There's also a playground and a horse show ring. | 803/385–2680 | Free | Daily 9–6.

Carolina Vineyards. You can visit and tour the vineyards and sample wines at this winery. | 1623 Woods Rd. | 803/377–3049 | Free | Mon.–Sat. 11–6, and by appointment.

ON THE CALENDAR
MAY: *Lily Festival.* This festival at Landsford Canal State Park, 25 mi northeast of town off Hwy 21, celebrates the peak blooming of the rare rocky shoals spider lilies with local musicians, children's activities, and guided walks to the lilies. | 2051 Park Dr., Catawba | 803/789–5800.

Dining
The Front Porch. American. A number of travelers en route from Canada to Miami stop at this restored farmhouse in Richburg, right off I–77 at Exit 65, 12 mi east of Chester. Homemade barbecue, baked chicken, apple cobbler, and pecan pie are served in the private dining room and front porch; there's now an ice cream parlor as well. | 3072 Lancaster Hwy., Richburg | 803/789–5029 | $6–$12 | No credit cards.

Lodging
Executive Inn. With a fishing camp next to it, this two-building motel seems particularly suited to fishermen. There are two restaurants across the street. Complimentary Continental breakfast. In-room data ports, some kitchenettes, some in-room hot tubs. Cable TV, room phones. Outdoor pool. Pets allowed (fee). | 1632 J.A. Cochran Bypass | 803/581–2525 | fax 803/581–4171 | 45 rooms, 2 suites | $43–$75 | AE, D, MC, V.

CLEMSON

MAP 9, C2

(Nearby towns also listed: Anderson, Greenville, Pendleton)

Clemson University and its well-known football team rule "Tiger" country. During fall weekends, the population often swells to nearly 10 times its norm as the town plays host not only to football but also to the accompanying tailgate parties. The university sits on the former plantation of Thomas Greene Clemson, who willed the land to the state for the site of an agricultural college for boys. His plantation home, Fort Hill, is at the center of the campus. The Blue Ridge mountains form a scenic backdrop for Clemson and hint at what's on hand at the 10 state parks in bordering counties: an abundance of hiking trails, majestic waterfalls, and dramatic overlooks.

Information: **Clemson Chamber of Commerce** | 398 College Ave., Clemson, SC 29633 | 864/654–1200 | fax 864/654–5096.

Attractions

Clemson University. Approximately 16,800 undergraduate and graduate students attend this state university, founded by Thomas Green Clemson in 1889. The 1,400-acre main campus is near the shores of Lake Hartwell. The university began as a small agricultural, mechanical, and military college; that heritage remains—more than 17,000 acres of farm and woodland surrounding the campus are devoted to research and the school provides Agricultural Extension Service operations in every South Carolina county. Student guides conduct walking tours (contact the university's Visitors Center). | 110 Daniel Dr. | 864/656–4789 | www.clemson.edu | Free | Daily; Visitors Center open daily 8–4:30, Sat. 9–4:30, Sun. 1–4:30.

People take the pigskin seriously in this town; 80,000 orange-clad fans turn out to see the **Clemson Tigers** play during football season. The green hills around campus and the "Death Valley" football field are awash with cars and tailgaters during Saturday home games. | Death Valley Stadium, Clemson University campus | 864/656–4789 | Ticket prices vary | Call for schedule.

Right in the center of campus stands **Fort Hill,** a National Historic Landmark and the antebellum plantation home of John C. Calhoun. The house contains items that once belonged to Calhoun and his son-in-law Thomas Clemson. | Fort Hill St. | 864/656–2475 | Donations accepted | Mon.–Sat. 10–noon and 1–5, Sun. 2–5.

Hanover House, the house museum in the South Carolina Botanical Gardens, was built by French Huguenots in 1716 and was moved from the Lowcountry to this spot. | 101 Garden Trail | 864/656–2241 | Free | Weekends only: Sat., 10–noon and 1–5 PM; Sun., 2–5.

The **South Carolina Botanical Gardens** cover 256 acres with a variety of azaleas, camellias, hostas, daffodils, and wildflowers; an arboretum; a dwarf conifer collection; a Therapeutic Horticulture Garden built to accommodate wheelchairs; vegetable and herb gardens; and several historic buildings. There are nature trails and a nature-based sculpture program. | 102 Garden Trail | 864/656–3405 | www.clemson.edu/scbg | Free | Daily 8 AM–dusk.

At **Uniquely Clemson Agricultural Sales Center,** you can buy agricultural products made in Clemson, including Clemson Blue Cheese and Blue Cheese Dressing, ice cream, and other dairy treats. The chocolate milk shake is not to be missed! | Hendrix Student Center | 864/656–3242 or 864/656–3663 | Free | Mon.–Sat., 9–9; Sun., 1–9.

Keowee–Toxaway State Park. A Cherokee Interpretive Center traces the history and culture of the Cherokee Nation. The 100-acre park also has camping, a large lakefront cabin, RV sites, and hiking and picnic areas along Lake Keowee. | Rte. 11 | 864/868–2605 | Free | Daylight savings months: daily, 9–9; rest of year: Sat.–Thurs., 9–6; Fri., 9–8; Interpretive Center, Wed.–Sun., or by appointment.

Oconee State Park. One of South Carolina's first state parks, this one has 19 fully furnished cabins with fireplaces, heat, and air-conditioning. You can keep occupied with the 20-acre lake, rental fishing boats and canoes, lake swimming, and picnic areas. The park makes a good base camp for trips on the Chattooga River or the 85-mi Foothills Trail. | 624 State Park Rd., Mountain Rest; 20 mi NW of Clemson, Rte. 28 to 107 | 864/638–5353 | fax 864/638–8776 | sp@prt.state.sc.us | $1.50 | Mar.–Dec.: Thurs.–Sun., 9–6.

Old Stone Church. This Presbyterian church was built with field stones and clay mortar in 1797. A number of interesting headstones lie in the cemetery, including that of Revolutionary War hero Andrew Pickens. | Hwy. 76 and Old Stone Church Rd. | 864/654–2061 | Free | Daily dawn to dusk.

Rafting Trips. You can raft down the Chattooga, Oconee, Nantahala, and Pigeon Rivers. | 800/451–9972 | www.wildwaterrafting.com | Call for prices | Mar.–Nov., trips available daily.

Stumphouse Tunnel Park. Only a partially sealed tunnel remains of an 1850s project attempting to link Charleston to the Midwest by rail. Scenic hiking opportunities abound, especially at the 200-ft Isaqueena Falls, and there are nearby picnic areas. | Hwy. 28, Walhalla; 8 mi NW of Clemson | 864/646–3782 or 800/862–1795 | fax 864/646–2506 | www.pendleton-district.org | Free | Daily 8 AM to dusk.

World of Energy. At Duke Power's education center next to the Oconee Nuclear Station on Lake Keowee, you can use a self-guided tour, computer games, and a nature trail to learn how electricity is generated by water. | 7812 Rochester Hwy., Seneca; 8 mi NW of Clemson | 864/885–4600 or 800/777–1004 | fax 864/885–4605 | Free | Mon.–Sat. 9–5, Sun. noon–5.

ON THE CALENDAR
EVERY OTHER MONTH: *Harvesting Our Heritage.* Fun, family-oriented workshops sponsored by the South Carolina Botanical Garden celebrate the area's rural traditions. | 102 Garden Trail | 864/656–3405 | fax 864/656–6230.
JULY: *ClemsonFest on the Lake.* Held on the YMCA beach and fields, this festival features a boat parade, games, food, and live entertainment. | July 4 | 864/646–6110.

Dining
Riviera. Mediterranean. Clemson's best kept secret is only ½ mile away from campus, and Clemson faculty usually make up this family-owned restaurant's clientele. Turkish paintings and pictures of Clemson students decorate the walls, and over 90 fresh Greek and Turkish dishes, made daily by the family matriarch, grace the menu. Chicken, seafood, and steak are also served, and you can eat outside on an enclosed patio. Local musicians perform occasionally. | 391 Old Greenville Hwy. | 864/653–8855 | $7–$11 | D, MC, V.

Tiger Town Tavern. American. A full wooden bar serves cheap beer on tap at this longtime college haunt, which also has club sandwiches, blackened chicken, and great hamburgers. | 368 College Ave. | 864/654–5901 | $5–$10 | AE, MC, V.

Lodging
Comfort Inn. This four-story chain hotel is 1 mi from the Clemson University campus and ½ mi from downtown in a commercial area close to several restaurants. Complimentary Continental breakfast. In-room data ports. Cable TV. Pool. Hot tub. Exercise equipment. | 1305 Tiger Blvd. | 864/653–3600 | fax 864/654–3123 | 122 rooms | $67–$130 | AE, D, DC, MC, V.

James F. Martin Inn. This contemporary inn on Lake Hartwell is connected to Clemson University's conference center. Restaurant, bar, picnic area, complimentary Continental breakfast, room service. In-room data ports, kitchenettes, microwaves, refrigerators, some hot tubs. Cable TV, in-room VCRs, room phones. Outdoor pool. 18-hole golf course. Gym. Laundry service. No pets. | 120 Madren Center Dr. | 888/654–9020 or 864/654–9020 | fax 864/654–9021 | www.clemson.edu/conference_center | 62 rooms, 27 suites | $125–$150 | AE, D, DC, MC, V.

Lake Hartwell Inn. Though 1½ mi from the downtown area and within walking distance of some restaurants, this lakeside hotel has a quiet, laid-back feel to it. Restaurant, bar, complementary buffet breakfast. In-room data ports. Cable TV. Pool. Laundry facilities. Business services. Some pets allowed. | 894 Tiger Blvd. | 864/654–4450 | fax 864/654–8451 | 219 rooms | $65 | AE, D, DC, MC, V.

COLUMBIA

MAP 9, F4

(Nearby towns also listed: Camden, Greenwood, Newberry)

In 1786, South Carolina's capital moved from Charleston to Columbia, in the center of the state along the banks of the Congaree River. One of the nation's first planned cities, Columbia has streets that are among the widest in America because it was then thought that stagnant air in narrow streets fostered the spread of malaria. The city soon grew into a center of political, commercial, cultural, and social activity, but in early 1865 General William Tecumseh Sherman invaded South Carolina and incinerated two-thirds of Columbia. A few homes and public buildings were spared, including the First Baptist Church, where secession was declared, which was saved when a janitor directed Sherman's troops to a Methodist church when asked directions. Today the city is a sprawling blend of modern office blocks, suburban neighborhoods, and the occasional antebellum home. Columbia is also home to the expansive main campus of the University of South Carolina.

Information: Columbia Metropolitan Convention Visitors Center | 1012 Gervais St., Columbia, SC 29202 | 803/254–0479 or 800/264–4884 | fax 803/799–6529 | www.columbiasc.net.

TRANSPORTATION INFORMATION

Airports: Columbia and the surrounding area are served by **Columbia Metro Airport** (3000 Aviation Way; 803/822–5000), approximately 10 mi west of downtown. American Eagle, ComAir/Delta, and US Air all service the area.
Amtrak (800/872–7245) serves the city from its station on Pulaski St.
South Carolina Transit Corporation: A local company provides city bus service in and around Columbia. Call 803/748–3019 for more information.

Attractions

ART AND ARCHITECTURE

Governor's Mansion and Governor's Green. The Governor's Mansion was built in 1855 as officers' housing for a military academy. You can tour the antiques-filled home, where South Carolina governors have lived since 1868. Also on the Green are the 1854 Lace House and the 1830 Caldwell-Boylston House. | 800 Richland St. | 843/737–1710 | Free | Tours by appointment.

Hampton–Preston Mansion. Confederate leader and South Carolina governor Gen. Wade Hampton lived here. The house, which dates from 1818, is filled with lavish furnishings collected by three generations of the Hampton and Preston families, two of the area's most influential. | 1615 Blanding St. | 803/252–1770 | $4; $14 combination ticket to Hampton–Preston Mansion, Robert Mills House, Mann–Simons Cottage, and Woodrow Wilson Boyhood Home | Tues.–Sat. 10:15–3:15, Sun. 1:15–4:15.

Robert Mills Historic House. This classic columned 1823 house was named for its architect, who later designed the Washington Monument. Opulent Regency furniture and marble mantels adorn the interior, and there are spacious grounds outside. At the Museum Shop, you can buy tickets to all four of the homes run by the Historic Columbia Foundation. | 1616 Blanding St. | 803/252–1770 | fax 803/929–7695 | $4; $14 combination ticket to Hampton–Preston Mansion, Robert Mills House, Mann–Simons Cottage, and Woodrow Wilson Boyhood Home | Tues.–Sat. 10:15–3:15, Sun. 1:15–4:15.

The State House. Started in 1855 and completed in 1950, the newly renovated Italian Renaissance–style capital building is made of native blue granite. Six bronze stars on the outer western wall mark direct hits by Sherman's cannons. Brass, marble, mahogany, and artwork decorate the interior, and a replica of Jean Antoine Houdon's statue of George Washington stands on the grounds. | Main and Gervais Sts. | 803/734–9400 | Free | Tours daily; call for times.

Tunnelvision. Make sure it's dark out when you drive by—or right up to—this optical illusion, painted on the wall of the Federal Land Bank Building by famous local artist Blue Sky. | Taylor and Marion Sts. | Free | Daily.

Woodrow Wilson Boyhood Home. Home to the future president from age 14 to 17, the house displays family photos and some original furnishings as well as the gaslights, arched doorways, and ornate furnishings of the Victorian period. | 1705 Hampton St. | 803/252–1770 | $4; $14 combination ticket to Hampton–Preston Mansion, Robert Mills House, Mann–Simons Cottage, and Woodrow Wilson Boyhood Home | Tues.–Sat. 10:15–3:15, Sun. 1:15–4:15.

BEACHES, PARKS, AND NATURAL SIGHTS

Lake Murray. You can have access to great fishing and water sports at this 50,000-acre lake, as well as marinas, camping, and outdoor recreation sites. | Visitors Center, 2184 North Lake Dr., Irmo | 803/781–5940 | Free | Daily.

Riverfront Park and Historic Columbia Canal. This park was created around the city's original waterworks and hydroelectric plant where the Broad and Saluda rivers meet to form the Congaree. Interpretive markers describe the area's plant and animal life and tell the history of the buildings. | 312 Laurel St. | 803/733–8613 | Free | Daily dawn–dusk.

Sesquicentennial State Park. A 1756 loghouse distinguishes this park, which also has camping, picnic shelters, lake swimming and fishing, nature trails, and pedal boat rentals. | 9564 Two Notch Rd.; I–20 to Exit 7 | 803/788–2706 | Free | Daily 7 AM–9 PM.

CULTURE, EDUCATION, AND HISTORY

Congaree Swamp National Monument. The Congaree's 22,000 acres provide shelter to more than 90 species of trees, as well as a handicap-accessible boardwalk and 18 mi of hiking trails, canoeing routes, and guided nature walks. | 200 Caroline Sims Rd., Hopkins; 20 mi SE of Columbia off Rte. 48 | 803/776–4396 | Free | Daily 10 AM–dusk.

South Carolina Archives and History Center. Official state and county records date from colonial days to modern times. | 8301 Parklane Rd. | 803/896–6201 | fax 803/896–6167 | www.state.sc.us/scdah | Free | Tues.–Fri. 9–9, Sat. 9–6, Sun. 1–6.

Town Theatre. Founded in 1919, this group stages six plays a year from September to late May, plus a special summer show. | 1012 Sumter St. | 803/799–2510 | Prices vary | Tues.–Sat., 8 PM; Sun., 3.

University of South Carolina. The sprawling campus of this state university, founded in 1801, serves 23,000 students. The Visitor Center showcases university programs, faculty, and students; tours by student ambassadors are available. | Pendleton and Assembly Sts. | 803/777–0169 or 800/922–9755 | www.sc.edu | Free | Mon.–Fri., 8:30–5; Sat., 9:30–2.

On the campus of the University of South Carolina, the **Carolina Coliseum** features men's and women's college basketball as well as live concerts. | Assembly and Blossom Sts. | 803/777–5113 | fax 803/251–6333 | Prices vary | Call for game times and performances.

Near the State House, a scenic cluster of Georgian buildings surrounded by trees and brick walkways makes up **The Horseshoe,** which dates to 1801, when the school was first established. It includes the South Carolina Library, dating to 1840, which has much sought-after state history and genealogy collections. | Sumter St. | 803/777–3131 | Free | Daily; call for library hours.

The massive **Koger Center for the Arts** presents national and international theater, ballet, and musical groups and individual performers throughout the year. | 1051 Greene St. | 803/777–7500 | fax 803/777–9774 | www.koger.sc.edu | Daily 8:30–5; call for show times.

The **McKissick Museum** on the historic Horseshoe has geology and gemstone exhibits and a fine display of silver. | Sumter St. | 803/777–7251 | fax 803/777–2829 | www.cls.sc.edu/mcks | Free | Weekdays 9–4, weekends 1–5.

MUSEUMS

Columbia Museum of Art. Contemporary paintings hang beside Baroque and Renaissance works and exhibitions include sculpture, decorative arts including art glass, and a collection of dolls. | Main and Hampton Sts. | 803/799–2810 | $4 | Tues., Thurs.–Sat. 10–5, Wed. 10–9, Sun. 1–5.

Fort Jackson Museum. Built in 1917 and named after President Andrew Jackson, the museum (on Fort Jackson's U.S. Army Training Center) exhibits artifacts relating to the history of the fort as well as Jackson memorabilia. | Fort Jackson Blvd. | 803/751–7419 or 803/751–7355 | Free | Tues.–Fri. 10–4, Sat. 1–4, closed Sun. and last 2 weeks Dec.

Lexington County Museum Complex. Fifteen historic buildings house collections of antebellum arts and crafts, including furniture, textiles, and decorative pieces. | Fox St. and U.S. 378, Lexington; 13 mi west of Columbia | 803/359–8369 | $1 | Tues.–Sun. 10–4.

Mann–Simons Cottage: Museum of African-American Culture. Celia Mann, a free slave, bought this house in 1850 after walking to Columbia from Charleston. This white frame cottage is now a historical heritage house museum. | 1403 Richland St. | 803/252–1770 | $4; $14 combination ticket to Hampton–Preston Mansion, Robert Mills House, Mann–Simons Cottage, and Woodrow Wilson Boyhood Home | Tues.–Sat. 10:15–3:15, Sun. 1:15–4:15.

South Carolina State Museum. Housed in a large, refurbished textile mill, this museum interprets the state's natural history, archaeology, historical development, and technological and artistic accomplishments. One exhibit (dedicated to South Carolina native Dr. Ronald McNair, who died on the *Challenger*) portrays noted black astronauts; another focuses on the cotton industry and slavery. An iron gate made for the museum by Phillip Simmons, the "dean of Charleston blacksmiths," is on display, as is the surfboard that physicist Kary Mullis was riding when he heard he'd won the Nobel prize. The Stringer Discovery Center is an interactive display for families. | 301 Gervais St. | 803/898–4921 | $4 | Mon.–Sat. 10–5, first Sun. of the month 1–5.

RELIGION AND SPIRITUALITY

First Baptist Church. Secessionists held their first convention at this 1859 church, where the original slave gallery, pulpit, and portico remain. Services are held on Sunday. | 1306 Hampton St. | 803/256–4251 | fax 803/343–8584 | Free | Sun.–Fri. 8:30–5.

Trinity Cathedral. Near the capital building, this 1847 church is one of the largest Episcopal churches in the nation. Six state governors are buried in the cemetery. | 1100 Sumter St. | 803/771–7300 | www.trinityepiscopalcathedral.org | Free | Tours mid-Mar.–May and Sept.–Nov., weekdays 10–2.

SIGHTSEEING TOURS/TOUR COMPANIES

Richland County Historic Preservation Commission. This organization runs guided tours and rents out historic properties. | 1616 Blanding St. | 803/252–3964 | Tues.–Sat. 10:15–3:15, Sun. 1:15–4:15.

OTHER POINTS OF INTEREST

Five Points Neighborhood. A few blocks from USC cluster an eclectic mix of coffee shops, book and music stores, restaurants, and nightspots frequented by the university community. | Harden and Green Sts. | Free.

★ **Riverbanks Zoological Park and Botanical Garden.** Many regard this popular zoo as one of the nation's finest. It contains more than 2,000 animals and birds. Pathways and landscaped gardens lead to polar bears, Siberian tigers, and black rhinos. The South American primate collection has won international acclaim, and the park is noted for its success in breeding endangered and fragile species, as well as the Endangered Species Carousel and the aquarium–reptile complex. A 70-acre botanical garden on the west bank of the Saluda River includes a forested section with trails past historic ruins and spectacular views of the river. A new Bird Pavilion is scheduled to open in summer 2000. | 500 Wildlife Pkwy. | 803/779–8717 | $6.25 | Daily 9–4.

ON THE CALENDAR

APR.: *South Carolina Oyster Festival.* As you might expect, you'll find lots of oysters as well as live music. | 2065 Blossom St. | 803/695–0676.
MAY: *Mayfest.* National, regional, and local entertainment, arts and crafts, plus vendors galore make this one of the state's largest festivals. | 722 Blanding St. | 803/343–8750.
OCT.: *South Carolina State Fair.* Fine art and livestock shows are some of the highlights of this large and varied fair. You can also find agricultural displays, educational exhibits, grandstand entertainment, and fair rides. | 1200 Rosewood Dr. | 803/799–3387 | fax 803/799–1760 | www.scstatefair.org.

Dining

INEXPENSIVE

Beulah's Bar and Grill. American. This bustling, casual pub serves lunch and dinner and specializes in fried appetizers. | 902–C Gervais St. | 803/779–4655 | $4–$7 | AE, D, MC, V.

California Dreaming. American. You can try the prime ribs and seafood at this contemporary American restaurant. | 401 South Main St. | 803/254–6767 | Closed Thanksgiving and Christmas | $10–$20 | AE, D, DC, MC, V.

Garibaldi's of Columbia, Inc. Italian. Both Italian dishes and seafood—such as fried flounder with apricot sauce—can be found at this art deco restaurant. | 2013 Green St. | 803/771–8888 | Closed Sun. No lunch | $10–$25 | AE, MC, V.

Gourmet Shop. Café. Music plays continuously at this bright, lively café–food shop that's popular with young people. You can sit on the sidewalk and enjoy their chicken salad, croissants, and dessert; the coffee is particularly good. | 724 Saluda St. | 803/779–3705 | No supper | $6–$8 | AE, MC, V.

Mr. Friendly's New Southern Cafe. Southern. Fried grits, herb goat cheese, salmon croquettes, strawberry shrimp, pecan crab cakes are some of the things you can get at this restaurant, which also has an extensive wine list. | 2001-A Greene St. | 803/254–7828 | Reservations not accepted | $9–$22 | AE, D, DC, MC, V.

★ **Piggie Park.** Southern. The mustard-based barbecue sauce at this bright, warm, family-style restaurant has a national following. You can try the barbecue sandwiches and ribs, hash over rice, or the daily made potato salad and coleslaw. | 1600 Charleston Hwy. | 803/796–0220 or 800/628–7423 (800/MAURICE) | 800 Elmwood Ave. | 803/256–4377 or 800/628–7423 (800/MAURICE) | www.mauricebbq.com | Reservations not accepted | $10–$20 | AE, D, DC, MC, V.

Yesterday's. American. Wooden booths and knickknacks decorate this college institution which has a lively bar and serves nachos, fried steak, mashed potatoes, and frozen wine coolers. | 2030 Devine St. | 803/799–0196 | $10–$12 | AE, D, DC, MC, V.

MODERATE

Al's Upstairs. Northern Italian. Candlelight along with the Congaree River and Columbia's skyline are big draws here. There is fresh fish daily and nightly seafood specials, as well as veal chops, filet mignon, pasta, and polenta, but you may want to try the smoked trout, a house specialty. | 304 Meeting St., West Columbia | 803/794–7404 | Closed Sun. | $13–$25 | AE, D, DC, MC, V.

Blue Marlin Seafood Kitchen. Seafood. Polished wooden booths and playful lighting now enhance what used to be a train station built in 1918; the five-table outdoor dining section used to be the walkway to the station. You can choose from six to eight fresh fish dishes offered nightly; the Blue Marlin Oscar, a house special, is mahi mahi stuffed with crab meat and served on a bed of garlic mashed potatoes with a citrus hollendaise sauce. Kids' menu. | 1200 Lincoln St. | 803/799–3838 | www.bluemarlinfood.com | $15–$25 | AE, D, DC, MC, V.

Dianne's on Devine. American. This cabaret-style restaurant serves steak and seafood specialties. On Wednesday evening, the Ross Holmes Band plays South Carolina beach music. | 2400 Devine St. | 803/254–3535 | Closed Sun. No lunch | $11–$24 | AE, DC, MC, V.

Hampton Street Vineyard. Contemporary. Crabcakes, veal chops, steaks, and grilled seafood have made this fine-dining restaurant a local haunt. | 1201 Hampton St. | 803/252–0850 | Closed Sun. No lunch Sat. | $15–$20 | AE, D, MC, V.

Hennessy's. Steak. This longtime club-type local favorite is known for its filet mignon and rib eye steak; there's also a full bar and beer on tap. | 1649 Main St. | 803/799–8280 | Closed Sun. No lunch Sat. | $15–25 | AE, D, DC, MC, V.

Motor Supply Company Bistro. Southern. High ceilings, archways, hardwood floors, and antiques furnish this semi-traditional bistro. You can sit at pub and bistro tables and try the crab cakes, quail, steak, grits, salsa, black-eyed peas, and fresh seafood. Sunday brunch. | 920 Gervais St. | 803/256–6687 | Closed Mon. | $13–$25 | AE, DC, MC, V.

Vista Brewing and Bistro. French. In keeping with the decidedly casual decor, the lively crowds have full views of the brewing equipment. | 936 Gervais St. | 803/799–2739 | Closed Sun. | $15–$24 | AE, D, DC, MC, V.

Lodging

INEXPENSIVE

Amerisuites. At the intersection of I–77 and I–20, this chain hotel has simple, modern decor. Complimentary Continental breakfast. Microwaves, refrigerators. Cable TV, in-room VCRs. Pool. Exercise equipment. Business services, free parking. | 7525 Two Notch Rd. | 803/736–6666 | fax 803/788–6011 | www.amerisuites.com | 112 suites | $78–$89 | AE, D, DC, MC, V.

Baymont Inn. This inn is centrally located, 10 mi from downtown and 5 mi from Fort Jackson. Complimentary Continental breakfast. In-room data ports. Cable TV. Pool. Laundry facilities. Business services, free parking. | 1538 Horseshoe Dr. | 803/736–6400 | fax 803/788–7875 | 102 rooms | $47–$74 | AE, D, DC, MC, V.

Best Western Riverside. Not nearly as old as the Horseshoe's historic buildings but closer than many other chain hotels, this one was built in 1950 and is 1 mi east of downtown. Complimentary Continental breakfast. In-room data ports. Cable TV. Pool. Putting green. Business services. | 111 Knox Abott Dr., Cayce | 803/939–4688 | fax 803/926–5547 | 64 rooms | $60 | AE, D, DC, MC, V.

Chestnut Cottage. Hardwood floors, four-poster antique beds, and Victoriana furnish the rooms at this 1850s inn. You can sit on the porches and relax or walk the five blocks to downtown. Complimentary breakfast. | 1718 Hampton St. | 803/256–1718 | jefsndavis@aol.com | www.bboline.com/sc-chestnut | 5 rooms | Rooms, $95; Suites, $225 | AE, D, DC, MC, V.

Clarion Town House Hotel. This contemporary hotel is within walking distance of the State Capitol, the University of South Carolina, and the Coliseum. It tends to host many business and professional meetings in its 8 conference rooms. Restaurant, lounge, room service. In-room data ports, some microwaves, some refrigerators, some hot tubs. Cable TV, room phones. Outdoor pool. Exercise equipment. Laundry service. Business services, free parking. No pets. | 1615 Gervais St. | 800/277–8711 or 803/771–8711 | fax 803/252–9347 | www.clariontownhouse.com | 163 rooms | $85–$95 | AE, D, DC, MC, V.

Claussen's Inn. An open, airy lobby welcomes you to this converted bakery warehouse built in 1928 in the Five Points neighborhood, which is right downtown. Complimentary Continental breakfast. Cable TV. | 2003 Greene St. | 803/765–0440 or 800/622–3382 | fax 803/799–7924 | 29 rooms | $125–$140 | AE, MC, V.

Comfort Inn and Suites. This chain hotel is next to Shoney's restaurant. All rooms have coffee pots, and some suites come with hot tubs. Complimentary Continental breakfast. In-room data ports, microwaves, refrigerators, some hot tubs. Cable TV, room phones. Indoor pool. Free parking. No pets. | 7337 Garner's Ferry Rd. | 803/695–5555 | fax 803/695–0009 | 67 suites | $69–$89 rooms, $110 suites | AE, D, DC, MC, V.

Courtyard by Marriott. Balconies and patios with courtyard views distinguish the rooms at this three-story standard chain 7 mi from downtown. Bar, complimentary breakfast. In-room data ports. Cable TV. Pool. Hot tub. Exercise equipment. Laundry facilities. Business services, free parking. | 347 Zimalcrest Dr. | 803/731–2300 | fax 803/772–6965 | www.mariot.com | 149 rooms | $59–$89 | AE, D, DC, MC, V.

Days Inn–Columbia. About a 15-min drive from Ft. Jackson, Williams–Brice Stadium, malls, and restaurants is this chain hotel, with extra parking for trucks. Complimentary Continental breakfast. In-room data ports. Cable TV, room phones. Outdoor pool. Free parking. Pets allowed (fee). | 133 Plumbers Rd. | 803/754–4408 | fax 803/786–2821 | www.daysinn.com | 42 rooms | $45 | AE, D, DC, MC, V.

Embassy Suites. This chain hotel is 2 mi from downtown. Restaurant, bar, complimentary breakfast. In-room data ports, microwaves, refrigerators. Cable TV. Indoor pool. Hot tub. Exercise equipment. Laundry facilities. Business services, airport shuttle. | 200 Stoneridge Dr. | 803/252–8700 | fax 803/256–8749 | www.embassysuites.com | 216 suites | $99–$144 | AE, D, DC, MC, V.

EconoLodge. This hotel is ½ mi from Ft. Jackson. Complimentary Continental breakfast. In-room data ports, microwaves, refrigerators. Cable TV, room phones. Free parking. No pets. | 4486 Ft. Jackson Blvd. | 803/738–0510 | fax 803/787–8558 | www.econolodge.com | 36 rooms | $42–$85 | AE, D, DC, MC, V.

Governor's House Hotel. This elegant mansion has nine guest bedrooms or suites, each with private baths and hardwood floors. The Grand Rooms have 12′ ceilings, a fireplace, and a private verandah. The Roofscape Rooms have a view of historic Charleston. The Kitchen House Suites have a separate living room, private porch, whirlpool, wet bar, and an original 1760 fireplace. The State Capitol is right across the street. 2 restaurants, complimentary Continental breakfast. In-room data ports, some microwaves, refrigerators, some hot tubs. Cable TV, room phones. Outdoor pool. Free parking. Pets allowed (fee). | 1301 Main St. | 803/779–7790 | fax 803/779–7856 | 9 rooms | $59–$119, $139–$189 suites | AE, D, DC, MC, V.

Hampton Inn. This well-maintained chain property has contemporary artwork and mahogany furniture. Complimentary Continental breakfast. In-room data ports, minibars in suites, microwaves, refrigerators, some in-room hot tubs. Cable TV. Pool. Exercise equipment. Business services. | 1551 Barbara Dr. | 803/865–8000 or 800/426–7866 | fax 803/865–8046 | www.hampton-inn.com | 111 rooms, 18 suites | $80 | AE, D, DC, MC, V.

Hampton Inn–Airport. This typical chain hotel is 4 mi east of downtown. Complimentary Continental breakfast. In-room data ports. Cable TV. Pool. Business services. | 1094 Chris

Dr., West Columbia | 803/791–8940 | fax 803/739–2291 | www.hampton-inn.com | 121 rooms | $72–$79 | AE, D, DC, MC, V.

Holiday Inn–Northeast. This hotel has a courtyard and the "Holidome"—a recreation area with an indoor basketball court, sauna, Ping-Pong, billiards, a swimming pool, and miniature golf. Restaurant, bar, room service. In-room data ports. Cable TV. Indoor/outdoor pool. Hot tub, sauna. Video Games. Laundry facilities. Business services. | 7510 Two Notch Rd. | 803/736–3000 | fax 803/736–6399 | 253 rooms | $109 | AE, D, DC, MC, V.

Knights Inn. This centrally located hotel is 8 mi from Columbia Metro Airport and 15 mi from Sesquicentennial State Park. Complimentary Continental breakfast. In-room data ports, some microwaves, some refrigerators, in-room hot tubs. Cable TV, room phones. Outdoor pool. Free parking. No pets. | 1803 Bush River Rd. | 803/772–0022 | fax 803/772–0022 | 106 rooms | $35–$40 | AE, D, DC, MC, V.

La Quinta. Large desks characterize the rooms at this otherwise-standard chain hotel, which is near the zoo and 3 mi from downtown. Complimentary Continental breakfast. Cable TV. Pool. Business services, free parking. | 1335 Garner La., off I–20 (Exit 65) | 803/798–9590 | fax 803/731–5574 | www.laquinta.com | 120 rooms | $52 | AE, D, DC, MC, V.

Ramada Plaza Hotel. This chain hotel is within 8 mi of movie theaters, the shopping mall, and restaurants. Restaurant, bar, service. In-room data ports, microwaves, refrigerators in suites. Cable TV. Pool. Hot tub. Exercise equipment. Business services, free parking. Some pets allowed. | 8105 Two Notch Rd. | 803/736–5600 | fax 803/736–1241 | www.ramada.com | 186 rooms | $89 | AE, D, DC, MC, V.

Red Roof Inn. Downtown is 10 mi east, and there are restaurants adjacent or ½ mi from this two-story standard. In-room data ports. Cable TV. Business services. | 7580 Two Notch Rd.; at the intersection of I–20 and I–77 | 803/736–0850 | fax 803/736–4270 | www.redroofinn.com | 108 rooms | $54 | AE, D, DC, MC, V.

Relax Inn. A large palm tree stands by the entrance to this chain hotel, which is within walking distance of shops and restaurants. Complimentary Continental breakfast. Cable TV. Pool. Business services, free parking. | 773 St. Andrews Rd., off I–26 (Exit 106) | 803/772–7275 | fax 803/750–1877 | 65 rooms | $49 | AE, D, DC, MC, V.

Residence Inn by Marriott. Fireplaces distinguish most of the rooms in this chain hotel. Complimentary Continental breakfast. In-room data ports, kitchenettes, microwaves. Cable TV. Pool. Hot tub. Exercise equipment. Laundry facilities. Business services, free parking. Some pets allowed. | 150 Stoneridge Dr. | 803/779–7000 or 800/331–3131 | fax 803/779–0408 | 128 suites | $114 | AE, D, DC, MC, V.

★ **Richland Street B&B.** Hardwood floors and four-poster beds grace the rooms and flower gardens blossom on the grounds at this colonial-style home. Complimentary breakfast. Cable TV. No kids under 12. No smoking. | 1425 Richland St. | 803/779–7001 | fax 803/256–3725 | 8 rooms, 1 suite | $89–$150, $150 suite | AE, MC, V.

Rose Hall B&B. A porch and decorative antiques keep it Victorian, but the hot tub makes life comfortable at this 1894 home. Complimentary Continental breakfast. Cable TV. Jacuzzis. No smoking. | 1006 Barnwell St. | 803/771–2288 | rosehallbb@infoave.net | 4 rooms | $65–$115 | AE, MC, V.

Travelodge Columbia West. Outlet shopping, restaurants, and movie theatres are 5 mi away from this modestly priced chain hotel. Cable TV. Pool. Business services, free parking. | 2210 Bush River Rd.; off I–20 (Exit 63) | 803/798–9665 | fax 803/798–9665 | 108 rooms | $45–$57 | AE, D, DC, MC, V.

The Whitney. All the suites in this seven-story building have balconies. Complimentary Continental breakfast. Microwaves, kitchenettes. Cable TV. Pool. Laundry facilities. Business services, airport shuttle, free parking. | 700 Woodrow St.; off of I–77 (Exit 10) | 803/252–0845 or 800/637–4008 | fax 803/771–0495 | www.thewhitney.com | 74 suites | $119 1–bedroom suite, $139 2–bedroom suite | AE, D, DC, MC, V.

MODERATE

Adams Mark Columbia. A warm, spacious lobby greets you at this hotel, within walking distance of the State Capitol, downtown shopping, and restaurants. Both guests and visitors can sit at the piano lounge and sports bar. Restaurant, 2 bars (with entertainment), room service. In-room data ports. Cable TV, room phones. Indoor pool. Health club. Laundry facilities, laundry service. Business services, airport shuttle, parking (fee). No pets. | 1200 Hampton St. | 800/444–ADAM or 803/771–7000 | fax 803/254–2911 | www.adamsmark.com | 301 rooms | $79–$154 | AE, D, DC, MC, V.

Sheraton Hotel and Conference Center. The fifth-floor "Club Level" has bigger rooms and more amenities than the other floors. This particular outpost of the hotel giant is 2 mi from shopping malls, 7 mi from the zoo, botanical gardens, and South Carolina State Museum. Restaurant, dance club (with entertainment). In-room data ports, some refrigerators. Cable TV. 2 pools (1 indoor). Hot tub. Exercise equipment. Business services, airport shuttle. | 2100 Bush River Rd. | 803/731–0300 | fax 803/731–4892 | 237 rooms | $135 | AE, D, DC, MC, V.

DARLINGTON

MAP 9, I3

(Nearby towns also listed: Bennettsville, Cheraw)

With a population of about 7,000, Darlington is best known for its twice-a-year 500-mi stock car races. In addition, the Stock Car Hall of Fame houses the largest collection of stock car racers in the world.

Information: Darlington Chamber of Commerce | 38 Public Square, Darlington, SC 29532 | 843/393–2641 | fax 843/393–8059.

Attractions

Darlington Raceway and NMPA Stock Car Hall of Fame/Joe Weatherly Stock Car Museum. The oldest superspeedway in the country, Darlington Raceway attracts champion drivers during the NASCAR TranSouth Financial 400 stock race each spring and the Mountain Dew Southern 500 on Labor Day weekend. The museum holds the largest collection of stock racing cars in the world, including those of Richard Petty and Fireball Roberts. | 1301 Harry Byrd Hwy. | 843/395–8821 | $3 | Daily 8:30–5.

ON THE CALENDAR

MAR.: *NASCAR Winston Cup Series TransSouth Financial 400.* The best NASCAR, Indy, and road racing drivers compete for the championship at Darlington Raceway. | 1301 Harry Byrd Hwy. | 843/395–8892.
SEPT.: *Mountain Dew Southern 500.* Drivers compete on Labor Day weekend at the Darlington Raceway's second of two stock car races. | 1301 Harry Byrd Hwy. | 843/395–8892.
OCT.: *South Carolina Sweet Potato Festival.* During the second weekend of the month, the sweet potato harvest provides the motive for celebration in the town square, with country music, a crafts exhibit, sweet potato recipes, mimes, clowns, and a barbecue. | 843/393–2641.

Dining

Ward Street Restaurant. Southern. Although grits, pancakes, hash browns, and barbecue are served, the homemade desserts—pecan pie, Boston cream pie, caramel cake, and chocolate cake—draw most customers. | 114 Ward St. | 843/395–0053 | fax 843/395–0053 | No supper | $4–$5 | No credit cards.

Lodging

Big Apple Inn. This independently owned motel is 1½ mi from Darlington's car track and ½ mi from restaurants and shopping. Some microwaves, some refrigerators. Cable TV, room phones. Free parking. | 705 Washington St. | 843/393–8990 | fax 843/395–0748 | 56 rooms | $25–$45 | AE, D, MC, V.

EDGEFIELD

MAP 9, D5

(Nearby town also listed: Aiken)

The entire town of Edgefield is listed in the National Register of Historic Places. Forty structures from the 19th century are laid out around the courthouse square; the elegant courthouse is still in use. This little town also spawned several South Carolina leaders: 10 governors and five lieutenant governors, including former Governor and longtime Senator Strom Thurmond. Edgefield's thick deposits of clay have long been a source of raw material for pottery. Potters began establishing small businesses in Edgefield shortly after 1800, supplying pioneers with jars, pitchers, pans, and bowls. The tradition lives on in the work of resident potters at Old Edgefield Pottery, a business created in 1992 by the Edgefield County Historical Society. Edgefield is also right in the middle of peach country, part of a strip of more than a million peach trees known as The Ridge.

Information: Edgefield County Chamber of Commerce | 416 Calhoun St., Box 23, Johnston, SC 29832 | 803/275–0010.

Attractions

Cedar Grove Plantation. Dating to 1790, this is one of the oldest plantations in the area. The home's original moldings, mantels, and hand-painted French wallpaper remain, as do the slave quarters and separate kitchen. | 1365 Hwy. 25N | 803/637–3056 | By appointment.

National Wild Turkey Federation. The Wild Turkey Federation, headquartered here, has a series of exhibits and artifacts on wild turkeys, including efforts to protect them. You should call ahead to arrange a tour. | 770 Augusta Rd. | 803/637–3106 | Free | Weekdays 9–5, or by appointment.

Old Edgefield Pottery. A resident potter demonstrates the making of alkaline-glazed traditional pottery, an art form dating to the 1800s. There are displays of old and new pottery, as well as items for sale. | 230 Simkins St. | 803/637–2060 | Donations accepted | Tues.–Sat. 10–6, or by appointment.

ON THE CALENDAR

OCT.: *Ten Governors Fall Festival.* This free festival, on the last Saturday of the month and held in the town square, honors the 10 governors of South Carolina who hailed from Edgefield. You can help celebrate among the food venders, rides, a crafts festival, bingo, and face painting. | 803/637–3800 or 803/637–1944.

Dining

Old Edgefield Grill. Southern. Chef Sean Wight specializes in preparing game, including lamb, quail, and rabbit. You can try his dishes in this 110-yr-old Victorian house (the first brick house built in the county), or out on the porch. | 202 Penn St. | 803/637–3222 | fax 803/637–3080 | Closed Sun., Mon. | $16–$24 | AE, MC, V.

Lodging

Cedar Grove Plantation. You can stay at one of the oldest plantations in the area (circa 1790) and savor its carved moldings, fireplaces, gardens, and porches. The restored slave quarters are the more disturbing remnants of South Carolina's history. Complimentary Continental breakfast. Some refrigerators, VCRs. Pool. Hot tub. | 1365 Hwy. 25N | 803/637–3056 | cdrgrvplan@aol.com | www.virtualcities.com | 2 rooms | $75–$95 | AE, D, DC, MC, V.

Edgefield Inn. Armchairs, game tables, and some desks furnish the rooms at this two-story hotel ½ mi from downtown. Complimentary Continental breakfast. Some microwaves, some refrigerators, some in-room hot tubs. Cable TV. Exercise equipment. | 702 Augusta Rd. | 803/637–2001 | fax 803/637–2020 | edgfiefield@jetbn.net | 42 rooms, 4 suites | $45–$85 | AE, D, MC, V.

Pleasant Lane Acres B&B. Trees line the driveway up to this 120-yr-old renovated farm house, which sits on 50 acres of land. Hard pine floors, antique heirlooms, and fireplaces romantically furnish the rooms, making this an ideal retreat for couples. There is a fishing pond on the land, as well as miles of bike trails; you can get a picnic to go if you plan to explore the area. Complimentary breakfast. Microwaves, refrigerators. Cable TV. Laundry facilities. Pets allowed. No kids. No smoking. | 318 Pleasant Lane Rd. | 888/771–3161 or 803/637–9387 | fax 803/637–9387 | pleasantlaneacresbb@jetbinn.net | www.bbonline.com/sc/pleasant-lane | 3 rooms | $135–$150 | Closed Mon.–Wed. | No credit cards.

EDISTO ISLAND

MAP 9, H8

(Nearby towns also listed: Charleston, Folly Beach, Kiawah Island)

Rural Edisto Island is off the beaten path, and it's not in any hurry to be discovered. Though settled in 1690, the island became notable for its Sea Island cotton throughout the 19th century and into the early 20th. You reach it via State Highway 174, where age-old oaks festooned with Spanish moss border quiet streams and side roads, and wild turkeys may still be spotted on open grasslands. If you turn off Highway 174 onto one of the byways, you may occasionally come to a private road leading to an antebellum plantation, in some cases still belonging to the same family as when the plantation grew indigo, rice, or cotton; many of the island's inhabitants are descendants of the slaves who worked these plantations. Some of Edisto's elaborate mansions have been restored; others brood in disrepair. Along Edisto Beach are unassuming older beach cottages (most are rentals); there isn't a single motel, nor is the "main drag" jammed with traffic on busy summer weekends. Many visitors have been coming back here for years, if not generations, staying in the same house.

Information: Edisto Chamber of Commerce | 430 Highway 174, Edisto Island, SC 29438 | 843/869–3867.

Attractions

ACE Basin National Wildlife Refuge. This 850,000-acre area, named for the rivers that bound it (the Ashepoo, Combahee, and Edisto), is one of the largest, most pristine estuarine ecosystems in North America. More than 100 bird species, sea turtles, otters, and other wildlife live here, 17 of which are endangered or threatened, including the wood stork and loggerhead sea turtle. The headquarters are within the preserve at Grove Plantation. | Grove Plantation, Jebossee Island Rd. | 843/889–3084 | Free | Daily 7:30–4.

Edisto Beach State Park. You can do some excellent shell collecting on the nearly 3 mi of beach at this park; there are also cabins and oceanside campsite. To get to the park from Charleston, take Highway 17 South, then Highway 174 East for 28 mi until it ends at the entrance to Edisto Beach. | Hwy. 174 E | 843/869–2756 | $2 | Daily 8–6.

Edisto Island Presbyterian Church. Though founded in 1685, the present church dates to 1830. The pink Legare mausoleum at the back of the cemetery is said to be haunted by the ghost of a young girl who was inadvertently buried alive in it. | 2164 Hwy. 174 | 843/869–2326 | Free | Grounds and cemetery, daily 9–5; church usually locked except during services.

Edisto Museum. This tiny museum houses artifacts and historical items about the history of Edisto. | 2343 Hwy. 174 | 843/869–1954 | $2 | Tues., Thurs., Sat. 1–4.

Edisto Water Sports and Tackle. You can sign up for tours of the ACE Basin, inshore and offshore fishing charters, parasailing, and boat, water bike, and Jet Ski rentals. | 3731 Dock-

© Artville

THE GULLAH CULTURE

In the Lowcountry, Gullah refers to several things: language, people, and a culture. The rhythmic Gullah language (the name itself is believed to be a version of the word Angola), an English-based dialect rooted in African languages, is the unique language of the African-Americans of the Sea Islands of South Carolina and Georgia. Its survival for more than 300 years stems in part from the geographic isolation of the people who speak it. Descended from thousands of slaves who were imported by planters in the Carolinas during the 18th century, the Gullah people have maintained not only their dialect but also their heritage.

Much of Gullah culture traces back to African rice coast culture and survives today in the art forms and skills, including sweetgrass basket making, of Sea Islanders. During the Colonial period, when rice was king, Africans from the West African rice kingdoms drew high premiums as slaves. Those with basket-making skills were especially valuable because baskets were needed for agricultural and household use. Still made by hand, sweetgrass baskets are intricate coils of a marsh grass called sweetgrass. Other Gullah art forms can be seen in hand-carved bateaus and gourds and in hand-tied nets used to catch shrimp in local creeks and rivers.

Nowhere is Gullah culture more evident than in the region's cuisine. Rice, of course, appears at nearly every meal—African slaves taught planters how to grow rice and how to cook and serve it as well. Lowcountry dishes use okra, peanuts, benne (sesame seeds), field peas, and hot peppers. Gullah food itself reflects the bounty of the islands: shrimp, crabs, oysters, fish, and vegetables such as greens, tomatoes, and corn. Many dishes are prepared in one pot, similar to the stew-pot cooking of West Africa. Frogmore stew, for example, calls for cooking shrimp, potatoes, sausage, and corn together. Hoppin' John—a one-pot mixture of rice and field peas traditionally served on New Year's Day—is similar to rice and pigeon peas, a mainstay in West Africa.

Some of the practices of plantation owners unwittingly helped Gullah culture survive. From praise houses—one-room houses of worship where Christianity was introduced in an effort to keep slaves from running away—came plantation melodies strongly influenced by Gullah music. These songs live on in performances by groups including the Hallelujah Singers, Sea Island Singers, Mt. Zion Spiritual Singers, and Ron and Natalie Daise, all of whom perform regularly in Charleston and Beaufort.

The Penn Center on St. Helena Island near Beaufort is the unofficial Gullah headquarters, preserving the culture and developing opportunities for Gullahs. Nearby on Daufuskie Island, as well as on Edisto, Wadmalaw, and Johns Islands near Charleston, Gullah communities can still be found, though development continues to encroach.

side Rd. | 843/869–0663 | Call ahead for prices | Apr.–Nov., daily 8–5; reduced hours the rest of the year.

Plantation and Island Tours. Native Edistonian Marie Elliott gives 2½-hr van tours of several plantations (most are private), churches, and other points of interest in the area. | 1914 Hwy. 174 | 843/869–1110 | $15 | By appointment.

ON THE CALENDAR

OCT.: *Plantation Tour.* On the second Saturday of the month, you can take a driving tour of the 18th- and 19th-century former plantations and old churches on the island. Docents at every location explain the history lived at each site. Tickets cost $20. | 843/869–1954.

Dining

Old Post Office. Contemporary. A former post office now houses a simple but elegant dining room where local artwork adorns the walls; old mailboxes decorate the entry. Try the shrimp and grits or the pecan coated quail with duck stock gravy and wash it down with a selection from the restaurant's extensive wine list. | 1442 Hwy. 174 | 843/869–2339 | Closed Sun.–Mon. No lunch | $16–$21 | MC, V.

Lodging

Fairfield Ocean Ridge Resort. You can still get all the resort amenities in a get-away-from-it-all setting near the beach. Restaurant, bar. Pool, wading pool. 18-hole golf course, miniature golf, 4 tennis courts. Hiking. Beach, boating. | 1 King Cotton Rd. | 843/869–2561 | fax 843/869–2384 | 100 rooms | $235 per 2 nights (minimum stay) | AE, D, MC, V.

Seaside Plantation. Rich woodwork, crown moldings, chandeliers, and antiques decorate this early 19th-century plantation house. The extensive grounds provide good opportunities for bird watching, and Edisto Beach, with canoeing, kayaking, and nature trails, is 1 mi away. Complimentary breakfast. Cable TV, in-room VCRs. No pets. No smoking. | 400 Highway 174, Box 359 | 843/869–0971 | fax 843/869–0971 | 2 rooms | $125 | Nov.–Feb. | No credit cards.

FLORENCE

MAP 9, I4

(Nearby town also listed: Darlington)

Florence lies at the center of the Pee Dee River region. Its growth began in the 1850s when three railroad lines converged on the settlement, making it a shipping hub to cotton docks in Charleston and North Carolina. Its location near two major interstates—I–20 and I–95—have now made it a hub of industrial development, with two major factories—Honda and Hoffman–Larouche—in the area. Florence is also the home of Francis Marion University.

Information: Florence Convention and Visitors Bureau | 3290 Radio Rd., Florence, SC 29502 | 843/664–0330 | fax 843/665–9580.

Attractions

Beauty Trail. Signs mark this 30-min driving trail, a project of the Florence Rotary Club; you can also get an accompanying cassette at the Convention and Visitors Center. The trail begins on Edisto Drive and meanders through Florence's neighborhoods, pointing out local history and color. | 3290 Radio Rd. | 843/664–0330 | Free | Visitors Center daily 9–5.

Florence Museum. The museum houses art and regional history displays, exhibits of Asian, African, Greek, and American cultures, and an interactive children's gallery. Next door is the one-room schoolhouse where Confederate poet laureate Henry Timrod once taught. | 558 Spruce St. | 843/662–3351 | Free | Tues.–Sat. 10–5, Sun. 2–5.

Jeffries Creek Nature Park. Jeffries Creek flows through this 55-acre park, which also has nature trails, playgrounds, and picnic areas. | Deberry Blvd. and Edisto Dr. | 843/665–3253 | Free | Daily dawn to dusk.

Lucas Park. These 12 acres include nature trails and gardens, a playground, a picnic area, and two tennis courts. | Santee Dr., Azalea La., and Park Ave. | 843/669–4597 | Free | Daily dawn to dusk.

Lynches River County Park. You can river fish, go birding, picnic, swim in the Olympic-size pool, or simply contemplate in the woods at this park, about 12 mi south of Florence off U.S. 52. | 1110 Ben Gause Rd., Coward | 843/389–2785 | Free | Daily 9–5.
On the first Saturday of every month, the Southeastern Blue Grass Association of South Carolina sponsors **Bluegrass Night,** with at least four live bluegrass bands, at Lynches River County Park in Coward. | 1110 Ben Gause Rd., Coward | 843/389–2785 or 843/659–2315 | $5.

McLeod Park. Sports enthusiasts can enjoy the five lighted baseball fields, four tennis courts, volleyball court, three horseshoe pits, and six basketball goals. The 50-acre park also has nature trails and picnic areas. | Santiago Dr. | 843/665–3253 | Free | Daily dawn to dusk.

National Military Cemetery. The veterans of five wars are buried here. | 803 E. National Cemetery Rd. | 843/669–8783 | Free | Daily.

Timrod Park. The 18 acres of this park contain 11 tennis courts, playgrounds, picnic areas, a gazebo, interpretive nature trails, gardens, and two fitness courses, one of which is handicap accessible. The Florence Museum is on the park's west end. | 400 Timrod Park Dr. | 843/669–4597 | Free | Daily dawn to dusk.

War Between the States Museum. This 81-yr-old two-story house contains Civil War artifacts, clothing, furniture, photographs, prints, letters and memorabilia from the Civil War period. It also has a model of the Florence prison stockade and gunboats on the Pee Dee River. | 107 South Guerry St. | 843/669–1266 | $2 | Wed., Sat. 10–5.

Woods Bay State Park. There are no campgrounds or playgrounds at this 1,541-acre all-nature state park, but you can rent canoes and follow the canoe trail into the swamp. There are also picnic tables and a 500-ft boardwalk reaching into the wetlands. | 11020 Woods Bay Rd., Olanta; 3 mi west of Olanta, off I-95 and U.S. 301 | 843/659–4445 | Free | Thurs.–Mon. 9–6.

ON THE CALENDAR

MAR.: *Skirmish of Gamble's Hotel.* During the first weekend of the month, players commemorate the March 5, 1865 routing of General Sherman's troops by a small Confederate militia by reenacting the Civil War skirmish. The original battle site, Gamble's Hotel, no longer exists, so the reenactment takes place at The Columns, a Greek revival home in town (admission $5). | 5001 Old Marion Hwy. | 843/393–7861.

APR.: *Arts Alive.* The town celebrates music and dance in an astonishing array of styles. | Francis Marion University | 843/661–1225.

JUNE: *Spring Festival.* On the first Saturday of the month, at Lynches River County Park, you can attend a blue grass music festival which forms part of the Spring Festival of Florence. Beginning in the afternoon and running well into the night, the festival ($10) features six bands, prize drawings, food vendors, and recreational entertainment. Admission to the Blue Grass concert costs $10 for adults, $5 for members of the South Carolina Blue Grass Association and children under 12 enter free. | Lynches River County Park, 1110 Bengause Road, Coward | 843/659–2315 or 843/386–3140.

OCT.: *Fall Festival.* The first Saturday in October there is a blue grass music festival which forms part of the Fall Festival of Florence held at Lynches River County Park the first Saturday in October from 1–10 PM. The festival presents drawings, door prizes, food and recreation. | 1110 Bengause Rd., Coward | 843/659–2315 or 843/386–3140.

Dining

P.A.'s Restaurant. Continental. Low, romantic lighting and a deep, richly colored decor set the mood at this quietly elegant restaurant known for steaks and chicken. | 1534 S. Irby St. | 843/665–0846 | No lunch | $12–$20 | D, MC, V.

Percy and Willie's Food and Spirits. Continental. A popular cocktail bar and booths make this a lively, casual spot to get steak, pasta, salads, or one of the huge desserts. Kids' menu. | 2401 David McLeod Blvd. | 843/669–1620 | $9–$13 | AE, MC, V.

Red Bone Alley. American. A streetscape mural of Charleston's Rainbow Row decorates this casual, colorful eatery known for its pastas, sandwiches, and salads. | 1903 W. Palmetto St. | 843/673–0035 | $7–$18 | AE, D, MC, V.

Roger's Bar-B-Q House. Barbecue. Try the pork barbecue at this laid-back, no-fuss barbecue joint's buffet. Kids' menu. | 2004 Second Loop Rd. | 843/667–9291 | Closed Sun.–Wed. | $10–$20 | No credit cards.

Lodging

Comfort Inn. This moderately priced chain hotel is 5 mi from shopping and restaurants. Complimentary Continental breakfast. Microwaves, some in-room hot tubs. Cable TV. Pool. Hot tub. Exercise equipment. | 1916 W. Lucas St.; I–95 Exit 164 | 843/665–4558 | fax 843/665–4558 | 162 rooms | $49–$79 | AE, D, DC, MC, V.

Days Inn. The rooms have exterior entrances at this standard two-story chain hotel 3 mi from downtown area. Complimentary Continental breakfast. Some microwaves, some refrigerators, some in-room hot tubs. Cable TV. Pool. Hot tub. Exercise equipment. Business services. Some pets allowed. | 2111 W. Lucas St. | 843/665–4444 | fax 843/665–4444 | 103 rooms | $63 | AE, D, DC, MC, V.

Fairfield Inn of Florence. This 11-yr-old hotel has spacious guest rooms with exterior entrances on the first two floors and an interior entrance on the top floor. In-room data ports, microwaves, refrigerators. Cable TV, in-room VCRs (and movies), room phones. Outdoor pool. No pets. | 140 Dunbarton Dr. | 843/669–1666 | fax 843/669–0942 | www.marriott.com | 135 rooms | $59–$69 | AE, D, DC, MC, V.

Ramada Inn. The commercial area of shopping malls and restaurants is 4 mi from this two-story chain hotel with simple rooms, some of which have exterior entrances. Restaurant, bar (with entertainment), room service. Microwaves. Cable TV. Pool. Hot tub. Exercise equipment. Business services. Some pets allowed. | 2038 W. Lucas St. | 843/669–4241 | fax 843/665–8883 | 179 rooms | $69 | AE, D, DC, MC, V.

Red Roof Inn. You can get budget accommodations across from the local shopping center. Some of the rooms have exterior entrances. Cable TV. Business services. Some pets allowed. | 2690 David McLeod Blvd. | 843/678–9000 | fax 843/667–1267 | 112 rooms | $48–$57 | AE, D, DC, MC, V.

Swamp Fox Inn. This standard motel has two double beds in each room. Restaurant. Cable TV, room phones. Outdoor pool. Pets allowed. | I–95 and U.S. 76 | 843/665–0803 | fax 843/665–0803 | 60 rooms | $24–$28 | AE, D, DC, MC, V.

FOLLY BEACH

MAP 9, 18

(Nearby towns also listed: Charleston, Edisto Island, Isle of Palms, Sullivans Island)

Ten miles to the south of Charleston lies Folly Beach, a traditional beach destination popular with area residents for its laid-back, unpolished style. Until the 1940s, it had a busy pavilion where big bands played. George Gershwin lived here when he wrote "Porgy and Bess" (which is set in Charleston). Today the island is a comfortable blend of unpretentious old beach homes (many for rent by the week during the season) and some new developments, with quiet streets shaded by cedar, cherry, laurel, and palmetto trees. The beach stretches more than 6 mi along the Atlantic on Folly Island. At its southwestern tip is Folly Beach County Park, with some of the best swimming in the area. There's also a handful of motels, restaurants, and shops, and a fishing pier. "The Washout" has long been a favorite surfing spot.

Information: **Charleston Area Convention and Visitors Bureau** | 81 Mary St., Box 975, Charleston, SC 29402 | 843/853–8000 or 800/868–8118 | fax 843/853–0444 | www.charlestoncvb.com.

Attractions
James Island County Park. This 660-acre park is open year-round. It has 4 miles of hiking and biking trails, along with bike, canoe, pedal boat, and kayak rentals, as well as a 50-ft climbing wall ($10). In summer, you can cool off at the Water Park/Splash Zone ($8 residents, $10 non-residents) inside the park. You can also stay overnight in the camping sites and vacation cottages. | 871 Riverland Dr., | 843/795–7275 | $1.

ON THE CALENDAR
NOV.–JAN.: *Festival of Lights in James Island County Park.* Over a million lights illuminate 125 displays, part of a 3-mi tour in the park on Thursday, Friday, and weekends that begins on the second Friday in November and lasts until January 2nd. You can visit the enchanted forest walking trail, and there are carousel rides, a gingerbread house competition, sand sculptures, life-size greeting cards, concerts, a marshmallow roast, and a train ride. | 871 Riverland Dr. | 843/795–7275.

Dining
Starfish Grille on Folly Pier. Seafood. Nautical motifs prevail at this restaurants overlooking the water. You can try some of the house favorites—grouper, snapper, mahi mahi, and crab cakes. | 101 East Artic Ave. | 843/588–2518 | AE, D, DC, MC, V.

Lodging
Holliday Inn of Folly Beach. This family-owned inn caters to families seeking rest and relaxation. Surfing, fishing, and kayaking are 1 block away. Kitchenettes, microwaves, refrigerators. Cable TV, room phones. Outdoor pool. Pets allowed (fee). | 116 West Ashley St. | 800/792–5270 or 843/588–2191 | fax 843/588–6645 | inn108@aol.co | www.hollidayinnfollybeach.com | 14 rooms | $95–$150 | AE, D, MC, V.

GEORGETOWN

MAP 9, J6

(Nearby towns also listed: Litchfield, McClellanville, Murrells Inlet, Pawleys Island)

Founded on Winyah Bay in 1729, Georgetown became the center of America's colonial rice empire. A rich plantation culture developed on a scale comparable to Charleston's, and the historic district, which can be walked in a couple of hours, is among the prettiest in the state. Today, ocean-going vessels still come to Georgetown's busy port, and the Harbor Walk, the restored waterfront, hums with activity.

Information: **Georgetown County Chamber of Commerce and Information Center** | 1005 Front St., Georgetown, SC 29440 | 843/546–8436 or 800/777–7705 | www.georgetown-sc.com/chamber.

Attractions

Harold Kaminski House. This house museum overlooking the Sampit River is especially notable for its collections of regional antiques and furnishings, Chippendale and Duncan Phyfe furniture, Royal Doulton vases, and silver. | 1003 Front St. | 843/546–7706 | $4 | Mon.–Sat. 10–5, Sun. 1–4.

Hobcaw Barony. Franklin D. Roosevelt and Winston Churchill came here to confer with the late Bernard M. Baruch, whose estate is now a vast 17,500-acre wildlife preserve. A museum is used for teaching and research in forestry and marine biology, and there are aquariums, terrariums, touch tanks, and video presentations. | 22 Hobcaw Rd. | 843/546–4623 | Free | Weekdays 10–5, Sat. 1–5.

Hopsewee Plantation. Surrounded by moss-draped live oaks, magnolias, and tree-size camellias, this plantation overlooks the North Santee River. A fine Georgian staircase and hand-carved Adam lighted-candle moldings reference the glorious past. | 494 Hopsewee Rd. | 843/546–7891 | Mansion $6, grounds $2 per car (parking fees apply toward tours) | Tues.–Fri. 10–4, or by appointment.

Prince George Winyah Church. Named after King George II, this church still serves the parish established in 1721. It was built in 1737 with bricks brought from England. | Broad and Highmarket Sts. | 843/546–4358 | Donations accepted | Mar.–Oct., weekdays 11:30–4:30, Sun. services at 8 and 10.

Rice Museum/Town Clock Building. This graceful market and meeting place, punctuated by an 1842 clock and tower, houses maps, tools, and dioramas. Next door, the Provost Gallery sells unique South Carolina glasswork, pearls, and pottery. | Front and Screven Sts. | 843/546–7423 | $3 | Mon.–Sat. 9:30–4:30.

Sightseeing Tours. A variety of themed tour companies operate out of Georgetown. You can take tram tours of the historic district, a ghostbusting tour, or an afternoon tea 'n' tour with the **Georgetown Tour Company.** | 627 Front St. | 843/546–6827 | Call for prices. Though Halloween lasts only a night, you can take a self-guided **Ghost Tour** of the "Ghost Capital of the World," with costumed reenactors, during the preceding week. | 1001 Front St. | 843/546–8437 | $7.50 | Oct. 26–Oct. 31, 10–5.
The Miss Nell of **Miss Nell's "Real South" Tours** offers walking tours of 8, 12, or 24 blocks; all leave from the front of the Mark Twain bookstore. | Tours depart from 723 Front St. | 843/527–3975 | Call for prices.
These hour-long **Tram Tours** give a rich history of the historic district. | Tours depart from the Chamber of Commerce, 1001 Front St. | 843/546–6827 | $7.50 | Tours depart hourly weekdays 10–4.

ON THE CALENDAR

APR.: *Chicora Indian Day Celebration.* A day of arts and crafts, music, dance, and food honors the Chicora Indian tribe. | Main St. | 803/264–3231.

Dining

Land's End Restaurant. Seafood. You can dine indoors or outside on the covered deck at this restaurant overlooking the Georgetown landing marina and the intracoastal waterway. Although known for its seafood, it also offers prime rib and chicken. Sunday brunch. | 444 Marina Dr., at Hwy. 17 | 843/527–1376 | No lunch Sat. No dinner Sun. | $9–$24 | AE, D, MC, V.

Rice Paddy. Contemporary. Works by local artists hang on the walls at this elegant eatery; you can also sit outside on the covered deck overlooking the river while you dine on fresh fish, lump crab cakes, or pan fried quail with country ham and cream grits. Veal and lamb are also available. | 819 Front St. | 843/546–2021 | Closed Sun. | $16–$25 | AE, D, MC, V.

River Room. Seafood. Candlelight and river views add to the dining experience at this restaurant in the oldest historical building in the area. Built in 1888, it used to be a store, a hat factory, and then a grain mill. Authentic antiques fill the restaurant and old photographs cover the walls. Though there are all kinds of grilled fish, rib-eye steak, chicken, and pasta dishes, try the popular soft shell crab sandwich and the crawfish dip served with tortillas. Kids' menu. | 801 Front St. | 843/527–4110 | Closed Sun. | $14–$25 | AE, MC, V.

Lodging

Alexandra's Inn. Working fireplaces and high ceilings distinguish the main house's five rooms. The carriage house, with two bedrooms and a full kitchen, is available for families— in fact, children and pets are not allowed in the main house. You can have access to golfing 5 mi away. Complimentary breakfast. Some in-room hot tubs. Cable TV, room phones. Outdoor pool. No smoking. | 620 Prince St. | 888/557–0233 or 843/527–0233 | fax 843/520–0718 | alexinn@sccoast.net | www.alexsandrasinn.com | 5 rooms; 2-bedroom carriage house | $95–$135 | AE, MC, V.

Clarion Carriage House–Carolinian Inn. This two-story chain hotel is 4 blocks from the cafés and restaurants of Main Street and the shopping area on the Waterfront. Restaurant, complimentary breakfast. Cable TV. Pool. Business services. | 706 Church St. (U.S. 17) | 843/546–5191 | fax 803/546–1514 | 89 rooms | $68–71 | AE, D, DC, MC, V.

Harbor House. Hard pine floors and antiques furnish the rooms at this family owned inn, built in 1765 and overlooking the working waterfront. The house is on the national historic register. Complimentary breakfast. In-room data ports, minibars, refrigerators. Cable TV, VCR in common area. No pets. No kids under 14. | 15 Cannon St. | 877/511–0101 or 843/546–6532 | info@harborhousebb.com | www.harborhousebb.com | 4 rooms | $105–$165 | Jan. | MC, V.

Mansfield Plantation. The original house and slave cabins are among the 11 buildings that remain on this 460-acre former rice plantation. Four-poster rice beds and 19th-century oil paintings decorate the guest rooms in the 1930s schoolhouse and renovated servants' quarters, all of which have private entrances. Complimentary breakfast. Boating, bicycles. Some pets allowed. | 1776 Mansfield Rd. | 843/546–6961 or 800/355–3223 | fax 843/546–5235 | www.bbonline.com/sc/mansfield | 8 rooms | $95–$135 | No credit cards.

1790 House. A covered porch wraps around this two-story colonial plantation house, and gardens bloom on the property. Handmade quilts cover the four-poster beds (with canopies), lace curtains grace the windows, and fireplaces warm the hardwood floors in the six bedrooms. The house is in Georgetown's Historical District and within walking distance of shops and restaurants. You can also use the house library. Complimentary breakfast. Cable TV in some rooms. Bicycles. No smoking. | 630 Highmarket St. | 843/546–4821 or 800/890–7432 | jwiley5211@aol.com | www.1790house.com | 6 rooms (4 with shower only), 1 suite | $95–$135 | AE, D, MC, V.

Shaw House Inn. Through built in 1975, this house seems colonial in more ways than simply architecturally: authentic and rare antiques, rice beds, and some queen-size canopies furnish the rooms, all of which have private baths. You can watch birds in the marsh from the glass-enclosed family room. Complimentary breakfast. Cable TV. | 613 Cypress Ct | 843/546–9663 | 3 rooms | $65–$80 | No credit cards.

GREENVILLE

MAP 9, C2

(Nearby towns also listed: Anderson, Clemson, Pendleton, Spartanburg)

Greenville is primarily known for its textile and manufacturing plants, but the town has a number of attractions and offers easy access to state parks such as Caesar's Head and Table Rock. Greenville is also home to Bob Jones University, which has a gallery of religious art and artifacts.

Information: Greenville Chamber of Commerce | 24 Cleveland St., Greenville, SC 29601 | 864/242–1050.

Attractions

BMW Zentrum Museum. At BMW's only North American auto manufacturing plant, you can see displays of BMW's impact on the automotive, motorcycle, and aviation industries. The virtual factory tour is almost as good as the real thing. | 1400 Hwy. 101 S, Greer; 10 mi NE of Greenville | 888/TOUR–BMW (868–7269) | Free | Tues.–Sat. 9:30–5:30.

Bob Jones University. Founded in 1947, this Christian liberal arts college offers 150 undergraduate and graduate majors and a controversial stumping ground for Republic presidential candidates. | 1700 Wade Hampton Blvd. | 864/242–5100 or 800/515–2233 | www.bju.edu | Free | Daily.
The **Bob Jones University Art Gallery and Museum** houses an international collection of religious art, including works by Dolci, Rembrandt, Rubens, Titian, and Van Dyck. Thirty galleries showcase sacred art from the 13th through the 19th centuries. | 1700 Wade Hampton Blvd. | 864/242–5100 | www.bju.edu/art.gallery | Free | Tues.–Sun. 2–5.
The **Mack Memorial Library** has 225,000 volumes, including a rare collection of bibles in the Jerusalem Chamber (a replica of the room in London's Westminster Abbey) and a number of historic hymnals and songbooks in the American Hymnody Collection. | 1700 Wade Hampton Blvd. | 864/242–5100 | fax 864/242–5100 | www.bju.edu/places | Free | Mon.–Thurs. 7:45 AM–10 PM, Fri. 7:45 AM–9 PM, Sat. 9–9.

Caesar's Head State Park. On a clear day, you can see the sweep of the Blue Ridge Mountains from the top of the Mountain Bridge Recreation and Wilderness Area (elevation 3,208 ft). The park has 50 mi of hiking trails, including a moderate 2⅕-mi hike to an overlook at Raven Cliff Falls. | 8155 Geer Hwy., Cleveland; 37 mi NW of Greenville | 864/836–6115 | Free | Daily 9–6.

Greenville County Museum of Art. One of the world's finest collections of Andrew Wyeth's watercolors comprises part of the museum's collection of Southern art. The Southern Collection features works from the 1700s to the present, including those by Georgia O'Keeffe and Jasper Johns. | 420 College St. | 864/271–7570 | Free | Tues.–Sat. 10–5, Sun. 1–5.

Greenville Zoo. Various creatures from around the world have found a home in Greenville, in natural, open-air exhibits. The zoo also has picnic shelters, playgrounds, and tennis courts. | 150 Cleveland Park Dr. | 864/467–4300 | $4 | Daily 10–4:30.

Nippon Center. Exquisite Japanese furniture and a rock garden help this cultural center successfully resemble the 14th-century Japanese mansion on which it was modeled. There's also an authentic Japanese restaurant and tea ceremony. | 500 Congaree Rd. | 864/987–9591 | www.nippon-center.org | Tours $3, tea ceremony $5 | Tours Mon.–Sat.; tea ceremony 3rd Wed. of month.

Paris Mountain. You can fish in the pond, swim in the lake, cruise around in pedal boats, hike the trails, camp, or just picnic. | 2401 State Park Rd. | 864/244–5565 | Free | Daily 9–6.

16th SC Volunteers Museum of Confederate History. This collection of personal and military Confederate memorabilia is in Greenville's Pettigru Historic District. There's a research library here, too. | 15 Boyce Ave. | 864/421–9039 | Donations accepted | Fri. 5–9, Sat. 10–5, Sun. 1–5.

Sightseeing Tours. Most tours are either of the countryside surrounding Greenville or the historic buildings in town.
The **Dark Corner Tour** takes you through the mountainous area of the Upcountry, stopping at several historic sites. | 302 Hwy. 11, Landrum | 864/242–5407 | Call for prices.
A Glimpse of Greenville is an award-winning volunteer tourism program that showcases the history of Greenville. | 103 Pebble Stone La., Taylors | 864/987–5572 | Call for prices.

Table Rock. One of the area's best-known landmarks, the rounded dome of Table Rock punctuates the skyline. The oldest and most popular state park in the Blue Ridge has 14 rustic cabins with fireplaces, 100 campsites, lake swimming, canoe and boat rentals, hiking trails, and a restaurant. | 158 E. Ellison La., Pickens; 20 mi west of Greenville | 864/878–9813 | $1.50 | Daily 7 AM–9:30 PM.

West End Market. This restored turn-of-the-20th-century cotton warehouse near Main Street has become the venue for trendy shops and restaurants, a coffee shop, and a jazz club. | 1 Augusta St. | 864/467–4412 | Free.

ON THE CALENDAR
MAY: *Freedom Weekend Aloft.* On Memorial Day, races of more than 100 hot-air balloons take place, accompanied by fireworks, entertainment, craft vendors, rides, and food. | 864/232–3700.
DEC.: *First Night Greenville.* This family-friendly New Year's Eve celebration in downtown Greenville includes performers and visual arts shows. | Main St. | Dec. 31 | 864/370–1795.

Dining
Bistro Europa. Contemporary. Seven tables sheltered by large umbrellas are outside on the sidewalk of Main Street; you can also sit inside. Grilled Long Island duck breast with garlic mashed potatoes or Ahi tuna with a seaweed salad and basmati rice are two of the most popular dishes served, though you can count on a good cup of coffee and fresh-baked bread as well. Sunday brunch. | 219 N. Main St. | 864/467–9975 | Closed Sun. | $14–22 | AE, D, DC, MC, V.

Brick Street Cafe. American. Fresh flowers and white tablecloths always decorate the tables here, which usually hold such specialties as sweet potato pie, coconut cake, cheese cake, and carrot cake. Lunch and dinner are also served. | 315 Augusta St. | 864/421–0111 | Closed Sun. | $9–$16 | AE, MC, V.

Melting Pot. French. Cheese, meat and chocolate fondues do the melting here, at this intimate restaurant near the Haywood Mall. | 475–5 Haywood Rd. | 864/297–5035 | No lunch | $14–$29 | AE, D, MC, V.

Occasionally Blues. Southern. In keeping with the area's cuisine, you can try shrimp and grits, baby back ribs, and swordfish at this restaurant. On Thursdays, Fridays, and Saturdays, a live band plays blues music ($10 cover charge on Fridays and Saturdays). | 1 Augusta St. | 864/242–6000 | Closed Sun., Mon. No lunch | $17–$22 | AE, D, DC, MC, V.

The Palms. Continental. Linen tablecloths, soft candlelight, and a piano bar make for a romantic evening at the elegant and formal dining room of Phoenix–Greenville's Inn. Duck and seafood are the specialties here. | 246 N. Pleasantburg Dr. | 864/233–4651 | Closed Sun. | AE, D, DC, MC, V.

Saskatoon: Steaks, Fish and Wildgame. Steak. This restaurant looks like a hunting lodge, with a working fireplace. You can try the specialty, usually a mixed grill, or sit at the popular bar. | 477 Haywood Rd. | 864/297–7244 | No lunch | $12–$19 | AE, D, DC, MC, V.

Seven Oaks. Continental. You can dine in the dining room with elegant curved ceilings and stained glass or in the courtyard adorned with candles and flowers. The restaurant serves fresh fish daily, as well as pasta and chicken, though you may want to try the popular filet mignon. You can also choose from an extensive wine list. | 104 Broadus Ave. | 864/232–1895 | Closed Sun. No lunch | $18–$29 | AE, DC, MC, V.

Stax's Omega. American. American, Greek, and Italian dishes are served late into the night at this diner. You can sit in booths or on stools at the half-circle counter. | 72 Orchard Park Dr. | 864/297–6639 | $8–$11 | AE, D, MC, V.

Stax's Peppermill. Seafood. The tables are covered in white linens and piano music sets the relaxing tone at this simple but elegant eatery serving fish, steak, pasta, and chicken dishes. There's a pianist Tuesday through Saturday. | 30 Orchard Park Dr. | 864/288–9320 | Closed Sun. No lunch | $20–$30 | AE, DC, MC, V.

Yagoto. Japanese. The Japanese cultural center, complete with imported fabrics, rugs, and furnishings, houses this Japanese restaurant. The tatami room overlooks a traditional Japanese rock garden. | 500 Congaree Rd. | 864/288–8471 | Closed Sun. | $15–$30 | AE, D, DC, MC, V.

Lodging

AmeriSuites. Three miles from downtown Greenville, 4 mi from Bob Jones University, and 15 mi from Furman University, this hotel is also convenient to downtown restaurants and shopping. Complimentary Continental breakfast. In-room data ports, kitchenettes, microwaves, refrigerators. Cable TV, in-room VCRs, room phones. Outdoor pool. Exercise equipment. Free parking. Pets allowed (fee). | 40 West Orchard Park Dr. | 800/833–1516 or 864/232–3000 | fax 864/271–4388 | www.amerisuites.com | 128 suites | $59–$89 | AE, D, DC, MC, V.

Courtyard by Marriott. Rooms in these three stories have balconies facing the courtyard. The hotel is 3 mi south of downtown. Restaurant (breakfast only). Refrigerators in suites. Cable TV. Pool. Hot tub. Exercise equipment. Laundry facilities. Business services, free parking. | 70 Orchard Park Dr.; off of I–385, Exit 39 | 864/234–0300 | fax 864/234–0296 | www.courtyard.com | 146 rooms | $95 | AE, D, DC, MC, V.

Crowne Plaza Greenville. This hotel is 5 mi from downtown Greenville, 8 mi from the airport, the Roper Mt. Science Center, and the Greenville Braves Ball Park. The rooms contain a hair dryer, iron, and ironing board. Restaurant, bar, room service. In-room data ports. Cable TV, room phones. Pool. Exercise equipment. Free parking. Pets allowed (fee). | 851 Congaree Rd. | 800/465–4329 or 864/297–6300 | fax 864/234–0747 | www.basshotels.com | 208 rooms | $129–$139 | AE, D, DC, MC, V.

Days Inn. The Greenville Expo Center is 7 mi away; downtown is 3 miles away. There's an adjoining restaurant. Complimentary Continental breakfast. In-room data ports. Cable TV. Pool. | 831 Congaree Rd. | 864/288–6221 | fax 864/288–2778 | 121 rooms | $55–$65 | AE, D, DC, MC, V.

Embassy Suites. The suites at this nine-story chain hotel have balconies. The Greenville Zoo, part of Cleveland Park, is 4 mi away, the Greenville County Museum is 6 mi away, and there are two shopping malls within a 2-mi radius of the hotel. Restaurant, bar, complimentary breakfast. In-room data ports, refrigerators. Cable TV. 2 pools (1 indoor). Hot tub. Driving range, putting green, 2 tennis courts. Exercise equipment. Laundry facilities. Business services, airport shuttle. | 670 Verdae Blvd. | 864/676–9090 | fax 864/676–0669 | www.embassysuites.com | 268 suites | $129–$144 | AE, D, DC, MC, V.

Fairfield Inn by Marriott. Three stories tall, this chain hotel in the nearby Bi-Lo Center has concerts, sporting events, and family fare. Two separate shopping malls lie within a 1-mi radius. Complimentary Continental breakfast. In-room data ports. Cable TV. Pool. Business services. Free parking. | 60 Roper Mountain Rd. | 864/297–9996 | fax 864/297–9965 | 132 rooms | $55 | AE, D, DC, MC, V.

Guesthouse Inn. Rooms come with a stove and coffee maker at this hotel, 5 mi from Bob Jones University, the airport, shops, and malls. In-room data ports, kitchenettes, microwaves, refrigerators. Cable TV, room phones. Free parking. No pets. | 2015 Wade Hampton Blvd. | 864/751–4500 or 864/751–4501 | fax 864/751–4502 | 170 rooms | $40–$65 | AE, D, MC, V.

GuestHouse International Suites Plus. The cozy and intimate suites here are within ½ mi from various shops and eateries. Complimentary Continental breakfast. Kitchenettes. Cable TV. Pool. Hot tub. Business services. Some pets allowed (fee). | 48 McPrice Ct. | 864/297–0099 | fax 864/288–8203 | 96 suites | $99–$129 | AE, D, DC, MC, V.

Hampton Inn. This typical chain hotel occupies four stories. You can find a shopping mall and restaurants nearby, and the hotel is 3 mi from downtown, off I–385 at Exit 39. Complimentary Continental breakfast. In-room data ports. Cable TV. Pool. Business services. | 246 Congaree Rd. | 864/288–1200 | fax 864/288–5667 | www.hampton-inn.com | 123 rooms | $69–$74 | AE, D, DC, MC, V.

Hilton. This hotel is located in the middle of the business district. Restaurant, bar. Refrigerators in suites. Cable TV. Indoor pool. Hot tub. Exercise equipment. Business services, airport shuttle. | 45 W. Orchard Park Dr.; off of I–385 Exit 39 | 864/232–4747 | fax 864/235–6248 | www.greenvillesc.hilton.com | 256 rooms | $159 | AE, D, DC, MC, V.

Holiday Inn. This familiar chain hotel is 6 mi from the park, an entertainment complex, and the Greenville Zoo. Restaurant, bar, room service. In-room data ports. Cable TV. Pool. Business services, airport shuttle, free parking. | 4295 Augusta Rd. | 864/277–8921 | fax 864/299–6066 | www.holiday-inn.com | 155 rooms | $69–$89 | AE, D, DC, MC, V.

Hyatt Regency. This standard chain hotel is in the center of Main Street, the heart of Greenville. The rooms are luxurious; the eight-story building has no balconies. Restaurants, bar. Room service. In-room data ports. Cable TV. Pool. Hot tub. Exercise equipment. Business services, airport shuttle. Valet parking. | 220 N. Main St. | 864/235–1234 | fax 864/232–7584 | www.hyatt.com | 327 rooms | $95–$159 | AE, D, DC, MC, V.

La Quinta. The Mediterranean decor matches the Spanish name of this two-story chain hotel. It's 7 mi from the airport. Complimentary Continental breakfast. Cable TV. Pool. Laundry facilities. Business services, free parking. Some pets allowed. | 31 Old Country Rd. | 864/297–3500 | fax 864/458–9818 | www.laquintainn.com | 122 rooms | $59–$66 | AE, D, DC, MC, V.

Marriott Airport. The closest hotel to the airport offers shuttle service to shopping areas and restaurants. Restaurant, bar. In-room data ports. Cable TV, 2 pools (1 indoor). Hot tub. Exercise equipment. Business services, airport shuttle. Free parking. | 1 Parkway E | 864/297–0300 or 800/441–1737 | fax 864/281–0801 | www.marriott.com | 204 rooms | $134 | AE, D, DC, MC, V.

Microtel Inn Greenville. One of the many budget options in Greenville, this motel is in the shopping district. Complimentary Continental breakfast. In-room data ports, some microwaves. Cable TV, room phones. Free parking. Pets allowed (fee). | 20 Interstate Ct. | 864/297–7866 | fax 864/297–7883 | 122 rooms | $32–$42 | AE, D, DC, MC, V.

Pettigru Place B&B. Different themes distinguish the rooms at this 1920s house on a quiet street downtown. Tropical fabrics, for example, decorate the rainforest room. Many rooms have four-poster beds and hardwood floors, and all have private baths. A fireplace warms the common room, and complimentary wine and cheese are served in the evening. You can relax outside on the two porches or in the three gardens. Complimentary breakfast. Cable TV. | 302 Pettigru St. | 864/242–4529 | fax 864/242–1231 | www.pettigruplace.com | 5 rooms | $95–$175 | AE, D, DC, MC, V.

Phoenix–Greenville's Inn. Renovations have converted a two-story 1971 motel into an elegant inn. Embellished with plantation shutters and four-poster beds, the rooms in two buildings overlook the courtyard. Restaurant (The Palms), bar (with entertainment), complimentary breakfast. Cable TV. Pool. | 246 N. Pleasantburg Dr. | 864/233–4651 | 800/257–3529 | 184 rooms | $88 | AE, D, DC, MC, V.

Quality Inn–Haywood. Though simply decorated, the rooms at this chain hotel have balconies. Restaurants are 1 mi away, and it's 6 mi to downtown. Complimentary Continental breakfast. Cable TV. Pool. Free parking. | 50 Orchard Park Dr. | 864/297–9000 | fax 864/297–8292 | www.conradusa.com | 147 rooms | $64 | AE, D, DC, MC, V.

Red Horse Inn. Fireplaces and hand-painted murals decorate these Victorian-style cottages, whose porches give out onto the 190 acres, with mountains in the distance. Complimentary Continental breakfast. Kitchenettes, some in-room hot tubs. Cable TV. | 310 N. Campbell Rd., Landrum; 28 mi NE of Greenville | 864/895–4968 | fax 864/895–4968 | www.thered-horseinn.com | 5 cottage suites | $110–$155 | AE, D, MC, V.

Travelodge. This hotel is ¼ mile from downtown Greenville, 2½ mi from Palmetto Center, 4 mi from Furman University, and within walking distance of Bob Jones University. Restaurant, complimentary Continental breakfast. In-room data ports, microwaves, refrigerators. Cable TV, room phones. Outdoor pool. Free parking. No pets. | 755 Wade Hampton Blvd. | 864/233–5393 | fax 864/233–6014 | www.travelodge.com | 78 rooms | $39–$69 | AE, D, DC, MC, V.

Travelodge. Five miles from downtown Greenville is this two-story hotel, which has special access for people with disabilities. In-room data ports, some microwaves, some refrigerators. Cable TV, room phones. Outdoor pool. Free parking. Pets allowed (fee). | 1465 S. Pleasantburg Dr. | 800/578–7878 or 864/277–8670 | fax 864/422–8960 | www.travelodge.com | 100 rooms | $39–$65 | AE, D, DC, MC, V.

GREENWOOD

MAP 9, D4

GREENWOOD

INTRO
ATTRACTIONS
DINING
LODGING

(Nearby town also listed: Abbeville)

Greenwood derives its name from the rolling landscape and dense forest that surrounded the site when it was founded by Irish settlers in 1802. Today, outdoor enthusiasts head for the 200-mi shore of Lake Greenwood, as well as to the nearby Sumter National Forest.

Attractions

Baker Creek State Park. Nature and bridle trails crisscross the 1,305–acre park. You can rent a pedal boat, fish, and swim on Thurmond Lake, camp, play golf, or relax on the sandy beach. | Route 3, Box 50,McCormick | 25 mi SW of Greenwood | 864/443–2457 or 864/443–5886 | Free; camping $17 | Daily, 6–6.

Emerald Farm. At this working goat farm with 75 acres of pastures, children can pet the Swiss goats, horses, cows, chickens, and rabbits. The farm produces milk for the handmade all-natural soaps also made here. | 409 Emerald Farm Rd. | 864/223–9747 | www.greenwood.net/~emeraldfarm | Free | Mon.–Sat. 9–5.

Gardens of Park Seed Co. One of the nation's largest seed supply houses, this company maintains colorful test gardens and greenhouses—the flower beds are especially vivid June 15 through July. The company's store sells seeds and bulbs. | Rte. 254 | 864/941–4213 or 800/845–3369 | Free | Gardens daily; store Mon.–Sat. 9–5; tours weekdays at 10 and 2.

Hickory Knob Resort. Nice accommodations—lakeside cottages, an 80-room lodge, and a 200-yr-old restored cottage—and a restaurant and conference center distinguish this 1,091–acre park. There's a lot more to it though: an 18-hole championship golf course, nature trails, tennis courts, a swimming pool, an archery range, boat slips, and a tackle shop, as well as fishing and swimming in Lake Thurmond. | Rte. 4, McCormick | 25 mi SW of Greenwood | 800/491–1764 | Free | Daily.

J. Strom Thurmond Lake. Most of the 1,200-mi shoreline of this lake, also known as Clarks Hill Lake, is within Sumter National Forest. You can do some great bass and catfish fishing in the waters. There's also an aquarium and interactive exhibits. | U.S. 221 | 864/333–1100 or 706/722–3770 | Swimming $1 fee, boating $2 launch fee | Daily 8–4:30.

Lake Greenwood. Anglers, swimmers, and boaters enjoy the 200-mi shore, but there are also hiking and mountain biking trails, camping, and picnic areas. The park, a project of the Depression-era Civilian Conservation Corps, has the stone work and landscaping of that period. | 302 State Park Rd., Ninety Six; 17 mi east of Greenwood | 864/543–3535 | Free | Daily, Daylight Savings Time, 6–9; Eastern Standard Time, 6–6.

The Museum. A replica of a village street with its one-room school and general store are among the more than 7,000 items on display here. There are also Native American artifacts, and natural history and geology exhibits. | 106 Main St. | 864/229–7093 | $2 | Wed.–Sat. 10–5.

Ninety Six National Historic Site. The first Revolutionary War land battle in the South was fought here in 1775; it's also the site of the longest Patriot army siege during the war. The visitor center's museum displays descriptive exhibits, remnants of the old village, a reconstructed French and Indian War stockade, and Revolutionary-era fortifications exist on the site. | Hwy. 248 | 864/543–4068 | Free | Daily 8–5.

Sumter National Forest. An amazing variety of wildlife live in this 118,000-acre woodland, which also has hiking trails and lake water sports. | 112 Andrew Pickens Circle (one of the ranger points), Mountain Rest | 864/561–4000 | Free | Daily.

ON THE CALENDAR

JUNE: *South Carolina Festival of Flowers.* Once a year, the George W. Park Seed Company opens their world-famous Trial Grounds to display several thousand varieties of flowers. Flower Day falls on a Saturday in late June and is at the heart of the festival which also hosts jazz and bluegrass concerts, plays, a crafts fair, and a photography competition. Some events are free, others charge admission of $10 and under. | 864/223–8431 | www.scfestivalofflowers.org.

Dining

O'Charleys. American. Families frequent this southern chain restaurant. Chicken tenders, Caesar salad, steak, and ribs are available for lunch and dinner. For dessert, you can try the Kentucky silk pie or the fudge brownie à la mode. | 452 Hwy. 72N | 864/227–0272 | $9–$17 | AE, D, DC, MC, V.

Regan's. American. This restaurant across the street from the Inn on the Square serves several chicken and steak dishes, as well as seafood and salads. Popular items include the honey-marinated and baked chicken Pooh, shrimp and grits, and the steak New Orleans, a blackened New York strip accompanied by spicy creole sauce. | 328 Main St. | 864/388–0565 | Closed Sun. No lunch Sat. | $8–$19 | AE, MC, V.

Lodging

Comfort Inn. Exterior entrances lead to the rooms at this two-story chain hotel, one block from restaurants and a movie theater, and 2 mi from the shopping mall. Complimentary Continental breakfast. Refrigerators. Cable TV. Pool. Hot tub. Exercise equipment. Business services. | 1215 NE U.S. 72 Bypass | 864/223–2838 | fax 864/942–0119 | 83 rooms | $68–$76 | AE, D, DC, MC, V.

Days Inn. Popular with business travelers, this chain hotel provides nice rooms in a quiet setting. The rooms come with hair dryers and alarm clocks and sometimes microwaves and refrigerators. Complimentary Continental breakfast. Some microwaves, some refrigerators. Cable TV, room phones, TV in common area. Laundry facilities. No pets. | 230 Birchtree Dr. | 864/223–1818 | fax 864/223–0513 | 62 rooms | $60 | AE, D, DC, MC, V.

Inn on the Square. The inn has spacious rooms decorated with antique reproductions. The hotel is in uptown Greenwood, and 50 mi from Greenville-Spartanburg Airport. Dining room, room service. Cable TV. Pool. Business services. | 104 Court St. | 864/223–4488 | fax 864/223–7067 | www.innonthesquare.com | 46 rooms | $80 | AE, D, DC, MC, V.

The Jameson Inn. Wood trim and magnolias decorate the lobby at this comfortable Southern colonial-style chain hotel. The rooms are clean and comfortable and you can relax at the pool or exercise in the gym. Dining room, complimentary Continental breakfast. Some in-room data ports, some microwaves, some refrigerators, some in-room hot tubs. Cable

TV, room phones, TV in common area. Outdoor pool. Gym. Laundry service. No pets. | 109 Enterprise Ct. | 864/942–0002 | fax 864/227–0040 | 66 rooms | $55–$62 | AE, D, DC, MC, V.

Ramada Inn. Though simply appointed, the rooms at this two-story chain are cozy and have balconies. You can cross the street to a shopping mall. Landers University is 3 mi away. Restaurant, bar, room service. In-room data ports. Cable TV. Pool. Laundry facilities. Business services. | 1014 Montague Ave. | 864/223–4231 | fax 864/223–6911 | www.ramada-inn.com | 100 rooms | $49–$55 | AE, D, DC, MC, V.

HARTSVILLE

(Nearby towns also listed: Bennettsville, Cheraw, Darlington, Florence)

Hartsville sits on the site of a former plantation and is home to Coker College. Brick-paved sidewalks line its revitalized downtown, with clean and tidy streets and a sprinkling of trendy shops and restaurants. Walking and canoe trails cross Kalmia Gardens, a natural oasis of swamp, thickets, and uplands. Hartsville is also well known as the headquarters for Sonoco Products Co., a Fortune 500 company that makes containers for industrial use.

Information: Greater Hartsville Chamber of Commerce | 214 N. 5th St., Hartsville, SC 29550 | 843/332–6401 | fax 843/332–8017.

Attractions

Elizabeth Boatwright Coker Performing Arts Center. This 40,000-square-ft state-of-the-art facility, the newest addition to Coker College, hosts performances most weekends. | Coker College, 300 E. College Ave. | 843/383–8018 | Call for performance schedule.

H. B. Robinson Nuclear Information Center. Carolina Power and Light Company has set up displays on how nuclear power works. There are also interactive activities and a slide show. | 3581 West Entrance Rd. | 843/857–1000 | Free | By appointment.

Hartsville Museum. A steam car, antique clothing, photographs, early household implements, and a Southern silver collection make up the exhibits at this museum, now in a restored 1930 post office. | 222 N. 5th St. | 843/383–3005 | Free | Mon.–Sat. 10–5.

Kalmia Gardens of Coker College. The plants in this 30-acre living laboratory represent vastly differing terrains and flora. Spring brings vivid blossoms and the *Kalmia latifolia* (mountain laurel), for which the gardens are famous. You can also walk the nature trails, take a canoe trip down the Black Creek River, or see the oldest home in Hartsville, that of Thomas Hart, the town's founding father. | Carolina Ave. | 843/383–8145 | Free | Daily 9–5.

Lee State Park. Cane fishing for redbreast bream is popular here, as are equestrian events, camping, and picnicking. | 487 Loop Rd., Bishopville; 17 mi SW of Hartsville | 843/428–3833.

ON THE CALENDAR

OCT.: *Jazz! Carolina Festival.* Downtown streets are closed off during performances by big-name and local jazz performers. There are also a festival, a parade, a Sunday gospel performance, and a blessing of the animals. Most of the action takes place at Centennial Park or the city parking lot. | 843/332–6401 or 888/427–8720.

Dining

Bizzell's. American. Local artwork decorates the walls of this downtown eatery serving soup, shrimp and grits, quiche, chicken, steak, and sandwiches. You can sit at the booths or on stools at the counter. | 137 E. Carolina Ave. | 843/857–9080 | Closed Sun. | $13–$30 | AE, D, MC, V.

Culinary Co. American. Friendly staff serve coffee, pancakes, and salads at this intimate café-style spot downtown. | 113 W. Carolina Ave. | 843/857–9511 | Breakfast also available. Closed Sun. | $8–$12 | AE, D, MC, V.

Grigg's Grocery/Miriam's Kitchen. American. This "restaurant" is a hard-to-find old grocery store, with a butcher and candy shop, that's known for its fried chicken, vegetables, biscuits, and potato salad. | 2541 Bethlehem Rd. | 843/332–6087 | Breakfast also available. No supper | $5–$15 | AE, D, MC, V.

Lodging

Fairfield Inn. It's 1 mi to Coker College and the Hartsville Museum from this business traveler's hotel. The complimentary breakfast includes your choice of waffles, pancakes, or french toast. Room rates double over weekends in early Sept. and mid-Mar. Complimentary breakfast. Some microwaves, some refrigerators, some in-room hot tubs. Cable TV, room phones, TV in common area. No pets. | 200 S. 4th St., at 5th St. | 843/332–9898 or 800/228–2800 | fax 843/332–1212 | www.fairfieldinn.com | 74 rooms in 3 stories | $69–$75 | AE, D, DC, MC, V.

Missouri Inn. Antiques and fireplaces furnish the interior and a porch fronts this clapboard house built circa 1900 in the downtown district, near Coker College. Complimentary Continental breakfast. Cable TV. Business services. | 314 E. Home Ave. | 843/383–9553 | fax 843/383–9553 | 5 rooms | $85 | AE, MC, V.

Nealcrest Farm B&B. Handmade quilts cover four-poster beds in spacious rooms with hardwood floors. The 47 acres of this property include a small kennel. Complimentary breakfast. Cable TV. Pool. Business services. Some pets allowed (fee). | 1248 Windfall Farm La. | 843/383–6677 | fax 843/383–4009 | 3 rooms, 1 apartment | $60–$80 | MC, V.

HILTON HEAD ISLAND

MAP 9, G9

(Nearby towns also listed: Beaufort)

Anchoring the southern tip of South Carolina's coastline is Hilton Head Island. Planters settled here in the 1700s and the island flourished until the Civil War. Thereafter, the economy declined and the island languished until Charles E. Fraser, a visionary South Carolina attorney, began developing the Sea Pines resort in 1956. Other developments followed, and today Hilton Head is one of the East Coast's most popular vacation getaways.

Lined by towering pines, palmetto trees, and wind-sculpted live oaks, Hilton Head's 12 mi of beaches are the major attraction, though oak and pine woodlands and meandering lagoons also cover the semitropical barrier island. Choice stretches are occupied by various resorts, or "plantations," among them Sea Pines, Shipyard, Palmetto Dunes, Port Royal, and Hilton Head. In these areas, you can find a mix of rental villas, lavish private houses, and luxury hotels. Though the resorts are private residential communities, many have public restaurants, marinas, shopping areas, and recreational facilities. A new, 5⅘-mi toll bridge ($1) makes it easy to bypass traffic and reach the southern end of the island, where most of the resort areas and hotels are.

Information: Hilton Head Island Chamber of Commerce | 1 Chamber Of Commerce, Hilton Head, SC 29928 | 843/785–3673.

Attractions

Audubon–Newhall Preserve. On 50 acres of pristine forest on the south of the island, you can find native plant life identified and tagged. There are also trails, a self-guided tour, and seasonal plant walks. | Palmetto Bay Rd. | 843/785–5775 | Free | Daily dawn to dusk.

Adventure Cruises. Boating excursions depart for Daufuskie Island; you can also charter a fishing trip. | Shelter Cove Marina | 843/785–4558.

Hilton Head Factory Stores 1 and 2. J. Crew, GAP, Brooks Brothers, Harry and David, and Timberland make up some of the more than 80 outlets here. | U.S. 78 | 843/837–4339 | Free | Mon.–Sat. 10–9, Sun. 11–6.

James M. Waddell Jr. Mariculture Research and Development Center. You can tour the 24 ponds and research building to see how methods of raising commercial seafood are studied. | Sawmill Creek Rd. | 843/837–3795 | Free | Tours weekdays at 10 AM and by appointment.

Museum of Hilton Head Island. A permanent collection depicts Native American life, and there are changing exhibits as well. Beach walks are conducted on weekdays, and tours of forts, plantations, and Native American sites are given randomly in season. | 100 William Hilton Pkwy. | 843/689–6767 | Free | Mon.–Sat. 10–5, Sun. noon–4.

Pinckney Island National Wildlife Refuge. Fourteen miles of biking and walking trails lace their way through more than 4,000 acres of salt marsh and small islands ½ mi west of Hilton Head Island. | U.S. 278 | 843/689–6767 | Free | Daily dawn to dusk.

Savannah National Wildlife Refuge. A nature drive winds through this 25,608-acre preserve that was once a community of rice plantations 8 mi south of Hardeeville. It's now a sanctuary for migratory birds and other wildlife. | U.S. 17 | 912/652–4415 | Free | Daily dawn to dusk.

Sea Pines Forest Preserve. This 605-acre public wilderness tract on Sea Pines Plantation has walking trails, a well-stocked fishing pond, a waterfowl pond, and a 3,400-yr-old

KODAK'S TIPS FOR PHOTOGRAPHING PEOPLE

Friends' Faces
- Pose subjects informally to keep the mood relaxed
- Try to work in shady areas to avoid squints
- Let kids pick their own poses

Strangers' Faces
- In crowds, work from a distance with a telephoto lens
- Try posing cooperative subjects
- Stick with gentle lighting—it's most flattering to faces

Group Portraits
- Keep the mood informal
- Use soft, diffuse lighting
- Try using a panoramic camera

People at Work
- Capture destination-specific occupations
- Use tools for props
- Avoid flash if possible

Sports
- Fill the frame with action
- Include identifying background
- Use fast shutter speeds to stop action

Silly Pictures
- Look for or create light-hearted situations
- Don't be inhibited
- Try a funny prop

Parades and Ceremonies
- Stake out a shooting spot early
- Show distinctive costumes
- Isolate crowd reactions
- Be flexible: content first, technique second

From Kodak Guide to Shooting Great Travel Pictures © 2000 by Fodor's Travel Publications

Native American shell ring. You can take self-guided or guided tours. | Sea Pines Recreation Department, 175 Greenwood Dr. | 843/842–1449 or 843/363–4530 | $3 per car for nonguests | Daily dawn to dusk; closed during Heritage Golf Classic in Apr.

Shelter Cove Marina, South Beach Marina, and Skull Creek Marina. All offer kayak nature trips, as well as boat rentals and fishing charters. | 843/671–2643, 800/686–6996, or 843/681–4234 | Call for prices | Daily.

ON THE CALENDAR

MAR.: *Springfest.* This festival of sports, art, and food is a month-long event on the island. | 800/424–3387.

MAR.–APR.: *Family Circle Magazine Cup Tennis Tournament.* Top players on the Corel WTA Tour compete in this national tennis tournament held at the Sea Pines Racquet Club. | 140A Lighthouse Rd. | 800/677–2293.

APR.: *MCI Heritage Classic.* More than 100 top golfers play at the Harbour Town Golf Links to win $1.4 million in prize money. | 11 Lighthouse La. | 800/234–1107.

SEPT.: *Hilton Head Island Celebrity Golf Tournament.* Celebrities and amateurs play for three days on three different courses during this annual Labor Day tournament to raise money for children's charities. | Box 7404, SC | 843/842–7711.

OCT.: *St. Luke's Tour of Homes.* You can take self-guided tours through beautiful homes and plantations. | Departure points vary. Call for details | 843/785–4099.

NOV.: *Hilton Head Island Bridge Run.* Runners and walkers of all ages and abilities can experience the beauty of the Intracoastal Waterway at the annual 5K walk and 8K run. The event benefits the Beaufort County Special Olympics. There's a Fitness Expo at The Mall at Shelter Cove the night before the run. | 843/689–3440.

Dining

Alexander's. Continental. Plants fill the screened-in porch, where you can dine on salmon Oscar, grilled Chilean sea bass, duck, steak, veal, and lamb. Kids' menu. | 76 Queens Folly Rd. | 843/785–4999 | No lunch | $18–$26 | AE, D, DC, MC, V.

Antonio's. Italian. White linen tablecloths cover the tables at this sophisticated but friendly, European café known for its pasta, seafood, and veal. Kids' menu. | G2 Village at Wexford | 843/842–5505 | No lunch | $16–$27 | AE, D, DC, MC, V.

Barony Grill. Continental. High-beamed ceilings, French doors, and high-back chairs make this dining room in the Westin Hotel sophisticated but unpretentious. You many want to try the oak-smoked rack of lamb, seared tuna with shiitake mushroom risotto, and prime rib with bourbon jus. Kids' menu. | 135 S. Port Royal Dr. | 843/681–4000 | Reservations essential | Closed Sun.–Mon. No lunch | $25–$29 | AE, D, DC, MC, V.

★ **Brick Oven Cafe.** American/Casual. Velvet drapes, massive chandeliers, and leather booths decorate this restaurant, which serves pizzas, salads, pastas, and appetizers. | 25 Park Plaza | 843/686–2233 | Reservations essential | No lunch | $9–$20 | AE, D, DC, MC, V.

Cafe Europa. Contemporary. You can watch the sunset or sit outside on the sidewalk and watch people on the boardwalk. Great coffee and desserts accompany pasta, sandwiches, and quiches. Kids' menu. | Lighthouse Rd. | 843/671–3399 | Closed late Oct.–mid-Feb. | $16–$27 | AE, MC, V.

Charlie's L'Etoile Verte. French. White linens and candles decorate the tables, but this bistro remains casual; there are also tables on the sidewalk. The menu changes daily to accommodate the fresh fish brought in, though fish encrusted with Parmesan is a popular item, as is the rack of lamb. No smoking. | 1000 Plantation Center | 843/785–9277 | Closed Sun.–Mon. | $19–$29 | AE, D, MC, V.

Gaslight. French. Artwork covers the peach color walls and plants fill the dining room at this restaurant serving fine French food, including rack of lamb and roasted chicken with garlic mashed potatoes. | 29 Park Plaza | 843/785–5814 | Closed Sun. No lunch Sat. | $17–$24 | AE, MC, V.

Harbourmaster's. Continental. Before eating in the formal dining room overlooking the water, you can sit at the cocktail lounge on the deck and have a drink. You can try the popular rack of New Zealand lamb, and for dessert, the Shelter Cove Diplomat (seasonal fruit in a chocolate shell with vanilla custard sauce). | 1 Shelter Cove La. | 843/785–3030 | Closed Sun. No lunch | $16–$25 | AE, DC, MC, V.

Hemingway's. Contemporary. This casual but elegant restaurant has white linens on the tables and a variety of dishes on the menu, including chicken, fish, pasta, and steak. Earlybird suppers. Sunday brunch. | 1 Hyatt Circle | 843/785–1234 | No lunch | $16–$27 | AE, D, DC, MC, V.

Hofbrauhaus. German. Bavarian decorations and pictures of Germany fill this restaurant. There's often live entertainment. Kids' menu. Earlybird suppers. | Pope Ave. and Executive Park | 843/785–3663 | No lunch | $10–$19 | AE, D, MC, V.

La Maisonette. French. Prix-fixe four-course dinners are served in a small, intimate dining room; the restaurant is known for its rack of lamb and filet mignon. | 20 Pope Ave. | 843/785–6000 | Reservations essential | Jacket required | No lunch | $16–$24 | AE, D, MC, V.

Little Venice. Italian. You can sit inside or outdoors on the canopy-covered porch overlooking the marina. The veal marsala and the Mediterranean angel hair are two popular dishes. | Shelter Cove Harbour | 843/785–3300 | Closed Jan. No lunch | $15–$22 | AE, D, DC, MC, V.

Longhorn Steak. Steak. Bulls' heads, antique pistols, chaps, and spurs decorate the walls, peanut shells cover the floor, and country music plays in the background. Jack Daniels whiskey flavors the baked beans, and besides its namesake steaks, fish and chicken are also served, prepared on a flat top grill. Kids' menu. | 841 U.S. 278 | 843/686–4056 | $9–$20 | AE, D, DC, MC, V.

Neno Il Toscano. Northern Italian. A granite-top bar and marble floor give this restaurant an upscale feel but it's actually pretty casual. Paintings hang on the gold color walls and you can take a look at their wine cellar instead of simply the wine list. The veal chops are particularly good, as is the home-made tiramisu. No smoking. | 105 Festival Center | 843/342–2400 | Closed Sun. No lunch Sat. | $15–$26 | AE, D, MC, V.

Old Fort Pub. Southern. This casual restaurant overlooks the marshlands of the Intracoastal Waterway. You can try the oyster stew, corn-encrusted pork chops, or mesquite-smoked filet mignon with mushroom cabernet sauce. Sunday brunch. | 65 Skull Creek Dr. | 843/681–2386 | $19–$29 | AE, D, DC, MC, V.

Old Oyster Factory. Seafood. You can sit on the outdoor deck over the water or inside by the bay windows overlooking Broad Creek. On Tuesday nights in summer, the restaurant has perfect views of the town's fireworks. Through steak and chicken are on the menu, the broiled scallops and the fresh salmon are popular dishes. Live music keeps the place hopping late into the night. Kids' menu. | 101 Marshland Rd. | 843/681–6040 | No lunch | $10–$24 | AE, D, DC, MC, V.

Reilley's. Irish. This pub claims to serve a "Perfect Guiness" to accompany such traditional Irish food as corn beef and cabbage, as well as American favorites such as sterling silver beef hamburgers and fresh lobster. Sports memorabilia decorates the walls inside, and the large deck seats 50. There's a prime rib special on Friday and Saturday. Kids' menu. Saturday, Sunday brunch. | 7-D Greenwood Dr. | 843/842–4414 | $10–$20 | AE, MC, V.

Scott's Fish Market. Seafood. This boat restaurant actually sits on the water; there's indoor dining with views of the water as well as outdoor dining, often with live music. Fresh fish is delivered daily; you can try pan seared yellow-fin tuna or barbecue grouper. Full bar. | Harbourside 1 | 803/785–7575 | Closed Jan. and Sun. No lunch | $17–$28 | AE, D, DC, MC, V.

Starfire Contemporary Bistro. Contemporary. Warm touches of wood accentuate the sunshine yellow walls of this small, somewhat formal bistro. The wild mushroom soup, salmon with spiced seed crust, and chocolate sorbet with homemade biscotti are made with ultrafresh ingredients. | 37 New Orleans Rd. | 843/785–3434 | No lunch | $18–$28 | AE, DC, MC, V.

Lodging

Best Western Inn. You can step onto the balconies at this centrally located three-story chain hotel surrounded by shops and restaurants. Restaurant, complimentary Continental breakfast. In-room data ports. Cable TV. Pool. Business services, free parking. | 40 Waterside Dr. | 843/842–8888 | fax 843/842–5948 | 92 rooms | $85 | AE, D, DC, MC, V.

Comfort Inn and Suites. This resort-style hotel on a seven-acre park with a lagoon opens a water park during the summer. It's across from the beach and 1 block from tennis courts. Restaurant, dining room, picnic area, complimentary Continental breakfast. In-room data ports, in-room safes, some microwaves, some refrigerators. Cable TV, room phones, TV in common area. Outdoor pool, wading pool. Golf privileges, miniature golf. Video games. Laundry facilities. Business services. Pets allowed (fee). | 2 Tanglewood Dr. | 843/842–6662 or 800/228–5150 | fax 843/842–6664 | www.comfortinn.com/hotel/sc173 | 153 rooms | $139–$179 | AE, D, DC, MC, V.

Crowne Plaza Resort. Tropical gardens and waterfalls flourish at this oceanfront luxury hotel. Private boats and guides will take you fishing, and you can rent bikes and other sporting equipment. Some rooms look out onto the ocean. Bar, dining rooms, room service. In-room data ports. Cable TV. 2 pools (1 indoor), wading pool. Hot tub. Driving range, 9-hole and 18-hole golf courses, putting green, tennis courts. Gym. Boating, bicycles. Video games. Kids' programs. Laundry facilities. Business services, free parking. | 130 Shipyard Dr. | 843/842–2400 | fax 843/842–9975 | 340 rooms | $279–$399 | AE, D, DC, MC, V.

Daufuskie Island Club and Resort. Bright blues, pinks and greens decorate the rooms and two-story cottages with ocean views on this private island, accessible only by boat. Much of the island remains undeveloped, with a strong Gullah culture. 3 restaurants, bar, dining room, room service. Some refrigerators. Cable TV, in-room movies. 2 pools (1 indoor). Hot tub. Driving range, golf course, putting green, tennis courts. Gym. Boating, bicycles. Video games. Free parking. | 1 Seabrook Dr. | 843/842–2000 or 800/648–6778 | fax 843/842–9975 | www.daufuskieresort.com | 37 cottages, 52 rooms | $195 | AE, D, DC, MC, V.

★ **Disney's Hilton Head Island Resort.** Vivid colors brighten the two-story cottages on the island's newest resort, all of which have patios with rocking chairs and views of the marina or the marsh. The cottages range from studios to three-bedrooms. Kitchenettes, microwaves. Cable TV, in-room VCRs and movies. Pool, wading pool. Hot tub. Driving range, three 18-hole golf courses, putting green, tennis courts. Exercise equipment. Boating, bicycles. Children's programs. Laundry service, free parking. | 22 Harborside La. | 843/341–4100 or 800/453–4911 | fax 843/341–4130 | www.dvcresorts.com | 102 cottages | $205–$325 | AE, D, DC, MC, V.

Fairfield Inn by Marriott. Hilton Head isn't all resorts; you can find simple, affordable rooms at this three-story standard chain hotel. Picnic area, complimentary Continental breakfast. In-room data ports, refrigerators in suites. Cable TV. Pool. Miniature golf. Business services. | 9 Marina Side Dr. | 843/842–4800 | fax 843/842–4800, ext. 709 | www.marriott.com | 119 rooms, 14 suites | $80 rooms, $125 suites | AE, D, DC, MC, V.

Hampton Inn. This chain hotel is in the middle of the island, ½ mi from a movie theater, 2 mi from shopping and restaurant areas (there are also five restaurants across the street), and 4 mi from the Coastal Discovery Museum. Complimentary Continental breakfast. In-room data ports, some kitchenettes, some refrigerators. Cable TV. Pool. Exercise equipment. Laundry facilities. Business services, airport shuttle. | 1 Dillon Rd. | 843/681–7900 | fax 843/681–4330 | www.hampton-inn.net | 124 rooms, 20 suites | $80–$110 | AE, D, DC, MC, V.

Hilton Head Island Hilton Resort. Beautifully landscaped gardens surround this oceanside hotel, where all the spacious and modern rooms face the ocean. Dining room, bar (with entertainment), room service. In-room data ports, some kitchenettes. Cable TV. 2 pools, wading pool. Hot tubs. Three 18-hole golf courses, tennis courts. Gym. Children's programs, playground. Laundry facilities. Business services, free parking. | 23 Ocean La. | 843/842–8000 |

fax 843/341–8033 | hiltonhh@hargray.com | www.hilton.com | 296 rooms, 28 suites | $219–$264, $350–$400 suites | AE, D, DC, MC, V.

Holiday Inn Oceanfront Resort. This five-story, late '70s-style beachfront hotel is within 3½ mi of restaurants, nightclubs, and a shopping plaza. Restaurant, bar, room service. In-room data ports. Cable TV. Pool, wading pool. Laundry facilities. Business services. | 1 S. Forest Beach Dr. | 843/785–5126 | fax 843/785–6678 | 200 rooms | $159–$219 | AE, D, DC, MC, V.

Howard Johnson. The rooms come with balconies at this two-story standard. It's 15 mi from Savannah Airport. Restaurant. Cable TV. Pool, wading pool. Business services. Some pets allowed (fee). | I–95, junction Hwy. 17, Hardeeville, SC; 24 mi east of Hilton Head | 843/784–2271 | fax 843/784–2271 | 128 rooms | $40–$45 | AE, D, DC, MC, V.

Hyatt Regency. The luxurious and spacious rooms here come with balconies, some of which look out onto the ocean. Bars (with entertainment), dining room, room service. In-room data ports. Cable TV, 2 pools (1 indoor), wading pool. Beauty salon, hot tub, massage. Three 18-hole golf courses, putting green, tennis courts. Gym. Boating, bicycles. Children's programs. Business services, free parking. | 1 Hyatt Circle | 843/785–1234 | fax 843/842–4695 | 505 rooms | $280 | AE, D, DC, MC, V.

Main Street Inn. Shuttered French doors and iron railings decorate this Italianate-style villa, complete with lovely gardens. Velvet and silk brocades cover the beds and hang from the windows of the pine-floored rooms. Bar, complimentary breakfast. In-room data ports, some in-room hot tubs. Cable TV. Pool. Hot tub, massage, spa. Business services. | 2200 Main St. | 843/681–3001 or 800/471–3001 | fax 843/681–5541 | www.mainstreetinn.com | 34 rooms | $210–$275 | AE, MC, V.

Marriott Barony Beach Club. Six buildings on part of Port Royal Plantation house hundreds of two-bedroom, two-bath villas that can accommodate up to eight people. Each villa has a kitchen, full living room and full dining room. Some units are on the beach and some have private balconies. Some in-room safes, microwaves, refrigerators, in-room hot tubs. Cable TV, in-room VCRs, room phones. 4 pools. Hot tub, outdoor hot tub, massage, sauna, spa, steam room. Golf privileges. Health club. Beach, water sports. Children's programs. Laundry facilities. No pets. | 4 Grasslawn Ave. | 800/845–5279 | fax 843/342–1606 | 240 villas | $175–$375 | AE, D, DC, MC, V.

Marriott Residence Inn. This typical chain hotel is near a shopping center, a fun park, and several restaurants. All the suites have balconies. Picnic area, complimentary Continental breakfast. Kitchenettes, microwaves. Cable TV. Pool. Hot tub. Tennis courts. Bicycles. Laundry facilities. Business services. | 12 Park La. | 843/686–5700 | fax 843/686–3952 | 156 suites | $99–$149 | AE, D, DC, MC, V.

Motel 6. Two blocks south of Shelter Cove Marina you'll find clean rooms typical of this chain. You can take advantage of the outdoor pool or walk to the beach. Some kitchenettes, some microwaves, some refrigerators. Cable TV, room phones. Outdoor pool. Laundry facilities. Pets allowed. | 830 William Hilton Pkwy. | 843/785–2700 or 800/466–8356 | fax 843/842–9543 | 116 rooms | $66–$76 | AE, D, DC, MC, V.

Palmetto Dunes Resort. This resort has 1- to 4-bedroom furnished villas, and rooms in the main five-story building. Fireplaces add a little warmth to many of the rooms. There is a 4,300-ft airstrip 4 mi from the hotel. Bars, dining rooms, picnic area. Microwaves. Cable TV. 28 pools, wading pools. Driving range, 3 golf courses, putting green, tennis courts. Beach, boating. Children's programs, playground. Business services, free parking. | 4 Queen's Folly Rd. | 843/785–7300 or 800/845–6130 | fax 843/842–4482 | sdmpdr@aol.com | www.palmettodunesresort.com | 500 villas | $105–$160 | AE, D, DC, MC, V.

Players Club Resort. A gravel path leads down to the beach and acres of gorgeous landscaping surround this hotel. All the rooms have private balconies. Picnic area. Some in-room data ports, refrigerators. Cable TV, room phones. Indoor pool, outdoor pool, wading pool. Hot tub, outdoor hot tub, massage, sauna, spa, steam room. Health club, racquetball. Bicycles. Baby-sitting, children's summer programs. Business services. No pets. | 35 Deallyon Ave. | 843/785–8000 or 800/497–7529 | fax 843/785–9185 | 96 rooms | $139–$216 | AE, D, MC, V.

Red Roof Inn. This chain hotel presents one of the cheaper options on the island; the simple, cozy rooms are about ½ mi from restaurants and a shopping area. Cable TV. Pool. Business services. | 5 Regency Pkwy. | 843/686–6808 | fax 843/842–3352 | www.redroofinn.com | 112 rooms | $80–$120 | AE, D, DC, MC, V.

Sea Pines. This classic 5,000–acre Lowcountry resort occupies most of Hilton Head Island. It has a sports director, and offers sailboat lessons and cookouts for guests. You can also charter your own boat. 4 restaurants. Kitchenettes in villas, microwaves. Cable TV, in-room VCRs. 19 pools (1 indoor-outdoor), wading pools. Driving range, three 18-hole golf courses, putting green, tennis courts. Gym. Beach, water sports, boating, bicycles. Children's programs, playgrounds. Laundry service. Business services. | 32 Greenwood Dr. | 843/785–3333 or 800/732–7463 | fax 843/842–1475 | www.seapines.com | 420 suites in villas, 60 houses | $189–$260 | AE, D, DC, MC, V.

South Beach Inn and Rentals. Between Braddock Cove and the Calibogue Sound is this hotel with one- and two-bedroom suites, villas, and condos on Sea Pines Plantation. You can walk across the street to watch for dolphins or spend a complimentary hour playing tennis. Restaurant, bar (with entertainment), picnic area. Kitchenettes, microwaves, refrigerators. Cable TV, some in-room VCRs, room phones, TV in common area. Outdoor pool. Tennis courts. Playground. Laundry facilities. No pets. No smoking. | 232 S. Sea Pines Dr. | 843/671–6498 | fax 843/671–7495 | www.southbeachvillage.com | 17 | $109–$169 | AE, D, DC, MC, V.

Quality Inn and Suites. The beach lies 3 mi away from this typical three-story chain hotel, which is also 2½ mi from the airport. Restaurant, bar. In-room data ports. Cable TV. Pool. Laundry facilities. Business services, free parking. | 200 Museum St. | 843/681–3655 | fax 843/681–3655, ext. 369 | 127 rooms; 2-rm suites available | $79–$129 | AE, D, DC, MC, V.

★ **Westin Resort.** Lushly landscaped gardens encircle one of the most luxurious beachfront properties in the area. Down pillows to nurture the head and wicker furniture to comfort the back appoint the rooms, most of which have balconies overlooking the ocean. 2 restaurants, room service. In-room data ports, refrigerators. Cable TV. 3 pools (1 indoor). Hot tub, massage. Driving range, golf courses, putting green, tennis courts. Gym. Children's programs, playground. Business services. | 2 Grasslawn Ave. | 843/681–4000 | fax 843/681–1087 | www.westin.com | 412 rooms, 88 cottages | $205–$450 rooms, $550–$2,000 cottages | AE, D, DC, MC, V.

ISLE OF PALMS

MAP 9, I7

(Nearby towns also listed: Charleston, Sullivans Island)

About 11 mi from downtown Charleston, the Isle of Palms community dates to just after World War II. It is mostly residential and has some of the area's most upmarket beach homes which are sometimes rented weekly in summer. Just down from the beachfront Isle of Palms County Park, on Ocean Boulevard, there is a small concentration of beach shops, bars, and restaurants. At the eastern point of the island is Wild Dunes Resort, a private, gated community.

Information: Mt. Pleasant/Isle of Palms Visitor Center | Hwy. 17N at McGrath Darby Blvd., Mt. Pleasant, SC 29464 | 800/868–8118.

Attractions

Isle of Palms County Park. Locals and tourists mingle at this public beach, where lifeguards are on duty seasonally. There are changing rooms, rest rooms, outdoor showers, vending machines and concession stand. You can picnic in the shade of wooden gazebos and rent boogie boards, beach chairs and umbrellas. | 114th Ave., at the foot of the Isle of Palms connector | 843/886–3863 | Free, parking $5 | May–Sept., daily 9–7; Oct.–Apr., daily 10–5.

ON THE CALENDAR
OCT.: *Halloween Carnival and Ghostly Tide Tales.* Haunted houses, hayrides, and costume contests are all part of the fun at the Isle of Palms Recreation Center. Popcorn and candy, carnival games, and a jumping castle add to the treating. Later in the evening, you can head to the beach to hear ghostly tales told around bonfires. | 24 28th Ave. | 843/886–8294.

Dining
One Eyed Parrot. Caribbean. You can eat amidst colorful, tropical decor in a second-floor dining room overlooking the ocean or on the deck outside. The restaurant is known for its seafood, chicken and rice, and stone crab claws. There is live entertainment on Fridays and weekends. Kids' menu. | 1130 Ocean Blvd. | 843/886–4360 | www.oneeyedparrot.com or dining@watersedge.com | No lunch | $13–$22 | AE, D, DC, MC, V.

Lodging
Seaside Inn. Lounge on the sundecks or hang out on the beach while you watch pelicans dive into the breaking waves in front of this less expensive alternative to beachfront condominiums. Restaurants and shopping are a few steps away. Complimentary Continental breakfast. Microwaves, refrigerators. Room phones. Beach. No pets. | 1004 Ocean Blvd. | 843/886–7000 or 888/999–6516 | fax 843/886–0921 | www.charlestownmanagement.com | 51 rooms | $99–$179 | AE, D, DC, MC, V.

Wild Dunes. There are several hundred one- to six-bedroom cottages and villas on this serene, 1,600-acre resort on the Isle of Palms, as well as a 93 room hotel. The rainbow colored Boardwalk Villas have separate entrances for each guest room and overlook a beachfront boardwalk. There are also two acclaimed golf courses on the property. Villas and cottages require a minimum one week stay. Bar (with entertainment), dining room, picnic area. Some kitchenettes in villas, microwaves. Cable TV. 20 Pools, wading pool. Beauty salon, hot tub. Driving range, two 18-hole golf courses, putting green, 17 tennis courts. Gym. Beach, boating, bicycles. Children's programs, playground. Laundry facilities. Business services. | 5757 Palm Blvd., Isle of Palms | 843/886–6000 or 888/845–8426 | fax 843/886–2916 | wilddunes@awod.com | www.wilddunes.com | 320 villas, 24 cottages, 83 rooms, 10 suites | Hotel rooms $199–$269, suites $349; villas and cottages weekly $1404–$1685 | AE, D, MC, V.

KIAWAH ISLAND

MAP 9, H8

(Nearby towns also listed: Charleston, Edisto Island, Folly Beach)

Twenty-one mi south of Charleston is Kiawah Island, a semi-tropical 10,000-acre island resort. Named after the Kiawah Indians, who inhabited the area until the 1600s, the island has about 5,000 homes and condos, championship golf courses (including the 1995 Ryder Cup's Ocean Course), tennis centers, a small shopping village, several restaurants, and the only hotel in the area. Despite such development, Kiawah Island has plenty of green space, including lagoons, marshes, estuaries, expanses of maritime forest, and miles of nature trails. It is home to 150 species of birds as well as deer, sea turtles, and alligators. Mostly residential, the resort offers low-key family activities and extensive children's programs to resort guests in summer.

Information: Kiawah Island Resorts | 12 Kiawah Beach Rd., Kiawah Island, SC 29455 | 843/768–2121 or 800/654–2924 | fax 843/768–9339 | www.kiawahisland-sc.com.

Attractions

Charleston Tea Plantation. This is the only tea plantation in America—American Classic tea is grown, harvested, dried, graded, and packaged here and used for official and ceremonial U.S. presidential events. You can take guided walking tours during the harvest season. | 6617 Maybank Hwy., Wadmalaw Island | 800/443–3049 | www.lionshouse.org/tea/tea2htm | Free | Tours May–Oct. on the first Sat. of each month.

ON THE CALENDAR

AUG.: *Rockville Regatta.* During the first Saturday of the month, this sailboat race and party brings locals and visitors together at the Sea Island Yacht Club in Rockville on Wadmalaw Island, 5 mi northeast of Kiawah Island. There's an evening dance, too. | 106 W. Main St., Rockville, Wadmalaw Island | 843/853–8000.

Dining

The Atlantic Room. Southern. Fresh flower arrangements, linen tablecloths, and an ocean view make this a local favorite. Chef Anthony Dibernardo experiments with New South cuisine, creating a remarkable Atlantic coast stew, excellent crab cakes, and wonderful specials every night. You can sip cocktails during happy hour or after dinner in the adjacent Charleston Bar. Sunday brunch. | 12 Kiawah Beach Dr. | 843/768–2768 | Reservations essential | Breakfast also available. No lunch | $15–$30 | AE, D, DC, MC, V.

Lodging

Holiday Inn Riverview. Although in Charleston, you have direct access to all the barrier islands and a complimentary shuttle to the area's attractions, as well as all the amenities. The restaurant and bar on the top floor have nice views of the Ashley River and Charleston Harbor. Restaurant, bar, dining room, room service. In-room data ports, some kitchenettes, some refrigerators. Cable TV, some in-room VCRs, room phones, TV in common area. Outdoor pool. Golf privileges. Gym. Laundry facilities, laundry service. Business services. Pets allowed. | 301 Savannah Hwy. | 843/556–7100 or 800/465–4329 | fax 843/556–6176 | www.holiday-inn.com | 181 rooms | $109–$139 | AE, D, DC, MC, V.

. . . .

Kiawah Island Resorts. Contemporary designs distinguish this island recreation retreat, with 10 mi of beach, 31 mi of bike trails, and a 21-acre park and nature center. A variety of lodging options, ranging from hotel-style rooms to luxury homes, are available on the private island. Rooms at the main inn are furnished in blond wood and have private balconies with views of the ocean, dunes, or landscaped grounds. The oceanside villas are arranged in duplex or multi-plex style units, and have full kitchens and screened-in porches that overlook the lagoon, tennis courts, or the ocean. A handful of luxury 1–6 bedroom homes are also available, many of which have full gourmet kitchens, ocean views, and multi-level sun decks. The resort boasts several restaurants and shopping areas, which are scattered throughout the 10 mi-long island; Kiawah Island is about a half hour from Charleston by car. Bar (with entertainment), 8 restaurants, picnic area, room service. Minibars, some microwaves, refrigerators. Cable TV. 5 pools, wading pool. Driving range, 5 18-hole golf courses, 28 tennis courts. Hiking. Beach, dock, boating, bicycles. Video games. Children's programs (3–11), playground. Business services. | 12 Kiawah Beach Dr. | 843/768–2121 or 800/654–2924 | fax 843/768–6099 | www.kiawah-island.com | 150 rooms, 600 villas, 50 houses | $195–$260, $155–$726 villas, $399–$1,699 houses | AE, D, DC, MC, V.

LATTA

MAP 9, J3

(Nearby towns also listed: Bennettsville, Florence)

There are 64 historic properties within a 1-mi radius of Latta, and most of them are Victorian, dating to the time when this was a railroad town with a prosperous tobacco community. The now quiet town is fast becoming a little artists' colony and has a handful of galleries on Main Street, where signs of creative revitalization are springing forth. The nearby tobacco towns of Marion, Mullins, and Dillon are scattered with historic sites and antiques shops, and you can kayak and fish on two blackwater rivers within a few miles of Latta.

Information: Dillon County Chamber of Commerce | 126 N. MacArthur Ave., Dillon, SC 29536 | 843/774–8551 | www.teamsc.com/PeeDeeFrame.htm.

Attractions

Dillon County Museum. This former medical office holds old dental and medical equipment, farm tools, historic flags, an indigo exhibit, and local historical items. | 101 S. Marion St. | 843/752–9457 | www.dillonsc.com | Free | Tues., Thurs., Sat. 10:30–noon, 1–4:30; Sun. 1:30–4:30.

Little Pee Dee State Park. Bream fishing in the Little Pee Dee River is the main draw to this 835-acre state park. There are also riverside picnic tables and campsites. | 2400 Park Access Rd. | 843/774–8872 | Free | Daily 9–9.

Marion County Museum. Housed in schoolhouse built circa 1887, the museum's collection includes Oriental and English rugs and local antiques. | 101 Wilcox Ave., Marion; 12 mi south of Latta on U.S. 301 | 843/423–8299 | Free | Tues.–Fri. 10–5, closed Sun.–Mon.

South of the Border. A sombrero-shape observation tower punctuates the skyline of this I–95 landmark, a complex of factory outlets, restaurants, and playgrounds, all with a Mexican motif. | U.S. 301, Exit 1 | 843/774–2411, 800/922–6064 in SC, or 800/845–6011 outside SC | Free | Daily 9 AM–10 PM, observation tower daily noon–7 PM.

Tobacco and Farm Life Museum. Housed in a restored train depot are intriguing exhibits on the planting, harvesting, curing, and auctioning of the "golden leaf" tobacco plant. | 104 N.E. Front St., Mullins | 843/464–8194 | Free | Sat.–Mon. 9–5 or by appointment.

ON THE CALENDAR
APR.: *Latta Springfest.* Entertainment at this local festival includes a judged art show, storytelling, a beauty pageant, and a chicken bog. | Main St. | 843/752–7242.
JULY–SEPT.: *Tobacco Auctions.* The sights, smells, and sounds of tobacco country can be experienced at late summer auctions in Hemingway, Kingstree, Lake City, Mullins, Lake City, Pamplico, and Timmonsville.
SEPT.: *Golden Leaf Festival.* A husband-hollerin' contest is one of the many draws of this festival, which celebrates the area's tobacco heritage with arts and crafts, a parade, and a food festival. | Smithaven Park, West Buck and Main Sts. | 843/464–6204.

Dining

1872, An American Bistro. Contemporary. A bright brick exterior and a wood interior make this restaurant, which opened in May 2000, look like an old tobacco barn. Open kitchen counter seating gives you a view of the cooks preparing seasonal menu items; you can also sit in the dining room. Appetizer favorites include pan-seared blue crab ravioli and fried green tomatoes. For dinner, try the chili-rubbed rib eye steak, sliced and rolled into a sun-dried tomato tortilla. | 3373 E. Highway 76, Mullins | 843/464–4460 | Closed Sun. No lunch Sat. | $11–$22 | AE, D, DC, MC, V.

Lodging

Abingdon Manor. A large lawn anchored by a papershell pecan tree surrounds this 1902 Greek Revival mansion in downtown Latta. The veranda, punctuated with wicker rockers, overlooks the inn's herb garden. Rooms are decorated in Italian Renaissance or traditional Southern styles and most have large Palladian windows and original shutters. The Blue Room has a collection of Russian nesting dolls; the Green Room has an antique writing desk. Complimentary breakfast. Cable TV in most rooms, in-room VCRs (and movies), no room phones. Hot tub. Exercise equipment. Business services. No kids under 12. No smoking. | 307 Church St. | 843/752–5090 or 888/752–5090 | abingdon@southtech.net | www.bbonline.com/sc/abingdon | 4 rooms, 1 suite | $105–$130, $140 suite | AE, D, DC, MC, V.

Ramada Limited. You'll find comfortable rooms and an outdoor pool at this chain hotel off I–95 at Exit 193. Dining room, complimentary Continental breakfast. Some microwaves, some refrigerators, some in-room hot tubs. Cable TV, room phones. Outdoor pool. No pets. | 823 Radford Blvd. | 843/841–0110 | fax 843/841–0110 | www.ramada.com | 50 rooms | $65 | AE, D, MC, V.

LITCHFIELD BEACH

MAP 9, K5

(Nearby towns also listed: Georgetown, Murrells Inlet, Myrtle Beach, Pawleys Island)

This town 20 mi south of Myrtle Beach is best known for its giant resort complex, the Litchfield Beach and Golf Resort. It also has private homes and many condominiums lining its mostly wide, sandy beach.

Information: **Myrtle Beach Chamber South Strand Office** | 3401 U.S. 17 South (Business), Murrells Inlet, SC 29576-0650 | 843/651–1010. | www.myrtlebeachlive.com.

Dining

Carriage House Club. Contemporary. A fireplace and library add to the stately atmosphere of this formal restaurant on the manicured lawns at Litchfield Plantation. The steak and grouper are particularly good. | Kings River Rd., Pawleys Island | 843/237–9322 | Reservations essential | Breakfast also available. No lunch | $30–$40 | AE, D, MC, V.

Pastaria 811. Abruzzi Italian. When you walk in, the deep burgundy decor and the smell of homemade bread and sauces send your heart to Italy. Owner/chef David Demer put palmoli sauce, named for his mother-in-law's hometown, into his eggplant Parmesan, said to be the best in the state. | 111 Litchfield Exchange Mall | 843/237–5811 | Closed Sun. No lunch Sat. | $7–$16 | AE, MC, V.

Lodging

Litchfield Beach and Golf Resort. The beachfront Litchfield Inn, with 140 motel-style rooms, is just one of the accommodation options at this sprawling resort with over 4,000 acres of expansive landscaped grounds. Restaurant, bar. Some minibars, some microwaves, some refrigerators. Indoor-outdoor pool. Hot tub, sauna. 3 18-hole golf courses, 19 tennis courts. Gym, racquetball. | U.S. 17 | 843/237–3000 or 800/845–1897 | fax 843/237–4282 | www.litchfieldbeach.com | 124 rooms, 112 suites, 254 apartments, 9 cottages | $59–$149, $109–$154 suites, $119–$159 apartments, $79–$329 cottages | AE, D, DC, MC, V.

Litchfield Plantation. A majestic live oaks–lined avenue fronts this restored 1750 rice plantation and manor house–turned–country inn, 17 mi from Myrtle Beach. Two rooms and two suites are available in the main plantation house, and include the Executive Suite, which has a king sleigh bed and wicker furniture, and the Gun room, with a canopy bed and a view of the Avenue of Live Oaks. The rest of the rooms are housed in cottages that dot the grounds; all of the cottages have shared common areas and full kitchens. Litchfield Plantation is also home to the Carriage House Club restaurant. Restaurant, bar, complimentary Continental breakfast. Pool. 2 tennis courts. Horseback riding. Boating. | On Kings River Rd., 5 mi south of Brookgreen Garden, Pawleys Island; Call for directions | 843/237–9121 or 800/869–1410 | fax 843/237–1041 | www.litchfieldplantation.com | 2 rooms and 2 suites in main house, 32 rooms and 2 suites in 8 cottages | $215–$350 rooms, $440–$620 suites | AE, D, MC, V.

Oceanfront Litchfield Inn. For 20 years people have been coming here to relax on the wide, uncrowded, pristine beach. The rooms, villas, and condos are furnished in pine, and in summer, kids can keep busy with an adventure camp. Restaurant, bar (with entertainment). Some kitchenettes, some microwaves, some refrigerators. Cable TV, room phones. Outdoor pool, wading pool. Beach, fishing, bicycles. Baby-sitting, children's programs (ages 5–15). Laundry facilities. Business services. No pets. | 1 Norris Dr., at Litchfield Blvd. | 843/237–4211 or 800/637–4211 | fax 843/237–4549 | info@litchfieldinn.com | www.litchfieldinn.com | 532 units | $124–$149 rooms, $260–$289 condos and villas | AE, D, DC, MC, V.

MCCLELLANVILLE

MAP 9, J6

(Nearby town also listed: Georgetown)

On the Intracoastal Waterway between Charleston and Georgetown, McClellanville is a sleepy fishing and shrimping village. Planters once retreated here during summers in the 1800s; they left their mark in the several historic homes and churches.

Information: McClellanville Town Hall | 405 Pinckney St., McClellanville, SC 29458 | 843/887–3712.

Attractions

Butterfly Barn. Local butterflies and moths fill this live butterfly zoo. | 816 Pinckney St. | 843/887–3939 | $4 | Apr.–Oct., Mon.–Sat. 10–4.

Cape Romain National Wildlife Refuge/ Seewee Visitor and Environmental Education Center. A grouping of barrier islands and salt marshes comprises this 60,000-acre refuge, one of the most outstanding in the country. At the Seewee Visitor and Environmental Education Center you can view exhibits about the refuge and arrange to take the ferry for a day trip to Bull's Island, a nearly untouched wilderness, and the only section of the refuge to which public transport is available. The beach there, strewn with bleached driftwood, is nicknamed Bone Beach. The ferry leaves from Moores Landing, 5 mi east of the Visitor Center. | 5821 U.S. 17N, Awendaw; 15 mi south of McClellanville on U.S. 17 | 843/928–3368 | Free; ferry to Bull's Island $20 | Tues.–Sun., 9–5; call for ferry departure times.

Francis Marion National Forest. This 256,000-acre, wildlife-dense forest was the site of a battle between the British forces and American General Francis Marion, nicknamed the "Swamp Fox." Activities available include hiking, horse, and motorcycle trails; camping, boating, and fishing. | 5821 U.S. 17N, Awendaw | 843/336–3248 | Free | Tues.–Sun. 9–5.

Hampton Plantation State Park. The park contains the home of Archibald Rutledge, poet laureate of South Carolina for 39 years until his death in 1973. The 18th-century plantation house is a good example of a Lowcountry mansion. The exterior has been restored; cutaway sections in the finely crafted interior show changes made through the centuries. There are picnic areas on the landscaped grounds. | 1950 Rutledge Rd. | 843/546–9361 | southcarolinaparks.com | Mansion $2, grounds free | Mansion, Thurs.–Mon. 1–4; grounds, Thurs.–Mon. 9–6.

ON THE CALENDAR

MAY: *Shrimp Festival.* The first McClellanville shrimp festival was held in 1976 as a fundraiser for Archibald Rutledge Academy. $1 suggested donation gains you entry to the festival, which includes the blessing of the fleet, arts and crafts vendors, live entertainment, and fun for the kids; plenty of fried shrimp and seafood chowder are also sold throughout the day. | 843/887–3323.

Dining

See Wee. Southern. This casual restaurant is halfway between McClellanville and Charleston. It's in a former 1920s general store and serves Lowcountry cuisine, including stuffed flounder, fried shrimp, fried green tomatoes, and home-cooked vegetables. Sunday brunch. | 4808 Hwy. 17, Awendaw | 843/928–3609 | No supper Sun. | $8–$19 | D, MC, V.

Lodging

Laurel Hill Plantation Bed and Breakfast. Down an unpaved, winding road off Highway 17, this inn almost effortlessly replaces the original 1850s plantation home that stood here until Hurricane Hugo demolished it in 1989. Wraparound porches overlook Cape Romain's salt marshes, islands, and waterways. A full country breakfast is served and refreshments, such as homemade cheese dip with tomatoes, are offered in the afternoon. Dining room, complimentary breakfast. Pond. Dock, fishing. No pets. No smoking. | 8913 N. Highway 17 | 843/887–3708 or 888/887–3708 | fax 843/887–3878 | laurelhill@prodigy.net | www.bbonline.com/sc/laurelhill/ | 4 rooms | $100–$125 | AE, D, DC, MC, V.

MURRELLS INLET

MAP 9, K5

(Nearby towns also listed: Georgetown, Litchfield Beach, Myrtle Beach, Pawleys Island)

Halfway between Pawleys Island and Myrtle Beach, Murrells Inlet is all about seafood. More than 40 restaurants crowd this little town, known for its fleet of commercial and charter fishing boats. Famous novelist Mickey Spillane lives here.

Information: **Myrtle Beach Area Chamber of Commerce and Info Center** | Box 2115, 1200 N. Oak St., Myrtle Beach, SC 29578-2115 | 800/356–3016 or 843/249–3519 | fax 843/626–0009 | www.mbchamber.com.

Attractions

★ **Brookgreen Gardens.** Begun in 1931 by railroad magnate and philanthropist Archer Huntington and his sculptor wife, Anna, these gardens have more than 500 sculptures by artists such as Frederic Remington and Daniel Chester French. The works are set amid beautifully landscaped grounds, with avenues of live oaks, reflecting pools, and more than 2,000 plant species. Also on the site are a wildlife park with deer, alligators, and two aviaries, as well as a cypress swamp, nature trails, an education center, and an excellent café. On summer evenings, the sculptures are illuminated, to magical effect, and the café serves three-course suppers. | West on U.S. 17, 3 mi south of Murrells Inlet | 843/235–6000 or 800/849–1931 | fax 843/237–1014 | www.brookgreen.org | $8.50 | May.–Sept., Sat.–Tue. 9:30–5:00, Wed.–Fri. 9:30–9:30; Oct.–Apr., daily 9:30–5:00.

Huntington Beach State Park. This is the 2,500-acre former estate of Archer and Anna Huntington, across the street from their Brookgreen Gardens. In addition to the splendid beach, there are nature trails, fishing, an interpretive center, a marsh boardwalk, picnic areas, a playground, concession stands, and a campground. | 16148 Ocean Hwy. (U.S. 17) | 843/237–4440 | www.southcarolinaparks.com | $4 | Nov.–Mar., daily 6–6; Apr.–Oct., daily 6 AM–10 PM.

Atalaya, which means watchtower, is the Huntingtons' Moorish 30-room winter home (built circa 1933) and is open to visitors year-round for self-guided tours. The fortress-like residence consists of two open courtyards surrounded by rooms, and is named for the tremendous watchtower that stands between the courtyard areas. Guided tours are available on a rotating basis– call ahead for schedule. | 912 Waccamaw Dr. | 843/237–4440 | Free with park admission | Nov.–Mar., daily 9–6; Apr.–Oct., daily 6 AM–10 PM.

SEPT.: *Atalaya Arts and Crafts Festival.* Every fall the Huntington Beach State Park invites all kinds of artists to exhibit their works, including paintings, sculpture, metal work, and jewelry; accompanied by live bands and food. | 843/237–4440.

Dining
Captain Dave's Dockside. Southern. Lowcountry specialties, fresh seafood, and aged beef are served up along with nautical decor and views of the marsh. You can dine on the deck, surrounded by palm trees, overlooking Murrell's Inlet. There is an outdoor gazebo bar, too. Kids' menu. | U.S. 17 Business | 843/651–5850 | Closed Mon. | $17–$24 | AE, D, MC, V.

Lodging
Barnacle Inn. The friendly staff and ocean view at this small motel keep the regulars coming back year after year. You can walk a half-mile to the center of town or across the street to fish at the Garden City Pier. Picnic area. Some kitchenettes, microwaves, refrigerators. Cable TV, some in-room VCRs, room phones. Outdoor pool. Laundry facilities. Pets allowed. | 215 S. Waccamaw Dr. | 843/651–2828 or 800/272–4222 | fax 843/651–2828 | 27 rooms, 3 apartments | $80 rooms, $108 apartments; 2–night minimum on weekends | AE, D, DC, MC, V.

MYRTLE BEACH

MAP 9, K5

(Nearby towns also listed: Litchfield Beach, Murrells Inlet, Pawleys Island)

Each year, more people visit Myrtle Beach, on South Carolina's north end coast, than Hawaii. Between North Myrtle Beach and Georgetown on a 60-mi stretch of coast on U.S. 17 known as the Grand Strand, the area draws an estimated 12 million tourists, more than any other East Coast destination except Orlando and Walt Disney World. On summer days, the year-round population of less than 40,000 often swells to 400,000 plus. More bus tours come here than to any other destination except Branson, Missouri, and Washington, D.C. Entertainment and shopping centers are so big they have their own visitor centers. There are nearly 20 theaters, more than 80 golf courses, as well as amusement rides and lots of showy putt-putt centers—Myrtle Beach is the miniature golf capital of America. By far the largest tourist attraction in South Carolina, this is one of the most highly developed beach resorts along the Eastern seaboard. There are miles of beaches, water sports, golf, tennis, and shopping; there are also hundreds of hotels, motels, time-shares, and condos along the beachfront. This is a high-energy destination with plenty to keep your entire family occupied. But the abundance of activity comes with a price: traffic along the main north–south arteries approaches gridlock at times during the summer, and the beaches are packed in good weather.

Information: Myrtle Beach Area Chamber of Commerce and Info Center | Box 2115, 1200 N. Oak St., Myrtle Beach, SC 29578-2115 | 800/356–3016 or 843/249–3519 | fax 843/626–0009 | www.mbchamber.com.

Attractions
Alligator Adventure. Interactive reptile shows, including an alligator-feeding demonstration, headline the activities at this 15-acre alligator park. Its boardwalks go through marshes and swamps on the 15-acre property, where you'll see wildlife of the wetlands, including the only known collection of rare white albino alligators; the gharial, an exotic crocodilian from Asia; giant Galápagos tortoises; and all manner of reptiles, including boas, pythons, and anacondas. Unusual plants and exotic birds also thrive here. | U.S. 17S at Barefoot Landing, North Myrtle Beach | 843/361–0789 | fax 843/361–0742 | $11.95 | Daily 9 AM–10 PM.

Broadway at the Beach. Anchored by a pyramid-shape Hard Rock Cafe, the Palace Theater, Planet Hollywood, and NASCAR Cafe, this is a glitzy entertainment and shopping complex with an IMAX theater, Hawaiian Rumble miniature golf, and restaurants galore. | 1325 Celebrity Circle | 843/444–3200 | Free | Daily.

Hawaiian Rumble. At this crown jewel of Myrtle Beach's miniature golf courses, a smoking mountain erupts fire and rumbles at timed intervals. Other courses mimic Jurassic Park and Never-Never Land. | 3210 33rd Ave. S | 843/272–7812 | www.mastersnationalchamps.com | $8 all day (9–5), $6 per round after 5 PM | Mar.–Dec., daily 9 AM–midnight.

Myrtle Beach Grand Prix. Formula 1 race cars, go-carts, bumper boats, mini-go-carts, kiddie cars, and mini-bumper boats make this automania heaven for adults and children age three and up. *Two locations:* | 3201 Hwy. 17 | 843/238–4783 | Windy Hill, 3900 U.S. 17S, North Myrtle Beach | 843/272–6010 or 843/238–4783 | www.mbgandprix.com | Rides $2–$6 each | Mar.–Oct., daily 10 AM–11 PM.

Myrtle Beach State Park. Pool and ocean swimming, pier fishing, and year-round nature programs make this a popular park. There are also cabins and camp sites throughout this 312-acre park. | 3205 Oak St. | 843/238–5325 | www.southcarolinaparks.com | Free | Daily 6 AM–10 PM.

Myrtle Beach Pavilion Amusement Park. The Carolinas' largest flume dominates this old-time beach-town amusement park. You'll also find thrill and kiddie rides, a Ferris wheel, roller coaster, merry-go-round, video games, a teen nightclub, specialty shops, antique cars, and sidewalk cafés. | 9th Ave. N. and Ocean Blvd. | 843/448–6456 | www.mbpavilion.com | Fees for individual attractions; $18.50 1-day pass for unlimited access to most rides | Daily 6 PM–midnight.

Ripley's Aquarium. An underwater tunnel exhibit at this attraction is longer than a football field, and exotic marine creatures range from poisonous lionfish to moray eels and an octopus. Children can touch horseshoe crabs and stingrays (minus the sting) in touch tanks. | 29th Ave. N, off U.S. 17 | 843/916–0888 or 800/734–8888 | $13.95 | Sun.–Thurs. 9–8, Fri.–Sat. 9–9.

Wild Water. The 25 rides and activities at this water park south of Myrtle Beach provide fun for water lovers of all ages. | 910 U.S. 17S, Surfside Beach | 843/238–9453 | www.wildwater.com | $21.95, $12.95 after 3 PM | Memorial Day weekend–Labor Day, daily 10–7.

ON THE CALENDAR
JUNE: *Sun Fun Festival.* In addition to a beauty pageant and a parade, there are beach games, sports events, jazz, and special shows around town. | 843/626–7444 or 800/356–3016.

Dining
The Bistro Cafe and Pub. Continental. Plants and paintings decorate this small, romantic restaurant known for its fresh fish and steak. Try the seafood cakes (shrimp, scallops, and whitefish seasoned and served with a light horseradish sauce), and for dessert go for the pecan-crusted snow pie. | 5101 N. Kings Hwy. (U.S. 17) | 843/449–5125 | Closed Sun. No lunch Sat. | $18.95–$28.95 | AE, D, DC, MC, V.

Cagney's Old Place. American. An odd assortment of collectibles, such as old bicycles, old gas tanks, and old plane parts, fill this colorful restaurant ¼ mi from the beach. The menu features typical American dishes, from pasta and steak to seafood, and dessert classics, such as Baked Alaska, are popular. There is entertainment on weekends. | 9911 N. Kings Hwy. (U.S. 17) | 843/449–3824 | Closed mid-Dec.–second week in Feb. and Sun. No lunch | $18–$25 | AE, D, MC, V.

Chesapeake House. Seafood. Out back there's a lake with live alligators, turtles, duck, and fish. Inside, you can choose from fresh seafood, steaks, pasta, chicken, and pork, though the restaurant is known for the fish stew of fresh flounder and rice. Baked spaghetti, lobster tails, and crab legs are other favorites. | 9918 N. Kings Hwy. (U.S. 17) | 843/449–7933 | fax 843/449–0373 | No lunch | $7–$28 | AE, D, MC, V.

★ **Collector's Cafe.** Contemporary. A restaurant, art gallery, and coffeehouse rolled into one, this is an unpretentiously arty spot three blocks from the beach, with bright, funky paintings and tile work covering the walls and tabletops. The menu changes seasonally and offers pasta to seafood to meat dishes, but the place is known for its coffee. | 7726 N. Kings Hwy. (U.S. 17) | 843/449–9370. | Closed Sun. | $15–$25 | AE, D, DC, MC, V.

Fiesta del Burro Loco. Mexican. Named after a Mexican cantina famous for its dancing donkey, this upbeat dining spot welcomes its clientele with salsa music and all your favorite dishes from south of the border. The crazy donkey feast, which feeds four, is a sizzling platter of shrimp, steak, chicken, ribs, rice, and beans. | 960 Jason Blvd. | 843/626–1756 | fax 843/626–1860 | $7–$12 | AE, D, DC, MC, V.

Fusco's. Continental. Crab cakes and lobster are the specialty in this casual dining room overlooking a pool and the ocean. The restaurant is a part of the Beach Colony. Kids' menu. | 5308 N. Ocean Blvd., North Myrtle Beach | 843/449–4010 | Breakfast also available. Closed first week in Jan. No lunch Labor Day–late Mar. | $18.95–$21.95 | AE, D, DC, MC, V.

Joe's Bar and Grill. Continental. Hanging ferns and palm trees decorate the open-air deck, which overlooks a salt marsh. Try blackened mahi mahi or the triple plate of rib eye steak, a crab cake, and blackened shrimp. Kids' menu. | 810 Conway Ave., North Myrtle Beach | 843/272–4666 | No lunch | $16–$40 | AE, D, MC, V.

Longhorn Steakhouse. Steak. This Southwestern steakhouse features a wide variety of American dishes including pastas and fish specials. Make yourself at home in one of the roomy booths or many tables in this busy family-style upscale restaurant. Salad bar. Kids' menu. | 7604 N. Kings Hwy. (U.S. 17) | 843/449–7013 | Closed 1 week during Christmas. No lunch | $30 | AE, D, DC, MC, V.

Mr. Fish. Seafood. Sit in Formica booths and chow down on the well-known fish sandwiches at this restaurant near the Pavillion. There's also a fish shop. Kids' menu. | 919 Broadway | 843/946–6869 | Closed Sun. | $15 | AE, DC, MC, V.

Nick's on 61st. Mediterranean. Specials change daily at this fine-dining restaurant featuring veal, pork, beef, duck, lamb, and fresh fish. Enjoy candle-lit elegance in the dining room or fresh air on the enclosed patio. | 503 61st Ave. N | 843/449–1716 | Closed Sun. | 16–$36 | AE, MC, V.

Oak Harbor. Contemporary. You can dine on the open-air patio overlooking the beach. The triple grill—lobster, shrimp, and steak—is a favorite, as is the blackened tuna. Kids' menu. | 1407 13th Ave. N, North Myrtle Beach | 843/249–4737 | No lunch | $15–$33 | AE, DC, MC, V.

Rosa Linda's Cafe. Eclectic. Local artists have hand-painted a mural on the wall of this lively, popular restaurant. Paella and calzones are house favorites. Kids' menu. | 4713 U.S. 17N, North Myrtle Beach | 843/272–6823 | Closed Dec.–Jan. | $9–$22 | AE, D, DC, MC, V.

Sea Captain's House. Seafood. Crab cakes and the popular she-crab soup are served in this 1930s building which overlooks the water. Kids' menu. | 3000 N. Ocean Blvd. | 843/448–8082 | Breakfast also available | $10–$20 | AE, D, MC, V.

Thoroughbreds. Continental. This traditional dinner house is set up to look like the clubhouse of a race track. It's known for prime rib, steaks, and veal, but the escargots are worth a try as well. | N. Kings Hwy. (U.S. 17) | 843/497–2636 | No lunch | $25–$35 | AE, D, DC, MC, V.

Tony's. Italian. Chianti bottles signed by patrons hang from the ceilings of the three large dining rooms with hardwood floors. Try the seafood combination—shrimp, clams, and lobster in marinara sauce over pasta—and the homemade cheesecake. Kids' menu. | 1407 U.S. 17, North Myrtle Beach | 843/249–1314 | Closed Sun. and Dec.–Jan. No lunch | $20–$30 | AE, D, DC, MC, V.

Lodging

Aloha Motel. Clean comfortable rooms make up this motel near a residential area. There's a snack bar on the premises and some bicycles are available for guests at no charge. Some kitchenettes, refrigerators. Cable TV, room phones. Outdoor pool, wading pool. Golf privileges. Bicycles. No pets. | 7307 N. Ocean Blvd. | 843/449–5444 | 40 rooms | $72 | D, MC, V.

Beach Colony. This oceanfront property is within walking distance of several restaurants and clubs, and 3 mi from Colonial Mall, one of the larger shopping centers in the area. Many rooms have balconies with patio furniture. Restaurant, bar. Kitchenettes, microwaves. Cable TV. Indoor pool, 2 outdoor pools, wading pool. Hot tub. Exercise equipment. Beach. Video games. Children's programs (5–12), (Jun.–Aug. only). Laundry facilities. | 5308 N. Ocean Blvd. | 843/449–4010 or 800/222–2141 | fax 843/449–2810 | www.beachcolony.com | 222 suites | $55–$125 1–bedroom suite, $69–$172 2–bedroom suite, $605–$1,403/week 3–bedroom suite, $665–$1,888/week 4–bedroom suite | AE, D, DC, MC, V.

Beach Cove Resort. The 1, 2, and 3-bedroom condominiums in this oceanside hotel are in three 15-story towers. All of the condos have ocean views, balconies, a living room, and modern furnishings, and all have either kitchenettes or full kitchens. The complex is 4 blocks from the ocean and from Barefoot Landing, a center with numerous theaters, restaurants, and shops. Restaurant, bar. Kitchenettes, microwaves. Cable TV. 4 pools (1 indoor). 3 hot tubs, sauna. Beach. Video games. Children's programs (5–12). Business services. | 4800 S. Ocean Blvd., North Myrtle Beach | 843/272–4044 or 800/331–6533 | fax 843/272–2294 | bch-cove@sccoast.net | www.beachcove.com | 340 condominium apartments | $47–$178 1–bedroom condominium, $73–$290 2–bedroom condominium, $89–$350 3–bedroom condominium | AE, D, MC, V.

Best Western Dayton House. This standard chain hotel is on the beach, and is a favorite with families. Kids enjoy the lazy river circulating pool, and a beachside lawn is ideal for picnics. Rooms are standard sized, and many have ocean views. Kitchenettes, microwaves, refrigerators. Cable TV. Indoor-outdoor pool. Hot tub. Exercise equipment. Laundry facilities. | 2400 N. Ocean Blvd. | 843/448–2441 or 800/258–7963 | fax 843/448–5957 | dayton@sccoast.net | www.daytonhouse.com | 328 apartments in 5 buildings | $44–$196 | AE, D, DC, MC, V.

The Breakers and North Tower. The rooms in this oceanfront hotel are airy and spacious, with contemporary decor. Restaurant, bar. Some kitchenettes, refrigerators. Cable TV. 3 pools (1 indoor-outdoor), wading pool. Hot tub. Exercise equipment. Children's programs (5–17). Laundry facilities. Airport shuttle. | 2006 N. Ocean Blvd. | 843/626–5000 or 800/845–0688 | fax 843/626–5001 | breakers@sccoast.net | www.breakers.com | 204 rooms and 186 suites in 3 buildings | $32–$205 | AE, D, DC, MC, V.

Brustman House. This pleasant B&B is 1 ½ blocks from the beach. Down comforters cover the beds, which are king- and queen-size; furnishings are Scandinavian. Complimentary breakfast. Some kitchenettes, many in-room hot tubs. Cable TV. Airport shuttle. No kids under 10. No smoking. | 400 25th Ave. S | 843/448–7699 or 800/448–7699 | fax 843/626–2478 | wcbrustman@worldnet.att.net | www.brustmanhouse.com | 5 rooms, 1 suite | $60–$115, $95–$190 suite | No credit cards.

Caravelle Resort and Villas. The rooms at this large beachside complex have ocean views. Most also have balconies and small sitting areas. Restaurant, room service. Some kitchenettes, refrigerators. Cable TV. 8 pools (2 indoor). Hot tub. Exercise equipment. Children's programs (3–12). Laundry facilities. Business services, airport shuttle. | 6900 N. Ocean Blvd. | 843/918–8000 or 800/845–0893 | fax 843/449–0643 | www.thecaravelle.com | 369 rooms, 210 villas | $59–$204, $69–$134 villas | AE, D, MC, V.

Caribbean Resort and Villas. On the beach, most of the standard rooms at this resort hotel have ocean views and balconies, and are decorated in floral pastels. Suites have full kitchens. Kitchens in suites, refrigerators. Cable TV. Pool. Hot tub. Video games. Laundry service. Business services. | 3000 N. Ocean Blvd. | 843/448–7181 or 800/845–0883 | fax 843/

448–3224 | caribr@sccoast.net | www.caribbeanresort.com | 316 rooms, 195 suites | $42–$124, $52–$124 suites | AE, D, DC, MC, V.

Chesterfield Inn. A throwback to the past, this oceanfront brick inn one block from the Pavilion has been in operation since 1937. There's also a motel wing, which is newer but with less character. The inn rooms have side views of the ocean, although the motel rooms have direct ocean views. Restaurant. Some kitchenettes, some refrigerators. Cable TV. Pool. | 700 N. Ocean Blvd. | 843/448–3177 or 800/392–3869 | fax 843/626–4736 | www.chesterfieldinn.mb.com | 64 rooms in 2 buildings | $59–$189 | Closed Dec.–mid-Feb. | AE, D, MC, V.

Courtyard by Marriott. A half-mile south of Barefoot Landing, a quarter-mile from the beach, and close to many of Myrtle Beach's attractions, this hotel opened in summer of 1999. Restaurant. Some in-room hot tubs. Cable TV, room phones, TV in common area. Indoor pool. Hot tub. Golf privileges. Gym. Laundry facilities, laundry service. No pets. Free parking. | 1000 Commons Blvd. | 843/361–1730 or 877/502–4653 | fax 843/361–1729 | 157 rooms | $79–$159 | AE, D, DC, MC, V.

Cypress Inn. Near Conway's riverwalk, this new inn with a historic look has porches that overlook the marina. Some rooms have sleigh beds, others four-poster beds, and many have details such as crystal collections, ceiling fans, and fireplaces. Complimentary breakfast. Refrigerators, some in-room hot tubs. Cable TV. | 16 Elm St., Conway | 843/248–8199 or 800/575–5307 | fax 843/248–0329 | www.acypressinn.com | 12 rooms | $100–$180 | AE, D, DC, MC, V.

Dunes Village Resort. All the oceanfront efficiencies at this beachside resort hotel, 3 mi from downtown, have private balconies and separate changing areas. Restaurant. Refrigerators. Cable TV. 2 pools (1 indoor). Hot tub. Tennis courts. Exercise room. Beach. Laundry facilities. | 5200 N. Ocean Blvd. | 843/449–5275 or 800/648–3539 | fax 843/449–2107 | www.dunesvillage.com | 93 rooms | $52–$135 | D, MC, V.

Embassy Suites Resort at Kingston Plantation. These luxurious, oceanside accommodations are on 145 acres. A 20-story, glass-sheathed tower is part of the complex of shops, restaurants, and condominiums that make up the resort. Villas have lakefront views, patios, or screened-in porches. Restaurant, bar (with entertainment). In-room data ports, kitchenettes, microwaves, refrigerators. Cable TV, in-room VCRs. 7 pools (1 indoor), wading pool. Hot tub, massage. Tennis courts. Gym. Children's programs. Business services. | 9800 Lake Dr. | 843/449–0006 | fax 843/497–1017 | www.kingstonplantation.com | 82 lodges, 255 suites, 137 apartments, 311 cottages | $159–$199 1–bedroom lodges, $129–$299 suites, $149–$409 apartments and cottages | AE, D, DC, MC, V.

Hampton Inn Northwood. This standard chain hotel is three blocks from the beach and next to a driving range. Complimentary Continental breakfast. In-room data ports, microwaves, minibars in suites, refrigerators, some in-room hot tubs. Cable TV. Indoor pool. Hot tub. Exercise equipment. Laundry facilities. Business services. | 620 75th Ave. N | 843/497–0077 or 800/543–4286 | fax 843/497–8845 | www.hamptoninn.com | 122 rooms, 20 suites | $114–$134, $216 suites | AE, D, DC, MC, V.

Hampton Inn–48th. Near the center of Myrtle Beach, this chain hotel is also 1½ blocks from the ocean. Restaurant, bar (with entertainment), complimentary Continental breakfast. In-room data ports, some refrigerators. Cable TV. Indoor pool. Laundry services. Business services. Free parking. | 4709 N. Kings Hwy. (U.S. 17) | 843/449–5231 | fax 843/449–1528 | www.mbhampton.com | 152 rooms | $99–$119 | AE, D, DC, MC, V.

Holiday Inn Oceanfront. All the rooms at this well-maintained, beach-side chain hotel downtown have balconies with picture windows and sliding glass doors that face the ocean. Restaurant, bar (with entertainment). Refrigerators. Cable TV. 2 pools (1 indoor). Hot tub. Exercise equipment. Business services. Children's programs (ages 3–12). Laundry facilities. | 415 S. Ocean Blvd. | 843/448–4481 or 800/845–0313 | fax 843/448–0086 | www.hioceanfront.com | 311 rooms | $169–$179 | AE, D, DC, MC, V.

Myrtle Beach Martinique. All the rooms at this oceanfront hotel have balconies overlooking the lawn or the ocean. Restaurant, bar (with entertainment). Some kitchenettes, microwaves, refrigerators. Cable TV. 2 pools (1 indoor). Hot tub. Exercise equipment, beach. Children's programs. Laundry service. Business services. | 7100 N. Ocean Blvd. | 843/449–4441 or 800/542–0048 | fax 843/497–3041 | martinq@sccoast.net | www.mbmartinique.com | 203 rooms | $135–$355 | AE, D, DC, MC, V.

Ocean Dunes Resort and Villas. This beach-side resort has all the amenities and is at the north end of Myrtle Beach, but is still close to restaurants and entertainment. Live plants in many rooms add a refreshing touch, and private terraces overlook the beach. Restaurant, bar (with entertainment). Refrigerators. Cable TV. 5 pools (1 indoor). Beauty salon, hot tub. Gym. Beach. Children's programs (2–12), (Jun.–Sept.). Laundry facilities. Business services, airport shuttle. | 201 75th Ave. N | 843/449–7441 or 800/845–0635 | fax 843/449–0558 | sands@sccoast.net | www.sandsresorts.com | 138 rooms, 165 tower suites, 10 town houses, 45 2-bedroom villas | $49–$155 rooms, $75–$340 suites, $240–$275 town houses, $245–$350 villas | AE, D, DC, MC, V.

Ocean Forest Plaza. Although about 3 mi from Myrtle Beach's main attractions and restaurants, this hotel is right across the street from the beach. Suites have wicker furnishings and glass-topped tables. Restaurant, bar. Kitchenettes, microwaves. Cable TV. 2 pools (1 indoor). Hot tub, sauna, steam room. Video games. Children's programs (4–12), (Jun.–Aug.). | 5523 N. Ocean Blvd. | 843/497–0044 or 800/522–0818 | fax 843/497–3051 | 190 suites | $46–$152 | AE, D, DC, MC, V.

The Palace. This resort-style hotel on the ocean has beachfront rooms with queen beds, queen sleeper sofas, and full-size kitchens. Restaurant. Kitchenettes, microwaves, refrigerators. Cable TV. 2 pools (1 indoor). Hot tub. Exercise equipment. Video games. Laundry facilities. | 1605 S. Ocean Blvd. | 843/448–4300 or 800/334–1397 | fax 843/448–6300 | 298 apartments | $50–$172 | AE, D, MC, V.

Pan American Motor Inn. This beachside motel is 10 mi from the airport and close to a number of restaurants. Many rooms have mahogany headboards and armoires. Restaurant, room service. Kitchenettes, refrigerators. Cable TV. Pool. Tennis courts. Gym. Laundry facilities. Business services. | 5300 N. Ocean Blvd. | 843/449–7411 or 800/845–4501 | fax 843/449–6031 | www.panamerican.com | 85 rooms | $40–$150 | D, MC, V.

Royal Inn. Surrounded by palm trees and across the street from the city park, this motel is four blocks from the Pavilion in a quiet neighborhood. Only couples and families may stay in its rooms and 2- and 3-bedroom suites. Picnic area. Some kitchenettes, refrigerators. Cable TV, room phones. 2 pools (1 indoor). Laundry facilities. Free Parking. Some pets allowed. | 1406 N. Chester St. | 843/448–7743 | 32 rooms, 8 suites | Rooms $67–$77, suites $85–$105 | Closed Dec.–Feb. | D, MC, V.

St. John's Inn. The rooms at this hotel across the street from the beach are decorated in bright colors and some have balconies. Restaurant. Kitchenettes, refrigerators. Cable TV. Pool. Hot tub. Some pets allowed. | 6803 N. Ocean Blvd. | 843/449–5251 or 800/845–0624 | fax 843/449–3306 | www.stjohnsinn.com/vacation.html | 90 rooms | $33–$105 | AE, D, MC, V.

Sandy Beach Resort. Once you're settled in your one-bedroom oceanfront suite, you can either grab an inner tube at the pool and float down the enclosed "lazy river" or walk to the nearby shops and Family Kingdom Amusement Park, all within ½ mi from the resort. Three-bedroom penthouse suites are also available. Some in-room safes, kitchens, refrigerators, some in-room hot tubs. Cable TV, room phones. 3 pools (1 indoor), hot tub, outdoor hot tub. Beach. Laundry facilities. No pets. Free parking. | 201 S. Ocean Blvd. | 843/448–5522 or 800/844–6534 | fax 843/916–4932 | www.beachtrips.com | 113 suites, 4 2-bedroom townhouses, 3 3-bedroom penthouses | $95–$175 1–bedroom suites, $195–$250 2–bedroom townhouses, $225–$300 3–bedroom penthouses | AE, D, MC, V.

Sea Island Inn. Floral bedspreads and curtains decorate the rooms, which all have views of a nice strip of Grand Strand beach and the ocean. Restaurant, room service. Some kitchenettes, refrigerators. Cable TV. Pool, 2 wading pools. Beach. Business services, airport shuttle. Free parking. | 6000 N. Ocean Blvd. | 843/449–6406 or 800/548–0767 | fax 843/449–4102 | www.seaislandinn.com | 90 rooms, 22 suites | $42–$102 rooms, $91–$306 suites | AE, D, MC, V.

Sea Mist Resort. The on-site water park is a draw at this 14½-acre resort on the south end of the beach. Restaurant, picnic area. Many kitchenettes, some refrigerators. Cable TV. 9 pools (1 indoor-outdoor), wading pools. Hot tub. Tennis courts. Exercise equipment. Beach. Video games. Children's programs (4–12), playground. Laundry facilities. Business services. Free parking. | 1200 S. Ocean Blvd. | 843/448–1551 or 800/732–6478 | fax 843/448–5858 | seamist@sccoast.net | www.seamist.com | 827 rooms | $110–$200; reservations are for 2–night minimum | AE, D, DC, MC, V.

Serendipity Bed and Breakfast. The rooms at this Spanish mission-style B&B range from antiqued—with four-poster beds—to modern—with wicker furnishings—and most have views of the beach, which is 300 yards away. It's surrounded by several restaurants, and within 6 blocks of movies and shopping. Picnic area, complimentary Continental breakfast. Some kitchenettes, refrigerators. Cable TV. Pool. Hot tub. Library. | 407 71st Ave. N | 843/449–5268 or 800/762–3229 | fax 843/449–3998 | serendipity-inn@worldnet.att.net | www.serendipityinn.com | 14 rooms, 2 suites | $89–$139, $149–$159 suites | D, MC, V.

Sheraton Myrtle Beach Resort. Modern rooms contribute to the freshness of this property, which is two blocks from Myrtle Beach State Park and 3 mi from the airport. Restaurant, bar. Some kitchenettes, refrigerators. Cable TV. 2 pools (1 indoor). Massage. Exercise equipment. Beach. Video games. Children's programs (5–12), (Jun.–Aug.). Laundry service. Business services, airport shuttle. Free parking. | 2701 S. Ocean Blvd. | 843/448–2518 or 800/992–1055 | fax 843/448–1506 | www.sheratonresort.com | 223 rooms, 9 suites | $85–$160 rooms, $209–$229 suites | AE, D, DC, MC, V.

Stardust Motel. The rooms are clean and comfortable at this motel four blocks from the Pavilion and a short walk to the beach. Some kitchenettes, some microwaves, refrigerators. Cable TV, room phones. Outdoor pool. Laundry facilities. Some pets allowed. | 501 5th Avenue N | 843/448–6717 | fax 843/626–8729 | 24 rooms | $68–$103 | MC, V.

Viking. Reasonably priced rooms on the beach, most of which face the ocean or a lawn-covered courtyard, are available at this locally-owned resort complex. The resort is within 7 blocks of restaurants, shopping, and nightlife. Refrigerators. Cable TV. Pool, wading pool. Beach. Laundry facilities. Business services. Free parking. | 1811 S. Ocean Blvd. | 843/448–4355 or 800/334–4876 (except SC) | fax 843/448–6174 | viking@sccoast.net | www.vikingmotel.com | 76 rooms, 67 suites | $82–$102 | AE, D, DC, MC, V.

Waikiki Village Motel. Two miles from the airport and across the street from the beach you'll find clean, comfortable rooms surrounded by palms trees and grassy areas. Some kitchenettes, some microwaves, refrigerators. Cable TV, room phones. Outdoor pool. Hot tub. Miniature golf, putting green. Laundry facilities. Free parking. No pets. | 1500 S. Ocean Blvd. | 843/448–8431 | fax 843/448–3870 | 46 rooms | $72 | MC, V.

NEWBERRY

MAP 9, E3

(Nearby towns also listed: Abbeville, Columbia)

An 1851 courthouse and surrounding square, brick-paved streets, and an 1882 opera house give Newberry its small-town charm. Settled in 1789 by German, English, and Scots–Irish, the town is enjoying increased popularity since the recent renovation of the Opera House, which hosts theater, music, and dance performances. Newberry is also home to Newberry College.

Information: Newberry Visitors Center | Box 396, 1109 Main St., Newberry, SC 29108 | 803/276–0513 | fax 803/276–4373.

Attractions

Carter and Homes Orchids. Eighteen greenhouses cover two acres with orchids, African violets, and other exotic plants. | 629 Mendenhall Rd. | 803/276–0579 | www.carter&homes.com | Free | Mon.–Fri. 8–5, Sat. 8–4.

Dreher Island State Park. Camping and fishing draw visitors to the 348 acres on Lake Murray, as do the five completely furnished lakeside villas, picnic facilities, nature trails, and marina. | 3677 State Park Rd. | 803/364–3530 or 803/364–4152 | www.southcarolinaparks.com | Free | Daily 6 AM–dusk.

Newberry Opera House. Renovated in 1998, this 1882 structure now hosts operas, concerts, plays, and lecture series. Its clock tower is a local landmark. | 1201 McKibben St. | 803/276–6264 | www.newberryoperahouse.com | Free | Daily 9–6.

Sumter National Forest. This 360,754-acre national forest is home to mountain waterfalls and a white-water river. | National Forest Service, main office, 4931 Broad River Rd., Columbia | 803/561–4000 | www.fs.fed.us/r8/fms | Free | Daily.

Wells Japanese Garden. The iris and lotus flowers, tranquil ponds, bridges, and pagodas make this an ideal spot for contemplation and peaceful conversation. | Lindsay St. | 803/276–0513 | Free | Daily dawn to dusk.

ON THE CALENDAR

APR.: *Agrifest.* Held at the fairgrounds on the third Saturday of the month, this event formerly known as the Newberry Egg and Dairy Festival celebrates the area's agricultural history with an arts and crafts fair, bands, and, among other entertainment, cloggers. Kids can enjoy petting zoo while you tinker around the antique cars and farm equipment. | 803/276–7101.

Dining

Steven W's. Contemporary. Steak, seafood, and pasta grace the tables at this elegant bistro across the street from the Opera House; it's often open late to accommodate events there. | 1100 Main St. | 803/276–7700 | Closed Mon. No lunch | $12–$30 | AE, D, DC, MC, V.

Lodging

Best Western Newberry Inn. The nearby lake draws people who like to fish, and since 1965, travelers have been staying at this chain motel off I–26 (Exit 74) and near the Newberry Opera House and Japanese Garden. Complimentary Continental breakfast. Some microwaves, some refrigerators. Cable TV, room phones. Outdoor pool. Pets allowed (fee). | 11701 S. Carolina Hwy. | 803/276–5850 or 800/528–1234 | fax 803/276–9851 | 113 rooms | $42–$55 | AE, D, DC, MC, V.

Days Inn. This standard chain motel is close to I–385 and Hwy. 56 as well as restaurants and shopping. Complimentary Continental breakfast. Some refrigerators. Cable TV. Pool. Exercise equipment. Laundry facilities. Some pets allowed. | 12374 Hwy. 56, North Clinton; 20 mi north of Newberry on Hwy. 56 | 864/833–6600 | fax 864/833–6600 | 54 rooms, 4 suites | $45–$85 | AE, D, DC, MC, V.

ORANGEBURG

MAP 9, G5

(Nearby town also listed: Santee)

German immigrants from Pennsylvania settled along the Edisto River in the 1730s; soon, Orangeburg boomed as a cotton market and is still the state's top cotton producer.

It's also home to two traditionally black schools: Claflin College and South Carolina State University. Edisto Memorial Gardens, the main draw, is one of only 26 All American Rose Society test gardens in the United States and many have have discovered the Edisto River to be a haven for fishing, boating, and canoeing.

Information: **Orangeburg County Chamber of Commerce** | 1570 John C. Calhoun Dr., Orangeburg, SC 29115 | 803/534–6821 or 800/545–6153 | www.orangeburgsc.net.

Attractions

Edisto Memorial Gardens. More than 4,000 roses of 75 varieties and a test rose garden line the banks of the Edisto River. Azaleas, wisteria, dogwoods, crab apples, and other flowering plants color the gardens throughout spring and fall. There's also a garden for the blind, plus a 2,600-ft boardwalk that carries visitors into the Horne Wetlands Park. | U.S. 301 | 803/533–6020 | www.orangeburgsc.net/quality/edisto.htm | Free | Daily 8 AM–8:30 PM.

Orangeburg National Fish Hatchery. Endangered shortnose sturgeon, bass, and sunfish fill the aquariums at this hatchery. | Rte. 21 Bypass (Stonewall Jackson Dr.) | 803/534–4828 | www.fws.gov | Free | Weekdays 8–4.

South Carolina State University. Founded in 1896 as the Colored Normal, Agricultural and Industrial College, this school remains a traditionally black university and is known in the state for its Education and Speech Pathology programs. | 300 College St. NE | 803/536–7000 | www.scsu.edu | Free | Daily.

I.P. Stanback Museum and Planetarium, the state's largest, crowns this museum, where African and African-American works are on display. Reservations to the planetarium are necessary, and viewings for the general public are limited. | 300 College St. NE | 803/536–7174 | www.draco.scsu.edu | Free | Weekdays 9–4; call for planetarium hours and reservations.

ON THE CALENDAR
SEPT.–OCT.: *Orangeburg County Fair.* Held at the Orangeburg County Fairgrounds, this event has been a part of Orangeburg tradition since 1910, and is the oldest continuosly running annual fair in the state. The fair focuses on good old-fashioned county fair favorites– livestock, canned goods, rides, and plenty of family entertainment. | 803/534–6821 or 800/545–6153.

Dining

Community House. Italian. Fresh local seafood, chicken, and pasta are served in country decor in a 1932 former schoolhouse. There are also homemade baked good. Kids' menu. | 10555 U.S. 17S | 843/237–8353 | Closed Sun. No lunch | $16–$24 | MC, V.

Lodging

Days Inn. The King Suites have hot tubs and work areas at this otherwise typical chain hotel 5 mi from Edisto Gardens and the museum. Complimentary Continental breakfast. Some refrigerators. Cable TV. Pool. | 3691 St. Matthews Rd. (U.S. 601 N) | 803/531–2590 | fax 803/531–2829 | www.thedaysinn.com/orangeburg | 74 rooms, 2 suites | $45–$75 rooms, $125 suites | AE, D, DC, MC, V.

Fairfield Inn. This chain hotel welcomes you with coffee, tea and juice, available 24 hours. It's off Interstate 26, Exit 145A, and is five minutes from South Carolina State University and Claflin College. Dining room, complimentary Continental breakfast. Some microwaves, some refrigerators, some in-room hot tubs. Cable TV, room phones, TV in common area. Outdoor pool. Outdoor hot tub. Airport shuttle. No pets. | 663 Citadel Rd. | 803/533–0014 or 800/228–2800 | fax 803/531–0144 | 65 rooms | $73–$79 | AE, D, DC, MC, V.

PAWLEYS ISLAND

MAP 9, K6

(Nearby towns also listed: Georgetown, Litchfield Beach, Murrells Inlet, Myrtle Beach)

Tiny, 3½-mi-long Pawleys Island still offers essentially the same summer escape it offered wealthy rice plantation families two centuries ago: laid-back relaxation on an unspoiled beach. Referred to as "arrogantly shabby" by locals, the island is made up of weathered old summer cottages (most dating to the 1800s) nestled in groves of oleander and oak trees. Hurricane Hugo and rising property values have brought new and upscale beach houses, too. Nearby, the famous Pawleys Island rope hammocks are hand-tied.

Information: Myrtle Beach Area Chamber of Commerce and Info Center | Box 2115, 1200 N. Oak St., Myrtle Beach, SC 29578-2115 | 800/356–3016 or 843/249–3519 | fax 843/626–0009 | www.mbchamber.com.

Attractions

Hammock Shops at Pawleys Island. You can shop for hammocks, jewelry, toys, antiques, and designer fashions in this complex of two dozen boutiques, shops, and restaurants. In the Hammock Weavers' Pavilion, craftspeople demonstrate the more than 100-yr-old art of weaving cotton-rope Pawleys Island hammocks. | 10880 Ocean Hwy. (U.S. 17) | 843/237–8448 | Free | Mon.–Sat. 10–6, Sun. 1–5.

ON THE CALENDAR
OCT.: *Pawleys Island Tour of Homes.* In the mid-19th century, wealthy rice planters built summer homes on the island to protect themselves from inland malaria-carrying mosquitoes. Although many were destroyed by Hurricane Hugo in 1989, you can take a self-guided tour of seventeen surviving homes that date back to 1843. The $20 fee goes to Habitat for Humanity. | 1907 Hapton Ct., Georgetown | 843/546–5685.

Dining

Frank's. Contemporary. You can dine on generous portions of seafood, beef and lamb cooked over an oak-burning grillbeef at this former 1930s grocery store with wood floors, framed French posters, and fireside seating. Out back is the more casual Frank's Outback Grill Room; try the crab cakes or the panfried grouper. The deck outdoors overlooks a lawn and Frank's beach-scene mural; there's an outdoor fireplace, too, and live music on the weekends. | 10434 Ocean Hwy. (U.S. 17) | 843/237–3030 | Reservations essential | No lunch. Closed Sun. | $17–$27 | D, MC, V.

Lodging

Ramada Inn. Motel-modern furnishings outfit spacious, bright, and airy rooms at this well-maintained inn on the first and ninth holes of the Seagull Golf Course. Room service. Some microwaves, some refrigerators. Cable TV, room phones, TV in common area. Outdoor pool. Golf privileges. No pets. | 7903 Ocean Hwy. (U.S. 17) | 843/237–4261 | fax 803/237–9703 | 99 rooms | $79–$89 | AE, D, DC, MC, V.

PENDLETON

MAP 9, C2

(Nearby towns also listed: Anderson, Clemson, Greenville)

The entire small town of Pendleton, plus the outlying area, is on the National Register of Historic Places, making it one of the largest historic districts in the nation. Established in 1790, Pendleton was popular with wealthy Lowcountry planters and politicians who built summer homes here, in sight of the Blue Ridge mountains. There are more than 45 historic buildings within a 1-mi radius, among them the Farmers Hall in the center of the town green; Clemson University is about 3 mi away.

Information: Pendleton Visitor Center and Pendleton District Historical, Recreational and Tourism Commission | Box 565, 125 E. Queen St., Pendleton, SC 29670 | 864/646–3782 or 800/862–1795 | fax 864/646–2506 | www.pendleton-district.org.

Attractions

Ashtabula. This two-story 1825 clapboard house on 10 acres of grounds has been restored and furnished to depict life on an Upcountry farm in the 1850s. | Hwy. 88 | 864/646–3782 | $5 | Apr.–Oct., Sun. 2–6 or by appointment.

Chatooga National Wild and Scenic River. Rapids, waterfalls, and steep cliffs as well as gentle bends and calm pools punctuate this mountain river—made famous in the movie *Deliverance*—that runs through Sumter National Forest. | National Park Service, 4931 Broad River Rd. | 803/561–4000 | www.fs.fed.us/r8/fms | Free | Daily dawn to dusk.

Farmers' Society Hall. Built in 1826 as the courthouse, this columned Greek Revival building stands in the center of the village green and is the oldest Farmers Hall still in continuous use in the United States. The meeting hall is on the second floor; the ground floor is now a restaurant. | 105 Exchange St. | 864/646–7024 | Free | Call for appointment.

Historic Homes. The entire town of Pendleton is on the National Register of Historic Places. You can pick up a self-guided walking tour brochure from the Pendleton Visitor Center, or stroll through town on your own to view these historic homes. | 864/646–3782 | Free | Daily.

Pendleton District Agricultural Museum. The first boll weevil found in South Carolina and a collection of antique farm tools and equipment commemorate the area's farming history. Also on display is a cotton gin that predates Eli Whitney's. | History La. | 864/646–3782 | www.pendleton-district.org | Free | By appointment.

Pendleton District Historical, Recreational, and Tourism Commission. Extensive genealogy archives and changing exhibits make this more than the typical tourist commission. The commission also has information on self-guided walking tours, including cassettes for rent, and is in the historic Hunter's Store. | 125 E. Queen St. | 864/646–3782 or 800/862–1795 | www.pendleton-district/org | Free | Weekdays 9–4:30.

Rafting Trips. A number of companies offer rafting tours on the Chatooga River.
Nantahala Outdoor Center is one of the companies that takes groups on rafting tours. | 851A Chatooga Ridge Rd., Mountain Rest | 800/232–7238 | www.noc.com | Call for prices | Mar.–Nov.
Southeastern Expeditions offers rafting tours of the Chatooga River. | Hwy. 76E, Clayton, GA | 800/868–7238 | www.southeasternraft.com | $47–$235 | Mar.–Nov.
Wildwater Ltd. can take you on rafting tours and provide you with overnight accommodations at cabins and bed-and-breakfasts. | 1251 Academy Rd., Long Creek | 800/451–9972 | www.wildwaterrafting.com | $25–$99 | Mar.–Oct.

Woodburn. The grand summer home (circa 1830) of the prominent Pinckney family has been restored and furnished with period antiques. | History La. | 864/646–3782 or 864/646–3655 | $5 | Apr.–Oct., Sun. 2–6; group tours by appointment all year.

ON THE CALENDAR

APR.: *Historic Pendleton Spring Jubilee.* Food vendors, art and craftspeople, and musicians gather at the village green to celebrate the beginning of tourist season and the opening of plantation homes and the Agricultural Museum. The bicycle race is on Saturday morning and costumed guided tours of the historic district are led all weekend. | 800/862–1795.

Dining

Confetti's. Contemporary. This airy café dining serving quiche, soups, and chicken salad also doubles as a gourmet basket/special-occasion shop. | 133 E. Queen St. | 864/646–6110 | Closed Mon. No supper Sun.–Wed. | $10–$20 | AE, D, DC, MC, V.

Farmer's Hall Restaurant. Contemporary. You can dine on lamb chops, steaks, and fish in this historic building built in 1824 on the town green. The desserts are delicious; try the homemade strawberry and chocolate crêpes. Additional sidewalk seating lets you look out onto the town center. | 105 Exchange St. | 864/646–7024 | Closed for supper Tues.–Wed., Sun. | $12–$25 | AE, MC, V.

Mac's Drive-In. American. Its location halfway between Clemson and Pendleton makes this restaurant popular with Clemson athletes, and it's filled with photographs of famous players. You can sit on stools at the counter and enjoy hamburgers, fries, and shakes. | 404 Pendelton Rd. | 864/654–2845 | Closed Sun. | $4–$6 | No credit cards.

Lodging

Liberty Hall Inn. Antiques and family heirlooms furnish the rooms at this country inn, which was built in the 1840s and used to be a dairy farm. It now caters to both business travelers and vacationers. Restaurant, complimentary Continental breakfast. Cable TV. | 621 S. Mechanic St. | 864/646–7500 or 800/643–7944 | fax 864/646–7500 | libertyhall@carol.net | www.bbonline.com/sc/liberty/ | 10 rooms | $85 | AE, D, DC, MC, V.

Rocky Retreat. In summer of 2000, Jim Ligon restored and re-opened this 150-yr-old Upcountry South Carolina farmhouse, which had been unoccupied for 15 years. This is the place to get away from it all—there are no TVs or phones in the rooms—and simply relax. There are 6½ acres of open grassy fields as well as a nature trail, and if you're interested in the people who lived here before, Jim will share his knowledge. Dining room, complimentary breakfast. No room phones, no TV. No pets. No kids under 10. | 1000 Millwee Creek Rd. | 864/225–3494 | 4 rooms | $75–$105 | AE, MC, V.

ROCK HILL

MAP 9, F2

(Nearby towns also listed: Chester, York)

Many think of Rock Hill, near the North Carolina border, as a bedroom community to Charlotte. One of South Carolina's newest cities, the town was established in 1852 as a railroad stop on the Charlotte–Columbia line. During the Industrial Revolution, it became a cotton mill town. The area has a rich Catawba Indian heritage and the Catawba Indians now have a reservation here.

Seven mi north of Rock Hill, the town of Fort Mill is on the site of a Colonial-era fort built by the British. Settled by Scotch-Irish in the 1750s, the town grew with the development of area textile mills, which maintain a presence in the area today. The Close Greenway, a 2,300-acre protected area 10 mi north of town on the U.S. 21 bypass, offers hiking, picnicking, horseback riding, and fishing.

Information: **Rock Hill Area Chamber of Commerce** | Box 590, 115 Dave Lyle Blvd., Rock Hill, SC 29731 | 803/324–7500 | fax 803/324–1889 | www.yorkcountychamber.com.

Attractions

Andrew Jackson State Park. A museum and one-room schoolhouse recall the pioneer era at this park, where Andrew Jackson was born. Along with camping, picnicking, and fishing, there are also nature trails, interpretive programs, and an amphitheater. | 196 Andrew Jackson Park Dr. | 803/285–3344 | www.southcarolinaparks.com | Free | Daily 8–6; museum, weekends 1–5, weekdays by appointment.

Catawba Cultural Center. The Catawba Indian Reservation preserves the Catawba Indian heritage through a variety of programs, exhibits, and craft stores. Call ahead for information on tours and special events. | 1536 Tom Steven Rd. | 803/328–2427 | www.ccppcrafts.com | Free | Mon.–Sat. 9–5.

Glencairn Garden. Trails wind through six acres of azaleas, winter honeysuckle, wisteria, dianthus, and daylilies that present a succession of blooms throughout the year. | 725 Crest St. | 803/329–5620 or 800/866–5200 | fax 803/329–8786 | www.ci.rock-hill.scus/rchl | Free | Daily dawn to dusk.

Historic Brattonsville. At this working farm, you can see a heritage farm program in action—the animals, crops, gardens, and orchards are historical varieties representative of South Carolina from the Revolution to the 19th century. Twenty-four historic buildings—including a pre-Revolutionary backwoodsman cabin, slave cabins, and a brick kitchen—recreate 18th- and 19th-century life. There's also a 10-mi hiking, biking, and equestrian trail. | 1444 Brattonsville Rd., McConnells; 11 mi southwest of Rock Hill on State Road 322 | 803/684–2327 | fax 803/684–0149 | $5 | Mon.–Sat. 10–5, Sun. 1–5.

Lake Wylie. Loads of bass, crappie, and catfish fill this 12,400-acre impoundment of the Catawba River, which also has a 325-mi shoreline. | Access from Mount Gallant Rd. | 803/324–7500 | Free | Daily.

Landsford Canal State Park. This is the best preserved of a series of old canals designed by Robert Mills in the 1820s. You can also fish on the Catawba River, walk the nature trails, or spend time at the museum and interpretive center. A rare species of spider lilies blooms extravagantly each spring. | 2051 Park Dr. | 803/789–5800 | www.southcarolinaparks.com | $1.50 | Thurs.–Mon. 9–6.

Museum of York County. One of the world's most diverse collections of mounted African mammals tops the displays. You'll also find hands-on exhibits and the art of Vernon Grant, creator of Kellogg's "Snap! Crackle! Pop!" characters. There's even a nature trail. | 4621 Mt. Gallant Rd. | 800/968–2726 or 803/329–2121 | www.yorkcounty.org | $4 | Daily 10–5.

Paramount's Carowinds. Motion pictures and television are brought to life at this 100-acre water and theme park, featuring rides (including the inverted coaster Top Gun and the Kids' playland Zoom Zone), shows, and life-size characters. | 14523 Carowinds Blvd. | 803/548–5300 or 800/888–4386 | $35 | Mon.–Thurs. 10 AM–8, Fri. 10AM–11PM, Sat. 10–10, Sun.10–9; hours may vary.

Winthrop University. Founded in 1886 as an all-girls college, Winthrop is now coeducational with 5,500 students and four colleges. | Oakland Ave. | 803/323–2211 | www.winthrop.edu | Free | Weekdays 8:30–5.

ON THE CALENDAR

APR.: *Come–See–Me.* More than 80 events, including an international food fair, an art exhibit, garden tours, road races, a parade, concerts, and fireworks, celebrate spring in the area. | 800/681–7635.

NOV.: *Yap Ye Iswa Festival.* Catawba Indians perform tribal dances, drumming, and storytelling for their annual festival at the Catawba Cultural Center on the reservation. There's also traditional foods and more. | 1536 Tom Steven Rd. | 803/328–2427.

DEC.: *Brattonsville Christmas Candlelight Tour.* On the first weekend of the month, costumed interpreters guide visitors through the historic homes of Brattonsville, which are decorated with traditional holiday fruit, greenery, and candles. | 803/684–2327.

Dining

Golden Corral. American. At the all-you-can-eat buffets, you can choose from a spread of salads, pizza, soup, burgers, and desserts. Wednesday has a steak and shrimp dinner buffet and Fridays are reserved for fish. | 1031 N. Anderson Rd. | 803/328–0327 | fax 803/328–9139 | $6–$9 | AE, D, MC, V.

Tam's Tavern. Continental. Greens, beiges, and bent wood furniture decorate this freestanding house. A large collection of animation cells fills the non-smoking room, where you can feast on seafood fettucine and creole-based dishes such as catfish stew. | 1027 Oakland Ave. | 803/329–2226 | Closed Sun. | $9–$17 | AE, DC, MC, V.

Thursdays Too. American. Owners Kathy and Larry Bigham have been running this local favorite since the late 1970s. Their all-are-welcome attitude has filtered down to the staff, who keep people coming back. The place is big enough to offer a quiet corner for two and a birthday celebration at the same time. | 147 Herlong Ave. | 803/366–6117 | fax 843/366–6584 | Closed Sun. | $8–$14 | AE, D, MC, V.

Lodging

Comfort Inn. This standard chain hotel is next door to a shopping area. It is 13 mi north of Rock Hill and less than a mile from the town of Carowinds. Restaurant, complimentary Continental breakfast. In-room data ports, refrigerators in suites. Cable TV. Pool. Exercise equipment. Airport shuttle. | 3725 Ave. of the Carolinas, Fort Mill | 704/339–0574 | fax 803/548–6692 | www.comfortinn.com | 138 rooms, 15 suites | $62–$71, $130–$160 suites | AE, D, DC, MC, V.

Courtyard by Marriott. Five miles from Cherry Park, this hotel provides the clean, comfortable rooms you would expect from Marriott. You can play video games in your room and the room service menu comes from Outback Steakhouse; a breakfast buffet is available in the morning. Dining room, bar, room service. In-room data ports, some microwaves, some refrigerators, some in-room hot tubs. Cable TV, room phones, TV in common area. Indoor pool. Hot tub. Gym. Laundry facilities, laundry service. No pets. | 1300 River Run Ct. | 803/324–1400 or 800/321–2211 | fax 803/324–1499 | 90 rooms | $79 | AE, DC, D, MC, V.

Days Inn. The reasonably priced rooms at this typical chain hotel are within walking distance of stores, cafés, and restaurants. Restaurant, complimentary Continental breakfast. Cable TV. Pool. Business services. | 914 Riverview Rd. | 803/329–6581 or 803/329–7466 | fax 803/366–4472 | www.daysinn.com | 113 rooms | $60–$65 | AE, D, DC, MC, V.

Days Inn Charlotte South/Carowinds. This chain hotel is ½ mi from Paramount's Carowinds amusement park and 3 mi from restaurants and shopping. Paintings of Carolina scenery decorate the rooms' walls. Complimentary Continental breakfast. Cable TV, in-room VCRs (and movies). Pool. Some pets allowed. | 3482 U.S. 21, Fort Mill | 803/548–8000 | fax 803/548–6058 | www.daysinn.com | 119 rooms | $35–$75 | AE, D, DC, MC, V.

Holiday Inn. Pastel-shaded bedspreads and walls decorate the rooms at this standard chain hotel, which is close to the bus station, shopping areas, and movie theatres. Restaurant, bar, complimentary breakfast. In-room data ports. Cable TV. Pool. Laundry facilities. Business services, airport shuttle. Some pets allowed. | 2640 Cherry Rd. | 803/329–1122 | fax 803/329–1072 | www.holiday-inn.com | 125 rooms | $89 | AE, D, DC, MC, V.

Ramada Plaza Hotel Carowinds. Rooms with pull-out sofas distinguish this otherwise typical chain hotel across the street from the amusement park and within 2 mi of restaurants. Restaurant, bar, complimentary Continental breakfast. In-room data ports. Cable TV. Pool. Gym. Laundry facilities. Business services, airport shuttle. Some pets allowed. | 225 Carowinds Blvd., Fort Mill | 803/548–2400 | fax 803/548–6382 | www.ramada.com | 205 rooms, 3 suites | $71–$105 rooms, $125–$145 suites | AE, D, DC, MC, V.

Wingate Inn. This business traveler's hotel opened in August 1999 and is across the street from the Rock Hill Galleria; it's also close to movie theaters and restaurants. Five miles down the road, you can play in the fields of Cherry Park. Picnic area, complimentary Continental breakfast. In-room safes, some kitchenettes, some microwaves, refrigerators. Cable TV, room phones, TV in common area. Outdoor pool. Hot tub. Gym. Business services. No pets. | 760 Galleria Blvd. | 803/324–9000 or 800/228–1000 | fax 803/324–9075 | www.wingateinn.com | 85 rooms, 5 suites | $99 rooms, $125–$140 suites | AE, D, MC, V.

SANTEE

(Nearby town also listed: Orangeburg)

In 1939, two rivers were connected for a hydroelectric project, creating Lakes Marion and Moultrie, now the center of Santee and Cooper counties. The lakeside community of Santee is a fisherman's and water sportsman's paradise, with a burgeoning retirement community and a scattering of golf enthusiasts.

Information: Santee Cooper Counties Promotion Commission | 9302 Old #6 Hwy., Santee, SC 29142 | 803/854–2131 or 800/227–8510 | fax 803/854–3906 | www.santeecoopercounty.org.

Attractions

Elloree Square Antique Mall. Elloree residents are proud of the renovations about town in the late 1990s. The Antique Mall, which opened in March 2000, houses 15 dealers from all over the state. You can find furniture, linens, books, toys, and many other goods from the 1800s. | 2724 Cleveland St.; 8 mi northwest of Santee on State Road 6 | 803/897–3642 | Free | Closed Sun.

Eutaw Springs Battlefield Site. The last major Revolutionary War battle in South Carolina was fought at this battle field 12 east of Santee. | Eutawville | 803/496–3831.

Fort Watson Battle Site and Indian Mound. British soldiers used this huge 30-ft Indian mound, now in Santee Wildlife Refuge, as a lookout point during the Revolutionary War. | Intersection of U.S. Hwy. 301 and Hwy. 15 | Free | Daily 8–5.

Santee National Wildlife Refuge. There are great views of the wintering flock of Canadian geese and other migratory fowl from the observation tower of this 15,000 acre refuge on the east bank of Lake Marion. You can walk on the 1-mi self-guided wildlife trail and visit the interpretive center. | Intersection of U.S. Hwy. 301 and Hwy. 15 | 803/478–2214 | Free | Daily 8–5.

Santee State Park. Popular with fishermen, this 2,500-acre park has 30 cabins (many on piers over the lake), campsites, boat rentals, lake swimming, a tackle shop, nature trails, tennis courts, and a restaurant. Nature-based boat tours are available in season. | Outside Moncks Corner, off Rembert Dennis Blvd. | 803/854–2408 or 803/854–4005 (boat tours) | $1.50 | Daily 8–7.

ON THE CALENDAR

MAR.: *Elloree Trials.* The mule race at the "drive-in" horse races at Elloree Training Center can be quite a crowd pleaser as the animals seldom behave. Food vendors, dog races, and other entertainment abound. Call ahead to get the best reserved space. | Route 1/ Racetrack Road, Elloree | 803/897–2616.

Dining

Clark's Inn. Contemporary. Its apple crisp and million-dollar bread have made Clark's, family-owned and -operated since 1946, famous. Fried green tomatoes, baked chicken, stir-fry and catfish fresh from Lake Marion add to its popularity. You can come to the lunch buffet to taste a little of everything. | 114 Bradford Blvd. | 803/854–2101 | $8–$21 | AE, D, DC, MC, V.

Lodging

Best Western. This chain hotel gives easy access to the outdoors; there are golfing and fishing right next door, and some rooms have views of the driving range or the water. Restaurant, complimentary Continental breakfast. Some in-room hot tubs. Cable TV. Pool. Business services. | Hwy. 6, I–95, Exit 98E | 803/854–3089 | fax 803/854–3093 | www.bestwestern.com | 108 rooms | $65 | AE, D, DC, MC, V.

Country Inn Suites. A lobby fireplace lends an individual touch to this chain hotel which opened in February 2000 and is 2 mi from Santee State Park. Seventy-five percent of the rooms are non-smoking. Complimentary Continental breakfast. In-room data ports, some microwaves, some refrigerators, some in-room hot tubs. Cable TV, room phones, TV in common area. Outdoor pool. Putting green. Gym. Laundry facilities. No pets. | 221 Britain St. | 803/854–4104 or 800/456–4000 | fax 803/854–4305 | 61 rooms | $72 | AE, D, DC, MC, V.

Days Inn. A fishing area and three golf courses next door make this typical chain hotel somewhat distinctive. Some rooms have lawn views, and the state park is 7 mi away. Restaurant, complimentary breakfast. Cable TV. Pool. Playground. Laundry service. Business services. Some pets allowed (fee). | 9074 Old Hwy. 6 | 803/854–2175 | fax 803/854–2835 | www.daysinn.com | 119 rooms | $50–$55 | AE, D, DC, MC, V.

SPARTANBURG

MAP 9, E2

(Nearby town also listed: Greenville)

Spartanburg was once the producer of the state's biggest peach crop. It's still part of the state's largest peach-producing area, but Spartanburg has transformed into an international business center. There are so many foreign corporations with plants in the area that some local attractions provide brochures in German, French, and Spanish. The drive down I–85 offers a view of the 20 German (including the new BMW plant), Swiss, and Austrian companies in Spartanburg County alone. As a result of all the activity, the town's turn-of-the-20th-century downtown is slowly being revitalized with a few trendy shops and cafés.

Information: Spartanburg Convention and Visitors Bureau | E298 Magnolia St., Spartanburg, SC 29306 | 864/594–5050 or 800/374–8326 | fax 864/594–5055.

YOUR FIRST-AID TRAVEL KIT

- ❏ Allergy medication
- ❏ Antacid tablets
- ❏ Antibacterial soap
- ❏ Antiseptic cream
- ❏ Aspirin or acetaminophen
- ❏ Assorted adhesive bandages
- ❏ Athletic or elastic bandages for sprains
- ❏ Bug repellent
- ❏ Face cloth

- ❏ First-aid book
- ❏ Gauze pads and tape
- ❏ Needle and tweezers for splinters or removing ticks
- ❏ Petroleum jelly
- ❏ Prescription drugs
- ❏ Suntan lotion with an SPF rating of at least 15
- ❏ Thermometer

Attractions

Arts Center. In addition to rotating art exhibitions, this building houses The Music Foundation as well as administrative offices for the theater and ballet. | 385 S. Spring St. | 864/583–2776 | Free | Weekdays 9–5, Sat. 10–2, Sun. 2–5.

Cowpens National Battlefield. Here, Virginian Daniel Morgan led a rustic militia against the British in a victory that made history. There's now a walking trail, a marked toad tour, picnic facilities, and a visitor center with exhibits and a slide show. | 4001 Chesnee Hwy. | 864/461–2828 | www.nps.gov/cowp | Free; fee for slide show | Daily 9–5.

Croft State Park. The equestrian facilities here make the park popular with horse lovers. You can also enjoy the swimming pool, 160-acre fishing lake, rental boats, tennis courts, campsites, picnic grounds, and nature trails. | 440 Croft State Park Rd. | 864/585–1283 | www.southcarolinaparks.com | Free | Daily 7–6.

Disney Catalog Outlet. You can find great prices, especially on clothes and other Disney-theme items for kids. | 3805 Furman L. Fendley Hwy. | 864/674–2031 | Free | Daily 7–6.

Peachoid Water Tower. The famous peach-shape and peach-color water tower lets you know you're in peach country. | Wilcox Ave. and Hwy. 105 | 864/489–5721.

Prime Outlets of Gaffney. Nike, GAP, Levi's, and Donna Karen represent a few of the more than 90 outlet shops here. There's also a playground for kids. | I–85N, Exit 90 | 864/902–9900 | Free | Mon.–Sat. 10–9, Sun. 1:30–6.

Regional Museum. Antique dolls contribute to the museum's collection of artifacts depicting regional history. | 501 Otis Blvd. | 864/596–3501 | $2 | Tues.–Sat. 10–5.

Rose Hill Plantation State Park. A rose garden and 44-acre lawn surround the 1832 mansion of William Gist, the "secession governor," at this park in the Sumter National Forest. The Federal-style home contains original Gist family furnishings and clothing; there are also a slave house and carriage house on the grounds of this former cotton plantation, which is 30 mi south of Spartanburg via U.S. 176. | 2677 Sardis Rd., Union | 864/427–5966 | www.southcarolinaparks.com or www.travelsouthcarolina.com | $2 | Thurs.–Mon. 9–6; tours 1–4, or by appointment.

Walnut Grove Plantation. The Moore family's pre-1830s antiques furnish this 18th-century plantation, where the smokehouse, barn, well house, and 1777 kitchen remain intact. | 1200 Otts Shoals Rd. | 864/576–6546 | $4.50 | Tues.–Sat. 11–5, Sun. noon–5.

ON THE CALENDAR

JULY: *South Carolina Peach Festival.* Peach desserts, concerts, sports events, and a parade mark this 10-day event. Since the location changes yearly, you can write or call to find out where it will be. | Box 549, Gaffney | 864/489–9066 | dfowler@cherco.net.

Dining

Abby's Grill. Continental. You can choose between the elegant, candlelit dining room and the casual, booth-filled lounge. A French influence marks seafood, pork, and steak. There is nightly entertainment. | 149 W. Main St. | 864/583–4660 | Closed Sun. | $13–$20 | DC, MC, V.

Bantam Chef. American. At this '50s-style diner, you can eat hot dogs, burgers, onion rings, and fries seated at a red vinyl booth surrounded by old cars and '50s memorabilia. The service is fast and friendly. | 418 S. Alabama Ave., Chesnee; 10 mi north of Spartanburg on Hwy. 221 A | 864/461–8403 | Breakfast also available. Closed Sun. | $5–$10 | AE, DC, MC, V.

Beacon Drive-In. American. This 54-yr-old Spartanburg institution with friendly staff and curbside service is known for its chili cheeseburgers, hot dogs, fish sandwiches, and onion rings. Try the 6-inch-high Beacon burger—½ lb of meat, with cheese, slaw, and mustard. The newly built ice-cream bar, with big-size desserts, is open daily. | 255 Reidville Rd. | 864/585–9387 | Breakfast also available. Restaurant closed Sun. | $2–$10 | No credit cards.

R.J. Rockers. American. College students and just-off-work business types enliven this brewpub, which brews its own beer on the premises. Appetizers, salads, and burgers are available. | 117 W. Main St. | 864/583–3100 | Closed Sun. | $10–$14 | AE, D, MC, V.

Stefano's. Northern Italian. Candles and linen tablecloths cover the tables at this upscale restaurant, and owner/chef Steve Tsoulos has dinner specials every night: fresh halibut and salmon, lamb chops, eight to ten different veal dishes, plenty of pasta, and new desserts every day. The pasta ecstasy fettucine with crab meat, broccoli, mushroom, and Alfredo sauce is a favorite. For dessert, you can try the strawberry fantasy cheesecake. | 1560 Union St. | 864/591–1941 | No lunch. Closed Sun. | $7–$18 | AE, D, DC, MC, V.

Lodging

Comfort Inn. You can get a simple, reasonably priced room at this chain hotel, which is 2 mi from the outlet shopping mall and 17 mi north of Spartanburg. Complimentary Continental breakfast. Refrigerators. Cable TV. Pool. Exercise equipment. | 143 Corona Dr., Gaffney | 864/487–4200 | fax 864/487–4637 | www.comfortinn.com | 83 rooms | $49–$68 | AE, D, DC, MC, V.

Comfort Inn–West. The zoo is 7 mi from this standard chain hotel, which is 6 mi from Spartanburg and 4 mi east of Westgate Mall, the largest mall in the state. There are also several restaurants within walking distance. Complimentary Continental breakfast. Cable TV. Pool. | 2070 New Cut Rd. | 864/576–2992 | fax 864/576–2992 | www.comfortinn.com | 99 rooms | $65 | AE, D, DC, MC, V.

Hampton Inn. This chain hotel's main draw is that it's 1 mi from the largest shopping mall in the state. The BMW Plant, which gives tours, is 6 mi away. Complimentary Continental breakfast. Cable TV. Pool. Business services. | 4930 College Dr. | 864/576–6080 | fax 864/587–8901 | www.hamptoninn.com | 112 rooms | $50–$74 | AE, D, DC, MC, V.

Inn at Merridun. The original stenciling has lasted on this antebellum columned 1855 home in Union, 30 mi southeast of Spartanburg. A large, curving staircase in the lobby leads up to rooms with brass beds and clawfoot bathtubs. You can explore the nine wooded acres, and picnic lunches and dinner are available. Complimentary breakfast. Cable TV. | 100 Merridun Pl., Union | 864/427–7052 or 888–892–6020 | fax 864/429–0373 | merridun@carol.net | www.bbonline.com/sc/merridun or www.merridun.com | 5 rooms | $89–$115 | AE, MC, V.

The Jameson Inn. The cathedral ceiling, glass foyer, and Old English lobby furniture make this chain hotel distinct. Maroon and green floral prints decorate the rooms and you can walk next door to restaurants. Picnic area, complimentary Continental breakfast. In-room data ports, some microwaves, some refrigerators, some in-room hot tubs. Cable TV, room phones, TV in common area. Outdoor pool. Gym. Some pets allowed. | 115 Rogers Commerce Blvd. | 864/814–0560 or 800/526–3766 | fax 864/814–0620 | 42 rooms | $56 | AE, D, DC, MC, V.

Juxa Plantation. A goldfish pond, waterfall, rose and azalea gardens, wooded paths, and a grape arbor dot the grounds of the 225-acre former plantation, complete with horse stable and pasture. Antiques fill the antebellum home, which was built in 1828 and still has its old kitchen and smokehouse. Picnic lunches and dinner are available. Complimentary breakfast. | 117 Wilson Rd., Union | 864/427–8688 | nolasjuxa@aol.com | 3 rooms | $85 | AE, MC, V.

Main Street Motel. You can check into a clean, quiet room at this family run hotel, in operation since the 1950s. Free coffee is available in the foyer in the morning, and reception is open 24 hours. Cable TV, room phones. Pets allowed (fee). | 700 W. Main St. | 864/583–8471 | 33 rooms | $45 | MC, V.

Quality Hotel and Conference Center. The University of South Carolina Spartanburg is only 1 mi away from this hotel, and there are many restaurants nearby. Restaurant, bar. In-room data ports, cable TV. Pool. Exercise equipment. Business services. Some pets allowed. | 7136 Asheville Hwy. | 864/503–0780 | fax 864/503–0780 | 143 rooms | $79–$149 | AE, D, DC, MC, V.

Ramada Plaza Hotel. This classic chain hotel is 3 mi from the university and a block to the nearest restaurants. Restaurant, bar (with entertainment), room service. In-room data ports. Cable TV. Indoor pool, wading pool. Hot tub. Exercise equipment. Laundry facilities. Business services. | 200 International Dr. | 864/576–5220 | fax 864/574–1243 | www.ramada.com | 225 rooms | $59–$89 rooms, $150–$200 suites | AE, D, DC, MC, V.

Wilson World Hotel & Suites. This large hotel is a popular spot for reunions, weddings and conferences. All rooms have a view of the countryside and open onto the expansive interior with a restaurant and lounge area. Most rooms have two king-size beds and a coffee maker. Restaurant, bar, room service. In-room data ports, some kitchenettes, some microwaves, refrigerators. Cable TV, room phones. Indoor pool. Putting green. Video games. Laundry facilities, laundry service. Business services. No pets. | 9027 Fairforest Rd. | 864/574–2111 or 800/945–7667 | fax 864/576–7602 | www.wilsonhotels.com | 200 | $79 | AE, D, DC, MC, V.

SULLIVANS ISLAND

(Nearby towns also listed: Charleston, Isle of Palms)

Charlestonians began building summer cottages and year-round homes on Sullivans Island in the 19th century. Edgar Allan Poe based his tale "The Gold Bug" on the island while he was in the army and stationed at Fort Moultrie in 1827–28. Today, the island is a middle-class, family-oriented residential area, with little commercial development on the beach. It has no hotels and only a few restaurants and bars. Many homes date to the 19th century, and Fort Moultrie, an important Revolutionary War site and part of the Fort Sumter National Monument Park, stands with its lighthouse at the southwest end of Sullivans Island.

Information: Charleston Area Convention and Visitors Bureau | Box 975, 81 Mary St., Charleston, SC 29402 | 843/853–8000 or 800/868–8118 | fax 843/853–0444.

Attractions
Patriots Point. The World War II submarine *Clamagore* is berthed at the world's largest naval and maritime museum, along with the aircraft carrier *Yorktown,* the destroyer *Laffey,* and the cutter *Ingham.* There's a Vietnam exhibit as well, and you can take a tour of any or all the vessels. | 40 Patriots Point Rd. | 843/884–2727 | $11 | Apr.–Sept., daily 9–7:30; Oct.–Mar., daily 9–6:30.

Dining
Slightly Up the Creek. Seafood. Chef Frank Lee refers to his cooking style as "Maverick," creating such dishes as mustard-crusted grouper and barbecue tuna with mustard sauce, topped with fried oysters, all of which you can enjoy while looking out the shrimping boats that dot Shem Creek. The specials change nightly; vegetarian entrées are available. The restaurant is 7 mi west of Sullivan's Island in Mt. Pleasant. | 130 Mill St., Mt. Pleasant | 843/884–5005 | No lunch | $16–$22 | AE, D, DC, MC, V.

Lodging
Hampton Inn at Patriot's Point. The clean, comfortable rooms at this modern hotel are 5 mi from the beach and a mile from downtown Charleston. Patriot's Point is about a mile away, and you can walk to restaurants. From downtown Charleston take the Cooper River Bridge and bear left on Hwy 17. Turn right on McGarth Darby Blvd, and the next right will be Johnny Dodd Blvd. Complimentary Continental breakfast. Cable TV, room phones, TV in common area. Outdoor pool. No pets. | 255 Johnnie Dodd Blvd., Mt. Pleasant | 843/881–

3300 or 800/426–7866 | fax 843/881–6288 | chsmt01@hi-hotel.com | 121 rooms | $59–$109 | AE, D, DC, MC, V.

Hilton Charleston Harbor Resort & Marina. You can hop on the hotel water taxi and be in downtown Charleston in five minutes. In the lobby of this stately Georgian building, you'll find a marlin that holds the state record for largest billfish. The property rents out six two-bedroom cottages in addition to the regular rooms. Restaurant, bar (with entertainment), picnic area, room service. In-room data ports, some kitchens, some microwaves, some refrigerators, some in-room hot tubs. Cable TV, some in-room VCRs, room phones, TV in common area. Outdoor pool. Outdoor hot tub, massage. Driving range, 18-hole golf course, putting green. Exercise equipment, volleyball. Baby-sitting. Laundry facilities, laundry service. No pets. | 20 Patriot's Point Rd., Mt. Pleasant | 843/856–0028 or 888/856–0028 | fax 843/856–8333 | www.hilton.com | 128 rooms; 6 cottages | $165–$245 rooms; $600 cottages | AE, D, DC, MC, V.

SUMTER

(Nearby town also listed: Camden)

Sumter is named after Revolutionary War hero Gen. Thomas Sumter. At the headwaters of the Pocotaligo River near the center of the state, Sumter grew as cotton grew. Cotton fortunes built many of the Victorian homes and buildings around town, including the Williams–Brice House. The palatial, clock-towered, 1890s stone Sumter Opera House is another landmark of the boom era. Today, Sumter is the state's number two cotton producer. The nearby Shaw Air Force Base also feeds into the town.

Information: Greater Sumter Convention and Visitors Bureau | 32 E. Calhoun St., Sumter, SC 29150 | 843/778–5434 or 800/688–4748 | fax 843/775–0915 | www.usc-sumter.edu/~sumter/tourism/home.html.

Attractions
Church of the Holy Cross. In the cemetery of this Gothic Revival church, made of *pise de terre* (rammed earth), many notables lie buried, including Joel Roberts Poinsett, the botanist who brought the poinsettia back from Mexico. | 335 N. Kings Hwy. | 803/494–8101 | Free | Daily dawn to dusk.

Poinsett Electronic Combat Range. At this 12,500-acre air-force training facility, you can watch from bleachers as pilots practice dropping bombs and shooting bullets. F-16s and F-18s practice their delivery systems targeting salvage vehicles and stationary parachutes. If you're lucky, you may be able to go up in the control tower. The practice schedule changes daily, so call ahead. | Hwy. 261, 4½ mi south of Wedgefield | 803/666–4272 | Free | Mon.–Thurs. 8–5, Fri. 8–1, closed weekends.

Poinsett State Park. You can camp, fish, hike, swim, and picnic among the nature trails and hills of this 1,000 acre park. | 6660 Poinsett Park Rd. | 803/494–8177 | www.southcarolina-parks.com | Free | Daily dawn to dusk.

Sumter County Museum. Housed in an 1845 Edwardian home and its outbuildings, this collection includes war artifacts and antique dolls, toys, and clothes. There's also an exhibit on the development of Sumter's agricultural and transport systems. | 122 N. Washington St. | 803/775–0908 | Free | Tues.–Sat. 10–5, Sun. 2–5.

Sumter Gallery of Art. The collection at this antebellum home includes local, state, and national exhibits, as well as a hands-on exhibit for the visually impaired. | 421 N. Main St. | 803/775–0543 | sumtergallery@sumter.net | Donations accepted | Aug.–June, Tues.–Fri. noon–5, weekends 2–5.

Swan Lake Iris Gardens. Eight species of swans glide across the inky waters of this lake in the middle of one the largest iris gardens in the nation. There are wooden walkways, a braille trail, picnic facilities, and play areas on the 150 acres. | W. Liberty and Brand Sts. | 803/775–1231 or 803/436–2555 | Daily 8 AM–dusk.

ON THE CALENDAR
MAY: *Sumter Iris Festival.* Concerts, arts and crafts, garden tours, and a parade at Swan Lake celebrate irises in full bloom. | W. Liberty and Brand Sts. | 800/688–4748.
OCT.: *Fall Fiesta of Arts.* The visual and performing arts are the focus of this celebration at Swan Lake, with music, dance, storytelling, and arts and crafts. | W. Liberty and Brand Sts. | 803/436–2260.

Dining
Caribbean Pepper Pot. Caribbean. Barbados Chef Clyde Licorish opened this unique little restaurant specializing in authentic West Indian cuisine in 1999. The eschoviched mahi mahi, red snapper, and swordfish are marinated in six fresh herbs. There is a daily twelve-item lunch buffet. | 20 W. Liberty | 803/934–8732 | $5–$13 | AE, D, DC, MC, V.

Casa Linda's. Mexican. Stucco walls and a mural of a street in a Mexican town surround you at this popular lunch spot where the combination fajita quesadilla exemplifies the small, simple dishes served. Other options include chimichangas, enchiladas and burritos. | 1029 Broad St. | 803/778–2939 | $6–$10 | AE, D, MC, V.

The Dragon. Chinese. Red silk seats complement the cherry wood and Chinese lanterns, and the menu offers both Cantonese and Szechuan dishes, almost all of which are prepared in a wok. Try the seafood delight, pepper steak, or boneless chicken. | 236 S. Pike W | 803/778–1807 | fax 803/778–5423 | Closed Mon. | $6–$10 | AE, D, MC, V.

Lodging
Bed and Breakfast of Sumter. A swing and rocking chairs embellish the front porch, while a soapstone fireplace with a stone mantel punctuates the Victorian parlor of this 1896 home. Antiques and crocheted bedspreads decorate the rooms, some of which also have fireplaces. Complimentary breakfast. No room phones, no TV in rooms. Cable TV in common area. No kids under 12. No smoking. | 6 Park Ave. | 803/773–2903 or 888/786–8372 | fax 803/775–6943 | www.bbonline.com/sc/sumter/index/html | 5 rooms | $80 | D, MC, V.

Best Western Sumter Inn. An outdoor pool and ceramic swans at the front desk individualize this motel across the street from the Jasmine mall. Complimentary Continental breakfast. Some microwaves, some refrigerators, some in-room hot tubs. Cable TV, room phones, TV in common area. Outdoor pool. No pets. | 1050 Broad St. | 803/773–8110 or 800/528–1234 | fax 803/773–1697 | www.bestwestern.com | 47 rooms | $56 | AE, D, DC, MC, V.

Comfort Suites. Centrally located on the Broad Street Extension, this hotel keeps all facilities open 24 hours, has "Evergreen" rooms with filtered air systems, and provides fax machines in some rooms. A racecar theme characterizes the lobby and breakfast areas, which are lined with framed prints signed by several big race winners. Picnic area, complimentary Continental breakfast. In-room data ports, microwaves, refrigerators, some in-room hot tubs. Cable TV, in-room VCRs, room phones, TV in common area. Indoor pool. Hot tub. Gym. Laundry facilities. Business services. No pets. | 2500 Broad St. | 803/469–0200 | fax 803/469–7880 | www.comfortsuitessumter.com | 65 rooms | $85–$115 | AE, D, DC, MC, V.

Holiday Inn. Simple, clean rooms comprise this well-maintained chain hotel 4 mi west of town, near Shaw Air Force Base. Restaurant, complimentary breakfast buffet, room service. In-room data ports. Cable TV. Pool. Exercise equipment. Business services. | 2390 Broad St. | 803/469–9001 | fax 803/469–9070 | www.basshotels.com/holiday-inn | 124 rooms | $59–$72 | AE, D, DC, MC, V.

Magnolia House. Built in 1907, this four-columned Greek revival house in Sumter's historic district makes a nice alternative to the region's many chain hotels. Antiques decorate the rooms, which also have inlaid oak floors and stained-glass windows. Complimentary breakfast. No room phones, cable TV in common area, VCR (and movies) in common area. No smoking. | 230 Church St. | 803/775–6694 or 888/666–0296 | magnoliahouse@sumter.net | 4 rooms, 1 suite | $80, $135 suite | AE, DC, MC, V.

Ramada Inn. Like the many chain hotels in the area, little distinguishes this one, though the rooms are clean and simple. Restaurant, bar, complimentary breakfast buffet, room service. In-room data ports, refrigerators. Cable TV. Pool. Business services. Some pets allowed. | 226 N. Washington St. | 803/775–2323 | fax 803/773–9500 | ramadagolf@aol.com | www.ramadagolf.com | 125 rooms in 2 buildings | $59–$109 | AE, D, DC, MC, V.

Travelers Inn. In the heart of town, this typical chain hotel is convenient to many shops and restaurants. Complimentary Continental breakfast. Cable TV. Pool. | 378 Broad St. | 803/469–9210 | fax 803/469–4306 | 104 rooms | $42–$65 | AE, D, DC, MC, V.

WALTERBORO

MAP 9, G7

(Nearby town also listed: Allendale)

Rice plantation owners began summering in the Walterboro area, about 50 mi west of Charleston, in 1784. The first nullification meeting in South Carolina was held in Colleton County's Greek Revival courthouse, still in use today and still an anchor of Walterboro's historic downtown. Many of the town's homes and churches date to the 19th century, trees shade the streets lined with historic buildings, and the old-fashioned, thriving main street has remained almost unchanged since the 1940s.

Information: Walterboro-Colleton Chamber of Commerce | 109C Benson St., Walterboro, SC 29488 | 843/549–9595 | fax 843/549–5775 | www.walterboro.org.

Attractions
Colleton County Courthouse. Believed to be designed by Robert Mills, this 1821 four-columned Greek Revival building in the center of downtown remains a courthouse. South Carolina held its first nullification meeting here in 1828. | 101 Hampton St. | 843/549–5791 | Free | Weekdays 9–5.

Colleton State Park and Edisto River Canoe and Kayak Trail. This park in a live oak forest on the Edisto River serves as headquarters for the Edisto River Canoe and Kayak Trail, a 56-mi black water river trail that travels through a wildlife-studded landscape. Camping facilities are also available. | Intersection of Rte. 61 and Hwy. 15 N | 843/538–8206 (11 AM–noon only) | colleton_sp@prt.state.sc.us | www.southcarolinaparks.com | Free | Daily.
Carolina Heritage Outfitters provides guided canoe and kayak tours of the Edisto River Canoe and Kayak Trail; they also rent out cabins. | Hwy. 15, Canadys | 843/563–5051 or 800/563–5053.

Old Colleton County Jail and Colleton Museum. The restored jail, dating from 1855, now houses the Colleton Museum, with exhibits on the county's history as a center for rice production as well as other heritage artifacts. | Jefferies Blvd. | 843/549–2303 | Free | Tues.–Fri. 9–1 and 2–5, Sat. 10–2, Sun. 2–4.

South Carolina Artisans Center. You can buy handcrafted items here, including jewelry, pottery, baskets, and glass made by South Carolina artists and craftspeople. | 334 Wichman St. | 843/549–0011 | www.southcarolinaartisanscenter.org | Free | Mon.–Sat. 9–6, Sun. 1–6.

APR.: *Rice Festival.* A parade, fireworks, a rice-cooking contest, and the world's largest pot of rice celebrate Walterboro's major crop. | Events take place all over town, but are concentrated at the intersection of Washington and Brown Sts. | 843/549–1079.

APR.: *World Grits Festival.* This popular event features rolling-in-the-grits and grits-eating contests, grits grinding, corn shelling, and grits cooked every which way. | Events take place all over town; call for specific locations | 843/563–4366 or 800/788–5646.

Dining

Dimitrio's. Mediterranean. In addition to pasta and submarine sandwiches, this restaurant in Dimitrio's plaza serves antipasto and seafood pasta salads. Greek specialties include gyros, moussaka, and Greek chicken. | 656 Bells Hwy. | 843/549–5597 | D, MC, V.

Glasshouse. Seafood. The shrimping boat on the roof gives you an idea of what's inside. Opened in September 2000, this candlelit restaurant specializes in Atlantic salmon, Lowcountry crab cakes, baked flounder and other fresh seafood. Pasta, ribs and steak are also available. For dessert, you can try the homemade seven layer chocolate cake. | 69 Downs La. | 843/538–6544 | No lunch. Closed Sun. | $8–$16 | MC, V.

Longhorn Family Steakhouse. American. Oldies music plays in the background of this family restaurant, which has an à la carte menu as well as a buffet with over 100 items. You can order chicken, sandwiches, or steaks, including a 24-oz T-bone. | 1366 Sniders Hwy. | 843/538–2921 | $5–$15 | AE, D, DC, MC, V.

Lodging

Best Western of Walterboro. Dark woodwork and floral patterns decorate the rooms at this motel chain, playing on a "Southern hospitality" theme. There are restaurants within walking distance; the motel is off I–95 on Exit 53. Restaurant, complimentary Continental breakfast. Cable TV, room phones, TV in common area. Outdoor pool. Exercise equipment. Pets allowed (fee). | 1428 Sniders Hwy. | 843/538–3600 or 800/528–1234 | fax 843/538–3600 | www.bestwestern.com | 112 rooms | $50–$70 | AE, D, DC, MC, V.

Bonnie Doone Plantation. You can stay on a former rice plantation, in a Georgian-style mansion and plantation caretaker's house, in the ACE (Ashepoo, Combahee, and Edisto rivers) basin. Complimentary Continental breakfast. | 5878 Bonnie Doone Rd. | 843/893–3396 | fax 843/893–2479 | Bonniedoone@lowcountry.com | 17 rooms | $90–$110 | AE, D, MC, V.

Days Inn. Framed floral art adorns the wall of rooms decorated in hunter green, mauve, and peach at this hotel 4 mi outside Walterboro. Complimentary Continental breakfast. Some microwaves, some refrigerators, some in-room hot tubs. Cable TV, room phones. Outdoor pool. Steam room. Gym. | 1787 Sniders Hwy. | 843/538–2933 or 800/325–2525 | fax 843/538–2158 | 61 rooms | $55–$70 | AE, D, DC, MC, V.

Econo Lodge. Budget accommodations can be found $4\frac{9}{10}$ mi south of Walterboro and within a few blocks of restaurants, movie theaters, and shopping. Complimentary Continental breakfast. Cable TV. | 1057 Sniders Hwy. | 843/538–3830 | fax 843/538–3341 | www.econolodge.com | 100 rooms | $45–$65 | AE, D, MC, V.

Holiday Inn. This chain hotel is near the historic district and within 2 mi of the museum; downtown is 3 mi away. Restaurant, room service. Cable TV. Pool, wading pool. Business services. Some pets allowed. | 1286 Sniders Hwy. | 843/538–5473 | fax 843/538–5473 | www.basshotels.com/holiday-inn | 171 rooms | $49–$69 | AE, D, DC, MC, V.

Town and Country Inn. This country inn features simple, very affordable rooms and is within a few blocks of shopping and restaurants. Restaurant, complimentary Continental breakfast. Cable TV. Pool. Playground. Business services. | 1139 Sniders Hwy. | 843/538–5911 | 96 rooms | $29–$43 | AE, D, DC, MC, V.

YORK

(Nearby town also listed: Chester)

The historic town of York, not far from the North Carolina border, grew up around what was once the intersection of two stagecoach routes in the late 18th century. The town prospered with the cotton industry and the coming of the railroad in the late 1800s. Wealthy planters built stately town houses and public buildings, which remain as the heart of York and part of one of the largest historic districts in the country.

Information: Greater York Chamber of Commerce | 23 E. Liberty St., York, SC 29745 | 803/684–2590 | www.yorkcountychamber.com.

Attractions

Historic District. Settled by Scotch–Irish, Scots, English, and Germans in the mid-1700s, the town of York was established as the county seat in 1785. Its historic district is one of the largest in the country and includes more than 70 structures. The Greater York Chamber of Commerce has maps for self-guided tours. | 803/684–2590 | Free | Daily.

Kings Mountain National Military and State Park. A Revolutionary War battle considered an important turning point was fought here on October 7, 1780, when ragtag Patriot forces from the southern Appalachians soundly defeated colonial Tories commanded by British major Patrick Ferguson. Visitor center exhibits, dioramas, and an orientation film describe the action, and a paved self-guided trail leads through the battlefield. The 6,000-acre state park, next to the national military park, has camping, swimming, fishing, boating, and nature and hiking trails. | 2625 Park Road, Blacksburg | 864/936–7921 or 803/222–3209 | www.southcarolinaparks.com | Free | Memorial Day–Labor Day, daily 9–6; rest of year, daily 9–5.

Dining

Garden Cafe. Contemporary. Prime rib, salads, soups, dessert, and coffee are served in an outdoor garden with live entertainment on Fridays and Saturdays. | 8-C N. Congress St. | 803/684–7019 | Closed Sun.–Mon. | $15–$17 | D, MC, V.

Index

Notes

Notes

Notes

Notes

Notes

Notes

Notes

Notes

Notes

Notes

TALK TO US
Fill out this quick survey and receive a free *Fodor's How to Pack* (while supplies last)

1 Which Road Guide did you purchase?
(Check all that apply.)
- ☐ AL/AR/LA/MS/TN
- ☐ AZ/CO/NM
- ☐ CA
- ☐ CT/MA/RI
- ☐ DE/DC/MD/PA/VA
- ☐ FL
- ☐ GA/NC/SC
- ☐ ID/MT/NV/UT/WY
- ☐ IL/IA/MO/WI
- ☐ IN/KY/MI/OH/WV
- ☐ KS/OK/TX
- ☐ ME/NH/VT
- ☐ MN/NE/ND/SD
- ☐ NJ/NY
- ☐ OR/WA

2 How did you learn about the Road Guides?
- ☐ TV ad
- ☐ Radio ad
- ☐ Newspaper or magazine ad
- ☐ Newspaper or magazine article
- ☐ TV or radio feature
- ☐ Bookstore display/clerk recommendation
- ☐ Recommended by family/friend
- ☐ Other:_____

3 Did you use other guides for your trip?
- ☐ AAA
- ☐ Compass American Guide
- ☐ Fodor's
- ☐ Frommer's
- ☐ Insiders' Guide
- ☐ Mobil
- ☐ Moon Handbook
- ☐ Other:_____

4 Did you use any of the following for planning?
- ☐ Tourism offices   ☐ Internet   ☐ Travel agent

5 Did you buy a Road Guide for (check one):
- ☐ Leisure trip
- ☐ Business trip
- ☐ Mix of business and leisure

6 Where did you buy your Road Guide?
- ☐ Bookstore
- ☐ Other store
- ☐ On-line
- ☐ Borrowed from a friend
- ☐ Borrowed from a library
- ☐ Other:_____

7 Why did you buy a Road Guide? (Check all that apply.)
- ☐ Number of cities/towns listed
- ☐ Comprehensive coverage
- ☐ Number of lodgings   ☐ Driving tours
- ☐ Number of restaurants ☐ Maps
- ☐ Number of attractions ☐ Fodor's brand name
- ☐ Other:_____

8 Did you use this guide primarily:
- ☐ For pretrip planning   ☐ While traveling
- ☐ For planning and while traveling

9 What was the duration of your trip?
- ☐ 2-3 days
- ☐ 4-6 days
- ☐ 7-10 days
- ☐ 11 or more days
- ☐ Taking more than 1 trip

10 Did you use the guide to select
- ☐ Hotels   ☐ Restaurants

11 Did you stay primarily in a
- ☐ Hotel
- ☐ Motel
- ☐ Resort
- ☐ Bed-and-breakfast
- ☐ RV/camper
- ☐ Hostel
- ☐ Campground
- ☐ Dude ranch
- ☐ With family or friends
- ☐ Other:_____

12 What sights and activities did you most enjoy?
- ☐ Historical sights   ☐ Shopping
- ☐ Sports   ☐ Theaters
- ☐ National parks   ☐ Museums
- ☐ State parks   ☐ Major cities
- ☐ Attractions off the beaten path

13 How much did you spend per adult for this trip?
- ☐ Less than $500   ☐ $751-$1,000
- ☐ $501-$750   ☐ More than $1,000

14 How many traveled in your party?
___ Adults   ___ Children   ___ Pets

15 Did you
- ☐ Fly to destination   ☐ Rent a van or RV
- ☐ Drive your own vehicle ☐ Take a train
- ☐ Rent a car   ☐ Take a bus

16 How many miles did you travel round-trip?
- ☐ Less than 100   ☐ 501-750
- ☐ 101-300   ☐ 751-1,000
- ☐ 301-500   ☐ More than 1,000

17 What items did you take on your vacation?
- ☐ Traveler's checks   ☐ Digital camera
- ☐ Credit card   ☐ Cell phone
- ☐ Gasoline card   ☐ Computer
- ☐ Phone card   ☐ PDA
- ☐ Camera   ☐ Other

18 Would you use Fodor's Road Guides again?
- ☐ Yes   ☐ No

19 How would you like to see Road Guides changed?

☐ More ☐ Less Dining
☐ More ☐ Less Lodging
☐ More ☐ Less Sports
☐ More ☐ Less Activities
☐ More ☐ Less Attractions
☐ More ☐ Less Shopping
☐ More ☐ Less Driving tours
☐ More ☐ Less Maps
☐ More ☐ Less Historical information
☐ Other:_____

20 Tell us about yourself.

☐ Male   ☐ Female

Age:

☐ 18-24   ☐ 35-44   ☐ 55-64
☐ 25-34   ☐ 45-54   ☐ Over 65

Income:

☐ Less than $25,000   ☐ $50,001-$75,000
☐ $25,001-$50,000   ☐ More than $75,0

Name:_____ E-mail:_____

Address:_____ City:_____ State:_____ Zip:_____

Fodor's Travel Publications
Attn: Road Guide Survey
280 Park Avenue
New York, NY 10017

Atlas

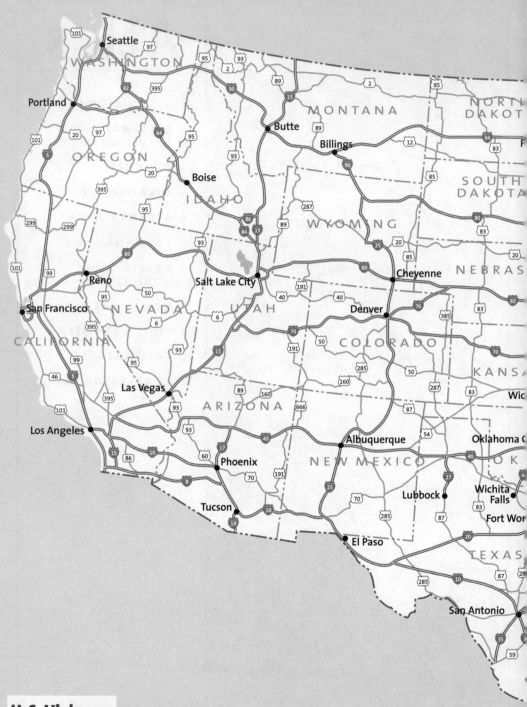

1

U. S. Highways

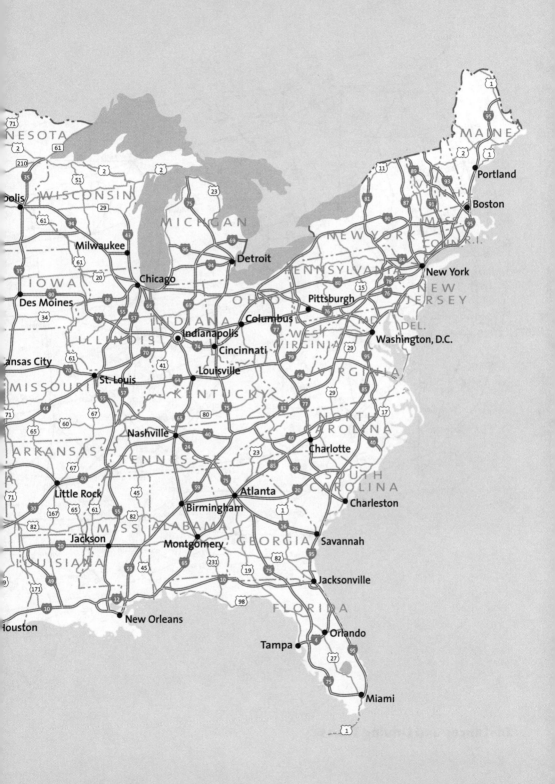

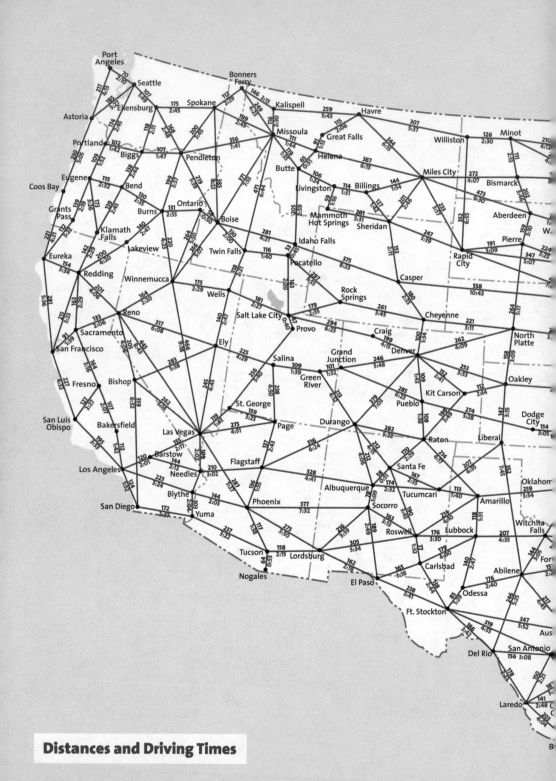

Distances and Driving Times

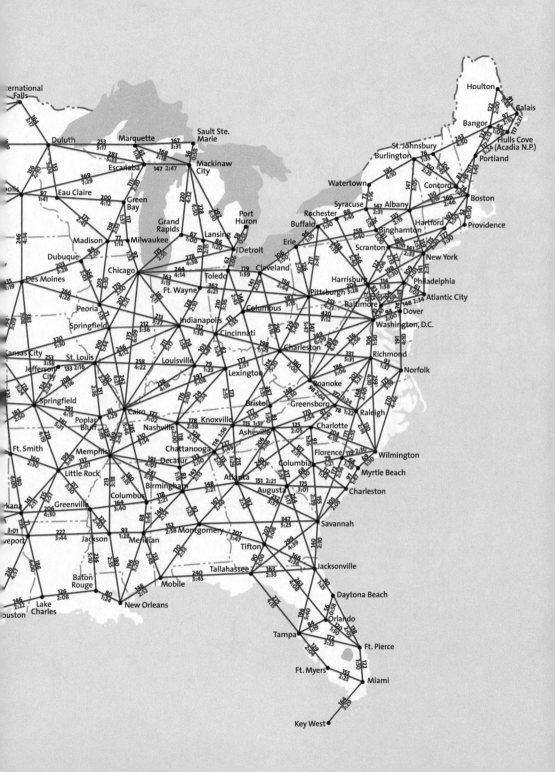

International Falls
Duluth
Marquette
Sault Ste. Marie
Mackinaw City
Escanaba
Eau Claire
Green Bay
Grand Rapids
Port Huron
Lansing
Madison
Milwaukee
Dubuque
Chicago
Des Moines
Toledo
Cleveland
Ft. Wayne
Peoria
Columbus
Springfield
Indianapolis
Cincinnati
Kansas City
St. Louis
Louisville
Jefferson City
Lexington
Springfield
Poplar Bluff
Cairo
Nashville
Knoxville
Ft. Smith
Memphis
Chattanooga
Decatur
Asheville
Little Rock
Birmingham
Atlanta
Columbus
Greenville
Columbus
Jackson
Meridian
Montgomery
Tifton
veport
Baton Rouge
Mobile
Tallahassee
Lake Charles
New Orleans
Houston

Houlton
Calais
Bangor
Hulls Cove (Acadia N.P.)
Portland
St. Johnsbury
Burlington
Concord
Boston
Watertown
Albany
Providence
Syracuse
Rochester
Hartford
Buffalo
Binghamton
Erie
Scranton
New York
Harrisburg
Philadelphia
Pittsburgh
Atlantic City
Baltimore
Dover
Washington, D.C.
Charleston
Richmond
Norfolk
Roanoke
Greensboro
Raleigh
Bristol
Charlotte
Florence
Wilmington
Columbia
Myrtle Beach
Augusta
Charleston
Savannah
Jacksonville
Daytona Beach
Orlando
Tampa
Ft. Pierce
Ft. Myers
Miami
Key West

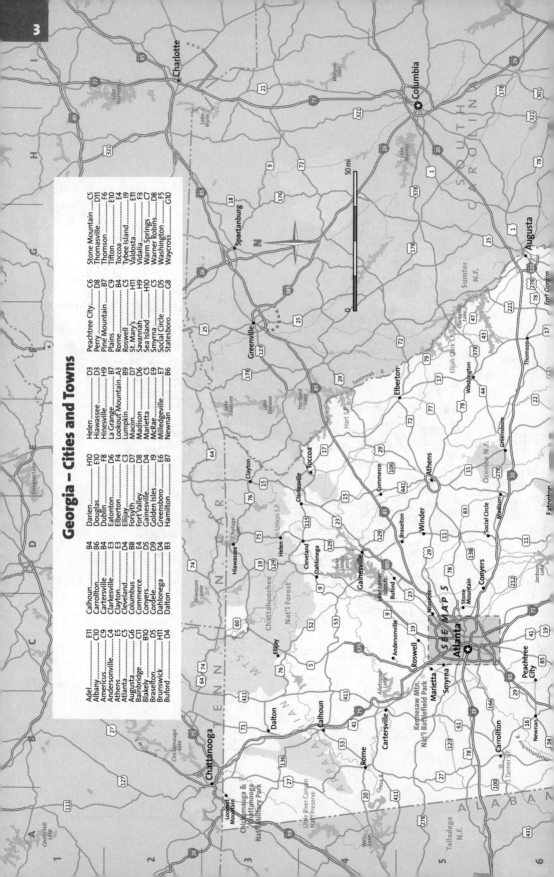

Georgia – Cities and Towns

Atlanta Area

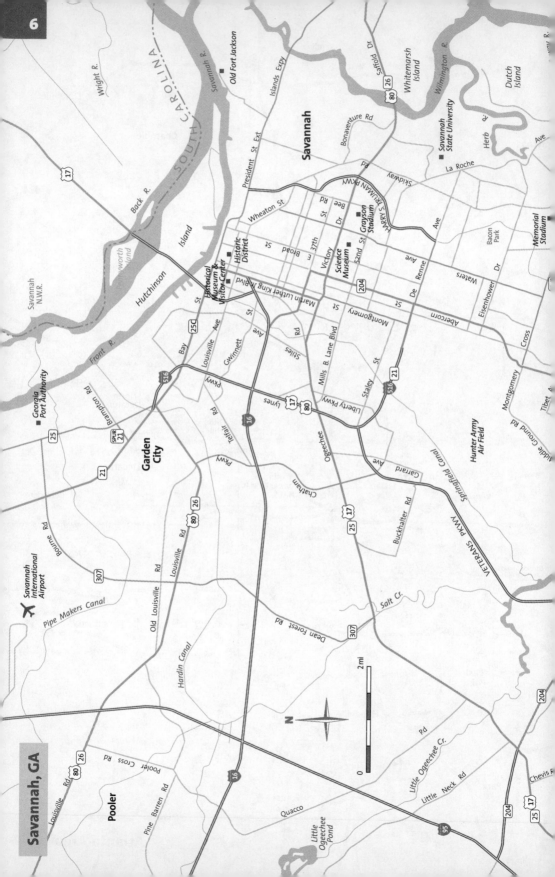

Savannah, GA

Raleigh/Durham, NC

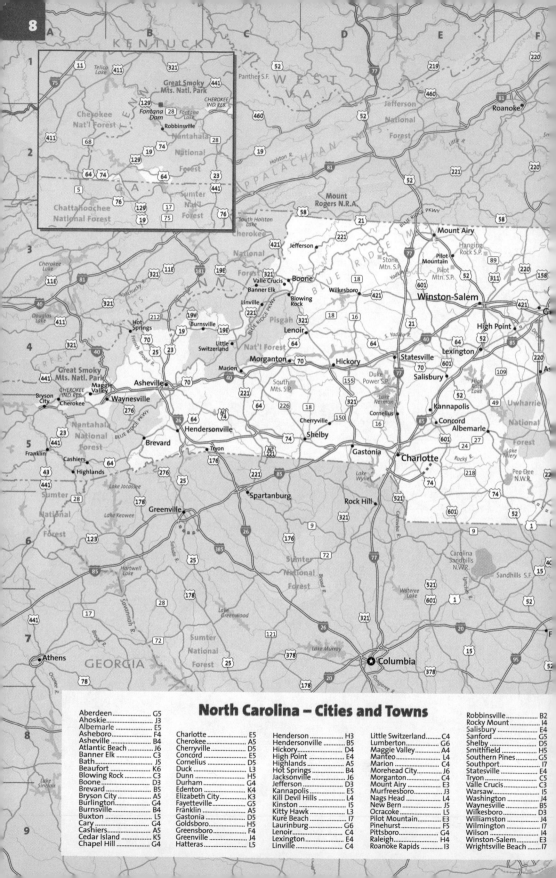

North Carolina – Cities and Towns

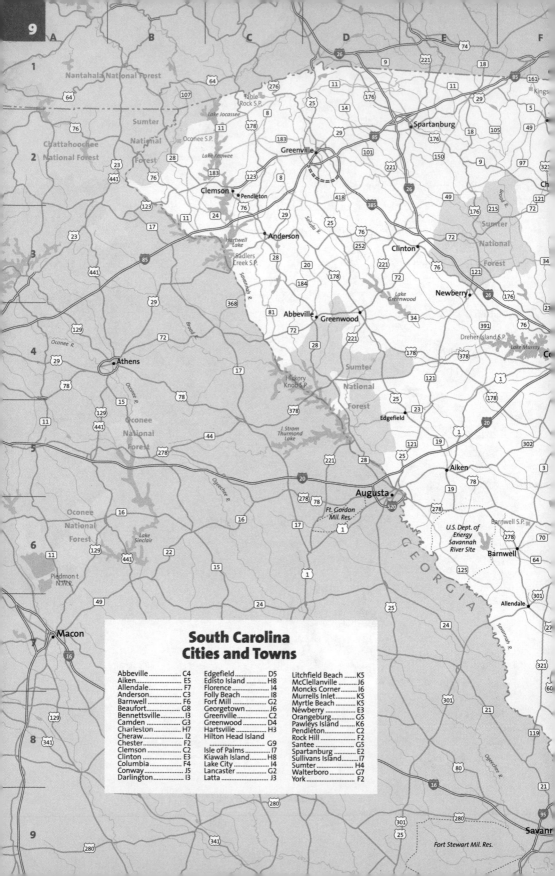

South Carolina
Cities and Towns

G   H   I   J   K   L

Charlotte

Uwharrie National Forest

Lake Tillery

Rocky R.

Pee Dee N.W.R.

Ft. Bragg Military Reserve

Fayetteville

Rockingham

Bladen Lakes S.F.

NORTH CAROLINA

Lancaster

Cheraw

Bennettsville

Carolina Sandhills N.W.R.

Sandhills S.F.

Whiteville

Cape Fear R.

Green Swamp

Hartsville

Darlington

Latta

Little Pee Dee S.P.

Camden

Florence

Pee Dee R.

Sumter

Lake City

Conway

Manchester S.F.

Myrtle Beach

Congaree R.

Myrtle Beach S.P.

ee Swamp t'l Mon.

Murrells Inlet

Orangeburg

Santee S.P.

Santee

Black R.

Litchfield Beach

Pawleys Island

Lake Marion

Santee R.

Georgetown

Lake Moultrie

Givhans Ferry S.P.

Moncks Corner

Francis Marion

National Forest

Tom Yawkey Wildlife Preserve

Cooper R.

McClellanville

Atlantic

Walterboro

Cape Romain N.W.R.

Edisto R.

Charleston

Isle of Palms

Sullivans Island

Ocean

Intracoastal Waterway

Folly Beach

Kiawah Island

Edisto Island

Edisto Beach S.P.

Beaufort

N

Hilton Head Island

0   50 mi

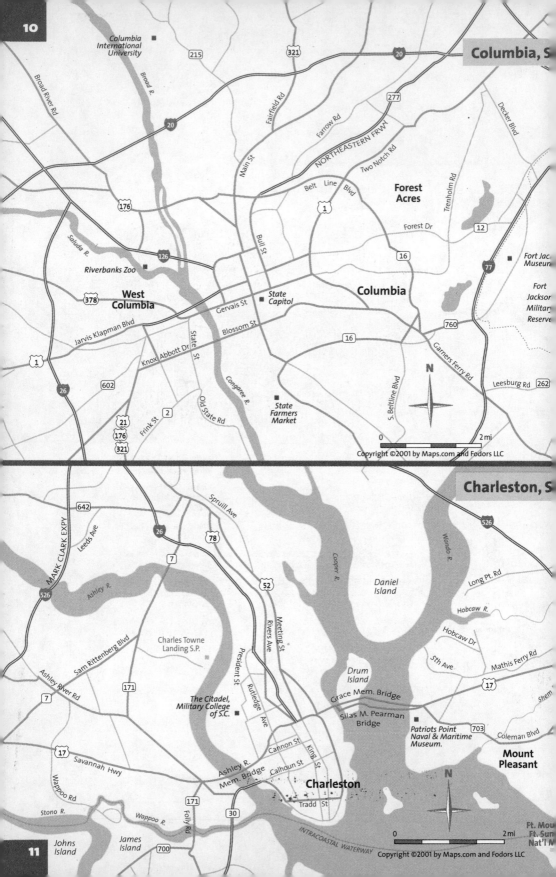

Columbia
International
University

215

321

20

277

Decker Blvd

NORTHEASTERN FRWY

Broad River Rd

Broad R.

Fairfield Rd

Farrow Rd

Two Notch Rd

Trenholm Rd

20

Main St

Belt Line Blvd

Forest
Acres

176

1

Forest Dr

12

Saluda R.

126

Bull St

16

Fort Jac.
Museum

77

Riverbanks Zoo

West
Columbia

Columbia

Fort
Jackson
Military
Reserve

378

State
Capitol

760

Gervais St

Garners Ferry Rd

1

Jarvis Klapman Blvd

Knox Abbott Dr

Blossom St

16

Leesburg Rd

262

State St

S. Beltline Blvd

N

26

602

Congaree R.

Old State Rd

Frink St

2

21

176

321

State
Farmers
Market

0   2 mi

642

Spruill Ave

526

MARK CLARK EXPY

Leeds Ave

26

78

Wando R.

7

Long Pt. Rd

Cooper R.

Daniel
Island

Hobcaw R.

52

Ashley R.

Rivers Ave

Hobcaw Dr

526

Sam Rittenberg Blvd

Charles Towne
Landing S.P.

Meeting St

5th Ave

Mathis Ferry Rd

Ashley River Rd

171

President St

Drum
Island

17

7

The Citadel,
Military College
of S.C.

Rutledge Ave

Grace Mem. Bridge

Shem

17

Savannah Hwy

Cannon St

Silas M. Pearman
Bridge

Patriots Point
Naval & Maritime
Museum.

703

King St

Coleman Blvd

Wappoo Rd

Ashley R.
Mem. Bridge

Calhoun St

Mount
Pleasant

Stono R.

171

Charleston

N

Johns
Island

James
Island

700

Wappoo R.

Folly Rd

30

Tradd St

INTRACOASTAL WATERWAY

Ft. Mou
Ft. Sum
Nat'l M

0   2 mi